Anthology of
BRITISH WOMEN
WRITERS

Anthology of
BRITISH WOMEN WRITERS

from the
MIDDLE AGES
to the
PRESENT DAY

EDITED BY

DALE JANET
SPENDER TODD

PANDORA

LONDON BOSTON SYDNEY WELLINGTON

First published by Pandora Press, an imprint of the
Trade Division of Unwin Hyman, in 1989.
Published in paperback by Pandora Press in 1990.

PANDORA PRESS
Unwin Hyman Limited
15/17 Broadwick Street
London W1V 1FP

Unwin Hyman Inc
8 Winchester Place, Winchester, MA 01890

Allen & Unwin Australia Pty Ltd
P.O.Box 764, 8 Napier Street, North Sydney, NSW 2060

Allen & Unwin NZ Ltd (in association with the Port Nicholson Press)
Compusales Building, 75 Ghuznee Street, Wellington 1, New Zealand

British Library Cataloguing in Publication Data

Anthology of British women writers.
1. English literature. British women
writers 1300–1987. Anthologies
I. Spender, Dale
820.8'09287
ISBN 0–04440–340–2

Typeset in 11 on 13 point Garamond
Printed and bound in Great Britain by
Hartnolls Ltd, Bodmin, Cornwall

Contents

CONTENTS   ix

x   CONTENTS

Acknowledgements

Janet Todd is grateful to Alison Hennegan for her generous assistance and for allowing use of her extensive library. She would like to thank Lucy Sloan for her help with preparing the manuscript, Julian and Clara Todd for their contribution to the typing, and Barry Nisbet and James Lynn for translations in the footnotes.

Dale Spender would like to thank Clare Sambrook for her assistance in tracing elusive details and dates, and Elizabeth Crawford for finding some of the buried texts. She would also like to thank David Doughan for his assistance with footnotes, the staff of the Fawcett Library and the London Library for their co–operation and support, and Candida Ann Lacey who has been a source of inspiration and an exemplary editor.

Janet Todd and Dale Spender both acknowledge their debt to Helen Gray who has so patiently and positively contributed to the organisation of the volume.

The authors and publisher would like to thank the following for permission to reproduce material in this anthology:

The extract from *A Testament of Youth* by Vera Brittain, published by Virago Press in 1978, copyright © Literary Executors of Vera Brittain 1970; 'Wolf-Alice' and 'The Company of Wolves' from *The Bloody Chamber and Other Stories* copyright © Angela Carter 1986, reprinted by permission of Victor Gollancz Ltd and Deborah Rogers Ltd; *Three More Sleepless Nights* copyright © Caryl Churchill 1988 (all rights whatsoever in this play are strictly reserved and application for performance should be made before rehearsal to Margaret Ramsay Ltd. No performance may be given unless a licence has been obtained); 'The Reunion' copyright © Margaret Drabble 1968, reprinted by permission of Macmillan Publishers Ltd; 'Fraulein Schwartz' from *Miss Ogilvy Finds Herself*, reprinted by permission of the Radclyffe Hall Estate; *How the Vote Was Won* by Cicely Hamilton, reprinted by permission of Sir Lesley Bower; 'An Old Woman and Her Cat', from *The Story of a Non-Marrying Man*, copyright © Doris Lessing 1972 and reprinted by permission of Jonathan Clowes Ltd on behalf of the author; extract from *Told by an Idiot*, published by Virago Press, copyright © the Estate of Rose Macaulay 1923; 'The Farmer's Bride', 'Beside the Bed', 'My Heart is Lame' from *Charlotte Mew: Collected Poems and Prose*, edited by Val Warner, published by Virago Press in 1982, copyright © 1981 the Estate of Charlotte Mew; 'The Poor Relation and the Secretary' copyright © Naomi Mitchison 1933, reprinted by permission of David Higham Associates Ltd; 'Ordeal' copyright © Dorothy Richardson 1930, reprinted by permission of the Estate of Dorothy Richardson; *Under His Roof* copyright © Elizabeth Robins 1908, reprinted by permission of the Estate of Elizabeth Robins; extract from *The Three Sisters* published by Virago Press 1982 copyright © Mrs M. L. Sinclair 1946; Edith Sitwell poems copyright ©

Edith Sitwell: 'The Sleeping Beauty' © 1924, 'Aubade' © 1924, 'Said King Pompey' © 1922, 'Waltz' © 1924 and 'Green Song' © 1944, reprinted by permission of David Higham Associates; 'Company', 'My Muse', 'A Dream of Comparison' and 'God the Eater' from *The Collected Poems of Stevie Smith*, originally published by Penguin, reprinted by permission of James McGibbon and New Directions Publishing Corporation; 'Surrounded by Children', 'I Forgive You', 'None of the Other Birds' and 'The Holiday' from *Me Again: Uncollected Writings of Stevie Smith*, published by Virago Press in 1981, copyright © James McGibbon 1981; 'Fanny Fitz's Gamble' copyright © Edith Somerville and Martin Ross 1903, reprinted with permission of the Executors of the Somerville and Ross Estate; 'The Dark Glasses' copyright © 1961 Muriel Spark and reprinted with permission; 'Taking Mother Out' and 'Nods and Becks and Wreathèd Smiles' from *Hester Lilly and Other Stories* published by Virago Press 1981 copyright © Elizabeth Taylor 1954 and reprinted with permission of the executors of the estate of Elizabeth Taylor; 'But at the Stroke of Midnight' from *The Innocent and the Guilty* copyright © Sylvia Townsend Warner 1971, reprinted by permission of the estate of the author and Chatto & Windus; 'IND AFF or Out of Love in Sarajevo' copyright © Fay Weldon 1988; 'Parthenope' by Rebecca West reprinted by permission of the Peters Fraser & Dunlop Group Ltd; 'The House of Clouds' copyright © Antonia White 1954 reprinted by permission of the Executors of the Antonia White Estate; extract from *A Room of One's Own* copyright © Quentin Bell and Angelica Garnett 1928 and reprinted by permission of the estate of Virginia Woolf, The Hogarth Press and Harcourt, Brace & Jovanovich.

Every effort has been made to trace the copyright holders of the material reprinted in this anthology. The authors and the publishers would be glad to hear from any copyright holders they have not been able to contact and to print due acknowledgements in the next edition.

Introduction

The reason for this anthology is simple; previously there has been no collection of the contributions of notable British women writers and as a result no easy opportunity to appreciate the range and richness of their work. A few anthologies including British women have appeared over the years, organised according to various periods or purposes,[1] but none has attempted methodically to provide an overview of the literary lineage as a whole. Yet without such a collection, it is difficult to identify the recurring themes and to trace the evolutionary and interconnecting patterns in British women's writing. This anthology aims to give samples so that a reader can become aware of the duration, development, and diversity of the literary achievements. With its appearance new links can be made and new insights forged, and in such a dynamic context new enthusiasm can, we hope, be generated and new directions pursued.

As no anthology of British women writers has been compiled before, and as women have been under-represented in the literary mainstream, many of the women who are included here will be unfamiliar to readers. Some of the contributors have been in print since they made their entry on the literary stage, but others who enjoyed acclaim in their own lifetimes, only to be later 'eclipsed', are being reprinted here for the first time. Their marginalisation in the past should not be taken to indicate their present worth; on the contrary, many of the works should prompt fundamental questions about their writers' former exclusion from the literary mainstream.

The anthology includes only women, both to compensate for exclusion and to celebrate achievement. An understanding of literature obviously requires the contributions of both men and women, and there is no absolute literary separation of the sexes at any time in history. Samuel Richardson had enormous influence on the novel by eighteenth-century women, George Eliot on the novel by nineteenth-century men. Yet, since purportedly inclusive anthologies exist that entirely exclude women and take no notice of the fact, this work exists in part as compensation. There is no complete continuity of female writing, nor any clear line of influence down the ages. But there is evidence that women read each other's work, and patterns and recurrent concerns do emerge. There is value in an anthology that brings many women together over time, whether as readers we wish to look for women's hidden messages, see a women's tradition or simply read what other women have written.

Given the quality of these contributions, there is no rational explanation for the way in which, over the centuries, a few women have found favour

---

[1] The most recent and relevant is the *Norton Anthology of Literature by Women: The Tradition in English*, edited by Sandra M. Gilbert and Susan Gubar: while an excellent overview of the English-speaking tradition, it is limited in its references to British women's writing in the late nineteenth and twentieth centuries.

enough to enter the literary canon, while the many have been dismissed. It would be difficult, for example, to determine the basis on which the work of Maria Edgeworth was allowed to go out of print, while that of her admirer, Jane Austen, should have been so consistently and readily available; why the recognition warranted by the extraordinary efforts of Aphra Behn should have been allowed to lapse, while those of Virginia Woolf (who in *A Room of One's Own* tried to reinstate Aphra Behn in the world of letters) should have been so widely published. This is not to detract from the outstanding contributions of Jane Austen or Virginia Woolf. But it is to point out that their visibility has been somewhat arbitrary; they have been removed from the matrix of women writers and singled out for praise, and, when they are re-placed alongside their peers, their achievements may stand out more clearly or they may be matched by those of women who have never been so isolated, and elevated.

By grouping all these women together, this anthology draws attention to some of the problematic principles of past selection at the same time as it extends the opportunities for examining the formation of literary traditions. With its presentation of both known and neglected women writers, it helps to suggest some of the dimensions of the stream from which the prominent authors have emerged, and it raises questions about judgement and justification in the literary establishment. It allows for the reappraisal of individual writers and facilitates appreciation of the collective whole.

   While the work of many writers has been selected for its representative nature, there are those whose efforts warrant recognition precisely because of their innovative qualities, which make them far from typical. A number of contributors have been included on the grounds that they are exceptional, and, while every attempt has been made to structure a unified and interconnected anthology, commonality has not been stressed at the expense of individual distinction.

   Even as claims are made, however, for the scope of this collection, qualifying statements must be introduced. Although the intention has been to reclaim and present the women writers of note, it must be acknowledged that not all the initial choices have found their way into this edition. Considerations of space have circumscribed selection, for it is simply not possible in the pages of a single volume to place all the women who obviously deserve inclusion. Difficult decisions have had to be made and the editors regret many of the omissions; however, in keeping with the principle of the need critically to examine the selective process, the attempt has been made to make explicit the criteria employed in selection.

1   Historical Representation

In order that the study of the themes and priorities in women's writing might be established over time, consideration has been given to the sampling from each century, so that trends and relationships can be readily traced.

On these grounds Julian of Norwich, Isabella Whitney and Lady Mary Wroth[2] have been included to provide some intimation of the origins of British women's literary heritage. Some of the seventeenth-century developments can be deduced from the substantial achievements of the prose of Margaret Cavendish, Duchess of Newcastle, the poems of Ann Finch, Countess of Winchilsea, and the plays of Aphra Behn. Unhappily excluded are the Commonwealth poets, prophetic women and the other playwrights who surround and follow Aphra Behn.

The evolution and expansion of women's writing in the eighteenth century is reflected in the increased number of contributors from this period with, for example, the work of Delarivier Manley,[3] Jane Barker, Sarah Fielding, and Frances Sheridan (whose Oriental tale *The History of Nourjahad* is reprinted here in its entirety) helping to map the directions in women's fiction-writing. While the prolific and popular Eliza Haywood could have been represented by her fiction, we have chosen instead her journalism; *The Female Spectator*, which she launched, well illustrates the early women's magazines of advice and entertainment. From the poems and essays of the aristocratic Lady Mary Wortley Montagu to those of the lowly cook-maid, Mary Leapor, conclusions might be drawn about women's literary freedom and constraints in this era. In Charlotte Smith, Fanny Burney, Mary Wollstonecraft, Mary Hays and Maria Edgeworth, we find the concern for women's education and the desire for self-expression clearly articulated, while the Gothic novels of Ann Radcliffe at the end of the century and the social satire of Jane Austen at the beginning of the next extend the realms of fiction still further.

But it is among the writers of the nineteenth century that some of the most difficult decisions had to be made about exclusion, particularly in relation to fiction. So numerous were the novelists of distinction that no one anthology could hope comprehensively to present them. For such a coverage would need to include contributions from, for example, Isabel Varley Banks, Rhoda Broughton, Mona Caird, Rosa Nouchette Carey, Mary Cholmondeley, Dinah Mulock Craik, Susan Ferrier, Violet Hunt, 'Vernon Lee' (Violet Paget), Caroline Norton, Flora Annie Steel, and Mrs Henry Wood (Ellen Wood) among others.

The Mad Willoughbys by Eliza Lynn Linton is here reprinted in full in the attempt to represent the nature, though not the extent, of this heritage of fiction. Other authors have been chosen to reflect the diversity and the development throughout the nineteenth century. The work of Lady Morgan (Sydney Owenson), written early in the period, illustrates the regional novel, for example, while that of 'Somerville and Ross' ('Fanny Fitz's Gamble'), written at a later stage, suggests the directions this form has taken. The fantasy contribution of Mary Shelley – *The Last Man* – marks the early development of science fiction by women, while the short story of Elizabeth Gaskell ('The Well of Pen Morfa') signals their growth of social awareness and political concern.

The related extracts from Charlotte Bronte's *The Professor* and *Villette* illustrate the achievements of a writer securely placed in the canon, while the extract

[2] Sometimes spelt Wro*a*th.
[3] Sometimes spelt Delariviere Manley, and sometimes referred to as Mary Delariviere Manley.

from *The Vixen*, by Mary Elizabeth Braddon, gives some indication of the calibre of popular writing.

The personal chronicles of Dorothy Wordsworth, Harriet Martineau, Geraldine Jewsbury, Margaret Oliphant and Mary Augusta Ward throw light on women's insights about self, community, nature and the writing process, and all help to set some of the parameters for the constant and controversial debate on 'the woman question'.

Travel writing of the period is illustrated by Fanny Trollope's *The Domestic Manners of the Americans*, and the popular essay by the contributions of George Eliot, Charlotte Yonge and Anne Thackeray, while the work of Elizabeth Barrett Browning, Emily Bronte and Christina Rossetti provides some of the reference points for poetic assessment in the nineteenth century.

Considerations change when the attempt is made to represent the major developments of the twentieth century: while more women have written during this period, it is also the case that they are more widely known and more readily available. So, with regret, the following writers of stature among other have been omitted, although they have a place in the contemporary literary consciousness; Jean Rhys, Vita Sackville-West, Margaret Kennedy, Elizabeth Bowen, Sheila Gibbon, Nancy Mitford, Barbara Pym, Iris Murdoch, Beryl Bainbridge, Anita Brookner, Ivy Compton Burnett, Lynne Reid Banks, Edna O'Brien and Eva Figes have made way for a small number of writers who must stand here for some of the significant achievements of the twentieth century.

2   Genre

Genre is another critical factor in the process of selection; if the literary traditions of British women are to be identified, then sufficient examples from within each genre are required in order to make connections and comparisons.

The inclusion of the letters of Margaret Cavendish, Duchess of Newcastle, Lady Mary Wortley Montagu, Mary Wollstonecraft and Geraldine Jewsbury help to indicate the extraordinary richness of the formal and informal letter written by women, while poetry, so important for women's self-expression and their entry into culturally privileged literature, is represented by the verse of Isabella Whitney, Lady Mary Wroth, Margaret Cavendish, Duchess of Newcastle, Anne Finch, Countess of Winchilsea, Mary Leapor, Charlotte Smith, Elizabeth Barrett Browning, Emily Bronte, Christina Rossetti, Charlotte Mew, Edith Sitwell and Stevie Smith. Three full-length plays are included: Aphra Behn's *The Rover* from the seventeenth century, the propagandist *How the Vote was Won* by Cicely Hamilton (and Christopher St John), and the very contemporary drama of Caryl Churchill, *Three More Sleepless Nights* (published here for the first time).

From the eighteenth and nineteenth centuries there are full-length works of previously unavailable fiction (Frances Sheridan and Eliza Lynn Linton); extracts from the work of Delarivier Manley and Jane Barker have also been included to bring into the arena contributions which have before been largely inaccessible. Along with the examples of the work of Sarah Fielding, Ann Radcliffe, Jane Austen, Lady Morgan (Sydney Owenson), Charlotte Bronte, Mary Elizabeth Braddon, May Sinclair, Dorothy Richardson and Rose Macaulay, these contributions give some idea of the innovations and consolidations that characterise women's command of fiction-writing, the genre in which they have most excelled. The growth and development of the short story is traced from one of its earliest and most talented exponents, Elizabeth Gaskell, through to some of its most outstanding contemporary exemplars, with Fay Weldon's 'IND AFF: or Out of Love in Sarajevo' being published for the first time. The achievements in this genre of Radclyffe Hall, Rebecca West, Naomi Mitchison, Muriel Spark, Doris Lessing, Elizabeth Taylor, Antonia White, Sylvia Townsend Warner, Margaret Drabble and Angela Carter, stand as a testimony to the range, resourcefulness and richness of women's short story heritage.

The diary and journal entries of women help to provide commentary on women's relationship to writing and their notions of self-expression. Extracts are taken from the formal meditations of Julian of Norwich, from the journals of Harriet Martineau, Dorothy Wordsworth and Vera Brittain, and from the diaries of Fanny Burney, Margaret Oliphant and Mary Augusta Ward. Because a predominant theme in women's non-fiction writing has been women's autonomy and literary legitimacy, most of the non-fiction pieces have been chosen with this theme in mind. So there is a unifying thread running through the contributions of Mary Hays, Maria Edgeworth, George Eliot, Anne Thackeray and Virginia Woolf, while the extract from Charlotte Yonge presents part of the case for the opposing side. Most of these contributions also point to the patterns which have prevailed in women's literary criticism, and put forward reasons for its secondary status.

Overall, the writers chosen here stand individually and together as a testimony to the various and valuable achievements of women in English literature; that this anthology is not comprehensive, and that the work of many more writers warrants attention is not a limitation, but an exciting prospect for the future.

Anthology of
BRITISH WOMEN
WRITERS

Julian of Norwich

c. 1343 – after 1416

*J*ulian of Norwich was one of the most profound of medieval spiritual writers.
*She is believed to have been a contemplative nun and later an anchoress
enclosed in a cell adjoining St Julian's Church, Norwich, from which she
took her name, her original one being irrelevant to her role as a medium
of God. During a severe illness in 1373 she claims to have received sixteen
visions which she recorded in a short text. After further contemplation over
many years, she expanded this text into a much longer work. Despite the usual
pious claims to being illiterate, Julian is clearly a skilful writer and theologian,
aware of rhetorical devices and of the Christian mystical tradition. Yet her work
is also highly original in its theological complexity and in its emphasis on the
mothering role of Christ derived from the mystery of the eucharist.*

The following extracts are taken from Julian of Norwich: Showings *(transl.,
Edmund College and James Walsh, Paulist Press, New York, 1978).*

From

Julian of Norwich: Showings

THE SECOND CHAPTER

THIS revelation was made to a simple, unlettered creature, living in this mortal
flesh, the year of our Lord one thousand, three hundred and seventy-three,
on the thirteenth day of May; and before this the creature had desired three
graces by the gift of God. The first was recollection of the Passion. The second
was bodily sickness. The third was to have, of God's gift, three wounds. As to the
first, it seemed to me that I had some feeling for the Passion of Christ, but still I
desired to have more by the grace of God. I thought that I wished that I had been
at that time with Magdalen and with the others who were Christ's lovers, so that I
might have seen with my own eyes the Passion which our Lord suffered for me,
so that I might have suffered with him as others did who loved him. Therefore
I desired a bodily sight, in which I might have more knowledge of our saviour's
bodily pains, and of the compassion of our Lady and of all his true lovers who
were living at that time and saw his pains, for I would have been one of them and
have suffered with them. I never desired any other sight of God or revelation,
until my soul would be separated from the body, for I believed that I should be

saved by the mercy of God. This was my intention, because I wished afterwards, because of that revelation, to have truer recollection of Christ's Passion. As to the second grace, there came into my mind with contrition—a free gift which I did not seek—a desire of my will to have by God's gift a bodily sickness. I wished that sickness to be so severe that it might seem mortal, so that I might in it receive all the rites which Holy Church has to give me, whilst I myself should think that I was dying, and everyone who saw me would think the same; for I wanted no comfort from any human, earthly life in that sickness. I wanted to have every kind of pain, bodily and spiritual, which I should have if I had died, every fear and temptation from devils, and every other kind of pain except the departure of the spirit. I intended this because I wanted to be purged by God's mercy, and afterwards live more to his glory because of that sickness; because I hoped that this would be to my reward when I should die, because I desired soon to be with my God and my Creator.

These two desires about the Passion and the sickness which I desired from him were with a condition, for it seemed to me that this was not the ordinary practice of prayer; therefore I said: Lord, you know what I want, if it be your will that I have it, and if it be not your will, good Lord, do not be displeased, for I want nothing which you do not want. When I was young I desired to have this sickness when I would be thirty years old.

As to the third, by the grace of God and the teaching of Holy Church I conceived a great desire to receive three wounds in my life, that is, the wound of true contrition, the wound of loving compassion and the wound of longing with my will for God. Just as I asked for the other two conditionally, so I asked urgently for this third without any condition. The two desires which I mentioned first passed from my mind, and the third remained there continually.

THE THIRD CHAPTER

A ND when I was thirty and a half years old, God sent me a bodily sickness in which I lay for three days and three nights, and on the third night I received all the rites of Holy Church, and did not expect to live until day. And after this I lay for two days and two nights, and on the third night I often thought that I was on the point of death, and those who were with me often thought so. And yet in this I felt a great reluctance to die, not that there was anything on earth which it pleased me to live for, or any pain of which I was afraid, for I trusted in the mercy of God. But it was because I wanted to live to love God better and longer, so that I might through the grace of that living have more knowledge and love of God in the bliss of heaven. Because it seemed to me that all the time that I had lived here was very little and short in comparison with the bliss which is everlasting, I thought: Good Lord, can my living no longer be to your glory? And I understood by my reason and the sensation of my pains that I should die; and with all the will of my heart I assented to be wholly as was God's will.

So I lasted until day, and by then my body was dead from the middle downwards, as it felt to me. Then I was helped to sit upright and supported, so that my heart might be more free to be at God's will, and so that I could think of him whilst my life would last. My curate was sent for to be present at my end; and before he came my eyes were fixed upwards, and I could not speak. He set the cross before my face, and said: I have brought the image of your saviour; look at it and take comfort from it. It seemed to me that I was well, for my eyes were set upwards towards heaven, where I trusted that I by God's mercy was going; but nevertheless I agreed to fix my eyes on the face of the crucifix if I could, and so I did, for it seemed to me that I would hold out longer with my eyes set in front of me rather than upwards. After this my sight began to fail. It grew as dark around me in the room as if it had been night, except that there was ordinary light trained upon the image of the cross, I did not know how. Everything around the cross was ugly and terrifying to me, as if it were occupied by a great crowd of devils.

After this the upper part of my body began to die, until I could scarcely feel anything. My greatest pain was my shortness of breath and the ebbing of my life. Then truly I believed that I was at the point of death. And suddenly at that moment all my pain was taken from me, and I was as sound, particularly in the upper part of my body, as ever I was before. I was astonished by this sudden change, for it seemed to me that it was by God's secret doing and not natural; and even so, in this ease which I felt, I had no more confidence that I should live, nor was the ease I felt complete for me, for I thought that I would rather have been delivered of this world, because that was what my heart longed for.

Then suddenly it came into my mind that I ought to wish for the second wound as a gift and a grace from our Lord, that my body might be filled full of recollection and feeling of his blessed Passion, as I had prayed before, for I wished that his pains might be my pains, with compassion which would lead to longing for God. So it seemed to me that I might with his grace have the wounds which I had before desired; but in this I never wanted any bodily vision or any kind of revelation from God, but the compassion which I thought a loving soul could have for our Lord Jesus, who for love was willing to become a mortal man. I desired to suffer with him, living in my mortal body, as God would give me grace.

THE FOURTH CHAPTER

A ND at this, suddenly I saw the red blood running down from under the crown, hot and flowing freely and copiously, a living stream, just as it was at the time when the crown of thorns was pressed on his blessed head. I perceived, truly and powerfully, that it was he who just so, both God and man, himself suffered for me, who showed it to me without any intermediary.

And in the same revelation, suddenly the Trinity filled my heart full of the greatest joy, and I understood that it will be so in heaven without end

to all who will come there. For the Trinity is God, God is the Trinity. The
Trinity is our maker, the Trinity is our protector, the Trinity is our everlasting
lover, the Trinity is our endless joy and our bliss, by our Lord Jesus Christ and
in our Lord Jesus Christ. And this was revealed in the first vision and in them
all, for where Jesus appears the blessed Trinity is understood, as I see it. And
I said: Blessed be the Lord! This I said with a reverent intention and in a loud
voice, and I was greatly astonished by this wonder and marvel, that he who is
so to be revered and feared would be so familiar with a sinful creature living
in this wretched flesh.

I accepted it that at that time our Lord Jesus wanted, out of his courteous
love, to show me comfort before my temptations began; for it seemed to
me that I might well be tempted by devils, by God's permission and with his
protection, before I would die. With this sight of his blessed Passion, with the
divinity which I saw in my understanding, I knew well that this was strength
enough for me, yes, and for all living creatures who were to be saved, against
all the devils of hell and against all their spiritual enemies.

In this he brought our Lady St. Mary to my understanding. I saw her
spiritually in her bodily likeness, a simple, humble maiden, young in years,
grown a little taller than a child, of the stature which she had when she
conceived. Also God showed me part of the wisdom and the truth of her soul,
and in this I understood the reverent contemplation with which she beheld
her God, who is her Creator, marvelling with great reverence that he was
willing to be born of her who was a simple creature created by him. And this
wisdom and truth, this knowledge of her Creator's greatness and of her own
created littleness, made her say very meekly to Gabriel: Behold me here, God's
handmaiden. In this sight I understood truly that she is greater, more worthy
and more fulfilled, than everything else which God has created, and which is
inferior to her. Above her is no created thing, except the blessed humanity of
Christ, as I saw.

THE FIFTY-EIGHTH CHAPTER

GOD the blessed Trinity, who is everlasting being, just as he is eternal from
without beginning, just so was it in his eternal purpose to create human
nature, which fair nature was first prepared for his own Son, the second person;
and when he wished, by full agreement of the whole Trinity he created us all
once. And in our creating he joined and united us to himself, and through this
union we are kept as pure and as noble as we were created. By the power of
that same precious union we love our Creator and delight in him, praise him
and thank him and endlessly rejoice in him. And this is the work which is
constantly performed in every soul which will be saved, and this is the godly will
mentioned before.

And so in our making, God almighty is our loving Father, and God all
wisdom is our loving Mother, with the love and the goodness of the Holy
Spirit, which is all one God, one Lord. And in the joining and the union he is

our very true spouse and we his beloved wife and his fair maiden, with which wife he was never displeased; for he says: I love you and you love me, and our love will never divide in two.

I contemplated the work of all the blessed Trinity, in which contemplation I saw and understood these three properties: the property of the fatherhood, and the property of the motherhood, and the property of the lordship in one God. In our almighty Father we have our protection and our bliss, as regards our natural substance, which is ours by our creation from without beginning; and in the second person, in knowledge and wisdom we have our perfection, as regards our sensuality, our restoration and our salvation, for he is our Mother, brother and saviour; and in our good Lord the Holy Spirit we have our reward and our gift for our living and our labour, endlessly surpassing all that we desire in his marvellous courtesy, out of his great plentiful grace. For all our life consists of three: In the first we have our being, and in the second we have our increasing, and in the third we have our fulfillment. The first is nature, the second is mercy, the third is grace.

As to the first, I saw and understood that the high might of the Trinity is our Father, and the deep wisdom of the Trinity is our Mother, and the great love of the Trinity is our Lord; and all these we have in nature and in our substantial creation. And furthermore I saw that the second person, who is our Mother, substantially the same beloved person, has now become our mother sensually, because we are double by God's creating, that is to say substantial and sensual. Our substance is the higher part, which we have in our Father, God almighty; and the second person of the Trinity is our Mother in nature in our substantial creation, in whom we are founded and rooted, and he is our Mother of mercy in taking our sensuality. And so our Mother is working on us in various ways, in whom our parts are kept undivided; for in our Mother Christ we profit and increase, and in mercy he reforms and restores us, and by the power of his Passion, his death and his Resurrection he unites us to our substance. So our Mother works in mercy on all his beloved children who are docile and obedient to him, and grace works with mercy, and especially in two properties, as it was shown, which working belongs to the third person, the Holy Spirit. He works, rewarding and giving. Rewarding is a gift for our confidence which the Lord makes to those who have laboured; and giving is a courteous act which he does freely, by grace, fulfilling and surpassing all that creatures deserve.

Thus in our Father, God almighty, we have our being, and in our Mother of mercy we have our reforming and our restoring, in whom our parts are united and all made perfect man, and through the rewards and the gifts of grace of the Holy Spirit we are fulfilled. And our substance is in our Father, God almighty, and our substance is in our Mother, God all wisdom, and our substance is in our Lord God, the Holy Spirit, all goodness, for our substance is whole in each person of the Trinity, who is one God. And our sensuality is only in the second person, Christ Jesus, in whom is the Father and the Holy Spirit; and in him and by him we are powerfully taken out of hell and out of the wretchedness on earth, and gloriously brought up into heaven, and blessedly united to our substance, increased in riches and nobility by all the power of Christ and by the grace and operation of the Holy Spirit.

THE FIFTY-NINTH CHAPTER

AND we have all this bliss by mercy and grace, and this kind of bliss we never could have had and known, unless that property of goodness which is in God had been opposed, through which we have this bliss. For wickedness has been suffered to rise in opposition to that goodness; and the goodness of mercy and grace opposed that wickedness, and turned everything to goodness and honour for all who will be saved. For this is that property in God which opposes good to evil. So Jesus Christ, who opposes good to evil, is our true Mother. We have our being from him, where the foundation of motherhood begins, with all the sweet protection of love which endlessly follows.

As truly as God is our Father, so truly is God our Mother, and he revealed that in everything, and especially in these sweet words where he says: I am he; that is to say: I am he, the power and goodness of fatherhood; I am he, the wisdom and the lovingness of motherhood; I am he, the light and the grace which is all blessed love; I am he, the Trinity, I am he, the unity; I am he, the great supreme goodness of every kind of thing; I am he who makes you to love; I am he who makes you to long; I am he, the endless fulfilling of all true desires. For where the soul is highest, noblest, most honourable, still it is lowest, meekest and mildest.

And from this foundation in substance we have all the powers of our sensuality by the gift of nature, and by the help and the furthering of mercy and grace, without which we cannot profit. Our great Father, almighty God, who is being, knows us and loved us before time began. Out of this knowledge, in his most wonderful deep love, by the prescient eternal counsel of all the blessed Trinity, he wanted the second person to become our Mother, our brother and our saviour. From this it follows that as truly as God is our Father, so truly is God our Mother. Our Father wills, our Mother works, our good Lord the Holy Spirit confirms. And therefore it is our part to love our God in whom we have our being, reverently thanking and praising him for our creation, mightily praying to our Mother for mercy and pity, and to our Lord the Holy Spirit for help and grace. For in these three is all our life: nature, mercy and grace, of which we have mildness, patience and pity, and hatred of sin and wickedness; for the virtues must of themselves hate sin and wickedness.

And so Jesus is our true Mother in nature by our first creation, and he is our true Mother in grace by his taking our created nature. All the lovely works and all the sweet loving offices of beloved motherhood are appropriated to the second person, for in him we have this godly will, whole and safe forever, both in nature and in grace, from his own goodness proper to him. I understand three ways of contemplating motherhood in God.[1] The first

---

[1] Julian is classifying the Trinitarian modes of divine motherhood.

is the foundation of our nature's creation; the second is his taking of our nature, where the motherhood of grace begins; the third is the motherhood at work. And in that, by the same grace, everything is penetrated, in length and in breadth, in height and in depth without end; and it is all one love.

THE SIXTIETH CHAPTER

BUT now I should say a little more about this penetration, as I understood our Lord to mean: How we are brought back by the motherhood of mercy and grace into our natural place, in which we were created by the motherhood of love, a mother's love which never leaves us.

Our Mother in nature, our Mother in grace, because he wanted altogether to become our Mother in all things, made the foundation of his work most humbly and most mildly in the maiden's womb. And he revealed that in the first revelation, when he brought that meek maiden before the eye of my understanding in the simple stature which she had when she conceived; that is to say that our great God, the supreme wisdom of all things, arrayed and prepared himself in this humble place, all ready in our poor flesh, himself to do the service and the office of motherhood in everything. The mother's service is nearest, readiest and surest: nearest because it is most natural, readiest because it is most loving, and surest because it is truest. No one ever might or could perform this office fully, except only him. We know that all our mothers bear us for pain and for death. O, what is that? But our true Mother Jesus, he alone bears us for joy and for endless life, blessed may he be. So he carries us within him in love and travail, until the full time when he wanted to suffer the sharpest thorns and cruel pains that ever were or will be, and at the last he died. And when he had finished, and had borne us so for bliss, still all this could not satisfy his wonderful love. And he revealed this in these great surpassing words of love: If I could suffer more, I would suffer more. He could not die any more, but he did not want to cease working; therefore he must nourish us, for the precious love of motherhood has made him our debtor.

The mother can give her child to suck of her milk, but our precious Mother Jesus can feed us with himself, and does, most courteously and most tenderly, with the blessed sacrament, which is the precious food of true life; and with all the sweet sacraments he sustains us most mercifully and graciously, and so he meant in these blessed words, where he said: I am he whom Holy Church preaches and teaches to you. That is to say: All the health and the life of the sacraments, all the power and the grace of my word, all the goodness which is ordained in Holy Church for you, I am he.

The mother can lay her child tenderly to her breast, but our tender Mother Jesus can lead us easily into his blessed breast through his sweet open side, and show us there a part of the godhead and of the joys of heaven, with inner certainty of endless bliss. And that he revealed in the tenth revelation, giving us the same understanding in these sweet words which he says: See, how I love you, looking into his blessed side, rejoicing.

This fair lovely word 'mother' is so sweet and so kind in itself that it cannot truly be said of anyone or to anyone except of him and to him who is the true Mother of life and of all things. To the property of motherhood belong nature, love, wisdom and knowledge, and this is God. For though it may be so that our bodily bringing to birth is only little, humble and simple in comparison with our spiritual bringing to birth, still it is he who does it in the creatures by whom it is done. The kind, loving mother who knows and sees the need of her child guards it very tenderly, as the nature and condition of motherhood will have. And always as the child grows in age and in stature, she acts differently, but she does not change her love. And when it is even older, she allows it to be chastised to destroy its faults, so as to make the child receive virtues and grace. This work, with everything which is lovely and good, our Lord performs in those by whom it is done. So he is our Mother in nature by the operation of grace in the lower part, for love of the higher part. And he wants us to know it, for he wants to have all our love attached to him; and in this I saw that every debt which we owe by God's command to fatherhood and motherhood is fulfilled in truly loving God, which blessed love Christ works in us. And this was revealed in everything, and especially in the great bounteous words when he says: I am he whom you love.

From

THE SIXTY-THIRD CHAPTER

SO in our true Mother Jesus our life is founded in his own prescient wisdom from without beginning, with the great power of the Father and the supreme goodness of the Holy Spirit. And in accepting our nature he gave us life, and in his blessed dying on the Cross he bore us to endless life. And since that time, now and ever until the day of judgment, he feeds us and fosters us, just as the great supreme lovingness of motherhood wishes, and as the natural need of childhood asks. Fair and sweet is our heavenly Mother in the sight of our soul, precious and lovely are the children of grace in the sight of our heavenly Mother, with gentleness and meekness and all the lovely virtues which belong to children by nature. For the child does not naturally despair of the mother's love, the child does not naturally rely upon itself, naturally the child loves the mother and either of them the other.

These, and all others that resemble them, are such fair virtues, with which our heavenly Mother is served and pleased. And I understood no greater stature in this life than childhood, with its feebleness and lack of power and intelligence, until the time that our gracious Mother has brought us up into our Father's bliss. And there it will truly be made known to us what he means in the sweet words when he says: All will be well, and you will see it yourself, that every kind of thing will be well. And then will the bliss of our motherhood in Christ be to begin anew in the joys of our Father, God, which new beginning will last, newly beginning without end.

Isabella Whitney

fl. 1567 – 73

*I*sabella Whitney may be the first professional woman poet in England.
Very little is known about her except that, contrary to most expectations of
female poets of the Elizabethan age, she seems to have come from the middle
class and to have been a working woman. Clearly she lived in London about
which she wrote in some detail. On the whole her verse is easy and colloquial,
concerned with worldly rather than religious and philosophical matters, and it
quotes much from the classics as well as from the Bible. One form of poetry that
she especially favoured was the verse epistle, usually addressed to relatives such
as sisters or cousins. In the following example it is directed to the city of London
to form a last will and testament. (For a later use of the will and testament
poem, see Mary Leapor in this volume).

The following extract is taken from Betty Travitsky's The Paradise of Women:
Writings by Englishwomen of the Renaissance of *Greenwood Press, (Westfield,
Conn., 1981).*

The Aucthour . . . Maketh Her Wyll and Testament

T HE time is come I must departe,
   From thee ah famous Citie:
I never yet to rue my smart,
   did finde that thou hadst pitie.
Wherefore small cause ther is, that I
   should greeve from thee to go:
But many women foolyshly,
   lyke me and other moe
Doe such a fyxed fancy set,
   on those which least desarve,
That long it is ere wit we get,
   away from them to swarve,
But tyme with pittie oft wyl tel
   to those that wil her try:
Whether it best be more to mell
   or utterly defye.
And now hath time me put in mind,

of thy great cruelnes:
That never once a help wold finde,
to ease me in distres.
Thou never yet, woldst credit geve
to boord me for a yeare:
Nor with Apparell me releve
except thou payed weare.
No, no, thou never didst me good,
nor ever wilt I know:
Yet am I in no angry moode,
but wyll, or ere I goe
In perfect love and charytie,
my Testament here write:
And leave to thee such Treasurye,
as I in it recyte.
Now stand a side and geve me leave
to write my latest Wyll
And see that none you do deceave,
of that I leave them tyl.

From

The Maner of Her Wyll, & What She Left to London: And to All Those in it: At Her Departing

I WHOLE in body and in minde,
but very weake in Purse:
Do make, and write my Testament
for feare it wyll be wurse.
And fyrst I wholy doo commend,
my Soule and Body eke:
To God The Father and the Son,
so long as I can speake.
And after speach: my Soule to hym,
And Body to the Grave:
Tyll time that all shall rise agayne,
their Judgement for to have.

***

And now let mee dispose such things,
as I shal leave behinde:
That those which shall receave the same,
may know my wylling minde.

I first of all to London leave
because I there was bred:
Brave buildyngs rare, of Churches store,
and Pauls to the head.
Betweene the same: fayre streats there bee,
and people goodly store:
Because their keeping craveth cost,
I yet wil leave him more.
First for their foode, I Butchers leave,
that every day shall kyll:
By Thames you shal have Brewers store,
and Bakers at your wyll.
And such as orders doo observe,
and eat fish thrice a weeke:
I leave two Streets, full fraught therwith
they neede not farre to seeke.

***

For Women shall you Taylors have,
by Bow, the chiefest dwel:
In every Lane you some shall finde,
can doo indifferent well.
And for the men, few Streetes or Lanes,
but Bodymakers[1] bee:
And such as make the sweeping cloakes,
with Gardes beneth the knee.

***

Now when thy folke are fed and clad
with such as I have namde:
For daynty mouthes, and stomachs weake
some Junckets must be framde.
Wherfore I Poticaries[2] leave,
with Banquets[3] in their Shop:
Phisicians also for the sicke,
Diseases for to stop.

***

Yf they that keepe what I you leave,
aske Mony: when they sell it:
At Mint there is such store, it is
unpossible to tell it.

[1] Makers of clothes covering the body.
[2] Apothecaries or druggists.
[3] Sweetmeats.

***

Now for the people in thee left,
I have done as I may:
And that the poore, when I am gone,
have cause for me to pray.
I wyll to prisons portions leave,
what though but very small:
Yet that they may remember me,
occasion be it shall:

***

Now London have I (for thy sake)
within thee, and without:
As coms into my memory,
dispearsed round about
Such needfull thinges, as they should have
herre left now unto thee,
When I am gon, with conscience
let them dispearsed bee.
And though I nothing named have,
to bury mee withall:
Consider that above the ground,
annoyance bee I shall.

***

Rejoice in God that I am gon,
out of this vale so vile.
And that of ech thing, left such store,
as may your wants exile,
I make thee sole executor, because
I lov'de thee best.
And thee I put in trust, to geve
the goodes unto the rest.

***

And (though I am perswade) that I
shall never more thee see:
Yet to the last, I shal not cease
to wish much good to thee.
This xx, of October,
in ANNO DOMINI
A thousand: v hundred seventy three
as Alminacks descry.
Did write this Wyll with mine owne hand
and it to London gave:

In witnes of the standers by,
whose names yf you wyll have,
Paper, pen and Standish were:
at that same present by:
With Time, who promised to reveale,
so fast as she cold hye
The same: least of my nearer kyn,
for any thing should vary:
So finally I make an end
no longer can I tary.

Lady Mary Wroth

fl. 1586 – 1651 or 1653

L*ady Mary Wroth was the niece of two poets, Sir Philip Sidney and Mary, Countess of Pembroke, and daughter of another, Sir Robert Sidney (later second Earl of Leicester) in the service of Elizabeth I. Brought up at Penshurst, she spent much time at Elizabeth's court. In 1604 she married Sir Robert Wroth and over the next years was conspicuous in various entertainments at the extravagant court of James I, where she was complimented by many of the writers of the day, including Ben Jonson who dedicated* The Alchemist *to her. Her husband's finances declined and on his death in 1614 he left his young wife with considerable debts. In 1621 her single published work appeared, a romance called* The Countesse of Mountgomeries Urania, *concerning the experiences in love of Pamphilia and Amphilanthus; similar to her uncles's* Arcadia, *it was darker in its picture of faithless love and more scandalous in its possible mockery of several court personages. She was accused of libel and the work was withdrawn under this pressure. Lady Mary spent the rest of her life in a fairly retired way, no doubt helped by her many relatives.*

Besides Urania, *her work consists of poems, some of which were published with or in* Urania, *while some remained unpublished until G. F. Waller's* Pamphilia to Amphilanthus (Elizabethan and Renaissance Studies,

Salzburg Studies in English Literature, *64, 1977), from which the texts below
below are taken.*

From

Pamphilia to Amphilanthus

I: 1

WHEN night's blacke Mantle could most darknesse prove,
And sleepe (deaths Image) did my senses hyre,
From Knowledge of my selfe, then thoughts did move
Swifter then those, most switnesse neede require?
In sleepe, a Chariot drawne by wind'd Desire,
I saw; where sate bright *Venus* Queene of Love,
And at her feete her Sonne, still adding Fire
To burning hearts, which she did hold above,

But one heart flaming more then all the rest,
The Goddesse held, and put it to my breast,
Dear Sonne now shut, said she, thus must we winne;

He her obeyd, and martyr'd my poore heart.
I waking hop'd as dreames it would depart,
Yet since, O me, a Lover I have beene.

LINDAMIRA'S COMPLAINT

LEAVE me vaine Hope, too long thou hast possest
My mind, made subject to thy flattring skill,
While Aprill mornings did my pleasures fill,
But cloudy dayes soone changd me from that rest;

And weeping afternoones to me adrest,
My utter ruine framd by Fortunes will,
When knowledge said Hope did but breed, and kill,
Producing only shadowes at the best.

Yet Hope tis true, thy faults did faire appeare ,
And therefore loth to thinke thou counseldst me
Or wilfully thy errors would not see
But catch at Sunne moates which I held most deare

Till now alas with true felt losse I know,
Thy selfe a Bubble each faire face can blow.

XXX: 26

DEARE cherish this and with it my soules will,
Nor for it ran away doe it abuse:
Alas it left (poore me) your brest to choose
As the best shrine, where it would harbour still.

Then favour shew, and not unkindly kill
The heart which fled to you, but doe excuse
That which for better did the worse refuse;
And pleas'd Ile be, though heartlesse my life spill.

But if you will bee kinde and just indeed,
Send me your heart, which in mine's place shall feede
On faithfull love to your devotion bound,

There shall it see the sacrifices made
Of pure and spotlesse Love, which shall not fade,
While soule and body are together found.

XLVIII: 42

IF ever love had force in humane brest,
If ever he could move in pensive heart:
Or if that he such powre could but impart,
To breed those flames, whose heat brings ioyes unrest.

Then looke on me; I am to these adrest,
I am the soule that feeles the greatest smart:
I am that heartlesse Trunck of hearts depart;
And I that One, by love, and griefe opprest.

None ever felt the truth of loves great misse
Of eyes till I deprived was of blisse;
For had he seene, he must have pitty show'd.

I should not have beene made this Stage of woe,
Where sad Disasters haue their open show:
O no, more pitty he had sure bestow'd.

X: 9

BEE you all pleas'd, your pleasures grive not me;
Doe you delight? I envy not your ioy:
Haue you content? contentment with you be;
Hope you for blisse? hope still, and still enjoy.

Let sad misfortune, haplesse me destroy,
Leave crosses to rule me, and still rule free:
While all delights their contraries imploy,
To keepe good backe, and I but torments see.

Ioyes are bereau'd me, harmes doe only tarry,
Despaire takes place, disdaine hath got the hand:
Yet firme love holds my senses in such band;
As since despised, I with sorrow marry.

Then if with griefe I now must coupled bee,
Sorrow Ile wed; Despaire thus governes mee.

Margaret Cavendish, Duchess of Newcastle

1623 – 73

Margaret Cavendish, Duchess of Newcastle, was born into a wealthy country family and educated at home. After the Civil War broke out she went to serve the Queen in Oxford and followed her into exile in France where she met her future husband, the Duke of Newcastle, thirty years her senior. The couple continued in impecunious exile for the next fifteen years, and, after the Restoration, returned to England where they lived on his family estates. The marriage was happy and childless, the Duke encouraging his wife's literary and scientific interests, even when they led to a reputation for eccentricity. The Duchess was very conscious of being an anomaly as a woman writer, but *she saw literature as the only way for a woman, barred from war and politics, to gain fame. She wrote plays, poems, autobiographical fantasies, scientific and philosophical works and a biography of her husband.*

The following poems and 'To All Writing Ladies' are taken from her book Poems and Fancies; Written by the Right Honourable, the Lady Newcastle *London, 1653). 'A True Relation of My Birth, Breeding, and Life' is taken from* Nature's Pictures Drawn by Fancies Pencil *(London, 1656). 'The Description of A New World Called The Blazing World' is taken from* Experimental Philosophy *(London, 1668).*

A Dialogue between Melancholy, and Mirth

A s I sate *Musing*, by my selfe alone,
My *Thoughts* on severall things did work upon.
Some did large *Houses* build, and *Stately Towers*,
Making *Orchards, Gardens*, and fine *Bowers*:
And *some* in *Arts*, and *Sciences* delight,
Some wars in Contradiction, *Reasons* fight.
And some, as *Kings*, do governe, rule a *State*;
Some as *Republickes*, which all *Monarches* hate.
Others, as *Lawyers*, pleading at the *Bar*,
Some privie Counsellors, and *Judges* are.
Some Priests, which do preach *Peace*, and *Godly life*,
Others *Tumultuous* are, and full of *strife*.
Some are *debauch'd*, do *wench, swagger*, and *sweare*,
And some poore *Thoughts* do tremble out of feare.
Some jealous are, and all things do suspect,
Others so *Carelesse*, every thing neglect.
Some Nymphes, Shepheards, and *Shepheardesses*,
Some so *kind*, as one another kisses,
All *sorts* of *Lovers*, and their *Passions*,
Severall waies of *Court-ship*, and fine *Fashions*.
Some take *strong Townes*, and *Battels* win,
Few do loose, but all must yeild to him.
Some are *Heroick, Generous*, and *Free*,
And some so base, do crouch with *Flattery*.
Some dying are, and in the *Grave* halfe lye,
And some *Repenting*, which for *sorrow* cry.
The *Mind* oppres'd with *Griefe, Thoughts Mourners* bee,
All cloath'd in *Black*, no light of *Joy* can see.
Some with *Despaire* do rage, are almost mad,
And some so merry, nothing makes them sad.
And many more, which were too long to tell,
Thoughts severall bee, in severall places dwell.

At last came two, which were in various dresse,
One *Melancholy*, th' other did *Mirth* expresse.
Melancholy was all in *black Array*,
And *Mirth* was all in *Colours fresh*, and *gay*.
Mirth laughing came, running unto me, flung
Her fat white Armes, about my *Neck* she hung:
Imbrac'd, and kis'd me oft, and strok't my *Cheek*,
Telling me, *shee* would no other *Lover* seek.
I'le sing you *Songs*, and please you every day,
Invent new *Sports*, to pass the time away.
I'le keep your *Heart*, and guard it from that *Theefe*,
Dull Melancholy Care, or *sadder Griefe*:
And make your *Eyes* with *Mirth* to over-flow,
With *springing blood*, your *Cheekes* they *fat* shall grow.
Your *Legs* shall nimble be, your *Body* light,
And all your *Spirits*, like to *Birds* in flight.
Mirth shall digest your *Meat*, and make you strong,
Shall give you *Health*, and your short daies prolong.
Refuse me not, but take me to your *Wife*,
For *I* shall make you happy all your *Life*.
If you take *Melancholy*, shee'l make you *leane*,
Your *Cheekes* shall hollow grow, your *Jawes* all seen:
Your *Eyes* shall buried be within your *Head*,
And look as *Pale*, as if you were quite dead.
Shee'l make you start at every noise you heare,
And *Visions strange* shall in your *Eyes* appeare.
Your *Stomack* cold, and raw, digesting nought,
Your *Liver* dry, your *Heart* with sorrow fraught.
Your *shriveled Skin*, and *Cloudy Browes, blood thick*,
Your long *lank Sides*, and *back* to *Belly* stick.
Thus would it be, if you to her were wed,
But better far it were, that you were dead.
Her Voice is low, and gives a *hollow sound*,
Shee hates the *Light*, in *darknesse* onely found:
Or set with *blinking Lampes*, or *Tapers* small,
Which *various Shadowes* make against a *Wall*.
She loves nought else but *Noise*, which *discords* make,
As *croaking Frogs* which do dwell in the *Lake*.
The *Ravens hoarse*, and so the *Mandrakes* groane,
And *shreeking Owles*, which in *Night* flye alone.
The *Tolling Bell*, which for the *dead* rings out,
A *Mill*, where *rushing waters* run about.
The *roaring windes*, which shake the *Cedars* tall,
Plow up the *Seas*, and beat the *Rocks* withall.
Shee loves to walk in the *still Moon-shine Night*,
Where in a *thick dark Grove* she takes delight.

In *hollow Caves, Houses thatcht*, or lowly *Cell*,
Shee loves to live, and there alone to dwell.
Her *Eares* are stopt with *Thoughts*, her *Eyes purblind*,
For all *shee heares*, or *sees*, is in the *Mind*.
But in her *Mind, luxuriously shee* lives,
Imagination severall pleasures gives.
Then leave *her* to *her selfe*, alone to dwell,
Let you and *I* in *Mirth* and pleasure swell:
And drink long lusty *Draughts* from *Bacchus Boule*,
Untill our *Braines* on *vaporous Waves* do roule.
Lets joy our selves in *Amorous Delights*.
There's none so happy, as the *Carpet Knights*.[1]

Melancholy.

Melancholy with *sad*, and *sober Face*,
Complexion pale, but of a *comely grace*:
With *modest Countenance, soft speech* thus spake.
May *I* so happy be, your *Love* to take?
True, *I* am dull, yet by me you shall know
More of your selfe, so wiser you shall grow.
I search the *depth*, and *bottome* of *Man-kind*,
Open the *Eye* of *Ignorance* that's blind.
I travell far, and view the *World* about,
I walk with *Reasons Staff* to find *Truth* out,
I watchfull am, all *dangers* for to shun,
And do prepare 'gainst *Evils* that may come.
I hange not on *Inconstant Fortunes wheele*,
Nor yet with *unresolving doubts* do reele.
I shake not with the *Terrours* of vaine feares,
Nor is my *Mind* fill'd with *unusefull Cares*.
I do not spend my time like *Idle Mirth*,
Which onely *happy* is just at her *Birth*.
Which seldome lives for to be *old*,
But, if she doth, can no *affections* hold.
For in short time *shee* troublesome will grow,
Though at the first *shee* makes a *pretty shew*.
But yet *shee* makes a *noise*, and keepes a *rout*,
And with *dislike* most commonly goes out.
Mirth good for nothing is, like *Weeds* do grow,
Such *Plants* cause *madnesse, Reason* doth not know.
Her face with *Laughter* crumples on a heap,
Which plowes deep *Furroughes*, making *wrinckles* great.
Her Eyes do water, and her *Skin* turnes red,
Her mouth doth gape, *Teeth* bare, like one that's *dead*.

---

[1] Stay-at-home soldier who avoids practical work.

Her sides do stretch, as set upon the *Last*,
Her Stomack heaving up, as if *shee'd* cast.[2]
Her Veines do swell, *Joynts* seem to be unset;
Her Pores are open, streaming out a *sweat*.
She fulsome is, and gluts the *Senses* all;
Offers her selfe, and comes before a *Call*:
Seekes *Company* out, hates to be alone.
Unsent-for Guests Affronts are throwne upon.
Her house is built upon the *golden Sandes*;
Yet no *Foundation* hath, whereon it stands.
A Palace tis, where comes a great Resort,
It makes a noise, and gives a loud report.
Yet underneath the *Roofe, Disasters* lye,
Beates downe the *house*, and many kills thereby.
I dwell in *Groves* that gilt are with the *Sun*,
Sit on the *Bankes*, by which cleare waters run.
In *Summers* hot, downe in a *Shade I* lye;
My *Musick* is the *buzzing* of a *Fly*:
Which in the *Sunny Beames* do dance all day,
And harmlesly do passe their time away.
I walk in *Meadowes*, where growes fresh green *Grasse*,
Or *Feilds*, where *Corne* is high, in which *I* passe:
Walk up the *Hills*, where round *I Prospects* see;
Some *Brushy Woods*, and some all *Champians* bee.
Returning back, in the *fresh Pasture* go,
To heare the *bleating Sheep*, and *Cowes* to *lowe*.
They gently feed, no *Evill* think upon,
Have no designes to do another *wrong*.
In *Winter Cold*, when *nipping Frosts* come on,
Then do *I* live in a small *House* alone.
The *littlenesse* doth make it warm, being close,
No *Wind*, nor *Weather cold*, can there have force.
Although tis plaine, yet cleanly tis within,
Like to a *Soule* that's pure, and cleare from *Sin*.
And there *I* dwell in quiet, and still *Peace*,
Not fill'd with *Cares*, for *Riches* to increase.
I wish, nor seek for vaine, and fruitlesse *Pleasures*,
No *Riches* are, but what the *Mind* intreasures.
Thus am *I solitary*, and live alone,
Yet better lov'd, the more that *I* am knowne.
And though my *Face* b'ill favoured at first sight
After Acquaintance it shall give delight.
For *I* am like a *Shade*, who sits in me,
Shall not come *wet*, nor yet *Sun-burned* be.

[2] Vomit.

I keep off *blustring Stormes*, from doing hurt,
When *Mirth* is often smutch'd with *dust* and *durt*,
Refuse me not, for *I* shall constant be,
Maintaine your *Credit*, keep up *Dignity*.

The Claspe

GIVE *Mee* the *Free*, and *Noble Stile*,
Which seems *uncurb'd*, though it be *wild*:
Though *It* runs wild about, *It* cares not where;
It shewes more *Courage*, then *It* doth of *Feare*.
Give me a *Stile* that *Nature* frames, not *Art*:
For *Art* doth seem to take the *Pedants* part.
And that seemes *Noble*, which is *Easie, Free*,
Not to be bound with ore-nice *Pedantry*.

The Hunting of the Hare

BETWIXT two *Ridges* of *Plowd-land*, lay Wat,[3]
Pressing his *Body* close to *Earth* lay squat.
His *Nose* upon his two *Fore-feet* close lies,
Glaring obliquely with his *great gray Eyes*.
His *Head* he alwaies sets against the *Wind*;
If turne his *Taile*, his *Haires* blow up behind:
Which *he* too cold will grow, but *he* is wise,
And keepes his *Coat* still downe, so warm *he* lies.
Thus resting all the *day*, till *Sun* doth set,
Then riseth up, his *Reliefe* for to get.
Walking about untill the *Sun* doth rise,
Then back returnes, downe in his *Forme he* lyes.
At last, *Poore Wat* was found, as *he* there lay,
By *Hunts-men*, with their *Dogs* which came that way.
Seeing, gets up, and fast begins to run,
Hoping some waies the *Cruell Dogs* to shun.
But they by *Nature* have so quick a *Sent*,
That by their *Nose* they trace, what way *he* went.
And with their deep, wide *Mouths* set forth a *Cry*,
Which answer'd was by *Ecchoes* in the *Skie*.
Then *Wat* was struck with *Terrour*, and with *Feare*,
Thinkes every *Shadow* still the *Dogs* they were.

---

[3] A dialect word for 'hare'.

And running out some distance from the *noise*,
To hide himselfe, his *Thoughts* he new imploies.
Under a *Clod* of *Earth* in *Sand-pit* wide,
Poore *Wat* sat close, hoping himselfe to hide.
There long he had not sat, but strait his *Eares*
The *Winding Hornes*, and crying *Dogs* he heares:
Starting with *Feare*, up leapes, then doth he run,
And with such speed, the *Ground* scarce treades upon.
Into a great thick *Wood he* strait way gets,
Where underneath a *broken Bough he* sits.
At every *Leafe* that with the *wind* did shake,
Did bring such *terrour*, made his *Heart* to ake.
That *Place he* left, to *Champian Plaines he* went,
Winding about, for to deceive their *Sent*.
And while they *snuffling* were, to find his *Track,*
Poore *Wat*, being weary, his swift pace did slack.
On his two *hinder legs* for ease did sit,
His *Fore-feet* rub'd his *Face* from *Dust*, and *Sweat*.
Licking his *Feet, he* wip'd his *Eares* so cleane,
That none could tell that *Wat* had hunted been.
But casting round about his *faire great Eyes*,
The *Hounds* in full *Careere he* neere him 'spies:
To *Wat* it was so terrible a *Sight*,
Feare gave him *Wings*, and made his *Body* light.
Though weary was before, by running long,
Yet now his *Breath* he never felt more strong.
Like those that *dying* are, think *Health* returnes,
When tis but a *faint Blast*, which *Life* out burnes.
For *Spirits* seek to guard the *Heart* about,
Striving with *Death*, but *Death* doth quench them out.
Thus they so fast came on, with such loud *Cries*,
That *he* no hopes hath left, nor *help* espies.
With that the *Winds* did pity *poore Wats* case,
And with their *Breath* the *Sent* blew from the *Place*.
Then every *Nose* is busily imployed,
And every *Nostrill* is set open wide:
And every *Head* doth seek a severall way,
To find what *Grasse*, or *Track*, the *Sent* on lay.
Thus quick Industry, that is not slack,
Is like to Witchery, brings lost things back.
For though the *Wind* had tied the *Sent* up close,
A *Busie Dog* thrust in his *Snuffling Nose*:
And drew it out, with it did foremost run,
Then *Hornes* blew loud, for th' *rest* to follow on.
The *great slow-Hounds*, their throats did set a *Base*,
The *Fleet swift Hounds*, as *Tenours* next in place;

The little *Beagles* they a *Trebble* sing,
And through the *Aire* their *Voice* a round did ring?
Which made a *Consort*, as they ran along;
If they but *words* could speak, might sing a *Song*,
The *Horses* kept time, the *Hunters* shout for *Joy*,
And valiant seeme, *poore Wat* for to destroy:
Spurring their *Horses* to a full *Careere*,
Swim Rivers deep, leap Ditches without feare;
Indanger *Life*, and *Limbes*, so fast will ride,
Onely to see how patiently *Wat* died.
For why, the *Dogs* so neere his *Heeles* did get,
That they their sharp *Teeth* in his *Breech* did set.
Then tumbling downe, did fall with *weeping Eyes*,
Gives up his *Ghost*, and thus poore *Wat he* dies.
Men hooping loud, such *Acclamations* make,
As if the *Devill* they did *Prisoner* take.
When they do but a *shiftlesse Creature* kill;
To hunt, there needs no *Valiant Souldiers* skill.
But *Man* doth think that *Exercise*, and *Toile*,
To keep their *Health*, is best, which makes most spoile.
Thinking that *Food*, and *Nourishment* so good,
And *Appetite*, that feeds on *Flesh*, and *blood*,
When they do *Lions, Wolves, Beares, Tigers* see,
To kill poore *Sheep*, strait say, they cruell be.
But for themselves all *Creatures* think too few,
For *Luxury* wish *God* would make them new.
As if that *God* made *Creatures* for *Mans meat*,
To give them *Life*, and *Sense*, for *Man* to eat;
Or else for *Sport*, or *Recreations* sake,
Destroy those *Lifes* that *God* saw good to make:
Making their *Stomacks, Graves*, which full they fill
With *Murther'd Bodies*, that in sport they kill.
Yet *Man* doth think himselfe so gentle, mild,
When *he* of *Creatures* is most cruell wild.
And is so *Proud*, thinks onely he shall live,
That *God* a *God*-like *Nature* did him give.
And that all *Creatures* for his sake alone,
Was made for him, to *Tyrannize* upon.

Nature's Cook

DEATH is the *Cook* of *Nature*; and we find
Meat drest severall waies to please her *Mind*.
Some *Meates shee* rosts with *Feavers, burning hot*,

And some *shee* boiles with *Dropsies* in a *Pot*.
Some for *Gelly* consuming by degrees,
And some with *Ulcers*, Gravie out to squeese.
Some *Flesh* as *Sage she* stuffs with *Gouts*, and *Paines*,
Others for tender *Meat* hangs up in *Chaines*.
Some in the *Sea she pickles* up to keep,
Others, as *Brawne* is sous'd, those in *Wine steep*.
Some with the *Pox*, chops *Flesh*, and *Bones* so small,
Of which *She* makes a *French Fricasse* withall.
Some on *Gridirons* of *Calenture*[4] is broyl'd
And some is trodden on, and so quite spoyl'd.
But those are *bak'd*, when smother'd they do dye,
By *Hectick Feavers* some *Meat* She doth *fry*.
In *Sweat* sometimes *she stues* with *savoury smell*,
A *Hodge-Podge* of *Diseases* tasteth well.
Braines drest with *Apoplexy* to *Natures* wish,
Or swimmes with *Sauce* of *Megrimes* in a *Dish*.
And *Tongues* she dries with *Smoak* from *Stomack's* ill,
Which as the second *Course* she sends up still.
Then *Death* cuts *Throats*, for *Blood-puddings* to make,
And puts them in the *Guts*, which *Collicks* rack.
Some hunted are by *Death*, for *Deere* that's red,
Or *Stal-fed Oxen*, knocked on the *Head*.
Some for *Bacon* by *Death* are *Sing'd*, or *scal'd*,
Then powdered up with *Flegme*, and *Rhume* that's salt.

To All Writing Ladies

I T is to be observed, that there is a secret working by Nature, as to cast an influence upon the mindes of men: like as in Contagions, when as the Aire is corrupted, it produces severall Diseases; so severall distempers of the minde, by the inflammations of the spirits. And as in healthfull Ages, bodies are purified, so wits are refined; yet it seemes to me as if there were severall invisible spirits, that have severall, but visible powers, to worke in severall Ages upon the mindes of men. For in many Ages men will be affected, and dis-affected alike: as in some Ages so strongly, and superstitiously devout, that they make many gods: and in another Age so Atheisticall, as they beleeve in no God at all, and live to those Principles. Some Ages againe have such strong faiths, that they will not only dye in their severall Opinions, but they will Massacre, and cut one anothers throats,

---

[4] Delirious tropical disease.

because their opinions are different. In some Ages all men seek absolute power, and every man would be Emperour of the World; which makes Civil Wars: for their ambition makes them restlesse, and their restlessnesse makes them seek change. Then in another Age all live peaceable, and so obedient, that the very Governours rule with obedient power. In some Ages againe, all run after Imitation, like a company of Apes, as to imitate such a Poet, to be of such a Philosophers opinion. Some Ages mixt, as Moralists, Poets, Philosophers, and the like: and in some Ages agen, all affect singularity; and they are thought the wisest, that can have the most extravagant opinions. In some Ages Learning flourisheth in Arts, and Sciences; other Ages so dull, as they loose what former Ages had taught. And in some Ages it seemes as if there were a Common-wealth of those governing spirits, where most rule at one time. Some Ages, as in Aristocracy, when some part did rule; and other Ages a pure Monarchy, when but one rules; and in some Ages, it seemes as if all those spirits were at defiance, who should have most power, which makes them in confusion, and War; so confused are some Ages, and it seemes as if there were spirits of the Fæminine Gender, as also the Masculine. There will be many Heroick Women in some Ages, in others very Propheticall; in some Ages very pious, and devout: For our Sex is wonderfully addicted to the spirits. But this Age hath produced many effeminate Writers, as well as Preachers, and many effeminate Rulers, as well as Actors. And if it be an Age when the effeminate spirits rule, as most visible they doe in every Kingdome, let us take the advantage, and make the best of our time, for feare their reigne should not last long; whether it be in the Amazonian Government, or in the Politick Common-wealth, or in flourishing Monarchy, or in Schooles of Divinity, or in Lectures of Philosophy, or in witty Poetry, or any thing that may bring honour to our Sex: for they are poore, dejected spirits, that are not ambitious of Fame. And though we be inferiour to Men, let us shew our selves a degree above Beasts; and not eate, and drink, and sleep away our time as they doe; and live only to the sense, not to the reason; and so turne into forgotten dust. But let us strive to build us Tombs while we live, of Noble, Honourable, and good Actions, at least harmlesse;

> That though our Bodies dye,
> Our Names may live to after memory.

From

A True Relation of My Birth, Breeding, and Life

...As for my humour, I was from my childhood given to contemplation, being more taken or delighted with thoughts than in conversation with a society, insomuch as I would walk two or three hours, and never rest, in a musing, considering, contemplating manner, reasoning with myself of everything my senses did present. But when I was in the company of my natural friends, I was very attentive of what they said or did; but for strangers I regarded not much what they said, but many times I did observe their actions, whereupon my reason as judge, and my thoughts as accusers, or excusers, or approvers and commenders, did plead, or appeal to accuse, or complain thereto. Also I never took delight in closets, or cabinets of toys, but in the variety of fine clothes, and such toys as only were to adorn my person. Likewise I had a natural stupidity towards the learning of any other language than my native tongue, for I could sooner and with more facility understand the sense, than remember the words, and for want of such memory makes me so unlearned in foreign languages as I am. As for my practice, I was never very active, by reason I was given so much to contemplation; besides my brothers and sisters were for the most part serious and staid in their actions, not given to sport or play, nor dance about, whose company I keeping, made me so too. But I observed, that although their actions were staid, yet they would be very merry amongst themselves, delighting in each other's company: also they would in their discourse express the general actions of the world, judging, condemning, approving, commending, as they thought good, and with those that were innocently harmless, they would make themselves merry therewith. As for my study of books it was little, yet I chose rather to read, than to employ my time in any other work, or practice, and when I read what I understood not, I would ask my brother, the Lord Lucas, he being learned, the sense or meaning thereof. But my serious study could not be much, by reason I took great delight in attiring, fine dressing, and fashions especially such fashions as I did invent myself, not taking that pleasure in such fashions as was invented by others. Also I did dislike any should follow my fashions, for I always took delight in a singularity, even in accoutrements of habits. But whatsoever I was addicted to, either in fashion of clothes, contemplation of thoughts, actions of life, they were lawful, honest, honourable, and modest, of which I can avouch to the world with a great confidence, because it is a pure truth. As for my disposition, it is more inclining to be melancholy than merry, but not crabbed or peevishly melancholy, but soft, melting, solitary, and contemplating melancholy. And I am apt to weep rather than laugh, not that I do often either of them. Also I am tender natured, for it troubles my conscience to kill a fly, and the groans of a dying beast strike my soul. Also where I place a particular affection, I love extraordinarily and constantly, yet not fondly, but soberly and observingly, not to hang about them as a trouble, but to wait upon them as a servant; but this affection will take no root, but where I think or find merit, and have leave both from divine and moral laws. Yet I find this passion too troublesome, as it is the only torment of my life, for fear any evil misfortune or accident, or sickness, or death, should come unto them, insomuch as I am never freely at rest. Likewise I am grateful, for I never received a courtesy—but I am impatient and troubled until I can return it. Also I am chaste, both by nature, and education, insomuch as I do abhor an unchaste thought. Likewise, I am seldom angry, as my servants may witness for me, for I rather choose to suffer some inconveniences than disturb my thoughts, which makes me wink many times at their faults; but when I am angry, I am very angry, but yet it is soon over, and I am easily pacified, if it be not such an injury as may create a hate. Neither am I apt to be exceptious or jealous, but if I have the least symptom of this passion, I declare it to those it concerns, for I never let it lie smothering in my breast to breed a malignant disease in the mind, which might break out into extravagant passions, or railing speeches, or indiscreet actions; but I examine moderately, reason soberly, and plead gently in my own behalf, through a desire to keep those affections I had, or at least thought to have. And truly I am so vain, as to be so self-conceited, or so naturally partial, to think my friends have as much reason to love me as another, since none can love more sincerely than I, and it were an injustice to prefer a fainter affection, or to esteem the body more than the mind. Likewise I am neither spiteful, envious, nor malicious. I repine not at the gifts that Nature or Fortune bestows upon others, yet I am a great emulator; for, though I wish none worse than they are, yet it is lawful for me to wish myself the best, and to do my honest endeavour thereunto. For I think it no crime to wish myself the exactest of Nature's works, my thread of life the longest, my chain of destiny the strongest, my mind the peaceablest, my life the pleasantest, my death the easiest, and the greatest saint in heaven; also to do my endeavour, so far as honour and honesty doth allow of, to be the highest on Fortune's wheel and to hold the wheel from turning, if I can. And if it be commendable to wish another's good, it were a sin not to wish my own; for as envy is a vice, so emulation is a virtue, but emulation is in the way to ambition, or indeed it is a noble ambition. But I fear my ambition inclines to vain-glory, for I am very ambitious; yet 'tis neither for beauty, wit, titles, wealth, or power, but as they are steps to raise me to Fame's tower, which is to live by remembrance in after-ages. Likewise I am that the vulgar call proud, not out of self-conceit, or to slight or condemn any, but scorning to do a base or mean act, and disdaining rude or unworthy persons; insomuch, that if I should find any that were rude, or too bold, I should be apt to be so passionate, as to affront them, if I can, unless discretion should get betwixt my passion and their boldness, which sometimes perchance it might if discretion should crowd hard for place. For though I am naturally bashful, yet in such a cause my spirits would be all on fire. Otherwise I am so well bred, as to be civil to all persons, of all degrees, or qualities. Likewise I am so proud, or rather just to my Lord, as to abate nothing of the quality of his wife, for if honour be the mark of merit, and his master's royal favour, who will favour none but those that have merit to deserve, it were a baseness for me to neglect the ceremony thereof. Also in some cases I am naturally a coward, and in other cases very valiant. As for example, if any of my nearest friends were in danger I should never consider my life in striving to help them though I were sure to do them no good, and would willingly, nay cheerfully, resign my life for their sakes: likewise I should not spare my life, if honour bids me die. But in a danger where my friends, or my honour is not concerned, or engaged, but only my life to be unprofitably lost, I am the veriest coward in nature, as upon the sea, or any dangerous places, or of thieves, or fire, or the like. Nay the shooting of a gun, although but a pot-gun will make me start, and stop my hearing, much less have I courage to discharge one; or if a sword should be held against me, although but in jest, I am afraid. Also as I am not covetous, so I am not prodigal, but of the two I am inclining to be prodigal, yet I cannot say to a vain prodigality, because I imagine it is to a profitable end; for perceiving the world is given, or apt to honour the outside more than the inside, worshipping show more than substance; and I am so vain (if it be a vanity) as to endeavour to be worshipped, rather than not to be regarded. Yet I shall never be so prodigal as to impoverish my friends, or go beyond the limits or facility of our estate. And though I desire to appear to the best advantage, whilst I live in the view of the public world, yet I could most willingly exclude myself, so as never to see the face of any creature but my Lord as long as I live, inclosing myself like an anchorite, wearing a frieze gown, tied with a cord about my waist. But I hope my readers will not think me vain for writing my life, since there have been many that have done the like, as Caesar, Ovid, and many more, both men and women, and I know no reason I may not do it as well as they: but I verily believe some censuring readers will scornfully say, why hath this Lady writ her own life? since none cares to know whose daughter she was or whose wife she is, or how she was bred, or what fortunes she had, or how she lived, or what humour or disposition she was of. I answer that it is true, that 'tis to no purpose to the readers, but it is to the authoress, because I write it for my own sake, not theirs. Neither did I intend this piece for to delight, but to divulge; not to please the fancy, but to tell the truth, lest after-ages should mistake, in not knowing I was daughter to one Master Lucas of St. Johns, near Colchester, in Essex, second wife to the Lord Marquis of Newcastle; for my Lord having had two wives; I might easily have been mistaken, especially if I should die and my Lord marry again.

The Description of a New World Called
The Blazing-World

[IN this fantasy the Duchess of Newcastle describes herself visiting the Empress of the Blazing World]

...WELL, said the Duchess, setting aside this dispute, my ambition is, that I would fain be as you are, that is, an Emperess of a World, and I shall never be at quiet until I be one. I love you so well, replied the Emperess, that I wish with all my soul, you had the fruition of your ambitious desire, and I shall not fail to give you my best advice how to accomplish it; the best informers are the Immaterial Spirits, and they'l soon tell you, whether it be possible to obtain your wish. But, said the Duchess, I have little acquaintance with them, for I never knew any before the time you sent for me. They know you, replied the Emperess; for they told me of you, and were the means and instrument of your coming hither: Wherefore I'le confer with them, and enquire whether there be not another World, whereof you may be Emperess as well as I am of this? No sooner had the Emperess said this, but some Immaterial Spirits came to visit her, of whom she inquired, whether there were but three Worlds in all, to wit, the Blazing-world where she was in, the World which she came from, and the World where the Duchess lived? The Spirits answered, That there were more numerous Worlds then the Stars which appeared in these three mentioned Worlds. Then the Emperess asked, whether it was not possible, that her dearest friend the Duchess of *Newcastle*, might be Emperess of one of them. Although there be numerous, nay, infinite Worlds, answered the Spirits, yet none is without Government. But is none of these Worlds so weak, said she, that it may be surprised or conquered. The Spirits answered, *That Lucian's* World of Lights,[5] had been for some time in a snuff, but of late years one *Helmont*[6] had got it, who since he was Emperour of it, had so strengthened the Immortal parts thereof with mortal out-works, as it was for the present impregnable. Said the Emperess, If there be such an Infinite number of Worlds, I am sure, not onely my friend, the Duchess, but any other might obtain one. Yes, answered the Spirits, if those Worlds were uninhabited; but they are as populous as this, your Majesty governs. Why, said the Emperess, it is not impossible to conquer a World. No, answered the Spirits, but, for the most part, Conquerers seldom enjoy their conquest, for they being more feared then loved, most commonly come to an untimely end. If you will but direct me, said the Duchess to the Spirits, which World is easiest to be conquered, her Majesty will assist me with means, and I will trust to Fate and Fortune; for I had rather die in the adventure of noble atchievements, then live in obscure and sluggish security; since by the one, I may live in a glorious Fame, and by the other I am buried in oblivion. The Spirits answered, That the lives of Fame were like other lives; for some lasted long, and some died soon. 'Tis true, said the Duchess; but yet the shortest-lived Fame lasts longer then the longest life of Man. But, replied the Spirits, if occasion does not serve you, you must content your self to live without such atchievements that may gain you a Fame: But we wonder, proceeded the Spirits, that you desire to be Emperess of a Terrestrial World, when as you can create your self a Celestial World if you please. What, said the Emperess, can any Mortal be a Creator? Yes, answered the Spirits; for every humane Creature can create an Immaterial World fully inhabited by immaterial Creatures, and populous of immaterial subjects, such as we are, and all this within the compass of the head or scull; nay, not onely so, but he may create a World of what fashion and Government he will, and give the Creatures thereof such

---

[5] A reference to the fantastical romance of the classical author Lucian who described a place called Lamptown where all the inhabitants were lamps and who gave a fabulous account of the moon as a country of lights.
[6] Johan van Helmont c1577–1644, Belgian chemist and mystic.

motions, figures, forms, colours, perceptions, etc. as he pleases, and make Whirl-pools, Lights, Pressures and Reactions, etc. as he thinks best; nay, he may make a World full of Veins, Muscles, and Nerves, and all these to move by one jolt or stroke: also he may alter that world as often as he pleases, or change it from a natural world, to an artificial; he may make a world of Ideas, a world of Atomes, a world of Lights, or whatsoever his fancy leads him to. And since it is in your power to create such a world, What need you to venture life, reputation and tranquility, to conquer a gross material world? For you can enjoy no more of a material world then a particular Creature is able to enjoy, which is but a small part, considering the compass of such a world; and you may plainly observe it by your friend the Emperess here, which although she possesses a whole world, yet enjoys she but a part thereof; neither is she so much acquainted with it, that she knows all the places, Countries and Dominions she Governs. The truth is, a Soveraign Monarch has the general trouble; but the Subjects enjoy all the delights and pleasures in parts; for it is impossible, that a Kingdom, nay, a County should be injoyed by one person at once, except he take the pains to travel into every part, and endure the inconveniencies of going from one place to another; wherefore, since glory, delight and pleasure lives but in other mens opinions, and can neither add tranquility to your mind, nor give ease to your body, why should you desire to be Emperess of a material world, and be troubled with the cares that attend Government? when as by creating a world within your self, you may enjoy all both in whole and in parts, without controle or opposition, and may make what world you please, and alter it when you please, and enjoy as much pleasure and delight as a world can afford you? You have converted me, said the Duchess to the Spirits, from my ambitious desire; wherefore I'le take your advice, reject and despise all the worlds without me, and create a world of my own. The Emperess said, If I do make such a world, then I shall be Mistress of two worlds, one within, and the other without me. That your Majesty may, said the Spirits; and so left these two Ladies to create two worlds within themselves: who did also part from each other, until such time as they had brought their worlds to perfection. . . .

***

. . . , when The Emperess's and Duchess's Soul were travelling into *Nottingham-shire*, for that was the place where the Duke did reside; passing through the forrest of *Sherewood*, the Emperess's soul was very much delighted with it, as being a dry, plain and woody place, very pleasant to travel in both in Winter and Summer; for it is neither much dirty, not dusty at no time: at last they arrived at *Welbeck*, a House where the Duke dwell'd, surrounded all with Wood, so close and full, that the Emperess took great pleasure and delight therein, and told the Duchess she never had observed more wood in so little a compass in any part of the Kingdom she had passed through; The truth is, said she, there seems to be more wood on the Seas, she meaning the Ships, then on the Land. The Duchess told her, the reason was, that there had been a long Civil War in that Kingdom, in which most of the best Timber-trees and

Principal Palaces were ruined and destroyed; and my dear Lord and Husband, said she, has lost by it half his Woods, besides many Houses, Land, and moveable Goods; so that all the loss out of his particular Estate, did amount to above half a Million of Pounds. I wish, said the Emperess, he had some of the Gold that is in the Blazing world, to repair his losses. The Duchess most humbly thank'd her Imperial Majesty for her kind wishes; but, said she, wishes will not repair his ruines: however, God has given my Noble Lord and Husband great Patience, by which he bears all his losses and misfortunes. At last, they enter'd into the Dukes House, an habitation not so magnificent, as useful; and when the Emperess saw it, Has the Duke, said she, no other house but this? Yes, answered the Duchess, some five miles from this place, he has a very fine Castle, called *Bolesover*. That place then, said the Emperess, I desire to see. Alas! replied the Duchess, it is but a naked house, and uncloath'd of all Furniture. However, said the Emperess, I may see the manner of its structure and building. That you may, replied the Duchess: and as they were thus discoursing, the Duke came out of the House into the Court, to see his Horses of mannage; whom when the Duchess's soul perceived, she was so overjoyed, that her aereal Vehicle became so splendorous, as if it had been enlightned by the Sun; by which we may perceive, that the passions of Souls or Spirits can alter their bodily Vehicles. Then these two Ladies Spirits went close to him, but he could not perceive them; and after the Emperess had observed the Art of Mannage, she was much pleased with it, and commended it as a noble pastime, and an exercise fit and proper for noble and heroick Persons: But when the Duke was gone into the house again, those two Souls followed him; where the Emperess observing, that he went to the exercise of the Sword, and was such an excellent and unparallell'd Master thereof, she was as much pleased with that exercise, as she was with the former: But the Duchess's soul being troubled, that her dear Lord and Husband used such a violent exercise before meat, for fear of overheating himself, without any consideration of the Emperess's soul, left her aereal Vehicle, and entered into her Lord. The Emperess's soul perceiving this, did the like: And then the Duke had three Souls in one Body; and had there been but some such Souls more, the Duke would have been like the Grand-Signior in his Seraglio, onely it would have been a Platonick Seraglio. But the Dukes soul being wise, honest, witty, complaisant and noble, afforded such delight and pleasure to the Emperess's soul by her conversation, that these two souls became enamoured of each other; which the Duchess's soul perceiving, grew jealous at first, but then considering that no Adultery could be committed amongst Platonick Lovers, and that Platonism was Divine, as being derived from Divine *Plato*, cast forth of her mind that Idea of Jealousie. Then the Conversation of these three souls was so pleasant, that it cannot be expressed; for the Dukes soul entertained the Emperesses soul with Scenes, Songs, Musick, witty Discourses, pleasant Recreations, and all kinds of harmless sports; so that the time passed away faster then they expected.

Aphra Behn

1640 – 89

A phra Behn was probably the daughter of a Kentish yeoman. She travelled to Surinam in her early twenties and later in London married a tradesman who seems to have died shortly afterwards. After a brief period as a spy in Antwerp for the English government she earned her living as a playwright, poet, novelist and translator, so becoming the first known professional woman writer in England. Over the next years many of her plays were produced, the most successful ones being in the witty bawdy style that characterized the theatre of Charles II's reign. Fiercely royalist, she used such works as The Rover (1677) to express her loyalty to the Stuart kings as well as to reveal her delight in sexual vitality and in the Restoration figure of the rake. Behn was famous in her day but, as the bourgeois morality stressing femininity grew in strength, her reputation declined and by the mid-eighteenth century she had become the antithesis of what a modest lady writer should be.

The following reprint of The Rover is taken from Frederick M. Link's edition (Edward Arnold, London, 1967).

The Rover

or

The Banished Cavaliers[1]

PROLOGUE

WITS, like physicians, never can agree,
When of a different society.
And Rabel's drops[2] were never more cried down

---

[1] The play is set during the Commonwealth period before the restoration of Charles II in 1660. Royalists or cavaliers had joined Charles in exile.
[2] A patent medicine.

By all the learned doctors of the town,
Than a new play whose author is unknown.
Nor can those doctors with more malice sue
(And powerful purses) the dissenting few,
Than those, with an insulting pride, do rail
At all who are not of their own cabal.
   If a young poet hit your humor right,
You judge him then out of revenge and spite.
So amongst men there are ridiculous elves,
Who monkeys hate for being too like themselves.
So that the reason of the grand debate
Why wit so oft is damned when good plays take,
Is that you censure as you love, or hate.
   Thus like a learned conclave poets sit,
Catholic judges both of sense and wit,
And damn or save as they themselves think fit.
Yet those who to others' faults are so severe,
Are not so perfect but themselves may err,
Some write correct, indeed, but then the whole
(Bating[3] their own dull stuff i'th'' play) is stole:
As bees do suck from flowers their honeydew,
So they rob others striving to please you.
   Some write their characters genteel and fine,
But then they do so toil for every line,
That what to you does easy seem, and plain,
Is the hard issue of their laboring brain.
And some th'effects of all their pains, we see,
Is but to mimic good extempore.
Others, by long converse about the town,
Have wit enough to write a lewd lampoon,
But their chief skill lies in a bawdy song.
In short, the only wit that's now in fashion,
Is but the gleanings of good conversation.
As for the author of this coming play,
I asked him what he thought fit I should say
In thanks for your good company today:
He called me fool, and said it was well known
You came not here for our sakes, but your own.
New plays are stuffed with wits, and with deboches,[4]
That crowd and sweat like cits[5] in May-Day coaches.
                    WRITTEN BY A PERSON OF QUALITY

[3] Excepting.
[4] Debauches.
[5] Middle-class citizens

THE ACTORS' NAMES

[Men]

DON ANTONIO, the Viceroy's son
DON PEDRO, a noble Spaniard, his friend
BELVILE, an English colonel in love with Florinda
WILLMORE, the Rover
FREDERICK, an English gentleman, and
   friend to Belvile and Blunt
BLUNT, an English country gentleman
STEPHANO, servant to Don Pedro
PHILIPPO, Lucetta's gallant
SANCHO, pimp to Lucetta
BISKEY *and* SEBASTIAN, two bravos to Angellica
OFFICER *and* SOLDIERS
[DIEGO,] Page to Don Antonio

[Women]

FLORINDA, sister to Don Pedro
HELLENA, a gay young woman designed for
   a nun, and sister to Florinda
VALERIA, a kinswoman to Florinda
ANGELLICA BIANCA, a famous courtesan
MORETTA, her woman
CALLIS, governess to Florinda and Hellena
LUCETTA, a jilting wench

SERVANTS, OTHER MASQUERADERS, MEN AND WOMEN
The scene: *Naples, in Carnival time*

ACT I

[I.i]   *A CHAMBER.*

Enter Florinda *and* Hellena.

FLORINDA.

What an impertinent thing is a young girl bred in a nunnery! How full
of questions! Prithee no more, Hellena; I have told thee more than thou
understand'st already.

HELLENA.

The more's my grief. I would fain know as much as you, which makes me so inquisitive; nor is't enough I know you're a lover, unless you tell me too who 'tis you sigh for.

FLORINDA.

When you're a lover I'll think you fit for a secret of that nature.

HELLENA.

'Tis true, I never was a lover yet, but I begin to have a shrewd guess what 'tis to be so, and fancy it very pretty to sigh, and sing, and blush, and wish, and dream and wish, and long and wish to see the man, and when I do, look pale and tremble, just as you did when my brother brought home the fine English colonel to see you. What do you call him? Don Belvile?

FLORINDA.

Fie, Hellena.

HELLENA.

That blush betrays you. I am sure 'tis so. Or is it Don Antonio the Viceroy's son? Or perhaps the rich old Don Vincentio, whom my father designs you for a husband? Why do you blush again?

FLORINDA.

With indignation; and how near soever my father thinks I am to marrying that hated object, I shall let him see I understand better what's due to my beauty, birth, and fortune, and more to my soul, than to obey those unjust commands.

HELLENA.

Now hang me, if I don't love thee for that dear disobedience. I love mischief strangely, as most of our sex do who are come to love nothing else. But tell me, dear Florinda, don't you love that fine *Anglese*? For I vow, next to loving him myself, 'twill please me most that you do so, for he is so gay and so handsome.

FLORINDA.

Hellena, a maid designed for a nun ought not to be so curious in a discourse of love.

HELLENA.

And dost thou think that ever I'll be a nun? Or at least till I'm so old I'm fit for nothing else? Faith no, sister; and that which makes me long to know whether you love Belvile, is because I hope he has some mad companion or other that will spoil my devotion. Nay, I'm resolved to provide myself this Carnival, if there be e'er a handsome proper fellow of my humor above ground, though I ask first.

FLORINDA.

Prithee be not so wild.

HELLENA.

Now you have provided yourself of a man you take no care of poor me. Prithee tell me, what dost thou see about me that is unfit for love? Have I not a world of youth? A humor gay? A beauty passable? A vigor desirable? Well shaped? Clean limbed? Sweet breathed? And sense enough to know how all these ought to be employed to the best advantage? Yes, I do and will; therefore lay aside your hopes of my fortune by my being a devote,[6] and tell me how you came acquainted with this Belvile. For I perceive you knew him before he came to Naples.

FLORINDA.

Yes, I knew him at the siege of Pamplona; he was then a colonel of French horse, who when the town was ransacked, nobly treated my brother and myself, preserving us from all insolences. And I must own, besides great obligations, I have I know not what that pleads kindly for him about my heart, and will suffer no other to enter. But see, my brother.

Enter Don Pedro, Stephano *with a masking habit,[7] and* Callis.

PEDRO.

Good morrow, sister. Pray when saw you your lover Don Vincentio?

FLORINDA.

I know not, sir. Callis, when was he here? For I consider it so little I know not when it was.

PEDRO.

I have a command from my father here to tell you you ought not to despise him, a man of so vast a fortune, and such a passion for you.—Stephano, my things.

Puts on his masking habi.

---

[6] A nun.
[7] Masquerade costume.

FLORINDA.

A passion for me? 'Tis more than e'er I saw, or he had a desire should be known. I hate Vincentio, sir, and I would not have a man so dear to me as my brother follow the ill customs of our country and make a slave of his sister. And, sir, my father's will I'm sure you may divert.

PEDRO.

I know not how dear I am to you, but I wish only to be ranked in your esteem equal with the English colonel Belvile. Why do you frown and blush? Is there any guilt belongs to the name of that cavalier?

FLORINDA.

I'll not deny I value Belvile. When I was exposed to such dangers as the licenced lust of common soldiers threatened when rage and conquest flew through the city, then Belvile, this criminal for my sake, threw himself into all dangers to save my honor. And will you not allow him my esteem?

PEDRO.

Yes, pay him what you will in honor, but you must consider Don Vincentio's fortune, and the jointure[8] he'll make you.

FLORINDA.

Let him consider my youth, beauty, and fortune, which ought not to be thrown away on his age and jointure.

PEDRO.

'Tis true, he's not so young and fine a gentleman as that Belvile. But what jewels will that cavalier present you with? Those of his eyes and heart?

HELLENA.

And are not those better than any Don Vincentio has brought from the Indies?

PEDRO.

Why, how now! Has your nunnery breeding taught you to understand the value of hearts and eyes?

HELLENA.

Better than to believe Vincentio's deserve value from any woman. He may perhaps increase her bags, but not her family.

---

[8] Income and estate intended for a woman in her widowhood.

PEDRO.

This is fine! Go! Up to your devotion! You are not designed for the conversation of lovers.

HELLENA (*aside*).

Nor saints yet a while, I hope.—Is't not enough you make a nun of me, but you must cast my sister away too, exposing her to a worse confinement than a religious life?

PEDRO.

The girl's mad! It is a confinement to be carried into the country to an ancient villa belonging to the family of the Vincentios these five hundred years, and have no other prospect than that pleasing one of seeing all her own that meets her eyes: a fine air, large fields, and gardens where she may walk and gather flowers?

HELLENA.

When, by moonlight? For I am sure she dares not encounter with the heat of the sun; that were a task only for Don Vincentio and his Indian breeding, who loves it in the dog days.[9] And if these be her daily divertissements, what are those of the night? To lie in a wide moth-eaten bedchamber with furniture in fashion in the reign of King Sancho the First; the bed, that which his forefathers lived and died in.

PEDRO.

Very well.

HELLENA.

This apartment, new furbrushed and fitted out for the young wife, he out of freedom makes his dressing room; and being a frugal and a jealous coxcomb, instead of a valet to uncase his feeble carcass, he desires you to do that office. Signs of favor, I'll assure you, and such as you must not hope for unless your woman be out of the way.

PEDRO.

Have you done yet?

HELLENA.

That honor being past, the giant stretches itself, yawns and sighs a belch or two loud as a musket, throws himself into bed, and expects you in his foul sheets; and ere you can get yourself undressed, calls you with a snore or two. And are not these fine blessings to a young lady?

9 Sultry part of summer when the dog-star was rising.

PEDRO.

Have you done yet?

HELLENA.

And this man you must kiss, nay you must kiss none but him too, and nuzzle through his beard to find his lips. And this you must submit to for threescore years, and all for a jointure.

PEDRO.

For all your character of Don Vincentio, she is as like to marry him as she was before.

HELLENA.

Marry Don Vincentio! Hang me, such a wedlock would be worse than adultery with another man. I had rather see her in the *Hostel de Dieu*,[10] to waste her youth there in vows, and be a handmaid to lazars[11] and cripples, than to lose it in such a marriage.

PEDRO.

You have considered, sister, that Belvile has no fortune to bring you to; banished his country, despised at home, and pitied abroad.

HELLENA.

What then? The Viceroy's son is better than that old Sir Fifty. Don Vincentio! Don Indian! He thinks he's trading to Gambo still, and would barter himself—that bell and bauble—for your youth and fortune.

PEDRO.

Callis, take her hence and lock her up all this Carnival, and at Lent she shall begin her everlasting penance in a monastery.

HELLENA.

I care not; I had rather be a nun than be obliged to marry as you would have me if I were designed for't.

PEDRO.

Do not fear the blessing of that choice. You shall be a nun.

HELLENA (*aside*).

Shall I so? You may chance to be mistaken in my way of devotion. A nun! Yes, I am like to make a fine nun! I have an excellent humor for

---

[10] Hospital run by a religious order.
[11] Paupers with diseases, especially leprosy.

a grate![12] No, I'll have a saint of my own to pray to shortly, if I like any that dares venture on me.

PEDRO.

Callis, make it your business to watch this wildcat.—As for you, Florinda, I've only tried you all this while and urged my father's will; but mine is that you would love Antonio: he is brave and young, and all that can complete the happiness of a gallant maid. This absence of my father will give us opportunity to free you from Vincentio by marrying here, which you must do tomorrow.

FLORINDA.

Tomorrow!

PEDRO.

Tomorrow, or 'twill be too late. 'Tis not my friendship to Antonio which makes me urge this, but love to thee and hatred to Vincentio; therefore resolve upon tomorrow.

FLORINDA.

Sir, I shall strive to do as shall become your sister.

PEDRO.

I'll both believe and trust you. Adieu.

Exeunt Pedro *and* Stephano.

HELLENA.

As becomes his sister! That is to be as resolved your way as he is his.
Hellena *goes to* Callis.

FLORINDA.

I ne'er till now perceived my ruin near.
I've no defence against Antonio's love,
For he has all the advantages of nature,
The moving arguments of youth and fortune.

HELLENA.

But hark you, Callis, you will not be so cruel to lock me up indeed, will you?

CALLIS.

I must obey the commands I have. Besides, do you consider what a life you are going to lead?

12 The barring of a convent window.

HELLENA.

Yes, Callis, that of a nun; and till then I'll be indebted a world of prayers to you if you'll let me now see what I never did, the divertissements of a Carnival.

CALLIS.

What, go in masquerade? 'Twill be a fine farewell to the world, I take it. Pray what would you do there?

HELLENA.

That which all the world does, as I am told: be as mad as the rest and take all innocent freedoms. Sister, you'll go too, will you not? Come, prithee be not sad. We'll outwit twenty brothers if you'll be ruled by me. Come, put off this dull humor with your clothes, and assume one as gay and as fantastic as the dress my cousin Valeria and I have provided, and let's ramble.

FLORINDA.

Callis, will you give us leave to go?

CALLIS. (*aside*).

I have a youthful itch of going myself.—Madam, if I thought your brother might not know it, and I might wait on you; for by my troth I'll not trust young girls alone.

FLORINDA.

Thou seest my brother's gone already, and thou shalt attend and watch us.

Enter Stephano

STEPHANO.

Madam, the habits are come, and your cousin Valeria is dressed and stays for you.

FLORINDA. [*aside*].

'Tis well. I'll write a note, and if I chance to see Belvile and want an opportunity to speak to him, that shall let him know what I've resolved in favor of him.

HELLENA.

Come, let's in and dress us.

Exeunt.

[I.ii]   *A LONG STREET*

Enter Belvile, *melancholy*; Blunt *and* Frederick.

FREDERICK.

Why, what the devil ails the colonel, in a time when all the world is gay to look like mere Lent thus? Hadst thou been long enough in Naples to have been in love, I should have sworn some such judgment had befallen thee.

BELVILE.

No, I have made no new amours since I came to Naples.

FREDERICK.

You have left none behind you in Paris?

BELVILE.

Neither.

FREDERICK.

I cannot divine the cause then, unless the old cause, the want of money.

BLUNT.

And another old cause, the want of a wench. Would not that revive you?

BELVILE.

You are mistaken, Ned.

BLUNT.

Nay, 'adsheartlikins, then thou'rt past cure.

FREDERICK.

I have found it out: thou has renewed thy acquaintance with the lady that cost thee so many sighs at the siege of Pamplona—pox on't, what d'ye call her—her brother's a noble Spaniard, nephew to the dead general. Florinda. Ay, Florinda. And will nothing serve thy turn but that damned virtuous woman, whom on my conscience thou lov'st in spite too, because thou seest little or no possibility of gaining her.

BELVILE.

Thou art mistaken; I have int'rest enough in that lovely virgin's heart to make me proud and vain, were it not abated by the severity of a brother, who perceiving my happiness—

FREDERICK.

Has civilly forbid thee the house?

BELVILE.

'Tis so, to make way for a powerful rival, the Viceroy's son, who has the advantage of me in being a man of fortune, a Spaniard, and her brother's friend; which gives him liberty to make his court, whilst I have recourse only to letters and distant looks from her window, which are as soft and kind as those which heaven sends down on penitents.

BLUNT.

Heyday! 'Adsheartlikins, simile! By this light the man is quite spoiled. Fred, what the devil are we made of that we cannot be thus concerned for a wench? 'Adsheartlikins, our Cupids are like the cooks of the camp: they can roast or boil a woman, but they have none of the fine tricks to set 'em off; no hogoes[13] to make the sauce pleasant and the stomach sharp.

FREDERICK.

I dare swear I have had a hundred as young, kind, and handsome as this Florinda; and dogs eat me if they were not as troublesome to me i'th morning as they were welcome o'er night.

BLUNT.

And yet I warrant he would not touch another woman if he might have her for nothing.

BELVILE.

That's thy joy, a cheap whore.

BLUNT.

Why, 'adsheartlikins, I love a frank soul. When did you ever hear of an honest woman that took a man's money? I warrant 'em good ones. But gentlemen, you may be free; you have been kept so poor with parliaments and protectors[14] that the little stock you have is not worth preserving. But I thank my stars I had more grace than to forfeit my estate by cavaliering.[15]

BELVILE.

Methinks only following the court should be sufficient to entitle 'em to that.

[13] Piquant flavours.
[14] A reference to Cromwell and the parliamentarians, victors of the English Civil War.
[15] Estates of cavaliers were confiscated during the Commonwealth.

BLUNT.

'Adsheartlikins, they know I follow it to do it no good, unless they pick a hole in my coat for lending you money now and then, which is a greater crime to my conscience, gentlemen, than to the commonwealth.

Enter Willmore.

WILLMORE.

Ha! Dear Belvile! Noble colonel!

BELVILE.

Willmore! Welcome ashore, my dear rover! What happy wind blew us this good fortune?

WILLMORE.

Let me salute my dear Fred, and then command me.—How is't, honest lad?

FREDERICK.

Faith, sir, the old compliment, infinitely the better to see my dear mad Willmore again. Prithee, why camest thou ashore? And where's the Prince?[16]

WILLMORE.

He's well, and reigns still lord of the wat'ry element. I must aboard again within a day or two, and my business ashore was only to enjoy myself a little this Carnival.

BELVILE.

Pray know our new friend, sir: he's but bashful, a raw traveler, but honest, stout, and one of us.

Embraces Blunt.

WILLMORE.

That you esteem him gives him an int'rest here.

BLUNT.

Your servant, sir.

[16] Later Charles II.

WILLMORE.

But well, faith, I'm glad to meet you again in a warm climate, where the kind sun has its godlike power still over the wine and women. Love and mirth are my business in Naples, and if I mistake not the place, here's an excellent market for chapmen[17] of my humor.

BELVILE.

See, here be those kind merchants of love you look for.

Enter several men in masking habits, some playing on music, others dancing after; women dressed like courtesans, with papers pinned on their breasts, and baskets of flowers in their hands.

BLUNT.

'Adsheartlikins, what have we here?

FREDERICK.

Now the game begins.

WILLMORE.

Fine pretty creatures! May a stranger have leave to look and love? What's here? "Roses for every month"?

Reads the papers.

BLUNT.

Roses for every month? What means that?

BELVILE.

They are, or would have you think they're courtesans, who here in Naples are to be hired by the month.

WILLMORE.

Kind and obliging to inform us, pray where do these roses grow? I would fain plant some of 'em in a bed of mine.

WOMAN.

Beware such roses, sir.

WILLMORE.

A pox of fear: I'll be baked with thee between a pair of sheets, and that's thy proper still; so I might but strew such roses over me and

---

[17] People who buy and sell.

under me. Fair one, would you would give me leave to gather at your
bush this idle month; I would go near to make somebody smell of it
all the year after.

BELVILE.

And thou hast need of such a remedy, for thou stink'st of tar and
ropes' ends like a dock or pesthouse.

The Woman puts herself into the hands of a man and exeunt.

WILLMORE.

Nay, nay, you shall not leave me so.

BELVILE.

By all means use no violence here.

WILLMORE.

Death! Just as I was going to be damnably in love, to have her led
off! I could pluck that rose out of his hand, and even kiss the bed the
bush grew in.

FREDERICK.

No friend to love like a long voyage at sea.

BLUNT.

Except a nunnery, Fred.

WILLMORE.

Death! But will they not be kind? Quickly be kind? Thou know'st I'm
no tame sigher, but a rampant lion of the forest.

*Advances from the farther end of the scenes two men dressed all over with
horns of several sorts, making grimaces at one another, with papers pinned
on their backs.*

BELVILE.

Oh the fantastical rogues, how they're dressed! 'Tis a satire against
the whole sex.

WILLMORE.

Is this a fruit that grows in this warm country?

BELVILE.

Yes, 'tis pretty to see these Italians start, swell, and stab at the word
cuckold, and yet stumble at horns on every threshold.

WILLMORE.

See what's on their back. (*Reads*). "Flowers of every night." Ah, rogue! And more sweet than roses of every month! This is a gardener of Adam's own breeding.

They dance.

BELVILE.

What think you of these grave people? Is a wake in Essex half so mad or extravagant?

WILLMORE.

I like their sober grave way; 'tis a kind of legal authorized fornication, where the men are not chid for't, nor the women despised, as amongst our dull English. Even the monsieurs want that part of good manners.

BELVILE.

But here in Italy, a monsieur is the humblest best-bred gentleman: duels are so baffled by bravos that an age shows not one but between a Frenchman and a hangman, who is as much too hard for him on the Piazza as they are for a Dutchman on the New Bridge.[18] But see, another crew.

Enter Florinda, Hellena, *and* Valeria, *dressed like gipsies;* Callis *and* Stephano, Lucetta, Philippo *and* Sancho *in masquerade.*

HELLENA.

Sister, there's your Englishman, and with him a handsome proper fellow. I'll to him, and instead of telling him his fortune, try my own.

WILLMORE.

Gipsies, on my life. Sure these will prattle if a man cross their hands. (*Goes to* Hellena.) —Dear, pretty, and, I hope, young devil, will you tell an amorous stranger what luck he's like to have?

HELLENA.

Have a care how you venture with me, sir, lest I pick your pocket, which will more vex your English humor than an Italian fortune will please you.

WILLMORE.

How the devil cam'st thou to know my country and humor?

[18] In 1673 the Dutch lost Nieuwerbrug to the French in a humiliating defeat.

HELLENA.

The first I guess by a certain forward impudence, which does not displease me at this time; and the loss of your money will vex you because I hope you have but very little to lose.

WILLMORE.

Egad, child, thou'rt i'th' right; it is so little I dare not offer it thee for a kindness. But cannot you divine what other things of more value I have about me that I would more willingly part with?

HELLENA.

Indeed no, that's the business of a witch, and I am but a gipsy yet. Yet without looking in your hand, I have a parlous guess 'tis some foolish heart you mean, an inconstant English heart, as little worth stealing as your purse.

WILLMORE.

Nay, then thou dost deal with the devil, that's certain. Thou hast guessed as right as if thou hadst been one of that number it has languished for. I find you'll be better acquainted with it, nor can you take it in a better time; for I am come from sea, child, and Venus not being propitious to me in her own element, I have a world of love in store. Would you would be good-natured and take some on't off my hands.

HELLENA.

Why, I could be inclined that way, but for a foolish vow I am going to make to die a maid.

WILLMORE.

Then thou art damned without redemption, and as I am a good Christian, I ought in charity to divert so wicked a design. Therefore prithee, dear creature, let me know quickly when and where I shall begin to set a helping hand to so good a work.

HELLENA.

If you should prevail with my tender heart, as I begin to fear you will, for you have horrible loving eyes, there will be difficulty in't that you'll hardly undergo for my sake.

WILLMORE.

Faith, child, I have been bred in dangers, and wear a sword that has been employed in a worse cause than for a handsome kind woman. Name the danger; let it be anything but a long siege, and I'll undertake it.

HELLENA.

Can you storm?

WILLMORE.

Oh, most furiously.

HELLENA.

What think you of a nunnery wall? For he that wins me must gain that first.

WILLMORE.

A nun! Oh, now I love thee for't! There's no sinner like a young saint. Nay, now there's no denying me; the old law had no curse to a woman like dying a maid: witness Jeptha's daugher.[19]

HELLENA.

A very good text this, if well handled; and I perceive, Father Captain, you would impose no severe penance on her who were inclined to console herself before she took orders.

WILLMORE.

If she be young and handsome.

HELLENA.

Ay, there's it. But if she be not—

WILLMORE.

By this hand, child, I have an implicit faith, and dare venture on thee with all faults. Besides, 'tis more meritorious to leave the world when thou hast tasted and proved the pleasure on't. Then 'twill be a virtue in thee, which now will be pure ignorance.

HELLENA.

I perceive, good Father Captain, you design only to make me fit for heaven. But if, on the contrary, you should quite divert me from it, and bring me back to the world again, I should have a new man to

[19] Judges 11; 37–40. Before sacrificing his daughter, Jephtha allowed her to lament her virginity.

seek, I find. And what a grief that will be; for when I begin, I fancy I shall love like anything; I never tried yet.

WILLMORE.

Egad, and that's kind! Prithee, dear creature, give me credit for a heart, for faith, I'm a very honest fellow. Oh, I long to come first to the banquet of love! And such a swinging appetite I bring. Oh, I'm impatient. Thy lodging, sweetheart, thy lodging, or I'm a dead man!

HELLENA.

Why must we be either guilty of fornication or murder if we converse with you men? And is there no difference between leave to love me, and leave to lie with me?

WILLMORE.

Faith, child, they were made to go together.

LUCETTA (*pointing to* Blunt).

Are you sure this is the man?

SANCHO.

When did I mistake your game?

LUCETTA.

This is a stranger, I know by his gazing; if he be brisk he'll venture to follow me, and then, if I understand my trade, he's mine. He's English, too, and they say that's a sort of good-natured loving people, and have generally so kind an opinion of themselves that a woman with any wit may flatter 'em into any sort of fool she pleases.

She often passes by Blunt *and gazes on him; he struts and cocks, and walks and gazes on her*.

BLUNT.

'Tis so, she is taken; I have beauties which my false glass at home did not discover.

FLORINDA (*aside*).

This woman watches me so, I shall get no opportunity to discover myself to him, and so miss the intent of my coming.—[*To* Belvile.] But as I was saying, sir, by this line you should be a lover.

Looking in his hand.

BELVILE.

I thought how right you guessed: all men are in love, or pretend to be so. Come, let me go; I'm weary of this fooling.

Walks away.

FLORINDA.

I will not, sir, till you have confessed whether the passion that you have vowed Florinda be true or false.

She holds him; he strives to get from her.

BELVILE.

Florinda!

Turns quick towards her.

FLORINDA.

Softly.

BELVILE.

Thou hast nam'd one will fix me here forever.

FLORINDA.

She'll be disappointed then, who expects you this night at the garden gate. And if you fail not, as— (*Looks on* Callis, *who observes 'em.*) Let me see the other hand—you will go near to do, she vows to die or make you happy.

BELVILE.

What canst thou mean?

FLORINDA.

That which I say. Farewell.

Offers to go.

BELVILE.

Oh charming sybil, stay; complete that joy which as it is will turn into distraction! Where must I be? At the garden gate? I know it. At night, you say? I'll sooner forfeit heaven than disobey.

Enter Don Pedro *and other maskers, and pass over the stage.*

CALLIS.

Madam, your brother's here.

FLORINDA.

Take this to instruct you farther.

Gives him a letter, and goes off.

FREDERICK.

Have a care, sir, what you promise; this may be a trap laid by her
brother to ruin you.

BELVILE.

Do not disturb my happiness with doubts.

Opens the letter.

WILLMORE.

My dear pretty creature, a thousand blessings on thee! Still in this
habit, you say? And after dinner at this place?

HELLENA.

Yes, if you will swear to keep your heart and not bestow it between
this and that.

WILLMORE.

By all the little gods of love, I swear; I'll leave it with you, and if you
run away with it, those deities of justice will revenge me.

Exeunt all the women [except Lucetta].

FREDERICK.

Do you know the hand?

BELVILE.

'Tis Florinda's.
All blessings fall upon the virtuous maid.

FREDERICK.

Nay, no idolatry; a sober sacrifice I'll allow you.

BELVILE.

Oh friends, the welcom'st news! The softest letter! Nay, you shall all
see it! And could you now be serious, I might be made the happiest
man the sun shines on!

WILLMORE.

The reason of this mighty joy?

BELVILE.

See how kindly she invites me to deliver her from the threatened
violence of her brother. Will you not assist me?

WILLMORE.

I know not what thou mean'st, but I'll make one at any mischief where a woman's concerned. But she'll be grateful to us for the favor, will she not?

BELVILE.

How mean you?

WILLMORE.

How should I mean? Thou know'st there's but one way for a woman to oblige me.

BELVILE.

Do not profane; the maid is nicely virtuous.

WILLMORE.

Who, pox, then she's fit for nothing but a husband. Let her e'en go, colonel.

FREDERICK.

Peace, she's the colonel's mistress, sir.

WILLMORE.

Let her be the devil; if she be thy mistress, I'll serve her. Name the way.

BELVILE.

Read here this postscript.

Give him a letter.

WILLMORE (*reads*).

"At ten at night, at the garden gate, of which, if I cannot get the key, I will contrive a way over the wall. Come attended with a friend or two." —Kind heart, if we three cannot weave a string to let her down a garden wall, 'twere pity but the hangman wove one for us all.

FREDERICK.

Let her alone for that; your woman's wit, your fair kind woman, will out-trick a broker or a Jew, and contrive like a Jesuit in chains. But see, Ned Blunt is stolen out after the lure of a damsel.

Exeunt Blunt *and* Lucetta.

BELVILE.

So, he'll scarce find his way home again unless we get him cried by the bellman in the market place. And 'twould sound prettily: "A lost English boy of thirty."

FREDERICK.

I hope 'tis some common crafty sinner, one that will fit him. It may be she'll sell him for Peru: the rogue's sturdy, and would work well in a mine. At least I hope she'll dress him for our mirth, cheat him of all, then have him well-favoredly banged, and turned out at midnight.

WILLMORE.

Prithee what humor is he of, that you wish him so well?

BELVILE.

Why, of an English elder brother's humor: educated in a nursery, with a maid to tend him till fifteen, and lies with his grandmother till he's of age; one that knows no pleasure beyond riding to the next fair, or going up to London with his right worshipful father in parliament time, wearing gay clothes, or making honorable love to his lady mother's laundry maid; gets drunk at a hunting match, and ten to one then gives some proofs of his prowess. A pox upon him, he's our banker, and has all our cash about him; and if he fail, we are all broke.

FREDERICK.

Oh, let him alone for that matter; he's of a damned stingy quality that will secure our stock. I know not in what danger it were indeed if the jilt should pretend she's in love with him, for 'tis a kind believing coxcomb; otherwise, if he part with more than a piece of eight, geld him—for which offer he may chance to be beaten if she be a whore of the first rank.

BELVILE.

Nay, the rogue will not be easily beaten; he's stout enough. Perhaps if they talk beyond his capacity he may chance to exercise his courage upon some of them, else I'm sure they'll find it as difficult to beat as to please him.

WILLMORE.

'Tis a lucky devil to light upon so kind a wench!

FREDERICK.

Thou hadst a great deal of talk with thy little gipsy; couldst thou do no good upon her? For mine was hardhearted.

WILLMORE.

Hang her, she was some damned honest person of quality, I'm sure, she was so very free and witty. If her face be but answerable to her wit and humor, I would be bound to constancy this month to gain her. In the meantime, have you made no kind acquaintance since you came to town? You do not use to be honest[20] so long, gentlemen.

FREDERICK.

Faith, love has kept us honest: we have been all fir'd with a beauty newly come to town, the famous Paduana Angellica Bianca.

WILLMORE.

What, the mistress of the dead Spanish general?

BELVILE.

Yes, she's now the only ador'd beauty of all the youth in Naples, who put on all their charms to appear lovely in her sight: their coaches, liveries, and themselves all gay as on a monarch's birthday to attract the eyes of this fair charmer, while she has the pleasure to behold all languish for her that see her.

FREDERICK.

'Tis pretty to see with how much love the men regard her, and how much envy the women.

WILLMORE.

What gallant has she?

BELVILE.

None; she's exposed to sale, and four days in the week she's yours, for so much a month.

WILLMORE.

The very thought of it quenches all manner of fire in me. Yet prithee, let's see her.

BELVILE.

Let's first to dinner, and after that we'll pass the day as you please. But at night ye must all be at my devotion.

[20] Chaste.

WILLMORE.

I will not fail you.

[*Exeunt.*]

The End of the First Act.

ACT II

[II.1]   *THE LONG STREET*

Enter Belvile *and* Frederick *in masking habits, and* Willmore *in his own clothes, with a vizard*[21] *in his hand.*

WILLMORE.

But why thus disguised and muzzled?

BELVILE.

Because whatever extravagances we commit in these faces, our own may not be obliged to answer 'em.

WILLMORE.

I should have changed my eternal buff,[22] too; but no matter, my little gipsy would not have found me out then. For if she should change hers, it is impossible I should know her unless I should hear her prattle. A pox on't, I cannot get her out of my head. Pray heaven, if ever I do see her again, she prove damnably ugly, that I may fortify myself against her tongue.

BELVILE.

Have a care of love, for o' my conscience she was not of a quality to give thee any hopes.

WILLMORE.

Pox on 'em, why do they draw a man in then? She has played with my heart so, that 'twill never lie still till I have met with some kind wench that will play the game out with me. Oh, for my arms full of soft, white, kind woman—such as I fancy Angellica.

BELVILE.

This is her house, if you were but in stock to get admittance. They have not dined yet; I perceive the picture is not out.

Enter Blunt.

---

21 Face mask.
22 Leather military coat.

WILLMORE.

I long to see the shadow of the fair substance; a man may gaze on that for nothing.

BLUNT.

Colonel, thy hand. And thine, Fred. I have been an ass, a deluded fool, a very coxcomb from my birth till this hour, and heartily repent my little faith.

BELVILE.

What the devil's the matter with thee, Ned?

BLUNT.

Oh, such a mistress, Fred! Such a girl!

WILLMORE.

Ha! Where?

FREDERICK.

Ay, where?

BLUNT.

So fond, so amorous, so toying, and so fine! And all for sheer love, ye rogue! Oh, how she looked and kissed! And soothed my heart from my bosom! I cannot think I was awake, and yet methinks I see and feel her charms still. Fred, try if she have not left the taste of her balmy kisses upon my lips.

Kisses him.

BELVILE.

Ha! Ha! Ha!

WILLMORE.

Death, man, where is she?

BLUNT.

What a dog was I to stay in dull England so long! How have I laughed at the colonel when he sighed for love! But now the little archer has revenged him! And by this one dart I can guess at all his joys, which then I took for fancies, mere dreams and fables. Well I'm resolved to sell all in Essex and plant here forever.

BELVILE.

What a blessing 'tis, thou hast a mistress thou dar'st boast of; for I know thy humor is rather to have a proclaimed clap than a secret amour.

WILLMORE.

Dost know her name?

BLUNT.

Her name? No, 'adsheartlikins. What care I for names? She's fair, young, brisk and kind, even to ravishment! And what a pox care I for knowing her by any other title?

WILLMORE.

Didst give her anything?

BLUNT.

Give her? Ha! Ha! Ha! Why, she's a person of quality. That's a good one! Give her? 'Adsheartlikins, dost think such creatures are to be bought? Or are we provided for such a purchase? Give her, quoth ye? Why, she presented me with this bracelet for the toy of a diamond I used to wear. No, gentlemen, Ned Blunt is not everybody. She expects me again tonight.

WILLMORE.

Egad, that's well; we'll all go.

BLUNT.

Not a soul! No, gentlemen, you are wits; I am a dull country rogue, I.

FREDERICK.

Well, sir, for all your person of quality, I shall be very glad to understand your purse be secure; 'tis our whole estate at present, which we are loath to hazard in one bottom.[23] Come sir, unlade.

BLUNT.

Take the necessary trifle useless now to me, that am beloved by such a gentlewoman. 'Adsheartlikins, money! Here, take mine too.

FREDERICK.

No, keep that to be cozened, that we may laugh.

[23] Ship's hold.

WILLMORE.

> Cozened? Death! Would I could meet with one that would cozen me of all the love I could spare tonight.

FREDERICK.

> Pox, 'tis some common whore, upon my life.

BLUNT.

> A whore? Yes, with such clothes, such jewels, such a house, such furniture, and so attended! A whore!

BELVILE.

> Why yes, sir, they are whores, though they'll neither entertain you with drinking, swearing, or bawdry; are whores in all those gay clothes and right jewels; are whores with those great houses richly furnished with velvet beds, store of plate, handsome attendance, and fine coaches; are whores, and errant ones.

WILLMORE.

> Pox on't, where do these fine whores live?

BELVILE.

> Where no rogues in office, ycleped constables, dare give 'em laws, nor the wine-inspired bullies of the town break their windows; yet they are whores though this Essex calf believe 'em persons of quality.

BLUNT.

> 'Adsheartlikins, y'are all fools. There are things about this Essex calf that shall take with the ladies, beyond all your wit and parts. This shape and size, gentlemen, are not to be despised; my waist, too, tolerably long, with other inviting signs that shall be nameless.

WILLMORE.

> Egad, I believe he may have met with some person of quality that may be kind to him.

BELVILE.

> Dost thou perceive any such tempting things about him that should make a fine woman, and of quality, pick him out from all mankind to throw away her youth and beauty upon; nay, and her dear heart, too? No, No, Angellica has raised the price too high.

WILLMORE.

> May she languish for mankind till she die, and be damned for that one sin alone.

Enter two Bravos[24] *and hang up a great picture of Angellica's against the balcony, and two little ones at each side of the door.*

BELVILE.

See there the fair sign to the inn where a man may lodge that's fool enough to give her price.

Willmore *gazes on the picture.*

BLUNT.

'Adsheartlikins, gentlemen, what's this?

BELVILE.

A famous courtesan, that's to be sold.

BLUNT.

How? To be sold? Nay, then I have nothing to say to her. Sold? What impudence is practiced in this country; with what order and decency whoring's established here by virtue of the Inquisition! Come, let's be gone; I'm sure we're no chapmen for this commodity.

FREDERICK.

Thou art none, I'm sure, unless thou couldst have her in thy bed at a price of a coach in the street.

WILLMORE.

How wondrous fair she is! A thousand crowns a month? By heaven, as many kingdoms were too little! A plague of this poverty, of which I ne'er complain but when it hinders my approach to beauty which virtue ne'er could purchase.

Turns from the picture.

BLUNT.

What's this? (*Reads.*) "A thousand crowns a month"! 'Adsheartlikins, here's a sum! Sure 'tis a mistake.—[*To one of the* Bravos.] Hark you, friend, does she take or give so much by the month?

FREDERICK.

A thousand crowns! Why, 'tis a portion for the Infanta!

BLUNT.

Hark ye, friends, won't she trust?

[24] Hired soldiers or villains.

BRAVO.

This is a trade, sir, that cannot live by credit.

Enter Don Pedro *in masquerade, followed by* Stephano.

BELVILE.

See, here's more company; let's walk off a while.

Exeunt English; Pedro *reads*.

PEDRO.

Fetch me a thousand crowns; I never wished to buy this beauty at
an easier rate.

Passes off.

Enter Angellica *and* Moretta *in the balcony, and draw a silk curtain*.

ANGELLICA.

Prithee, what said those fellows to thee?

BRAVO.

Madam, the first were admirers of beauty only, but no purchasers;
they were merry with your price and picture, laughed at the sum,
and so passed off.

ANGELLICA.

No matter, I'm not displeased with their rallying; their wonder feeds
my vanity, and he that wishes but to buy gives me more pride than
he that gives my price can make my pleasure.

BRAVO.

Madam, the last I knew through all his disguises to be Don Pedro,
nephew to the general, and who was with him in Pamplona.

ANGELLICA.

Don Pedro? My old gallant's nephew? When his uncle died he left
him a vast sum of money; it is he who was so in love with me at
Padua, and who used to make the general so jealous.

MORETTA.

Is this he that used to prance before our window, and take such
care to show himself an amorous ass? If I am not mistaken, he is the
likeliest man to give your price.

ANGELLICA.

The man is brave and generous, but of a humor so uneasy and
inconstant that the victory over his heart is as soon lost as won; a slave

that can add little to the triumph of the conqueror. But inconstancy's the sin of all mankind, therefore I'm resolved that nothing but gold shall charm my heart.

MORETTA.

I'm glad on't; 'tis only interest that women of our profession ought to consider, though I wonder what has kept you from that general disease of our sex so long; I mean, that of being in love.

ANGELLICA.

A kind but sullen star under which I had the happiness to be born. Yet I have had no time for love; the bravest and noblest of mankind have purchased my favors at so dear a rate, as if no coin but gold were current with our trade. But here's Don Pedro again; fetch me my lute, for 'tis for him or Don Antonio the Viceroy's son that I have spread my nets.

Enter at one door Don Pedro, *Stephano*; Don Antonio *and* Diego [*his page*] *at the other door, with people following him in masquerade, anticly attired, some with music. They both go up to the picture.*

ANTONIO.

A thousand crowns! Had not the painter flattered her, I should not think it dear.

PEDRO.

Flattered her? By heaven, he cannot. I have seen the original, nor is there one charm here more than adorns her face and eyes; all this soft and sweet, with a certain languishing air that no artist can represent.

ANTONIO.

What I heard of her beauty before had fired my soul, but this confirmation of it has blown it to a flame.

PEDRO.

Ha!

PAGE.

Sir, I have known you throw away a thousand crowns on a worse face, and though y'are near your marriage, you may venture a little love here; Florinda will not miss it.

PEDRO (*aside*).

Ha! Florinda! Sure 'tis Antonio.

ANTONIO.

Florinda! Name not those distant joys; there's not one thought of her
will check my passion here.

PEDRO [*aside*].

Florinda scorned! (*A noise of a lute above.*) And all my hopes defeated
of the possession of Angellica! (Antonio *gazes up.*) Her injuries, by
heaven, he shall not boast of!

Song to a lute above.

SONG

I

When Damon first began to love
He languished in a soft desire,
And knew not how the gods to move,
To lessen or increase his fire.
For Caelia in her charming eyes
Wore all love's sweets, and all his cruelties.

II

But as beneath a shade he lay,
Weaving of flowers for Caelia's hair,
She chanced to lead her flock that way,
And saw the am'rous shepherd there.
She gazed around upon the place,
And saw the grove, resembling night,
To all the joys of love invite,
Whilst guilty smiles and blushes dressed her face.
At this the bashful youth all transport grew,
And with kind force he taught the virgin how
To yield what all his sighs could never do.

Angellica *throws open the curtains and bows to* Antonio, *who pulls off his*
vizard and bows and blows up kisses. Pedro, *unseen, looks in's face. [The*
curtains close.]

ANTONIO.

By heaven, she's charming fair!

PEDRO (*aside*).

'Tis he, the false Antonio!

ANTONIO (*to the bravo*).

> Friend, where must I pay my off'ring of love?
> My thousand crowns I mean.

PEDRO.

> That off'ring I have designed to make,
>
> And yours will come too late.

ANTONIO.

> Prithee begone; I shall grow angry else,
> And then thou art not safe.

PEDRO.

> My anger may be fatal, sir, as yours,
> And he that enters here may prove this truth.

ANTONIO.

> I know not who thou art, but I am sure thou'rt worth my killing, for
> aiming at Angellica.   *They draw and fight.*

> *Enter* Willmore *and* Blunt, *who draw and part 'em.*

BLUNT.

> 'Adsheartlikins, here's fine doings.

WILLMORE.

> Tilting for the wench, I'm sure. Nay, gad, if that would win her I have
> as good a sword as the best of ye. Put up, put up, and take another
> time and place, for this is designed for lovers only.
>
>   *They all put up.*

PEDRO.

> We are prevented; dare you meet me tomorrow on the Molo?
> For I've a title to a better quarrel,
> That of Florinda, in whose credulous heart
> Thou'st made an int'rest, and destroyed my hopes.

ANTONIO.

> Dare!
> I'll meet thee there as early as the day.

PEDRO.

> We will come thus disguised, that whosoever chance to get the better,
> he may escape unknown.

ANTONIO.

It shall be so.   *Exeunt* Pedro *and* Stephano.
—Who should this rival be? Unless the English colonel, of whom
I've often heard Don Pedro speak. It must be he, and time he were
removed who lays a claim to all my happiness.

Willmore, *having gazed all this while on the picture, pulls down a little
one*.

WILLMORE.

This posture's loose and negligent;
The sight on't would beget a warm desire
In souls whom impotence and age had chilled.
This must along with me.

BRAVO.

What means this rudeness, sir? Restore the picture.

ANTONIO.

Ha! Rudeness committed to the fair Angellica! —Restore the picture,
sir.

WILLMORE.

Indeed I will not, sir.

ANTONIO.

By heaven, but you shall.

WILLMORE.

Nay, do not show your sword; if your do, by this dear beauty, I will
show mine too.

ANTONIO.

What right can you pretend to't?

WILLMORE.

That of possession, which I will maintain. You, perhaps, have a
thousand crowns to give for the original.

ANTONIO.

No matter sir, you shall restore the picture.

          [*The curtains open*;] Angellica *and* Moretta *above*.

ANGELLICA.

Oh, Moretta, what's the matter?

ANTONIO.

Or leave your life behind.

WILLMORE.

Death! You lie; I will do neither.

They fight. The Spaniards join with Antonio, Blunt *laying on like mad.*

ANGELLICA.

Hold, I command you, if for me you fight.

They leave off and bow.

WILLMORE [*aside*].

How heavenly fair she is! Ah, plague of her price!

ANGELLICA.

You sir, in buff, you that appear a soldier, that first began this insolence—

WILLMORE.

'Tis true, I did so, if you call it insolence for a man to preserve himself. I saw your charming picture and was wounded; quite through my soul each pointed beauty ran; and wanting a thousand crowns to procure my remedy, I laid this little picture to my bosom, which, if you cannot allow me, I'll resign.

ANGELLICA.

No, you may keep the trifle.

ANTONIO.

You shall first ask me leave, and this. *Fight again as before.*

Enter Belvile *and* Frederick, *who join with the English.*

ANGELLICA.

Hold! Will you ruin me?—Biskey! Sebastian! Part 'em!

The Spaniards are beaten off.

MORETTA.

Oh, madam, we're undone. A pox upon that rude fellow; he's set on to ruin us. We shall never see good days again till all these fighting poor rogues are sent to the galleys.

Enter Belvile, Blunt, Frederick, *and* Willmore *with's shirt bloody.*

BLUNT.

'Adsheatlikins, beat me at this sport and I'll ne'er wear sword more.

BELVILE (*to* Willmore).

The devil's in thee for a mad fellow; thou art always one at an unlucky adventure. Come, let's be gone whilst we're safe, and remember these are Spaniards, a sort of people that know how to revenge an affront.

FREDERICK.

You bleed! I hope you are not wounded.

WILLMORE.

Not much. A plague on your dons; if they fight no better they'll ne'er recover Flanders. What the devil was't to them that I took down the picture?

BLUNT.

Took it! 'Adsheartlikins, we'll have the great one too; 'tis ours by conquest. Prithee help me up and I'll pull it down.

ANGELLICA [*to* Willmore].

Stay, sir, and ere you affront me farther let me know how you durst commit this outrage. To you I speak, sir, for you appear a gentleman.

WILLMORE.

To me, madam?—Gentlemen, your servant.

                                      Belvile *stays him.*

BELVILE.

Is the devil in thee? Dost know the danger of ent'ring the house of an incensed courtesan?

WILLMORE.

I thank you for your care, but there are other matters in hand, there are, though we have no great temptation. Death! Let me go!

FREDERICK.

Yes, to your lodging if you will, but not in here. Damn these gay harlots; by this hand I'll have as sound and handsome a whore for a patacoon.[25] Death, man, she'll murder thee!

WILLMORE.

Oh, fear me not. Shall I not venture where a beauty calls? A lovely charming beauty! For fear of danger? When, by heaven, there's none so great as to long for her whilst I want money to purchase her.

[25] Spanish silver coin of little value.

FREDERICK.

Therefore 'tis loss of time unless you had the thousand crowns to pay.

WILLMORE.

It may be she may give a favor; at least I shall have the pleasure of saluting her when I enter and when I depart.

BELVILE.

Pox, she'll as soon lie with thee as kiss thee, and sooner stab than do either. You shall not go.

ANGELLICA.

Fear not, sir, all I have to wound with is my eyes.

BLUNT.

Let him go. 'Adsheartlikins, I believe the gentlewoman means well.

BELVILE.

Well, take thy fortune; we'll expect you in the next street. Farewell, fool, farewell.

WILLMORE.

'Bye, colonel.

Goes in.

FREDERICK.

The rogue's stark mad for a wench.

Exeunt.

[II.ii]   *A FINE CHAMBER*

Enter Willmore, Angellica, *and* Moretta.

ANGELLICA.

Insolent sir, how durst you pull down my picture?

WILLMORE.

Rather, how durst you set it up to tempt poor am'rous mortals with so much excellence, which I find you have but too well consulted by the unmerciful price you set upon't. Is all this heaven of beauty shown to move despair in those that cannot buy? And can you think th'effects of that despair should be less extravagant than I have shown?

ANGELLICA.

I sent for you to ask my pardon, sir, not to aggravate your crime. I thought I should have seen you at my feet imploring it.

WILLMORE.

You are deceived. I came to rail at you, and rail such truths too, as shall let you see the vanity of that pride which taught you how to set such price on sin.
For such it is whilst that which is love's due
Is meanly bartered for.

ANGELLICA.

Ha! Ha! Ha! Alas, good captain, what pity 'tis your edifying doctrine will do no good upon me. Moretta, fetch the gentleman a glass, and let him survey himself to see what charms he has.—(*Aside, in a soft tone.*) And guess my business.

MORETTA.

He knows himself of old: I believe those breeches and he have been acquainted ever since he was beaten at Worcester.[26]

ANGELLICA.

Nay, do not abuse the poor creature.

MORETTA.

Good weatherbeaten corporal, will you march off? We have no need of your doctrine, though you have of our charity. But at present we have no scraps; we can afford no kindness for God's sake. In fine, sirrah, the price is too high i'th' mouth for you, therefore troop, I say.

WILLMORE.

Here, good forewoman of the shop, serve me and I'll be gone.

MORETTA.

Keep it to pay your laundress; your linen stinks of the gun room. For here's no selling by retail.

WILLMORE.

Thou has sold plenty of thy stale ware at a cheap rate.

MORETTA.

Ay, the more silly kind heart I, but this is an age wherein beauty is at higher rates. In fine, you know the price of this.

---

[26] The decisive defeat of the royalists by Cromwell in 1651.

WILLMORE.

I grant you 'tis here set down, a thousand crowns a month. Pray, how much may come to my share for a pistole? Bawd, take your black lead[27] and sum it up, that I may have a pistole's worth of this vain gay thing, and I'll trouble you no more.

MORETTA.

Pox on him, he'll fret me to death! Abominable fellow, I tell thee we only sell by the whole piece.

WILLMORE.

'Tis very hard, the whole cargo or nothing. Faith, madam, my stock will not reach it; I cannot be your chapman. Yet I have countrymen in town, merchants of love like me; I'll see if they'll put in for a share. We cannot lose much by it, and what we have no use for, we'll sell upon the Friday's mart at "Who gives more?"—I am studying, madam, how to purchase you, though at present I am unprovided of money.

ANGELLICA (*aside*).

Sure this from any other man would anger me; nor shall he know the conquest he has made.—Poor angry man, how I despise this railing.

WILLMORE.

Yes, I am poor. But I'm a gentleman,
And one that scorns this baseness which you practice.
Poor as I am I would not sell myself,
No, not to gain your charming high-prized person.
Though I admire you strangely for your beauty,
Yet I contemn your mind.
And yet I would at any rate enjoy you;
At your own rate; but cannot. See here
The only sum I can command on earth:
I know not where to eat when this is gone.
Yet such a slave I am to love and beauty
This last reserve I'll sacrifice to enjoy you.
Nay, do not frown, I know you're to be bought,
And would be bought by me. By me,
For a meaning trifling sum, if I could pay it down.
Which happy knowledge I will still repeat,
And lay it to my heart: it has a virtue in't,
And soon will cure those wounds your eyes have made.
And yet, there's something so divinely powerful there—
Nay, I will gaze, to let you see my strength.

[27] Spanish gold coin.

Holds her, looks on her, and pauses and sighs.

By heav'n, bright creature, I would not for the world
Thy fame were half so fair as is thy face.

Turns her away from him.

ANGELLICA (*aside*).

His words go through me to the very soul.—
If you have nothing else to say to me—

WILLMORE.

Yes, you shall hear how infamous you are—
For which I do not hate thee—
But that secures my heart, and all the flames it feels
Are but so many lusts:
I know it by their sudden bold intrusion.
The fire's impatient and betrays; 'tis false.
For had it been the purer flame of love,
I should have pined and languished at your feet,
Ere found the impudence to have discovered it.
I now dare stand your scorn and your denial.

MORETTA.

Sure she's bewitched, that she can stand thus tamely and hear his
saucy railing. —Sirrah, will you be gone?

ANGELLICA (*to* Moretta).

How dare you take this liberty! Withdraw! —Pray tell me, sir, are not
you guilty of the same mercenary crime? When a lady is proposed to
you for a wife, you never ask how fair, discreet, or virtuous she is,
but what's her fortune; which, if but small, you cry "She will not do
my business," and basely leave her, though she languish for you. Say,
is not this as poor?

WILLMORE.

It is a barbarous custom, which I will scorn to defend in our sex, and
do despise in yours.

ANGELLICA.

Thou'rt a brave fellow! Put up thy gold, and know,
That were thy fortune as large as is thy soul,
Thou shouldst not buy my love
Couldst thou forget those mean effects of vanity
Which set me out to sale,
And as a lover prize my yielding joys.
Canst thou believe they'll be entirely thine,
Without considering they were mercenary?

WILLMORE.

>I cannot tell, I must bethink me first.
>(*Aside*). Ha! Death, I'm going to believe her.

ANGELLICA.

>Prithee confirm that faith, or if thou canst not,
>Flatter me a little: 'twill please me from thy mouth.

WILLMORE (*aside*).

>Curse on thy charming tongue! Dost thou return
>My feigned contempt with so much subtlety?—
>Thou'st found the easiest way into my heart,
>Though I yet know that all thou say'st is false.
>>*Turning from her in rage.*

ANGELLICA.

>By all that's good, 'tis real;
>I never loved before, though oft a mistress.
>Shall my first vows be slighted?

WILLMORE (*aside*).

>What can she mean?

ANGELLICA (*in an angry tone*).

>I find you cannot credit me.

WILLMORE.

>I know you take me for an errant ass,
>An ass that may be soothed into belief,
>And then be used at pleasure;
>But, madam, I have been so often cheated
>By perjured, soft, deluding hypocrites,
>That I've no faith left for the cozening sex,
>Especially for women of your trade.

ANGELLICA.

>The low esteem you have of me perhaps
>May bring my heart again:
>For I have pride that yet surmounts my love.
>>*She turns with pride; he holds her.*

WILLMORE.

>Throw off this pride, this enemy to bliss,
>And show the power of love: 'tis with those arms
>I can be only vanquished, made a slave.

ANGELLICA.

> Is all my mighty expectation vanished?
> No, I will not hear thee talk; thou hast a charm
> In every word that draws my heart away,
> And all the thousand trophies I designed
> Thou hast undone. Why art thou soft?
> Thy looks are bravely rough, and meant for war.
> Couldst thou not storm on still?
> I then perhaps had been as free as thou.

WILLMORE.

> Death, how she throws her fire about my soul!—
> Take heed, fair creature, how you raise my hopes,
> Which once assumed pretends to all dominion:
> There's not a joy thou hast in store
> I shall not then command.
> For which I'll pay you back my soul, my life!
> Come, let's begin th'account this happy minute!

ANGELLICA.

> And will you pay me then the price I ask?

WILLMORE.

> Oh, why dost thou draw me from an awful worship,
> By showing thou art no divinity.
> Conceal the fiend, and show me all the angel!
> Keep me but ignorant, and I'll be devout
> And pay my vows forever at this shrine.
>
> *Kneels and kisses her hand.*

ANGELLICA.

> The pay I mean is but thy love for mine.
> Can you give that?

WILLMORE.

> Entirely. Come, let's withdraw where I'll renew my vows, and breathe
> 'em with such ardor thou shalt not doubt my zeal.

ANGELLICA.

> Thou hast a power too strong to be resisted.
>
> *Exeunt* Willmore *and* Angellica.

MORETTA.

> Now my curse go with you! Is all our project fallen to this? To love
> the only enemy to our trade? Nay, to love such a shameroon; a very

beggar; nay, a pirate beggar, whose business is to rifle and be gone;
a no-purchase, no-pay tatterdemalion, and English picaroon; a rogue
that fights for daily drink, and takes a pride in being loyally lousy?
Oh, I could curse now, if I durst. This is the fate of most whores.

> *Trophies, which from believing fops we win,*
> *Are spoils to those who cozen us again.*   [*Exit.*]

The End of the Second Act.

ACT III

[III.i]   *A STREET*

Enter Florinda, Valeria, Hellena, *in antic different dresses from what they were
in before*; Callis *attending*.

FLORINDA.

I wonder what should make my brother in so ill a humor? I hope he
has not found out our ramble this morning.

HELLENA.

No, if he had, we should have heard on't at both ears, and have been
mewed up this afternoon, which I would not for the world should
have happened. Hey ho, I'm as sad as a lover's lute.

VALERIA.

Well, methinks we have learnt this trade of gipsies as readily as if
we had been bred upon the road to Loretto; and yet I did so fumble
when I told the stranger his fortune that I was afraid I should have
told my own and yours by mistake. But methinks Hellena has been
very serious ever since.

FLORINDA.

I would give my garters she were in love, to be revenged upon her
for abusing me. How is't, Hellena?

HELLENA.

Ah, would I had never seen my mad monsieur. And yet, for all your
laughing, I am not in love. And yet this small acquaintance, o' my
conscience, will never out of my head.

VALERIA.

Ha! Ha! Ha! I laugh to think how thou art fitted with a lover, a fellow that I warrant loves every new face he sees.

HELLENA.

Hum, he has not kept his word with me here, and may be taken up. That thought is not very pleasant to me. What the deuce should this be now that I feel?

VALERIA.

What is't like?

HELLENA.

Nay, the Lord knows, but if I should be hanged I cannot choose but be angry and afraid when I think that mad fellow should be in love with anybody but me. What to think of myself I know not: would I could meet with some true damned gipsy, that I might know my fortune.

VALERIA.

Know it! Why there's nothing so easy: thou wilt love this wand'ring inconstant till thou find'st thyself hanged about his neck, and then be as mad to get free again.

FLORINDA.

Yes, Valeria, we shall see her bestride his baggage horse and follow him to the campaign.

HELLENA.

So, so, now you are provided for there's no care taken of poor me. But since you have set my heart a-wishing, I am resolved to know for what; I will not die of the pip,[28] so I will not.

FLORINDA.

Art thou mad to talk so? Who will like thee well enough to have thee, that hears what a mad wench thou art?

HELLENA.

Like me? I don't intend every he that likes me shall have me, but he that I like. I should have stayed in the nunnery still if I had liked my

---

[28] Slight disease or depression.

lady abbess as well as she liked me. No, I came thence not, as my wise brother imagines, to take an eternal farewell of the world, but to love and to be beloved; and I will be beloved, or I'll get one of your men, so I will.

VALERIA.

Am I put into the number of lovers?

HELLENA.

You? Why, coz, I know thou'rt too good-natured to leave us in any design; thou wouldst venture a cast though thou comest off a loser, especially with such a gamester. I observed your man, and your willing ear incline that way; and if you are not a lover, 'tis an art soon learnt—that I find.

Sighs.

FLORINDA.

I wonder how you learnt to love so easily. I had a thousand charms to meet my eyes and ears ere I could yield, and 'twas the knowledge of Belvile's merit, not the surprising person, took my soul. Thou art too rash, to give a heart at first sight.

HELLENA.

Hang your considering lover! I never thought beyond the fancy that 'twas a very pretty, idle, silly kind of pleasure to pass one's time with: to write little soft nonsensical billets, and with great difficulty and danger receive answers in which I shall have my beauty praised, my wit admired, though little or none, and have the vanity and power to know I am desirable. Then I have the more inclination that way because I am to be a nun, and so shall not be suspected to have any such earthly thoughts about me; but when I walk thus—and sigh thus—they'll think my mind's upon my monastery, and cry, "How happy 'tis she's so resolved." But not a word of man.

FLORINDA.

What a mad creature's this!

HELLENA.

I'll warrant, if my brother hears either of you sigh, he cries gravely, "I fear you have the indiscretion to be in love, but take heed of the honor of our house, and your own unspotted fame"; and so he conjures on till he has laid the soft winged god in your hearts, or broke the bird's nest. But see, here comes your lover, but where's my inconstant? Let's step aside, and we may learn something.

Go aside.

Enter Belvile, Frederick, *and* Blunt.

BELVILE.

What means this! The picture's taken in.

BLUNT.

It may be the wench is good-natured, and will be kind gratis. Your friend's a proper handsome fellow.

BELVILE.

I rather think she has cut his throat and is fled; I am mad he should throw himself into dangers. Pox on't, I shall want him, too, at night. Let's knock and ask for him.

HELLENA.

My heart goes a-pit, a-pat, for fear 'tis my man they talk of.

Knock; Moretta *above.*

MORETTA.

What would you have?

BELVILE.

Tell the stranger that entered here about two hours ago that his friends stay here for him.

MORETTA.

A curse upon him for Moretta: would he were at the devil! But he's coming to you.

Enter Willmore.

HELLENA.

Ay, ay 'tis he. Oh, how this vexes me!

BELVILE.

And how and how, dear lad, has fortune smiled? Are we to break her windows, or raise up altars to her, hah?

WILLMORE.

Does not my fortune sit triumphant on my brow? Dost not see the little wanton god there all gay and smiling? Have I not an air about my face and eyes that distinguish me from the crowd of common lovers? By heaven, Cupid's quiver has not half so many darts as her eyes! Oh, such a *bona roba*! To sleep in her arms is lying *in fresco*, all perfumed air about me.

HELLENA (*aside*).

Here's fine encouragement for me to fool on!

WILLMORE.

Hark'ee, where didst thou purchase that rich Canary[29] we drank today? Tell me, that I may adore the spigot and sacrifice to the butt. The juice was divine; into which I must dip my rosary, and then bless all things that I would have bold or fortunate.

BELVILE.

Well, sir, let's go take a bottle and hear the story of your success.

FREDERICK.

Would not French wine do better?

WILLMORE.

Damn the hungry balderdash! Cheerful sack has a generous virtue in't inspiring a successful confidence, gives eloquence to the tongue and vigor to the soul, and has in a few hours completed all my hopes and wishes! There's nothing left to raise a new desire in me. Come, let's be gay and wanton. And, gentlemen, study; study what you want, for here are friends that will supply gentlemen. [*Jingles gold.*] Hark what a charming sound they make! 'Tis he and she gold whilst here, and shall beget new pleasures every moment.

BLUNT.

But hark'ee, sir, you are not married, are you?

WILLMORE

All the honey of matrimony but none of the sting, friend.

BLUNT.

'Adsheartlikins, thou'rt a fortunate rogue!

[29] Sweet wine from the Canary Islands.

WILLMORE.

I am so, sir: let these inform you! Ha, how sweetly they chime! Pox of poverty: it makes a man a slave, makes wit and honor sneak. My soul grew lean and rusty for want of credit.

BLUNT.

'Adsheartlikins, this I like well; it looks like my lucky bargain! Oh, how I long for the approach of my squire, that is to conduct me to her house again. Why, here's two provided for!

FREDERICK.

By this light, y'are happy men.

BLUNT.

Fortune is pleased to smile on us, gentlemen, to smile on us.

Enter Sancho *and pulls down* Blunt *by the sleeve; they go aside.*

SANCHO.

Sir, my lady expects you. She has removed all that might oppose your will and pleasure, and is impatient till you come.

BLUNT.

Sir, I'll attend you.—Oh the happiest rogue! I'll take no leave, lest they either dog me or stay me.

Exit with Sancho.

BELVILE.

But then the little gipsy is forgot?

WILLMORE.

A mischief on thee for putting her into my thoughts! I had quite forgot her else, and this night's debauch had drunk her quite down.

HELLENA.

Had it so, good captain!

Claps him on the back.

WILLMORE (*aside*).

Ha! I hope she did not hear me!

HELLENA.

What, afraid of such a champion?

WILLMORE.

Oh, you're a fine lady of your word, are you not? To make a man languish a whole day—

HELLENA.

In tedious search of me.

WILLMORE.

Egad, child, thou'rt in the right. Hadst thou seen what a melancholy dog I have been ever since I was a lover, how I have walked the streets like a Capuchin, with my hands in my sleeves—faith, sweetness, thou wouldst pity me.

HELLENA [*aside*].

Now if I should be hanged I can't be angry with him, he dissembles so heartily. —Alas, good captain, what pains you have taken; now were I ungrateful not to reward so true a servant.

WILLMORE.

Poor soul, that's kindly said; I see thou barest a conscience. Come then, for a beginning show me thy dear face.

HELLENA.

I'm afraid, my small acquaintance, you have been staying that swinging stomach you boasted of this morning. I then remember my little collation would have gone down with you without the sauce of a handsome face. Is your stomach so queasy now?

WILLMORE.

Faith, long fasting, child, spoils a man's appetite. Yet if you durst treat, I could so lay about me still—

HELLENA.

And would you fall to before a priest says grace?

WILLMORE.

Oh fie, fie, what an old out-of-fashioned thing has thou named? Thou couldst not dash me more out of countenance shouldst thou show me an ugly face.

Whilst he is seemingly courting Hellena, *enter* Angellica, Moretta, Biskey, *and* Sebastian, *all in masquerade.* Angellica *sees* Willmore *and stares.*

ANGELLICA.

Heavens, 'tis he! And passionately fond to see another woman!

MORETTA.

What could you less expect from such a swaggerer?

ANGELLICA.

Expect? As much as I paid him: a heart entire,
Which I had pride enough to think when'er I gave,
It would have raised the man above the vulgar,
Made him all soul, and that all soft and constant.

HELLENA.

You see, captain, how willing I am to be friends with you, till time
and ill luck make us lovers; and ask you the question first rather than
put your modesty to the blush by asking me. For alas, I know you
captains are such strict men, and such severe observers of your vows
to chastity, that 'twill be hard to prevail with your tender conscience
to marry a young willing maid.

WILLMORE.

Do not abuse me, for fear I should take thee at thy word and marry
thee indeed, which I'm sure will be revenge sufficient.

HELLENA.

O' my conscience, that will be our destiny, because we are both of
one humor: I am as inconstant as you, for I have considered, captain,
that a handsome woman has a great deal to do whilst her face is good.
For then is our harvest-time to gather friends, and should I in these
days of my youth catch a fit of foolish constancy, I were undone: 'tis
loitering by daylight in our great journey. Therefore, I declare I'll
allow but one year for love, one year for indifference, and one year
for hate; and then go hang yourself, for I profess myself the gay, the
kind, and the inconstant. The devil's in't if this won't please you!

WILLMORE.

Oh, most damnably. I have a heart with a hole quite through it too;
no prison mine, to keep a mistress in.

ANGELLICA (*aside*).

Perjured man! How I believe thee now!

HELLENA.

Well, I see our business as well as humors are alike: yours to cozen
as many maids as will trust you, and I as many men as have faith. See

if I have not as desperate a lying look as you can have for the heart of you. (*Pulls off her vizard; he starts.*) How do you like it, captain?

WILLMORE.

Like it! By heaven, I never saw so much beauty! Oh, the charms of those sprightly black eyes! That strangely fair face, full of smiles and dimples! Those soft round melting cherry lips and small even white teeth! Not to be expressed, but silently adored! [*She replaces her mask.*] Oh, one look more, and strike me dumb, or I shall repeat nothing else till I'm mad.

He seems to court her to pull off her vizard; she refuses.

ANGELLICA.

I can endure no more. Nor is it fit to interrupt him, for if I do, my jealousy has so destroyed my reason I shall undo him. Therefore I'll retire, and you, Sebastian (*to one of her bravos*), follow that woman and learn who 'tis; while you (*to the other bravo*) tell the fugitive I would speak to him instantly.

Exit.

This while Florinda *is talking to* Belvile, *who stands sullenly*; Frederick *courting* Valeria.

VALERIA [*to* Belvile].

Prithee, dear stranger, be not so sullen, for though you have lost your love you see my friend frankly offers you hers to play with in the meantime.

BELVILE.

Faith, madam, I am sorry I can't play at her game.

FREDERICK [*to* Valeria].

Pray leave your intercession and mind your own affair. They'll better agree apart: he's a modest sigher in company, but alone no woman 'scapes him.

FLORINDA [*aside*].

Sure he does but rally. Yet, if it should be true? I'll tempt him farther. —Believe me, noble stranger, I'm no common mistress. And for a little proof on't, wear this jewel. Nay, take it, sir, 'tis right, and bills of exchange may sometimes miscarry.

BELVILE

Madam, why am I chose out of all mankind to be the object of your bounty?

VALERIA.

There's another civil question asked.

FREDERICK [*aside*].

Pox of's modesty; it spoils his own markets and hinders mine.

FLORINDA.

Sir, from my window I have often seen you, and women of my quality have so few opportunities for love that we ought to lose none.

FREDERICK [*to* Valeria].

Ay, this is something! Here's a woman! When shall I be blest with so much kindness from your fair mouth?—(*Aside to* Belvile.) Take the jewel, fool!

BELVILE.

You tempt me strangely, madam, every way—

FLORINDA (*aside*).

So, if I find him false, my whole repose is gone.

BELVILE.

And but for a vow I've made to a very fair lady, this goodness had subdued me.

FREDERICK [*aside to* Belvile].

Pox on't, be kind, in pity to me be kind. For I am to thrive here but as you treat her friend.

HELLENA.

Tell me what you did in yonder house, and I'll unmask.

WILLMORE.

Yonder house? Oh, I went to a—to—why, there's a friend of mine lives there.

HELLENA.

What, a she or a he friend?

WILLMORE.

A man, upon honor, a man. A she friend? No, no, madam, you have done my business, I thank you.

HELLENA.

And was't your man friend that had more darts in's eyes than Cupid carries in's whole budget of arrows?

WILLMORE.

So—

HELLENA.

"Ah, such a *bona roba*! To be in her arms is lying *in fresco*, all perfumed air about me." Was this your man friend too?

WILLMORE.

So—

HELLENA.

That gave you the he and the she gold, that begets young pleasures?

WILLMORE.

Well, well, madam, then you can see there are ladies in the world that will not be cruel. There are, madam, there are.

HELLENA.

And there be men, too, as fine, wild, inconstant fellows as yourself. There be, captain, there be, if you go to that now. Therefore, I'm resolved—

WILLMORE.

Oh!

HELLENA.

To see your face no more—

WILLMORE.

Oh!

HELLENA.

Till tomorrow.

WILLMORE.

Egad, you frighted me.

HELLENA.

Nor then neither, unless you'll swear never to see that lady more.

WILLMORE.

See her! Why, never to think of womankind again.

HELLENA.

Kneel, and swear.

Kneels; she gives him her hand.

WILLMORE.

I do, never to think, to see, to love, nor lie, with any but thyself.

HELLENA.

Kiss the book.

WILLMORE.

Oh, most religiously.

Kisses her hand.

HELLENA.

Now what a wicked creature am I, to damn a proper fellow.

CALLIS (*to* Florinda).

Madam, I'll stay no longer: 'tis e'en dark.

FLORINDA [*to* Belvile].

However, sir, I'll leave this with you, that when I'm gone you may repent the opportunity you have lost by your modesty.

Gives him the jewel, which is her picture, and exit. He gazes after her.

WILLMORE [*to* Hellena].

'Twill be an age till tomorrow, and till then I will most impatiently expect you. Adieu, my dear pretty angel.

Exeunt all the women.

BELVILE.

Ha! Florinda's picture! 'Twas she herself. What a dull dog was I! I would have given the world for one minute's discourse with her.

FREDERICK.

This comes of your modesty. Ah, pox o' your vow; 'twas ten to one but we had lost the jewel by't.

BELVILE.

Willmore, the blessed'st opportunity lost! Florinda, friends, Florinda!

WILLMORE.

Ah, rogue! Such black eyes! Such a face! Such a mouth! Such teeth! And so much wit!

BELVILE.

All, all, and a thousand charms besides.

WILLMORE.

Why, dost thou know her?

BELVILE.

Know her! Ay, ay, and a pox take me with all my heart for being so modest.

WILLMORE.

But hark'ee, friend of mine, are you my rival? And have I been only beating the bush all this while?

BELVILE.

I understand thee not. I'm mad! See here—

Shows the picture.

WILLMORE.

Ha! Whose picture's this? 'Tis a fine wench!

FREDERICK.

The colonel's mistress, sir.

WILLMORE.

Oh, oh, here. (*Gives the picture back.*) I thought't had been another prize. Come, come, a bottle will set thee right again.

BELVILE.

I am content to try, and by that time 'twill be late enough for our design.

WILLMORE.

Agreed.

Love does all day the soul's great empire keep,
But wine at night lulls the soft god asleep.

                                                    Exeunt.

[III.ii]   *LUCETTA'S HOUSE.*

Enter Blunt *and* Lucetta *with a light.*

LUCETTA.

Now we are safe and free: no fears of the coming home of my old
jealous husband, which made me a little thoughtful when you came
in first. But now love is all the business of my soul.

BLUNT.

I am transported!—(*Aside.*) Pox on't, that I had but some fine things
to say to her, such as lovers use. I was a fool not to learn of Fred a
little by heart before I came. Something I must say. —'Adsheartlikins,
sweet soul, I am not used to compliment, but I'm an honest gentleman,
and thy humble servant.

LUCETTA.

I have nothing to pay for so great a favor, but such a love as cannot
but be great, since at first sight of that sweet face and shape it made
me your absolute captive.

BLUNT (*aside*).

Kind heart, how prettily she talks! Egad, I'll show her husband a Spanish
trick: send him out of the world and marry her; she's damnably in love
with me, and will ne'er mind settlements, and so there's that saved.

LUCETTA.

Well, sir, I'll go and undress me, and be with you instantly.

BLUNT.

Make haste then, for 'adsheartlikins, dear soul, thou canst not guess
at the pain of a longing lover when his joys are drawn within the
compass of a few minutes.

LUCETTA.

You speak my sense, and I'll make haste to prove it.

                                                    Exit.

BLUNT.

'Tis a rare girl, and this one night's enjoyment with her will be worth
all the days I ever passed in Essex. Would she would go with me into
England, though to say truth, there's plenty of whores already. Put a
box on 'em, they are such mercenary prodigal whores that they want
such a one as this, that's free and generous, to give 'em good examples.
Why, what a house she has, how rich and fine!

Enter Sancho.

SANCHO.

Sir, my lady has sent me to conduct you to her chamber.

BLUNT.

Sir, I shall be proud to follow. —(*Aside.*) Here's one of her servants
too; 'adsheartlikins, by this garb and gravity he might be a justice of
peace in Essex, and is but a pimp here.

Exeunt.

[III.iii]

The scene changes to a chamber with an alcove bed in't, a table, etc.; Lucetta *in
bed. Enter* Sancho *and* Blunt, *who takes the candle of Sancho at the door.*

SANCHO.

Sir, my commission reaches no farther.

BLUNT.

Sir, I'll excuse your compliment.   [*Exit* Sancho.]
—What, in bed, my sweet mistress?

LUCETTA.

You see, I still outdo you in kindness.

BLUNT.

And thou shalt see what haste I'll make to quit scores. Oh, the
luckiest rogue!

He undresses himself.

LUCETTA.

Should you be false or cruel now—

BLUNT.

False! 'Adsheartlikins, what dost thou take me for, a Jew? An insensible heathen? A pox of thy old jealous husband: an he were dead, egad, sweet soul, it should be none of my fault if I did not marry thee.

LUCETTA.

It never should be mine.

BLUNT.

Good soul! I'm the fortunatest dog!

LUCETTA.

Are you not undressed yet?

BLUNT.

As much as my impatience will permit.
Goes toward the bed in his shirt, drawers, etc.

LUCETTA.

Hold, sir, put out the light; it may betray us else.

BLUNT.

Anything; I need no other light but that of thine eyes. —(*Aside.*) 'Adsheartlikins, there I think I had it.

Puts out the candle; the bed descends; he gropes about to find it.

Why, why, where am I got? What, not yet? Where are you, sweetest—Ah, the rogue's silent now. A pretty love-trick this; how she'll laugh at me anon! —You need not, my dear rogue, you need not! I'm all on fire already; come, come, now call me, in pity. —Sure I'm enchanted! I have been round the chamber, and can find neither woman nor bed. I locked the door; I'm sure she cannot go that way, of if she could, the bed could not. —Enough, enough, my pretty wanton; do not carry the jest too far! (*Lights on a trap, and is let down.*) —Ha! Betrayed! Dogs! Rogues! Pimps! Help! Help!

Enter Lucetta, Phillipo, *and* Sancho *with a light.*

PHILLIPO.

Ha! Ha! Ha! He's dispatched finely.

LUCETTA.

Now, sir, had I been coy, we had missed of this booty.

PHILLIPO.

Nay, when I saw 'twas a substantial fool, I was mollified. But when you dote upon a serenading coxcomb, upon a face, fine clothes, and a lute, it makes me rage.

LUCETTA.

You know I was never guilty of that folly, my dear Phillipo, but with yourself. But come, let's see what we have got by this.

PHILLIPO.

A rich coat; sword and hat; these breeches, too, are well lined! See here, a gold watch! A purse— Ha! Gold! At least two hundred pistoles! A bunch of diamond rings, and one with the family arms! A gold box, with a medal of his king, and his lady mother's picture! These were sacred relics, believe me. See, the waistband of his breeches have a mine of gold—old queen Bess's! We have a quarrel to her ever since eighty-eight.[30] and may therefore justify the theft: the Inquisition might have committed it.

LUCETTA.

See, a bracelet of bowed gold! These his sisters tied about his arm at parting. But well, for all this, I fear his being a stranger may make a noise and hinder our trade with them hereafter.

PHILLIPO.

That's our security: he is not only a stranger to us, but to the country too. The common shore[31] into which he is descended, thou know'st, conducts him into another street, which this light will hinder him from ever finding again. He knows neither your name, nor that of the street where your house is; nay, nor the way to his own lodgings.

LUCETTA.

And art thou not an unmerciful rogue, not to afford him one night for all this? I should not have been such a Jew.

PHILLIPO.

Blame me not, Lucetta, to keep as much of thee as I can to myself. Come, that thought makes me wanton; let's to bed. —Sancho, lock up these.

[30] The Spanish Armada invading England was destroyed in 1588.
[31] Sewer.

> *This is the fleece which fools do bear,*
> *Designed for witty men to shear.*

Exeunt.

[III.iv]

The scene changes, and discovers Blunt *creeping out of a common shore; his face, etc., all dirty.*

BLUNT (*climbing up*).

Oh, Lord, I am got out at last, and, which is a miracle, without a clue. And now to damning and cursing! But if that would ease me, where shall I begin? With my fortune, myself, or the quean that cozened me? What a dog was I to believe in woman! Oh, coxcomb! Ignorant conceited coxcomb! To fancy she could be enamored with my person! At first sight enamored! Oh, I'm a cursed puppy! 'Tis plain, fool was writ upon my forehead! She perceived it; saw the Essex calf there. For what allurements could there be in this countenance, which I can endure because I'm acquainted with it. Oh dull, silly dog, to be thus soothed into a cozening! Had I been drunk, I might fondly have credited the young quean; but as I was in my right wits to be thus cheated, confirms it: I am a dull believing English country fop. But my comrades! Death and the devil, there's the worst of all! Then a ballad will be sung tomorrow on the Prado, to a lousy tune of the enchanted squire and the annihilated damsel. But Fred—that rogue—and the colonel will abuse me beyond all Christian patience. Had she left me my clothes, I have a bill of exchange at home would have saved my credit. But now all hope is taken from me. Well, I'll home, if I can find the way, with this consolation: that I am not the first kind believing coxcomb; but there are, gallants, many such good natures amongst ye.

> *And though you've better arts to hide your follies,*
> *'Adsheartlikins, y'are all as errant cullies.*

Exit.

[III.v]   *Scene, the Garden in the Night.*

Enter Florinda *in an undress, with a key and a little box.*

FLORINDA.

Well, thus far I'm in my way to happiness. I have got myself free from Callis; my brother too, I find my yonder light, is got into his cabinet, and thinks not of me; I have by good fortune got the key of the garden back door. I'll open it to prevent Belvile's knocking: a little noise will now alarm my brother. Now am I as fearful as a young thief. (*Unlocks the door.*) Hark! What noise is that? Oh, 'twas the wind that played amongst the boughs. Belvile stays long, methinks; it's time. Stay, for fear of a surprise, I'll hide these jewels in yonder jasmine.

She goes to lay down the box.

Enter Willmore, *drunk.*

WILLMORE.

What the devil is become of these fellows Belvile and Frederick? They promised to stay at the next corner for me, but who the devil knows the corner of a full moon? Now, whereabouts am I? Ha, what have we here? A garden! A very convenient place to sleep in. Ha! What has God sent us here? A female! By this light, a woman! I'm a dog if it be not a very wench!

FLORINDA.

He's come! Ha! Who's there?

WILLMORE.

Sweet soul, let me salute thy shoestring.

FLORINDA [*aside*].

'Tis not my Belvile. Good heavens, I know him not!—Who are you, and from whence come you?

WILLMORE.

Prithee, prithee, child, not so many hard questions! Let it suffice I am here, child. Come, come kiss me.

FLORINDA.

Good gods! What luck is mine?

WILLMORE.

Only good luck, child, parlous good luck. Come hither.—'Tis a delicate shining wench. By this hand, she's perfumed, and smells like any nosegay.—Prithee, dear soul, let's not play the fool and lose time—precious time. For as God shall save me, I'm as honest a fellow as breathes, though I'm a little disguised at present. Come, I say. Why, thou mayst be free with me: I'll be very secret. I'll not boast who 'twas obliged me, not I; for hang me if I know thy name.

FLORINDA.

Heavens! What a filthy beast is this!

WILLMORE.

I am so, and thou ought'st the sooner to lie with me for that reason. For look you, child, there will be no sin in't, because 'twas neither designed nor premeditated: 'tis pure accident on both sides. That's a certain thing now. Indeed, should I make love to you, and you vow fidelity, and swear and lie till you believed and yielded—that were to make it wilful fornication, the crying sin of the nation. Thou art, therefore, as thou art a good Christian, obliged in conscience to deny me nothing. Now, come be kind without any more idle prating.

FLORINDA.

Oh, I am ruined! Wicked man, unhand me!

WILLMORE.

Wicked? Egad, child, a judge, were he young and vigorous, and saw those eyes of thine, would know 'twas they gave the first blow, the first provocation. Come, prithee let's lose no time, I say. This is a fine convenient place.

FLORINDA.

Sir, let me go, I conjure you, or I'll call out.

WILLMORE.

Ay, ay, you were best to call witness to see how finely you treat me. Do!

FLORINDA.

I'll cry murder, rape, or anything, if you do not instantly let me go!

WILLMORE.

A rape! Come, come, you lie, you baggage, you lie. What! I'll warrant you would fain have the world believe now that you are not so forward as I. No, not you. Why at this time of night was your cobweb door set open, dear spider, but to catch flies? Ha! Come, or I shall be damnably angry. Why, what a coil is here!

FLORINDA.

Sir, can you think—

WILLMORE.

That you would do't for nothing? Oh, oh, I find what you would be at. Look here, here's a pistole for you. Here's a work indeed! Here, take it, I say!

FLORINDA.

For heaven's sake, sir, as you're a gentleman—

WILLMORE.

So now, now, she would be wheedling me for more! What, you will not take it then? You are resolved you will not? Come, come, take it or I'll put it up again, for look ye, I never give more. Why, how now, mistress, are you so high i'th' mouth a pistole won't down with you? Ha! Why, what a work's here! In good time! Come, no struggling to be gone. But an y'are good at a dumb wrestle, I'm for ye. Look ye, I'm for ye.

She struggles with him.

Enter Belvile *and* Frederick.

BELVILE.

The door is open. A pox of this mad fellow! I'm angry that we've lost him; I durst have sworn he had followed us.

FREDERICK.

But you were so hasty, colonel, to be gone.

FLORINDA.

Help! Help! Murder! Help! Oh, I am ruined!

BELVILE.

Ha! Sure that's Florinda's voice! (*Comes up to them.*) A man!—Villain, let go that lady!

A noise; Willmore *turns and draws;* Frederick *interposes.*

FLORINDA.

Belvile! Heavens! My brother too is coming, and 'twill be impossible to escape. Belvile, I conjure you to walk under my chamber window, from whence I'll give you some instructions what to do. This rude man has undone us.

Exit.

WILLMORE.

Belvile!

Enter Pedro, Stephano, *and other servants, with lights.*

PEDRO.

I'm betrayed! Run, Stephano, and see if Florinda be safe.

Exit Stephano.

They fight, and Pedro's *party beats 'em out.*

—So, who'er they be, all is not well. I'll to Florinda's chamber.
Going out, meets Stephano.

STEPHANO.

You need not, sir: the poor lady's fast asleep, and thinks no harm.
I would not awake her, sir, for fear of frighting her with your
danger.

PEDRO.

I'm glad she's there. —Rascals, how came the garden door open?

STEPHANO.

That question comes too late, sir. Some of my fellow servants masquerading, I'll warrant.

PEDRO.

Masquerading! A lewd custom to debauch our youth! There's something more in this than I imagine.

Exeunt.

[III.vi]   *Scene changes to the street.*

Enter Belvile *in rage,* Frederick *holding him,* Willmore *melancholy.*

WILLMORE.

Why, how the devil should I know Florinda?

BELVILE.

Ah, plague of your ignorance! If it had not been Florinda, must you
be a beast? A brute? A senseless swine?

WILLMORE.

Well, sir, you see I am endued with patience: I can bear. Though
egad, y'are very free with me, methinks. I was in good hopes the
quarrel would have been on my side, for so uncivilly interrupting
me.

BELVILE.

Peace, brute, whilst thou'rt safe. Oh, I'm distracted!

WILLMORE.

Nay, nay, I'm an unlucky dog, that's certain.

BELVILE.

Ah, curse upon the star that ruled my birth, or whatsoever other influence that makes me still so wretched.

WILLMORE.

Thou break'st my heart with these complaints. There is no star in fault, no influence but sack, the cursed sack I drunk.

FREDERICK.

Why, how the devil came you so drunk?

WILLMORE.

Why, how the devil came you so sober?

BELVILE.

A curse upon his thin skull, he was always beforehand that way.

FREDERICK.

Prithee, dear colonel, forgive him; he's sorry for his fault.

BELVILE.

He's always so after he has done a mischief. A plague on all such brutes!

WILLMORE.

By this light, I took her for an errant harlot.

BELVILE.

Damn your debauched opinion! Tell me, sot, hadst thou so much sense and light about thee to distinguish her woman, and couldst not see something about her face and person to strike an awful reverence into thy soul?

WILLMORE.

Faith no, I considered her as mere a woman as I could wish.

BELVILE.

'Sdeath, I have no patience. Draw, or I'll kill you!

WILLMORE.

Let that alone till tomorrow, and if I set not all right again, use your pleasure.

BELVILE.

Tomorrow! Damn it,
The spiteful light will lead me to no happiness.
Tomorrow is Antonio's, and perhaps
Guides him to my undoing. Oh, that I could meet
This rival, this powerful fortunate!

WILLMORE.

What then?

BELVILE.

Let thy own reason, or my rage, instruct thee.

WILLMORE.

I shall be finely informed then, no doubt. Hear me, colonel, hear me;
show me the man and I'll do his business.

BELVILE.

I know him no more than thou, or if I did I should not need
thy aid.

WILLMORE.

This you say is Angellica's house; I promised the kind baggage to lie
with her tonight.

Offers to go in.

Enter Antonio *and his* Page. Antonio *knocks on the hilt of's sword.*

ANTONIO.

You paid the thousand crowns I directed?

PAGE.

To the lady's old woman, sir, I did.

WILLMORE.

Who the devil have we have?

BELVILE.

I'll now plant myself under Florinda's window, and if I find no
comfort there, I'll die.

Exeunt Belvile *and* Frederick.

Enter Moretta.

MORETTA.

Page?

PAGE.

Here's my lord.

WILLMORE.

How is this? A picaroon[32] going to board my frigate? —Here's one chase gun for you!
Drawing his sword, justles Antonio, *who turns and draws. They fight;* Antonio *falls.*

MORETTA.

Oh, bless us! We're all undone!

Runs in and shuts the door.

PAGE.

Help! Murder!

Belvile *returns at the noise of fighting.*

BELVILE.

Ha! The mad rogue's engaged in some unlucky adventure again.

Enter two or three Masqueraders.

MASQUERADER.

Ha! A man killed!

WILLMORE.

How, a man killed? Then I'll go home to sleep.
Puts up and reels out. Exeunt Masqueraders *another way.*

BELVILE.

Who should it be? Pray heaven the rogue is safe, for all my quarrel to him.

As Belvile *is groping about, enter an* Officer *and six* Soldiers.

SOLDIER.

Who's there?

OFFICER.

So, here's one dispatched. Secure the murderer.

BELVILE.

Do not mistake my charity for murder! I came to his assistance!

Solders sieze on Belvile.

OFFICER.

That shall be tried, sir. St. Jago! Swords drawn in the Carnival time!

Goes to Antonio.

32 A rogue or pirate.

ANTONIO.

Thy hand, prithee.

OFFICER.

Ha! Don Antonio! Look well to the villain there.—How is it, sir?

ANTONIO.

I'm hurt.

BELVILE.

Has my humanity made me a criminal?

OFFICER.

Away with him!

BELVILE.

What a curst chance is this!

Exeunt soldiers with Belvile.

ANTONIO [*aside*].

This is the man that has set upon me twice. —(*To the officer.*) Carry him to my apartment till you have farther orders from me.

Exit Antonio, *led*.

The End of the Third Act.

ACT IV

[IV.i] *A FINE ROOM.*

Discovers Belvile *as by dark alone.*

BELVILE.

When shall I be weary of railing on fortune, who is resolved never to turn with smiles upon me? Two such defeats in one night none but the devil and that mad rogue could have contrived to have plagued me with. I am here a prisoner. But where, heaven knows. And if there be murder done, I can soon decide the fate of a stranger in a nation without mercy. Yet this is nothing to the torture my soul bows with when I think of losing my fair, my dear Florinda. Hark, my door opens. A light! A man, and seems of quality. Armed, too, Now shall I die like a dog, without defense.

Enter Antonio *in a nightgown, with a light; his arm in a scarf, and a sword under his arm. He sets the candle on the table.*

ANTONIO.

Sir, I come to know what injuries I have done you, that could provoke you to so mean an action as to attack me basely without allowing time for my defense?

BELVILE.

Sir, for a man in my circumstances to plead innocence would look like fear. But view me well, and you will find no marks of coward on me, nor anything that betrays that brutality you accuse me with.

ANTONIO.

In vain, sir, you impose upon my sense. You are not only he who drew on me last night, but yesterday before the same house, that of Angellica. Yet there is something in your face and mien that makes me wish I were mistaken.

BELVILE.

I own I fought today in the defense of a friend of mine with whom you, if you're the same, and your party were first engaged. Perhaps you think this crime enough to kill me, but if you do, I cannot fear you'll do it basely.

ANTONIO.

No sir, I'll make you fit for a defense with this.

Gives him the sword.

BELVILE.

This gallantry surprises me, nor know I how to use this present, sir, against a man so brave.

ANTONIO.

You shall not need. For know, I come to snatch you from a danger that is decreed against you: perhaps your life, or long imprisonment. And 'twas with so much courage you offended, I cannot see you punished.

BELVILE.

How shall I pay this generosity?

ANTONIO.

It had been safer to have killed another than have attempted me. To show your danger, sir, I'll let you know my quality: and 'tis the Viceroy's son whom you have wounded.

BELVILE.

The Viceroy's son! —(*Aside.*) Death and confusion! Was this plague reserved to complete all the rest? Obliged by him, the man of all the world I would destroy!

ANTONIO.

You seem disordered, sir.

BELVILE.

Yes, trust me, I am, and 'tis with pain that man receives such bounties who wants the power to pay 'em back again.

ANTONIO.

To gallant spirits 'tis indeed uneasy, but you may quickly overpay me, sir.

BELVILE (*aside*).

Then I am well. Kind heaven, but set us even, that I may fight with him and keep my honor safe. —Oh, I'm impatient, sir, to be discounting the mighty debt I owe you. Command me quickly.

ANTONIO.

I have a quarrel with a rival, sir, about the maid we love.

BELVILE (*aside*).

Death, 'tis Florinda he means! That thought destroys my reason, and I shall kill him.

ANTONIO.

My rival, sir, is one has all the virtues man can boast of—

BELVILE (*aside*).

Death, who should this be?

ANTONIO.

He challenged me to meet him on the Molo as soon as day appeared, but last night's quarrel has made my arm unfit to guide a sword.

BELVILE.

I apprehend you, sir. You'd have me kill the man that lays a claim to the maid you speak of. I'll do't. I'll fly to do't!

ANTONIO.

Sir, do you know her?

BELVILE.

No, sir, but 'tis enough she is admired by you.

ANTONIO.

Sir, I shall rob you of the glory on't, for you must fight under my name and dress.

BELVILE.

That opinion must be strangely obliging that makes you think I can personate the brave Antonio, whom I can but strive to imitate.

ANTONIO.

You say too much to my advantage. Come, sir, the day appears that calls you forth. Within, sir, is the habit.

Exit Antonio.

BELVILE.

Fantastic fortune, thou deceitful light,
That cheats the wearied traveler by night,
Though on a precipice each step you tread,
I am resolved to follow where you lead.

Exit.

[IV.ii]   *THE MOLO*.

Enter Florinda *and* Callis *in masks, with* Stephano.

FLORINDA (*aside*).

I'm dying with my fears: Belvile's not coming as I expected under my window makes me believe that all those fears are true. —Canst thou not tell with whom my brother fights?

STEPHANO.

No, madam, they were both in masquerade. I was by when they challenged one another, and they had decided the quarrel then, but were prevented by some cavaliers; which made 'em put it off till now. But I am sure 'tis about you they fight.

FLORINDA (*aside*).

Nay, then, 'tis with Belvile, for what other lover have I that dares fight for me except Antonio, and he is too much in favor with my brother. If it be he, for whom shall I direct my prayers to heaven?

STEPHANO.

Madam, I must leave you, for if my master see me, I shall be hanged for being your conductor. I escaped narrowly for the excuse I made for you last night i'th' garden.

FLORINDA.

And I'll reward thee for't. Prithee, no more.

Exit Stephano.

Enter Don Pedro *in his masking habit.*

PEDRO.

Antonio's late today; the place will fill, and we may be prevented.

Walks about.

FLORINDA (*aside*).

Antonio? Sure I heard amiss.

PEDRO.

But who will not excuse a happy lover
When soft fair arms confine the yielding neck,
And the kind whisper languishingly breathes
"Must you be gone so soon?"
Sure I had dwelt forever on her bosom—
But stay, he's here.

Enter Belvile *dressed in Antonio's clothes.*

FLORINDA [*aside*].

'Tis not Belvile; half my fears are vanished.

PEDRO.

Antonio!

BELVILE (*aside*).

This must be he. —You're early, sir; I do not use to be outdone this way.

PEDRO.

The wretched, sir, are watchful, and 'tis enough you've the advantage
of me in Angellica.

BELVILE (*aside*).

Angellica! Or I've mistook my man, or else Antonio! Can he forget his
interest in Florinda and fight for common prize?

PEDRO.

Come, sir, you know our terms.

BELVILE (*aside*).

By heaven, not I. —No talking; I am ready, sir.

Offers to fight; Florinda *runs in.*

FLORINDA (*to* Belvile).

Oh, hold! Whoe'er you be, I do conjure you hold! If you strike here, I die!

PEDRO.

Florinda!

BELVILE.

Florinda imploring for my rival!

PEDRO.

Away; this kindness is unseasonable.

Puts her by; they fight; she runs in just as Belvile *disarms* Pedro.

FLORINDA.

Who are you, sir, that dares deny my prayers?

BELVILE.

Thy prayers destroy him; if thou wouldst preserve him, do that thou'rt unacquainted with, and curse him.

She holds him.

FLORINDA.

By all you hold most dear, by her you love,
I do conjure you, touch him not.   .

BELVILE.

By her I love?
See, I obey, and at your feet resign
The useless trophy of my victory.

Lays his sword at her feet.

PEDRO.

Antonio, you've done enough to prove you love Florinda.

BELVILE.

Love Florinda! Does heaven love adoration, prayer, or penitence? Love her? Here, sir, your sword again.

Snatches up the sword and gives it to him.
Upon this truth I'll fight my life away.

PEDRO.

No, you've redeemed my sister, and my friendship.

He gives him Florinda, *and pulls off his vizard to show his face, and puts it on again.*

BELVILE.

Don Pedro!

PEDRO.

Can you resign your claims to other women, and give your heart entirely to Florinda?

BELVILE.

Entire, as dying saints' confessions are!
I can delay my happiness no longer:
This minute let me make Florinda mine.

PEDRO.

This minute let it be. No time so proper: this night my father will arrive from Rome, and possibly may hinder what we purpose.

FLORINDA.

Oh, heavens! This minute?

Enter masqueraders and pass over.

BELVILE.

Oh, do not ruin me!

PEDRO.

The place begins to fill, and that we may not be observed, do you walk off to St. Peter's church, where I will meet you and conclude your happiness.

BELVILE.

I'll meet you there. —(*Aside.*) If there be no more saints' churches in Naples.

FLORINDA.

Oh, stay, sir, and recall your hasty doom!
Alas, I have not yet prepared my heart
To entertain so strange a guest.

PEDRO.

Away; this silly modesty is assumed too late.

BELVILE.

Heaven, madam, what do you do?

FLORINDA.

Do? Despise the man that lays a tyrant's claim
To what he ought to conquer by submission.

BELVILE.

You do not know me. Move a little this way.

Draws her aside.

FLORINDA.

Yes, you may force me even to the altar,
But not the holy man that offers there
Shall force me to be thine.

Pedro *talks to* Callis *this while.*

BELVILE.

Oh, do not lose so blest an opportunity!   *Pulls off his vizard.*
See, 'tis your Belvile, not Antonio,
Whom your mistaken scorn and anger ruins.

FLORINDA.

Belvile!
Where was my soul it could not meet thy voice,
And take this knowledge in.

As they are talking, enter Willmore, *finely dressed, and* Frederick.

WILLMORE.

No intelligence? No news of Belvile yet? Well, I am the most unlucky
rascal in nature. Ha! Am I deceived, or is it he? Look, Fred! 'Tis he,
my dear Belvile!

Runs and embraces him; Belvile's vizard falls out on's hand.

BELVILE.

Hell and confusion seize thee!

PEDRO.

    Ha! Belvile! I beg your pardon, sir.

Takes Florinda from him.

BELVILE.

    Nay, touch her not. She's mine by conquest, sir;
    I won her by my sword.

WILLMORE.

    Didst thou so? And egad, child, we'll keep her by the sword.

Draws in Pedro; Belvile goes between.

BELVILE.

    Stand off!
    Thou'rt profanely lewd, so curst by heaven,
    All quarrels thou espousest must be fatal.

WILLMORE.

    Nay, an you be so hot, my valor's coy,
    And shall be courted when you want it next.

Puts up his sword.

BELVILE (to Pedro).

    You know I ought to claim a victor's right,
    But you're the brother to divine Florinda,
    To whom I'm such a slave. To purchase her
    I durst not hurt the man she holds so dear.

PEDRO.

    'Twas by Antonio's, not by Belvile's sword
    This question should have been decided, sir.
    I must confess much to your bravery's due,
    Both now and when I met you last in arms;
    But I am nicely punctual in my word,
    As men of honor ought, and beg your pardon:
    For this mistake another time shall clear.

Aside to Florinda as they are going out.

    —This was some plot between you and Belvile,
    But I'll prevent you.

[Exeunt Pedro and Florinda.]

Belvile *looks after her and begins to walk up and down in rage.*

WILLMORE.

Do not be modest now and lose the woman. But if we shall fetch her back so—

BELVILE.

Do not speak to me!

WILLMORE.

Not speak to you? Egad, I'll speak to you, and will be answered, too.

BELVILE.

Will you, sir?

WILLMORE.

I know I've done some mischief, but I'm so dull a puppy that I'm the son of a whore if I know how or where. Prithee inform my understanding.

BELVILE.

Leave me, I say, and leave me instantly!

WILLMORE.

I will not leave you in this humor, nor till I know my crime.

BELVILE.

Death, I'll tell you, sir—

Draws and runs at Willmore; *he runs out,* Belvile *after him*; Frederick *interposes.*

Enter Angellica, Moretta, *and* Sebastian.

ANGELLICA.

Ha! Sebastian, is that not Willmore? Haste! haste and bring him back.
                                                    [*Exit* Sebastian].

FREDERICK [*aside*].

The colonel's mad: I never saw him thus before. I'll after 'em lest he do some mischief, for I am sure Willmore will not draw on him.
                                                              Exit.

ANGELLICA.

> I am all rage! My first desires defeated!
> For one for aught he knows that has no
> Other merit than her quality,
> Her being Don Pedro's sister. He loves her!
> I know 'tis so, Dull, dull, insensible,
> He will not see me now, though oft invited,
> And broke his word last night. False perjured man!
> He that but yesterday fought for my favors,
> And would have made his life a sacrifice
> To've gained one night with me,
> Must now be hired and courted to my arms.

MORETTA.

> I told you what would come on't, but Moretta's an old doting fool. Why
> did you give him five hundred crowns, but to set himself out for other
> lovers? You should have kept him poor if you had meant to have had
> any good from him.

ANGELLICA.

> Oh, name not such mean trifles! Had I given
> Him all my youth has earned from sin,
> I had not lost a thought nor sigh upon't.
> But I have given him my eternal rest,
> My whole repose, my future joys, my heart!
> My virgin heart, Moretta! Oh, 'tis gone!

MORETTA.

> Curse on him, here he comes. How fine she has made him, too.

> *Enter* Willmore *and* Sebastian; Angellica *turns and walks away.*

WILLMORE.

> How now, turned shadow?
> Fly when I pursue, and follow when I fly?

> *Sings.*

> *Stay, gentle shadow of my dove,*
> *And tell me ere I go,*
> *Whether the substance may not prove*
> *A fleeting thing like you.*

> *As she turns she looks on him.*
> There's a soft kind look remaining yet.

ANGELLICA.

> Well, sir, you may be gay: all happiness, all joys pursue you still.
> Fortune's your slave, and gives you every hour choice of new hearts

and beauties, till you are cloyed with the repeated bliss which others vainly languish for. But know, false man, that I shall be revenged.

Turns away in rage.

WILLMORE.

So, gad, there are of those faint-hearted lovers, whom such a sharp lesson next their hearts would make as impotent as fourscore. Pox o' this whining; my business is to laugh and love. A pox on't, I hate your sullen lover: a man shall lose as much time to put you in humor now as would serve to gain a new woman.

ANGELLICA.

I scorn to cool that fire I cannot raise,
Or do the drudgery of your virtuous mistress.

WILLMORE.

A virtuous mistress? Death, what a thing thou hast found out for me! Why, what the devil should I do with a virtuous woman, a sort of ill-natured creatures that take a pride to torment a lover. Virtue is but an infirmity in woman, a disease that renders ever the handsome ungrateful; whilst the ill-favored, for want of solicitations and address, only fancy themselves so. I have lain with a woman of quality who has all the while been railing at whores.

ANGELLICA.

I will not answer for your mistress's virtue.
Though she be young enough to know no guilt;
And I could wish you would persuade my heart
'Twas the two hundred thousand crowns you courted.

WILLMORE.

Two hundred thousand crowns! What story's this? What trick? What woman, ha?

ANGELLICA.

How strange you make it. Have you forgot the creature you entertained on the Piazzo last night?

WILLMORE (*aside*).

Ha! My gipsy worth two hundred crowns! Oh, how I long to be with her! Pox, I knew she was of quality.

ANGELLICA.

> False man! I see my ruin in thy face.
> How many vows you breathed upon my bosom
> Never to be unjust. Have you forgot so soon?

WILLMORE.

> Faith, no; I was just coming to repeat 'em. But here's a humor indeed
> would make a man a saint. —(*Aside.*) Would she would be angry
> enough to leave me, and command me not to wait on her.
>   *Enter* Hellena *dressed in man's clothes.*

HELLENA.

> This must be Angellica: I know it by her mumping[33] matron here.
> Ay, ay, 'tis she. My mad captain's with her, too, for all his swearing.
> How this unconstant humor makes me love him! —Pray, good grave
> gentlewoman, is not this Angellica?

MORETTA.

> My too young sir, it is.—[*Aside.*] I hope 'tis one from Don Antonio.
>   *Goes to* Angellica.

HELLENA (*aside.*)

> Well, something I'll do to vex him for this.

ANGELLICA.

> I will not speak with him. Am I in humor to receive a lover?

WILLMORE.

> Not speak with him? Why, I'll be gone, and wait your idler minutes.
> Can I show less obedience to the thing I love so fondly?
>   *Offers to go.*

ANGELLICA.

> A fine excuse this! Stay—

WILLMORE.

> And hinder your advantage? Should I repay your bounties so ungrate-
> fully?

ANGELLICA [*to* Hellena].

> Come hither, boy. —[*To* Willmore.] That I may let you see
> How much above the advantages you name
> I prize one minute's joy with you.

[33] Sullen.

WILLMORE (*impatient to be gone*).

> Oh, you destroy me with this endearment. —[*Aside.*] Death, how shall
> I get away?—Madam, 'twill not be fit I should be seen with you. Besides,
> it will not be convenient. And I've a friend—that's dangerously sick.

ANGELLICA.

> I see you're impatient. Yet you shall stay.

WILLMORE (*aside*).

> And miss my assignation with my gipsy.

Walks about impatiently; Moretta *brings* Hellena, *who addresses herself to*
Angellica.

HELLENA.

> Madam,
> You'll hardly pardon my instrusion
> When you shall know my business,
> And I'm too young to tell my tale with art;
> But there must be a wondrous store of goodness
> Where so much beauty dwells.

ANGELLICA.

> A pretty advocate, whoever sent thee.
> Prithee proceed.
>
> > *To* Willmore, *who is stealing off.*
>
> —Nay, sir, you shall not go.

WILLMORE (*aside*).

> Then I shall lose my dear gipsy forever. Pox on't, she stays me
> out of spite.

HELLENA.

> I am related to a lady, madam,
> Young, rich, and nobly born, but has the fate
> To be in love with a young English gentleman.
> Strangely she loves him, at first sight she loved him,
> But did adore him when she heard him speak;
> For he, she said, had charms in every word
> That failed not to surprise, to wound and conquer.

WILLMORE (*aside*).

> Ha! Egad, I hope this concerns me.

ANGELLICA (*aside*).

> 'Tis my false man he means. Would he were gone:
> This praise will raise his pride, and ruin me.
>
> >   (*To* Willmore.) —Well,
> Since you are so impatient to be gone,
> I will release you, sir.

WILLMORE (*aside*).

> Nay, then I'm sure 'twas me he spoke of: this cannot be the effects of
> kindness in her. —No, Madam, I've considered better on't, and will
> not give you cause of jealousy.

ANGELLICA.

> But sir, I've business that—

WILLMORE.

> This shall not do; I know 'tis but to try me.

ANGELLICA.

> Well, to your story, boy. —(*Aside*). Though 'twill undo me.

HELLENA.

> With this addition to his other beauties,
> He won her unresisting tender heart.
> He vowed, and sighed, and swore he loved her dearly;
> And she believed the cunning flatterer,
> And thought herself the happiest maid alive.
> Today was the appointed time by both
> To consummate their bliss:
> The virgin, altar, and the priest were dressed;
> And whilst she languished for th'expected bridegroom,
> She heard he paid his broken vows to you.

WILLMORE (*aside*).

> So, this is some dear rogue that's in love with me, and this way
> lets me know it. Or, if it be not me, he means someone whose place
> I may supply.

ANGELLICA.

> Now I perceive
> The cause of thy impatience to be gone,
> And all the business of this glorious dress.

WILLMORE.

> Damn the young prater; I know not what he means.

HELLENA.

> Madam,
> In your fair eyes I read too much concern
> To tell my farther business.

ANGELLICA.

> Prithee, sweet youth, talk on: thou mayst perhaps
> Raise here a storm that may undo my passion,
> And then I'll grant thee anything.

HELLENA.

> Madam, 'tis to entreat you (oh unreasonable)
> You would not see this stranger.
> For if you do, she vows you are undone;
> Though nature never made a man so excellent,
> And sure he 'ad been a god, but for inconstancy.

WILLMORE (*aside*).

> Ah, rogue, how finely he's instructed! 'Tis plain, some woman that has seen me *en passant*.

ANGELLICA.

> Oh, I shall burst with jealousy! Do you know the man you speak of?

HELLENA.

> Yes, madam, he used to be in buff and scarlet.

ANGELLICA (*to* Willmore).

> Thou false as hell, what canst thou say to this?

WILLMORE.

> By heaven—

ANGELLICA.

> Hold, do not damn thyself—

HELLENA.

> Nor hope to be believed.

He walks about; they follow.

ANGELLICA.

> Oh perjured man!
> Is't thus you pay my generous passion back?

HELLENA.

> Why would you, sir, abuse my lady's faith?

ANGELLICA.

And use me so unhumanely.

HELLENA.

A maid so young, so innocent—

WILLMORE.

Ah, young devil!

ANGELLICA.

Dost thou not know thy life is in my power?

HELLENA.

Or think my lady cannot be revenged?

WILLMORE (*aside*).

So, so, the storm comes finely on.

ANGELLICA.

Now thou art silent: guilt has struck thee dumb.
Oh, hadst thou still been so, I'd lived in safety.

> *She turns away and weeps.*

WILLMORE (*aside* to Hellena).

Sweetheart, the lady's name and house—quickly! I'm impatient to
be with her.

Looks toward Angellica *to watch her turning, and as she comes towards them
he meets her.*

HELLENA (*aside*).

So, now is he for another woman.

WILLMORE.

The impudent'st young thing in nature: I cannot persuade him out of
his error, madam.

ANGELLICA.

I know he's in the right; yet thou'st a tongue
That would persuade him to deny his faith.

> *In rage walks away.*

WILLMORE (*said softly to* Hellena).

Her name, her name, dear boy!

HELLENA.

Have you forgot it, sir?

WILLMORE (*aside*).

Oh, I perceive he's not to know I am a stranger to his lady. —Yes, yes, I do know, but I have forgot the— (Angellica *turns*.)—By heaven, such early confidence I never saw.

ANGELLICA.

Did I not charge you with this mistress, sir?
Which you denied, though I beheld your perjury.
This little generosity of thine has rendered back my heart.

Walks away.

WILLMORE (*to* Hellena).

So, you have made sweet work here, my little mischief. Look your lady be kind and good-natured now, or I shall have but a cursed bargain on't. (Angellica *turns toward them*.)—The rogue's bred up to mischief: art thou so great a fool to credit him?

ANGELLICA.

Yes, I do, and you in vain impose upon me. Come hither, boy. Is not this he you spake of?

HELLENA.

I think it is. I cannot swear, but I vow he has just such another lying lover's look.

Hellena looks in his face; he gazes on her.

WILLMORE (*aside*).

Ha! Do I not know that face? By heaven, my little gipsy! What a dull dog was I: had I but looked that way I'd known her. Are all my hopes of a new woman banished? —Egad, if I do not fit thee for this, hang me.—[*To* Angellica.] Madam, I have found out the plot.

HELLENA [*aside*].

Oh lord, what does he say? Am I discovered now?

WILLMORE.

Do you see this young spark here?

HELLENA [*aside*].

He'll tell her who I am.

WILLMORE.

Who do you think this is?

HELLENA [*aside*].

Ay, ay, he does know me. —Nay, dear captain, I am undone if you discover me.

WILLMORE.

Nay, nay, no cogging;[34] she shall know what a precious mistress I have.

HELLENA.

Will you be such a devil?

WILLMORE.

Nay, nay, I'll teach you to spoil sport you will not make. —This small ambassador comes not from a person of quality, as you imagine and he says, but from a very errant gipsy: the talking'st prating'st, canting'st little animal thou ever saw'st.

ANGELLICA.

What news you tell me, that's the thing I mean.

HELLENA (*aside*).

Would I were well off the place! If ever I go a-captain-hunting again—

WILLMORE.

Mean that thing? That gipsy thing? Thou mayst as well be jealous of thy monkey or parrot as of her. A German motion[35] were worth a dozen of her, and a dream were a better enjoyment—a creature of a constitution fitter for heaven than man.

HELLENA (*aside*).

Though I'm sure he lies, yet this vexes me.

ANGELLICA.

You are mistaken: she's a Spanish woman made up of no such dull materials.

WILLMORE.

Materials? Egad, an she be made of any that will either dispense or admit of love, I'll be bound to continence.

[34] Wheedling and fawning.
[35] Puppet show.

HELLENA (*aside to him*).

Unreasonable man, do you think so?

WILLMORE.

You may return, my little brazen head, and tell your lady, that till she be handsome enough to be beloved, or I dull enough to be religious, there will be small hopes of me.

ANGELLICA.

Did you not promise, then, to marry her?

WILLMORE.

Not I, by heaven.

ANGELLICA.

You cannot undeceive my fears and torments, till you have vowed you will not marry her.

HELLENA (*aside*).

If he swears that, he'll be revenged on me indeed for all my rogueries.

ANGELLICA.

I know what arguments you'll bring against me: fortune and honor.

WILLMORE.

Honor! I tell you, I hate it in your sex; and those that fancy themselves possessed of that foppery are the most impertinently troublesome of all womankind, and will transgress nine commandments to keep one. And to satisfy your jealousy, I swear—

HELLENA (*aside to him*).

Oh, no swearing, dear captain.

WILLMORE.

If it were possible I should ever be inclined to marry, it should be some kind young sinner: one that has generosity enough to give a favor handsomely to one that can ask it discreetly, one that has wit enough to manage an intrigue of love. Oh, how civil such a wench is to a man that does her the honor to marry her.

ANGELLICA.

By heaven, there's no faith in anything he says.

                              Enter Sebastian.

SEBASTIAN.

    Madam, Don Antonio—

ANGELLICA.

    Come hither.

HELLENA [*aside*].

    Ha! Antonio! He may be coming hither, and he'll certainly discover me. I'll therefore retire without a ceremony.

                                          Exit Hellena.

ANGELLICA.

    I'll see him. Get my coach ready.

SEBASTIAN.

    It waits you, madam.

WILLMORE [*aside*].

    This is lucky. —What, madam, now I may be gone and leave you to the enjoyment of my rival?

ANGELLICA.

    Dull man, that canst not see how ill, how poor,
    That false dissimulation looks. Be gone,
    And never let me see thy cozening face again.
    Lest I relapse and kill thee.

WILLMORE.

    Yes, you can spare me now. Farewell, till you're in better humor.
    —[*Aside.*] I'm glad of this release. Now for my gipsy:
    For though to worse we change, yet still we find
    New joys, new charms, in a new miss that's kind.

                                          Exit Willmore.

ANGELLICA.

    He's gone, and in this ague of my soul
    The shivering fit returns.
    Oh, with what willing haste he took his leave,
    As if the longed-for minute were arrived
    Of some blest assignation.
    In vain I have consulted all my charms,
    In vain this beauty prized, in vain believed
    My eyes could kindle any lasting fires;
    I had forgot my name, my infamy,
    And the reproach that honor lays on those

That dare pretend a sober passion here.
Nice reputation, though it leave behind
More virtues than inhabit where that dwells,
Yet that once gone, those virtues shine no more.
Then since I am not fit to be beloved,
I am resolved to think on a revenge
On him that soothed me thus to my undoing.

Exeunt.

[IV.iii]   *A STREET*

Enter Florinda *and* Valeria *in habits different from what they have been seen in.*

FLORINDA.

We're happily escaped, and yet I tremble still.

VALERIA.

A lover, and fear? Why, I am but half an one, and yet I have courage
for any attempt. Would Hellena were here: I would fain have had her
as deep in this mischief as we; she'll fare but ill else, I doubt.

FLORINDA.

She pretended a visit to the Augustine nuns; but I believe some other
design carried her out; pray heaven we light on her. Prithee, what didst
do with Callis?

VALERIA.

When I saw no reason would do good on her, I followed her into
the wardrobe, and as she was looking for something in a great chest, I
toppled her in by the heels, snatched the key of the apartment where
you were confined, locked her in, and left her bawling for help.

FLORINDA.

'Tis well you resolve to follow my fortunes, for thou darest never
appear at home again after such an action.

VALERIA.

That's according as the young stranger and I shall agree. But to
our business. I delivered your note to Belvile when I got out under
pretense of going to mass. I found him at his lodging, and believe me
it came seasonably, for never was man in so desperate a condition.
I told him of your resolution of making your escape today if your
brother would be absent long enough to permit you; if not, to die
rather than be Antonio's.

FLORINDA.

Thou should'st have told him I was confined to my chamber upon my brother's suspicion that the business on the Molo was a plot laid between him and I.

VALERIA.

I said all this, and told him your brother was now gone to his devotion; and he resolves to visit every church till he find him, and not only undeceive him in that, but caress him so as shall delay his return home.

FLORINDA.

Oh heavens! He's here, and Belvile with him too.

They put on their vizards.

Enter Don Pedro, Belvile, Willmore; Belvile *and* Don Pedro *seeming in serious discourse.*

VALERIA.

Walk boldly by them, and I'll come at a distance, lest he suspect us.

She walks by them and looks back on them.

WILLMORE.

Ha! A woman, and of excellent mien!

PEDRO.

She throws a kind look back on you.

WILLMORE.

Death, 'tis a likely wench, and that kind look shall not be cast away. I'll follow her.

BELVILE.

Prithee do not.

WILLMORE.

Do not? By heavens, to the antipodies, with such an invitation.

She goes out, and Willmore *follows her.*

BELVILE.

'Tis a mad fellow for a wench.

Enter Frederick.

FREDERICK.

Oh, colonel, such news!

BELVILE.

Prithee what?

FREDERICK.

News that will make you laugh in spite of fortune.

BELVILE.

What, Blunt has had some damned trick put upon him? Cheated, banged, or clapped?[36]

FREDERICK.

Cheated, sir, rarely cheated of all but his shirt and drawers; the unconscionable whore turned him out before consummation, so that, traversing the streets at midnight, the watch found him in this *fresco* and conducted him home. By heaven, 'tis such a sight, and yet I durst as well been hanged as laughed at him or pity him: he beats all that do but ask him a question, and is in such an humor.

PEDRO.

Who is't has met with this ill usage, sir?

BELVILE.

A friend of ours whom you must see for mirth's sake. —(*Aside*.) I'll employ him to give Florinda time for an escape.

PEDRO.

What is he?

BELVILE.

A young countryman of ours, one that has been educated at so plentiful a rate he yet ne'er knew the want of money; and 'twill be a great jest to see how simply he'll look without it. For my part, I'll lend him none: and the rogue know not how to put on a borrowing face and ask first, I'll let him see how good 'tis to play our parts whilst I play his. Prithee, Fred, do you go home and keep him in that posture till we come.

Exeunt.

Enter Florinda *from the farther end of the scene, looking behind her.*

FLORINDA

I am followed still. Ha! My brother too advancing this way! Good heavens defend me from being seen by him!

She goes off.

---

[36] Infected with venereal disease.

Enter Willmore, *and after him* Valeria, *at a little distance*.

WILLMORE.

Ah, there she sails! She looks back as she were willing to be boarded;
I'll warrant her prize.

He goes out, Valeria *following*.

Enter Hellena, *just as he goes out, with a page*.

HELLENA.

Ha, is not that my captain that has a woman in chase? 'Tis not Angellica.
—Boy, follow those people at a distance, and bring me an account
where they go in.   *Exit page*.
—I'll find his haunts, and plague him everywhere. Ha! My brother!

Belvile, Willmore, Pedro *cross the stage*; Hellena *runs off*.

[IV.iv]   *Scene changes to another street*.
                              Enter Florinda

FLORINDA.

What shall I do? My brother now pursues me. Will no kind power
protect me from his tyranny? Ha! Here's a door open; I'll venture in,
since nothing can be worse than to fall into his hands. My life and
honor are at stake, and my necessity has no choice.

She goes in.

Enter Valeria, *and Hellena's* Page *peeping after Florinda*.

PAGE.

Here she went in; I shall remember this house.

Exit boy.

VALERIA.

This is Belvile's lodging; she's gone in as readily as if she knew it.
Ha! Here's that mad fellow again; I dare not venture in. I'll watch my
opportunity.

Goes aside.

Enter Willmore, *gazing about him*.

WILLMORE.

I have lost her hereabouts. Pox on't, she must not 'scape me so.

Goes out.

[IV.v] *Scene changes to* Blunt's *chamber, discovers him sitting on a couch in his shirt and drawers, reading.*

BLUNT.

So, now my mind's a little at peace, since I have resolved revenge. A pox on this tailor, though, for not bringing home the clothes I bespoke. And a pox of all poor cavaliers: a man can never keep a spare suit for 'em, and I shall have these rogues come in and find me naked, and then I'm undone. But I'm resolved to arm myself: the rascals shall not insult over me too much. (*Puts on an old rusty sword and buff belt.*) Now, how like a morris dancer I am equipped! A fine ladylike whore to cheat me thus without affording me a kindness for my money! A pox light on her, I shall never be reconciled to the sex more; she has made me as faithless as a physician, as uncharitable as a churchman, and as ill-natured as a poet. Oh, how I'll use all womankind hereafter! What would I give to have one of 'em within my reach now! Any mortal thing in petticoats, kind fortune, send me, and I'll forgive thy last night's malice. —Here's a cursed book, too—a warning to all young travelers—that can instruct me how to prevent such mischiefs now 'tis too late. Well, 'tis a rare convenient thing to read a little now and then, as well as hawk and hunt.

Sits down again and reads.

Enter to him Florinda.

FLORINDA.

This house is haunted, sure: 'tis well furnished, and no living thing inhabits it. Ha! A man! Heavens, how he's attired! Sure 'tis some rope dancer, or fencing master. I tremble now for fear, and yet I must venture now to speak to him.—Sir, if I may not interrupt your meditations—

He starts up and gazes.

BLUNT.

Ha, what's here? Are my wishes granted? And is not that a she creature? 'Adsheartlikins, 'tis. —What wretched thing art thou, ha?

FLORINDA.

Charitable sir, you've told yourself already what I am: a very wretched maid, forced by a strange unlucky accident to seek a safety here, and must be ruined if you do not grant it.

BLUNT.

Ruined! Is there any ruin so inevitable as that which now threatens thee? Dost thou know, miserable woman, into what den of mischiefs thou art fallen; what abyss of confusion, ha? Dost not see something in my looks that frights thy guilty soul, and makes thee wish to change that shape of woman for any humble animal, or devil? For those were safer for thee, and less mischievous.

FLORINDA.

Alas, what mean you, sir? I must confess, your looks have something in 'em makes me fear, but I beseech you, as you seem a gentleman, pity a harmless virgin that takes your house for sanctuary.

BLUNT.

Talk on, talk on; and weep, too, till my faith return. Do, flatter me out of my senses again. A harmless virgin with a pox; as much one as t'other, 'adsheartlikins. Why, what the devil, can I not be safe in my house for you, not in my chamber? Nay, not even being naked too cannot secure me? This is an impudence greater than has invaded me yet. Come, no resistance.

Pulls her rudely.

FLORINDA.

Dare you be so cruel?

BLUNT.

Cruel? 'Adsheartlikins, as a galley slave, or a Spanish whore. Cruel? Yes, I will kiss and beat thee all over, kiss and see thee all over; thou shalt lie with me too, not that I care for the enjoyment, but to let thee see I have ta'en deliberated malice to thee, and will be revenged on one whore for the sins of another. I will smile and deceive thee; flatter thee, and beat thee; embrace thee and rob thee, as she did me; fawn on thee, and strip thee stark naked; then hang thee out at my window by the heels, with a paper of scurvy verses fastened to thy breast in praise of damnable women. Come, come, along.

FLORINDA.

Alas, sir, must I be sacrificed for the crimes of the most infamous of my sex? I never understood the sins you name.

BLUNT.

Do, persuade the fool you love him, or that one of you can be just or honest; tell me I was not an easy coxcomb, or any strange impossible tale: it will be believed sooner than thy false showers or protestations. A generation of damned hypocrites! To flatter my very clothes from my back! Dissembling witches! Are these the returns you make an honest gentleman that trusts, believe, and loves you? But if I be not even with you—Come along, or I shall—

Pulls her again.

Enter Frederick.

FREDERICK.

Ha, what's here to do?

BLUNT.

'Adsheartlikins, Fred, I am glad thou art come, to be a witness of my dire revenge.

FREDERICK.

What's this, a person of quality too, who is upon the ramble to supply the defects of some grave impotent husband?

BLUNT.

No, this has another pretense: some very unfortunate accident brought her hither, to save a life pursued by I know not who or why, and forced to take sanctuary here at fool's haven. 'Adsheartlikins, to me of all mankind for protection? Is the ass to be cajoled again, think ye? No, young one, no prayers or tears shall mitigate my rage; therefore prepare for both my pleasures of enjoyment and revenge. For I am resolved to make up my loss here on thy body: I'll take it out in kindness and in beating.

FREDERICK.

Now, mistress of mine, what do you think of this?

FLORINDA.

I think he will not, dares not be so barbarous.

FREDERICK.

Have a care, Blunt, she fetched a deep sigh; she is enamoured with thy shirt and drawers. She'll strip thee even of that; there are of her calling such unconscionable baggages and such dexterous thieves, they'll flea a man and he shall ne'er miss his skin till he feels the cold. There was a countryman of ours robbed of a row of teeth whilst he was a-sleeping, which the jilt made him buy again when he waked. You see, lady, how little reason we have to trust you.

BLUNT.

'Adsheartlikins, why this is most abominable!

FLORINDA.

Some such devils there may be, but by all that's holy, I am none such. I entered here to save a life in danger.

BLUNT.

For no goodness, I'll warrant her.

FREDERICK.

Faith, damsel, you had e'en confessed the plain truth, for we are
fellows not to be caught twice in the same trap. Look on that wreck:
a tight vessel when he set out of haven, well trimmed and laden. And
see how a female picaroon of this island of rogues has shattered him,
and canst thou hope for any mercy?

BLUNT.

No, no, gentlewoman, come along; 'adsheartlikins, we must be better
acquainted. —We'll both lie with her, and then let me alone to
bang her.

FREDERICK.

I'm ready to serve you in matters of revenge that has a double
pleasure in't.

BLUNT.

Well said. —You hear, little one, how you are condemned by public
vote to the bed within; there's no resisting your destiny, sweetheart.

Pulls her.

FLORINDA.

Stay, sir. I have seen you with Belvile, an English cavalier. For his sake,
use me kindly. You know him, sir.

BLUNT.

Belvile? Why yes, sweeting, we do know Belvile, and wish he were
with us now. He's a cormorant at whore and bacon:[37] he'd have a limb
or two of thee, my virgin pullet. But 'tis no matter; we'll leave him the
bones to pick.

FLORINDA.

Sir, if you have any esteem for that Belvile, I conjure you to treat me
with more gentleness; he'll thank you for the justice.

FREDERICK.

Hark'ee, Blunt, I doubt we are mistaken in this matter.

FLORINDA.

Sir, if you find me not worth Belvile's care, use me as you please. And
that you may think I merit better treatment than you threaten, pray
take this present.

Gives him a ring; he looks on it.

[37] Greedy and sexually insatiable.

BLUNT.

Hum, a diamond! Why, 'tis a wonderful virtue now that lies in this ring, a mollifying virtue. 'Adsheartlikins, there's more persuasive rhetoric in't than all her sex can utter.

FREDERICK.

I begin to suspect something, and 'twould anger us vilely to be trussed up for a rape upon a maid of quality, when we only believe we ruffle a harlot.

BLUNT.

Thou art a credulous fellow, but 'adsheartlikins, I have no faith yet. Why, my saint prattled as parlously as this does; she gave me a bracelet, too, a devil on her! But I sent my man to sell it today for necessaries, and it proved as counterfeit as her vows of love.

FREDERICK.

However, let it reprieve her till we see Belvile.

BLUNT.

That's hard, yet I will grant it.

Enter a Servant.

SERVANT.

Oh, sir, the colonel is just come in with his new friend and a Spaniard of quality, and talks of having you to dinner with 'em.

BLUNT.

'Adsheartlikins, I'm undone! I would not see 'em for the world. Hark'ee, Fred, lock up the wench in your chamber.

FREDERICK.

Fear nothing, madam: whate'er he threatens, you are safe whilst in my hands.

Exeunt Frederick *and* Florinda.

BLUNT.

And sirrah, upon your life, say I am not at home, or that I'm asleep, or—or—anything. Away, I'll prevent their coming this way.

Locks the door, and exeunt.

The End of the Fourth Act.

ACT V

BLUNT'S CHAMBER.

After a great knocking as at his chamber door, enter Blunt *softly crossing the stage, in his shirt and drawers as before.*

[VOICES] (*call within*).
Ned! Ned Blunt! Ned Blunt!

BLUNT.

The rogues are up in arms. 'Adsheartlikins, this villainous Frederick has betrayed me: they have heard of my blessed fortune.

[VOICES] (*and knocking within*).
Ned Blunt! Ned! Ned!

BELVILE [*within*].

Why, he's dead, sir, without dispute dead; he has not been seen today. Let's break open the door. Here boy—

BLUNT.

Ha, break open the door? 'Adsheartlikins, that mad fellow will be as good as his word.

BELVILE [*within*].

Boy, bring something to force the door..
                              A great noise within, at the door again.

BLUNT.

So, now must I speak in my own defense; I'll try what rhetoric will do.
—Hold, hold! What do you mean, gentlemen, what do you mean?

BELVILE (*within*).

Oh, rogue, art alive? Prithee open the door and convince us.

BLUNT.

Yes, I am alive, gentlemen, but at present a little busy.

BELVILE (*within*).

How, Blunt grown a man of business? Come, come, open and let's see this miracle.

BLUNT.

No, no, no, no, gentlemen, 'tis no great business. But—I am—at—my devotion. 'Adsheartlikins, will you not allow a man time to pray?

BELVILE (*within*).

Turned religious? A greater wonder than the first! Therefore open quickly, or we shall unhinge, we shall.

BLUNT [*aside*].

This won't do. —Why hark'ee, colonel, to tell you the truth, I am about a necessary affair of life: I have a wench with me. You apprehend me? —The devil's in't if they be so uncivil as to disturb me now.

WILLMORE [*within*].

How, a wench? Nay then, we must enter and partake. No resistance. Unless it be your lady of quality, and then we'll keep our distance.

BLUNT.

So, the business is out.

WILLMORE [*within*].

Come, come, lend's more hands to the door. Now heave, all together. (*Breaks open the door.*) So, well done, my boys.

Enter Belvile [*and his* Page], Willmore, Frederick *and* Pedro. Blunt *looks simply, they all laugh at him; he lays his hand on his sword, and comes up to* Willmore.

BLUNT.

Hark'ee, sir, laugh out your laugh quickly, d'ye hear, and be gone. I shall spoil your sport else, 'adsheartlikins, sir, I shall. The jest has been carried on too long. —(*Aside.*) A plague upon my tailor!

WILLMORE.

'Sdeath, how the whore has dressed him! Faith, sir, I'm sorry.

BLUNT.

Are you so, sir? Keep't to yourself then, sir, I advise you, d'ye hear, for
I can as little endure your pity as his mirth.

Lays his hand on's sword.

BELVILE.

Indeed, Willmore, thou wert a little too rough with Ned Blunt's mistress. Call a person of quality whore, and one so young, so handsome,
and so eloquent? Ha, ha, he.

BLUNT.

Hark'ee, sir, you know me, and know I can be angry. Have a care, for
'adsheartlikins, I can fight, too, I can, sir. Do you mark me? No more.

BELVILE.

Why so peevish, good Ned? Some disappointments, I'll warrant. What,
did the jealous count, her husband, return just in the nick?

BLUNT.

Or the devil, sir. (*They laugh.*) D'ye laugh? Look ye settle me a good
sober countenance, and that quickly, too, or you shall know Ned
Blunt is not—

BELVILE.

Not everybody, we know that.

BLUNT.

Not an ass to be laughed at, sir.

WILLMORE.

Unconscionable sinner! To bring a lover so near his happiness—a vigorous passionate lover—and then not only cheat him of his movables,
but his very desires, too.

BELVILE.

Ah, sir, a mistress is a trifle with Blunt; he'll have a dozen the next
time he looks abroad. His eyes have charms not to be resisted; there
needs no more than to expose that taking person to the view of the
fair, and he leads 'em all in triumph.

PEDRO.

Sir, though I'm a stranger to you, I am ashamed at the rudeness of my
nation; and could you learn who did it, would assist you to make an
example of 'em.

BLUNT.

Why ay, there's one speaks sense now, and handsomely. And let me tell
you, gentlemen, I should not have showed myself like a jack pudding[38]
thus to have made you mirth, but that I have revenge within my power.
For know, I have got into my possession a female, who had better have
fallen under any curse than the ruin I design her. 'Adsheartlikins, she
assaulted me here in my own lodgings, and had doubtless committed
a rape upon me, had not this sword defended me.

FREDERICK.

I know not that, but o' my conscience thou had ravished her, had she
not redeemed herself with a ring. Let's see't, Blunt.

Blunt shows the ring.

BELVILE [*aside*.]

Ha! The ring I gave Florinda when we exchanged our vows! —Hark'ee,
Blunt—

Goes to whisper to him.

WILLMORE.

No whispering, good colonel, there's a woman in the case. No whispering.

BELVILE [*aside to* Blunt].

Hark'ee, fool, be advised, and conceal both the ring and the story for
your reputation's sake. Do not let people know what despised cullies
we English are; to be cheated and abused by one whore, and another
rather bribe thee than be kind to thee, is an infamy to our nation.

WILLMORE.

Come, come, where's the wench? We'll see her; let her be what she
will, we'll see her.

PEDRO.

Ay, ay, let us see her. I can soon discover whether she be of quality,
or for your diversion.

38 A fool.

BLUNT.

She's in Fred's custody.

WILLMORE.

Come, come, the key—
                    To Frederick, *who gives him the key; they are going.*

BELVILE.

Death, what shall I do? —Stay, gentlemen. —[*Aside.*] Yet if I hinder 'em, I shall discover all. —Hold, let's go one at once. Give me the key.

WILLMORE.

Nay, hold there, colonel, I'll go first.

FREDERICK.

Nay, no dispute, Ned and I have the propriety of her.

WILLMORE.

Damn propriety! Then we'll draw cuts. (Belvile *goes to whisper* Willmore.) Nay, no corruption, good colonel. Come, the longest sword carries her.

They all draw, forgetting Don Pedro, *being a Spaniard, had the longest.*

BLUNT.

I yield up my interest to you, gentlemen, and that will be revenge sufficient.

WILLMORE (*to* Pedro).

The wench is yours. —[*Aside.*] Pox of his Toledo,[39] I had forgot that.

FREDERICK.

Come, sir, I'll conduct you to the lady.
                    Exeunt Frederick *and* Pedro.

BELVILE.

To hinder him will certainly discover her. —Dost know, dull beast, what mischief thou hast done?
                    Willmore *walking up and down, out of humor.*

---

[39] Sword blade from Toledo.

WILLMORE.

Ay, ay, to trust our fortune to lots! A devil on't, 'twas madness, that's the truth on't.

BELVILE.

Oh, intolerable sot—

Enter Florinda *running, masked*, Pedro *after her*; Willmore *gazing round her.*

FLORINDA (*aside*).

Good heaven defend me from discovery!

PEDRO.

'Tis but in vain to fly me; you're fallen to my lot.

BELVILE [*aside*].

Sure she's undiscovered yet, but now I fear there is no way to bring her off.

WILLMORE [*aside*].

Why, what a pox, is not this my woman, the same I followed but now?
                    Pedro *talking to* Florinda, *who walks up and down.*

PEDRO.

As if I did not know ye, and your business here.

FLORINDA (*aside*).

Good heaven, I fear he does indeed!

PEDRO.

Come, pray be kind; I know you meant to be so when you entered here, for these are proper gentlemen.

WILLMORE.

But sir, perhaps the lady will not be imposed upon: she'll choose her man.

PEDRO.

I am better bred than not to leave her choice free.
                    Enter Valeria, *and is surprised at sight of* Don Pedro.

VALERIA (*aside*).

Don Pedro here! There's no avoiding him.

FLORINDA (*aside*).

Valeria! Then I'm undone.

VALERIA (to Pedro, *running to him*).

Oh, I have found you, sir! The strangest accident—if I had breath—to tell it.

PEDRO.

Speak! Is Florinda safe? Hellena well?

VALERIA.

Ay, ay, sir. Florinda is safe. —[*Aside*.] From any fears of you.

PEDRO.

Why, where's Florinda? Speak!

VALERIA.

Ay, where indeed, sir; I wish I could inform you. But to hold you no longer in doubt—

FLORINDA (*aside*).

Oh, what will she say?

VALERIA.

She's fled away in the habit—of one of her pages, sir. But Callis thinks you may retrieve her yet, if you make haste away. She'll tell you, sir, the rest. —(*Aside*.) If you can find her out.

PEDRO.

Dishonourable girl, she has undone my aim. —[*To* Belvile.] Sir, you see my necessity of leaving you, and I hope you'll pardon it. My sister, I know, will make her flight to you; and if she do, I shall expect she should be rendered back.

BELVILE.

I shall consult my love and honor, sir.

Exit Pedro.

FLORINDA (*to* Valeria).

My dear preserver, let me embrace thee.

WILLMORE.

What the devil's all this?

BLUNT.

Mystery, by this light.

VALERIA.

Come, come, make haste and get yourselves married quickly, for your brother will return again.

BELVILE.

I'm so surprised with fears and joys, so amazed to find you here in safety, I can scare persuade my heart into a faith of what I see.

WILLMORE.

Hark'ee, colonel, is this that mistress who has cost you so many sighs, and me so many quarrels with you?

BELVILE.

It is. —[To Florinda.] Pray give him the honor of your hand.

WILLMORE.

Thus it must be received, then. (*Kneels and kisses her hand.*) And with it give your pardon, too.

FLORINDA.

The friend to Belvile may command me anything.

WILLMORE (*aside*).

Death, would I might; 'tis a surprising beauty.

BELVILE.

Boy, run and fetch a father instantly.

Exit Boy.

FREDERICK.

So, now do I stand like a dog, and have not a syllable to plead my own cause with. By this hand, madam, I was never thoroughly confounded before, nor shall I ever more dare look up with confidence, till you are pleased to pardon me.

FLORINDA.

Sir, I'll be reconciled to you on one condition: that you'll follow the example of your friend in marrying a maid that does not hate you, and whose fortune, I believe, will not be unwelcome to you.

FREDERICK.

Madam, had I no inclinations that way, I should obey your kind commands.

BELVILE.

Who, Fred marry? He has so few inclinations for womankind that had he been possessed of paradise he might have continued there to this day, if no crime but love could have disinherited him.

FREDERICK.

Oh, I do not use to boast of my intrigues.

BELVILE.

Boast! Why, thou dost nothing but boast. And I dare swear, wert thou as innocent from the sin of the grape as thou art from the apple, thou might'st yet claim that right in Eden which our first parents lost by too much loving.

FREDERICK.

I wish this lady would think me so modest a man.

VALERIA.

She would be sorry then, and not like you half so well. And I should be loath to break my word with you, which was, that if your friend and mine agreed, it should be a match between you and I.

She gives him her hand.

FREDERICK.

Bear witness, colonel, 'tis a bargain.

Kisses her hand.

BLUNT (*to* Florinda).

I have a pardon to beg, too; but 'adsheartlikins, I am so out of countenance that I'm a dog if I can say anything to purpose.

FLORINDA.

Sir, I heartily forgive you all.

BLUNT.

That's nobly said, sweet lady. —Belvile, prithee present her her ring again, for I find I have not courage to approach her myself.

Gives him the ring; he gives it to Florinda.

Enter Boy.

BOY.

Sir, I have brought the father that you sent for.

[*Exit* Boy.]

BELVILE.

'Tis well. And now, my dear Florinda, let's fly to complete that mighty joy we have so long wished and sighed for. —Come, Fred, you'll follow?

FREDERICK.

Your example, sir, 'twas ever my ambition in war, and must be so in love.

WILLMORE.

And must not I see this juggling knot tied?

BELVILE.

No, thou shalt do us better service and be our guard, lest Don Pedro's sudden return interrupt the ceremony.

WILLMORE.

Content; I'll secure this pass.

Exeunt Belvile, Florinda, Frederick, *and* Valeria.

Enter Boy.

BOY (*to* Willmore).

Sir, there's a lady without would speak to you.

WILLMORE.

Conduct her in; I dare not quit my post.

BOY [*to* Blunt].

And sir, your tailor waits you in your chamber.

BLUNT.

Some comfort yet: I shall not dance naked at the wedding.

Exeunt Blunt *and* Boy.

Enter again the Boy, *conducting in* Angellica *in a masking habit and a vizard*. Willmore *runs to her*.

WILLMORE [*aside*].

> This can be none but my pretty gipsy. —Oh, I see you can follow as well as fly. Come, confess thyself the most malicious devil in nature; you think you have done my business with Angellica—

ANGELLICA.

> Stand off, base villain!

> > *She draws a pistol and holds it to his breast.*

WILLMORE.

> Ha, 'tis not she! Who art thou, and what's thy business?

ANGELLICA.

> One thou has injured, and who comes to kill thee for't.

WILLMORE.

> What the devil canst thou mean?

ANGELLICA.

> By all my hopes to kill thee—

Holds still the pistol to his breast; he going back, she following still.

WILLMORE.

> Prithee, on what acquaintance? For I know thee not.

ANGELLICA.

> Behold this face so lost to thy remembrance,
> > > *Pulls off her vizard.*
> And then call all thy sins about thy soul,
> And let 'em die with thee.

WILLMORE.

> Angellica!

ANGELLICA.

> Yes, traitor! Does not thy guilty blood run shivering through thy veins? Hast thou no horror at this sight, that tells thee thou hast not long to boast thy shameful conquest?

WILLMORE.

> Faith, no, child. My blood keeps its ebbs and flows still, and that usual heat too, that could oblige thee with a kindness, had I but opportunity.

ANGELLICA.

   Devil! Dost wanton with my pain? Have at thy heart!

WILLMORE.

   Hold, dear virago![40] Hold thy hand a little; I am not now at leisure to be
   killed. Hold and hear me. —(*Aside.*) Death, I think she's in earnest.

ANGELLICA (*aside, turning from him*).

   Oh, if I take not heed, my coward heart will leave me to his mercy.
   —What have you, sir, to say? —But should I hear thee, thoud'st talk
   away all that is brave about me, and I have vowed thy death by all
   that's sacred.

                                   Follows him with the pistol to his breast.

WILLMORE.

   Why then, there's an end of a proper handsome fellow, that might 'a
   lived to have done good service yet. That's all I can say to't.

ANGELLICA (*pausingly*).

   Yet—I would give thee time for—penitence.

WILLMORE.

   Faith, child, I thank God I have ever took care to lead a good, sober,
   hopeful life, and am of a religion that teaches me to believe I shall
   depart in peace.

ANGELLICA.

   So will the devil! Tell me,
   How many poor believing fools thou hast undone?
   How many hearts thou hast betrayed to ruin?
   Yet these are little mischiefs to the ills
   Thou'st taught mine to commit: thou'st taught it love.

WILLMORE.

   Egad, 'twas shrewdly hurt the while.

ANGELLICA.

   Love, that has robbed it of its unconcern,
   Of all that pride that taught me how to value it.
   And in its room

[40] A female warrior.

A mean submissive passion was conveyed,
That made me humbly bow, which I ne'er did
To anything but heaven.
Thou, perjured man, didst this; and with thy oaths,
Which on thy knees thou didst devoutly make,
Softened my yielding heart, and then I was a slave.
Yet still had been content to've worn my chains,
Worn 'em with vanity and joy forever,
Hadst thou not broke those vows that put them on.
'Twas then I was undone.

All this while follows him with the pistol to his breast.

WILLMORE.

Broke my vows? Why, where hast thou lived? Amongst the gods? For I never heard of mortal man that has not broke a thousand vows.

ANGELLICA.

Oh, impudence!

WILLMORE.

Angellica, that beauty has been too long tempting, not to have made a thousand lovers languish; who, in the amorous fevor, no doubt have sworn like me. Did they all die in that faith, still adoring? I do not think they did.

ANGELLICA.

No, faithless man; had I repaid their vows, as I did thine, I would have killed the ingrateful that had abandoned me.

WILLMORE.

This old general has quite spoiled thee: nothing makes a woman so vain as being flattered. Your old lover ever supplies the defects of age with intolerable dotage, vast charge, and that which you call constancy; and attributing all this to your own merits, you domineer, and throw your favors in's teeth, upbraiding him still with the defects of age, and cuckold him as often as he deceives your expectations. But the gay, young, brisk lover, that brings his equal fires, and can give you dart for dart, you'll find will be as nice as you sometimes.

ANGELLICA.

All this thou'st made me know, for which I hate thee.
Had I remained in innocent security,
I should have thought all men were born my slaves,
And worn my power like lightning in my eyes,
To have destroyed at pleasure when offended.

But when love held the mirror, the undeceiving glass
Reflected all the weakness of my soul, and made me know
My richest treasure being lost, my honor,
All the remaining spoil could not be worth
The conqueror's care or value.
Oh, how I fell, like a long-worshipped idol,
Discovering all the cheat.
Would not the incense and rich sacrifice
Which blind devotion offered at my altars
Have fallen to thee?
Why wouldst thou then destroy my fancied power?

WILLMORE.

By heaven, thou'rt brave, and I admire thee strangely.
I wish I were that dull, that constant thing
Which thou wouldst have, and nature never meant me.
I must, like cheerful birds, sing in all groves,
And perch on every bough,
Billing the next kind she that flies to meet me;
Yet, after all, could build my nest with thee,
Thither repairing when I'd loved my round,
And still reserve a tributary flame.
To gain your credit, I'll pay you back your charity,
And be obliged for nothing but for love.

Offers her a purse of gold.

ANGERLLICA.

Oh, that thou wert in earnest!
So mean a thought of me
Would turn my rage to scorn, and I should pity thee,
And give thee leave to live;
Which for the public safety of our sex,
And my own private injuries, I dare not do.
Prepare—   *Follows still, as before.*
I will no more be tempted with replies.

WILLMORE.

    Sure—

ANGELLICA.

    Another word will damn thee! I've heard thee talk too long.
She follows him with the pistol ready to shoot; he retires, still amazed. Enter Don
Antonio, *his arm in a scarf, and lays hold on the pistol.*

ANTONIO.

    Ha! Angellica!

ANGELLICA.

Antonio! What devil brought thee hither?

ANTONIO.

Love and curiosity, seeing your coach at door. Let me disarm you of this unbecoming instrument of death. (*Takes away the pistol.*) Amongst the number of your slaves was there not one worthy the honor to have fought your quarrel? —[*To* Willmore.] Who are you, sir, that are so very wretched to merit death from her?

WILLMORE.

One, sir, that could have made a better end of an amorous quarrel without you, than with you.

ANTONIO.

Sure 'tis some rival. Ha! The very man took down her picture yesterday; the very same that set on me last night! Blessed opportunity—
                                                                    Offers to shoot him.

ANGELLICA.

Hold, you're mistaken, sir.

ANTONIO.

By heaven, the very same! —Sir, what pretensions have you to this lady?

WILLMORE.

Sir, I do not use to be examined, and am ill at all disputes but this—
                                                   Draws; Antonio *offers to shoot.*

ANGELLICA (*to* Willmore).

Oh, hold! You see he's armed with certain death.

—And you, Antonio, I command you hold,
By all the passion you've so lately vowed me.

                 Enter Don Pedro, *sees* Antonio, *and stays.*

PEDRO (*aside*).

Ha! Antonio! And Angellica!

ANTONIO.

When I refuse obedience to your will,
May you destroy me with your mortal hate.

By all that's holy, I adore you so,
That even my rival, who has charms enough
To make him fall a victim to my jealousy,
Shall live; nay, and have leave to love on still.

PEDRO (*aside*).

What's this I hear?

ANGELLICA (*pointing to* Willmore).

Ah thus, 'twas thus he talked, and I believed.
Antonio, yesterday
I'd not have sold my interest in his heart
For all the sword has won and lost in battle.
—But now, to show my utmost of contempt,
I give thee life; which, if thou wouldst preserve,
Live where my eyes may never see thee more.
Live to undo someone whose soul may prove
So bravely constant to revenge my love.

> *Goes out*, Antonio *follows, but* Pedro *pulls him back*.

PEDRO.

Antonio, stay.

ANTONIO.

Don Pedro!

PEDRO.

What coward fear was that prevented thee from meeting me this
morning on the Molo?

ANTONIO.

Meet thee?

PEDRO.

Yes, me; I was the man that dared thee to't.

ANTONIO.

Hast thou so often seen me fight in war, to find no better cause to
excuse my absence? I sent my sword and one to do thee right, finding
myself uncapable to use a sword.

PEDRO.

But 'twas Florinda's quarrel that we fought, and you, to show how little
you esteemed her, sent me your rival, giving him your interest. But I
have found the cause of this affront, and when I meet you fit for the
dispute, I'll tell you my resentment.

ANTONIO.

I shall be ready, sir, ere long, to do you reason.

Exit Antonio.

PEDRO.

If I could find Florinda, now whilst my anger's high, I think I should be kind, and give her to Belvile in revenge.

WILLMORE.

Faith, sir, I know not what you would do, but I believe the priest within has been so kind.

PEDRO.

How? My sister married?

WILLMORE.

I hope by this time he is, and bedded too, or he has not my longings about him.

PEDRO.

Dares he do this? Does he not fear my power?

WILLMORE.

Faith, not at all; if you will go in and thank him for the favor he has done your sister, so; if not, sir, my power's greater in this house than yours: I have a damned surly crew here that will keep you till the next tide, and then clap you on board for prize. My ship lies but a league off the Molo, and we shall show your donship a damned Tramontana[41] rover's trick.

Enter Belvile.

BELVILE.

This rogue's in some new mischief. Ha! Pedro returned!

PEDRO.

Colonel Belvile, I hear you have married my sister.

BELVILE.

You have heard truth then, sir.

PEDRO.

Have I so? Then, sir, I wish you joy.

[41] From north of the Alps.

BELVILE.

How?

PEDRO.

By this embrace I do, and I am glad on't.

BELVILE.

Are you in earnest?

PEDRO.

By our long friendship and my obligations to thee, I am; the sudden change I'll give you reasons for anon. Come, lead me to my sister, that she may know I now approve her choice.

Exit Belvile *with* Pedro.

Willmore *goes to follow. Enter* Hellena, *as before in boy's clothes, and pulls him back.*

WILLMORE.

Ha! My gipsy! Now a thousand blessings on thee for this kindness. Egad, child, I was e'en in despair of ever seeing thee again; my friends are all provided for within, each man his kind woman.

HELLENA.

Ha! I thought they had served me some such trick!

WILLMORE.

And I was e'en resolved to go abroad, and condemn myself to my lone cabin, and the thoughts of thee.

HELLENA.

And could you have left me behind? Would you have been so ill natured?

WILLMORE.

Why, 'twould have broke my heart, child. But since we are met again, I defy foul weather to part us.

HELLENA.

And would you be a faithful friend now, if a maid should trust you?

WILLMORE.

For a friend I cannot promise: thou art of a form so excellent, a face and humor too good for cold dull friendship. I am parlously afraid of being in love, child; and you have not forgotten how severely you have used me?

HELLENA.

That's all one; such usage you must still look for: to find out all your haunts, to rail at you to all that love you, till I have made you love only me in your own defense, because nobody else will love you.

WILLMORE.

But hast thou no better quality to recommend thyself by?

HELLENA.

Faith, none, captain.Why, 'twill be the greater charity to take me for thy mistress. I am a lone child, a kind of orphan lover; and why I should die a maid, and in a captain's hands too, I do not understand.

WILLMORE.

Egad, I was never clawed away with broadsides from any female before. Thou hast one virtue I adore—good nature. I hate a coy demure mistress, she's as troublesome as a colt; I'll break none. No, give me a mad mistress when mewed, and in flying, one I dare trust upon the wing, that whilst she's kind will come to the lure.[42]

HELLENA.

Nay, as kind as you will, good captain, whilst it lasts. But let's lose no time.

WILLMORE.

My time's as precious to me as thine can be. Therefore, dear creature, since we are so well agreed, let's retire to my chamber; and if ever thou wert treated with such savory love! Come, my bed's prepared for such a guest all clean and sweet as thy fair self. I love to steal a dish and a bottle with a friend, and hate long graces. Come, let's retire and fall to.

HELLENA.

'Tis but getting my consent, and the business is soon done. Let but old gaffer Hymen and his priest say amen to't, and I dare lay my mother's daughter by as proper a fellow as your father's son, without fear or blushing.

WILLMORE.

Hold, hold, no bug words, child. Priest and Hymen? Prithee add a hangman to 'em to make up the consort.[43] No, no, we'll have no

[42] Will return to him as long as she is satisfied.
[43] Company, usually of musicians.

vows but love, child, nor witness but the lover: the kind deity enjoins naught but love and enjoy. Hymen and priest wait still upon portion and jointure; love and beauty have their own ceremonies. Marriage is as certain a bane to love as lending money is to friendship. I'll neither ask nor give a vow, though I could be content to turn gipsy and become a left-handed bridegroom to have the pleasure of working that great miracle of making a maid a mother, if you durst venture. 'Tis upse gipsy that, and if I miss I'll lose my labor.

HELLENA.

And if you do not lose, what shall I get? A cradle full of noise and mischief, with a pack of repentance at my back? Can you teach me to weave incle[44] to pass my time with? 'Tis upse gipsy that, too.

WILLMORE.

I can teach thee to weave a true love's knot better.

HELLENA.

So can my dog.

WILLMORE.

Well, I see we are both upon our guards, and I see there's no way to conquer good nature but by yielding. Here, give me thy hand: one kiss, and I am thine.

HELLENA.

One kiss! How like my page he speaks! I am resolved you shall have none, for asking such a sneaking sum. He that will be satisfied with one kiss will never die of that longing. Good friend single-kiss, is all your talking come to this? A kiss, a caudle![45] Farewell, captain single-kiss.

Going out; he stays her.

WILLMORE.

Nay, if we part so, let me die like a bird upon a bough, at the sherrif's charge. By heaven, both the Indies shall not buy thee from me. I adore thy humor and will marry thee, and we are so of one humor it must be a bargain. Give me thy hand. (*Kisses her hand.*) And now let the blind ones, love and fortune, do their worst.

HELLENA.

Why, god-a-mercy, captain!

---

[44] Linen thread.
[45] Warm drink given to sick people.

WILLMORE.

But hark'ee: the bargain is now made, but is it not fit we should know each other's names, that when we have reason to curse one another hereafter, and people ask me who 'tis I give to the devil, I may at least be able to tell what family you came of?

HELLENA.

Good reason, captain; and where I have cause, as I doubt not but I shall have plentiful, that I may know at whom to throw my—blessings, I beseech ye your name.

WILLMORE.

I am called Robert the Constant.

HELLENA.

A very fine name! Pray was it your faulkner or butler that christened you? Do they not use to whistle when they call you?

WILLMORE.

I hope you have a better, that a man may name without crossing himself—you are so merry with mine.

HELLENA.

I am called Hellena the Inconstant.

> *Enter* Pedro, Belvile, Florinda, Frederick, Valeria.

PEDRO.

Ha! Hellena!

FLORINDA.

Hellena!

HELLENA.

The very same. Ha! My brother! Now, captain, show your love and courage; stand to your arms and defend me bravely, or I am lost forever.

PEDRO.

What's this, I hear? False girl, how came you hither, and what's your business? Speak!

> *Goes roughly to her.*

WILLMORE.

Hold off, sir; you have leave to parley only.

> *Puts himself between.*

HELLENA.

I had e'en as good tell it, as you guess it. Faith, brother, my business is the same with all living creatures of my age: to love and be beloved—and here's the man.

PEDRO.

Perfidious maid, hast thou deceived me too; deceived thyself and heaven?

HELLENA.

'Tis time enough to make my peace with that;
Be you but kind, let me alone with heaven.

PEDRO.

Belvile, I did not expect this false play from you. Was't not enough you'd gain Florinda, which I pardoned, but your lewd friends too must be enriched with the spoils of a noble family?

BELVILE.

Faith, sir, I am as much surprised at this as you can be. Yet, sir, my friends are gentlemen, and ought to be esteemed for their misfortunes, since they have the glory to suffer with the best of men and kings. 'Tis true, he's a rover of fortune, yet a prince aboard his little wooden world.

PEDRO.

What's this to the maintenance of a woman of her birth and quality?

WILLMORE.

Faith, sir, I can boast of nothing but a sword which does me right where'er I come, and has defended a worse cause than a woman's; and since I loved her before I either knew her birth or name, I must pursue my resolution and marry her.

PEDRO.

And is all your holy intent of becoming a nun debauched into a desire of man?

HELLENA.

Why, I have considered the matter, brother, and find the three hundred thousand crowns my uncle left me, and you cannot keep from me, will be better laid out in love than in religion, and turn to as good an account. Let most voices carry it: for heaven or the captain?

ALL CRY.

A captain! A captain!

HELLENA.

Look ye, sir, 'tis a clear case.

PEDRO.

Oh, I am mad! —(*Aside.*) If I refuse, my life's in danger. —Come, there's one motive induces me. Take her; I shall now be free from fears of her honor. Guard it you now, if you can; I have been a slave to't long enough.

Gives her to him.

WILLMORE.

Faith, sir, I am of a nation that are of opinion a woman's honor is not worth guarding when she has a mind to part with it.

HELLENA.

Well said, captain.

PEDRO (*to* Valeria).

This was your plot, mistress, but I hope you have married one that will revenge my quarrel to you.

VALERIA.

There's no altering destiny, sir.

PEDRO.

Sooner than a woman's will; therefore I forgive you all, and wish you may get my father's pardon as easily, which I fear.

Enter Blunt *dressed in a Spanish habit, looking very ridiculously; his* Man *adjusting his band.*

MAN.

'Tis very well, sir.

BLUNT.

Well, sir! 'Adsheartlikins, I tell you 'tis damnable ill, sir. A Spanish habit! Good Lord! Could the devil and my tailor devise no other punishment for me but the mode of a nation I abominate?

BELVILE.

What's the matter, Ned?

BLUNT.

Pray view me round, and judge.

Turns round.

BELVILE.

I must confess thou art a kind of an odd figure.

BLUNT.

In a Spanish habit with a vengeance! I had rather be in the Inquisition for Judaism than in this doublet and breeches; a pillory were an easy collar to this, three handfuls high; and these shoes, too, are worse than the stocks, with the sole an inch shorter than my foot. In fine, gentlemen, methinks I look like a bag of bays[46] stuffed full of fool's flesh.

BELVILE.

Methinks 'tis well, and makes thee look e'en cavalier. Come, sir, settle your face and salute our friends. Lady—

BLUNT (*to* Hellena).

Ha! Sayst thou so, my little rover? Lady, if you be one, give me leave to kiss your hand, and tell you, 'adsheartlikins, for all I look so, I am your humble servant. A pox of my Spanish habit!

Music is heard to play.

WILLMORE.

Hark! What's this?

Enter Boy.

BOY.

Sir, as the custom is, the gay people in masquerade, who make every man's house their own, are coming up.

Enter several men and women in masking habits, with music; they put themselves in order and dance.

BLUNT.

'Adsheartlikins, would 'twere lawful to pull off their false faces, that I might see if my doxy[47] were not amongst 'em.

BELVILE (*to the maskers*).

Ladies and gentlemen, since you are come so *a propos*, you must take a small collation with us.

WILLMORE (*to* Hellena).

Whilst we'll to the good man within, who stays to give us a cast of his office. Have you no trembling at the near approach?

[46] Bag of spices used for cooking.
[47] Sweetheart.

HELLENA.

No more than you have in an engagement or a tempest.

WILLMORE.

Egad, thou'rt a brave girl, and I admire thy love and courage.
Lead on; no other dangers they can dread,
Who venture in the storms o'th' marriage bed.
Exeunt.

THE END

EPILOGUE

The banished cavaliers! A roving blade!
A popish carnival! A masquerade!
The devil's in't if this will please the nation
In these our blessed times of reformation,
When conventickling[48] is so much in fashion.
And yet—
That mutinous tribe[49] less factions do beget,
Than your continual differing in wit.
Your judgment's, as your passion's, a disease;
Nor muse nor miss your appetite can please;
You're grown as nice as queasy consciences,
Whose each convulsion, when the spirit moves,
Damns everything that maggot[50] disapproves.

With canting rule you would the stage refine,
And to dull method all our sense confine.
With th'insolence of commonwealths you rule,
Where each gay fop and politic grave fool
On monarch wit impose, without control.
As for the last, who seldom sees a play,
Unless it be the old Blackfriars way;
Shaking his empty noddle o'er bamboo,[51]
He cries. "Good faith, these plays will never do!
Ah, sir, in my young days, what lofty wit,
What high-strained scenes of fighting there were writ.

[48] A pun; a conventicle was a Dissenting meeting.
[49] Dissenters.
[50] Whimsical fancy.
[51] A cane.

These are slight airy toys. But tell me, pray,
What has the House of Commons done today?"
Then shows his politics, to let you see
Of state affairs he'll judge as notably
As he can do of wit and poetry.
The younger sparks, who hither do resort,
Cry,
"Pox o' your genteel things! Give us more sport!
Damn me, I'm sure 'twill never please the court."

    Such fops are never pleased, unless the play
Be stuffed with fools as brisk and dull as they.
Such might the half-crown spare, and in a glass
At home behold a more accomplished ass.
Where they may set their cravats, wigs, and faces,
And practice all their buffoonry grimaces:
See how this huff becomes, this damny, stare,
Which they at home may act because they dare,
But must with prudent caution do elsewhere.
Oh that our Nokes, or Tony Lee,[52] could show
A fop but half so much to th' life as you.

Anne Finch
Countess of Winchilsea
1661 – 1720

Anne Finch, Countess of Winchilsea, came from a royalist family. Remaining loyal to the Stuart King James II, after he was deposed she retired from court life to Kent with her husband, Heneage Finch, later the Earl of Winchilsea, with whom she had a happy, childless marriage. She lived in Kent for thirty years and her reflective pastoral verse draws on her secluded life in

[52] The best low comedians of the day.

nature, while her satiric poetry often derives from her knowledge of the frivolous Restoration court. Authorship still being a dubious state for a lady, she circulated her poems in manuscript, publishing a volume only in 1713. Her main themes are external nature described in fresh, evocative images, and women, especially their friendships and the disparity between their rational potential and their debased reality as sexual objects for men.

The following poems are reprinted from her book Miscellany Poems on Several Occasions, Written by a Lady *(1713).*

The Introduction

DID I, my lines intend for publick view,
How many censures, wou'd their faults persue,
Some wou'd, because such words they do affect,
Cry they're insipid, empty, uncorrect.
And many, have attain'd, dull and untaught
The name of Witt, only by finding fault.
True judges, might condemn their want of witt,
And all might say, they're by a Woman writt.
Alas! a woman that attempts the pen,
Such an intruder on the rights of men,
Such a presumptuous Creature, is esteem'd,
The fault, can by no vertue be redeem'd.
They tell us, we mistake our sex and way;
Good breeding, fassion, dancing, dressing, play
Are the accomplishments we shou'd desire;
To write, or read, or think, or to enquire
Wou'd cloud our beauty, and exaust our time,
And interrupt the Conquests of our prime;
Whilst the dull mannage, of a servile house
Is held by some, our outmost art, and use.
    Sure 'twas not ever thus, nor are we told
Fables, of Women that excell'd of old;
To whom, by the diffusive hand of Heaven
Some share of witt, and poetry was given.
On that glad day, on which the Ark return'd,
The holy pledge, for which the Land had mourn'd,
The joyfull Tribes, attend itt on the way,
The Levites do the sacred Charge convey,
Whilst various Instruments, before itt play;
Here, holy Virgins in the Concert joyn,
The louder notes, to soften, and refine,
And with alternate verse, compleat the Hymn Devine.

Loe! the yong Poet, after God's own heart,
By Him inspired, and taught the Muses Art,
Return'd from Conquest, a bright Chorus meets,
That sing his slayn ten thousand in the streets.
In such loud numbers they his acts declare,
Proclaim the wonders, of his early war,
That Saul upon the vast applause does frown,
And feels, itts mighty thunder shake the Crown.
What, can the threat'n'd Judgment now prolong?
Half of the Kingdom is already gone;
The fairest half, whose influence guides the rest,
Have David's Empire, o're their hearts confess't.
    A Woman here, leads fainting Israel on,
She fights, she wins, she tryumphs with a song,
Devout, Majestick, for the subject fitt,
And far above her arms, exalts her witt,
Then, to the peacefull, shady Palm withdraws,
And rules the rescu'd Nation, with her Laws.
How are we fal'n, fal'n by mistaken rules?
And Education's, more then Nature's fools,
Debarr'd from all improve-ments of the mind,
And to be dull, expected and dessigned;
And if some one, wou'd Soar above the rest,
With warmer fancy, and ambition press't,
So strong, th' opposing faction still appears,
The hopes to thrive, can ne're outweigh the fears,
Be caution'd then my Muse, and still retir'd;
Nor be dispis'd, aiming to be admir'd;
Conscious of wants, still with contracted wing,
To some few friends, and to thy sorrows sing;
For groves of Lawrel, thou wert never meant;
Be dark enough thy shades, and be thou there content.

Friendship between Ephelia and Ardelia

E PH.   What friendship is, Ardelia, show.
  Ard.   'Tis to love, as I love you.
    Eph.   This account, so short (though kind)
              Suits not my inquiring mind.
              Therefore farther now repeat:
              What is friendship when complete?
    Ard.   'Tis to share all joy and grief;
              'Tis to lend all due relief

From the tongue, the heart, the hand;
'Tis to mortgage house and land;
For a friend be sold a slave;
'Tis to die upon a grave,
If a friend therein do lie.

Eph.   This indeed, though carried high,
This, though more than e'er was done
Underneath the rolling sun,
This has all been said before.
Can Ardelia say no more?

Ard.   Words indeed no more can show:
But 'tis to love, as I love you.

A Nocturnal Reverie

I N such a night, when every louder wind
Is to its distant cavern safe confined;
And only gentle Zephyr[1] fans his wings,
And lonely Philomel,[2] still waking, sings;
Or from some tree, famed for the owl's delight,
She, hollowing clear, directs the wand'rer right;
In such a night, when passing clouds give place,
Or thinly veil the heaven's mysterious face;
When in some river overhung with green,
The waving moon and trembling leaves are seen;
When freshened grass now bears itself upright,
And makes cool banks to pleasing rest invite,
Whence springs the woodbind and the bramble-rose,
And where the sleepy cowslip sheltered grows;
Whilst now a paler hue the foxglove takes,
Yet chequers still with red the dusky brakes;[3]
When scattered glow-worms, but in twilight fine,
Show trivial beauties, watch their hour to shine;
Whilst Salisb'ry stands the test of every light,
In perfect charms and perfect virtue bright;
When odours, which declined repelling day,
Through temp'rate air uninterrupted stray;
When darkened groves their softest shadows wear,
And falling waters we distinctly hear;

[1] West wind.
[2] Poetic name for a nightingale.
[3] Clumps of bushes or briers.

When through the gloom more venerable shows
Some ancient fabric, awful in repose,
While sunburnt hills their swarthy looks conceal,
And swelling haycocks thicken up the vale;
When the loosed horse now, as his pasture leads,
Comes slowly grazing through th' adjoining meads,
Whose stealing pace and lengthened shade we fear,
Till torn-up forage in his teeth we hear;
When nibbling sheep at large pursue their food,
And unmolested kine[4] rechew the cud;
When curlews cry beneath the village walls,
And to her straggling brood the partridge calls;
Their short-lived jubilee the creatures keep,
Which but endures whilst tyrant man does sleep;
When a sedate content the spirit feels,
And no fierce light disturbs, whilst it reveals,
But silent musings urge the mind to seek
Something too high for syllables to speak;
Till the free soul to a compos'dness charmed,
Finding the elements of rage disarmed,
O'er all below a solemn quiet grown,
Joys in th' inferior world and thinks it like her own:
In such a night let me abroad remain,
Till morning breaks, and all's confused again:
Our cares, our toils, our clamours are renewed,
Or pleasures, seldom reached, again pursued.

Delarivier Manley
1663 – 1724

D*elarivier Manley, daughter of the royalist lieutenant-governor of Jersey,
wrote plays, poems, political tracts and, above all, 'scandal novels' which,
using fictitious names, implicated her various political opponents and*

[4] Cows.

*personal enemies in sexual scandals. Although one aim was to discredit those
who did not share her royalist, conservative views, such as the powerful Duchess
of Marlborough, another was to provide a series of short tales describing the
struggle between the sexes. A favourite plot of the early woman writer was that
of virtue in distress, a plot that would later be elaborated and sentimentalized
in women's fiction throughout the eighteenth century. In the vaguely incestuous
early version of the plot, an innocent girl is debauched and ruined by an older
or more sophisticated man who may be an uncle or stepfather. In Manley's case
the repeated story probably had some autobiographical basis since she claimed
that she herself had, as a young girl, been lured into a bigamous marriage
by her guardian.*

   *The New Atalantis (1709) from which this extract comes was her
most notorious work; it is a* roman à clef, *the incidents of which are
based on real scandals. In the case of this extract, they refer to events
in the life of the first Earl of Portland, who in the reign of William III
was said to have seduced and deserted a friend's daughter of whom he
was the guardian.*

From

The New Atalantis

... To return to the Duke. He spar'd for no expence in the Education of
young *Charlot*; she was brought up at his own House with his Children;
but having something the advantage in Age of his Daughters, the Precepts were
proportionably advanced. He design'd her (in those early Days of his Power) as
a Wife for his Son, before the increase of his own Ambition, and Riches taught
him other desires; that is to say, to look out a Lady for the young Lord with
more than six times *Charlot's* Fortune: And indeed he was not to blame in
that, for certainly all that Fable has ever reported of *Adonis, Narcissus,*[1] the most
beautiful of the *Hero's*, the united Sweetness and Graces of Mankind, are to be
found in his Person! with an unknown Goodness of Temper! an Air of perfect
Behaviour and accomplish'd Courtship! neither has he shown us an Inclination
to any Vice, that might balance these Perfections! but as Malice loves to mingle
in the Characters ev'n of the most deserving; not being able to find a fault from
without, have recourse to the inside, and assure us there of a Genius no way
proportionable to the Greatness of his Fathers; a softness of Conversation, which
they otherways term a weakness of Intellects: But the Ladies find no such fault

---

[1] Adonis was a youth loved by Venus, goddess of love, because of his exceptional beauty;
Narcissus was a beautiful youth who fell in love with his own reflection.

with the charming Youth; he has all things in his Person, Voice and Discourse, that
prove him indeed irresistable! besides, occasion calls not upon him to exert his
Faculties, as they did the Duke; his Fortune is made, his Father was Born before
him, and so happily too, as from a meer Gentleman to make himself one of the
Richest and most Potent Subjects in *Europe*.

Charlot was no great Beauty, her Shape was the best; but Youth and Dress
make all things agreeable. To have prepossessed you in her favour, I shou'd,
as I was inclin'd, have advanc'd a System of her Charms; but *Truth*, who too well
foresaw my Intentions, has repell'd 'em with a Frown; not but *Charlot* had
many Admirers; there's something so touching in the *agreeable*, that I know
not whether it does not enchant us deeper than Beauty; we are oftentimes
upon our guard against the attack of that, whilst the unwary Heart, careless
and defenceless, as. dreading no surprize, permits the *agreeable* to manage
as they please.

The Duke had a seeming Admiration for *Virtue*, wherever he found it, but
he was a Statesman, and held it incompatable (in an Age like this) with a Mans
making his Fortune, *Ambition, desire of Gain, Dissimulation, Cunning*, all these
were meritoriously serviceable to him: 'Twas enough he always applauded Virtue
and in his Discourse decry'd Vice; as long as he stuck close in his Practice, no
matter what became of his Words, these are not times where the Heart and the
Tongue do not agree! However, young *Charlot* was to be educated in the high
road to applause and Virtue, he banish'd far from her Conversation[2] whatever
would not edify, Airy *Romances, Plays*, dangerous *Novels, loose* and *insinuating
Poetry*, artificial Introductions of *Love*, well-painted Landskips[3] of that dangerous
Poyson; her Diversions were always among the sort that were most Innocent and
Simple, such as Walking, but not in publick Assemblies; Musick in Airs all Divine;
reading and improving Books of Education and Piety; as well knowing, that if a
Lady be too early us'd to violent Pleasures, it debauches their Tastes for ever to
any others, he taught her to beware of *Hopes* and *Fears*; never to desire any thing
with too much eagerness; to guard herself from those dangerous Convulsions
of the Mind; that upon the least Disappointment precipitates into a Million of
Inconveniencies; he endeavour'd to cure her of those number of Affections and
Aversions so natural to young People, by shewing her that nothing truly deserved
to be passionately belov'd, but the *Gods*, because they alone were perfect, though
nothing on the other Hand ought to be hated but Vice, because we are all the
Image of their Divinities; he wisely and early forewarn'd her, from what seem'd
too natural to her, a desire of being applauded for her Wit, she had a brightness
of Genius, that would often break out in dangerous Sparkle; he shew'd her that
true Wit consisted not in much speaking, but in speaking much in few Words,
that whatever carried her beyond the knowledge of her Duty; carried her too
far; all other Embelishments of the Mind were more dangerous than useful,
and to be avoided as her Ruin; that the possession of 'em was attended with
Self-Love, Vanity and *Coquettry*, things incomparable and never mingled in the

---

2 Society.
3 Landscapes.

Character of a Woman of true Honour, he recommended *Modesty* and *Silence*; that she should shun all occasions of speaking upon Subjects not necessary to a Ladies Knowledge, tho' it were true that she spoke never so well; he remembred her, that so Great, so Wise a Man as *Zeno*, of all the Virtues made choice of Silence, for by it he heard other Mens Imperfections, and conceal'd his own; that the more Wit she was Mistress of, the less occasion she had to show it; that if want of it gave a disgust, too much does not generally please better, *That* assuming Air that generally accompanies it, is distasteful to the Company, where all pretend an equal right to be heard; the weakness of Human Nature is such, the chiefest Pleasure of Conversation lies in the speaking, not the hearing part, and if a presumptious Person (though with never so great a Capacity) pretends to usurp once upon that Priviledge, they look upon her as a Tyrant, that would ravish from 'em the Freedom of their Votes. But his strongest Battery was united against *Love*, that invader of the *Heart*; he show'd her how shameful it was, for a young Lady ever so much as to think of any tenderness for a Lover, 'till he was become her Husband; that true Piety and Duty would instruct her in all that was necessary for a good Wife to feel of that dangerous Passion; that she should not so much as ever seek to know what was meant by that shameful Weakness call'd Jealousy; 'twas abominable in us to give others occasion to be Jealous, and painful to be so our selves; that 'tis generally attended with *Slander* and *Hatred*, two base and contemptible Qualities; That that violent *inborn* desire of pleasing so natural to Ladies is the pest of Virtue, they would by the Charms of their Beauty, and their sweet and insinuating way of Conversation, assume that native Empire over Mankind, which seems to be politically deny'd them, because the way to Authority and Glory is stop'd up: Hence it is that, with their aquir'd Arts and languishing Charms, they risque their *Virtue* to gain a little contemptible Dominion over a Heart that at the same time it surrenders it self a Slave; refuses to bestow esteem upon the Victor; that Friendship was far nobler in its Nature, and much to be prefer'd to Love, because a *Friend loves always, a Lover but for a time*; that under the most flattering appearances is conceal'd inevitable Ruin; the very first Impressions were dreadful, and to be carefully suppressed. *Pythagoras, Taught, the assaults of Love were to be beaten back at the first Sight, least they undermine at the second. And* Plato *that the first step to Wisdom was not to love; the second so to love, as not to be perceived.*

Fraught with these, and a number more of such Precepts such as these, the young *Charlot* seem'd to intend her self a Pattern for the Ladies of this degenerate Age, who divide their Hours between the *Toylet* and *Basset*[4] Table; wich is grown so totally the Business of the Fair; that even the Diversions of the *Opera, Gallantry* and *Love*, are but secondary Pleasures: A Person who has once given her self up to Gaming, neglects all her Duties, disorders her Family, breaks her Rest, forgets her Husband, and by her Expence often inconveniences him irreparably, together with their waste of time: The Passions of Anger and Avarice, concur to make her odious to all, but those who ingage with her at that dangerous Diversion; not to instance, who have compounded for the loss

[4] A gambling game with cards.

of Mony, with the loss of their Chastity and Honour; nor is it a new, tho' frequent way of paying of Play-Debts, in this entirely corrupted Age.

The Duke had a magnificent *Villa* within five Leagues of the Capital, adorn'd with all that's imaginable Beautiful, either in Art or Nature; the pride of Conquest, the plunder of Victory, the homage of the Vanquish'd, the presents of Neighbouring Monarchs, and whatever Curiosity could inform, or Mony recover, were the Ornaments of this Palace. *Henriquez*,[5] had received a new Favourite into his Bosom, but it was a Favourite not at all interfering with the Duke, who was ever trusted and esteemed; by this means he oftner found a recess from Court; his great Master would sometimes in Goodness dismiss him to his *Villa*, to taste a rest from Power, a calm of Greatness, a suspense of Business, a respiration of Glory; here it was, that he us'd to confirm the young *Charlot* in that early love of Virtue that had been taught her, to unbend her Mind from the more serious Studies; he sometimes permitted her those of *Poetry*, not loose Descriptions, lascivious Joys or wanton heightnings of the Passions; they sung and acted the History of the *Gods*, the Rape of *Proserpine*,[6] the descent of *Ceres*, the Chastity of *Diana*, and such pieces that tended to the instruction of the Mind. One Evening at a Representation, where *Charlot* personated the Goddess, and the Duke's Son *Acteon*,[7] she Acted with so animated a Spirit, and cast such Rays of Divinity about her, gave every Word so twanging, yet so sweet an Accent, that awaken'd the Duke's Attention, and so admirably she varied the Passions that gave Birth in his Breast, to what he had never felt before; he applauded, embrac'd, and even kiss'd the charming *Diana*; 'twas Poyson to his Peace, the cleaving sweetness thrill'd swiftly to his Heart, thence tingled in his Blood, and cast Fire throughout his whole Person; he Sigh'd with Pleasure! he wondered what those Sighs meant! he repeats his Kisses, to find if *Charlot* were the occasion of his Disorder. Confirm'd by this new taste of Joy, he throws the young Charmer hastily from him, folds his Arms, and walks off with continu'd Sighs! the innocent Beauty makes after him modest and afraid, insinuatingly and with trembling she enquires, if she have not offended? Begs to know her Fault, and that she will endeavour to repair it. He answers her not but with his Eyes, which have but too tender an Aspect; the Maid (by them) improving her Courage, comes nearer, spreads her fond Arms about him, and in her usual fawning Language calls him dear *Pappa*, joins her Face, her Eyes, her Cheeks, her Mouth close to his; by this time the Duke was fallen upon a Chair that stood next him, he was fully in her reach, and without any opposition she had leisure to difuse the irremediable Poison through his Veins: he sat immoveable to all her Kindness, but with the greatest taste of Joy, he had ever been sensible of. Whilst he was thus dangerously entertain'd, the young *Acteon*, and the rest of the Company, join 'em, the Duke was forc'd to rouse himself from his Love-sick Lethargy; *Charlot* wou'd leave him, till he wou'd tell her in what she had done amiss?

[5] William III.
[6] Proserpine, the daughter of Ceres by Jupiter, who became enamoured of her. She was carried off by Pluto, god of the underworld.
[7] Acteon, the hunter, was turned into a stag for watching the chaste goddess Diana bathing.

He only answer'd her, that he had nothing to object, she had acted her part but too well. The young Lady had been taught (in her cold Precepts of Education) that it was a degree of fault to excel, even in an Accomplishment. Occasion was not to be sought of eminently distinguishing one's self in any thing but solid Virtue; she fear'd she had shown too great a Transport in representing *Diana*; that the Duke wou'd possibly think she was prepossessed more than she ought with that diversion, and in this despondence she took resolutions to regulate herself hereafter more to his satisfaction.

That fatal Night the Duke felt hostile Fires in his Breast, *Love* was entred with all his dreadful Artillery; he took possession in a moment of the Avenues that lead to the Heart! neither did the resistance he found there serve for any thing but to make his Conquest more illustrious. The Duke try'd every corner of his uneasie Bed! whether shut or open, *Charlot* was still before his Eyes! his Lips and Face retain'd the dear Impression of her Kisses! the Idea of her innocent and charming Touches, wander'd o'er his Mind! he wish'd again to be so bless'd but then, with a deep and dreadful Sigh, he remembred who she was, the Daughter of his Friend! of a Friend who had at his Death left the charge of her Education to him! his Treaty with the Princess Dowager, wou'd not admit him to think of marrying of her, Ambition came in to rescue him (in that particular) from the Arms of Love. To possess her without, was a villanous detestable Thought! but not to possess her at all, was loss of Life! was Death inevitable! Not able to gain one wink of Sleep, he arose with the first Dawn, and posted back to *Angela*.[8] He hop'd the hurry of Business, and the Pleasures of the Court, wou'd stifle so guilty a Passion; he was too well perswaded of his Distemper, the Symptoms were right, the Malignity was upon him! he was regularly posses'd! Love, in all its forms, had took in that formidable Heart of his! he began to be jealous of his Son, whom he had always design'd for *Charlot's* Husband; he cou'd not bear the thoughts that he shou'd be belov'd by her, tho' all beautiful, as the lovely Youth was. She had never had any tender Inclinations for him, nothing that exceeded the warmth of a Sister's love! whether it were that he were designed for, or that the Precepts of Education had warn'd her from too precipitate a liking: She was bred up with him, accustom'd to his Charms, they made no impression upon her Heart! neither was the Youth more sensible. The Duke cou'd distress neither of 'em by his love of that side, but this he was not so happy to know. He wrote up for the young Lord to come to Court, and gave immediate orders for forming his Equipage, that he might be sent to Travel: Mean time *Charlot* was never from his Thoughts. Who knows not the violence of beginning Love! especially a Love that we hold opposite to our Interest and Duty? *'Tis an unreasonable excess of Desire, which enters swiftly, but departs slowly. The love of Beauty, is the loss of Reason. Neither is it to be suppress'd by Wisdom, because it is not to be comprehended with Reason.* And the Emperor *Aurelius; Love is a cruel Impression of that wonderful Passion, which to define is impossible, because no Words reach to the strong Nature of it, and only they know which inwardly feel it.*

[8] London.

The Duke vainly strugled in the Snare; he wou'd live, without seeing *Charlot*,
but then he must live in Pain, in inexplicable Torture! he applies the relief of
Business, the Pleasures of Woman! *Charlot's* Kisses were still upon his Lips,
and made all others insipid to him. In short, he try'd so much to divert his
Thoughts from her, that it but more perfectly confirm'd him of the vanity and
the unsuccessfulness of the attempt: He could neither eat or sleep! love and
restlessness rais'd Vapours[9] in him to that degree, he was no longer Master of
his Business! Wearied with all things, hurry'd by a secret Principle of *Self-Love*,
and *Self-Preservation*, the Law of Nature! he orders his Coach to carry him
down once more to his *Villa*, there to see his Dear! this dangerous *Charlot*! that
little innocent Sweetness! that imbitter'd his Happiness. She lov'd him tenderly,
as a Benefactor, a Father, or something more; that she had been us'd to love
without that severe mixture of Fear that mingles in the love we bear to Parents:
She ran to meet him as he alighted; her young Face, over-spread with blushing
Joys! his transport exceeded hers! he took her in his Arms with eagarness! he
exchang'd all his Pains for Pleasures! there was the Cure of his past Anguish!
her Kisses were the Balm to his wounded Mind! he wonder'd at the immediate
alteration! she caress'd and courted him; shew'd him all things that cou'd divert
or entertain. He knew not what to resolve upon; he cou'd not prudently marry
her, and how to attempt to corrupt her! those excellent Principles that had been
early infused into her, were all against him; but yet he must love her! he found
he cou'd not live without her! he open'd a *Machiavel*, and read there a Maxim,
That none but great Souls can be compleatly Wicked.[10] He took it for a kind of
Oracle to him: He wou'd be loath to tell himself, his *Soul was not great enough
for any attempt*. He clos'd the Book, took some turns about the Gallery to digest
what he had read, and from thence concluded, that neither *Religion, Honour,
Gratitude* nor *Friendship*, were ties sufficient to deprive us of an essential Good!
Charlot was necessary to his very Being! all his Pleasures faded without her! and,
which was worse, he was in torture! in actual pain as well as want of pleasure!
therefore *Charlot* he would have; he had strugled more than sufficient, Virtue
ought to be satisfied with the terrible Conflict he had suffered! but Love was
become Master, and 'twas time for her to abscond. After he had settled his
Thoughts, he grew more calm and quiet; nothing shou'd now disturb him, but
the manner how to corrupt her. He was resolv'd to change her whole Form of
Living to bring her to Court, to show her the World; *Balls, Assemblies, Opera's,
Comedies, Cards*, and *Visits*, every thing that might enervate the Mind, and fit
it for the soft play and impression of Love. One thing he a little scrupled, lest
in making her susceptible of that Passion, it shou'd be for another, and not for
him; he did not doubt, but upon her first appearance at Court she wou'd have
many Admirers; Lovers have this opinion peculiar to themselves, they believe
that others see with their Eyes: He knew that were she less agreeable, the gloss
of Novelty was enough to recommend her; but the remedy he found for this,

[9] Exhalations dangerous to health which were thought to be developed in the body.
[10] The Florentine writer, Machiavelli, was renowned for advocating expediency and
fulfillment of desire over morality.

was, to caress and please her above all others; to shew such a particular regard
for her, that shou'd frighten any new pretender. Few are willing to cross a first
Minister, especially in such a tender Point, where all Mankind are tenacious of
their Pretensions.

He had observ'd, that *Charlot* had been, but with disgust, deny'd the gay
Part of reading: 'Tis natural for young People to chuse the diverting, before
the instructive; he sent for her into the Gallery, where was a noble Library in
all Languages, a Collection of the most valuable Authors, with a mixture of the
most Amorous. He told her, that now her Understanding was increas'd, with her
Statue, he resolv'd to make her Mistress of her own Conduct; and as the first thing
that he intended to oblige her in, that *Governante* who had hitherto had the
care of her Actions, should be dismiss'd; because he had observ'd the severity of
her Temper had sometimes been displeasing to her; that she shou'd henceforward have none above her, that she shou'd need to stand in awe of; and to confirm to her that good opinion he seem'd to have, he presented her with the
Key of that Gallery, to improve her Mind, and seek her Diversion, amongst
those Authors he had formerly forbid her the use of. *Charlot* made him a
very low Curtsie, and, with a blushing Grace, return'd him Thanks for the two
favours he bestow'd upon her. She assur'd him, that no Action of hers shou'd
make him repent the distinction; that her whole endeavour should be to walk
in that Path he made familiar to her; and that Virtue shou'd ever be her
only Guide. Tho' this was not what the Duke wanted, 'twas nothing but what
he expected: He observ'd formerly, that she was a great lover of Poetry, especially when 'twas forbid her; he took down an *Ovid*, and opening it just
at the love of *Myrra*[11] for her Father, conscious red overspread his Face; he
gave it her to read, she obey'd him with a visible delight; nothing is more
pleasing to young Girls, than in being first consider'd as Women. *Charlot* saw
the Duke entertain'd her with an Air of Consideration more than usual, passionate and respectful; this taught her to refuge in the native Pride and Cunning
of the Sex, she assum'd an Air more haughty. The leaving a Girl just beginning to believe herself capable of attaining that Empire over Mankind, which
they are all born and taught by Instinct to expect. She took the Book, and
plac'd herself by the Duke, his Eyes, Feasted themselves upon her Face, thence
wander'd over her snowy Bosom, and saw the young swelling Breasts just
beginning to distinguish themselves, and which were gently heav'd at the
Impression *Myrra's* Sufferings made upon her Heart, by this dangerous reading,
he pretended to shew her, that there were Pleasures her Sex were born for,
and which she might consequently long to taste! Curiosity is an early and
dangerous Enemy to Virtue, the young *Charlot*, who had by a noble Incli[nation]
of Gratitude a strong propension of Affection for the Duke, whom she call'd
and estem'd her *Papa*, being a Girl of wonderful reflection, and consequently
Application, wrought her Imagination up to such a lively heighth at the Fathers
Anger after the possession of his Daughter, which she judg'd highly unkind and
unnatural, that she drop'd her Book, Tears fill'd her Eyes, Sobs rose to oppress

---

[11] In Ovid's *Metamorphosis* Myrrha falls in love with her father and bears a son to him.

her, and she pull'd out her Handkerchief to cover the Disorder. The Duke, who was Master of all Mankind, could trace 'em in all the *Meanders* of Dissimulation and Cunning, was not at a loss how to interpret the Agitation of a Girl who knew no Hipocrisy, all was Artless, the beautiful product of Innocence and Nature; he drew her gently to him, drunk her Tears with his Kisses, suck'd her Sighs and gave her by that dangerous Commerce (her Soul before prepar'd to softness) new and unfelt Desires; her Virtue was becalm'd, or rather unapprehensive of him for an Invader; he prest her Lips with his, the nimble beatings of his Heart, apparently seen and felt thro' his open Breast! the glowings! the tremblings of his Limbs! the glorious Sparkles from his guilty Eyes! his shortness of Breath, and eminent Disorder, were things all new to her, that had never seen, heard, or read before of those powerful Operations, struck from the Fire of the two meeting Sex; nor had she leisure to examine his disorders, possess'd by greater of her own! greater! because that Modesty opposing Nature, forc'd a struggle of Dissimulation. But the Duke's pursuing Kisses overcame the very Thoughts of any thing, but that new and lazy Poison stealing to her Heart, and spreading swiftly and imperceptibly thro' all her Veins, she clos'd her Eyes with languishing Delight! deliver'd up the possession of her Lips and Breath to the amorous Invader; return'd his eagar grasps, and, in a word, gave her whole Person into his Arms, in meltings full of delight! The Duke by that lovely Extasie, carry'd beyond himself, sunk over the expiring Fair, in Raptures too powerful for description! calling her his admirable *Charlot*! his charming Angel! his adorable Goddess! but all was so far modest, that he attempted not beyond her Lips and Breast, but cry'd that she shou'd never be anothers. The Empire of his Soul was hers; enchanted by inexplicable, irresistable Magick! she had Power beyond the Gods themselves! *Charlot* return'd from that amiable Disorder, was a new charm'd at the Duke's Words; Words that set her so far above what was mortal, the Woman assum'd in her, and she wou'd have no notice taken of the Transports she had shown. He saw and favour'd her modesty, secure of that fatal Sting he had fix'd within her Breast, that Taste of delight, which powerful Love and Nature wou'd call upon her to repeat. He own'd he lov'd her; that he never cou'd love any other; that 'twas impossible for him to live a day, an hour, without seeing her; that in her absence he had felt more than ever had been felt by Mortal; he begg'd her to have pity on him, to return his Love, or else he shou'd be the most lost, undone thing alive. *Charlot*, amaz'd and charm'd, felt all those dangerous perturbations of Nature that arise from an amorous Constitution, with Pride and Pleasure, she saw herself necessary to the happiness of one, that she had hitherto esteemed so much above her, ignorant of the Power of Love, that Leveller of Mankind; that blender of Distinction and Hearts. Her soft Answer was, That she was indeed reciprocally Charm'd, she knew not how; all he had said and done was wonderful and pleasing to her; and if he wou'd still more please her (if there were a more) it shou'd be never to be parted from her. The Duke had one of those violent Passions, where, to heighten it, resistance was not at all necessary; it had already reach'd the ultimate, it cou'd not be more ardent; yet was he loth to rush upon the possession of the Fair, lest the too early pretension might disgust her: He wou'd steal himself into her Soul, he wou'd make himself necessary to her quiet, as she was to his.

From the Library he led her to his Cabinet,[12] from forth his strong Box he took a set of Jewels that had been her Mothers; he told her, she was now of an Age to expect the Ornaments, as well as Pleasures of a Woman. He was pleas'd to see her look down, with a seeming contempt, upon what most other Girls wou'd have been transported with: He had taught her other Joys, those of the Mind and Body. She sigh'd, she rav'd to herself, she was all charm'd and uneasie! The Duke casting over the rest of his Jewels, made a Collection of such as were much more valuable than her Mothers; he presented her with, and wou'd force her to accept 'em; but *Charlot*, as tender and gallant as the Duke, seeing his Picture in little, set round with Diamonds, begg'd that he wou'd only honour her with that mark of his Esteem. The ravish'd Duke consented, conditionally, that she wou'd give him hers in return.

After this tender, dangerous Commerce, *Charlot* found every thing insipid, nothing but the Duke's kisses cou'd relish with her; all those Conversations she had formerly delighted in, were insupportable: He was oblig'd to return to Court; and had recommended to her reading the most dangerous Books of Love, *Ovid, Petrarch, Tibullus*, those moving Tragedies that so powerfully expose the force of Love, and corrupt the Mind; he went even farther, and left her such as explain'd the Nature, Manner, and Raptures of Enjoyment. Thus he infus'd Poison into the Ears of the lovely Virgin. She easily (from those emotions she had found in herself) believ'd as highly of those Delights as was imaginable; her waking Thoughts, her golden Slumber, ran all of a Bliss only imagin'd but never prov'd: She even forgot, as one that wakes from sleep, and the Vissions of the Night, all those Precepts of airy Virtue, which she found had nothing to do with Nature: She long'd again to renew those dangerous Delights. The Duke was an Age absent from her, she cou'd only in imagination possess what she believ'd so pleasing. Her Memory was prodigious, she was indefatigable in Reading. The Duke had left orders she shou'd not be controul'd in any thing: Whole Nights were wasted by her in that Gallery; she had too well inform'd herself of the speculative Joys of Love. There are Books dangerous to the Community of Mankind; abominable for Virgins, and destructive to Youth; such as explain the Mysteries of Nature, the congregated Pleasures of *Venus*, the full Delights of mutual Lovers, and which rather ought to pass the Fire than the Press. The Duke had laid in her way such as made no mention of *Virtue* or *Hymen*, but only advanced native, generous and undissembled Love. She was become so great a Proficient, that nothing of the Theory was a stranger to her.

Whilst *Charlot* was thus employ'd, the Duke was not idle; he had prepar'd her a Post at Court with *Henriquez's* Queen. The young Lady was sent for; neither Art, Money, nor Industry was wanting, to make her appearance glorious. The Duke aw'd and trembling with his Passion, approach'd her as a Goddess; conscious of his and her own desires, the mantling Blood wou'd smile upon her Cheeks, sometimes glowing with delight, then afterwards, by a feeble recollection of Virtue, sink apace, to make room for a guilty succeeding Paleness. The Duke knew all the motions of her Heart, he debated with himself, whether it were best

---

[12] Small chamber.

to attempt the possession of her whilst so young, or permit her time to know and set a value upon what she granted. His Love was highly impatient, but respectful; he long'd to be happy, but he dreaded to displease her. The Ascendant she had over him was wonderful; he had let slip those first Impressions, which strike deepest in the Hearts of Women, to be successful; *One ought never to allow 'em time to Think, their vivacity being prodigious, and their forsight exceeding short, and limited; the first hurry of their Passions, if they are but vigorously follow'd, is what is generally most favourable to Lovers.* Charlot by this time had inform'd herself, that there were such terrible things as Perfidy and Inconstancy, in Mankind; that even the very Favours they receiv'd, often disgusted; and that to be entirely Happy, one ought never to think of the faithless Sex. This brought her back to those Precepts of Virtue that had embellish'd her dawn of Life; but alas! these Admonitions were too feeble, the Duke was all submissive, passionate, eager to obey, and to oblige. He watch'd her uprisings, scarce cou'd eat without her; she was Mistress of his Heart and Fortune; his own Family, and the whole Court, imagin'd that he resolv'd her for his Duchess; they almost look'd upon her as such; she went often to his Palace, where all were devoted to her Service; the very glance of her Eyes commanded their attention, at her least request, as soon as her Mouth was open'd to speak, before her Words were half form'd, they started to obey her.

She had learnt to manage the Duke, and to distrust herself; she wou'd no more permit of Kisses, that sweet and dangerous Commerce. The Duke had made her wise at his own cost, and vainly languish'd for a repetition of Delight. He guess'd at the Interest he had in her Heart, had prov'd the warmth of her Constitution, and was resolv'd he wou'd no more be wanting to his own Happiness; he omitted no occasion by which he might express his love; pressing her to crown his Longings. Her courage did not reach to ask him that honourable Proof of his Passion, which 'tis believ'd he wou'd not have refused, if she had but insisted of it. The Treaty was still depending, he might marry the Princess Dowager; *Charlot* tenderly drop'd a word that spoke her apprehensions of it; he assured her there was nothing in it, all he aim'd at was to purchase the Succession, that he might make her a Princess, as she deserv'd. Indeed the hopes his Agent had given the Lady, of becoming her Husband, was not the smallest inducement to the Treaty; therefore he delay'd his Marriage with *Charlot*; for if that were but once confirm'd, the Princess; (by resenting, as she ought, the abuse that had been lain upon her) wou'd put an end to it, infinitely to his prejudice.

Charlot, very well satisfied with these Reasons, and unwilling to do any thing against the Interest of a Man whom she tenderly lov'd, accustom'd herself to hear his eager Sollicitations: He cou'd no longer contend with a Fire that consumed him, he must be gratified, or die. She languished under the same disquiets. The Season of the Year was come that he must make the Campaign with the King; he cou'd not resolve to depart unbless'd; *Charlot* still refus'd him that last proof of her Love. He took a tender and passionate Farewel. *Charlot*, drown'd in Tears, told him, 'twas impossible she shou'd support his absence; all the Court wou'd ridicule her Melancholy. This was what he wanted; he bid her take care of that, a Maid was but an ill Figure, that brought herself to be the sport of Laughters; but since her Sorrow (so pleasing and glorious to him) was like to be visible, he advised her to pass some days at his *Villa*, till the height of Melancholy shou'd be over, under the pretence of Indisposition; he wou'd take care that the Queen shou'd be satisfied of the necessity of her absence; he advis'd her even to depart that hour; since the King was already on his Journey, he must be gone that moment, and endeavour to overtake him. He assur'd her he wou'd write by every Courier, and beg'd her not to admit of another Lover, tho' he was sensible there were many (taking the advantage of his absence, wou'd endeavour to please her). To all this she answer'd so as to quiet his distrust and fears, her Tears drowned her Sighs, her Words were lost in Sobs and Groans! The Duke did not show less concern, but led her all trembling, to put her in a Coach that was to carry her to his *Villa*; where he had often wish'd to have her, but she distrusted her self, and wou'd not go with him, nor had she ventur'd now, but that she thought he was to follow the King, who cou'd not be without him.

Charlot no sooner arriv'd, but the Weather being very hot, she order'd a Bath to be prepar'd for her. Soon as she was refresh'd with that, she threw her self down upon a Bed, with only one thin Petticoat and a loose Nightgown, the Bosom of her Gown and Shift open; her Night-clothes tied carefully together with a Cherry-colour'd Ribon, which answer'd well to the yellow and silver Stuff of her Gown. She lay uncover'd, in a melancholy careless Posture, her Head resting upon one of her Hands, the other held a Handkerchief, that she employ'd to dry those Tears that sometimes fell from her Eyes; when raising herself a little, at a gentle noise she heard from the opening of a Door that answer'd to the Bed-side, she was quite astonished to see enter the amorous Duke. Her first emotions were all Joy, but in a minute she recollected herself, thinking he was not come there for nothing: She was going to rise, but he prevented her, by flying to her Arms, where, as we may call it, he nail'd her down to the Bed with Kisses; his love and resolution gave him a double vigour, he wou'd not stay a moment to capitulate with her; whilst yet her surprise made her doubtful of his designs, he took advantage of her confusion to accomplish 'em; neither her prayers, tears, nor struglings, cou'd prevent him, but in her Arms he made himself a full amends for all those pains he had suffered for her.

Thus was *Charlot* undone! thus ruin'd by him that ought to have been her Protector! 'Twas very long before he cou'd appease her; but so artful, so amorous, so submissive was his Address, so violent his Assurances, he told her, that he must have dy'd without the Happiness. *Charlot* espous'd his Crime, by stealing his Forgiveness. He pass'd the whole Night in her Arms, pleas'd, transported, and out of himself; whilst the ravish'd Maid was not all behind-hand in Extasies and guilty Transports. He staid a whole Week with *Charlot*, in a Surfeit of Love and Joy! that Week more inestimable than all the Pleasures of his Life before! whilst the Court believed him with the King, posting to the Army; he neglected *Mars* to devote himself wholly to *Venus*;[13] abstracted from all Business, that happy Week sublim'd him almost to an Immortal. *Charlot* was form'd to give and take all

---

[13] Substituted love for war.

those Raptures necessary to accomplish the Lover's happiness; none were ever more Amorous! none were ever more Happy!

The two Lovers separated, the Duke for the Army, *Charlot* return'd to Court; one of the Royal-Secretaries fell in Love with her, but his being of the precise Party,[14] and a marry'd Man, it behov'd to carry himself discreetly: He omitted no private Devoirs to please her, but her Heart entirely fix'd upon the Duke, neglected the Attempt. She had made an intimate Friendship with a young Countess, who was a lovely Widow, full of Air, Life and Fire; her Lord purchas'd her from his Rival, by the Point of his Sword, but he did not long survive to enjoy the Fruits of his Victory; he made her Circumstances as easie as he cou'd, but that was not extraordinary, however, she appear'd well at Court; knew the Management of Mankind, and how to procure her self universal Love and Admiration. *Charlot* made her the unwary Confidant of her Passion for the Duke; the Countess had the Goodness, or Complaisance, which you please, to hearken to the over-flowings[15] of a Love-sick-Heart: She imparted to her all the Letters she receiv'd from him, and took her Approbation for the Answer; that *never dying Fire!* those *racking Uneasiness's! Languors! Expectations! Impatiencies!* that the two Lovers express'd, were all *Greek* and *Hebrew* to the Countess, who was bred up in the fashionable way of making Love, wherein the Heart has little or no part, quite another turn of Amour. She would often tell *Charlot*, that no Lady ever suffer'd her self to be truly touch'd, but from that moment she was blinded and undone; the first thing a Woman ought to consult was her Interest, and Establishment in the World; that Love shou'd only be a handle towards it; when she left the pursuit of that to give up her self to her Pleasures, Contempt and Sorrow were sure to be her Companions: No Lover was yet ever known so ardent, but time abated of his Transport; no Beauty so ravishing, but that her Sweetness wou'd cloy; nor did Men any longer endeavour to please, when nothing was wanting to their Wishes: Love the most generous, and yet the most mercenary of all the Passions, does not care what he lavishes, provided there be something still in view to repay his Expence; but that once over, the Lover possess'd of what ever his Mistress can bestow, he hangs his Head, the *Cupid* drops his Wings, and seldom feels their native Energy return, but to carry him to new Conquests.

Charlot knew not how to digest this System of Amour; she was sure the Countess knew the World, but thought she knew not the Duke, who had not a Soul like other Men: She said, she would, at his return, convince her, (all Infidel as she was) that he had not the same Cast of Mind as the rest of his Sex; the Countess said she should be glad to see it, but that he had took exactly the same Methods to make his Fortune: She would advise her as a good Friend, (if it were strangely true, that his Ardors were yet unallayed) to push her Interest with him, that he might marry her; advis'd her to bestow no more Favours, till he paid her price; made her read the History of *Roxalana*, who by her wise Address, brought an imperious *Sultan*, contrary to the establish'd Rules of the

[14] Strict and correct in behaviour.
[15] Too revealing communications.

Seraglio, to divide with her the Royal Throne, *Charlot* said she would try what she could do; at the same time she receiv'd certain Advice, that the Treaty was broke off with the *Princess Dowager*. *Charlot* thought it was for her sake, and from thence (flatter'd by Love) took it into her Head, that it would not be long before she should be the Dutchess of——.

The Queen prepar'd a Ball to be danced the King's Birth-Night, which happen'd to be that of his Return from a fortunate Campaign. *Charlot* had, since the Duke's absence, (to render her self conspicuous to him) been practising an Accomplishment, which a certain great Author calls *excelling in a Mistake*. She danc'd that Night to the satisfaction of all who beheld her: the Duke's Return and Presence re-animated her; she seem'd born to new Life, and more Vivacity: He was charm'd with the Performance, and long'd for nothing so much, as to tell her he was more in Love with her than ever. Those *Duena's* that Guard the fair Maids belonging to the Queen, would not permit him all the Happiness he wish'd: How impatient they were to lose themselves in unnumber'd Kisses and Joys! the Duke proposed to her to go down to his *Villa* the next Day; that he would ask the King's leave to retire to put his Affairs in order, and immediately follow. There was no Body that wonder'd she shou'd pay her Compliment whilst he was in the Country, her Guardian, the Trustee of her Family; all the Duke's Children caress'd and lov'd her, they even wish'd their Father would marry her; for so 'twas receiv'd and believ'd at Court, that she shou'd be the Dutchess of——. They were no Strangers to his Love, he never pretended to dissemble; but not one imagin'd his guilty Passion had carry'd him that length it had: He was so charm'd with her, that he told her, she must resolve to pretend a distant Journey to her Relations, and remain conceal'd near *Angela*, where he might have the freedom of seeing her twice a Day, at least, unknown to all the Court; that if she could devote her self to such a Solitude, he would endeavour to do all things that were in his power to make it agreeable to her; the Love-sick Maid consented with joy; then was her time to push for what he possibly might have consented to, rather than not have possessed her undisturbed; but she was afraid that he shou'd think her Love was the result of Interest, and believ'd so well of his Honour, as not to distrust his Care of hers.

Behold her then settled in a pleasing Solitude, within a short Mile of the *Capitol*; the Servants that were put about her were all Strangers, her Name chang'd, and not a Mortal suspected but *Charlot* was gone into the Country to her Relations. The Duke saw her twice or thrice every Day, sometimes eat with her, and because he could not be so often lost, without being found by some body, they reported that he had a new Mistress, and had sent *Charlot* away, not to discompose her with the Report; no body could tell who she was, yet many pretended to have seen her, and ev'n gave Descriptions of her Height, Features, and Complexion, all by guess, and not likely to agree; some would have her the *fair*, some the *brunet*, and not a few the *black* Beauty. Every one spoke of what was most agreeable to themselves, but a Beauty to be sure she must be, because the Duke was so attach'd to her.

Charlot, tho' she possess'd all she cou'd desire in the Duke's Company, yet had many Hours of Solitude upon her Hands, the great Hurry of Affairs, the Business of the State, which lay heavy upon the Duke, engross'd too much of his time: To alleviate the Pains his Absence gave her, *Charlot* begg'd the Countess might be let into the Secret, to help her pass away, more agreeably those Moments that he was not with her: She urg'd this so earnestly, that the Duke knew not how to deny her, but bid her take it for her pains, if she one day repented of it; that if he was not mistaken in the Countess, she was none of those few Ladies that possess the retentive Faculty; but shou'd their Secret not suffer by her Tongue, (which indeed wou'd be wonderful) her being known to visit there, (as all things of that Nature are quickly known) wou'd blow the Suspicion of it abroad, to the prejudice of *Charlot's* Honour, which was dearer to him than his Life. She might easily have believ'd this last Asseveration, if he had had any Sense of his own, for there's no body but what would condemn him for corrupting hers.

Charlot cou'd not evade her Destiny; she wou'd have the Countess with her. Pride concurr'd with Diversion; she long'd to shew the Countess (who had so slender an Opinion of the Constancy of Mankind) how much and faithfully she was belov'd. The Countess came, and they met on both sides over-joy'd; she boasted of her good Fortune; the Widow told her, all that was very fine, but why did she not think of marrying of him, then they might be all Day and Night, and every Day and Night together, without interruption, and hiding; that other Diversions ought to have their turn with a Lady of her age. *Charlot* told her, she found all she desir'd in the Duke's Love, and her Friendship, she had nothing further to wish, if she wou'd but have the Goodness to see her as often as she cou'd. The Countess pitied the Love-sick Maid, but finding she was incorrigible, resolv'd to speak to her no more of her marrying the Duke: She saw, by his Delays, that he did not design it, and look'd upon *Charlot* as a *pauvre Fille trompez*.[16]

Almost the whole Winter pass'd away in an agreeable Cabal; the Countess had Wit enough, and a pleasant manner of relating things; her Intelligence was universal; she knew all that was done both at Court, and in the City: The Duke, who came to unbend himself with these two fair Ladies, seem'd to relish the Countess's Conversation: Not to disgrace Love, he was sometimes beholden to this gay Widow, for keeping up the Diversion. 'Tis not possible always to love, or to bear up to the extravagant height of a beginning Flame, without new Supplies it must decay, at least abate of its first Vigour, when not a Look, or Touch, but are Fuel to it. The Countess was not displeas'd at being heard; she remark'd his Attention; saw his Eyes were less on *Charlot*, and more on her; that he wou'd turn away, with a gentle Sigh, when she catch'd him looking at her; who does not know that undisturb'd possession makes Desire languish. *Charlot* believ'd nothing of this, but the Countess knew all the Maxims of Mankind. She presently guess'd how things went, and was not surpriz'd to hear the Duke tell the young Lady, that the time drawing on to take the Field; he would have her think of returning to Court; but that she might do it with the more Honour, and free from all suspicion of their Commerce, he advis'd her, in reallity, to take a Journey down to her Relations, from whence she might give notice of

---

[16] Poor deceived girl.

her return, as if she had been there the whole Winter. *Charlot* look'd tenderly upon the Duke, her Eyes fill'd with Tears; some drops of Blood fell from her Nose upon her Handkerchief, as she was reaching it to her Eyes, the Omen startled her, she was going to withdraw, to weep alone, when her Spirits fail'd her, and she fell in a fainting Fit upon the Countess's Bosom; the Duke had Affairs that urg'd his departure; he call'd her Women, and left her to their Care: Nothing is able to express the Despair she was in, when she found he could depart and leave her in that Condition. His date of Love is out, says the unfortunate *Charlot*, Oh Madam! that I had but believ'd you! What is to be done? Shall I see my self complaining, and neglected, scorn'd and yet fawning upon my Undoer? tho' my Heart burst with Grief and Tenderness, I will never have that little Spirit. The Countess confirm'd her in those Heroick Thoughts, and ev'n advis'd her to depart as soon as she cou'd, and without taking her Leave of him; for if he still lov'd her, that Indifferency would distract him, and cause him to fetch her back; if otherwise, prevent her from being his Triumph. *Charlot* judg'd the Advice good, and order'd all things for her departure on the morrow: She might, and ought to have gone early in the Morning, as the Countess would have had her, but lazy, lingering Love, made her trifle away the time, till the usual hour of the Duke's Visit. As he entred the Chamber, a mortal Paleness, and universal Trembling was seen in poor *Charlot*: He tenderly ran to support her; when she was a little recover'd, he ask'd her what those Preparations meant? She told him 'twas for her Journey, as he had advis'd her. The Duke told her he was glad of it, 'twas prudently resolv'd, but he wish'd, for both their sakes, she wou'd make no long stay in the Country, because he hop'd to be thus bless'd again, before he departed. She burst out into a Passion of Tears, at his approbation of a thing, when she thought the suddenness of it would have startled him. Let us go, let us go for ever, said she, sobbing, my Lord Duke, I wish your Eminence all Happiness, wretched *Charlot* shall never disturb it. Farewel, my dear Countess, I was not born to taste the Sweets of Love and Friendship: Here she hasted out of the Room, and got into the Coach that waited, without taking her Leave in Form, either of the one or the other. They made after her to the Gate; she briskly order'd the Coachman to drive on, and with six good Horses was presently out of sight.

The Duke gave his Hand to the Countess, to lead her back into the House; they continued in mutual Silence till the Duke broke it, by Words to these effect. "You doubtless condemn me, Madam, for my Indifference to *Mademoiselle Charlot*, I would remove so strong an Evidence as your self, by making you equally guilty. I know you are a Woman of the World, fully acquainted with your own Charms, and what they can do upon the Hearts of others. You have Wit, understand your own Interest, therefore if you have no Aversion for my Person, 'tis in your power to do what you please with me. For your sake I have advis'd *Mademoiselle* to this Journey: I cou'd not say what I wou'd before so troublesome a Witness; I have good Nature, and cou'd not see a Creature who loves me in pain, when nothing but Esteem and Pity remain for her: Not that I am naturally Inconstant, but your superior Charms have imperceptibly made their way, I had doubtless lov'd her a long time, if the

Vivacity of your Wit and Conversation had not interfer'd: However, I will omit
nothing for her Establishment in the World. Her Fault is yet a Secret between
us Two, and that I may bribe you to keep it inviolably, I offer to share
Interests; whatever is mine may be yours, nay Honour as well as Interest will
oblige you to it, for it cannot be unknown, that we see one another often at
this House, when we are married, that will be suppos'd to be the Secret: 'Tis
your own Fault if it be not done this Night: In giving you that ultimate Proof
of my Love, I spare both you and my self the trouble of Words: I have took
time to weigh the Design, all things plead for you, *Beauty, Merit, Sense*, and
every thing that can render a Woman charming, whilst I pretend nothing to
plead for me, but making it your own Interest to make me happy. As I
have avoided the tedious Forms, by which our Sex think they must engage
yours, so I beg that you will use none to me, that relate in any sort to
Mademoiselle Charlot, that is a tender Point, I wou'd not so much as remember,
(in the Joys I prepare my self for with you) that there is such a Person
in the World."

This Harangue put the Countess to her Reflections. She begg'd his Eminency
wou'd be pleas'd to give her time till to morrow Night, before she pretended
to answer him; and then she would do herself the Honour to expect him alone
at her House to Supper. The Duke kiss'd her Hand with a respective Assent to
what she had said, then led her to her Chair, and departed to prepare himself
for his Marriage with the Countess.

He did not fail to wait upon her at the usual Hour: The Lady was in
a gentile *Dishabile*, ev'n to the very Night-cloaths that she intended to lie
in. After a well order'd Supper, she carry'd him into a little Drawing-Room,
and told him, in a few Words, she was ready to receive the Honour of what
he had offer'd; his Inconstancy had held her for some Moments in suspence,
but as to that, she assur'd her self, that religiously performing her own Duty,
would oblige his Eminence to a Tenderness in his; that as the Distance was
so infinitely great, both in their Title, and other Circumstances, she would
not pretend to capitulate with him, but left all her Interest in his, as the
best Hands, who was so much her Friend, as to raise her to a Rank and
Fortune she could not without the highest Vanity have expected. The Duke
receiv'd her Consent with a wonderful deal of Joy and Gallantry; they were
immediately marry'd, and bedded. That very Night 'twas known at Court,
and some of poor *Charlot's* Friends, did her the Diskindness to send the
News of it into the Country, already Heart-broke with the Imagination of
the Duke's Indifferency. This but confirm'd her in her Resolution, of not
surviving the Loss of his Kindness: Her Solitude was Nourishment to those
black and corroding Thoughts that incessantly devour'd her: We may be sure
she often exclaim'd against *breach* of *Trust*, and *Friendship* in the Countess,
as well as Ingratitude and Faithlesness in the Duke: The remainder of her
Life was one continu'd Scene of Horror, Sorrow, and Repentance: She dy'd a
true Landmark: to warn all believing Virgins from shipwracking their Honour
upon (that dangerous Coast of Rocks) the Vows and pretended Passion of
Mankind.

Jane Barker

fl. 1688 – 1726

*J*ane Barker, who was writing between 1688 and 1726, was a Catholic from
a royalist family. Her poems treat political matters such as the changes of
monarch, as well as personal themes such as female friendship and religious
faith. In 1723 she published a prose work interspersed with poems, A Patch-work
Screen for the Ladies; *it tells loosely connected anecdotes and stories which often*
indicate startling psychological problems and insights. Through the character of
Galesia, Barker investigates her own failure to marry and the seductive but
socially injurious nature of learning and literature for a woman.

The following extract is taken from A Patch-work Screen for the Ladies, *and*
begins as Galesia is overturned in a coach on a bridge.

From

A *Patch-work Screen for the Ladies*

INTRODUCTION

...**B**Y good Luck, this Bridge was at the Entry of a little Village, so that People
hastened to their Assistance; some helping the Horses, some the Coach,
and some with Difficulty getting out *Galesia*; Who however, when she was got
out, found no Hurt, only was very wet: She was much pity'd by the good People;
amongst whom there was a poor Woman took her under the Arm, and told her,
she would conduct her to a House, where she might be accommodated with all
Manner of Conveniences.

All wet and dropping, she got to this House, which was a poor Village
Ale-house; and a poor one indeed it was; It being Evening, the Woman of
the House was gone out a Milking, so that the good Man could come at no Sheets,
that she might have got rid of her wet Cloaths, by going to Bed; However, he laid
on a large Country Faggot;[1] so she sat and snoaked in her wet Cloaths, till the
good Woman came; who hasten'd and got the Bed Sheeted, into which she gladly
laid herself; but the poorest that her Bones ever felt, there being a few Flocks[2] that

[1] Bundle of sticks bound together for burning.
[2] Coarse tuft of wool.

stank; and so thin of the same, that she felt the Cords cut through. The Blankets were of Thread-bare Home-spun Stuff, which felt and smelt like a Pancake fry'd in Grease; There were Four Curtains at the Four Corners, from whence they could no more stir, than Curtains in a Picture; for there were neither Rods nor Ropes for them to run upon; no Testern,[3] but the Thatch of the House; A Chair with a Piece of a Bottom, and a brown Chamber-pot, furr'd as thick as a Crown Piece.

However, all this was a better Lodging than the Bottom of the River; and great and many Thanks were due to God for it. The good Woman was kind, and brought *Galesia* a good wooden Dish-full of boil'd Milk, well crumb'd with brown Barley-Bread; which she persuaded her to eat, to drive out the Cold. She took Care to get her Cloaths dry, and brought them to her, e'er she went a Milking. And not-withstanding all these Hardships, she got no Cold, Cough or Lameness; but arose well-refresh'd; took Leave of her Landlord and departed, directing her Steps and Intentions towards the Town were the Stage-Coach'd Inn'd.

But it so happen'd, in this her Journey, that she lost her Way, and got, she knew not how, into a fine Park, amongst Trees, Firs, Thickets, Rabbet-burrows, and such like; nor knew she where she was, nor which Way to go; but standing still a little while to consider, she heard a *Tomtit* sing in a Tree, as her musing Fancy made her imagine,

Sit thee down, sit thee down, sit thee down, sit.

At the same time looking on one Side, she saw a handsome Seat at a very little Distance, to which she went, and obey'd the threefold Advice. As she sat there to rest herself, revolving divers Thoughts, a little Hedge-Sparrow in a Bush, sung, *Chear-up, Chear-up*; Ah! poor Bird! said she, thou givest me good Counsel; but that is all thou hast to give; and bare Words help little to a hungry Stomach, and I know not where to fill mine, unless I could eat Grass like the Four-footed Beasts.

As she was in these Thoughts, a Crow sitting in a Tree, with a hoarse Voice, seem'd to say *Good-Luck, Good-Luck*! If thou art a true Prophet, said *Galesia*, the Birds of thy Colour, shall no more be counted Birds of Ill Omen, but the Painters shall put a long Tail to you, and the Poets shall call you *Birds of Paradise*.

As she was thus musing on the Language of the Birds, she heard a Noise of Hunting in the Park, Horns winding, Men hollowing, and calling *Ringwood, Rockwood, ho! Boman! Blossom, ho*.[4]She then began to reflect how necessary this Diversion was: Alas! said she, if it was not for this, we might all lodge as bad as I did last Night. We are beholden to *Ringwood* and *Jowler*, for many a Dainty Morsel which *Reynard*[5] would deprive us of, if it were not for this Pack of Allies, who oppose his Tyranny; Who otherwise would not only over-run the Woods, and Farmers Yards, 'till there is neither Cocks nor Hens, but would also ravage the Fens and Islands, the Habitations of Ducks and Geese; Then long live *Ringwood, Rockwood, Boman* and *Jowler*, by whose Industry we eat good Bits, and lie on good Beds.

3 Canopy of a bed.
4 Hounds for hunting.
5 A fox.

Whilst *Galesia* was in these Cogitations, the Dogs and Hunters came very near where she was sitting; amongst whom, was a Lady, mounted on a beautiful Steed, who beginning to grow weary of the Chace, order'd her Servants to stop, and help her off her Horse, resolving to walk home over the Park, it being a fine smooth Walk betwixt two Rows of Lime trees, planted and grown in exact Form, agreeable to the Eye, pleasing to the Smell, and making a most delightful Shade. The Lady directing her Eyes and Steps towards this Walk, she saw *Galesia* sitting in the disconsolate Posture aforesaid, and being not a little surpriz'd to see a Gentlewoman all alone in that desolate Place, could not avoid interrogating her thereupon.

Galesia, in few and respectful Words, inform'd the Lady of her Disaster of being overthrown into the River the Day before, and her bad Lodging at Night, and her losing her Way that Morning, all which made her betake herself to that Seat. The Lady most courteously and charitably took her along with her to her House, which was a Noble Structure, situate in the midst of that Park. Here she entertain'd her very kindly; assuring her of all Assistance to convey her to the Place to which she was design'd, when she had rested and recover'd her Fatigue. In the mean Time, she diverted her, by shewing *Galesia* her Gardens, House, and glorious Appartments, adorn'd with rich Furniture of all Sorts; some were the Work of hers and her Husband's Ancestors, who delighted to imploy poor Gentlewomen, thereby to keep them from Distress, and evil Company, 'till Time and Friends could dispose Things for their better Settlement.

At last, the Lady shew'd her an Appartment embellish'd with Furniture of her own making, which was PATCH-WORK, most curiously compos'd of rich Silks, and Silver and Gold Brocades: The whole Furniture was compleated excepting a SCREEN, which the Lady and her Maids were going about. Her Ladyship told *Galesia*, She would take it kindly if her Affairs would permit her to stay with her some time, and assist her in her SCREEN. Which Invitation *Galesia* most gladly accepted, begging the Lady to send to the next Stage of the Coach and Carrier, for her Trunks and Boxes, which contained her Wearing-Cloaths. The Lady forthwith sent for the Things, hoping that therein they might find some Bits of one thing or other, that might be useful to place in the SCREEN. But when the Trunks and Boxes came, and were opened, alas! they found nothing but Pieces of *Romances, Poems, Love-Letters*, and the like: At which the good Lady smil'd, saying, She would not have her Fancy balk'd, and therefore resolved to have these ranged and mixed in due Order, and thereof compose a SCREEN.

And thus it came to pass, that the following SCREEN was compos'd.

LEAF I

THE CONTINUATION OF THE HISTORY OF GALESIA

G ALESIA *tells episodes from her life. After an unfortunate involvement with a man named Bosvil, she recovers and resumes her social activities and her studies.*

...I began to delight my-self in Dressing, Visiting, and other Entertainments, befitting a young Gentlewoman; nevertheless, did not omit my Study, in which my Brother continued to oblige my Fancy, and assisted me in *Anatomy* and *Simpling*,[6] in which we took many a pleasing Walk, and gather'd many Patterns of different Plants, in order to make a large natural Herbal.[7] I made such Progress in *Anatomy*, as to understand *Harvey's*[8] Circulation of the Blood, and *Lower's*[9] Motion of the Heart. By these and the like Imployments, I began to forget and scorn *Bosvil*. If I thought on him at all, it was with Contempt; and I wonder'd how it came to pass that I ever lov'd him, and thought myself secure the rest of my Days from that Weakness.

As I thus betook myself to an Amusement different from my Sex and Years, my other young Companions, began to look grave upon me; or I, perhaps, look'd so upon them. Our little Follies of telling our Dreams; laying Things under each other's Heads to dream of our Amours; counting Specks on our Nails, who should have the most Presents from Friends or Lovers; tying Knots in the Grass; pinning Flowers on our Breasts, to know the Constancy of our Pretenders; drawing Husbands in the Ashes; St. *Agnes's* Fast;[10] and all such childish Auguries, were now no more any Diversion to me; so that I became an useless Member in our rural Assemblies. My Time and Thoughts were taken up in *Harvey, Willis,*[11] and such-like Authors, which my Brother help'd me to understand and relish, which otherwise might have seemed harsh or insipid: And these serv'd to make me unfit Company for every body; for the Unlearned fear'd, and the Learned scorn'd my Conversation; at least, I fancy'd so: A Learned Woman, being at best but like a Forc'd-Plant, that never has its due or proper Relish, but is wither'd by the first Blast that Envy or Tribulation blows over her Endeavours. Whereas every Thing, in its proper Place and Season, is graceful, beneficial, and pleasant. However, my dear Brother humouring my Fancy, I pass'd my Time in great Satisfaction. His Company was my Recreation, and his wise Documents my Instruction; even his Reproofs were but as a poignant Sauce, to render his good Morals the more savoury, and easier digested. Thus we walk'd and talk'd; we laugh'd and delighted our-selves; we dress'd and visited; we received our Friends kindly and by them were generously treated in their turn: all which was to the Satisfaction of our endearing tender Parents. But alas! short was the Continuance of this Happiness; for my dear Brother died. And now, Madam, forgive these flowing Tears, which interrupt my Discourse.

Galesia having discharg'd a Torrent of Tears, the usual Effect of any Discourse for so great a Loss, she endeavoured to compose herself, dry'd her Eyes, and return'd to her Story.

[6] The study and gathering of medicinal plants.
[7] Book containing names and descriptions of plants.
[8] William Harvey (1578–1657) an English physician, famous for his discovery of the circulation of the blood.
[9] Richard Lower (1631–91) an anatomist who isolated and described various sections of the heart.
[10] On St. Agnes's eve maids were supposed to have visions of their lovers.
[11] Thomas Willis (1621–75) an eminent physician who described the anatomy of the brain.

This, Madam, was such a Grief as I had never felt; for though I had suffer'd much in the Transactions of *Bosvil*; yet those Sorrows were allay'd, in some degree, by the Mixture of other Passions, as Hope, Fear, Anger, Scorn, Revenge, etc. But this was Grief in Abstract, Sorrow in pure Element. I griev'd without ceasing; my Sighs alternatively blew up my Tears, and my Tears allay'd my Sighs, 'till fresh Reflections rais'd new Gusts of Sorrow. My Solitude was fill'd with perpetual Thoughts of Him; and Company was entertain'd with nothing but Discourses of this my irreparable Loss. My sleeping, as well as waking Hours, were fill'd with Ideas of him! Sometimes I dream'd I saw his Ghost, come to visit me from the other World; sometimes I thought I assisted him in his Sickness; sometimes attending at his Funeral; then awake in a Flood of Tears; when, waking, I cou'd form no Thought or Idea, but what Grief suggested. In my Walks and Studies, it was still the same, the Remembrance of some wise Documents, or witty Entertainment, roused up my Grief, by reflecting on my great Loss. No Book or Paper cou'd I turn over, but I found *Memorandums* of his Wisdom and Learning, which served to continue and augment my Grief; and so far transported me sometimes, that I even wish'd for that which is *the Horror of Nature*, that I might see his *Ghost*. I experienced what the Philosophers assert, *That much reflecting on* Death, *is the way to make it less terrible*; and 'tis certain, I reflected so much on his, that I wish'd for nothing more; wish'd to be with him; wish'd to be in that happy State, in which I assur'd my self his Vertues had plac'd him. But in vain I wish'd for Death; I was ordain'd to struggle with the Difficulties of Life; which were to be many, as I have since experienced; Heaven having taken away from me, Him, who seem'd by Nature ordain'd to conduct me through the Labyrinth of this World, when the Course of Nature should take my dear indulgent Parents from me, to their Repose in *Elysium*. And now, instead of being a Comfort to them in this their great Affliction, my Griefs added Weight to theirs, such as they could hardly sustain. ...

[*Galesia surmounts her grief in time*]

...being one Day where there was a young Gentleman, who did not think me so much a *Stoick* as I thought my self, he so far lik'd my Person and Humour, that altho' he had been a very loose Liver, he began to think he could endure to put on Shackles, and be confin'd to *one*: But being perfectly a Stranger, and knowing not well how to introduce himself into my farther Acquaintance, he took this odd Method.

There was a certain Gossip in those Parts, that used to go between the Ladies and Gentlewomen, with Services, and How-d'ye's; always carrying with her the little prattling News of Transactions where she frequented. This Woman coming to our House, was receiv'd with a good Mien, and the best Chear our Larder would afford, which was my Office to perform. She took the Opportunity to tell me, that her coming at that Time was particularly to Me, from Mr. *Bellair*, who had seen me the other Day at such a Place, since which time he had had no Repose, nor none could have, 'till I gave him Leave to make me a Visit, which he begg'd most earnestly. To which I reply'd, That though Mr. *Bellair* had seen me, he was perfectly a Stranger to me, otherwise he had not sent such a Message; he knowing that I lived in my Father's House, not in my own; therefore had no right to invite or receive any body unknown to my Parents, much less young Gentlemen; that being an Irregularity misbecoming my Sex and Station, and the Character of a dutiful Daughter: This I desir'd her to tell him, with my Service; which Answer I utter'd with a little Sharpness, that the Woman could not but see her Errand was disobliging, as it was, and ought to be; such a Message looking more like a dishonourable Intrigue, than an Address to a vertuous Maiden-Gentlewoman. The Truth is, I always had an Aversion to those secret Addresses, as all vertuous Maids ought, and was resolved as carefully to avoid them as Mariners do Rocks; for'tis certain, that Parents are naturally willing to promote their Childrens Happiness; and therefore, that Lover who desires to keep the Parents in the Dark, is conscious to himself of something that has need to shun the Light; for his Concealing his Pretensions from the Mother, looks as if he meant an unworthy Conquest on the Daughter; and especially those of Mr. *Bellair's* Character.

However, I mistook my young Gentleman, his Intentions being more sincere than I expected: For upon that Answer to my Gossip, he took the first Occasion to discover his Sentiments to his Father; who did not only approve, but rejoyced thereat, hoping that he was in a Disposition to reclaim himself from his loose Way of Living; and that the Company of a Wife, and Care of a Family, wou'd totally wean him from those wild Companions, in whom he too much delighted: Not but that his Father had divers times offered, and earnestly persuaded him, to dispose himself for a Married Life, having no Son but him, to inherit his Riches, and continue his Family. To which the young Man was ever averse; counting Marriage as Fetters and Shackles, a Confinement not to be borne by the Young and the Witty; a Wife being suppos'd to be the Destruction of all Pleasure and good Humour, and a Death to all the Felicities of Life; only good in the Declension of Years, when Coughs and Aches oblige a Man to his own Fire-side: then a Nurse is a most necessary Utensil in a House. These and the like, us'd to be the wild Notions, wherewith he oppos'd his Father's indulgent Care, whenever he went about to provide for his happy Establishment: So the good old Gentleman was overjoy'd at his Son's own Proposal, and took the first Opportunity with my Father, over a Bottle, to deliver his Son's Errand. To which my Father answer'd, like a plain Country Gentleman, as he was (who never gilded his Actions with fraudulent Words, nor painted his Words with deceitful or double Meanings;) and told him, "That he was very sensible of the Honour he did him in this Proposal; but that he cou'd not make his Daughter a Fortune suitable to his Estate: For, continued he, that becoming Way in which we live, is more the Effect of prudent Management, than any real Existence of Riches." To which the old Gentleman reply'd, "That Riches were not what he sought in a Wife for his Son; Fortune having been so propitious to him, that he needed not to make that his greatest Care: A prudent, vertuous Woman, was what he most aim'd at, in his Son's Espousals, hoping that such an one, would reclaim and wean him from all those wild Excursions to which Youth and Ill-Company had drawn him, to his great Affliction. But, methinks, continu'd he, I spy a Dawn of Reformation in the Choice he has made of your Daughter; who, amongst all the young Gentlewomen of these Parts, I value, she having a distinguishing Character for Prudence and Vertue, capable to command Respect and Esteem from all the World; as well as does her amiable Person ingage my Son's Affections. Wherefore, said he, I hope you will not refuse your Concurrence, thereby to make my Son happy." My Father making him a grateful Acknowledgment, told him, "He wou'd propose it to my Mother and me; and added, That his Daughter having been always dutiful and tenderly observant, he resolv'd to be indulgent, and impose nothing contrary to her Inclinations. Her Mother also, continu'd he, has been a Person of that Prudence and Vertue, that I should not render the Justice due to her Merit, if I did any thing of this kind, without her Approbation."

This my Father related to me, with an Air full of Kindness, telling me, That he wou'd leave the Affair wholly to my Determination; adding, That there was an Estate, full Coffers, and a brisk young Gentleman; So that I think (said he) I need say no more to a Person of common Sense, to comply with what is so advantageous.

To which I reply'd, "That these or any of these, were above my Desert; and your Recommendations, Sir, redouble the Value; upon whose Wisdom and paternal Care I ought wholly to depend: But his particular loose Way of Living, I hope will justify me, when I lay that before you, as a Cause of Hesitation." To which my Mother reply'd, "That it must be my Part, with Mildness and Sweetness, to reclaim him: That he having now *Sow'd his wild Oats*, (according to the Proverb) wou'd see his Folly; and finding there is nothing to be reap'd but Noise, Vanity, and Disgrace, in all Probability, wou'd apply himself to another Way of Living; especially having made the Proposal to his Father of settling with a Person of his own choosing, where no Interest nor Family-Necessity had any Hand in the Election."

These and the like Discourses and Considerations, pass'd among us; we having his Father's serious Proposal for our Foundation; which, join'd with the Message he himself had sent me by the Gossip, we had Reason to believe the Superstructure would not be defective.

Nevertheless, though I was but an innocent Country Girl, yet I was not so ignorant of the World, but to know or believe, that often those Beau Rakes, have the Cunning and Assurance to make Parents on both sides, Steps to their Childrens Disgrace, if not Ruin: For very often, good Country Ladies, who reflect not on the Vileness of the World, permit their Daughters to give private Audiences, to their Lovers, in some obscure Arbour or Distant Drawing-room; where the Spark has Opportunity to misbehave himself to the Lady; which, if she resent, there is a ready Conveniency for him to bespatter her with Scandal. And I did not know but *Bellair* might have some such thing in his Thoughts, out of Malice for my having rejected his Intrigue by the Gossip. For I could not fancy my-self endow'd with Charms sufficient to hold fast such a Volage;[12] however, I knew myself safe under my Mother's Prudence, and my own Resolution.

[12] Inconstant person.

And thus I expected my pretended Lover some Days; But instead of his personal Appearance, News came, That he was taken in a Robbery on the High-way, and committed to the County-Gaol: And all this out of a Frolick; for tho' he had all Things necessary, both for Conveniency and Diversion, nevertheless, this detestable Frolick must needs be put in Practice, with some of his lewd Companions; for which at the next Assizes, he receiv'd the Reward of his Crimes at the Place of publick Execution.

I have told you this Transaction, that your Ladyship may not be ignorant of any thing that appertains to me, though this was an Affair utterly unknown to all the World; I mean his Proposal of Marriage; nor does any of my Poems take the least Notice, or give any Hint of it; for there was no Progress made by any personal Correspondence, nor can I persuade my-self he meant any thing but Mischief.

I cou'd recount to your Ladyship another Story or two of odd Disappointments; but, they will take up too great a Place in your SCREEN, and render the View disagreeable.

LEAF II

T HESE Amours affected me but little, or rather not at all; For the Troubles ... of the World lighting upon me, a thousand Disappointments attended me, when deprived of my Father. Alas! we know not the real Worth of indulgent, tender Parents, 'till the Want of them teach us by a sad Experience: And none experienc'd this more than myself: deceitful Debtors, impatient Creditors, distress'd Friends, peevish Enemies, Law-suits, rotten Houses, Eye-servants,[13] spightful Neighbours, impertinent and interested Lovers, with a thousand such Things to terrify and vex me, nothing to consolate or assist me, but Patience and God's Providence.

When my Mother and I had accommodated our Affairs, we endeavour'd to make ourselves easy, by putting off our Country Incumbrance, and so went to live at *London*.

Here I was, as if I was born again: This was a new life to me, and very little fitted the Shape of my Rural Fancy; for I was wholly form'd to the Country in Mind and Manners; as unfit for the Town, as a Tarpaulin[14] for a States-man; the Town to me was a Wilderness, where, methought, I lost my self and my Time; and what the World there calls Diversion, to me was Confusion. The Park, Plays, and Operas, were to me but as so much Time thrown away. I was a Stranger to every-body, and their Way of Living; and, I believe, my stiff Air and awkward Mien, made every-body wish to remain a Stranger to me. The *Assemblèes, Ombre*, and *Basset-Tables*,[15] were all *Greek* to me; and I believe my Country Dialect, to them, was as unintelligible; so that we were neither serviceable nor pleasant to each other. Perhaps some or other of the Company, either out of Malice

13 People who work only when under the eye of their masters.
14 Tarred canvas worn by sailors.
15 Public assemblies and places for card games.

to expose me, or Complaisance to entertain me in my own Way, would enter
into the Praise of a Country Life, and its plentiful Way of Living, amongst our
Corn, Dairies, and Poultry, till by Degrees, these bright *Angels* would make
the *Ass* open its Mouth, and upon their Demand, tell how many Pounds of
Butter a good *Cow* would make in a week; or how many Bushels of *Wheat*
a good *Acre* of *Land* would produce; Things quite out of their Sphere or
Element: And amongst the rest, the Decay of the *Wooll Trade* is not to be
omitted; and, like a true Country Block-head, grumble against the *Parliament*,
for taking no better Care of the *Country-Trade*, by prohibiting *Cane-Chairs* and
Wainscot,[16] by which means the *Turkey-work, Tapistry*, and *Kidderminster trades*
were quite lost;[17] and in them the great Manufacture of the Nation; and not
only so, but perpetual Fires intail'd on the City of *London*. Thus I, one of the
free-born People of *England*, thought I had full Privilege to rail at my *Betters*.
Sometimes, and in some Places, perhaps, Part of the Company, who knew a little
of my Bookish Inclinations, would endeavour to relieve that Silence which the
Ignorance of the Town laid upon me; and enter into a Discourse of Receipts,[18]
Books, and Reading. One ask'd me, If I lik'd Mrs. *Phillips*, or Mrs. *Behn* best?[19]
To whom I reply'd, with a blunt Indignation, That *they ought not to be nam'd
together*: And so, in an unthinking, unmannerly Way, reproach'd the Lady that
endeavour'd to divert and entertain me; she having that Moment been pleased
to couple them. By this Blunder, Madam, said *Galesia*, you see how far one is
short, in Conversation acquired only by Reading; for the many Plays and pretty
Books I had read, stood me in little stead at that Time, to my great Confusion;
for though Reading inriches the Mind, yet it is Conversation that inables us to
use and apply those Riches or Notions gracefully.
    At the *Toilet*, I was as ignorant a Spectator as a Lady is an Auditor at an
Act-Sermon[20] in the University, which is always in *Latin*; for I was not capable
to distinguish which Dress became which Face; or whether the *Italian, Spanish*,
or *Portugal* Red, best suited such or such Features; nor had I a Catalogue of
the Personal or Moral Defects of such or such Ladies, or Knowledge of their
Gallantries, whereby to make my *Court* to the *Present*, at the *Cost* of the *Absent*;
and so to go the World round, 'till I got thereby the Reputation of *ingaging* and
agreeable Company. However, it was not often that the whole Mystery of the *Toilet*,
was reveal'd to my Country Capacity; but now and then some Aunt, or Governess,
would call me to a Dish of Chocolate, or so; whilst the Lady and her officious
Madamoiselle,[21] were putting on those secret Imbellishments which illustrated
her Beauties in the Eyes of most of the fine bred Beholders. But some petulant,
antiquated Tempers, despised such Ornaments, as not having been used in good
Queen BESS'S Days; nor yet in the more Modern Court of *Oliver Cromwel*.[22] As

[16] Cane and wainscot (oak) were imported.
[17] Tapestries imitating Turkish ones and Kidderminster carpets, i.e. native goods.
[18] Prescriptions and formulae.
[19] Aphra Behn the playwright was notorious for her frank language, Katherine Phillips,
the poet, famous for her propriety and sentiment.
[20] A sermon preached by a new Doctor of Divinity to show proficiency.
[21] French maid.
[22] Time of Queen Elizabeth I (1658–63) and the Commonwealth (1649–60).

to myself, I was like a *Wild Ass* in a Forest, and liv'd alone in the midst of this great Multitude, even the great and populous City of *London*.

When Duty and good Days call'd me to Church, I thought I might find there some Compeeresses, or Persons of my own Stamp, and amongst the Congregation behave my self like others of my Sex and Years; But, alas! there were Locks and Keys, Affronts from Pew-keepers,[23] crowding and pushing by the Mob, and the gathering Congregation gazing upon me as a Monster; at least I fancied so. When patient waiting, and Pocket opening[24] to the Pew-Keeper, had got me a Place, I thought to exercise the Duty that call'd me thither: But, alas! the Curtesies, the Whispers, the Grimaces, the Pocket Glasses, Ogling, Sighing, Fleating,[25] Glancing, with a long &c. so discompos'd my thoughts, that I found I was as unfit for those Assemblies, as those others before nam'd, where a verbal Conversation provided against those mute Entertainments; which my Clownish Breeding made me think great Indecencies in that Sacred Place; where nothing ought to be thought on, much less acted, but what tended to Devotion, and God's Glory; so that I was here likewise alone in the midst of a great Congregation. Thus you see, Madam, how an Education, purely Country, renders one unfit to live in the great World, amongst People of refin'd and nice Breeding; and though I had bestow'd Time and Pains in Book-Acquests,[26] a little more than usual; yet it was but *lost Labour* to say the *best of it*: However, I did not repent; for though it had suppress'd and taken Place of that nice Conversation belonging to the Ladies, yet it furnish'd me with Notions above the Trifles of my Sex, wherewith to entertain my self in *Solitude*; and likewise, when Age and Infirmities confin'd my dear Mother within-doors, and very much to her Chamber, I paid my Duty to her with Pleasure, which otherwise might have seem'd a Constraint, if not in some Degree omitted, had my Thoughts been levell'd at those gaudy Pleasures of the Town, which intangle and intoxicate the greater Part of Woman-kind. ...

...I began to believe Providence had ordain'd for me a *Single Life. Began*, did I say? No, rather *continued* in that Sentiment ever since the Disappointment of *Bosvil*. And I think here are a few Lines something tending to that Subject:

A VIRGIN LIFE

S INCE, O good Heavens! you have bestow'd on me
  So great a Kindness for *Virginity*,
Suffer me not to fall into the Powers
Of Man's almost Omnipotent Amours.
But let me in this happy State remain,

[23] Enclosed pews were kept for richer or more important worshippers.
[24] Paying money.
[25] Grinning and laughing.
[26] Knowledge.

And in chaste Verse my chaster Thoughts explain;
Fearless of *Twenty-five*, and all its Rage,
When Time with Beauty lasting Wars ingage.
When once *that Clock has struck*, all Hearts retire,
Like *Elves* from *Day-break*, or like *Beasts* from Fire,
'Tis Beauty's *Passing-Bell*; no more are slain;
But dying Lovers all revive again.
Then every Day some new Contempt we find,
As if the Scorn and Lumber of Mankind.
These frightful Prospects, oft our Sex betray;
Which to avoid, some fling themselves away;
Life harmless *Kids*, who when pursu'd by *Men*,
For Safety, run into a *Lyon's Den*.
   Ah! *happy State*! how strange it is to see,
What mad Conceptions some have had of *Thee*!
As if thy Being was all Wretchedness,
Or foul Deformity, in vilest Dress:
Whereas thy Beauty's pure Celestial,
Thy Thoughts Divine, thy Words Angelical:
And such ought all thy Votaries to be,
Or else they're so but for Necessity.
A *Virgin* bears the Impress of all Good,
Under that Name, all Verture's understood.
So equal all her Looks, her Mien, her Dress,
That nought but Modesty is in Excess;
The Business of her Life to this extends,
To serve her God, her Neighbour and her Friends.

  Indeed, said the Lady, the Transactions of thy Life hitherto seem a perfect Chain of Disappointments. However, the Almighty has been gracious in giving thee a Mind submissive and resign'd; for which thou art bound to glorify his Goodness, and hope for more prosperous Days for the Time to come....

THE NECESSITY OF FATE

I

IN vain, in vain it is, I find,
   To strive against our Fate;
  We may as well command the Wind,
The Sea's rude Waves, to gentle Manners bind,
Or to Eternity prescribe a Date;
As frustrate ought that Fortune has design'd:
For when we think we're Politicians grown,
   And live by Methods of our own,

We then obsequiously obey
Fate's Dictates, and a blindfold Homage pay.

II

WERE it not so, I surely could not be
     Still Slave to Rhime, and lazy Poetry:
     I, who so oft have strove
     My Freedom to regain;
And sometimes too, for my Assistance took
     Obedience, and sometimes a Book;
     Company, and sometimes Love:
     All which, still proves in vain;
For I can only shake, but not cast off my Chain.

III

ALL this, my *Fate*, all this thou didst fore show,
     Ev'n when I was a Child,
     When in my *Picture's* Hand,
     My Mother did command,
There should be drawn a *Lawrel Bough*.
Lo! then my *Muse* sat by, and smil'd,
To hear how some the Sentence did oppose,
     Saying an *Apple, Bird*, or *Rose*,
Were Objects which did more befit
My childish Years, and no less childish Wit.

IV

FOR then my *Muse* well knew, that *constant Fate*
     Her Promise would compleat:
     For *Fate* at my Initiation
     Into the Muses Congregation,
As my Reponsor promis'd then for me,
     I should forsake those *Three*;[27]
Soaring Honours, vain Persuits of Pleasure,
     And vainer Fruits of worldly Treasure,
All for the Muses *melancholy Tree*,
E'er I knew ought of its *great Mystery*.

---

[27] Referring to the Apple, Bird or Rose (author).

> Since, O my Fate! thou needs wilt have it so,
> Let thy kind Hand exalt it to my Brow.

To which my Mother reply'd, I think, *Fate* would be more kind to set a Basket, or a Milk-pail, on thy Head; thereby to suppress those foolish Vapours that thus intoxicate thy Brain: But if there be a *fatal Necessity* that it must be so, e'en go on, and make thyself easy with thy fantastick Companions the Muses: I remember, continued she, I have been told, that one of the ancient Poets says:

> Thrust *Nature* off, with Fork, by Force,
> She'll still return to her old Course:

And so I find it in the whole Course of thy Life. And, as thou sayest in this Poem, thou hast tryed divers means to chase away this unlucky Genius that attends thee; and, I am sensible, out of a true design'd Obedience to me: But since it will not do, I shall no more oppose thy Fancy, but comply and indulge so innocent a Diversion. As I was about to return her my Thanks, a Gentleman that had married our Kinswoman, came in. ...

...This Gentleman, said Galesia, had married a young Gentlewoman of Distinction, against the Consent of her Friends; which she accomplish'd by the Help of her Mother's Maid-Servant. To say the Truth, though her Birth was very considerable, yet her Person was not at all agreeable; and her Fortune but indifferent: her Parents, I suppose, thinking, that more than just enough to support her, would but betray her to an unhappy Marriage. In short, married she was to the foresaid young Man, whose Person was truly handsome; and with Part of her Fortune he plac'd himself in the Army, bestow'd another Part in furnishing her a house, and so liv'd very decently; and notwithstanding her indifferent Person, he had Children by her, though they did not live long. Thus they made a pretty handsome Shift in the World, 'till a vile Wretch, her Servant, overturn'd all; as follows. This Servant, whether she was a Creature of her Master's before she came to her Mistress, is not known; but she became very fruitful, and had every Year a Child; pretending that she was privately married to an Apprentice. Whether the Wife knew the whole of the Matter, or was impos'd upon, is uncertain; but which way soever it was, she was extremely kind to this Woman, to a degree unheard of; became a perfect Slave to her, and, as if she was the Servant, instead of the Mistress, did all the Household-Work, made the Bed, clean'd the House, wash'd the Dishes; nay, farther than so, got up in the Morning, scour'd the Irons, made the fire, &c. leaving this vile Strumpet in Bed with her Husband; for they lay all Three together every Night. All this her Friends knew, or at least suspected; but thought it Complaisance, not Choice in her; and that she consider'd her own Imperfections, and Deformity; and therefore was willing to take no Notice of her Husband's Fancy in the Embraces of this Woman her Servant. But the sequel opens quite another Scene: And now I come to that Part of the Story, where he came to my Mother. His Business was, to desire her to come to his Wife, and endeavour to persuade her to part with this Woman; For, said he, she has already Three Children living, and God knows how many more she

may have: Which indeed, Madam, said he, is a Charge my little Substance is
not able to sustain; and I have been using all Endeavours to persuade my Wife
to part with her, but cannot prevail: Wherefore I beg you, as a Friend, Relation,
and her Senior in Years, to come, and lay before her the Reasonableness of what I
desire, and the ridiculousness of her proceeding. Good Heaven! said my Mother,
can you think thus to bore my Nose with a Cushion? Can you imagine me so
stupid, as to believe your Wife can persist in such a condition of Nature? It is
impossible a Wife should oppose her Husband's Desire in parting with such a
Woman. Madam, reply'd he, I beg you once more to be so good as to come to
my Wife, and then condemn me if I have advanc'd a Falshood. Well, reply'd my
Mother, I will come; though I doubt not but upon due Inspection, the whole, will
prove a Farce compos'd amongst you, in which your Wife is to act her Part just
as you between you think fit to teach her; which she, out of Fear, or some other
Delusion, is to perform. But he averr'd again and again, that, without Fraud or
Trick, the Thing was as he said. In short, my Mother went; and there she found
the Servant sitting in a handsome Velvet Chair, dress'd up in very good lac'd
Linnen, having clean Gloves on her Hands, and the Wife washing the Dishes.
This sight put my Mother into such a violent Passion, that she had much ado
to refrain from laying Hands on her. However, she most vehemently chid the
Mistress; telling her, that she offended God, disgrac'd her Family, scandaliz'd
her Neighbours, and was a Shame to Woman-kind. All which she return'd with
virulent Words; amongst other Things, she stood Buff[28] in Favour of that Woman;
saying, That she had been not only a faithful Servant, but the best of Friends, and
those that desir'd to remove such a Friend from her, deserved not the Name of
Friends, neither did she desire they should come into her House: All which she
utter'd with such an Air of Vehemency, that there was no Room left to doubt of
the Sincerity of her Words; but that all proceeded from an Interiour thoroughly
degenerated. All which my Mother related to me with great Amazement: But
withal, told me, that she would have me go to her on the Morrow; and with
calm and friendly Words, endeavour to persuade her to Reason; for, said she,
I was in a Passion at the disagreeable View; but you, who have naturally more
Patience than my-self, pray put on the best Resolutions you can to keep your
Temper, whatsoever Provocations shall occur. This instructed, thus resolved, I
went next Day, hoping that a Night's Repose would calm the Storm my Mother's
Anger might have rais'd. But when I came, I found it all the same: Though I
took her apart, and with the utmost Mildness, persuaded her, and us'd the best
Reasons I could think on to inforce those Persuasions, yet all was in vain; and she
said, We all join'd with her Husband to make her miserable, by removing from
her, the only Friend she had in the World; and passionately swore by Him that
made her, that if we combin'd to send that Woman away, she would go with her.
I would try that, reply'd I, were I in your Husband's Place: At which her Passion
redoubled; and she, with violent Oaths, repeated her Resolution; desiring, that
her Friends would meddle with their own Business, and let her alone, to remain
in Quiet in her house, and not come to give her Disturbance. After these uncouth

[28] Firm.

Compliments, I left her, carrying with me the greatest Amazement possible. After this, the Husband came to us, and ask'd, if we did not find true what he had told us? Indeed, replied I, true, and doubly true; such a Truth as I believe never was in the World before, nor never will be again. In this Case, said he, What would you counsel me to do? Truly, said my Mother, it is hard to advise; for to let the Woman live there still, is not proper; nor can your Circumstances undergo the Charge: And if your Wife should do as she says, and go with her; I should in some Degree be accessary to the parting Man and Wife. I would venture, said I, for when it comes to the Push, I warrant her she will not go. Hereupon the Man said he would try; and accordingly, hired a Place in a Waggon to carry the Creature into her own Country;[29] hoping, as I suppose, that his Wife would have rested herself contented with him, when the Woman had been gone; but instead thereof, she acted as she said, and went along with her.

This Transaction was so extraordinary, that every-body was amazed at it; and when they had been gone some time, there arose a Murmuring, amongst Friends, Neighbours and Acquaintance, as if he had made his Wife away; and when he told them the Manner of her Departure, they would not believe him, the thing in itself being so incredible.

But as we will leave him to make his Party good, as well as he can, amidst the Censure of his Neighbours, the Threats of her Friends, and the Ridicule of his Acquaintance; and follow the Travellers, into the Country whither they were gone.

They arrived safe at the Woman's Father's, where they found as kind Reception as a poor Cottage could afford; and a very poor one it was, there being no Light but what came in at the Door, no Food but from the Hands of Charity, nor Fewel but what they pilfer'd from their Neighbours Hedges.

Now what this unaccountable Creature thought of this kind of Being, is unknown, or what Measures she and her Companion thought to take, or what Schemes they form'd to themselves, is not conceivable: But whatever they were, the discreet Neighbourhood put a Period to their Projects; for they got a Warrant to have them before a Justice, in order to prevent a Parish Charge;[30] there being two Children there already, which they had sent some time before; and now two helpless Women being come, they knew not where the Charge might light, and therefore proceeded as aforesaid. It happen'd as the Constable was conducting them to the Justice, with a mob at their heels, that they passed by the house of a Lady of Quality; who looking out of her Window, saw in the midst of this Throng, this unfortunate Wife, whom she immediately knew to be the Daughter of her Friend; knew to be the Child of an honourable Family. It is impossible to describe what Amazement seiz'd her: She call'd out to the Constable and other Neighbours there, bidding them bring that Gentlewoman to her, which they immediately did. This good Lady, out of Respect to her old Friends, a worthy Family, bid them discharge her, telling them, That her-self would be bound that she should be no Parish Charge; so took her into her house, treated her kindly,

29 District.
30 An expense to the parish.

and offer'd her all she could do on such an Occasion: For all which she return'd the Lady but cold Thanks, and begg'd her Ladyship's Assistance to convey her to London along with the other Woman, who, she said, was the truest Friend in the World. The Lady knowing nothing of her Story, with much Goodness provided for her Departure, together with her Companion. In this manner, loaden with Disgrace, they came back to London, to her Husband, from whom, no doubt, she found Reproaches suitable to her Folly.

Long it was not, e'er Deth made a true and substantial Separation, by carrying the Husband into the other World. Now was the time to make manifest, whether Promises, Flatteries or Threatnings had made her act the foresaid Scene: But it appear'd all voluntary; for when he was dead, her Friends and Relations invited and persuaded her to leave that Creature and her Children, and come to live with them, suitable to her Birth and Education. But all in vain; she absolutely adher'd to this Woman and her Children, to the last Degree of Folly, insomuch, that being reduc'd to Poverty, she begg'd in the Streets to support them. At last, some Friend of her Family told the Queen of the distressed way she was in; and in some Degree, how it came to pass, that neither her dead Husband nor her Relations might be blameable. The Queen, with much Goodness, told her Friend, That if she would leave that Woman, and go live with some Relation, she would take Care she should not want; and withal sent her Five Guineas, as an Earnest of a Monthly Pension; but notwithstanding, this infatuated Creature refus'd the Queen's Favour, rather than part with this Family: And so, for their Support, begg'd in the Streets, the remainder of her Days.

Sure, said the Lady, This poor Creature was under some Spell or Inchantment, or she could never have persisted, in so strange a manner, to oppose her Husband, and all her nearest Friends, and even her Sovereign.

Lady Mary Wortley Montagu

1689 – 1762

Lady Mary Wortley Montagu was the daughter of the Earl of Kingston and Lady Mary Fielding. She eloped with Edward Wortley in 1712 and in 1716 journeyed with him to Constantinople where she wrote *her* Embassy Letters. *Back in England she became involved in political and literary controversies and wrote satires and pamphlets to intervene. In 1736 she became infatuated with a twenty-four year old Italian man with whom she planned to live in Italy. The plan did not materialize but for twenty years she lived abroad alone, mainly in Italy, writing many letters about her life and her reading and revealing her increasing alienation from her native country. Her letters to her daughter Lady Bute are much concerned with the education of her grandchildren. Lady Mary was keenly aware of her rank and she despised middle-class vulgarity and sentimentality in literature. Disappointed in marriage, she saw clearly the difficulty of the intelligent woman within the family and wider society, doomed to silence or to mockery for her 'masculine' wit.*

The following poems are taken from Lady Mary Wortley Montagu: Essays and Poems *(R. Halsband and I. Grundy (eds), Clarendon Press, Oxford, 1977, pp. 200–3). The letters are taken from* Selected Letters of Lady Mary Wortley Montagu *(R. Halsband (ed.), Longman, 1970).*

Satturday:
The Small Pox:
Flavia

THE wretched Flavia, on her Couch reclin'd,
Thus breath'd the Anguish of a wounded mind.
A Glass revers'd in her right hand she bore;
For now she shunn'd the Face she sought before.
    How am I chang'd! Alas, how am I grown
A frightfull Spectre to my selfe unknown!
Where's my Complexion, where the radiant bloom
That promis'd Happyness for Years to come?
Then, with what Pleasure I this Face survey'd!
To look once more, my Visits oft delay'd!
Charm'd with the veiw, a fresher red would rise,
And a new Life shot sparkling from my Eyes.
Ah Faithless Glass, my wonted bloom restore!
Alas, I rave! that bloom is now no more!
    The Greatest Good the Gods on Men bestow,
Even Youth it selfe to me is useless now.
There was a Time, (Oh that I could forget!)
When Opera Tickets pour'd before my Feet,

And at the Ring[1] where brightest Beauties shine,
The earliest Cherrys of the Park were mine.
Wittness oh Lilly![2] and thou Motteux[3] tell!
How much Japan[4] these Eyes have made you sell,
With what contempt you saw me oft despise
The humble Offer of the raffled Prize:
For at each raffle still the Prize I bore,
With Scorn rejected, or with Triumph wore:
Now Beautie's Fled, and Presents are no more.
    For me, the Patriot has the House[5] forsook,
And left debates to catch a passing look,
For me, the Soldier has soft verses writ,
For me, the Beau has aim'd to be a Wit,
For me, the Wit to Nonsense was betraid,
The Gamester has for me his Dun[6] delaid,
And overseen the Card, I would have paid.
The bold and Haughty, by Success made vain,
Aw'd by my Eyes has trembled to complain,
The bashful 'Squire touch'd with a wish unknown
Has dar'd to speak with Spirit not his own,
Fir'd by one Wish, all did alike Adore,
Now Beauty's fled, and Lovers are no more.
    As round the Room I turn my weeping Eyes,
New unaffected Scenes of Sorrow rise;
Far from my Sight that killing Picture bear,
The Face disfigure, or the Canvas tear!
That Picture, which with Pride I us'd to show,
The lost ressemblance but upbraids me now.
And thou my Toilette! where I oft have sate,
While Hours unheeded pass'd in deep Debate,
How Curls should fall, or where a Patch[7] to place,
If Blue or Scarlet best became my Face;
Now on some happier Nymph thy Aid bestow,
On Fairer Heads, ye useless Jewells, glow!
No borrow'd Lustre can my Charms restore,
Beauty is fled, and Dress is now no more.
    Ye meaner Beauties, I permit you, shine,
Go triumph in the Hearts, that once were mine,

---

[1] The Ring in Hyde Park was used for social riding and driving.
[2] Charles Lilly kept a shop for perfumes in the Strand.
[3] Peter Anthony Motteux, a French shopkeeper.
[4] Japanese painted work.
[5] House of Commons.
[6] Demand for payment.
[7] Piece of black silk or plaster used to adorn the face.

But midst your Triumphs, with Confusion know,
'Tis to my Ruin all your Charms ye owe.
Would pitying Heaven restore my wonted mein,
You still might move, unthought of, and unseen—
But oh, how vain, how wretched is the boast,
Of Beauty faded, and of Empire lost!
What now is left, but weeping to Deplore
My Beauty fled, and Empire now no more!
   Ye cruel Chymists,[8] what with held your Aid?
Could no Pomatums[9] save a trembling Maid?
How false and triffling is that Art you boast;
No Art can give me back my Beauty lost!
In tears surrounded by my Freinds I lay,
Mask'd o're, and trembling at the light of Day,
Mirmillo[10] came my Fortune to deplore
(A golden headed Cane, well carv'd he bore),
Cordials, he cry'd, my Spirits must restore,—
Beauty is fled, and Spirit is no more!
Galen the Grave,[11] Officious Squirt was there,
With fruitless Greife and unavailing Care;
Machaon too, the Great Machaon,[12] known
By his red Cloak, and his Superior frown,
And why (he cry'd) this Greife, and this Dispair?
You shall again be well, again be fair,
Beleive my Oath (with that an Oath he swore),
False was his Oath! my Beauty is no more.
   Cease hapless Maid, no more thy Tale persue,
Forsake Mankind, and bid the World Adieu.
Monarchs, and Beauties rule with equal sway,
All strive to serve, and Glory to obey,
Alike unpity'd when depos'd they grow,
Men mock the Idol of their Former vow.
   'Adieu, ye Parks—in some obscure recess,
Where Gentle streams will weep at my distress,
Where no false Freind will in my Greife take part,
And mourn my Ruin with a Joyful Heart,
There let me live, in some deserted Place,
There hide in shades this lost Inglorious Face.
Operas, Circles, I no more must view!
My Toilette, Patches, all the World, Adieu!'

[8] Pharmacists.
[9] Scented ointment.
[10] Possibly Richard Mead who wrote on smallpox.
[11] Physician of the second century AD whose name was given to other doctors.
[12] Name of the doctor in the *Dispensary*; used also for its author Samuel Garth, physician to Lady Mary's family.

From

The Letters of Lady Mary Wortley Montagu

TO LADY—

ADRIANOPLE, 1 APRIL 1717

I AM now got into a new world where everything I see appears to me a change of scene, and I write to your Ladyship with some content of mind, hoping at least that you will find the charm of novelty in my letters and no longer reproach me that I tell you nothing extraordinary. I won't trouble you with a relation of our tedious journey, but I must not omit what I saw remarkable at Sophia, one of the most beautiful towns in the Turkish Empire and famous for its hot baths that are resorted to both for diversion and health. I stopped here one day on purpose to see them. Designing to go incognito, I hired a Turkish coach. These *voitures* are not at all like ours, but much more convenient for the country, the heat being so great that glasses would be very troublesome. They are made a good deal in the manner of the Dutch coaches, having wooden lattices painted and gilded, the inside being painted with baskets and nosegays of flowers, intermixed commonly with little poetical mottoes. They are covered all over with scarlet cloth, lined with silk and very often richly embroidered and fringed. This covering entirely hides the persons in them, but may be thrown back at pleasure and the ladies peep through the lattices. They hold four people very conveniently, seated on cushions, but not raised.

In one of these covered wagons I went to the bagnio about ten o'clock. It was already full of women. It is built of stone in the shape of a dome with no windows but in the roof, which gives light enough. There was five of these domes joined together, the outmost being less than the rest and serving only as a hall where the porteress stood at the door. Ladies of quality generally give this woman the value of a crown or ten shillings, and I did not forget that ceremony. The next room is a very large one, paved with marble, and all round it raised two sofas of marble, one above another. There were four fountains of cold water in this room, falling first into marble basins and then running on the floor in little channels made for that purpose, which carried the streams into the next room, something less than this, with the same sort of marble sofas, but so hot with steams of sulphur proceeding from the baths joining to it, 'twas impossible to stay there with one's clothes on. The two other domes were the hot baths, one of which had cocks of cold water turning into it to temper it to what degree of warmth the bathers have a mind to.

I was in my travelling habit, which is a riding dress, and certainly appeared very extraordinary to them, yet there was not one of 'em that showed the least surprise or impertinent curiosity, but received me with all the obliging civility possible. I know no European court where the ladies would have behaved themselves in so polite a manner to a stranger. I believe in the

whole there were two hundred women and yet none of those disdainful
smiles or satiric whispers that never fail in our assemblies when anybody
appears that is not dressed exactly in fashion. They repeated over and over
to me, 'Uzelle, pek uzelle', which is nothing but, 'Charming, very charming'.
The first sofas were covered with cushions and rich carpets, on which sat the
ladies, and on the second their slaves behind 'em, but without any distinction
of rank by their dress, all being in the state of nature, that is, in plain English,
stark naked, without any beauty or defect concealed, yet there was not the
least wanton smile or immodest gesture amongst 'em. They walked and moved
with the same majestic grace which Milton describes of our General Mother.
There were many amongst them as exactly proportioned as ever any goddess
was drawn by the pencil of Guido or Titian, and most of their skins shiningly
white, only adorned by their beautiful hair divided into many tresses hanging
on their shoulders, braided either with pearl or riband, perfectly representing
the figures of the Graces.

I was here convinced of the truth of a reflection that I had often made, that
if 'twas the fashion to go naked the face would be hardly observed. I perceived
that the ladies with the finest skins and most delicate shapes had the greatest
share of my admiration, though their faces were sometimes less beautiful than
those of their companions. To tell you the truth, I had wickedness enough to
wish secretly that Mr. Jervas[13] could have been there invisible. I fancy it would
have very much improved his art to see so many fine women naked in different
postures, some in conversation, some working, others drinking coffee or sherbet,
and many negligently lying on their cushions while their slaves (generally pretty
girls of seventeen or eighteen) were employed in braiding their hair in several
pretty manners. In short, 'tis the women's coffee-house, where all the news of
the town is told, scandal invented, etc. They generally take this diversion once a
week, and stay there at least four or five hours without getting cold by immediate
coming out of the hot bath into the cool room, which was very surprising to
me. The lady that seemed the most considerable amongst them entreated me
to sit by her and would fain have undressed me for the bath. I excused myself
with some difficulty, they being all so earnest in persuading me. I was at last
forced to open my skirt and show them my stays, which satisfied 'em very well,
for I saw they believed I was so locked up in that machine that it was not in
my own power to open it, which contrivance they attributed to my husband. I
was charmed with their civility and beauty and should have been very glad to
pass more time with them, but Mr. Wortley resolving to pursue his journey the
next morning early I was in haste to see the ruins of Justinian's church, which
did not afford me so agreeable a prospect as I had left, being little more than
a heap of stones.

Adieu, madam. I am sure I have now entertained you with an account
of such a sight as you never saw in your life and what no book of travels
could inform you of. 'Tis no less than death for a man to be found in one
of these places.

13 Charles Jervas, the portrait painter of London.

TO LADY MAR

ADRIANOPLE, 1 APRIL 1717

I WISH to God (dear sister) that you was as regular in letting me have the pleasure of knowing what passes on your side of the globe, as I am careful in endeavouring to amuse you by the account of all I see that I think you care to hear of. You content yourself with telling me over and over that the town is very dull. It may possibly be dull to you when everyday does not present you with something new, but for me that am in arrear at least two months' news, all that seems very stale with you would be fresh and sweet here; pray let me into more particulars. I will try to awaken your gratitude by giving you a full and true relation of the novelties of this place, none of which would surprise you more than a sight of my person as I am now in my Turkish habit, though I believe you would be of my opinion that 'tis admirably becoming. I intend to send you my picture; in the meantime accept of it here.

The first piece of my dress is a pair of drawers, very full, that reach to my shoes and conceal the legs more modestly than your petticoats. They are of a thin, rose-colour damask brocaded with silver flowers, my shoes of white kid leather embroidered with gold. Over this hangs my smock of a fine white silk gauze edged with embroidery. This smock has wide sleeves hanging half-way down the arm and is closed at the neck with a diamond button, but the shape and colour of the bosom very well to be distinguished through it. The *antery* is a waistcoat made close to the shape, of white and gold damask, with very long sleeves falling back and fringed with deep gold fringe, and should have diamond or pearl buttons. My caftan of the same stuff with my drawers is a robe exactly fitted to my shape and reaching to my feet, with very long strait falling sleeves. Over this is the girdle of about four fingers broad, which all that can afford have entirely of diamonds or other precious stones. Those that will not be at that expense have it of exquisite embroidery on satin, but it must be fastened before with a clasp of diamonds. The *curdée* is a loose robe they throw off or put on according to the weather, being of a rich brocade (mine is green and gold) either lined with ermine or sables; the sleeves reach very little below the shoulders.

The head-dress is composed of a cap called *talpack*, which is in winter of fine velvet embroidered with pearls or diamonds and in summer of a light, shining silver stuff. This is fixed on one side of the head, hanging a little way down with a gold tassel and bound on either with a circle of diamonds (as I have seen several) or a rich embroidered handkerchief. On the other side of the head the hair is laid flat, and here the ladies are at liberty to show their fancies, some putting flowers, others a plume of heron's feathers, and, in short, what they please, but the most general fashion is a large bouquet of jewels made like natural flowers, that is, the buds of pearl, the roses of different coloured rubies, the jasmines of diamonds, jonquils of topazes, etc., so well set and enamelled 'tis hard to imagine anything of that kind so beautiful. The hair hangs at its full length behind, divided into tresses braided with pearl or riband, which is always in great quantity.

I never saw in my life so many fine heads of hair. I have counted one hundred and ten of these tresses of one lady's, all natural; but it must be owned that every beauty is more common here than with us. 'Tis surprising to see a young woman that is not very handsome. They have naturally the most beautiful complexions in the world and generally large black eyes. I can assure you with great truth that the Court of England (though I believe it the fairest in Christendom) cannot show so many beauties as are under our protection here. They generally shape their eyebrows, and the Greeks and Turks have a custom of putting round their eyes on the inside a black tincture that, at a distance or by candlelight, adds very much to the blackness of them. I fancy many of our ladies would be overjoyed to know this secret, but 'tis too visible by day. They dye their nails rose colour; I own I cannot enough accustom myself to this fashion to find any beauty in it.

As to their morality or good conduct, I can say like Harlequin, 'Tis just as 'tis with you'; and the Turkish ladies don't commit one sin the less for not being Christians. Now I am a little acquainted with their ways, I cannot forbear admiring either the exemplary discretion or extreme stupidity of all the writers that have given accounts of 'em. 'Tis very easy to see they have more liberty than we have, no woman of what rank soever being permitted to go in the streets without two muslins, one that covers her face all but her eyes and another that hides the whole dress of her head and hangs half-way down her back; and their shapes are wholly concealed by a thing they call a *ferigée*, which no woman of any sort appears without. This has strait sleeves that reach to their fingers' ends and it laps all round 'em, not unlike a riding hood. In winter 'tis of cloth, and in summer, plain stuff or silk. You may guess how effectually this disguises them, that is no distinguishing the great lady from her slave, and 'tis impossible for the most jealous husband to know his wife when he meets her, and no man dare either touch or follow a woman in the street.

This perpetual masquerade gives them entire liberty of following their inclinations without danger of discovery. The most usual method of intrigue is to send an appointment to the lover to meet the lady at a Jew's shop, which are as notoriously convenient as our Indian houses, and yet even those that don't make that use of 'em do not scruple to go to buy penn'orths and tumble over rich goods, which are chiefly to be found amongst that sort of people. The great ladies seldom let their gallants know who they are, and 'tis so difficult to find it out that they can very seldom guess at her name they have corresponded with above half a year together.

You may easily imagine the number of faithful wives very small in a country where they have nothing to fear from their lovers' indiscretion, since we see so many that have the courage to expose themselves to that in this world and all the threatened punishment of the next, which is never preached to the Turkish damsels. Neither have they much to apprehend from the resentment of their husbands, those ladies that are rich having all their money in their own hands, which they take with 'em upon a divorce with an addition which he is obliged to give 'em. Upon the whole, I look upon the Turkish women as the only free people in the empire. The very Divan pays a respect to 'em, and the Grand Signior

himself, when a pasha is executed, never violates the privileges of the harem
(or women's apartment) which remains unsearched entire to the widow. They
are queens of their slaves, which the husband has no permission so much as
to look upon, except it be an old woman or two that his lady chooses. 'Tis true
their law permits them four wives, but there is no instance of a man of quality
that makes use of this liberty, or of a woman of rank that would suffer it. When
a husband happens to be inconstant (as those things will happen) he keeps his
mistress in a house apart and visits her as privately as he can, just as 'tis with
you. Amongst all the great men here I only know the *tefterdar* (*i.e.* treasurer)
that keeps a number of she slaves for his own use (that is, on his own side of
the house, for a slave once given to serve a lady is entirely at her disposal), and
he is spoke of as a libertine, or what we should call a rake, and his wife won't
see him, though she continues to live in his house.

   Thus you see, dear sister, the manners of mankind do not differ so widely
as our voyage writers would make us believe. Perhaps it would be more
entertaining to add a few surprising customs of my own invention, but nothing
seems to me so agreeable as truth, and I believe nothing so acceptable to you.
I conclude with repeating the great truth of my being, dear sister, etc.

TO LADY BUTE

GOTTOLENGO, BRESCIA, 5 JANUARY 1748

D EAR Child,
   I am glad to hear that yourself and family are in good health. As to
the alteration you say you find in the world, it is only owing to your being
better acquainted with it. I have never, in all my various travels, seen but two
sorts of people (and those very like one another); I mean men and women,
who always have been, and ever will be, the same. The same vices and the same
follies have been the fruit of all ages, though sometimes under different names.
I remember (when I returned from Turkey) meeting with the same affectation
of youth amongst my acquaintance that you now mention amongst yours, and I
do not doubt but your daughter will find the same twenty years hence amongst
hers. One of the greatest happinesses of youth is the ignorance of evil, though
it is often the ground of great indiscretions, and sometimes the active part of
life is over before an honest mind finds out how one ought to act in such a
world as this. I am as much removed from it as it is possible to be on this side
the grave, which is from my own inclination, for I might have even here a great
deal of company, the way of living in this province being what I believe it is
now in the sociable part of Scotland and was in England a hundred years ago.

   I had a visit in the beginning of these holidays of thirty horse of ladies
and gentlemen with their servants (by the way, the ladies all ride like the
late Duchess of Cleveland).[14] They came with the kind intent of staying with

---

[14] i.e. astride.

me at least a fortnight, though I had never seen any of them before; but they were all neighbours within ten mile round. I could not avoid entertaining them at supper, and by good luck had a large quantity of game in the house, which with the help of my poultry furnished out a plentiful table. I sent for the fiddles; and they were so obliging to dance all night, and even dine with me next day, though none of them had been in bed, and were much disappointed I did not press them to stay, it being the fashion to go in troops to one another's houses, hunting and dancing together, a month in each castle. I have not yet returned any of their visits, nor do not intend it of some time, to avoid this expensive hospitality. The trouble of it is not very great, they not expecting any ceremony. I left the room about one o'clock, and they continued their ball in the salon above stairs without being at all offended at my departure. The greatest diversion I had was to see a lady of my own age comfortably dancing with her own husband some years older, and I can assure you she jumps and gallops with the best of them.

May you always be as well satisfied with your family as you are at present, and your children return in your age the tender care you have of their infancy. I know no greater happiness that can be wished for you by your most affectionate mother,

M. Wortley

My compliments to Lord Bute and blessing to my grandchildren.

TO LADY BUTE

GOTTOLENGO, 27 NOVEMBER 1749

DEAR Child,
By the account you give me of London I think it very much reformed. At least you have one sin the less (and it was a very reigning one in my time): I mean scandal. It must be literally reduced to a whisper since the custom of living altogether. I hope it has also banished the fashion of talking all at once (which was very prevailing when I was in town) and may perhaps contribute to brotherly love and unity, which was so much declined in my memory that it was hard to invite six people that would not, by cold looks or piqueing reflections, affront one another. I suppose parties are at an end, though I fear it is the consequence of the old almanac prophecy – poverty brings peace – and I fancy you really follow the French mode, and the lady keeps an assembly, that the assembly may keep the lady, and card money pay for clothes and equipage as well as cards and candles. I find I should be as solitary in London as I am here in the country, it being impossible for me to submit to live in a drum, which I think so far from a cure of uneasiness that it is, in my opinion, adding one more to the heap. There are so many attached to humanity, 'tis impossible to fly from them all, but experience has confirmed to me (what I always thought), that the pursuit of pleasure will be ever attended with pain, and the study of ease be most certainly accompanied with pleasures.

I have had this morning as much delight in a walk in the sun as ever I felt formerly in the crowded Mall even when I imagined I had my share of the admiration of the place, which was generally soured before I slept by the informations of my female friends, who seldom failed to tell me it was observed I had showed an inch above my shoe heels, or some other criticism of equal weight, which was construed affectation, and utterly destroyed all the satisfaction my vanity had given me. I have now no other but in my little housewifery, which is easily gratified in this country, where (by the help of my receipt book) I make a very shining figure amongst my neighbours by the introduction of custards, cheese-cakes and minced pies, which were entirely unknown in these parts and are received with universal applause, and I have reason to believe will preserve my memory even to future ages, particularly by the art of butter-making, in which I have so improved them that they now make as good as in any part of England.

My paper is at an end, which I do not doubt you are glad of. I have hardly room for my compliments to Lord Bute, blessing to my grandchildren, and to assure you that I am ever your most affectionate mother,

M.W.

TO LADY BUTE

GOTTOLENGO, JANUARY 1750

M Y dear Child,
I am extremely concerned to hear you complain of ill health at a time of life when you ought to be in the flower of your strength. I hope I need not recommend to you the care of it. The tenderness you have for your children is sufficient to enforce you to the utmost regard for the preservation of a life so necessary to their well-being. I do not doubt your prudence in their education; neither can I say anything particular relating to it at this distance, different tempers requiring different management. In general, never attempt to govern them (as most people do) by deceit. If they find themselves cheated (even in trifles) it will so far lessen the authority of their instructor as to make them neglect all their future admonitions. And (if possible) breed them free from prejudices; those contracted in the nursery often influence the whole life after, of which I have seen many melancholy examples.

I shall say no more of this subject, nor would have said this little if you had not asked my advice. 'Tis much easier to give rules than to practise them. I am sensible my own natural temper is too indulgent. I think it the least dangerous error, yet still it is an error. I can only say with truth that I do not know in my whole life having ever endeavoured to impose on you or give a false colour to anything that I represented to you. If your daughters are inclined to love reading, do not check their inclination by hindering them of the diverting part of it. It is as necessary for the amusement of women as the reputation of men; but teach them not to expect or desire any applause from it. Let their brothers shine, and let them content themselves with making their lives easier by it, which I experimentally know is more effectually done by study than any other way. Ignorance is as much the fountain of vice as idleness, and indeed generally produces it. People that do not read or work for a livelihood have many hours they know not how to employ, especially women, who commonly fall into vapours or something worse. I am afraid you'll think this letter very tedious. Forgive it as coming from your most affectionate mother,

M.W.

My compliments to Lord Bute and blessing to my grandchildren.

TO LADY BUTE

GOTTOLENGO, 19 FEBRUARY 1750

MY dear Child,
I gave you some general thoughts on the education of your children in my last letter, but fearing you should think I neglected your request by answering it with too much conciseness, I am resolved to add to it what little I know on that subject, and which may perhaps be useful to you in a concern with which you seem so nearly affected.

People commonly educate their children as they build their houses, according to some plan they think beautiful, without considering whether it is suited to the purposes for which they are designed. Almost all girls of quality are educated as if they were to be great ladies, which is often as little to be expected as an immoderate heat of the sun in the north of Scotland. You should teach yours to confine their desires to probabilities, to be as useful as is possible to themselves, and to think privacy (as it is) the happiest state of life.

I do not doubt your giving them all the instructions necessary to form them to a virtuous life, but 'tis a fatal mistake to do this without proper restrictions. Vices are often hid under the name of virtues, and the practice of them followed by the worst of consequences. Sincerity, friendship, piety, disinterestedness, and generosity are all great virtues, but pursued without discretion become criminal. I have seen ladies indulge their own ill humour by being very rude and impertinent, and think they deserved approbation by saying, 'I love to speak truth'. One of your acquaintance made a ball the next day after her mother died, to show she was sincere. I believe your own reflection will furnish you with but too many examples of the ill effects of the rest of the sentiments I have mentioned, when too warmly embraced. They are generally recommended to young people without limits or distinction, and this prejudice hurries them into great misfortunes while they are applauding themselves in the noble practice (as they fancy) of very eminent virtues.

I cannot help adding (out of my real affection to you) I wish you would moderate that fondness you have for your children. I do not mean you should abate any part of your care, or not do your duty to them in its utmost extent, but I would have you early prepare yourself for disappointments, which are heavy in proportion to their being surprising. It is hardly possible in such a number that none should be unhappy. Prepare yourself against a misfortune of that kind. I confess there is hardly any more difficult to support, yet it is certain imagination has a great share in the pain of it, and it is more in our power (than it is commonly believed) to soften whatever ills are founded or augmented by fancy. Strictly speaking, there is but one real evil: I mean acute pain. All other complaints are so considerably diminished by time that it is plain the grief is owing to our passion, since the sensation of it vanishes when that is over.

There is another mistake I forgot to mention usual in mothers. If any of their daughters are beauties they take great pains to persuade them that they are ugly, or at least that they think so, which the young woman never fails to believe springs from envy, and is (perhaps) not much in the wrong. I would, if possible, give them a just notion of their figure, and show them how far it is valuable. Every advantage has its price, and may be either over or undervalued. It is the common doctrine of (what are called) good books to inspire a contempt of beauty, riches, greatness etc., which has done as much mischief amongst the young of our sex as an over-eager desire of them. They should look on these things as blessings where they are bestowed, though not necessaries that it is impossible to be happy without. I am persuaded the ruin of Lady Frances Meadows was in great measure owing to the notions given her by the sillily good people that had the care of her.[15] 'Tis true her circumstances and your daughters' are very different. They should be taught to be content with privacy, and yet not neglect good fortune if it should be offered them.

I am afraid I have tired you with my instructions. I do not give them as believing my age has furnished me with superior wisdom, but in compliance with your desire, and being fond of every opportunity that gives a proof of the tenderness with which I am ever your affectionate mother,

M.Wortley

TO LADY BUTE

GOTTOLENGO, 22 JUNE 1752

M Y dear Child,
Since you tell me my letters (such as they are) are agreeable to you I shall for the future indulge myself in thinking upon paper when I write to you.

I cannot believe Sir John's advancement is owing to his merit, though he certainly deserves such a distinction, but I am persuaded the present disposers of such dignities are neither more clear-sighted or more disinterested than their predecessors.[16] Ever since I knew the world, Irish patents have been

---

[15] Lady Frances Pierrepont, Lady Mary's niece and a great heiress, had lived with Lady Cheyne until 1732. She was living with Lady Mary when she eloped with the impecunious Philip Meadows.

[16] In 1750 Sir John Rawdon had become Baron Rawdon of Moira, an Irish peer.

hung out to sale like the laced and embroidered coats in Monmouth Street,[17] and bought up by the same sort of people; I mean those who had rather wear shabby finery than no finery at all, though I don't suppose this was Sir John's case. That good creature (as the country saying is) has not a bit of pride in him. I dare swear he purchased his title for the same reason he used to purchase pictures in Italy, not because he wanted to buy, but because somebody or other wanted to sell. He hardly ever opened his mouth but to say: 'What you please, sir – at your service – your humble servant,' or some gentle expression to the same effect. It is scare credible that with this unlimited complaisance he should draw a blow upon himself, yet it so happened that one of his own countrymen was brute enough to strike him. As it was done before many witnesses Lord Mansell heard of it, and thinking that if poor Sir John took no notice of it he would suffer daily insults of the same kind, out of pure good nature resolved to spirit him up, at least to some show of resentment, intending to make up the matter afterwards in as honourable a manner as he could for the poor patient. He represented to him very warmly that no gentleman could take a box o' th' ear. Sir John answered with great calmness: 'I know that, but this was not a box o' th' ear; it was only a slap o' th' face.' I was as well acquainted with his two first wives as the difference of our ages permitted. I fancy they have broke their hearts by being chained to such a companion.

'Tis really terrible for a well-bred virtuous young woman to be confined to the conversation of the object of their contempt. There is but one thing to be done in that case, which is a method I am sure you have observed practised with success by some ladies I need not name. They associate the husband and the lap-dog, and manage so well that they make exactly the same figure in the family. My Lord and Dell tag after Madam to all indifferent places, and stay at home together whenever she goes into company where they would be troublesome.

I pity Lady F. Meadows if the Duke of Kingston marries.[18] She will then know that her mean compliances will appear as despicable to him as they do now to other people. Who would have thought that all her nice notions and pious meditations would end in being the humble companion of Madame de La Touche?[19] I do not doubt she has been forced to it by necessity, and is one proof (amongst many I have seen) of what I always thought, that nobody should trust their virtue with necessity, the force of which is never known till it is felt, and it is therefore one of the first duties to avoid the temptation of it. I am not pleading for avarice, far from it. I can assure you I equally contemn Lady Caroline Brand, who can forget she was born a gentlewoman for the sake of money she did not want.[20] That is indeed the only sentiment that properly deserves the name of avarice. A prudential care of one's affairs or (to go further) a desire of being in circumstances to be useful to one's friends is

[17] The street where second-hand clothes were sold.
[18] Lady Frances, the Duke's sister, lived with him and his mistress at Thoresby.
[19] Marie Therese de Fontaine was a married French lady whose liaison with the Duke provoked much gossip.
[20] Lady Mary's half-sister married Thomas Brand, a wealthy MP.

not only excusable but highly laudable, never blamed but by those who would persuade others to throw away their money in hopes to pick up a share of it. The greatest declaimers for disinterestedness I ever knew have been capable of the vilest actions on the least view of profit, and the greatest instances of true generosity given by those who were regular in their expenses and superior to the vanities in fashion.

I believe you are heartily tired of my dull moralities. I confess I am in very low spirits. It is hotter weather than has been known for some years, and I have got an abominable cold, which has drawn after it a troop of complaints I will not trouble you with reciting. I hope all your family are in good health. I am humble servant to Lord Bute. I give my blessing to my grandchildren and am ever your most affectionate mother,

M. Wortley

TO LADY BUTE

GOTTOLENGO, 28 JANUARY 1753

D EAR Child,
You have given me a great deal of satisfaction by your account of your eldest daughter. I am particularly pleased to hear she is a good arithmetician; it is the best proof of understanding. The knowledge of numbers is one of the chief distinctions between us and brutes. If there is anything in blood you may reasonable expect your children should be endowed with an uncommon share of good sense. Mr Wortley's family and mine have both produced some of the greatest men that have been born in England. I mean Admiral Sandwich, and my great-grandfather who was distinguished by the name of Wise William. I have heard Lord Bute's father mentioned as an extraordinary genius (though he had not many opportunities of showing it), and his uncle the present Duke of Argyle has one of the best heads I ever knew.

I will therefore speak to you as supposing Lady Mary not only capable but desirous of learning. In that case, by all means let her be indulged in it. You will tell me, I did not make it a part of your education. Your prospect was very different from hers, as you had no defect either in mind or person to hinder, and much in your circumstances to attract, the highest offers. It seemed your business to learn how to live in the world, as it is hers to know how to be easy out of it. It is the common error of builders and parents to follow some plan they think beautiful (and perhaps is so) without considering that nothing is beautiful that is misplaced. Hence we see so many edifices raised that the raisers can never inhabit, being too large for their fortunes. Vistas are laid open over barren heaths, and apartments contrived for a coolness very agreeable in Italy but killing in the north of Britain. Thus every woman endeavours to breed her daughter a fine lady, qualifying her for a station in which she will never appear, and at the same time incapacitating her for that retirement to which she is destined. Learning (if she has a real taste for it) will not only make her contented but happy in it. No entertainment is so cheap as reading, nor any pleasure so lasting. She will not want new fashions nor regret the loss of expensive diversions or variety of company if she can be amused with an author in her closet. To render this amusement extensive, she should be permitted to learn the languages. I have heard it lamented that boys lose so many years in mere learning of words. This is no objection to a girl, whose time is not so precious. She cannot advance herself in any profession, and has therefore more hours to spare; and as you say her memory is good she will be very agreeably employed this way.

There are two cautions to be given on this subject: first, not to think herself learned when she can read Latin or even Greek. Languages are more properly to be called vehicles of learning than learning itself, as may be observed in many schoolmasters, who though perhaps critics in grammar are the most ignorant fellows upon earth. True knowledge consists in knowing things, not words. I would wish her no further a linguist than to enable her to read books in their originals, that are often corrupted and always injured by translations. Two hours application every morning will bring this about much sooner than you can imagine, and she will have leisure enough beside to run over the English poetry, which is a more important part of a woman's education than it is generally supposed. Many a young damsel has been ruined by a fine copy of verses, which she would have laughed at if she had known it had been stolen from Mr Waller. I remember when I was a girl I saved one of my companions from destruction, who communicated to me an epistle she was quite charmed with. As she had a natural good taste she observed the lines were not so smooth as Prior's or Pope's, but had more thought and spirit than any of theirs. She was wonderfully delighted with such a demonstration of her lover's sense and passion, and not a little pleased with her own charms, that had force enough to inspire such elegancies. In the midst of this triumph I showed her they were taken from Randolph's *Poems*,[21] and the unfortunate transcriber was dismissed with the scorn he deserved. To say truth, the poor plagiary was very unlucky to fall into my hands; that author, being no longer in fashion, would have escaped anyone of less universal reading than myself. You should encourage your daughter to talk over with you what she reads, and as you are very capable of distinguishing, take care she does not mistake pert folly for wit and humour, or rhyme for poetry, which are the common errors of young people, and have a train of ill consequences.

The second caution to be given her (and which is most absolutely necessary) is to conceal whatever learning she attains, with as much solicitude as she would hide crookedness or lameness. The parade of it can only serve to draw on her the envy, and consequently the most inveterate hatred of all he and she fools, which will certainly be at least three parts in four of all her acquaintance. The use of knowledge in our sex (beside the amusement of solitude) is to moderate the passions and learn to be contented with a small expense, which are the certain effects of a studious life and, it may be, preferable even to that

---

[21] Thomas Randolph, *Poems* (1638).

fame which men have engrossed to themselves and will not suffer us to share. You will tell me I have not observed this rule myself, but you are mistaken; it is only inevitable accident that has given me any reputation that way. I have always carefully avoided it, and ever thought it a misfortune.

The explanation of this paragraph would occasion a long digression, which I will not trouble you with, it being my present design only to say what I think useful for the instruction of my granddaughter, which I have much at heart. If she has the same inclination (I should say passion) for learning that I was born with, history, geography, and philosophy will furnish her with materials to pass away cheerfully a longer life than is allotted to mortals. I believe there are few heads capable of making Sir Isaac Newton's calculations, but the result of them is not difficult to be understood by a moderate capacity. Do not fear this should make her affect the character of Lady——, or Lady——, or Mrs——. Those women are ridiculous not because they have learning but because they have it not. One thinks herself a complete historian after reading Echard's *Roman History*,[22] another a profound philosopher having got by heart some of Pope's unintelligible essays[23] and a third an able divine on the strength of Whitefield's sermons.[24] Thus you hear them screaming politics and controversy. It is a saying of Thucydides: Ignorance is bold, and knowledge reserved.[25] Indeed it is impossible to be far advanced in it without being more humbled by a conviction of human ignorance than elated by learning.

At the same time I recommend books I neither exclude work nor drawing. I think it as scandalous for a woman not to know how to use a needle, as for a man not to know how to use a sword. I was once extreme find of my pencil, and it was a great mortification to me when my father turned off my master, having made a considerable progress for the short time I learned. My over-eagerness in the pursuit of it had brought a weakness on my eyes that made it necessary to leave if off, and all the advantage I got was the improvement of my hand. I see by hers that practice will make her a ready writer. She may attain it by serving you for a secretary when your health or affairs make it troublesome to you to write yourself, and custom will make it an agreeable amusement to her. She cannot have too many for that station of life which will probably be her fate. The ultimate end of your education was to make you a good wife (and I have the comfort to hear that you are one); hers ought to be, to make her happy in a virgin state. I will not say it is happier, but it is undoubtedly safer than any marriage. In a lottery where there is (at the lowest computation) ten thousand blanks to a prize it is the most prudent choice not to venture.

I have always been so thoroughly persuaded of this truth that notwithstanding the flattering views I had for you (as I never intended you a sacrifice to my vanity) I thought I owed you the justice to lay before you all the hazards

[22] Lawrence Echard, *The Roman History* (1695–98).
[23] Alexander Pope's *Essay on Man* (1733–34.
[24] George Whitefield, famous Calvinist evangelical preacher.
[25] The sentiment occurs in Thucydides' *Peloponnesian War*.

attending matrimony. You may recollect I did so in the strongest manner. Perhaps you may have more success in the instructing your daughter. She has so much company at home she will not need seeking it abroad, and will more readily take the notions you think fit to give her. As you were alone in my family, it would have been thought a great cruelty to suffer you no companions of your own age, especially having so many near relations, and I do not wonder their opinions influenced yours. I was not sorry to see you not determined on a single life, knowing it was not your father's intention, and contented myself with endeavouring to make your home so easy that you might not be in haste to leave it.

I am afraid you will think this a very long and insignificant letter. I hope the kindness of the design will excuse it, being willing to give you every proof in my power that I am your most affectionate mother,

M. Wortley

TO LADY BUTE

GOTTOLENGO, 6 MARCH 1753

I CANNOT help writing a sort of apology for my last letter, foreseeing that you will think it wrong, or at least Lord Bute will be extremely shocked at the proposal of a learned education for daughters, which the generality of men believe as great a profanation as the clergy would do if the laity should presume to exercise the functions of the priesthood. I desire you would take notice I would not have learning enjoined them as a task, but permitted as a pleasure if their genius leads them naturally to it. I look upon my granddaughters as a sort of lay nuns. Destiny may have laid up other things for them, but they have no reason to expect to pass their time otherwise than their aunts do at present, and I know by experience it is in the power of study not only to make solitude tolerable but agreeable. I have now lived almost seven years in a stricter retirement than yours in the Isle of Bute,[26] and can assure you I have never had half an hour heavy on my hands for want of something to do.

Whoever will cultivate their own mind will find full employment. Every virtue does not only require great care in the planting, but as much daily solicitude in cherishing as exotic fruits and flowers; the vices and passions (which I am afraid are the natural product of the soil) demand perpetual weeding. Add to this the search after knowledge (every branch of which is entertaining), and the longest life is too short for the pursuit of it, which, though in some regards confined to very strait limits, leaves still a vast variety of amusements to those capable of tasting them, which is utterly impossible for those that are blinded by prejudices, which are the certain effect of an ignorant education. My own was one of the worst in the world, being exactly the same as Clarissa Harlowe's, her

---

[26] Because of their small means, the Butes lived on the Isle of Bute for ten years after their marriage.

pious Mrs Norton so perfectly resembling my governess (who had been nurse to my mother) I could almost fancy the author was acquainted with her.[27] She took so much pains from my infancy to fill my head with superstitious tales and false notions, it was none of her fault I am not at this day afraid of witches and hobgoblins, or turned Methodist.

Almost all girls are bred after this manner. I believe you are the only woman (perhaps I might say person) that never was either frighted or cheated into anything by your parents. I can truly affirm I never deceived anybody in my life excepting (which I confess has often happened undesignedly) by speaking plainly. As Earl Stanhope used to say (during his ministry), he always imposed on the foreign ministers by telling them the naked truth, which, as they thought impossible to come from the mouth of a statesman, they never failed to write informations to their respective courts directly contrary to the assurances he gave them, most people confounding the ideas of sense and cunning, though there are really no two things in nature more opposite. It is in part from this false reasoning, the unjust custom prevails of debarring our sex from the advantages of learning, the men fancying the improvement of our understandings would only furnish us with more art to deceive them, which is directly contrary to the truth. Fools are always enterprising, not seeing the difficulties of deceit or the ill consequences of detection. I could give many examples of ladies whose ill conduct has been very notorious, which has been owing to that ignorance which has exposed them to idleness, which is justly called the mother of mischief.

There is nothing so like the education of a woman of quality as that of a prince. They are taught to dance and the exterior part of what is called good breeding, which if they attain they are extraordinary creatures in their kind, and have all the accomplishments required by their directors. The same characters are formed by the same lessons, which inclines me to think (if I dare say it) that nature has not placed us in an inferior rank to men, no more than the females of other animals, where we see no distinction of capacity, though I am persuaded if there was a commonwealth of rational horses (as Doctor Swift has supposed) it would be an established maxim amongst them that a mare could not be taught to pace.[28] I could add a great deal on this subject, but I am not now endeavouring to remove the prejudices of mankind. My only design is to point out to my granddaughters the method of being contented with that retreat to which probably their circumstances will oblige them, and which is perhaps preferable to all the show of public life. It has always been my inclination. Lady Stafford (who knew me better than anybody else in the world, both from her own just discernment, and my heart being ever as open to her as myself) used to tell me my true vocation was a monastery, and I now find by experience more sincere pleasures with my books and garden than all the flutter of a court could give me.

[27] Reference to Samuel Richardsons's novel *Clarissa* (1748).
[28] Reference to the society of the rational horses in Book IV of Jonathan Swift's *Gulliver's Travels* (1726).

If you follow my advice in relation to Lady Mary, my correspondence may be of use to her, and I shall very willingly give her those instructions that may be necessary in the pursuit of her studies. Before her age I was in the most regular commerce with my grandmother, though the difference of our time of life was much greater, she being past forty-five when she married my grandfather. She died at ninety-six, retaining to the last the vivacity and clearness of her understanding, which was very uncommon. You cannot remember her, being then in your nurse's arms. I conclude with repeating to you, I only recommend but am far from commanding, which I think I have no right to do. I tell you my sentiments because you desired to know them, and hope you will receive them with some partiality as coming from your most affectionate mother,

M. Wortley

TO LADY BUTE

GOTTOLENGO, 30 NOVEMBER [?1753]

M Y dear Child,
I received your agreeable letter of Sept. 24 yesterday, Nov. 29, and am very glad our daughter (for I think she belongs to us both) turns out so much to your satisfaction; may she ever do so. I hope she has by this time received my token. I am afraid I have lost some of your letters. In last April you wrote me word the box directed to me was to set out in a week's time. Since that I have had no news of it, and apprehend very much that the bill which I suppose you sent me has miscarried. If so, I am in danger of losing the cargo.

You please me extremely in saying my letters are of any entertainment to you. I would contribute to your happiness in every shape I can, but in my solitude there are so few subjects present themselves, it is not easy to find one that would amuse you, though as I believe you have some leisure hours at Kenwood, when anything new is welcome, I will venture to tell you a small history in which I had some share.

I have already informed you of the divisions and subdivisions of estates in this country, by which you will imagine there is a numerous gentry of great names and little fortunes. Six of those families inhabit this town. You may fancy this forms a sort of society, but far from it, as there is not one of them that does not think (for some reason or other) they are far superior to all the rest. There is such a settled aversion amongst them, they avoid one another with the utmost care, and hardly ever meet except by chance at the castle (as they call my house), where their regard for me obliges them to behave civilly, but it is with an affected coldness that is downright disagreeable, and hinders me from seeing any of them often.

I was quietly reading in my closet when I was interrupted by the chamber-maid of the Signora Laura Bono, who flung herself at my feet, and in an agony of sobs and tears begged me for the love of the Holy Madonna to hasten to her master's house, where the two brothers would certainly murder one another if my presence did not stop their fury. I was very much surprised, having always heard them spoke of as a pattern of fraternal union. However, I made all possible speed thither, without staying for hoods or attendance. I was soon there (the house touching my garden wall) and was directed to the bedchamber by the noise of oaths and execrations, but on opening the door was astonished to a degree you may better guess than I describe, by seeing the Signora Laura prostrate on the ground, melting in tears, and her husband standing with a drawn stiletto in his hand, swearing she should never see tomorrow's sun. I was soon let into the secret.

The good man, having business of consequence at Brescia, went thither early in the morning, but as he expected his chief tenant to pay his rent that day, he left orders with his wife that if the farmer (who lived two mile off) came himself or sent any of his sons, she should take care to make him very welcome. She obeyed him with great punctuality. The money coming in the hand of a handsome lad of eighteen she did not only admit him to her own table and produced the best wine in the cellar, but resolved to give him *chère entière*. While she was exercising this generous hospitality, the husband met midway the gentleman he intended to visit, who was posting to another side of the country. They agreed on another appointment, and he returned to his own house, where, giving his horse to be led round to the stable by the servant that accompanied him, he opened his door with the *passe-partout* key, and proceeded to his chamber without meeting anybody, where he found his beloved spouse asleep on the bed with her gallant. The opening of the door waked them. The young fellow immediately leaped out of the window, which looked into the garden and was open (it being summer), and escaped over the fields, leaving his breeches on a chair by the bedside, a very striking circumstance. In short, the case was such I do not think the Queen of the Fairies herself could have found an excuse, though Chaucer tells us she has made a solemn promise to leave none of her sex unfurnished with one, to all eternity.[29] As to the poor criminal, she had nothing to say for herself but what I dare swear you will hear from your youngest daughter if ever you catch her stealing of sweetmeats: pray, pray, she would do so no more, and indeed it was the first time.

This last article found no credit with me. I can not be persuaded that any woman who had lived virtuous till forty (for such was her age) could suddenly be endowed with such consummate impudence to solicit a youth at first sight, there being no probability, his age and station considered, that he would have made any attempt of that kind. I must confess I was wicked enough to think the unblemished reputation she had hitherto maintained, and did not fail to put us in mind of, was owing to a series of such frolics; and to say truth, they are the only *amours* that can reasonably hope to remain undiscovered. Ladies that can resolve to make love thus *ex tempore* may pass unobserved, especially if they can content themselves with low life, where fear may oblige their favourites

29 Chaucer, 'The Merchant's Tale', *Canterbury Tales*.

to secrecy. There wants only a very lewd constitution, a very bad heart, and a moderate understanding to make this conduct easy, and I do not doubt it has been practised by many prudes beside her I am now speaking of.

You may be sure I did not communicate these reflections. The first word I spoke was to desire Signor Carlo to sheathe his poniard, not being pleased with its glittering. He did so very readily, begging my pardon for not having done it on my first appearance, saying he did not know what he did; and indeed he had the countenance and gesture of a man distracted. I did not endeavour a defence that seemed to me impossible, but represented to him as well as I could the crime of a murder which, if he could justify before men, was still a crying sin before God, the disgrace he would bring on himself and posterity, and irreparable injury he would do his eldest daughter (a pretty girl of fifteen, that I knew he was extreme fond of). I added that if he thought it proper to part from his lady he might easily find a pretext for it some months hence, and that it was as much his interest as hers to conceal this affair from the knowledge of the world. I could not presently make him taste these reasons, and was forced to stay there near five hours (almost from five to ten at night) before I durst leave them together, which I would not do till he had sworn in the most serious manner he would make no future attempt on her life. I was content with his oath, knowing him to be very devout, and found I was not mistaken.

How the matter was made up between them afterwards I know not, but 'tis now two year since it happened, and all appearances remaining as if it had never been. The secret is in very few hands; his brother, being at that time at Brescia, I believe knows nothing of it to this day. The chambermaid and myself have preserved the strictest silence; and the lady retains the satisfaction of insulting all her acquaintance on the foundation of a spotless character that only she can boast in the parish, where she is most heartily hated, from these airs of impertinent virtue, and another very essential reason, being the best dressed woman amongst them, though one of the plainest in her figure.

The discretion of the chambermaid in fetching me, which possibly saved her mistress's life, and her taciturnity since, I fancy appears very remarkable to you, and is what would certainly never happen in England. The first part of her behaviour deserves great praise, coming of her own accord and inventing so decent an excuse for her admittance; but her silence may be attributed to her knowing very well that any servant that presumes to talk of his master will most certainly be incapable of talking at all in a short time, their lives being entirely in the power of their superiors. I do not mean by law but by custom, which has full as much force. If one of them was killed it would either never be inquired into at all or very slightly passed over; yet it seldom happens and I know no instance of it, which I think is owing to the great submission of domestics, who are sensible of their dependence, and the national temper not being hasty and never enflamed by wine, drunkness being a vice abandoned to the vulgar and spoke of with greater detestation than murder, which is mentioned with as little concern as a drinking bout in England, and is almost as frequent. It was extreme shocking to me at my first coming, and still gives me a sort of horror, though custom has in some degree familiarized it to my imagination. Robbery would be pursued with great vivacity and punished with the utmost rigour, therefore is very rare, though stealing is in daily practice; but as all the peasants are suffered the use of firearms the slightest provocation is sufficient to shoot, and they see one of their own species lie dead before them with as little remorse as a hare or a partridge, and when revenge spurs them on, with much pleasure. A dissertation on this subject would engage me in a discourse not proper for the post.

My compliments to Lord Bute. His kindness to you ought to obtain the friendship of all that love you. My blessing to your little ones. Think of me as ever your most affectionate mother,

M. Wortley

Eliza Haywood
1693 – 1756

E liza Haywood was a prolific novelist, playwright and translator, as well as a writer of periodicals. She was the daughter of a shopkeeper in London and married a clergyman. She went on the stage and began writing racy novels, a successful example of which is Love in Excess (1719). By 1721 she had left her husband and was supporting herself by acting and writing fiction and plays. Through the 1720s she produced a succession of works, sometimes depending on contemporary scandals, and she was attacked by Pope as licentious in The Dunciad in 1728. By the 1740s Haywood had responded to the changing taste and was working far more decorously and moralistically. In April 1744, she established the periodical, The Female Spectator, and made a significant contribution to the tradition of women's magazines. The Female Spectator was published monthly until May 1746 and revealed her continued liking for tales of seduction and passion, but these are now told without her earlier risqué extravagance and are surrounded by commonsensical moralizing.

The following extracts are taken from The Female Spectator, vol. 1 (T. Gardner, London, 1745).

From

The Female Spectator

BOOK 1

I T is very much by the Choice we make of Subjects for our Entertainment, that the refined Taste distinguishes itself from the vulgar and more gross: Reading is universally allowed to be one of the most improving, as well as agreeable Amusements; but then to render it so, one should, among the Number of Books which are perpetually issuing from the Press, endeavour to single out such as promise to be most conducive to those Ends. In order to be as little deceived as possible, I, for my own part, love to get as well acquainted as I can with an Author, before I run the risque of losing my Time in perusing his Work; and as I doubt not but most People are of this way of thinking, I shall, in imitation of my learned Brother of ever precious Memory;[1] give some Account of what I am, and those concerned with me in this Undertaking; and likewise of the chief Intent of the *Lucubrations* hereafter communicated, that the Reader, on casting his Eye over the four or five first Pages, may judge how far the Book may, or may not be qualified to entertain him; and either accept; or throw it aside as he thinks proper: And here I promise, that in the Pictures I shall give of myself and Associates, I will draw no flattering Lines, assume no Perfection that we are not in reality possessed of, nor attempt to shadow over any Defect with an artificial Gloss.

As a Proof of my Sincerity, I shall, in the first place, assure him, that for my own Part I never was a Beauty, and am now very far from being young; (a Confession he will find few of my Sex ready to make:) I shall also acknowledge, that I have run through as many Scenes of Vanity and Folly as the greatest Coquet of them all. — Dress, Equipage, and Flattery, were the Idols of my Heart. — I should have thought that Day lost which did not present me with some new Opportunity of shewing myself. —— My Life, for some Years, was a continued Round of what I then called Pleasure, and my whole Time engrossed by a Hurry of promiscuous Diversions. — But whatever Inconveniences such a manner of Conduct has brought upon myself, I have this Consolation, to think that the Public may reap some Benefit from it. —— The Company I kept was not, indeed, always so well chosen as it ought to have been, for the sake of my own Interest or Reputation; but then it was general, and by Consequence furnished me, not only with the Knowledge of many Occurrences, which otherwise I had been ignorant of, but also enabled me, when the too great Vivacity of my Nature became tempered with Reflection, to see into the secret Springs which gave rise to the Actions I had either heard, or been Witness of, — to judge of the various Passions of the human Mind, and distinguish those imperceptible Degrees by

---

[1] Joseph Addison began vol. 1 of *The Spectator* in 1710–11 with a description of his life and character.

which they become Masters of the Heart, and attain the Dominion over Reason.
—— A thousand odd Adventures, which at the Time they happened made slight
Impression on me, and seemed to dwell no longer on my Mind than the Wonder
they occasioned, now rise fresh to my Remembrance, with this Advantage, that
the Mystery I then, for want of Attention, imagined they contained, is entirely
vanished, and I find it easy to account for the Cause by the Consequence.

With this Experience, added to a Genius tolerably extensive, and an Education
more liberal than is ordinarily allowed to Persons of my Sex, I flattered myself that
it might be in my Power to be in some measure both useful and entertaining to
the Public; and this Thought was so soothing to those Remains of Vanity, not yet
wholly extinguished in me, that I resolved to pursue it, and immediately began to
consider by what Method I should be most likely to succeed: To confine myself
to any one Subject, I knew, could please but one kind of Taste, and my Ambition
was to be as universally read as possible: From my Observations of human
Nature, I found that Curiosity had, more or less, a Share in every Breast; and my
Business, therefore, was to hit this reigning Humour in such a manner, as that the
Gratification it should receive from being made acquainted with other People's
Affairs, should at the same time teach every one to regulate their own.

Having agreed within myself on this important Point, I commenced Author, by
setting down many Things, which, being pleasing to myself, I imagined would be
so to others; but on examining them the next Day, I found an infinite Deficiency
both in Matter and Stile, and that there was an absolute Necessity for me to call
in to my Assistance such of my Acquaintance as were qualified for that Purpose.
—— The *first* that occured to me, I shall distinguish by the Name of *Mira*, a Lady
descended from a Family to which Wit seems hereditary, married to a Gentleman
every way worthy of so excellent a Wife, and with whom she lives in so perfect
a Harmony, that having nothing to ruffle the Composure of her Soul, or disturb
those sparkling Ideas she received from Nature and Education, left me no room
to doubt if what she favoured me with would be acceptable to the Public. ——
The *next* is a Widow of Quality, who not having buried her Vivacity in the Tomb
of her Lord, continues to make one in all the modish Diversions of the Times,
so far, I mean, as she finds them consistent with Innocence and Honour; and as
she is far from having the least Austerity in her Behaviour, nor is rigid to the
Failings she is wholly free from herself, those of her Acquaintance, who had
been less circumspect, scruple not to make her the Confidante of Secrets they
conceal from all the World beside. — The *third* is the Daughter of a wealthy
Merchant, charming as an Angel, but endued with so many Accomplishments,
that to those who know her truly, her Beauty is the least distinguished Part of
her. — This fine young Creature I shall call *Euphrosine*, since she has all the
Chearfulness and Sweetness ascribed to that Goddess.

These *three* approved my Design, assured me of all the Help they could
afford, and soon gave a Proof of it in bringing their several Essays; but as the
Reader, provided the Entertainment be agreeable, will not be interested from
which Quarter it comes, whatever Productions I shall be favoured with from
these Ladies, or any others I may hereafter correspond with, will be exhibited
under the general Title of *The Female Spectator*; and how many Contributors

soever there may happen to be to the Work, they are to be considered only as several Members of one Body, of which I am the Mouth.

It is also highly proper I should acquaint the Town, that to secure an eternal Fund of Intelligence, Spies are placed not only in all the Places of Resort in and about this great Metropolis, but at *Bath, Tunbridge*, and the *Spaw*, and Means found out to extend my Speculations even as far as *France, Rome, Germany*, and other foreign Parts, so that nothing curious or worthy of Remark can escape me; and this I look upon to be a more effectual way of penetrating into the Mysteries of the Alcove, the Cabinet, or Field, than if I had the Power of Invisibility, or could with a Wish transport myself wherever I pleased, since with the Aid of those supernatural Gifts, I could still be in no more than one Place at a Time; whereas now, by tumbling over a few Papers from my Emissaries, I have all the Secrets of *Europe*, at least such of them as are proper for my Purpose, laid open at one View.

I would, by no means, however, have what I say be construed into a Design of gratifying a vicious Propensity of propagating Scandal: — Whoever sits down to read me with this View, will find themselves mistaken; for tho' I shall bring real Facts on the Stage, I shall conceal the Actors Names under such as will be conformable to their Characters; my Intention being only to expose the Vice, not the Person. — Nor shall I confine myself to modern Transactions:—Whenever I find any Example among the Antients which may serve to illustrate the Topic I shall happen to be upon, I shall make no scruple to insert it. — An Instance of shining Virtue in any Age, can never be too often proposed as a Pattern, nor the Fatality of Misconduct too much impressed on the Minds of our Youth of both Sexes; and as the sole Aim of the following Pages is to reform the Faulty, and give an innocent Amusement to those who are not so, all possible Care will be taken to avoid every thing that might serve as Food for the Venom of Malice and Ill-nature. Whoever, therefore, shall pretend to fix on any particular Person the Blame of Actions they may happen to find recorded here, or make what they call a Key to these Lucubrations, must expect to see themselves treated in the next Publication with all the Severity so unfair a Proceeding merits.

And now having said as much as I think needful of this Undertaking, I shall, without being either too greatly confident, or too anxious for the Success, submit it to the Publick Censure.

> *Of all the Passions giv'n us from Above,*
> *The noblest, softest, and the best is Love,*

Says a justly celebrated Poet; and I readily agree that Love in itself, when under the Direction of Reason, harmonizes the Soul, and gives it a gentle, generous Turn; but I can by no means approve of such Definitions of that Passion as we generally find in Romances, Novels, and Plays: In most of those Writings, the Authors seem to lay out all their Art in rendering that Character most interesting, which most sets at Defiance all the Obligations, by the strict Observance of which Love can alone become a Virtue. — They dress their *Cupid* up in Roses, call him the God of soft Desires, and ever-springing Joys,

yet at the same time give him the vindictive Fury, and the Rage of *Mars*. — Shew
him impatient of Controul, and trampling over all the Ties of Duty, Friendship,
or natural Affection, yet make the Motive sanctify the Crime. — How fatal, how
pernicious to a young and unexperienced Mind must be such Maxims, especially
when dressed up in all the Pomp of Words! The Beauty of the Expression steals
upon the Senses, and every Mischief, every Woe that Love occasions, appears a
Charm. — Those who feel the Passion are so far from endeavouring to repel
its Force, or being ashamed of their Attachment, however opposite to Reason,
that they indulge and take a Pride in turning into Ridicule the Remonstrances
of their more discerning Friends. But what is yet more preposterous, and more
evidently shews the ill Effects of writing in this manner is, that we often see Girls
too young, either to be addressed to on the Score of Love, or even to know what
is meant by the Passion, affect the Languishment they read of, — roll their Eyes,
sigh, fold their Arms, neglect every useful Learning, and attend to nothing but
acquiring the Reputation of being enough a Woman to know all the Pains and
Delicacies of Love.

Miss *Tenderilla* is one of those I have described: She was the other Day invited
to a Concert, and as soon as the Music began to strike up, cried out in a kind of
dying Tone, yet loud enough to be heard by a great Part of the Assembly,

If Music be the Food of Love, play on.[2]

A young Lady happened to be near her, who is supposed to be very near entering
into the Marriage-State, but contents herself with discovering what Sentiments she
is possessed of in favour of her intended Bridegroom only to those interested
in them.—She blushed extremely at the Extravagance of her Companion, and
the more so, as she found the Eyes of every one turned upon her, and by their
Smiles and Whispers to each other, shewed that they imagined *Miss* had burst
into this Exclamation merely on her Account. A smart Gentleman, on the next
Bench to them, took this Opportunity of rallying her very wittily, as he thought,
on the Discovery the young Confidante had made; and the poor Lady was in the
utmost Confusion, 'till she who had occasioned it being vexed to find what she
had said so much mistaken, and that no Notice was taken of herself, behaved
in such a manner as left no room to doubt which of them was the proper
Object for Ridicule.

How easy were it now for a designing Fortune-Hunter to make a Prey of
this Bib-and-Apron Heroine! — The less qualified he was to render her Choice
of him approved, and the more averse her Friends appeared to such a Match,
the more would she glory in a noble Obstinacy of contemning their Advice,
and sacrificing her Person and Fortune to an imaginary Passion for him; and
one has no need of being a very great Prophet to foretel, that if she is not
speedily removed from those who at present have the Care of her, and some
other Methods taken than such as hitherto have been made use of, to give her
a more rational way of thinking, that Wealth her frugal Parents hoarded up, in

2 *Twelfth Night* I, 1.

order to purchase for her a lasting Happiness, will only prove the Bait for her Destruction.

I am sorry to observe, that of late Years this Humour has been strangely prevalent among our young Ladies, some of whom are scarce entered into their Teens before they grow impatient for Admiration, and to be distinguished in Love-Songs and Verses, expect to have a great Bustle made about them, and he that first attempts to perswade them he is a Lover, bids very fair for carrying his Point. — The Eagerness of their Wishes to be addressed, gives Charms to the Address itself, which otherwise it would not have; and hence it follows, that when a young Creature has suffered herself to fall a Victim to the Artifices of her pretended Lover, and her own giddy Whim, and is afterwards convinced of her Error, she looks back with no less Wonder than Shame on her past Conduct, detests the Object of her former imaginary Passion, and wishes nothing more than to be eternally rid of the Presence of him she once with so much Eagerness pursued.

It is not, therefore, from the Inconstancy of Nature which the Men charge upon our Sex, but from that romantic Vein which makes us sometimes imagine ourselves Lovers before we are so, that we frequently run such Lengths to shake off a Yoke we have so precipitately put on. — When once we truly love, we rarely change: We bear the Frowns of Fortune with Fortitude and Patience: — We repent not of the Choice we have made, whatever we suffered by it; and nothing but a long continued Series of Slights and ill Usage from the Object of our Affection can render him less dear.

To be well convinced of the Sincerity of the Man they are about to marry, is a Maxim, with great Justice, always recommended to a young Lady; but I say it is no less material for her future Happiness, as well as that of her intended Partner, that she should be well assured of her own Heart, and examine, with the utmost Care, whether it be real Tenderness, or a bare Liking she at present feels for him; and as this is not to be done all at once, I cannot approve of hasty Marriages, or before Persons are of sufficient Years to be supposed capable of knowing their own Minds.

Could fourteen have the Power of judging of itself, or for itself, who that knew the beautiful *Martesia* at that Age, but would have depended on her Conduct! — *Martesia*, descended of the most illustrious Race, possessed of all that Dignity of Sentiment befitting her high Birth, endued by Nature with a surprizing Wit, Judgment, and Penetration, and improved by every Aid of Education. — *Martesia*, the Wonder and Delight of all who saw or heard her, gave the admiring World the greatest Expectations that she would one Day be no less celebrated for all those Virtues which render amiable the conjugal State, than she at that Time was for every other Perfection that do Honour to the Sex.

Yet how, alas, did all these charming Hopes vanish into Air! Many noble Youths, her Equals in Birth and Fortune, watched her Increase of Years for declaring a Passion, which they feared as yet would be rejected by those who had the Disposal of her; but what their Respect and Timidity forbad them to attempt, a more daring and unsuspected Rival ventured at, and succeeded in. — Her unexperienced Heart approved his Person, and was pleased with the

Protestations he made her of it. — In fine, the Novelty of being addressed in
that manner, gave a double Grace to all he said and she never thought herself
so happy as in his Conversation. His frequent Visits at length were taken notice
of; he was denied the Privilege of seeing her, and she was no longer permitted
to go out without being accompanied by some Person who was to be a Spy upon
her Actions.—She had a great Spirit, impatient of Controul, and this Restraint served
only to heighten the Inclination she before had to favour him: — She indulged
the most romantic Ideas of his Merit and his Love: — Her own flowing Fancy
invented a thousand melancholly and tender Soliloquies, and set them down as
made by him in this Separation: It is not, indeed, to be doubted, but that he
was very much mortified at the Impediment he found in the Prosecution of
his Courtship; but whether he took this Method of disburthening his Affliction,
neither she nor any body else could be assured. It cannot, however, be denied,
but that he pursued Means much more efficacious for the Attainment of his
Wishes. By Bribes, Promises, and Entreaties, he prevailed on a Person who
came frequently to the House to convey his Letters to her, and bring back her
Answers.— This Correspondence was, perhaps, of greater Service to him, than
had the Freedom of their Interviews not been prevented: — She consented to be
his, and to make good her Word, ventured her Life, by descending from a two
Pair of Stairs Window, by the Help of Quilt, Blankets, and other Things fastened
to it, at the Dead of Night. — His Coach and Six waited to receive her at the End
of the Street, and conveyed her to his Country Seat, which reaching soon after
Break of Day, his Chaplain made them too fast for any Authority to separate.

As he was of an antient honourable Family and his Estate very considerable,
her Friends in a short time were reconciled to what was now irremedible,
and they were looked upon as an extreme happy Pair. — But soon, too
soon the fleeting Pleasures fled, and in their room Anguish and Bitterness of
Heart succeeded.

Martesia, in a Visit she made to a Lady of her intimate Acquaintance, unfortunately happened to meet the young *Clitander*; he was just returned from his
Travels, had a handsome Person, an Infinity of Gaiety and a certain Something in
his Air and Deportment which had been destructive to the Peace and Reputation
of many of our Sex. — He was naturally of an amorous Disposition, and being
so, felt all the Force of Charms, which had some Effect even on the most Cold
and Temperate. — Emboldened by former Successes, the Knowledge *Martesia*
was another's, did not hinder him from declaring to her the Passion she had
inspired him with. — She found a secret Satisfaction in hearing him, which she
was yet too young to consider the Dangers of, and therefore endeavoured not
to suppress 'till it became too powerful for her to have done so, even had she
attempted it with all her Might; but the Truth is, she now experienced in *reality*
a Flame she had but *imagined* herself possessed of for him who was now her
Husband, and was too much averse to the giving herself Pain to combat with an
Inclination which seemed to her fraught only with Delights.

The House where their Acquaintance first began, was now the Scene of their
future Meetings: — The Mistress of it was too great a Friend to Gallantry herself
to be any Interruption to the Happiness they enjoyed in entertaining each

other without Witnesses. — How weak is Virtue when Love and Opportunity combine! — Tho' no Woman could have more refined and delicate Notions than *Martesia*, yet all were ineffectual against the Sollicitations of her adored *Clitander*. — One fatal Moment destroyed at once all her own exalted Ideas of Honour and Reputation, and the Principles early instilled into her Mind by her virtuous Preceptors.

The Consequence of this Amour was a total Neglect of Husband, House, and Family. — Herself abandoned, all other Duties were so too. — So manifest a Change was visible to all that knew her, but most to her Husband, as most interested in it. — He truly loved, and had believed himself truly beloved by her. — Loth he was to think his Misfortune real, and endeavoured to find some other Motive for the Aversion she now expressed for staying at Home, or going to any of those Places where they had been accustomed to visit together; but she either knew not how to dissemble, or took so little Pains to do it, that he was, in spite of himself, convinced all that Affection she so lately had professed, and given him Testimonies of, was now no more. — He examined all his Actions, and could find nothing in any of them that could give occasion for so sad a Reverse. — He complained to her one Day, in the tenderest Terms, of the small Portion she had of late allowed him of her Conversation:— Entreated, that if by any Inadvertency he had offended her, she would acquaint him with his Fault, which he assured her he would take care never to repeat. — Asked if there was any thing in her Settlement or Jointure she could wish to have altered, and assured her she need but let him know her Commands to be instantly obeyed.

To all this she replied with the most stabbing Indifference.— That she knew not what he meant. — That as she had accused him with nothing, he had no Reason to think she was dissatisfied. — But that People could not be always in the same Humour, and desired he would not give himself nor her the Trouble of making any farther Interrogatories.

He must have been as insensible, as he is known to be the contrary, had such a Behaviour not opened his Eyes; he no longer doubted of his Fate, and resolving, if possible, to find out the Author of it, he caused her Chair to be watched wherever she went, and took such effectual Methods, as soon informed him of the Truth.

In the first Emotions of his Rage he was for sending a Challenge to this Destroyer of his Happiness; but in his cooler Moments he rejected that Design as too injurious to the Reputation of *Martesia*, who was still dear to him, and whom he flattered himself with being able one Day to reclaim.

It is certain he put in Practice every tender Stratagem that Love and Wit could furnish him with for that Purpose; but she appearing so far from being moved at any thing he either said or did, that, on the contrary, her Behaviour was every Day more cold; he at last began to expostulate with her, gave some Hints that her late Conduct was not unknown to him, and that tho' he was willing to forgive what was past, yet as a Husband, it was not consistent with his Character to bear any future Insults of that nature. This put her beyond all Patience. — She reproached him in the bitterest Terms for daring to harbour the least Suspicion of her Virtue, and censuring her innocent Amusements as Crimes; and perhaps was glad of this Opportunity of testifying her Remorse for having ever listened to his Vows, and cursing before his Face the Hour that joined their Hands.

They now lived so ill a Life together, that not having sufficient Proofs for a Divorce, he parted Beds, and tho' they continued in one House, behaved to each other as Strangers; never eat at the same Table but when Company was there, and then only to avoid the Questions that would naturally have been otherwise; neither of them being desirous the World should know any thing of their Disagreement.

But while they continued to treat each other in a manner so little conformable to their first Hopes, or their Vows pledged at the Holy Altar, *Martesia* became pregnant: This gave the first Alarm to that Indolence of Nature she hitherto had testified; her Husband would now have it in his Power to sue out a Divorce; and tho' she would have rejoiced to have been separated from him on any other Terms, yet she could not support the Thoughts of being totally deprived of all Reputation in the World. — She was not ignorant of the Censures she incurr'd; but had Pride and Spirit enough to enable her to despise whatever was said of her, while it was not backed by Proof; but the glaring one she was now about to give struck Shame and Confusion to her Soul. —She left no Means untried to procure an Abortion; but failing in that, she had no other Resource than to that Friend who was the sole Confidante of her unhappy Passion, who comforted her as well as she could, and assured her, that when the Hour approached she need have no more to do than to come directly to her House, where every thing should be prepared for the Reception of a Woman in her Condition.

To conceal the Alteration in her Shape, she pretended Indisposition, saw little Company, and wore only loose Gowns. — At length the so much dreaded Moment came upon her at the dead of Night; and in the midst of all that Rack Nature, made yet more horrible by the Agonies of her Mind, she rose, rung for her Woman, and telling her she had a frightful Dream concerning that Lady, whom she knew she had the greatest Value for of any Person upon Earth, ordered her to get a Chair, for she could not be easy unless she went and saw her herself. The Woman was strangely surprized, but her Lady was always absolute in her Commands. — A Chair was brought, and without any other Company or Attendance than her own distracted Thoughts, she was conveyed to the only Asylum where she thought her Shame might find a Shelter.

A Midwife being prepared before, she was safely delivered of a Daughter, who expired almost as soon as born; and to prevent as much as possible all Suspicion of the Truth, she made herself be carried Home the next Morning, where she went to Bed, and lay several Days under Pretence of having sprained her Ancle.

But not all the Precautions she had taken were effectual enough to prevent some People from guessing and whispering what had happened. — Those whose Nearness in Blood gave them a Privilege of speaking their Minds, spared not to tell her all that was said of her; and those who dared not take that Liberty, shewed by their distant Looks and reserved Behaviour, whenever she came in Presence, how little they approved her Conduct. —She was too discerning not to see into their Thoughts, nor was her innate Pride of any Service to keep up her Spirits on this Occasion. — To add to her Discontents, *Clitander* grew every

Day more cool in his Respects, and she soon after learned he was on the Point of Marriage with one far inferior to herself in every Charm both of Mind and Person. — In short, finding herself deserted by her Relations, and the greatest Part of her Acquaintance, without Love, without Respect, and reduced to the Pity of those, who, perhaps, had nothing but a greater Share of Circumspection to boast of, she took a Resolution to quit *England* for ever, and having settled her Affairs with her Husband, who by this Time had entered into other Amusements, and, it is probable, was very well satisfied to be eased of the Constraint her Presence gave him, readily agreed to remit her the Sum agreed between them, to be paid yearly to whatever Part of the World she chose to reside in, she then took leave of a Country of which she had been the Idol, and which now seemed to her as too unjust in not being blind to what she desired should be concealed.

Behold her now in a voluntary Banishment From Friends and Country, and roaming round the World in fruitless Search of that Tranquillity she could not have failed enjoying at Home in the Bosom of a Consort equally beloved as loving.—Unhappy charming Lady, born and endued with every Quality to attract universal Love and Admiration, yet by one inadvertent Step undone and lost to every thing the World holds dear, and only more conspicuously wretched by having been conspicuously amiable.

BOOK IV

How glorious a Privilege has Man beyond all other sublunary Beings! who, tho' indigent, unpitied, forsaken by the World, and even chain'd in a Dungeon, can by the Aid of Divine Contemplation, enjoy all the Charms of Pomp, Respect, and Liberty! — Transport himself in Idea to whatever Place he wishes, and grasp in Theory imagin'd Empires!

Unaccountable is it, therefore, that so many People find an Irksomeness in being alone, tho' for never so small a Space of Time!—Guilt indeed creates Perturbations, which may well make Retirement horrible, and drive the self-tormented Wretch into any Company to avoid the Agonies of Remorse; but I speak not of those who are *afraid* to reflect, but of those who seem to me not to have the *Power* to do it.

There are several of my Acquaintance of both Sexes, who lead Lives perfectly inoffensive, and when in Company appear to have a Fund of Vivacity capable of enlivening all the Conversation they come into; yet if you happen to meet them after half an Hour's Solitude, are for some Minutes the most heavy lumpish Creatures upon Earth: — Ask them if they are indispos'd? they will drawl out—*No, they are well enough.*— If any Misfortune has befallen them? still they answer — *No*, in the same stupid Tone as before, and look like Things inanimate till something is said or done to reinspire them.—One would imagine they were but half awoke from a deep Sleep, and indeed their Minds, during this Lethargy, may be said to have been in a more inactive State than even that of Sleep, for they have not so much as dream'd; but I think they may justly enough be compar'd to Clock-work, which has Power to do nothing of itself till wound up by another.

Whatever Opinion the World may have of the Wit of Persons of this Cast, I cannot help thinking there is a Vacuum in the Mind: — that they have no Ideas of their own, and only through Custom and a genteel Education are enabled to talk agreeably on those of other People.—A real fine Genius can never want Matter to entertain itself, and tho' on the Top of a Mountain without Society, and without Books, or any *exterior* Means of Employment, will always find that *within* which will keep it from being idle: — *Memory* and *Recollection* will bring the Transactions of *past* Times to View: — *Observation* and *Discernment* point out the *present* with their Causes; and *Fancy*, temper'd with *Judgment*, anticipate the *future*,—This Power of Contemplation and Reflection it is that chiefly distinguishes the *Human* from the *Brute* Creation, and proves that we have Souls which are in reality Sparks of that Divine, Omniscient, Omnipresent Being whence we all boast to be deriv'd.

The Pleasures which an agreeable Society bestows are indeed the most elegant we can taste; but even that Company we like best would grow insipid and tiresome were we to be for ever in it; and to a Person who knows how to think justly, it would certainly be as great a Mortification never to be alone, as to be always so.

Conversation, in effect, but furnishes Matter for Contemplation; — it exhilerates the Mind, and fits it for Reflection afterward: — Every new thing we hear in Company raises in us new Ideas in the Closet or on the Pillow; and as there are few People but one may gather something from, either to divert or improve, a good Understanding will, like the industrious Bee, suck out the various Sweets, and digest them in Retirement. But those who are perpetually hurrying from one Company to another, and never suffer themselves to be alone but when weary Nature summonses them to Repose, will be little amended, tho' the Maxims of a *Seneca*[3] were to be deliver'd to them in all the enchanting Eloquence of a *Tully*.[4]

But not to be more improved, is not the worst Mischief that attends an immoderate Aversion to Solitude.—People of this Humour, rather than be alone, fly into all Company indiscriminately, and sometimes fall into such as they have Reason to repent their whole Lives of having ever seen; for tho' they may not possibly reap any Advantage from the *Good*, their Reputations must certainly, and perhaps their Morals and Fortunes too, will suffer very much from the *Bad*; and where we do not give ourselves Leisure to chuse, it is rarely we happen on the former, as they being infinitely the smaller Number, and also less easy of Access to those whose Characters they are unacquainted with.

Many young Persons of both Sexes owe their Ruin to this one unfortunate Propensity of loving to be always in Company; and it is the more dangerous, as nobody takes any Pains to conquer it in themselves, but on the contrary are

3 A first-century Roman philosopher and moralist, famous for his virtuous sayings.
4 Marcus Tullius Cicero (106–43 B.C.) a renowned Roman orator.

apt to mistake it for a laudable Inclination, and look on those who preach up the Happiness of a more retir'd Life, as phlegmatic and vaporish.— I doubt not but I shall pass for such in the Opinion of many of my Readers, who are too volatile to consider that it is not a sullen, *cynical*, total avoiding of Society that I recommend, but a proper Love of Solitude at *some Times*, to enable us to relish with more Pleasure, as well as to be essentially the better for Conversation at *others*, and also to select such for our Companions as may be likely to answer both these Ends.

Nor is it only where there is a Difference of Sex that I think Youth ought to be upon its Guard: — The Dangers in that Case are too universally allowed to stand in need of any Remonstrances, and yet perhaps are not greater than others which both may happen to fall into among those of their own.—Are not almost all the Extravagancies Parents with so much Grief behold their Children guilty of, owing to ill-chosen Company?— Great is the Privilege of Example, and some are so weak as to think they must do as they see others do.—The Fear of being laughed at has made many a young Gentleman run into Vices to which his Inclination was at first averse; but, alas! by Habitude become more pleasing to him: He has in his Turn too play'd the Tempter's Part, and made it his Glory to seduce others as himself had been seduced.—It is this Love of Company, more than the Diversions mentioned in the Bills, that makes our Ladies run galloping in Troops every Evening to Masquerades, Balls and Assemblies in Winter, and in the Summer to *Vaux-Hall, Ranelagh, Cuper's-Gardens, Mary le Bon, Sadler's-Wells*, both old and new, *Goodman's Fields*, and twenty other such Places, which, in this Age of Luxury, serve as Decoys to draw the Thoughtless and Unwary together, and, as it were, prepare the Way for other more vicious Excesses: For there are, and of Condition too, not a few (as I am informed by the *Gnomes* who preside over Midnight Revels) that, going with no other Intention than to partake what seems an innocent Recreation, are prevail'd upon by the Love of Company either to remain in these Houses, or adjourn to some other Place of Entertainment till the sweet Harbinger of Day, *Aurora*, wakes, and blushes to behold the Order of Nature thus perverted; nor then perhaps would separate, did not wearied Limbs, heavy languid Eyes, and *dirty Linnen* remind them of repairing to their respective Habitation, where having lain a while, they rise, they dress, and go again in quest of new Company and new Amusements.

Heaven forbid, and I am far from suggesting that to run such Lengths as these should be common to all who hate Retirement and Reflection: Fortune is sometimes kinder than our Endeavours merit, and by not throwing any Temptations in our way, renders our Carelesness of no worse Consequence than being deprived of those solid Pleasures which flow from a Consciousness of having behaved according to the Dictates of Honour and Reason.

But suppose we make some Allowances to a few of the very Young and Gay, especially the Beautiful and High-born, who, by a mistaken Fondness in their Parents, from the Moment they were capable of understanding what was said to them, heard nothing but Flattery, and are made to believe they came into the World for no other Purpose than to be adored and indulged, what can we say for those who had a different Education, and are of riper Years?—How little Excuse is there for a gadding Matron, or for a Woman who ought to have the Care of a House and Family at Heart!—How odd a Figure does the Mother of five or six Children make at one of these nocturnal Rambles; and how ridiculous is it for a Person in any Trade or Avocation, to be, or affect to be, above the Thought of all Economy, and make one in every Party of Pleasure that presents itself?—Yet such as these are no Prodigies.—All kinds of Regulation and Management require some small Reflection and Recess from Company, and these are two Things so terrible to some People, that they will rather suffer every thing to be ruined than endure the Fatigue of Thought.

A Young Widow of my Acquaintance, rich, beautiful and gay, had scare sully'd the Blackness of her Weeds, before she ventur'd to take for a second Husband a Man, who, had she once consider'd on what she was about to do, she would have found had no one Quality that could promise her any Felicity with him.—He had not been married a Month before he loaded her with the most gross Abuse, turned her innocent Babes out of Doors, and affronted all her Friends who came to reason with him on the Injustice and Cruelty of his Behaviour.—The unadvised Step she had taken indeed but little merited Compassion for the Event, but the Sweetness of Disposition with which she had always treated all who knew her, render'd it impossible not to have a Fellow-feeling of the Calamities she labour'd under. A particular Friend of her's, however, took one Day the Liberty of asking how she could throw away herself on a Person so every way undeserving of her? To which she made this short, but sincere Reply:—*Ah*! said she, *it is a sad thing to live alone.* To this the other might have returned, that she could not be said to be *alone* who had a Mother to advise, and three sweet Children to divert her most melancholly Hours; but this would have been only adding to her Affliction, and her Condition being now irremidable required Consolation.

Perhaps the reading this short Detail of the Misfortune her Inadvertency had brought upon her, may give her some Palpitations which I should be sorry to occasion; but as she is a much-lamented Instance of the Danger to which any one may be subjected through want of a due Reflection, I could not forbear mentioning it as a Warning to others.

When this immoderate Desire of Company remains in Persons of an advanced Age, tho' it threatens less Mischief, is more ridiculous than in the younger sort. I know a Lady, who by her own Confession, is no less than fifty-five, yet in all that long Length of Time has treasured up nothing in her Mind wherewith she can entertain herself two Minutes.—She has been a Widow for several Years, has a Jointure sufficient to support a handsome Equipage, is without Children, or any other Incumbrance, and might live as much respected by the World as she is really contemned, could she prevail on herself to reflect what sort of Behaviour would be most becoming in a Woman of her Age and Circumstances.

But instead of living in a regular decent manner, she roams from Place to Place,—hires Lodgings at three or four different Houses at the same time, lies one Night at *St. James's*, another at *Covent-Garden*, a third perhaps at *Westminster*, and a fourth in the *City*:—Nor does she look on this as a sufficient Variety:—She has at this Moment Apartments at *Richmond,—Hammersmith,— Kensington* and *Chelsea*, each of which she visits two or three times at least every Month, so that her Time is pass'd in a continual Whirl from one *Home* to another if any can be justly called so; but it seems as if she had an Aversion to the very Name, for the Rooms she pays for, she dwells in the least; seldom eats in any of them, and forces herself as it were into those of other People, where she sends in a Stock of Provision sufficient for the whole Family, in order to purchase for herself a Welcome. But as People of any Figure in the World would not accept of such Favours, and those of good Sense not endure to be depriv'd of the Privilege of thinking their own Thoughts and entertaining their own Friends, it can be only the extremely Necessitous, or those who have as little in their Heads as herself, that will submit to have their Lodgings and Time taken up in this manner.

Poor Woman! How does she lavish away a handsome Income?—How forfeit all Pretensions to good Understanding and good Breeding, merely for the sake of being permitted to talk as much as she pleases without Contradiction, and being never alone but when asleep. — I have been told by those who are to be depended upon, that the Moment she is out of Bed, she runs with her Stays and Petticoats into the next Neighbour's Chamber, not being able to live without Company even till she is dress'd.

There are People so uncharitable, as to believe some latent Crime hangs heavy on the Minds of all those who take so much Pains to avoid being alone; but I am far from being of that Number:—It is my Opinion that neither this old Rattle I have mentioned, nor many others who act in the same manner, ever did a real Hurt to any one.—Those who are incapable of *Thinking*, are certainly incapable of any *premeditated* Mischief; and, as I have already said, seem to me a Set of Insensibles, who never act of themselves, but are acted upon by others.

Before one passes so cruel a Censure, one should therefore examine, I mean not the Lives and Characters, for they may deceive us, but at what Point of Time this Aversion to Solitude commenced:—If from Childhood, and so continued even to the extremest old Age, it can proceed only from a Weakness in the Mind, and is deserving our Compassion; but if from taking that Satisfaction in Contemplation and Retirement, which every reasonable Soul finds in it, one sees a Person has turned to the reverse,—starts even while in Company at the bare mention of quitting it, and flies Solitude as a House on Fire, one may very well suspect some secret Crime has wrought so great a Transition, and that any Conversation, tho' the most insipid and worthless, seems preferable to that which the guilty Breast can furnish to itself.

I am well aware that there is another Motive besides either a Want of Power to think, or a Consciousness of having done what renders Thought a Pain, that induces many People to avoid being alone as much as possible;

and that is, when the Mind is oppress'd with any very severe Affliction.—To be able to reflect on our Misfortunes, goes a great way towards bearing them with that Fortitude which is becoming the Dignity of human Nature; but all have not Courage to do it, and those who have not would sink beneath the Weight of Grief, were they to indulge the Memory of what occasion'd it.

This I am sensible is the Case of many who pass for Persons of very good Understanding, and the Excuse is allowed by the Generality of the World as a reasonable one; but yet I must beg their Pardon when I say, that whatsoever Share of fine Sense they may shew in other Things, they betray a very great Deficiency in this:—The Relaxation which Noise and Hurry may afford is but short-liv'd, and are so far from removing that Burthen which the Spirit labours under, that they afterward make it felt with double Weight.

Some are so madly stupid as to attempt to lose the Thoughts of one Evil by running into others of perhaps worse Consequence,—I mean that of Drinking, and some other Excesses equally pernicious both to Fortune and Constitution; but how false a Relief this gives I need only appeal to those who have made the Trial.

Would such People be prevail'd upon to make a little Reflection before it is too late, they would certainly have Recourse to more solid Consolations:—Would not the Works of some of our celebrated Poets divert a melancholly Hour much more than all the Rhodomontades of a vague idle Conversation!—Would not the Precepts of Philosophy, of which so many excellent Treaties have been wrote, give them more true Courage than all the Bottle can inspire!—And above all, would not the Duties of an entire Submission and Resignation to the Almighty Disposer of all Things, so often and so strenuously recommended, be infinitely more efficacious to quiet all Perturbations of the Mind than any vain Amusements of what kind soever!

It is not that I would perswade any one to a continual poreing over Books, too much Reading, tho' of the best Authors, is apt to dull the Spirits, and destroy that Attention which alone can render this Employment profitable.—A few good Maxims, well digested by Reflection, dwell upon the Memory, and are not only a Remedy for present Ills, but also a kind of Antidote against any future ones that Fate may have in Store.

But it may be said that this Advice can only be complied with by Persons of Condition; and as for the meaner Part, it cannot be imagined that they have either Time or Capacities to enable them to square themselves by such Rules:—This indeed must be allowed; but then it must also be allowed, that they can the least afford to waste what Time they have in such fruitless Attempts as they generally make use of for forgetting their Cares; and as to their Capacities, we are to suppose that every one understands the Trade or Business to which he has been bred, and in my Opinion, nothing is more plain than that an industrious Application to that would be his best Relief for any Vexation he is involved in, as well as the surest Means of avoiding falling into others.

Upon the whole, it denotes a Meanness of Soul, not to be forgiven even in the lowest Rank of People, much less in those of a more refined Education, when to shun the Remembrance of perhaps a trifling Affliction, they rush into Irregularities, each of which their Reason might inform them would be productive of greater Ills than any they yet had to lament; and is so far from affording any Relief, that it serves only to give new Additions to their former Disquiets, according to the Poet, justly describing this Fever of the Mind.

> Restless they toss, and turn about their feavorish Will,
> When all their Ease must come by lying still.

But what can be more amazing, than that Persons, who have no one thing on Earth to incommode them, should not be able to take any Pleasure in contemplating on the Tranquillity of their Situation!—Yet so it is: There are those in the World, and in the great World too, who being possessed of every thing they can wish, and frequently much more than either they deserve or could ever expect, seem altogether insensible of the Benefits they receive from Heaven, or any Obligations they may have to Man.—This, methinks, is an Indolence of Nature which can never be too much guarded against, because whoever is guilty of it becomes ungrateful and unjust without knowing he is so, and incurs the Censure of all who are acquainted with him for Omissions which himself is wholly ignorant of, and if he were not so, would perhaps be very far from meriting.

The beautiful and noble Widow, who is so good never to fail making one in our little Society, was inclinable to impute this thoughtless Behaviour in many People to the Negligence of those who, having the Care of their Education, did not inspire them with proper Notions of the Necessity there is for every body to enter sometimes into themselves: But we were all against her in this Point, and she was easily convinced, that tho' this was certainly a Duty incumbent on all who had the Government of Youth, yet without some Share of a natural Bent that way, no Lessons would be effectual; and that where the Spirits were too volatile, any Confinement, tho' for never so short a Space of Time, would rather mope than render them profitably serious.

But after all that has, or can be said, the World is more inclinable to excuse this Defect than any other I know of:—A Person who loves to be always in Company, and accept of any sort rather than be alone, is accounted a good-natur'd harmless Creature; and tho' it is impossible they can be magnified for any extraordinary Virtues or Qualifications, what they lose in *Respect* is for the most Part made up with *Love*. — They have rarely any Enemies, and the Reason is plain, they are generally merry, never contradict whatever is said or done, nor refuse any thing that is asked of them:— People of a middling Understanding like their Conversation;—the most Weak are in no Awe of them; and the Wisest will sometimes suffer themselves to be diverted by them.—In fine, every body is easy with them, and how easy they are to themselves in all Events there are innumerable Instances.

Sarah Fielding

1710 – 68

*S**arah Fielding came from a landed family in Dorset. She went to a boarding school but gained most of her education on her own. Her income was too small to allow independence and she relied on her brother, the novelist Henry Fielding, for some financial support and for assistance with the publication of her work, as the preface to* The Adventures of David Simple *(1744) reveals. In the 1740s and 1750s she lived with her brother and her sisters in London, contributing to her brother's works, defending Richardson's* Clarissa, *collaborating with her friend Jane Collier on* The Cry, *and writing novels marked less by realistic characterization than by wittily and pithily expressed moral sentiments and by acute psychological insight.*

The following extract is taken from The Adventures of David Simple, *(Oxford University Press, 1969). The book tells of the search by a naive, virtuous man for friends whom he can trust. Cynthia appears to be one of these and in this extract she tells him her life story.*

From

The Adventures of David Simple

CHAPTER VI

'I CANNOT say, I ever had any Happiness in my Life; for while I was young, I was bred up with my Father and Mother, who, without designing me any harm, were continually teazing me. I loved reading, and had a great Desire of attaining Knowledge; but whenever I asked Questions of any kind whatsoever I was always told, *such Things were not proper for Girls of my Age to know*: If I was pleased with any Book above the most silly Story or Romance, it was taken from me. For *Miss must not enquire too far into things, it would turn her Brain; she had better mind her Needle-work, and such Things as were useful for Women; reading and poring on Books, would never get me a Husband.* Thus was I condemned to spend my Youth, the Time when our Imagination is at the highest, and we are capable of most Pleasure, without being indulged in any one thing I liked; and obliged to employ myself, in what was fancied by my mistaken Parents to be for my improvement, altho' in reality it was nothing more than what any Person, a degree above a natural Fool, might learn as well in a very small time, as in a thousand Ages. And what yet aggravated my Misfortunes was, my having a Brother who hated reading to such a degree, he had a perfect Aversion to the very Sight of a Book; and he must be cajoled or whipp'd into Learning, while it was denied me, who had the utmost Eagerness for it. Young, and unexperienced as I was in the World, I could not help observing the Error of this Conduct, and the Impossibility of ever making him get any Learning, that could be of use to him, or of preventing my loving it.

'I had two Sisters, whose Behaviour was more shocking to me than that of my Father and Mother; because as we were more of an Age, we were more constantly together. I should have loved them with the sincerest Affection, if they had behaved to me in a manner I could have borne with Patience: They neither of them were to be reckon'd amongst the silliest of Women; and had both some small glimmering Rays of Parts and Wit. To this was owing all their Faults, for they were so partial to themselves, they mistook this faint Dawn of Day, for the Sun in its Meridian; and from grasping at what they could not attain, obscured, and rendered useless all the Understanding they really had. From hence, they took an inveterate Hatred to me, because most of our Acquaintance allowed me to have more Wit than they had; and when I spoke, I was generally listened to with most Attention. I don't speak this from Vanity; for I have been so teazed and tormented about *Wit*, I really wish there was no such thing in the World. I am very certain, the Woman who is possessed of it, unless she can be so peculiarly happy as to live with People void of Envy, had better be without it. The Fate of those Persons who have Wit, is no where so well described, as in those excellent Lines in the *Essay on Criticism*, which are so exactly suited to my present Purpose, I cannot forbear repeating them to you:

> *Unhappy Wit, like most mistaken Things,*
> *Atones not for that Envy which it brings;*
> *In Youth alone its empty Praise we boast,*
> *But soon the short-liv'd Vanity is lost:*
> *Like some fair Flower, the early Spring supplies,*
> *That gayly blooms, but even in blooming dies.*
> *What is this Wit, which must our Cares employ?*
> *The Owner's Wife, that other Men enjoy:*
> *The most our Trouble still, when most admir'd,*
> *The more we give, the more is still requir'd.*
> *The Fame with Pains we gain, but lose with Ease;*
> *Sure some to vex, but never all to please:*
> *'Tis what the Vicious fear, the Virtuous shun,*
> *By Fools 'tis hated, and by Knaves undone.*[1]

'I never spoke, but I was a *Wit*; if I was silent, it was Contempt. I *certainly would not deign to converse with such People as they were*. Thus whatever I did, disobliged them; and it was impossible to be otherwise, as the Cause of

---

[1] Alexander Pope, *An Essay on Criticism* (1711) pp 494–507.

their Displeasure was what I could not remove. I should have been very well pleased with their Conversation, if they had been contented to have been what Nature design'd them; for Good-humour, and a Desire to please, is all I wish for in a Companion; for, in my Opinion, being inoffensive goes a great way in rendering any Person agreeable; but so little did they shew to me, that every Word I spoke was misunderstood, and turned to my Disadvantage. I remember once on my saying, I would follow my Inclinations while they were innocent, and no ill Consequences attended them; my eldest Sister made me so absurd an Answer, I cannot help relating it to you: for she said, *she did not at all doubt, but I would follow my Inclinations, she was really afraid what I should come to, as she saw, I fancied it a Sign of* Wit *to be a* Libertine; a Word which she chose to thunder often in my Ears, as she had heard me frequently express a particular Aversion to those of our Sex who deserve it. Indeed she always exulted, in saying any thing she thought could hurt me: If I dropt an unguarded Word or Expression, they could possibly lay hold on, to turn into what they thought *Ridicule*, the Joy it gave them was incredible; if I took up a Book, they could not comprehend, they suddenly grew very modest, and did not pretend to know what was only *fit for the Learned*. It is really entertaining to see the shifts People make to conceal from themselves their own want of Capacities: for whoever really has Sense, will understand whatever is writ in their own Language, altho' they are intirely ignorant of all others, with an Exception only of the Technical Terms of Sciences. But I was once acquainted with an old Man, who, from a small Suspicion, that he was not thought by the World to be extremely wise, was always considering which way he should flatter himself that the Fault was not in him, but owing to some Accident; till at last, he hit on the Thought that his Folly was caused by his Father's Neglect of him; for he did not at all seem to doubt, but he should have had as much Sense as another if he had but understood *Greek* and *Latin*. As if Languages had a Charm in them, which could banish all *Stupidity and Nonsense* from those who understood them. But to proceed in my Story:

'If Youth and Liveliness sometimes led me into any Action, which they, in their *riper Judgments*, (for the youngest of them was five Years older than myself) termed Indiscretions, they immediately *thanked God, tho' they had no* Wit, *they had* common Sense, *and knew how to conduct themselves in Life, which they thought much more valuable; but* these Wits *had never any Judgment*. This is a Mistake which prevails generally in the World, and, I believe, arises from the strong Desire most Men have to be thought witty; but when they find it's impossible, they would willingly be thought to have a Contempt for it; and perhaps they sometimes have the Art of flattering themselves to such a Degree, as really to believe they do despise it: *For Men often impose so much on their own Understandings, as to triumph in those very Things they would be ashamed of, if their Self-Love would but permit them for a Moment, to see things clearly as they are. They go beyond the Jack-daw in the Fables,[2] who never went farther than to strut about in the Peacock's Feathers, with a design of imposing on others. For they endeavour so long to blind other Men's Eyes, that at last they*

[2] *Phaedrus* I.iii.

quite darken their own; and altho' in their Nature they are certainly Daws, yet they find a Method of persuading themselves that they are Peacocks. But notwithstanding all the Industry People may make use of to blind themselves, *if Wit consists,* as Mr. *Locke* says, *in the Assemblage of Ideas, and Judgment in the separating them;*[3] I really believe the Person who can join them with the most Propriety, *will separate them with the greatest Nicety.* A Metaphor from Mechanism, I think, will very plainly illustrate my Thoughts on this Subject: for let a Machine, of any kind, be joined together by an ingenious Artist, and I dare say, he will be best able to take it apart again: a Bungler, or an ignorant Person, perhaps, may pull it asunder, or break it to pieces; but to separate it nicely, and know how to divide it in the right Places, will certainly be the best performed, by the Man who had Skill enough to set it together. But with strong Passions, and lively Imaginations, People may sometimes be led into Errors, altho' their Judgments are ever so good; and when Persons, who are esteemed by the World to have Wit, are guilty of any Failing, all *the Envious,* (and I am afraid they are too great a part of the human Species) set up a general Outcry against them.'

David, into whose Head not one envious Thought ever entered, could easily comprehend the Reasonableness of what *Cynthia* said, tho' he was at a loss for Examples of such Behaviour, but was too well pleased with her Manner of talking to interrupt her: And she thus continued her Story:

'We had a young Cousin lived with us, who was the Daughter of my Father's Brother, she was the oddest Character I ever knew; for she certainly could not be said to have any Understanding, and yet she had one of the strongest signs of Sense that could be: For she was so conscious of her Defect that way, that it made her so bashful, she never spoke but with Fear and Trembling, lest she should make herself ridiculous. This poor Creature would have been made a perfect *Mope,* had it not been for me; for she was the only Person I ever submitted to flatter. I always approved whatever she said, and never failed asking her Opinion, whenever I could contrive to do it without appearing to make a Jest of her. This was the highest Joy to my Sisters, who thought that in this Instance, at least, they could prove my want of Sense and their own *Superiority*; for their Delight was in making a *Butt* of this poor Girl, by *rallying,* as they were pleased to term it, and putting her out of countenance.'

'Pray, Madam, (said *David*) what is the meaning of making a Butt of any one?' *Cynthia* replied, 'It is setting up a Person as a Mark to be scorned, and pointed at for some Defect of Body or Mind, and this without any Offence committed, to provoke such Treatment: Nay, on the contrary, it generally falls on the Bashful and Innocent; and when a poor Creature is thus undeservedly put to the Torment of feeling the uneasy Sensation of Shame, these *Railliers* exult in the Thoughts of their own *Wit.* To be witty without either Blasphemy, Obscenity, or Ill-nature, requires a great deal more than every Person, who heartily desires the Reputation of being so, can come up to; but I have made it my Observation, in all the Families I have ever seen, that if any one Person in it is more remarkably silly than the rest, those who approach in the next

---

[3] John Locke, *An Essay Concerning Human Understanding* (1690) II.xi.2.

degree to them, always despise them the most; they are as glad to find any
one below them, whom they may triumph over and laugh at, as they are
envious and angry to see any one above them; *as Cowards kick and abuse
the Person who is known to be a Degree more timorous than themselves, as
much as they tremble at the Frown of any one, who has more Courage.* Thus
my Sisters always treated my Cousin as a *Fool*, while they upbraided me with
being a *Wit*; little knowing, that if that Term has any Meaning at all, when it
is used by way of Contempt, they were the very People who deserved to be
called so. For if I understand it, it is then used to signify a Person with but a
very moderate Share of Understanding, who from Affectation, and an insatiable
Desire of being thought witty, grows impertinent, and says all the ill natured
things he can think of. For my part, I conceive all manner of Raillery to be the
most disagreeable Conversation in the World, unless it be amongst those People
who have Politeness and Delicacy enough to railly in the manner *La Bruyere*[4]
speaks of; that is to fall only on such Frailties as People of Sense voluntarily give
up to Censure: these are the best Subjects to display Humour, as it turns into a
Compliment to the Person raillied, being a sort of Insinuation that they have
no greater Faults to be fallen upon.

'When I was about sixteen, I became acquainted with a young Lady, in whose
Conversation I had the utmost Pleasure; but I had not often an Opportunity of
seeing her: for as she too was fond of Reading, my Mother was frighten'd out
of her Wits, to think what would become of us, if we were much together. I
verily believe, she thought we should draw *Circles*, and turn *Conjurers*. Every
new Acquaintance we had, increased my Sisters' Aversion to me; for as I was
generally liked best, they were in a continual Rage at seeing I was taken so
much notice of. But the only Proof of their Sense they ever gave me, was the
being irritated more than usual, at the Fondness which was shewn me by this
young Woman: for since they could be so low as to be envious, there was
more Understanding in being so at my attaining what was really valuable, than
at what was of no consequence, and gave me no other Pleasure but finding
it was in my power to give it; which was the Case with most of the People I
conversed with.

'When I was seventeen, my Mother died, and after that, I got with more
Freedom to my Companion; for my Father did not trouble himself much about
me, he had given way to my Mother's Method of educating me, as indeed he
always complied with her in every thing; not that he had any extraordinary
Affection for her, but she was one of those *sort of Women*, who, if they once
take any thing in *their Heads*, will never *be quiet* till they have attained it; and
as he was of a Disposition which naturally loved Quietness, he would sooner
consent to any thing, than hear a Noise.

'One Day, at Dinner, my Father told me, *if I would be a* good Girl, *I should
be* married *very soon*. I laugh'd and said, I hoped, I should see the Man who
was to be my Husband, at least an Hour before-hand. *Yes, yes*, replied he, *you
shall see him time enough; but it suffices I have an Offer for you, which I think to*

---

[4] Jean de La Bruyère (1645–96), ironist, essayist and epigrammatist.

your Advantage, and I expect your Obedience; you know, your Mother always obeyed me, and I will be Master of my own Family. I really could hardly forbear laughing in his face; but as I thought that would be very unbecoming in me to my Father, I turned the Discourse as fast as possible. My Sisters both fell out a laughing; one cried, *Oh! now we shall have fine Diversion,* Cynthia *will be a charming* Mistress of a Family. *I wonder which of her* Books *will teach her to be a* Housewife. *Yes,* says the other, *undoubtedly her Husband will be mightily pleased, when he wants his Dinner, to find she has been all the Morning diverting herself with* Reading, *and forgot to order any; which I dare say will be the Case.* I had now been so long used to them that what they said gave me no manner of Concern, and I was seldom at the trouble of answering them.

'The next day my Father brought a Country Gentleman home to dinner with him, who was a perfect Stranger to me: I did not take much notice of him, for he had nothing remarkable in him; he was neither handsome nor ugly, tall nor short, old nor young; he had something, indeed, of a Rusticity in his Person; what he said, had nothing entertaining in it, either in a serious or merry way, and yet it was neither silly nor ridiculous. In short, I might be in Company with a thousand such sort of Men, and quite forget I had ever seen them: but I was greatly surprized after dinner, at my Father's calling me out of the Room, and telling me, *that was the Gentleman he designed for my Husband; that he expected me to receive him as such, and he would take the first Opportunity to leave us together, that my Lover might explain himself.* Which, as soon as he could contrive it, he did, by sending my Sisters and Cousin, one after another, out of the Room, and then withdrawing himself. I had so ridiculous an Idea of being thus shut up with a Stranger, in order to be made Love to, that I could not resist the Temptation of making a little Diversion with a Person who appeared to me in so despicable a Light. The Gentleman took three or four strides across the Room, looked out of the Window once or twice, and then turned to me, with an *aukward* Bow, and an *irresistable* Air, (as I fancy he thought it) and made me the polite Compliment, of telling me, *that he supposed my Father had informed me that they two were agreed on a Bargain.* I replied, I did not know my Father was of any Trade, or had any Goods to dispose of; but if he had, and they could agree on their Terms, he should have my Consent, for I never interfered with any Business of my Father's: And went on rattling a good while, till he was quite out in his Catechism, and knew not what to say. But he soon recollected himself, for he had all the Assurance of a Man, who from knowing he has a good *Fortune,* thinks he does every Woman an *Honour* he *condescends* to speak to; and *assured me, I must interfere in* this *Business, as it more particularly concerned me. In short, Madam,* continued he, *I have seen you two or three times, altho' you did not know it; I like your Person, hear you have had a sober Education, think it time to have an* Heir to my Estate, *and am willing, if you consent to it, to make you my Wife; notwithstanding your Father tells me, he can't lay you down above two thousand Pounds. I am none of those nonsensical Fools that can whine and make romantick Love, I leave that to* younger Brothers, *let my Estate speak for me; I shall expect nothing from you, but that you will retire into the Country with me, and take care of my Family. I must inform you, I shall desire to have every thing in order; for I love good* Eating and Drinking, *and have been used to have my own Humour from my Youth, which, if you will observe and comply with, I shall be very kind to you, and take care of the* main Chance *for you and your Children.* I made him a low Court'sey, and thanked him for the Honour he intended me; but told him, I had no kind of Ambition to be his *upper Servant*: Tho', indeed, I could not help wondring how it was possible for me to escape being charmed with his *genteel Manner* of addressing me. I then asked him how many Offices he had allotted for me to perform, for those great Advantages he had offered me, of suffering me to humour him in all his Whims, and to receive Meat, Drink, and Lodging at his hands; but hoped he would allow me some *small Wages*, that I might now and then recreate myself with my *Fellow-Servants*. In short, my Youth led me into indulging myself in a foolish Ridicule, for which I now condemn myself. He grew angry at my laughing at him, and left me, saying, *he should let my Father know in what manner I had used him; that I might very likely repent the refusing him, for such* Estates *as his were not to be met with every day*.

'I could not help reflecting on the Folly of those Women who *prostitute* themselves, (*for I shall always call it Prostitution, for a Woman who has Sense, and has been tolerably educated, to marry a Clown and a Fool*) and give up that Enjoyment, which every one who has taste enough to know how to employ their time, can procure for themselves, tho' they should be obliged to live ever so retired, only to know they have married a Man who has an Estate; for they very often have no more Command of it, than if they were perfect Strangers. Some Men, indeed, delight in seeing their Wives finer than their Neighbours; which to those Women, whose whole Thoughts are fixed on fine Clothes, may be a Pleasure; but, for my part, I should in that case think myself just in the Situation of the Horse who wears *gaudy Trappings* only to gratify his *Master's Vanity*, whilst he himself is not at all considered in them. I was certain I could live much more to my Satisfaction on the Interest of my own little Fortune, than I could do with subjecting myself to the Humours of a Man I must have always disliked and despised.

'I don't know how it was brought about, but this Man married my second Sister, and she took the other away with her, so that I was happily rid of them both. My Father was very angry with me for the present; but I thought that would be soon over, and did not at all doubt his being reconciled to me again. I now began to flatter myself, that I should lead a Life perfectly suitable to my Taste; my Cousin was very fond of me, for I was the only Woman she had ever met with, who had not shewn a Contempt for her. I carried her with me where-ever I went, and had the Pleasure of seeing I was the Cause of her being happy. I conversed as much as I pleased with my beloved Companion, and *Books and Friendship shared my peaceful Hours*. But this lasted but a very short time; for my Father, in the heat of his Anger against me, made a *Will*, in which he left me nothing; and before his Rage abated enough for him to alter it, he died of an Apoplexy. As soon as my Sisters heard of his Death, they hurried to Town; when the *Will* was opened, and they found I was excluded

from having any share in my Father's Fortune; they triumphed over me with
all the Insolence imaginable, and vented all their usual Reproaches; saying, *it
was impossible but that a Person of my great* Wit *and* Genius *must be able to
provide for myself, they did not doubt but I could shift very well without Money.*
Thus this unpardonable Crime of being thought to have more Sense than they
had, was never to be forgiven; they staid no longer in town, than while they
were settling their Affairs, and left me with but five Guineas, which I happened
to have saved out of my Pocket-Money, while my Father was alive. The young
Woman I have so often mentioned to you, was so generous as to let me have
all the the little Money she was mistress of. I wish nothing so much as to see
her again; but while I was abroad, she and her Brother went from their Father's
House, on his bringing home a Mother-in-law, and I cannot hear what is become
of them. Whilst I was in this Situation, my Lady——, with whom I had had a small
Acquaintance for some time, took such a fancy to me, she invited me to come
and live with her; she seemed as if she loved me, and I was ignorant enough
of the World to think she did so. She was going abroad, and as I had a great
Desire to see more Countries than my own, I proposed to myself a great deal
of Pleasure in going with her: the only Regret I had, was in leaving my dear
Companion, but I was not in Circumstances to refuse my Lady——'s Offer.

'And now I am come to the Conclusion of my History, whilst I went
under the Denomination of a *Wit*, and am really quite tired of talking; but if
you have a Curiosity to know the rest of my History, and will favour me with
your Company to-morrow, I will resume it.' *David* assured her, nothing could
oblige him more, and in a little while took his leave of her for that Night.

CHAPTER VII

DAVID went exactly at the Time appointed the next Day, and after some little
Discourse, *Cynthia* went on with her Story, as follows:
'I think I left off at my going abroad with my Lady. My Cousin went home
to live with her Mother; as they had but a very small Income to keep them,
I should have been heartily glad if it had been in my power to have increased
it. I forgot to tell you, that my Brother died at School, when he was fifteen; for
he had but a weakly Constitution, and the continual tormenting and whipping
him, to make him learn his Book (which was utterly impossible) had such an
Effect on the poor Boy, it threw him into a Consumption, of which he died. I
shall not undertake to give you a Description of the Countries through which
we passed for as we were only to make the Tour of *France* and *Italy*, I suppose
you have read a hundred Descriptions of them already. The Lady I went with, had
something very amiable in her Manner, and at first behaved to me with so much
Good-nature, that I loved her with the utmost Sincerity. I dwelt with pleasure
on the Thoughts of the Obligations I owed her, as I fancied she was generous
enough to delight in conferring them; and I had none of that sort of *Pride, by
Fools mistaken for Greatness of Mind*, which makes People disdain the receiving

Obligations: for I think the only Meanness consists in accepting, and not gratefully acknowledging them. I had learned *French*, that is, I had read some *French* Books with the help of a Dictionary, to satisfy my own Curiosity; for no body had ever taught me any thing: On the contrary, I was to be kept back as much as possible, for fear I should *know too much*. But the little I had learned by myself, helped me when I came into the Country, to talk it tolerable well. My Lady————could not speak it at all, and as she did not care to take much pains while we were in *Paris*, which was a whole Winter, we herded mostly amongst the *English*.

'I was now in the place of the World I had often most wished to go to, where I had every thing in great plenty, and yet I was more miserable than ever. Perhaps you will wonder what caused my Unhappiness; but I was to appear in a Character I could not bear, namely, that of a *Toad-eater*: and what hurt me most, was, that my Lady herself soon began to take pains to throw me into it as much as possible.'

David *begged an Explanation of what she meant by a* Toad-eater; *for he said it was a Term he had never heard before*. On which *Cynthia* replied, 'I don't wonder, Sir, you never heard of it, I wish I had spent my Life without knowing the Meaning of it: It is a Metaphor taken from a Mountebank's Boy who eats Toads, in order to shew his Master's Skill in expelling Poison: It is built on a Supposition, (which I am afraid is too generally true) that People who are so unhappy as to be in a State of Dependance, are forced to do the most nauseous things that can be thought on, to please and humour their Patrons. And the Metaphor may be carried on yet farther, for most People have so much the Art of tormenting, that every time they have made the poor Creatures they have in their power *swallow a Toad*, they give them something to expel it again, that they may be ready to swallow the next they think proper to prepare for them: that is, when they have abused and fooled them, as *Hamlet* says, *to the top of their bent*,[5] they grow soft and good to them again, on purpose to have it in their power to *plague them the more*. The *Satire* of the Expression, in reality, falls on the Person who is mean enough to act in so cruel a manner to their Dependent; but as it is no uncommon thing for People to make use of Terms they don't understand, it is generally used, by way of *Derision*, to the unfortunate Wretch who is thrown into such a miserable Situation.

'I remember once I went with my Lady————to visit some *English* Ladies, where there happened to be a great deal of Company: As we went out of the Room, I heard some-body mention the word *Toad-eater*; I thought it was me they were speaking of, and dropt my Fan, for an Excuse to make a stop at the Door; when I heard one Lady say to another,—*What a* creature it is! *I* believe she *is* dumb, *for she has not spoke one Word since she has been here; but yet I don't dislike to see her, for I love* Ridicule of all things, *and there is certainly nothing so* ridiculous as a Toad-eater. I could not stay to hear any more; but I despised both these Women too much to let it be in their power to give me any Pain, for I knew by their manner of talking they were *fine Ladies*; and that is the Character in Life I have the greatest Contempt for.'

5 *Hamlet*, III, 2.

David *begged her to let him know what she meant by fine Ladies.* On which she replied, 'Indeed, Sir, you have imposed on me the hardest Task in the World: I know them when I meet with them; but they have so little of what we call Character, that I don't know how to go about the describing them. They are made up of *Caprice* and *Whim*; they *love* and *hate*, are angry and pleased, without being able to assign a Reason for any of these Passions. If they have a *Characteristick*, it is *Vanity*, to which every thing else seems to be subservient; they always affect a great deal of *Good-nature*, are frightened out of their Wits at the sight of any Object in bodily Pain, and yet value not how much they rack People's Minds. But I must justify them so far as to say, I believe this is owing to their Ignorance; for as they have no *Minds of their own, they have no Idea of others Sensations.* They cannot, I think, well be liable to the Curse attending *Eve's* Transgression, as they do not enjoy the Benefit proposed by it, of knowing *Good from Evil.* They are so very *wise*, as to think a Person's being ignorant of what is utterly impossible they should know, is a perfect sign of *Folly. Congreve* seems to me to have know them the best of any one: My Lady *Wish-for't* at her Toilette[6] is a perfect Picture of them, where she insults over, and thinks herself witty on a poor ignorant Wench, because she does not know what she has never been taught, or used to. That fine Ridicule of the *Brass-Thimble*, and the *Nutmeg jingling in her Pocket*, with the Hands dangling like Bobbins, is exactly their sort of Wit; and then they never call any one by their right Names, *Creatures, Animals, Things*, all the Words of Contempt they can think of, are what they delight in. *Shakespear* has made *Hamlet* give the best Description imaginable of them, in that one Line which he addresses to *Ophelia;—Ye lisp—and ye amble,—and ye nick-name God's Creatures.*[7] An Expression I never understood, till I knew the World enough to have met with some of those sort of Women. They are not confined to any Station; for I have known, while the Lady has been insulting her Waiting-woman in the Dressing-Room, the Chamber-Maid has been playing just the same Part below stairs, with the Person she thought her inferior, only with a small Variation of Terms. But I will dwell no longer on them; for I am tired of them, as I have often been in Life.

'But this would have had no Effect on me, had my Lady behaved well herself. To her Usage was owing all my Misery; for by that time I had remained with her two or three Months, she began to treat me as a *Creature* born to be her *Slave*: whenever I spoke, I was sure to offend her; if I was *silent*, I was *out of humour*; if I said any thing in the softest Terms, to complain of the Alteration of her Affection, I was *whimsical* and *ungrateful.* I think it impossible to be in a worse Situation. She had raised my Love, by the Obligations she had confer'd on me, and yet continually provoked my Rage by her Ill-nature: I could not, for a great while, any way account for this Conduct: I thought, if she did not love me, she had no Reason to have given herself any trouble about me; and yet I could not think she could have used one for whom she had had the least Regard

[6] In Congreve's *The Way of the World* (1700), III, 1, Lady Wishfort mocks her maid Peg for her lack of sophistication and quickness.
[7] *Hamlet*, III, ii.

in so cruel a manner. At last, I reflected, it must be owing to a love of *Tyranny*, and as we are born in a Country where there is no such thing as public, legal Slavery, People lay Plots to draw in others to be their Slaves, with the pretence of having an Affection for them: And what is yet more unfortunate, they always chuse the Persons who are least able to bear it. It's the fierce mettled Courser (who must be brought to their Lure by fawning and stroaking) that they love to wring, and gird the Saddle on; whilst the Mule, which seems born to bear their Burdens, passes by them unheeded and neglected. I was caught, like the poor Fish, by the Bait which was treacherously extended for me, and did not observe the *Hook* which was to pierce *my Heart*, and be my Destruction. You cannot imagine what I felt; for to be used ungratefully, by any one I had confer'd Favours on, would have been nothing to me, in comparison of being ill used by the Person I thought myself obliged to. I was to have no *Passions*, no *Inclinations* of my own; but was to be turned into a piece of Clock-work, which her Ladyship was to wind up or let down, as she pleased. I had Resolution enough to have borne any Consequence that might have attended my leaving her; but I could not bear the Thoughts of even the Imputation of Ingratitude; *for there are very few People, who have any Notion of Obligations which are not pecuniary*. But, in my Opinion, those Persons who give up their Time, and sacrifice all their own Inclinations, to the Humours of others, cannot be over-paid by any thing they can do for them. Men never think a Slave obliged to them for giving him Bread, when he has performed his Task. And certainly it is a double Slavery to be made *servile* under the pretence of *Friendship*; for no Labour of the Body could have been so painful to me, as the having my Mind thus teazed and tortured. My *Wit*, which I had heard so much of, was now all fled; for I was looked on in so contemptible a Light, that nobody would hearken to me: The only Comfort I had, was in the Conversation of a *led Captain*,[8] who came abroad with a Gentleman of my Lady's Acquaintance. There are two sorts of led Captains; the one is taken a fancy to by somebody much above him, seated at his Superior's Table, and can *cringe and flatter, fetch and carry Nonsense for my Lord*; thinking himself happy in being thus admitted into Company, whom his Sphere of Life gives him no Pretensions to keep. The other is a sort of Male Toad-eater, who by some Misfortune in Life is thrown down below his proper Station, meets with a Patron who pretends to be *his Friend*; and who by that means draws him in to be sincerely his. This Gentleman's Case and mine were so much alike, that our greatest Pleasure was in comparing them; but I was much more astonished at his Patron's Behaviour than at my Lady——'s, for altho' she had a tolerable Understanding, yet it was not of that sort, which would make one wonder at her Frailties. But he was remarkable for his Sense and Wit, and yet could not forbear making this poor Gentleman feel all the weight of *Dependance*. He was so inconsistent with himself, he could not bear he should see his *Tyranny*, because he was very *fond* of gaining every body's Esteem; not considering his Aim would have been lost, if the other had not been sensible of his Behaviour: but because he saw him uneasy under it, he took a perfect Aversion to him. I have heard of a Gentleman, who would

[8] A hanger-on or dependant.

never go to another's House, if he had ever so many Coaches and Six to carry
him in, without Horses of *his own*: saying, *the only Way to be treated well, was
to shew People he had it in his power to* leave them whenever he pleased. And
I think he was perfectly in the right; for melancholy Experience has taught me
how miserable it is to abandon one's self to another's Power. But now to shew
you the unaccountable Caprice of Human Nature, I must tell you, that this very
Gentleman, who had thus *groaned* under the Affliction of another's using him
ill, coming to an Estate which was entailed on him by a Cousin's dying without
Children, became the greatest *Tyrant in the World*; and kept a *led Captain*, whom
he used much worse than his former Patron had ever done him: And instead
of avoiding the treating another in a manner he himself had found so difficult
to bear, he seemed as if he was resolved to revenge his former Sufferings, on a
Person who was perfectly innocent of them.

'I know not to what Malignity it is owing, but I have observed, in all
the Families I have ever been acquainted with, that one part of them spend
their whole time in oppressing and teazing the other; and all this they do like
Drawcansir, only *because they dare*, and to shew their power: While the other
Part languish away their Days, in bemoaning their own hard Fate, which has
thus subjected them to the Whims and Tyranny of *Wretches*, who are so *totally
void of Taste, as not to desire the Affection of the very People they appear willing
to oblige*. It's late to-night; but if you have a Curiosity to hear the Remainder of
my Story, to-morrow I will proceed.'

David, who never desired any one to do what was the least irksome, took
his leave for that Evening, and returned the next day, according to *Cynthia's*
own Appointment.

CHAPTER VIII

THE next Evening, after the usual Civilities had passed between *David* and
Cynthia, she, at his Request, went on with her Story.

'I spent the whole time I was abroad in Misery; because my Lady——chose
to see me *unhappy*, and *sighing* at her *Tyranny*, instead of viewing me always
(which she might have done) with *cheerful Looks*, and a Countenance expressive
of the most *grateful Acknowledgments*, for owing a Life of *Ease* and *Plenty* to
her *Benevolence*.'

David, whose only Pleasure was in giving it others, was more amazed
at this Account of my Lady——'s Behaviour, than he would have been at
the most surprizing Phænomenon in Nature: But he had so much Curiosity
to know the End of *Cynthia's* Story, that he would not interrupt her: And she
went on as follows.

'Since our Arrival in *England*, an Accident has happened to me, which
was as little thought on as wish'd for. My Lady——has a Nephew of about
seventeen Years of Age, who after the Death of his Father, will be Earl of——,
with a great Estate. This young Man took such a Fancy to me, that the very
first Opportunity he had of speaking to me alone, he made me a Proposal of

Marriage. This is, in my Opinion, a very odd way of proceeding; but it is not very uncommon amongst Men who think themselves so much *above us*, that there is no danger of a Refusal; and consequently that they may be excused the *usual Forms* on such Occasions. I was, at first, so surprized, I knew not what to answer; but as soon as I could recollect my Thoughts, and revolve in my Mind the Situation I was in, I told him that I was infinitely obliged to him, for his good Opinion of me; but that as I lived in my Lady——'s House, I should think myself guilty of the utmost *Treachery*, to marry so near a Relation of her's without her Consent; and as in my Circumstances I was not likely to obtain that, I begged him to give up all Thoughts of it. The more I refused him, the more earnest he was with me to comply: But while we were talking, my Lady——entered the Room. I could not help blushing and looking confused, and my Lord —— was almost as much so as myself. She has very penetrating Eyes, and immediately saw something extraordinary had happened. However, she said nothing till my Lord —— was gone, when she insisted on knowing the whole Truth, and was so very pressing, that at last I told it her; as I had done nothing I had any reason to be ashamed of, but acted (as I thought) with great *Honour* towards my Lady—— I had no Suspicion, that letting her know her Nephew liked me, could possibly turn out to my Disadvantage. But the Moment I had complied with her Desire, in openly declaring the Cause of that Confusion she had observed in us both, at her Entrance, she flew into as great a *Rage*, as if I had been guilty of the worst of Crimes; talked in her usual Style, of my *Ingratitude*; said, *It was a fine Return for all her Kindness, to endeavour to draw in her Nephew to marry me*. All I could say or do, could not pacify her. She immediately sent to my Lord's Father, who carried his Son out of town, and intends to send him abroad, in order to prevent his seeing me any more.

'And now I am to be used ten times worse than ever I was: But I shall not bear it much longer; for let the Consequence be what it will, I am sure I cannot lead a more unhappy Life than I do at present. I verily believe, if my Lord —— was to marry *any other Woman*, without a *Fortune*, it would not give her half the Uneasiness; but to think that a Person, whom she has so long looked on as her *Subject*, should have an Opportunity of becoming her *Equal*, is more than she can bear. Thus, Sir, I am come to the End of my Story: I wish there was any thing more entertaining in it; but your desiring to know it, appeared to me to arise from so much Good-nature and Compassion for the Afflicted, I could not refuse to gratify your Curiosity.'

David assured her, 'if it was any way in his Power to serve her, he should have the utmost Pleasure in doing it; and that if she thought it proper to leave my Lady——, and go into a Lodging by herself, he would supply her with whatever she wanted: That she had no Reason to be afraid, that he should upbraid her with being *obliged* to him; for that, on the contrary, he should be thankful to her for giving him an Opportunity of being any ways useful to a Person of her *Merit*: For that he had observed the World in general was so very mercenary, he could not help being at once pleased and surprized, to find a Person of her Age, and in her Circumstances, who had Resolution enough to think of refusing any Offer that was for her advantage, from a Notion of Honour.'

Whilst they were in this Discourse, my Lady——, who had altered her Mind, and did not stay out of town as long as she at first intended, returned home. *David* thinking he might be troublesome at her first coming off her Journey, soon retired, and the Moment he was gone, my Lady——vented all the most ill-natured Reproaches on poor *Cynthia*, she could think on; saying, 'she supposed, now her House was to be made the Receptacle for all the *young Fellows* in town:— That she was sure there must be something very *forward in her Behaviour*, for it could not be her *Beauty* that drew Men after her.'—In short, she treated her as if she had been the most *infamous* Creature alive; nor did she scruple to do this before all the Servants in her House. I suppose, besides her natural Love of Tyranny, she was one of those sort of Women, who, like *Venus* in *Telemachus*,[9] lose the Pleasure of their numberless *Votaries*, if one Mortal escapes their Snares. Besides, she thought it insupportable, that *a Wretch*, whom she looked upon to be so much *below* her as *Cynthia*, should have any Charms at all.

The next Day, *David* went to see her again, and as my Lady——was gone to make a Visit, he met with *Cynthia* alone: He found her dissolved in Tears, and in such an Agony, that she was hardly able to speak to him: At last, however, she informed him in what manner my Lady——had used her, because he happened to be there when she came home. *David* begged her not to bear this Treatment any longer, but to accept his Offer; and assured her, he would both protect and support her, if she would give him leave. *Cynthia* was charmed with his generous manner of offering to assist her, but said, her case was the most to be lamented in the world; for that if she accepted what he with so much Good-nature offered her, it would be in my Lady——'s Power (and she was certain it would be in her Will) to make her infamous. But on an Assurance from *David*, that he would submit to what Rules she pleased, supply her with whatever she wanted, and at the same time deny himself even the Pleasure of seeing her, if she thought it proper, she at last consented, and they consulted together the Method they should take. They agreed that *Cynthia* should leave a place she so much detested, as the House where she then was, the next day. But she said, she would acquaint my Lady——with her Resolution, that it might not look like running away from her: She was very sensible, she must bear great Invectives and Reproaches; but however, she thought she should be able to go through them, as she hoped it would be the last time.

David was to take her a Lodging, and send her word by some Woman, where it was, that she might go to it without his appearing in the Affair. When they had settled every thing to their Satisfaction, he took his leave, that he might not be there when my Lady——came home. Now the Anxiety was over, *for the Perplexity which is caused by not knowing how to act, is the greatest Torment imaginable*; but as *Cynthia* had fixed her Resolution, her Mind was calmer and her Countenance more cheerful than it had been for some time. My Lady——designed that Evening to use her very well, which she generally did once a week or fortnight, as if she laid a plot sometimes just to give her a

---

[9] Fenelon's didactic play, *Télémaque* (1699) in which Venus persecutes Telemachus for disdaining her worship.

taste of Pleasure, only to make her feel the want of it the more. But when she saw her look pleased, and on inquiry found that *David* had been there, her Designs were altered, and she could not forbear abusing her. But the moment she began, *Cynthia*, instead of keeping her usual Silence, intreated her to give her one quarter of an Hour's Attention; which, after two or three Speeches, which my Lady——thought *Witticisms*, (such as, *That what she said must be worth hearkening to; That may be, her new Gallant had put some fresh Nonsense in her Head*;) was at last obtained: When *Cynthia* began as follows.

'I confess, Madam, you took me from *Poverty* and *Distress*, and gave me *Plenty*; I own the Obligation, nor have I ever, even in my Thoughts, tried to lessen it. *The moment Pride makes any of us wish or endeavour, by the Power of Imagination and Fallacy, to lose the Sense of Favours conferred on us, all Gratitude must necessarily be at an end.* Had you behaved to me, as I first flattered myself you intended, your Ladyship in me might have had a *willing Slave*: I should have thought my Life would have been but a small Sacrifice, could any Interest of your's have required it. Nay, I have already done more, I have given up my Youth, the time which is the most valuable in Life, to please all your *Whims*, and comply with all your *Humours*. You have chose, that instead of looking on you as my *generous Benefactress*, I should find you an *arbitrary Tyrant*: the Laws of *England* will not suffer you to make *Slaves of your Servants*, nor will I bear it any longer. I am certain, the meanest Person in your House has not gone thro' half what I have done for *Bread*: And, in short, Madam, here your Power is at an end, to-morrow I shall take my leave of you; I cannot help wishing you happy, but must own, I heartily hope you will never have any body so much in your *Power* again.'

My Lady, who had been used to be treated by every thing in her House, (*her Husband not excepted*) with the greatest deference, swelled and reddened at this Discourse of *Cynthia's*, till at last, for want of Words to vent her Rage, she *burst into Tears. Cynthia*, whose Good-nature nothing could exceed, thinking this arose from my Lady's *Consciousness* of her own wrong Behaviour, was softened, and threw herself at her Feet, asked ten thousand Pardons, said *if she could have guessed the Effect what she said would have had on her, she would sooner have been for ever dumb, than have utter'd a Word to offend her.* But, alas! how was she mistaken? For as soon as my Lady——'s Tears had made way for her Words, she fell upon her with all the most bitter *Invectives* she could think of, and even descended so far as to forget her Quality, (*which was seldom out of her Thoughts*) and use the most vulgar Terms, in order to abuse her. *Cynthia*, who had a great Aversion to all Broils and Quarrels, seeing her Passion was so high, said no more, but let her rail on, till it was time to go to bed.

When *Cynthia* waked the next Morning, she thought she had now per- formed her Duty in informing my Lady —— of her Design to leave her, and therefore *chose* not to bear any farther Abuses from her: so that as soon as *David's* Messenger came, which was very early, she went with her, without any more *Ceremony*, to the Lodging he had taken for her. And here, I doubt not, but the graver sort of my Female Readers will be as ready to condemn *Cynthia* for taking such a Step, and thus putting herself in the power of a Man, with whom she had had so short an Acquaintance, as my Lady —— herself was. I do not pretend wholly to justify her; *but, without doubt, there are some Circumstances in Life, where the Distress is so high, and the Mind in such an Anxiety, that a Person may be pardoned the being thrown so much off their guard, as to be drawn into Actions, which, in the common Occurrences of Life, would admit of no Alleviation.*

Mary Leapor
1722 – 46

*M*ary Leapor was one of a long line of peasant or working-class poets who responded to the vogue for primitive and spontaneous art. The most famous female example was probably Ann Yearsley in the late eighteenth century, partly because she quarrelled very publicly with her patron Hannah More and partly because she emphasized her own status as victimized woman and marginal writer. On the whole the peasant poets wrote conventional verse and were eager to show competence in the standard literary genres of their day, but many also wrote about their sorry position as both female and poor. Mary Leapor, the daughter of a gardener, died when she was only twenty-four.

The following poems appear in Poems upon Several Occasions, which was published posthumously in 1748 and 1751.

An Essay on Woman

WOMAN, a pleasing but a short-lived flow'r,
    Too soft for business and too weak for pow'r:
A wife in bondage, or neglected maid;

Despised, if ugly; if she's fair, betrayed.
'Tis wealth alone inspires ev'ry grace,
And calls the raptures to her plenteous face.
What numbers for those charming features pine,
If blooming acres round her temples twine!
Her lip the strawberry, and her eyes more bright
Than sparkling Venus in a frosty night;
Pale lilies fade and, when the fair appears,
Snow turns a negro and dissolves in tears,
And, where the charmer treads her magic toe,
On English ground Arabian odours grow;
Till mighty Hymen lifts his sceptred rod,
And sinks her glories with a fatal nod,
Dissolves her triumphs, sweeps her charms away,
And turns the goddess to her native clay.
    But, Artemisia,[1] let your servant sing
What small advantage wealth and beauties bring.
Who would be wise, that knew Pamphilia's fate?
Or who be fair, and joined to Sylvia's mate?
Sylvia, whose cheeks are fresh as early day,
As ev'ning mild, and sweet as spicy May:
And yet that face her partial husband tires,
And those bright eyes, that all the world admires.
Pamphilia's wit who does not strive to shun,
Like death's infection or a dog-day's sun?[2]
The damsels view her with malignant eyes,
The men are vexed to find a nymph so wise:
And wisdom only serves to make her know
The keen sensation of superior woe.
The secret whisper and the list'ning ear,
The scornful eyebrow and the hated sneer,
The giddy censures of her babbling kind,
With thousand ills that grate a gentle mind,
By her are tasted in the first degree,
Though overlooked by Simplicus and me.
Does thirst of gold a virgin's heart inspire,
Instilled by nature or a careful sire?
Then let her quit extravagance and play,
The brisk companion and expensive tea,
To feast with Cordia in her filthy sty
On stewed potatoes or on mouldy pie;

---

[1] A poetic name for Bridget Freemantle, a rector's daughter, who was trying to raise a subscription for Leapor when the poet died of measles after a long period of ill health.
[2] The days when the dog-star (Sirius) was rising, thought to be the hottest and most unwholesome period of the year.

Whose eager eyes stare ghastly at the poor,
And fright the beggars from her hated door;
In greasy clouts she wraps her smoky chin,
And holds that pride's a never-pardoned sin.
   If this be wealth, no matter where it falls;
But save, ye Muses, save your Mira's[3] walls:
Still give me pleasing indolence and ease,
A fire to warm me and a friend to please.
   Since, whether sunk in avarice or pride,
A wanton virgin or a starving bride;
Or wond'ring crowds attend her charming tongue,
Or, deemed an idiot, ever speaks the wrong;
Though nature armed us for the growing ill
With fraudful cunning and a headstrong will;
Yet, with ten thousand follies to her charge,
Unhappy woman's but a slave at large.

An Epistle to a Lady

IN vain, dear Madam, yes, in vain you strive,
  Alas! to make your luckless Mira thrive,
For Tycho and Copernicus agree,
No golden planet bent its rays on me.
   'Tis twenty winters, if it is no more,
To speak the truth it may be twenty-four:
As many springs their 'pointed space have run,
Since Mira's eyes first opened on the sun.
'Twas when the flocks on slabby[4] hillocks lie,
And the cold Fishes rule the watry sky:
But though these eyes the learned page explore,
And turn the pond'rous volumes o'er and o'er,
I find no comfort from their systems flow,
But am dejected more as more I know.
Hope shines a while, but like a vapour flies
(The fate of all the curious and the wise),
For, ah! cold Saturn triumphed on that day,
And frowning Sol denied his golden ray.
   You see I'm learned, and I show't the more,
That none may wonder when they find me poor.

[3] Poetic name for herself.
[4] Damp and muddy.

Yet Mira dreams, as slumb'ring poets may,
And rolls in treasures till the breaking day,
While books and pictures in bright order rise,
And painted parlours swim before her eyes:
Till the shrill clock impertinently rings,
And the soft visions move their shining wings:
Then Mira wakes—her pictures are no more,
And through her fingers slides the vanished ore.
Convinced too soon, her eye unwilling falls
On the blue curtains and the dusty walls:
She wakes, alas! to business and to woes,
To sweep her kitchen, and to mend her clothes.
   But see pale Sickness with her languid eyes,
At whose appearance all delusion flies:
The world recedes, its vanities decline,
Clorinda's features seem as faint as mine;
Gay robes no more the aching sight admires,
Wit grates the ear, and melting music tires.
Its wonted pleasures with each sense decay,
Books please no more, and paintings fade away,
The sliding joys in misty vapours end:
Yet let me still, ah! let me grasp a friend:
And when each joy, when each loved object flies,
Be you the last that leaves my closing eyes.
   But how will this dismantled soul appear,
When stripped of all it lately held so dear,
Forced from its prison of expiring clay,
Afraid and shiv'ring at the doubtful way?
   Yet did these eyes a dying parent see,
Loosed from all cares except a thought for me,
Without a tear resign her short'ning breath,
And dauntless meet the ling'ring stroke of death.
Then at th' Almighty's sentence shall I mourn,
'Of dust thou art, to dust shalt thou return'?
Or shall I wish to stretch the line of fate,
That the dull years may bear a longer date,
To share the follies of succeeding times
With more vexations and with deeper crimes?
Ah no—though heav'n brings near the final day,
For such a life I will not, dare not pray;
But let the tear for future mercy flow,
And fall resigned beneath the mighty blow.
Nor I alone—for through the spacious ball,
With me will numbers of all ages fall:
And the same day that Mira yields her breath,
Thousands may enter through the gates of death.

Mira's Will

*I*MPRIMIS—My departed shade I trust
To heav'n—My body to the silent dust;
My name to public censure I submit,
To be disposed of as the world thinks fit;
My vice and folly let oblivion close,
The world already is o'erstocked with those;
My wit I give, as misers give their store,
To those who think they had enough before.
Bestow my patience to compose the lives
Of slighted virgins and neglected wives;
To modish lovers I resign my truth,
My cool reflection to unthinking youth;
And some good-nature give ('tis my desire)
To surly husbands, as their needs require;
And first discharge my funeral—and then
To the small poets I bequeath my pen.
  Let a small sprig (true emblem of my rhyme)
Of blasted laurel on my hearse recline;
Let some grave wight, that struggles for renown
By chanting dirges through a market-town,
With gentle step precede the solemn train;
A broken flute upon his arm shall lean.
Six comic poets may the corse surround,
And all free-holders, if they can be found:
Then follow next the melancholy throng,
As shrewd instructors, who themselves are wrong.
The virtuoso, rich in sun-dried weeds,
The politician, whom no mortal heeds,
The silent lawyer, chambered all the day,
And the stern soldier that receives no pay.
But stay—the mourners should be first our care:
Let the freed 'prentice lead the miser's heir;
Let the young relict wipe her mournful eye,
And widowed husbands o'er their garlic cry.
  All this let my executors fulfil,
And rest assured that this is Mira's will,
Who was, when she these legacies designed,
In body healthy, and composed in mind.

Frances Sheridan

1724 – 66

F rances Sheridan, a novelist and a playwright, was born in Dublin, the daughter of an archdeacon. She published a pamphlet supporting the actor and theatre manager, Thomas Sheridan, in a dispute over the Dublin playhouse; in 1747 she married him and bore four children, one of whom was the playwright and politician Richard Brinsley Sheridan. In 1754 the couple moved to London where they struggled to earn a living through literature and where they came into contact with many of the most famous literary people of their day, including Samuel Richardson who encouraged Frances to write fiction. Her popular novel The Memoirs of Miss Sidney Bidulph was published in 1761. She also wrote sentimental comedies which were performed by David Garrick. She was very much concerned that literature should not come in the way of her domestic duties and she frequently stressed her roles of wife and mother.

The following reprint of The History of Nourjahad was Frances Sheridan's last completed work, published posthumously in 1767 and intended as the first in a series of didactic tales. It was translated into several languages and turned into both a melodrama and a musical play.

The History of Nourjahad

S CHEMZEDDIN was in his two and twentieth year when he mounted the throne of Persia. His great wisdom and extraordinary endowments rendered him the delight of his people, and filled them with expectations of a glorious and happy reign. Amongst the number of persons who stood candidates for the young sultan's favour, in the new administration, which was now going to take place, none seemed so likely to succeed, as Nourjahad the son of Namarand. This young man was about the age of Schemzeddin, and had been bred up with him from his infancy. To a very engaging person was added a sweetness of temper, a liveliness of fancy, and a certain agreeable manner of address, that engaged every one's affections who approached him. The sultan loved him, and every one looked on Nourjahad as the rising star of the Persian court, whom his master's partial fondness would elevate to the highest pinnacle of honour. Schemzeddin indeed was desirous of promoting his favourite, yet notwithstanding his attachment to him, he was not blind to his faults; but they appeared to him only such as are almost inseparable from youth and inexperience; and he made no doubt but that Nourjahad, when time had a little more subdued his youthful passions, and matured his judgment, would be able to fill the place of his first minister, with abilities equal to any of his predecessors. He would not, however, even in his own private thoughts, resolve on so important a step, without first consulting with some old lords of his court, who had been the constant friends and counsellors of the late sultan his father. Accordingly having called them into his closet one day, he proposed the matter to them, and desired their opinion. But before they delivered it, he could easily discover by the countenances of these grave and prudent men, that they disapproved his choice. What have you to object to Nourjahad? said the sultan, finding that they all continued silent, looking at each other. His youth, replied the eldest of the counsellors. That objection, answered Schemzeddin, will grow lighter every day. His avarice, cried the second. Thou art not just, said the sultan, in charging him with that; he has no support but from my bounty, nor did he ever yet take advantage of that interest which he knows he has in me, to desire an encrease of it. What I have charged him with, is in his nature notwithstanding, replied the old lord. What hast thou to urge? cried the sultan, to his third adviser. His love of pleasure, answered he. That, cried Schemzeddin, is as groundless an accusation as the other; I have known him from his childhood, and think few men of his years are so temperate. Yet would he indulge to excess, if it were in his power, replied the old man. The sultan now addressed the fourth: What fault hast thou to object to him? cried he. His irreligion, answered the sage. Thou art even more severe, replied the sultan, than the rest of thy brethren, and I believe Nourjahad as good a Mussulman[1] as thyself. He dismissed them coldly from his closet;[2] and the four counsellors saw how impolitic a thing it was to oppose the will of their sovereign.

Though Schemzeddin seemed displeased with the remonstrances of the old men, they nevertheless had some weight with him. It is the interest of Nourjahad, said he, to conceal his faults from me; the age and experience of these men doubtless has furnished them with more sagacity than my youth can boast of; and he may be in reality what they have represented him. This thought disquieted the sultan, for he loved Nourjahad as his brother. Yet who knows, cried he, but it may be envy in these old men? they may be provoked at having a youth raised to that honour to which each of them perhaps in his own heart aspires. We can sometimes form a better judgment of a man's real disposition, from an unguarded sally of his own lips, than from a close observation of years, where the person, conscious of being observed, is watchful and cautious of every look and expression that falls from him. I will sound Nourjahad when he least suspects that I have any such design, and from his own mouth will I judge him.

It was not long before the sultan had an opportunity of executing his purpose. Having passed the evening with his favourite at a banquet, where they had both indulged pretty freely, he invited Nourjahad to a walk by moon-light in the gardens of the seraglio. Schemzeddin leaned on his shoulder as they rambled from one delicious scene to another; scenes rendered still more enchanting

[1] Mohammedan.
[2] Small private room.

by the silence of the night, the mild lustre of the moon now at full, and the exhalations which arose from a thousand odoriferous shrubs. The spirits of Nourjahad were exhilarated by the mirth and festivity in which he had passed the day. The sultan's favour intoxicated him; his thoughts were dissipated by a variety of agreeable sensations, and his whole soul as it were rapt in a kind of pleasing delirium. Such was the frame of Nourjahad's mind, when the sultan, with an assumed levity, throwing himself down on a bank of violets, and familiarly drawing his favourite to sit by him, said, *Tell me, Nourjahad, and tell me truly, what would satisfy thy wishes, if thou wert certain of possessing whatsoever thou shouldst desire?* Nourjahad remaining silent for some time, the sultan, smiling, repeated his question. My wishes, answered the favourite, are so boundless, that it is impossible for me to tell you directly; but in two words, I should desire to be possessed of inexhaustible riches, and to enable me to enjoy them to the utmost, to have my life prolonged to eternity. Wouldst thou then, said Schemzeddin, forego thy hopes of paradise? I would, answered the favourite, make a paradise of this earthly globe whilst it lasted, and take my chance for the other afterwards.

The sultan, at hearing these words, started up from his seat, and knitting his brow, Be gone, said he, sternly, thou art no longer worthy of my love or my confidence: I thought to have promoted thee to the highest honours, but such a wretch does not deserve to live. Ambition, though a vice, is yet the vice of great minds; but avarice, and an insatiable thirst for pleasure, degrades a man below the brutes.

Saying this, he turned his back on Nourjahad, and was about to leave him; when the favourite catching him by the robe, and falling on his knees, Let not my lord's indignation, said he, be kindled against his slave, for a few light words, which fell from him only in sport: I swear to thee, my prince, by our holy prophet, that what I said is far from being the sentiments of my heart; my desire for wealth extends not farther than to be enabled to procure the sober enjoyments of life; and for length of years, let not mine be prolonged a day beyond that in which I can be serviceable to my prince and my country.

It is not, replied the sultan, with a mildness chastened with gravity, it is not for mortal eyes to penetrate into the close recesses of the human heart; thou hast attested thy innocence by an oath; it is all that can be required from man to man; but remember thou hast called our great prophet to witness; him thou canst not deceive, though me thou mayest.

Schemzeddin left him without waiting for his reply; and Nourjahad, exceedingly mortified that his unguarded declaration had so much lessened him in his master's esteem, retired to his own house, which immediately joined the sultan's palace.

He passed the rest of the night in traversing his chamber, being unable to take any rest. He dreaded the thoughts of losing the sultan's favour, on which alone he depended for his future advancement; and tormenting himself all night with apprehensions of his disgrace, he found himself so indisposed in the morning, that he was unable to leave his chamber. He spent the day in gloomy reflections without suffering any one to come near him, or taking any repast: and when night came, wearied with painful thoughts, and want of sleep, he threw himself on his bed. But his slumbers were disturbed by perplexing dreams. What had been the subject of his anxiety when awake, served now to imbitter and distract his rest: his fancy represented the sultan to him as he had last seen him in the garden, his looks severe, and his words menacing. 'Go, wretch,' he thought he heard him cry, 'go seek thy bread in a remote country, thou hast nothing to expect from me but contempt.'

Nourjahad awoke in agonies: Oh Heaven, cried he aloud, that I could now inherit the secret wish I was fool enough to disclose to thee, how little should I regard thy threats! And thou shalt, Oh Nourjahad, replied a voice, possess the utmost wishes of thy soul! Nourjahad started up in his bed, and rubbed his eyes, doubting whether he was really awake, or whether it was not his troubled imagination which cheated him with this delusive promise; when behold! to his unutterable astonishment, he saw a refulgent light in his chamber, and at his bed's side stood a youth of more than mortal beauty. The lustre of his white robes dazzled his eyes; his long and shining hair was incircled with a wreath of flowers that breathed the odours of paradise.

Nourjahad gazed at him, but had not power to open his mouth. Be not afraid, said the divine youth, with a voice of ineffable sweetness; I am thy guardian genius, who have carefully watched over thee from thy infancy, though never till this hour have I been permitted to make myself visible to thee. I was present at thy conversation in the garden with Schemzeddin, I was a witness to thy unguarded declaration, but found thee afterwards awed by his frowns to retract what thou hadst said: I saw too the rigour of the sultan's looks as he departed from thee, and know that they proceeded from his doubting thy truth. I, though an immortal spirit, am not omniscient; to God only are the secrets of the heart revealed; speak boldly then, thou highly favoured of our prophet, and know that I have power from Mahomet to grant thy request, be it what it will. Wouldst thou be restored to the favour and confidence of thy master, and receive from his friendship and generosity the reward of thy long attachment to him, or dost thou really desire the accomplishment of that extravagant wish, which thou didst in the openness of thy heart avow to him last night?

Nourjahad, a little recovered from his amazement, and encouraged by the condescension of his celestial visitant, bowed his head low in token of adoration.

Disguise to thee, Oh son of paradise, replied he, were vain and fruitless; if I dissembled to Schemzeddin it was in order to reinstate myself in his good opinion, the only means in my power to secure my future prospects: from thee I can have no reason to conceal my thoughts; and since the care of my happiness is consigned to thee my guardian angel, let me possess that wish, extravagant as it may seem, which I first declared.

Rash mortal, replied the shining vision, reflect once more, before you receive the fatal boon; for once granted, you will wish perhaps, and wish in vain, to have it recalled. What have I to fear, answered Nourjahad, possessed of endless riches and of immortality? Your own passions, said the heavenly youth. I will submit to all the evils arising from them, replied Nourjahad, give me but the power of gratifying them in their full extent. Take thy wish then, cried the genius, with a look of discontent. The contents of this vial will confer immortality on thee, and to-morrow's sun shall behold thee richer than all the kings of the East. Nourjahad stretched his hands out eagerly to receive a vessel of gold, enriched with precious stones, which the angel took from under his mantle. Stop, cried the aerial being, and hear the condition, with which thou must accept the wondrous gift I am now about to bestow. Know then, that your existence here shall equal the date of this sublunary globe; yet to enjoy life all that while, is not in my power to grant. Nourjahad was going to interrupt the celestial, to desire him to explain this, when he prevented him, by proceeding thus: Your life, said he, will be frequently interrupted by the temporary death of sleep. Doubtless, replied Nourjahad, nature would languish without that sovereign balm. Thou misunderstandest me, cried the genius; I do not mean that ordinary repose which nature requires: The sleep thou must be subject to, at certain periods, will last for months, years, nay, for a whole revolution of Saturn[3] at a time, or perhaps for a century. Frightful! cried Nourjahad, with an emotion that made him forget the respect which was due to the presence of his guardian angel. He seemed suspended, while the radiant youth proceeded: It is worth considering, resolve not too hastily. If the frame of man, replied Nourjahad, in the usual course of things, requires for the support of that short span of life which is allotted to him, a constant and regular portion of sleep, which includes at least one third of his existence; my life, perhaps, stretched so much beyond its natural date, may require a still greater proportion of rest, to preserve my body in due health and vigour. If this be the case, I submit to the conditions; for what is thirty or fifty years out of eternity? Thou art mistaken, replied the genius; and though thy reasoning is not unphilosophical, yet is it far from reaching the true cause of these mysterious conditions which are offered thee; know that these are contingencies which depend entirely on thyself. Let me beseech you, said Nourjahad, to explain this. If thou walkest, said the genius, in the paths of virtue, thy days will be crowned with gladness, and the even tenor of thy life undisturbed by any evil; but if, on the contrary, thou pervertest the good which is in thy power, and settest thy heart on iniquity, thou wilt thus be occasionally punished by a total privation of thy faculties. If this be all, cried Nourjahad, then am I sure I shall never incur the penalty; for though I mean to enjoy all the pleasures that life can bestow, yet am I a stranger to my own heart, if it ever lead me to the wilful commission of a crime. The genius sighed. Vouchsafe then, proceeded Nourjahad, vouchsafe, I conjure you, most adorable and benign spirit, to fulfil your promise, and keep me not longer in suspence. Saying this, he again reached forth his hand for the golden vessel, which the genius no longer with-held from him. Hold thy nostrils over that viol, said he, and let the fumes of the liquor which it contains ascend to thy brain. Nourjahad opened the vessel, out of which a vapour issued of a most exquisite fragrance; it formed a thick atmosphere about his head, and sent out such volatile and sharp effluvia, as made his eyes smart exceedingly, and he was obliged to shut them whilst he snuffed up the essence. He remained not long in this situation, for the

---

[3] A remote planet, the revolution of which signified a long period.

subtle spirit quickly evaporating, the effects instantly ceased, and he opened his eyes; but the apparition was vanished, and his apartment in total darkness. Had not he still found the viol in his hands, which contained the precious liquor, he would have looked on all this as a dream; but so substantial a proof of the reality of what had happened leaving no room for doubts, he returned thanks to his guardian genius, whom he concluded, though invisible, to be still within hearing, and putting the golden vessel under his pillow, filled as he was with the most delightful ideas, composed himself to sleep.

The sun was at his meridian height when he awoke next day; and the vision of the preceding night immediately recurring to his memory, he sprung hastily from his bed; but how great was his surprise, how high his transports, at seeing the accomplishment of the genius's promise! His chamber was surrounded with several large urns of polished brass, some of which were filled with gold coin of different value and impressions; others with ingots of fine gold; and others with precious stones of prodigious size and lustre.

Amazed, enraptured at the sight, he greedily examined his treasures, and looking into each of the urns one after the other, in one of them he found a scroll of paper, with these words written on it.

'I have fulfilled my promise to thee, Oh Nourjahad. Thy days are without number, thy riches inexhaustible, yet cannot I exempt thee from the evils to which all the sons of Adam are subject. I cannot screen thee from the machinations of envy, nor the rapaciousness of power: thy own prudence must henceforth be thy guard. There is a subterraneous cave in thy garden where thou mayst conceal thy treasure; I have marked the place, and thou wilt easily find it. Farewel, my charge is at an end.'

And well hast thou acquitted thyself of this charge, most munificent and benevolent genius, cried Nourjahad; ten thousand thanks to thee for this last friendly warning; I should be a fool indeed if I had not sagacity enough to preserve myself against rapaciousness or envy; I will prevent the effects of the first, by concealing thee, my precious treasure, thou source of all felicity, where no mortal shall discover thee; and for the other, my bounty shall disarm it of its sting. Enjoy thyself, Nourjahad, riot in luxurious delights, and laugh at Schemzeddin's impotent resentment.

He hastened down into his garden, in order to find the cave, of which he was not long in search. In a remote corner stood the ruins of a small temple, which in former days, before the true religion prevailed in Persia, had been dedicated to the worship of the Gentiles. The vestiges of this little building were so curious, that they were suffered to remain, as an ornament, where they stood. It was raised on a mount, and according to the custom of idolaters, surrounded with shady trees. On a branch of one of these, Nourjahad perceived hanging a scarf of fine white taffety,[4] to which was suspended a large key of burnished steel.

Nourjahad's eager curiosity soon rendered his diligence successful in finding the door, to which this belonged; it was within-side the walls of the temple, and under what formerly seemed to have been the altar. He descended by a few

---

[4] Taffeta, glossy silk.

steps into a pretty spacious cavern, and by groping about, for there was scarce any light, he judged it large enough to contain his treasures.

Whether his guardian genius had contrived it purely for his use, or whether it had been originally made for some other purpose, he did not trouble himself to enquire; but glad to have found so safe a place, in which to deposite his wealth, he returned to his house; and having given orders that no visitors should approach him, he shut himself up in his chamber for the rest of the day, in order to contemplate his own happiness, and without interruption, to lay down plans of various pleasures and delights for ages to come.

Whilst Nourjahad was rich only in speculation, he really thought that he should be able to keep his word with the genius. That the employing his wealth to noble and generous purposes would have constituted great part of his happiness; and that without plunging into guilt, he could have gratified the utmost of his wishes. But he soon found that his heart had deceived him, and that there is a wide difference between the fancied and actual possession of wealth. He was immediately absorbed in selfishness, and thought of nothing but the indulgence of his own appetites. My temper, said he, as he lay stretched at length on a sopha, does not much incline me to take any trouble; I shall therefore never aspire at high employments, nor would I be the sultan of Persia, if I might; for what addition would that make to my happiness? None at all; it would only disturb my breast with cares, from which I am now exempt. And which of the real, substantial delights of life, could I then possess, that are not now within my power? I will have a magnificent house in town, and others in the country, with delicious parks and gardens. What does it signify whether or not they are dignified with the names of palaces? or whether I am attended by princes or slaves? The latter will do my business as well, and be more subservient to my will. There are three particulars indeed, in which I will exceed my master. In the beauties of my seraglio; the delicacies of my table; and the excellence of my musicians. In the former of these especially, King Solomon himself shall be outdone. All parts of the earth shall be explored for women of the most exquisite beauty; art and nature shall combine their utmost efforts, to furnish the boundless variety and elegance of my repasts; the sultan's frigid temperance shall not be a pattern to me. Then no fear of surfeits; I may riot to excess, and bid defiance to death. Here he started, on recollection that he had not requested the genius to secure him against the attacks of pain or sickness. I shall not however be impaired by age, said he, and this too perhaps is included in his gift. But no matter; since I cannot die, a little temporary pain will make me the more relish my returning health. Then, added he, I will enjoy the charms of music in its utmost perfection. I will have the universe searched for performers of both sexes, whose exquisite skill, both in instrumental and vocal harmony, shall ravish all hearts. I shall see the line of my posterity past numeration, and all the while enjoy a constant succession of new delights. What more is there wanting to consummate happiness, and who would ever wish to change such an existence, for one of which we are entirely ignorant? Here he paused. But are there not, he proceeded, some things called intellectual pleasures? Such as Schemzeddin used to talk of to me, and for which, when I was poor, I fancied

I had a sort of relish. They may have their charms, and we will not leave them quite out of our plan. I will certainly do abundance of good; besides, I will retain in my family half a score of wise and learned men, to entertain my leisure hours with their discourse. Then when I am weary of living in this country, I will set out with some chosen companions to make a tour through the whole earth. There shall not be a spot of the habitable world, which contains any thing worthy of my curiosity, that I will not visit; residing longest in those places which I like best: and by this means I may pass through two or three centuries, even before I have exhausted the variety of my prospects: after that I must content myself with such local enjoyments, as may fall in my way.

With such thoughts as these he entertained himself, waiting for the hour when his slaves should be retired to rest, as he had resolved to take that opportunity of burying his treasure.

He had tried the weight of the urns one by one; those which contained the gold he found so extremely heavy that it was impossible for him to lift them. Those which held the jewels, he could easily carry. Accordingly, when every one in his house was asleep, he loaded himself with his pleasing burdens; and having, from each of the repositories which held the gold, filled several large purses for his immediate expences, he conveyed the rest by many journeys to and from the cave, all safe to his subterranean treasury; where having locked them up securely, he retired to his apartment, and went to bed.

For the three succeeding days his thoughts were so perplexed and divided, that he knew not which of his favourite schemes he should first enter upon. Satisfied with having the means in his power, he neglected those ends for which he was so desirous of them. Shall I, said he, purchase or set about building for myself a magnificent palace? Shall I dispatch emissaries in search of the most beautiful virgins that can be obtained? and others, at the same time, to procure for me the rarest musicians? My household, meanwhile, may be established, and put on a footing suitable to the grandeur in which I purpose to live. I will directly hire a number of domestics, amongst which shall be a dozen of the best cooks in Persia, that my table at least may be immediately better supplied than that of the sultan. I am bewildered with such a multiplicity of business, and must find out some person, who, without giving me any trouble, will undertake to regulate the oeconomy of all my domestic concerns.

In these thoughts he was so immersed, that he intirely forgot to pay his court to Schemzeddin; and without any other enjoyment of his riches, than the pleasure of thinking of them, he sat for whole days alone, alternately improving on, or rejecting, such systems of happiness as arose in his mind.

The sultan, mean time, offended at his absenting himself, without offering any excuse for it, especially as their last parting had been a cold one, was so disgusted at his behaviour, that he sent one of his officers to forbid him his presence, and charge him never more to appear at court. Tell him, however, said he, that I have not so far forgot my former friendship for him, as to see him want a decent support; that house, therefore, in which he now lives, I freely bestow on him; and shall moreover allow him a pension of a thousand crowns yearly. Bid him remember that this is sufficient to supply him with all the sober enjoyments of life. These being his favourite's own words, the sultan thought proper to remind him of them.

Nourjahad received this message with the utmost indifference; but without daring to shew any mark of disrespect. Tell my lord the sultan, said he, that I would not have been thus long without prostrating myself at his feet, but that I was hastily sent for to visit a kinsman, whose dwelling was some leagues from Ormuz; and who in his last hours was desirous of seeing me. He died very rich, and has made me his heir. The thousand crowns a year therefore, my royal master may please to bestow on some one who wants them more, and is more deserving of his bounty, than I; wretch that I am, to have forfeited my prince's favour! The house that his goodness bestows on me, with all gratitude I thankfully accept, as it will daily remind me that Schemzeddin does not utterly detest his slave. Saying this, he presented the officer with a handsome diamond, which he took from his finger, and begged him to accept of it as a token of his respect for him, and submission to the sultan's pleasure. Though Nourjahad had given such a turn to his acceptance of the house, his true reason was, that having his treasure buried in the garden, he thought he could not without great difficulty, and the hazard of a discovery, remove it. Thus had he already, in two instances, been obliged to depart from truth, in consequence of his ill judged and pernicious choice.

The house which the sultan had given him was handsome and commodious; and he thought by enlarging and furnishing it magnificently, it would sufficiently answer the purpose of his town residence; besides, as it was a royal grant, he was sure of remaining unmolested in the possession of it.

He now bent his thoughts on nothing but in giving a loose to his appetites, and indulging without controul in every delight which his passions or imagination could suggest to him. As he was not of an active temper, he put the conduct of his pleasures into the hands of one, whom he had lately received into his service. This man, whose name was Hasem, he found had good sense, and a quickness of parts, which he thought qualified him for the trust he reposed in him. To him he committed the care of regulating his family, and appointed him the director of his household. In short, under Hasem's inspection, who on this occasion displayed an admirable taste, his house was soon furnished with every thing that could charm the senses, or captivate the fancy. Costly furniture, magnificent habits, sumptuous equipages, and a grand retinue, fully gratified his vanity. By Hasem's diligence his seraglio was soon adorned with a number of the most beautiful female slaves, of almost every nation, whom he purchased at a vast expence. By Hasem's care, his board was replenished with the most delicious products of every climate; and by Hasem's management he had a chosen band of the most skilful musicians of the age; and by Hasem's judgment and address, he had retained in his house some of the most learned and ingenious men of all Persia, skilled in every art and science. These were received into his family for the instruction and entertainment of his hours of reflection, if he should chance to be visited with any such.

Behold him now arrived at the height of human felicity; for, to render his happiness incapable of addition, he had distinguished amongst the beauties of his seraglio, a young maid, so exquisitely charming and accomplished, that he gave her the intire possession of his heart; and preferring her to the rest of his women, passed whole days in her apartment. By Mandana he found himself equally beloved; a felicity very rare amongst Eastern husbands; and longing to unbosom himself to one, on whose tenderness and fidelity he could rely, to her he disclosed the marvellous story of his destiny. His mind thus disburthened of this important secret, which he had often longed to divulge, but could find none whom he dared to trust with the discovery, he had not one anxious thought remaining. He gave himself up to pleasures, he threw off all restraint, he plunged at once into a tide of luxurious enjoyments; he forgot his duty towards God, and neglected all the laws of his prophet. He grew lazy and effeminate; and had not his pride now and then urged him to display to the wondering eyes of the public the magnificence of his state, he would seldom have been inclined to go out of his house.

Thus possessed of every thing that his soul could wish, he continued for the space of three moons, without any interruption, to wallow in voluptuousness: When one morning just as he was preparing to set out for a beautiful villa, which Hasem had recommended to him for his rural retirement, and which he purposed to buy if it answered his description, he was prevented by a messenger from the sultan. It was the same person who once before had been sent to him, to forbid him the court. I am sorry, my lord, said he, on entering Nourjahad's apartment, to be a second time the bearer of unwelcome tidings; but Schemzeddin, hearing of the extraordinary grandeur and magnificence in which you live, a magnificence indeed equal to that of the sultan himself, would needs know whence you derive your wealth, which seems so much to surpass that of any of his subjects; and has commanded me to conduct you to his presence, in order to give an account of it.

Nourjahad was exceedingly startled at this unexpected summons; but it was in vain to dispute the sultan's orders, and he was forced, though with great reluctance, to accompany the officer to the palace of Schemzeddin.

He entered it trembling, fearful to declare a falsehood to his sovereign, yet still more unwilling to confess the truth.

In this suspence the officer left him, to acquaint the sultan of his arrival. He waited not long before he was admitted to the royal presence.

Whence is it, Nourjahad, said the sultan, that thy imprudence hath drawn on thee the attention of my whole empire, insomuch that the representations made to me of thy pomp and luxury, now render it necessary to enquire into thy riches. They seem indeed to be immense. Who was that relation that bequeathed them to thee, and wherein do they consist?

Though Nourjahad had endeavoured to prepare himself with proper answers to all those questions, which he naturally expected would be asked on the occasion, he was nevertheless confounded; he could not utter the lies he had framed with the unabashed look of sincerity; his speech faltered, and his colour changed. Schemzeddin saw his confusion. I perceive, said he, there is some mystery in this affair which thou hast no mind to discover; I pray heaven that thou hast used no sinister means to come at the great wealth which I am told thou possessest! Confess the truth, and beware of prevaricating with thy prince.

Nourjahad, frightened at the difficulties he found himself involved in, fell at the sultan's feet. If my lord, said he, will give me a patient hearing, and forgive the presumption of his servant, I will unfold such wonders as will amaze him, and at the same time utter nothing but the strictest truth. The sultan turned coldly towards him; but by seeming to attend to his explanation, encouraged him to proceed.

He then gave a faithful relation of the vision he had seen, with all the consequences of that miraculous event. Schemzeddin suffered him to conclude his narration without interruption; but instead of shewing any marks of surprise, or appearing to credit what he said, looking at him with the utmost indignation, Audacious wretch, cried he, how darest thou presume thus to abuse my patience, and affront my understanding with the relation of so ridiculous a forgery? Go tell thy incredible tales to fools and children, but dare not to insult thy sovereign with such outrageous falsehoods.

Though Nourjahad was terrified at the sultan's anger, he nevertheless persisted in his declaration, confirming all he had said by the most solemn oaths. The sultan commanded him to be silent. Thou art mad, said he; I perceive now that the riches thou hast acquired, let the means be what they may, have turned thy brain; and I am now more than ever convinced of the sordidness of thy mind, when the unexpected acquisition of a little wealth could thus pervert thy judgment, and teach thee to impose on thy master for truth the monstrous chimeras of thy wild fancy. Thy folly be on thy head; for a little, a very little time must, with the unbounded extravagance of which thou art guilty, dissipate what thy friend hath left thee; and when thou art again reduced to thy former state, thou wilt be glad to sue to my bounty for that which thou didst lately with so much arrogance reject. Go, unhappy Nourjahad, continued he, (his voice a little softened) the remembrance of what thou once wert to me will not permit me to see thee fall a victim to thy own desperate folly. Should it be publickly known that thou hast thus endeavoured by lies and profanation to abuse the credulity of thy prince, thou wouldst find that thy boasted immortality would not be proof against that death, which he should think himself obliged, in justice to his own honour and dignity, to inflict on so bold an impostor. Hence, miserable man, pursued he, retire to thy house; and if thou art not quite abandoned, endeavour by a sober and regular conduct to expiate thy offences against heaven and thy sovereign; but as a punishment for thy crime, presume not, without my leave, to stir beyond the limits of thy own habitation, on pain of a more rigorous and lasting confinement.

Nourjahad, thunder-struck at this unexpected sentence, was unable to reply; and the sultan, having ordered the captain of his guards to be called, committed his prisoner to his hands; telling him if he suffered Nourjahad to escape, his head should answer it.

Filled with resentment and discontent, Nourjahad was conducted back to his own house; at all the avenues of which he had the mortification to see guards posted, agreeably to the charge given by the sultan.

He retired pensively to his closet, where, shutting himself up, he now for the first time repented of his indiscretion in the choice he had made.

Unfortunate that I am, cried he, what will riches or length of days avail me, if I am thus to be miserably immured within the walls of my own dwelling? Would it not have been better for me to have requested the genius to restore me to the favour of my prince? Schemzeddin always loved me, and would not fail to have promoted me to wealth and honours; mean while I should have enjoyed my liberty, which now methinks, as I am debarred of it, appears to me a greater blessing than any I possess. Unhappy Nourjahad, what is become of all thy schemes of felicity! He was even weak enough to shed tears, and gave himself up to vexation for the remainder of the day.

His mind, however, was by pleasure rendered too volatile to suffer any thing to make a lasting impression on him; and he had still too many resources of happiness in his power, to give himself up to despair. It is true, said he, I am debarred of my liberty, but have I not still a thousand delights in my possession? The incredulous sultan, satisfied with punishing me, will give himself no farther concern about me, provided I do not attempt to escape; and thus withdrawn from the public eye, envy will not endeavour to penetrate into the recesses of a private dwelling. I will secure the fidelity of my servants, by my liberality towards them. Schemzeddin's resentment will not last; or if it should, even as long as he lives, what is his life, the scanty portion of years allotted to common men, to my promised immortality?

Having thus reconciled his thoughts to his present situation, he resolved, in order to make himself amends for the restraint on his person, to indulge himself with an unbounded freedom in his most voluptuous wishes. He commanded a banquet to be prepared for him that night, which exceeded in luxury and profusion any of the preceding. He ordered all his women, of which he had a great number, adorned with jewels and dressed in their richest habits, to attend on him whilst he was at supper, permitting none but Mandana the favour to sit down with him. The magnificence of his apartments were heightened by a splendid illumination of a thousand torches, composed of odoriferous gums, which cast a blaze of light that vied with the glories of the sun. His musicians, both vocal and instrumental, were ordered to exert the utmost stretch of their art, and to sooth his mind with all the enchanting powers of harmony. Himself attired in robes, such as the kings of Persia were used to wear, was seated under a canopy of silver tissue, which he had put up for the purpose; and assuming the pomp of an Eastern monarch, suffered the illusion to take such possession of his mind, that if he were not before mad, he now seemed to be very near distraction.

Intoxicated with pleasure, the historian who writes his life, affirms that this night Nourjahad for the first time got drunk.

Be that as it may, it is certain that having retired to rest, he slept sounder and longer than usual; for on his awaking, and missing Mandana from his side, whom he had made the partner of his bed, he called out to the slave who always attended in his anti-chamber, in order to enquire for her, resolving to chide her tenderly for leaving him.

He called loud and often, but nobody answering him, as he was naturally choleric, he jumped out of bed, and stepping hastily into the outer chamber, he found that none of the slaves were in waiting. Enraged at this neglect, he called several of his domestics by their names, one after another; when at length, after he was almost out of breath with passion, a female slave appeared, who was one of those appointed to wait on Mandana.

The damsel no sooner perceived him, than giving a loud shriek, she was about to run away; when Nourjahad, provoked at her behaviour, catching her roughly by the arm, Where is thy mistress, said he, and whence arises that terror and amazement in thy countenance? Alas! my lord, answered the slave, pardon my surprise, which is occasioned by my seeing you so unexpectedly. Nourjahad now perceiving that in his hurry he had forgot to put on his cloaths, concluded that it was that circumstance which had alarmed the damsel, and turning from her, Foolish woman, said he, go tell Mandana that I desire to see her. Ah, my lord, replied the maid, I would she were in a condition to come to you. Why, what is the matter, said Nourjahad, no ill I hope has befallen the dear light of my life? Is she sick? Methinks she went to bed last night in perfect health. Last night! my lord, replied the slave, and shook her head. Trifler, cried Nourjahad, what means that motion? Where is thy mistress? Speak! She is, I hope, said the slave, gone to receive the reward of her goodness! Here she began to weep. Oh Heaven, cried Nourjahad, is my dear Mandana dead? She is, answered the damsel, redoubling her tears, and I shall never have so kind a mistress.

Alas! replied Nourjahad, by what fatal accident am I thus suddenly deprived of the adorable creature?

It was not suddenly, my lord, replied the slave, Mandana died in childbed. Ah traitress, cried Nourjahad, how darest thou thus mock the sorrow of thy master, and traduce the chastity of my beloved. Thou knowest it is not more than three moons since I received her a virgin to my arms, and doest thou presume to impose so ridiculous a story on me as that of her having died in childbed? My lord, answered the slave, it is more than three years since Mandana died. Audacious wretch, cried Nourjahad, wouldst thou persuade me out of my senses? With this he pinched the slave so hard by the arm, that she screamed out.

The noise she made brought several of the servants into the room, who, on seeing Nourjahad, all shewed manifest tokens of fear and surprise. What is the reason of all this, cried he out in a rage, are ye all leagued in combination against me? Be quick and explain to me the cause of this distraction which appears amongst you.

Hasem, who had run in amongst the other domestics, took upon him to answer for the rest. It is not to be wondered at, my lord, said he, that your slaves seem surprised at seeing you thus as it were raised from the dead; but if they are amazed, their joy doubtless is equal to their wonder; mine I am sure is unutterable, to behold my lord once more restored to his faithful servants, after we had almost despaired of your ever more unclosing your eyes.

You talk strangely, said Nourjahad, a little staggered at what he saw and heard. He just then recollected the terms on which he had received the important gift from the genius; and began to suspect that he had endured one of those preternatural slumbers, to which he had subjected himself. How long may I have slept, said he? Four years and twenty days exactly, answered Hasem; I have reason to know, for I counted the melancholy hours as they passed, and seldom quitted your bed-side. It may be so, said Nourjahad, I have been subject to these trances from a boy, but this has lasted rather longer than usual. He then commanded all his slaves to withdraw, retaining only Hasem, with whom he wanted to have some discourse.

Tell me now, said he, (when they were alone) and tell me truly, is all I have heard real, and is Mandana actually dead? Too true, my lord, replied Hasem, Mandana died in childbed, and dying left her infant son to my care. Is my child alive? said Nourjahad eagerly. He is, my lord, answered Hasem, and you shall see him presently: Mandana called me to her, continued he, when she found herself dying.

Hasem, said she, be careful of your lord; Heaven will one day restore him to you again. See that you manage his household with the same prudence and regularity that you would if he himself were to inspect into your conduct; for be assured he will sooner or later exact a just account of your proceedings. Here are the keys of his coffers. I ventured to take them from under his pillow, where I knew he kept them. I have husbanded his fortune with oeconomy, and have hitherto kept order and harmony in his family: On you it rests to preserve it in the same condition. Nourjahad will not fail to reward your diligence and fidelity. It is not expedient that any one should know the condition to which he is reduced. His life is governed by a strange fatality. You have nothing to do therefore, but to give out that he is seized with a lingering distemper, which confines him to his bed. Let no impertinent enquirers see him, and all curiosity about him will soon cease. These, proceeded Hasem, were almost the last words that my beloved mistress spoke. I have punctually complied with her orders. Your condition has been kept a profound secret from every one but your own family, and they all love you too well to betray their trust. Your women are all immured within the sacred wall of your seraglio, and though they murmur at their situation, they fail not to offer up their daily prayers that Heaven would restore you to them. I will now, continued he, present your son to you; it will be some consolation to you to see that charming pledge of Mandana's love. Saying this, he withdrew, but soon returned leading in the child, who was as beautiful as a little cherub.

Nourjahad melted into tears at the sight of him, and renewed his complaints for the loss of his adored Mandana. He saw that the child's age seemed to agree exactly with the account he had received; and now fully convinced of the truth of his misfortune, Oh Heaven, cried he, clasping the young boy to his bosom, what would I give that my dear Mandana were now here to partake of the pleasure I feel in this infant's caresses; gladly would I consent to have three ages cut off from the number of my years, to have her more precious life restored. But my felicity would then be too great, and I must submit to the destiny which I myself have chosen. Prudent Hasem, said he, observing he looked surprised, thou dost wonder at the words which thou hast heard me speak, but I will not conceal from thee the marvellous story of my life. Thy fidelity and zeal deserve this confidence; besides, it is requisite that I should trust some discreet person with my important secret, since Mandana, on whose tenderness and loyalty I could depend, is no more.

Nourjahad then acquainted Hasem with the wonderful mystery of his life. He did not, however, divulge the circumstance of his concealed treasure; he judged from his own heart, that it would not be altogether advisable to lay such a tempting bait in the way even of the most virtuous and steady mind; but contented himself with telling him that his genius constantly supplied him with riches, as his occasions required. Hasem listened to him with astonishment; but assured him, after what had already passed, he doubted not a tittle of the truth of what he had been told, amazing and almost incredible as it appeared.

My lord, said he, you may securely rely on my zeal and diligence, so long as you are pleased to entertain me in your service. That I shall do during your life, interrupted Nourjahad. But, replied Hasem, what if one of those unmerciful long trances should continue for a length of time much beyond that from which you are but now awakened, and that I should happen to die before you recover your senses, who knows in that case what might be the consequences? It is an accident exceedingly to be dreaded, replied Nourjahad; Heaven knows to what indignities I might be exposed, perhaps to be buried alive, and condemned to pass a century or two in a dismal sepulchre. The thought makes me shudder, and I almost repent of having accepted life on such conditions. As I have no warning, continued he, when those fatal slumbers will overpower me, (for who can always be guarded against the starts of passion, or what man is so attentive to that impertinent monitor within, as to hear his whispers amidst the hurry of tumultuous pleasures?) As I know not, I say, when I am to be condemned to that state of insensibility, or how long I shall continue in it, I can only conjure thee if I should happen to be seized with another trance during thy life, (which, considering my disposition, is not impossible) that thou wilt observe the same conduct which thou hast lately done; and if the angel of death should summon thee away before my senses are loosed from their mysterious bands, that thou wilt with thy dying breath, commit the secret to some one faithful person of my family, whom thou thinkest most fit to be relied on, for a punctual discharge of their duty. As I shall never part with any of my servants, till the inevitable stroke of death separates them from me, and shall constantly supply their places with the worthiest persons that can be found, I think I cannot fail of a succession of people, from amongst whom, one at least may always be found, in whose secrecy and truth I may safely confide.

Without doubt, my lord, answered Hasem, you may by such wise measures as these, be always guarded against the worst that may befal you.

Though Nourjahad had, by thus providing against evil events, exceedingly relieved his mind from the fears by which it was agitated, lest any ill should happen to him during his slumbers; yet was his heart far from being at ease. The loss of Mandana preyed upon his spirits. He had no relish for the charms of his other women. Mandana's superior loveliness was always present to his eyes: The delicacies of his table grew tasteless; Mandana's sprightly wit was wanting to give a relish to the feast. The melodious concerts of music with which he was wont to be so delighted now only served to overwhelm him with melancholy: Mandana's enchanting voice was not heard, which used to swell his heart to rapture.

In short, for a time he took pleasure in nothing but the caresses and innocent prattle of his little son, whom by his tenderness and endearments he had taught to love him.

I am unhappy, my dear Hasem, would he often say; the loss of Mandana imbitters all my joys, and methinks I begin to look forward with disgust.

My lord, said Hasem, there is nothing which has befallen you but what is common to all. Every one may naturally expect to see the death of some person or other whom they love; but you who are endowed with so miraculous a life must needs look to drop a tear over a thousand graves.

Melancholy reflection! said Nourjahad; it occurred not to me in this light when I made my choice. I knew indeed I must of necessity bury hundreds of succeeding generations; but, said I to myself, I shall insensibly contract new amities, as I perceive the old ones are likely to be dissolved by the hand of time. My heart, said I, shall never feel a vacuity, for want of fit objects of desire. A new beauty will naturally take place of her whose charms begin to decline; thus the ardors of love will be supplied with perpetual fewel; and upon the same principle will the social joys of friendship be unremitting. I considered the world as a flower garden, the product of which was to delight my senses for a certain season. The bloom is not made to last, thought I, but it will be succeeded by a fresh blow, whose sweetness and variety will equal the former, and intirely obliterate them from my memory. I thought not, alas, that before the spring ended, a cruel blast might suddenly destroy my fairest flower.

Would you, my lord, said Hasem, if it were in your power, absolve your genius from his promise, seeing your life must be perpetually subject to such misfortunes?

Not so neither, answered Nourjahad; time is a never-failing remedy for grief; I shall get over this, and be better prepared against the next assault of evil.

In effect, Nourjahad kept his word, and soon returned to his former way of living.

He had the mortification, however, to find himself still a prisoner. Hasem told him that the sultan had not yet taken off the restraint, under which he had formerly laid him; and whether it was through forgetfulness or design, the guards still maintained their posts about his house. This Nourjahad was himself convinced of, by seeing them from his windows.

It is strange, said he, that Schemzeddin should retain his resentment against me for so long a time; especially as he might have been convinced of the truth of what I asserted, by the extraordinary state in which I have lain all this while. You forget, my lord, said Hasem, that this was an absolute secret, no one from under your own roof knowing a word of the matter. Such was Mandana's last injunction, and your faithful servants never divulged a tittle of it.

Did not my friends come to visit me, said Nourjahad, during that interval in which I slept? Those whom you called your friends, answered Hasem, came as usual, during the first month of your dormant state; but being refused admittance, under pretence that your health was so much declined, that you were not in a condition to receive them, they soon desisted from their visits; and finding they could no more be entertained with feasting and jollity, they have never since inquired after you.

Ungrateful wretches! said Nourjahad; I cast them off for ever. Yet it is an irksome thing to live without friends. You, Hasem, are a prudent and honest man, but still you are my servant; I cannot therefore consider you on that footing of equality which friendship requires. There is one man, said Hasem, who has shewn himself grateful and compassionate; and those two virtues never come alone, but are ever found attended with many others. Oh name him, said Nourjahad. It is Zamgrad, replied Hasem, that officer of the sultan's whom you once obliged by a trifling present of a ring; he never fails sending every day to enquire after your welfare. Nay, he has often called himself, and expressed an honest sorrow for the ill state of health to which I told him you were reduced; tenderly blaming the sultan for his rigorous confinement of you.

Worthy Zamgrad, said Nourjahad, thou, thou alone shalt be the chosen friend of my heart; the rest of my worthless acquaintance I from this minute discard.

I will write to Schemzeddin, pursued he; perhaps he may now relent and restore me to my liberty. I long to shift the scene, and remove to some place where Mandana's image may not be so often revived in my memory. Wert thou not, Hasem, about to procure for me a noble seat in the country, which I was going to take a view of that day on which the good Zamgrad came to carry me before the sultan? If I might but retire thither, I should think myself happy.

Alas, my lord, replied Hasem, that fine seat cannot now be your's. You may remember I made only a conditional agreement with the owner of it, depending on your approbation of the place after your having seen it. I recollect it, said Nourjahad, but may it not still be mine? By no means, answered Hasem; the owner has long since disposed of it to another.

That is unlucky, said Nourjahad; but we can easily find another. Be it your care to look out for one, whilst I endeavour to move the sultan in my favour.

Hasem was not slow in executing his master's orders. In three days he told him he had seen a villa, which seemed to him to surpass all the descriptions of Eden in its primary state of beauty. It is but at the distance of ten leagues from Ormuz, said he. The house and gardens are in compleat order, and you may purchase the whole for fifty thousand pieces of gold. The sultan himself hath not in his possession any thing more delightful. I will have it, said Nourjahad: Get the money ready, you have the keys of my coffers, and they contain more than that sum.

My lord, answered Hasem, when you last saw them they did contain much more; but you will be pleased to recollect that it is above four years since, and that your household has been maintained during that time; which, notwithstanding I have used the utmost oeconomy, must needs have somewhat diminished your treasury. I had forgot, replied Nourjahad, but I will soon supply you with the gold you want.

Accordingly he paid a visit to the subterraneous cave that very night; where finding every thing as he had left it, he loaded himself with a quantity of gold, sufficient to prevent the necessity of drawing from his hidden store of wealth for a considerable time.

Intent now on the pursuit of his pleasures, he neglected not applying to the sultan for a repeal, or at least a mitigation of his sentence. He writ to Schemzeddin a letter in terms full of humility; thinking if he could remove his incredulity by convincing him that the extraordinary fact he had related, was nothing more than the truth, that the sultan would no longer deny him his liberty. He scrupled not to acquaint him, that he had been for more than four years in a profound sleep, for the confirmation of which fact, strange as it might seem to his majesty, he desired leave to appeal to every one of his own household, and conjured the sultan to take the trouble of informing himself more fully from some of his people, whom he might cause to be brought into his presence and privately examined, as he confessed he did not wish to have so uncommon an event divulged.

Nourjahad from this expedient had great hopes of obtaining his desire; but the event turned out contrary to his expectations.

Zamgrad two days after brought him an answer from the sultan in writing: Nourjahad laid the paper on his head, then, kissing the seals, he broke them open, and read as follows.

"I have not been unmindful of thy motions, and I was pleased to hear from time to time, that for these four years past, order and decency have been preserved in thy dwelling. I flattered myself that this was owing to thy having returned to a sense of thy duty. But my hope deceived me, when I found that Nourjahad was by a violent malady which seized him (doubtless the effects of his intemperance) disqualified from indulging in those excesses in which he was wont to riot.

"This visitation from heaven I thought would have produced salutary effects on thy mind, and hoped if the angel of health were again to revisit thy pillow, that thou wouldst make a different use of thy recovered strength. How must my indignation then be roused against thee, abandoned as thou art to perdition, to find thou persistest in thy enormous folly and wickedness; and continuest to abuse the patience of thy benefactor and sovereign master, with such unparalleled falsehoods. A prince less merciful than myself would no longer delay to punish thee with death: But I give thee thy wretched life. Spend it if thou canst in penitence. Nay, I will so far indulge thee, as to permit thee, for the more perfect recovery of thy health, to retire to thy house in the country; but at the peril of thy head presume not to stir beyond the bounds of thy own habitation."

Nourjahad now too late found his error in endeavouring to force belief of a thing which appeared so incredible; and wished he had rather availed himself of the sultan's prepossessions in favour of the story propagated by his servants, as he found that would have been the wiser course.

What a world is this, said he to Zamgrad, (after having read the letter) where he who ought to be the rewarder of truth, and the dispenser of justice, shuts his ears against conviction, and condemns an innocent man for endeavouring to set him right! But I will not involve you in the punishment imposed on my imaginary guilt, by requiring your belief of what I have in vain endeavoured to convince the incredulous Schemzeddin.

I know not, my lord, replied Zamgrad, what has passed between the sultan and you; of this only I am certain, that he seems exceedingly enraged against you. I would it were in my power, from the respect I bear you, to mitigate his resentment.

I thank thee, gentle Zamgrad, said Nourjahad; I find thou, of all my numerous acquaintance, art the only man who has shewn any attachment to me. If the friendship of one labouring under the displeasure of his prince be worth thy accepting, I offer thee mine, and conjure thee to grant me yours in return. The base ingratitude I have already experienced from the rest of my pretended friends has determined me to disclaim all society with them: if thou wilt sometimes visit me in my retirement thou wilt find Nourjahad not undeserving of thy kindness.

Zamgrad promised to see him as often as he could, and took his leave.

However vexed Nourjahad was at his disappointment, in finding himself, by being still debarred of his liberty, deprived for a time at least from executing one of his favourite purposes, that of travelling all over the world, he yet contented himself with the reflection, that this project was only postponed to another opportunity; and that he should have time enough for executing his design, after Schemzeddin and many of his posterity were in their graves. I will not waste my hours, said he, in fruitless languishment for what I cannot at present attain, but make the most of the good which now offers itself to my acceptance.

He ordered Hasem to pay down the money forthwith, for that fine seat: I will remove thither, said he, immediately; and make myself some recompence by all the means that art can devise, for that cruel long trance, which overpowered me so unseasonably: I hope I shall not be visited by another for these fifty or sixty years at least.

Hasem's diligence kept pace with his lord's impatience: He got every thing in readiness for his reception at his rural mansion; and to avoid the notice which might be taken of so numerous a seraglio, and such a train of domestics, the prudent Hasem advised that they should set out and travel by night. This precaution, said he, will prevent the malice of your enemies from making ill-natured representations of your conduct to the sultan; and as you yourself are supposed by every body in Ormuz to have laboured under a long and painful illness, I think, to give colour to this report, it would be most advisable for you to be carried in a litter. As Nourjahad loved his ease, he readily enough consented to this proposal, and in this manner suffered himself to be conveyed to his new habitation.

On his arrival he found Hasem had not exaggerated in his description of this place. The house, or rather palace, for such it might be called, infinitely exceeded his expectations; but above all, the gardens were so delicious that his senses were ravished with delight. He declared that those mansions of joy prepared for the reception of the faithful could not exceed them; and forgetting that this paradise was to be his prison, he ordered that a pavilion of light brocade should be reared for him in the midst of his garden, where he purposed to enjoy the cool hours of the evening, amidst the noise of falling waters, and the wild notes of innumerable birds, who had taken up their residence in this terrestrial paradise.

Behold him now once more, in the possession of every thing, for which the heart of man in the wildest wishes of Epicurean phrenzy could paint. He gave the reins to his passions; he again became the slave of voluptuous appetites: He submitted a second time to the power of beauty; he invented new modes of luxury; and his delightful abode became the scene of every licentious pleasure.

The delicacies and profusion in which he himself wallowed made him forget that there were wants or miseries amongst his fellow-creatures; and as he had but little intercourse with mankind, except with those who flattered his follies, or administered to his loose pleasures, he became hardened to all the social affections. He ceased to relieve the poor, because they never came in his way; and with a heart naturally generous and benevolent, he lived only for himself.

Immersed in sensual gratifications, he lost all relish for any others. The poets and sages whom he entertained in his house began to grow irksome to him. He derided the wisdom and philosophy of the latter; and if they attempted to entertain him with learned or grave discourses, he laughed at them; and at length thinking their company tedious, he turned them out of his house.

His bards would have shared the same fate, if they had not by a timely address rendered their art subservient to his depraved inclinations. They composed nothing but pieces filled with adulation on himself, or light verses in praise of one or other of his mistresses; these were set to melting airs, and sung accompanied by the lute.

Thus did Nourjahad pass his days. Every rising sun beheld some fresh outrage on the laws of temperance and decency; and the shades of every night descended on his unatoned offences.

The delightful season of the year, winged with pleasures, was now almost fled, when one of the most extravagant projects came into the head of Nourjahad, that ever entered the imagination of man.

As the gardens of his palace were exceedingly delicious, he vainly fancied that they must be very like the regions of paradise (where all good Mussulmen are received after death) and that in order to make the resemblance perfectly complete he would cause the women of his seraglio to personate the Houriis;[5] those beautiful virgins who are given as a reward to all true believers. He himself would needs represent Mahomet; and one of his mistresses whom he loved best, and who was indeed the handsomest of them, he would have to appear under the name and character of Cadiga, the favourite wife of the great Prophet.

The idea, wild and profane as it was, was notwithstanding readily adopted by all the people about him, no one presuming to dispute his will. Nor were the women on this occasion much inclined to do so, as it served them for a very agreeable amusement.

[5] Nymphs in the Mohammedan heaven.

Some debates however arose amongst them on account of the dresses proper to be worn on this occasion; as none of them remembered to have read in the Koran what sort of habits the Houriis wore; and some of the ladies gave it as their opinion that those beauties went naked.

After many disputes on the subject, however, they struck a sort of medium, and agreed to be attired in loose robes of the thinnest Persian gauze, with chaplets of flowers on their heads.

Nourjahad approved of the invention, and gave orders to Hasem to prepare for this celestial masquerade, with all possible diligence; charging him to leave nothing out, that could render the entertainment worthy of Mahomet himself.

Neither art nor expence were spared on this extraordinary occasion. He gave commandment that the fountains which adorned his garden should be so contrived, that instead of water, they should pour forth milk and wine; that the seasons should be anticipated, and the early fragrance of the spring should be united with the more vivid colours of the glowing summer. In short, that fruits, blossoms, and flowers, should at once unite their various beauties, to imbellish this terrestrial paradise.

The diligence of Hasem was so active, that every thing was got in readiness, even sooner than Nourjahad expected. He descended into his garden to take a survey of these wondrous preparations; and finding all exactly to his mind, he gave orders to his women to hold themselves prepared to act their parts; telling them that on that very evening he would give them a foretaste of the ravishing pleasures they were to enjoy, in the happy regions of light.

The weather was extremely hot, and Nourjahad, in order to take a view of the magnificent decorations, having fatigued himself with wandering through his elysium,[6] retired to his apartment, and threw himself down on a sopha, with intent to take a short repose, the better to prepare himself for the excesses of the night: leaving orders with Hasem and Cadiga to awake him from sleep before sunset.

Nourjahad, however, opened his eyes without any one's having roused him from his slumbers; when perceiving that the day was almost closed, and finding that his commands had been neglected, he flew into a violent passion, suspecting that his women had prevailed on Hasem, to grant them this opportunity whilst he slept, of indulging themselves in liberties without that restraint to which they were accustomed in his presence.

Enraged at the thought, he resolved to have them called before him, and after severely reprimanding them, and punishing Hasem proportionally to his fault, to have his women all locked up, and postpone his festivity till he was in a better humour to relish it.

Impatient, and even furious at his disappointment, he stamped on the floor with his foot; when immediately a black eunuch presented himself at the door. Go, said he, his words almost choaked with indignation, go and bid my women one and all hasten directly into my presence.

[6] In classical mythology the place where the virtuous went after death.

The slave retired in respectful silence; and presently all the ladies of his seraglio entered his apartment. They were, according to the custom, covered with vails, but on appearing in their lord's presence, they threw them off. But, Oh Heaven! what was Nourjahad's anger and astonishment, when instead of the beautiful Houriis whom he expected to see, he beheld a train of wrinkled and deformed old hags.

Amazement and rage for a while suspended the power of speech: When the foremost of the old women approaching, and offering to embrace him, he thrust her rudely from him: Detestable fiend, said he, whence this presumption? where are my slaves? Where is Hasem? and the women of my seraglio? The traitoresses! they shall pay dearly for thus abusing my indulgence.

The old women at this all fell upon their faces to the ground; but the first who had advanced addressing herself to speak, Avaunt! cried Nourjahad, begone, wretches, and rid my sight of such hideous aspect.

Alas, my lord, replied the old woman, have you intirely forgot me? has time left no traces to remind you of your once beloved Cadiga? Cadiga! thou Cadiga? do not provoke me, said Nourjahad, or by Allah I'll spurn thee with my foot.

The old women now all set up a lamentable cry; Miserable wretches that we are, said they, beating their withered breasts, it had been happy for us if we had all died in our youth, rather than have thus outlived our lord's affections!

Evil betide ye, said Nourjahad, who in the name of deformity are ye all? Hereupon the beldames cried out with one voice, Your mistresses! the once admired and loved partners of your bed, but the relentless hand of time has made such cruel ravage on our charms, that we do not wonder thou shouldst find it impossible to recollect us.

Nourjahad now began to suspect that he had been overpowered by a second trance. Why, how long, in the devil's name, have I then slept, said he?

Forty years and eleven moons, answered the lady who called herself Cadiga. Thou liest, I am sure, said Nourjahad, for it appears to me but as yesterday since I ordered thee (if thou really art Cadiga) to awake me at a certain hour, that I might enjoy the glorious entertainment prepared for me in the gardens of the Houriis.

I do remember it, said Cadiga, and we your faithful slaves were to personate those beautiful virgins. Alas, alas, we are not now fit to represent those daughters of paradise! Thou art fitter, said Nourjahad, to represent the furies. I tell thee again, it cannot be many hours since I first fell into a slumber.

It may well seem so, answered Cadiga, buried as your senses have been in forgetfulness, and every faculty consigned to oblivion, that the interval of time so past must be quite annihilated; yet it is most certain that you have slept as long as I tell you.

Nourjahad upon this examined the faces of the old women one after the other, but finding them so totally different from what they once were, he swore that he did not believe a word they said. Thou Cadiga! said he, the black-browed Cadiga, whose enchanting smiles beguiled all hearts; thou art wonderously like her, I confess!

Yet that I am that identical fair one, answered she, I shall be able to convince you, from a remarkable signature which I bear on my bosom, and which still remains, though the rest of my person is so intirely changed.

Saying this, she uncovered her breast, on which the figure of a rose-bud was delineated by the hand of nature. Nourjahad well remembered the mark; he had once thought it a beauty, and made it the subject of an amorous sonnet, when the bosom of the fair Cadiga was as white and as smooth as alabaster.

Convinced by this proof, that these women were really what they pretended to be, Nourjahad could not conceal his vexation. By the Temple of Mecca, said he, this genius of mine is no better than he should be, and I begin to suspect he is little less than an evil spirit, or he could not thus take delight in persecuting me for nothing.

Ah, my lord, said Cadiga, I am not ignorant of the strange fate by which your life is governed. Hasem, your faithful Hasem, communicated the secret to me with his dying breath. Is Hasem dead? cried Nourjahad. He is, my lord, answered Cadiga, and so is the worthy Zamgrad. What is become of my son? said Nourjahad; I hope he has not shared the same fate. It were better that he had, replied Cadiga, for it is now some five and twenty years since he ran away from the governor in whose hands the wise Hasem had placed him for his education; and having in vain endeavoured to prevail on that honest man to bury you, that giving out you were deceased, he might take possession of all your wealth, finding he could not succeed in his unnatural design, he took an opportunity of breaking open your cabinet, and securing all the treasure he could find, stole secretly away, and has never been heard of since.

Ungrateful viper! exclaimed Nourjahad; and thou cruel genius, thus to imbitter a life, which was thy own voluntary gift; for thou camest to me unasked.

Had not, proceeded Cadiga, myself and the rest of your women consented to give up all our jewels to Hasem, who turned them into money, we must long ere this have been reduced to want; for your unworthy son stripped you of all your wealth; but Hasem conducted every thing with the same regularity and care as if you had been awake, discharging such of your domestics as he thought unnecessary, and replacing such as died in your service; and it is not many days since the good old man was himself summoned away by the angel of death.

Tell me, said Nourjahad, does Schemzeddin still live?

He does, replied Cadiga, but bending under the weight of age and infirmities, he is become so intolerably peevish that no one dares speak to him. Indeed he is at times so fantastical and perverse, that it is secretly whispered he is not perfectly in his senses. It may very well be, said Nourjahad, that he is doating by this time, for he cannot be much less than seventy years old. The genius has in this article been faithful to his promise; for I, though nearly of the same age, find myself as vigorous and healthy as ever, but I give him little thanks for this, seeing he has defrauded me of such an unconscionable portion of my life.

My lord, said Cadiga, there is one circumstance which may in some measure reconcile you to what has already happened. You know, by the severity of the sultan, you have been the greatest part of your days a prisoner; which condition, however it might have been alleviated by the pleasures which surrounded you, must nevertheless have by this time grown exceedingly irksome, had you all the while been sensible of your restraint; and you would now probably have been so palled with the repetition of the same enjoyments, that I know not whether your good genius has not, instead of cruelty, shewn an extreme indulgence, in rendering you for such a number of years unconscious of your misfortune; especially as the sultan, by what I learnt from Hasem, has, notwithstanding the length of time since he first deprived you of your liberty, never reversed the barbarous sentence.

What thou hast said has some colour, replied Nourjahad, and I am very much inclined to think thou hast hit upon the truth. Sage Cadiga, pursued he, what thou hast lost in beauty, thou hast gained in wisdom; and though I can no longer regard thee with tenderness, I will still retain thee in my service, and constitute thee governess over my female slaves; for I must have my seraglio supplied with a new race of beauties. For the rest of those hags, as I do not know of any thing they are now good for, I desire to see them no more. Be gone, said he to them, I shall give orders to Cadiga concerning you.

When Nourjahad was left alone, he began seriously to reflect on his condition. How unhappy I am, said he, thus to find myself at once deprived of every thing that was dear to me; my two faithful friends, Hasem and Zamgrad, all the blooming beauties of my seraglio, who used to delight my eyes; but above all, my son, whose ingratitude and cruelty pierces me more deeply than all my other losses; and that rigid spirit who presides over my life, to take advantage of those hours of insensibility, to deprive me of all my comforts! Yet why do I reproach my protector for that? the same ills might have befallen me, had the progress of my life been conducted by the common laws of nature. I must have seen the death of my friends, and they might possibly have been snatched from me in a manner equally sudden and surprising as their loss now appears.

My women, had I seen them every day, must necessarily by this time have grown old and disgustful to me; and I should certainly before now have discarded two or three generations of beauties. My son too, would, in his heart, have been the same thankless and perfidious creature that he has now shewn himself, had the eye of watchful authority been constantly open on his conduct; and there is only this difference perhaps, between me and every other parent, that I have lived to see my offspring trampling on filial duty, riotously seizing on my wealth, leaving my family to poverty, and not so much as bestowing a grateful thought on him who gave him being, and by whose spoils he is enriched; whilst other fathers, deceived by a specious outside, in the full persuasion of the piety, justice, and affection of their children, have descended to the grave in peace, whilst their heirs, with as little remorse as my graceless child, have laughed at their memories.

I see it is in vain, proceeded he, to escape the miseries that are allotted to human life. Fool that I was to subject myself to them more by ten thousand fold than any other can possibly experience! But stop, Nourjahad, how weak are thy complaints! thou knowest the conditions of thy existence, and that thou must of necessity behold the decay and dissolution of every thing that is mortal; take comfort then, and do not imbitter thy days by melancholy reflections, but resolve for the future to let no events disturb thy peace, seize every fleeting joy as it passes, and let variety be thy heaven, for thou seest there is nothing permanent.

As Nourjahad was never used, but on occasions of distress, to make use of his reason or philosophy, he no sooner found an alleviation of the evil, than he put them both to flight, as impertinent intruders. He did not therefore long disturb himself with disagreeable reflections, but resolved as soon as possible to return to those pleasures which he thought constituted the felicity of man's life.

He gave himself but little concern about those treasures of which his son had robbed him, knowing he had an inexhaustible fund of wealth, of which, agreeably to the genius's promise, he could not be deprived.

From Cadiga he learnt that his house at Ormuz was in the same condition he had left it; Hasem having taken care to place a diligent and faithful servant there, on whom he might rely with equal security as on himself; and he had the farther precaution, added Cadiga, not long before his death, to solicit, through Zamgrad's means, the sultan's permission for your return thither. This, said he, may be necessary in case our lord awakes before Schemzeddin's decease, and should have a desire to quit this place, he may do it without the trouble of a fresh application.

And has the sultan granted this? cried Nourjahad.

He has, answered Cadiga, as a matter of great indulgence: for having, as he said, heard that your profusion was unbounded, finding there were no hopes of reclaiming you, he had determined to confine you for the remainder of your life, with this liberty, however, that you might make choice either of this palace or your house at Ormuz for your prison.

Fool, cried Nourjahad, he little imagines how impotent are his threats, when he speaks of confining me for life! I would however *he* were dead, that I might be rid of this irksome restraint; but it cannot last much longer, for the days of Schemzeddin must needs draw towards a period. I will not, mean while, bestow any farther thought on him, but avail myself of that liberty which he has allowed me, and return to Ormuz; for I am weary of this solitude, seeing I have lost every thing that could render my retirement agreeable.

Do thou, said he, see that every thing is prepared for my reception. I would have my seraglio filled once more, otherwise my house, when I enter it, will appear a desert to me, and I shall be at a loss how to divert the tedious hours which may yet remain of my confinement. I will depend on thy experience and skill in beauty, to make choice of such virgins, as you think will well supply the place of those I have lost.

I have a friend, said Cadiga, a merchant, who deals in female slaves; and he has always such a number, that it will be easy to select from amongst them some whose charms cannot fail to please you. I will order him to repair to your house, and bring with him a collection of the rarest beauties he has in his possession; you may then chuse for yourself.

Be it so, said Nourjahad, I leave the conduct of every thing to thee; if I approve of the damsels, I shall not scruple at any price for their purchase.

The day being come for his return to Ormuz, full of pleasing eagerness to behold the divine creatures which he was told waited his arrival, he set out with a splendid equipage, but had the mortification to behold his chariot surrounded by a party of the sultan's guards, with drawn sabres in their hands, to repress the curiosity of those who might approach the chariot to gaze at the person who was conducted in so unusual a manner.

I could well excuse this part of my retinue, said Nourjahad, as he passed along, but there is no resisting the commands of this whimsical old fellow Schemzeddin. Being thus conducted to his house, the guards as before posted themselves round it.

However chagrined Nourjahad was at this circumstance, he was resolved it should not interrupt his pleasures.

He found the young slaves whom Cadiga had prepared all waiting his arrival. They were richly cloathed, and standing together in a row, in a long gallery through which he was to pass. On his entering, the merchant to whom they belonged ordered the women to unveil.

Nourjahad examined them one after the other, but none of them pleased him. One had features too large, and another's were too small; the complexion of this was not brilliant, and the air of that wanted softness; this damsel was too tall, and the next was ill proportioned.

Dost thou call these beauties, said Nourjahad, angrily? By my life they are a pack of as awkward damsels as ever I beheld.

Surely, my lord, cried the merchant, you do not speak as you think. These young maids are allowed by all good judges to be the most perfect beauties that ever were seen in Persia: The sultan himself has none equal to them in his seraglio.

I tell thee, man, said Nourjahad, they are not worthy even to wait on those of whom I myself was formerly master. I know not that, my lord, answered the merchant, but this I am sure of, that I can have any sum which I shall demand for their purchase. Then thou must carry them to some other market, cried Nourjahad, for to me they appear fit for nothing but slaves.

Cadiga, who was present, now taking Nourjahad aside, said, These, my lord, these damsels are less charming than those of which you were formerly possessed, but the taste for beauty is quite altered since that time: You may assure yourself that none will be offered to your acceptance that will exceed these. Were I and my companions, whom you once so much admired, to be restored to our youth again, we should not now be looked upon; such is the fantastic turn of the age.

If this be so, said Nourjahad, I shall be very unfashionable in my amours; for the present, however, I shall content myself with some of the most tolerable of these maidens, till I have time and opportunity of supplying myself with better.

Saying this, he selected half a dozen of those young slaves, whom he thought the most agreeable, and having paid the merchant what he demanded for them, dismissed the rest.

Nourjahad having now once more established his household, and perceiving that these damsels upon a longer acquaintance were really amiable, expected to find himself restored to his former contentment and alacrity of spirits. But in this he was deceived. He was seized with a lassitude that rendered his days tiresome. The vacancy he found in his heart was insupportable. Surrounded by new faces, he saw nobody for whom he could entertain either love or friendship. This is a comfortless life, would he exclaim to himself, yet how often, during the date of my existence, must this situation, melancholy as it is, recur to me. A friend shall no sooner be endeared to me by long experience of kindness and fidelity, without which it is impossible I should regard him; than death will deprive me of him, as it has already done of Hasem and Zamgrad; and how many bright eyes am I doomed to see for ever closed, or what is as mortifying to behold, their faded lustre. There is but one way, said he, to guard against those evils: I will no more contract friendships amongst men, nor ever again suffer my mind to be subdued by female charms. I will confound all distinction by variety, nor permit one woman to engross my heart; for I find by sad experience, even after such an amazing length of time, that the bare idea of my dear Mandana inspires me with more tenderness, than ever I experienced from the fondest blandishments of all the beauties I have since possessed.

Nourjahad endeavoured to banish those melancholy thoughts by others more agreeable; but he had no resources within himself. He had nothing to reflect on, from which he could derive any satisfaction. My life, said he, appears like a dream of pleasure, that has passed away without leaving any substantial effects: and I am even already weary of it, though in fact, notwithstanding my advanced age, I have enjoyed it but a short time, dating from that period whence my immortality commenced.

He tried to read to divert his distempered thoughts; but from books he could receive no entertainment. If he turned over the pages of philosophers, moralists, or expounders of the mysteries of his religion, What have I to do with thy tedious lessons, or dry precepts? said he. Thou writest to men like thyself, subject to mortality; thou teachest them how to live, that they may learn how to die; but what is this to me? as I am not subject to the latter, thy advice can be of little use to me in regard to the former.

He had next recourse to the poets; but their works gave him as little pleasure as the others. Absorbed as he had been in the grosser pleasures of sense, he had lost those fine feelings, which constitute that delicate and pleasing perception we have, of such images, as are addressed to the heart. He knew the fallacy and even essence of all sensual enjoyments; and to the most warm descriptions of love and the most pathetic pictures of grief he was equally insensible.

Poor wretch, said he, on reading a fine elegy written by a lover on the death of his mistress, doomed as thou wert to a short span of life, and a narrow circle of enjoyments, thou magnifiest every thing within thy confined sphere. One single object having engrossed thy whole heart, and inspired thee with transports, thou dost immortalize her charms. Her death (despairing to supply her place) filled thy eyes with tears, and taught thee to record thy own sorrows with her praises. I partake not of thy pleasures or thy pains; none but such as are liable to the same fate can be affected by thy sentiments.

When he read of the death of heroes and kings, and the destruction of cities, or the revolution of empires, How circumscribed, said he, is the knowledge of a paltry historian! Who is at the pains of collecting the scanty materials which a life of forty or fifty years perhaps affords him, and then he makes a mighty parade of learning, with the poor pittance for which he has been drudging all his days. How infinitely superior will my fund of information be, who shall myself be an eye-witness to events as extraordinary as these, and numbered a thousand times over; for doubtless the same things which have happened, will happen again. What curiosity can you incite in me, who shall infallibly see the same chain of causes and effects take place over and over again, in the vast round of eternity?

The accounts of travellers, descriptions of the manners and customs of various countries, and books of geography, afforded him a little more entertainment. All these places, said he, I shall visit in my own proper person, and shall then be able to judge whether these accounts are just.

Whilst he endeavoured to fill up the vacuity he found in his mind, his time was spent at best but in a sort of insipid tranquillity. The voluptuary has no taste for mental pleasures.

He every now and then returned to his former excesses, but he had not the same relish for them as before. Satiety succeeded every enjoyment. In vain did his slaves torture their invention to procure new delights for him. The powers of luxury were exhausted, and his appetites palled with abundance.

He grew peevish, morose, tyrannical; cruelty took possession of his breast; he abused his women and beat his slaves, and seemed to enjoy no satisfaction but that of tormenting others.

In vain did the prudent Cadiga, who had still some little influence over him, expostulate with him on the enormity of his behaviour.

How darest thou, said he, presume to dictate to thy master, or to censure his conduct! To whom am I accountable for my actions? To God and our prophet, answered Cadiga, with a boldness that provoked Nourjahad's wrath. Thou liest, said he; as I am exempt from death, I never can be brought to judgment: what then have I to fear from the resentment, or hope from the favour of the powers whom thou namest?

But hast thou no regard, said Cadiga, for the laws of society, nor pity for the sufferings of thy fellow creatures, whom thou makest to groan every day under thy cruelty?

Foolish woman, said Nourjahad, dost thou talk to me of laws, who think myself bound by none? Civil and religious laws are so interwoven, that you cannot pluck out a single thread without spoiling the whole texture, and if I cut the woof, thinkest thou that I will spare the weft, when I can do it with impunity? The privilege of immortality which I enjoy would be bestowed on me to little purpose, if I were to suffer the weak prejudices of religion, in which I am no way concerned, to check me in any of my pursuits. And what can the feeble laws of man do? My life they cannot reach. Yet thou art a prisoner notwithstanding, answered Cadiga. True, replied Nourjahad, but even in my confinements I have surfeited with delights. Schemzeddin's death must soon give that liberty, which considering the race of uncontrouled freedom I have before me, I do not now think worth attempting. I shall then expatiate freely all over the globe; mean while I tell thee, woman, I am weary of the dull round of reiterated enjoyments which are provided for me; my sensual appetites are cloyed, I have no taste for intellectual pleasures, and I must have recourse to those which gratify the malevolent passions.

Thou art not fit to live, cried Cadiga, with a warmth of which she had cause to repent; for Nourjahad, enraged at her reply, plucked a poniard from his girdle: Go tell thy prophet so, said he, and plunged it into the side of the unfortunate slave, who fell at his feet weltering in blood.

The brutal Nourjahad, so far from being moved with this spectacle, turned from her with indifference, and quitting the chamber, entered the apartments of his women, to whom with barbarous mirth he related what he had done.

Though he had now lost all relish for delicate pleasures, or even for the more gross enjoyments of sense, he nevertheless indulged himself in them to excess; and knowing he was not accountable to any one for the death of his slave, he thought no more of Cadiga; but after a day spent in extravagant debauchery sunk to repose.

But his eyes were opened to a different scene from that on which he had closed them. He no sooner awoke than he perceived a man sitting at his bed's-foot, who seemed to be plunged in sorrow; he leaned pensively on his arm, holding a handkerchief before his eyes.

What mockery is this, said Nourjahad, didst thou suppose me dead, and art thou come to mourn over me?

Not so, my lord, replied the man, I knew that you still lived; but the sultan is dead, the good Schemzeddin is no more! I am glad of it, replied Nourjahad, I shall now obtain my liberty. Who then is to reign in Ormuz? Doubtless, my lord, answered the man, the prince Schemerzad, the eldest son of Schemzeddin. Thou ravest, cried Nourjahad, Schemzeddin has no son. Pardon me, my lord, said the man, the sultana Nourmahal was delivered of this prince the very hour on which the unfortunate Cadiga died by your hand. Thou art insolent, replied Nourjahad, to mention that circumstance; but if so, we have indeed got a very young successor to the throne. My lord, answered the man, Schemerzad is allowed to be one of the most accomplished and wise young princes in all Persia. That is marvellous, cried Nourjahad, bursting into a fit of laughter, a sultan of four and twenty hours old must needs be wonderously wise and accomplished. Nay, my lord, replied the man, the prince is this day exactly twenty years of age.

(Nourjahad, on hearing this, looked in the face of the man, whom, from his dress, supposing he had been one of his slaves, he had not regarded before, but now perceived he was a stranger.) Twenty years old! cried he, starting up, thou dost not tell me so! Most certain, said the man. Schemzeddin was so far advanced in years before the birth of the prince, that he despaired of ever having a child; yet had the righteous monarch the satisfaction to see his beloved son arrive at manhood, and adorned with such virtues as made him worthy to fill his father's throne. When did the old sultan die? cried Nourjahad. His funeral obsequies were performed last night, answered the man, and the people of Ormuz have not yet wiped the tears from their eyes. It should seem then, said Nourjahad, that I have slept about twenty years! if so, prithee, who art thou? for I do not remember ever to have seen thy face before.

My name, answered the stranger, is Cozro, and I am the brother of Cadiga, that faithful creature whom thy ungoverned fury deprived of life. How darest thou mention her again? cried Nourjahad; art thou not afraid to share the same fate thyself for thy presumption?

I do not value my life, answered Cozro; having acquitted myself well of my duty here, I am sure of my reward in those blessed mansions, where avarice, luxury, cruelty and pride, can never enter. Strike then, Nourjahad, if thou darest; dismiss me to endless and uninterrupted joys, and live thyself a prey to remorse and disappointment, the slave of passions never to be gratified, and a sport to the vicissitudes of fortune.

Nourjahad was confounded at the undaunted air with which Cozro pronounced these words; he trembled with indignation, but had not courage to strike the unarmed man who thus insulted him; wherefore, dissembling his anger, I see, said he, that thou partakest of thy sister Cadiga's spirit; but answer me, How camest thou hither, and in what condition are the rest of my family? I will tell thee, answered Cozro. When Cadiga found herself dying, she sent for me: I was then a page to one of the emirs of Schemzeddin's court. She made me kneel by her bed-side and take a solemn oath, to perform with fidelity and secrecy what she should enjoin me. She then told me the secret of your life, and conjured me to watch and attend you carefully. I have hitherto, said she, had the conduct of his house; do you supply my place, and do not let Nourjahad, when he awakes from his trance, be sensible of the loss of the unfortunate Cadiga.

She then called in your principal slaves, and delivering to me in their presence the keys with which you had entrusted her, she told them they were henceforth to obey me, as they had done her. Tell my lord, said she to me, that I forgive him the death which his cruelty inflicted on a woman who loved him to the latest minute of her life. In pronouncing these words, she expired.

I knew not till then, pursued Cozro, that thou hadst been the murderer of my sister; but she was no sooner dead, than the slaves informed me of the manner of her death. My resentment against thee was proportioned to the horror of thy guilt; and had I thrown myself at the feet of Schemzeddin, and implored justice on thy crimes, neither thy riches nor thy immortality would have availed thee, but thou wouldst have been condemned by a perpetual decree, to have languished out thy wretched existence in a vile dungeon.

And what hindered thee, cried Nourjahad, from pursuing thy revenge, seeing I was not in a condition to resist thee? My reverence for the oath I had taken, answered Cozro, and fear of offending the Almighty!

Nourjahad, at this reply, was struck with a secret awe which he could not repel; he remained silent whilst Cozro proceeded.

I obtained permission of the master whom I served, to leave him, and entered immediately on my new employment; but I found I had undertaken a difficult task. Thou hadst rendered thyself so odious to thy women, that not one of them retained the smallest degree of love or fidelity towards thee. In spite of my vigilance they made thy hated seraglio the scene of their unlawful pleasures; and at length having bribed the eunuchs who guarded them, they all in one night fled from thy detested walls, taking with them the slaves who had assisted them in their purpose. Pernicious spirit, exclaimed Nourjahad, are these the fruits I am to reap from thy fatal indulgence! The rest of your servants, pursued Cozro, I endeavoured to keep within the bounds of their duty. And how didst thou succeed? cried Nourjahad. But ill, replied Cozro; they all declared that nothing could have induced them to stay so long with a master of so capricious and tyrannical a humour, but the luxury and idleness in which thou permittedst them to live; and finding I managed your affairs with oeconomy, they one after the other left your house; neither promises nor threats having power to prevent those who stayed longest in thy service, from following the example of the first who deserted thee; so that I alone of all thy numerous household have remained faithful to thee: I, who of all others, had the most reason to abhor thee! But I have now acquitted myself of the trust which was reposed in me, and I leave thee as one condemned to wander in an unknown land, where he is to seek out for new associates, and to endeavour by the power of gold to bribe that regard from men which his own worth cannot procure for him.

Unfortunate wretch that I am, cried Nourjahad, pierced to the quick with what he had just been told, what benefit have I hitherto received from my long life, but that of feeling by miserable experience the ingratitude and frailty of man's nature? How transitory have been all my pleasures! the recollection of them dies on my memory, like the departing colours of the rainbow, which fades under the eye of the beholder, and leaves not a trace behind. Whilst on the other hand, every affliction with which I have been visited has imprinted a deep and lasting wound on my heart, which not even the hand of time itself has been able to heal.

What have thy misfortunes been, said Cozro, that are not common to all the race of man? Oh, I have had innumerable griefs, said Nourjahad. After a short enjoyment (during my fatal slumbers) the grave robbed me of Mandana, whilst she was yet in the bloom of youth and beauty. I lamented her death—tears and heaviness of heart were my portion for many days. Yet remembering that sorrow would not recall the dead, I suffered myself to be comforted, and sought for consolation in the society of my other women, and the fond and innocent caresses of an infant son, whom Mandana left me. Joy and tranquillity revisited my dwelling, and new pleasures courted my acceptance; but they again eluded my grasp, and in one night (for so it appeared to me) my son like an unnatural viper, forgetting all my tenderness, plundered and deserted me. The two faithful friends in whom I most confided had closed their eyes for ever; and the beauties of my seraglio, whom I had last beheld fresh and charming as the lilies of the field, I now saw deformed with wrinkles and bending under the infirmities of age.

Yet these afflictions I surmounted; and resolved once more to be happy. And wert thou so? interrupted Cozro. No, replied Nourjahad, the treacherous joys deceived me; yet I still looked forward with hope, but now awake to fresh disappointment. I find myself abandoned by those whose false professions of love had lulled me into security, and I rouse myself like a savage beast in the desart, whose paths are shunned by all the children of men.

Nourjahad could not conclude this speech without a groan, that seemed to rend his heart.

As thou art, said Cozro, exempt from punishment hereafter, dost thou think also to escape the miseries of this life? Mistaken man, know, that the righteous Being, whose ordinances thou defyest, will even here take vengeance on thy crimes. And if thou wilt look back on thy past life, thou wilt find (for I have heard thy story) that every one of those several ills of which thou complainest was sent as a scourge to remind thee of thy duty, and inflicted immediately after the commission of some notorious breach of it.

The death of Mandana was preceded by a brutal fit of drunkenness, by which, contrary to the laws of our prophet, thou sufferedst thyself to be overtaken. Then it was thy good genius, to punish thee, plunged thee into that temporary death, from which thou didst awake to grief and disappointment: But thou madest no use of the admonition, but didst permit thyself to be again swallowed up by intemperance; and not content to tread the ordinary paths of vice, thou turnedst out of the road, to the commission of a crime, to which thou couldst have no temptation, but the pride and licentiousness of thy heart. Thy profanation of our holy religion, in presuming to personate our great prophet, and make thy concubines represent the virgins of paradise, was immediately chastised as it deserved, by a second time depriving thee of those faculties, which thou didst prostitute to such vile purposes.

The ills with which thou foundest thyself surrounded on awaking from thy trance served to no other purpose than to stir up thy resentment against the power who governed thy life. And instead of reforming thy wickedness, thou soughtest out new ways of rendering thyself still more obnoxious to the wrath of Heaven. In the wantonness of thy cruelty, thou stainedst thy hand in blood; and that same night were thy eyelids sealed up by the avenging hand of thy watchful genius, and thy depraved senses consigned for twenty years to oblivion! See then, continued Cozro, if a life which is to be a continued round of crimes and punishments in alternate succession is a gift worthy to be desired by a wise man? for assure thyself, Oh Nourjahad, that by the immutable laws of Heaven one is to be a constant concomitant of the other, and that either in this world or the next, vice will meet its just reward.

Alas, replied Nourjahad, thou hast awakened in me a remorse of which I was never sensible before; I look back with shame on the detested use I have made of those extraordinary gifts vouchsafed me by my guardian spirit.

What shall I do, Oh Cozro, to expiate the offences I have committed? For though I have no dread of punishment hereafter, yet does that ætherial spark within inspire me with such horror for my former crimes, that all the vain delights which this world can afford me will not restore my mind to peace, till by a series of good actions I have atoned for my past offences.

If thou art sincere in thy resolutions, replied Cozro, the means, thou knowest, are amply in thy power. Thy riches will enable thee to diffuse blessings amongst mankind, and thou wilt find more true luxury in that, than in all the gratifications wherewith thou hast indulged thy appetites.

It shall be so, replied Nourjahad; my treasures shall be open to thee, thou venerable old man, and do thou make it thy business to find out proper objects, whereon charity and benevolence may exert their utmost powers.

Enquire out every family in Ormuz whom calamity hath overtaken, and provided they did not bring on their distress by their own wilful misconduct, restore them to prosperity. Seek out the helpless and the innocent; and by a timely supply of their wants, secure them against the attacks of poverty, or temptations of vice. Search for such as you think have talents which will render them useful to society; but who, for want of the goods of fortune, are condemned to obscurity; relieve their necessities, and enable them to answer the purposes for which nature designed them. Find out merit wherever it lies concealed, whether with-held from the light by diffidence, chained down and clogged by adversity, obscured by malice, or overborne by power; lift it up from the dust, and let it shine conspicuous to the world.

Glorious task! cried Cozro; happy am I in being the chosen instrument of Nourjahad's bounty, and still more happy shall he be in seeing the accomplishment of his good designs.

We must not stop here, said Nourjahad; I will have hospitals built for the reception of the aged and the sick; and my tables shall be spread for the refreshment of the weary traveller. No virtuous action shall pass by me unrewarded, and no breach of the laws of temperance, justice, or mercy, shall escape unreproved. My own example, so far as it can influence, shall henceforth countenance the one, and discourage the other.

Blessed be the purpose of thy heart, said Cozro, and prosperous be the days of thy life!

Nourjahad now found the anxiety under which he had but a little before laboured exceedingly relieved. My mind, said he, is much more at ease than it was; let us not delay to put our design in execution. I will lead you to the place where my treasure is concealed, which I never yet discovered to any one. Saying this, he took Cozro by the hand, and conducted him to the cave.

Thou seest here, said he, riches which can never be exhausted; thou mayest perceive that I have not yet sunk a third part of one of these urns which contain my wealth; yet have I with monstrous profusion lavished away immense sums. Five more such urns as these are yet untouched. Those six which thou seest on the right hand contain wedges of the finest gold, which must be equal in value to the others. These six, which are ranged on the left, are filled with precious stones, whose worth must be inestimable: the wealth of Ormuz would not purchase a single handful. Judge then, my friend, if I need be sparing in my liberality.

Cozro expressed his astonishment at the sight of these wonders. If thou wouldst be advised by me, said he, thou wouldst secretly remove from Ormuz, and carry thy treasures with thee. Thou mayest deposit part of them in each of the different countries through which thou passest in thy progress all over the earth. By this means thou mayest have it in thy power to distribute with more ease thy bounty wherever thou goest; and be always provided with riches in what part soever of the world thou shalt chuse for a time to take up thy residence. Thy long abode in this city will draw observations on thee sooner or later; and thy person's not having undergone any change from length of time, will bring on thee the suspicion of magic; for tradition will not fail to inform posterity of thy strange history.

You counsel well, replied Nourjahad; as I am now at liberty, I will retire from Ormuz. You, my dear Cozro, shall accompany me; your prudent counsel shall be my guide; and when I shall be deprived of you by death, I will still endeavour to follow your wise precepts.

Come, continued he, I am in haste to enter on my new course of life; let us both go into the city and try to find out proper objects on which to exert our charity. I shall pass without observation, and unknown, as few of my contemporaries can now be living, and I will not leave the country which gave me birth, without first making it feel the effects of that beneficence which thou hast awakened in my heart.

Deserving of praise as thou art, said Cozro, thou for the present must suppress thy ardour to do good; for though by the death of Schemzeddin thou art no longer a prisoner, thou art not nevertheless yet at liberty to leave thy house. Why not? answered Nourjahad, who is there now to prevent me?

The young sultan, replied Cozro, deeply afflicted for the death of his father, and out of a pious regard to his memory, has given strict commandment, that all his subjects should observe a solemn mourning for him, during the space of twenty days; in which time all the shops, and places of public resort (except the mosques) are to be shut up, and no business of any kind transacted; nor are any persons to be seen in the streets, excepting those who visit the sick, and the slaves who must necessarily be employed to carry provisions, on pain of the sultan's heavy displeasure.

This edict was published yesterday, and the people of Ormuz all love the memory of Schemzeddin and the person of their present sultan too well not to pay an exact obedience to it.

If so, said Nourjahad, I will not by my example encourage others to infringe their duty; yet as the relieving of the poor is in itself meritorious, I would not wish to be with-held from doing it so long as twenty days. How many virtuous people may be during that time pining for want! more especially as this prohibition must cut off all intercourse between man and man, and deprive many poor wretches of the charitable succour they might otherwise receive. I think therefore that thou, Cozro, in thy slave's habit, mayst go forth unsuspected; and by privately seeking out, and alleviating the miseries of our fellow-citizens, do an act of more real benefit, than can result from the strictest conformity to this pageant of sorrow, which many in their hearts I am sure must condemn.

Cozro approving of these sentiments, readily agreed to the expedient, and taking a large purse of gold with him to distribute as occasion might serve, immediately set out in order to execute his lord's demands.

Nourjahad now entered on a total reformation in his way of living. He rose at day break, and spent the morning in study or meditation. Luxury and intemperance were banished from his board; his table was spread with the plainest dishes, and he wholly abstained from excess in wine. His slumbers were sweet, and he found his health more vigorous.

I will no more, said he, enslave myself to the power of beauty. I have lived to see the decay of a whole seraglio of the fairest faces in Persia, and have sighed for the ingratitude of the next generation that succeeded them. I will not then seek out for those destroyers of my quiet, for whose death or infidelity I must for ever complain. Mandana was the only woman who ever really deserved my love; could I recal her from the grave, and endue her with the same privilege of which I am myself possessed, I would confine myself to her arms alone; but since that is impossible, I will devote myself to the charms of virtue, which of all things she most resembled.

Whilst Nourjahad was thus resolving to correct the errors of his past life, his virtue was not merely in speculation. He never laid him down to rest, without the satisfaction of having made some one the better for him. Cozro, who constantly spent the day in enquiring out and relieving the distressed, failed not to return every night to give an account of his charitable mission, and to infuse into his master's bosom the (till now unfelt) joy which springs from righteous deeds.

The heart of Nourjahad was expanded, and glowed with compassion for those sufferings which Cozro feelingly described as the lot of so many of his fellow-creatures. As charity and benevolence rose in his breast, he found his pride subside. He was conscious of his own unworthiness. He kneeled, he prayed, he humbled himself before the Almighty, and returned thanks to God for enabling him to succour the unfortunate.

In this happy frame of mind he continued for eighteen days; there wanted but two more to the expiration of the mourning for the sultan, when Nourjahad was to be at full liberty to pursue in his own person the dictates of his reformed, and now truly generous and benevolent heart.

He was sitting alone in his apartment, waiting the arrival of Cozro, in the pleasing expectation of receiving some fresh opportunity of doing good. The hour of his usual return was already past, and Nourjahad began to fear some accident had happened to him; but he little knew that a black cloud hung over him, which was ready to pour down all its malignity on his own head.

As he mused on what might be the occasion of Cozro's long stay, he heard a loud knocking at his door. It was immediately opened by one of his slaves, and a man, whom by his habit he knew to be one of the cady's[7] officers, rudely entered his chamber.

How comes it, said the stranger, that thou hast had the temerity, in contempt of our sovereign lord's commands, to employ thy emissary about the city at a time when thou knowest that so strict an injunction has been laid on all people to keep within their houses, none being permitted to stir abroad but for the absolute necessities of life, or in cases of imminent danger?

Far be it from me, replied Nourjahad, to disobey our mighty sultan's orders; but I understood that slaves had permission to go unquestioned on their master's

7 A Middle Eastern civil judge.

business. And what business, answered the man, can thy slave have from morning to night in so many different quarters of the city?

Nourjahad, who did not care to be himself the trumpeter of his own good deeds, hesitated to give an answer.

Ha, ha, cried the stranger, I see plainly there is something dangerous in thy mystery, and that the money which thy slave has been distributing amongst such a variety of people is for a purpose very different from that which he pretends. A likely matter it is indeed that a private man should bestow in charity such sums as Cozro acknowledges he has within these few days distributed!

Yet nothing is more certain, replied Nourjahad, than that Cozro has spoke the truth. We shall see that, replied the officer, in a tone of insolence; Cozro is already in prison, and my orders are to conduct thee to him.

Nourjahad, exceedingly troubled at hearing this, replied, He was ready to go with him; and the officer led him out of his house.

It was now late at night; they passed along the streets without meeting any one, and soon reached the place wherein Cozro was confined. It was the prison where such persons were shut up as were accused of treason against the state.

Here he found the unfortunate Cozro in a dungeon. Alas, cried he, as soon as his master entered, why do I see thee here? Say rather, my dear Cozro, replied Nourjahad, what strange fatality has brought *thee* to this dismal place?

I can give no other account, answered Cozro, but that in returning home this night, I was seized on in the street by some of those soldiers who were employed to patrol about the city, to see that the sultan's orders were punctually observed; and being questioned concerning my business, I told them that I had been relieving the wants of indigent people, and saving even from perishing some poor wretches who had not wherewithal to buy food.

That is an idle errand, replied one of them, and might have been deferred till the term of mourning was expired; however, if you will give me a piece of gold, I will let you pass for this time, otherwise both you and your employer may happen to repent of having transgressed the sultan's commands. I made no scruple, pursued Cozro, to take out my purse, in which there were ten sequins[8] left. I gave one of them to the soldier, but the rapacious wretches seeing I had more money, were not content with this, but insisted on my giving the whole amongst them. I refused; some angry words ensued; one of the miscreants struck me, and I returned the blow. Enraged at this, they hurried me before the cady, to whom they accused me of having disobeyed the edict and assaulted the sultan's officers in the discharge of their duty. I was not heard in my defence, having four witnesses against me, but was immediately dragged to this horrid prison; and the sultan himself, they say, is to take cognizance of my offence.

Oh, Heaven, cried Nourjahad, to what mischiefs does not the love of gold expose us! See, my friend, into what misfortunes thou art plunged by the sordid avarice of those vile soldiers. But why, why didst thou hesitate to give up that paltry sum which thou hadst in thy purse, to obtain thy liberty? I do not repent

[8] A Venetian gold coin.

what I have done, answered Cozro, and shall contentedly suffer the penalty I
have incurred, since it was in so good a cause.

If the sultan is just, replied Nourjahad, the punishment ought only to fall on
me, who alone am guilty, since what thou didst was by my command.

Here the officer who had conducted Nourjahad to prison, and who was present
at this discourse, interposed, and addressing himself to Nourjahad, Thou hast
not as yet been accused to the sultan, said he, and it is not too late to extricate
even thy slave from this troublesome affair; it is but making a handsome present
to the cady, and I will undertake this matter will go no farther. I am willing to
do so, replied Nourjahad, eagerly; name your demand, and you shall have it.
Provided I am allowed to go home to my own house, I will fetch the money;
and if you are afraid of my escaping, you yourself may bear me company.

I will not consent to it, replied Cozro; neither liberty nor life are worth purchasing on base conditions. I will submit my cause to Schemerzad's justice—the
cause of uprightness and truth; my own innocence shall be my support, and I
will dare the worst that fraud and malice can suggest against me.

In vain did Nourjahad urge him to accept the proffered terms; he remained
inflexible to all the arguments he could use to persuade him; wherefore, finding
him determined, he was obliged to desist; and Cozro, after passing the remainder
of the night in quiet and profound sleep, though without any other bed than
the bare earth, was at dawn of day called forth to appear before the sultan.

The reflections Nourjahad made on the resolute behaviour of Cozro served
not a little to fortify his mind. How noble must this man's soul be, said he, which
sets him thus above the reach of adversity! and with what contempt he looks
down on the glorious prospects he has before him, when put in the balance
with his integrity. Surely it is not in this life he places his happiness, since he is
so ready to forego the pleasures he might enjoy with me, in that participation
of wealth and liberty which I have promised him. How superior is my servant
to me, who but for his example, should now sink under my fears; but he has
resources which I have not. Alas, why did I barter my hopes of paradise for the
vain, the transitory, the fallacious joys which this vile world bestows! Already I
have tried them; what do they inspire but satiety and disgust? I never experienced
true contentment, but during the time, short as it is, since I abjured those follies in
which I once delighted: And I am now persuaded, that after having passed a few,
a very few years more in the enjoyment of such gratifications as I have not yet
had an opportunity of tasting, that I shall grow even weary of the light, and wish
to be dismissed to that place, where we are told no sorrows can approach.

Nourjahad was buried in these reflections, when he was roused by the return
of Cozro. The glimmering light which a lamp afforded struck full on the face of
his friend (for he no longer considered him as a servant) and he rejoiced to see
Cozro's chearful countenance, by which he judged that he had nothing to fear.

I am come, said Cozro, approaching Nourjahad, and kissing his hand, to bid
thee adieu, for from this day, we are to be for ever divided! It is that thought
only which makes our separation grievous: Had I hopes of ever beholding thy
face in the mansions of light, I should go to death with the same alacrity with
which I close my eyes in slumber.

Good Heaven, cried Nourjahad, doest thou talk of death? Can it be, is it possible that thy life is in danger?

What is the life, about which thou art anxious? replied Cozro; our being here is but a shadow; that only is real existence which the blessed enjoy after their short travel here. And know, Oh Nourjahad, I would not yield up my expectations of the humblest place in paradise for the sovereign rule of the whole earth, though my days were to be extended to the date of thy life, and every wish of my soul gratified to the utmost. Think then, with how little reluctance I shall leave a world, wherein I am sure of meeting nothing but oppression, treachery, and disappointment, where mercy is construed into treason, and charity is called sedition!

And art thou then doomed to die? said Nourjahad, pale and trembling at the thought, though convinced it was a predicament in which he could never stand.

I am, answered Cozro, my offence was found capital. Disobedience to the sultan's edict alone incurred a heavy punishment; but my crime was, by the malice of my accusers, so highly aggravated, that the penalty became death. They charged me with having distributed money for evil purposes, amongst persons disaffected to the state, and with having beat and abused those officers who first detected me. In vain did I offer all the pleas that truth could suggest; my enemies, exasperated at losing the sum which they hoped to have extorted from you, swore to the facts of which I was accused, and the rigid sultan condemned me to death. What thy fate is to be, I know not; but since it is thy misfortune to be doomed to perpetual life, better purchase thy freedom on any terms, than be condemned to languish for years in a prison, for such probably will be thy lot.

Oh that I could die with thee! said Nourjahad; miserable that I am, thus to be deprived of thy counsel and friendship, at a time when I so much stood in need of them; but wherefore, my friend, why should we submit to the tyranny of the sultan? though thou art condemned, there may yet be found means to deliver thee. The keeper of the prison will gladly set a price on thy liberty; a hundred thousand pieces of gold shall be thy ransom; and I shall think myself rich by the purchase! And what is to become of thee, replied Cozro? I will buy my own freedom at the same rate, answered Nourjahad, and we will both fly from Ormuz together. And leave your treasures behind you, cried Cozro, for it will be impossible to convey from hence such a vast mass of riches without discovery.

I value them no longer, said Nourjahad; they can never yield me any permanent enjoyment. The saving thy life is the only good turn I now expect from them. That once accomplished, I shall desire to retain no more of them than what will support me above want, and I will leave the rest to be for ever hid in the bosom of the earth, where they now lie, that they may never more become a snare to others as they have been to me.

Praised be our holy prophet, said Cozro, that has at length endued the heart of Nourjahad with wisdom. Pursue the purposes of thy soul; effect thy own freedom as soon as possible, since no comfort can visit thee in the gloom of this frightful prison; but tempt not Cozro back to a life which he despises. I tell thee again, there is nothing in this world to be put in competition with the glories I have in prospect in that state to which I am now hastening. Why then, Nourjahad, wouldst thou retard my felicity, or wish me to hazard, for the sake of delusive pleasures, those transcendent joys which await the virtuous?

The energy with which Cozro delivered himself pierced Nourjahad to the inmost soul. A holy ardor was kindled in his breast, which he had never felt before; he found his faculties enlarged, his mind was transported above this world; he felt as it were unimbodied, and an involuntary adjuration burst from his lips. Oh, holy prophet, said he, take, take back the gift, that I in the ignorance and presumption of my heart so vainly sought, and which too late I find a punishment instead of a blessing! I contemn riches, and for ever cast them from me; suffer me then to yield up my life; for there can be no true happiness but in beholding thee, Oh Mahomet, face to face, in the neverfading fields of paradise!

Saying this, he prostrated himself on the ground, and continued for some time in mental prayer.

Cozro observed an awful silence whilst he continued in this posture. When Nourjahad arose from the earth, May our great prophet, said Cozro, hear your prayers; and were he even now to grant them, all the favours he has already bestowed on you would be poor and contemptible to this last best boon. Farewel, said he; I must now leave thee: I was only permitted to come and bid thee adieu. May the Supreme grant thy petition: then shall we again meet in the mansions of happy spirits. Nourjahad embraced him, and Cozro withdrew.

Being now left at liberty to his own thoughts, he made bitter reflections on the strangeness of his fate. Fool, fool that I was, cried he aloud, beating his breast, to prefer so rash, so impious a petition to the prophet, as to desire the everlasting laws of nature to be overturned, to gratify my mad luxurious wishes. I thought the life of man too short for the enjoyment of those various and unbounded pleasures which wealth could procure; but it is long since I have found my error. Well did my guardian spirit say I should repent of the gift I had implored, when it should be too late. I do indeed repent; but Oh, thou benign intelligence, if thou hast remaining any favour for thy inconsiderate unhappy charge, descend once more to my relief, and if possible restore me to that state, for which I was designed by my creator; a poor mortal, liable to and now longing for the friendly stroke of death.

He had scarce pronounced these words, when his prison doors flew open; a refulgent light flashed in, which illuminated the whole dungeon, and he beheld his guardian genius standing before him, exactly as he had appeared to him before. Thy prayers are heard, said he, Oh son of frailty, and thy penitence is accepted in the sight of the Most High. I am sent down again by our prophet to reassume that gift which thou art now satisfied must make thee miserable. Yet examine thy heart once more before I pronounce thy irrevocable doom; say, art thou willing again to become subject to the common lot of mortals?

Most willing, replied Nourjahad; yet I wonder not, my seraphic guide, that thou shouldst doubt the stability of my mind; but in this last purpose of it I am sure I shall remain unshaken.

If so, replied the shining vision, thy guardian angel consigns thee to the arms of death, with much more joy than he conferred on thee riches and immortality. Thou hast nothing more to do, than to prostrate thyself with thy face to the earth. Remain this evening in fervent prayer, and await what shall befal thee to-morrow.

Nourjahad made no reply, but falling with his face to the ground, he soon found the dungeon restored to its former gloom, the light and the guardian spirit vanishing together in an instant.

He continued in devout prayer till night; when the keeper of the prison entered his dungeon to bring him some refreshment.

The sultan, said he, purposes to examine you tomorrow, and much I fear you will have as rigorous a sentence passed on you, as that which has been already executed on Cozro. Is he then dead? cried Nourjahad, mournfully. He is, replied the keeper; it is but an hour since I saw him deprived of breath; but he received the blow with such an heroic firmness, that thou wouldst have thought he rather enjoyed a triumph, than suffered an ignominious death.

Happy, happy Cozro! cried Nourjahad; thou art now beyond the reach of misfortune, whilst I, perhaps, may be doomed to sustain for years a wretched life.

Thy life, said the keeper, may be nearer a period than thou art aware of. The sultan is covetous, and surrounded by needy favourites, whom the report of your immense wealth has made eager for your destruction; for you cannot be ignorant, that should you die, involved as it is said you are, in Cozro's guilt, your treasures would be confiscated to the sultan. From this circumstance I have heard it whispered, your head is already devoted; and this perhaps was the true cause of Cozro's death, and will give the better colour to your's. It is not, however, added he, even yet too late to prevent the danger; had not your slave been obstinate, he might now have been alive, and out of the reach of harm. You have the same means of preservation in regard to your own person, still in your power; and if you will make it worth my while to run the risque, I will this night set you at liberty.

And dost thou think, said Nourjahad, that I have profited so little by the example of my noble friend, as to accept of thy offer, sordid and treacherous as thou art? If thou art base enough to betray thy trust for gold, know that the mind of Nourjahad is above receiving a favour from such a wretch. As for my wealth, let the sultan take it; my only wish is to part with that and my life also.

That wish may speedily be accomplished, said the keeper, in an angry tone, and to-morrow perhaps you may repent of your folly, when you find yourself condemned to follow your noble friend to the other world. Nourjahad made no reply; and the keeper sullenly departed.

Nourjahad spent the night in prayers and meditation; he found peace and tranquillity restored to his breast, and, perfectly resigned to the will of the prophet, he waited the event of the next day with the utmost composure.

In the morning the keeper of the prison entered to him. Follow me, said he; thou art going to appear before the sultan, who himself is to be thy judge; a rigorous one thou wilt find him, but thy folly be on thy own head, who didst proudly refuse the proffer I made thee of liberty and life.

Lead on, said Nourjahad, it is not for such men as thou art, to censure a conduct, to which thou dost not know the motive.

He was now carried out of the dungeon, and ordered to ascend a chariot, in which the captain of the sultan's guards was already placed, to receive his prisoner. The chariot was surrounded by soldiers; and in this manner he was conducted to the presence of the sultan.

Schemerzad was seated on a throne, in the hall of his palace, wherein he was used to distribute justice. The emirs, and great officers of his court, were standing round him.

Nourjahad stood before him with his eyes bent to the ground; and however awed he might be at the presence of his royal master, and the august assembly which surrounded him, yet the dignity of conscious innocence, and the perfect reliance he had on the Supreme Judge of *his* judge, rendered him superior to every thing. His deportment was modest and respectful, yet did he discover no symptom of fear.

The sultan made a sign for every one present to withdraw, but one person who stood on the lower step of his throne, and whom Nourjahad judged to be his prime visier.

What hast thou to say, presumptuous man, said Schemerzad, in a stern voice, what excuse canst thou offer for daring, in contempt of my edict, to employ thy agent (during the time set apart for mourning) in going about the city from day to day; ostentatiously displaying thy ill-timed liberality amongst my subjects; endeavouring, as I am informed, to conciliate their affections, for purposes dangerous to me, and the safety of my crown? What hast thou to offer in answer to this charge?

Nourjahad prostrated himself to the ground. Mighty sultan, said he, I have nothing to offer in extenuation of my fault, with regard to the first part of the charge. I acknowledge that I distributed money amongst your majesty's subjects, and that at a time too when every act (but those of absolute necessity) was interdicted. I offer not to palliate this breach of my duty.—

Audacious wretch, interrupted the sultan, to what end was thy profusion employed?

To obtain a blessing from Heaven, answered Nourjahad; and by relieving the wants and afflictions of others, to make some atonement for my own riotous and intemperate abuse of that wealth, which ought to have been employed to better purposes.

Wouldst thou persuade me then, cried Schemerzad, that charity was thy motive! It was, illustrious sultan, replied Nourjahad; I have spoke the truth, and to convince your majesty that I have no sinister designs against the ever sacred person of my sovereign, I will now voluntarily yield up that treasure to thee, which had I been vile enough to have so employed, would have bought the fidelity of more than half thy subjects, though every man of them had stood near the heart and throne of Schemerzad.

The undaunted manner in which Nourjahad spoke these words, made Schemerzad shake on his imperial seat; but quickly reassuming the majesty of his station, Do then as thou has spoken, said he, and I will believe thee.

If your majesty will permit me, said Nourjahad, to go to my house, and will send a proper person with me, I will deliver up into his hands all my wealth, requesting no more than will supply my wants so long as heaven permits me to live.

I will not trust thee out of my sight, said Schemerzad; thou mayest as well instruct some one in my presence where to find the riches of which I hear thou art possessed, and I will send for them.

Nourjahad then informed the sultan of the subterraneous cave in his garden; and delivering him the key, told him he would there find all the wealth of which he was master.

Schemerzad immediately dispatched his visier, ordering him to have the riches he should find immediately conveyed to his treasury. He then commanded Nourjahad to retire into a saloon, that was separated from the hall only by a curtain, and there wait the return of the visier; before whom, the sultan said he had some farther questions to put to him.

As the gardens of Nourjahad joined to those belonging to the royal palace, the visier was not long in going and returning. Nourjahad heard him talk to Schemerzad, and straight he was called on to come forth, and stand before the sultan: But Schemerzad now accosted him in a voice like thunder. Perfidious and insolent slave, said he, art thou not afraid of instant death falling on thee, for daring thus to falsify before thy sovereign lord and master? Say, before thou art cut off by torture from the face of the earth, where thou hast concealed thy wealth! for well thou knowest, there is nothing contained in that cave, which thou pretendest with so much care to lock up.

Nothing! replied Nourjahad, in amazement. By the heart of our prophet, when I last was there, it contained more than would purchase thy whole empire a thousand times over. It was but the very day on which I was dragged to prison, that I saw it; the key has never since been out of my pocket; who then could possibly have conveyed away my treasure?

As Nourjahad applied himself to the visier whilst he spoke, that minister thinking himself reflected on by his words, replied scornfully, Thou thinkest perhaps it is I who have robbed thee, and that I have framed this story to deceive the sultan, and ruin thee. I do not say so, answered Nourjahad; but this I am sure of, that no human being but thyself knew where to find my treasure. Some dæmon, perhaps, replied the visier, with an air of contempt, has removed it thence.

Nourjahad now recollecting suddenly, that his guardian spirit had probably reclaimed this, as well as the other gift, replied coolly, It is not at all unlikely; a certain genius, who watches over my motions, has undoubtedly carried away my wealth.

Do not think, said the sultan, that affecting to be out of thy senses, shall preserve thee from my wrath.

Your majesty, said the visier, had best order that his head be instantly struck off, for daring to impose on your credulity and abuse your clemency in suffering him to out-live that slave, who obstinately persisted in refusing to discover his master's riches.

Did Cozro do so? cried Nourjahad. He did, answered the visier; but we will see whether thou wilt persevere in the denial, and to the latest minute of thy life preserve the firmness of thy slave.

And who is it that thou callest a slave, thou minister of cruelty? said Nourjahad boldly: The soul of Cozro raised him infinitely more above thee, than the rank of the sultan of Persia lifts him above the meanest of his subjects.—My lord, pursued he, throwing himself at Schemerzad's feet, I have no other plea to offer for my life; I call Heaven to witness I have spoken nothing but the truth; the severest tortures you can inflict on me will extort no more. I was willing to make a voluntary sacrifice of my riches; I am now as ready to yield my life.

Art thou not then afraid to die? said Schemerzad.

No, mighty sultan, answered Nourjahad, I look upon death to a virtuous man, as the greatest good the Almighty can bestow!

The sultan, instead of making any reply, clapped his hands; and Nourjahad supposing it was a signal to have him seized and carried to execution, rose up, and stood with an intrepidity in his looks, that shewed how little he was affected with the near prospect of death.

But instead of the slaves whom he expected to see coming to lay hold on him, he beheld standing close to the throne of Schemerzad, his guardian genius, just in the same celestial form in which he had twice before appeared to him!

Awed and amazed, Nourjahad started back, and gazed at the heavenly vision. Not daring to trust his senses, he remained mute, and motionless, for some minutes; but he was roused from his deep attention, by a loud burst of laughter which broke at once from the sultan, the visier, and the guardian genius.

This new and extraordinary incident threw Nourjahad into fresh astonishment; when, without giving him time to recover himself, the angelic youth, snatching from his head a circlet of flowers intermixed with precious stones, which encompassed his brows, and shaded a great part of his forehead; and at the same time throwing off a head of artificial hair which flowered in golden ringlets down his shoulders; a fine fall of brown hair which was concealed under it succeeded, dropping in light curls on his neck and blushing cheeks; and Nourjahad, in the person of his seraphic guide, discovered his beloved and beautiful Mandana!

Whatever transports the sight of her would at another time have inspired in the breast of Nourjahad, his faculties were now too much absorbed in wonder, to leave room for any other passion. Wherefore, not daring to approach her, the sultan, willing to put an end to his suspence, cried out, Look up, Nourjahad, raise thy eyes to thy master's face, no longer the angry Schemerzad, thy offended prince, but the real Schemzeddin, thy friend and kind protector.

Nourjahad, who before, out of respect and awful distance, had not ventured to look in the sultan's face, now fixed his eyes earnestly upon him. By the life of Schemerzad, said he, if I were not certain that all this is illusion, and that thy illustrious father, my royal and once beloved master, is dead, thou art so very like him, that I should swear that thou wert the real sultan Schemzeddin himself; such at thy years was his countenance and features.

The sultan at this burst into a second fit of laughter. And for whom, said the visier, (who had by this time taken off his turban, and a false beard which he wore) for whom wouldst thou take me?

By Mahomet, cried Nourjahad, falling back a step or two, I should take thee for my old friend Hasem, if I were not convinced that the good man died above twenty years ago.

It is time, said the sultan, descending from his throne, and taking Nourjahad by the hand, it is now time to undeceive thee, and explain to thee the mystery of all those extraordinary events, which seem to have bewildered thy senses.

Know then, Nourjahad, that the adventure of thy guardian genius was all a deception, and a piece of machinery of my contrivance. You are now convinced, by the evidence of your own eyes, that your celestial intelligence was no other than this young damsel.

I had a mind to make trial of thy heart, and for this purpose made choice of this charming virgin, for whom I own I had entertained a passion, but found I could not gain her affections. She had seen you from the windows of the women's apartments, walking with me in the gardens of the seraglio, and had conceived a tenderness for you, which she frankly confessed to me, declaring at the same time, she would never give her love to any other. Though she was my slave, I would not put a constraint upon her inclinations; but told her, if she would assist me faithfully in a design I had formed, I would reward her, by bestowing her on you.

She readily assented to my proposal, and having previously prepared every thing for my purpose, I equipped her as you see.

It was not difficult for me to introduce her into your chamber, by a private door which you know communicates between your apartments, and certain lodgings in my palace.

I myself stood at the door, whilst she entered as you slept, and contrived to throw that light into your chamber, which disclosed to you the wonderful vision. I overheard all your discourse, and could scarce contain my laughter, when you so greedily received that marvellous essence from Mandana; which you supposed would confer immortality; but which was in reality nothing more than a soporific drug, of so potent a nature, that the fumes of it alone were capable of throwing the person who smelt them into a profound sleep. It had quickly this effect on you; and I took that opportunity of conveying into your chamber those coffers which you thought contained such immense treasures; but which in truth were as great counterfeits as your guardian angel. The supposed precious stones were nothing more than false gems, which I procured from a skilful lapidary, who had given them such an extraordinary polish and lustre, that they might well pass for jewels of inestimable value, on one better skilled in those matters than you were.

The ingots of gold were all base metal, which I got from the same artist. Nothing, in short, was real, but the money, part of which I was very willing to sacrifice to my experiment; though, as I have managed it, the largest sums which thou in thy extravagance hast expended were returned into my coffers.

As I naturally supposed that so long as the money lasted you would not have recourse to the other treasures, I was not afraid of having the fraud detected. The cave, which was an accidental circumstance, but which I had long known, was by my contrivance made the repository of thy riches.

When thou wert settled in the full possession of thy imaginary felicity, thou mayst remember that Hasem was first recommended to thy service; Mandana too was amongst other slaves presented to thy view. No wonder that her charms captivated thy heart. Her love to thee was as pure as it was fervent; but thy boundless wishes were not to be restrained; and forgetting all the rational principles that thou didst at first lay down to regulate thy conduct, thou gavest thyself up to all manner of vile excesses, and didst shew the depravity of the human heart, when unrestrained by divine laws.

It was now time, I thought, to punish thee, and to shew thee the vanity of all earthly enjoyments. By opiates infused into thy wine that night on which thou didst debase thyself by drunkenness, I threw thee into a sound sleep; and though it lasted not much longer than the usual term of ordinary repose, it yet gave me an opportunity of making such farther dispositions, as I thought necessary for the carrying on of my design.

I laid hold of this juncture to withdraw Mandana from thy arms, promising however to restore her to thee, if I found thee ever worthy of her.

I believe it is needless to inform you, that the confinement I laid you under was for no other end than to cut off all intercourse between you and any others than those of your own household, every one of whom were of my placing about you, even to the ladies of your seraglio, who were no others than the prettiest slaves I could find, amongst those who attended my own women.

Every one entrusted with my secret, were tied down by the most solemn oaths to keep it inviolably; and this with a promise of reward, served, as the event has shewn, to secure their fidelity.

There was not an action of thy life but I was made acquainted with; and whilst thou didst triumph in the joys of my successful illusion, I sometimes pitied thy weakness, and sometimes laughed at thy extravagance.

That magnificent palace of which thou thoughtest thyself master, was one which I had borrowed for the purpose from an emir who was in my secret, and who was himself often present in disguise amongst your slaves, a witness to your extravagancies. I will not encrease thy confusion by reminding thee of the inordinate excesses thou wert guilty of in thy retirement. Thou canst not have forgot the project of creating for thyself an earthly paradise. This was the second crisis I laid hold on to punish thee; and by tearing thee from thy impious pleasures, to remind thee that crimes cannot be committed with impunity. A second sleep, procured as the former was, but of somewhat longer duration, gave me full opportunity to make a total change in the face of thy affairs. Hasem (whom thou didst suppose to be dead) remained still secretly concealed in thy house, to be as it were the grand spring to move all the rest of thy domestics. The hags whom thou hadst imposed upon thee for the decayed beauties of thy seraglio, were really a set of notable old dames, whom he had tutored for the purpose: Thy former mistresses, who were insignificant slaves, were dismissed.

She who personated the feigned Cadiga, acted her part to admiration, and with the artful contrivance of having a rose-bud painted on her breast, a mark which your young favourite really bore from nature, she had cunning and address enough to impose herself on you for the very Cadiga whom you formerly loved.

I believe, proceeded the sultan, you are by this time convinced, that there was nothing supernatural in the several events of your life, and that you were in reality nothing more than the dupe of your own folly and avarice.

Thou mayst remember after this period, that, sated with voluptuousness, thy licentious heart began to grow hardened; and from rioting without controul in pleasures, which, however criminal in themselves, carry at least with them the excuse of temptation, thou wantonly didst stir up and indulge the latent cruelty of thy nature. Thy ungoverned passions led thee to an act of blood! thou piercedst with thy poniard the honest creature who remonstrated with thee on thy evil works; but Heaven did not, however, permit thee to deprive her of life.

See, Nourjahad, of what the heart of man is capable, when he shuts his eyes against the precepts of our holy prophet. Thou stoodst as it were alone in the creation, and self-dependent for thy own happiness or misery, thou lookedst not for rewards or punishments in that invisible world, from which thou thoughtest thyself by thy own voluntary act excluded.

This last barbarous deed, however, called aloud for chastisement; and thou wast for the third time deceived with a belief that thou hadst slept a number of years, in which many mortifying revolutions had happened in thy family.

I was now resolved to be myself an eye-witness of thy behaviour, and to try if there was any spark of virtue remaining in thy soul which could possibly be rekindled.

I disguised myself in the habit of a slave; and having altered my face, and my voice, I presented myself to thee under the name of Cozro. Thou knowest what passed between us on thy first awaking from thy compelled slumbers, and that I heard and saw with what indifference thou receivedst the news of my supposed death. But I will not reproach thee with ingratitude—let the memory of *that* be buried with the rest of thy errors.

I had soon the satisfaction to find that thou wast as it were a new man. The natural goodness of thy disposition, thy reason, thy experience of the deceitfulness of worldly enjoyments, joined to the remorse which thou couldst not help feeling for a series of vice and folly, at length roused thee to a just sense of what thou owedst to the dignity of thy own nature, and to the duties incumbent on thee towards the rest of thy fellow-creatures.

I now discovered, with joy, that thou hadst intirely divested thyself of that insatiable love of pleasure, to which thou hadst before addicted thyself, and that thou no longer didst regard wealth, but as it enabled thee to do good. There was but one trial more remained. If, said I, his repentance be sincere, and he has that heroism of mind which is inseparable from the truly virtuous, he will not shrink at death; but, on the contrary, will look upon it as the only means by which he can obtain those refined enjoyments suited to the divine part of his nature, and which are as much superior in their essence, as they are in their duration to all the pleasures of sense.

I made the trial—The glorious victory, Oh Nourjahad, is thine! By thy contempt of riches, thou hast proved how well thou deservedst them; and thy readiness to die shews how fit thou art to live.—

In the space of fourteen moons (for it is no longer since I first imposed on thy credulity the belief of thy miraculous state) thou hast had the experience of four times so many years. Such assuredly would be the vicissitudes of thy life, hadst thou in reality possessed what thou didst in imagination. Let this dream of existence then be a lesson to thee for the future, never to suppose that riches can ensure happiness; that the gratification of our passions can satisfy the human heart; or that the immortal part of our nature will suffer us to taste unmixed felicity, in a world which was never meant for our final place of abode. Take thy amiable Mandana to thee for a wife, and receive the fixed confidence and love of Schemzeddin.

The history says that Nourjahad was from that minute raised to be the first man in power next to the sultan; that his wisdom and virtue proved an ornament and support to the throne of Persia during the course of a long and prosperous life; and that his name was famous throughout the Eastern world.

FINIS

Charlotte Smith
1749 – 1806

C harlotte Smith was a prolific novelist and poet who responded to a harsh life by writing to express her feelings and to make money. Having married young and produced ten children, she found herself in extreme financial difficulties when her husband fell into debt, for which he was imprisoned, and an inheritance which he expected was dissolved in legal wrangling. Charlotte Smith was forced to support herself and her children by writing for money. Elegiac Sonnets (1784) made a profit and, with additions, went through several editions. Yet, despite this moderate success and her own preference for poetry, she had to turn to the far more popular form of the long novel to provide an adequate living. Over a decade as her children grew up she managed to produce one novel a year, several of them achieving considerable success, especially the first, Emmeline *(1788), which drew on the growing appetite for Gothic settings. But her later novels were frequently regarded by reviewers as too political for a woman and too approving of French revolutionary principles. In her last years the financial pressures did not diminish and her children's various misfortunes weighed heavily on her. She suffered ten years of illness before she died.*

Charlotte Smith's poems are written in the sentimental style of the day, self-conscious, sometimes self-pitying, and much concerned with humanitarian subjects like slaves and beggars; several were written in the sonnet form just beginning to come into fashion again. They reveal a melancholy that is both conventional and deeply personal; as she said, 'It was unaffected sorrows drew them forth; I wrote mournfully because I was unhappy.'

From

Elegiac Sonnets

I

THE partial Muse, has from my earliest hours
   Smiled on the rugged path I'm doomed to tread,
And still with sportive hand has snatch'd wild flowers,
   To weave fantastic garlands for my head:
But far, far happier is the lot of those
   Who never learn'd her dear delusive art;
Which, while it decks the head with many a rose,
   Reserves the thorn, to fester in the heart.
For still she bids soft Pity's melting eye
   Stream o'er the ills she knows not to remove,
Points every pang, and deepens every sigh
   Of mourning friendship, or unhappy love.
Ah! then, how dear the Muse's favours cost,
   If those paint sorrow best—who feel it most![1]

IV

'To the Moon'

QUEEN of the silver bow!—by thy pale beam,
   Alone and pensive, I delight to stray,
And watch thy shadow trembling in the stream,

[1] An allusion to Pope's *Eloisa to Abelard* I 366 (Smith's note).

Or mask the floating clouds that cross thy way.
And while I gaze, thy mild and placid light
   Sheds a soft calm upon my troubled breast;
And oft I think—fair planet of the night,
   That in thy orb, the wretched may have rest:
The sufferers of the earth perhaps may go,
   Released by death—to thy benignant sphere,
And the sad children of despair and woe
   Forget in thee, their cup of sorrow here.
Oh! that I soon may reach thy world serene,
Poor wearied pilgrim—in this toiling scene!

VIII

'To Spring'

AGAIN the wood, and long-withdrawing vale,
   In many a tint of tender green are drest,
Where the young leaves, unfolding, scarce conceal
   Beneath their early shade, the half-form'd nest
Of finch or woodlark; and the primrose pale,
   And lavish cowslip, wildly scatter'd round,
Give their sweet spirits to the sighing gale.
   Ah! season of delight!—could aught be found
   To sooth awhile the tortured bosom's pain,
Of Sorrows' rankling shaft to cure the wound,
   And bring life's first delusions once again,
'Twere surely met in thee!—thy prospect fair,
Thy sounds of harmony, thy balmy air,
Have power to cure all sadness—but despair.[2]

XLIII

THE unhappy exile, whom his fates confine
   To the bleak coast of some unfriendly isle,
Cold, barren, desart, where no harvests smile,
   But thirst and hunger on the rocks repine;
When, from some promontory's fearful brow,
   Sun after sun he hopeless sees decline

---

[2] An allusion to *Paradise Lost* Book IV: 'Vernal delight and joy, able to drive/All sadness but despair' (Smith's note).

In the broad shipless sea—perhaps may know
   Such heartless pain, such blank despair as mine:
And, if a flattering cloud appears to show
   The fancied semblance of a distant sail,
   Then melts away—anew his spirits fail,
While the lost hope but aggravates his woe!
Ah! so for me delusive Fancy toils,
Then, from contrasted truth—my feeble soul recoils.

LVIII

'The Glow-worm'

WHEN on some balmy-breathing night of Spring
   The unhappy child, to whom the world is new,
Pursues the evening moth, of mealy wing,
   Or from the heath-bell beats the sparkling dew;
He sees before his inexperienced eyes
   The brilliant Glow-worm, like a meteor, shine
On the turf-bank;—amazed, and pleased, he cries,
   "Star of the dewy grass![3]—I make thee mine!"
Then, ere he sleep, collects "the moisten'd" flower,[4]
   And bids soft leaves his glittering prize enfold,
And dreams that Fairy-lamps illume his bower:
   Yet with the morning shudders to behold
His lucid treasure, rayless as the dust!
—So turn the World's bright joys to cold and blank disgust.

LXXIII

'To a Querulous Acquaintance'

"THOU! whom Prosperity has always led
   O'er level paths, with moss and flow'rets strewn;
For whom she still prepares a downy bed
   With roses scatter'd, and to thorns unknown,
Wilt thou yet murmur at a mis-placed leaf?[5]

---

[3] Allusion to Dr Darwin (Smith's note). Erasmus Darwin was famous for his botanical poems including *The Botanic Garden* (1789–91).
[4] Allusion to Walcot's 'Ode to the Glow-worm' (Smith's note).
[5] From a story (I know not where told) of a fastidious being, who on a bed of rose leaves complained that his or her rest was destroyed because one of those leaves was doubled (Smith's note).

Think, ere thy irritable nerves repine,
    How many, born with feelings keen as thine,
Taste all the sad vicissitudes of grief;
How many steep in tears their scanty bread;
    Or, lost to reason, Sorrow's victims! rave:
How many know not where to lay their head;
    While some are driven by anguish to the grave!
Think; nor impatient at a feather's weight,
Mar the uncommon blessings of thy fate!

'Verses Intended to have been Prefixed to the Novel of Emmeline, but then Suppressed.'

O'erwhelm'd with sorrow, and sustaining long
    "The proud man's contumely, th'oppressor's wrong,"[6]
Languid despondency, and vain regret,
Must my exhausted spirit struggle yet?
Yes!—Robb'd myself of all that fortune gave,
Even of all hope—but shelter in the grave,
Still shall the plaintive lyre essay its powers
To dress the cave of Care with Fancy's flowers,
Maternal Love the fiend Despair withstand,
Still animate the heart and guide the hand.
—May you, dear objects of my anxious care,
Escape the evils I was born to bear!
Round *my* devoted head while tempests roll,
Yet there, where I have treasured up my soul,
May the soft rays of dawning hope impart
Reviving Patience to my fainting heart;—
And when its sharp solicitudes shall cease,
May I be conscious in the realms of peace
That every tear which swells my children's eyes,
From sorrows past, not present ills arise.
Then, with some friend who loves to share your pain,
For 'tis my boast that *some* such friends remain,
By filial grief, and fond remembrance prest,
You'll seek the spot where all my sorrows rest;
Recal my hapless days in sad review,
The long calamities I bore for you,
And—with an happier fate—resolve to prove
How well you merited your mother's love.

6 *Hamlet* III,1.

'The Dead Beggar, an Elegy addressed to a Lady, who was affected at seeing the Funeral of a nameless Pauper, buried at the Expence of the Parish, in the Church-Yard at Brighthelmstone, in November 1792.'

SWELLS then thy feeling heart, and streams thine eye
    O'er the deserted being, poor and old,
Whom cold, reluctant, Parish Charity
    Consigns to mingle with his kindred mould?

Mourn'st thou, that *here* the time-worn sufferer ends
    Those evil days still threatening woes to come;
Here, where the friendless feel no want of friends,
    Where even the housless wanderer finds an home?

What tho' no kindred crowd in sable forth,
    And sigh, or seem to sigh, around his bier;
Tho' o'er his coffin with the humid earth
    No children drop the unavailing tear?
Rather rejoice that *here* his sorrows cease,
    Whom sickness, age, and poverty oppress'd;
Where Death, the Leveller, restores to peace
    The wretch who living knew not where to rest.

Rejoice, that tho' an outcast spurn'd by fate,
    Thro' penury's rugged path his race he ran;
In earth's cold bosom, equall'd with the great,
    Death vindicates the insulted rights of Man.

Rejoice, that tho' severe his earthly doom,
    And rude, and sown with thorns the way he trod,
Now, (where unfeeling Fortune cannot come)
    He rests upon the mercies of his God.[7]

---

[7] A long note follows this poem in which Smith states, 'I have been told that I have incurred blame for having used in this short composition, terms that have become obnoxious to certain persons.' But she claims that liberty of thought is a right and that it remains true that the poor should not die of want.

Fanny Burney

1752–1840

F anny Burney was one of the many children of an author and musician who belonged to high social and intellectual circles in London. She began a diary when still in her teens and in 1778 anonymously published her novel Evelina; as her diary reveals, she derived much enjoyment from hearing speculation about the authorship of what proved to be a sensationally successful work. Her next more substantial novel, Cecilia, followed in 1782. In 1786 she was offered the prestigious post at court of Second Keeper of the Robes to the Queen, which she accepted to please her father but the restrictions of which she thoroughly detested. After five years she fell ill and her illness helped to extricate her from the position. A few years later she married a French emigré without income and in 1796 published the lengthy and moralistic Camilla to earn money. One son was born who proved a considerable worry to his mother and who died in early adulthood. Burney's diary gives a lively sense of London society in the late eighteenth century and of court life during the dramatic period of the King's increasing mental disorder.

The following extract is reprinted from The Diary of Fanny Burney (Lewis Gibbs (ed.), Everyman Library, Dent, London, 1971).

From

The Diary of Fanny Burney

PART ONE

JANUARY, 1778–DECEMBER, 1784

THIS year was ushered in by a grand and most important event! At the latter end of January, the literary world was favoured with the first publication of the ingenious, learned, and most profound Fanny Burney! I doubt not but this memorable affair will, in future times, mark the period whence chronologers will date the zenith of the polite arts in this island!

This admirable authoress has named her most elaborate performance, *Evelina; or, a Young Lady's Entrance into the World.*

Perhaps this may seem a rather bold attempt and title for a female whose knowledge of the world is very confined, and whose inclinations, as well as situation, incline her to a private and domestic life. All I can urge is, that I have only presumed to trace the accidents and adventures to which a 'young woman' is liable; I have not pretended to show the world what it actually *is*, but what it *appears* to a girl of seventeen: and so far as that, surely any girl who is past seventeen may safely do?

My little book, I am told, is now at all the circulating libraries. I have an exceeding odd sensation when I consider that it is now in the power of *any* and *every* body to read what I so carefully hoarded even from my best friends, till this last month or two; and that a work which was so lately lodged, in all privacy, in my bureau, may now be seen by every butcher and baker, cobbler and tinker, throughout the three kingdoms, for the small tribute of threepence.

My aunt and Miss Humphries being settled at this time at Brompton, I was going thither with Susan[1] to tea, when Charlotte acquainted me that they were then employed in reading *Evelina* to the invalid, my cousin Richard.

This intelligence gave me the utmost uneasiness—I foresaw a thousand dangers of a discovery—I dreaded the indiscreet warmth of all my confidants. In truth, I was quite sick with apprehension, and was too uncomfortable to go to Brompton, and Susan carried my excuses.

Upon her return, I was somewhat tranquillized, for she assured me that there was not the smallest suspicion of the author, and that they had concluded it to be the work of a *man*!

Finding myself more safe than I had apprehended, I ventured to go to Brompton next day. On my way upstairs, I heard Miss Humphries in the midst of Mr Villars's letter of consolation upon Sir John Belmont's rejection of his daughter;[2] and just as I entered the room, she cried out: 'How pretty that is!'

How much in luck would she have thought herself, had she known *who* heard her!

In a private confabulation which I had with my Aunt Anne, she told me a thousand things that had been said in its praise, and assured me they had not for a moment doubted that the work was a *man's*.

I must own I suffered great difficulty in refraining from laughing upon several occasions—and several times, when they praised what they read, I was on the point of saying: 'You are very good!' and so forth, and I could scarcely keep myself from making acknowledgments, and bowing my head involuntarily. However, I got off perfectly safe.

It seems, to my utter amazement, Miss Humphries has guessed the author to be Anstey,[3] who wrote the *Bath Guide*! How improbable and how extraordinary a supposition! But they have both of them done it so much honour, that, but for Richard's anger at Evelina's bashfulness, I never could believe they did not suspect me.

CHESINGTON, JUNE 18th

[1] Fanny Burney's younger sister Susan knew the secret of *Evelina's* authorship.
[2] In *Evelina* Mr Villars is the virtuous elderly guardian of the heroine; Sir John Belmont is her natural father.
[3] Christopher Anstey (1724–1805) was the author of *The New Bath Guide, or Memoirs of the Blunderhead Family*.

Here I am, and here I have been this age; though too weak to think of journalizing; however, as I never had so many curious anecdotes to record, I will not, at least this year, the first of my appearing in public—give up my favourite old hobby-horse.

I came hither the first week in May. My recovery, from that time to this, has been slow and sure; but as I could walk hardly three yards in a day at first, I found so much time to spare, that I could not resist treating myself with a little private sport with *Evelina*, a young lady whom I think I have some right to make free with. I had promised *Hetty*[4] that *she* should read it to Mr Crisp,[5] at her own particular request; but I wrote my excuses, and introduced it myself.

I told him it was a book which Hetty had taken to Brompton, to divert my cousin Richard during his confinement. He was so indifferent about it, that I thought he would not give himself the trouble to read it, and often embarrassed me by unlucky questions, such as, 'If it was reckoned clever?' and 'What I thought of it?' and 'Whether folks laughed at it?' I always evaded any direct or satisfactory answer; but he was so totally free from any idea of suspicion, that my perplexity escaped his notice.

At length, he desired me to begin reading to him. I dared not trust my voice with the little introductory ode,[6] for as *that* is no romance, but the sincere effusion of my heart, I could as soon read aloud my own letters, written in my own name and character: I therefore skipped it, and have so kept the book out of his sight, that, to this day, he knows not it is there. Indeed, I have, since, heartily repented that I read *any* of the book to him, for I found it a much more awkward thing than I had expected: my voice quite faltered when I began it, which, however, I passed off for the effect of remaining weakness of lungs; and, in short, from an invincible embarrassment, which I could not for a page together repress, the book, by my reading, lost all manner of spirit.

Nevertheless, though he has by no means treated it with the praise so lavishly bestowed upon it from other quarters, I had the satisfaction to observe that he was even greedily eager to go on with it; so that I flatter myself the *story* caught his attention: and, indeed, allowing for my *mauling* reading, he gave it quite as much credit as I had any reason to expect. But, now that I was sensible of my error in being my own mistress of the ceremonies, I determined to leave to Hetty the third volume, and therefore pretended I had not brought it. He was in a delightful ill-humour about it, and I enjoyed his impatience far more than I should have done his forbearance. Hetty, therefore, when she comes, has undertaken to bring it.

Well, I cannot but rejoice that I published the book, little as I ever imagined how it would fare; for hitherto it has occasioned me no small diversion, and *nothing* of the disagreeable sort. But I often think a change *will* happen, for

[4] The eldest daughter of Dr Burney.
[5] Samuel Crisp was a close friend of the Burney family, especially of Fanny who refers to him as Daddy Crisp.
[6] The ode, To ——— , is addressed to her father; it begins, 'O Author of my being!'

I am by no means so sanguine as to suppose such success will be uninterrupted. Indeed, in the midst of the greatest satisfaction that I feel, an inward *something* which I cannot account for, prepares me to expect a reverse; for the more the book is drawn into notice, the more exposed it becomes to criticism and remark.

JULY 25

MRS Cholmondeley has been reading and praising *Evelina*, and my father is quite delighted at her approbation, and told Susan that I could not have had a greater compliment than making two such women my friends as Mrs Thrale and Mrs Cholmondeley,[7] for they were severe and knowing, and afraid of praising *à tort et à travers*,[8] as their opinions are liable to be quoted.

Mrs Thrale said she had only to complain it was too short. She recommended it to my mother to read!—how droll!—and she told her she would be much entertained with it, for there was a great deal of human life in it, and of the manners of the present times, and added that it was written 'by somebody who knows the top and the bottom, the highest and the lowest of mankind.' She has even lent her set to my mother, who brought it home with her!

AUGUST 3

I NOW come to last Saturday evening, when my beloved father came to Chesington, in full health, charming spirits, and all kindness, openness, and entertainment.

In his way hither he had stopped at Streatham, and he settled with Mrs Thrale that he would call on her again in his way to town, and carry me with him! and Mrs Thrale said: 'We all long to know her.'

I have been in a kind of twitter ever since, for there seems something very formidable in the idea of appearing as an authoress! I ever dreaded it, as it is a title which must raise more expectations than I have any chance of answering. Yet I am highly flattered by her invitation, and highly delighted in the prospect of being introduced to the Streatham society.

My dear father communicated this intelligence, and a great deal more, with a pleasure that almost surpassed that with which I heard it, and he seems quite eager for me to make another attempt. He desired to take upon himself the communication to my Daddy Crisp, and as it is now in so many hands that it is possible accident might discover it to him, I readily consented.

Sunday evening, as I was going into my father's room, I heard him say: 'The variety of characters—the variety of scenes—and the language—why she has had very little education but what she has given herself—less than any of the others!' and Mr Crisp exclaimed: 'Wonderful!—it's wonderful!'

[7] Mrs Cholmondeley was a society lady, sister of the actress Peg Woffington; Mrs Thrale, wife of a wealthy brewer, was an author and hostess at her house in Streatham where she frequently entertaned the most famous author and man of letters of his day, Samuel Johnson, sixty-eight at the time Fanny Burney met him.
[8] At random.

I now found what was going forward, and therefore deemed it most fitting to decamp.

About an hour after, as I was passing through the hall, I met my daddy [Crisp]. His face was all animation and archness; he doubled his fist at me, and would have stopped me, but I ran past him into the parlour.

Before supper, however, I again met him, and he would not suffer me to escape; he caught both my hands, and looked as if he would have looked me through, and then exclaimed: 'Why, you little hussy—you young devil!—an't you ashamed to look me in the face, you *Evelina*, you! Why, what a dance have you led me about it! Young friend, indeed! Oh, you little hussy, what tricks have you served me!'

LONDON, AUGUST

I HAVE now to write an account of the most consequential day I have spent since my birth; namely, my Streatham visit.

Our journey to Streatham was the least pleasant part of the day, for the roads were dreadfully dusty, and I was really in the fidgets from thinking what my reception might be, and from fearing they would expect a less awkward and backward kind of person than I was sure they would find.

Mr Thrale's house is white, and very pleasantly situated, in a fine paddock. Mrs Thrale was strolling about, and came to us as we got out of the chaise.

She then received me, taking both my hands, and with mixed politeness and cordiality welcoming me to Streatham. She led me into the house, and addressed herself almost wholly for a few minutes to my father, as if to give me an assurance she did not mean to regard me as a show, or to distress or frighten me by drawing me out. Afterwards she took me upstairs, and showed me the house, and said she had very much wished to see me at Streatham, and should always think herself much obliged to Dr Burney for his goodness in bringing me, which she looked upon as a very great favour.

But though we were some time together, and though she was so very civil, she did not *hint* at my book, and I love her much more than ever for her delicacy in avoiding a subject which she could not but see would have greatly embarrassed me.

When we returned to the music room, we found Miss Thrale was with my father. Miss Thrale is a very fine girl, about fourteen years of age, but cold and reserved, though full of knowledge and intelligence.

Soon after, Mrs Thrale took me to the library; she talked a little while upon common topics, and then, at last, she mentioned *Evelina*.

'Yesterday at supper,' said she, 'we talked it all over, and discussed all your characters; but Dr Johnson's favourite is Mr Smith. He declares the fine gentleman *manqué* was never better drawn, and he acted him all the evening, saying "he was all for the ladies"! He repeated whole scenes by heart. I declare I was astonished at him. Oh, you can't imagine how much he is pleased with the book; he "could not get rid of the rogue," he told me. But was it not droll,' said she, 'that I should recommend to Dr Burney? and tease him so innocently to read it?'

I now prevailed upon Mrs Thrale to let me amuse myself, and she went to dress. I then prowled about to choose some book, and I saw, upon the reading-table, *Evelina*—I had just fixed upon a new translation of Cicero's *Laelius*, when the library door was opened, and Mr Seward entered. I instantly put away my book, because I dreaded being thought studious and affected. He offered his service to find anything for me, and then, in the same breath, ran on to speak of the book with which I had myself 'favoured the world'!

The exact words he began with I cannot recollect, for I was actually confounded by the attack; and his abrupt manner of letting me know he was *au fait* equally astonished and provoked me. How different from the delicacy of Mr and Mrs Thrale!

When we were summoned to dinner, Mrs Thrale made my father and me sit on each side of her. I said that I hoped I did not take Dr Johnson's place—for he had not yet appeared.

'No,' answered Mrs Thrale, 'he will sit by you, which I am sure will give him great pleasure.'

Soon after we were seated, this great man entered. I have so true a veneration for him, that the very sight of him inspires me with delight and reverence, notwithstanding the cruel infirmities to which he is subject; for he has almost perpetual convulsive movements either of his hands, lips, feet, or knees, and sometimes all together.

Mrs Thrale introduced me to him, and he took his place. We had a noble dinner, and a most elegant dessert. Dr Johnson, in the middle of dinner, asked Mrs Thrale what was in some little pies that were near him.

'Mutton,' answered she, 'so I don't ask you to eat any, because I know you despise it.'

'No, madam, no,' cried he; 'I despise nothing that is good of its sort; but I am too proud now to eat of it. Sitting by Miss Burney makes me very proud to-day!'

'Miss Burney,' said Mrs Thrale, laughing, 'you must take great care of your heart if Dr Johnson attacks it; for I assure you he is not often successless.'

'What's that you say, madam?' cried he; 'are you making mischief between the young lady and me already?'

A little while after he drank Miss Thrale's health and mine, and then added:

''Tis a terrible thing that we cannot wish young ladies well without wishing them to become old women!'

'But some people,' said Mr Seward, 'are old and young at the same time, for they wear so well that they never look old.'

'No, sir, no,' cried the doctor, laughing; 'that never yet was; you might as well say they are at the same time tall and short. I remember an epitaph to that purpose, which is in——'
(I have quite forgot what—and also the name it was made upon, but the rest I recollect exactly:)

'——lies buried here;
So early wise, so lasting fair,

> That none, unless her years you told,
> Thought her a child, or thought her old."

Mrs Thrale then repeated some lines in French, and Dr Johnson some more in Latin. An epilogue of Mr Garrick's[9] to *Bonduca* was then mentioned, and Dr Johnson said it was a miserable performance, and everybody agreed it was the worst he had ever made.

'And yet,' said Mr Seward, 'it has been very much admired; but it is in praise of English valour, and so I suppose the subject made it popular.'

'I don't know, sir,' said Dr Johnson, 'anything about the subject, for I could not read on till I came to it; I got through half a dozen lines, but I could observe no other subject than eternal dullness. I don't know what is the matter with David; I am afraid he is grown superannuated, for his prologues and epilogues used to be incomparable.'

'Nothing is so fatiguing,' said Mrs Thrale, 'as the life of a wit; he and Wilkes[10] are the two oldest men of their ages I know, for they have both worn themselves out by being eternally on the rack to give entertainment to others.'

'David, madam,' said the doctor, 'looks much older than he is; for his face has had double the business of any other man's; it is never at rest; when he speaks one minute, he has quite a different countenance to what he assumes the next; I don't believe he ever kept the same look for half an hour together in the whole course of his life; and such an eternal, restless, fatiguing play of the muscles must certainly wear out a man's face before its real time.'

'Oh, yes,' cried Mrs Thrale; 'we must certainly make some allowance for such wear and tear of a man's face.'

We left Streatham at about eight o'clock, and Mr Seward, who handed me into the chaise, added his interest to the rest, that my father would not fail to bring me again next week to stay with them for some time. In short, I was loaded with civilities from them all. And my ride home was equally happy with the rest of the day, for my kind and most beloved father was so happy in *my* happiness, and congratulated me so sweetly, that he could, like myself, think on no other subject.

Yet my honours stopped not here; for Hetty, who, with her *sposo*, was here to receive us, told me she had lately met Mrs Reynolds, sister of Sir Joshua;[11] and that she talked very much and very highly of a new novel called *Evelina*; though without a shadow of suspicion as to the scribbler; and not contented with her own praise, she said that Sir Joshua, who began it one day when he was too much engaged to go on with it, was so much caught, that he could think of nothing else, and was quite absent all the day, not knowing a word that was said to him: and, when he took it up again, found himself so much interested in it, that he sat up all night to finish it!

[9] David Garrick (1717-79), former pupil of Dr Johnson, was the foremost actor of his day.
[10] John Wilkes (1727-97) was a political agitator and popular hero in the cause of liberty.
[11] Sir Joshua Reynolds (1723-92), famous portrait painter and first president of the Royal Academy.

Sir Joshua, it seems, vows he would give fifty pounds to know the author! I have also heard, by the means of Charles, that other persons have declared they *will* find him out!

MONDAY, FEBRUARY 2nd [1789]

WHAT an adventure had I this morning! one that has occasioned me the severest personal terror I ever experienced in my life.

Sir Lucas Pepys persisting that exercise and air were absolutely necessary to save me from illness, I have continued my walks, varying my gardens from Richmond to Kew, according to the accounts I received of the movements of the King. For this I had her Majesty's permission, in the representation of Sir Lucas.

This morning, when I received my intelligence of the King from Dr John Willis, I begged to know where I might walk in safety? 'In Kew Gardens,' he said, 'as the King would be in Richmond.'

'Should any unfortunate circumstance,' I cried, 'at any time, occasion my being seen by his Majesty, do not mention my name, but let me run off without call or notice.'

This he promised. Everybody, indeed, is ordered to keep out of sight.

Taking, therefore, the time I had most at command, I strolled into the gardens. I had proceeded, in my quick way, nearly half the round, when I suddenly perceived, through some trees, two or three figures. Relying on the instructions of Dr John, I concluded them to be workmen and gardeners; yet tried to look sharp, and in so doing, as they were less shaded, I thought I saw the person of his Majesty!

Alarmed past all possible expression, I waited not to know more, but turning back, ran off with all my might. But what was my terror to hear myself pursued!—to hear the voice of the King himself loudly and hoarsely calling after me: 'Miss Burney! Miss Burney!'

I protest I was ready to die. I knew not in what state he might be at the time; I only knew the orders to keep out of his way were universal; that the Queen would highly disapprove of any unauthorized meeting, and that the very action of my running away might deeply, in his present irritable state, offend him. Nevertheless, on I ran, too terrified to stop, and in search of some short passage, for the garden is full of little labyrinths, by which I might escape.

The steps still pursued me, and still the poor hoarse and altered voice rang in my ears—more and more footsteps resounded frightfully behind me—the attendants all running, to catch their eager master, and the voices of the two Doctor Willises loudly exhorting him not to heat himself so unmercifully.

Heavens, how I ran! I do not think I should have felt the hot lava from Vesuvius—at least not the hot cinders—had I so run during its eruption. My feet were not sensible that they even touched the ground.

Soon after, I heard other voices, shriller, though less nervous, call out: 'Stop! stop! stop!'

I could by no means consent; I knew not what was purposed, but I recollected fully my agreement with Dr John that very morning, that I should decamp if surprised, and not be named.

My own fears and repugnance, also, after a flight and disobedience like this, were doubled in the thought of not escaping: I knew not to what I might be exposed, should the malady be then high, and take the turn of resentment. Still, therefore, on I flew; and such was my speed, so almost incredible to relate or recollect, that I fairly believe no one of the whole party could have overtaken me, if these words, from one of the attendants, had not reached me: 'Doctor Willis begs you to stop!'

'I cannot! I cannot!' I answered, still flying on, when be called out: 'You must, ma'am; it hurts the King to run.'

Then, indeed, I stopped—in a state of fear really amounting to agony. I turned round, I saw the two Doctors had got the King between them and three attendants of Dr Willis's were hovering about. They all slackened their pace, as they saw me stand still; but such was the excess of my alarm, that I was wholly insensible to the effects of a race which, at any other time, would have required an hour's recruit.

As they approached, some little presence of mind happily came to my command: it occurred to me that, to appease the wrath of my flight, I must now show some confidence: I therefore faced them as undauntedly as I was able, only charging the nearest of the attendants to stand by my side.

When they were within a few yards of me, the King called out: 'Why did you run away?'

Shocked at a question impossible to answer, yet a little assured by the mild tone of his voice, I instantly forced myself forward, to meet him, though the internal sensation, which satisfied me this was a step the most proper to appease his suspicions and displeasure, was so violently combated by the tremor of my nerves, that I fairly think I may reckon it the greatest effort of personal courage I have ever made.

The effort answered: I looked up, and met all his wonted benignity of countenance, though something still of wildness in his eyes. Think, however, of my surprise, to feel him put both his hands round my two shoulders, and then kiss my cheek!

I wonder I did not really sink, so exquisite was my affright when I saw him spread out his arms! Involuntarily, I concluded he meant to crush me: but the Willises, who have never seen him till this fatal illness, not knowing how very extraordinary an action this was from him, simply smiled and looked pleased, supposing, perhaps, it was his customary salutation!

He now spoke in such terms of his pleasure in seeing me, that I soon lost the whole of my terror; astonishment to find him so nearly well, and gratification to see him so pleased, removed every uneasy feeling, and the joy that succeeded, in my conviction of his recovery, made me ready to throw myself at his feet to express it.

What a conversation followed! When he saw me fearless, he grew more and more alive, and made me walk close by his side, away from the attendants, and even the Willises themselves, who, to indulge him, retreated. I own myself not completely composed, but alarm I could entertain no more.

Everything that came uppermost in his mind he mentioned; he seemed to have just such remains of his flightiness as heated his imagination without deranging his reason, and robbed him of all control over his speech, though nearly in his perfect state of mind as to his opinions.

What did he not say! He opened his whole heart to me—expounded all his sentiments, and acquainted me with all his intentions.

He assured me he was quite well—as well as he had ever been in his life; and then inquired how I did, and how I went on? and whether I was more comfortable?

If these questions, in their implication, surprised me, imagine how that surprise must increase when he proceeded to explain them! He asked after the coadjutrix, laughing, and saying: 'Never mind her—don't be oppressed—I am your friend! don't let her cast you down! I know you have a hard time of it—but don't mind her!'[12]

Almost thunderstruck with astonishment, I merely curtsied to his kind 'I am your friend,' and said nothing.

Then presently he added: 'Stick to your father—stick to your own family—let them be your objects.'

How readily I assented!

Again he repeated all I have just written, nearly in the same words, but ended it more seriously: he suddenly stopped, and held me to stop too, and putting his hand on his breast, in the most solemn manner, he gravely and slowly said: 'I will protect you!—I promise you that—and therefore depend upon me!'

I thanked him; and the Willises, thinking him rather too elevated, came to propose my walking on. 'No, no, no!' he cried, a hundred times in a breath; and their good humour prevailed, and they let him again walk on with his new companion.

He then gave me a history of his pages, animating almost into a rage, as he related his subjects of displeasure with them, particularly with Mr Ernst, who, he told me, had been brought up by himself. I hope his ideas upon these men are the result of the mistakes of his malady.

Then he asked me some questions that very greatly distressed me, relating to information given him in his illness, from various motives, but which he suspected to be false, and which I knew he had reason to suspect: yet was it most dangerous to set anything right, as I was not aware what might be the views of their having been stated wrong. I was as discreet as I knew how to be, and I hope I did no mischief; but this was the worst part of the dialogue.

He next talked to me a great deal of my dear father, and made a thousand inquiries concerning his *History of Music*. This brought him to his favourite theme, Handel; and he told me innumerable anecdotes of him, and particularly that celebrated tale of Handel's saying of himself, when a boy: 'While that

[12] Burney's life at the court was rendered especially miserable by the jealous and exacting Keeper of the Robes, Mrs Schwellenberg.

boy lives, my music will never want a protector.' And this, he said, I might relate to my father.

Then he ran over most of his oratorios, attempting to sing the subjects of several airs and choruses, but so dreadfully hoarse that the sound was terrible.

Dr Willis, quite alarmed at this exertion, feared he would do himself harm, and again proposed a separation. 'No! no! no!' he exclaimed, 'not yet; I have something I must just mention first.'

Dr Willis, delighted to comply, even when uneasy at compliance, again gave way.

The good King then greatly affected me. He began upon my revered old friend, Mrs Delany;[13] and he spoke of her with such warmth—such kindness! 'She was my friend!' he cried, 'and I loved her as a friend! I have made a memorandum when I lost her—I will show it you.'

He pulled out a pocket-book, and rummaged some time, but to no purpose.

The tears stood in his eyes—he wiped them, and Dr Willis again became very anxious. 'Come, sir,' he cried, 'now do you come in and let the lady go on her walk—come, now, you have talked a long while—so we'll go in—if your Majesty pleases.'

No, no!' he cried, 'I want to ask her a few questions; I have lived so long out of the world, I know nothing!'

He then told me he was very much dissatisfied with several of his state officers, and meant to form an entire new establishment. He took a paper out of his pocket-book, and showed me his new list.

This was the wildest thing that passed; and Dr John Willis now seriously urged our separating; but he would not consent; he had only three more words to say, he declared, and again he conquered.

He now spoke of my father, with still more kindness, and told me he ought to have had the post of Master of the Band, and not that little poor musician Parsons, who was not fit for it: 'But Lord Salisbury,' he cried, 'used your father very ill in that business, and so he did me! However, I have dashed out his name, and I shall put your father's in—as soon as I get loose again!'

This again—how affecting was this!

'And what,' cried he, 'has your father got, at last? Nothing but that poor thing at Chelsea?[14] Oh, fie! fie! fie! But never mind! I will take care of him! I will do it myself!'

Then presently he added: 'As to Lord Salisbury, he is out already, as this memorandum will show you, and so are many more. I shall be much better served; and when once I get away, I shall rule with a rod of iron!'

This was very unlike himself, and startled the two good doctors, who could not bear to cross him, and were exulting at my seeing his great amendment, but yet grew quite uneasy at his earnestness and volubility.

[13] Mary Delany (1700–88), a Bluestocking and a lively letter writer, had been a friend of both Burney and the royal family.
[14] Dr. Burney hoped for a post of Master of the Band but became organist of Chelsea Hospital instead.

Finding we now must part, he stopped to take leave, and renewed again his charges about the coadjutrix. 'Never mind her!' he cried, 'depend upon me! I will be your friend as long as I live!—I here pledge myself to be your friend!' And then he saluted me again just as at the meeting, and suffered me to go on.

What a scene! How variously was I affected by it! But upon the whole, how inexpressibly thankful to see him so nearly himself—so little removed from recovery!

I went very soon after to the Queen, to whom I was most eager to avow the meeting, and how little I could help it. Her astonishment, and her earnestness to hear every particular, were very great. I told her almost all. Some few things relating to the distressing questions I could not repeat; nor many things said of Mrs Schwellenberg, which would much, and very needlessly, have hurt her.

Mary Wollstonecraft
1759 – 97

Mary Wollstonecraft, daughter of an unsuccessful gentleman farmer, was a polemical writer and novelist. After an unstable childhood in which she deeply resented the favouritism shown to her eldest brother, she tried to achieve independence by becoming a companion, teacher, and governess before taking the unusual step of joining the publisher Joseph Johnson in London as editorial assistant on his new radical magazine. She responded to the French Revolution by becoming a political writer, first with A Vindication of the Rights of Men (1790) and then with her most famous work, A Vindication of the Rights of Woman (1792), in which she argued that women should be allowed to prove their equality in reason with men. At the height of the Revolution she went to France where she fell in love with an American commercial adventurer, Gilbert Imlay. Soon after she bore a child, she sensed Imlay's withdrawal and responded with a suicide attempt. To relieve the situation, Imlay dispatched her (with the baby) to Scandinavia as his business representative in an effort to recover some lost merchandise.

The following letters are reprinted from Letters Written during a Short Residence in Sweden, Norway, and Denmark *(1796). Prepared for publication by Wollstonecraft, they chronicled her travels and her emotional odyssey.*

From

Letters Written during a Short Residence in Sweden, Norway and Denmark

From LETTER V

ARRIVING at Fredericshall, at the siege of which Charles XII lost his life,[1] we had only time to take a transient view of it, wilst they were preparing us some refreshment.

Poor Charles! I thought of him with respect. I have always felt the same for Alexander; with whom he has been classed as a madman, by several writers, who have reasoned superficially, confounding the morals of the day with the few grand principles on which unchangeable morality rests. Making no allowance for the ignorance and prejudices of the period, they do not perceive how much they themselves are indebted to general improvement for the acquirements, and even the virtues, which they would not have had the force of mind to attain, by their individual exertions in a less advanced state of society.

The evening was fine, as is usual at this season; and the refreshing odour of the pine woods became more perceptible; for it was nine o'clock when we left Fredericshall. At the ferry we were detained by a dispute relative to our Swedish passport, which we did not think of getting countersigned in Norway. Midnight was coming on; yet it might with such propriety have been termed the noon of night, that had Young ever travelled towards the north, I should not have wondered at his becoming enamoured of the moon.[2] But it is not the queen of night alone who reigns here in all her splendour, though the sun, loitering just below the horizon, decks her with a golden tinge from his car, illuminating the cliffs that hide him; the heavens also, of a clear softened blue, throw her forward, and the evening star appears a lesser moon to the naked eye. The huge shadows of the rocks, fringed with firs, concentrating the views, without darkening them, excited that tender melancholy which, sublimating the imagination, exalts, rather than depresses the mind.

My companions fell asleep:—fortunately they did not snore; and I contemplated, fearless of idle questions, a night such as I had never before seen or felt

---

[1] Charles XII, King of Sweden (1697–1718), was a famous military leader.
[2] Edward Young's *Night Thoughts*, published between 1742 and 1745, was an example of the 'graveyard' school of poetry; book 3 contains an invocation to the moon.

to charm the senses, and calm the heart. The very air was balmy, as it freshened into morn, producing the most voluptuous sensations. A vague pleasurable sentiment absorbed me, as I opened my bosom to the embraces of nature; and my soul rose to its author, with the chirping of the solitary birds, which began to feel, rather than see, advancing day. I had leisure to mark its progress. The grey morn, streaked with silvery rays, ushered in the orient beams,—how beautifully varying into purple!—yet, I was sorry to lose the soft watry clouds which preceded them, exciting a kind of expectation that made me almost afraid to breathe, lest I should break the charm. I saw the sun—and sighed.

One of my companions, now awake, perceiving that the postillion had mistaken the road, began to swear at him, and roused the other two, who reluctantly shook off sleep.

We had immediately to measure back our steps, and did not reach Stromstad before five in the morning.

The wind had changed in the night, and my boat was ready.

A dish of coffee, and fresh linen, recruited my spirits; and I directly set out again for Norway; purposing to land much higher up the coast.

Wrapping my great coat round me, I lay down on some sails at the bottom of the boat, its motion rocking me to rest, till a discourteous wave interrupted my slumbers, and obliged me to rise and feel a solitariness which was not so soothing as that of the past night.

From LETTER VI

As the Norwegians do not frequently see travellers, they are very curious to know their business, and who they are—so curious that I was half tempted to adopt Dr Franklin's[3] plan, when travelling in America, where they are equally prying, which was to write on a paper, for public inspection, my name, from whence I came, where I was going, and what was my business. But if I were importuned by their curiosity, their friendly gestures gratified me. A woman, coming alone, interested them. And I know not whether my weariness gave me a look of peculiar delicacy; but they approached to assist me, and enquire after my wants, as if they were afraid to hurt, and wished to protect me. The sympathy I inspired, thus dropping down from the clouds in a strange land, affected me more than it would have done, had not my spirits been harassed by various causes—by much thinking—musing almost to madness—and even by a sort of weak melancholy that hung about my heart at parting with my daughter[4] for the first time.

You know that as a female I am particularly attached to her—I feel more than a mother's fondness and anxiety, when I reflect on the dependent and oppressed state of her sex. I dread lest she should be forced to sacrifice her heart to her principles, or principles to her heart. With trembling hand I shall

---

[3] The American statesman and writer, Benjamin Franklin (1706–90), was much admired in English radical circles.
[4] The baby Fanny had been left in Gothenberg because of the dangers of the later journey.

cultivate sensibility, and cherish delicacy of sentiment, lest, whilst I lend fresh blushes to the rose, I sharpen the thorns that will wound the breast I would fain guard—I dread to unfold her mind, lest it should render her unfit for the world she is to inhabit—Hapless woman! what a fate is thine!

But whither am I wandering? I only meant to tell you that the impression the kindness of the simple people made visible on my countenance increased my sensibility to a painful degree. I wished to have had a room to myself; for their attention, and rather distressing observation, embarrassed me extremely. Yet, as they would bring me eggs, and make my coffee, I found I could not leave them without hurting their feelings of hospitality.

It is customary here for the host and hostess to welcome their guests as master and mistress of the house.

My clothes, in their turn, attracted the attention of the females; and I could not help thinking of the foolish vanity which makes many women so proud of the observation of strangers as to take wonder very gratuitously for admiration. This error they are very apt to fall into; when arrived in a foreign country, the populace stare at them as they pass: yet the make of a cap, or the singularity of a gown, is often the cause of the flattering attention, which afterwards supports a fantastic superstructure of self-conceit . . . .

Amongst the Norwegians I had the arrangements of my own time; and I determined to regulate it in such a manner, that I might enjoy as much of their sweet summer as I possibly could:—short, it is true; but "passing sweet."[5]

I never endured a winter in this rude clime; consequently it was not the contrast, but the real beauty of the season which made the present summer appear to me the finest I had ever seen. Sheltered from the north and eastern winds, nothing can exceed the salubrity, the soft freshness of the western gales. In the evening they also die away; the aspen leaves tremble into stillness, and reposing nature seems to be warmed by the moon, which here assumes a genial aspect: and if a light shower has chanced to fall with the sun, the juniper the underwood of the forest, exhales a wild perfume, mixed with a thousand nameless sweets, that, soothing the heart, leave images in the memory which the imagination will ever hold dear.

Nature is the nurse of sentiment,—the true source of taste;—yet what misery, as well as rapture, is produced by a quick perception of the beautiful and sublime, when it is exercised in observing animated nature, when every beauteous feeling and emotion excites responsive sympathy, and the harmonized soul sinks into melancholy, or rises to extasy, just as the chords are touched, like the aeolian harp agitated by the changing wind. But how dangerous is it to foster these sentiments in such an imperfect state of existence; and how difficult to eradicate them when an affection for mankind, a passion for an individual, is but the unfolding of that love which embraces all that is great and beautiful.

When a warm heart has received strong impressions, they are not to be effaced. Emotions become sentiments; and the imagination renders even transient sensations permanent, by fondly retracing them. I cannot, without a thrill of

<hr />

[5] A reference to William Cowper's poem 'The Retirement' (1782).

delight, recollect views I have seen, which are not to be forgotten,—nor looks I have felt in every nerve which I shall never more meet. The grave has closed over a dear friend, the friend of my youth;[6] still she is present with me, and I hear her soft voice warbling as I stray over the heath. Fate has separated me from another, the fire of whose eyes, tempered by infantine tenderness, still warms my breast; even when gazing on these tremendous cliffs, sublime emotions absorb my soul. And, smile not, if I add, that the rosy tint of morning reminds me of a suffusion, which will never more charm my senses, unless it reappears on the cheeks of my child. Her sweet blushes I may yet hide in my bosom, and she is still too young to ask why starts the tear, so near akin to pleasure and pain?

I cannot write any more at present. Tomorrow we will talk of Tonsberg.

From LETTER VII ·

THE Norwegians are fond of music; and every little church has an organ. In the church I have mentioned, there is an inscription importing that a king,[7] James the sixth, of Scotland, and first of England, who came with more than princely gallantry, to escort his bride home, stood there, and heard divine service.

There is a little recess full of coffins, which contains bodies embalmed long since—so long, that there is not even a tradition to lead to a guess at their names.

A desire of preserving the body seems to have prevailed in most countries of the world, futile as it is to term it a preservation, when the noblest parts are immediately sacrificed merely to save the muscles, skin and bone from rottenness. When I was shewn these human petrifactions, I shrunk back with disgust and horror. "Ashes to ashes!" thought I—"Dust to dust!"—If this be not dissolution, it is something worse than natural decay. It is treason against humanity, thus to lift up the awful veil which would fain hide its weakness. The grandeur of the active principle is never more strongly felt than at such a sight; for nothing is so ugly as the human form when deprived of life, and thus dried into stone, merely to preserve the most disgusting image of death. The contemplation of noble ruins produces a melancholy that exalts the mind.—We take a retrospect of the exertions of man, the fate of empires and their rulers; and marking the grand destruction of ages, it seems the necessary change of time

[6] Fanny Blood, Wollstonecraft's close friend who died after childbirth in 1785.
[7] 'Anno 1589, St. Martin's Day, which was the 11th Day of November, on a Tuesday, came the high-born Prince and Lord Jacob Stuart, King in Scotland, to this Town, and the 25th Sunday after Trinity (Sunday) which was the 16th Day of November, stood his Grace in this Pew, and heard Scotch Preaching from the 23rd Psalm, "The Lord is my Shepherd," etc. which Mr. David Lentz, Preacher in Lith, then preached between 10 and 12.'
    The above is an inscription which stands in St Mary's church in Tonsburg [Norway].
    It is known that King James VI went to Norway, to marry Princess Anna, the daughter of Frederick II, and sister to Christian IV; and that the wedding was performed at Opslo (now Christiania), where the princess, by contrary winds, was detained; but that the king, during this voyage, was at Tonsberg, nobody would have known, if an inscription, in remembrance of it, had not been placed in this church.—(Wollstonecraft's note).

leading to improvement.—Our very soul expands, and we forget our littleness; how painfully brought to our recollection by such vain attempts to snatch from decay what is destined so soon to perish. Life, what art thou? Where goes this breath? this *I*, so much alive? In what element will it mix, giving or receiving fresh energy?—What will break the enchantment of animation?—For worlds, I would not see a form I loved—embalmed in my heart—thus sacrilegiously handled!—Pugh! my stomach turns.—Is this all the distinction of the rich in the grave?—They had better quietly allow the scythe of equality to mow them down with the common mass, than struggle to become a monument of the instability of human greatness.

The teeth, nails and skin were whole, without appearing black like the Egyptian mummies; and some silk, in which they had been wrapt, still preserved its colour, pink, with tolerable freshness.

I could not learn how long the bodies had been in this state, in which they bid fair to remain till the day of judgment, if there is to be such a day; and before that time, it will require some trouble to make them fit to appear in company with angels, without disgracing humanity.—God bless you! I feel a conviction that we have some perfectible principle in our present vestment, which will not be destroyed just as we begin to be sensible of improvement; and I care not what habit it next puts on, sure that it will be wisely formed to suit a higher state of existence. Thinking of death makes us tenderly cling to our affections—with more than usual tenderness, I therefore assure you that I am yours, wishing that the temporary death of absence may not endure longer than is absolutely necessary.

From LETTER VIII

TONSBERG was formerly the residence of one of the little sovereigns of Norway; and on an adjacent mountain the vestiges of a fort remain, which was battered down by the Swedes; the entrance of the bay lying close to it.

Here I have frequently strayed, sovereign of the waste, I seldom met any human creature; and sometimes, reclining on the mossy down, under the shelter of a rock, the prattling of the sea amongst the pebbles has lulled me to sleep—no fear of any rude satyr's approaching to interrupt my repose. Balmy were the slumbers, and soft the gales, that refreshed me, when I awoke to follow, with an eye vaguely curious, the white sails, as they turned the cliffs, or seemed to take shelter under the pines which covered the little islands that so gracefully rose to render the terrific ocean beautiful. The fishermen were calmly casting their nets; whilst the seagulls hovered over the unruffled deep. Every thing seemed to harmonize into tranquillity—even the mournful call of the bittern was in cadence with the tinkling bells on the necks of the cows, that, pacing slowly one after the other, along an inviting path in the vale below, were repairing to the cottages to be milked. With what ineffable pleasure have I not gazed—and gazed again, losing my breath through my eyes—my very soul diffused itself in the scene—and, seeming to become all senses, glided in the scarcely-agitated waves, melted in the freshening breeze, or, taking its flight with fairy wing, to the misty mountains which bounded the prospect, fancy tript over new lawns, more beautiful even than the lovely slopes on the winding shore before me.—I pause, again breathless, to trace, with renewed delight, sentiments which entranced me, when, turning my humid eyes from the expanse below to the vault above, my sight pierced the fleecy clouds that softened the azure brightness; and, imperceptibly recalling the reveries of childhood, I bowed before the awful throne of my Creator, whilst I rested on its footstool.

You have sometimes wondered, my dear friend, at the extreme affection of my nature—But such is the temperature of my soul—It is not the vivacity of youth, the hey-day of existence. For years have I endeavoured to calm an impetuous tide—labouring to make my feelings take an orderly course.—It was striving against the stream.—I must love and admire with warmth, or I sink into sadness. Tokens of love which I have received have rapt me in elysium—purifying the heart they enchanted.—My bosom still glows.—Do not saucily ask, repeating Sterne's question, "Maria, is it still so warm?"[8] Sufficiently, O my God! has it been chilled by sorrow and unkindness—still nature will prevail—and if I blush at recollecting past enjoyment, it is the rosy hue of pleasure heightened by modesty; for the blush of modesty and shame are as distinct as the emotions by which they are produced.

I need scarcely inform you, after telling you of my walks, that my constitution has been renovated here; and that I have recovered my activity, even whilst attaining a little *embonpoint*.[9] My imprudence last winter, and some untoward accidents just at the time I was weaning my child, had reduced me to a state of weakness which I never before experienced. A slow fever preyed on me every night, during my residence in Sweden, and after I arrived at Tonsberg. By chance I found a fine rivulet filtered through the rocks, and confined in a bason for the cattle. It tasted to me like a chalybeat;[10] at any rate it was pure; and the good effect of the various waters which invalids are sent to drink, depends, I believe, more on the air, exercise and change of scene, than on their medicinal qualities. I therefore determined to turn my morning walks towards it, and seek for health from the nymph of the fountain; partaking of the beverage offered to the tenants of the shade.

Chance likewise led me to discover a new pleasure, equally beneficial to my health. I wished to avail myself of my vicinity to the sea, and bathe; but it was not possible near the town; there was no convenience. The young woman whom I mentioned to you, proposed rowing me across the water, amongst the rocks; but as she was pregnant, I insisted on taking one of the oars, and learning to row. It was not difficult; and I do not know a pleasanter exercise. I soon became expert, and my train of thinking kept time, as it were, with the oars, or I suffered the boat to be carried along by the current, indulging a pleasing forgetfulness,

[8] In Laurence Sterne's *A Sentimental Journey*, the traveller Yorick cries so profusely over Maria's misfortunes that he drenches his handkerchief. She says she will dry it in her bosom, to which Yorick replies, 'And is your heart still so warm Maria?'
[9] Plumpness.
[10] Mineral water impregnated with iron, often used as a tonic.

or fallacious hopes.—How fallacious! yet, without hope, what is to sustain life, but the fear of annihilation—the only thing of which I have ever felt dread—I cannot bear to think of being no more—of losing myself—though existence is often but a painful consciousness of misery; nay, it appears to me impossible that I should cease to exist, or that this active, restless spirit, equally alive to joy and sorrow, should only be organized dust—ready to fly abroad the moment the spring snaps, or the spark goes out, which kept it together. Surely something resides in this heart that is not perishable—and life is more than a dream.

Sometimes, to take up my oar, once more, when the sea was calm, I was amused by disturbing the innumerable young star fish which floated just below the surface: I had never observed them before; for they have not a hard shell, like those which I have seen on the sea-shore. They look like thickened water, with a white edge; and four purple circles, of different forms, were in the middle, over an incredible number of fibres, or white lines. Touching them, the cloudy substance would turn or close, first on one side, then on the other, very gracefully; but when I took one of them up in the ladle with which I heaved the water out of the boat, it appeared only a colourless jelly.

I did not see any of the seals, numbers of which followed our boat when we landed in Sweden; for though I like to sport in the water, I should have had no desire to join in their gambols.

From LETTER IX

As the farmers cut away the wood, they clear the ground. Every year, therefore, the country is becoming fitter to support the inhabitants. Half a century ago the Dutch, I am told, only paid for the cutting down of the wood, and the farmers were glad to get rid of it without giving themselves any trouble. At present they form a just estimate of its value; nay, I was surprised to find even fire wood so dear, when it appears to be in such plenty. The destruction, or gradual reduction, of their forests, will probably meliorate the climate; and their manners will naturally improve in the same ratio as industry requires ingenuity. It is very fortunate that men are, a long time, but just above the brute creation, or the greater part of the earth would never have been rendered habitable; because it is the patient labour of men, who are only seeking for a subsistence, which produces whatever embellishes existence, affording leisure for the cultivation of the arts and sciences, that lift man so far above his first state. I never, my friend, thought so deeply of the advantages obtained by human industry as since I have been in Norway. The world requires, I see, the hand of man to perfect it; and as this task naturally unfolds the faculties he exercises, it is physically impossible that he should have remained in Rousseau's golden age of stupidity.[11] And, considering the question of human happiness, where, oh! where does it reside? Has it taken up its abode with unconscious ignorance, or with the high-wrought mind? Is it the offspring

---

[11] Wollstonecraft is mocking the popular version of Jean-Jacques Rousseau's idea of the state of nature, in which a person was free and alone, without social limitation.

of thoughtless animal spirits, or the elve of fancy continually flitting round the expected pleasure?

The increasing population of the earth must necessarily tend to its improvement, as the means of existence are multiplied by invention....

From LETTER XI

THE view of this wild coast, as we sailed along it, afforded me a continual subject for meditation. I anticipated the future improvement of the world, and observed how much man had still to do, to obtain of the earth all it could yield. I even carried my speculations so far as to advance a million or two of years to the moment when the earth would perhaps be so perfectly cultivated, and so completely peopled, as to render it necessary to inhabit every spot; yes; these bleak shores. Imagination went still farther, and pictured the state of man when the earth could no longer support him. Where was he to fly to from universal famine? Do not smile: I really became distressed for these fellow creatures, yet unborn. The images fastened on me, and the world appeared a vast prison. I was soon to be in a smaller one—for no other name can I give to Rusoer. It would be difficult to form an idea of the place, if you have never seen one of these rocky coasts.

We were a considerable time entering amongst the islands, before we saw about two hundred houses crowded together, under a very high rock—still higher appearing above. Talk not of bastilles! To be born here, was to be bastilled by nature—shut out from all that opens the understanding, or enlarges the heart. Huddled one behind another, not more than a quarter of the dwellings even had a prospect of the sea. A few planks formed passages from house to house, which you must often scale, mounting steps like a ladder, to enter.

The only road across the rocks leads to a habitation, sterile enough, you may suppose, when I tell you that the little earth on the adjacent ones was carried there by the late inhabitant. A path, almost impracticable for a horse, goes on to Arendall, still further to the westward.

I enquired for a walk, and mounting near two hundred steps made round a rock, walked up and down for about a hundred yards, viewing the sea, to which I quickly descended by steps that cheated the declivity. The ocean, and these tremendous bulwarks, enclosed me on every side. I felt the confinement, and wished for wings to reach still loftier cliffs, whose slippery sides no foot was so hardy as to tread; yet what was it to see?—only a boundless waste of water—not a glimpse of smiling nature—not a patch of lively green to relieve the aching sight, or vary the objects of meditation.

I felt my breath oppressed, though nothing could be clearer than the atmosphere. Wandering there alone, I found the solitude desirable; my mind was stored with ideas, which this new scene associated with astonishing rapidity. But I shuddered at the thought of receiving existence, and remaining here, in the solitude of ignorance, till forced to leave a world of which I had seen so little; for the character of the inhabitants is as uncultivated, if not as picturesquely wild, as their abode.

Having no employment but traffic, of which a contraband trade makes the basis of their profit, the coarsest feelings of honesty are quickly blunted. You may suppose that I speak in general terms; and that, with all the disadvantages of nature and circumstances, there are still some respectable exceptions, the more praiseworthy, as tricking is a very contagious mental disease that dries up all the generous juices of the heart. Nothing genial, in fact, appears around this place, or within the circle of its rocks. And, now I recollect, it seems to me that the most genial and humane characters I have met with in life, were most alive to the sentiments inspired by tranquil country scenes. What, indeed, is to humanise these beings, who rest shut up, for they seldom even open their windows, smoaking, drinking brandy, and driving bargains? I have been almost stifled by these smoakers. They begin in the morning, and are rarely without their pipe till they go to bed. Nothing can be more disgusting than the rooms and men towards the evening: breath, teeth, clothes, and furniture, all are spoilt. It is well that the women are not very delicate, or they would only love their husbands because they were their husbands. Perhaps, you may add, that the remark need not be confined to so small a part of the world; and, *entre nous*, I am of the same opinion. You must not term this inuendo fancy, for it does not come home.

If I had not determined to write, I should have found my confinement here, even for three or four days, tedious. I have no books; and to pace up and down a small room, looking at tiles, overhung by rocks, soon becomes wearisome. I cannot mount two hundred steps, to walk a hundred yards, many times in the day. Besides, the rocks, retaining the heat of the sun, are intolerably warm. I am nevertheless very well; for though there is a shrewdness in the character of these people, depraved by a sordid love of money which repels me, still the comparisons they force me to make keep my heart calm, by exercising my understanding.

Every where wealth commands too much respect; but here, almost exclusively; and it is the only object pursued—not through brake and briar, but over rocks and waves—yet of what use would riches be to me? I have sometimes asked myself, were I confined to live in such a spot. I could only relieve a few distressed objects, perhaps render them idle, and all the rest of life would be a blank.

My present journey has given fresh force to my opinion, that no place is so disagreeable and unimproving as a country town. I should like to divide my time between the town and country; in a lone house, with the business of farming and planting, where my mind would gain strength by solitary musing; and in a metropolis to rub off the rust of thought, and polish the taste which the contemplation of nature had rendered just. Thus do we wish as we float down the stream of life, whilst chance does more to gratify a desire of knowledge than our best-laid plans. A degree of exertion, produced by some want, more or less painful, is probably the price we must all pay for knowledge. How few authors or artists have arrived at eminence who have not lived by their employment?

From LETTER XII

I LEFT East Rusoer the day before yesterday. The weather was very fine; but so calm that we loitered on the water near fourteen hours, only to make about six and twenty miles.

It seemed to me a sort of emancipation when we landed at Helgeraac. The confinement which every where struck me whilst sojourning amongst the rocks, made me hail the earth as a land of promise; and the situation shone with fresh lustre from the contrast—from appearing to be a free abode. Here it was possible to travel by land—I never thought this a comfort before, and my eyes, fatigued by the sparkling of the sun on the water, now contentedly reposed on the green expanse, half persuaded that such verdant meads had never till then regaled them.

I rose early to pursue my journey to Tonsberg. The country still wore a face of joy—and my soul was alive to its charms. Leaving the most lofty, and romantic of the cliffs behind us, we were almost continually descending to Tonsberg, through elysian scenes; for not only the sea, but mountains, rivers, lakes, and groves, gave an almost endless variety to the prospect. The cottagers were still leading home the hay; and the cottages, on this road, looked very comfortable. Peace and plenty—I mean not abundance, seemed to reign around—still I grew sad as I drew near my old abode. I was sorry to see the sun so high; it was broad noon. Tonsberg was something like a home—yet I was to enter without lighting-up pleasure in any eye—I dreaded the solitariness of my apartment, and wished for night to hide the starting tears, or to shed them on my pillow, and close my eyes on a world where I was destined to wander alone. Why has nature so many charms for me—calling forth and cherishing refined sentiments, only to wound the breast that fosters them? How illusive, perhaps the most so, are the plans of happiness founded on virtue and principle; what inlets of misery do they not open in a half civilized society? The satisfaction arising from conscious rectitude, will not calm an injured heart, when tenderness is ever finding excuses; and self-applause is a cold solitary feeling, that cannot supply the place of disappointed affection, without throwing a gloom over every prospect, which, banishing pleasure, does not exclude pain. I reasoned and reasoned; but my heart was too full to allow me to remain in the house, and I walked, till I was wearied out, to purchase rest—or rather forgetfulness.

Employment has beguiled this day, and tomorrow I set out for Moss, in my way to Stromstad. At Gothenburg I shall embrace my *Fannikin*; probably she will not know me again—and I shall be hurt if she do not. How childish is this! still it is a natural feeling. I would not permit myself to indulge the "thick coming fears" of fondness, whilst I was detained by business.—Yet I never saw a calf bounding in a meadow, that did not remind me of my little frolicker. A calf, you say. Yes; but a *capital* one, I own.

I cannot write composedly—I am every instant sinking into reveries—my heart flutters, I know not why. Fool! It is time thou wert at rest.

Friendship and domestic happiness are continually praised; yet how little is there of either in the world, because it requires more cultivation of mind to keep awake affection, even in our own hearts, than the common run of people suppose. Besides, few like to be seen as they really are; and a degree of simplicity, and of undisguised confidence, which, to uninterested observers, would almost border on weakness, is the charm, nay the essence of love or friendship: all the bewitching graces of childhood again appearing. As objects merely to exercise my taste, I therefore like to see people together who have an affection for each other; every turn of their features touches me, and remains pictured on my imagination in indelible characters. The zest of novelty is, however, necessary to rouse the languid sympathies which have been hacknied in the world; as is the factitious behaviour, falsely termed good-breeding, to amuse those, who, defective in taste, continually rely for pleasure on their animal spirits, which not being maintained by the imagination, are unavoidably sooner exhausted than the sentiments of the heart. Friendship is in general sincere at the commencement, and lasts whilst there is any thing to support it; but as a mixture of novelty and vanity is the usual prop, no wonder if it fall with the slender stay. The fop in the play, payed a greater compliment than he was aware of, when he said to a person, whom he meant to flatter, "I like you almost as well as a *new acquaintance*."[12] Why am I talking of friendship, after which I have had such a wild-goose chace.—I thought only of telling you that the crows, as well as wild geese, are here birds of passage.

From LETTER XIX

BUSINESS having obliged me to go a few miles out of town this morning, I was surprised at meeting a crowd of people of every description; and inquiring the cause, of a servant who spoke French, I was informed that a man had been executed two hours before, and the body afterwards burnt. I could not help looking with horror around—the fields lost their verdure—and I turned with disgust from the well-dressed women, who were returning with their children from this sight. What a spectacle for humanity! The seeing such a flock of idle gazers, plunged me into a train of reflections, on the pernicious effects produced by false notions of justice. And I am persuaded that till capital punishments be entirely abolished, executions ought to have every appearance of horrour given to them; instead of being, as they are now, a scene of amusement for the gaping crowd, where sympathy is quickly effaced by curiosity.

I have always been of opinion that the allowing actors to die, in the presence of the audience, has an immoral tendency; but trifling when compared with the ferocity acquired by viewing the reality as a show; for it seems to me, that in all countries the common people go to executions to see how the poor wretch plays his part, rather than to commiserate his fate, much less to think of the breach of morality which has brought him to such

12 'For though I have known thee a great while, never go, if I do not love thee as well as a new acquaintance,' says Sparkish in William Wycherley's satiric play *The Country Wife* (1675).

a deplorable end. Consequently executions, far from being useful examples to the survivors, have, I am persuaded, a quite contrary effect, by hardening the heart they ought to terrify. Besides, the fear of an ignominious death, I believe, never deterred any one from the commission of a crime; because, in committing it, the mind is roused to activity about present circumstances. It is a game at hazard, at which all expect the turn of the die in their own favour; never reflecting on the chance of ruin, till it comes. In fact, from what I saw, in the fortresses of Norway, I am more and more convinced that the same energy of character, which renders a man a daring villain, would have rendered him useful to society, had that society been well organized. When a strong mind is not disciplined by cultivation, it is a sense of injustice that renders it unjust . . . .

Wealth does not appear to be sought for, amongst the Danes, to obtain the elegant luxuries of life; for a want of taste is very conspicuous at Copenhagen; so much so, that I am not surprised to hear that poor Matilda[13] offended the rigid Lutherans, by aiming to refine their pleasures. The elegance which she wished to introduce, was termed lasciviousness: yet I do not find that the absence of gallantry renders the wives more chaste, or the husbands more constant. Love here seems to corrupt the morals, without polishing the manners, by banishing confidence and truth, the charm as well as cement of domestic life. A gentleman, who has resided in this city some time, assures me that he could not find language to give me an idea of the gross debaucheries into which the lower order of people fall; and the promiscuous amours of the men of the middling class with their female servants, debases both beyond measure, weakening every species of family affection.

I have every where been struck by one characteristic difference in the conduct of the two sexes; women, in general, are seduced by their superiors, and men jilted by their inferiors; rank and manners awe the one, and cunning and wantonness subjugate the other; ambition creeping into the woman's passion, and tyranny giving force to the man's; for most men treat their mistresses as kings do their favourites: *ergo* is not man then the tyrant of the creation?

Still harping on the same subject, you will exclaim—How can I avoid it, when most of the struggles of an eventful life have been occasioned by the oppressed state of my sex: we reason deeply, when we forcibly feel.

From LETTER XXII

A RRIVING at Sleswick, the residence of prince Charles of Hesse-Cassel, the sight of the soldiers recalled all the unpleasing ideas of German despotism, which

[13] Queen Caroline Matilda, (1751–75), the sister of George III, was married while still in her teens to the cruel unstable Danish King, Christian VII. Her affair with the court physician led to her imprisonment and his execution.

imperceptibly vanished as I advanced into the country. I viewed, with a mixture of pity and horrour, these beings training to be sold to slaughter, or be slaughtered,[14] and fell into reflections, on an old opinion of mine, that it is the preservation of the species, not of individuals, which appears to be the design of the Deity throughout the whole of nature. Blossoms come forth only to be blighted; fish lay their spawn where it will be devoured: and what a large portion of the human race are born merely to be swept prematurely away. Does not this waste of budding life emphatically assert, that it is not men, but man, whose preservation is so necessary to the completion of the grand plan of the universe? Children peep into existence, suffer, and die; men play like moths about a candle, and sink into the flame: war, and "the thousand ills which flesh is heir to,"[15] mow them down in shoals, whilst the more cruel prejudices of society palsies existence, introducing not less sure, though slower decay.

Mary Hays
1760 – 1843

M*ary Hays came from a Dissenting family. She was disappointed in love: her fiancé died before the wedding and her later passion for a Unitarian philosopher was unrequited. She described some of her bitter feelings in her novel* The Memoirs of Emma Courtney *(1796). She was a friend of Mary Wollstonecraft, whose* Vindication of the Rights of Woman *(1792) she greatly admired. Her position on women was similar to Wollstonecraft's except that she more strongly emphasized their Christian status and, living longer and experiencing more thoroughly the anti-feminist reaction of the late 1790s, she sometimes softened her political assertions with apology.*

The following extract, reprinted from Appeal to the Men of Great Britain in Behalf of Women *(1798), appeared anonymously and was ascribed to Mary Hays.*

[14] German princes frequently hired their subjects out as soldiers to foreign and neighbouring powers as, for example, to England in the American War of Independence.
[15] 'the thousand natural shocks/That flesh is heir to.' *Hamlet* III.i.

From

Appeal to the Men of Great Britain in Behalf of Women

Implicit faith, all hail! Imperial Man
Exacts submission.

YEARSLEY[1]

WHAT MEN WOULD HAVE WOMEN TO BE

OF all the systems,—if indeed a bundle of contradictions and   absurdities may be called a system,—which human nature in its moments of intoxication has produced; that which men have contrived with a view to forming the minds, and regulating the conduct of women, is perhaps the most completely absurd. And, though the consequences are often very serious to both sexes, yet if one could for a moment forget these, and consider it only as a system, it would rather be found a subject of mirth and ridicule than serious anger.

What a chaos!—What a mixture of strength and weakness,—of greatness and littleness,—of sense and folly,—of exquisite feeling and total insensibility,—have they jumbled together in their imaginations,—and then given to their pretty darling the name of woman! How unlike the father of gods and men, the gay, the gallant Jupiter, who on producing wisdom the fruit of his brains, presented it to admiring worlds under the character of a female.[2]

But in the composition of Man's woman, wisdom must not be spoken of, nay nor even hinted at, yet strange to tell! there it must be in full force, and come forth upon all convenient occasions. This is a mystery which, as we are not allowed to be amongst the initiated, we may admire at an awful distance, but can never comprehend.

Again how great in some parts of their conduct, and how insignificant upon the whole, would men have women to be! For one example;—when their love, their pride, their delicacy; in short, when all the finest feelings of humanity are insulted and put to the rack, what is the line of conduct, then expected from them?

I need not explain that the situation I here allude to is,—when a woman finds that the husband of her choice, the object of her most sincere and constant love, abandons himself to other attachments; and not only this, but when,—the natural consequences of these,—estrangement of affection and estrangement of confidence follow, which are infinitely cutting to a woman of sensibility and soul; what I say is the line of conduct then expected from a creature declared to be,—weak by nature, and who is rendered still weaker by education?

Now here is one of those absurdities of which I accuse men in their system of contradictions. They expect that this poor weak creature, setting aside in a

---

[1] Ann Yearsley (1752–1806) a working-class poet and novelist.
[2] Minerva, goddess of wisdom, was produced from Jupiter's brain.

moment, love, jealousy, and pride, the most powerful and universal passions interwoven in the human heart, and which even men, clothed in wisdom and fortitude, find so difficult to conquer, that they seldom attempt it—that she shall notwithstanding lay all these aside as easily as she would her gown and petticoat, and plunge at once into the cold bath of prudence, of which though the wife only is to receive the shock, and make daily use of, yet if she does so, it has the virtue of keeping both husband and wife in a most agreeable temperament. Prudence being one of those rare medicines which affect by sympathy, and this being likewise one of those cases, where the husbands have no objections to the wives acting as principals, nor to their receiving all the honors and emoluments of office; even if death should crown their martyrdom, as has been sometimes known to happen.

Dear, generous creatures!

This reminds me of a singular circumstance which I heard the other day, of a poor man who had the misfortune to have a cataract on each eye. The one was cut, or extracted, or what you please to call it, and suffered as one may suppose the most extreme anguish. The other immediately wore off, or, I really don't know well how to express myself, dispersed, nobody knows how, except by the power of sympathy; but certainly without any operation being performed upon it. Now this last eye,—this not guiltless though unsuffering luminary, is what learned physicians call the *male* eye; and this operation when followed by such consequences, in honor of those consequences they have been pleased to distinguish by a most expressive name, which I have however entirely forgot; but under it they mean in future to class, all those cases, where one part only suffers, and the other receives all the benefit. For, I had almost forgot to mention, that the poor eye on which the experiment was made, soon 'Closed in endless night.'

But to return to our subject; the situations before alluded to, though perhaps the most trying for human nature in general, and to minds of sensibility in particular, are not the only ones prepared for women upon which to exercise their patience and temper. For, there are no vices to which a man addicts himself, no follies he can take it into his head to commit, but his wife and his nearest female relations are expected to connive at, are expected to look upon, if not with admiration, at least with respectful silence, and at awful distance. Any other conduct is looked upon, as a breach of that fanciful system of arbitrary authority, which men have so assiduously erected in their own favor; and any other conduct is accordingly resisted, with the most acrimonious severity.

A man, for example, is addicted to the destructive vice of drinking. His wife sees with terror and anguish the approach of this pernicious habit, and by anticipation beholds the evils to be dreaded to his individual health, happiness, and consequence; and the probable misery to his family. Yet with this melancholy prospect before her eyes, it is reckoned an unpardonable degree of harshness and imprudence, if she by any means whatever endeavour to check in the bud, this baleful practice; and she is in this case accused at all hands of driving him to pursue in worse places, that which he cannot enjoy in peace at home. And, when this disease gains ground, and ends in an established habit, she is treated as a fool for attempting a cure for what is incurable.

Thus there is no stage of this disorder, or any other to which man is morally liable, when it is accounted necessary or proper for women to interfere; or if they do so, men suppose themselves fully justified to plunge deeper and deeper into those vices, which create most misery to their wives, in order to punish their presumption. And thus it is that the designs of Providence seem to be counteracted, by the pride and obstinacy of man. For, the design of Providence seems evidently to be,—that the sexes should restrain, discourage, and prevent vice in each other; as much as they should encourage, promote, and reward virtue.

Again, women are often connected with men, whose shameful extravagance leave little for their families to hope for, but poverty, and the consequent neglect of a hard-hearted world. In this case perhaps, in the little sphere in which she is permitted to move, a wife may likewise be permitted to economise; but the fruits of her economy are still at the mercy of an imperious master, who thinks himself entitled to spend upon his unlawful pleasures, what might have procured her, innocent enjoyment, and rational delight. And, I am sorry to add, that the men in general are but too apt in these cases, as well as upon most other occasions, to take the part of their own sex; and to consider nothing as blameable in them to such a degree, as to justify opposition from the women connected with them.

Again, women of liberal sentiments and expanded hearts,—and surely there are such, in consequence of good, or in spite of bad education,—who would willingly employ fortune in acts of benevolence and schemes of beneficence; are connected with men, sordid in principle, rapacious in acquiring riches, and contemptibly mean in restraining them from returning again into society, through their proper channels. Woman here again is the sport, of the vices and infirmities of her tyrant: and however formed by nature to virtue and benevolence,—however trained by education,—here she finds all this against her. Here she finds that her time and endeavours would have been much more happily employed, in strengthening the opposite habits of selfishness, and uncharitableness. Since, the highest pitch of virtue, to which a woman can possibly aspire on the present system of things; is to please her husband, in whatever line of conduct pleasing him consists. And, to this great end, this one thing needful, men are impolitic enough to advance, and to expect, that every thing else should be sacrificed. Reason, religion,—or at least many of the most important maxims of religion,—private judgment, prejudices; all these, and much more than these must be swallowed up in the gulph of authority; which requiring every thing as a right, disdains to return any thing but as a concession.

I wish not however to be misunderstood, if even but for a moment; for though this is not the place to enlarge upon the subject, it must be acknowledged, that to please a reasonable and worthy husband,—let me repeat my own words,—in whatever pleasing him consists, is one of the most heartfelt, and purest pleasures, which a woman such as she ought to be, can possibly enjoy. But for women to be obliged to humor the follies, the caprice, the vices of men of a very different stamp, and to be obliged to consider this as their duty; is perhaps as unfortunate a system of politics in morals, as ever was introduced for degrading the human species.

I could here enumerate numberless instances, of WHAT MEN WOULD HAVE WOMEN TO BE, under circumstances the most trying and the most humiliating; but as I neither wish to tire out the reader nor myself with what may be well imagined without repetition, I shall only say; that though they are allowed, and even expected, to assume upon proper occasions, and when it happens to indulge the passions, or fall in with the humors of men, all that firmness of character, and greatness of mind commonly esteemed masculine; yet this is in so direct opposition, and so totally inconsistent with that universal weakness, which men first endeavour to affix upon women for their own convenience, and then for their own defence affect to admire; that really it requires more than female imbecility and credulity to suppose that such extremes can unite with any degree of harmony, in such imperfect beings as we all of us, men and women, must acknowledge ourselves to be. And therefore, except a woman has some schemes of her own to accomplish by this sort of management,—which necessity is most galling to an ingenuous mind; or except she is herself a mere nothing,—in which case her merit is next to nothing; these violent extremes,—these violent exertions of the mind,—are by no means natural or voluntary ones; but are on the contrary at variance with nature, with reason, and with common sense.

Indeed by preparatory tortures any mode of conduct, however unnatural, may be forced upon individuals.

Even inferior animals are taught not only to dance, but to dance to appearance in time, and with alacrity, when their tyrant pipes. Bears and Turkeys for example. But we ought not to forget, that to produce these wonderful exertions; the first have had their eyes put out, to render them more docile to the cruel caprice of man; and that nothing less than hot iron applied to the feet of the latter, had furnished that singular spectacle, with which many had the barbarity to be amused.

So alas! women often go through scenes with apparent cheerfulness, that did the most indifferent spectators, but consider what such appearances must have previously cost them, they would execrate the mean and sordid system; and join in endeavouring to expel from society those errors in theory, which produce such consequences in practice. For, from exertions made under such circumstances;—against nature,—against reason,—and against common sense;—can good be expected? Can such mend the understanding, or purify the heart? No, never! On the contrary they debase the one, and they corrupt the other. But it is a melancholy truth, that the whole system raised and supported by the men, tends to, nay I must be honest enough to say hangs upon, degrading the understandings, and corrupting the hearts of women; and yet! they are unreasonable enough to expect, discrimination in the one, and purity in the other.

Ann Radcliffe

1764 – 1823.

Ann Radcliffe came from a business family. She married a political journalist and led an outwardly uneventful life, remaining childless and largely separate from the literary society of her day. In 1789 she published the first of her Gothic stories which culminated in the extremely successful Mysteries of Udolpho in 1794, enjoyed by educated men as well as by the much despised female readership. This novel, together with her equally successful The Italian (1797) presents the Gothic setting and machinery which would become so popular with the reading public of the time and would give rise to a host of imitations. In the typical story, young and innocent female protagonists enter the Gothic place, which may be a castle, a dungeon, cave or monastery, controlled by a threatening and tyrannical older man. The novels were famous for their achievement of suspense and for their lengthy descriptions of picturesque and romantic scenery.

The following extract is reprinted from The Italian (F. Garber (ed.), Oxford University Press, 1981).

From

The Italian

CHAPTER VII

The Italian *is set in Naples dominated by the Inquisition. The noble hero Vivaldi wishes to marry Ellena from an obscure family. His mother opposes the match and, with the help of a villainous monk Schedoni, causes the couple to be separated and Ellena to be kidnapped.*

Ellena, meanwhile, when she had been carried from the chapel of San Sebastian, was placed upon a horse in waiting, and, guarded by the two men who had seized her, commenced a journey, which continued with little interruption during two nights and days. She had no means of judging whither she was going, and listened in vain expectation, for the feet of horses, and the voice of Vivaldi, who, she had been told, was following on the same road.

The steps of travellers seldom broke upon the silence of these regions, and, during the journey, she was met only by some market-people passing to a neighbouring town, or now and then by the vine-dressers or labourers in the olive grounds; and she descended upon the vast plains of Apulia, still ignorant of her situation. An encampment, not of warriors, but of shepherds, who were leading their flocks to the mountains of Abruzzo, enlivened a small tract of these levels, which were shadowed on the north and east by the mountainous ridge of the Garganus, stretching from the Apennine far into the Adriatic.

The appearance of the shepherds was nearly as wild and savage as that of the men, who conducted Ellena; but their pastoral instruments of flageolets and tabors spoke of more civilized feelings, as they sounded sweetly over the desert. Her guards rested, and refreshed themselves with goat's milk, barley cakes, and almonds, and the manners of these shepherds, like those she had formerly met with on the mountains, proved to be more hospitable than their air had indicated.

After Ellena had quitted this pastoral camp, no vestige of a human residence appeared for several leagues, except here and there the towers of a decayed fortress, perched upon the lofty acclivities she was approaching, and half concealed in the woods. The evening of the second day was drawing on, when her guards drew near the forest, which she had long observed in the distance, spreading over the many-rising steeps of the Garganus. They entered by a track, a road it could not be called, which led among oaks and gigantic chestnuts, apparently the growth of centuries, and so thickly interwoven, that their branches formed a canopy which seldom admitted the sky. The gloom which they threw around, and the thickets of cystus, juniper, and lenticus, which flourished beneath the shade, gave a character of fearful wildness to the scene.

Having reached an eminence, where the trees were more thinly scattered. Ellena perceived the forests spreading on all sides among hills and vallies, and descending towards the Adriatic, which bounded the distance in front. The coast, bending into a bay, was rocky and bold. Lofty pinnacles, wooded to their summits, rose over the shores, and cliffs of naked marble of such gigantic proportions, that they were awful even at a distance, obtruded themselves far into the waves, breasting their eternal fury. Beyond the margin of the coast, as far as the eye could reach, appeared pointed mountains, darkened with forests, rising ridge over ridge in many successions. Ellena, as she surveyed this wild scenery, felt as if she was going into eternal banishment from society. She was tranquil, but it was with the quietness of exhausted grief, not of resignation; and she looked back upon the past, and awaited the future, with a kind of out-breathed despair.

She had travelled for some miles through the forest, her guards only now and then uttering to each other a question, or an observation concerning the changes which had taken place in the bordering scenery, since they last passed it, when night began to close in upon them.

Ellena perceived her approach to the sea, only by the murmurs of its surge upon the rocky coast, till, having reached an eminence, which was, however, no more than the base of two woody mountains that towered closely over it, she saw dimly its gray surface spreading in the bay below. She now ventured to ask how much further she was to go, and whether she was to be taken on board one of the little vessels apparently fishing smacks, that she could just discern at anchor.

'You have not far to go now,' replied one of the guards, surlily; 'you will soon be at the end of your journey, and at rest.'

They descended to the shore, and presently came to a lonely dwelling, which stood so near the margin of the sea, as almost to be washed by the waves. No light appeared at any of the lattices; and, from the silence that reigned within, it seemed to be uninhabited. The guard had probably reason to know otherwise, for they halted at the door, and shouted with all their strength. No voice, however, answered to their call, and, while they persevered in efforts to rouse the inhabitants, Ellena anxiously examined the building, as exactly as the twilight would permit. It was of an ancient and peculiar structure, and, though scarcely important enough for a mansion, had evidently never been designed for the residence of peasants.

The walls, of unhewn marble, were high, and strengthened by bastions; and the edifice had turretted corners, which, with the porch in front, and the sloping roof, were falling fast into numerous symptoms of decay. The whole building, with its dark windows and soundless avenues, had an air strikingly forlorn and solitary. A high wall surrounded the small court in which it stood, and probably had once served as a defence to the dwelling; but the gates, which should have closed against intruders, could no longer perform their office; one of the folds had dropped from its fastenings, and lay on the ground almost concealed in a deep bed of weeds, and the other creaked on its hinges to every blast, at each swing seeming ready to follow the fate of its companion.

The repeated calls of the guard, were, at length, answered by a rough voice from within; when the door of the porch was lazily unbarred, and opened by a man, whose visage was so misery-struck, that Ellena could not look upon it with indifference, though wrapt in misery of her own. The lamp he held threw a gleam athwart it, and shewed the gaunt ferocity of famine, to which the shadow of his hollow eyes added a terrific wildness. Ellena shrunk while she gazed. She had never before seen villainy and suffering so strongly pictured on the same face, and she observed him with a degree of thrilling curiosity, which for a moment excluded from her mind all consciousness of the evils to be apprehended from him.

It was evident that this house had not been built for his reception; and she conjectured, that he was the servant of some cruel agent of the Marchesa di Vivaldi.

From the porch, she followed into an old hall, ruinous, and destitute of any kind of furniture. It was not extensive but lofty, for it seemed to ascend to the roof of the edifice, and the chambers above opened around it into a corridor.

Some half-sullen salutations were exchanged between the guard and the stranger, whom they called Spalatro, as they passed into a chamber, where, it appeared that he had been sleeping on a mattress laid in a corner. All the other furniture of the place, were two or three broken chairs and a table. He eyed Ellena with a shrewd contracted brow, and then looked significantly at the guard, but was silent, till he desired them all to sit down, adding, that he would

dress some fish for supper. Ellena discovered that this man was the master of
the place; it appeared also that he was the only inhabitant; and, when the guard
soon after informed her their journey concluded here, her worst apprehensions
were confirmed. The efforts she made to sustain her spirits were no longer
successful. It seemed that she was brought hither by ruffians to a lonely house
on the sea-shore, inhabited by a man, who had 'villain' engraved in every line
of his face, to be the victim of inexorable pride and an insatiable desire of
revenge. After considering these circumstances, and the words, which had just
told her, she was to go no further, conviction struck like lightning upon her
heart; and, believing she was brought hither to be assassinated, horror chilled
all her frame, and her senses forsook her.

On recovering, she found herself surrounded by the guard and the stranger,
and she would have supplicated for their pity, but that she feared to exasperate
them by betraying her suspicions. She complained of fatigue, and requested to
be shewn to her room. The men looked upon one another, hesitated, and then
asked her to partake of the fish that was preparing. But Ellena having declined
the invitation with as good a grace as she could assume, they consented that
she withdraw. Spalatro, taking the lamp, lighted her across the hall, to the
corridor above, where he opened the door of a chamber, in which he said
she was to sleep.

'Where is my bed?' said the afflicted Ellena fearfully as she looked round.

'It is there—on the floor,' replied Spalatro, pointing to a miserable mattress,
over which hung the tattered curtains of what had once been a canopy. 'If you
want the lamp,' he added, 'I will leave it, and come for it in a minute or two.'

'Will you not let me have a lamp for the night,' she said in a supplicating
and timid voice.

'For the night!' said the man gruffly; 'What! to set fire to the house.'

Ellena still entreated that he would allow her the comfort of a light.

'Ay, ay,' replied Spalatro, with a look she could not comprehend, 'it would be
a great comfort to you, truly! You do not know what you ask.'

'What is it that you mean?' said Ellena, eagerly; 'I conjure you, in the name
of our holy church, to tell me!'

Spalatro stepped suddenly back, and looked upon her with surprise, but
without speaking.

'Have mercy on me!' said Ellena, greatly alarmed by his manner; 'I am
friendless, and without help!'

'What do you fear,' said the man, recovering himself; and then, without waiting
her reply, added—'Is it such an unmerciful deed to take away a lamp?'

Ellena, who again feared to betray the extent of her suspicions, only replied,
that it would be merciful to leave it, for that her spirits were low, and she
required light to cheer them in a new abode.

'We do not stand upon such conceits here,' replied Spalatro, 'we have other
matters to mind. Besides, it's the only lamp in the house, and the company below
are in darkness while I am losing time here. I will leave it for two minutes, and
no more.' Ellena made a sign for him to put down the lamp; and, when he left
the room, she heard the door barred upon her.

She employed these two minutes in examining the chamber, and the possibility it might afford of an escape. It was a large apartment, unfurnished and unswept of the cobwebs of many years. The only door she discovered was the one, by which she had entered, and the only window a lattice, which was grated. Such preparation for preventing escape seemed to hint how much there might be to escape from.

Having examined the chamber, without finding a single circumstance to encourage hope, tried the strength of the bars, which she could not shake, and sought in vain for an inside fastening to her door, she placed the lamp beside it, and awaited the return of Spalatro. In a few moments he came, and offered her a cup of sour wine with a slice of bread; which, being somewhat soothed by this attention, she did not think proper to reject.

Spalatro then quitted the room, and the door was again barred. Left once more alone, she tried to overcome apprehension by prayer; and after offering up her vespers with a fervent heart, she became more confiding and composed.

But it was impossible that she could so far forget the dangers of her situation, as to seek sleep, however wearied she might be, while the door of her room remained unsecured against the intrusion of the ruffians below; and, as she had no means of fastening it, she determined to watch during the whole night.Thus left to solitude and darkness, she seated herself upon the mattress to await the return of morning, and was soon lost in sad reflection; every minute occurrence of the past day, and of the conduct of her guards, moved in review before her judgment; and, combining these with the circumstances of her present situation, scarcely a doubt as to the fate designed for her remained. It seemed highly improbable, that the Marchesa di Vivaldi had sent her hither merely for imprisonment, since she might have confined her in a convent, with much less trouble; and still more so, when Ellena considered the character of the Marchesa, such as she had already experienced it. The appearance of this house, and of the man who inhabited it, with the circumstance of no woman being found residing here, each and all of these signified, that she was brought hither, not for long imprisonment, but for death. Her utmost efforts for fortitude or resignation could not overcome the cold tremblings, the sickness of heart, the faintness and universal horror, that assailed her. How often, with tears of mingled terror and grief, did she call upon Vivaldi—Vivaldi, alas! far distant—to save her; how often exclaim in agony, that she should never, never see him more!

She was spared, however, the horror of believing that he was an inhabitant of the Inquisition. Having detected the imposition, which had been practised towards herself, and that she was neither on the way to the Holy Office, nor conducted by persons belonging to it, she concluded, that the whole affair of Vivaldi's arrest, had been planned by the Marchesa, merely as a pretence for confining him, till she should be placed beyond the reach of his assistance. She hoped, therefore, that he had only been sent to some private residence belonging to his family, and that, when her fate was decided, he would be released, and she be the only victim. This was the sole consideration, that afforded any degree of assuagement to her sufferings.

The people below sat till a late hour. She listened often to their distant voices, as they were distinguishable in the pauses of the surge, that broke loud and hollow on the shore; and every time the creaking hinges of their room door moved, apprehended they were coming to her. At length, it appeared they had left the apartment, or had fallen asleep there, for a profound stillness reigned whenever the murmur of the waves sunk. Doubt did not long deceive her, for, while she yet listened, she distinguished footsteps ascending to the corridor. She heard them approach her chamber, and stop at the door; she heard, also, the low whisperings of their voices, as they seemed consulting on what was to be done, and she scarcely ventured to draw breath, while she intensely attended to them. Not a word, however, distinctly reached her, till, as one of them was departing, another called out in a half-whisper, 'It is below on the table, in my girdle; make haste.' The man came back, and said something in a lower voice, to which the other replied, 'she sleeps,' or Ellena was deceived by the hissing consonants of some other words. He then descended the stairs; and in a few minutes she perceived his comrade also pass away from the door; she listened to his retreating steps, till the roaring of the sea was alone heard in their stead.

Ellena's terrors were relieved only for a moment. Considering the import of the words, it appeared that the man who had descended, was gone for the stiletto[1] of the other, such an instrument being usually worn in the girdle, and from the assurance, 'she sleeps,' he seemed to fear that his words had been overheard; and she listened again for their steps; but they came no more.

Happily for Ellena's peace, she knew not that her chamber had a door, so contrived as to open without sound, by which assassins might enter unsuspectedly at any hour of the night. Believing that the inhabitants of this house had now retired to rest, her hopes and her spirits began to revive; but she was yet sleepless and watchful. She measured the chamber with unequal steps, often starting as the old boards shook and groaned where she passed; and often pausing to listen whether all was yet still in the corridor. The gleam, which a rising moon threw between the bars of her window, now began to shew many shadowy objects in the chamber, which she did not recollect to have observed while the lamp was there. More than once, she fancied she saw something glide along towards the place where the mattress was laid, and, almost congealed with terror, she stood still to watch it; but the illusion, if such it was, disappeared where the moon-light faded, and even her fears could not give shape to it beyond. Had she not known that her chamber-door remained strongly barred, she would have believed this was an assassin stealing to the bed where it might be supposed she slept. Even now the thought occurred to her, and vague as it was, had power to strike an anguish, almost deadly, through her heart, while she considered that her immediate situation was nearly as perilous as the one she had imagined. Again she listened, and scarcely dared to breathe; but not the lightest sound occurred in the pauses of the waves, and she believed herself convinced that no person except herself was in the room. That she was deceived in this belief, appeared from her unwillingness to approach the mattress, while it was yet involved in

[1] A short dagger.

shade. Unable to overcome her reluctance, she took her station at the window, till the strengthening rays should allow a clearer view of the chamber, and in some degree restore her confidence; and she watched the scene without as it gradually became visible. The moon, rising over the ocean, shewed its restless surface spreading to the wide horizon; and the waves, which broke in foam upon the rocky beach below, retiring in long white lines far upon the waters. She listened to their measured and solemn sound, and, somewhat soothed by the solitary grandeur of the view, remained at the lattice till the moon had risen high into the heavens; and even till morning began to dawn upon the sea, and purple the eastern clouds.

Re-assured, by the light that now pervaded her room, she returned to the mattress; where anxiety at length yielded to her weariness, and she obtained a short repose.

CHAPTER VIII

ELLENA was awakened from profound sleep, by a loud noise at the door of her chamber; when, starting from her mattress, she looked around her with surprise and dismay, as imperfect recollections of the past began to gather on her mind. She distinguished the undrawing of iron bars, and then the countenance of Spalatro at her door, before she had a clear remembrance of her situation—that she was a prisoner in a house on a lonely shore, and that this man was her jailor. Such sickness of the heart returned with these convictions, such faintness and terror, that unable to support her trembling frame, she sunk again upon the mattress, without demanding the reason of this abrupt intrusion.

'I have brought you some breakfast,' said Spalatro, 'if you are awake to take it; but you seem to be asleep yet. Surely you have had sleep sufficient for one night; you went to rest soon enough.'

Ellena made no reply, but, deeply affected with a sense of her situation, looked with beseeching eyes at the man, who advanced, holding forth an oaten cake and a bason of milk. 'Where shall I set them?' said he, 'you must needs be glad of them, since you had no supper.'

Ellena thanked him, and desired he would place them on the floor, for there was neither table nor chair in the room. As he did this, she was struck with the expression of his countenance, which exhibited a strange mixture of archness and malignity. He seemed congratulating himself upon his ingenuity, and anticipating some occasion of triumph; and she was so much interested, that her observation never quitted him while he remained in the room. As his eyes accidentally met hers, he turned them away, with the abruptness of a person who is conscious of evil intentions, and fears lest they should be detected; nor once looked up till he hastily left the chamber, when she heard the door secured as formerly.

The impression, which his look had left on her mind, so wholly engaged her in conjecture, that a considerable time elapsed before she remembered that he had brought the refreshment she so much required; but, as she now lifted it to her lips, a horrible suspicion arrested her hand; it was not, however, before she had swallowed a small quantity of the milk. The look of Spalatro, which occasioned her surprise, had accompanied the setting down of the breakfast, and it occurred to her, that poison was infused in this liquid. She was thus compelled to refuse the sustenance, which was become necessary to her, for she feared to taste even the oaten cake, since Spalatro had offered it, but the little milk she had unwarily taken, was so very small that she had no apprehension concerning it.

The day, however, was passed in terror, and almost in despondency; she could neither doubt the purpose, for which she had been brought hither, nor discover any possibility of escaping from her persecutors; yet that propensity to hope, which buoys up the human heart, even in the severest hours of trial, sustained, in some degree, her fainting spirits.

During these miserable hours of solitude and suspense, the only alleviation to her suffering arose from a belief, that Vivaldi was safe, at least from danger, though not from grief; but she now understood too much of the dexterous contrivances of the Marchesa, his mother, to think it was practicable for him to escape from her designs, and again restore her to liberty.

All day Ellena either leaned against the bars of her window, lost in reverie, while her unconscious eyes were fixed upon the ocean, whose murmurs she no longer heard; or she listened for some sound from within the house, that might assist her conjectures, as to the number of persons below, or what might be passing there. The house, however, was profoundly still, except when now and then a footstep sauntered along a distant passage, or a door was heard to close; but not the hum of a single voice arose from the lower rooms, nor any symptom of there being more than one person, beside herself, in the dwelling. Though she had not heard her former guards depart, it appeared certain that they were gone, and that she was left alone in this place with Spalatro. What could be the purport of such a proceeding, Ellena could not imagine; if her death was designed, it seemed strange that one person only should be left to the hazard of the deed, when three must have rendered the completion of it certain. But this surprise vanished, when her suspicion of poison returned; for it was probable, that these men had believed their scheme to be already nearly accomplished, and had abandoned her to die alone, in a chamber from whence escape was impracticable, leaving Spalatro to dispose of her remains. All the incongruities she had separately observed in their conduct, seemed now to harmonize and unite in one plan; and her death, designed by poison, and that poison to be conveyed in the disguise of nourishment, appeared to have been the object of it. Whether it was that the strength of this conviction affected her fancy, or that the cause was real, Ellena, remembering at this moment that she had tasted the milk, was seized with an universal shuddering, and thought she felt that the poison had been sufficiently potent to affect her, even in the inconsiderable quantity she might have taken.

While she was thus agitated, she distinguished footsteps loitering near her door, and attentively listening, became convinced, that some person was in the corridor. The steps moved softly, sometimes stopping for an instant, as if to allow time for listening, and soon after passed away.

'It is Spalatro!' said Ellena; 'he believes that I have taken the poison, and he comes to listen for my dying groans! Alas! he is only come somewhat too soon, perhaps!'

As this horrible supposition occurred, the shuddering returned with encreased violence, and she sunk, almost fainting, on the mattress; but the fit was not of long continuance. When it gradually left her, and recollection revived, she perceived, however, the prudence of suffering Spalatro to suppose she had taken the beverage he brought her, since such belief would at least procure some delay of further schemes, and every delay afforded some possibility for hope to rest upon. Ellena, therefore, poured through the bars of her window, the milk, which she believed Spalatro had designed should be fatal in its consequence.

It was evening, when she again fancied footsteps were lingering near her door, and the suspicion was confirmed, when, on turning her eyes, she perceived a shade on the floor, underneath it, as of some person stationed without. Presently the shadow glided away, and at the same time she distinguished departing steps treading cautiously.

'It is he!' said Ellena; 'he still listens for my moans!'

This further confirmation of his designs affected her nearly as much as the first; when anxiously turning her looks towards the corridor, the shadow again appeared beneath the door, but she heard no step. Ellena now watched it with intense solicitude and expectation; fearing every instant that Spalatro would conclude her doubts by entering the room. 'And O! when he discovers that I live,' thought she, 'what may I not expect during the first moments of his disappointment! What less than immediate death!'

The shadow, after remaining a few minutes stationary, moved a little, and then glided away as before. But it quickly returned, and a low sound followed, as of some person endeavouring to unfasten bolts without noise. Ellena heard one bar gently undrawn, and then another; she observed the door begin to move, and then to give way, till it gradually unclosed, and the face of Spalatro presented itself from behind it. Without immediately entering, he threw a glance round the chamber, as if he wished to ascertain some circumstance before he ventured further. His look was more than usually haggard as it rested upon Ellena, who apparently reposed on her mattress.

Having gazed at her for an instant, he ventured towards the bed with quick and unequal steps; his countenance expressed at once impatience, alarm, and the consciousness of guilt. When he was within a few paces, Ellena raised herself, and he started back as if a sudden spectre had crossed him. The more than usual wildness and wanness of his looks, with the whole of his conduct, seemed to confirm all her former terrors; and, when he roughly asked her how she did, Ellena had not sufficient presence of mind to answer that she was ill. For some moments, he regarded her with an earnest and sullen attention, and then a sly glance of scrutiny, which he threw round the chamber, told her that he was enquiring whether she had taken the poison. On perceiving that the bason was empty, he lifted it from the floor, and Ellena fancied a gleam of satisfaction passed over his visage.

'You have had no dinner,' said he, 'I forgot you; but supper will soon be ready; and you may walk up the beach till then, if you will.'

Ellena, extremely surprised and perplexed by this offer of a seeming indulgence, knew not whether to accept or reject it. She suspected that some treachery lurked within it. The invitation appeared to be only a stratagem to lure her to destruction, and she determined to decline accepting it; when again she considered, that to accomplish this, it was not necessary to withdraw her from the chamber, where she was already sufficiently in the power of her persecutors. Her situation could not be more desperate than it was at present, and almost any change might make it less so.

As she descended from the corridor, and passed through the lower part of the house, no person appeared but her conductor; and she ventured to enquire, whether the men who had brought her hither were departed. Spalatro did not return an answer, but led the way in silence to the court, and, having passed the gates, he pointed toward the west, and said she might walk that way.

Ellena bent her course towards the 'many-sounding waves,' followed at a short distance by Spalatro, and, wrapt in thought, pursued the windings of the shore, scarcely noticing the objects around her; till, on passing the foot of a rock, she lifted her eyes to the scene that unfolded beyond, and observed some huts scattered at a considerable distance, apparently the residence of fishermen. She could just distinguish the dark sails of some skiffs turning the cliffs, and entering the little bay, where the hamlet margined the beach; but, though she saw the sails lowered, as the boats approached the shore, they were too far off to allow the figures of the men to appear. To Ellena, who had believed that no human habitation, except her prison, interrupted the vast solitudes of these forests and shores, the view of the huts, remote as they were, imparted a feeble hope, and even somewhat of joy. She looked back, to observe whether Spalatro was near; he was already within a few paces; and, casting a wistful glance forward to the remote cottages, her heart sunk again.

It was a lowering evening, and the sea was dark and swelling; the screams of the sea-birds too, as they wheeled among the clouds, and sought their high nests in the rocks, seemed to indicate an approaching storm. Ellena was not so wholly engaged by selfish sufferings, but that she could sympathise with those of others, and she rejoiced that the fishermen, whose boats she had observed, had escaped the threatening tempest, and were safely sheltered in their little homes, where, as they heard the loud waves break along the coast, they could look with keener pleasure upon the social circle, and the warm comforts around them. From such considerations however, she returned again to a sense of her own forlorn and friendless situation.

'Alas!' said she, 'I have no longer a home, a circle to smile welcomes upon me! I have no longer even one friend to support, to rescue me! I—a miserable wanderer on a distant shore! tracked, perhaps, by the footsteps of the assassin, who at this instant eyes his victim with silent watchfulness, and awaits the moment of opportunity to sacrifice her!'

Ellena shuddered as she said this, and turned again to observe whether Spalatro was near. He was not within view; and, while she wondered, and congratulated herself on a possibility of escaping, she perceived a Monk walking silently beneath the dark rocks that overbrowed the beach. His black garments were folded round him; his face was inclined towards the ground, and he had the air of a man in deep meditation.

'His, no doubt, are worthy musings!' said Ellena, as she observed him, with mingled hope and surprise. 'I may address myself, without fear, to one of his order. It is probably as much his wish, as it is his duty, to succour the unfortunate. Who could have hoped to find on this sequestered shore so sacred a protector! his convent cannot be far off.'

He approached, his face still bent towards the ground, and Ellena advanced slowly, and with trembling steps, to meet him. As he drew near, he viewed her askance, without lifting his head; but she perceived his large eyes looking from under the shade of his cowl, and the upper part of his peculiar countenance. Her confidence in his protection began to fail, and she faultered, unable to speak, and scarcely daring to meet his eyes. The Monk stalked past her in silence, the lower part of his visage still muffled in his drapery, and as he passed her looked neither with curiosity, nor surprise.

Ellena paused, and determined, when he should be at some distance, to endeavour to make her way to the hamlet, and throw herself upon the humanity of its inhabitants, rather than solicit the pity of this forbidding stranger. But in the next moment she heard a step behind her, and, on turning, saw the Monk again approaching. He stalked by as before, surveying her, however, with a sly and scrutinizing glance from the corners of his eyes. His air and countenance were equally repulsive, and still Ellena could not summon courage enough to attempt engaging his compassion; but shrunk as from an enemy. There was something also terrific in the silent stalk of so gigantic a form; it announced both power and treachery. He passed slowly on to some distance, and disappeared among the rocks.

Ellena turned once more with an intention of hastening towards the distant hamlet, before Spalatro should observe her, whose strange absence she had scarcely time to wonder at; but she had not proceeded far, when suddenly she perceived the Monk again at her shoulder. She started, and almost shrieked; while he regarded her with more attention than before. He paused a moment, and seemed to hesitate; after which he again passed on in silence. The distress of Ellena encreased; he was gone the way she had designed to run, and she feared almost equally to follow him, and to return to her prison. Presently he turned, and passed her again, and Ellena hastened forward. But, when fearful of being pursued, she again looked back, she observed him conversing with Spalatro. They appeared to be in consultation, while they slowly advanced, till, probably observing her rapid progress, Spalatro called on her to stop, in a voice that echoed among all the rocks. It was a voice, which would not be disobeyed. She looked hopelessly at the still distant cottages, and slackened her steps. Presently the Monk again passed before her, and Spalatro had again disappeared. The frown, with which the former now regarded Ellena, was so terrific, that she shrunk trembling back, though she knew him not for her persecutor, since she had never consciously seen Schedoni. He was agitated, and his look became darker.

'Whither go you?' said he in a voice that was stifled by emotion.

'Who is it, father, that asks the question?' said Ellena, endeavouring to appear composed.

'Whither go you, and who are you?' repeated the Monk more sternly.

'I am an unhappy orphan,' replied Ellena, sighing deeply, 'If you are, as your habit denotes, a friend to the charities, you will regard me with compassion.'

Schedoni was silent, and then said—'Who, and what is it that you fear?'

'I fear—even for my life,' replied Ellena, with hesitation. She observed a darker shade pass over his countenance. 'For your life!' said he, with apparent surprise, 'who is there that would think it worth the taking.'

Ellena was struck with these words.

'Poor insect!' added Schedoni, 'who would crush thee?'

Ellena made no reply; she remained with her eyes fixed in amazement upon his face. There was something in his manner of pronouncing this, yet more extraordinary than in the words themselves. Alarmed by his manner, and awed by the encreasing gloom, and swelling surge, that broke in thunder on the beach, she at length turned away, and again walked towards the hamlet which was yet very remote.

He soon overtook her; when rudely seizing her arm, and gazing earnestly on her face, 'Who is it, that you fear?' said he, 'say who!'

'That is more than I dare say,' replied Ellena, scarcely able to sustain herself.

'Hah! is it even so!' said the Monk, with encreasing emotion. His visage now became so terrible, that Ellena struggled to liberate her arm, and supplicated that he would not detain her. He was silent, and still gazed upon her, but his eyes, when she had ceased to struggle, assumed the fixt and vacant glare of a man, whose thoughts have retired within themselves, and who is no longer conscious to surrounding objects.

'I beseech you to release me!' repeated Ellena, 'it is late, and I am far from home.'

'That is true,' muttered Schedoni, still grasping her arm, and seeming to reply to his own thoughts rather than to her words,—'that is very true.'

'The evening is closing fast,' continued Ellena, 'and I shall be overtaken by the storm.'

Schedoni still mused, and then muttered—'The storm, say you? Why ay, let it come.'

As he spoke, he suffered her arm to drop, but still held it, and walked slowly towards the house. Ellena, thus compelled to accompany him, and yet more alarmed both by his looks, his incoherent answers, and his approach to her prison, renewed her supplications and her efforts for liberty, in a voice of piercing distress, adding, 'I am far from home, father; night is coming on. See how the rocks darken! I am far from home, and shall be waited for.'

'That is false!' said Schedoni, with emphasis; 'and you know it to be so.'

'Alas! I do,' replied Ellena, with mingled shame and grief, 'I have no friends to wait for me!'

'What do those deserve, who deliberately utter falsehoods,' continued the Monk, 'who deceive, and flatter young men to their destruction?'

'Father!' exclaimed the astonished Ellena.

'Who disturb the peace of families—who trepan,[2] with wanton arts, the heirs of noble houses—who—hah! what do such deserve?'

Overcome with astonishment and terror, Ellena remained silent. She now understood that Schedoni, so far from being likely to prove a protector, was an agent of her worst, and as she had believed her only enemy; and an apprehension of the immediate and terrible vengeance, which such an agent seemed willing to accomplish, subdued her senses; she tottered, and sunk upon the beach. The weight, which strained the arm Schedoni held, called his attention to her situation.

As he gazed upon her helpless and faded form, he became agitated. He quitted it, and traversed the beach in short turns, and with hasty steps; came back again, and bent over it—his heart seemed sensible to some touch of pity. At one moment, he stepped towards the sea, and taking water in the hollows of his hands, threw it upon her face; at another, seeming to regret that he had done so, he would stamp with sudden fury upon the shore, and walk abruptly to a distance. The conflict between his design and his conscience was strong, or, perhaps, it was only between his passions. He, who had hitherto been insensible to every tender feeling, who, governed by ambition and resentment had contributed, by his artful instigations, to fix the baleful resolution of the Marchesa di Vivaldi, and who was come to execute her purpose,—even he could not now look upon the innocent, the wretched Ellena, without yielding to the momentary weakness, as he termed it, of compassion.

While he was yet unable to baffle the new emotion by evil passions, he despised that which conquered him. 'And shall the weakness of a girl,' said he, 'subdue the resolution of a man! Shall the view of her transient sufferings unnerve my firm heart, and compel me to renounce the lofty plans I have so ardently, so laboriously imagined, at the very instant when they are changing into realities! Am I awake! Is one spark of the fire, which has so long smouldered within my bosom, and consumed my peace, alive! Or am I tame and abject as my fortunes? hah! as my fortunes! Shall the spirit of my family yield for ever to circumstances? The question rouses it, and I feel its energy revive within me.'

He stalked with hasty steps towards Ellena, as if he feared to trust his resolution with a second pause. He had a dagger concealed beneath his Monk's habit; as he had also an assassin's heart shrouded by his garments. He had a dagger—but he hesitated to use it, the blood which it might spill, would be observed by the peasants of the neighbouring hamlet, and might lead to a discovery. It would be safer, he considered, and easier, to lay Ellena, senseless as she was, in the waves; their coldness would recal her to life, only at the moment before they would suffocate her.

[2] Ensnare.

As he stooped to lift her, his resolution faultered again, on beholding her innocent face, and in that moment she moved. He started back, as if she could have known his purpose, and, knowing it, could have avenged herself. The water, which he had thrown upon her face, had gradually revived her; she unclosed her eyes, and, on perceiving him, shrieked and attempted to rise. His resolution was subdued, so tremblingly fearful is guilt in the moment when it would execute its atrocities. Overcome with apprehensions, yet agitated with shame and indignation against himself for being so, he gazed at her for an instant in silence, and then abruptly turned away his eyes and left her. Ellena listened to his departing steps, and, raising herself, observed him retiring among the rocks that led towards the house. Astonished at his conduct, and surprised to find that she was alone, Ellena renewed all her efforts to sustain herself, till she should reach the hamlet so long the object of her hopes; but she had proceeded only a few paces, when Spalatro again appeared swiftly approaching. Her utmost exertion availed her nothing; her feeble steps were soon overtaken, and Ellena perceived herself again his prisoner. The look with which she resigned herself, awakened no pity in Spalatro, who uttered some taunting jest upon the swiftness of her flight, as he led her back to her prison, and proceeded in sullen watchfulness. Once again, then, she entered the gloomy walls of that fatal mansion, never more, she now believed, to quit them with life, a belief, which was strengthened when she remembered that the Monk on leaving her, had taken the way hither; for, though she knew not how to account for his late forbearance, she could not suppose that he would long be merciful. He appeared no more, however, as she passed to her chamber, where Spalatro left her again to solitude and terror, and she heard that fateful door again barred upon her. When his retreating steps had ceased to sound, a stilness, as of the grave, prevailed in the house; like the dead calm, which sometimes precedes the horrors of a tempest.

CHAPTER IX

S CHEDONI had returned from the beach to the house, in a state of perturbation, that defied the controul of even his own stern will. On the way thither he met Spalatro, whom, as he dispatched him to Ellena, he strictly commanded not to approach his chamber till he should be summoned.

Having reached his apartment, he secured the door, though not any person, except himself, was in the house, nor any one expected, but those who he knew would not dare to intrude upon him. Had it been possible to have shut out all consciousness of himself, also, how willingly would he have done so! He threw himself into a chair, and remained for a considerable time motionless, and lost in thought, yet the emotions of his mind were violent and contradictory. At the very instant when his heart reproached him with the crime he had meditated, he regretted the ambitious views he must relinquish if he failed to perpetrate it, and regarded himself with some degree of contempt for having hitherto hesitated on the subject. He considered the character of his own mind with astonishment, for circumstances had drawn forth traits, of which, till now, he had no suspicion. He knew not by what doctrine to explain the inconsistencies, the contradictions, he experienced, and, perhaps, it was not one of the least that in these moments of direful and conflicting passions, his reason could still look down upon their operations, and lead him to a cool, though brief examination of his own nature. But the subtlety of self-love still eluded his enquiries, and he did not detect that pride was even at this instant of self-examination, and of critical import, the master-spring of his mind. In the earliest dawn of his character this passion had displayed its predominancy, whenever occasion permitted, and its influence had led to some of the chief events of his life.

The Count di Marinella, for such had formerly been the title of the Confessor,[3] was the younger son of an ancient family, who resided in the duchy of Milan, and near the feet of the Tyrolean Alps, on such estates of their ancestors, as the Italian wars of a former century had left them. The portion, which he had received at the death of his father, was not large, and Schedoni was not of a disposition to improve his patrimony by slow diligence, or to submit to the restraint and humiliation, which his narrow finances would have imposed. He disdained to acknowledge an inferiority of fortune to those, with whom he considered himself equal in rank; and, as he was destitute of generous feeling, and of sound judgment, he had not that loftiness of soul, which is ambitious of true grandeur. On the contrary, he was satisfied with an ostentatious display of pleasures and of power, and, thoughtless of the consequence of dissipation, was contented with the pleasures of the moment, till his exhausted resources compelled him to reflect. He perceived, too late for his advantage, that it was necessary for him to dispose of part of his estate, and to confine himself to the income of the remainder. Incapable of submitting with grace to the reduction, which his folly had rendered expedient, he endeavoured to obtain by cunning, the luxuries that his prudence had failed to keep, and which neither his genius or his integrity could command. He withdrew, however, from the eyes of his neighbours, unwilling to submit his altered circumstances to their observation.

Concerning several years of his life, from this period, nothing was generally known; and, when he was next discovered, it was in the Spirito Santo convent at Naples, in the habit of a Monk, and under the assumed name of Schedoni. His air and countenance were as much altered as his way of life; his looks had become gloomy and severe, and the pride, which had mingled with the gaiety of their former expression, occasionally discovered itself under the disguise of humility, but more frequently in the austerity of silence, and in the barbarity of penance.

The person who discovered Schedoni, would not have recollected him, had not his remarkable eyes first fixed his attention, and then revived remembrance. As he examined his features, he traced the faint resemblance of what Marinella had been, to whom he made himself known.

[3] i.e. Schedoni.

The Confessor affected to have forgotten his former acquaintance, and assured him, that he was mistaken respecting himself, till the stranger so closely urged some circumstances, that the former was no longer permitted to dissemble. He retired, in some emotion, with the stranger, and, whatever might be the subject of their conference, he drew from him, before he quitted the convent, a tremendous vow, to keep secret from the brotherhood his knowledge of Schedoni's family, and never to reveal without those walls, that he had seen him. These requests he had urged in a manner, that at once surprised and awed the stranger, and which at the same time that it manifested the weight of Schedoni's fears, bade the former tremble for the consequence of disobedience; and he shuddered even while he promised to obey. Of the first part of the promise he was probably strictly observant; whether he was equally so of the second, does not appear; it is certain, that after this period, he was never more seen or heard of at Naples.

Schedoni, ever ambitious of distinction, adapted his manners to the views and prejudices of the society with whom he resided, and became one of the most exact observers of their outward forms, and almost a prodigy for self-denial and severe discipline. He was pointed out by the fathers of the convent to the juniors as a great example, who was, however, rather to be looked up to with reverential admiration, than with an hope of emulating his sublime virtues. But with such panegyrics their friendship for Schedoni concluded. They found it convenient to applaud the austerities, which they declined to practise; it procured them a character for sanctity, and saved them the necessity of earning it by mortifications of their own; but they both feared and hated Schedoni for his pride and his gloomy austerities, too much, to gratify his ambition by any thing further than empty praise. He had been several years in the society, without obtaining any considerable advancement, and with the mortification of seeing persons, who had never emulated his severity, raised to high offices in the church. Somewhat too late he discovered, that he was not to expect any substantial favour from the brotherhood, and then it was that his restless and disappointed spirit first sought preferment by other avenues. He had been some years Confessor to the Marchesa di Vivaldi, when the conduct of her son awakened his hopes, by showing him, that he might render himself not only useful but necessary to her, by his councils. It was his custom to study the characters of those around him, with a view of adapting them to his purposes, and, having ascertained that of the Marchesa, these hopes were encouraged. He perceived that her passions were strong, her judgment weak; and he understood, that, if circumstances should ever enable him to be serviceable in promoting the end at which any one of those passions might aim, his fortune would be established.

At length, he so completely insinuated himself into her confidence, and became so necessary to her views, that he could demand his own terms, and this he had not failed to do, though with all the affected delicacy and finesse that his situation seemed to require. An office of high dignity in the church, which had long vainly excited his ambition, was promised him by the Marchesa, who had sufficient influence to obtain it; her condition was that of his preserving the honour of her family, as she delicately termed it, which she was careful to make him understand could be secured only by the death of Ellena. He acknowledged, with the Marchesa, that the death of this fascinating young woman was the only means of preserving that honour, since, if she lived, they had every evil to expect from the attachment and character of Vivaldi, who would discover and extricate her from any place of confinement, however obscure or difficult of access, to which she might be conveyed. How long and how arduously the Confessor had aimed to oblige the Marchesa, has already appeared. The last scene was now arrived, and he was on the eve of committing that atrocious act, which was to secure the pride of her house, and to satisfy at once his ambition and his desire of vengeance; when an emotion new and surprising to him, had arrested his arm, and compelled his resolution to falter. But this emotion was transient, it disappeared almost with the object that had awakened it; and now, in the silence and retirement of his chamber, he had leisure to recollect his thoughts, to review his schemes, to re-animate his resolution, and to wonder again at the pity, which had almost won him from his purpose. The ruling passion of his nature once more resumed its authority, and he determined to earn the honour, which the Marchesa had in store for him.

After some cool, and more of tumultuous, consideration, he resolved that Ellena should be assassinated that night, while she slept, and afterwards conveyed through a passage of the house communicating with the sea, into which the body might be thrown and buried, with her sad story, beneath the waves. For his own sake, he would have avoided the danger of shedding blood, had this appeared easy; but he had too much reason to know she had suspicions of poison, to trust to a second attempt by such means; and again his indignation rose against himself, since by yielding to a momentary compassion, he had lost the opportunity afforded him of throwing her unresistingly into the surge.

Spalatro, as has already been hinted, was a former confident of the Confessor, who knew too truly, from experience, that he could be trusted, and had, therefore, engaged him to assist on this occasion. To the hands of this man he consigned the fate of the unhappy Ellena, himself recoiling from the horrible act he had willed; and intending by such a step to involve Spalatro more deeply in the guilt, and thus more effectually to secure his secret.

The night was far advanced before Schedoni's final resolution was taken, when he summoned Spalatro to his chamber to instruct him in his office. He bolted the door, by which the man had entered, forgetting that themselves were the only persons in the house, except the poor Ellena, who, unsuspicious of what was conspiring, and her spirits worn out by the late scene, was sleeping peacefully on her mattress above. Schedoni moved softly from the door he had secured, and, beckoning Spalatro to approach, spoke in a low voice, as if he feared to be overheard. 'Have you perceived any sound from her chamber lately?' said he. 'Does she sleep, think you?'

'No one has moved there for this hour past, at least,' replied Spalatro, 'I have been watching in the corridor, till you called, and should have heard if she had stirred, the old floor shakes so with every step.'

'Then hear me, Spalatro,' said the Confessor. 'I have tried, and found thee faithful, or I should not trust thee in a business of confidence like this.

Recollect all I said to thee in the morning, and be resolute and dexterous, as I have ever found thee.'

Spalatro listened in gloomy attention, and the Monk proceeded, 'It is late; go, therefore, to her chamber; be certain that she sleeps. Take this,' he added, 'and this,' giving him a dagger and a large cloak—'You know how you are to use them.'

He paused, and fixed his penetrating eyes on Spalatro, who held up the dagger in silence, examined the blade, and continued to gaze upon it, with a vacant stare, as if he was unconscious of what he did.

'You know your business,' repeated Schedoni, authoritatively, 'dispatch! time wears; and I must set off early.'

The man made no reply.

'The morning dawns already,' said the Confessor, still more urgently, 'Do you faulter? do you tremble? Do I not know you?'

Spalatro put up the poinard in his bosom without speaking, threw the cloak over his arm, and moved with a loitering step towards the door.

'Dispatch!' repeated the Confessor, 'why do you linger?'

'I cannot say I like this business, Signor,' said Spalatro surlily. 'I know not why I should always do the most, and be paid the least.'

'Sordid villain!' exclaimed Schedoni, 'you are not satisfied then!'

'No more a villain than yourself, Signor,' retorted the man, throwing down the cloak, 'I only do your business; and 'tis you that are sordid, for you would take all the reward, and I would only have a poor man have his dues. Do the work yourself, or give me the greater profit.'

'Peace!' said Schedoni, 'dare no more to insult me with the mention of reward. Do you imagine I have sold myself! 'Tis my will that she dies; this is sufficient; and for you—the price you have asked has been granted.'

'It is too little,' replied Spalatro, 'and besides, I do not like the work.—What harm has she done me?'

'Since when is it, that you have taken upon you to moralize?' said the Confessor, 'and how long are these cowardly scruples to last? This is not the first time you have been employed; what harm had others done you! You forget that I know you, you forget the past.'

'No, Signor, I remember it too well, I wish I could forget; I remember it too well.—I have never been at peace since. The bloody hand is always before me! and often of a night, when the sea roars, and storms shake the house, *they* have come, all gashed as I left them, and stood before my bed! I have got up, and ran out upon the shore for safety!'

'Peace!' repeated the Confessor, 'where is this frenzy of fear to end? To what are these visions, painted in blood, to lead? I thought I was talking with a man, but find I am speaking only to a baby, possessed with his nurse's dreams! Yet I understand you,—you shall be satisfied.'

Schedoni, however, had for once misunderstood this man, when he could not believe it possible that he was really averse to execute what he had undertaken. Whether the innocence and beauty of Ellena had softened his heart, or that his conscience did torture him for his past deeds, he persisted in refusing to murder her. His conscience, or his pity, was of a very peculiar kind however; for, though he refused to execute the deed himself, he consented to wait at the foot of a back stair-case, that communicated with Ellena's chamber, while Schedoni accomplished it, and afterward to assist in carrying the body to the shore. 'This is a compromise between conscience and guilt, worthy of a demon,' muttered Schedoni, who appeared to be insensible that he had made the same compromise with himself not an hour before; and whose extreme reluctance at this moment, to perpetrate with his own hand, what he had willingly designed for another, ought to have reminded him of that compromise.

Spalatro, released from the immediate office of an executioner, endured silently the abusive, yet half-stifled, indignation of the Confessor, who also bade him remember, that, though he now shrunk from the most active part of this transaction, he had not always been restrained, in offices of the same nature, by equal compunction; and that not only his means of subsistence, but his very life itself, was at his mercy. Spalatro readily acknowledged that it was so; and Schedoni knew, too well, the truth of what he had urged, to be restrained from his purpose, by any apprehension of the consequence of a discovery from this ruffian.

'Give me the dagger, then,' said the Confessor, after a long pause, 'take up the cloak and follow to the stair-case. Let me see, whether your valour will carry you thus far.'

Spalatro resigned the stiletto, and threw the cloak again over his arm. The Confessor stepped to the door, and, trying to open it, 'It is fastened!' said he in alarm, 'some person has got into the house,—it is fastened!'

'That well may be, Signor,' replied Spalatro, calmly, 'for I saw you bolt it yourself, after I came into the room.'

'True,' said Schedoni, recovering himself; 'that is true.'

He opened it, and proceeded along the silent passages, towards the private stair-case, often pausing to listen, and then stepping more lightly;—the terrific Schedoni, in this moment of meditative guilt, feared even the feeble Ellena. At the foot of the stair-case, he again stopped to listen. 'Do you hear any thing?' said he in a whisper.

'I hear only the sea,' replied the man.

'Hush! it is something more!' said Schedoni; 'that is the murmur of voices!'

They were silent. After a pause of some length, 'It is, perhaps, the voice of the spectres I told you of, Signor,' said Spalatro, with a sneer. 'Give me the dagger,' said Schedoni.

Spalatro, instead of obeying, now grasped the arm of the Confessor, who, looking at him for an explanation of this extraordinary action, was still more surprised to observe the paleness and horror of his countenance. His starting eyes seemed to follow some object along the passage, and Schedoni, who began to partake of his feelings, looked forward to discover what occasioned this dismay, but could not perceive any thing that justified it. 'What is it you fear?' said he at length.

Spalatro's eyes were still moving in horror, 'Do you see nothing!' said he pointing. Schedoni looked again, but did not distinguish any object in the remote gloom of the passage, whither Spalatro's sight was now fixed.

'Come, come,' said he, ashamed of his own weakness, 'this is not a moment for such fancies. Awake from this idle dream.'

Spalatro withdrew his eyes, but they retained all their wildness. 'It was no dream,' said he, in the voice of a man who is exhausted by pain, and begins to breathe somewhat more freely again. 'I saw it as plainly as I now see you.'

'Dotard! what did you see!' enquired the Confessor.

'It came before my eyes in a moment, and shewed itself distinctly and outspread.'

'What shewed itself?' repeated Schedoni.

'And then it beckoned—yes, it beckoned me, with that blood-stained finger! and glided away down the passage, still beckoning——till it was lost in the darkness.'

'This is very frenzy!' said Schedoni, excessively agitated. 'Arouse yourself, and be a man!'

'Frenzy! would it were, Signor. I saw that dreadful hand—I see it now—it is there again!—there!'

Schedoni, shocked, embarrassed, and once more infected with the strange emotions of Spalatro, looked forward expecting to discover some terrific object, but still nothing was visible to him, and he soon recovered himself sufficiently to endeavour to appease the fancy of this conscience-struck ruffian. But Spalatro was insensible to all he could urge, and the Confessor, fearing that his voice, though weak and stifled, would awaken Ellena, tried to withdraw him from the spot, to the apartment they had quitted.

'The wealth of San Loretto should not make me go that way, Signor,' replied he, shuddering—'that was the way *it* beckoned, it vanished that way!'

Every emotion now yielded with Schedoni, to that of apprehension lest Ellena, being awakened, should make his task more horrid by a struggle, and his embarrassment encreased at each instant, for neither command, menace, or entreaty could prevail with Spalatro to retire, till the Monk luckily remembered a door, which opened beyond the stair-case, and would conduct them by another way to the opposite side of the house. The man consented so to depart, when, Schedoni unlocking a suit of rooms, of which he had always kept the keys, they passed in silence through an extent of desolate chambers, till they reached the one, which they had lately left.

Here, relieved from apprehension respecting Ellena, the Confessor expostulated more freely with Spalatro, but neither argument or menace could prevail, and the man persisted in refusing to return to the stair-case, though protesting, at the same time, that he would not remain alone in any part of the house; till the wine, with which the Confessor abundantly supplied him, began to overcome the terrors of his imagination. At length, his courage was so much re-animated, that he consented to resume his station, and await at the foot of the stairs the accomplishment of Schedoni's dreadful errand, with which agreement they returned thither by the way they had lately passed. The wine, with which Schedoni also had found it necessary to strengthen his own resolution, did not secure him from severe emotion, when he found himself again near

Ellena; but he made a strenuous effort for self-subjection, as he demanded the dagger of Spalatro.

'You have it already, Signor,' replied the man.

'True,' said the Monk; 'ascend softly, or our steps may awaken her.'

'You said I was to wait at the foot of the stairs, Signor, while you'——

'True, true, true!' muttered the Confessor, and had begun to ascend, when his attendant desired him to stop. 'You are going in darkness, Signor, you have forgotten the lamp. I have another here.'

Schedoni took it angrily, without speaking, and was again ascending, when he hesitated, and once more paused. 'The glare will disturb her,' thought he, 'it is better to go in darkness.—Yet——'. He considered, that he could not strike with certainty without light to direct his hand, and he kept the lamp, but returned once more to charge Spalatro not to stir from the foot of the stairs till he called, and to ascend to the chamber upon the first signal.

'I will obey, Signor, if you, on your part, will promise not to give the signal till all is over.'

'I do promise,' replied Schedoni, 'No more!'

Again he ascended, nor stopped till he reached Ellena's door, where he listened for a sound; but all was as silent as if death already reigned in the chamber. This door was, from long disuse, difficult to be opened; formerly it would have. yielded without sound, but now Schedoni was fearful of noise from every effort he made to move it. After some difficulty, however, it gave way, and he perceived, by the stillness within the apartment, that he had not disturbed Ellena. He shaded the lamp with the door for a moment, while he threw an enquiring glance forward, and when he did venture farther, held part of his dark drapery before the light, to prevent the rays from spreading through the room.

As he approached the bed, her gentle breathings informed him that she still slept, and the next moment he was at her side. She lay in deep and peaceful slumber, and seemed to have thrown herself upon the mattress, after having been wearied by her griefs; for, though sleep pressed heavily on her eyes, their lids were yet wet with tears.

While Schedoni gazed for a moment upon her innocent countenance, a faint smile stole over it. He stepped back. 'She smiles in her murderer's face!' said he, shuddering. 'I must be speedy.'

He searched for the dagger, and it was some time before his trembling hand could disengage it from the folds of his garment; but, having done so, he again drew near, and prepared to strike. Her dress perplexed him; it would interrupt the blow, and he stooped to examine whether he could turn her robe aside, without waking her. As the light passed over her face, he perceived that the smile had vanished—the visions of her sleep were changed, for tears stole from beneath her eye-lids, and her features suffered a slight convulsion. She spoke! Schedoni, apprehending that the light had disturbed her, suddenly drew back, and, again irresolute, shaded the lamp, and concealed himself behind the curtain, while he listened. But her words were inward and indistinct, and convinced him that she still slumbered.

His agitation and repugnance to strike encreased with every moment of delay, and, as often as he prepared to plunge the poinard in her bosom, a shuddering horror restrained him. Astonished at his own feelings, and indignant at what he termed a dastardly weakness, he found it necessary to argue with himself, and his rapid thoughts said, 'Do I not feel the necessity of this act! Does not what is dearer to me than existence—does not my consequence depend on the execution of it? Is she not also beloved by the young Vivaldi?—have I already forgotten the church of the Spirito Santo?[4] This consideration re-animated him; vengeance nerved his arm, and drawing aside the lawn from her bosom, he once more raised it to strike; when, after gazing for an instant, some new cause of horror seemed to seize all his frame, and he stood for some moments aghast and motionless like a statue. His respiration was short and laborious, chilly drops stood on his forehead, and all his faculties of mind seemed suspended. When he recovered, he stooped to examine again the miniature, which had occasioned this revolution, and which had lain concealed beneath the lawn that he withdrew. The terrible certainty was almost confirmed, and forgetting, in his impatience to know the truth, the imprudence of suddenly discovering himself to Ellena at this hour of the night, and with a dagger at his feet, he called loudly 'Awake! awake! Say, what is your name? Speak! speak quickly!'

Ellena, aroused by a man's voice, started from her mattress, when, perceiving Schedoni, and by the pale glare of the lamp, his haggard countenance, she shrieked, and sunk back on the pillow. She had not fainted; and believing that he came to murder her, she now exerted herself to plead for mercy. The energy of her feelings enabled her to rise and throw herself at his feet. 'Be merciful, O father! be merciful!' said she, in a trembling voice.

'Father!' interrupted Schedoni, with earnestness; and then, seeming to restrain himself, he added, with unaffected surprise, 'Why are you thus terrified?' for he had lost, in new interests and emotions, all consciousness of evil intention, and of the singularity of his situation. 'What do you fear?' he repeated.

'Have pity, holy father!' exclaimed Ellena in agony.

'Why do you not say whose portrait that is?' demanded he, forgetting that he had not asked the question before.

'Whose portrait?' repeated the Confessor in a loud voice.

'Whose portrait!' said Ellena, with extreme surprise.

'Ay, how came you by it? Be quick—whose resemblance is it?'

'Why should you wish to know?' said Ellena.

'Answer my question,' repeated Schedoni, with encreasing sternness.

'I cannot part with it, holy father,' replied Ellena, pressing it to her bosom, 'you do not wish me to part with it!'

'Is it impossible to make you answer my question!' said he, in extreme perturbation, and turning away from her, 'has fear utterly confounded you!' Then, again stepping towards her, and seizing her wrist, he repeated the demand in a tone of desperation.

4 In this church Vivaldi had insulted Schedoni and called him a hypocrite.

'Alas! he is dead! or I should not now want a protector,' replied Ellena, shrinking from his grasp, and weeping.

'You trifle,' said Schedoni, with a terrible look, 'I once more demand an answer—whose picture?'——

Ellena lifted it, gazed upon it for a moment, and then pressing it to her lips said, 'This was my father.'

'Your father!' he repeated in an inward voice, 'your father!' and shuddering, turned away.

Ellena looked at him with surprise. 'I never knew a father's care,' she said, 'nor till lately did I perceive the want of it.—But now.'——

'His name?' interrupted the Confessor.

'But now' continued Ellena—'if you are not as a father to me—to whom can I look for protection?'

'His name?' repeated Schedoni, with sterner emphasis.

'It is sacred,' replied Ellena, 'for he was unfortunate!'

'His name?' demanded the Confessor, furiously.

'I have promised to conceal it, father.'

'On your life, I charge you tell it; remember, on your life!'

Ellena trembled, was silent, and with supplicating looks implored him to desist from enquiry, but he urged the question more irresistibly. 'His name then,' said she, 'was Marinella.'

Schedoni groaned and turned away; but in a few seconds, struggling to command the agitation that shattered his whole frame, he returned to Ellena, and raised her from her knees, on which she had thrown herself to implore mercy.

'The place of his residence?' said the Monk.

'It was far from hence,' she replied; but he demanded an unequivocal answer, and she reluctantly gave one.

Schedoni turned away as before, groaned heavily, and paced the chamber without speaking; while Ellena, in her turn, enquired the motive of his questions, and the occasion of his agitation. But he seemed not to notice any thing she said, and, wholly given up to his feelings, was inflexibly silent, while he stalked, with measured steps, along the room, and his face, half hid by his cowl, was bent towards the ground.

Ellena's terror began to yield to astonishment, and this emotion encreased, when, Schedoni approaching her, she perceived tears swell in his eyes, which were fixt on hers, and his countenance soften from the wild disorder that had marked it. Still he could not speak. At length he yielded to the fulness of his heart, and Schedoni, the stern Schedoni, wept and sighed! He seated himself on the mattress beside Ellena, took her hand, which she affrighted attempted to withdraw, and when he could command his voice, said, 'Unhappy child!——behold your more unhappy father!' As he concluded, his voice was overcome by groans, and he drew the cowl entirely over his face.

'My father!' exclaimed the astonished and doubting Ellena—'my father!' and fixed her eyes upon him. He gave no reply, but when, a moment after, he lifted his head, 'Why do you reproach me with those looks!' said the conscious Schedoni.

'Reproach you!—reproach my father!' repeated Ellena, in accents softening into tenderness. '*Why* should I reproach my father!'

'*Why!*' exclaimed Schedoni, starting from his seat, 'Great God!'

As he moved, he stumbled over the dagger at his foot; at that moment it might be said to strike into his heart. He pushed it hastily from sight. Ellena had not observed it; but she observed his labouring breast, his distracted looks, and quick steps, as he walked to and fro in the chamber; and she asked, with the most soothing accents of compassion, and looks of anxious gentleness, what made him so unhappy, and tried to assuage his sufferings. They seemed to encrease with every wish she expressed to dispel them; at one moment he would pause to gaze upon her, and in the next would quit her with a frenzied start.

'Why do you look so piteously upon me, father?' Ellena said, 'why are you so unhappy? Tell me, that I may comfort you.'

This appeal renewed all the violence of remorse and grief, and he pressed her to his bosom, and wetted her cheek with his tears. Ellena wept to see him weep, till her doubts began to take alarm. Whatever might be the proofs, that had convinced Schedoni of the relationship between them, he had not explained these to her, and, however strong was the eloquence of nature which she witnessed, it was not sufficient to justify an entire confidence in the assertion he had made, or to allow her to permit his caresses without trembling. She shrunk, and endeavoured to disengage herself; when immediately understanding her, he said, 'Can you doubt the cause of these emotions? these signs of paternal affection?'

'Have I not reason to doubt,' replied Ellena, timidly, 'since I never witnessed them before?'

He withdrew his arms, and fixing his eyes earnestly on hers, regarded her for some moments in expressive silence. 'Poor Innocent!' said he, at length, 'you know not how much your words convey!—It is too true, you never have known a father's tenderness till now!'

His countenance darkened while he spoke, and he rose again from his seat. Ellena, meanwhile, astonished, terrified and oppressed by a variety of emotions, had no power to demand his reasons for the belief that so much agitated him, or any explanation of his conduct; but she appealed to the portrait, and endeavoured, by tracing some resemblance between it and Schedoni, to decide her doubts. The countenance of each as as different in character as in years. The miniature displayed a young man rather handsome, of a gay and smiling countenance; yet the smile expressed triumph, rather than sweetness, and his whole air and features were distinguished by a consciousness of superiority that rose even to haughtiness.

Schedoni, on the contrary, advanced in years, exhibited a severe physiognomy, furrowed by thought, no less than by time, and darkened by the habitual indulgence of morose passions. He looked as if he had never smiled since the portrait was drawn; and it seemed as if the painter, prophetic of Schedoni's future disposition, had arrested and embodied that smile, to prove hereafter that cheerfulness had once played upon his features.

Though the expression was so different between the countenance, which Schedoni formerly owned, and that he now wore, the same character of haughty pride was visible in both; and Ellena did trace a resemblance in the bold outline of the features, but not sufficient to convince her, without farther evidence, that each belonged to the same person, and that the Confessor had ever been the young cavalier in the portrait. In the first tumult of her thoughts, she had not had leisure to dwell upon the singularity of Schedoni's visiting her at this deep hour of the night, or to urge any questions, except vague ones, concerning the truth of her relationship to him. But now, that her mind was somewhat recollected, and that his looks were less terrific, she ventured to ask a fuller explanation of these circumstances, and his reasons for the late extraordinary assertion. 'It is past midnight, father,' said Ellena, 'you may judge then how anxious I am to learn, what motive led you to my chamber at this lonely hour?'

Schedoni made no reply.

'Did you come to warn me of danger?' she continued, 'had you discovered the cruel designs of Spalatro? Ah! when I supplicated for your compassion on the shore this evening, you little thought what perils surrounded me! or you would——'

'You say true!' interrupted he, in a hurried manner, 'but name the subject no more. Why will you persist in returning to it?'

His words surprized Ellena, who had not even alluded to the subject till now; but the returning wildness of his countenance, made her fearful of dwelling upon the topic, even so far as to point out his error.

Another deep pause succeeded, during which Schedoni continued to pace the room, sometimes stopping for an instant, to fix his eyes on Ellena, and regarding her with an earnestness that seemed to partake of frenzy, and then gloomily withdrawing his regards, and sighing heavily, as he turned away to a distant part of the room. She, meanwhile, agitated with astonishment at his conduct, as well as at her own circumstances, and with the fear of offending him by further questions, endeavoured to summon courage to solicit the explanation which was so important to her tranquillity. At length she asked, how she might venture to believe a circumstance so surprising, as that of which he had just assured her, and to remind him that he had not yet disclosed his reason for admitting the belief.

The Confessor's feelings were eloquent in reply; and, when at length they were sufficiently subdued, to permit him to talk coherently, he mentioned some circumstances concerning Ellena's family, that proved him at least to have been intimately acquainted with it; and others, which she believed were known only to Bianchi[5] and herself, that removed every doubt of his identity.

This, however, was a period of his life too big with remorse, horror, and the first pangs of parental affection, to allow him to converse long; deep solitude was necessary for his soul. He wished to plunge where no eye might restrain his emotions, or observe the overflowing anguish of his heart. Having obtained sufficient proof to convince him that Ellena was indeed his child, and assured her that she should be removed from this house on the following day, and be restored to her home, he abruptly left the chamber.

[5] Ellena's aunt and guardian.

As he descended the stair-case, Spalatro stepped forward to meet him, with the cloak which had been designed to wrap the mangled form of Ellena, when it should be carried to the shore. 'Is it done?' said the ruffian, in a stifled voice, 'I am ready;' and he spread forth the cloak, and began to ascend.

'Hold! villain, hold!' said Schedoni, lifting up his head for the first time, 'Dare to enter that chamber, and your life shall answer for it.'

'What!' exclaimed the man, shrinking back astonished—'will not *her's* satisfy you!'

He trembled for the consequence of what he had said, when he observed the changing countenance of the Confessor. But Schedoni spoke not; the tumult in his breast was too great for utterance, and be pressed hastily forward. Spalatro followed. 'Be pleased to tell me what I am to do,' said he, again holding forth the cloak.

'Avaunt!' exclaimed the other, turning fiercely upon him; 'leave me.'

'How!' said the man, whose spirit was now aroused, 'has *your* courage failed too, Signor? If so, I will prove myself no dastard, though you called me one; I'll do the business myself.'

'Villain! fiend!' cried Schedoni, seizing the ruffian by the throat, with a grasp that seemed intended to annihilate him; when, recollecting that the follow was only willing to obey the very instructions he had himself but lately delivered to him, other emotions succeeded to that of rage; he slowly liberated him, and in accents broken, and softening from sternness, bade him retire to rest. 'Tomorrow,' he added, 'I will speak further with you. As for this night——I have changed my purpose. Begone!'

Spalatro was about to express the indignation, which astonishment and fear had hitherto overcome, but his employer repeated his command in a voice of thunder, and closed the door of his apartment with violence, as he shut out a man, whose presence was become hateful to him. He felt relieved by his absence, and began to breathe more freely, till, remembering that his accomplice had just boasted that he was no dastard, he dreaded lest, by way of proving the assertion, he should attempt to commit the crime, from which he had lately shrunk. Terrified at the possibility, and even apprehending that it might already have become a reality, he rushed from the room, and found Spalatro in the passage leading to the private stair-case; but, whatever might have been his purpose, the situation and looks of the latter were sufficiently alarming. At the approach of Schedoni, he turned his sullen and malignant countenance towards him, without answering the call, or the demand as to his business there; and with slow steps obeyed the order of his master, that he should withdraw to his room. Thither Schedoni followed, and, having locked him in it for the night, he repaired to the apartment of Ellena, which he secured from the possibility of intrusion. He then returned to his own, not to sleep, but to abandon himself to the agonies of remorse and horror; and he yet shuddered like a man, who has just recoiled from the brink of a precipice, but who still measures the gulf with his eye.

Maria Edgeworth

1768 – 1849

Born in Oxfordshire, Maria Edgeworth was the daughter of Anna Maria Ellers and Richard Lovell Edgeworth, and she endured some unhappy periods in her childhood. In 1743 her mother died and her father married the second of his four wives and moved his family to his estate in Ireland. One of the eldest in the increasing family, Maria Edgeworth's literary leanings were influenced by parental requirements; she assumed some of the responsibility for the education of the younger children who were to be taught according to her father's enlightened educational methods – which were set out in their joint publication, Practical Education, in 1798. Maria Edgeworth also wrote many of her own teaching materials; the author of some of the first and best 'reading schemes', her educational stories served as models for future generations.

In 1795 she published Letters for Literary Ladies and revealed her commitment to feminist themes; in 1800 Castle Rackrent established her reputation as the originator of the regional novel; it was followed by Belinda in 1801. A prolific author, Maria Edgeworth ranges in her works from educational tracts to explorations in fiction of the human psyche; consciously a woman writer, she claimed dignity and equality for members of her own sex and portrayed men who were concerned with rearing children, and women who were interested in politics. Among her many novels are Popular Tales (1804), The Modern Griselda (1805), Leonora (1806), Tales of Fashionable Life (1809, 1812), Patronage (1814), Ormond (1817) and Helen (1834).

The following extract is reprinted from Letters for Literary Ladies (Joseph Johnson, London, 1795).

From

Letters for Literary Ladies

LETTER FROM A GENTLEMAN TO HIS FRIEND
UPON THE BIRTH OF A DAUGHTER

I CONGRATULATE you, my dear Sir, upon the birth of your daughter; and I wish that some of the Fairies of ancient times were at hand to endow the damsel with health, wealth, wit, and beauty—Wit?——I should make a long pause before I accepted of this gift for a daughter—you would make none.

As I know it to be your opinion, that it is in the power of education, more certainly than it was ever believed to be in the power of Fairies, to bestow all mental gifts; and as I have heard you say that education should begin as early as possible, I am in haste to offer you my sentiments, lest my advice should come too late.

Your general ideas of the habits and virtues essential to the perfection of the female character nearly agree with mine; but we differ materially as to the cultivation, which it is necessary or expedient to bestow upon the understandings of women: you are a champion for the rights of woman, and insist upon the equality of the sexes. But since the days of chivalry are past, and since modern gallantry permits men to speak, at least to one another, in less sublime language of the fair, I may confess to you that I see neither in experience or analogy much reason to believe that, in the human species alone, there are no marks of inferiority in the female;—curious and admirable exceptions there may be, but many such have not fallen within my observation. I cannot say that I have been much enraptured either on a first view or on a closer inspection with female prodigies. Prodigies are scarcely less offensive to my taste than monsters; humanity makes us refrain from expressing disgust at the awkward shame of the one, whilst the intemperate vanity of the other justly provokes ridicule and indignation. I have always observed in the understandings of women who have been too much cultivated, some disproportion between the different faculties of their minds. One power of the mind undoubtedly may be cultivated at the expence of the rest, as we see that one muscle or limb may acquire excessive strength and an unnatural size at the expence of the health of the whole body: I cannot think this desirable either for the individual or for society.—The unfortunate people in certain mountains in Switzerland are, some of them, proud of the excrescence by which they are deformed.[1] I have seen women vain of exhibiting mental deformities, which to me appeared no less disgusting. In the course of my life it has never been my good fortune to meet with a female whose mind, in strength, just proportion, and activity, I could compare to that of a sensible man.—

Allowing, however, that women are equal to our sex in natural abilities, from their situation in society, from their domestic duties, their taste for dissipation, their love of romance, poetry, and all the lighter parts of literature, their time must be so fully occupied, that they could never have leisure, even supposing that they had inclination, for that severe application to which our sex submit.—Between persons of equal genius, and equal industry, time becomes the only measure of their acquirements——Now calculate the time, which is wasted by the fair sex, and tell me how much the start of us they ought to have in the beginning of the race, if they are to reach the goal before us?—It is not possible that women should ever be our equals in knowledge, unless you assert that they are far our superiors in natural capacity.——Not only time but opportunity must be wanting to complete female studies—we mix with the

[1] The Swiss in the Alps of Savoy frequently had goitres because of a lack of iodine in the water, essential for the thyroid gland.

world without restraint, we converse freely with all classes of people, with men of wit, of science, of learning, with the artist, the mechanic, the labourer; every scene of life is open to our view;—every assistance, that foreign or domestic ingenuity can invent, to encourage literary studies, is ours almost exclusively. From academies, colleges, public libraries, private associations of literary men, women are excluded, if not by law, at least by custom, which cannot easily be conquered.——Whenever women appear, even when we seem to admit them as our equals in understanding, every thing assumes a different form; our politeness, delicacy, habits towards the sex forbid us to argue, or to converse with them as we do with one another—we see things as they are, but women must always see things through a veil, or cease to be women.—With these insuperable difficulties in their education and in their passage through life, it seems impossible that their minds should ever acquire that vigour and *efficiency*, which accurate knowledge and various experience of life and manners can bestow.

Much attention has lately been paid to the education of the female sex, and you will say, that we have been amply repaid for our care—That ladies have lately exhibited such brilliant proofs of genius as must dazzle and confound their critics. I do not ask for proofs of genius,—I ask for solid proofs of utility. In which of the useful arts, in which of the exact sciences have we been assisted by female sagacity or penetration?—I should be glad to see a list of discoveries, of inventions, of observations, evincing patient research, of truths established upon actual experiment, or deduced by just reasoning from previous principles—If these or any of these can be presented by a female champion for her sex, I shall be the first to clear the way for her to the Temple of Fame.

I must not speak of my contemporaries, else candor might oblige me to allow, that there are some few instances of great talents applied to useful purposes—But, except these, what have been the literary productions of women?—In poetry, plays and romances, in the art of imposing upon the understanding by means of the imagination, they have excelled—but to useful literature they have scarcely turned their thoughts—I have never heard of any female proficients in science—few have pretended to science till within these few years.—I know of none of their inventions, and few of their discoveries.

You will tell me, that in the most difficult and most extensive science of politics women have succeeded—you will cite the names of some illustrious queens—I am inclined to think, with the Duke of Burgundy, that "queens who reigned well were governed by men, and kings who reigned ill were governed by women."

The isolated examples of a few heroines cannot convince me that it is safe or expedient to trust the sex with power—their power over themselves has regularly been found to diminish, in proportion as their power over others has been encreased.—I should not refer you to the scandalous chronicles of modern times, to volumes of private anecdotes, or to the abominable secret histories of courts, where female influences, and female depravity are synonymous terms, but I appeal to the open equitable page of history, to a body of evidence collected from the testimony of ages, for experiments tried upon the grandest scale of which nature admits, registered by various hands without the possibility of collusion and without a view to any particular system—from these you must be convinced, that similar consequences have uniformly resulted from the same causes in nations the most unlike, and at periods the most distant. Follow the history of female nature from the court of Augustus,[2] to the court of Lewis the Fourteenth,[3] and tell me whether you can hesitate to acknowledge, that the influence, the liberty, and the *power* of women have been constant concomitants of the moral and political decline of empires—I say the concomitants: where events are thus invariably connected I might be justified in saying, that they were *causes*—you would call them *effects*, but we need not dispute about the momentary precedence of evils, which are found to be inseparable companions—they may be alternately cause and effect,—the reality of the connexion is established, it may be difficult to ascertain precisely its nature.

You will assert, that the fatal consequences which have resulted from our trusting the sex with liberty and power, have been originally occasioned by the subjection and ignorance in which they had previously been held, and of our subsequent folly and imprudence in *throwing the reins of dominion into hands unprepared and uneducated to guide them.* I am at a loss to conceive any system of education that can properly prepare women for the exercise of power:—Cultivate their understandings, "cleanse the visual orb with Euphrasy and Rue,"[4] till they can with one comprehensive glance take in "one half at least of round eternity," still you have no security that their reason shall govern their conduct. The moral character seems, even amongst men of superior strength of mind, to have no certain dependence upon the reasoning faculty;—habit, prejudice, taste, example, and the different strength of various passions, form the moral character. We are impelled to action frequently contrary to the belief of our sober reason, and we pursue what we could, in the hour of deliberation, demonstrate to be inconsistent with *that greatest possible share of happiness*, which it is the object of every rational creature to secure. We frequently "think with one species of enthusiasm, and act with another:" and can we expect from women more consistency of conduct, if they are allowed the same liberty. No one can feel more strongly than you do the necessity and the value of female integrity; no one can more clearly perceive how much in society depends upon the honour of women, and how much it is the interest of every individual, as well as of every state, to guard their virtue, and to preserve inviolate the purity of their manners. Allow me, then, to warn you of the danger of talking in loud strains to the sex of the noble contempt of prejudice. You would look with horrour at one who should go to sap the foundations of the building; beware then how you venture to tear away the ivy which clings to the walls, and braces the loose stones together.

[2] First Roman Emperor, reigned 27BC–14AD.
[3] Louis XIV reigned 1643–1715, France's 'Sun King'.
[4] Milton's *Paradise Lost*, Book XI, line 414, '...Then purg'd with euphrasy and rue/The visual nerve, for he had much to see.'

I am by no means disposed to indulge in the fashionable ridicule of prejudice. There is a sentimental, metaphysical argument, which, independently of all others, has lately been used to prevail upon us to relinquish that superiority which strength of body in savage, and strength of mind in civilized, nations secures to man. We are told, that as women are reasonable creatures, they should be governed only by reason; and that we *disgrace* ourselves, and *enslave* them when we instil even the most useful truths as prejudices.—Morality should, we are told, be founded upon demonstration, not upon sentiment; and we should not require human beings to submit to any laws or customs, without convincing their understandings of the universal utility of these political conventions. When are we to expect this conviction? We cannot expect it from childhood, scarcely from youth; but, from the maturity of the understanding, we are told that we may expect it with certainty.—And of what use can it then be to us? When the habits are fixed, when the character is decided, when the manners are formed, what can be done by the bare conviction of the understanding? What could we expect from that woman whose moral education was to begin at the moment when she was called upon to *act*; and who without having imbibed in her early years any of the salutary prejudices of her sex, or without having been educated in the amiable acquiescence to well-established maxims of female prudence, should boldly venture to conduct herself by the immediate conviction of her understanding? I care not for the names or titles of my guides; all that I shall enquire is, which is best acquainted with the road. Provided women be conducted quietly to their good, it is scarcely worth their while to dispute about the pompous, metaphysical names or precedency of their motives. Why should they deem it disgraceful to be induced to pursue their interest by what some philosophers are pleased to call *weak* motives? Is it not much less disgraceful to be peaceably governed by weak reasons, than to be incapable of being restrained by the strongest? The dignity of human nature, and the boasted free-will of rational agents, are high-sounding words, likely to impose upon the vanity of the fair sex, as well as upon the pride of our's; but if we analyse the ideas annexed to these terms, to what shall we reduce them? Reason in its highest perfection seems just to arrive at the certainty of instinct; and truth, impressed upon the mind in early youth by the united voice of affection and authority, gives all the real advantages of the most investigating spirit of philosophy. If the result of the thought, experience, and sufferings of one race of beings is (when inculcated upon the belief of the next) to be stigmatised as prejudice, there is an end to all the benefits of history and of education. The mutual intercourse of individuals and of nations must be only for the traffic or amusement of the day. Every age must repeat the same experiments; every man and every nation must make the same mistakes, and suffer the same miseries, whilst the civilization and happiness of the world, if not retrograde in their course, must for ever be stationary.

Let us not, then, despise or teach the other sex to despise the traditional maxims of experience, or those early prepossessions, which may be termed prejudices, but which in reality serve as their moral instinct. I can see neither tyranny on our part, nor slavery on theirs, in this system of education. This sentimental or metaphysical appeal to our candour and generosity has then no

real force, and every other argument for the *literary* and *philosophical* education
of women, and for the extraordinary cultivation of their understandings, I
have examined.

You probably imagine, that, by the superior ingenuity and care you propose
to bestow on your daughter's education, you shall make her an exception to
general maxims, you shall give her all the blessings of a literary cultivation, and
at the same time preserve her from all the follies and faults, and evils which
have been found to attend the character of a literary lady.

Systems produce projects; and as projects in education are of all others the most
hazardous, they should not be followed till after the most mature deliberation:
though it may be natural, is it wise for any man to expect extraordinary success,
from his efforts or his precautions, beyond what has ever been the share of those
who have had motives as strong for care and for exertion, and some of whom
were possibly his equals in ability? Is it not incumbent upon you, as a parent and
as a philosopher, to calculate accurately what you have to fear, as well as what
you have to hope. You can at present, with a sober degree of interest, bear to
hear me enumerate the evils, and ridicule the foibles, incident to literary ladies;
but if your daughter were actually in this class, you would not think it friendly
if I were to attack them. In this favourable moment, then, I beg you to hear
me with temper; and as I touch upon every danger and every fault, consider
cautiously whether you have a specific remedy or a certain preventative in store
for each of them.

Women of literature are much more numerous of late than they were a few
years ago. They make a class in society, they fill the public eye, and have acquired
a degree of consequence and an appropriate character. The esteem of private
friends, and the admiration of the public for their talents, are circumstances
highly flattering to their vanity, and as such I will allow them to be substantial
pleasures. I am also ready to acknowledge that a taste for literature adds much
to the happiness of life, and women may enjoy to a certain degree this happiness
as well as men. But with literary women this silent happiness seems at best but a
subordinate consideration; it is not by the treasures they possess, but by those
which they have an opportunity of displaying, that they estimate their wealth. To
obtain public applause, they are betrayed too often into a miserable ostentation
of their learning.

Coxe[5] tells us, that certain Russian ladies split their pearls, in order to
make a greater display of finery. The pleasure of being admired for wit or
erudition, I cannot exactly measure in a female mind, but state it to be as great
as you reasonably can suppose it, there are evils attendant upon it, which, in
the estimation of a prudent father, may overbalance the good. The intoxicating
effect of wit upon the brain, has been well remarked by a poet, who was
a friend to the fair sex, and too many ridiculous, and too many disgusting,
examples confirm the truth of the observation. The deference that is paid to
genius sometimes makes the fair sex forget, that genius will be respected only

[5] William Coxe (1747–1828), travel writer. The reference is to his *Travels into Poland,
Russia, Sweden and Denmark* (1784).

when united with discretion. Those who have acquired fame, fancy that they can afford to sacrifice reputation. I will suppose, however, that their heads shall be strong enough to bear inebriating admiration; and that their conduct shall be essentially irreproachable, yet they will shew in their manners and conversation that contempt of inferior minds, and that neglect of common forms and customs, which will provoke the indignation of fools, and which cannot escape the censure of the wise. Even whilst we are secure of their innocence, we dislike that daring spirit in the female sex, which delights to oppose the common opinions of society, and from apparent trifles we draw unfavourable omens, which experience too often confirms. You will ask me why I should suppose that wits are more liable to be spoiled by admiration than beauties, who have usually a larger share of it, and who are not more exempt from vanity? Those who are vain of trifling accomplishments, of rank, of riches, or of beauty, depend upon the world for their immediate gratification. They are sensible of their dependence; they listen with deference to the maxims, and attend with anxiety to the opinions of those from whom they expect their reward and their daily amusements. In their subjection consists their safety, whilst women, who neither feel dependent for amusement or for self-approbation upon company and public places, are apt to consider this subjection as humiliating, if not insupportable: perceiving their own superiority, they despise, and even set at defiance, the opinions of their acquaintance of inferior abilities: contempt, where it cannot be openly retorted, produces aversion, not the less to be dreaded, because constrained to silence: envy, considered as the involuntary tribute, extorted by merit, is flattering to pride; and I know, that many women delight to excite envy, even whilst they affect to fear its consequences. But they who imprudently provoke it, are little aware of the torments they prepare for themselves—"cover your face well before you disturb the hornet's nest", was a maxim of the *experienced* Catharine de Medicis.[6]

Men of literature, if we may trust to the bitter expressions of anguish in their writings, and in their private letters, feel acutely all the stings of envy. Women, who have more susceptibility of temper, and less strength of mind, and who, from the delicate nature of their reputation, are more exposed to attack, are also less able to endure it. Malignant critics, when they cannot attack an author's peace in his writings, frequently scrutinize his private life; and every personal anecdote is published without regard to truth or propriety. How will the delicacy of the female character endure this treatment? how will her friends bear to see her pursued even in domestic retirement, if she should be wise enough to make that retirement her choice? how will they like to see premature memoirs and spurious collections of familiar letters published by needy booksellers or designing enemies? Yet to all these things men of letters are subject; and such must literary ladies expect, if they attain to any degree of eminence.—Judging, then, from the experience of our sex, I may pronounce envy to be one of the evils which women of uncommon genius have to dread.

[6] Catharine de Medicis (1519–89), queen of Henry II of France; she exercised considerable political influence during the reign of her sons Francis II, Charles IX and Henry III.

"Censure", says a celebrated writer, "is a tax which every man must pay to the public who seeks to be eminent." Women must expect to pay it doubly.

Your daughter, perhaps, shall be above scandal. She shall despise the idle whisper, and the common tattle of her sex; her soul shall be raised above the ignorant and the frivolous; she shall have a relish for higher conversation, and a taste for higher society. But where is she to find this society? how is she to obtain this society? You make her incapable of friendship with her own sex. Where is she to look for friends, for companions, for equals? Amongst men? Amongst what class of men? Not amongst men of business, or men of gallantry, but amongst men of literature?

I think it is Stuart,[7] who, in speaking of Rousseau,[8] observes that learned men have usually chosen for their wives, or for their companions, women who were rather below than above the standard of mediocrity: this seems to me natural and reasonable. Such men, probably, feel their own incapacity for the daily business of life, their ignorance of the world, their slovenly habits, and neglect of domestic affairs. They do not want wives who have precisely their own defects; they rather desire to find such as shall, by the opposite habits and virtues, supply their deficiencies. I do not see why two books should marry, any more than two estates. Some few exceptions might be quoted against Stuart's observations. I have just seen, under the article "A Literary Wife", in D'Israeli's[9] Curiosities of Literature, an account of Francis Phidelphus, a great scholar in the fifteenth century, who was so desirous of acquiring the Greek language in perfection, that he travelled to Constantinople in search of a *Grecian wife*: the lady proved a scold. "But to do justice to the name of Theodora", as this author adds, "she has been honourably mentioned in the French Academy of Sciences." I hope this proved an adequate compensation to her husband for his domestic broils.

Happy Madame Dacier![10] you found a husband suited to your taste! "You and Monsieur Dacier, if D'Alembert[11] tells the story rightly, once cooked a dish in concert, by a receipt, which you found in Apicius, and you both sat down and eat of your learned ragout till you were both like to die."

Were I sure, my dear friend, that every literary lady would be equally fortunate in finding in a husband a man who would sympathise in her tastes, I should diminish my formidable catalogue of evils. But alas! Monsieur Dacier is no more! "and we shall never live to see his fellow." Literary ladies will, I am afraid, be losers in love as well as in friendship, by their superiority.—Cupid[12] is a timid, playful child, and is frightened at the helmet of Minerva.[13] It has been

---

7 Daniel Stuart (1766–1846), Scottish journalist and political radical.
8 Jean-Jacques Rousseau (1712–78), extremely influential political philosopher and educationist. He had a lifelong liaison with Thérèse Levasseur, an uneducated servant.
9 D'Israeli (1766–1848), author of *Curiosities of Literature*, 1791.
10 Anne Dacier (c.1654–1720) was a learned lady and translator, married to a similarly learned man, André Dacier (1651–1722).
11 Jean Le Rond d'Alembert (1717–83), French mathematician and encyclopaedist.
12 Roman god of love.
13 Roman warrior goddess of wisdom.

observed, that gentlemen are not apt to admire a prodigious quantity of learning, and masculine acquirements in the fair sex—our sex usually consider a certain degree of weakness, both of mind and body, as friendly to female grace. I am not absolutely of this opinion, yet I do not see the advantage of supernatural force, either of body or mind, to female excellence. Hercules-Spinster[14] found his strength rather an incumbrance than an advantage.

Superiority of mind must be united with great temper and generosity to be tolerated by those who are forced to submit to its influence. I have seen witty and learned ladies, who did not seem to think it at all incumbent upon them to sacrifice any thing to the sense of propriety. On the contrary, they seemed to take both pride and pleasure in shewing the utmost stretch of their strength, regardless of the consequences, panting only for victory. Upon such occasions, when the adversary has been a husband or a father, I must acknowledge that I have felt sensations, which few ladies can ever believe they excite. Airs and graces I can bear as well as another—but airs without graces, no man thinks himself bound to bear—and learned airs least of all. Ladies of high rank, in the Court of Parnassus,[15] are apt, sometimes, to claim precedency out of their own dominions, which creates much confusion, and generally ends in their being affronted. That knowledge of the world, which keeps people in their proper places, they will never learn from the Muses.

As Moliere[16] has pointed out with all the force of comic ridicule, in the Femmes Savantes, a lady who aspires to the sublime delights of philosophy and poetry, must forego the simple pleasures, and will despite the duties of domestic life. I should not expect that my house affairs would be with haste dispatched by a Desdemona,[17] weeping over some unvarnished tale, petrified with some history of horrors, deep in a new theory of the earth, or seriously inclined to hear of "Antres vast, and desarts idle"—"and men whose heads do grow beneath their shoulders"—at the very time when she should be ordering dinner, or paying the butcher's bill—I should have the less hope of rousing her attention to my culinary concerns and domestic grievances, because I should probably incur her contempt for hinting at these sublunary matters, and her indignation for supposing that she ought to be employed in such degrading occupations. I have heard that if these sublime geniuses are wakened from their reveries by the *appulse*[18] of external circumstances, they start and exhibit all the perturbation and amazement of *cataleptic* patients.

Sir Charles Harrington, in the days of Queen Elizabeth, addressed a copy of verses to his wife, "on Women's Virtues"—these he divides into "the private,

---

[14] According to legend, Hercules became besotted with the nymph Omphale, who made him spin her wool. The name 'Omphale' is related to the Greek for 'navel' and would seem to refer to the Great Goddess. The story appears a warning against matriarchy.

[15] Greek mountain, supposed to be the seat of the Muses.

[16] Pen-name of Jean-Baptiste Poquelin (1622–73), French dramatist. His *Femmes Savantes* (= learned women) mocks the pretensions of women to learning.

[17] Tragic heroine of Shakespeare's *Othello*; her courtship included the telling of traveller's tales.

[18] Literally a driving against; here intrusion.

civill, and heroyke; the private belong to the country housewife, whom it
concerneth chiefly—

> The fruit, malt, hops, to tend, to dry, to utter,
>   To beat, strip, spin the wool, the hemp, the flax,
>   Breed poultry, gather honey, try the wax,
> And more than all, to have good cheese and
>   butter.
> Then next a step, but yet a large step higher,
>   Came civill virtue fitter for the citty,
>   With modest looks, good cloths, and answers
>   witty;
> These baser things not done, but guided by her."

As for heroyke vertue, and heroyke dames, honest Sir Charles would have
nothing to do with them.

Allowing, however, that you could combine all these virtues—that you could
form a perfect whole, a female wonder from every creature's best, dangers still
threaten you. How will you preserve your daughter from that desire of universal
admiration, which will ruin all your work? How will you, along with all the pride
of knowledge, give her that "retiring modesty" which is supposed to have more
charms for our sex than the fullest display of wit and beauty.

The *fair Thoulouse* was so called, because she was so fair that no one could
live either with or without beholding her—whenever she came forth from her
own mansion, which history observes she did very seldom, such impetuous
crowds rushed to obtain a sight of her, that limbs were broken and lives
were lost wherever she appeared. She ventured abroad less frequently—the evil
encreased—till at length the magistrates of the city issued an edict commanding
the fair Thoulouse, under the pain of perpetual imprisonment to appear in broad
day-light for one hour, every week, in the public market-place.

Modern ladies, by frequenting public places so regularly, declare their approbation of the wholesome regulations of these prudent magistrates. Very different
was the crafty policy of the Prophet Mahomet, who forbad his worshippers even
to paint his picture. The Turks have pictures of the hand, the foot, the features,
of Mahomet, but no representation of the whole face or person is allowed.
The portraits of our beauties, in our exhibition-room, shew a proper contempt
of this insidious policy; and those learned and ingenious ladies, who publish
their private letters, select maxims, secret anecdotes, and family memoirs, are
entitled to our thanks for thus presenting us with full lengths of their minds.

Can you expect, my dear Sir, that your daughter, with all the genius and learning
which you intend to give her, should refrain from these imprudent exhibitions?
Will she "yield her charms of mind with sweet delay?" Will she, in every moment
of her life, recollect that the fatal desire for universal admiration always defeats its
own purpose, especially if the purpose be to win love as well as admiration? It is
in vain to tell me that more enlarged ideas in our sex would alter our tastes, and
alter even the associations which now influence our passions. The captive who

has numbered the links of his chains, and who has even discovered how those chains are constructed, is not therefore nearer to the recovery of his liberty.

Besides, it must take a length of time to alter associations and opinions, which, if not *just*, are at least *common* in our sex. You cannot expect even that conviction should operate immediately upon the public taste. You will, in a few years, have educated your daughter; and if the world be not educated exactly at the right time to judge of her perfections, to admire and love them, you will have wasted your labour, and you will have sacrificed your daughter's happiness: that happiness, analyse it as a man of the world or as a philosopher, must depend on friendship, love, the exercise of her virtues, the just performance of all the duties of life, and the self-approbation arising from the consciousness of good conduct..

I am, my dear friend,
Yours sincerely.

ANSWER TO THE PRECEDING LETTER

I F I were not naturally of a sanguine temper, your letter, my dear friend, would fill my mind with so many melancholy fears for the fate of literary women, that I should be tempted to educate my daughter in the secure "bliss of ignorance."

I am sensible that we have no right to try new experiments and fanciful theories at the expence of our fellow-creatures, especially on those who are helpless, and immediately under our protection. Who can estimate the anguish which a parent must feel from the ruin of his child, when joined to the idea that it may have been caused by imprudent education: but reason should never be blinded by sentiment, when it is her proper office to guide and enlighten. There is scarcely any family, I hope, which does not feel within itself the happy effects of the improvements in modern education; but we could never have felt these advantages, if we had resisted all attempts at alteration.

Do not, my dear Sir, call me "*a champion for the rights of women*"; I am more intent upon their happiness than ambitious to enter into a metaphysical discussion of their rights. Their happiness is so nearly connected with ours, that it seems to me absurd to manage any argument so as to set the two sexes at variance by vain contention for superiority. It is not our object to make an invidious division of rights and privileges, but to determine what is most for our general advantage.

I shall not, therefore, examine with much anxiety how far women are naturally inferior to us either in strength of mind or body. The strength of the one has no necessary connection with the other, I may observe; and intellectual ability has ever conquered mere bodily strength, from the times of Ajax and Ulysses to the present day. In civilized society, that species of superiority which belongs to superior force, is reduced to little in the lowest classes, to less in the higher classes of life.

The invention of fire-arms renders address and presence of mind more than a match for force, or at least reduces to an affair of chance the pretensions of the feeble and the strong. The art of printing has extended the dominion of the mind, as much by facilitating the intercourse and combination of persons of literature, as by the rapid and universal circulation of knowledge. Both these inventions have tended to alter the relative situation of women in modern society.

I acknowledge that, with respect to the opportunities of acquiring knowledge, institution and manners are much in favour of our sex; but your argument concerning *time* appears to me to be inaccurate. Whilst the knowledge of the learned languages continues to form an indispensable part of a gentleman's education, many years of childhood and youth must be devoted to their attainment. During these studies, the general cultivation of the understanding is in some degree retarded. All the intellectual powers are cramped, except the memory, which is sufficiently exercised, but which is overloaded with words, and with words which are seldom understood. The genius of living and of dead languages differs so much, that the pains which are taken to write elegant Latin, frequently spoil the English style. Girls usually write much better than boys: they think and express their thoughts clearly at an age when young men can scarcely write an easy letter upon any common occasion. Women do not read the best authors of antiquity as school books; but they can have excellent translations of most of them, when they are capable of tasting their beauties. I know that it is supposed no one can judge of the classics by translations; and I am sensible that much of the merit of the originals may be lost; but I think the difference in pleasure is more than overbalanced to women, by the *time* they save, and by the labour and misapplication of abilities which is spared. If they do not acquire a classic taste, neither do they acquire classic prejudices: nor are they early disgusted with literature, by pedagogues, lexicons, grammars, and all the melancholy apparatus of learning. Field-sports, travelling, gaming, lounging, and what is called pleasure in various shapes, usually fill the interval between quitting the college and settling for life: this period is not lost by the other sex. Women begin to taste the real pleasures of reading just at the age when young men, disgusted with their studies, begin to be ashamed amongst their companions of alluding to literature. When this period is past, business, the necessity of pursuing a profession, the ambition of shining in parliament, or of rising in public life, occupy a large portion of their lives. The understanding is but partially cultivated for these purposes; men of genius must contract their enquiries, and concentrate their powers; they must pursue *the expedient*, even when they distinguish that it is not *the right*, and they are degraded to "*literary artisans*".[19] The other sex have no such constraint upon their understandings; neither the necessity of earning their bread, nor the ambition to shine in public life, hurry or prejudice their minds; in domestic life, "they have leisure to be wise." Women, who do not love dissipation, must have more time for the cultivation of their understandings, than men can have if you compute the whole of life.

You apprehend that knowledge must be hurtful to the sex, because it will be the means of their acquiring power. It seems to me impossible that

[19] Quoted from Stuart (Edgeworth).

women can acquire the species of direct power which you dread: the manners of society must totally change before women can mingle with men in the busy and public scenes of life. They must become Amazons before they can effect this change; they must cease to be women before they can desire it. The happiness of neither sex could be increased by this metamorphosis: the object cannot be worth the price. Power, supposing it to be a certain good to its possessor, is like all our other pleasures, capable of being appreciated; and if women are taught to estimate their pleasures, they will be governed in their choice by the real, not by the imaginary, value. They will be convinced, not by the voice of the moralist alone, but by their own observation and experience, that power is an evil in most cases; and to those who really wish to do good to their fellow-creatures, it is at best but a painful trust. If, my dear Sir, it be your object to monopolize power for our sex, you cannot possibly better secure it from the wishes of the other, than by enlightening their minds, and enlarging their view of human affairs. The common fault of ignorant and ill-educated women is a love for dominion: this they shew in every petty struggle where they are permitted to act in private life. You are afraid that the same disposition should have a larger field for its display; and you believe this temper to be inherent in the sex. I doubt whether any temper be *natural*, as it is called: certainly this disposition need not be attributed to any innate cause; it is the consequence of their erroneous education. The belief that pleasure is necessarily connected with the mere exercise of free-will, is a false and pernicious association of ideas, arising from the tyranny of those who have had the management of their childhood, from their having frequently discovered that they have been more happy in chusing about trifles, when they have acted in opposition to the maxims of those who govern them, than when they have followed their advice. I shall endeavour to prevent this from happening in my daughter's early education, and shall thus, I hope, prevent her acquiring any unconquerable prejudice in favour of her own wishes, or any unreasonable desire to influence the opinions of others. People, who have reasons for their preferences and aversions, are never so zealous in the support of their own tastes, as those are who have no arguments either to convince themselves or others that they are in the right. *Power* over the minds of others will not, therefore, in domestic, any more than in public life, be an object of ambition to women of enlarged understandings.

You appeal to history to prove to me that great calamities have ensued whenever the female sex has been indulged with liberty, yet you acknowledge that we cannot be certain whether these evils have been the effects of our trusting them with liberty, or of our not having previously instructed them in the use of it: upon the decision of this rests your whole argument. Women have not erred from having knowledge, but from not having had experience: they may have grown vain and presumptuous when they have learned but little, they will be sobered into good sense when they shall have learned more.

But you fear that knowledge should injure the delicacy of female manners, that truth would not keep so firm a hold upon the mind as prejudice, and that the conviction of the understanding will never have a permanent, good effect upon the conduct. I agree with you in thinking, that the strength of mind, which makes people govern themselves by reason, is not always connected with abilities in their most cultivated state. I deplore the instances I have seen of this truth; but I do not despair: I am, on the contrary, excited to examine into the causes of this phænomenon in the human mind: nor, because I see some evil, would I sacrifice the good on a motive of bare suspicion. It is a contradiction to say, that to give the power of discerning what is good, is to give a disposition to prefer what is bad. All that you prove when you say that prejudice, passion, habit, often impel us to act in opposition to our reason, is, that there exist enemies to reason, which have not yet been subdued. Would you destroy her power because she has not been always victorious? rather think on the means by which you may extend her dominion, and secure to her in future the permanent advantages of victory.

Women, whose talents have been much cultivated, have usually had their attention distracted by subordinate pursuits, and they have not been taught that the grand object of life is to be happy; to be prudent and virtuous that they may be happy: their ambition has been directed to the acquisition of knowledge and learning, merely as other women have been excited to acquire accomplishments, for the purposes of ostentation, not with a view to the real advantage of the acquisition. But, from the abuse, you are not to argue against the use of knowledge. Place objects in a just view before the understanding, shew their different proportions, and the mind will make a wise choice. "You think yourself happy because you are wise", said a philosopher; "I think myself wise because I am happy."

No woman can be happy in society who does not preserve the peculiar virtues of her sex. When this is demonstrated to the understanding, must not those virtues, and the means of preserving them, become objects of the first and most interesting importance to a sensible woman? I would not rest her security entirely upon this conviction, when I can increase it by all the previous habits of early education: these things are not, as you seem to think, incompatible. Whilst a child has not the use of reason, I would guide it by my reason, and give it such habits as my experience convinces me will tend to its happiness. As the child's understanding is enlarged, I can explain the meaning of my conduct, and habit will then be confirmed by reason: I lose no time, I expose myself to no danger by this system. On the contrary, those who depend merely on the force of habit and of prejudice alone, expose themselves to perpetual danger. If once their pupils begin to reflect upon their own hood-winked education, if once their faith is shaken in the dogmas which have been imposed upon them, they will probably believe that they have been deceived in every thing which they have been taught, and they will burst their former bonds with indignation: credulity is always rash in the moment of detection.

You dislike in the female sex that daring spirit which despises the common forms of society, and which breaks through the delicacy and reserve of female manners. So do I. And the best method to make my pupil respect these things, is to shew her how they are indispensably connected with the largest interests of society, and with their highest pleasures. Surely this perception, this view of the utility of forms, apparently trifling, must be a strong security to the sex, and far superior to the automatic habits of those who submit to the conventions of the world, without consideration or conviction. Habit, improved by reason, assumes the rank of virtue. The motives which restrain from vice must be encreased, by the clear conviction that vice and wretchedness are inseparably united.

It is too true that women, who have been but half instructed, who have seen only superficially the relations of moral and political ideas, and who have obtained but an imperfect knowledge of the human heart, have conducted themselves so as to disgrace their talents and their sex: these are conspicuous and melancholy examples, cited oftener with malice than with pity. The benevolent and the wise point out the errors of genius with more care than those of folly, because there is more danger from the example.

I appeal to examples, which every man of literature will immediately recollect amongst our contemporaries, to prove, that where the female understanding has been properly cultivated, women have not only obtained admiration by their useful abilities, but respect by their exemplary conduct.

You very prudently avoid alluding to your contemporaries, but you must excuse me if I cannot omit instances essential to my cause. Modern education has been improved; the fruits of these improvements appear, and you must not forbid me to point them out.

Instead of being ashamed that so little has been hitherto done by female abilities, in science and in useful literature, I am surprised that so much has been effected. Till of late, women were kept in Turkish ignorance; every means of acquiring knowledge was discountenanced by fashion, and impracticable even to those who despised fashion. Our books of science were full of unintelligible jargon, and mystery veiled pompous ignorance from public contempt; but now, writers must offer their discoveries to the public in distinct terms, which every body may understand; technical language will no longer supply the place of knowledge, and the art of teaching has been carried to great perfection by the demand for learning: all this is in favour of women. Many things, which were thought to be above their comprehension, or unsuited to their sex, have now been found to be perfectly within the compass of their abilities, and peculiarly suited to their situation. Botany has become *fashionable*; in time it may become useful, if it be not so already. Science has *"been enlisted under the banners of imagination"*, by the irresistible charms of genius; by the same power her votaries will be led *from the looser analogies which dress out the imagery of poetry, to the stricter ones which form the ratiocination of philosophy.*[20]

Chemistry will follow botany; chemistry is a science particularly suited to women, suited to their talents and to their situation. Chemistry is not a science of parade, it affords occupation and infinite variety; it demands no bodily strength, it can be pursued in retirement, it applies immediately to useful and domestic purposes; and whilst the ingenuity of the most inventive mind may be exercised, there is no danger of inflaming the imagination; the judgment is improved, the mind is intent upon realities, the knowledge that is acquired is exact, and the pleasure of the pursuit is a sufficient reward for the labour.

[20] Preface to Dr Darwin's *Botanic Garden*. Erasmus Darwin (1731–1802), scientist, philosopher and grandfather of Charles.

Dr Johnson[21] says, that "nothing is ever well done that is done by a receipt."[22] Were I attempting to recommend chemistry to certain *Epicurean philosophers*, I should say that a good cook was only an empirical chemist, and that the study of this science would produce a salutary reform in receipt books, and must improve the accomplishments of every lady who unites in her person the offices of housekeeper and wife.

Sir Anthony Absolute,[23] the inveterate foe to literary ladies, declares, that "were he to chuse another helpmate, the extent of her erudition should consist in her knowing her simple letters without their mischievous combinations; and the summit of her science be—her ability to count as far as twenty: the first would enable her to work A.A. upon his linen, and the latter would be quite sufficient to prevent her giving him a shirt No.1. and a stock No.2."

Sir Anthony's helpmate would, by the proper application of chemistry, mark A.A. upon his linen, with an ease and expedition unknown to the persevering practitioners of cross-stitch; and the oeconomy of his wardrobe and of his house would be benefitted by the science of arithmetic and the taste for order. Economy is not the mean, "penny-wise and pound-foolish policy" which some suppose it to be; it is the art of calculation, joined to the habit of order, and the power of proportioning our wishes to the means of gratifying them. "The little pilfering temper of a wife"[24] is despicable and odious to every husband of sense and taste. But, far from despising domestic duties, women, who have been well educated, will hold them in high respect, because they will see that the whole happiness of life is made up of the happiness of each particular day and hour, and that the enjoyment of these must depend upon the punctual practice of those virtues which are more valuable than splendid. Taste, ingenuity, judgment, are all applicable to the arts of domestic life; and domestic life will be most preferred by those who have within their own minds a perpetual flow of fresh ideas, who cannot be tempted to dissipation, and who are most capable of enjoying all the real pleasures of friendship and of love.

Since I began this letter, I met with the following pathetic passage, which I cannot forbear transcribing:—

"The greatest part of the observations contained in the foregoing pages were derived from a lady, who is now beyond the reach of being affected by any thing in this sublunary world. Her beneficence of disposition induced her never to overlook any fact or circumstance that fell within the sphere of her observation, which promised to be in any respect beneficial to her fellow-creatures. To her gentle influence the public are indebted, if they be indeed indebted at all, for whatever useful hints may at any time have dropt from my pen; a being, she thought, who must depend so much as man does on the assistance of others, owes, as a debt to his fellow-creatures, the communication of the little useful knowledge that chance may have thrown in his way. Such has been my constant

[21] Samuel Johnson (1709–84), man of letters, poet and lexicographer.
[22] i.e. recipe.
[23] Character in Sheridan's play, *The Rivals*.
[24] Quoted from Parnell (Edgeworth's note). Thomas Parnell (1679–1718), poet essayist and associate of Swift and Pope.

aim; such were the views of the wife of my bosom, the friend of my heart, who supported and assisted me in all my pursuits. I now feel a melancholy satisfaction in contemplating those objects she once delighted to elucidate."[25]

The elegant Lord Lyttleton,[26] the benevolent Haller,[27] the amiable Dr Gregory,[28] have all, in the language of affection, poetry, and truth, described the pleasures which men of genius and literature enjoy in a union with women who can sympathise in all their thoughts and feelings; who can converse with them as equals, live with them as friends; who can assist them in the important and delightful duty of educating their children; who can make their family their most agreeable society, and their home the attractive centre of happiness.

Can women of uncultivated understandings make such wives?

Women have not the privilege of choice as we have; but they have the power to determine. Women cannot precisely force the tastes of the person with whom they may be connected, yet their happiness will greatly depend upon their being able to conform their tastes to his. For this reason, I should rather, in female education, cultivate the general powers of the mind than any particular faculty. I do not desire to make my daughter a musician, a painter, or a poetess; I do not desire to make her a botanist, a mathematician, or a chemist; but I wish to give her the habit of industry and attention, the love of knowledge and the power of reasoning: these will enable her to attain excellence in any pursuit of science or of literature. Her tastes and her occupations will, I hope, be determined by her situation, and by the wishes of her friends: she will consider all accomplishments and all knowledge as subordinate to her first object, the contributing to their happiness and her own.

I am, my dear friend,
Yours sincerely.

---

[25] J. Anderson—Essay on the Management of a Dairy (Edgeworth's note).
[26] George, first Baron Lyttleton (1709–73), politician and writer; author of *Advice to a Lady*.
[27] Albrecht von Haller (1708–77), Swiss biologist and poet.
[28] John Gregory (1724–73), Professor of Medicine at Edinburgh and author of *A Father's Legacy to his Daughters*.

Dorothy Wordsworth

1771 – 1855

D orothy Wordsworth was orphaned at an early age and she and her brothers were raised by relatives. In 1795 she went to live with her brother, the poet William Wordsworth, whom she adored and with whom she stayed for the rest of her life, even after William's marriage. Following a period in the South of England, Dorothy and William settled in the Lake District, the changing appearance of which under different seasons and lights she described in minute and vivid detail. Although she produced little specifically for publication, she wrote frequently, mainly journals and letters; her descriptions influenced the poetry both of her brother and their friend, Samuel Taylor Coleridge. Dorothy Wordsworth's Grasmere Journal was begun in May 1800 to 'give William pleasure' and ends in January 1803 shortly after his marriage.

The following extract from Grasmere Journal is taken from Dove Cottage: The Wordsworths at Grasmere 1799–1803 (Kingsley Hart (ed.), Folio Society, London, 1966).

From

Grasmere Journal

MAY 14TH, 1800 [WEDNESDAY]

WM and John[1] set off into Yorkshire after dinner at 1/2 past 2 o'clock, cold pork in their pockets. I left them at the turning of the Lowwood bay under the trees. My heart was so full that I could hardly speak to W when I gave him a farewell kiss. I sate a long time upon a stone at the margin of the lake, and after a flood of tears my heart was easier. The lake looked to me, I knew not why, dull and melancholy, and the weltering on the shores seemed a heavy sound. I walked as long as I could amongst the stones of the shore. The wood rich in flowers; a beautiful yellow, palish yellow, flower, that looked thick, round, and double, and smelt very sweet—I supposed it was a ranunculus. Crowfoot, the grassy-leaved rabbit-toothed white flower, strawberries, geranium, scentless violets, anemones

---

[1] Her brothers.

two kinds, orchises, primroses. The heckberry very beautiful, the crab coming out as a low shrub. Met a blind man, driving a very large beautiful Bull, and a cow—he walked with two sticks. Came home by Clappersgate. The valley very green; many sweet views up to Rydale head, when I could juggle away the fine houses; but they disturbed me, even more than when I have been happier; one beautiful view of the Bridge, without Sir Michael's.[2] Sate down very often, though it was cold. I resolved to write a journal of the time till W and J return, and I set about keeping my resolve, because I will not quarrel with myself, and because I shall give Wm pleasure by it when he comes home again. At Rydale, a woman of the village, stout and well dressed, begged a half-penny; she had never she said done it before, but these hard times! Arrived at home with a bad headach, set some slips of privett, the evening cold, had a fire, my face now flame-coloured. It is nine o'clock. I shall soon go to bed. A young woman begged at the door—she had come from Manchester on Sunday morn. with two shillings and a slip of paper which she supposed a Bank note—it was a cheat. She had buried her husband and three children within a year and a half—all in one grave—burying very dear—paupers all put in one place—20 shillings paid for as much ground as will bury a man—a stone to be put over it or the right will be lost—11/6 each time the ground is opened. Oh! that I had a letter from William!

MAY 15TH, THURSDAY

A coldish dull morning—hoed the first row of peas, weeded etc. etc., sat hard to mending till evening. The rain which had threatened all day came on just when I was going to walk.

[MAY 16TH] FRIDAY MORNING

Warm and mild, after a fine night of rain. Transplanted radishes after breakfast, walked to Mr Gell's with the books, gathered mosses and plants. The woods extremely beautiful with all autumnal variety and softness. I carried a basket for mosses, and gathered some wild plants. Oh! that we had a book of botany. All flowers now are gay and deliciously sweet. The primrose still pre-eminent among the later flowers of the spring. Foxgloves very tall, with their heads budding. I went forward round the lake at the foot of Loughrigg Fell. I was much amused with the business of a pair of stone-chats; their restless voices as they skimmed along the water following each other, their shadows under them, and their returning back to the stones on the shore, chirping with the same unwearied voice. Could not cross the water, so I went round by the stepping-stones. The morning clear but cloudy, that is the hills were not overhung by mists. After dinner Aggy[3] weeded onions and carrots. I helped for a little—wrote to Mary Hutchinson[4]—washed my head—worked. After tea went

[2] Rydal Hall, the home of Sir Michael le Fleming.
[3] Aggy (Agnes) Fisher, her husband John Fisher and his sister Molly (Mary Fisher) all lived in the house opposite Dove Cottage. Molly was the Wordsworths' servant during the early years at Grasmere.
[4] Later William's wife.

to Ambleside—a pleasant cool but not cold evening. Rydale was very beautiful, with spear-shaped streaks of polished steel. No letters!—only one newspaper. I returned by Clappersgate. Grasmere was very solemn in the last glimpse of twilight; it calls home the heart to quietness. I had been very melancholy in my walk back. I had many of my saddest thoughts, and I could not keep the tears within me. But when I came to Grasmere I felt that it did me good. I finished my letter to M.H. Ate hasty pudding and went to bed. As I was going out in the morning I met a half crazy old man. He shewed me a pin-cushion and begged a pin, afterwards a half-penny. He began in a kind of indistinct voice in this manner: 'Matthew Jobson's lost a cow. Tom Nichol has two good horses strayed. Jim Jones's cow's brokken her horn, etc. etc.' He went into Aggy's and persuaded her to give him some whey, and let him boil some porridge. She declares he ate two quarts.

[MAY 17TH] SATURDAY

Incessant rain from morning till night. T. Ashburner brought us coals. Worked hard, and read *Midsummer Night's Dream*,[5] [and] Ballads—sauntered a little in the garden. The Skobby[6] sate quietly in its nest, rocked by the wind, and beaten by the rain.

[MAY] 18TH, SUNDAY

Went to church, slight showers, a cold air. The mountains from this window look much greener, and I think the valley is more green than ever. The corn begins to shew itself. The ashes are still bare, went part of the way home with Miss Simpson. A little girl from Coniston came to beg. She had lain out all night—her step-mother had turned her out of doors. Her father could not stay at home 'she flights[7] so'. Walked to Ambleside in the evening round the lake, the prospect exceedingly beautiful from Loughrigg Fell. It was so green that no eye could be weary of reposing upon it. The most beautiful situation for a house in the field next to Mr Benson's. It threatened rain all the evening but was mild and pleasant. I was overtaken by 2 Cumberland people on the other side of Rydale who complimented me upon my walking. They were going to sell cloth, and odd things which they make themselves, in Hawkshead and the neighbourhood. The post was not arrived, so I walked thro' the town, past Mrs Taylor's, and met him. Letters from Coleridge and Cottle. John Fisher overtook me on the other side of Rydale. He talked much about the alteration in the times, and observed that in a short time there would be only two ranks of people, the very rich and the very poor, 'for those who have small estates,' says he, 'are forced to sell, and all the land goes into one hand'. Did not reach home till 10 o'clock.

[5] Over the next three weeks Dorothy Wordsworth appears to be working her way through Shakespeare's plays.
[6] Dialect name for the chaffinch.
[7] Scolds and quarrels.

[MAY 19TH] MONDAY

Sauntered a good deal in the garden, bound carpets, mended old clothes. Read *Timon of Athens*. Dried linen. Molly weeded the turnips, John stuck the peas. We had not much sunshine or wind, but no rain till about 7 o'clock, when we had a slight shower just after I had set out upon my walk. I did not return but walked up into the Black Quarter.[8] I sauntered a long time among the rocks above the church. The most delightful situation possible for a cottage, commanding two distinct views of the vale and of the lake, is among those rocks. I strolled on, gathered mosses etc. The quietness and still seclusion of the valley affected me even to producing the deepest melancholy. I forced myself from it. The wind rose before I went to bed. No rain—Dodwell and Wilkinson called in my absence.

[MAY 20TH] TUESDAY MORNING

A fine mild rain. After breakfast the sky cleared and before the clouds passed from the hills I went to Ambleside. It was a sweet morning. Everything green and overflowing with life, and the streams making a perpetual song, with the thrushes and all little birds, not forgetting the stonechats. The post was not come in. I walked as far as Windermere, and met him there. No letters! no papers. Came home by Clappersgate. I was sadly tired, ate a hasty dinner and had a bad headach—went to bed and slept at least 2 hours. Rain came on in the evening—Molly washing.

[MAY 21ST] WEDNESDAY

Went often to spread the linen which was bleaching—a rainy day and very wet night.

[MAY 22ND] THURSDAY

A very fine day with showers—dried the linen and starched. Drank tea at Mr Simpson's. Brought down Batchelor's Buttons (Rock Ranunculus) and other plants—went part of the way back, a showery mild evening—all the peas up.

[MAY] 23RD, FRIDAY

Ironing till tea time. So heavy a rain that I could not go for letters—put by the linen, mended stockings etc.

MAY 24TH, SATURDAY

Walked in the morning to Ambleside. I found a letter from Wm and from Mary Hutchinson and Douglas. Returned on the other side of the lakes—wrote

---

[8] Easedale.

to William after dinner, nailed up the beds, worked in the garden, sate in the evening under the trees. I went to bed soon with a bad headach. A fine day.

[MAY 25TH] SUNDAY

A very fine warm day, had no fire. Read *Macbeth* in the morning, sate under the trees after dinner. Miss Simpson came just as I was going out and she sate with me. I wrote to my brother Christopher, and sent John Fisher to Ambleside after tea. Miss Simpson and I walked to the foot of the lake—her Brother met us. I went with them nearly home and on my return found a letter from Coleridge and from Charles Lloyd, and three papers.

MAY 26TH, MONDAY

A very fine morning, worked in the garden till after 10 when old Mr Simpson came and talked to me till after 12. Molly weeding—wrote letters to J.H., Coleridge, C.L1., and W. I walked towards Rydale, and turned aside at my favorite field. The air and the lake were still—one cottage light in the vale, and so much of day left that I could distinguish objects, the woods, trees and houses. Two or three different kinds of birds sang at intervals on the opposite shore. I sate till I could hardly drag myself away, I grew so sad. 'When pleasant thoughts,' etc. ...[9]

[MAY] 27TH, TUESDAY

I walked to Ambleside with letters—met the post before I reached Mr Partridge's, one paper, only a letter for Coleridge. I expected a letter from Wm. It was a sweet morning, the ashes in the valley nearly in full leaf, but still to be distinguished, quite bare on the higher ground. I was warm in returning, and becoming cold with sitting in the house. I had a bad headach—went to bed after dinner, and lay till after 5. Not well after tea. I worked in the garden, but did not walk further. A delightful evening before the sun set, but afterwards it grew colder—mended stockings etc.

[MAY 28TH] WEDNESDAY

In the morning walked up to the rocks above Jenny Dockeray's, sate a long time upon the grass, the prospect divinely beautiful. If I had three hundred pounds, and could afford to have a bad interest for my money, I would buy that estate, and we would build a cottage there to end our days in. I went into her garden and got white and yellow lilies, periwinkle, etc., which I planted. Sate under the trees with my work. No fire in the morning. Worked till between 7 and 8, and then watered the garden, and was about to go up to Mr Simpson's, when Miss S and her visitors passed the door. I went home with them, a beautiful evening, the crescent moon hanging above Helm Crag.

[9] William Wordsworth's 'Lines Written in Early Spring': 'In that sweet mood when pleasant thoughts/Bring sad thoughts to the mind.'

[MAY 29TH] THURSDAY

In the morning worked in the garden a little, read *King John*. Miss Simpson and Miss Falcon and Mr S came very early. Went to Mr Gell's boat before tea. We fished upon the lake, and amongst us caught 13 Bass. Miss Simpson brought gooseberries *and cream*. Left the water at near nine o'clock, very cold. Went part of the way home with the party.

[MAY 30TH] FRIDAY

In the morning went to Ambleside, forgetting that the post does not come till the evening. How was I grieved when I was so informed. I walked back, resolving to go again in the evening. It rained very mildly and sweetly in the morning as I came home, but came on a wet afternoon and evening, but chilly. I caught Mr Olliff's lad as he was going for letters, he brought me one from Wm and 12 papers. I planted London Pride upon the well, and many things on the borders. John sodded the wall. As I came past Rydale in the morning, I saw a Heron swimming with only its neck out of the water; it beat and struggled amongst the water, when it flew away, and was long in getting loose.

[MAY 31ST] SATURDAY

A sweet mild rainy morning. Grundy the carpet man called. I paid him 1-10/-. Went to the blind man's for plants. I got such a load that I was obliged to leave my basket in the road, and send Molly for it. Planted till after dinner when I was putting up vallances. Miss Simpson and her visitors called. I went with them to Brathay Bridge. We got Broom on returning, strawberries etc., came home by Ambleside. Grasmere looked divinely beautiful. Mr and Miss Simpson and Tommy drank tea at 8 o'clock. I walked to the Potters with them.

JUNE 1ST, SUNDAY

Rain in the night—a sweet mild morning. Read Ballads; went to church. Singers from Wytheburn, went part of the way home with Miss Simpson. Walked upon the hill above the house till dinner time—went again to church—Christening and singing which kept us very late. The pew-side came down with me. Walked with Mr Simpson nearly home. After tea, went to Ambleside, round the lakes—a very fine warm evening. I lay upon the steep of Loughrigg, my heart dissolved in what I saw, when I was not startled but re-called from my reverie by a noise as of a child paddling without shoes. I looked up and saw a lamb close to me. It approached nearer and nearer, as if to examine me, and stood a long time. I did not move. At last it ran past me, and went bleating along the pathway, seeming to be seeking its mother. I saw a hare on the high road. The post was not come in; waited in the road till John's apprentice came with a letter from Coleridge and 3 papers. The moon shone upon the water—reached home at 10 o'clock, went to bed immediately. Molly brought daisies etc. which we planted.

[JUNE 2ND] MONDAY

A cold dry windy morning. I worked in the garden, and planted flowers, etc. Sate under the trees after dinner till tea time. John Fisher stuck the peas, Molly weeded and washed. I went to Ambleside after tea, crossed the stepping-stones at the foot of Grasmere, and pursued my way on the other side of Rydale and by Clappersgate. I sate a long time to watch the hurrying waves, and to hear the regularly irregular sound of the dashing waters. The waves round about the little Island seemed like a dance of spirits that rose out of the water, round its small circumference of shore. Inquired about lodgings for Coleridge, and was accompanied by Mrs Nicholson as far as Rydale. This was very kind, but God be thanked, I want not society by a moonlight lake. It was near 11 when I reached home. I wrote to Coleridge, and went late to bed.

[JUNE 3RD] TUESDAY

I sent off my letter by the Butcher. A boisterous drying day. I worked in the garden before dinner. Read *R[ichar]d Second*—was not well after dinner and lay down. Mrs Simpson's grandson brought me some gooseberries. I got up and walked with him part of the way home, afterwards went down rambling by the lake side—got Lockety[10] Goldings, strawberries etc., and planted. After tea the wind fell. I walked towards Mr Simpson's, gave the newspapers to the Girl, reached home at 10. No letter, no William—a letter from R[ichar]d to John.

[JUNE 4TH] WEDNESDAY

A very fine day. I sate out of doors most of the day, wrote to Mr Jackson. Ambleside Fair. I walked to the lake-side in the morning, took up plants, and sate upon a stone reading Ballads. In the evening I was watering plants when Mr and Miss Simpson called. I accompanied them home, and we went to the waterfall at the head of the valley. It was very interesting in the Twilight. I brought home lemon thyme, and several other plants, and planted them by moonlight. I lingered out of doors in the hope of hearing my Brother's tread.

[JUNE 5TH] THURSDAY

I sate out of doors great part of the day and worked in the garden—had a letter from Mr Jackson,[11] and wrote an answer to Coleridge. The little birds busy making love, and pecking the blossoms and bits of moss off the trees; they flutter about and about, and thrid the trees as I lie under them. Molly went out to tea, I would not go far from home, expecting my Brothers. I rambled on the hill above the house, gathered wild thyme, and took up roots of wild columbine.

---

[10] Dialect name for the globeflower.
[11] The owner of Greta Hall, Keswick. The Wordsworths were arranging for Coleridge to rent the house.

Just as I was returning with my load, Mr and Miss Simpson called. We went again upon the hill, got more plants, set them, and then went up with them as far as the Blacksmith's, a fine lovely moonlight night.

[JUNE 6TH] FRIDAY

Sate out of doors reading the whole afternoon, but in the morning I wrote to my aunt Cookson. In the evening I went to Ambleside with Coleridge's letter—it was a lovely night as the day had been. I went by Loughrigg and Clappersgate and just met the post at the turnpike; he told me there were two letters but none for me, so I was in no hurry and went round again by Clappersgate, crossed the stepping-stones and entered Ambleside at Matthew Harrison's. A letter from Jack Hutchinson, and one from Montagu, enclosing a 3£ note. No William! I slackened my pace as I came near home, fearing to hear that he was not come. I listened till after one o'clock to every barking dog, cock-fighting, and other sports: it was Mr Borwick's opening. Foxgloves just coming into blossom.

[JUNE 7TH] SATURDAY

A very warm cloudy morning, threatening to rain. I walked up to Mr Simpson's to gather gooseberries—it was a very fine afternoon. Little Tommy came down with me, ate gooseberry pudding and drank tea with me. We went up the hill, to gather sods and plants, and went down to the lake side, and took up orchises, etc. I watered the garden and weeded. I did not leave home, in the expectation of Wm and John, and sitting at work till after 11 o'clock I heard a foot go to the front of the house, turn round, and open the gate. It was William! After our first joy was over, we got some tea. We did not go to bed till 4 o'clock in the morning, so he had an opportunity of seeing our improvements. The birds were singing, and all looked fresh, though not gay. There was a greyness on earth and sky. We did not rise till near 10 in the morning. We were busy all day in writing letters to Coleridge, Montagu, Douglas, Richard. Mr and Miss Simpson called in the evening, the little boy carried our letters to Ambleside. We walked with Mr and Miss S home, on their return. The evening was cold and I was afraid of the tooth-ach for William. We met John on our return home. ...

[JUNE] 9TH, MONDAY

In the morning W cut down the winter cherry tree. I sowed French beans and weeded. A coronetted Landau went by, when we were sitting upon the sodded wall. The ladies (evidently Tourists) turned an eye of interest upon our little garden and cottage. We went to R. Newton's for pike floats and went round to Mr Gell's boat, and on to the lake to fish. We caught nothing—it was extremely cold. The reeds and bullrushes or bullpipes of a tender soft green, making a plain whose surface moved with the wind. The reeds not yet tall. The lake clear to the bottom, but saw no fish. In the evening I stuck peas, watered the garden, and planted brocoli. Did not walk, for it was very cold. A poor girl called to beg,

who had no work at home, and was going in search of it to Kendal. She slept in
Mr Benson's, and went off after breakfast in the morning with 7d. and a letter
to the Mayor of Kendal.

[JUNE] 10TH, TUESDAY

A cold, yet sunshiny morning. John carried letters to Ambleside. I made tarts,
pies, etc. Wm stuck peas. After dinner he lay down. John not at home. I stuck
peas alone. Molly washing. Cold showers with hail and rain, but at half-past five,
after a heavy rain, the lake became calm and very beautiful. Those parts of the
water which were perfectly unruffled lay like green islands of various shapes.
W and I walked to Ambleside to seek lodgings for C. No letters. No papers.
It was a very cold chearless evening. John had been fishing in Langdale and
was gone to bed.

On Tuesday, May 27th, a very tall woman, tall much beyond the measure of
tall women, called at the door. She had on a very long brown cloak and a very
white cap, without bonnet; her face was excessively brown, but it had plainly
once been fair. She led a little bare-footed child about 2 years old by the hand,
and said her husband, who was a tinker, was gone before with the other children.
I gave her a piece of bread. Afterwards on my road to Ambleside, beside the
bridge at Rydale, I saw her husband sitting by the roadside, his two asses feeding
beside him, and the two young children at play upon the grass. The man did
not beg. I passed on and about 1/4 of a mile further I saw two boys before
me, one about 10, the other about 8 years old, at play chasing a butterfly. They
were wild figures, not very ragged, but without shoes and stockings; the hat of
the elder was wreathed round with yellow flowers, the younger whose hat was
only a rimless crown, had stuck it round with laurel leaves. They continued at
play till I drew very near, and then they addressed me with the begging cant and
the whining voice of sorrow. I said 'I served your mother this morning'. (The
Boys were so like the woman who had called at the door that I could not be
mistaken.) 'O!' says the elder, 'you could not serve my mother for she's dead,
and my father's on at the next town—he's a potter.' I persisted in my assertion,
and that I would give them nothing. Says the elder, 'Come, let's away', and away
they flew like lightning. They had however sauntered so long in their road that
they did not reach Ambleside before me, and I saw them go up to Matthew
Harrison's house with their wallet upon the elder's shoulder, and creeping with
a beggar's complaining foot. On my return through Ambleside I met in the street
the mother driving her asses; in the two panniers of one of which were the two
little children, whom she was chiding and threatening with a wand which she
used to drive on her asses, while the little things hung in wantonness over the
pannier's edge. The woman had told me in the morning that she was of Scotland
which her accent fully proved, but that she had lived (I think) at Wigton, that
they could not keep a house and so they travelled.

JUNE 11TH, WEDNESDAY

A very cold morning—we went on the lake to set pike floats with John's
fish. W and J went first alone. Mr Simpson called, and I accompanied him to

the lake side. My Brothers and I again went upon the water, and returned to
dinner. We landed upon the Island where I saw the whitest hawthorn I have
seen this year, the generality of hawthorns are bloomless. I saw wild roses in
the hedges. Went to bed in the afternoon and slept till after six—a threatening
of the toothach. Wm and John went to the pike floats—they brought in 2 pikes.
I sowed kidney-beans and spinnach. A cold evening. Molly stuck the peas. I
weeded a little. Did not walk. ...

[NOVEMBER] 18TH, WEDNESDAY [1802]

We sate in the house in the morning reading Spenser. I was unwell and lay in
bed all the afternoon. Wm and Mary walked to Rydale. Very pleasant moonlight.
The Lakes beautiful. The church an image of peace. Wm wrote some lines upon
it in bed when they came home. Mary and I walked as far as Sara's Gate before
supper. We stood there a long time, the whole scene impressive, the mountains
indistinct, the Lake calm and partly ruffled. Large Island, a sweet sound of water
falling into the quiet Lake. A storm was gathering in Easedale, so we returned;
but the moon came out, and opened to us the church and village. Helm Crag
in shade, the larger mountains dappled like a sky. We stood long upon the
bridge. Wished for Wm, he had stayed at home being sickish—found him better;
we went to bed.

NOV[EMBE]R 19TH, THURSDAY

A beautiful sunny, frosty morning. We did not walk all day. Wm said he would
put it off till the fine moonlight night, and then it came on a heavy rain and
wind. Charles and Olivia Lloyd called in the morning.

[NOVEMBER] 20TH, FRIDAY

We walked in the morning to Easedale. In the evening we had chearful letters
from Coleridge and Sara.

[NOVEMBER] 21ST, SATURDAY

We walked in the morning, and paid one pound and 4d. for letters. William
out of spirits. We had a pleasant walk and spent a pleasant evening. There was
a furious wind and cold at night. Mr Simpson drank tea with us, and helped
William out with the boat. Wm and Mary walked to the Swan, homewards, with
him. A keen clear frosty night. I went into the orchard while they were out.

[NOVEMBER] 22ND, SUNDAY

We wrote to Coleridge and sent our letter by the boy. Mr and Miss Simpson
came in at tea time. We went with them to the Blacksmith's and returned
by Butterlip How—a frost and wind with bright moonshine. The vale looked

spacious and very beautiful—the level meadows seemed very large and some nearer us, unequal ground, heaving like sand, the Cottages beautiful and quiet, we passed one near which stood a cropped ash with upright forked branches like the Devil's horns frightening a guilty conscience. We were happy and chearful when we came home—we went early to bed.

NOV[EMBER] 23RD, MONDAY

A beautiful frosty morning. Mary was making William's woollen waistcoat. Wm unwell, and did not walk. Mary and I sate in our cloaks upon the bench in the orchard. After dinner I went to bed unwell. Mary had a headach at night. We all went to bed soon.

[NOVEMBER] 24TH, TUESDAY

A rainy morning. We all were well except that my head ached a little, and I took my breakfast in bed. I read a little of Chaucer, prepared the goose for dinner, and then we all walked out. I was obliged to return for my fur tippet and spencer, it was so cold. We had intended going to Easedale, but we shaped our course to Mr Gell's cottage. It was very windy, and we heard the wind everywhere about us as we went along the lane, but the walls sheltered us. John Green's house looked pretty under Silver How. As we were going along we were stopped at once, at the distance perhaps of 50 yards from our favourite birch tree. It was yielding to the gusty wind with all its tender twigs, the sun shone upon it, and it glanced in the wind like a flying sunshiny shower. It was a tree in shape, with stem and branches, but it was like a Spirit of water. The sun went in, and it resumed its purplish appearance, the twigs still yielding to the wind, but not so visibly to us. The other birch trees that were near it looked bright and chearful, but it was a creature by its own self among them. We could not get into Mr Gell's grounds—the old tree fallen from its undue exaltation above the gate. A shower came on when we were at Benson's. We went through the wood—it became fair. There was a rainbow which spanned the lake from the island-house to the foot of Bainriggs. The village looked populous and beautiful. Catkins are coming out; palm trees budding; the alder, with its plumb-coloured buds. We came home over the stepping-stones. The lake was foamy with white waves. I saw a solitary butter-flower in the wood. I found it not easy to get over the stepping-stones. Reached home at dinner time. Sent Peggy Ashburner some goose. She sent me some honey, with a thousand thanks. 'Alas! the gratitude of men has', etc.[12] I went in to set her right about this, and sate a while with her. She talked about Thomas's having sold his land. 'Ay,' says she, 'I said many a time he's not come fra London to buy our land, however.' Then she told me with what pains and industry they had made up their taxes, interest, etc. etc., how they all got up at 5 o'clock in the morning to spin and Thomas carded, and that they had paid off a hundred pounds of the interest. She said she used to take

12 William Wordsworth's 'Simon Lee' ii.75–6.

such pleasure in the cattle and sheep. 'O how pleased I used to be when they fetched them down, and when I had been a bit poorly I would gang out upon a hill and look ower 't fields and see them, and it used to do me so much good you cannot think.' Molly said to me when I came in, 'Poor body! she's very ill, but one does not know how long she may last. Many a fair face may gang before her.' We sate by the fire without work for some time, then Mary read a poem of Daniel upon Learning. After tea Wm read Spenser, now and then a little aloud to us. We were making his waistcoat. We had a note from Mrs C, with bad news from poor C—very ill. William went to John's Grove, I went to meet him. Moonlight, but it rained. I met him before I had got as far as John Baty's—he had been surprized and terrified by a sudden rushing of winds, which seemed to bring earth sky and lake together, as if the whole were going to enclose him in; he was glad he was in a high road.

In speaking of our walk on Sunday evening, the 22nd November, I forgot to notice one most impressive sight. It was the moon and the moonlight seen through hurrying driving clouds immediately behind the Stone-Man upon the top of the hill on the Forest Side. Every tooth and every edge of rock was visible, and the Man stood like a Giant watching from the roof of a lofty castle. The hill seemed perpendicular from the darkness belòw it. It was a sight that I could call to mind at any time, it was so distinct.

Jane Austen
1775 – 1817

Jane Austen, one of the major novelists in English, came from a well-connected family in the South of England. She was the daughter of a country rector and, although she never married, she was by no means isolated, spending much of her time in the company of her brothers and sisters and her many relatives. A great reader of novels, she began her literary career in her teens with clever parodies of contemporary sentimental fiction aimed at women; the first three of her six major books, sketched out when she was still a young girl, have parodic elements. Of these three, the most popular has been Pride and Prejudice, published in 1813. It has the usual Austen plot based on the *conventional women's plot of the time, in which a young unguided girl learns to reject the unsuitable and welcome the suitable man and, in the process, adapts to the adult social scene while holding to a firm morality. Like all Austen's novels,* Pride and Prejudice *has a narrator whose tart ironic comments provide much of the humour and social commentary.*

The following extract is reprinted from Pride and Prejudice *(1813).*

From

Pride and Prejudice

VOLUME 1

CHAPTER 1

I T is a truth universally acknowledged, that a single man in possession of a good fortune, must be in want of a wife.

However little known the feelings or views of such a man may be on his first entering a neighbourhood, this truth is so well fixed in the minds of the surrounding families, that he is considered as the rightful property of some one or other of their daughters.

"My dear Mr. Bennet," said his lady to him one day, "have you heard that Netherfield Park is let at last?"

Mr Bennet replied that he had not.

"But it is," returned she; "for Mrs. Long has just been here, and she told me all about it."

Mr Bennet made no answer.

"Do not you want to know who has taken it?" cried his wife impatiently.

"You want to tell me, and I have no objection to hearing it."

This was invitation enough.

"Why, my dear, you must know, Mrs. Long says that Netherfield is taken by a young man of large fortune from the north of England; that he came down on Monday in a chaise and four to see the place, and was so much delighted with it that he agreed with Mr. Morris immediately; that he is to take possession before Michaelmas, and some of his servants are to be in the house by the end of next week."

"What is his name?"

"Bingley."

"Is he married or single?"

"Oh! single, my dear, to be sure! A single man of large fortune; four or five thousand a year. What a fine thing for our girls!"

"How so? how can it affect them?"

"My dear Mr. Bennet," replied his wife, "how can you be so tiresome! You must know that I am thinking of his marrying one of them."

"Is that his design in settling here?"

"Design! nonsense, how can you talk so! But it is very likely that he *may* fall in love with one of them, and therefore you must visit him as soon as he comes."

"I see no occasion for that. You and the girls may go, or you may send them by themselves, which perhaps will be still better, for as you are as handsome as any of them, Mr. Bingley might like you the best of the party."

"My dear, you flatter me. I certainly *have* had my share of beauty, but I do not pretend to be any thing extraordinary now. When a woman has five grown up daughters, she ought to give over thinking of her own beauty."

"In such cases, a woman has not often much beauty to think of."

"But, my dear, you must indeed go and see Mr. Bingley when he comes into the neighbourhood."

"It is more than I engage for, I assure you."

"But consider your daughters. Only think what an establishment it would be for one of them. Sir William and Lady Lucas are determined to go, merely on that account, for in general you know they visit no new comers. Indeed you must go, for it will be impossible for *us* to visit him, if you do not."

"You are over scrupulous surely. I dare say Mr. Bingley will be very glad to see you; and I will send a few lines by you to assure him of my hearty consent to his marrying which ever he chuses of the girls; though I must throw in a good word for my little Lizzy."

"I desire you will do no such thing. Lizzy is not a bit better than the others; and I am sure she is not half so handsome as Jane, nor half so good humoured as Lydia. But you are always giving *her* the preference."

"They have none of them much to recommend them," replied he; "they are all silly and ignorant like other girls; but Lizzy has something more of quickness than her sisters."

"Mr. Bennett, how can you abuse your own children in such a way? You take delight in vexing me. You have no compassion on my poor nerves."

"You mistake me, my dear. I have a high respect for your nerves. They are my old friends. I have heard you mention them with consideration these twenty years at least."

"Ah! you do not know what I suffer."

"But I hope you will get over it, and live to see many young men of four thousand a year come into the neighbourhood."

"It will be no use to us, if twenty such should come since you will not visit them."

"Depend upon it, my dear, that when there are twenty, I will visit them all."

Mr Bennet was so odd a mixture of quick parts, sarcastic humour, reserve, and caprice, that the experience of three and twenty years had been insufficient to make his wife understand his character. *Her* mind was less difficult to develop. She was a woman of mean understanding, little information, and uncertain temper. When she was discontented she fancied herself nervous.

The business of her life was to get her daughters married; its solace was visiting and news.

CHAPTER II

Mr. Bennet was among the earliest of those who waited on Mr. Bingley. He had always intended to visit him, though to the last always assuring his wife that he should not go; and till the evening after the visit was paid, she had no knowledge of it. It was then disclosed in the following manner. Observing his second daughter employed in trimming a hat, he suddenly addressed her with,

"I hope Mr. Bingley will like it, Lizzy."

"We are not in a way to know *what* Mr. Bingley likes," said her mother resentfully, "since we are not to visit."

"But you forget, mama," said Elizabeth, "that we shall meet him at the assemblies, and that Mrs. Long has promised to introduce him."

"I do not believe Mrs. Long will do any such thing. She has two neices of her own. She is a selfish, hypocritical woman, and I have no opinion of her."

"No more have I," said Mr. Bennet; "and I am glad to find that you do not depend on her serving you."

Mrs. Bennet deigned not to make any reply; but unable to contain herself, began scolding one of her daughters.

"Don't keep coughing so, Kitty, for heaven's sake! Have a little compassion on my nerves. You tear them to pieces."

"Kitty has no discretion in her coughs," said her father; "she times them ill."

"I do not cough for my own amusement," replied Kitty fretfully.

"When is your next ball to be, Lizzy?"

"To-morrow fortnight."

"Aye, so it is," cried her mother, "and Mrs. Long does not come back till the day before; so, it will be impossible for her to introduce him, for she will not know him herself."

"Then, my dear, you may have the advantage of your friend, and introduce Mr. Bingley to *her*."

"Impossible, Mr. Bennet, impossible, when I am not acquainted with him myself; how can you be so teazing?"

"I honour your circumspection. A fortnight's acquaintance is certainly very little. One cannot know what a man really is by the end of a fortnight. But if *we* do not venture, somebody else will; and after all, Mrs. Long and her neices must stand their chance; and therefore, as she will think it an act of kindness, if you decline the office, I will take it on myself."

The girls stared at their father. Mrs. Bennet said only, "Nonsense, nonsense!"

"What can be the meaning of that emphatic exclamation?" cried he. "Do you consider the forms of introduction, and the stress that is laid on them, as nonsense? I cannot quite agree with you *there*. What say you, Mary? for you are a young lady of deep reflection I know, and read great books, and make extracts."

Mary wished to say something very sensible, but knew not how.

"While Mary is adjusting her ideas," he continued, "let us return to Mr. Bingley."

"I am sick of Mr. Bingley," cried his wife.

"I am sorry to hear *that*; but why did you not tell me so before? If I had known as much this morning, I certainly would not have called on him. It is very unlucky; but as I have actually paid the visit, we cannot escape the acquaintance now."

The astonishment of the ladies was just what he wished; that of Mrs. Bennet perhaps surpassing the rest; though when the first tumult of joy was over, she began to declare that it was what she had expected all the while.

"How good it was in you, my dear Mr. Bennet! But I knew I should persuade you at last. I was sure you loved your girls too well to neglect such an acquaintance. Well, how pleased I am! and it is such a good joke, too, that you should have gone this morning, and never said a word about it till now."

"Now, Kitty, you may cough as much as you chuse," said Mr. Bennet; and, as he spoke, he left the room, fatigued with the raptures of his wife.

"What an excellent father you have, girls," said she, when the door was shut. "I do not know how you will ever make him amends for his kindness; or me either, for that matter. At our time of life, it is not so pleasant I can tell you, to be making new acquaintance every day; but for your sakes, we would do any thing. Lydia, my love, though you *are* the youngest, I dare say Mr. Bingley will dance with you at the next ball."

"Oh!" said Lydia stoutly, "I am not afraid; for though I *am* the youngest, I'm the tallest."

The rest of the evening was spent in conjecturing how soon he would return Mr. Bennet's visit, and determining when they should ask him to dinner.

CHAPTER III

Not all that Mrs. Bennet, however, with the assistance of her five daughters, could ask on the subject was sufficient to draw from her husband any satisfactory description of Mr. Bingley. They attacked him in various ways; with barefaced questions, ingenious suppositions, and distant surmises; but he eluded the skill of them all; and they were at last obliged to accept the second-hand intelligence of their neighbour Lady Lucas. Her report was highly favourable. Sir William had been delighted with him. He was quite young, wonderfully handsome, extremely agreeable, and to crown the whole, he meant to be at the next assembly with a large party. Nothing could be more delightful! To be fond of dancing was a certain step towards falling in love; and very lively hopes of Mr. Bingley's heart were entertained.

"If I can but see one of my daughters happily settled at Netherfield," said Mrs. Bennet to her husband, "and all the others equally well married, I shall have nothing to wish for."

In a few days Mr. Bingley returned Mr. Bennet's visit, and sat about ten minutes with him in his library. He had entertained hopes of being admitted to a sight of the young ladies, of whose beauty he had heard much; but he saw only the father. The ladies were somewhat more fortunate, for they had the advantage of ascertaining from an upper window, that he wore a blue coat and rode a black horse.

An invitation to dinner was soon afterwards dispatched; and already had Mrs. Bennet planned the courses that were to do credit to her housekeeping, when an answer arrived which deferred it all. Mr. Bingley was obliged to be in town the following day, and consequently unable to accept the honour of their invitation, &c. Mrs Bennet was quite disconcerted. She could not imagine what business he could have in town so soon after his arrival in Hertfordshire; and she began to fear that he might be always flying about from one place to another, and never settled at Netherfield as he ought to be. Lady Lucas quieted her fears a little by starting the idea of his being gone to London only to get a large party for the ball; and a report soon followed that Mr. Bingley was to bring twelve ladies and seven gentlemen with him to the assembly. The girls grieved over such a number of ladies; but were comforted the day before the ball by hearing, that instead of twelve, he had brought only six with him from London, his five sisters and a cousin. And when the party entered the assembly room, it consisted of only five altogether; Mr. Bingley, his two sisters, the husband of the eldest, and another young man.

Mr. Bingley was good looking and gentlemanlike; he had a pleasant countenance, and easy, unaffected manners. His sisters were fine women, with an air of decided fashion. His brother-in-law, Mr. Hurst, merely looked the gentleman; but his friend Mr. Darcy soon drew the attention of the room by his fine, tall person, handsome features, noble mien; and the report which was in general circulation within five minutes after his entrance, of his having ten thousand a year. The gentlemen pronounced him to be a fine figure of a man, the ladies declared he was much handsomer than Mr. Bingley, and he was looked at with great admiration for about half the evening, till his manners gave a disgust which turned the tide of his popularity; for he was discovered to be proud, to be above his company, and above being pleased; and not all his large estate in Derbyshire could then save him from having a most forbidding, disagreeable countenance, and being unworthy to be compared with his friend.

Mr. Bingley had soon made himself acquainted with all the principal people in the room; he was lively and unreserved, danced every dance, was angry that the ball closed so early, and talked of giving one himself at Netherfield. Such amiable qualities must speak for themselves. What a contrast between him and his friend! Mr. Darcy danced only once with Mrs. Hurst and once with Miss Bingley, declined being introduced to any other lady, and spent the rest of the evening in walking about the room, speaking occasionally to one of his own party. His character was decided. He was the proudest, most disagreeable man in the world, and every body hoped that he would never come there again. Amongst the most violent against him was Mrs Bennet, whose dislike of his general behaviour, was sharpened into particular resentment, by his having slighted one of her daughters.

Elizabeth Bennet had been obliged, by the scarcity of gentlemen, to sit down for two dances; and during part of that time, Mr. Darcy had been standing near enough for her to overhear a conversation between him and Mr. Bingley, who came from the dance for a few minutes, to press his friend to join it.

"Come, Darcy," said he, "I must have you dance. I hate to see you standing about by yourself in this stupid manner. You had much better dance."

"I certainly shall not. You know how I detest it, unless I am particularly acquainted with my partner. At such an assembly as this, it would be insupportable. Your sisters are engaged, and there is not another woman in the room, whom it would not be a punishment to me to stand up with."

"I would not be so fastidious as you are," cried Bingley, "for a kingdom! Upon my honour, I never met with so many pleasant girls in my life, as I have this evening; and there are several of them you see uncommonly pretty."

"*You* are dancing with the only handsome girl in the room," said Mr. Darcy, looking at the eldest Miss Bennet.

"Oh! she is the most beautiful creature I ever beheld! But there is one of her sisters sitting down just behind you, who is very pretty, and I dare say very agreeable. Do let me ask my partner to introduce you."

"Which do you mean?" and turning round, he looked for a moment at Elizabeth, till catching her eye, he withdrew his own and coldly said, "She is tolerable; but not handsome enough to tempt *me*; and I am in no humour at present to give consequence to young ladies who are slighted by other men. You had better return to your partner and enjoy her smiles, for you are wasting your time with me."

Mr. Bingley followed his advice. Mr. Darcy walked off; and Elizabeth remained with no very cordial feelings towards him. She told the story however with great spirit among her friends; for she had a lively, playful disposition, which delighted in any thing ridiculous.

The evening altogether passed off pleasantly to the whole family. Mrs. Bennet had seen her eldest daughter much admired by the Netherfield party. Mr. Bingley had danced with her twice, and she had been distinguished by his sisters. Jane was as much gratified by this, as her mother could be, though in a quieter way. Elizabeth felt Jane's pleasure. Mary had heard herself mentioned to Miss Bingley as the most accomplished girl in the neighbourhood; and Catherine and Lydia had been fortunate enough to be never without partners, which was all that they had yet learnt to care for at a ball. They returned therefore in good spirits to Longbourn, the village where they lived, and of which they were the principal inhabitants. They found Mr. Bennet still up. With a book he was regardless of time; and on the present occasion he had a good deal of curiosity as to the event of an evening which had raised such splendid expectations. He had rather hoped that all his wife's views on the stranger would be disappointed; but he soon found that he had a very different story to hear.

"Oh! my dear Mr. Bennet," as she entered the room, "we have had a most delightful evening, a most excellent ball. I wish you had been there. Jane was so admired, nothing could be like it. Every body said how well she looked; and Mr. Bingley thought her quite beautiful, and danced with her twice. Only think of *that* my dear; he actually danced with her twice; and she was the only creature in the room that he asked a second time. First of all, he asked Miss Lucas. I was so vexed to see him stand up with her; but, however, he did not admire her at all: indeed, nobody can, you know; and he seemed quite struck with Jane as she was going down the dance. So, he enquired who she was, and got introduced, and asked her for the two next. Then, the two third he danced with Miss King, and the two fourth with Maria Lucas, and the two fifth with Jane again, and the two sixth with Lizzy, and the Boulanger——"[1]

"If he had had any compassion for *me*," cried her husband impatiently, "he would not have danced half so much! For God's sake, say no more of his partners. Oh! that he had sprained his ancle in the first dance!"

"Oh! my dear," continued Mrs Bennet, "I am quite delighted with him. He is so excessively handsome! and his sisters are charming women. I never in my life saw any thing more elegant than their dresses. I dare say the lace upon Mrs. Hurst's gown——"

Here she was interrupted again. Mr. Bennet protested against any description of finery. She was therefore obliged to seek another branch of the subject, and related, with much bitterness of spirit and some exaggeration, the shocking rudeness of Mr. Darcy.

"But I can assure you," she added, "that Lizzy does not lose much by not suiting *his* fancy; for he is a most disagreeable, horrid man, not at all worth pleasing. So high and so conceited that there was no enduring him! He walked here, and he walked there, fancying himself so very great! Not handsome enough to dance with! I wish you had been there, my dear, to have given him one of your set downs. I quite detest the man."

CHAPTER IV

When Jane and Elizabeth were alone, the former, who had been cautious in her praise of Mr. Bingley before, expressed to her sister how very much she admired him.

"He is just what a young man ought to be," said she, "sensible, good humoured, lively; and I never saw such happy manners!—so much ease, with such perfect good breeding!"

"He is also handsome," replied Elizabeth, "which a young man ought likewise to be, if he possibly can. His character is thereby complete."

"I was very much flattered by his asking me to dance a second time. I did not expect such a compliment."

"Did not you? *I* did for you. But that is one great difference between us. Compliments always take *you* by surprise, and *me* never. What could be more

[1] A round dance.

natural than his asking you again? He could not help seeing that you were about five times as pretty as every other woman in the room. No thanks to his gallantry for that. Well, he certainly is very agreeable, and I give you leave to like him. You have liked many a stupider person."

"Dear Lizzy!"

"Oh! you are a great deal too apt you know, to like people in general. You never see a fault in any body. All the world are good and agreeable in your eyes. I never heard you speak ill of a human being in my life."

"I would wish not to be hasty in censuring any one; but I always speak what I think."

"I know you do; and it is *that* which makes the wonder. With *your* good sense, to be so honestly blind to the follies and nonsense of others! Affectation of candour is common enough;—one meets it every where. But to be candid without ostentation or design—to take the good of every body's character and make it still better, and say nothing of the bad—belongs to you alone. And so, you like this man's sisters too, do you? Their manners are not equal to his."

"Certainly not; at first. But they are very pleasing women when you converse with them. Miss Bingley is to live with her brother and keep his house; and I am much mistaken if we shall not find a very charming neighbour in her."

Elizabeth listened in silence, but was not convinced; their behaviour at the assembly had not been calculated to please in general; and with more quickness of observation and less pliancy of temper than her sister, and with a judgment too unassailed by any attention to herself, she was very little disposed to approve them. They were in fact very fine ladies; not deficient in good humour when they were pleased, nor in the power of being agreeable where they chose it; but proud and conceited. They were rather handsome, had been educated in one of the first private seminaries in town, had a fortune of twenty thousand pounds, were in the habit of spending more than they ought, and of associating with people of rank; and were therefore in every respect entitled to think well of themselves, and meanly of others. They were of a respectable family in the north of England; a circumstance more deeply impressed on their memories than that their brother's fortune and their own had been acquired by trade.

Mr. Bingley inherited property to the amount of nearly an hundred thousand pounds from his father, who had intended to purchase an estate, but did not live to do it.—Mr. Bingley intended it likewise, and sometimes made choice of his county; but as he was now provided with a good house and the liberty of a manor,[2] it was doubtful to many of those who best knew the easiness of his temper, whether he might not spend the remainder of his days at Netherfield, and leave the next generation to purchase.

His sisters were very anxious for his having an estate of his own; but though he was now established only as a tenant, Miss Bingley was by no means unwilling to preside at his table, nor was Mrs. Hurst, who had married a man of more fashion than fortune, less disposed to consider his house as her home when it suited her. Mr. Bingley had not been of age two years, when he

---

[2] Right to hunt on its fields.

was tempted by an accidental recommendation to look at Netherfield House. He did look at it and into it for half an hour, was pleased with the situation and the principal rooms, satisfied with what the owner said in its praise, and took it immediately.

Between him and Darcy there was a very steady friendship, in spite of a great opposition of character.—Bingley was endeared to Darcy by the easiness, openness, ductility of his temper, though no disposition could offer a greater contrast to his own, and though with his own he never appeared dissatisfied. On the strength of Darcy's regard Bingley had the firmest reliance, and of his judgment the highest opinion. In understanding Darcy was the superior. Bingley was by no means deficient, but Darcy was clever. He was at the same time haughty, reserved, and fastidious, and his manners, though well bred, were not inviting. In that respect his friend had greatly the advantage. Bingley was sure of being liked wherever he appeared, Darcy was continually giving offence.

The manner in which they spoke of the Meryton assembly was sufficiently characteristic. Bingley had never met with pleasanter people or prettier girls in his life; every body had been most kind and attentive to him, there had been no formality, no stiffness, he had soon felt acquainted with all the room; and as to Miss Bennet, he could not conceive an angel more beautiful. Darcy, on the contrary, had seen a collection of people in whom there was little beauty and no fashion, for none of whom he had felt the smallest interest, and from none received either attention or pleasure. Miss Bennet he acknowledged to be pretty, but she smiled too much.

Mrs. Hurst and her sister allowed it to be so—but still they admired her and liked her, and pronounced her to be a sweet girl, and one whom they should not object to know more of. Miss Bennet was therefore established as a sweet girl, and their brother felt authorised by such commendation to think of her as he chose.

*   *   *

CHAPTER XV

Mr. Collins[3] was not a sensible man, and the deficiency of nature had been but little assisted by education or society; the greatest part of his life having been spent under the guidance of an illiterate and miserly father; and though he belonged to one of the universities, he had merely kept the necessary terms, without forming at it any useful acquaintance. The subjection in which his father had brought him up, had given him originally great humility of manner, but it was now a good deal counteracted by the self-conceit of a weak head, living in retirement, and the consequential feelings of early and unexpected prosperity. A fortunate chance had recommended him to Lady Catherine de Bourgh when the living[4] of Hunsford was vacant; and the respect which he felt for her high rank,

---

[3] The heir to the Bennets' house of Longbourn since Mr Bennet has no son.
[4] The position of clergyman which was within the patronage of the landowning Lady Catherine de Bourgh.

and his veneration for her as his patroness, mingling with a very good opinion of himself, of his authority as a clergyman, and his rights as a rector, made him altogether a mixture of pride and obsequiousness, self-importance and humility.

Having now a good house and very sufficient income, he intended to marry; and in seeking a reconciliation with the Longbourn family he had a wife in view, as he meant to chuse one of the daughters, if he found them as handsome and amiable as they were represented by common report. This was his plan of amends—of atonement—for inheriting their father's estate; and he thought it an excellent one, full of eligibility and suitableness, and excessively generous and disinterested on his own part.

His plan did not vary on seeing them.—Miss Bennet's lovely face confirmed his views, and established all his strictest notions of what was due to seniority; and for the first evening *she* was his settled choice. The next morning, however, made an alteration; for in a quarter of an hour's tête-à-tête with Mrs. Bennet before breakfast, a conversation beginning with his parsonage-house, and leading naturally to the avowal of his hopes, that a mistress for it might be found at Longbourn, produced from her, amid very complaisant smiles and a general encouragement, a caution against the very Jane he had fixed on.—"As to her *younger* daughters she could not take upon her to say—she could not positively answer—but she did not *know* of any prepossession;—her *eldest* daughter, she must just mention—she felt it incumbent on her to hint, was likely to be very soon engaged."

Mr. Collins had only to change from Jane to Elizabeth—and it was soon done—done while Mrs. Bennet was stirring the fire. Elizabeth, equally next to Jane in birth and beauty, succeeded her of course.

Mrs. Bennet treasured up the hint, and trusted that she might soon have two daughters married; and the man whom she could not bear to speak of the day before, was now high in her good graces. ...

CHAPTER XIX

The next day opened a new scene at Longbourn. Mr. Collins made his declaration in form. Having resolved to do it without loss of time, as his leave of absence extended only to the following Saturday, and having no feelings of diffidence to make it distressing to himself even at the moment, he set about it in a very orderly manner, with all the observances which he supposed a regular part of the business. On finding Mrs. Bennet, Elizabeth, and one of the younger girls together, soon after breakfast, he addressed the mother in these words,

"May I hope, Madam, for your interest with your fair daughter Elizabeth, when I solicit for the honour of a private audience with her in the course of this morning?"

Before Elizabeth had time for any thing but a blush of surprise, Mrs. Bennet instantly answered,

"Oh dear!—Yes—certainly.—I am sure Lizzy will be very happy—I am sure she can have no objection.—Come, Kitty, I want you up stairs." And gathering her work together, she was hastening away, when Elizabeth called out,

"Dear Ma'am, do not go.—I beg you will not go.—Mr. Collins must excuse me. —He can have nothing to say to me that any body need not hear. I am going away myself."

"No, no, nonsense, Lizzy.—I desire you will stay where you are."—And upon Elizabeth's seeming really, with vexed and embarrassed looks, about to escape, she added, "Lizzy, I *insist* upon your staying and hearing Mr. Collins."

Elizabeth would not oppose such an injunction—and a moment's considera- tion making her also sensible that it would be wisest to get it over as soon and as quietly as possible, she sat down again, and tried to conceal by incessant employ- ment the feelings which were divided between distress and diversion. Mrs. Bennet and Kitty walked off, and as soon as they were gone Mr. Collins began.

"Believe me, my dear Miss Elizabeth, that your modesty, so far from doing you any disservice, rather adds to your other perfections. You would have been less amiable in my eyes had there *not* been this little unwillingness; but allow me to assure you that I have your respected mother's permission for this address. You can hardly doubt the purport of my discourse, however your natural delicacy may lead you to dissemble; my attentions have been too marked to be mistaken. Almost as soon as I entered the house I singled you out as the companion of my future life. But before I am run away with by my feelings on this subject, perhaps it will be advisable for me to state my reasons for marrying—and moreover for coming into Hertfordshire with the design of selecting a wife, as I certainly did."

The idea of Mr. Collins, with all his solemn composure, being run away with by his feelings, made Elizabeth so near laughing that she could not use the short pause he allowed in any attempt to stop him farther, and he continued:

"My reasons for marrying are, first, that I think it a right thing for every clergyman in easy circumstances (like myself) to set the example of matrimony in his parish. Secondly, that I am convinced it will add very greatly to my happiness; and thirdly—which perhaps I ought to have mentioned earlier, that it is the particular advice and recommendation of the very noble lady whom I have the honour of calling patroness. Twice has she condescended to give me her opinion (unasked too!) on this subject; and it was but the very Saturday night before I left Hunsford—between our pools at quadrille, while Mrs. Jenkinson was arranging Miss de Bourgh's foot-stool, that she said, 'Mr. Collins, you must marry. A clergyman like you must marry.—Chuse properly, chuse a gentlewoman for *my* sake; and for your *own*, let her be an active, useful sort of person, not brought up high, but able to make a small income go a long way. This is my advice. Find such a woman as soon as you can, bring her to Hunsford, and I will visit her.' Allow me, by the way, to observe, my fair cousin, that I do not reckon the notice and kindness of Lady Catherine de Bourgh as among the least of the advantages in my power to offer. You will find her manners beyond any thing I can describe; and your wit and vivacity I think must be acceptable to her, especially when tempered with the silence and respect which her rank will inevitably excite. Thus much for my general intention in favour of matrimony; it remains to be told why my views were directed to Longbourn instead of my own neighbourhood, where I assure you there are many amiable young women. But the fact is, that being, as I am, to inherit this estate after the death of your honoured father, (who, however, may live many years longer,) I could not satisfy myself without resolving to chuse a wife from among his daughters, that the loss to them might be as little as possible, when the melancholy event takes place—which, however, as I have already said, may not be for several years. This has been my motive, my fair cousin, and I flatter myself it will not sink me in your esteem. And now nothing remains for me but to assure you in the most animated language of the violence of my affection. To fortune I am perfectly indifferent, and shall make no demand of that nature on your father, since I am well aware that it could not be complied with; and that one thousand pounds in the 4 per cents.[5] which will not be yours till after your mother's decease, is all that you may ever be entitled to. On that head, therefore, I shall be uniformly silent; and you may assure yourself that no ungenerous reproach shall ever pass my lips when we are married."

It was absolutely necessary to interrupt him now.

"You are too hasty, Sir," she cried. "You forget that I have made no answer. Let me do it without farther loss of time. Accept my thanks for the compliment you are paying me. I am very sensible of the honour of your proposals, but it is impossible for me to do otherwise than decline them."

"I am not now to learn," replied Mr. Collins, with a formal wave of the hand, "that it is usual with young ladies to reject the addresses of the man whom they secretly mean to accept, when he first applies for their favour; and that sometimes the refusal is repeated a second or even a third time. I am therefore by no means discouraged by what you have just said, and shall hope to lead you to the altar ere long."

"Upon my word, Sir," cried Elizabeth, "your hope is rather an extraordinary one after my declaration. I do assure you that I am not one of those young ladies (if such young ladies there are) who are so daring as to risk their happiness on the chance of being asked a second time. I am perfectly serious in my refusal.—You could not make *me* happy, and I am convinced that I am the last woman in the world who would make *you* so.—Nay, were your friend Lady Catherine to know me, I am persuaded she would find me in every respect ill qualified for the situation."

"Were it certain that Lady Catherine would think so," said Mr. Collins very gravely—"but I cannot imagine that her ladyship would at all disapprove of you. And you may be certain that when I have the honour of seeing her again I shall speak in the highest terms of your modesty, economy, and other amiable qualifications."

"Indeed, Mr. Collins, all praise of me will be unnecessary. You must give me leave to judge for myself, and pay me the compliment of believing what I say. I wish you very happy and very rich, and by refusing your hand, do all in my power to prevent your being otherwise. In making me the offer, you must have satisfied the delicacy of your feelings with regard to my family, and may take possession of Longbourn estate whenever it falls, without any self-reproach. This matter may be considered, therefore, as finally settled." And rising as she thus spoke, she would have quitted the room, had not Mr. Collins thus addressed her.

[5] Government stock.

"When I do myself the honour of speaking to you next on this subject I shall hope to receive a more favourable answer than you have now given me; though I am far from accusing you of cruelty at present, because I know it to be the established custom of your sex to reject a man on the first application, and perhaps you have even now said as much to encourage my suit as would be consistent with the true delicacy of the female character."

"Really, Mr. Collins," cried Elizabeth with some warmth, "you puzzle me exceedingly. If what I have hitherto said can appear to you in the form of encouragement, I know not how to express my refusal in such a way as may convince you of its being one."

"You must give me leave to flatter myself, my dear cousin, that your refusal of my address is merely words of course. My reasons for believing it are briefly these:—It does not appear to me that my hand is unworthy your acceptance, or that the establishment I can offer would be any other than highly desirable. My situation in life, my connections with the family of De Bourgh, and my relationship to your own, are circumstances highly in my favour; and you should take it into farther consideration that in spite of your manifold attractions, it is by no means certain that another offer of marriage may ever be made you. Your portion is unhappily so small that it will in all likelihood undo the effects of your loveliness and amiable qualifications. As I must therefore conclude that you are not serious in your rejection of me, I shall chuse to attribute it to your wish of increasing my love by suspense, according to the usual practice of elegant females."

"I do assure you, Sir, that I have no pretension whatever to that kind of elegance which consists in tormenting a respectable man. I would rather be paid the compliment of being believed sincere. I thank you again and again for the honour you have done me in your proposals, but to accept them is absolutely impossible. My feelings in every respect forbid it. Can I speak plainer? Do not consider me now as an elegant female intending to plague you, but as a rational creature speaking the truth from her heart."

"You are uniformly charming!" cried he, with an air of awkward gallantry; "and I am persuaded that when sanctioned by the express authority of both your excellent parents, my proposals will not fail of being acceptable."

To such perseverance in wilful self-deception Elizabeth would make no reply, and immediately and in silence withdrew; determined, if he persisted in considering her repeated refusals as flattering encouragement, to apply to her father, whose negative might be uttered in such a manner as must be decisive, and whose behaviour at least could not be mistaken for the affectation and coquetry of an elegant female.

CHAPTER XX

Mr. Collins was not left long to the silent contemplation of his successful love; for Mrs. Bennet, having dawdled about in the vestibule to watch for the end of the conference, no sooner saw Elizabeth open the door and with quick step pass her towards the staircase, than she entered the breakfast-room, and congratulated both him and herself in warm terms on the happy prospect of their nearer connection. Mr. Collins received and returned these felicitations with equal pleasure, and then proceeded to relate the particulars of their interview, with the result of which he trusted he had every reason to be satisfied, since the refusal which his cousin had stedfastly given him would naturally flow from her bashful modesty and the genuine delicacy of her character.

This information, however, startled Mrs. Bennet;—she would have been glad to be equally satisfied that her daughter had meant to encourage him by protesting against his proposals, but she dared not to believe it, and could not help saying so.

"But depend upon it, Mr. Collins," she added, "that Lizzy shall be brought to reason. I will speak to her about it myself directly. She is a very headstrong foolish girl, and does not know her own interest; but I will *make* her know it."

"Pardon me for interrupting you, Madam," cried Mr. Collins; "but if she is really headstrong and foolish, I know not whether she would altogether be a very desirable wife to a man in my situation, who naturally looks for happiness in the marriage state. If therefore she actually persists in rejecting my suit, perhaps it were better not to force her into accepting me, because if liable to such defects of temper, she could not contribute much to my felicity."

"Sir, you quite misunderstand me," said Mrs. Bennet, alarmed. "Lizzy is only headstrong in such matters as these. In every thing else she is as good natured a girl as ever lived. I will go directly to Mr. Bennet, and we shall very soon settle it with her, I am sure."

She would not give him time to reply, but hurrying instantly to her husband, called out as she entered the library,

"Oh! Mr. Bennet, you are wanted immediately; we are all in an uproar. You must come and make Lizzy marry Mr. Collins, for she vows she will not have him, and if you do not make haste he will change his mind and not have *her*."

Mr. Bennet raised his eyes from his book as she entered, and fixed them on her face with a calm unconcern which was not in the least altered by her communication.

"I have not the pleasure of understanding you," said he, when she had finished her speech. "Of what are you talking?"

"Of Mr. Collins and Lizzy. Lizzy declares she will not have Mr. Collins, and Mr. Collins begins to say that he will not have Lizzy."

"And what am I to do on the occasion?—It seems an hopeless business."

"Speak to Lizzy about it yourself. Tell her that you insist upon her marrying him."

"Let her be called down. She shall hear my opinion."

Mrs. Bennet rang the bell, and Miss Elizabeth was summoned to the library.

"Come here, child," cried her father as she appeared. "I have sent for you on an affair of importance. I understand that Mr. Collins has made you an offer of marriage. Is it true?" Elizabeth replied that it was. "Very well—and this offer of marriage you have refused?"

"I have, Sir."

"Very well. We now come to the point. Your mother insists upon your accepting it. Is not it so, Mrs. Bennet?"

"Yes, or I will never see her again."

"An unhappy alternative is before you, Elizabeth. From this day you must be a stranger to one of your parents.—Your mother will never see you again if you do *not* marry Mr. Collins, and I will never see you again if you *do*."

Lady Morgan (Sydney Owenson)

? – 1859

Lady Morgan was born Sydney Owenson in about 1776; there is some debate about the time and place of her birth but the version that she adhered to was that she was born on the Irish Sea, halfway between England and Ireland when her parents were returning to her father's native land. She led an extraordinary life: her mother died when she was young, her father was an impoverished itinerant actor, and from an early age she found it necessary to supplement the family finances. Her first career choice was to be a poet but the publication of the remarkable Poems by a Young Lady Between the Ages of 12 and 14 (1801) convinced her that the financial rewards from this form of writing were insufficient; and she became a governess. But she found time to write as well as teach and she enjoyed considerable public attention on the appearance of her novels St Clair or The Heiress of Desmond (1803) and The Novice of St Dominick (1804). It was, however, The Wild Irish Girl: A National Tale (1805) that established her reputation as a significant regional novelist. Because of the passionate way that she presented the Irish Cause she was treated with hostility by some members of the English literary elite, but she was celebrated in Ireland where her powerful blend of politics and romance proved to be extremely popular. She created a lively and influential salon in Dublin which she transferred to London after her marriage to Charles Morgan. Talented, witty, self-reliant – and very successful – she was William Thackeray's model for Becky Sharpe in Vanity Fair. Her contribution to the world of letters was finally acknowledged when she became the first woman to be granted a literary pension of £300 p.a.

*The author of approximately seventy volumes, she wrote travel documen-
taries and social histories as well as religious and philosophical exposés.
In 1840* Woman and Her Master: A History of the Female Sex from the
Earliest Period *(2 vols) was published.*

The following is an extract from O'Donnel: A National Tale, *first published
in 1814 (Irish Novelists Library, London, 1896).*

From

O'Donnel: A National Tale

CHAPTER 1

TO THE RIGHT REV. THE LORD BISHOP OF——PALACE OF——.

DEAR BISHOP,
If our most serious resolutions are sometimes broken, may we not reasonably expect forgiveness, when occasionally found wanting in the discharge
of our duties of ceremony, or engagements of etiquette? I feel that I ought
long since to have congratulated you on your advancement from your English
Rectory to an Irish See. I have done it in fact; and for forms, you know how
little I deal in them.

Since my arrival on my Irish estate, which I have now visited for the first
time, I have been deeply involved in business. The renewal of old leases,
reclamation of neglected rights, repair of highways, and restoration of all kinds
of dilapidations, both in the house and demesne (the consequence of many
years' absence and neglect), together with almost endless labouring through
the labyrinth of minor law transactions, exclusively incidental, I believe, to
Irish property, have scarcely left me breathing-time. So different is all this from
the quiet tenor of my life at Glentworth Hall, that I scarcely know myself in my
novel character. However, my affairs are now nearly brought to a close; and
though I should certainly prefer (being now in Ireland) a longer residence at
Ballynogue, in order to become better acquainted with my tenants on this side
the water, and more effectually to study their interests, yet so anxious is Lady
Singleton to be off, that I think we shall return home early in the ensuing month.
Lady Singleton, who is, as you know, a traveller by profession, wishes to return
by Scotland, in preference to retracing our steps by Holyhead. I have therefore
to beg a night's lodging at your palace for myself and family *en passant*, for I
understand the sleeping stage within a few miles of your residence is execrably
bad. But should we change our minds, and not go by Port Pa—

Dear Bishop,—Patrick, Mr. Glentworth would have written, but I have
snatched the pen from his hand, in the conviction that I shall come more
immediately to the point. I know of old, that his head is by no means *bien*

timbré[1] for this sort of negotiation: there is nobody so clever as Mr. Glentworth; but, as I used to say to poor dear Lord Singleton, men always fail when they come to details. I need not tell you how difficult it is to move Mr. Glentworth out of Derbyshire. During his twenty years' marriage with his first wife, he never (as he boasts) slept one night away from Glentworth Hall, except while he was attending Parliament: and though I have been constantly urging him since the day of our union to visit his Irish estates (for I heard there was everything to do), I never could prevail upon him, until the falling in of his leases gave him no alternative; and so—here we are.

Oh, my poor dear Bishop, what a country! What room for change and improvement! or rather what a necessity for a total upsetting of everything! I have done a little; that is, I have undone everything: but, for the present, I shall not have time to complete anything. My plans (most of them drawn out myself) have quite astonished Mr. Glentworth's Irish agent; but, as is usual among the semi-barbarous, improvement is resisted as innovation. Mr. O'Grady has an obstacle to oppose to everything I have suggested, because the old muddling system must go on for ever in the old muddling way.

There is nothing so much wanted here as a canal from Ballynogue to Dublin: I have drawn out a plan upon the Newcastle system, and——but we will talk all these things over when we meet. Now that Mr. Glentworth is here, it is quite as difficult to get him back to England as it was to induce him to leave it. We propose, however, bidding farewell to Ballynogue on or about the 18th of September; and as we shall go slowly (for we intend to travel with a set of horses we have made up since we came here), we may expect to be with you by the 21st. We left Charles Glentworth at Oxford, with your quondam pupil, Lord Boston. Our party therefore consists of Mr. G., myself, my two daughters, their governess, and five servants. Apropos of Lord B.: we met his mother, Lady Llanberis, in Wales, on her way to what I call her principality. There never was so bored a woman: though she talked in raptures of her 'native mountains,' when in London. They say she is capricious—but she has an excellent heart. She expects the Savills at Llanberis; they are amazingly intimate. What can it mean? She talks with great delight of her son; and, considering the care you took of his education, she might have done something better than placing you in a poor bishopric in the north of Ireland: however, she will do more and better in time, for her five boroughs must carry everything before them. I wish, however, you had consulted me before you accepted the See: I will not pledge myself that my brother would or could do better at present for you; but at least he would have done as well.

Farewell, my dear Bishop: we all unite in congratulations, etc.

I am just going to walk to our little town of Ballynogue, with a new friend of ours (whom we found here, and who was quite, what is vulgarly called, a Godsend)—a Mr. Dexter, an amazing safe person, quite of the right side, and with a quantity of good sense: he agrees with me in everything, but particularly on the state of this wretched country. He is settled at Ballynogue, and has promised in my absence to keep a certain watch over things here, which is a great matter. By

---

[1] Well suited.

the bye, you have no idea what a sensation I create when I go into the town of Ballynogue; for I make it a rule to enter every house *sans façon*,[2] as lady of the manor. It is a sort of feudal privilege, you know; and I go on examining, changing, correcting, and improving, according to exigencies. In fact, a radical reform is called for; and I will lend my little aid to its completion. But Mr. Glentworth remains inert; he listens and smiles, and is not a bit the more complying; so that (plan as I may) the means are still denied me to execute. Once more adieu.

Yours truly,

C. SINGLETON.

August the 28th,
Ballynogue Castle, Ballynogue.

TO THE LADY VISCOUNTESS SINGLETON, BALLYNOGUE CASTLE, BALLYNOGUE

MY DEAR MADAM,
I return your Ladyship, Mr. Glentworth, and the Misses Singleton my most unfeigned and hearty thanks for your kind congratulations on my unmerited promotion to the distinguished situation which I now unworthily hold. My elevation to the See of——took place shortly after you left our ever, by me, esteemed and regretted neighbourhood in Derbyshire. The event was unexpected, but the solicitude of my noble friends got the start of my humble desires. I trust I was contented with my former state; nor, indeed, was an Irish bishopric, with so small a revenue, and such limited patronage, an object greatly to be coveted: but I left everything to the Countess of Llanberis.

I must certainly rejoice in any circumstance which may bring your ladyship and Mr. Glentworth to this remote part of the world; and the best accommodation my poor episcopal residence (by courtesy called palace) can afford, is at your ladyship's service. The house, though old, is capacious; and you may judge that I have a tolerable number of lodging-rooms, when I inform your ladyship that at the time when I hope to have the honour of seeing your family, I expect also as my guests, Commodore and Lady Florence Grandville, their friend Mr. Vandeleur, and Colonel Percy Moclere, Lord B——'s second son, who is quartered in my neighbourhood. Commodore Grandville (with whose eldest brother, the present Earl Grandville, I was travelling when I first had the honour of meeting your ladyship and your respected late lord at Florence) is stationed off Lough Swilly. He has, I hear, taken, for the time being, a house prettily situated on the coast, and Lady Florence intends (as it is right she should) to spend the three ensuing months with him: she comes from her father's near Edinburgh; and the Commodore meets her at —— palace, to give her convoy to Lough Swilly.

Mr. Vandeleur, at one of whose unrivalled dinners in Portman Square I had the honour of meeting your ladyship, when I was last in town, is come over merely to see his friends the Grandville's; and Lady Florence wrote me word she had appointed him to meet them at my place. I sincerely rejoice, therefore, that I have something to offer your ladyship which may serve as an inducement to you and Mr. Glentworth to remain a few days under my roof;

[2] Without ceremony.

and I hope Lady Singleton will believe that I am, with every sentiment of respect, and the highest consideration,

Her Ladyship's servant and friend,

RICHARD ——.

Palace of ——,
September the 1st.
P.S.—I have been sadly oppressed with my old complaint in the chest ever since I came to Ireland. The moisture of the climate is much against me. I have, however, found relief for the present from a newly discovered medicine, a balsam I have got over from London, recommended by my friend Judge ——. I find here ample room for my little agricultural tastes, and I have a spot of ground near the palace, which I call my Pet Farm: it is, indeed, a nice thing in its way. Game is plentiful and excellent just about me; the salmon abundant and very good: but, as your ladyship observes, there is much to do to make things endurable. I hear but bad accounts of our friend the Archbishop. Poor Mrs. B——! I pity her most sincerely. If Lord —— should succeed there, for his friend, I wonder who would get Lincoln.

TO THE RIGHT REV. THE LORD BISHOP OF ——, PALACE OF ——.

D EAR BISHOP,
We have received yours of the first, and thank you for your offered hospitality. I happen to know all the party you mention particularly well, and shall be glad to meet them. How Lady Florence will get on at Lough Swilly I don't very well understand, except the officers of the Commodore's squadron go for something; however, her joining her husband is amazingly like her. She professes great respect for the *bienséances*,[3] and she is quite right: it is that which precisely draws the line. I have often told her so: and when she was doing all sorts of foolish things, a few years back, I first gave her the hint. She has not let it lie idle, and gets on amazingly well in consequence.

Mr. Vandeleur's going so far from London surprises me; for though he always lies by at the right season, I never knew him before get so completely out of the way of the world. I should like to know his real motive for this journey to Ireland. As to his friendship for Lady Florence, that is an understood thing to be merely a matter *de convenance*[4] on both sides. I don't at all agree with you that his dinners are good. He likes to *afficher*[5] the thing, I know, beyond any man in town; and any one may toady him by praising his cook, who, after all (as I told him the last day I dined with him), would at Paris be considered only fit for a tavern. We had a dispute about him that day. He sent up (in his *menu*) '*Filets à la Berri*', for the famous '*Filets de Bellevue, à la Pompadour.*' Now, when my brother went on his first embassy, we happened to have this precise dish, dressed by the son of Mad. de Pompadour's cook; for it was she that invented

---

3 Proprieties.
4 Of form, of respectability.
5 Advertise.

them for the '*petits appartements*' at Bellevue;[6] whereas the other was a thing quite obsolete, and invented by the famous Duchess of Berry for her father, the Regent, ages before.[7] I have been amazingly unpopular ever since with Mr. Vandeleur; and, indeed, I have more than once got myself into scrapes with my English friends by setting them right on subjects, of which, from the very nature and character of the country, they must be ignorant. Although, now and then, you will find things pretty fair at some of our best nobility's houses, yet upon the whole England is, on this chapter, pretty much where it was in the days of *Louis Quatorze*, whose ambassador exclaimed, on his return to Paris: 'Ah! quel pays étrange – vingt religions, et une sauce!'[8]

You used to have a good deal of *savoir* about these things yourself, at least in West India cookery. I remember, when you were travelling with Lord Grandville, you dressed for us at Florence some *pilau*, which poor dear Lord Singleton voted supreme. It was not, however, strictly West Indian; but it was a good thing in its way.

You may certainly expect us about the middle of September; Mr. Glentworth says the eighteenth; I say the twentieth. Mr. Dexter has the horses in training every day under my inspection. We have cured, between us, Mr. Glentworth's favourite mare of a disease, which Thompson, as usual, denies she ever had. You know Mr. Glentworth's way of going on for ever with his old servants, and suffering himself to be imposed on by them. I am convinced he is afraid of Thompson. What a quiet, half-alive person the late poor Mrs. Glentworth must have been! Charles is like neither of them; he is a most headstrong boy. His getting a curricle[9] was quite against my consent; for he happens to know just nothing at all about driving, and will take no hints.

Adieu, my dear Bishop—you will say I am *véritable causeuse*[10] to-day. I am, nevertheless, sincerely yours,

C. SINGLETON.

Sept. 4th,
Ballynogue Castle.

P.S.—I proposed to Mr. O'Grady to enrich the soil of the demesne with marl,[11] as we did in Derbyshire; but he at once declined the experiment: first, because it was not adapted to this soil; next, because, if it were, there is no marl-pit in the neighbourhood. How Irish! If I remained here I would carry my point, however, as I should about a road which I wanted to have proposed at the next county meeting. Mr. O'Grady says it is not to be done, unless the bog, across which I want to run it (to meet the new canal we were talking of), were drained. I told him of the artificial banks in Holland and other places; but

---

[6] Little apartments; Madame de Pompadour (1721–1764) famous mistress of Louis XV who built Bellevue for her.
[7] Duchess of Berry, the daughter of the Duke of Orleans, Regent for Louis XV, was famous for her wit and eccentricity.
[8] Ah! What a strange country – twenty religions and one sauce!
[9] Carriage.
[10] A real chatter-box.
[11] Mixture of lime and clay formerly used as a fertiliser.

he is *entête*[12] beyond everything. I must say, Mr. Glentworth bears him out in all, because he is one of his 'plain, honest, straight-forward men;' which means, you know, persons who have not the ingenuity to be rogues, if they were ever so well inclined. Adieu once more. Oh! by the bye, throw all your quackeries out of the window, and adopt my prescription, the simple, single sheet of paper laid on the chest, my old remedy, which you may remember never failed. I long to see your Pet Farm; but if you don't know the merits and property of *fiorin*[13] grass, you know nothing. *We* shall make hay at Christmas. I only heard of it this day myself, and have not yet mentioned it to Mr. Glentworth or Mr O'Grady. I am a great stickler for wooden shoes instead of the horrible *brogues*[14] they wear here. I got some made, and these miserable people will not be prevailed on to adopt them. In everything, how unlike the peasantry of France and Switzerland—at least what they were!

On the afternoon of the fourteenth of September, Mr. Glentworth, Lady Single-ton, and suite arrived before the palace gates of the Right Rev. the Bishop of——, almost at the same moment that Commodore and Lady Florence Grandville, Mr. Vandeleur, and Colonel Moclere were in the act of mounting their horses for a morning ride. While the obsequious prelate stood upon the steps of his episcopal residence, bowing out one party and bowing in the other, his guests exchanged their greetings and salutations *en passant*, with all the careless recognition with which people of the world hail people of the world, but somewhat enlivened by exclamations of surprise at the remoteness of the scene in which they had met.

'Good heavens, how extraordinary! I should as soon have expected we should have met in the deserts of Arabia.'

'Only think of a particular set from the neighbourhood of St. James's finding themselves accidentally re-assembled in the wilds of Ireland.'

'Do you know, Lady Florence, it is quite a *coup de théatre*,[15] a thing for a comedy.'

'Or a pantomime,' added the Colonel; '*hi presto popolorum!*[16] and here we are!'

''Tis quite ridiculous.'

The party then separated: the travellers to repose in their apartments after the fatigue of their journey; the loungers to pursue their morning's amusements; and the Bishop to extend his pastoral care over his Pet Farm.

CHAPTER II

THE party, thus accidentally brought together, were of that class in society vaguely designated people of fashion; and though no one individual was sufficiently distinguished to be placed at the head of his subdivision, yet were

[12] Stubborn.
[13] A type of coarse grass.
[14] Shoes of untanned hide, formerly worn in rural Ireland.
[15] A dramatic effect.
[16] Pseudo Latin, nonsense incantation.

they all so far 'fair specimens', that there could be little difficulty in determining their respective places in the arrangement of notoriety.

Mr. Glentworth alone was a variety; chance had included him in the general classification. He was a rich English commoner, and represented that best and most enlightened order in the population of the country, from which England drew her statesmen, her patriots, and her heroes in her Augustan days; and which still holds her up to the rest of the world as a nation where political liberty is best understood, and moral probity best represented. His character, firm but mild, decided but tranquil, was of an even temperature, remote from extremes. A certain constitutional indolence rendered him passive and yielding to the trivial impediments or the petty concerns of everyday life. He desired no supremacy in trifles; in essentials he admitted no influence. In the latter his actions were invariably the result of his principles; and to them he adhered with a tenacity which set opposition at defiance and made persuasion hopeless. His own life had been so prosperous, that, though he was prompt to relieve distress, he could scarcely be supposed to sympathise with misfortune; and so little had the varieties of human character been exhibited to his observation, that to their finer shades he was totally insensible; his discrimination was applied only to their extremes. The villain could not have escaped him; the rascal might have gone on imposing upon him for ever; but the candid and fair, the enlightened and liberal, would at all times have attracted his attention and challenged his respect.

Lady Singleton had been the object of his first love, when she was young and handsome; but he was then a younger brother, and ambition decided against him. This lady, with all the importance of an ambassadress, accompanied her brother, Lord B., in his successive embassies to the courts of Florence, Vienna, and Paris. Poor, though well born, her object was to make a brilliant alliance; and while her diplomatic brother was assisting at councils which were to decide the fate of nations, she was, with no less exertion of political sagacity, endeavouring to determine the destiny of Viscount Singleton, a rich and highly connected nobleman, devotedly attentive to his health, which he preserved by living abroad. Lord S. was wholly averse from the state of matrimony, but he at last embraced it, merely to rid himself of the importunities of the woman he made his wife. His property was entailed on the male heir; and he died, leaving two daughters and his widow inadequately provided for. During life his health had been his only concern, the supporting the family grandeur his only passion; and he died true to the principles in which he had lived. Lady Singleton was more than disappointed; she was mortified and indignant. She thought she must have had paramount influence over her husband, because she believed she had married a fool; and she failed, perhaps, because she was right in her conviction.

While Lady Singleton was pursuing matrimony and politics abroad, Mr. Glentworth succeeded to twenty thousand per annum, and married at home; and when, at the expiration of twenty years, both parties accidentally met, free from the respective engagements they had formed in the interim, Lady Singleton again put her political sagacity into motion, and took into consideration the scantiness of her own jointure, and the value of Mr. Glentworth's estates. At the age when she had been susceptible of preference, Mr. Glentworth had been its sole object; and interest and inclination alike combined in urging her views on the heart and hand of her former lover. Lady Singleton was a fine woman, and a diplomatist: Mr. Glentworth was an English country gentleman, who knew no more of what is called life than was to be learned during his annual attendance on parliament: the odds were of course against him; and he lost his game, even before he suspected he had been drawn in to play it.

A long session favoured her ladyship's political arrangements: she talked of old times, and old feelings returned with old remembrances, till the senses and the imagination became the dupes of memory. Time was not challenged to account for the thefts he had committed, while prepossession supplied their loss; and on the day parliament rose, Lady Singleton went down to Glentworth Hall, as the bride of its excellent master. Dissimilar in every point of character, the pair, by a happy *discordia concors*,[17] went on well together. Her fussiness was well opposed to his quietude. Her interference sometimes amused, if it occasionally annoyed him; and her judicious attention to his habits and comforts ensured his patience for her whims, his indulgence for her follies. An only son was the fruit of his first marriage; by his second he had no issue.

The force of health and high spirits had given to Lady Singleton the semblance of that energy which belongs to genuine talent alone. Habits and manners (acquired in countries where woman is called upon to take a part in all the interests of society), blended with her own constitutional activity, made of her that kind of person which the French have aptly termed '*une femme affairée*'.[18] Idle from circumstance, restless by disposition; loving indolence, yet hating quiet; she was officious without being useful, and busy without being occupied. Always struggling for authority, she spoke only to dictate, and moved only to meddle; while, in her desire for influence, she had not the tact to discern whether attention or neglect followed her counsels, or waited on her orders. To obvious contradiction, however, she was intemperately alive; and to obsequious flattery weakly susceptible: easy to dupe, but difficult to convince, she was sought for by the cunning, and avoided by the wise. Gay, dissipated, and amusing,—the giddy, the frivolous, and the inconsequent found their account in her society; and her foreign connections, knowledge of the world, and (more than all else) the immense size of her house in town, gave her a distinguished place in the circle of fashion.

One eminent person in a family generally produces a proportionate degree of mediocrity in the succeeding members: and extraordinarily clever mothers do not always produce extraordinarily clever daughters. The Honourable Caroline and the Honourable Horatia Singleton were as vapid and as dull as their mamma was animated and sagacious. Destitute of common intelligence, they were overburthened with accomplishments; but, old enough to take their parts in society among the *corps de ballet* of exhibited young ladies, they were kept in the background, on some principle which maternal wisdom had not chosen to

17 Harmony by discord.
18 A busy woman, a busybody.

divulge to them: and to this wisdom, which was feared without being respected, they bowed implicitly,—submissive, but not resigned.

The Honorable Misses Singleton belonged to a large class of young ladies to be found in almost all societies, who have for their prototype that intelligent young lady of other times, who wrote to the *Spectator*[19] to inquire whether 'dimple' was spelled with two *p*s. Their minds had never elaborated a query more important, or admitted a doubt more abstruse. No lowly consciousness of their own unimportance disturbed the confidence of their self-sufficiency. Dull and giddy, conceited and flippant, they sneered, winked, and whispered to each other their contempt of all who were excluded from their own little mysteries; of all whom they had been taught to regard as inferior, or to laugh at as quizzical. But the person whom they held in most thorough contempt was their governess, by whom, it must be confessed, they were seldom instructed, though they were sometimes entertained. Passiveness, and seeming inanity, with some other prominent points in her character favourable to their turn for a sort of maudlin ridicule, rendered her the perpetual object of their derision. To their attempts at ridicule, however, this lady, if she felt them, never replied, when alone with her pupils in their study; but when, in the presence of others, they endeavoured to show off their 'pretty wit' at her expense, she had the art, or the artlessness (it was impossible to say which), by some unexpected look or word, to throw them into situations ludicrous beyond their power to extricate themselves; and then they wondered how a person, whom mamma called '*bête*,'[20] should blunder upon such things, and make them feel so uncomfortable. Still, however, they did not complain, lest they should get somebody in her place less indulgent, less facile, and (as they expressed it) less quizzical than herself.

This governess, who was half Irish, half foreign, had passed the first fourteen years of her life in Ireland and the last ten in Italy, and was the only person who had ever retained a similar situation in Lady Singleton's family beyond the first six months. She had now held her post for nearly a year, and stood indebted, not to her merits, but to her deficiencies, for the circumstance.

When Lady Singleton was engaging her, a few weeks after her arrival in England, she observed that she did not want a governess to meddle with the education of her daughters further than as she directed; that she did not particularly desire to bring into her family *une illustre malheureuse*,[21] blessed with fine talents and superfine feelings; nor did she require a governess to outdress herself and her daughters, to play the agreeable, and to make one of her society. To each clause of these stipulations implicit assent had been given by the submissive duenna. 'In short, Miss O'Halloran,' continued her ladyship, 'my daughters do not now want a governess so much as a companion, and my object in engaging you is, that I am told you speak "*La lingua Toscana, nella bocca Romana.*"[22] Not that I quite think so myself, for your *u* is French; how—ever, I know nobody that speaks it better, and therefore I take you, and, *par*

[19] Popular weekly paper of the early eighteenth century.
[20] Stupid.
[21] A well-bred misfit.
[22] Literally, the Italian tongue in a Roman mouth; the most authentic sort of Italian.

consequence,[23] we must have nothing but Italian: French always goes on, one does not know how; but observe, we must have none of your Doric English.[24] Your brogue[25] is as pure as if you only left Ireland yesterday; as indeed has always been the case with every Irish person I ever met on the Continent.'

Miss O'Halloran had not hitherto violated this treaty; and the result of her docility and implicit obedience was that Lady Singleton said she was '*bête*', and the young ladies believed it.

Though all governesses are interesting by prescriptive right, yet Miss O'Halloran had so wholly neglected her privilege that Lady Singleton and her daughters had as little to fear from her attractions as to expect from her resistance: she had, however, a youthfulness of appearance which is sometimes deemed beauty in itself, but this juvenile air was counteracted by inertness and indolence of motion. The abruptness of her manner might, perhaps, under the influence of prepossession, have passed for *naïveté*, had it not always been followed by a certain vacancy of countenance, which changed the promised charm into an actual defect; while her smiles, which were 'few and far between', alone threw a ray of intelligence over her features, and seemed to struggle with their own acuteness lest they should shame the stupor of her vacant eye. Either from a sense of her situation, a most arduous one, or from natural gravity, her conduct was distinguished by reserve almost amounting to sullenness, and yet she had the habit of bursting into an abrupt laugh whenever circumstances called upon her risible faculties; this she did, 'not wisely, but too well,' for her laugh, though always ill-timed, was ever well-directed. Lady Singleton had in vain rebuked her for this obedience to a natural impulse: nature was more powerful than her ladyship; but as this was evidently a fault beyond cure, Lady Singleton contented herself by telling every one who witnessed the incorrigible propensity that the girl was *rieuse par constitution*;[26] and having no other fault to find with her, she thought it a pity to part with her for that. For the rest, Miss O'Halloran was a mere dead letter in the splendid volume of society with which she was accidentally bound up, and she has only obtained her place in this *catalogue raisonnée*[27] from the accident of association.

Commodore the Honourable Augustus Grandville was a brave, thoughtless, good-natured sea officer, destitute of domestic feelings and domestic habits; he admired his wife as a fine woman (for which reason he had married her), and confided in her as a heartless one, for he knew her cold, and believed her prudent. He loved his only son passionately, because he had nothing else to love: being almost always on service, he considered his ship as his home, and on shore felt himself only a visitor.

Lady Florence Grandville was a woman of fashion by *état*,[28] an observer of the decencies by profession, and a coquette by every charter, right, and

---

[23] Therefore.
[24] Substandard, rural dialect.
[25] Irish accent.
[26] Naturally inclined to laughing.
[27] Systematic catalogue.
[28] Rank, social status.

privilege with which nature, circumstances, and education could endow her: like the glow-worm, shining without heat, at once vain and insensible, she was not to be misled by fancy or committed by passion; as a wife and a mother she was attentive without being affectionate, and gave to her family only what the superfluities of self-gratification could spare. With some reputation for being brilliant, or at least attractive in conversation, she had in fact but just sufficient intelligence to lead her to the means by which her own views could be best effected; and she had early discovered the secret of purchasing, by well-directed bribes to the vanity of others, that distinction indispensably necessary to her own. The men who followed her were unconscious of the lure which led them, and knew not that they were less attracted by the admiration they felt for her than by the self-love flattered in themselves.

A French philosopher, in a metaphysical work (a French philosopher only would think of mingling love with metaphysics), has declared a platonic love to be the only love for a rich *desoeuvré*;[29] and a coquette the only mistress—'*Et pour ce dernier, une coquette est une maitresse delicieuse,*'[30] he observes. Tried by this rule, Lady Florence Grandville was the fittest person in the world to be the platonic friend of Mr. Vandeleur: such in fact she was.

Mr. Vandeleur was English by birth and education, Dutch by descent, dull by nature, rich by inheritance, and gallant by assumption. Labouring under the embarrassment of his opulence, which no extravagance of youth or of passion had decreased, he sought to extricate himself from his difficulties by a boundless indulgence in his dominant propensity. *Gourmand*[31] by habit, he became by principle

'Un véritable Amphitryon:'[32]

and the science of his dinners obtained him notoriety in London, where such science boasts disciples as numerous and distinguished as any in the range of human acquirement. It also obtained for him the notice of Lady Florence Grandville, whose bon-ton gave the finish to his rising fashion, and who admitted him into the legion of her 'thousand and one' friends on the merits of his entertainments. Time, habit, and an unsuccessful winter's campaign, favoured his promotion: from being an '*amant de parade,*'[33] he became a friend by profession. Lady Florence afforded him her attention, without according him her preference; and he continued to follow in a kind of blind but tranquil devotion, which passion had never disturbed, nor had love exalted; he was at once the most obsequious and most indifferent of men.

The Honourable Colonel Percy Moclere was a 'young man upon town whom everybody knew.' To give some little distinction to a character which

[29] Person of leisure.
[30] And for the latter, a flirt is a delightful mistress.
[31] Glutton.
[32] A real Amphitryon, a good host.
[33] A lover for show.

naturally had none, he affected the subordinate and innocent, but tiresome, branch of ridicule called quizzing;[34] and as some excellence in that art can be worked out of the smallest possible quantity of ideas which can go to the formation of a human mind, there was no insuperable bar to the success of his attempts.

Such was the party which a six o'clock dinner-bell summoned, and re-united at the well-furnished table of the Bishop.

The soups and fish were scarcely removed, and something like conversation was beginning to circulate, by Lady Singleton's attacking Mr. Vandeleur on the subject of his cook's want of science, when one of Mr. Glentworth's servants approached her ladyship, and delivered a message in a low voice. 'Oh, very well,' she replied. 'Edwards, go and see if you can be of any assistance to Mr. Dexter; tell him dinner has been served up some time;' then, turning to the Bishop, she added, 'Oh, my dear Bishop, I entirely forgot to mention that our friend Mr. Dexter accompanies us, and that I must beg you will extend your hospitality to him.'

The Bishop returned a 'neat and appropriate speech,' expressive of the pleasure he must feel in receiving any friend of her ladyship's; and Lady Singleton continued, interrupting something that Mr. Glentworth intended to say—

'I can assure you, Bishop, you will like Mr. Dexter of all things: he is an extremely sensible and obliging person, of the right way of thinking, and plays all sorts of games. He offered to accompany us as far as Donaghadee, merely to be of use to us on the road; for he says 'tis impossible to guard against imposition on Irish roads except one has been long resident in the country, which is his case; and he knows exactly how to deal with the people. He is our purse-bearer; but, further than that, I am pretty equal myself to all the exigencies of a journey in any country.'

Mr. Glentworth smiled, and said, 'I am sure, my dear, I wish that in the present instance you had relied upon your own abilities, and not taken advantage of Mr. Dexter's civil and accommodating disposition. I protested from the first starting of the project against bringing a man such a distance, merely to be of use to us, when it must, undoubtedly, be a great inconvenience to himself.'

'Oh, but then, my dear Mr. Glentworth, you know you oppose every scheme in the first blush of its proposal.'

'But where has this gallant convoy been detained,' asked Lady Florence, 'that he has suffered his charge to come on without his protection?'

'Why,' said Lady Singleton, 'he was so obliging as to ride back to the last stage, for a very valuable paper which I left behind in my reticule; a draft of the plan and elevation of an aqueduct for Ballynogue, and a drawing of my Lancasterian schoolhouses.'

'Does this Mr. Dexter live in the world?' asked Lady Florence.

Before the question could be answered, the subject of the conversation entered, with an air of effrontery rather than ease. He was a spruce, smart, dapper

[34] Teasing.

person, and received the Bishop's welcome with a jerking bow, as obsequious as it was inelegant.

'Here, Mr. Dexter, cried Lady Singleton, 'here is a seat between Lady Florence Grandville and me.'

Mr. Dexter smirked and smiled, and wriggled to his chair, then rose, and bowed profoundly, as he received the honour of presentation to his noble and distinguished neighbour; and, while his soup was preparing at the sideboard, he presented Lady Singleton's reticule, observing, in an affected tone of voice,—

'I have had the good fortune to recover your ladyship's valuable—or, indeed, I should say, invaluable, drawings; not, however, till I had recourse to some little artifice when threats failed; for, after all, you must ever meet the lower Irish with their own cunning. I know them well; and I am sure your la'ship would be much amused if you knew the little stratagem I had recourse to.'

'*Politique aux choux et aux raves*,[35] eh! Mr. Dexter?' said Lady Singleton, laughing.

'Critically, Lady Singleton,' said Mr. Dexter, with the air of one who really understood what she said.

'Well, but do let us hear, Mr. Dexter; I should like amazingly to know what use they could make of such drawings.'

'That is exactly what I said, ma'am, to the innkeeper; and, to tell the truth, the moment I saw the sign of St Patrick over his door, I—but oh! Lady Singleton, such an affecting sight as I beheld since!!—the state of this country is too deplorable. A poor old woman, scarcely able to crawl!—such a venerable countenance, too! seated weeping on the side of a ditch. I alighted, and inquired into the cause of her affliction, offering to carry her behind me to the next village. Poor soul! her little story was short and sad. She had been stopped, and ill-treated, and robbed, by a rebel.'[36]

'A rebel!' repeated the Bishop, 'God bless me!'

'Yes, my lord, a rebel. The wretch took from her, her little tobacco, and her poor snuff-box; what further he would have done I will not presume to say, but that I appeared in view. Government, it must be owned, is obstinately lenient, and strangely blind to the internal state of this unhappy country. The lower orders are ripe, at this moment, for rebellion; and even the public roads are unsafe, except one goes in a kind of caravan, as I may say.'

'Well, I must confess,' observed Mr. Glentworth, 'that I do not agree with you, Mr. Dexter, in this instance. The common people about and on my estate seem thinking of anything, poor people, but rebellion; and as for the roads we have lately passed through, I would ride back alone, as far as we have come, without the smallest apprehension.'

'I can very well understand, Mr. Glentworth, that you do not, and indeed ought not, to agree with me on this subject, for you must and ought, naturally,

[35] Cabbage and celery.

[36] In some of the Dublin prints this is a general epithet for all sorts of criminals. A few days previously to the writing of this note, it appeared in a morning paper, that a *rebel* had fired at a soldier, but, happily, the *rebel* missed his aim. This note was written in 1814 [Lady Morgan's note.]

to judge of the rest of the country by your own flourishing estate, and your town of Ballynogue (for I may well call it yours), where, by your extraordinary liberality and benevolence to your tenants, and the unexampled activity and spirit of reform which my Lady Singleton has——'

'Nay, we must cry for quarter, Mr. Dexter,' interrupted Mr. Glentworth, laughing.

'I believe, however,' said the Bishop, 'Mr. Dexter is quite right, generally speaking, with respect to the real state of this country, for a clergyman in my diocese gives pretty much the same account, and he has some right to know, for he acts in his district and parish, in the three capacities, civil, military, and clerical.'

'My lord, I am highly flattered by your lordship's condescension in agreeing with me upon any subject, and, after all, who better than your lordship should know the real state of things in this unfortunate country, particularly that part of it in which your lordship holds so distinguished and so sacred a situation? But I must be permitted to say, Mr. Glentworth, that all great English landholders have not your confidence, on first coming to this country; indeed, so much is the case the contrary, that a young gentleman, a friend of mine, who has an immensely fine estate in Leinster, and who for the first time came from England to visit it last summer, had the precaution to apply in Dublin for a guard of soldiers to protect him on the journey. Strange, however, to say, he was refused, and he had then recourse to a simpler means of protection: he engaged a celebrated piper, and made him play the whole way before him on the dickey-box,[37] wishing to try conciliation, and being well aware that the lower Irish are addicted to music, and that sort of idle things—and——'

Here Mr. Dexter was interrupted by Miss O'Halloran's bursting into a violent fit of laughter, in which she was joined by every one at table except Lady Singleton; for Mr. Dexter, not to be discountenanced by any event, joined the laughers himself, until, observing the displeasure of Lady Singleton's countenance, he abruptly composed his own, and with great gravity asked her to take wine.

Lady Singleton threw a look at her governess, and murmured 'bête!' Mr. Glentworth endeavoured to give another turn to the conversation; and Mr. Dexter addressed himself to Lady Florence, who, though she affected to give him a flattering and undivided attention, threw a sly glance of quizzing intelligence at the colonel, who was only waiting for his moment.

Meantime Mr. Vandeleur had stood up to dress his salad at the sideboard, calling for trenchers[38] and wooden spoons, and accusing the Bishop of being not orthodox, because he profaned his endive and cos[39] with china and plate.

When the ladies withdrew, Mr. Dexter and the Bishop renewed the subject of Irish affairs; for the Bishop was a timid man, and Mr. Dexter soon discovered that fact. So far as Mr. Dexter stood himself related, or in any way connected

[37] The driver's seat of a carriage.
[38] Wooden dishes.
[39] A type of lettuce.

with Ireland, it is sufficient to say, that he lived by the country he reviled, like the noxious weed that preys on the stately ruin out of which it draws its existence.

The gentlemen broke up early; the Commodore accompanied Mr. Dexter to the stable, he having told Mr. Glentworth that he would just take a peep at his favourite mare, before she was done up for the night. The rest of the gentlemen proceeded to the drawing-room.

'I wonder who this quiz of a person is,' said the Colonel, addressing Mr. Vandeleur, 'that Lady Singleton has picked up?'

'I don't know at all,' yawned Mr. Vandeleur; 'but I rather patronise any one who makes the *frais*[40] of conversation after dinner, and saves one the trouble of talking. I have a theory that silence aids digestion.'

'Pray, Mr. Glentworth,' said the Bishop, 'is Mr. Dexter an Irishman?'

'I have not the least idea, Bishop. Lady Singleton can tell you more of him than I can: my acquaintance with him was quite accidental. Riding into Ballynogue one day, my whip broke in the market-place: a gentleman perceiving it, stepped up, offered me his, and insisted on taking mine to mend. The next day he called at the Castle with it. We asked him to dinner, and—here he is. Lady S. has found him extremely useful and good-natured. He has kept our table in game, and been very attentive to a mare of mine, whom he cured of a vice, which, indeed, I never suspected she had, till Mr. Dexter found it out. I understand he is a man of small but independent fortune, and has accepted an appointment in the revenue, in our district, merely to have something to do.'

'Upon my word,' said the Bishop, 'he appears to me to be a very sensible, intelligent man, and of a very right way of thinking.'

'Indeed I believe he is,' returned Mr. Glentworth, smiling; 'and I have but one fault to find with him. He makes his responses so loud at our little church at Ballynogue, that he puts out the clerk, and disturbs the congregation.'

The gentlemen had now reached the drawing-room, and coffee was served. Shortly after a bell rang for evening prayers; but no one followed his lordship to the chapel except Mr. Dexter, and (by Lady Singleton's desire) the Misses Singleton and their governess.

---

[40] Expenditure, effort.

Frances Trollope

1780 – 1863

Frances Trollope (1779–1863) was the daughter of a clergyman; she married a barrister in 1809 and settled first in London and then on a farm in Harrow. She had seven children, including the novelist Anthony Trollope. When nearly fifty she was led by her husband's financial difficulties to seek means of support for herself and family. In 1827 with three of her children she travelled to America to investigate Frances Wright's settlement for emancipated slaves in Tennessee. Disliking the place, she soon left for Cincinnati where she opened a shop which failed. Returning to England desperate for money, Frances Trollope began her writing career with her impressions of America, Domestic Manners of the Americans. Her crusty criticism annoyed American readers but pleased the English and the book proved a great success. For the rest of her life, thirty-four novels – including the first anti-slavery novel – and five more travel books provided a comfortable living.

   The following extract is taken from The Domestic Manners of the Americans (Herbert Van Thal (ed.), Folio Society, London, 1974)

From

The Domestic Manners of the Americans

CHAPTER VI

SERVANTS—SOCIETY—EVENING PARTIES

THE greatest difficulty in organizing a family establishment in Ohio, is getting servants, or, as it is there called, 'getting help', for it is more than petty treason to the Republic, to call a free citizen a *servant*. The whole class of young women, whose bread depends upon their labour, are taught to believe that the most abject poverty is preferable to domestic service. Hundreds of half-naked girls work in the paper-mills, or in any other manufactory, for less than half the wages they would receive in service; but they think their equality is compromised by the latter, and nothing but the wish to obtain some particular article of finery will ever induce them to submit to it. A kind friend, however, exerted herself so effectually for me, that a tall stately lass soon presented herself, saying, 'I be come to help you'. The intelligence was very agreeable, and I welcomed her in the most gracious manner possible, and asked what I should give her by the year.

'Oh Gimini!' exclaimed the damsel, with a loud laugh, 'you be a downright Englisher, sure enough. I should like to see a young lady engage by the year in America! I hope I shall get a husband before many months, or I expect I shall be an outright old maid, for I be most seventeen already; besides, mayhap I may want to go to school. You must just give me a dollar and half a week, and mother's slave, Phillis, must come over once a week, I expect, from t'other side the water, to help me clean.'

I agreed to the bargain, of course, with all dutiful submission; and seeing she was preparing to set to work in a yellow dress parsemé with red roses, I gently hinted, that I thought it was a pity to spoil so fine a gown, and that she had better change it.

''Tis just my best and my worst,' she answered, 'for I've got no other.'

And in truth, I found that this young lady had left the paternal mansion with no more clothes of any kind than what she had on. I immediately gave her money to purchase what was necessary for cleanliness and decency, and set to work with my daughters to make her a gown. She grinned applause when our labour was completed, but never uttered the slightest expression of gratitude for that, or for any thing else we could do for her. She was constantly asking us to lend her different articles of dress, and when we declined it, she said, 'Well, I never seed such grumpy folks as you be; there is several young ladies of my acquaintance what goes to live out now and then with the old women about the town, and they and their gurls always lends them what they asks for; I guess you Inglish thinks we should poison your things, just as bad as if we was Negurs.' And here I beg to assure the reader, that whenever I give conversations they were not made *à loisir*,[1] but were written down immediately after they occurred, with all the verbal fidelity my memory permitted.

This young lady left me at the end of two months, because I refused to lend her money enough to buy a silk dress to go to a ball, saying, 'Then, 'tis not worth my while to stay any longer.'

I cannot imagine it possible that such a state of things can be desirable, or beneficial to any of the parties concerned. I might occupy a hundred pages on the subject, and yet fail to give an adequate idea of the sore, angry, ever wakeful pride that seemed to torment these poor wretches. In many of them it was so excessive, that all feeling of displeasure, or even of ridicule, was lost in pity. One of these was a pretty girl, whose natural disposition must have been gentle and kind; but her good feelings were soured, and her gentleness turned to morbid sensitiveness, by having heard a thousand and a thousand times that she was as good as any other lady, that all men were equal, and women too, and that it was a sin and a shame for a free-born American to be treated like a servant.

When she found she was to dine in the kitchen, she turned up her pretty lip, and said, 'I guess that's 'cause you don't think I'm good enough to eat with you. You'll find that won't do here.' I found afterwards that she rarely ate any dinner at all, and generally passed the time in tears. I did every thing in my power to conciliate and make her happy, but I am sure she hated me. I gave her

[1] At leisure.

very high wages, and she staid till she had obtained several expensive articles of dress, and then, *un beau matin*,[2] she came to me full dressed, and said, 'I must go.' 'When shall you return, Charlotte?' 'I expect you'll see no more of me.' And so we parted. Her sister was also living with me, but her wardrobe was not yet completed, and she remained some weeks longer, till it was.

I fear it may be called bad taste to say so much concerning my domestics, but, nevertheless, the circumstances are so characteristic of America that I must recount another history relating to them. A few days after the departure of my ambitious belle, my cries for 'Help' had been so effectual that another young lady presented herself, with the usual preface 'I'm come to help you.' I had been cautioned never to ask for a reference for character, as it would not only rob me of that help, but entirely prevent my ever getting another; so, five minutes after she entered she was installed, bundle and all, as a member of the family. She was by no means handsome, but there was an air of simple frankness in her manner that won us all. For my own part, I thought I had got a second Jeanie Deans,[3] for she recounted to me histories of her early youth, wherein her plain good sense and strong mind had enabled her to win her way through a host of cruel step-mothers, faithless lovers, and cheating brothers. Among other things, she told me, with the appearance of much emotion, that she had found, since she came to town, a cure for all her sorrows, 'Thanks and praise for it, I have got religion!' and then she asked if I would spare her to go to Meeting every Tuesday and Thursday evening; 'You shall not have to want me, Mrs Trollope, for our minister knows that we have all our duties to perform to man, as well as to God, and he makes the Meeting late in the evening that they may not cross one another.' Who could refuse? Not I, and Nancy had leave to go to Meeting two evenings in the week, besides Sundays.

One night, that the mosquitoes had found their way under my net, and prevented my sleeping, I heard some one enter the house very late; I got up, went to the top of the stairs, and, by the help of a bright moon, recognized Nancy's best bonnet. I called to her; 'You are very late,' said I, 'what is the reason for it?' 'Oh, Mrs Trollope,' she replied, 'I am late, indeed! We have this night had seventeen souls added to our flock. May they live to bless this night! But it has been a long sitting, and very warm; I'll just take a drink of water, and get to bed; you shan't find me later in the morning for it.' Nor did I. She was an excellent servant, and performed more than was expected from her; moreover, she always found time to read the Bible several times in the day, and I seldom saw her occupied about any thing without observing that she had placed it near her.

At last she fell sick with the cholera, and her life was despaired of. I nursed her with great care, and sat up the greatest part of two nights with her. She was often delirious, and all her wandering thoughts seemed to ramble to heaven. 'I have been a sinner,' she said, 'but I am safe in the Lord Jesus.' When she recovered, she asked me to let her go into the country for a few days, to change the air, and begged me to lend her three dollars.

[2] One fine morning.
[3] A reference to the self-reliant and sensible heroine of Walter Scott's *The Heart of Midlothian*.

While she was absent a lady called on me, and enquired, with some agitation, if my servant, Nancy Fletcher, were at home. I replied that she was gone into the country. 'Thank God,' she exclaimed, 'never let her enter your doors again, she is the most abandoned woman in the town: a gentleman who knows you, has been told that she lives with you, and that she boasts of having the power of entering your house at any hour of the night.' She told many other circumstances, unnecessary to repeat, but all tending to prove that she was a very dangerous inmate.

I expected her home the next evening, and I believe I passed the interval in meditating how to get rid of her without an *eclaircissement*. At length she arrived, and all my study having failed to supply me with any other reason than the real one for dismissing her, I stated it at once. Not the slightest change passed over her countenance, but she looked steadily at me, and said, in a very civil tone, 'I should like to know who told you.' I replied that it could be of no advantage to her to know, and that I wished her to go immediately. 'I am ready to go,' she said, in the same quiet tone, 'but what will you do for your three dollars?' 'I must do without them, Nancy; good morning to you.' 'I must just put up my things,' she said, and left the room. About half an hour afterwards, when we were all assembled at dinner, she entered with her usual civil composed air. 'Well, I am come to wish you all good bye,' and with a friendly good-humoured smile she left us.

This adventure frightened me so heartily, that, notwithstanding I had the dread of cooking my own dinner before my eyes, I would not take any more young ladies into my family without receiving some slight sketch of their former history. At length I met with a very worthy French woman, and soon after with a tidy English girl to assist her; and I had the good fortune to keep them till a short time before my departure: so, happily, I have no more misfortunes of this nature to relate.

Such being the difficulties respecting domestic arrangements, it is obvious, that the ladies who are brought up amongst them cannot have leisure for any great development of the mind: it is, in fact, out of the question; and, remembering this, it is more surprising that some among them should be very pleasing, than that none should be highly instructed.

Had I passed as many evenings in company in any other town that I ever visited as I did in Cincinnati, I should have been able to give some little account of the conversations I had listened to; but, upon reading over my notes, and then taxing my memory to the utmost to supply the deficiency, I can scarcely find a trace of any thing that deserves the name. Such as I have, shall be given in their place. But, whatever may be the talents of the persons who meet together in society, the very shape, form, and arrangement of the meeting is sufficient to paralyse conversation. The women invariably herd together at one part of the room, and the men at the other; but, in justice to Cincinnati, I must acknowledge that this arrangement is by no means peculiar to that city, or to the western side of the Alleghanies. Sometimes a small attempt at music produces a partial reunion; a few of the most daring youths, animated by the consciousness of curled hair and smart waistcoats, approach the piano-forte, and begin to mutter a little to the half-grown pretty things, who are comparing with one another 'how many quarters' music they have had'. Where the mansion is of sufficient dignity to have two drawing-rooms, the piano, the little ladies, and the slender gentlemen are left to themselves, and on such occasions the sound of laughter is often heard to issue from among them. But the fate of the more dignified personages, who are left in the other room, is extremely dismal. The gentlemen spit, talk of elections and the price of produce, and spit again. The ladies look at each other's dresses till they know every pin by heart; talk of Parson Somebody's last sermon on the day of judgment, on Dr T'otherbody's new pills for dyspepsia, till the 'tea' is announced, when they all console themselves together for whatever they may have suffered in keeping awake, by taking more tea, coffee, hot cake and custard, hoe cake, johnny cake, waffle cake and dodger cake, pickled peaches, and preserved cucumbers, ham, turkey, hung beef, apple sauce, and pickled oysters than ever were prepared in any other country in the known world. After this massive meal is over, they return to the drawing-room, and it always appeared to me that they remained together as long as they could bear it, and then they rise *en masse*, cloak, bonnet, shawl, and exit.

CHAPTER X

REMOVAL TO THE COUNTRY—WALK IN THE FOREST—EQUALITY[4]

AT length my wish of obtaining a house in the country was gratified. A very pretty cottage, the residence of a gentleman who was removing into town, for the convenience of his business as a lawyer, was to let, and I immediately secured it. It was situated in a little village about a mile and a half from the town, close to the foot of the hills formerly mentioned as the northern boundary of it. We found ourselves much more comfortable here than in the city. The house was pretty and commodious, our sitting-rooms were cool and airy; we had got rid of the detestable mosquitoes, and we had an ice-house that never failed. Besides all this, we had the pleasure of gathering our tomatoes from our own garden, and receiving our milk from our own cow. Our manner of life was infinitely more to my taste than before; it gave us all the privileges of rusticity, which are fully as incompatible with a residence in a little town of Western America as with a residence in London. We lived on terms of primaeval intimacy with our cow, for if we lay down on our lawn she did not scruple to take a sniff at the book we were reading, but then she gave us her own sweet breath in return. The verge of the cool-looking forest that rose opposite our windows was so near, that we often used it as an extra drawing-room, and there was no one to wonder if we went out with no other preparation than our parasols, carrying books and work enough to while away a long summer day in the shade; the meadow that divided us from it was covered with a fine short grass, that continued for a little way under the trees, making a beautiful carpet, while sundry logs and stumps furnished our sofas and

[4] Mrs Trollope was at this time in the neighbourhood of Cincinnati.

tables. But even this was not enough to satisfy us when we first escaped from the city, and we determined upon having a day's enjoyment of the wildest forest scenery we could find. So we packed up books, albums, pencils, and sandwiches, and, despite a burning sun, dragged up a hill so steep that we sometimes fancied we could rest ourselves against it by only leaning forward a little. In panting and in groaning we reached the top, hoping to be refreshed by the purest breath of heaven; but to have tasted the breath of heaven we must have climbed yet farther, even to the tops of the trees themselves, for we soon found that the air beneath them stirred not, nor ever had stirred, as it seemed to us, since first it settled there, so heavily did it weigh upon our lungs.

Still we were determined to enjoy ourselves, and forward we went, crunching knee deep through aboriginal leaves, hoping to reach some spot less perfectly air-tight than our landing-place. Wearied with the fruitless search, we decided on reposing awhile on the trunk of a fallen tree; being all considerably exhausted, the idea of sitting down on this tempting log was conceived and executed simultaneously by the whole party, and the whole party sunk together through its treacherous surface into a mass of rotten rubbish that had formed part of the pith and marrow of the eternal forest a hundred years before.

We were by no means the only sufferers by the accident; frogs, lizards, locusts, katiedids, beetles, and hornets, had the whole of their various tenements disturbed, and testified their displeasure very naturally by annoying us as much as possible in return; we were bit, we were stung, we were scratched; and when, at last, we succeeded in raising ourselves from the venerable ruin, we presented as woeful a spectacle as can well be imagined. We shook our (not ambrosial) garments, and panting with heat, stings, and vexation, moved a few paces from the scene of our misfortune, and again sat down; but this time it was upon the solid earth.

We had no sooner began to 'chew the cud' of the bitter fancy that had beguiled us to these mountain solitudes than a new annoyance assailed us. A cloud of mosquitoes gathered round, and while each sharp proboscis sucked our blood, they teased us with their humming chorus, till we lost all patience, and started again on our feet, pretty firmly resolved never to try the *al fresco* joys of an American forest again. The sun was now in its meridian splendour, but our homeward path was short, and down hill, so again packing up our preparations for felicity, we started homeward, or, more properly speaking, we started, for in looking for an agreeable spot in this dungeon forest we had advanced so far from the verge of the hill that we had lost all trace of the precise spot where we had entered it. Nothing was to be seen but multitudes of tall, slender, melancholy stems, as like as peas, and standing within a foot of each other. The ground, as far as the eye could reach (which certainly was not far), was covered with an unvaried bed of dried leaves; no trace, no track, no trail, as Mr Cooper would call it,[5] gave us a hint which way to turn; and having paused for a moment to meditate, we remembered that chance must decide for us at last, so we set

[5] A reference to the descriptions of early America in the novels of Fenimore Cooper being published at this time.

forward, in no very good mood, to encounter new misfortunes. We walked about a quarter of a mile, and coming to a steep descent, we thought ourselves extremely fortunate, and began to scramble down, nothing doubting that it was the same we had scrambled up. In truth, nothing could be more like, but alas! things that are like are not the same; when we had slipped and stumbled down to the edge of the wood, and were able to look beyond it, we saw no pretty cottage with the shadows of its beautiful acacias coming forward to meet us: all was different; and, what was worse, all was distant from the spot where we had hoped to be. We had come down the opposite side of the ridge, and had now to win our weary way a distance of three miles round its base. I believe we shall none of us ever forget that walk. The bright, glowing, furnace-like heat of the atmosphere seems to scorch as I recall it. It was painful to tread, it was painful to breathe, it was painful to look round; every object glowed with the reflection of the fierce tyrant that glared upon us from above.

We got home alive, which agreeably surprised us; and when our parched tongues again found power of utterance, we promised each other faithfully never to propose any more parties of pleasure in the grim stove-like forests of Ohio.

We were now in daily expectation of the arrival of Mr T.; but day after day, and week after week passed by, till we began to fear some untoward circumstance might delay his coming till the Spring; at last, when we had almost ceased to look out for him, on the road which led from the town, he arrived, late at night, by that which leads across the country from Pittsburgh. The pleasure we felt at seeing him was greatly increased by his bringing with him our eldest son, which was a happiness we had not hoped for. Our walks and our drives now became doubly interesting. The young men, fresh from a public school, found America so totally unlike all the nations with which their reading had made them acquainted, that it was indeed a new world to them. Had they visited Greece or Rome they would have encountered objects with whose images their minds had been long acquainted; or had they travelled to France or Italy they would have seen only what daily conversation had already rendered familiar; but at our public schools America (except perhaps as to her geographical position) is hardly better known than Fairy Land; and the American character has not been much more deeply studied than that of the Anthropophagi;[6] all, therefore, was new, and every thing amusing.

The extraordinary familiarity of our poor neighbours startled us at first, and we hardly knew how to receive their uncouth advances, or what was expected of us in return; however, it sometimes produced very laughable scenes. Upon one occasion two of my children set off upon an exploring walk up the hills; they were absent rather longer than we expected, and the rest of our party determined upon going out to meet them; we knew the direction they had taken, but thought it would be as well to enquire at a little public-house at the bottom of the hill, if such a pair had been seen to pass. A woman, whose appearance more resembled a Covent Garden market-woman than any thing else I can remember, came out and answered my question with the most jovial good humour in the affirmative,

[6] Legendary cannibals.

and prepared to join us in our search. Her look, her voice, her manner, were so exceedingly coarse and vehement, that she almost frightened me; she passed her arm within mine, and to the inexpressible amusement of my young people, she dragged me on, talking and questioning me without ceasing. She lived but a short distance from us, and I am sure intended to be a very good neighbour; but her violent intimacy made me dread to pass her door; my children, including my sons, she always addressed by their Christian names, excepting when she substituted the word 'honey'; this familiarity of address, however, I afterwards found was universal throughout all ranks in the United States.

My general appellation amongst my neighbours was 'the English old woman', but in mentioning each other they constantly employed the term 'lady'; and they evidently had a pleasure in using it, for I repeatedly observed, that in speaking of a neighbour, instead of saying Mrs Such-a-one, they described her as 'the lady over the way what takes in washing', or as 'that there lady, out by the Gulley, what is making dip-candles'. Mr Trollope was as constantly called 'the old man', while draymen, butchers' boys, and the labourers on the canal were invariably denominated 'them gentlemen'; nay, we once saw one of the most gentlemanlike men in Cincinnati introduce a fellow in dirty shirt sleeves, and all sorts of detestable et cetera, to one of his friends, with this formula, 'D---- let me introduce this gentleman to you.'

Our respective titles certainly were not very important; but the eternal shaking hands with these ladies and gentlemen was really an annoyance, and the more so, as the near approach of the gentlemen was always redolent of whiskey and tobacco.

But the point where this republican equality was the most distressing was in the long and frequent visitations that it produced. No one dreams of fastening a door in Western America; I was told that it would be considered as an affront by the whole neighbourhood. I was thus exposed to perpetual, and most vexatious interruptions from people whom I had often never seen, and whose names still oftener were unknown to me.

Those who are native there, and to the manner born, seem to pass over these annoyances with more skill than I could ever acquire. More than once I have seen some of my acquaintance beset in the same way, without appearing at all distressed by it; they continued their employment or conversation with me, much as if no such interruption had taken place; when the visitor entered, they would say, 'How do you do?' and shake hands.

'Tolerable, I thank ye, how be you?' was the reply.

If it was a female, she took off her hat; if a male, he kept it on, and then taking possession of the first chair in their way, they would retain it for an hour together, without uttering another word; at length, rising abruptly, they would again shake hands, with, 'Well, now I must be going, I guess,' and so take themselves off, apparently well contented with their reception.

I could never attain this philosophical composure; I could neither write nor read, and I always fancied I must talk to them. I will give the minutes of a conversation which I once set down after one of their visits, as a specimen of their tone and manner of speaking and thinking. My visitor was a milkman.

'Well now, so you be from the old country? Ay—you'll see sights here, I guess.'

'I hope I shall see many.'

'That's a fact. I expect your little place of an island don't grow such dreadful fine corn as you sees here?'

'It grows no corn at all, sir.'

'Possible! no wonder, then, that we reads such awful stories in the papers of your poor people being starved to death.'

'We have wheat, however.'

'Ay, for your rich folks, but I calculate the poor seldom gets a belly full.'

'You have certainly much greater abundance here.'

'I expect so. Why they do say, that if a poor body contrives to be smart enough to scrape together a few dollars, that your King George always comes down upon 'em, and takes it all away. Don't he?'

'I do not remember hearing of such a transaction.'

'I guess they be pretty close about it. Your papers ben't like ourn, I reckon? Now we says and prints just what we likes.'

'You spend a good deal of time in reading the newspapers.'

'And I'd like you to tell me how we can spend it better. How should freemen spend their time, but looking after their government, and watching that them fellers as we gives offices to, doos their duty, and gives themselves no airs?'

'But I sometimes think, sir, that your fences might be in more thorough repair, and your roads in better order, if less time was spent in politics.'

'The Lord! to see how little you knows of a free country! Why, what's the smoothness of a road, put against the freedom of a free-born American? And what does a broken zig-zag signify, comparable to knowing that the men what we have been pleased to send up to Congress, speaks handsome and straight, as we chooses they should?'

'It is from a sense of duty, then, that you all go to the liquor store to read the papers?'

'To be sure it is, and he'd be no true born American as didn't. I don't say that the father of a family should always be after liquor, but I do say that I'd rather have my own son drunk three times a week, than not look after the affairs of his country.'

Our autumn walks were delightful; the sun ceased to scorch; the want of flowers was no longer peculiar to Ohio; and the trees took a colouring, which in richness, brilliance, and variety, exceeded all description. I think it is the maple, or sugar-tree, that first sprinkles the forest with rich crimson; the beech follows, with all its harmony of golden tints, from pale yellow up to brightest orange. The dog-wood gives almost the purple colour of the mulberry; the chestnut softens all with its frequent mass of delicate brown, and the sturdy oak carries its deep green into the very lap of winter. These tints are too bright for the landscape painter; the attempt to follow nature in an American autumn scene must be abortive. The colours are in reality extremely brilliant, but the medium through which they are seen increases the effect surprisingly. Of all the points in which America has the advantage of England, the one I felt most sensibly was the clearness and brightness of the atmosphere. By day and by night this exquisite purity of air gives tenfold beauty to every object. I could hardly believe the stars were the same; the Great Bear looked like a constellation of suns; and Jupiter justified all the fine things said of him in those beautiful lines, from I know not what spirited pen, beginning,

I looked on thee, Jove! till my gaze
Shrunk, smote by the pow'r of thy blaze.

I always remarked that the first silver line of the moon's crescent attracted the eye on the first day, in America, as strongly as it does here on the third. I observed another phenomenon in the crescent moon of that region, the cause of which I less understood. That appearance which Shakespeare describes as 'the new moon, with the old moon in her lap',[7] and which I have heard ingeniously explained as the effect of *earth light*, was less visible there than here.

Cuyp's[8] clearest landscapes have an atmosphere that approaches nearer to that of America than any I remember on canvas; but even Cuyp's *air* cannot reach the lungs, and, therefore, can only give an idea of half the enjoyment; for it makes itself felt as well as seen, and is indeed a constant source of pleasure.

Our walks were, however, curtailed in several directions by my old Cincinnati enemies, the pigs; immense droves of them were continually arriving from the country by the road that led to most of our favourite walks; they were often fed and lodged in the prettiest valleys, and worse still, were slaughtered beside the prettiest streams. Another evil threatened us from the same quarter, that was yet heavier. Our cottage had an ample piazza, (a luxury almost universal in the country houses of America), which, shaded by a group of acacias, made a delightful sitting-room; from this favourite spot we one day perceived symptoms of building in a field close to it; with much anxiety we hastened to the spot, and asked what building was to be erected there.

''Tis to be a slaughter-house for hogs,' was the dreadful reply. As there were several gentlemen's houses in the neighbourhood, I asked if such an erection might not be indicted as a nuisance.

'A what?'

'A nuisance,' I repeated, and explained what I meant.

'No, no,' was the reply, 'that may do very well for your tyrannical country, where a rich man's nose is more thought of than a poor man's mouth; but hogs be profitable produce here, and we be too free for such a law as that, I guess.'

During my residence in America, little circumstances like the foregoing often recalled to my mind a conversation I once held in France with an old gentleman on the subject of their active police, and its omnipresent gens d'armerie; 'Croyez moi, Madame, il n'y a que ceux à qui ils ont à faire, qui les trouvent de trop.'[9]

---

[7] Not from Shakespeare, but from the ballad, 'Sir Patrick Spens'.
[8] Aelbert Cuyp (1620–91), a Dutch artist famous for his paintings of rivers and towns in the early morning or evening sun.
[9] Believe me, Madame, only those with whom they are involved, find them unnecessary.

And the old gentleman was right, not only in speaking of France, but of the whole human family, as philosophers call us. The well disposed, those whose own feeling of justice would prevent their annoying others, will never complain of the restraints of the law. All the freedom enjoyed in America, beyond what is enjoyed in England, is enjoyed solely by the disorderly at the expense of the orderly; and were I a stout knight, either of the sword or of the pen, I would fearlessly throw down my gauntlet, and challenge the whole Republic to prove the contrary; but being, as I am, a feeble looker on, with a needle for my spear, and 'I talk' for my device, I must be contented with the power of stating the fact, perfectly certain that I shall be contradicted by one loud shout from Maine to Georgia.

CHAPTER XI

RELIGION

I HAD often heard it observed before I visited America, that one of the great blessings of its constitution was the absence of a national religion, the country being thus exonerated from all obligation of supporting the clergy; those only contributing to do so whose principles led them to it. My residence in the country has shewn me that a religious tyranny may be exerted very effectually without the aid of the government,[10] in a way much more oppressive than the paying of tithe, and without obtaining any of the salutary decorum, which I presume no one will deny is the result of an established mode of worship.

[10] I shall not expect to escape the charge of impossible exaggeration if I describe the species of petty persecution that I have seen exercised on religious subjects in America. The whole people appear to be divided into an almost endless variety of religious factions; I was told in Cincinatti that to be well received in society it was indispensably necessary to declare that you belonged to some one of these factions – it did not much matter which – as far as I could make out, the Methodists were considered as the most pious, the Presbyterians as the most powerful, the Episcopalians and the Catholics as the most genteel, the Universalists as the most liberal, the Swedenborgians as the most musical, the Unitarians as the most enlightened, the Quakers the most amiable, the dancing Shakers the most amusing, and the Jews as the most interesting. Besides these there are dozens more of fancy religions whose designations I cannot remember, but declaring yourself to belong to any one of them as far as I could learn was sufficient to constitute you a respectable member of society. Having thus declared yourself, your next submission must be that of unqualified obedience to the will and pleasure of your elected pastor, or you will run a great risk of being 'passed out of the church'. This was a phrase that I perpetually heard, and upon enquiry I found that it did not mean being passed neck and heels out of the building at the discretion of the sexton, but a sort of congregational excommunication which infallibly betides those who venture to [do] any thing that their pastor and master disapproves. I once heard a lady say 'I must not wear high bows on my bonnet, or I shall be passed out of our church' and another 'I must not go to see the dancing at the theatre or I shall be passed out of our church' and another 'I must not confess that I visit Mrs J. or I shall be passed out of our church, for they say that she does not belong to any church in the town.' I think I am tolerant not only in religion but of all opinions that differ from my own, but this does not prevent my seeing that the end of a true and rational religion is better obtained when the government of the church is confided to the hands of those who act in conformity & obedience to it. [Trollope's note]

As it was impossible to remain many weeks in the country without being struck with the strange anomalies produced by its religious system, my early notes contain many observations on the subject; but as nearly the same scenes recurred in every part of the country, I state them here, not as belonging to the west alone, but to the whole Union, the same cause producing the same effect every where.

The whole people appear to be divided into an almost endless variety of religious factions, and I was told, that to be well received in society, it was necessary to declare yourself as belonging to some one of these. Let your acknowledged belief be what it may, you are said to be *not a Christian*, unless you attach yourself to a particular congregation. Besides the broad and well-known distinctions of Episcopalian, Catholic, Presbyterian, Calvinist, Baptist, Quaker, Swedenborgian, Universalist, Dunker, etc. etc. etc.; there are innumerable others springing out of these, each of which assumed a church government of its own; of this, the most intriguing and factious individual is invariably the head; and in order, as it should seem, to shew a reason for this separation, each congregation invests itself with some queer variety of external observance that has the melancholy effect of exposing *all* religious ceremonies to contempt.

It is impossible, in witnessing all these unseemly vagaries, not to recognize the advantages of an established church as a sort of headquarters for quiet unpresuming Christians, who are contented to serve faithfully, without insisting upon having each a little separate banner, embroidered with a device of their own imagining.

The Catholics alone appear exempt from the fury of division and sub-division that has seized every other persuasion. Having the Pope for their common head, regulates, I presume, their movements, and prevents the outrageous display of individual whim which every other sect is permitted.

I had the pleasure of being introduced to the Catholic bishop of Cincinnati, and have never known in any country a priest of a character and bearing more truly apostolic.[11] He was an American, but I should never have discovered it from his pronunciation or manner. He received his education partly in England, and partly in France. His manners were highly polished; his piety active and sincere, and infinitely more mild and tolerant than that of the factious Sectarians who form the great majority of the American priesthood.

I believe I am sufficiently tolerant; but this does not prevent my seeing that the object of all religious observances is better obtained, when the government of the church is confided to the wisdom and experience of the most venerated among the people, than when it is placed in the hands of every tinker and tailor who chooses to claim a share in it. Nor is this the only evil attending the want of a national religion, supported by the State. As there is no legal and fixed provision for the clergy, it is hardly surprising that their services are confined to those who can pay them. The vehement expressions of insane or hypocritical zeal, such as were exhibited during 'the Revival', can but ill atone for the want of

[11] Edward Dominic Fenwick (b. 1768 in Maryland) studied in Bulgaria and returned to America in 1805 to help introduce the Dominican Order.

village worship, any more than the eternal talk of the admirable and unequalled government, can atone for the continual contempt of social order. Church and State hobble along, side by side, notwithstanding their boasted independence. Almost every man you meet will tell you, that he is occupied in labours most abundant for the good of his country; and almost every woman will tell you, that besides those things that are within (her house) she has coming upon her daily the care of all the churches. Yet spite of this universal attention to the government, its laws are half asleep; and spite of the old women and their Dorcas societies, atheism is awake and thriving.

In the smaller cities and towns prayer-meetings take the place of almost all other amusements; but as the thinly scattered population of most villages can give no parties, and pay no priests, they contrive to marry, christen, and bury without them. A stranger taking up his residence in any city in America must think the natives the most religious people upon earth; but if chance lead him among her western villages, he will rarely find either churches or chapels, prayer or preacher; except, indeed, at that most terrific saturnalia, 'a camp-meeting'. I was much struck with the answer of a poor woman, whom I saw ironing on a Sunday. 'Do you make no difference in your occupations on a Sunday?' I said, 'I beant a Christian, Ma'am; we have got no opportunity,' was the reply. It occurred to me, that in a country where 'all men are equal', the government would be guilty of no great crime, did it so far interfere as to give them all *an opportunity* of becoming Christians if they wished it. But should the federal government dare to propose building a church, and endowing it, in some village that has never heard 'the bringing home of bell and burial', it is perfectly certain that not only the sovereign state where such an abomination was proposed, would rush into the Congress to resent the odious interference, but that all the other states would join the clamour, and such an intermeddling administration would run great risk of impeachment and degradation.

Where there is a church-government so constituted as to deserve human respect, I believe it will always be found to receive it, even from those who may not assent to the dogma of its creed; and where such respect exists, it produces a decorum in manners and language often found wanting where it does not. Sectarians will not venture to rhapsodize, nor infidels to scoff, in the common intercourse of society. Both are injurious to the cause of rational religion, and to check both must be advantageous.

It is certainly possible that some of the fanciful variations upon the ancient creeds of the Christian Church, with which transatlantic religionists amuse themselves, might inspire morbid imaginations in Europe as well as in America; but before they can disturb the solemn harmony *here*, they must prelude by a defiance, not only to common sense, but what is infinitely more appalling, to common usage. They must at once rank themselves with the low and illiterate, for only such prefer the eloquence of the tub to that of the pulpit. The aristocracy must ever, as a body, belong to the established Church, and it is but a small proportion of the influential classes who would be willing to allow that they do not belong to the aristocracy. That such feelings influence the professions of men it were ignorance or hypocrisy to deny; and that nation is wise who knows how to turn even such feelings into a wholesome stream of popular influence.

As a specimen of the tone in which religion is mixed in the ordinary intercourse of society, I will transcribe the notes I took of a conversation, at which I was present, at Cincinnati; I wrote them immediately after the conversation took place.

DR A. 'I wish, Mrs M., that you would explain to me what a revival is. I hear it talked of all over the city, and I know it means something about Jesus Christ and religion; but that is all I know, will you instruct me farther?'

MRS M. 'I expect, Dr A., that you want to laugh at me. But that makes no difference. I am firm in my principles, and I fear no one's laughter.'

DR A. 'Well, but what is a revival?'

MRS M. 'It is difficult, very difficult, to make those see who have no light; to make those understand whose souls are darkened. A revival means just an elegant kindling of the spirit; it is brought about to the Lord's people by the hands of the saints, and it means salvation in the highest.'

DR A. 'But what is it the people mean by talking of feeling the revival? and waiting in spirit for the revival? and the extacy of the revival?'

MRS M. 'Oh Doctor! I am afraid that you are too far gone astray to understand all that. It is a glorious assurance, a whispering of the everlasting covenant, it is the bleating of the lamb, it is the welcome of the shepherd, it is the essence of love, it is the fullness of glory, it is being in Jesus, it is Jesus being in us, it is taking the Holy Ghost into our bosoms, it is sitting ourselves down by God, it is being called to the high places, it is eating, and drinking, and sleeping in the Lord, it is becoming a lion in the faith, it is being lowly and meek, and kissing the hand that smites, it is being mighty and powerful, and scorning reproof, it is—'

DR A. 'Thank you, Mrs M., I feel quite satisfied; and I think I understand a revival now almost as well as you do yourself.'

MRS A. 'My! Where can you have learnt all that stuff, Mrs M.?'

MRS M. 'How benighted you are! From the holy book, from the Word of the Lord, from the Holy Ghost, and Jesus Christ themselves.'

MRS A. 'It does seem so droll to me, to hear you talk of "the Word of the Lord". Why, I have been brought up to look upon the Bible as nothing better than an old newspaper.'

MRS O. 'Surely you only say this for the sake of hearing what Mrs M. will say in return—you do not mean it?'

MRS A. 'La, yes! to be sure I do.'

DR A. 'I profess that I by no means wish my wife to read all she might find there.—What says the Colonel, Mrs M.?'

MRS M. 'As to that, I never stop to ask him. I tell him every day that I believe in Father, Son, and Holy Ghost, and that it is his duty to believe in them too, and then my conscience is clear, and I don't care what he believes. Really, I have no notion of one's husband interfering in such matters.'

DR A. 'You are quite right. I am sure I give my wife leave to believe just what she likes; but she is a good woman, and does not abuse the liberty; for she believes nothing.'

It was not once, nor twice, nor thrice, but many many times, during my residence in America, that I was present when subjects which custom as well as principle had taught me to consider as fitter for the closet than the tea-table, were thus lightly discussed. I hardly know whether I was more startled at first hearing, in little dainty namby pamby tones, a profession of Atheism over a teacup, or at having my attention called from a Johnny cake, to a rhapsody on election and the second birth.

But, notwithstanding this revolting license, persecution exists to a degree unknown, I believe, in our well-ordered land since the days of Cromwell. I had the following anecdote from a gentleman perfectly well acquainted with the circumstances. A tailor sold a suit of clothes to a sailor a few moments before he sailed, which was on a Sunday morning. The corporation of New York prosecuted the tailor, and he was convicted, and sentenced to a fine greatly beyond his means to pay. Mr F., a lawyer of New York, defended him with much eloquence, but in vain. His powerful speech, however, was not without effect, for it raised him such a host of Presbyterian enemies as sufficed to destroy his practice. Nor was this all: his nephew was at the time preparing for the bar, and soon after the above circumstance occurred his certificates were presented, and refused, with this declaration, 'that no man of the name and family of F. should be admitted.' I have met this young man in society; he is a person of very considerable talent, and being thus cruelly robbed of his profession, has become the editor of a newspaper.

CHAPTER XII

PEASANTRY, COMPARED TO THAT OF ENGLAND—EARLY MARRIAGES —CHARITY—INDEPENDENCE AND EQUALITY— COTTAGE PRAYER-MEETING

MOHAWK, as our little village was called, gave us an excellent opportunity of comparing the peasants of the United States with those of England, and of judging the average degree of comfort enjoyed by each. I believe Ohio gives as fair a specimen as any part of the Union; if they have the roughness and inconveniences of a new state to contend with, they have higher wages and cheaper provisions; if I err in supposing it a mean state in point of comfort, it certainly is not in taking too low a standard.

Mechanics, if good workmen, are certain of employment, and good wages, rather higher than with us; the average wages of a labourer throughout the

Union is ten dollars a month, with lodging, boarding, washing, and mending; if he lives at his own expense he has a dollar a day. It appears to me that the necessaries of life, that is to say, meat, bread, butter, tea, and coffee, (not to mention whiskey), are within the reach of every sober, industrious, and healthy man who chooses to have them; and yet I think that an English peasant, with the same qualifications, would, in coming to the United States, change for the worse. He would find wages somewhat higher, and provisions in Western America considerably lower; but this statement, true as it is, can lead to nothing but delusion if taken apart from other facts, fully as certain, and not less important, but which require more detail in describing, and which perhaps cannot be fully comprehended, except by an eye-witness. The American poor are accustomed to eat meat three times a day; I never enquired into the habits of any cottagers in Western America, where this was not the case. I found afterwards in Maryland, Pennsylvania, and other parts of the country, where the price of meat was higher, that it was used with more economy; yet still a much larger portion of the weekly income is thus expended than with us. Ardent spirits, though lamentably cheap, still cost something, and the use of them among the men, with more or less of discretion, according to the character, is universal. Tobacco also grows at their doors, and is not taxed; yet this too costs something, and the air of heaven is not in more general use among the men at America, than chewing tobacco. I am not now pointing out the evils of dram-drinking, but it is evident, that where this practice prevails universally, and often to the most frightful excess, the consequence must be, that the money spent to obtain the dram is less than the money lost by the time consumed in drinking it. Long, disabling, and expensive fits of sickness are incontestably more frequent in every part of America, than in England, and the sufferers have no aid to look to, but what they have saved, or what they may be enabled to sell. I have never seen misery exceed what I have witnessed in an American cottage where disease has entered.

But, if the condition of the labourer be not superior to that of the English peasant, that of his wife and daughters is incomparably worse. It is they who are indeed the slaves of the soil. One has but to look at the wife of an American cottager, and ask her age, to be convinced that the life she leads is one of hardship, privation, and labour. It is rare to see a woman in this station who has reached the age of thirty, without losing every trace of youth and beauty. You continually see women with infants on their knee, that you feel sure are their grand-children, till some convincing proof of the contrary is displayed. Even the young girls, though often with lovely features, look pale, thin, and haggard. I do not remember to have seen in any single instance among the poor, a specimen of the plump, rosy, laughing physiognomy so common among our cottage girls. The horror of domestic service, which the reality of slavery, and the fable of equality, have generated, excludes the young women from that sure and most comfortable resource of decent English girls; and the consequence is, that with a most irreverend freedom of manner to the parents, the daughters are, to the full extent of the word, domestic slaves. This condition, which no periodical merry-making, no village *fête*, ever occurs to cheer, is only changed for the still sadder burdens of a teeming wife. They marry very young; in fact, in no rank of life do you meet with young women in that delightful period of existence between childhood and marriage, wherein, if only tolerably well spent, so much useful information is gained, and the character takes a sufficient degree of firmness to support with dignity the more important parts of wife and mother. The slender, childish thing, without vigour of mind or body, is made to stem a sea of troubles that dims her young eye and makes her cheek grow pale, even before nature has given it the last beautiful finish of the full-grown woman.

'We shall get along,' is the answer in full, for all that can be said in way of advice to a boy and girl who take it into their heads to go before a magistrate and 'get married'. And they do get along, till sickness overtakes them, by means perhaps of borrowing a kettle from one and a tea-pot from another; but intemperance, idleness, or sickness will, in one week, plunge those who are even getting along well, into utter destitution; and where this happens, they are completely without resource.

The absence of poor-laws is, without doubt, a blessing to the country, but they have not that natural and reasonable dependence on the richer classes which, in countries differently constituted, may so well supply their place. I suppose there is less alms-giving in America than in any other Christian country on the face of the globe. It is not in the temper of the people either to give or to receive.

I extract the following pompous passage from a Washington paper of Feb. 1829, (a season of uncommon severity and distress), which, I think, justifies my observation.

'Among the liberal evidences of sympathy for the suffering poor of this city, two have come to our knowledge which deserve to be especially noticed: the one a donation by the President of the United States to the committee of the ward in which he resides of fifty dollars; the other the donation by a few of the officers of the war department to the Howard and Dorcas Societies,[12] of seventy-two dollars.' When such mention is made of a gift of about nine pounds sterling from the sovereign magistrate of the United States, and of thirteen pounds sterling as a contribution from one of the state departments, the inference is pretty obvious, that the sufferings of the destitute in America are not liberally relieved by individual charity.

I had not been three days at Mohawk-cottage before a pair of ragged children came to ask for medicine for a sick mother; and when it was given to them, the eldest produced a handful of cents, and desired to know what he was to pay. The superfluous milk of our cow was sought after eagerly, but every new comer always proposed to pay for it. When they found out that 'the English old woman' did not sell any thing, I am persuaded they by no means liked her the better for it; but they seemed to think, that if she were a fool it was no reason they should be so too, and accordingly the borrowing, as they called it, became very constant, but always in a form that shewed their dignity and freedom. One

12 John Howard (1726–90) was concerned for the sufferings of prisoners; Howard Associations were formed after his death. Dorcas Societies, named after the biblical Dorcas who made 'coats and garments for widows', were circles of women sewing clothes for charity.

woman sent to borrow a pound of cheese; another half a pound of coffee; and more than once an intimation accompanied the milk-jug, that the milk must be fresh, and unskimmed: on one occasion the messenger refused milk, and said, 'Mother only wanted a little cream for her coffee.'

I could never teach them to believe, during above a year that I lived at this house, that I would not sell the old clothes of the family; and so pertinacious were they in bargain-making, that often, when I had given them the articles which they wanted to purchase, they would say, 'Well, I expect I shall have to do a turn of work for this; you may send for me when you want me.' But as I never did ask for the turn of work, and as this formula was constantly repeated, I began to suspect that it was spoken solely to avoid uttering that most un-American phrase 'I thank you'.

There was one man whose progress in wealth I watched with much interest and pleasure. When I first became his neighbour, himself, his wife, and four children, were living in one room, with plenty of beefsteaks and onions for breakfast, dinner, and supper, but with very few other comforts. He was one of the finest men I ever saw, full of natural intelligence and activity of mind and body, but he could neither read nor write. He drank but little whiskey, and but rarely chewed tobacco, and was therefore more free from that plague spot of spitting which rendered male colloquy so difficult to endure. He worked for us frequently, and often used to walk into the drawing-room and seat himself on the sofa, and tell me all his plans. He made an engagement with the proprietor of the wooded hill before mentioned, by which half the wood he could fell was to be his own. His unwearied industry made this a profitable bargain, and from the proceeds he purchased the materials for building a comfortable frame (or wooden) house; he did the work almost entirely himself. He then got a job for cutting rails, and, as he could cut twice as many in a day as any other man in the neighbourhood, he made a good thing of it. He then let half his pretty house, which was admirably constructed, with an ample portico, that kept it always cool. His next step was contracting for the building a wooden bridge, and when I left Mohawk he had fitted up his half of the building as an hotel and grocery store; and I have no doubt that every sun that sets sees him a richer man than when it rose. He hopes to make his son a lawyer, and I have little doubt that he will live to see him sit in congress; when this time arrives, the wood-cutter's son will rank with any other member of congress, not of courtesy, but of right, and the idea that his origin is a disadvantage, will never occur to the imagination of the most exalted of his fellow-citizens.

This is the only feature in American society that I recognize as indicative of the equality they profess. Any man's son may become the equal of any other man's son, and the consciousness of this is certainly a spur to exertion; on the other hand, it is also a spur to that coarse familiarity, untempered by any shadow of respect, which is assumed by the grossest and lowest in their intercourse with the highest and most refined. This is a positive evil, and, I think, more than balances its advantages.

And here again it may be observed, that the theory of equality may be very daintily discussed by English gentlemen in a London dining-room, when the servant, having placed a fresh bottle of cool wine on the table, respectfully shuts the door, and leaves them to their walnuts and their wisdom; but it will be found less palatable when it presents itself in the shape of a hard, greasy paw, and is claimed in accents that breathe less of freedom than of onions and whiskey. Strong, indeed, must be the love of equality in an English breast if it can survive a tour through the Union.

There was one house in the village which was remarkable from its wretchedness. It had an air of *in*decent poverty about it, which long prevented my attempting an entrance; but at length, upon being told that I could get chicken and eggs there whenever I wanted them, I determined upon venturing. The door being opened to my knock, I very nearly abandoned my almost blunted purpose; I never beheld such a den of filth and misery: a woman, the very image of dirt and disease, held a squalid imp of a baby on her hip bone while she kneaded her dough with her right fist only. A great lanky girl, of twelve years old, was sitting on a barrel, gnawing a corn cob; when I made known my business, the woman answered, 'No, not I; I got no chickens to sell, nor eggs neither; but my son will, plenty I expect. Here, Nick,' (bawling at the bottom of a ladder), 'here's an old woman what wants chickens'. Half a moment brought Nick to the bottom of the ladder, and I found my merchant was one of a ragged crew, whom I had been used to observe in my daily walk, playing marbles in the dust, and swearing lustily; he looked about ten years old.

'Have you chicken to sell, my boy?'

'Yes, and eggs too, more nor what you'll buy'

Having enquired price, condition, and so on, I recollected that I had been used to give the same price at market, the feathers plucked, and the chicken prepared for the table, and I told him that he ought not to charge the same.

'Oh for that, I expect I can fix 'em as well as ever them was, what you got in market.'

'You fix them?'

'Yes to be sure, why not?'

'I thought you were too fond of marbles.'

He gave me a keen glance, and said, 'You don't know I.—When will you be wanting the chickens?'

He brought them at the time directed, extremely well 'fixed', and I often dealt with him afterwards. When I paid him, he always thrust his hand into his breeches pocket, which I presume, as being *the keep*, was fortified more strongly than the dilapidated outworks, and drew from thence rather more dollars, half-dollars, levies, and fips, than his dirty little hand could well hold. My curiosity was excited, and though I felt an involuntary disgust towards the young Jew, I repeatedly conversed with him.

'You are very rich, Nick,' I said to him one day, on his making an ostentatious display of the change, as he called it; he sneered with a most unchildish expression of countenance, and replied, 'I guess 'twould be a bad job for I, if that was all I'd got to shew.'

I asked him how he managed his business. He told me that he bought eggs by the hundred, and lean chicken by the score, from the waggons that passed their door on the way to market; that he fatted the latter in coops he had made himself, and could easily double their price, and that his eggs answered well too, when he sold them out by the dozen.

'And do you give the money to your mother?' 'I expect not,' was the answer, with another sharp glance of his ugly blue eyes.

'What do you do with it, Nick?'

His look said plainly, what is that to you? but he only answered, quaintly enough, 'I takes care of it'.

How Nick got his first dollar is very doubtful; I was told that when he entered the village store, the person serving always called in another pair of eyes; but having obtained it, the spirit, activity, and industry, with which he caused it to increase and multiply, would have been delightful in one of Miss Edgeworth's dear little clean bright-looking boys, who would have carried all he got to his mother;[13] but in Nick it was detestable. No human feeling seemed to warm his young heart, not even the love of self-indulgence, for he was not only ragged, and dirty, but looked considerably more than half starved, and I doubt not his dinners and suppers half fed his fat chickens.

I by no means give this history of Nick, the chicken merchant, as an anecdote characteristic in all respects of America; the only part of the story which is so, is the independence of the little man, and is one instance out of a thousand, of the hard, dry, calculating character that is the result of it. Probably Nick will be very rich; perhaps he will be President. I once got so heartily scolded for saying, that I did not think all American citizens were equally eligible to that office, that I shall never again venture to doubt it.

Another of our cottage acquaintance was a market-gardener, from whom we frequently bought vegetables; from the wife of this man we one day received a very civil invitation to 'please to come and pass the evening with them in prayer'. The novelty of the circumstance, and its great dissimilarity to the way and manners of our own country, induced me to accept the invitation, and also to record the visit here.

We were received with great attention, and a place was assigned us on one of the benches that surrounded the little parlour. Several persons, looking like mechanics and their wives, were present; every one sat in profound silence, and with that quiet subdued air, that serious people assume on entering a church. At length, a long, black, grim-looking man entered; his dress, the cut of his hair, and his whole appearance, strongly recalled the idea of one of Cromwell's fanatics. He stepped solemnly into the middle of the room, and took a chair that stood there, but not to sit upon it; he turned the back towards him, on which he placed his hands, and stoutly uttering a sound between a hem and a cough, he deposited freely on either side of him a considerable portion of masticated tobacco. He then began to preach. His text was 'Live in hope', and he continued to expound it for two hours in a drawling, nasal tone, with no other respite than what he allowed himself for expectoration. If I say that he

[13] Reference to Maria Edgeworth (1768–1849), who provided popular lessons and stories for and about children.

repeated the words of his text a hundred times, I think I shall not exceed the truth, for that allows more than a minute for each repetition, and in fact the whole discourse was made up of it. The various tones in which he uttered it might have served as a lesson on emphasis; as a question—in accents of triumph—in accents of despair—of pity—of threatening—of authority—of doubt—of hope—of faith. Having exhausted every imaginable variety of tone, he abruptly said, 'Let us pray', and twisting his chair round, knelt before it. Every one knelt before the seat they had occupied, and listened for another half hour to a rant of miserable, low, familiar jargon, that he presumed to *improvisé* to his Maker as a prayer. In this, however, the cottage apostle only followed the example set by every preacher throughout the Union, excepting those of the Episcopalian and Catholic congregations; *they* only do not deem themselves privileged to address the Deity in strains of crude and unweighed importunity. These ranters may sometimes be very much in earnest, but surely the least we can say of it is, that they

Praise their God amiss.

I enquired afterwards of a friend, well acquainted with such matters, how the grim preacher of 'Hope' got paid for his labours, and he told me that the trade was an excellent one, for that many a gude wife bestowed more than a tithe of what her gude man trusted to her keeping, in rewarding the zeal of these self-chosen apostles. These sable ministers walk from house to house, or if the distance be considerable, ride on a comfortable ambling nag. They are not only as empty as wind, but resemble it in other particulars; for they blow where they list, and no man knoweth whence they come, nor whither they go. When they see a house that promises comfortable lodging and entertainment, they enter there, and say to the good woman of the house, 'Sister, shall I pray with you?' If the answer be favourable, and it is seldom otherwise, he instals himself and his horse till after breakfast the next morning. The best meat, drink, and lodging are his, while he stays, and he seldom departs without some little contribution in money for the support of the crucified and suffering church. Is it not strange that 'the most intelligent people in the world' should prefer such a religion as this, to a form established by the wisdom and piety of the ablest and best among the erring sons of men, solemnly sanctioned by the nation's law, and rendered sacred by the use of their fathers?

It would be well for all reasoners on the social system to observe steadily, and with an eye obscured by no beam of prejudice, the result of the experiment that is making on the other side of the Atlantic. If I mistake not, they might learn there, better than by any abstract speculation, what are the points on which the magistrates of a great people should dictate to them, and on what points they should be left freely to their own guidance. I sincerely believe, that if a fire-worshipper, or an Indian Brahmin, were to come to the United States, prepared to preach and pray in English, he would not be long without a 'very respectable congregation'.

The influence of a religion, sanctioned by the government, could in no country, in the nineteenth century, interfere with the speculations of a philosopher in his closet, but it might, and must, steady the weak and wavering opinions of the multitude. There is something really pitiable in the effect produced by the want of this rudder oar. I knew a family where one was a Methodist, one a Presbyterian, and a third a Baptist; and another, where one was a Quaker, one a declared Atheist, and another an Universalist. These are all females, and all moving in the best society that America affords; but one and all of them as incapable of reasoning on things past, present, and to come, as the infants they nourish, yet one and all of them perfectly fit to move steadily and usefully in a path marked out for them. But I shall be called an itinerant preacher myself if I pursue this theme.

As I have not the magic power of my admirable friend, Miss Mitford, to give grace and interest to the humblest rustic details,[14] I must not venture to linger among the cottages that surrounded us; but before I quit them I must record the pleasing recollection of one or two neighbours of more companionable rank, from whom I received so much friendly attention, and such unfailing kindness, in all my little domestic embarrassments, that I shall never recall the memory of Mohawk, without paying an affectionate tribute to these far distant friends. I wish it were within the range of hope, that I might see them again, in my own country, and repay, in part, the obligations I owe them.

CHAPTER XXVI

QUAKERS—PRESBYTERIANS—ITINERANT METHODIST PREACHER —MARKET—INFLUENCE OF FEMALES IN SOCIETY

I HAD never chanced, among all my wanderings, to enter a Quaker Meeting-house; and as I thought I could no where make my first visit better than at Philadelphia, I went under the protection of a Quaker lady to the principal *orthodox* meeting of the city. The building is large, but perfectly without ornament; the men and women are separated by a rail which divides it into two equal parts; the meeting was very full on both sides, and the atmosphere almost intolerably hot. As they glided in at their different doors, I spied many pretty faces peeping from the prim head gear of the females, and as the broad-brimmed males sat down, the welcome Parney[15] supposes prepared for them in heaven, recurred to me,

Entre donc, et garde ton chapeau.[16]

The little bonnets and the large hats were ranged in long rows, and their stillness was for a long time so unbroken, that I could hardly persuade myself the figures they surmounted were alive. At length a grave square man arose, laid aside his ample beaver, and after another solemn interval of silence, he gave a

[14] Mary Russell Mitford (1787–1855), novelist and dramatist, author of *Our Village* (1832).
[15] Evariste Desire de Forges Parny (1753–1814) wrote religious and political burlesque.
[16] Come in then, and hold onto your hat.

deep groan, and as it were by the same effort uttered, 'Keep they foot'. Again
he was silent for many minutes, and then he continued for more than an hour
to put forth one word at a time, but at such an interval from each other that
I found it quite impossible to follow his meaning, if, indeed, he had any. My
Quaker friend told me she knew not who he was, and that she much regretted
I had heard so poor a preacher. After he had concluded, a gentleman-like old
man (a physician by profession) arose, and delivered a few moral sentences in
an agreeable manner; soon after he had sat down, the whole congregation rose,
I know not at what signal, and made their exit. It is a singular kind of worship,
if worship it may be called, where all prayer is forbidden; yet it appeared to
me, in its decent quietness, infinitely preferable to what I had witnessed at the
Presbyterian and Methodist meeting-houses. A great schism had lately taken
place among the Quakers of Philadelphia; many objecting to the over-strict
discipline of the orthodox. Among the seceders there are again various shades
of difference; I met many who called themselves Unitarian Quakers, others
were Hicksites,[17] and others again, though still wearing the Quaker habit, were
said to be Deists.

We visited many churches and chapels in the city, but none that would
elsewhere be called handsome, either internally or externally.

I went one evening, not a Sunday, with a party of ladies to see a Presbyterian
minister inducted. The ceremony was woefully long, and the charge to the young
man awfully impossible to obey, at least if he were a man, like unto other men.
It was matter of astonishment to me to observe the deep attention, and the
unwearied patience with which some hundreds of beautiful young girls who
were assembled there, (not to mention the old ladies), listened to the whole of
this tedious ceremony; surely there is no country in the world where religion
makes so large a part of the amusement and occupation of the ladies. Spain, in its
most catholic days, could not exceed it: besides, in spite of the gloomy horrors
of the Inquisition, gaiety and amusement were not there offered as a sacrifice
by the young and lovely.

The religious severity of Philadelphian manners is in nothing more conspicuous than in the number of chains thrown across the streets on a Sunday to prevent
horses and carriages from passing. Surely the Jews could not exceed this country
in their external observances. What the gentlemen of Philadelphia do with
themselves on a Sunday, I will not pretend to guess, but the prodigious majority
of females in the churches is very remarkable. Although a large proportion of
the population of this city are Quakers, the same extraordinary variety of faith
exists here, as every where else in the Union, and the priests have, in some
circles, the same unbounded influence which has been mentioned elsewhere.

One history reached me, which gave a terrible picture of the effect this power
may produce; it was related to me by my mantua-maker; a young woman highly
estimable as a wife and mother, and on whose veracity I perfectly rely. She told
me that her father was a widower, and lived with his family of three daughters,

[17] Followers of the liberal American Quaker, Elias Hicks (1748–1830) who seceded from
the orthodox Quaker movement.

at Philadelphia. A short time before she married, an itinerant preacher came to
the city, who contrived to obtain an intimate footing in many respectable families.
Her father's was one of these, and his influence and authority were great with
all the sisters, but particularly with the youngest. The young girl's feelings for
him seem to have been a curious mixture of spiritual awe and earthly affection.
When she received a hint from her sisters that she ought not to give him too
much encouragement till he spoke out, she shewed as much holy resentment
as if they had told her not to say her prayers too devoutly. At length the father
remarked the sort of covert passion that gleamed through the eyes of his godly
visitor, and he saw too, the pallid anxious look which had settled on the young
brow of his daughter; either this, or some rumours he had heard abroad, or
both together, led him to forbid this man his house. The three girls were present
when he did so, and all uttered a deprecating 'Oh father!' but the old man added
stoutly, 'If you shew yourself here again, reverend sir, I will not only teach you
the way out of my house, but out of the city also.' The preacher withdrew, and
was never heard of in Philadelphia afterwards; but when a few months had
passed, strange whispers began to creep through the circle which had received
and honoured him, and, in due course of time; no less than seven unfortunate
girls produced living proofs of the wisdom of my informant's worthy father. In
defence of this dreadful story I can only make the often repeated quotation, 'I
tell the tale as 'twas told to me'; but, in all sincerity I must add, that I have no
doubt of its truth.

I was particularly requested to visit the market of Philadelphia, at the hour
when it presented the busiest scene; I did so, and thought few cities had any
thing to shew better worth looking at; it is indeed, the very perfection of a
market, the *beau ideal* of a notable housewife, who would confide to no deputy
the important office of caterer. The neatness, freshness, and entire absence of
every thing disagreeable to sight or smell, must be witnessed to be believed.
The stalls were spread with snow-white napkins; flowers and fruit, if not quite
of Paris or London perfection, yet bright fresh, and fragrant; with excellent
vegetables in the greatest variety and abundance, were all so delightfully
exhibited, that objects less pleasing were overlooked and forgotten. The dairy,
the poultry-yard, the forest, the river, and the ocean, all contributed their spoil;
in short, for the first time in my life, I thought a market a beautiful object. The
prices of most articles were, as nearly as I could calculate between dollars and
francs, about the same as at Paris; certainly much cheaper than in London, but
much dearer than at Exeter.

My letters of introduction brought me acquainted with several amiable and
interesting people. There is something in the tone of manners at Philadelphia
that I liked; it appeared to me that there was less affectation of ton there than
elsewhere. There is a quietness, a composure in a Philadelphia drawing-room,
that is quite characteristic of a city founded by William Penn. The dress of
the ladies, even those who are not Quakers, partakes of this; they are most
elegantly neat, and there was a delicacy and good taste in the dress of the
young ladies that might serve as a model to the whole Union. There can hardly

be a stronger contrast in the style of dress between any two cities than may be remarked between Baltimore and Philadelphia; both are costly, but the former is distinguished by gaudy splendour, the latter by elegant simplicity.

It is said that this city has many gentlemen distinguished by their scientific pursuits; I conversed with several well-informed and intelligent men, but there is a cold dryness of manner and an apparent want of interest in the subjects they discuss, that, to my mind, robs conversation of all its charm. On one occasion I heard the character and situation of an illustrious officer discussed, who had served with renown under Napoleon, and whose high character might have obtained him favour under the Bourbons, could he have abandoned the principles which led him to dislike their government. This distinguished man had retreated to America after the death of his master, and was endeavouring to establish a sort of Polytechnic academy at New York: in speaking of him, I observed, that his devotion to the cause of freedom must prove a strong recommendation in the United States. 'Not the least in the world, madam,' answered a gentleman who ranked deservedly high among the *literati* of the city, 'it might avail him much in England, perhaps, but here we are perfectly indifferent as to what people's principles may be.'

This I believe to be exactly true, though I never before heard it avowed as a national feature.

The want of warmth, of interest, of feeling, upon all subjects which do not immediately touch their own concerns, is universal, and has a most paralysing effect upon conversation. All the enthusiasm of America is concentrated to the one point of her own emancipation and independence; on this point nothing can exceed the warmth of her feelings. She may, I think, be compared to a young bride, a sort of Mrs Major Waddle; her independence is to her as a newly-won bridegroom; for him alone she has eyes, ears, or heart;—the honeymoon is not over yet;—when it is, America will, perhaps, learn more coquetry, and know better how to *faire l'aimable*[18] to other nations.

I conceive that no place in the known world can furnish so striking a proof of the immense value of literary habits as the United States, not only in enlarging the mind, but what is of infinitely more importance, in purifying the manners. During my abode in the country I not only never met a literary man who was a tobacco chewer or a whiskey drinker, but I never met any who were not, that had escaped these degrading habits. On the women, the influence is, if possible, still more important; unfortunately, the instances are rare, but they are to be found. One admirable example occurs in the person of a young lady of Cincinnati: surrounded by a society totally incapable of appreciating or even of comprehending her, she holds a place among it, as simply and unaffectedly as if of the same species; young, beautiful, and gifted by nature with a mind singularly acute and discriminating, she has happily found such opportunities of cultivation as might distinguish her in any country; it is, indeed, that best of all cultivation which is only to be found in domestic habits of literature, and in that hourly education which the daughter of a man of letters receives when she

[18] Be pleasing to.

is made the companion and friend of her father. This young lady is the more admirable as she contrives to unite all the multifarious duties which usually devolve upon American ladies, with her intellectual pursuits. The companion and efficient assistant of her father's literary labours, the active aid in all the household cares of her mother, the tender nurse of a delicate infant sister, the skilful artificer of her own always elegant wardrobe, ever at leisure, and ever prepared to receive with the sweetest cheerfulness her numerous acquaintance, the most animated in conversation, the most indefatigable in occupation, it was impossible to know her, and study her character without feeling that such women were 'the glory of all lands', and, could the race be multiplied, would speedily become the reformers of all the grossness and ignorance that now degrade her own. Is it to be imagined, that if fifty modifications of this charming young woman were to be met at a party, the men would dare to enter it reeking with whiskey, their lips blackened with tobacco, and convinced, to the very centre of their hearts and souls, that women were made for no other purpose than to fabricate sweetmeats and gingerbread, construct shirts, darn stockings, and become mothers of possible presidents? Assuredly not. Should the women of America ever discover what their power might be, and compare it with what it is, much improvement might be hoped for. While, at Philadelphia, among the handsomest, the wealthiest, and the most distinguished of the land, their comparative influence in society, with that possessed in Europe by females holding the same station, occurred forcibly to my mind.

Let me be permitted to describe the day of a Philadelphia lady of the first class, and the inference I would draw from it will be better understood.

It may be said that the most important feature in a woman's history is her maternity. It is so; but the object of the present observation is the social, and not the domestic influence of woman.

This lady shall be the wife of a senator and a lawyer in the highest repute and practice. She has a very handsome house, with white marble steps and door-posts, and a delicate silver knocker and door-handle; she has very handsome drawing-rooms, very handsomely furnished, (there is a sideboard in one of them, but it is very handsome and has very handsome decanters and cut glass water-jugs upon it); she has a very handsome carriage, and a very handsome free black coachman; she is always very handsomely dressed; and, moreover, she is very handsome herself.

She rises, and her first hour is spent in the scrupulously nice arrangement of her dress; she descends to her parlour neat, stiff, and silent; her breakfast is brought in by her free black footman; she eats her fried ham and her salt fish, and drinks her coffee in silence, while her husband reads one newspaper, and puts another under his elbow; and then, perhaps, she washes the cups and saucers. Her carriage is ordered at eleven; till that hour she is employed in the pastry-room, her snow-white apron protecting her mouse-coloured silk. Twenty minutes before her carriage should appear, she retires to her chamber, as she calls it, shakes, and folds up her still snow-white apron, smooths her rich dress, and with nice care, sets on her elegant bonnet, and all the handsome *et caetera*; then walks down stairs, just at the moment that her free black coachman announces to her free black footman that the carriage waits. She steps into it, and gives the word, 'Drive to the Dorcas society'. Her footman stays at home to clean the knives, but her coachman can trust his horses while he opens the carriage door, and his lady not being accustomed to a hand or an arm, gets out very safely without, though one of her own is occupied by a work-basket, and the other by a large roll of all those indescribable matters which ladies take as offerings to Dorcas societies. She enters the parlour appropriated for the meeting, and finds seven other ladies, very like herself, and takes her place among them; she presents her contribution, which is accepted with a gentle circular smile, and her parings of broad cloth, her ends of ribbon, her gilt paper, and her minikin pins, are added to the parings of broad cloth, the ends of ribbon, the gilt paper, and the minikin pins with which the table is already covered; she also produces from her basket three ready-made pincushions, four ink-wipers, seven paper-matches, and a paste-board watch-case; these are welcomed with acclamations, and the youngest lady present deposits them carefully on shelves, amid a prodigious quantity of similar articles. She then produces her thimble, and asks for work; it is presented to her, and the eight ladies all stitch together for some hours. Their talk is of priests and of missions; of the profits of their last sale, of their hopes from the next; of the doubt whether young Mr This, or young Mr That should receive the fruits of it to fit him out for Liberia; of the very ugly bonnet seen at church on Sabbath morning, of the very handsome preacher who performed on Sabbath afternoon, and of the very large collection made on Sabbath evening. This lasts till three, when the carriage again appears, and the lady and her basket return home; she mounts to her chamber, carefully sets aside her bonnet and its appurtenances, puts on her scolloped black silk apron, walks into the kitchen to see that all is right, then into the parlour, where, having cast a careful glance over the table prepared for dinner, she sits down, work in hand, to await her spouse. He comes, shakes hands with her, spits and dines. The conversation is not much, and ten minutes suffices for the dinner; fruit and toddy, the newspaper and the work-bag succeed. In the evening the gentleman, being a savant, goes to the Wistar society,[19] and afterwards plays a snug rubber at a neighbour's. The lady receives at tea a young missionary and three members of the Dorcas society.—And so ends her day.

For some reason or other, which English people are not very likely to understand, a great number of young married persons board by the year, instead of 'going to house-keeping', as they call having an establishment of their own. Of course this statement does not include persons of large fortune, but it does include very many whose rank in society would make such a mode of life quite impossible with us. I can hardly imagine a contrivance more effectual for ensuring the insignificance of a woman, than marrying her at seventeen, and placing her in a boarding-house. Nor can I easily imagine a life of more uniform dulness for the lady herself; but this certainly is a matter of taste. I have heard many ladies declare that it is 'just quite the perfection of comfort to have nothing to fix for oneself'. Yet despite these assurances I always experienced a

[19] A small circle meeting for literary and scientific discussions.

feeling which hovered between pity and contempt, when I contemplated their mode of existence.

How would a newly-married Englishwoman endure it, her head and her heart full of the one dear scheme—

Well ordered home, his *dear delight to make?*

She must rise exactly in time to reach the boarding table at the hour appointed for breakfast, or she will get a stiff bow from the lady president, cold coffee, and no egg. I have been sometimes greatly amused upon these occasions by watching a little scene in which the bye-play had much more meaning than the words uttered. The fasting, but tardy lady, looks round the table, and having ascertained that there was no egg left, says distinctly, 'I will take an egg if you please'. But as this is addressed to no one in particular, no one in particular answers it, unless it happen that her husband is at table before her, and then he says, 'There are no eggs, my dear'. Whereupon the lady president evidently cannot hear, and the greedy culprit who has swallowed two eggs (for there are always as many eggs as noses) looks pretty considerably afraid of being found out. The breakfast proceeds in sombre silence, save that sometimes a parrot, and sometimes a canary bird, ventures to utter a timid note. When it is finished, the gentlemen hurry to their occupations, and the quiet ladies mount the stairs, some to the first, some to the second, and some to the third stories, in an inverse proportion to the number of dollars paid, and ensconce themselves in their respective chambers. As to what they do there is not very easy to say; but I believe they clear-starch a little, and iron a little, and sit in a rocking-chair, and sew a great deal. I always observed that the ladies who boarded wore more elaborately worked collars and petticoats than any one else. The plough is hardly a more blessed instrument in America than the needle. How could they live without it? But time and the needle wear through the longest morning, and happily the American morning is not very long, even though they breakfast at eight.

It is generally about two o'clock that the boarding gentlemen meet the boarding ladies at dinner. Little is spoken, except a whisper between the married pairs. Sometimes a sulky bottle of wine flanks the plate of one or two individuals, but it adds nothing to the mirth of the meeting, and seldom more than one glass to the good cheer of the owners. It is not then, and it is not there, that the gentlemen of the Union drink. Soon, very soon, the silent meal is done, and then, if you mount the stairs after them, you will find from the doors of the more affectionate and indulgent wives, a small of cigars steam forth, which plainly indicates the felicity of the couple within. If the gentleman be a very polite husband, he will, as soon as he has done smoking and drinking his toddy, offer his arm to his wife, as far as the corner of the street, where his store, or his office is situated, and there he will leave her to turn which way she likes. As this is the hour for being full dressed, of course she turns the way she can be most seen. Perhaps she pays a few visits; perhaps she goes to chapel; or, perhaps, she enters some store where her husband deals, and ventures to order a few notions; and then she goes home again—no, not home—I will not give that name to a boarding-house, but she re-enters the cold heartless atmosphere in which she dwells, where hospitality can never enter, and where interest takes the management instead of affection. At tea they all meet again, and a little trickery is perceptible to a nice observer in the manner of partaking the pound-cake, etc. After this, those who are happy enough to have engagements, hasten to keep them; those who have not, either mount again to the solitude of their chamber, or, what appeared to me much worse, remain in the common sitting-room, in a society cemented by no tie, endeared by no connection, which choice did not bring together, and which the slightest motive would break asunder. I remarked that the gentlemen were generally obliged to go out every evening on business, and, I confess, the arrangement did not surprise me.

It is not thus that the women can obtain that influence in society which is allowed to them in Europe, and to which, both sages and men of the world have agreed in ascribing such salutary effects. It is in vain that 'collegiate institutes' are formed for young ladies, or that 'academic degrees' are conferred upon them. It is after marriage, and when these young attempts upon all the sciences are forgotten, that the lamentable insignificance of the American women appears, and till this be remedied, I venture to prophesy that the tone of their drawing-rooms will not improve.

Whilst I was at Philadelphia a great deal of attention was excited by the situation of two criminals, who had been convicted of robbing the Baltimore mail, and were lying under sentence of death. The rare occurrence of capital punishment in America makes it always an event of great interest; and the approaching execution was repeatedly the subject of conversation at the boarding table. One day a gentleman told us he had that morning been assured that one of the criminals had declared to the visiting clergyman that he was certain of being reprieved, and that nothing the clergyman could say to the contrary made any impression upon him. Day after day this same story was repeated, and commented upon at table, and it appeared that the report had been heard in so many quarters, that not only was the statement received as true, but it began to be conjectured that the criminal had some ground for his hope. I learnt from these daily conversations that one of the prisoners was an American, and the other an Irishman, and it was the former who was so strongly persuaded he should not be hanged. Several of the gentlemen at table, in canvassing the subject, declared, that if the one were hanged and the other spared, this hanging would be a murder, and not a legal execution. In discussing this point, it was stated that very nearly all the white men who had suffered death since the Declaration of Independence had been Irishmen. What truth there may be in this general statement I have no means of ascertaining; all I know is, that I heard it made. On this occasion, however, the Irishman was hanged, and the American was not.

Mary Shelley
1797 – 1851

M ary Shelley was the daughter of the philosopher William Godwin and of the feminist author Mary Wollstonecraft who died a few days after her birth. In 1814 she eloped with the poet Percy Bysshe Shelley whose wife subsequently killed herself. With Percy, Mary Shelley came to know Lord Byron and it was while staying near him in Switzerland that she conceived the idea of her first, immensely popular novel Frankenstein (1818). After her husband's death, Mary Shelley edited his works and wrote novellas, short stories and plays, as well as five more novels, including The Last Man (1826).

The Last Man is set in the future and describes the end of humanity through a general plague. The theme of the destruction of the world was a common one in Romantic poetry, including that of Byron, whose personality, along with Shelley's, informs the novel's characterization. The narrator of the work is Lionel Verney, the last man, whose close friend Adrian dies towards the conclusion of the account.

The following extract is reprinted from The Last Man (University of Nebraska Press, Lincoln, 1965).

From

The Last Man

[Volume two, Chapter five]

... O N the eighteenth of this month news arrived in London that the plague was in France and Italy. These tidings were at first whispered about town; but no one dared express aloud the soul-quailing intelligence. When any one met a friend in the street, he only cried as he hurried on, "You know!"—while the other, with an ejaculation of fear and horror, would answer,—"What will become of us?" At length it was mentioned in the newspapers. The paragraph was inserted in an obscure part: "We regret to state that there can be no longer a doubt of the plague having been introduced at Leghorn, Genoa, and Marseilles." No word of comment followed; each reader made his own fearful one. We were as a man who hears that his house is burning, and yet hurries through the streets, borne along by a lurking hope of a mistake, till he turns the corner, and sees his sheltering roof enveloped in a flame. Before it had been a rumour; but now in words uneraseable, in definite and undeniable print, the knowledge went forth. Its obscurity of situation rendered it the more conspicuous: the diminutive letters grew gigantic to the bewildered eye of fear: they seemed graven with a pen of iron, impressed by fire, woven in the clouds, stamped on the very front of the universe.

The English, whether travellers or residents, came pouring in one great revulsive stream, back on their own country; and with them crowds of Italians and Spaniards. Our little island was filled even to bursting. At first an unusual quantity of specie[1] made its appearance with the emigrants; but these people had no means of receiving back into their hands what they spent among us. With the advance of summer, and the increase of the distemper, rents were unpaid, and their remittances failed them. It was impossible to see these crowds of wretched, perishing creatures, late nurslings of luxury, and not stretch out a hand to save them. As at the conclusion of the eighteenth century, the English unlocked their hospitable store, for the relief of those driven from their homes by political revolution; so now they were not backward in affording aid to the victims of a more widespreading calamity. We had many foreign friends whom we eagerly sought out, and relieved from dreadful penury. Our Castle became an asylum for the unhappy. A little population occupied its halls. The revenue of its possessor, which had always found a mode of expenditure congenial to his generous nature, was now attended to more parsimoniously, that it might embrace a wider portion of utility. It was not however money, except partially, but the necessaries of life, that became scarce. It was difficult to find an immediate remedy. The usual one of imports was entirely cut off. In this emergency, to feed the very people to whom we had given refuge, we were obliged to yield to the plough and the mattock our pleasure-grounds and parks. Live stock diminished sensibly in the country, from the effects of the great demand in the market. Even the poor deer, our antlered protégés, were obliged to fall for the sake of worthier pensioners. The labour necessary to bring the lands to this sort of culture, employed and fed the offcasts of the diminished manufactories.

Adrian did not rest only with the exertions he could make with regard to his own possessions. He addressed himself to the wealthy of the land; he made proposals in parliament little adapted to please the rich; but his earnest pleadings and benevolent eloquence were irresistible. To give up their pleasure-grounds to the agriculturist, to diminish sensibly the number of horses kept for the purposes of luxury throughout the country, were means obvious, but unpleasing. Yet, to the honour of the English be it recorded, that, although natural disinclination made them delay awhile, yet when the misery of their fellow-creatures became glaring, an enthusiastic generosity inspired their decrees. The most luxurious were often the first to part with their indulgencies. As is common in communities, a fashion was set. The high-born ladies of the country would have deemed themselves disgraced if they had now enjoyed, what they before called a necessary, the ease of a carriage. Chairs, as in olden

[1] Coin or money.

time, and Indian palanquins were introduced for the infirm; but else it was nothing singular to see females of rank going on foot to places of fashionable resort. It was more common, for all who possessed landed property to secede to their estates, attended by whole troops of the indigent, to cut down their woods to erect temporary dwellings, and to portion out their parks, parterres and flower-gardens, to necessitous families. Many of these, of high rank in their own countries, now, with hoe in hand, turned up the soil. It was found necessary at last to check the spirit of sacrifice, and to remind those whose generosity proceeded to lavish waste, that, until the present state of things became permanent, of which there was no likelihood, it was wrong to carry change so far as to make a reaction difficult. Experience demonstrated that in a year or two pestilence would cease; it were well that in the mean time we should not have destroyed our fine breeds of horses, or have utterly changed the face of the ornamented portion of the country.

It may be imagined that things were in a bad state indeed, before this spirit of benevolence could have struck such deep roots. The infection had now spread in the southern provinces of France. But that country had so many resources in the way of agriculture, that the rush of population from one part of it to another, and its increase through foreign emigration, was less felt than with us. The panic struck appeared of more injury, than disease and its natural concomitants.

Winter was hailed, a general and never-failing physician. The embrowning woods, and swollen rivers, the evening mists, and morning frosts, were welcomed with gratitude. The effects of purifying cold were immediately felt; and the lists of mortality abroad were curtailed each week. Many of our visitors left us: those whose homes were far in the south, fled delightedly from our northern winter, and sought their native land, secure of plenty even after their fearful visitation. We breathed again. What the coming summer would bring, we knew not; but the present months were our own, and our hopes of a cessation of pestilence were high. . . .

[Volume three, Chapter one]

[*But the plague continues*]

Plague is the companion of spring, of sunshine, and plenty. We no longer struggle with her. We have forgotten what we did when she was not. Of old navies used to stem the giant ocean-waves betwixt Indus and the Pole for slight articles of luxury. Men made perilous journies to possess themselves of earth's splendid trifles, gems and gold. Human labour was wasted—human life set at nought. Now life is all that we covet; that this automaton of flesh should, with joints and springs in order, perform its functions, that this dwelling of the soul should be capable of containing its dweller. Our minds, late spread abroad through countless spheres and endless combinations of thought, now retrenched themselves behind this wall of flesh, eager to preserve its well-being only. We were surely sufficiently degraded.

At first the increase of sickness in spring brought increase of toil to such of us, who, as yet spared to life, bestowed our time and thoughts on our fellow creatures. We nerved ourselves to the task: "in the midst of despair we performed the tasks of hope." We went out with the resolution of disputing with our foe. We aided the sick, and comforted the sorrowing; turning from the multitudinous dead to the rare survivors, with an energy of desire that bore the resemblance of power, we bade them—live. Plague sat paramount the while, and laughed us to scorn.

Have any of you, my readers, observed the ruins of an anthill immediately after its destruction? At first it appears entirely deserted of its former inhabitants; in a little time you see an ant struggling through the upturned mould; they reappear by twos and threes, running hither and thither in search of their lost companions. Such were we upon earth, wondering aghast at the effects of pestilence. Our empty habitations remained, but the dwellers were gathered to the shades of the tomb.

As the rules of order and pressure of laws were lost, some began with hesitation and wonder to transgress the accustomed uses of society. Palaces were deserted, and the poor man dared at length, unreproved, intrude into the splendid apartments, whose very furniture and decorations were an unknown world to him. It was found, that, though at first the stop put to to all circulation of property, had reduced those before supported by the factitious wants of society to sudden and hideous poverty, yet when the boundaries of private possession were thrown down, the products of human labour at present existing were more, far more, than the thinned generation could possibly consume. To some among the poor this was matter of exultation. We were all equal now; magnificent dwellings, luxurious carpets, and beds of down, were afforded to all. Carriages and horses, gardens, pictures, statues, and princely libraries, there were enough of these even to superfluity; and there was nothing to prevent each from assuming possession of his share. We were all equal now, but near at hand was an equality still more levelling, a state where beauty and strength, and wisdom, would be as vain as riches and birth. The grave yawned beneath us all, and its prospect prevented any of us from enjoying the ease and plenty which in so awful a manner was presented to us.

Still the bloom did not fade on the cheeks of my babes; and Clara sprung up in years and growth, unsullied by disease. We had no reason to think the site of Windsor Castle peculiarly healthy, for many other families had expired beneath its roof; we lived therefore without any particular precaution; but we lived, it seemed, in safety. If Idris became thin and pale, it was anxiety that occasioned the change; an anxiety I could in no way alleviate. She never complained, but sleep and appetite fled from her, a slow fever preyed on her veins, her colour was hectic, and she often wept in secret; gloomy prognostications, care, and agonizing dread, ate up the principle of life within her. I could not fail to perceive this change. I often wished that I had permitted her to take her own course, and engage herself in such labours for the welfare of others as might have distracted her thoughts. But it was too late now. Besides that, with the nearly extinct race of man, all our toils grew near a conclusion, she was too weak; consumption, if so it might be called, or rather the over active life within her, which, as with Adrian, spent the vital oil in the early morning hours, deprived her limbs of strength. At night, when she could leave me unperceived, she wandered through the house, or hung over the couches of her children; and in the day time would sink into a perturbed sleep, while her murmurs and starts betrayed the unquiet dreams that vexed her. As this state of wretchedness became more confirmed, and, in spite of her endeavours at concealment more apparent, I strove, though vainly, to awaken in her courage and hope. I could not wonder at the vehemence of her care; her very soul was tenderness; she trusted indeed that she should not outlive me if I became the prey of the vast calamity, and this thought sometimes relieved her. We had for many years trod the highway of life hand in hand, and still thus linked, we might step within the shades of death; but her children, her lovely, playful animated children—beings sprung from her own dear side—portions of her own being—depositories of our loves—even if we died, it would be comfort to know that they ran man's accustomed course. But it would not be so; young and blooming as they were, they would die, and from the hopes of maturity, from the proud name of attained manhood, they were cut off for ever. Often with maternal affection she had figured their merits and talents exerted on life's wide stage. Alas for these latter days! The world had grown old, and all its inmates partook of the decrepitude. Why talk of infancy, manhood, and old age? We all stood equal sharers of the last throes of time-worn nature. Arrived at the same point of the world's age—there was no difference in us; the name of parent and child had lost their meaning; young boys and girls were level now with men. This was all true; but it was not less agonizing to take the admonition home.

Where could we turn, and not find a desolation pregnant with the dire lesson of example? The fields had been left uncultivated, weeds and gaudy flowers sprung up,—or where a few wheat-fields shewed signs of the living hopes of the husbandman, the work had been left halfway, the ploughman had died beside the plough; the horses had deserted the furrow, and no seedsman had approached the dead; the cattle unattended wandered over the fields and through the lanes; the tame inhabitants of the poultry yard, baulked of their daily food, had become wild—young lambs were dropt in flower-gardens, and the cow stalled in the hall of pleasure. Sickly and few, the country people neither went out to sow nor reap; but sauntered about the meadows, or lay under the hedges, when the inclement sky did not drive them to take shelter under the nearest roof. Many of those who remained, secluded themselves; some had laid up stores which should prevent the necessity of leaving their homes;—some deserted wife and child, and imagined that they secured their safety in utter solitude. Such had been Ryland's plan, and he was discovered dead and half-devoured by insects, in a house many miles from any other, with piles of food laid up in useless superfluity. Others made long journies to unite themselves to those they loved, and arrived to find them dead.

London did not contain above a thousand inhabitants; and this number was continually diminishing. Most of them were country people, come up for the sake of change; the Londoners had sought the country. The busy eastern part

of the town was silent, or at most you saw only where, half from cupidity, half
from curiosity, the warehouses had been more ransacked than pillaged: bales
of rich India goods, shawls of price, jewels, and spices, unpacked, strewed the
floors. In some places the possessor had to the last kept watch on his store, and
died before the barred gates. The massy portals of the churches swung creaking
on their hinges; and some few lay dead on the pavement. The wretched female,
loveless victim of vulgar brutality, had wandered to the toilet of high-born
beauty, and, arraying herself in the garb of splendour, had died before the
mirror which reflected to herself alone her altered appearance. Women whose
delicate feet had seldom touched the earth in their luxury, had fled in fright
and horror from their homes, till, losing themselves in the squalid streets of
the metropolis, they had died on the threshold of poverty. The heart sickened
at the variety of misery presented; and, when I saw a specimen of this gloomy
change, my soul ached with the fear of what might befall my beloved Idris and my
babes. Were they, surviving Adrian and myself, to find themselves protectorless
in the world? As yet the mind alone had suffered—could I for ever put off the
time, when the delicate frame and shrinking nerves of my child of prosperity,
the nursling of rank and wealth, who was my companion, should be invaded by
famine, hardship, and disease? Better die at once—better plunge a poinard in
her bosom, still untouched by drear adversity, and then again sheathe it in my
own! But, no; in times of misery we must fight against our destinies, and strive
not to be overcome by them. I would not yield, but to the last gasp resolutely
defended my dear ones against sorrow and pain; and if I were vanquished at
last, it should not be ingloriously. I stood in the gap, resisting the enemy—the
impalpable, invisible foe, who had so long beseiged us—as yet he had made
no breach: it must be my care that he should not, secretly undermining,
burst up within the very threshold of the temple of love, at whose altar
I daily sacrificed.

The hunger of Death was now stung more sharply by the diminution of
his food: or was it that before, the survivors being many, the dead were less
eagerly counted? Now each life was a gem, each human breathing form of far,
O! far more worth than subtlest imagery of sculptured stone; and the daily, nay,
hourly decrease visible in our numbers, visited the heart with sickening misery.
This summer extinguished our hopes, the vessel of society was wrecked, and
the shattered raft, which carried the few survivors over the sea of misery, was
riven and tempest tost. Man existed by twos and threes; man, the individual who
might sleep, and wake, and perform the animal functions; but man in himself
weak, yet more powerful in congregated numbers than wind or ocean; man,
the queller of the elements, the lord of created nature, the peer of demi-gods,
existed no longer.

Farewell to the patriotic scene, to the love of liberty and well earned meed
of virtuous aspiration!—farewell to crowded senate, vocal with the councils
of the wise, whose laws were keener than the sword blade tempered at
Damascus,—farewell to kingly pomp and warlike pageantry; the crowns are in
the dust, and the wearers are in their graves!—farewell to the desire of rule,
and the hope of victory; to high vaulting ambition, to the appetite for praise,

and the craving for the suffrage of their fellows! The nations are no longer! No senate sits in council for the dead; no scion of a time honoured dynasty pants to rule over the inhabitants of a charnel house; the general's hand is cold, and the soldier has his untimely grave dug in his native fields, unhonoured, though in youth. The market-place is empty, the candidate for popular favour finds none whom he can represent. To chambers of painted state farewell!—To midnight revelry, and the panting emulation of beauty, to costly dress and birth-day shew, to title and the gilded coronet farewell!

Farewell to the giant powers of man,—to knowledge that could pilot the deep-drawing bark through the opposing waters of shoreless ocean,—to science that directed the silken balloon through the pathless air,—to the power that could put a barrier to mighty waters, and set in motion wheels, and beams, and vast machinery, that could divide rocks of granite or marble, and make the mountains plain!

Farewell to the arts,—to eloquence, which is to the human mind as the winds to the sea, stirring, and then allaying it;—farewell to poetry and deep philosophy, for man's imagination is cold, and his enquiring mind can no longer expatiate on the wonders of life, for "there is no work, nor device, nor knowledge, nor wisdom in the grave, whither thou goest!"[2]—to the graceful building, which in its perfect proportion transcended the rude forms of nature, the fretted gothic and massy saracenic pile, to the stupendous arch and glorious dome, the fluted column with its capital, Corinthian, Ionic, or Doric, the peristyle and fair entablature, whose harmony of form is to the eye as musical concord to the ear!—farewell to sculpture, where the pure marble mocks human flesh, and in the plastic expression of the culled excellencies of the human shape, shines forth the god!—farewell to painting, the high wrought sentiment and deep knowledge of the artist's mind in pictured canvas—to paradisaical scenes, where trees are ever vernal, and the ambrosial air rests in perpetual glow:—to the stamped form of tempest, and wildest uproar of universal nature encaged in the narrow frame, O farewell! Farewell to music, and the sound of song; to the marriage of instruments, where the concord of soft and harsh unites in sweet harmony, and gives wings to the panting listeners, whereby to climb heaven, and learn the hidden pleasures of the eternals!—Farewell to the well-trod stage; a truer tragedy is enacted on the world's ample scene, that puts to shame mimic grief: to high-bred comedy, and the low buffoon, farewell!—Man may laugh no more.

Alas! to enumerate the adornments of humanity, shews, by what we have lost, how supremely great man was. It is all over now. He is solitary; like our first parents expelled from Paradise, he looks back towards the scene he has quitted. The high walls of the tomb, and the flaming sword of plague, lie between it and him. Like to our first parents, the whole earth is before him, a wide desart. Unsupported and weak, let him wander through fields where the unreaped corn stands in barren plenty, through copses planted by his fathers, through towns built for his use. Posterity is no more; fame, and ambition, and

[2] Ecclesiastes 12:5.

love, are words void of meaning; even as the cattle that grazes in the field, do thou, O deserted one, lie down at evening-tide, unknowing of the past, careless of the future, for from such fond ignorance alone canst thou hope for ease!

Joy paints with its own colours every act and thought. The happy do not feel poverty—for delight is as a gold-tissued robe, and crowns them with priceless gems. Enjoyment plays the cook to their homely fare, and mingles intoxication with their simple drink. Joy strews the hard couch with roses, and makes labour ease.

Sorrow doubles the burthen to the bent-down back; plants thorns in the unyielding pillow; mingles gall with water; adds saltness to their bitter bread; cloathing them in rags, and strewing ashes on their bare heads. To our irremediable distress every small and pelting inconvenience came with added force; we had strung our frames to endure the Atlean weight thrown on us; we sank beneath the added feather chance threw on us, "the grass-hopper was a burthen." Many of the survivors had been bred in luxury—their servants were gone, their powers of command vanished like unreal shadows: the poor even suffered various privations; and the idea of another winter like the last, brought affright to our minds. Was it not enough that we must die, but toil must be added?—must we prepare our funeral repast with labour, and with unseemly drudgery heap fuel on our deserted hearths—must we with servile hands fabricate the garments, soon to be our shroud?

Not so! We are presently to die, let us then enjoy to its full relish the remnant of our lives. Sordid care, avaunt! menial labours, and pains, slight in themselves, but too gigantic for our exhausted strength, shall make no part of our ephemeral existences. In the beginning of time, when, as now, man lived by families, and not by tribes or nations, they were placed in a genial clime, where earth fed them untilled, and the balmy air enwrapt their reposing limbs with warmth more pleasant than beds of down. The south is the native place of the human race; the land of fruits, more grateful to man than the hard-earned Ceres of the north,—of trees, whose boughs are as a palace-roof, of couches of roses, and of the thirst-appeasing grape. We need not there fear cold and hunger.

Look at England! the grass shoots up high in the meadows; but they are dank and cold, unfit bed for us. Corn we have none, and the crude fruits cannot support us. We must seek firing in the bowels of the earth, or the unkind atmosphere will fill us with rheums and aches. The labour of hundreds of thousands alone could make this inclement nook fit habitation for one man. To the south then, to the sun!—where nature is kind, where Jove has showered forth the contents of Amalthea's horn,[3] and earth is a garden.

England, late birth-place of excellence and school of the wise, thy children are gone, thy glory faded! Thou, England, wert the triumph of man! Small favour was shewn thee by thy Creator, thou Isle of the North; a ragged canvas naturally, painted by man with alien colours; but the hues he gave are faded, never more

---

3 Known as the horn of plenty, taken by Jove from the goat Amalthea, who fed him with her milk.

to be renewed. So we must leave thee, thou marvel of the world; we must bid farewell to thy clouds, and cold, and scarcity for ever! Thy manly hearts are still; thy tale of power and liberty at its close! Bereft of man, O little isle! the ocean waves will buffet thee, and the raven flap his wings over thee; thy soil will be birth-place of weeds, thy sky will canopy barrenness. It was not for the rose of Persia thou wert famous, nor the banana of the east; not for the spicy gales of India, nor the sugar groves of America; not for thy vines nor thy double harvests, nor for thy vernal airs, nor solstitial sun—but for thy children, their unwearied industry and lofty aspiration. They are gone, and thou goest with them the oft trodden path that leads to oblivion,—

> Farewell, sad Isle, farewell, thy fatal glory
> Is summed, cast up, and cancelled in this story[4]

[Volume three, Chapter ten]

[*Lionel, now the only human being left alive, journeys to Rome where he contemplates the past.*]

I was long wrapt by such ideas; but the soul wearies of a pauseless flight; and, stooping from its wheeling circuits round and round this spot, suddenly it fell ten thousand fathom deep, into the abyss of the present—into self-knowledge—into tenfold sadness. I roused myself—I cast off my waking dreams; and I, who just now could almost hear the shouts of the Roman throng, and was hustled by countless multitudes, now beheld the desart ruins of Rome sleeping under its own blue sky; the shadows lay tranquilly on the ground; sheep were grazing untended on the Palatine, and a buffalo stalked down the Sacred Way that led to the Capitol. I was alone in the Forum; alone in Rome; alone in the world. Would not one living man—one companion in my weary solitude, be worth all the glory and remembered power of this time-honoured city? Double sorrow—sadness, bred in Cimmerian caves, robed my soul in a mourning garb. The generations I had conjured up to my fancy, contrasted more strongly with the end of all—the single point in which, as a pyramid, the mighty fabric of society had ended, while I, on the giddy height, saw vacant space around me.

From such vague laments I turned to the contemplation of the minutiae of my situation. So far, I had not succeeded in the sole object of my desires, the finding a companion for my desolation. Yet I did not despair. It is true that my inscriptions were set up for the most part, in insignificant towns and villages; yet, even without these memorials, it was possible that the person, who like me should find himself alone in a depopulate land, should, like me, come to Rome. The more slender my expectation was, the more I chose to build on it, and to accommodate my actions to this vague possibility.

[4] From *The Character of London-Diurnall; with Severall Select Poems* (1644) by John Cleveland.

It became necessary therefore, that for a time I should domesticate myself at Rome. It became necessary, that I should look my disaster in the face—not playing the school-boy's part of obedience without submission; enduring life, and yet rebelling against the laws by which I lived.

Yet how could I resign myself? Without love, without sympathy, without communion with any, how could I meet the morning sun, and with it trace its oft repeated journey to the evening shades? Why did I continue to live—why not throw off the weary weight of time, and with my own hand, let out the fluttering prisoner from my agonized breast?—It was not cowardice that withheld me; for the true fortitude was to endure; and death had a soothing sound accompanying it, that would easily entice me to enter its demesne. But this I would not do. I had, from the moment I had reasoned on the subject, instituted myself the subject to fate, and the servant of necessity, the visible laws of the invisible God—I believed that my obedience was the result of sound reasoning, pure feeling, and an exalted sense of the true excellence and nobility of my nature. Could I have seen in this empty earth, in the seasons and their change, the hand of a blind power only, most willingly would I have placed my head on the sod, and closed my eyes on its loveliness for ever. But fate had administered life to me, when the plague had already seized on its prey—she had dragged me by the hair from out the strangling waves—By such miracles she had bought me for her own; I admitted her authority, and bowed to her decrees. If, after mature consideration, such was my resolve, it was doubly necessary that I should not lose the end of life, the improvement of my faculties, and poison its flow by repinings without end. Yet how cease to repine, since there was no hand near to extract the barbed spear that had entered my heart of hearts? I stretched out my hand, and it touched none whose sensations were responsive to mine. I was girded, walled in, vaulted over, by seven-fold barriers of loneliness. Occupation alone, if I could deliver myself up to it, would be capable of affording an opiate to my sleepless sense of woe. Having determined to make Rome my abode, at least for some months, I made arrangements for my accommodation—I selected my home. The Colonna Palace was well adapted for my purpose. Its grandeur—its treasure of paintings, its magnificent halls were objects soothing and even exhilarating.

I found the granaries of Rome well stored with grain, and particularly with Indian corn; this product requiring less art in its preparation for food, I selected as my principal support. I now found the hardships and lawlessness of my youth turn to account. A man cannot throw off the habits of sixteen years. Since that age, it is true, I had lived luxuriously, or at least surrounded by all the conveniences civilization afforded. But before that time, I had been "as uncouth a savage, as the wolf-bred founder of old Rome"—and now, in Rome itself, robber and shepherd propensities, similar to those of its founder, were of advantage to its sole inhabitant. I spent the morning riding and shooting in the Campagna—I passed long hours in the various galleries—I gazed at each statue, and lost myself in a reverie before many a fair Madonna or beauteous nymph. I haunted the Vatican, and stood surrounded by marble forms of divine beauty. Each stone deity was possessed by sacred gladness, and the eternal fruition of love. They looked on me with unsympathizing complacency, and often in wild accents I reproached them for their supreme indifference—for they were human shapes, the human form divine was manifest in each fairest limb and lineament. The perfect moulding brought with it the idea of colour and motion; often, half in bitter mockery, half in self-delusion, I clasped their icy proportions, and, coming between Cupid and his Psyche's lips, pressed the unconceiving marble.

I endeavoured to read. I visited the libraries of Rome. I selected a volume, and, choosing some sequestered, shady nook, on the banks of the Tiber, or opposite the fair temple in the Borghese Gardens, or under the old pyramid of Cestius, I endeavoured to conceal me from myself, and immerse myself in the subject traced on the pages before me. As if in the same soil you plant nightshade and a myrtle tree, they will each appropriate the mould, moisture, and air administered, for the fostering their several properties—so did my grief find sustenance, and power of existence, and growth, in what else had been divine manna, to feed radiant meditation. Ah! while I streak this paper with the tale of what my so named occupations were—while I shape the skeleton of my days—my hand trembles—my heart pants, and my brain refuses to lend expression, or phrase, or idea, by which to image forth the veil of unutterable woe that clothed these bare realities. O, worn and beating heart, may I dissect thy fibres, and tell how in each unmitigable misery, sadness dire, repinings, and despair, existed? May I record my many ravings—the wild curses I hurled at torturing nature—and how I have passed days shut out from light and food—from all except the burning hell alive in my own bosom?

I was presented, meantime, with one other occupation, the one best fitted to discipline my melancholy thoughts, which strayed backwards, over many a ruin, and through many a flowery glade, even to the mountain recess, from which in early youth I had first emerged.

During one of my rambles through the habitations of Rome, I found writing materials on a table in an author's study. Parts of a manuscript lay scattered about. It contained a learned disquisition on the Italian language; one page an unfinished dedication to posterity, for whose profit the writer had sifted and selected the niceties of this harmonious language—to whose everlasting benefit he bequeathed his labours.

I also will write a book, I cried—for whom to read?—to whom dedicated? And then with silly flourish (what so capricious and childish as despair?) I wrote,

DEDICATION
TO THE ILLUSTRIOUS DEAD.
SHADOWS, ARISE, AND READ YOUR FALL!
BEHOLD THE HISTORY OF THE
LAST MAN.

Yet, will not this world be re-peopled, and the children of a saved pair of lovers, in some to me unknown and unattainable seclusion, wandering to these prodigious relics of the ante-pestilential race, seek to learn how beings so wondrous in their achievements, with imaginations infinite, and powers godlike, had departed from their home to an unknown country?

I will write and leave in this most ancient city, this "world's sole monument," a record of these things. I will leave a monument of the existence of Verney, the Last Man. At first I thought only to speak of plague, of death, and last, of desertion; but I lingered fondly on my early years, and recorded with sacred zeal the virtues of my companions. They have been with me during the fulfilment of my task. I have brought it to an end—I lift my eyes from my paper—again they are lost to me. Again I feel that I am alone.

A year has passed since I have been thus occupied. The seasons have made their wonted round, and decked this eternal city in a changeful robe of surpassing beauty. A year has passed; and I no longer *guess* at my state or my prospects—loneliness is my familiar, sorrow my inseparable companion. I have endeavoured to brave the storm—I have endeavoured to school myself to fortitude—I have sought to imbue myself with the lessons of wisdom. It will not do. My hair has become nearly grey—my voice, unused now to utter sound, comes strangely on my ears. My person, with its human powers and features, seems to me a monstrous excrescence of nature. How express in human language a woe human being until this hour never knew! How give intelligible expression to a pang none but I could ever understand!—No one has entered Rome. None will ever come. I smile bitterly at the delusion I have so long nourished, and still more, when I reflect that I have exchanged it for another as delusive, as false, but to which I now cling with the same fond trust.

Winter has come again; and the gardens of Rome have lost their leaves—the sharp air comes over the Campagna, and has driven its brute inhabitants to take up their abode in the many dwellings of the deserted city—frost has suspended the gushing fountains—and Trevi has stilled her eternal music. I had made a rough calculation, aided by the stars, by which I endeavoured to ascertain the first day of the new year. In the old out-worn age, the Sovereign Pontiff was used to go in solemn pomp, and mark the renewal of the year by driving a nail in the gate of the temple of Janus. On that day I ascended St. Peter's, and carved on its topmost stone the era 2100, last year of the world!

My only companion was a dog, a shaggy fellow, half water and half shepherd's dog, whom I found tending sheep in the Campagna. His master was dead, but nevertheless he continued fulfilling his duties in expectation of his return. If a sheep strayed from the rest, he forced it to return to the flock, and sedulously kept off every intruder. Riding in the Campagna I had come upon his sheep-walk, and for some time observed his repetition of lessons learned from man, now useless, though unforgotten. His delight was excessive when he saw me. He sprung up to my knees; he capered round and round, wagging his tail, with the short, quick bark of pleasure: he left his fold to follow me, and from that day has never neglected to watch by and attend on me, shewing boisterous gratitude whenever I caressed or talked to him. His pattering steps and mine alone were heard, when we entered the magnificent extent of nave and aisle of St. Peter's. We ascended the myriad steps together, when on the summit I achieved my design, and in rough figures noted the date of the last year. I then turned to gaze on the country, and to take leave of Rome. I have long determined to quit it, and I now formed the plan I would adopt for my future career, after I had left this magnificent abode.

A solitary being is by instinct a wanderer, and that I would become. A hope of amelioration always attends on change of place, which would even lighten the burthen of my life. I had been a fool to remain in Rome all this time: Rome noted for Mal'aria, the famous caterer for death. But it was still possible, that, could I visit the whole extent of earth, I should find in some part of the wide extent a survivor. Methought the sea-side was the most probable retreat to be chosen by such a one. If left alone in an inland district, still they could not continue in the spot where their last hopes had been extinguished; they would journey on, like me, in search of a partner for their solitude, till the watery barrier stopped their further progress.

To that water—cause of my woes, perhaps now to be their cure, I would betake myself. Farewell, Italy!—farewell, thou ornament of the world, matchless Rome, the retreat of the solitary one during long months!—to civilized life—to the settled home and succession of monotonous days, farewell! Peril will now be mine; and I hail her as a friend—death will perpetually cross my path, and I will meet him as a benefactor; hardship, inclement weather, and dangerous tempests will be my sworn mates. Ye spirits of storm, receive me! ye powers of destruction, open wide your arms, and clasp me for ever! if a kinder power have not decreed another end, so that after long endurance I may reap my reward, and again feel my heart beat near the heart of another like to me.

Tiber, the road which is spread by nature's own hand, threading her continent, was at my feet, and many a boat was tethered to the banks. I would with a few books, provisions, and my dog, embark in one of these and float down the current of the stream into the sea; and then, keeping near land, I would coast the beauteous shores and sunny promontories of the blue Mediterranean, pass Naples, along Calabria, and would dare the twin perils of Scylla and Charybdis;[5] then, with fearless aim, (for what had I to lose?) skim ocean's surface towards Malta and the further Cyclades.[6] I would avoid Constantinople, the sight of whose well-known towers and inlets belonged to another state of existence from my present one; I would coast Asia Minor, and Syria, and, passing the seven-mouthed Nile, steer northward again, till losing sight of forgotten Carthage and deserted Lybia, I should reach the pillars of Hercules.[7] And then—no matter where—the oozy caves, and soundless depths of ocean may be my dwelling, before I accomplish this long-drawn voyage, or the arrow of disease find my heart as I float singly on the weltering Mediterranean; or, in some place I touch at, I may find what I seek—a companion; or if this may not be—to endless time, decrepid and grey headed—youth already in the grave with those I love—the lone wanderer will still unfurl his sail, and clasp the tiller—and, still obeying the

[5] Scylla and Charybdis are rocks and a whirlpool off the coast of Crete, renowned for the danger they present to ships.
[6] Islands in the Ægæan Sea.
[7] The rocks of Gibraltar and Centa on either side of the Strait of Gibraltar.

breezes of heaven, for ever round another and another promontory, anchoring in another and another bay, still ploughing seedless ocean, leaving behind the verdant land of native Europe, adown the tawny shore of Africa, having weathered the fierce seas of the Cape, I may moor my worn skiff in a creek, shaded by spicy groves of the odorous islands of the far Indian ocean.

These are wild dreams. Yet since, now a week ago, they came on me, as I stood on the height of St. Peter's, they have ruled my imagination. I have chosen my boat, and laid in my scant stores. I have selected a few books; the principal are Homer and Shakespeare—But the libraries of the world are thrown open to me—and in any port I can renew my stock. I form no expectation of alteration for the better; but the monotonous present is intolerable to me. Neither hope nor joy are my pilots—restless despair and fierce desire of change lead me on. I long to grapple with danger, to be excited by fear, to have some task, however slight or voluntary, for each day's fulfilment. I shall witness all the variety of appearance, that the elements can assume—I shall read fair augury in the rainbow—menace in the cloud—some lesson or record dear to my heart in everything. Thus around the shores of deserted earth, while the sun is high, and the moon waxes or wanes, angels, the spirits of the dead, and the ever-open eye of the Supreme, will behold the tiny bark, freighted with Verney—the LAST MAN.

THE END

Harriet Martineau

1802 – 76

arriet Martineau, novelist and political and social commentator, had an unhappy childhood in East Anglia; she used her childhood experiences not only in her Autobiography (1877) but also in Household Education (1849) and in her novel Deerbrook (1839). In 1834 and 1837 she visited America and wrote critically of the treatment of women and blacks in a country professedly devoted to liberty. She had a formidable reputation as an economist and a journalist, and wrote more than one thousand leader articles for major newspapers of her day. Much of her fame derived from the nine volumes of her Illustrations of Political Economy (1832–34); an outstanding *success, the volumes educated the public in the economic principles of the emerging individualistic and capitalist system.*

The following extract is reprinted from Harriet Martineau's Autobiography, *vol. I (Smith, Elder & Co., 3rd edn, 1877).*

From

Harriet Martineau's Autobiography

FIRST PERIOD
TO EIGHT YEARS
OLD

SECTION I
[1802–1807]

MY first recollections are of some infantile impressions which were in abeyance for a long course of years, and then revived in an inexplicable way,—as by a flash of lightning over a far horizon in the night. There is no doubt of the genuineness of the remembrance, as the facts could not have been told me by any one else. I remember standing on the threshold of a cottage, holding fast by the doorpost, and putting my foot down, in repeated attempts to reach the ground. Having accomplished the step, I toddled (I remember the uncertain feeling) to a tree before the door, and tried to clasp and get round it; but the rough bark hurt my hands. At night of the same day, in bed, I was disconcerted by the coarse feel of the sheets,—so much less smooth and cold than those at home; and I was alarmed by the creaking of the bedstead when I moved. It was a turn-up bedstead in a cottage, or small farm-house at Carleton, where I was sent for my health, being a delicate child. My mother's account of things was that I was all but starved to death in the first weeks of my life,—the wetnurse being very poor, and holding on to her good place after her milk was going or gone. The discovery was made when I was three months old, and when I was fast sinking under diarrhoea. My bad health during my whole childhood and youth, and even my deafness, was always ascribed by my mother to this. However it might be about that, my health certainly was very bad till I was nearer thirty than twenty years of age; and never was poor mortal cursed with a more beggarly nervous system. The long years of indigestion by day and night-mare terrors are mournful to think of now.—Milk has radically disagreed with me, all my life: but when I was a child, it was a thing unheard of for children not to be fed on milk: so, till I was old enough to have tea at breakfast, I went on having a horrid lump at my throat for hours of every morning, and the most terrific oppressions in the night. Sometimes the dim light of the windows in the night seemed to advance till it pressed upon my eyeballs, and then the windows would seem to recede to an infinite distance. If I laid my hand under my head on the pillow, the hand seemed to vanish almost to a point, while the head grew as big as a mountain. Sometimes I was panic struck at the head of the stairs, and was sure I could never get down; and I could never cross the yard to the garden without flying and panting, and fearing to look behind, because a wild beast was after me. The starlight sky was the worst; it was always coming down, to stifle and crush me, and rest upon my head. I do not remember any dread of thieves or ghosts in particular; but things as I actually saw them were dreadful to me; and it now appears to me that I had scarcely any respite from the terror. My fear of persons was as great as any other. To the best of my belief, the first person I was ever not afraid of was Aunt Kentish, who won my heart and my confidence when I was sixteen. My heart was ready enough to flow out; and it often did: but I always repented of such expansion, the next time I dreaded to meet a human face.—It now occurs to me, and it may be worth while to note it,—what the extremest terror of all was about. We were often sent to walk on the Castle Hill at Norwich. In the wide area below, the residents were wont to expose their feather-beds, and to beat them with a stick. That sound,—a dull shock,—used to make my heart stand still: and it was no use my standing at the rails above, and seeing the process. The striking of the blow and the arrival of the sound did not correspond; and this made matters worse. I hated that walk; and I believe for that reason. My parents knew nothing of all this. It never occurred to me to speak of any thing I felt most: and I doubt whether they ever had the slightest idea of my miseries. It seems to me now that a little closer observation would have shown them the causes of the bad health and fitful temper which gave them so much anxiety on my account; and I am sure that a little more of the cheerful tenderness which was in those days thought bad for children, would have saved me from my worst faults, and from a world of suffering.

My hostess and nurse at the above-mentioned cottage was a Mrs. Merton, who was, as was her husband, a Methodist or melancholy Calvinist of some sort. The family story about me was that I came home the absurdest little preacher of my years (between two and three) that ever was. I used to nod my head emphatically, and say 'Never ky for tyfles:' 'Dooty fust, and pleasure afterwards,' and so forth: and I sometimes got courage to edge up to strangers, and ask them to give me—'a maxim.' Almost before I could join letters, I got some sheets of paper, and folded them into a little square book, and wrote, in double lines, two or three in a page, my beloved maxims. I believe this was my first effort at book-making. It was probably what I picked up at Carleton that made me so intensely religious as I certainly was from a very early age. The religion was of a bad sort enough, as might be expected from the urgency of my needs; but I doubt whether I could have got through without it. I pampered my vain-glorious propensities by dreams of divine favour, to make up for my utter deficiency of self-respect: and I got rid of otherwise incessant remorse by a most convenient confession and repentance, which relieved my nerves without at all, I suspect, improving my conduct.

To revert to my earliest recollections:—I certainly could hardly walk alone when our nursemaid took us,—including my sister Elizabeth, who was eight years older than myself,—an unusual walk; through a lane, (afterwards called by us the 'Spinner's Lane') where some Miss Taskers, acquaintances of Elizabeth's and her seniors, were lodging, in a cottage which had a fir grove behind it. Somebody set me down at the foot of a fir, where I was distressed by the slight rising of the ground at the root, and by the long grass, which seemed a terrible entanglement. I looked up the tree, and was scared at its height, and at that of so many others. I was comforted with a fir-cone; and then one of the Miss Taskers caught me up in her arms and kissed me; and I was too frightened to cry till we got away.—I was not more than two years old when an impression of touch occurred to me which remains vivid to this day. It seems indeed as if impressions of touch were at that age more striking than those from the other senses. I say this from observation of others besides myself; for my own case is peculiar in that matter. Sight, hearing and touch were perfectly good in early childhood; but I never had the sense of smell; and that of taste was therefore exceedingly imperfect.—On the occasion I refer to, I was carried down a flight of steep back stairs, and Rachel (a year and half older than I) clung to the nursemaid's gown, and Elizabeth was going before, (still quite a little girl) when I put down my finger ends to feel a flat velvet button on the top of Rachel's bonnet. The rapture of the sensation was really monstrous, as I remember it now. Those were our mourning bonnets for a near relation; and this marks the date, proving me to have been only two years old.

I was under three when my brother James was born. That day was another of the distinct impressions which flashed upon me in after years. I found myself within the door of the best bedroom,—an impressive place from being seldom used, from its having a dark, polished floor, and from the awful large gay figures of the chintz bed hangings. That day the curtains were drawn, the window blinds were down, and an unknown old woman, in a mob cap, was at the fire, with a bundle of flannel in her arms. She beckoned to me, and I tried to go, though it seemed impossible to cross the slippery floor. I seem to hear now the pattering of my feet. When I arrived at her knee, the nurse pushed out with her foot a tiny chair, used as a foot-stool, made me sit down on it, laid the bundle of flannel across my knees, and opened it so that I saw the little red face of the baby. I then found out that there was somebody in the bed,—seeing a nightcap on the pillow. This was on the 21st of April, 1805. I have a distinct recollection of some incidents of that summer. My mother did not recover well from her confinement, and was sent to the sea, at Yarmouth. On our arrival there, my father took me along the old jetty,—little knowing what terror I suffered. I remember the strong grasp of his large hand being some comfort; but there were holes in the planking of the jetty quite big enough to let my foot through; and they disclosed the horrible sight of waves flowing and receding below, and great tufts of green weeds swaying to and fro. I remember the sitting-room at our lodgings, and my mother's dress as she sat picking shrimps, and letting me try to help her.—Of all my many fancies, perhaps none was so terrible as a dream that I had at four years old. The impression is as fresh as possible now; but I cannot at all understand what the fright was about. I know nothing more strange than this power of re-entering, as it were, into the narrow mind of an infant, so as to compare it with that of maturity; and therefore it may be worth while to record that piece of precious nonsense,—my dream at four years old. I imagine I was learning my letters then from cards, where each letter had its picture,—as a stag for S. I dreamed that we children were taking our walk with our nursemaid out of St. Austin's Gate (the nearest bit of country to our house). Out of the public-house there came a stag, with prodigious antlers. Passing the pump, it crossed the road to us, and made a polite bow, with its head on one side, and with a scrape of one foot, after which it pointed with its foot to the public-house, and spoke to me, inviting me in. The maid declined, and turned to go home. Then came the terrible part. By the time we were at our own door, it was dusk, and we went up the steps in the dark; but in the kitchen it was bright sunshine. My mother was standing at the dresser, breaking sugar; and she lifted me up, and set me in the sun, and gave me a bit of sugar. Such was the dream which froze me with horror! Who shall say why?—But my panics were really unaccountable. They were a matter of pure sensation, without any intellectual justification whatever, even of the wildest kind. A magic-lantern was exhibited to us on Christmas-day, and once or twice in the year besides. I used to see it cleaned by daylight, and to handle all its parts,—understanding its whole structure; yet, such was my terror of the white circle on the wall, and of the moving slides, that, to speak the plain truth, the first apparition always brought on bowel-complaint; and, at the age of thirteen, when I was pretending to take care of little children during the exhibition, I could never look at it without having the back of a chair to grasp, or hurting myself, to carry off the intolerable sensation. My bitter shame may be conceived; but then, I was always in a state of shame about something or other. I was afraid to walk in the town, for some years, if I remember right, for fear of meeting two people. One was an unknown old lady who very properly rebuked me one day for turning her off the very narrow pavement of London Lane, telling me, in an awful way, that little people should make way for their elders. The other was an unknown farmer, in whose field we had been gleaning (among other trespassers) before the shocks were carried. This man left the field after us, and followed us into the city,—no doubt, as I thought, to tell the Mayor, and send the constable after us. I wonder how long it was before I left off expecting that constable. There were certain little imps, however, more alarming still. Our house was in a narrow street; and all its windows, except two or three at the back, looked eastwards. It had no sun in the front rooms, except before breakfast in summer. One summer morning, I went into the drawing-room, which was not much used in those days, and saw a sight which made me hide my face in a chair, and scream with terror. The drops of the lustres on the mantlepiece, on which the sun was shining, were somehow set in motion, and the prismatic colours danced vehemently on the walls. I thought they were alive,—imps of some sort; and I never dared to into that room alone in the morning, from that time forward. I am afraid I must own that my heart has beat, all my life long, at the dancing of prismatic colours on the wall.

I was getting some comfort, however, from religion by this time. The Sundays began to be marked days, and pleasantly marked, on the whole. I do not know why crocuses were particularly associated with Sunday at that time; but probably my mother might have walked in the garden with us, some early spring Sunday. My idea of Heaven was of a place gay with yellow and lilac crocuses. My love of gay colours was very strong. When I was sent with the keys to a certain bureau in my mother's room, to fetch miniatures of my father and grandfather, to be shown to visitors, I used to stay an unconscionable time, though dreading punishment for it, but utterly unable to resist the fascination of a certain watch-ribbon kept in a drawer there. This ribbon had a pattern in floss silk, gay and beautifully shaded; and I used to look at it till I was sent for, to be questioned as to what I had been about. The young wild parsley and other weeds in the hedges used to make me sick with their luscious green in spring. Once crimson and purple sunrise I well remember, when James could hardly walk alone, and I could not therefore have been more than five. I awoke very early, that summer morning, and saw the maid sound asleep in her bed, and 'the baby' in his crib. The room was at the top of the house; and some rising ground beyond the city could be seen over the opposite roofs. I crept out of bed, saw James's pink toes showing themselves invitingly through the rails of his crib, and gently pinched them, to wake him. With a world of trouble I got him over the side, and helped him to the window, and upon a chair there. I wickedly opened the window, and the cool air blew in; and yet the maid did not wake. Our arms were smutted with the blacks on the window-sill, and our bare feet were corded with the impression of the rush-bottomed chair; but we were not found out. The sky was gorgeous, and I talked very religiously to the child. I remember the mood, and the pleasure of expressing it, but nothing of what I said.

I must have been a remarkably religious child, for the only support and pleasure I remember having from a very early age was from that source. I was just seven when the grand event of my childhood took place,—a journey to Newcastle to spend the summer (my mother and four of her children) at my grandfather's; and I am certain that I cared more for religion before and during that summer than for anything else. It was after our return, when Ann Turner, daughter of the Unitarian Minister there, was with us, that my piety first took a practical character; but it was familiar to me as an indulgence long before. While I was afraid of everybody I saw, I was not in the least afraid of God. Being usually very unhappy, I was constantly longing for heaven, and seriously, and very frequently planning suicide in order to get there. I was sure that suicide would not stand in the way of my getting there. I knew it was considered a crime; but I did not feel it so. I had a devouring passion for justice;—justice, first to my own precious self, and then to other oppressed people. Justice was precisely what was least understood in our house, in regard to servants and children. Now and then I desperately poured out my complaints; but in general I brooded over my injuries, and those of others who dared not speak; and then the temptation to suicide was very strong. No doubt, there was much vindictiveness in it. I gloated over the thought that I would make somebody

care about me in some sort of way at last: and, as to my reception in the other
world, I felt sure that God could not be very angry with me for making haste
to him when nobody else cared for me, and so many people plagued me. One
day I went to the kitchen to get the great carving knife, to cut my throat; but
the servants were at dinner; and this put it off for that time. By degrees, the
design dwindled down into running away. I used to lean out of the window,
and look up and down the street, and wonder how far I could go without being
caught. I had no doubt at all that if I once got into a farm-house, and wore
a woollen petticoat, and milked the cows, I should be safe, and that nobody
would inquire about me any more.—It is evident enough that my temper must
have been very bad. It seems to me now that it was downright devilish, except
for a placability which used to annoy me sadly. My temper might have been
early made a thoroughly good one, by the slightest indulgence shown to my
natural affections, and any rational dealing with my faults: but I was almost the
youngest of a large family, and subject, not only to the rule of severity to which
all were liable, but also to the rough and contemptuous treatment of the elder
children, who meant no harm, but injured me irreparably. I had no self-respect,
and an unbounded need of approbation and affection. My capacity for jealousy
was something frightful. When we were little more than infants, Mr. Thomas
Watson, son of my father's partner, one day came into the yard, took Rachel up
in his arms, gave her some grapes off the vine, and carried her home, across
the street, to give her Gay's Fables,[1] bound in red and gold. I stood with a
bursting heart, beating my hoop, and hating every body in the world. I always
hated Gay's Fables, and for long could not abide a red book. Nobody dreamed
of all this; and the 'taking down' system was pursued with me as with the rest,
issuing in the assumed doggedness and wilfulness which made me desperately
disagreeable during my youth, to every body at home. The least word or tone
of kindness melted me instantly, in spite of the strongest predeterminations to
be hard and offensive. . . .

[1818]

. . . ONE of our school-fellows was a clever, mischievous girl,—so clever,
and so much older than myself as to have great influence over me
when she chose to try her power, though I disapproved her ways very heartily.
She one day asked me, in a corner, in a mysterious sort of way, whether I did
not perceive that Rachel was the favourite at home, and treated with manifest
partiality. Everybody else, she said, observed it. This had never distinctly occurred
to me. Rachel was handy and useful, and not paralysed by fear, as I was; and,
very naturally, our busy mother resorted to her for help, and put trust in her
about matters of business, not noticing the growth of an equally natural habit in
Rachel of quizzing[2] or snubbing me, as the elder ones did. From the day of this
mischievous speech of my school-fellow, I was on the watch, and with the usual

[1] John Gay's popular *Fables* appeared in 1727, the second series in 1738.
[2] Teasing.

result to the jealous. Months,—perhaps a year or two—passed on while I was brooding over this, without a word to any one; and then came the explosion, one winter evening after tea, when my eldest sister was absent, and my mother, Rachel and I were sitting at work. Rachel criticised something that I said, in which I happened to be right. After once defending myself, I sat silent. My mother remarked on my 'obstinacy,' saying that I was 'not a bit convinced.' I replied that nothing convincing had been said. My mother declared that she agreed with Rachel, and that I ought to yield. Then I passed the verge, and got wrong. A sudden force of daring entering my mind, I said, in the most provoking way possible, that this was nothing new, as she always did agree with Rachel against me. My mother put down her work, and asked me what I meant by that. I looked her full in the face, and said that what I meant was that every thing that Rachel said and did was right, and every thing that I said and did was wrong. Rachel burst into a insulting laugh, and was sharply bidden to 'be quiet.' I saw by this that I had gained some ground; and this was made clearer by my mother sternly desiring me to practise my music. I saw that she wanted to gain time. The question now was how I should get through. My hands were clammy and tremulous: my fingers stuck to each other; my eyes were dim, and there was a roaring in my ears. I could easily have fainted; and it might have done no harm if I had. But I made a tremendous effort to appear calm. I opened the piano, lighted a candle with a steady hand, began, and derived strength from the first chords. I believe I never played better in my life. Then the question was—how was I ever to leave off? On I went for what seemed to me an immense time, till my mother sternly called to me to leave off and go to bed. With my candle in my hand, I said, 'Good night.' My mother laid down her work, and said, 'Harriet, I am more displeased with you to-night than ever I have been in your life.' Thought I, 'I don't care: I have got it out, and it is all true.' 'Go and say your prayers,' my mother continued; 'and ask God to forgive you for your conduct to-night; for I don't know that I can. Go to your prayers.' Thought I,—'No, I shan't.' And I did not: and that was the only night from my infancy to mature womanhood that I did not pray. I detected misgiving in my mother's forced manner; and I triumphed. If the right was on my side (as I entirely believed) the power was on hers; and what the next morning was to be I could not conceive. I slept little, and went down sick with dread. Not a word was said, however, then or ever, of the scene of the preceding night; but henceforth, a most scrupulous impartiality between Rachel and me was shown. If the occasion had been better used still,—if my mother had but bethought herself of saying to me, 'My child, I never dreamed that these terrible thoughts were in your mind. I am your mother. Why do you not tell me every thing that makes you unhappy?' I believe this would have wrought in a moment that cure which it took years to effect, amidst reserve and silence. . . .

[1826]

A ND now my own special trial was at hand. It is not necessary to go into detail about it. The news which got abroad that we had grown comparatively poor,—and the evident certainty that we were never likely to be rich, so wrought

upon the mind of one friend as to break down the mischief which I have referred
to as caused by ill-offices. My friend had believed me rich, was generous about
making me a poor man's wife, and had been discouraged in more ways than one.
He now came to me, and we were soon virtually engaged. I was at first very anxious
and unhappy. My veneration for his *morale* was such that I felt that I dared not
undertake the charge of his happiness: and yet I dared not refuse, because I saw
it would be his death blow. I was ill,—I was deaf,—I was in an entangled state
of mind between conflicting duties and some lower considerations; and many a
time did I wish, in my fear that I should fail, that I had never seen him. I am far
from wishing that now;—now that the beauty of his goodness remains to me,
clear of all painful regrets. But there was a fearful period to pass through. Just
when I was growing happy, surmounting my fears and doubts, and enjoying his
attachment, the consequences of his long struggle and suspense overtook him. He
became suddenly insane; and after months of illness of body and mind, he died.
The calamity was aggravated to me by the unaccountable insults I received from
his family, whom I had never seen. Years afterwards, when his sister and I met,
the mystery was explained. His family had been given to understand, by cautious
insinuations, that I was actually engaged to another, while receiving my friend's
addresses! There has never been any doubt in my mind that, considering what I
was in those days, it was happiest for us both that our union was prevented by any
means. I am, in truth, very thankful for not having married at all. I have never since
been tempted, nor have suffered any thing at all in relation to that matter which is
held to be all-important to woman,—love and marriage. Nothing, I mean, beyond
occasional annoyance, presently disposed of. Every literary woman, no doubt, has
plenty of importunity of that sort to deal with; but freedom of mind and coolness
of manner dispose of it very easily: and since the time I have been speaking
of, my mind has been wholly free from all idea of love-affairs. My subsequent
literary life in London was clear from all difficulty and embarrassment,—no
doubt because I was evidently too busy, and too full of interest of other kinds
to feel any awkwardness,—to say nothing of my being then thirty years of age;
an age at which, if ever, a woman is certainly qualified to take care of herself. I
can easily conceive how I might have been tempted,—how some deep springs
in my nature might have been touched, then as earlier; but, as a matter of
fact, they never were; and I consider the immunity a great blessing, under the
liabilities of a moral condition such as mine was in the olden time. If I had
had a husband dependent on me for his happiness, the responsibility would
have made me wretched. I had not faith enough in myself to endure avoidable
responsibility. If my husband had *not* depended on me for his happiness,
I should have been jealous. So also with children. The care would have so
overpowered the joy,—the love would have so exceeded the ordinary chances
of life,—the fear on my part would have so impaired the freedom on theirs,
that I rejoice not to have been involved in a relation for which I was, or
believed myself unfit. The veneration in which I hold domestic life has always
shown me that that life was not for those whose self-respect had been early
broken down, or had never grown. Happily, the majority are free from this
disability. Those who suffer under it had better be as I,—as my observation

of married, as well as single life assures me. When I see what conjugal love is, in the extremely rare cases in which it is seen in its perfection, I feel that there is a power of attachment in me that has never been touched. When I am among little children, it frightens me to think what my idolatry of my own children would have been. But, through it all, I have ever been thankful to be alone. My strong will, combined with anxiety of conscience, makes me fit only to live alone; and my taste and liking are for living alone. The older I have grown, the more serious and irremediable have seemed to me the evils and disadvantages of married life, as it exists among us at this time: and I am provided with what it is the bane of single life in ordinary cases to want—substantial, laborious and serious occupation. My business in life has been to think and learn, and to speak out with absolute freedom what I have thought and learned. The freedom is itself a positive and never-failing enjoyment to me, after the bondage of my early life. My work and I have been fitted to each other, as is proved by the success of my work and my own happiness in it. The simplicity and independence of this vocation first suited my infirm and ill-developed nature, and then sufficed for my needs, together with family ties and domestic duties, such as I have been blessed with, and as every woman's heart requires. Thus, I am not only entirely satisfied with my lot, but think it the very best for me,—under my constitution and circumstances: and I long ago came to the conclusion that, without meddling with the case of the wives and mothers, I am probably the happiest single woman in England. Who could have believed, in that awful year 1826, that such would be my conclusion a quarter of a century afterwards!

Elizabeth Barrett Browning

1806 – 61

E lizabeth Barrett Browning was the oldest of the twelve children of the notoriously possessive Edward Barrett Moulton-Barrett and his wife Mary. Educated at home, she became an invalid in her teens. She began *writing poetry early in life and by 1838 had published three volumes. Her famous courtship by the poet Robert Browning was expressed in numerous letters and in her extremely popular* Sonnets from the Portuguese *(1850). In 1846, knowing her father's hostility to his children's marrying, she eloped with Browning; the couple settled in Florence where her health improved. They remained there, with frequent visits to England, for the rest of her life. Barrett Browning's later poems often concern political and social issues: Italian politics, American slavery and, in the lengthy* Aurora Leigh *(1856), women's place in patriarchal culture.*

The following poems are reprinted from Selections from the Poetry of Elizabeth Barrett Browning *(1883).*

Sonnets from the Portuguese[1]

I

I THOUGHT once how Theocritus[2] had sung
Of the sweet years, the dear and wished-for years,
Who each one in a gracious hand appears
To bear a gift for mortals, old or young:
And, as I mused it in his antique tongue,
I saw, in gradual vision through my tears,
The sweet, sad years, the melancholy years,
Those of my own life, who by turns had flung
A shadow across me. Straightway I was 'ware,
So weeping, how a mystic Shape did move
Behind me, and drew me backward by the hair;
And a voice said in mastery, while I strove,—
'Guess now who holds thee?'—'Death,' I said. But, there,
The silver answer rang,—'Not Death, but Love.'

III

UNLIKE are we, unlike, O princely Heart!
Unlike our uses and our destinies.
Our ministering two angels look surprise
On one another, as they strike athwart

---

[1] The title was chosen to hide the autobiographical nature of the poems by suggesting that they were translated from the Portuguese. Browning call Elizabeth Barrett 'the Portuguese' in reference to her poem 'Catarina to Camoens' which described a woman's devoted love for the Portuguese poet.
[2] Greek pastoral poet from the third century BC.

Their wings in passing. Thou, bethink thee, art
A guest for queens to social pageantries,
With gages from a hundred brighter eyes
Than tears even can make mine, to play thy part
Of chief musician. What hast *thou* to do
With looking from the lattice-lights at me,
A poor, tired, wandering singer, singing through
The dark, and leaning up a cypress tree?
The chrism[3] is on thine head,—on mine, the dew,—
And Death must dig the level where these agree.

VI

GO from me. Yet I feel that I shall stand
Henceforward in thy shadow. Nevermore
Alone upon the threshold of my door
Of individual life, I shall command
The uses of my soul, nor lift my hand
Serenely in the sunshine as before,
Without the sense of that which I forbore—
Thy touch upon the palm. The widest land
Doom takes to part us, leaves thy heart in mine
With pulses that beat double. What I do
And what I dream include thee, as the wine
Must taste of its own grapes. And when I sue
God for myself, He hears that name of thine,
And sees within my eyes the tears of two.

VIII

WHAT can I give thee back, O liberal
And princely giver, who hast brought the gold
And purple of thine heart, unstained, untold,
And laid them on the outside of the wall
For such as I to take or leave withal,
In unexpected largesse? am I cold,
Ungrateful, that for these most manifold
High gifts, I render nothing back at all?
Not so; not cold,—but very poor instead.
Ask God who knows. For frequent tears have run
The colours from my life, and left so dead
And pale a stuff, it were not fitly done

[3] A mixture of oil and balm used in a sacramental anointing.

To give the same as pillow to thy head.
Go farther! let it serve to trample on.

X

YET, love, mere love, is beautiful indeed
    And worthy of acceptation. Fire is bright,
Let temple burn, or flax; an equal light
Leaps in the flame from cedar-plank or weed:
And love is fire. And when I say at need
I love thee ... mark! ... *I love thee*—in thy sight
I stand transfigured, glorified aright,
With conscience of the new rays that proceed ·
Out of my face toward thine. There's nothing low
In love, when love the lowest: meanest creatures
Who love God, God accepts while loving so.
And what I *feel*, across the inferior features
Of what I *am*, doth flash itself, and show
How that great work of Love enhances Nature's.

XIII

AND wilt thou have me fashion into speech
    The love I bear thee, finding words enough,
And hold the torch out, while the winds are rough,
Between our faces, to cast light on each?—
I drop it at thy feet. I cannot teach
My hand to hold my spirit so far off
From myself—me—that I should bring thee proof
In words, of love hid in me out of reach.
Nay, let the silence of my womanhood
Commend my woman-love to thy belief,—
Seeing that I stand unwon, however wooed,
And rend the garment of my life, in brief,
By a most dauntless, voiceless fortitude,
Lest one touch of this heart convey its grief.

XIV

IF thou must love me, let it be for nought
    Except for love's sake only. Do not say
'I love her for her smile—her look—her way
Of speaking gently,—for a trick of thought

That falls in well with mine, and certes brought
A sense of pleasant ease on such a day'—
For these things in themselves, Belovëd, may
Be changed, or change for thee,—and love, so wrought,
May be unwrought so. Neither love me for
Thine own dear pity's wiping my cheeks dry,—
A creature might forget to weep, who bore
Thy comfort long, and lose thy love thereby!
But love me for love's sake, that evermore
Thou may'st love on, through love's eternity.

XXII

WHEN our two souls stand up erect and strong,
     Face to face, silent, drawing nigh and nigher,
Until the lengthening wings break into fire
At either curvëd point,—what bitter wrong
Can the earth do to us, that we should not long
Be here contented? Think. In mounting higher,
The angels would press on us and aspire
To drop some golden orb of perfect song
Into our deep, dear silence. Let us stay
Rather on earth, Belovëd,—where the unfit
Contrarious moods of men recoil away
And isolate pure spirits, and permit
A place to stand and love in for a day,
With darkness and the death-hour rounding it.

XXVI

I LIVED with visions for my company
  Instead of men and women, years ago,
And found them gentle mates, nor thought to know
A sweeter music than they played to me.
But soon their trailing purple was not free
Of this world's dust, their lutes did silent grow,
And I myself grew faint and blind below
Their vanishing eyes. Then THOU didst come—to be,
Belovëd, what they seemed. Their shining fronts,
Their songs, their splendours, (better, yet the same,
As river-water hallowed into fonts)
Met in thee, and from out thee overcame
My soul with satisfaction of all wants:
Because God's gifts put man's best dreams to shame.

XXXI

THOU comest! all is said without a word.
  I sit beneath thy looks, as children do
In the noon-sun, with souls that tremble through
Their happy eyelids from an unaverred
Yet prodigal inward joy. Behold, I erred
In that last doubt! and yet I cannot rue
The sin most, but the occasion—that we two
Should for a moment stand unministered
By a mutual presence. Ah, keep near and close,
Thou dove-like help! and, when my fears would rise,
With thy broad heart serenely interpose:
Brood down with thy divine sufficiencies
These thoughts which tremble when bereft of those,
Like callow birds left desert to the skies.

XLIII

HOW do I love thee? Let me count the ways.
  I love thee to the depth and breadth and height
My soul can reach, when feeling out of sight
For the ends of Being and ideal Grace.
I love thee to the level of everyday's
Most quiet need, by sun and candlelight.
I love thee freely, as men strive for Right;
I love thee purely, as they turn from Praise.
I love thee with the passion put to use
In my old griefs, and with my childhood's faith.
I love thee with a love I seemed to lose
With my lost saints,—I love thee with the breath,
Smiles, tears, of all my life!—and, if God choose,
I shall but love thee better after death.

Geraldine Jewsbury

1812 – 80

A novelist, essayist and letter writer, Geraldine Jewsbury was born in Measham, Derbyshire, the daughter of a Manchester merchant and the younger sister of another successful author (Maria Jane Jewsbury). Much of her life was taken up with domestic responsibilities; she cared for her father's household after her sister's marriage in 1832, and, on her father's death, for her brother's household until his marriage in 1853. She then became friendly with Jane Welsh Carlyle and her husband, and she visited the couple frequently in London where she made the acquaintance of many of the literary figures of the day. When apart, Geraldine Jewsbury kept in touch with Jane Carlyle through a continuous and intense correspondence.

It was Jane Carlyle who found the publisher for Geraldine Jewsbury's first novel, Zoe; The History of Two Lives (1845); from this time, until 1859, she published six novels and two stories for children. She was a popular writer, a regular reviewer for The Athenaeum, and contributor to Household Words and The Westminster Review. She was also a reader for the publishers Hurst and Blackett, and for Bentley; she helped to edit Lady Morgan's Memoirs (1858).

The following letters are reprinted from A Selection from the Letters of Geraldine Jewsbury to Jane Welsh Carlyle (Mrs Alexander Ireland (ed.), Longmans, Green & Co., 1892).

From

The Letters
of Geraldine Jewsbury
to Jane Welsh Carlyle

LETTER 2

Friday—Monday (Postmark, April 19), 1841

DEAREST Jane,—I don't know that I have anything to tell you, specially worth writing down. But my eyes are still too weak to allow me to read; writing does not try them so much, and you are the only person I feel tempted to talk to just now! What would I have given to be with you this last week! though, after all, quietness and rest were the best things for you. Still, I would have liked to join my rest to yours, for I also have attained to the 'Giaour's'[1] beatitude, and feel just now uncertain whether I am alive or dead! Lying on a sofa as I am, half dreaming, half dozing, in a light that is neither light nor darkness—except for occasional twinges of recollection I should have altogether attained to a highly pacified and vegetative state, which will be changed, perhaps not for the better, so soon as I can bear the light of day. This was to have been a gay week. I was engaged to two grand parties—not fine, stilted 'conversation affairs,' but regular unsophisticated dances!—and I was obliged to send back-word to both. I had rather set my heart on one of them, at the house of one of the nicest women I know down here. It is a German family; and she is such a charming, natural, kind-hearted creature, just cultivated up (to) the most agreeable point, and stops short of any pretensions! Only to think what harlequinade tricks fate sometimes play one! The other day Mr. —— sent up word by my brother that he was in town, and should come up to see me. He has not been since our memorable conversation; and whilst I was rather wondering what turn things would take this time, there arrived, not him, but a most sober and reputable matron of my acquaintance, who came, she said, 'just to teach me how to net,' thinking that it would be a nice amusement for me now that I could not see to read or work! and she stayed all afternoon. —— did not come at all for some reason or another, and on the whole I was not sorry, for seeing him now is like the meeting of two ghosts on the other side Styx.[2] Each has been connected so strangely with the history of so many feelings and incidents, which at the time seemed as if their memory could never pass away. And what has been the end of so much passionate suffering, so much love which all the parties thought would endure for ever? The woman he loved so madly—of whom he declared (to one he trusted) that he would rather obtain her friendship even, than have possession of her whole sex—died of a broken heart, or, rather, of a cancer, which Sir Astley Cooper[3] said had been brought on by grief and anxiety of mind. She was a fine creature. I never saw her but once; but I heard of her from many quarters, and from those who knew her best. She was married to a man who did not care for her, and she, till she met ——, did not know what affection meant. His own testimony, and the way he spoke of her to me (that time we had our conversation), was enough to absolve her from all censure except the deepest commiseration. Her sister (who knew nothing of the matter) said, after her death, that she used to sit for hours gazing on the wall without seeing anything or speaking a word. When asked, What are you thinking about?—'Oh, many things; don't talk to me!' He, for whom she had risked everything—very soon after he had obtained everything—began to grow, not indifferent exactly, but satisfied. Unfortunately for her, she and her husband were obliged to leave this country; in absence she lost her influence over him. In a very short time he forced her to break with him; he married for

---

[1] A Christian under Muslim rule; a poem by Lord Byron.
[2] In Greek mythology, the river of death.
[3] Sir Astley Cooper (1788–1841): famous surgeon.

convenance,[4] and is now the father of a family, is a respectable man, and in prosperous circumstances. Since her death he professes, to those who knew the facts, bitterly to regret the past; but it is somewhat dubious whether these brave sentiments are real, or assumed as a piece of his respectability.

I, who was a bystander, have the recollection of the faith I then had in his good qualities, and the strong feeling I had for him, and the firm belief in his chivalrous, honourable dealing towards her, and the undoubting trust in her submission to duty, honour, and so forth. I did believe, then, in many fine things, and even now I only doubt their durability, or rather it now seems unreasonable to expect high-pressure efforts except from a steam-engine, and even that wears out; and why should we regret that things are so constituted? The fact of all that is worth having, and even life itself, being precarious, gives it a value beyond its own, and those who have an eternity to trust to, little know the desperate tenacity of those who have to make the most of Time! I cannot explain to you the superstitious value I set on those I ever love, and the sort of religious feeling with which I try to guard every word or thought which might raise a shade between us.

No, my dear, you must first have no hope of anything beyond this world, before you can know how very precious is a friend we really love. This letter has been written *à plusieurs reprises*,[5] for my eyes are rather worse, if anything, to-day than they were this day week, so that now I can hardly write, and what is to become of me I don't know!

I have more time for thinking than is at all agreeable. All this while I have never thanked you for your letter—it made me feel very sad. Those efforts after strength are weary things, and I doubt whether they do much good. They go to exhaust what strength we may possess. On the whole, I cannot help thinking it is the wisest to let ourselves be drifted along. Time brings quiet and strength naturally; in fact, the very change he works in us and in our feelings is equivalent to strength. There are two lines in Coleridge's translation of 'Wallenstein' that haunt me from morning to night, and have done so ever since I began to know what endurance meant. 'What pang is permanent with man? From the highest as from the vilest things he learns to wean himself, and the strong hours conquer him!'

If you will, from time to time, send me word how you go on, it will be a great favour. Just now I am especially anxious to hear from you; if you cannot guess why, I won't tell you. Do not plague yourself to write long letters, but say how you are in every way; patronise the pronoun 'I' as much as I do myself! Never mind telling me anything, except inasmuch as it affects or interests you! I have not said a tithe of what I have thought of when lying on the sofa. You little know the comfort it is to me to have you to think of, nor how much I think of you. If you take an interest in my friend ——, she is rather better, at least was last Tuesday. She had a scheme in her head which had quite roused her. Heaven only knows whether it will prove wise and feasible, but even the power of hoping is no small blessing to her!

---

[4] Expediency.
[5] At several sittings.

She did talk of going to the the seaside in a few weeks, and it was settled that I should go with her when she went, but all is yet in a state of uncertainty.

Is your husband returned from his excursion?

I heartily hope he will be the better for it.

Will you give my love to him? He has had splendid weather. So soon as I have eyes to see to write a reputable letter, there are several knotty points I want him to solve for me, but I cannot venture to send him the sort of scrawl I bestow on you. 'Les sept cordes'[6] are waiting for me at the bookseller's, I expect, but they will not get touched yet awhile, hélas! I am too cross this morning to write any more. I am in an ill humour with my doctor, too, which is almost as bad in a patient as it would be for a hungry man to quarrel with his bread and butter! Offer my respects to your brother-in-law, and you may tell him that I have about as little to contend with as a young woman of 'my sort' could hope to find anywhere. To the immortal credit of all the people here be it spoken, they take me as I am, which is a great virtue in my eyes of course; and then they hang up Nymphs, and Cupids, and Psyches, &c., &c., in their dining-rooms, so that, 'sans peur et sans reproche,'[7] as I told you before, I have said ten thousand things to you in my own mind which are not written in this letter. I wish you were here to-day. An individual I once named to you is coming here this evening. It is well for us that we cannot solve all the problems presented to us in this world; for my own part, I am quite reconciled that my heart should be deceitful sometimes. I don't want to know the truth of what it means, and if 'Job' had been a wise man he would never have asked the question. Give my remembrances to ——, your damsel, and believe me, most affectionately yours,

G. E. J.

P.S.—I began a little tale called the 'Lune de Lait' in one of your French newspapers. Could you spare me some of the succeeding numbers to finish it? for I took great interest in it. I will return them by post—if it is not convenient, never mind, however.

LETTER 4

Monday, June 15, 1841

DEAREST Jane,—There is a great deal I want to say to you, but when I begin to write to you it seems difficult, almost impossible, to put it down as it really is.

I would give the world—that is, all my expectations in it—for the space between four walls where I might talk to you in peace for an hour, so many things occur every day which I should like you to know at the time, but I cannot patronise 'small beer' so far as to chronicle them, and besides, they are only interesting for the minute—like newspapers. But there is not a day that I do not most sadly want you. Your letters tell me little or nothing about yourself,

[6] The seven strings, reference appears obscure.
[7] Without fear and without fault (the traditional attributes of a mediaeval knight).

and, besides, you don't like writing, and I cannot find the heart to plague you to write, and then there is so little connection between the world you live in and that which I live in, every day seems to separate us more, and these stiff documents are the only substitute for speech and sight; I want to see you more than I can tell you. I cannot write half I want to say, and I dare not write even a quarter of what could be written, so these letters are very unsatisfactory all ways. One thing you may do, however—tell me how you are, and how you go on; never mind other people or news of any sort, it is you I want to hear about. I think of you a great deal, and with an anxiety I cannot account for. I can't express my feelings even to myself, only by tears; but I am no good to you, and I, who wish to be and do anything that might be a comfort to you, can give you nothing but vague, undefined yearnings to be yours in some way. I can use no expressions of affection. I don't like using them. I am jealous of giving you what I have ever offered to another, and, besides, talk as much as I will, it's the same thing said over and over; you will let me be yours, and think of me as such, will you not? How are you? Do you sleep well still? That is my *summum bonum*[8] of felicity. I can get through any given amount of plague if I may sleep all night without dreaming. I am come home again ten days since, and, after all, I am best here, though it is not much I do. My eyes are, I suppose, well, but I cannot use them for long together, and the green spectacles are still in requisition. They are weak, my dear, and weakness in all things is the worst sort of ailment; *au reste* I am well and have nothing to plague me just now, but I suppose that is a beatific state which never lasts long.

My friend —— is much better, and I am relieved from much anxiety about her. I have begun to do something, and I have a strong notion that it will have to be undone again. I think we are both of us mad; but there is a sort of instinct sometimes which leads one to do things that seem to have no profit in them beyond the fact that they ought not to be done! What I am after now is something of the kind you once suggested. One day, as we were walking in the grounds, Mrs. —— exclaimed, looking at the house, 'If we could but make those walls tell all they have ever seen or heard for the last seven years, they would teach (to women especially) more than they have ever been taught yet.' This had no reference to anything previous, but we began settling all the various affairs that had been transacted there, and the fierce passages of life and suffering we had seen pass, and our philosophy on the same! Well, we agreed to make it into a history in letters. The actual letters that were written from time to time have been destroyed; but now that some of the persons are dead, and others married or removed far away, there is a strange sort of pleasure in working out one's own peculiar notions on certain subjects. I should like you to see it, but I much fear that it would be objected to if I asked leave. I wonder whether you would agree with us! Do you remember in one of your letters you tell me that 'I am clever, but wrong on certain points'? How much I wish that you would give me some of your own philosophy some time! One day, whilst at Seaforth, a youth I have known a long time took it into his head to be very confidential, and preached

8 Highest good.

his own gospel for the space of a whole afternoon! He had been thrown on the world very young to shift for himself, and a real little youth of the world he had become. He looked so young—though he is twenty-five—that one could not call him a man! The mere facts that he told me were not disguised and beautified, yet the *morale* that stood out clear was to the effect that men cannot afford to be very long or very much in earnest in their intercourse with women; that when a woman got thoroughly earnest and engrossed, a man who had any regard for himself or her would break off at once! That *une grande passion* 'was an embarrassing affair, and was very dangerous to people who had to get a living,' and that he had always 'broken off' as soon as he came to his senses; that women seemed to think it was the only object of interest in life, and it was a desperate thing to let them go too far. One thing specially struck me—though this was not said to me, only repeated to me—viz., that all men who have received an English education hate a woman in proportion as she commits herself for them, though a woman cares for a man exactly in the proportion in which she has made sacrifices for him, evidently thinking and showing, he thought, that all that was in the world—business and riches and success and so forth—were the only realities, and the only things worth making objects! He is neither better nor worse, but an average specimen of the generality of men. He once did me a material piece of kindness, and he was not in love with me; he had taken a fit of kindness to a friend of mine, and he raised himself in my opinion, and showed more real feeling than I had supposed in him. To be sure, the fact that my friend did not care about him would account for his good behaviour; it was not put in his power to behave ill! This will seem stupid to you, not knowing the people and the circumstances; but it had a great interest for me, and it set me moralising to think how much more miserable we should be than we are if we had our eyes opened to discern always true from make-believe. I have great sympathy with that prayer of the Ancient Mariner,[9] 'O let me be awake, my God, or let me sleep away!' There is something else I long very much to tell you, but I dare not in a letter.

I wish there were some photographic process by which one's mind could be struck off and transferred to that of the friend we wish to know it, without the medium of this confounded letter-writing!

I want your counsel, and I cannot even ask for it! Well, my dear, I must not omit to tell you that, by way of natural female occupation, I am engaged in preparing a 'baby basket' for my sister-in-law, who is expecting her first little one next month. This is the 'ha'penny worth of bread to so much sack.'[10]

I am going to drink tea and take my work to a very nice lady, one who interests me much—a real specimen of an English woman. She is married, and devoted to her husband, who is also a real specimen of an English *mari*.[11] I am sure she is not happy, by several little observations she has dropped, though she would start to think she had given such an impression; but there is a great

[9] Poem by Coleridge.
[10] A reference to Shakespeare's *King Henry IV*, Pt 1, Act 2, Scene 4 ('sack' here means 'sherry').
[11] Husband.

deal that wants saying about matrimony. Who dare say it? I have read the 'Sept Cordes' at last, and full of genius it is—more so, I think, than any other of the writer's works. No one but herself could have written it; but what a pity that such splendid truths should be buried in the earth! She might do so much more than she has done.

Why will she do nothing but write novels? I am also deep in a very different book, and am equally chained to it, though I had to begin by an odd volume. It is altogether fascinating, and there is such a fine, healthy feeling through it all, and so much human sympathy, and wit enough to endow all the libraries of useful (?) knowledge 'ever inflicted on the world.'

It was a volume of 'Rabelais'[12] I got hold of the other day, and shall not rest till I have got the beginning of him. I cannot give you an idea of the delight it has given me. The Old French is a great bore; but it is well worth the plague of it.

A poor lady of my acquaintance is in great trouble; she has just lost a daughter, of whom I was very fond, under most painful circumstances, and I must go and see her. It makes my heart sick to see her. Her husband is a great scoundrel; he left his family, after tormenting them to death, and now he increases their trouble by all sorts of vexations, and it makes me mad to hear people coolly say, 'I understand Mrs. —— has a violent temper,' as if a woman was to be steel and marble under the most unprovoked outrages! I wish I might say my say about matrimony. This is a tremendously long letter.

God bless you, dear love. Take care of yourself, and write as soon as you can.

Ever yours
G. E. J.

LETTER 16[13]

Seaforth: Friday (Postmark, May 30, 1842)

MY Darling,—Your note has made me very sad. There is nothing to be said to it, as you cannot be comforted, but time—time, that is the only hope and refuge for all of us! I know full well what it is to cease to see the necessity of struggling; it would puzzle the wisest of us to point it out at the best of times, but the inscrutableness does not always press upon us so heavily—it does not come till we see into some deep trouble, and then are like to go mad. To all of us life is a riddle put more or less unintelligibly, and death is the only end we can see—for we may die, and that is a strong consolation, of which nothing can defraud us. We cannot well be more dark or miserable than we are; we shall all die—no exception, no fear of exemption. Every morning I say this to myself. When I am in sorrow, it is the only comfort that has strength in it. Why, indeed,

[12] François Rabelais (1495–1553), French humorous (and scatological) writer.
[13] Jane Carlyle is grieving over the death of her mother.

must we go on struggling, rising up early and late and taking rest? 'Behold, He giveth His beloved sleep!' And yet it is not well that you feel this so constantly that it swallows up all other feelings. Life is not strong in you when you are thus—it will not be so always. There is a strength in life to make us endure it. I am astonished sometimes to find that I am glad to be alive—that the instinct of feeling that 'it is a pleasant thing to behold the sun, and that light is good.' And this is a feeling that will spring up in your heart after a while, crushed and dead as it seems now. When my father died I cannot tell you the horrible sense of desolateness and insecurity that struck through me. I had friends to love me, who would do anything for me, but I had no right to count on their endurance. I had lost the one on whose love I could depend as on the earth itself—the one whose relationship seemed to revoke the law of change pronounced against all other things in this world. Our parents and relations are given us by the same unknown Power which sent us into this world, given to us like our own bodies, without our knowing how or where, and when they are taken from us our ties to this life are loosened, and all seems tottering—nothing can supply their place. But yet even this gets blunted after a while; we can and do live, when we are put to it, on wonderfully little, without all we at first fancied indispensable, and then for ever after the love of such friends as are left or raised up to us becomes strangely precious in a way no one else can understand. We strain them to us with all our force, to try to supply the place of that natural necessity which united us without effort on our part to those who are gone! We have always a fear that the friends we have made for ourselves will leave us; we were only afraid for the others that they would be taken away. Dear love, this present strange, stunned state you will recover from. No fear of your sinking down into apathy—there is too much for you to do. You are necessary to the welfare of too many; your life will take shape again, though now it seems nothing but confused hopelessness. The thought of you brings tears to my eyes any moment it comes. Do not be so very wretched. I can give you no comfort—there is none—but from time to time write when you can, but don't plague yourself. I also will write without waiting. I am most thankful the dear little cousin still stays with you. Give my love to her. I am glad that your husband is well, and that he has his book to busy himself in. It is like a child to him. I am here since a week. I go home in a few days. Mrs. —— sends her love to you. I wish you could be within reach of her; she would be a comfort to you, as she has been to me. Good bye, dear love; take care of yourself for the sake of others besides yourself!

LETTER 19

(Postmark, October 17, 1843)

DEAREST Jane,—As you know of old, I generally contrive to get done all I feel disposed to do. You will have decided that I am a most shameful and unfeeling person, but you will be wrong. I shall say nothing of the 'kicks over kicks' to which we have fallen victims since I wrote last, and especially since your letter came, because those ought not to count for preventive checks. But, to say nothing of my fits of nervous sleeplessness, which have kept me in a sort of mesmeric state when ordinary mortals are alive and brisk, we have had company in the house, who, however, might all (with one exception) have gone and hanged themselves before they should have hindered me. All these have been hindrances and snares of the Evil One, to keep me from writing to you, and to make you expect and get disappointed, but the real cause has been that poor —— has been very ill, and two or three times when I have sat down and fairly begun to write to you she has been so ill and in so much pain that I could not find in my heart to do anything but sit beside her—for, as my father used to say when he was suffering, 'It is a comfort if you will look at one as if you were sorry!' And she has taken a fancy that rubbing her feet and hands soothes the nervous feeling that torments her, and it often gives her ease when nothing else does, and as, from practice, I do not feel tired, I am rather in request. But all this time I have been horribly uneasy about you, for though you laugh and make witty speeches, I know the state you are in. I fear still more the state you will be in, my poor darling. I could have sworn, I was so provoked on reading your letter. You have no one who has any sort of consideration for you, and then, forsooth, you and your comfort are to be sacrificed to getting things made as comfortable as Heaven, and at small outlay of anything besides. My dear child, you ought to know your value better, and not to allow your life to be worried away for no earthly good—It is a sort of quixotism you have for sacrificing yourself, never thinking that when you are at last fairly used up the state of ruin and desolation to which all will be reduced that you have most wished to benefit, as 'Faust' says, will come all the same, and 'cursed be patience!' You have had patience and endurance till I am sick of the virtues, and what have they done for you? Half-killed you! I can do you no good, but I am very unhappy about you. I will not plague you to write to me, but if you can get anybody to be scribe enough to indite two lines to say whether you are dead or alive, or quite mad, I shall be very glad and thankful. I had a note from —— yesterday, which I cannot too well read, but she talks of getting home this week, so I shall see her before I leave here. We are rather expecting Dr. Wiseman[14] this week: this you feel no sympathy with, though I can assure you that the Catholic Church goes for nothing in the matter. But I shall make you laugh if I were with you to tell you all our plots, and schemes, and wickednesses—for it is a sort of historical style of wickedness that peculiarly takes my fancy. Also, on my own account I have indulged in a matrimonial scheme, but the gentleman is so dreadfully in love with himself that I have not patience, energy, hope, or inclination enough to persevere. Indeed, those things are not much in my way; it was only the eligibility that put it into my head. Sheridan Knowles[15] is down here trying to pick up a few pounds by lecturing on oratory. We went to hear him last night, and I brought back a stiff neck. We have met him several times, and he is by far the most lamentable tragedy I have seen either on or off the stage. He is very good and affectionate in his nature, but so dismally merry. Such deep depression

[14] Nicholas Wiseman (1802–65), prominent Roman Catholic and later Cardinal.
[15] James Sheridan Knowles (1784–1862), Irish dramatist.

and anxiety under all sorts of puns and jokes! This letter is written in haste, and is good for nothing, but you shall have another soon. —— has asked me at least half a dozen times 'whether I have done yet?' and now the
man is waiting to take it to the post, and I am only too lucky to get the chance of its going in time. Mrs. —— is in Liverpool shopping, or would send love.

    God bless you!

Ever your own
G. E. J.

LETTER 77

[Presumably from Mrs. Salis-Schwabe's house]

Crumpsall House, March 29, 1849

MY dear Jane,—Here is an hour in which I am left to myself entirely, so I give you the benefit of it—to comfort my soul by abusing you; for if I don't get a better letter from you, or at least a letter with something in it, you may pass 'a month of Sundays' at breakfast without any letter from me. I want to know how you are in bodily health. You are going on pretty well in your worldly matters, I can see; you always have a certain tone when you are 'well-to-do in Zion' which is good for telling that, if it is for nothing else; but still I would have been as glad to have some news of you after such a long silence as to be scolded about a matter which was a harmless caricature. Never abuse 'surfaces'; cream lies at the top, and there is nothing but skimmed milk underneath; and, besides, the surface is the result of all that is gone before, and is generally the best worth seeing. As far as I am concerned, my surface is like those strata which go down all the same as deep as people can dig below, so it is not much worth exploring. I could not help laughing at your assertion that I keep all sealed up with Solomon's seal. I have actually and literally told you all there has been to tell, what has filled up my days and my hours, and because it has been simply barren, you think I have secreted the crops, when in fact none have been grown. I come here much of my time, and shall do so as long as the Chevalier stays, and when he goes I shall be very sorry. He has begun the almost impracticable task of making me speak French correctly, a feat I have never achieved in English, and when I am at home I have often been in a dead-fix about my writing. I think the simple mystery of my existence just now—(your letter forced me to a self-examination)—is that I am 'bone lazy,' as my nurse used to phrase it. But I have great faith in 'lying fallow,' and when I have a spell of laziness on me I follow it religiously, looking on it as the Orientals do on idiots—as an inscrutable manifestation of the Deity. I am sure I am glad to hear that a good novel is coming out. I want to read one sadly. I was not grateful for 'Jane Eyre.' I did not take to it somehow. I wish Lewes would write another. I like his very much. He is coming back again for his play, which is to come out after Easter, and I shall be quite glad to see him again. I took to him like a relation. He and —— have sworn everlasting friendship. You really ought to come down amongst us again; you would see how the warmth of your presence would dry up all the marshy exhalations. And how you would enjoy it! As for me, be quite sure we should prosper; we are always glad in each other when we see one another. It is in absence that all the mischief arises—in the night the enemy sows tares; so just come, and send obstacles to the Devil; but you will be seeing Mrs. ——. I had an advent the other night. I went to hear the 'Creation',[16] the very grandest thing in the shape of music I can conceive. It seemed to take one into a new world of sound, it broke one up altogether, and called one out of oneself, possessed one like a new spirit. It was music that had nothing to do with passion or emotion, but when it was over one felt as if one had been banished to a realm of common things, without sunshine, and nothing but an east wind. I have been miserable ever since, as I used to be, when a child, after a great pleasure. Jenny Lind[17] sang very wonderfully, but the music itself swallowed up all she did. One never thought of her, at least I did not. She seemed to do what she was wanted to do, nothing more. The music was too grand to let anything else be thought of. There was a prayer, an old Catholic one, which I wish you could have heard. It was Pergolesi's 'Lord, have mercy upon me, for I am in trouble.' It went down to one's inmost soul. Jenny sang a very wonderful song, a sort of 'Cheval de Bataille,' about the 'Bright Seraphin,' but it did not touch anything but my organ of wonder. Here I am interrupted, so good-bye, and write me a good letter, and not a perverse one!

Yours,
G. E. J.

LETTER 96

[Undated—1849?]
(About women and the Corn Law League)

Sunday

D EAREST Jane,—I have been 'looking, and better looking'[18] for a letter from you all the week, and wondering what could have befallen you. This morning the postman came before I was out of bed, and brought your letter, which makes me fancy you are better, and that makes me more comfortable without any fancy at all! But, my dear, I am in a real fright; my eyes (confound them!) are threatening just as they began before. I can see to do nothing by candle-light, and not too much by daylight. I hope they will be stopped in time, but this damp weather is against me. I was so sick of my doctor last time, that I could not find either faith or patience to begin again with him, and I have a sort of Faust's revelation, and on the strength of it set off to a lady, a very clever woman of my acquaintance who is wild after homoeopathy. She has got a book and a medicine-chest, and doctors herself and her friends with great zeal. She looked at me, and read in her book,

---

[16] Haydn's oratorio.
[17] Jenny Lind (1820–1887): famous Swedish soprano.
[18] A Scotch expression, meaning 'looking and looking again.'—A.E.I. [orig. edn]

and finally brought out a little box the size and shape of a tiny tea-caddy, all full of miraculous-looking little bottles filled with what seemed pure water, but they were all deadly essences. She mixed me two drops of one in a phial of water; so now I am taking an infinitesimal dose of belladonna. Whether it is for good or harm I don't know, but it affects me very uncomfortably, and my eyes are rather worse to-day, but I do expect it will do me good. She promised to come and see me to-morrow, however. Meanwhile the medicine affects my head, and I am as limp, and washed out, and miserable to-day as anyone could wish me to be; it is a foggy, drizzling day, and I am neither dead nor alive. And I am vowed not to touch either tea or coffee, nor anything more comfortable than milk-and-water, which is very nasty, and I am cross. O ye gods! how cross! —— was in dismay with me, thinking me gone mad, yesterday, and made a most touching admission that 'being a missis I might say what I pleased.' But only fancy, my dear, the vexation of being able to do nothing but shut my eyes the minute the candles come; but, en revanche,[19] I sleep! Well, now, here I am, inflicting complaints on you as if you were my doctor, and God knows the poor man got plenty! But to talk of something else (now I have said my say). Well, perhaps, we are better off now than they used to be in old Greek times, when it was only slaves who were taught anything. God knows they are very uncomfortable, that's certain, but I believe we are touching on better days, when women will have a genuine, normal life of their own to lead. There, perhaps, will not be so many marriages, and women will be taught not to feel their destiny manqué[20] if they remain single. They will be able to be friends and companions in a way they cannot be now. All the strength of their feelings and thoughts will not run into love; they will be able to associate with men, and make friends of them, without being reduced by their position to see them as lovers or husbands. Instead of having appearances to attend to, they will be allowed to have their virtues, in any measure which it may please God to send, without being diluted down to the tepid 'rectified spirit' of 'feminine grace' and 'womanly timidity'—in short, they will make themselves women, as men are allowed to make themselves men. I think matters are tending to this, and I think that to this, in spite of that dreadful Mrs. ——, they will come before long; not in the present 'rising generation,' but in the one after. Except when my health is out of order, I do not feel that either you or I are to be called failures. We are indications of a development of womanhood which as yet is not recognised. It has, so far, no ready-made channels to run in, but still we have looked, and tried, and found that the present rules for women will not hold us—that something better and stronger is needed. And as for us, individually, women a thousand times commoner, both in intellect and aspirations after doing right, may have made something apparently better out of their lives—still, I would prefer my own imperfect accomplishment. There are women to come after us, who will approach nearer the fulness of the measure of the stature of a woman's nature. I regard myself as a mere faint indication, a rudiment of the idea, of certain higher qualities and possibilities that lie in women, and all the

19 On the other hand.
20 Failed, missed the mark.

eccentricities and mistakes and miseries and absurdities I have made are only the consequences of an imperfect formation, an immature growth. Where I am not wiser than the general run of women I am a much greater fool, and when I do not succeed in doing better than they, I do infinitely worse, and that is the general occurrence, *hélas*! But will you lay your hand on your heart, and say that, in your 'fifteen years' long illness,' as you call your life, you have not both felt and shown qualities infinitely higher and nobler than all the 'Mrs. Ellis-code'[21] can dream of? You know you have. If you consider yourself as the 'be-all and the end-all' of what a superior woman can be, the balance of actual respectable facts might perchance be on the other side, but the power and possibility is with you, and it is that which is to be looked to. A 'Mrs. Ellis' woman is developed to the extreme of her little possibility; but I can see there is a precious mine of a species of womanhood yet undreamed of by the professors and essayists on female education, and I believe also that we belong to it. So there is a modest climax! I fear I shall never be available to any actual purposes except 'to point a moral and adorn a tale,' and even of that I feel dubious. I don't know what has possessed me to give you the benefit of this long 'settle,' except that your letter suggested it. Talking of practical matters, my bedroom is done (all but some of the hangings, for which the stuff has had to be made to match, and has not come home), and you must have yearned after a pretty bedroom all your life before you can understand the pleasure of getting it. I hope you will come and sleep in it some time. It will be such a nice room to write in. My visitor has not come. She is detained in Dublin, which will cut down her stay to a very short space. I must tell you a story. The other night the Lord-Lieutenant went in state to the theatre. Something had put the audience out of humour, or they were in an excited state, or something, but they began to give vent to their feelings by calling out for 'three cheers' to different people, pit and gallery taking it in turns. After three cheers for 'O'Connell,'[22] the others insisted on three for 'Lord ——,' and then began a dreadful row, all the noises possible for *in*humanity to make. At last they grew more and more uproarious, and they were proceeding to tear up the benches when one fellow, seeing that he was likely in this way to lose his shilling's worth of the play, shouted at the top of his voice, during a momentary lull, 'Boys, three cheers for the Devil, entirely!' They were given, and peace was restored. That is quite true—gospel! By-the-way, talking of the Devil, do you remember ages ago that I wrote an article for ——, which he rejected with ignominious disdain. Well, then, I wrote it over again, and Carlyle was at the pains of sending it to 'Fraser,'[23] as you told him to, who would not have it, but refused it in its amended state just as much. Well, it lay tossing about for a full twelvemonth, when I took it in hand once more, wrote it over again, and

---

[21] Mrs Ellis (1810?–72) wrote many books deploring the agitation for women's emancipation and lauding the 'feminine' virtues of home and hearth. *The Women of England* (1839) is probably her best known work.
[22] Daniel O'Connell (1775–1847), Irish nationalist leader.
[23] *Fraser's Magazine* (a popular monthly).

sent it to Douglas Jerrold,[24] by way of calming down the little one that went
with it. And lo! when the Magazine came yesterday, the first thing I saw was
my poor little thing, flourishing in good legible print. I was quite pleased to
see it. Whether it was that I had such trouble with it, or whether I was glad of
my own way at last, I don't know; but I fancied it read very decently. I have not
heard from —— for a long while. She has been to Manchester, but did not come
near me. I spent last Monday with the Smiths. He—Mr. J. B. Smith—was one of
the originators of the 'League.'[25] He brought the first resolution for repeal of the
Corn Laws, twenty years ago, before the Chamber of Commerce in Manchester,
and could get no one to second it, till at last one man did for the sake of
discussion, and was horrified when he found Mr. Smith was in earnest. After a
while Cobden[26] joined, and about five of them kept fighting to get a petition
sent to Parliament; and there was such difficulty to get it agreed to, and such
little trembling resolutions proposed! I think he said they were three
years before they could get the petition sent. My word, to hear him talk!
It gave me some notion of what perseverance means. He afterwards was
secretary to the League. He is a little wizened, uninteresting-looking man; gives
no idea of any sort of what you call either greatness or cleverness, but he was so
in earnest. They all speak of Cobden as a sort of martyr; they say he has ruined
his health, and made all sorts of sacrifices, injuring his worldly affairs terribly.
His house was doing infinitely more business ten years ago than it is now; it
has dwindled down, and everybody who knows him speaks of his modesty and
disinterestedness. There was another man, Alderman ——, at dinner, remarkable
here for having been an 'ultra-Liberal' when Liberals were only thought fit to send
to prison. A very uninteresting man—tyrannical I am certain, for I felt as if sitting
beside a thumb-screw. But he has done good work, and is now recognised as
a respectable man; and it was curious to meet a man who could talk of Hone[27]
and Godwin,[28] and all those people. He knew them, and he has spent money
on his principles, so now he proses like a Patriarch. This is a letter and a-half.
Write to me very soon.

Ever your own
G. E. J.

[24] Douglas Jerrold (1803–57), journalist, editor and writer who, from 1854, ran *Douglas Jerrold's Shilling Magazine*.
[25] Anti-Corn Law League.
[26] Richard Cobden (1804–65), Liberal politician and leader of campaign against the corn laws.
[27] William Hone (1780–1842), radical publisher and bookseller.
[28] William Godwin (1756–1836), radical philosopher and novelist, briefly husband of Mary Wollstonecraft.

Elizabeth Gaskell

1810 – 65

Elizabeth Gaskell was the daughter and wife of Unitarian clergymen. As a married woman she lived in Manchester and began her career as a political/social novelist and short story writer with Mary Barton (1848), in which she roused the English conscience with her depiction of the industrial poor and the plight of women. Shortly after her friend Charlotte Brontë died, Elizabeth Gaskell wrote a sympathetic biography of her in which she revealed aspects of Charlotte Brontë's spiritual development and family life, as well as her growth as a writer. Elizabeth Gaskell used fiction to investigate women's situation, especially the risks and rewards of motherhood (she had four daughters); some of her fiction which focused on the predicament of unsupported and 'fallen' woman was considered provocative, and in poor taste. But despite her decision to pursue some of the controversial political and moral issues of her day in fiction, she earned for herself a substantial literary reputation.

The following short story, 'The Well of Pen-orfa', was first published in Household Words in 1850 and is representative of her work. It is reprinted from Elizabeth Gaskell: Four Short Stories (Pandora Press, London, 1983).

The Well of Pen-Morfa

CHAPTER I

OF a hundred travellers who spend a night at Trê-Madoc, in North Wales, there is not one, perhaps, who goes to the neighbouring village of Pen-Morfa. The new town, built by Mr Maddocks, Shelley's friend, has taken away all the importance of the ancient village—formerly, as its name imports, 'the head of the marsh;' that marsh which Mr Maddocks drained and dyked, and reclaimed from the Traeth Mawr, till Pen-Morfa, against the walls of whose cottages the winter tides lashed in former days, has come to stand high and dry, three miles from the sea, on a disused road to Caernarvon. I do not think there has been a new cottage built in Pen-Morfa this hundred years; and many an old one has dates in some obscure corner which tell of the fifteenth century. The joists of timber, where they meet overhead, are blackened with the smoke of centuries. There is one large room, round which the beds are built like cupboards, with wooden doors to open and shut; somewhat in the old Scotch fashion, I imagine; and below the bed (at least in one instance I can testify that this was the case, and I was told it was not uncommon), is a great wide wooden drawer, which contained the oat-cake, baked for some months' consumption by the family. They call the promontory of Llyn (the point at the end of Caernarvonshire), *Welsh* Wales: I think they might call Pen-Morfa a Welsh Welsh village; it is so national in its ways, and buildings, and inhabitants, and so different from the towns and hamlets into which the English throng in summer. How these said inhabitants of Pen-Morfa ever are distinguished by their names, I, uninitiated, cannot tell. I only know for a fact, that in a family there with which I am acquainted, the eldest son's name is John Jones, because his father's was John Thomas; that the second son is called David Williams, because his grandfather was William Wynn, and that the girls are called indiscriminately by the names of Thomas and Jones. I have heard some of the Welsh chuckle over the way in which they have baffled the barristers at Caernarvon Assizes, denying the name under which they had been subpoenaed to give evidence, if they were unwilling witnesses. I could tell you of a great deal which is peculiar and wild in these true Welsh people, who are what I suppose we English were a century ago; but I must hasten on to my tale.

I have received great, true, beautiful kindness, from one of the members of the family of whom I just now spoke as living at Pen-Morfa; and when I found that they wished me to drink tea with them, I gladly did so, though my friend was the only one in the house who could speak English at all fluently. After tea, I went with them to see some of their friends; and it was then I saw the interiors of the houses of which I have spoken. It was an autumn evening; we left mellow sunset-light in the open air when we entered the houses, in which all seemed dark, save in the ruddy sphere of the firelight, for the windows were very small, and deep-set in the thick walls. Here were an old couple, who welcomed me in Welsh; and brought forth milk and oat-cake with patriarchal hospitality. Sons and daughters had married away from them; they lived alone; he was blind, or nearly so; and they sat one on each side of the fire, so old and so still (till we went in and broke the silence) that they seemed to be listening for death. At another house lived a woman stern and severe-looking. She was busy hiving a swarm of bees, alone and unassisted. I do not think my companion would have chosen to speak to her, but seeing her out in her hill-side garden, she made some inquiry in Welsh, which was answered in the most mournful tone I ever heard in my life; a voice of which the freshness and 'timbre' had been choked up by tears long years ago. I asked who she was. I dare say the story is common enough, but the sight of the woman, and her few words had impressed me. She had been the beauty of Pen-Morfa; had been in service; had been taken to London by the family whom she served; had come down, in a year or so, back to Pen-Morfa, her beauty gone into that sad, wild, despairing look which I saw; and she about to become a mother. Her father had died during her absence, and left her a very little money; and after her child was born she took the little cottage where I saw her, and made a scanty living by the produce of her bees. She associated with no one. One event had made her savage and distrustful to her kind. She kept so much aloof that it was some time before it became known that her child was deformed, and had lost the use of its lower limbs. Poor thing! When I saw the mother, it had been for fifteen years bed-ridden. But go past when you would, in the night, you saw a light burning; it was often that of the watching mother, solitary and friendless, soothing the moaning child; or you might hear her crooning some old Welsh air, in hopes to still the pain with the loud monotonous music. Her sorrow was so dignified, and her mute endurance and her patient love won her such respect, that the neighbours would fain have been friends; but she kept alone and solitary. This a most true story. I hope that woman and her child are dead now, and their souls above.

Another story which I heard of these old primitive dwellings I mean to tell at somewhat greater length:-

There are rocks high above Pen-Morfa; they are the same that hang over Trê-Madoc, but near Pen-Morfa they sweep away, and are lost in the plain. Everywhere they are beautiful. The great sharp ledges, which would otherwise look hard and cold, are adorned with the brightest-coloured moss, and the golden lichen. Close to, you see the scarlet leaves of the crane's-bill, and the tufts of purple heather, which fill up every cleft and cranny; but in the distance you see only the general effect of infinite richness of colour, broken here and there by great masses of ivy. At the foot of these rocks come a rich verdant meadow or two; and then you are at Pen-Morfa. The village well is sharp down under the rocks. There are one or two large sloping pieces of stone in that last field, on the road leading to the well, which are always slippery; slippery in the summer's heat, almost as much as in the frost of winter, when some little glassy stream that runs over them is turned into a thin sheet of ice. Many, many years back—a lifetime ago—there lived in Pen-Morfa a widow and her daughter. Very little is required in those out-of-the-way Welsh villages. The wants of the people are very simple. Shelter, fire, a little oat-cake and buttermilk, and garden produce; perhaps some pork and bacon from the pig in winter; clothing, which is principally of home manufacture, and of the most enduring kind: these take very little money to purchase, especially in a district into which the large capitalists have not yet come, to buy up two or three acres of the peasants; and nearly every man about Pen-Morfa owned, at the time of which I speak, his dwelling and some land beside.

Eleanor Gwynn inherited the cottage (by the road-side, on the left-hand as you go from Trê-Madoc to Pen-Morfa), in which she and her husband had lived all their married life, and a small garden sloping southwards, in which her bees lingered before winging their way to the more distant heather. She took rank among her neighbours as the possessor of a moderate independence—not rich, and not poor. But the young men of Pen-Morfa thought her very rich in the possession of a most lovely daughter. Most of us know how very pretty Welsh women are; but from all accounts, Nest Gwynn (Nest, or Nesta, is the Welsh for Agnes) was more regularly beautiful than any one for miles around. The Welsh are still fond of triads, and 'as beautiful as a summer's morning at sun-rise, as a white sea-gull on the green sea-wave, and as Nest Gwynn,' is yet a saying in that district. Nest knew she was beautiful, and delighted in it. Her mother sometimes checked her in her happy pride, and sometimes reminded her that beauty was a great gift of God (for the Welsh are a very pious people); but when she began her little homily, Nest came dancing to her, and knelt down before her, and put her face up to be kissed, and so with a sweet interruption she stopped her mother's lips. Her high spirits made some few shake their heads, and some called her a flirt and a coquette; for she could not help trying to please all, both old and young, both men and women. A very little from Nest sufficed for this; a sweet glittering smile, a word of kindness, a merry glance, or a little sympathy, all these pleased and attracted; she was like the fairy-gifted child, and dropped inestimable gifts. But some who had interpreted her smiles and kind words rather as their wishes led them than as they were really warranted, found that the beautiful, beaming Nest could be decided and saucy enough, and so they revenged themselves by calling her a flirt. Her mother heard it and sighed; but Nest only laughed.

It was her work to fetch water for the day's use from the well I told you about. Old people say it was the prettiest sight in the world to see her come stepping lightly and gingerly over the stones with the pail of water balanced on her head; she was too adroit to need to steady it with her hand. They say, now that they can afford to be charitable and speak the truth, that in all her changes to other people, there never was a better daughter to a widowed mother than Nest. There is a picturesque old farmhouse under Moel Gwynn, on the road from Trê-Madoc to Criccaeth, called by some Welsh name which I now forget; but its meaning in English is 'The End of Time;' a strange, boding, ominous name. Perhaps the builder meant his work to endure till the end of time. I do not know; but there the old house stands, and will stand for many a year. When Nest was young, it belonged to one Edward Williams; his mother was dead, and people said he was on the look-out for a wife. They told Nest so, but she tossed her head and reddened, and said she thought he might look long before he got one; so it was not strange that one morning when she went to the well, one autumn morning when the dew lay heavy on the grass, and the thrushes were busy among the mountain-ash berries, Edward Williams happened to be there, on his way to the coursing match near, and somehow his greyhounds threw her pail of water over in their romping play, and she was very long in filling it again; and when she came home she threw her arms round her mother's neck, and in a passion of joyous tears told her that Edward Williams of The End of Time had asked her to marry him, and that she had said 'Yes.'

Eleanor Gwynn shed her tears too; but they fell quietly when she was alone. She was thankful Nest had found a protector—one suitable in age and apparent character, and above her in fortune; but she knew she should miss her sweet daughter in a thousand household ways; miss her in the evenings by the fireside; miss her when at night she wakened up with a start from a dream of her youth, and saw her fair face lying calm in the moonlight, pillowed by her side. Then she forgot her dream, and blessed her child, and slept again. But who could be so selfish as to be sad when Nest was so supremely happy? She danced and sang more than ever; and then sat silent, and smiled to herself: if spoken to, she started and came back to the present with a scarlet blush, which told what she had been thinking of.

That was a sunny, happy, enchanted autumn. But the winter was nigh at hand; and with it came sorrow. One fine frosty morning, Nest went out with her lover—she to the well, he to some farming business, which was to be transacted at the little inn of Pen-Morfa. He was late for his appointment; so he left her at the entrance of the village, and hastened to the inn; and she, in her best cloak and new hat (put on against her mother's advice; but they were a recent purchase, and very becoming), went through the Dol Mawr, radiant with love and happiness. One who lived until lately, met her going down towards the well, that morning; and said he turned round to look after her, she seemed unusually lovely. He wondered at the time at her wearing her Sunday clothes; for the pretty, hooded blue-cloth cloak is kept among the Welsh women as a church and market garment, and not commonly used even on the coldest days of winter for such household errands as fetching water from the well. However, as he said, 'It was not possible to look in her face, and "fault" anything she wore.' Down the sloping stones the girl went blithely with her pail. She filled it at the well: and then she took off her hat, tied the strings together, and slung it over her arm; she lifted the heavy pail and balanced it on her head. But alas! in going up the smooth, slippery, treacherous rock, the encumbrance of her cloak—it might be such a trifle as her slung hat—something, at any rate, took away her evenness of poise; the freshet had frozen on the slanting stone, and was one coat of ice; poor Nest fell, and put out her hip. No more flushing rosy colour on that sweet face—no more look of beaming innocent happiness;—instead, there was deadly pallor, and filmy eyes, over which dark shades seemed to chase each other as the shoots of agony grew more and more intense. She screamed once or twice; but the exertion (involuntary, and forced out of her by excessive pain) overcame her, and she fainted. A child coming an hour or so afterwards on the same errand, saw her lying there, ice-glued to the stone, and thought she was dead. It flew crying back.

'Nest Gwynn is dead! Nest Gwynn is dead!' and, crazy with fear, it did not stop until it had hid its head in its mother's lap. The village was alarmed, and all who were able went in haste towards the well. Poor Nest had often thought she was dying in that dreary hour; had taken fainting for death, and struggled against it; and prayed that God would keep her alive till she could see her lover's face once more; and when she did see it, white with terror, bending over her, she gave a feeble smile, and let herself faint away into unconsciousness.

Many a month she lay on her bed unable to move. Sometimes she was delirious, sometimes worn-out into the deepest depression. Through all, her mother watched her with tenderest care. The neighbours would come and offer help. They would bring presents of country dainties; and I do not suppose that there was a better dinner than ordinary cooked in any household in Pen-Morfa parish, but a portion of it was sent to Eleanor Gwynn, if not for her sick daughter, to try and tempt her herself to eat and be strengthened; for to no one would she delegate the duty of watching over her child. Edward Williams was for a long time most assiduous in his inquiries and attentions;

but by-and-by (ah! you see the dark fate of poor Nest now), he slackened, so little at first that Eleanor blamed herself for her jealousy on her daughter's behalf, and chid her suspicious heart. But as spring ripened into summer, and Nest was still bedridden, Edward's coolness was visible to more than the poor mother. The neighbours would have spoken to her about it, but she shrunk from the subject as if they were probing a wound. 'At any rate,' thought she, 'Nest shall be strong before she is told about it. I will tell lies—I shall be forgiven—but I must save my child; and when she is stronger, perhaps I may be able to comfort her. Oh! I wish she would not speak to him so tenderly and trustfully, when she is delirious. I could curse him when she does.' And then Nest would call for her mother, and Eleanor would go, and invent some strange story about the summonses Edward had had to Caernarvon assizes, or to Harlech cattle market. But at last she was driven to her wits' end; it was three weeks since he had even stopped at the door to inquire, and Eleanor, mad with anxiety about her child, who was silently pining off to death for want of tidings of her lover, put on her cloak, when she had lulled her daughter to sleep one fine June evening, and set off to 'The End of Time.' The great plain which stretches out like an amphitheatre, in the half-circle of hills formed by the ranges of Moel Gwynn and the Trê-Madoc Rocks, was all golden-green in the mellow light of sunset. To Eleanor it might have been black with winter frost, she never noticed outward things till she reached The End of Time; and there, in the little farm-yard, she was brought to a sense of her present hour and errand by seeing Edward. He was examining some hay, newly stacked; the air was scented by its fragrance, and by the lingering sweetness of the breath of the cows. When Edward turned round at the footstep and saw Eleanor, he coloured and looked confused; however, he came forward to meet her in a cordial manner enough.

'It's a fine evening,' said he. 'How is Nest? But, indeed, you're being here is a sign she is better. Won't you come in and sit down?' He spoke hurriedly, as if affecting a welcome which he did not feel.

'Thank you. I'll just take this milking-stool and sit down here. The open air is like balm after being shut up so long.'

'It is a long time,' he replied, 'more than five months.'

Mrs Gwynn was trembling at heart. She felt an anger which she did not wish to show; for, if be any manifestations of temper or resentment she lessened or broke the waning thread of attachment which bound him to her daughter, she felt she should never forgive herself. She kept inwardly saying, 'Patience, patience! he may be true and love her yet;' but her indignant convictions gave her words the lie.

'It's a long time, Edward Williams, since you've been near us to ask after Nest;' said she. 'She may be better, or she may be worse, for aught you know.' She looked up at him reproachfully, but spoke in a gentle quiet tone.

'I—you see the hay has been a long piece of work. The weather has been fractious—and a master's eye is needed. Besides,' said he, as if he had found the reason for which he sought to account for his absence, 'I have heard of her from Rowland Jones. I was at the surgery for some horse-medicine—he told me about her:' and a shade came over his face, as he remembered what the doctor had said. Did he think that shade would escape the mother's eye?

'You saw Rowland Jones! Oh, man-alive, tell me what he said of my girl! He'll say nothing to me, but just hems and haws the more I pray him. But you will tell me. You *must* tell me.' She stood up and spoke in a tone of command, which his feeling of independence, weakened just then by an accusing conscience, did not enable him to resist. He strove to evade the question, however.

'It was an unlucky day that ever she went to the well!'

'Tell me what the doctor said of my child,' repeated Mrs Gwynn. 'Will she live, or will she die?' He did not dare to disobey the imperious tone in which this question was put.

'Oh, she will live, don't be afraid. The doctor said she would live.' He did not mean to lay any peculiar emphasis on the word 'live,' but somehow he did, and she, whose every nerve vibrated with anxiety, caught the word.

'She will live!' repeated she. 'But there is something behind. Tell me, for I will know. If you won't say, I'll go to Rowland Jones to-night and make him tell me what he has said to you.'

There had passed something in this conversation between himself and the doctor, which Edward did not wish to have known; and Mrs Gwynn's threat had the desired effect. But he looked vexed and irritated.

'You have such impatient ways with you, Mrs Gwynn,' he remonstrated.

'I am a mother asking news of my sick child,' said she. 'Go on. What did he say? She'll live—' as if giving the clue.

'She'll live, he has no doubt of that. But he thinks—now don't clench your hands so—I can't tell you if you look in that way; you are enough to frighten a man.'

'I'm not speaking,' said she in a low husky tone. 'Never mind my looks: she'll live—'

'But she'll be a cripple for life.—There! you would have it out,' said he, sulkily.

'A cripple for life,' repeated she, slowly. 'And I'm one-and-twenty years older than she is!' She sighed heavily.

'And, as we're about it, I'll just tell you what is in my mind,' said he, hurried and confused. 'I've a deal of cattle; and the farm makes heavy work, as much as an able healthy woman can do. So you see—' He stopped, wishing her to understand his meaning without words. But she would not. She fixed her dark eyes on him, as if reading his soul, till he flinched under her gaze.

'Well,' said she, at length, 'say on. Remember I've a deal of work in me yet, and what strength is mine is my daughter's.'

'You're very good. But, altogether, you must be aware, Nest will never be the same as she was.'

'And you've not yet sworn in the face of God to take her for better, for worse; and, as she is worse'—she looked in his face, caught her breath, and went on—'as she is worse, why, you cast her off, not being church-tied to her. Though her body may be crippled, her poor heart is the same—alas!—and full of love for you. Edward, you don't mean to break it off because of our sorrows. You're only trying me, I know,' said she, as if begging him to assure her that her fears were false. 'But, you see, I'm a foolish woman—a poor foolish woman—and ready to take fright at a few words.' She smiled up in his face; but it was a forced doubting smile, and his face still retained its sullen dogged aspect.

'Nay, Mrs Gwynn,' said he, 'you spoke truth at first. Your own good sense told you Nest would never be fit to be any man's wife—unless indeed, she could catch Mr Griffiths of Tynwntyrybwlch; he might keep her a carriage, may-be.' Edward really did not mean to be unfeeling; but he was obtuse, and wished to carry off his embarrassment by a kind of friendly joke, which he had no idea would sting the poor mother as it did. He was startled at her manner.

'Put it in words like a man. Whatever you mean by my child, say it for yourself, and don't speak as if my good sense had told me any thing. I stand here, doubting my own thoughts, cursing my own fears. Don't be a coward. I ask you whether you, and Nest are troth-plight?'

'I am not a coward. Since you ask me, I answer, Nest, and I *were* troth-plight; but we *are* not. I cannot—no one would expect me to wed a cripple. It's your own doing I've told you now; I had made up my mind, but I should have waited a bit before telling you.'

'Very well,' said she, and she turned to go away; but her wrath burst the flood-gates, and swept away discretion and forethought. She moved, and stood in the gateway. Her lips parted, but no sound came; with an hysterical motion she threw her arms suddenly up to heaven, as if bringing down lightning towards the grey old house to which she pointed as they fell, and then she spoke:-

'The widow's child is unfriended. As surely as the Saviour brought the son of a widow from death to life, for her tears and cries, so surely will God and His angels watch over my Nest, and avenge her cruel wrongs.' She turned away weeping, and wringing her hands.

Edward went in-doors: he had no more desire to reckon his stores; he sat by the fire, looking gloomily at the red ashes. He might have been there half-an-hour or more, when some one knocked at the door. He would not speak. He wanted no one's company. Another knock sharp and loud. He did not speak. Then the visitor opened the door; and, to his surprise—almost to his affright—Eleanor Gwynn came in.

'I knew you were here. I knew you could not go out into the clear holy night, as if nothing had happened. Oh! did I curse you? If I did, I beg you to forgive me; and I will try and ask the Almighty to bless you, if you will but have a little mercy—a very little. It will kill my Nest if she knows the truth now—she is so very weak. Why, she cannot feed herself, she is so low and feeble. You would not wish to kill her, I think, Edward!' She looked at him as if expecting an answer; but he did not speak. She went down on her knees on the flags by him.

'You will give me a little time, Edward, to get her strong, won't you, now? I ask it on my bended knees! Perhaps, if I promise never to curse you again, you will come sometimes to see her, till she is well enough to know how all is over, and her heart's hopes crushed. Only say you'll come for a month, or so, as if you still loved her—the poor cripple—forlorn of the world. I'll get her strong, and not tax you long.' Her tears fell too fast for her to go on.

'Get up, Mrs Gwynn,' Edward said. 'Don't kneel to me. I have no objection to come and see Nest, now and then, so that all is clear between you and me. Poor thing! I'm sorry, as it happens, she's so taken up with the thought of me.'

'It was likely, was not it? and you to have been her husband before this time, if—Oh, miserable me! to let my child go and dim her bright life! But you'll forgive me, and come sometimes, just for a little quarter of an hour, once or twice a-week. Perhaps she'll be asleep sometimes when you call, and then, you know, you need not come in. If she were not so ill, I'd never ask you.'

So low and humble was the poor widow brought, through her exceeding love for her daughter.

CHAPTER II

NEST revived during the warm summer weather. Edward came to see her, and stayed the allotted quarter of an hour; but he dared not look her in the face. She was indeed a cripple: one leg was much shorter than the other, and she halted on a crutch. Her face, formerly so brilliant in colour, was wan and pale with suffering: the bright roses were gone, never to return. Her large eyes were sunk deep down in their hollow, cavernous sockets; but the light was in them still, when Edward came. Her mother dreaded her returning strength—dreaded, yet desired it; for the heavy burden of her secret was most oppressive at times, and she thought Edward was beginning to weary of his enforced attentions. One October evening she told her the truth. She even compelled her rebellious heart to take the cold, reasoning side of the question; and she told her child that her disabled frame was a disqualification for ever becoming a farmer's wife. She spoke hardly, because her inner agony and sympathy was such, she dared not trust herself to express the feelings that were rending her. But Nest turned away from cold reason; she revolted from her mother; she revolted from the world. She bound her sorrow tight up in her breast, to corrode and fester there.

Night after night, her mother heard her cries and moans—more pitiful, by far, than those wrung from her by bodily pain a year before; and night after night, if her mother spoke to soothe, she proudly denied the existence of any pain but what was physical, and consequent upon her accident.

'If she would but open her sore heart to me—to me, her mother,' Eleanor wailed forth in prayer to God, 'I would be content. Once it was enough to have my Nest all my own. Then came love, and I knew it would never be as before; and then I thought the grief I felt, when Edward spoke to me, was as sharp a sorrow as could be; but this present grief, Oh Lord, my God, is worst of all; and Thou only, Thou, canst help!'

When Nest grew as strong as she was ever likely to be on earth, she was anxious to have as much labour as she could bear. She would not allow her mother to spare her anything. Hard work—bodily fatigue—she seemed to crave. She was glad when she was stunned by exhaustion into a dull insensibility of feeling. She was almost fierce when her mother, in those first months of convalescence, performed the household tasks which had formerly been hers; but she shrank from going out of doors. Her mother thought that she was unwilling to expose her changed appearance to the neighbours' remarks; but Nest was not afraid of that: she was afraid of their pity, as being one deserted and cast off. If Eleanor gave way before her daughter's imperiousness, and sat by while Nest 'tore' about her work with the vehemence of a bitter heart, Eleanor could have cried, but she durst not; tears, or any mark of commiseration, irritated the crippled girl so much, she even drew away from caresses. Everything was to go on as it had been before she had known Edward; and so it did, outwardly; but they trod carefully, as if the ground on which they moved was hollow—deceptive. There was no more careless ease; every word was guarded, and every action planned. It was a dreary life to both. Once, Eleanor brought in a little baby, a neighbour's child, to try and tempt Nest out of herself, by her old love of children. Nest's pale face flushed as she saw the innocent child in her mother's arms; and, for a moment, she made as if she would have taken it; but then, she turned away, and hid her face behind her apron, and murmured, 'I shall never have a child to lie in my breast, and call me mother!' In a minute she arose, with compressed and tightened lips, and went about her household work, without her noticing the cooing baby again, till Mrs Gwynn, heart-sick at the failure of her little plan, took it back to its parents.

One day the news ran through Pen-Morfa that Edward Williams was about to be married. Eleanor had long expected this intelligence. It came upon her like no new thing; but it was the filling-up of her cup of woe. She could not tell Nest. She sat listlessly in the house, and dreaded that each neighbour who came in would speak about the village news. At last some one did. Nest looked round from her employment, and talked of the event with a kind of cheerful curiosity as to the particulars, which made her informant go away, and tell others that Nest had quite left off caring for Edward Williams. But when the door was shut, and Eleanor and she were left alone, Nest came and stood before her weeping mother like a stern accuser.

'Mother, why did not you let me die? Why did you keep me alive for this?' Eleanor could not speak, but she put her arms out towards her girl. Nest turned away, and Eleanor cried aloud in her soreness of spirit. Nest came again.

'Mother, I was wrong. You did your best. I don't know how it is I am so hard and cold. I wish I had died when I was a girl and had a feeling heart.'

'Don't speak so, my child. God has afflicted you sore, and your hardness of heart is but for a time. Wait a little. Don't reproach yourself, my poor Nest. I understand your ways. I don't mind them, love. The feeling heart will come back to you in time. Anyways, don't think you're grieving me, because, love, that may sting you when I'm gone; and I'm not grieved, my darling. Most times we're very cheerful, I think.'

After this, mother, and child were drawn more together. But Eleanor had received her death from these sorrowful, hurrying events. She did not conceal the truth from herself; nor did she pray to live, as some months ago she had done, for her child's sake; she had found out that she had no power to console the poor wounded heart. It seemed to her as if her prayers had been of no avail; and then she blamed herself for this thought.

There are many Methodist preachers in this part of Wales. There was a certain old man, named David Hughes, who was held in peculiar reverence because he had known the great John Wesley. He had been captain of a Caernarvon slate-vessel; he had traded in the Mediterranean, and had seen strange sights. In those early days (to use his own expression) he had lived without God in the world; but he went to mock John Wesley, and was converted by the white-haired patriach, and remained to pray. Afterwards he became one of the earnest, self-denying, much-abused band of itinerant preachers who went forth under Wesley's direction, to spread abroad a more earnest and practical spirit of religion. His rambles, and travels were of use to him. They extended his knowledge of the circumstances in which men are sometimes placed, and enlarged his sympathy with the tried and tempted. His sympathy, combined with the thoughtful experience of fourscore years, made him cognisant of many of the strange secrets of humanity; and when younger preachers upbraided the hard hearts they met with, and despaired of the sinners, he 'suffered long, and was kind.'

When Eleanor Gwynn lay low on her death-bed, David Hughes came to Pen-Morfa. He knew her history, and sought her out. To him she imparted the feelings I have described.

'I have lost my faith, David. The tempter has come, and I have yielded. I doubt if my prayers have been heard. Day, and night have I prayed that I might comfort my child in her great sorrow; but God has not heard me. She has turned away from me, and refused my poor love. I wish to die now; but I have lost my faith, and have no more pleasure in the thought of going to God. What must I do, David?'

She hung upon his answer; and it was long in coming.

'I am weary of earth,' said she, mournfully, 'and can I find rest in death even, leaving my child desolate and broken-hearted?'

'Eleanor,' said David, 'where you go all things will be made clear; and you will learn to thank God for the end of what now seems grievous and heavy to be borne. Do you think your agony has been greater than the awful agony in the Garden—or your prayers more earnest than that which He prayed in that hour when the great drops of blood ran down his face like sweat? We know that God heard Him, although no answer came to Him through the dread silence of that night. God's times are not our times. I have lived eighty and one years, and never yet have I known an earnest prayer fall to the ground unheeded. In an unknown way, and when no one looked for it, may be, the answer came; a fuller, more satisfying answer than heart could conceive of, although it might be different to what was expected. Sister you are going where in His light you will see light; you will learn there that in very faithfulness he has afflicted you!'

'Go on—you strengthen me,' said she.

After David Hughes left that day, Eleanor was calm as one already dead, and past mortal strife. Nest was awed by the change. No more passionate weeping—no more sorrow in the voice; though it was low and weak, it sounded with a sweet composure. Her last look was a smile; her last word a blessing.

Nest, tearless, streeked the poor worn body. She laid a plate with salt upon it on the breast, and lighted candles for the head and feet. It was an old Welsh custom; but when David Hughes came in, the sight carried him back to the time when he had seen the chapels in some old Catholic cathedral. Nest sat gazing on the dead with dry, hot eyes.

'She is dead,' said David, solemnly, 'she died in Christ. Let us bless God, my child. He giveth and He taketh away.'

'She is dead,' said Nest, 'my mother is dead. No one loves me now.'

She spoke as if she were thinking aloud, for she did not look at David, or ask him to be seated.

'No one loves you now? No human creature, you mean. You are not yet fit to be spoken to concerning God's infinite love. I, like you, will speak of love for human creatures. I tell you if no one loves you, it is time for you to begin to love.' He spoke almost severely (if David Hughes ever did); for, to tell the truth, he was repelled by her hard rejection of her mother's tenderness, about which the neighbours had told him.

'Begin to love!' said she, her eyes flashing. 'Have I not loved? Old man, you are dim, and worn-out. You do not remember what love is.' She spoke with a scornful kind of pitying endurance. 'I will tell you how I have loved by telling you the change it has wrought in me. I was once the beautiful Nest Gwynn; I am now a cripple, a poor, wan-faced cripple, old before my time. That is a change; at least people think so.' She paused and then spoke lower. 'I tell you, David Hughes, that outward change is as nothing compared to the change in my nature caused by the love I have felt—and have had rejected. I was gentle once, and if you spoke a tender word, my heart came towards you as natural as a little child goes to its mammy. I never spoke roughly, even to the dumb creatures, for I had a kind feeling for all. Of late (since I loved, old man), I have been cruel in my thoughts to every one. I have turned away from tenderness with bitter indifference, Listen!' she spoke in a hoarse whisper, 'I will own it. I have spoken hardly to her,' pointing towards the corpse. 'Her who was ever patient, and full of love for me. She did not know,' she muttered, 'she is gone to the grave without knowing how I loved her—I had such strange, mad, stubborn pride in me.'

'Come back, mother! Come back,' said she, crying wildly to the still, solemn corpse; 'come back as a spirit or a ghost—only come back, that I may tell you how I have loved you.'

But the dead never come back.

The passionate adjuration ended in tears—the first she had shed. When they ceased, or were absorbed into long quivering sobs, David knelt down. Nest did not kneel, but bowed her head. He prayed, while his own tears fell fast. He rose up. They were both calm.

'Nest,' said he, 'your love has been the love of youth; passionate, wild, natural to youth. Henceforward you must love like Christ; without thought of self, or wish for return. You must take the sick and the weary to your heart, and love them. That love will lift you up above the storms of the world into God's own peace. The very vehemence of your nature proves that you are capable of this. I do not pity you. You no not require pity. You are powerful enough to trample down your own sorrows into a blessing for others; and to others you will be a blessing; I see it before you; I see in it the answer to your mother's prayer.'

The old man's dim eyes glittered as if they saw a vision; the fire-light sprang up, and glinted on his long white hair. Nest was awed as if she saw a prophet, and a prophet he was to her.

When next David Hughes came to Pen-Morfa, he asked about Nest Gwynn with a hovering doubt as to the answer. The inn-folk told him she was living still in the cottage, which was now her own.

'But would you believe it, David,' said Mrs Thomas, 'she has gone and taken Mary Williams to live with her? You remember Mary Williams, I'm sure.'

No! David Hughes remembered no Mary Williams at Pen-Morfa.

'You must have seen her, for I know you've called at Thomas Griffiths', where the parish boarded her?'

'You don't mean the half-witted woman—the poor crazy creature?'

'But I do!' said Mrs Thomas.

'I have seen her sure enough, but I never thought of learning her name. And Nest Gwynn has taken her to live with her.'

'Yes! I thought I should surprise you. She might have had many a decent girl for companion. My own niece, her that is an orphan, would have gone, and been thankful. Besides, Mary Williams is a regular savage a times; John Griffiths says there were days when he used to beat her till she howled again, and yet she would not do as he told her. Nay, once, he says, if he had not seen her eyes glare like a wild beast, from under the shadow of the table where she had taken shelter, and got pretty quickly out of her way, she would have flown upon him, and throttled him. He gave Nest fair warning of what she must expect, and he thinks some day she will be found murdered.'

David Hughes thought a while. 'How came Nest to take her to live with her?' asked he.

'Well! Folk say John Griffiths did not give her enough to eat. Half-wits, they tell me, take more to feed them than others, and Eleanor Gwynn had given her oat-cake, and porridge a time or two, and most likely spoken kindly to her (you know Eleanor spoke kind to all), so some months ago, when John Griffiths had been beating her, and keeping her without food to try, and tame her, she ran away, and came to Nest's cottage in the dead of night, all shivering, and starved, for she did not know Eleanor was dead, and thought to meet with kindness from her, I've no doubt; and Nest remembered how her mother used to feed and comfort the poor idiot, and made her some gruel, and wrapped her up by the fire. And in the morning when John Griffiths came in search of Mary, he found her with Nest, and Mary wailed so piteously at the sight of him, that Nest went to the parish officers, and offered to take her to board with her for the same money they gave to him. John says he was right glad to be off his bargain.'

David Hughes knew there was a kind of remorse which sought relief in the performance of the most difficult and repugnant tasks. He thought he could understand how, in her bitter repentance for her conduct towards her mother, Nest had taken in the first helpless creature that came seeking shelter in her name. It was not what he would have chosen, but he knew it was God that had sent the poor wandering idiot there.

He went to see Nest the next morning. As he drew near the cottage—it was summer time, and the doors and windows were all open—he heard an angry passionate kind of sound that was scarcely human. That sound prevented his approach from being heard; and standing at the threshold, he saw poor Mary Williams pacing backwards, and forwards in some wild mood. Nest, cripple as she was, was walking with her, speaking low soothing words, till the pace was slackened, and time and breathing was given to put her arm around the crazy woman's neck, and soothe her by this tender caress into the quiet luxury of tears; tears which give the hot brain relief. Then David Hughes came in. His first words, as he took off his hat, standing on the lintel, were—'The peace of God be upon this house.' Neither he nor Nest recurred to the past; though solemn recollections filled their minds. Before he went, all three knelt and prayed; for, as Nest told him, some mysterious influence of peace came over the poor half-wit's mind, when she heard the holy words of prayer; and often when she felt a paroxysm coming on, she would kneel and repeat a homily rapidly over, as if it were a charm to scare away the Demon in possession; sometimes, indeed, the control over herself requisite for this effort was enough to dispel the fluttering burst. When David rose up to go, he drew Nest to the door.

'You are not afraid, my child?' asked he.

'No,' she replied. 'She is often very good and quiet. When she is not, I can bear it.'

'I shall see your face on earth no more;' said he. 'God bless you!' He went on his way. Not many weeks after, David Hughes was borne to his grave.

The doors of Nest's heart were opened—opened wide by the love she grew to feel for crazy Mary, so helpless, so friendless, so dependent upon her. Mary loved her back again, as a dumb animal loves its blind master. It was happiness enough to be near her. In general she was only too glad to do what she was bidden by Nest. But there were times when Mary was overpowered by the glooms and fancies of her poor disordered brain. Fearful times! No one knew how fearful. On those days, Nest warned the little children who loved to come, and play around her, that they must not visit the house. The signal was a piece of white linen hung out of the side-window. On those days the sorrowful, and sick waited in vain for the sound of Nest's lame approach. But what she had to endure was only known to God, for she never complained. If she had given up the charge of Mary, or if the neighbours had risen out of love, and care for her life, to compel such a step, she knew what hard curses and blows—what starvation and misery, would await the poor creature.

She told of Mary's docility, and her affection, and her innocent little sayings; but she never told the details of the occasional days of wild disorder, and driving insanity.

Nest grew old before her time, in consequence of her accident. She knew that she was as old at fifty as many are at seventy. She knew it partly by the vividness with which the remembrance of the days of her youth came back to her mind, while the events of yesterday were dim, and forgotten. She dreamt of her girlhood, and youth. In sleep she was once more the beautiful Nest Gwynn, the admired of all beholders, the light-hearted girl, beloved by her mother. Little circumstances connected with those early days, forgotten since the very time when they occurred, came back to her mind, in her waking hours. She had a scar on the palm of her left hand, occasioned by the fall of a branch of a tree, when she was a child; it had not pained her since the first two days after the accident; but now it began to hurt her slightly; and clear in her ears was the crackling sound of the treacherous, rending wood; distinct before her rose the presence of her mother tenderly binding up the wound. With these remembrances came a longing desire to see the beautiful fatal well, once more before her death. She had never gone so far since the day when, by her fall there, she lost love, and hope, and her bright glad youth. She yearned to look upon its waters once again. This desire waxed as her life waxed. She told it to poor crazy Mary.

'Mary!' said she, 'I want to go to the Rock Well. If you will help me, I can manage it. There used to be many a stone in the Dol Mawr on which I could sit and rest. We will go to-morrow morning before folks are astir.'

Mary answered briskly, 'Up, up! To the Rock Well: Mary will go. Mary will go.' All day long she kept muttering to herself, 'Mary will go.'

Nest had the happiest dream that night. Her mother stood beside her—not in the flesh, but in the bright glory of a blessed spirit. And Nest was no longer young—neither was she old—'they reckon not by days, nor years where she was gone to dwell;' and her mother stretched out her arms to her with a calm glad look of welcome. She awoke; the woodlark was singing in the near copse—she little birds were astir, and rustling in their leafy nests. Nest arose, and called Mary. The two set out through the quiet lane. They went along slowly, and silently. With many a pause they crossed the broad Dol Mawr; and carefully descended the sloping stones, on which no trace remained of the hundreds of feet that had passed over them since Nest was last there. The clear water sparkled and quivered in the early sun-light, the shadows of the birch-leaves were stirred on the ground; the ferns—Nest could have believed that they were the very same ferns which she had seen thirty years before, hung wet and dripping where the water over-flowed—a thrush chanted matins from a holly bush near—and the running stream made a low, soft, sweet accompaniment. All was the same; Nature was as fresh and young as ever. It might have been yesterday that Edward Williams had overtaken her, and told her his love—she thought of his words—his handsome looks—(he was a grey hard-featured man by this time), and then she recalled the fatal wintry morning when joy, and youth had fled; and as she remembered that faintness of pain, a new, a real faintness—no echo of the memory—came over her. She leant her back against a rock, without a moan or sigh, and died! She found immortality by the well side, instead of her fragile perishing youth. She was so calm, and placid that Mary (who had been dipping her fingers in the well, to see the waters drop off in the gleaming sun-light), thought she was asleep, and for some time continued her amusement in silence. At last she turned, and said,

'Mary is tired. Mary wants to go home.' Nest did not speak, though the idiot repeated her plaintive words. She stood and looked till a strange terror came over her—a terror too mysterious to be borne.

'Mistress, wake! Mistress, wake!' she said, wildly, shaking the form.

But Nest did not awake. And the first person who came to the well that morning found crazy Mary sitting, awe-struck, by the poor dead Nest. They had to get the poor creature away by force, before they could remove the body.

Mary is in Trê-Madoc workhouse; they treat her pretty kindly, and in general she is good and tractable. Occasionally the old paroxysms come on; and for a time she is unmanageable. But some one thought of speaking to her about Nest. She stood arrested at the name; and since then, it is astonishing to see what efforts she makes to curb her insanity; and when the dread time is past, she creeps up to the matron, and says, 'Mary has tried to be good. Will God let her go to Nest now?'

Charlotte Brontë

1816 – 55

Charlotte Brontë *grew up in Haworth parsonage in Yorkshire, with her surviving siblings, Emily, Anne and Branwell. Among themselves the children created fantasy worlds about which they wrote stories and poems. Their life together was interrupted when they left for various teaching positions; Charlotte went to Brussels where she suffered an unrequited passion for her Belgian employer. The women were reunited at Haworth. Their first publication, under male pseudonyms, was a volume of poems; they then submitted a novel each. Charlotte Brontë's production was* The Professor *which was rejected and only published in 1857 after her death. However she rapidly finished another novel,* Jane Eyre. An Autobigraphy, *which was immediately published to considerable acclaim in 1847. The experiences of Belgium which had been used in* The Professor, *with its male narrator, were more successfully reworked in* Villette *(1853)*

with a female one. By the time of Villette's *publication, all the Brontë siblings
except Charlotte were dead; shortly afterwards she married her father's curate
and became pregnant, only to die herself a few months later.*

The following extracts are from The Professor *and* Villette.

From

The Professor

...KNOW, O incredulous reader! that a master stands in a somewhat different
relation towards a pretty, light-headed, probably ignorant girl, to that
occupied by a partner at a ball, or a gallant on the promenade. A professor does
not meet his pupil to see her dressed in satin and muslin, with hair perfumed
and curled, neck scarcely shaded by aërial lace, round white arms circled with
bracelets, feet dressed for the gliding dance. It is not his business to whirl her
through the waltz, to feed her with compliments, to heighten her beauty by the
flush of gratified vanity. Neither does he encounter her on the smooth-rolled,
tree-shaded Boulevard, in the green and sunny park, whither she repairs clad in her
becoming walking dress, her scarf thrown with grace over her shoulders, her little
bonnet scarcely screening her curls, the red rose under its brim adding a new tint to
the softer rose on her cheek: her face and eyes, too, illumined with smiles, perhaps
as transient as the sunshine of the gala-day, but also quite as brilliant; it is not his
office to walk by her side, to listen to her lively chat, to carry her parasol, scarcely
larger than a broad green leaf, to lead in a ribbon her Blenheim spaniel or Italian
greyhound. No, he finds her in the schoolroom, plainly dressed, with books before
her. Owing to her education or her nature books are to her a nuisance, and she
opens them with aversion, yet her teacher must instil into her mind the contents
of these books; that mind resists the admission of grave information, it recoils, it
grows restive, sullen tempers are shown, disfiguring frowns spoil the symmetry
of the face, sometimes coarse gestures banish grace from the deportment, while
muttered expressions, redolent of native and ineradicable vulgarity, desecrate
the sweetness of the voice. Where the temperament is serene though the intellect
be sluggish, an unconquerable dulness opposes every effort to instruct. Where
there is cunning but not energy, dissimulation, falsehood, a thousand schemes
and tricks are put in play to evade the necessity of application; in short, to the
tutor, female youth, female charms, are like tapestry hangings, of which the wrong
side is continually turned towards him; and even when he sees the smooth, neat
external surface he so well knows what knots, long stitches, and jagged ends are
behind that he has scarce a temptation to admire too fondly the seemly forms and
bright colours exposed to general view.

Our likings are regulated by our circumstances. The artist prefers a hilly
country because it is picturesque; the engineer a flat one because it is convenient; the man of pleasure likes what he calls "a fine woman"—she suits him;

the fashionable young gentleman admires the fashionable young lady—she is of his kind; the toil-worn, fagged, probably irritable tutor, blind almost to beauty, insensible to airs and graces, glories chiefly in certain mental qualities: application, love of knowledge, natural capacity, docility, truthfulness, gratefulness are the charms that attract his notice and win his regard. These he seeks, but seldom meets; these if by chance he finds, he would fain retain for ever, and when separation deprives him of them he feels as if some ruthless hand had snatched from him his only ewe-lamb. Such being the case, and the case it is, my readers will agree with me that there was nothing either very meritorious or very marvellous in the integrity and moderation of my conduct at Mdlle. Reuter's pensionnat de demoiselles.[1]

My first business this afternoon consisted in reading the list of places for the month, determined by the relative correctness of the compositions given the preceding day. The list was headed, as usual, by the name of Sylvie, that plain, quiet little girl I have described before as being at once the best and ugliest pupil in the establishment; the second place had fallen to the lot of a certain Léonie Ledru, diminutive, sharp-featured, and parchment-skinned creature of quick wits, frail conscience, and indurated feelings; a lawyer-like thing, of whom I used to say that, had she been a boy, she would have made a model of an unprincipled, clever attorney. Then came Eulalie, the proud beauty, the Juno of the school, whom six long years of drilling in the simple grammar of the English language had compelled, despite the stiff phlegm of her intellect, to acquire a mechanical acquaintance with most of its rules. No smile, no trace of pleasure or satisfaction appeared in Sylvie's nun-like and passive face as she heard her name read first. I always felt saddened by the sight of that poor girl's absolute quiescence on all occasions, and it was my custom to look at her, to address her, as seldom as possible; her extreme docility, her assiduous perseverance, would have recommended her warmly to my good opinion; her modesty, her intelligence, would have induced me to feel most kindly—most affectionately towards her, notwithstanding the almost ghastly plainness of her features, the disproportion of her form, the corpse-like lack of animation in her countenance, had I not been aware that every friendly word, every kindly action, would be reported by her to her confessor, and by him misinterpreted and poisoned. Once I laid my hand on her head in token of approbation; I thought Sylvie was going to smile, her dim eye almost kindled; but, presently, she shrank from me; I was a man and a heretic; she, poor child! a destined nun and devoted Catholic; thus a fourfold wall of separation divided her mind from mine. A pert smirk, and a hard glance of triumph, was Léonie's method of testifying her gratification; Eulalie looked sullen and envious—she had hoped to be first. Hortense and Caroline exchanged a reckless grimace on hearing their names read out somewhere near the bottom of the list; the brand of mental inferiority was considered by them as no disgrace, their hopes for the future being based solely on their personal attractions.

This affair arranged, the regular lesson followed. During a brief interval, employed by the pupils in ruling their books, my eye, ranging carelessly over

[1] Establishment for young ladies.

the benches, observed, for the first time, that the farthest seat in the farthest row—a seat usually vacant—was again filled by the new scholar, the Mdlle. Henri so ostentatiously recommended to me by the directress. To-day I had on my spectacles; her appearance, therefore, was clear to me at the first glance; I had not to puzzle over it. She looked young; yet, had I been required to name her exact age, I should have been somewhat nonplussed: the slightness of her figure might have suited seventeen; a certain anxious and preoccupied expression of face seemed the indication of riper years. She was dressed, like all the rest, in a dark stuff gown and a white collar; her features were dissimilar to any there, not so rounded, more defined, yet scarcely regular. The shape of her head too was different, the superior part more developed, the base considerably less. I felt assured, at first sight, that she was not a Belgian; her complexion, her countenance, her lineaments, her figure, were all distinct from theirs, and, evidently, the type of another race—of a race less gifted with fulness of flesh and plenitude of blood; less jocund, material, unthinking. When I first cast my eyes on her, she sat looking fixedly down, her chin resting on her hand, and she did not change her attitude till I commenced the lesson. None of the Belgian girls would have retained one position, and that a reflective one, for the same length of time. Yet, having intimated that her appearance was peculiar, as being unlike that of her Flemish companions, I have little more to say respecting it; I can pronounce no encomiums on her beauty, for she was not beautiful; nor offer condolence on her plainness, for neither was she plain; a careworn character of forehead, and a corresponding moulding of the mouth, struck me with a sentiment resembling surprise, but these traits would probably have passed unnoticed by any less crotchety observer.

Now, reader, though I have spent more than a page in describing Mdlle. Henri, I know well enough that I have left on your mind's eye no distinct picture of her; I have not painted her complexion, nor her eyes, nor her hair, nor even drawn the outline of her shape. You cannot tell whether her nose was aquiline or retroussé, whether her chin was long or short, her face square or oval; nor could I the first day, and it is not my intention to communicate to you at once a knowledge I myself gained by little and little.

I gave a short exercise which they all wrote down. I saw the new pupil was puzzled at first with the novelty of the form and language; once or twice she looked at me with a sort of painful solicitude, as not comprehending at all what I meant; then she was not ready when the others were, she could not write her phrases so fast as they did; I would not help her, I went on relentless. She looked at me; her eye said most plainly, "I cannot follow you." I disregarded the appeal, and, carelessly leaning back in my chair, glancing from time to time with a *nonchalant* air out of the window, I dictated a little faster. On looking towards her again, I perceived her face clouded with embarrassment, but she was still writing on most diligently; I paused a few seconds; she employed the interval in hurriedly re-perusing what she had written, and shame and discomfiture were apparent in her countenance; she evidently found she had made great nonsense of it. In ten minutes more the dictation was complete, and, having allowed a brief space in which to correct it, I took their books; it was with a reluctant hand Mdlle. Henri gave up hers, but, having once yielded it to my possession, she composed her anxious face, as if, for the present, she had resolved to dismiss regret, and had made up her mind to be thought unprecedentedly stupid. Glancing over her exercise, I found that several lines had been omitted, but what was written contained very few faults; I instantly inscribed "Bon" at the bottom of the page, and returned it to her; she smiled, at first incredulously, then as if reassured, but did not lift her eyes; she could look at me, it seemed, when perplexed and bewildered, but not when gratified; I thought that scarcely fair.

Villette

From *Chapter Eight*

'YOU will not expect aid from me, or from any one,' said madame. 'That would at once set you down as incompetent for your office.'

I opened the door, let her pass with courtesy, and followed her. There were three school-rooms, all large. That dedicated to the second division, where I was to figure, was considerably the largest, and accommodated an assemblage more numerous, more turbulent, and infinitely more unmanageable than the other two. In after days, when I knew the ground better, I used to think sometimes (if such a comparison may be permitted), that the quiet, polished, tame first division, was to the robust, riotous demonstrative second division, what the English House of Lords is to the House of Commons.

The first glance informed me that many of the pupils were more than girls —quite young women; I knew that some of them were of noble family (as nobility goes in Labassecour[2]); and I was well convinced that not one amongst them was ignorant of my position in madame's household. As I mounted the estrade (a low platform, raised a step above the flooring), where stood the teacher's chair and desk, I beheld opposite to me a row of eyes and brows that threatened stormy weather—eyes full of an insolent light, and brows hard and unblushing as marble. The continental 'female' is quite a different being to the insular 'female' of the same age and class: I never saw such eyes and brows in England. Madame Beck introduced me in one cool phrase, sailed from the room, and left me alone in my glory.

I shall never forget that first lesson, nor all the under-current of life and character it opened up to me. Then first did I begin rightly to see the wide difference that lies between the novelist's and poet's ideal 'jeune fille,' and the said 'jeune fille' as she really is.

It seems that three titled belles in the first row had sat down predetermined that a *bonne d'enfants*[3] should not give them lessons in English. They knew

2 Belgium.
3 Nursery maid.

they had succeeded in expelling obnoxious teachers before now; they knew that madame would at any time throw overboard a professeur or maîtresse who became unpopular with the school—that she never assisted a weak official to retain his place—that if he had not strength to fight, or tact to win his way—down he went: looking at 'Miss Snowe' they promised themselves an easy victory.

Mesdemoiselles Blanche, Virginie, and Angélique opened the campaign by a series of titterings and whisperings; these soon swelled into murmurs and short laughs, which the remoter benches caught up and echoed more loudly. This growing revolt of sixty against one, soon became oppressive enough; my command of French being so limited, and exercised under such cruel constraint.

Could I but have spoken in my own tongue, I felt as if I might have gained a hearing; for, in the first place, though I knew I looked a poor creature, and in many respects actually was so, yet nature had given me a voice that could make itself heard, if lifted in excitement or deepened by emotion. In the second place, while I had no flow, only a hesitating trickle of language, in ordinary circumstances, yet—under stimulus such as was now rife through the mutinous mass—I could, in English, have rolled out readily phrases stigmatizing their proceedings as such proceedings deserved to be stigmatized; and then with some sarcasm, flavoured with contemptuous bitterness, for the ring-leaders, and relieved with easy banter for the weaker, but less knavish followers, it seemed to me that one might possibly get command over this wild herd and bring them into training, at least. All I could now do was to walk up to Blanche—Mademoiselle de Melcy, a young baronne—the eldest, tallest, handsomest, and most vicious—stand before her desk, take from under her hand her exercise-book, remount the estrade, deliberately read the composition, which I found very stupid, and as deliberately, and in the face of the whole school, tear the blotted page in two.

This action availed to draw attention and check noise. One girl alone, quite in the background, persevered in the riot with undiminished energy. I looked at her attentively. She had a pale face, hair like night, broad strong eyebrows, decided features and a dark, mutinous, sinister eye: I noted that she sat close by a little door, which door, I was well aware, opened into a small closet where books were kept. She was standing up for the purpose of conducting her clamour with freer energies. I measured her stature and calculated her strength. She seemed both tall and wiry; but, so the conflict were brief and the attack unexpected, I thought I might manage her.

Advancing up the room, looking as cool and careless as I possibly could, in short, *ayant l'air de rien*,[4] I slightly pushed the door and found it was ajar. In an instant, and with sharpness, I had turned on her. In another instant she occupied the closet, the door was shut, and the key in my pocket.

It so happened that this girl, Dolores by name and a Catalonian by race, was the sort of character at once dreaded and hated by all her associates; the act of summary justice above noted, proved popular: there was not one present but, in her heart, liked to see it done. They were stilled for a moment; then a smile—not a laugh—passed from desk to desk: then—when I had gravely and tranquilly

[4] Seeming unconcerned.

returned to the estrade, courteously requested silence, and commenced a dictation as if nothing at all had happened—the pens travelled peacefully over the pages, and the remainder of the lesson passed in order and industry.

'C'est bien,' said Madame Beck, when I came out of class, hot and a little exhausted. 'Ça ira.'[5]

She had been listening and peeping through a spy-hole the whole time.

From that day I ceased to be nursery-governess, and became English teacher. Madame raised my salary; but she got thrice the work out of me she had extracted from Mr Wilson, at half the expense.

From *Chapter 9*

My time was now well and profitably filled up. What with teaching others and studying closely myself, I had hardly a spare moment. It was pleasant. I felt I was getting on; not lying the stagnant prey of mould and rust, but polishing my faculties and whetting them to a keen edge with constant use. Experience of a certain kind lay before me, on no narrow scale. Villette is a cosmopolitan city, and in this school were girls of almost every European nation, and likewise of very varied rank in life. Equality is much practised in Labassecour; though not republican in form, it is nearly so in substance, and at the desks of Madame Beck's establishment the young countess and the young bourgeoise sat side by side: nor could you always by outward indications decide which was noble and which plebeian; except that, indeed, the latter had often franker and more courteous manners, while the former bore away the bell for a delicately balanced combination of insolence and deceit. In the former there was often quick French blood mixed with their marsh-phlegm: I regret to say that the effect of this vivacious fluid chiefly appeared in the oilier glibness with which flattery and fiction ran from the tongue, and in a manner lighter and livelier, but quite heartless and insincere.

To do all parties justice, the honest aboriginal Labassecouriennes had an hypocrisy of their own too; but it was of a coarse order, such as could deceive few. Whenever a lie was necessary for their occasions, they brought it out with a careless ease and breadth altogether untroubled by the rebuke of conscience. Not a soul in Madame Beck's house, from the scullion to the directress herself, but was above being ashamed of a lie; they thought nothing of it: to invent might not be precisely a virtue, but it was the most venial of faults. 'J'ai menti plusieurs fois'[6] formed an item of every girl's and woman's monthly confession: the priest heard unshocked, and absolved unreluctant. If they had missed going to mass, or read a chapter of a novel, that was another thing: these were crimes whereof rebuke and penance were the unfailing meed.

[5] That's fine. It will do.
[6] I've lied many times.

While yet but half-conscious of this state of things, and unlearned in its results, I got on in my new sphere very well. After the first few difficult lessons, given amidst peril and on the edge of a moral volcano, that rumbled under my feet and sent sparks and hot fumes into my eyes, the eruptive spirit seemed to subside, as far as I was concerned. My mind was a good deal bent on success: I could not bear the thought of being baffled by mere undisciplined disaffection and wanton indocility, in the first attempt to get on in life. Many hours of the night I used to lie awake, thinking what plan I had best adopt to get a reliable hold on these mutineers, to bring this stiff-necked tribe under permanent influence. In the first place, I saw plainly that aid in no shape was to be expected from Madame: her righteous plan was to maintain an unbroken popularity with the pupils, at any and every cost of justice or comfort to the teachers. For a teacher to seek her alliance in any crisis of insubordination was equivalent to securing her own expulsion. In intercourse with her pupils, Madame only took to herself what was pleasant, amiable, and recommendatory; rigidly requiring of her lieutenants sufficiency for every annoying crisis, where to act with adequate promptitude was to be unpopular. Thus, I must look only to myself.

Imprimis[7]—it was clear as the day that this swinish multitude were not to be driven by force. They were to be humoured, borne with very patiently: a courteous though sedate manner impressed them; a very rare flash of raillery did good. Severe or continuous mental application they could not, or would not, bear: heavy demand on the memory, the reason, the attention, they rejected point-blank. Where an English girl of not more than average capacity and docility, would quietly take a theme and bind herself to the task of comprehension and mastery, a Labassecourienne would laugh in your face, and throw it back to you with the phrase,—'Dieu que c'est difficile! Je n'en veux pas. Cela m'ennuie trop.'[8]

A teacher who understood her business would take it back at once, without hesitation, contest, or expostulation—proceed with even exaggerated care to smoothe every difficulty, to reduce it to the level of their understandings, return it to them thus modified, and lay on the lash of sarcasm with unsparing hand. They would feel the sting, perhaps wince a little under it, but they bore no malice against this sort of attack, provided the sneer was not *sour* but *hearty*, and that it held well up to them, in a clear light and bold type, so that she who ran might read, their incapacity, ignorance, and sloth. They would riot for three additional lines to a lesson; but I never knew them rebel against a wound given to their self-respect: the little they had of that quality was trained to be crushed, and it rather liked the pressure of a firm heel, than otherwise.

By degrees, as I acquired fluency and freedom in their language, and could make such application of its more nervous idioms as suited their case, the elder and more intelligent girls began rather to like me, in their way: I noticed that whenever a pupil had been roused to feel in her soul the stirring of worthy emulation, or the quickening of honest shame, from that date she was won. If I could but once make their (usually large) ears burn under their thick, glossy hair,

---

[7] In the first place.
[8] Gracious, how difficult that is! I don't want any more of it. It makes me so tired.

all was comparatively well. By-and-by bouquets began to be laid on my desk in the morning: by way of acknowledgment for this little foreign attention, I used sometimes to walk with a select few during recreation. In the course of conversation it befel once or twice that I made an unpremeditated attempt to rectify some of their singularly distorted notions of principle, especially I expressed my ideas of the evil and baseness of a lie. In an unguarded moment, I chanced to say that, of the two errors, I considered falsehood worse than an occasional lapse in church-attendance. The poor girls were tutored to report in Catholic ears whatever the Protestant teacher said. An edifying consequence ensued. Something—an unseen, an indefinite, a nameless something—stole between myself and these my best pupils: the bouquets continued to be offered, but conversation thenceforth became impracticable. As I paced the alleys or sat in the berceau, a girl never came to my right hand but a teacher, as if by magic, appeared at my left. Also, wonderful to relate, Madame's shoes of silence brought her continually to my back, as quick, noiseless, and unexpected, as some wandering zephyr.

The opinion of my Catholic acquaintance concerning my spiritual prospects was somewhat naïvely expressed to me on one occasion. A pensionnaire, to whom I had rendered some little service, exclaimed one day as she sat beside me:

'Mademoiselle, what a pity you are a Protestant!'

'Why, Isabelle?'

'Parceque, quand vous serez morte—vous brûlerez tout de suite dans l'Enfer.'

'Croyez-vous?'

'Certainement que j'y crois: tout le monde le sait; et d'ailleurs le prêtre me l'a dit.'

Isabelle was an odd, blunt little creature. She added, *sotto voce*:

'Pour assurer votre salut là-haut, on ferait bien de vous brûler toute vive ici-bas.'[9]

I laughed, as, indeed, it was impossible to do otherwise.

***

Has the reader forgotten Miss Ginevra Fanshawe? If so, I must be allowed to re-introduce that young lady as a thriving pupil of Madame Beck's, for such she was. On her arrival in the Rue Fossette, two or three days after my sudden settlement there, she encountered me with very little surprise. She must have had good blood in her veins, for never was any duchess more perfectly, radically, unaffectedly *nonchalante* than she: a weak, transient amaze was all she knew of the sensation of wonder. Most of her other faculties seemed to be in the same flimsy condition: her liking and disliking, her love and hate, were mere cobweb and gossamer; but she had one thing about her that seemed strong and durable enough, and that was—her selfishness.

---

9 'Because, when you die—you will immediately burn in hell.'
  'Do you believe that?'
  'Certainly I believe it: everyone knows it, besides, the priest told me so.'
  'To ensure your salvation in the next world, they should burn you alive in this one.'

She was not proud; and—*bonne d'enfants* as I was—she would forthwith have made of me a sort of friend and confidant. She teased me with a thousand vapid complaints about school-quarrels and household economy: the cookery was not to her taste—the people about her, teachers and pupils, she held to be despicable, because they were foreigners. I bore with her abuse of the Friday's salt-fish and hard eggs—with her invective against the soup, the bread, the coffee–with some patience for a time; but at last, wearied by iteration, I turned crusty and put her to rights—a thing I ought to have done in the very beginning, for a salutary setting down always agreed with her.

Much longer had I to endure her demands on me in the way of work. Her wardrobe, so far as concerned articles of external wear, was well and elegantly supplied; but there were other habiliments not so carefully provided: what she had, needed frequent repair. She hated needle-drudgery herself, and she would bring her hose, &c., to me in heaps, to be mended. A compliance of some weeks threatening to result in the establishment of an intolerable bore—I at last distinctly told her she must make up her mind to mend her own garments. She cried on receiving this information, and accused me of having ceased to be her friend; but I held by my decision, and let the hysterics pass as they could.

Notwithstanding these foibles, and various others needless to mention—but by no means of a refined or elevating character—how pretty she was! How charming she looked, when she came down on a sunny Sunday morning, well-dressed and well-humoured, robed in pale lilac silk, and with her fair long curls reposing on her white shoulders.

Emily Brontë

1818 – 48

E mily Brontë grew up in Haworth parsonage with her sisters, Charlotte and Anne, and her brother Branwell. Like her siblings she wrote prose and poetry from a young age, much of it connected with an imaginary realm named Gondal, full of passionate and romantic characters. In 1842 she went with Charlotte to Belgium, but returned home when her aunt died; she stayed at Haworth for the rest of her short life, writing poetry and, in 1847, *publishing her only novel* Wuthering Heights *under a pseudonym. An intense and religious woman, she guarded her inner life and the references in some of her poems, extracted here, remain obscure.*

    The following poems are reprinted from Selected Brontë Poems *(Edward Chitham and Tom Winnifrith (eds), Basil Blackwell, Oxford, 1985).*

'How still, how happy!'

'How still, how happy!' Those are words
That once would scarce agree together;
I loved the plashing of the surge—
The changing heaven, the breezy weather

More than smooth seas and cloudless skies
And solemn, soothing, softened airs
That in the forest woke no sighs
And from the green spray shook no tears.

'How still, how happy!' Now I feel
Where silence dwells is sweeter far
Than laughing mirth's most joyous swell
However pure its raptures are.

Come sit down on this sunny stone:
'Tis wintery light o'er flowerless moors—
But sit—for we are all alone
And clear expand heaven's breathless shores.

I could think in the withered grass
Spring's budding wreaths we might discern;
The violet's eye might shyly flash
And young leaves shoot among the fern.

It is but thought—full many a night
The snow shall clothe those hills afar
And storms shall add a drearier blight
And winds shall wage a wilder war

Before the lark may herald in
Fresh foliage twined with blossoms fair
And summer days again begin
Their glory-haloed crown to wear.

Yet my heart loves December's smile
As much as July's golden beam;
Then let us sit and watch the while
The blue ice curdling on the stream.

'Fair sinks the summer evening now'

FAIR sinks the summer evening now
In softened glory round my home;
The sky upon its holy brow
Wears not a cloud that speaks of gloom.

The old tower, shrined in golden light,
Looks down on the descending sun—
So gently evening blends with night
You scarce can say that day is done—

And this is just the joyous hour
When we were wont to burst away,
To 'scape from labour's tyrant power
And cheerfully go out to play.

Then why is all so sad and lone?
No merry footstep on the stair—
No laugh—no heart-awaking tone,
But voiceless silence everywhere.

I've wandered round our garden-ground
And still it seemed at every turn
That I should greet approaching feet
And words upon the breezes borne.

In vain—they will not come to-day
And morning's beam will rise as drear;
Then tell me—are they gone for aye
Our sun-blinks through the mists of care?

Ah no, reproving Hope doth say
Departed joys 'tis fond to mourn
When every storm that hides their ray
Prepares a more divine return.

'The wind, I hear it sighing'

THE wind, I hear it sighing
With Autumn's saddest sound;
Withered leaves as thick are lying
As spring-flowers on the ground—

This dark night has won me
To wander far away—
Old feelings gather fast upon me
Like vultures round their prey.

Kind were they once, and cherished
But cold and cheerless now—
I would their lingering shades had perished
When their light left my brow.

'Tis like old age pretending
The softness of a child,
My altered hardened spirit bending
To meet their fancies wild.

Yet could I with past pleasures
Past woe's oblivion buy—
That by the death of my dearest treasures
My deadliest pains might die,

O then another daybreak
Might haply dawn above—
Another summer gild my cheek,
My soul, another love.

Sympathy

THERE should be no despair for you
      While nightly stars are burning;
While evening pours its silent dew
And sunshine gilds the morning.
There should be no despair—though tears
May flow down like a river:
Are not the best beloved of years
Around your heart for ever?

They weep, you weep, it must be so;
Winds sigh as you are sighing,
And Winter sheds his grief in snow
Where Autumn's leaves are lying:
Yet, these revive, and from their fate
Your fate cannot be parted:
Then, journey on, if not elate,
Still, *never* broken-hearted!

The Old Stoic

RICHES I hold in light esteem
      And Love I laugh to scorn

And Lust of Fame was but a dream
That vanished with the morn—

And if I pray—the only prayer
That moves my lips for me
Is—'Leave the heart that now I bear
And give me liberty.'

Yes, as my swift days near their goal
'Tis all that I implore—
In life and death, a chainless soul
With courage to endure!

'Shall Earth no more inspire thee'

S HALL Earth no more inspire thee,
  Thou lonely dreamer now?
Since passion may not fire thee
Shall Nature cease to bow?

Thy mind is ever moving
In regions dark to thee;
Recall its useless roving—
Come back and dwell with me.

I know my mountain breezes
Enchant and soothe thee still—
I know my sunshine pleases
Despite thy wayward will.

When day with evening blending
Sinks from the summer sky,
I've seen thy spirit bending
In fond idolatry.

I've watched thee every hour—
I know my mighty sway—
I know my magic power
To drive thy griefs away.

Few hearts to mortals given
On earth so wildly pine,
Yet none would ask a Heaven
More like the Earth than thine.

Then let my winds caress thee—
Thy comrade let me be—

Since nought beside can bless thee,
Return and dwell with me.

Self-Interrogation

'THE evening passes fast away,
    'Tis almost time to rest—
What thoughts has left the vanished day,
What feelings, in thy breast?'

'The vanished day? It leaves a sense
Of labour hardly done;
Of little gained with vast expense—
A sense of grief alone!

'Time stands before the door of Death
Upbraiding bitterly;
And Conscience with exhaustless breath
Pours black reproach on me;

'And though I've said that Conscience lies,
And Time should Fate condemn;
Still, sad Repentance clouds my eyes,
And makes me yield to them!'

'Then art thou glad to seek repose?
Art glad to leave the sea,
And anchor all thy weary woes
In calm Eternity?

'Nothing regrets to see thee go—
Not one voice sobs "farewell",
And where thy heart has suffered so,
Canst thou desire to dwell?'

'Alas! The countless links are strong
That bind us to our clay;
The loving spirit lingers long
And would not pass away!

'And rest is sweet, when laurelled fame
Will crown the soldier's crest;
But a brave heart with a tarnished name
Would rather fight than rest.'

'Well thou hast fought for many a year,
Hast fought thy whole life through,

Hast humbled Falsehood, trampled Fear;
What is there left to do?'

''Tis true, this arm has hotly striven,
Has dared what few would dare;
Much have I done, and freely given,
But little learnt to bear!'

'Look on the grave, where thou must sleep,
Thy last and strongest foe—
It is endurance not to weep
If that repose seem woe.

'The long war closing in defeat,
Defeat serenely borne,
Thy midnight rest may still be sweet,
And break in glorious morn!'

The Philosopher

'ENOUGH of Thought, Philosopher;
Too long hast thou been dreaming
Unlightened, in this chamber drear
While summer's sun is beaming—
Space-sweeping soul, what sad refrain
Concludes thy musings once again?

'O for the time when I shall sleep
Without identity—
And never care how rain may steep
Or snow may cover me!

'No promised Heaven, these wild Desires
Could all or half fulfil—
No threatened Hell—with quenchless fires,
Subdue this quenchless will!'

—So said I, and still say the same,
—Still to my Death will say—
Three Gods within this little frame
Are warring night and day—

Heaven could not hold them all, and yet
They all are held in me
And must be mine till I forget
My present entity—

O, for the time, when in my breast
Their struggles will be o'er—
O for the day when I shall rest
And never suffer more!

'I saw a Spirit standing, Man,
Where thou dost stand—an hour ago,
And round his feet, three rivers ran
Of equal depth and equal flow—

'A Golden Stream, and one like blood
And one like Sapphire, seemed to be,
But where they joined their triple flood
It tumbled in an inky sea—

'The Spirit bent his dazzling gaze
Down on that Ocean's gloomy night,
Then—kindling all with sudden blaze,
The glad deep sparkled wide and bright—
White as the sun; far, far more fair
Than its divided sources were!'

—And even for that Spirit, Seer,
I've watched and sought my lifetime long;
Sought him in Heaven, Hell, Earth and Air,
An endless search—and always wrong!

Had I but seen his glorious eye
Once light the clouds that 'wilder me,
I ne'er had raised this coward cry
To cease to think and cease to be—

I ne'er had called oblivion blest,
Nor stretching eager hands to Death
Implored to change for lifeless rest
This sentient soul, this living breath.

O let me die, that Power and Will
Their cruel strife may close,
And vanquished Good, victorious Ill
Be lost in one repose.

'No coward soul is mine'

No coward soul is mine,
No trembler in the world's storm-troubled sphere;
I see Heaven's glories shine
And Faith shines equal arming me from Fear.

O God within my breast,
Almighty ever-present Deity
Life, that in me has rest
As I, Undying Life, have power in Thee.

Vain are the thousand creeds
That move men's hearts, unutterably vain,
Worthless as withered weeds
Or idlest froth amid the boundless main

To waken doubt in one
Holding so fast by thy infinity,
So surely anchored on
The steadfast rock of Immortality.

With wide-embracing love
Thy Spirit animates eternal years,
Pervades and broods above,
Changes, sustains, dissolves, creates and rears.

Though Earth and moon were gone
And suns and universes ceased to be
And thou wert left alone
Every Existence would exist in thee.

There is not room for Death
Nor atom that his might could render void
Since thou are Being and Breath
And what thou art may never be destroyed.

George Eliot

1819 – 80

George Eliot (Mary Ann Evans) was the daughter of an estate manager from Warwickshire and his second wife, Christiana Pearson. She
developed intellectual interests at an early age, reading widely in

*religious and philosophical literature. After translating and contributing for
some years to* The Westminster Review, *she began writing fiction at the beginning
of her union with the married but separated George Henry Lewes. The publication
of* Adam Bede *(1859) established her status as a leading novelist, a position
which was confirmed by her subsequent books, including the highly acclaimed*
Middlemarch *(1871–72). George Eliot contributed to some of the literary issues
of her day (as the following extract indicates), and by the time of her death she
was considered the leading English novelist, praised for the moral seriousness
of her works, and for her commanding intelligence.*

*'Silly Novels by Lady Novelists' was first published in October 1856,
in* The Westminster Review.

Silly Novels by Lady Novelists

SILLY novels by Lady Novelists are a genus with many species, determined by
the particular quality of silliness that predominates in them—the frothy, the
prosy, the pious, or the pedantic. But it is a mixture of all these—a composite
order of feminine fatuity, that produces the largest class of such novels, which
we shall distinguish as the *mind-and-millinery* species. The heroine is usually
an heiress, probably a peeress in her own right, with perhaps a vicious baronet,
an amiable duke, and an irresistible younger son of a marquis as lovers in the
foreground, a clergyman and a poet sighing for her in the middle distance, and
a crowd of undefined adorers dimly indicated beyond. Her eyes and her wit
are both dazzling; her nose and her morals are alike free from any tendency to
irregularity; she has a superb *contralto* and a superb intellect; she is perfectly
well-dressed and perfectly religious; she dances like a sylph, and reads the Bible
in the original tongues. Or it may be that the heroine is not an heiress—that rank
and wealth are the only things in which she is deficient; but she infallibly gets into
high society, she has the triumph of refusing many matches and securing the best,
and she wears some family jewels or other as a sort of crown of righteousness at
the end. Rakish men either bite their lips in impotent confusion at her repartees,
or are touched to penitence by her reproofs, which, on appropriate occasions,
rise to a lofty strain of rhetoric; indeed, there is a general propensity in her
to make speeches, and to rhapsodize at some length when she retires to her
bedroom. In her recorded conversations she is amazingly eloquent, and in her
unrecorded conversations, amazingly witty. She is understood to have a depth of
insight that looks through and through the shallow theories of philosophers, and
her superior instincts are a sort of dial by which men have only to set their clocks
and watches, and all will go well. The men play a very subordinate part by her side.
You are consoled now and then by a hint that they have affairs, which keeps you
in mind that the working-day business of the world is somehow being carried
on, but ostensibly the final cause of their existence is that they may accompany
the heroine on her 'starring' expedition through life. They see her at a ball, and

are dazzled; at a flower-show, and they are fascinated; on a riding excursion, and they are witched by her noble horsemanship; at church, and they are awed by the sweet solemnity of her demeanour. She is the ideal woman in feelings, faculties, and flounces. For all this, she as often as not marries the wrong person to begin with, and she suffers terribly from the plots and intrigues of the vicious baronet; but even death has a soft place in his heart for such a paragon, and remedies all mistakes for her just at the right moment. The vicious baronet is sure to be killed in a duel, and the tedious husband dies in his bed requesting his wife, as a particular favour to him, to marry the man she loves best, and having already dispatched a note to the lover informing him of the comfortable arrangement. Before matters arrive at this desirable issue our feelings are tried by seeing the noble, lovely, and gifted heroine pass through many *mauvais moments*, but we have the satisfaction of knowing that her sorrows are wept into embroidered pocket-handkerchiefs, that her fainting form reclines on the very best upholstery, and that whatever vicissitudes she may undergo, from being dashed out of her carriage to having her head shaved in a fever, she comes out of them all with a complexion more blooming and locks more redundant than ever.

We may remark, by the way, that we have been relieved from a serious scruple by discovering that silly novels by lady novelists rarely introduce us into any other than very lofty and fashionable society. We had imagined that destitute women turned novelists, as they turned governesses, because they had no other 'lady-like' means of getting their bread. On this supposition, vacillating syntax and improbable incident had a certain pathos for us, like the extremely supererogatory pincushions and ill-devised nightcaps that are offered for sale by a blind man. We felt the commodity to be a nuisance, but we were glad to think that the money went to relieve the necessitous, and we pictured to ourselves lonely women struggling for a maintenance, or wives and daughters devoting themselves to the production of 'copy' out of pure heroism,—perhaps to pay their husband's debts, or to purchase luxuries for a sick father. Under these impressions we shrank from criticising a lady's novel: her English might be faulty, but, we said to ourselves, her motives are irreproachable; her imagination may be uninventive, but her patience is untiring. Empty writing was excused by an empty stomach, and twaddle was consecrated by tears. But no! This theory of ours, like many other pretty theories, has had to give way before observation. Women's silly novels, we are now convinced, are written under totally different circumstances. The fair writers have evidently never talked to a tradesman except from a carriage window; they have no notion of the working-classes except as 'dependents'; they think five hundred a-year a miserable pittance; Belgravia and 'baronial halls' are their primary truths; and they have no idea of feeling interest in any man who is not at least a great landed proprietor, if not a prime minister. It is clear that they write in elegant boudoirs, with violet-coloured ink and a ruby pen; that they must be entirely indifferent to publishers' accounts, and inexperienced in every form of poverty except poverty of brains. It is true that we are constantly struck with the want of verisimilitude in their representations of the high society in which they seem to live; but then they betray no closer acquaintance with any other form of life. If their peers and peeresses are improbable, their literary men, tradespeople, and cottagers are impossible; and their intellect seems to have the peculiar impartiality of reproducing both what they *have* seen and heard, and what they have *not* seen and heard, with equal unfaithfulness.

There are few women, we suppose, who have not seen something of children under five years of age, yet in 'Compensation',[1] a recent novel of the mind-and-millinery species, which calls itself a 'story of real life', we have a child of four and a half years old talking in this Ossianic[2] fashion—

> 'Oh, I am so happy, dear gran'mamma;—I have seen,—I have seen such a delightful person: he is like everything beautiful,—like the smell of sweet flowers, and the view from Ben Lomond;—or no, *better than that*—he is like what I think of and see when I am very, very happy; and he is really like mamma, too, when she sings; and his forehead is like *that distant sea*,' she continued, pointing to the blue Mediterranean; 'there seems no end—no end; or like the clusters of stars I like best to look at on a warm fine night. . . .Don't look so. . .your forehead is like Loch Lomond, when the wind is blowing and the sun is gone in; I like the sunshine best when the lake is smooth. . . .So now—I like it better than ever. . .it is more beautiful still from the dark cloud that has gone over it, *when the sun suddenly lights up all the colours of the forests and shining purple rocks, and it is all reflected in the waters below.*'

We are not surprised to learn that the mother of this infant phenomenon, who exhibits symptoms so alarmingly like those of adolescence repressed by gin, is herself a phoenix. We are assured, again and again, that she had a remarkably original mind, that she was a genius, and 'conscious of her originality,' and she was fortunate enough to have a lover who was also a genius, and a man of 'most original mind.'

This lover, we read, though 'wonderfully similar' to her 'in powers and capacity,' was 'infinitely superior to her in faith and development,' and she saw in him the '"Agape"—so rare to find—of which she had read and admired the meaning in her Greek Testament; having, *from her great facility in learning languages*, read the Scriptures in their original *tongues*.' Of course! Greek and Hebrew are mere play to a heroine; Sanscrit is no more than *a b c* to her; and she can talk with perfect correctness in any language except English. She is a polking polyglott, a Creuzer[3] in crinoline. Poor men! There are so few of you who know even Hebrew; you think it something to boast of if, like Bolingbroke, you only 'understand that sort of learning, and what is writ about it';[4] and you are perhaps adoring women who can think slightingly of you in all the Semitic languages successively. But, then, as we are almost invariably told, that a heroine has a 'beautifully small head,' and as her intellect has probably been early invigorated by an attention to costume and deportment, we may conclude

---

1 Lady Chatterton, '*Compensation*'. *A Story of Real Life Thirty Years Ago* (1856).
2 A reference to the style of Macpherson's *Fingal* (1762) which the author claimed was a translation from Ossian, an ancient Scottish poet.
3 Georg Friedrich Creuzer, author of *Symbolik* (1810–12), a history of ancient religions.
4 Pope's answer to the question as to whether Bolingbroke knew Hebrew.

that she can pick up the Oriental tongues, to say nothing of their dialects, with the same aërial facility that the butterfly sips nectar. Besides, there can be no difficulty in conceiving the depth of the heroine's erudition, when that of the authoress is so evident.

In 'Laura Gay,'[5] another novel of the same school, the heroine seems less at home in Greek and Hebrew, but she makes up for the deficiency by a quite playful familiarity with the Latin classics—with the 'dear old Virgil,' 'the graceful Horace, the humane Cicero, and the pleasant Livy;' indeed, it is such a matter of course with her to quote Latin, that she does it at a pic-nic in a very mixed company of ladies and gentlemen, having, we are told, 'no conception that the nobler sex were capable of jealousy on this subject. And if, indeed,' continues the biographer of Laura Gay, 'the wisest and noblest portion of that sex were in the majority, no such sentiment would exist; but while Miss Wyndhams and Mr. Redfords abound, great sacrifices must be made to their existence.' Such sacrifices, we presume, as abstaining from Latin quotations, of extremely moderate interest and applicability, which the wise and noble minority of the other sex would be quite as willing to dispense with as the foolish and ignoble majority. It is as little the custom of well-bred men as of well-bred women to quote Latin in mixed parties; they can contain their familiarity with 'the humane Cicero' without allowing it to boil over in ordinary conversation, and even references to 'the pleasant Livy' are not absolutely irrepressible. But Ciceronian Latin is the mildest form of Miss Gay's conversational power. Being on the Palatine with a party of sightseers, she falls into the following vein of well-rounded remark: 'Truth can only be pure objectively, for even in the creeds where it predominates, being subjective, and parcelled out into portions, each of these necessarily receives a hue of idiosyncrasy, that is, a taint of superstition more or less strong; while in such creeds as the Roman Catholic, ignorance, interest, the bias of ancient idolatries, and the force of authority, have gradually accumulated on the pure truth, and transformed it, at last, into a mass of superstition for the majority of its votaries; and how few are there, alas! whose zeal, courage, and intellectual energy are equal to the analysis of this accumulation, and to the discovery of the pearl of great price which lies hidden beneath this heap of rubbish.' We have often met with women much more novel and profound in their observations than Laura Gay, but rarely with any so inopportunely long winded. A clerical lord, who is half in love with her, is alarmed by the daring remarks just quoted, and begins to suspect that she is inclined to free-thinking. But he is mistaken; when in a moment of sorrow he delicately begs leave to 'recal to her memory, *a depôt* of strength and consolation under affliction, which, until we are hard pressed by the trials of life, we are too apt to forget,' we learn that she really has 'recurrence to that sacred depôt,' together with the tea-pot. There is a certain flavour of orthodoxy mixed with the parade of fortunes and fine carriages in 'Laura Gay', but it is an orthodoxy mitigated by study of 'the humane Cicero,' and by an 'intellectual disposition to analyse.'

[5] *Laura Gay* (Anon., Hurst & Blackett, London, 1856).

'Compensation' is much more heavily dosed with doctrine, but then it has a treble amount of snobbish worldliness and absurd incident to tickle the palate of pious frivolity. Linda, the heroine, is still more speculative and spiritual than Laura Gay, but she has been 'presented,' and has more, and far grander, lovers; very wicked and fascinating women are introduced—even a French *lionne*; and no expense is spared to get up as exciting a story as you will find in the most immoral novels. In fact, it is a wonderful *pot pourri* of Almack's, Scotch second-sight, Mr. Rogers's breakfasts,[6] Italian brigands, death-bed conversions, superior authoresses, Italian mistresses, and attempts at poisoning old ladies, the whole served up with a garnish of talk about 'faith and development,' and 'most original minds.' Even Miss Susan Barton, the superior authoress, whose pen moves in a 'quick decided manner when she is composing,' declines the finest opportunities of marriage; and though old enough to be Linda's mother (since we are told that she refused Linda's father), has her hand sought by a young earl, the heroine's rejected lover. Of course, genius and morality must be backed by eligible offers, or they would seem rather a dull affair; and piety, like other things, in order to be *comme il faut*, must be in 'society,' and have admittance to the best circles.

'Rank and Beauty'[7] is a more frothy and less religious variety of the mind-and-millinery species. The heroine, we are told, 'if she inherited her father's pride of birth and her mother's beauty of person, had in herself a tone of enthusiastic feeling that perhaps belongs to her age even in the lowly born, but which is refined into the high spirit of wild romance only in the far descended, who feel that it is their best inheritance.' This enthusiastic young lady, by dint of reading the newspaper to her father, falls in love with the *prime minister*, who, through the medium of leading articles and 'the *resumé* of the debates,' shines upon her imagination as a bright particular star, which has no parallax for her, living in the country as simple Miss Wyndham. But she forthwith becomes Baroness Umfraville in her own right, astonishes the world with her beauty and accomplishments when she bursts upon it from her mansion in Spring Gardens, and, as you foresee, will presently come into contact with the unseen *objet aimé*. Perhaps the words 'prime minister' suggest to you a wrinkled or obese sexagenarian; but pray dismiss the image. Lord Rupert Conway has been 'called while still almost a youth to the first situation which a subject can hold in the *universe*,' and even leading articles and a *resumé* of the debates have not conjured up a dream that surpasses the fact.

The door opened again, and Lord Rupert Conway entered. Evelyn gave one glance. It was enough; she was not disappointed. It seemed as if a picture on which she had long gazed was suddenly instinct with life, and had stepped from its frame before her. His tall figure, the distinguished simplicity of his air—it was a living Vandyke, a cavalier, one of his noble cavalier ancestors, or one to whom

6 Almack's Assembly rooms in St James's, London; Samuel Rogers (1763–1855) poet, art collector and, for over forty years, a giver of 'breakfasts'.
7 *Rank and Beauty, or the Young Baroness* (Anon., Hurst & Blackett, London, 1856).

her fancy had always likened him, who long of yore had, with an Umfraville, fought
the Paynim far beyond sea. Was this reality?

Very little like it, certainly.

By-and-by, it becomes evident that the ministerial heart is touched. Lady
Umfraville is on a visit to the Queen at Windsor, and,

The last evening of her stay, when they returned from riding, Mr. Wyndham
took her and a large party to the top of the Keep, to see the view. She was leaning
on the battlements, gazing from that 'stately height' at the prospect beneath her,
when Lord Rupert was by her side. 'What an unrivalled view!' exclaimed she.

'Yes, it would have been wrong to go without having been up here. You are
pleased with your visit?'

'Enchanted! A Queen to live and die under, to live and die for!'

'Ha!' cried he, with sudden emotion, and with a *eureka* expression of countenance, as if he had *indeed found a heart in unison with his own*.

The '*eureka* expression of countenance,' you see at once to be prophetic of
marriage at the end of the third volume; but before that desirable consummation,
there are very complicated misunderstandings, arising chiefly from the vindictive
plotting of Sir Luttrell Wycherley, who is a genius, a poet, and in every way a most
remarkable character indeed. He is not only a romantic poet, but a hardened rake
and a cynical wit; yet his deep passion for Lady Umfraville has so impoverished
his epigrammatic talent, that he cuts an extremely poor figure in conversation.
When she rejects him, he rushes into the shrubbery, and rolls himself in the
dirt; and on recovering, devotes himself to the most diabolical and laborious
schemes of vengeance, in the course of which he disguises himself as a quack
physician, and enters into general practice, foreseeing that Evelyn will fall ill,
and that he shall be called in to attend her. At last, when all his schemes are
frustrated, he takes leave of her in a long letter, written, as you will perceive
from the following passage, entirely in the style of an eminent literary man:

'Oh, lady, nursed in pomp and pleasure, will you ever cast one thought upon
the miserable being who addresses you? Will you ever, as your gilded galley is
floating down the unruffled stream of prosperity, will you ever, while lulled by
the sweetest music—thine own praises,—hear the far-off sigh from that world to
which I am going?'

On the whole, however, frothy as it is, we rather prefer 'Rank and Beauty'
to the other two novels we have mentioned. The dialogue is more natural and
spirited; there is some frank ignorance, and no pedantry; and you are allowed
to take the heroine's astounding intellect upon trust, without being called on
to read her conversational refutations of sceptics and philosophers, or her
rhetorical solutions of the mysteries of the universe.

Writers of the mind-and-millinery school are remarkably unanimous in their
choice of diction. In their novels, there is usually a lady or gentleman who is
more or less of a upas tree: the lover has a manly breast; minds are redolent

of various things; hearts are hollow; events are utilized; friends are consigned to the tomb; infancy is an engaging period; the sun is a luminary that goes to his western couch, or gathers the rain-drops into his refulgent bosom; life is a melancholy boon; Albion and Scotia are conversational epithets. There is a striking resemblance, too, in the character of their moral comments, such, for instance, as that 'It is a fact, no less true than melancholy, that all people, more or less, richer or poorer, are swayed by bad example;' that 'Books, however trivial, contain some subjects from which useful information may be drawn;' that 'Vice can too often borrow the language of virtue;' that 'Merit and nobility of nature must exist, to be accepted, for clamour and pretension cannot impose upon those too well read in human nature to be easily deceived;' and that, 'In order to forgive, we must have been injured.' There is, doubtless, a class of readers to whom these remarks appear peculiarly pointed and pungent; for we often find them doubly and trebly scored with the pencil, and delicate hands giving in their determined adhesion to these hardy novelties by a distinct *très vrai*, emphasized by many notes of exclamation. The colloquial style of these novels is often marked by much ingenious inversion, and a careful avoidance of such cheap phraseology as can be heard every day. Angry young gentlemen exclaim—''Tis ever thus, methinks;' and in the half-hour before dinner a young lady informs her next neighbour that the first day she read Shakspeare she 'stole away into the park, and beneath the shadow of the greenwood tree, devoured with rapture the inspired page of the great magician.' But the most remarkable efforts of the mind-and-millinery writers lie in their philosophic reflections. The authoress of 'Laura Gay,' for example, having married her hero and heroine, improves the event by observing that 'if those sceptics, whose eyes have so long gazed on matter that they can no longer see aught else in man, could once enter with heart and soul into such bliss as this, they would come to say that the soul of man and the polypus are not of common origin, or of the same texture.' Lady novelists, it appears, can see something else besides matter; they are not limited to phenomena, but can relieve their eyesight by occasional glimpses of the *noumenon*, and are, therefore, naturally better able than any one else to confound sceptics, even of that remarkable, but to us unknown school, which maintains that the soul of man is of the same texture as the polypus.

The most pitiable of all silly novels by lady novelists are what we may call the *oracular* species—novels intended to expound the writer's religious, philosophical, or moral theories. There seems to be a notion abroad among women, rather akin to the superstition that the speech and actions of idiots are inspired, and that the human being most entirely exhausted of common sense is the fittest vehicle of revelation. To judge from their writings, there are certain ladies who think that an amazing ignorance, both of science and of life, is the best possible qualification for forming an opinion on the knottiest moral and speculative questions. Apparently, their recipe for solving all such difficulties is something like this: Take a woman's head, stuff it with a smattering of philosophy and literature chopped small, and with false notions of society baked hard, let it hang over a desk a few hours every day, and serve up hot in feeble English, when not required. You will rarely meet with a lady novelist of the oracular

class who is diffident of her ability to decide on theological questions,—who has
any suspicion that she is not capable of discriminating with the nicest accuracy
between the good and evil in all church parties,—who does not see precisely
how it is that men have gone wrong hitherto,—and pity philosophers in general
that they have not had the opportunity of consulting her. Great writers, who
have modestly contented themselves with putting their experience into fiction,
and have thought it quite a sufficient task to exhibit men and things as they are,
she sighs over as deplorably deficient in the application of their powers. 'They
have solved no great questions'—and she is ready to remedy their omission by
setting before you a complete theory of life and manual of divinity, in a love story,
where ladies and gentlemen of good family go through genteel vicissitudes, to
the utter confusion of Deists, Puseyites,[8] and ultra-Protestants, and to the perfect
establishment of that particular view of Christianity which either condenses itself
into a sentence of small caps, or explodes into a cluster of stars on the three
hundred and thirtieth page. It is true, the ladies and gentlemen will probably
seem to you remarkably little like any you have had the fortune or misfortune to
meet with, for, as a general rule, the ability of a lady novelist to describe actual life
and her fellow-men, is in inverse proportion to her confident eloquence about
God and the other world, and the means by which she usually chooses to conduct
you to true ideas of the invisible is a totally false picture of the visible.

As typical a novel of the oracular kind as we can hope to meet with,
is 'The Enigma: a Leaf from the Chronicles of the Wolchorley House.'[9] The
'enigma' which this novel is to solve, is certainly one that demands powers no
less gigantic than those of a lady novelist, being neither more nor less than the
existence of evil. The problem is stated, and the answer dimly foreshadowed
on the very first page. The spirited young lady, with raven hair, says, 'All life is
an inextricable confusion;' and the meek young lady, with auburn hair, looks
at the picture of the Madonna which she is copying, and—'*There* seemed the
solution of that mighty enigma.' The style of this novel is quite as lofty as its
purpose; indeed, some passages on which we have spent much patient study
are quite beyond our reach, in spite of the illustrative aid of italics and small
caps; and we must await further 'development' in order to understand them. Of
Ernest, the model young clergyman, who sets every one right on all occasions,
we read, that 'he held not of marriage in the marketable kind, after a social
desecration;' that, on one eventful night, 'sleep had not visited his divided heart,
where tumultuated, in varied type and combination, the aggregate feelings of
grief and joy;' and that, 'for the *marketable* human article he had no toleration,
be it of what sort, or set for what value it might, whether for worship or class,
his upright soul abhorred it, whose ultimatum, the self-deceiver, was to him
THE *great spiritual lie*, "living in a vain show, deceiving and being deceived;"
since he did not suppose the phylactery and enlarged border on the garment

---

8 Followers of Edward Pusey (1800–82), who was part of the High Church Movement within
the Church of England and a believer in the union of the English and Roman Churches.
9 *The Enigma: A Leaf from the Archives of Wolchorley House* (Anon., John W. Parker &
Son, London, 1856)

to be *merely* a social trick.' (The italics and small caps are the author's, and we hope they assist the reader's comprehension.) Of Sir Lionel, the model old gentleman, we are told that 'the simple ideal of the middle age, apart from its anarchy and decadence, in him most truly seemed to live again, when the ties which knit men together were of heroic cast. The first-born colours of pristine faith and truth engraven on the common soul of man, and blent into the wide arch of brotherhood, where the primæval law of *order* grew and multiplied, each perfect after his kind, and mutually inter-dependent.' You see clearly, of course, how colours are first engraven on a soul, and then blent into a wide arch, on which arch of colours—apparently a rainbow— the law of order grew and multiplied, each—apparently the arch and the law—perfect after his kind? If, after this, you can possibly want any further aid towards knowing what Sir Lionel was, we can tell you, that in his soul 'the scientific combinations of thought could educe no fuller harmonies of the good and the true, than lay in the primæval pulses which floated as an atmosphere around it!' and that, when he was sealing a letter, 'Lo! the responsive throb in that good man's bosom echoed back in simple truth the honest witness of a heart that condemned him not, as his eye, bedewed with love, rested, too, with something of ancestral pride, on the undimmed motto of the family—"LOIAUTÉ".'

The slightest matters have their vulgarity fumigated out of them by the same elevated style. Commonplace people would say that a copy of Shakspeare lay on a drawing-room table; but the authoress of 'The Enigma,' bent on edifying periphrasis, tells you that there lay on the table, 'that fund of human thought and feeling, which teaches the heart through the little name, "Shakspeare."' A watchman sees a light burning in an upper window rather longer than usual, and thinks that people are foolish to sit up late when they have an opportunity of going to bed; but, lest this fact should seem too low and common, it is presented to us in the following striking and metaphysical manner: 'He marvelled—as man *will* think for others in a necessarily separate personality, consequently (though disallowing it) in false mental premise,—how differently *he* should act, how gladly *he* should prize the rest so lightly held of within.' A footman—an ordinary Jeames, with large calves and aspirated vowels—answers the door-bell, and the opportunity is seized to tell you that he was a 'type of the large class of pampered menials, who follow the curse of Cain—"vagabonds" on the face of the earth, and whose estimate of the human class varies in the graduated scale of money and expenditure. . . . These, and such as these, O England, be the false lights of thy morbid civilization!' We have heard of various 'false lights,' from Dr. Cumming to Robert Owen,[10] from Dr. Pusey to the Spirit-rappers,[11] but we never before heard of the false light that emanates from plush and powder.

In the same way very ordinary events of civilized life are exalted into the most awful crises, and ladies in full skirts and *manches à la Chinoise*,[12]

[10] Dr John Cummings was an evangelical preacher; Robert Owen was a social philanthropist and reformer.
[11] Spiritualists, who believed spirits 'rapped out' messages on tables during séances.
[12] Chinese sleeves.

conduct themselves not unlike the heroines of sanguinary melodramas. Mrs. Percy, a shallow woman of the world, wishes her son Horace to marry the auburn-haired Grace, she being an heiress; but he, after the manner of sons, falls in love with the raven-haired Kate, the heiress's portionless cousin; and, moreover, Grace herself shows every symptom of perfect indifference to Horace. In such cases, sons are often sulky or fiery, mothers are alternately manoeuvring and waspish, and the portionless young lady often lies awake at night and cries a good deal. We are getting used to these things now, just as we are used to eclipses of the moon, which no longer set us howling and beating tin kettles. We never heard of a lady in a fashionable 'front' behaving like Mrs. Percy under these circumstances. Happening one day to see Horace talking to Grace at a window, without in the least knowing what they are talking about, or having the least reason to believe that Grace, who is mistress of the house and a person of dignity, would accept her son if he were to offer himself, she suddenly rushes up to them and clasps them both, saying, 'with a flushed countenance and in an excited manner'—'This is indeed happiness; for, may I not call you so, Grace?—my Grace—my Horace's Grace!—my dear children!' Her son tells her she is mistaken, and that he is engaged to Kate, whereupon we have the following scene and tableau:

> Gathering herself up to an unprecedented height,(!) her eyes lightning forth the fire of her anger:—
> 'Wretched boy!' she said, hoarsely and scornfully, and clenching her hand, 'Take then the doom of your own choice! Bow down your miserable head and let a mother's—'
> 'Curse not!' spake a deep low voice from behind, and Mrs. Percy started, scared, as though she had seen a heavenly visitant appear, to break upon her in the midst of her sin.
> Meantime, Horace had fallen on his knees at her feet, and hid his face in his hands.
> Who, then, is she—who!Truly his 'guardian spirit' hath stepped between him and the fearful words, which, however unmerited, must have hung as a pall over his future existence;—a spell which could not be unbound— which could not be unsaid.
> Of an earthly paleness, but calm with the still, iron-bound calmness of death—the only calm one there,—Katherine stood; and her words smote on the ear in tones whose appallingly slow and separate intonation rung on the heart like the chill, isolated tolling of some fatal knell.
> 'He would have plighted me his faith, but I did not accept it; you cannot, therefore—you *dare* not curse him. And here,' she continued, raising her hand to heaven, whither her large dark eyes also rose with a chastened glow, which, for the first time, *suffering* had lighted in those passionate orbs,—'here I promise, come weal, come woe, that Horace Wolchorley and I do never interchange vows without his mother's sanction—without his mother's blessing'!

Here, and throughout the story, we see that confusion of purpose which is so characteristic of silly novels written by women. It is a story of quite modern drawing-room society—a society in which polkas are played and

Puseyism discussed; yet we have characters, and incidents, and traits of manner introduced, which are mere shreds from the most heterogeneous romances. We have a blind Irish harper 'relic of the picturesque bards of yore,' startling us at a Sunday-school festival of tea and cake in an English village; we have a crazy gipsy, in a scarlet cloak, singing snatches of romantic song, and revealing a secret on her deathbed which, with the testimony of a dwarfish miserly merchant, who salutes strangers with a curse and a devilish laugh, goes to prove that Ernest, the model young clergyman, is Kate's brother; and we have an ultra-virtuous Irish Barney, discovering that a document is forged, by comparing the date of the paper with the date of the alleged signature, although the same document has passed through a court of law, and occasioned a fatal decision. The 'Hall' in which Sir Lionel lives is the venerable country-seat of an old family, and this, we suppose, sets the imagination of the authoress flying to donjons and battlements, where 'lo! the warder blows his horn;' for, as the inhabitants are in their bedrooms on a night certainly within the recollection of Pleaceman X., and a breeze springs up, which we are at first told was faint, and then that it made the old cedars bow their branches to the greensward, she falls into this mediæval vein of description (the italics are ours): 'The banner *unfurled it* at the sound, and shook its guardian wing above, while the startled owl *flapped her* in the ivy; the firmament looking down through her "argus eyes,"—

'Ministers of heaven's· mute melodies'.
And lo! two strokes tolled from out the warder tower, and "Two o'clock" re-echoed its interpreter below.'

Such stories as this of 'The Enigma' remind us of the pictures clever children sometimes draw 'out of their own head', where you will see a modern villa on the right, two knights in helmets fighting in the foreground, and a tiger grinning in a jungle on the left, the several objects being brought together because the artist thinks each pretty, and perhaps still more because he remembers seeing them in other pictures.

But we like the authoress much better on her mediæval stilts than on her oracular ones,—when she talks of the *Ich* and of 'subjective' and 'objective', and lays down the exact line of Christian verity, between 'right-hand excesses and left-hand declensions.' Persons who deviate from this line are introduced with a patronizing air of charity. Of a certain Miss Inshquine she informs us, with all the lucidity of italics and small caps, that '*function*, not *form*, AS *the inevitable outer expression of the spirit in this tabernacled age*, weakly engrossed her.' And *à propos* of Miss Mayjar, an evangelical lady who is a little too apt to talk of her visit to sick women and the state of their souls, we are told that the model clergyman is 'not one to disallow, through the *super* crust, the undercurrent towards good in the *subject*, or the positive benefits, nevertheless, to the *object*.' We imagine the double-refined accent and protrusion of chin which are feebly represented by the italics in this lady's sentences! We abstain from quoting any of her oracular doctrinal passages, because they refer to matters too serious for our pages just now.

The epithet 'silly' may seem impertinent, applied to a novel which indicates so much reading and intellectual activity as 'The Enigma;' but we use this epithet advisedly. If, as the world has long agreed, a very great amount of instruction will not make a wise man, still less will a very mediocre amount of instruction make a wise woman. And the most mischievous form of feminine silliness is the literary form, because it tends to confirm the popular prejudice against the more solid education of women. When men see girls wasting their time in consultations about bonnets and ball dresses, and in giggling or sentimental love-confidences, or middle-aged women mismanaging their children, and solacing themselves with acrid gossip, they can hardly help saying, 'For Heaven's sake, let girls be better educated; let them have some better objects of thought—some more solid occupations.' But after a few hours' conversation with an oracular literary woman, or a few hours' reading of her books, they are likely enough to say, 'After all, when a woman gets some knowledge, see what use she makes of it! Her knowledge remains acquisition, instead of passing into culture; instead of being subdued into modesty and simplicity by a larger acquaintance with thought and fact, she has a feverish consciousness of her attainments; she keeps a sort of mental pocket-mirror, and is continually looking in it at her own "intellectuality"; she spoils the taste of one's muffin by questions of metaphysics; "puts down" men at a dinner table with her superior information; and seizes the opportunity of a *soirée* to catechise us on the vital question of the relation between mind and matter. And then, look at her writings! She mistakes vagueness for depth, bombast for eloquence, and affectation for originality; she struts on one page, rolls her eyes on another, grimaces in a third, and is hysterical in a fourth. She may have read many writings of great men, and a few writings of great women; but she is as unable to discern the difference between her own style and theirs as a Yorkshireman is to discern the difference between his own English and a Londoner's: rhodomontade is the native accent of her intellect. No—the average nature of women is too shallow and feeble a soil to bear much tillage; it is only fit for the very lightest crops.'

It is true that the men who come to such a decision on such very superficial and imperfect observation may not be among the wisest in the world; but we have not now to contest their opinion—we are only pointing out how it is unconsciously encouraged by many women who have volunteered themselves as representatives of the feminine intellect. We do not believe that a man was ever strengthened in such an opinion by associating with a woman of true culture, whose mind had absorbed her knowledge instead of being absorbed by it. A really cultured woman, like a really cultured man, is all the simpler and the less obtrusive for her knowledge; it has made her see herself and her opinions in something like just proportions; she does not make it a pedestal from which she flatters herself that she commands a complete view of men and things, but makes it a point of observation from which to form a right estimate of herself. She neither spouts poetry nor quotes Cicero on slight provocation; not because she thinks that a sacrifice must be made to the prejudices of men, but because that mode of exhibiting her memory and Latinity does not present itself to her as edifying or graceful. She does not write books to confound philosophers, perhaps because she is able to write books that delight them. In conversation she is the least formidable of women, because she understands you, without wanting to make you aware that you *can't* understand her. She does not give you information, which is the raw material of culture,—she gives you sympathy, which is its subtlest essence.

A more numerous class of silly novels than the oracular, (which are generally inspired by some form of High Church, or transcendental Christianity,) is what we may call the *white neck-cloth* species, which represent the tone of thought and feeling in the Evangelical party. This species is a kind of genteel tract on a large scale, intended as a sort of medicinal sweetmeat for Low Church young ladies; an Evangelical substitute for the fashionable novel, as the May Meetings[13] are a substitute for the Opera. Even Quaker children, one would think, can hardly have been denied the indulgence of a doll; but it must be a doll dressed in a drab gown and a coal-scuttle bonnet—not a worldly doll, in gauze and spangles. And there are no young ladies, we imagine,—unless they belong to the Church of the United Brethren, in which people are married without any love-making—who can dispense with love stories. Thus, for Evangelical young ladies there are Evangelical love stories, in which the vicissitudes of the tender passion are sanctified by saving views of Regeneration and the Atonement. These novels differ from the oracular ones, as a Low Churchwoman often differs from a High Churchwoman: they are a little less supercilious, and a great deal more ignorant, a little less correct in their syntax, and a great deal more vulgar.

The Orlando of Evangelical literature is the young curate, looked at from the point of view of the middle class, where cambric bands are understood to have as thrilling an effect on the hearts of young ladies as epaulettes have in the classes above and below it. In the ordinary type of these novels, the hero is almost sure to be a young curate, frowned upon, perhaps, by worldly mammas, but carrying captive the hearts of their daughters, who can 'never forget *that* sermon;' tender glances are seized from the pulpit stairs instead of the opera-box; *tête-à-têtes* are seasoned with quotations from Scripture, instead of quotations from the poets; and questions as to the state of the heroine's affections are mingled with anxieties as to the state of her soul. The young curate always has a background of well-dressed and wealthy, if not fashionable society;—for Evangelical silliness is as snobbish as any other kind of silliness; and the Evangelical lady novelist, while she explains to you the type of the scapegoat on one page, is ambitious on another to represent the manners and conversation of aristocratic people. Her pictures of fashionable society are often curious studies considered as efforts of the Evangelical imagination; but in one particular the novels of the White neck-cloth School are meritoriously realistic,—their favourite hero, the Evangelical young curate is always rather an insipid personage.

The most recent novel of this species that we happen to have before us, is 'The Old Grey Church.'[14] It is utterly tame and feeble; there is no one set of

13 The Church of England Missionary Society's annual May Meetings.
14 By Lady Caroline Scott (1856).

objects on which the writer seems to have a stronger grasp than on any other; and we should be entirely at a loss to conjecture among what phases of life her experience has been gained, but for certain vulgarisms of style which sufficiently indicate that she has had the advantage, though she has been unable to use it, of mingling chiefly with men and women whose manners and characters have not had all their bosses and angles rubbed down by refined conventionalism. It is less excusable in an Evangelical novelist, than in any other, gratuitously to seek her subjects among titles and carriages. The real drama of Evangelicalism—and it has abundance of fine drama for any one who has genius enough to discern and reproduce it—lies among the middle and lower classes; and are not Evangelical opinions understood to give an especial interest in the weak things of the earth, rather than in the mighty? Why then, cannot our Evangelical lady novelists show us the operation of their religious views among people (there really are many such in the world) who keep no carriage, 'not so much as a brassbound gig,' who even manage to eat their dinner without a silver fork, and in whose mouths the authoress's questionable English would be strictly consistent? Why can we not have pictures of religious life among the industrial classes in England, as interesting as Mrs. Stowe's pictures of religious life among the negroes?[15] Instead of this, pious ladies nauseate us with novels which remind us of what we sometimes see in a worldly woman recently 'converted';—she is as fond of a fine dinner table as before, but she invites clergymen instead of beaux; she thinks as much of her dress as before, but she adopts a more sober choice of colours and patterns; her conversation is as trivial as before, but the triviality is flavoured with gospel instead of gossip. In 'The Old Grey Church,' we have the same sort of Evangelical travesty of the fashionable novel, and of course the vicious, intriguing baronet is not wanting. It is worth while to give a sample of the style of conversation attributed to this high-born rake—a style that in its profuse italics and palpable innuendoes, is worthy of Miss Squeers.[16] In an evening visit to the ruins of the Colosseum, Eustace, the young clergyman, has been withdrawing the heroine, Miss Lushington, from the rest of the party, for the sake of a *tête-à-tête*. The baronet is jealous, and vents his pique in this way:

There they are, and Miss Lushington, no doubt, quite safe; for she is under the holy guidance of Pope Eustace the First, who has, of course, been delivering to her an edifying homily on the wickedness of the heathens of yore, who, as tradition tells us, in this very place let loose the wild *beastises* on poor St. Paul!—Oh, no! by-the-bye, I believe I am wrong, and betraying my want of clergy, and that it was not at all St. Paul, nor was it here. But no matter, it would equally serve as a text to preach from, and from which to diverge to the degenerate *heathen* Christians of the present day, and all their naughty practices, and so end with an exhortation to 'come out from among them, and be separate;'—and I am sure, Miss Lushington, you have most scrupulously

[15] Harriet Beecher Stowe's *Uncle Tom's Cabin* (1851–2) and *Dred* (1856).
[16] A vicious young woman who writes sneering letters in Charles Dickens's *Nicholas Nickleby* (1838–9).

conformed to that injunction this evening, for we have seen nothing of you since our arrival. But every one seems agreed it has been a *charming party of pleasure*, and I am sure we all feel *much indebted* to Mr. Grey for having *suggested* it; and as he seems so capital a cicerone, I hope he will think of something else equally agreeable to *all*.

This drivelling kind of dialogue, and equally drivelling narrative, which, like a bad drawing, represents nothing, and barely indicates what is meant to be represented, runs through the book; and we have no doubt is considered by the amiable authoress to constitute an improving novel, which Christian mothers will do well to put into the hands of their daughters. But everything is relative; we have met with American vegetarians whose normal diet was dry meal, and who, when their appetite wanted stimulating, tickled it with *wet* meal; and so, we can imagine that there are Evangelical circles in which 'The Old Grey Church' is devoured as a powerful and interesting fiction.

But, perhaps, the least readable of silly women's novels, are the *modern-antique* species, which unfold to us the domestic life of Jannes and Jambres,[17] the private love affairs of Sennacherib, or the mental struggles and ultimate conversion of Demetrius the silversmith.[18] From most silly novels we can at least extract a laugh; but those of the modern antique school have a ponderous, a leaden kind of fatuity, under which we groan. What can be more demonstrative of the inability of literary women to measure their own powers, than their frequent assumption of a task which can only be justified by the rarest concurrence of acquirement with genius? The finest effort to reanimate the past is of course only approximative—is always more or less an infusion of the modern spirit into the ancient form,

> Was ihr den Geist der Zeiten heisst,
> Das ist im Grund der Herren eigner Geist,
> In dem die Zeiten sich bespiegeln.[19]

Admitting that genius which has familiarized itself with all the relics of an ancient period can sometimes, by the force of its sympathetic divination, restore the missing notes in the 'music of humanity,'[20] and reconstruct the fragments into a whole which will really bring the remote past nearer to us, and interpret it to our duller apprehension,—this form of imaginative power must always be among the very rarest, because it demands as much accurate and minute knowledge as creative vigour. Yet we find ladies constantly choosing to make their mental mediocrity more conspicuous, by clothing it in a masquerade of ancient names; by putting their feeble sentimentality into the mouths of Roman

[17] St. Paul's names for the Egyptian magicians who contended against Moses at the Pharaoh's court (2 *Tim* 3:8).
[18] *Acts* 19:24 ff.
[19] What you call the spirit of the age is in reality the spirit of those men in whom their time is reflected, Goethe's *Faust* 1, 'Nacht' 577–9.
[20] Wordsworth, 'Tintern Abbey', 1,91.

vestals or Egyptian princesses, and attributing their rhetorical arguments to Jewish high-priests and Greek philosophers. A recent example of this heavy imbecility is, 'Adonijah, a Tale of the Jewish Dispersion,'[21] which forms part of a series, 'uniting,' we are told, 'taste, humour, and sound principles.' 'Adonijah,' we presume, exemplifies the tale of 'sound principles;' the taste and humour are to be found in other members of the series. We are told on the cover, that the incidents of this tale are 'fraught with unusual interest,' and the preface winds up thus: 'To those who feel interested in the dispersed of Israel and Judea, these pages may afford, perhaps, information on an important subject, as well as amusement.' Since the 'important subject' on which this book is to afford information is not specified, it may possibly lie in some esoteric meaning to which we have no key; but if it has relation to the dispersed of Israel and Judea at any period of their history, we believe a tolerably well-informed school-girl already knows much more of it than she will find in this 'Tale of the Jewish Dispersion.' 'Adonijah' is simply the feeblest kind of love story, supposed to be instructive, we presume, because the hero is a Jewish captive, and the heroine a Roman vestal; because they and their friends are converted to Christianity after the shortest and easiest method approved by the 'Society for Promoting the Conversion of the Jews;' and because, instead of being written in plain language, it is adorned with that peculiar style of grandiloquence which is held by some lady novelists to give an antique colouring, and which we recognise at once in such phrases as these: 'the splendid regnal talents undoubtedly possessed by the Emperor Nero'—'the expiring scion of a lofty stem'—'the virtuous partner of his couch'—'ah, by Vesta!'—and 'I tell thee, Roman.' Among the quotations which serve at once for instruction and ornament on the cover of this volume, there is one from Miss Sinclair,[22] which informs us that 'Works of imagination are *avowedly* read by men of science, wisdom, and piety'; from which we suppose the reader is to gather the cheering inference that Dr. Daubeny, Mr. Mill, or Mr. Maurice,[23] may openly indulge himself with the perusal of 'Adonijah', without being obliged to secrete it among the sofa cushions, or read it by snatches under the dinner table.

'Be not a baker if your head be made of butter,' says a homely proverb, which, being interpreted, may mean, let no woman rush into print who is not prepared for the consequences. We are aware that our remarks are in a very different tone from that of the reviewers who, with a perennial recurrence of precisely similar emotions, only paralleled, we imagine, in the experience of monthly nurses,[24] tell one lady novelist after another that they 'hail' her productions 'with delight.' We are aware that the ladies at whom our criticism is pointed are accustomed to be told, in the choicest phraseology of puffery, that their pictures of life are brilliant, their characters well drawn, their style fascinating, and their sentiments lofty. But if they are inclined to resent our plainness of speech, we ask them to

[21] By Jane Margaret Strickland? (1856)
[22] Catherine Sinclair (1800–64), novelist, philanthropist and writer for children.
[23] Charles Daubeny (1795–1867), chemist and naturalist; John Stuart Mill (1806–73), philosopher and political economist; F. D. Maurice (1805–72), socialist theologian.
[24] A nurse who attends a woman for the first month after the birth of a child.

reflect for a moment on the chary praise, and often captious blame, which their panegyrists give to writers whose works are on the way to become classics. No sooner does a woman show that she has genius or effective talent, than she receives the tribute of being moderately praised and severely criticised. By a peculiar thermometric adjustment, when a woman's talent is at zero, journalistic approbation is at the boiling pitch; when she attains mediocrity, it is already at no more than summer heat; and if ever she reaches excellence, critical enthusiasm drops to the freezing point. Harriet Martineau, Currer Bell, and Mrs. Gaskell[25] have been treated as cavalierly as if they had been men. And every critic who forms a high estimate of the share women may ultimately take in literature, will, on principle, abstain from any exceptional indulgence towards the productions of literary women. For it must be plain to every one who looks impartially and extensively into feminine literature, that its greatest deficiencies are due hardly more to the want of intellectual power than to the want of those moral qualities that contribute to literary excellence—patient diligence, a sense of the responsibility involved in publication, and an appreciation of the sacredness of the writer's art. In the majority of women's books you see that kind of facility which springs from the absence of any high standard; that fertility in imbecile combination or feeble imitation which a little self-criticism would check and reduce to barrenness; just as with a total want of musical ear people will sing out of tune, while a degree more melodic sensibility would suffice to render them silent. The foolish vanity of wishing to appear in print, instead of being counter balanced by any consciousness of the intellectual or moral derogation implied in futile authorship, seems to be encouraged by the extremely false impression that to write *at all* is a proof of superiority in a woman. On this ground, we believe that the average intellect of women is unfairly represented by the mass of feminine literature, and that while the few women who write well are very far above the ordinary intellectual level of their sex, the many women who write ill are very far below it. So that, after all, the severer critics are fulfilling a chivalrous duty in depriving the mere fact of feminine authorship of any false prestige which may give it a delusive attraction, and in recommending women of mediocre faculties—as at least a negative service they can render their sex—to abstain from writing.

The standing apology for women who become writers without any special qualification is, that society shuts them out from other spheres of occupation. Society is a very culpable entity, and has to answer for the manufacture of many unwholesome commodities, from bad pickles to bad poetry. But society, like 'matter,' and Her Majesty's Government, and other lofty abstractions, has its share of excessive blame as well as excessive praise. Where there is one woman who writes from necessity, we believe there are three women who write from vanity; and, besides, there is something so antiseptic in the mere healthy fact of working for one's bread, that the most trashy and rotten kind of feminine literature is not likely to have been produced under such circumstances. 'In all

[25] Harriet Martineau (1802–76) novelist, writer on political economy, and autobiographer; Charlotte Bronte (Currer Bell) (1816–55) novelist; Mrs. Gaskell (1810–65) novelist.

labour there is profit;'[26] but ladies' silly novels, we imagine, are less the result of labour than of busy idleness.

Happily, we are not dependent on argument to prove that Fiction is a department of literature in which women can, after their kind, fully equal men. A cluster of great names, both living and dead, rush to our memories in evidence that women can produce novels not only fine, but among the very finest;—novels, too, that have a precious speciality, lying quite apart from masculine aptitudes and experience. No educational restrictions can shut women out from the materials of fiction, and there is no species of art which is so free from rigid requirements. Like crystalline masses, it may take any form, and yet be beautiful; we have only to pour in the right elements—genuine observation, humour, and passion. But it is precisely this absence of rigid requirement which constitutes the fatal seduction of novel-writing to incompetent women. Ladies are not wont to be very grossly deceived as to their power of playing on the piano; here certain positive difficulties of execution have to be conquered, and incompetence inevitably breaks down. Every art which has its absolute *technique* is, to a certain extent, guarded from the intrusions of mere left-handed imbecility. But in novel-writing there are no barriers for incapacity to stumble against, no external criteria to prevent a writer from mistaking foolish facility for mastery. And so we have again and again the old story of La Fontaine's[27] ass, who puts his nose to the flute, and, finding that he elicits some sound, exclaims, 'Moi, aussi, je joue de la flute;'—a fable which we commend, at parting, to the consideration of any feminine reader who is in danger of adding to the number of 'silly novels by lady novelists.'

Eliza Lynn Linton

1822 – 98

T*he daughter of Charlotte Goodenough and James Lynn, she was the youngest of twelve children; her mother lived only a few months after her birth and the children – of whom the eldest was only sixteen – were*

[26] Proverbs 14:23.
[27] La Fontaine's *Fables* were published between 1668 and 1694.

of little interest to their father. In her childhood home at Keswick, Cumberland,
she educated herself and even took up Hebrew, Latin and Greek. At the
age of twenty-three she decided upon a literary life and, with characteristic
determination, took herself to London where she spent a great deal of time in the
Reading Room of the British Museum undertaking the research for her first two
learned historical novels, Azeth the Egyptian *(1847) and* Amymone, A Romance
of the Days of Pericles *(1848). But her novels alone could not provide sufficient*
remuneration and she turned to other forms of writing as well. By 1851 she
was the first full-time woman journalist, earning the impressive salary of twenty
guineas a month at The Morning Chronicle. *She then spent a short period of time*
in Paris as a correspondent for the London papers. Her marriage in 1858 was
soon followed by an amiable separation.

She became a staff member of the Monthly Review *in 1866 and*
continued to be a prolific writer; she wrote highly successful novels and
in 1870–71, for example, she contributed at least 225 stories or essays
to The Saturday Review, All the Year Round, *and* Queens.

There are many contradictions in the woman and her work. While
independent herself she publicly supported the Victorian image of ideal
womanhood, but this did not prevent her heroines from enjoying a most
exciting life. Her highly influential 'Girl of the Period' pieces, published from 1866
to 1877, and which were ostensibly an endorsement of womanliness, could be
seen to depict some of the advantages of emancipation.

Eliza Lynn Linton was a contributor to the novel of ideas and helped
to fictionalise some of the major religious debates of her day; Sowing the
Wind *(1867) is an illuminating account of a young woman's attempt to*
become a journalist and The Autobiography of Christopher Kirkland *(1885) is*
a fascinating 'autobiography' in which the author adopts a male persona.

'The Mad Willoughbys' is taken from The Mad Willoughbys and Other
Tales *(Ward, Lock and Taylor, London, 1875).*

The Mad Willoughbys

CHAPTER I

OUT OF THE DUST

I T was the general belief in the neighbourhood that Mr. Willoughby, of Longmire Hall, was mad. It was in the family. His father before him had been held
mad, or worse; for what else could be said of a man who gave his time to dissecting
mice and moles, and made his shrubbery a pest-place by the dead things hung up
in the trees to dry? Comparative anatomy was a science in no good repute when
old Willoughby took it in hand to discover its secrets; and the skinless bodies and
bleaching bones of bird and beast dangling from the branches of a gentleman's

ornamental wood, made a ghastly and revolting desecration of pleasant property that set every local aristocrat against the evil-doer, and gave the place a bad name it never lost. The amateur anatomist was the Ishmaelite[1] of his locality; and if he escaped graver suspicion than that of a very uncomfortable form of insanity from the gentry, the commonalty, more uncompromising, made up for it by crediting him with every sin under heaven, of which atheism, sorcery, and dealings with the resurrection-men[2] were about the most distinct.

When his son therefore, the present John Willoughby, became the owner of Longmire Hall, and began his career of "plain living and high thinking," he found himself dedicated to suspicion and derision beforehand by the neighbours; and every plan that he proposed for the advancement of knowledge or the regeneration of society was received with distrust and dismissed with contempt. The world, as Longmire knew it, was good enough for its inhabitants before he came into it, they said; and they were in no wise minded to be drilled into ways which ended in such results as were to be seen at Longmire Hall.

For Mr. Willoughby, in his pursuit after the ideal of philosophic simplicity, gave up one after another of the ordinary conditions of a gentleman's mode of living; till, after having successively laid down his carriages, discharged his men and reduced the number of his female servants to two—then to one, and as time went on to none at all—sowed his flower-beds with pot-herbs, made his conservatory into a hen-house and his hot-houses into infirmaries for his sick live-stock, he found himself reduced to a state of simplicity which was next thing to savagery, with a house and grounds given up to decay, desolation, and neglect. It was his idea of righteous living and a philosopher's befitting environment; but it did not please the people of the place; and the breach existing between the man of original ideas and the world of stereotyped habits in which he lived, grew so wide that for all practical purposes the owner of Longmire Hall was an exile in his own house, cut off from society as too disturbing in his views and too audacious in his impiety for the recognition of sober citizens and professing Christians.

Meanwhile, three children had been born to him; one son and two daughters; and his wife had died abroad. No one knew much about this last fact, however; for one of his principles being, the absolute authority of a man over the members of his own family, more especially the female members, it never occurred to him that he owed any account to society of his wife's death and burial. If he had thought good to have had her embalmed as an Egyptian mummy, that he might keep her for ever in his sight, or if he had chosen to fling her dead body uncoffined and unsanctified into the river, he would have done so, with the most entire indifference as to what the world would think. It might think as it liked for John Willoughby, provided it left him to do as he liked. Liberty for himself and authority over others were the twin deities of his personal sphere; and so long as he could retain these he let the rest go.

[1] An outcast after Ishmael, the son of Abraham and Hagar, handmaid of his wife, Sarah, *Genesis* xvi, 12.
[2] Grave-robbers who sold fresh corpses to anatomists.

If the owner of Longmire Hall had odd notions about the simplicity of life as a philosophic grace, he had strong notions about obedience as a womanly glory. He used to say that he took his stand on the elemental principle of sex, and he defied, and divided, the world from that vantage-ground. From this elemental principle he had deduced a whole code of morals and manners, neatly tabulated under the several heads of Difference in Duties; Apportionment of Work; Natural Arrangements; and the Righteousness of Feminine Subjection. To man he gave the root and the flower, the wine and the oil of life; to woman he gave—man; and he always maintained that her portion was the best. For her activities he assigned her the care of the children, the painstaking distribution of the money allowed her by her master, and, no matter what her social condition, practical and personal fulfilment of all domestic duties. Hence, his wife in her time and now his daughters in theirs had the whole of the house work on their hands, as the duty belonging to their feminine condition and the crown of glory prepared for them by the eternal fitness of things. He was thus, as may easily be seen, as entirely out of harmony with his period as his father before him had been with his; and his social status only made matters worse. Had he been a mere nobody, his crotchets would have attracted no attention; being one of the county families, it was a scandal that more than one magnate said, "should be put down."

His two daughters, Marian and Ellen, handsome, high-spirited girls, with strong cravings after pleasure and the flesh-pots, had never reconciled themselves to their father's peculiar views of life. They called his philosophic simplicity "disgraceful stinginess," "abominable shabbiness," and a host of other epithets more strong than euphonious; and they pitied themselves as the victims of capricious tyranny and parental despotism. But they indemnified themselves in the best way they could—a way, by the bye, pleasant but dangerous;—and as in country places lights are not hidden under bushels and all things come to all ears, when the neighbours said sneeringly, that "if report spoke true, old Willoughby had better look to home and hold his own in hand instead of trying to drive other folk's teams," they had only too much reason for their words.

Report said strange things of these two young ladies, who could not be brought to accept their crown of glory with becoming appreciation. It said, *inter alia*, that neither by preachments nor punishments could their father instil into them so much feminine instinct as went to make a pudding that could be eaten, or a bed that could be slept in. It was their method of retaliation for being put to work, unworthy ladies and the daughters of a county family, as they were. Report said, moreover, that many a day when they ought to have been at home seeing to the kitchen fire and "seconding the little things in soak," they were careering about the lanes and fields, sometimes alone, but oftener with two young men of the district—the one of whom was Harry Marsden, the son of the rich distiller of Marsden Folly, and the other Julius Stanford, the heir of Dutton End.

To both of these young men, as ill luck would have it, Mr. Willoughby bore the most passionate, if unreasonable, aversion; to the one because he was the son of an uneducated parvenu whose h's were sometimes shaky, and the blue blood of the aristocratic Liberal disdained parvenus—to the other because he was the son of a bigoted Tory squire who denied the doctrine of human equality and kept his ladies like drawing-room dolls; to both because they held no high principle of life, as the arbitrary philosopher counted principle, but cared only for pleasure and the present hour, personal success and material advantages. Do grapes grow from thorns? neither then from such fathers could spring sons worthy of the name and destinies of men with brains wherewith to think and souls to be saved!

This he had said loftily one day when Marian, to break ground and try the lay of the paternal land, had spoken of the young fellows carelessly, and asked her father why they never came to the Hall?

But a parent's private reasons for liking or disliking young people of either sex seldom affect the children. Especially did their father's, in this case, seem to the two Misses Willoughby utterly absurd; for, if they had had to give an opinion, they would have said, judging by results, that the Marsden and Stanford parental stems were surely, so far from being thorns or thistles, vines of the most splendid fruitage! To Marian, Henry, and to Ellen, Julius, were young Apollos good against the world; and it is doubtful if a voice from heaven would have changed their opinion. They were in the believing age, and objects for love ran short in their lives. They clung therefore with all the more tenacity to those they had met with in the dark.

On their side, the beauty, the courage, and the home hardships of the girls bound the young men with a double chain of loving pity and chivalrous desire to release them. They would have had no hesitation in releasing them now at this very moment, but for the absurd prejudices of mothers and sisters at home, and the shameful power of fathers over the family cheque-book. Still, these secret interviews begun in sport by the men and for the very recklessness of weariness by the girls, were assuredly destined to become matters of grave import as time went on, and romance should ripen into the sober possibilities of reality.

Beside these two girls left to their father's autocracy at home there was, as we have said, a son. But he, following Mr. Willoughby's ideas of sex and apportionment on the other side, had been educated at Eton, and was now at Oxford;—theoretically that his cup might be dipped deep in all sorts of pure wells, and his mind become a magazine of good things fitting him for his future important *rôle* in life as the head of a house, the owner of Longmire Hall—man the ruler of woman, and man the brother of men. In reality young Claude was mainly occupied in qualifying himself to pull stroke in the University boat, defying the Proctor, dodging his bull-dogs,[3] and making his college tutor's life a burden to him by reason of his unconquerable idleness and manifold misdeeds. It was not the best or most harmonious kind of training perhaps, for the future wise ownership of Longmire Hall—not one that would lead him to value its carved oak cabinets full of carefully-mounted skeletons, its shelves loaded with natural curiosities preserved in spirits, and its

[3] The two men who assisted the Proctor in his task of enforcing university discipline over uproarious undergraduates.

rare old library, where the books were rotting under accumulated decades of dust. The dust, the handsome, self-willed, pleasure-loving lad would be pretty sure to sweep away as his contribution to the better ordering of the world; but for the skeletons and the curiosities in spirits, the black-letter books and early editions, and all that these represented, they would fall into uncongenial hands enough when they should come into his; for, of the special veins of intellectual "madness" traversing his father and grandfather, not the smallest fragment, the thinnest lamina, could be found in him.

It was a question however, with those who knew both, if the lad would ever live at Longmire Hall when he had it. And it was a question with those who knew all three, if his father would leave it to him. The boy, perhaps unwisely if truthfully, always professed the most uncompromising aversion to the place, for all that it was his birthright, the home of his childhood, and his presumed ancestral inheritance.

And it was a gloomy old tenement enough. It was a worm-eaten, weather-stained house, set in the heart of a dense wood which no Willoughby had yet dared to thin. The race had been neither spendthrift nor grasping; consequently, though not entailed and the absolute property of each successive owner, its oaks and elms had been respected as things inalienable and belonging to the title-deeds as much as the land itself.

Marking the boundary of the home wood flowed the swift and sullen Mortey; a river that never broke into scudding spray nor laughed in running ripples over sunny pools; a river that never leaped from rock to rock like a creature rejoicing in its strength; where no fish darted in silvery shoals from their hiding-places of sheltering rock or mossy green; and where no growths of stately water-plants were borne like gold and silver treasures on its breast; but a river that flowed with a strong and steady current, silent, oily, black, like the river of death flowing down to eternal night. There were places in it of unknown depth which seemed as if they hid all manner of awful secrets and nameless crimes—places full of terrible traditions of suicide and murder, where the doomed bodies of strong men waited for the eternal judgment, and the helpless hands of women and their children had been stretched in vain for pity. Gloomy, soddened, matted with poisonous weeds and barren of all beautiful life, its banks seemed to swarm with the ghosts of the dead things below. They were to be seen in the thick vapours that stole up in the evening, as the pall that covered their graves; they were to be heard in the muttering of the wind among the dank alders and the rotting weeds—that funeral dirge which never ceased;—in the howl of the winter storm and the soft moan of the summer air they were ever and always to be heard, sighing out their sorrows, calling vainly on God for help; witnesses of crime, victims of despair, who sent men mad from horror of what they told and revealed.

Set full over this stream of evil history, built on the top of a mass of rock that overhung the water, was a small Gazebo of four rooms. It was a place which no one now, save Ralph Rowsley the surly old handy-man about the Hall who chopped wood and moved heavy weights, was ever seen to enter; and he but seldom. The anatomist had used it as a dissecting-place for his bats and creatures; and the present Mr. Willoughby had been accustomed to sit there in the first years of his marriage, when he wished to meditate in peace on the perfectibility of humanity. But since his wife's death he had given up the keys to Ralph; and the place had been abandoned to a bad name and mildew.

If the Hall itself was considered but a doubtful kind of abode for a Christian gentleman and his family, this special offshoot was held in infinite horror. Not the bravest poacher of the district would have ventured near it after nightfall, were the trees set as thick with birds as the bushes are with berries; and had the river been teeming with fish, every fin would have been safe in that special stretch of water overshadowed by this desolate erection. For it was haunted. Sure every one knew that! Indeed, there were many who swore to having seen the ghost that haunted it—an awful thing with its white face pressed against the dirt-encrusted panes, and some added blood on its waving hands and across its spectral breast; and some swore they had seen lights in the upper rooms, where the ghost mostly showed itself—corpse lights,[4] burning dimly at midnight, and fruitful of evil to the wretch who saw them. There were many who could tell you all about it; how the godless old anatomist had once decoyed a poor maid there and murdered her for the sake of her bones. Those bones, of which he was so fain, were reputed to have strange properties belonging to them for those who could use them aright; and what the skulls and vertebræ of moles and mice could do, naturally enough a full-grown human being's could do by just so much the more. This was logic, though not called by the schoolman's name; and, to the average mind about Longmire, unanswerable. Wherefore they gave you chapter and verse of ocular demonstration, and moral reason why, the Gazebo was and must be haunted by the ghost of the poor murdered maid about whom everyone knew something, but no two the same thing.

For all these reasons then, young Claude Willoughby might be almost excused his intense hatred of home, connected too as it was with the remembrance of a repressed and unnatural childhood, dull and gloomy holidays, and, as time had gone on and his knowledge of men and manners had increased, with a state of things for his two sisters for which his young indignation had no bounds and his disgust could find no name hard enough.

All that was best, as well as all that was worst, in Claude, was wakened into anger at the life marked out for his sisters by his father; and the only thing that ever roused him to exertion, or sent him to the lecture-room with a determination to profit by what he heard, was his desire to "get on" for their sakes, so that he might have a home where he could take them from the tyranny and mismanagement of Longmire Hall.

It was seldom that Mr. Willoughby left either the house or grounds. His longest walk was rarely farther than to the great elm-tree that stood in the midst of the tangled shrubbery, where he would go sometimes on a hot summer's day to discuss wood-craft with old Ralph; who also had his ideas—master and man often disagreeing, but the man as often getting the better of the master. One day, however (it was one first of May) stung by some oestrum of unrest,

[4] Flames or light seen inexplicably, often in churchyards, and believed to herald a death.

or led by some unseen spirit for a purpose, he departed so far from the habits of years as to drift beyond the gate of his own property, over the bridge that spanned the sullen river, and into the road.

He made a striking picture as he sauntered down the road, his long white hair lying in feathery curls far on his shoulders; his blue linen blouse, open at the neck, showing his delicate white chest as a brawny navvy or a weather-beaten sailor might show his; his keen light-grey eyes searching the hedges for a new flower, the sky for a rare bird—a peripatetic philosopher of a not quite new sort, seeking to dragoon men and women into virtue as interpreted by him, and holding it as a personal affront when they abjured his leadership and preferred their own. So far as he had gone yet, most people had so abjured. Even his own children had been recalcitrant with the rest, and had disdained his favourite formula of "Ladies in the parlour and queens in the kitchen," as now hypocrisy, now an insult, and always nonsense. Still he never doubted but that he should be victorious in the end, and make them what he wished them to be.

"They are young yet, and have no power of prevision. They never think that I have their future in my own hands, and that I can make them rich or leave them beggars by my will. If they had as much sense as that dear robin there, they would remember that I am all-powerful, so far as they are concerned, and they would be careful to avoid the wrong path where they are walking now, and to take the right which hitherto they have refused. Sad! sad! but no doubt they will find it before too late."

He was thinking this with his fine benevolent air, and taking comfort in the thought, just as he passed a turn in the road and came upon a girl sitting on the wayside bank, resting.

She was evidently very poor and had walked far, for her naked feet were dusty and her threadbare clothes travel-stained. She looked hungry too, and forlorn; but she was substantially clean in spite of dust and travel-stain, and, though hungry and forlorn, poor and in want, she was as beautiful as one of Guido's angels, and her face was almost as pure in its expression.

She looked up as Mr. Willoughby came near—a yearning dumb beast kind of look shining with prayer in her soft eyes; but she did not beg. Her parched lips moved mechanically, and her pale face flushed with sudden hope as she pushed the hair from her forehead wearily; but she made no overt sign. And her very silence charmed where maybe the most eloquent prayer would have repelled.

"Who are you, and where do you come from?" asked Mr. Willoughby, suddenly stopping before her.

She tottered to her swollen bleeding feet.

"My name is Jessie," she said simply, folding her hands in a childlike attitude behind her back.

"And what are you doing here?" he asked again.

She glanced round her dejectedly. "Seeking for work," she said; and looked at road and river as if the answer to her wants lay written in visible words on each.

"You are young to be alone; have you no one to take care of you?" He said this almost sternly. Interested as he was in this young creature who was evidently no common beggar, he could not tamper with his conscience so far as to shut his eyes to the fact that she was alone, hence a woman under no restraint, and looking for the work she ought to have found lying to her hand at home prepared by the eternal fitness of things.

Tears came up into her eyes.

"My mother died this week," she said; "and I am nothing but myself now."

"What can you do?" asked the philanthropist. A sudden idea of remunerative benevolence struck him.

"Nothing," said Jessie; then she added, with a pretty air of profound conviction, as if it was a discovery she had just made; "and that makes it hard."

"Yes, that makes it hard as you say," he answered; "and great blame rests on those who should have taught you better. Merciful powers! what are women fit for if they cannot go through their appointed tasks? Man is a meat-eating animal, and it devolves on woman to cook the food he provides. He to take scalps and hunt buffalo, she to seethe flesh and sew skins."

"I can cook a little," she said timidly. "When there was any to do I did it; and all the sewing. My mother made me sew, and always said I was handy at my needle."

"You can cook and sew? Then you .ave got your fortune in your own hands. And what more you want you can learn," cried Mr Willoughby almost enthusiastically.

"Yes, I can learn," she repeated with a patient smile. "I can learn anything I am put to."

"Well, come with me, and we will see what can be done," said Mr. Willoughby, drawing the beggar girl's hand in his arm.

And in this strange guise he walked back along the road and through the grand old rusty gates with their quaint carvings and twisted iron-work, and so up the broad carriage drive, through the wilderness and to the desert he called his home. But to poor Jessie, waif and stray of humanity as she was, the companion of penury and the house-mate of hunger, it was all as fine as the finest palace, and not a want was to be seen anywhere.

In the hall, which was made into an odd but picturesque sitting-room to save space and economize labour, were two girls sitting by a table, as the master entered with his fine air of old-world courtesy, to introduce and protect the pretty, shrinking, dusty beggar-girl on his arm. One of these girls was peeling potatoes, the other scraping carrots. It was an odd occupation for both place and persons, but Jessie was too untaught to see its strangeness. To her indeed, it was no more strange than it would have been to a passing Greek had he seen Nausicäa with her handmaidens at the brook, washing her royal father's linen.

Mr. Willoughby smiled approvingly. There was a broad dash of the histrionic temperament in the man, and he liked the several scenes of life to be well rounded off.

Marian, the elder, looked up as the pair crossed the threshold, her dark brows knit and her eyes scornful at what she saw. Ellen looked up too and laughed. It was not a pleasant laugh, being of the kind by which certain natures express the same feeling which others make manifest by curses. This was the way in which they generally divided their manifestations; Marian frowned and Ellen laughed; but both meant the same thing.

"My children," said Mr. Willoughby loftily, still holding Jessie's hand in his, "I have brought you a companion—a sister to love and to cherish—a wild flower gathered by the wayside, but a flower out of the Eternal Garden like yourselves. Take her to your rooms; cleanse, feed, and clothe her. She will repay your care; and you will have the satisfaction that comes upon the conscience from the performance of a meritorious action."

This address was delivered well, and the effect, as a mere bit of elocution, was superb. One might have thought it would have moved the typical heart of stone, but Miriam knit her handsome brows afresh and tossed her head impatiently before the paternal lips had half concluded their peroration. She had an untamable kind of nature, this Marian of his, and the contest of wills between them was daily growing stronger.

For a moment she seemed about to refuse. He read it in her face, and wondered how he should force her if she did. But the mood passed. With a quick glance to her sister that meant "Do as I do," she rose from her seat and made a step forward.

"Very well, papa," she said; "we will take her in and make her as comfortable as we can. Who is she?"

"Jessie," answered Mr. Willoughby, as if Jessie expressed everything that was needed in the way of biography, and no more need be said in excuse or explanation.

On which Marian, taking her cue and giving it to her sister, said with a very creditable assumption of condescension: "Come, Jessie, you look tired and hungry. Let us see what we can do for you."

"Postponed," said Mr. Willoughby to himself; "and every outpost gained is so much to the good of future victory."

But if the two girls received the wayfarer graciously, old Ralph did not, and did not scruple to tell his master what he thought of his folly the next time they were alone and he could speak his mind freely. Mischief would come of it, he said; he felt sure of that; and there never was a tramp taken into a respectable house yet who didn't bring worse than the plague with her. If the master wanted a servant, good lord, why couldn't he get one of respectable parents! But to go out into the high road and bring in a dusty trollop like that, it was rank foolishness, that it was; and he wouldn't be doing his duty not to say so!

To all of which Mr. Willoughby listened with his eyes half shut; when the old man had finished contenting himself by answering mildly: "Have you ever heard of King Cophetua, my faithful old friend? He married a beggar girl—I have only sheltered one."

"King Cophetua, who was he? He ain't in the Bible!" answered Ralph irreverently; "and what a king may do ain't no rule for us. We are not kings!"

"Thank heaven, no!" said Mr. Willoughby. "Uneasy lies the head that wears a crown! I would rather be as I am."

"It ain't only crowned heads as lie uneasy, when all's said and done," said Ralph a little significantly.

"True, Ralph, very true; but philosophy, divine philosophy—the love of wisdom—makes the rough smooth, and the bitter sweet, and wipes over the slate with a damp sponge, enabling one to forget all that is unpleasant and refuse to be reminded. *Verbum sap!* my dear old friend; which, being interpreted means; a word to the wise. Good day!"

To himself he said, as he wandered towards the house: "If that old man was not necessary to me I would wring his neck for his insolence!"

CHAPTER II

CINDERELLA'S PRINCE

M R. WILLOUGHBY'S whimsies had seldom led him to a better outfall than this of taking poor homeless Jessie into his house as one of his restricted family. True, she was a beggar, uneducated, and so far as could be seen, of such mental quality as forbad the possibility of satisfactory training of a high class, even if she had had it. She was of the kind which can be taught mechanical work fairly well, but which is utterly incapable of understanding abstract propositions, or of using its brains in metaphysical thought. She had a natural aptitude for cooking, for sewing, for scrubbing; and in fact she had been already grounded in these elements of homely science, so far as had been possible with means of such poor dimensions as never excluded hunger, cold, and privation all round.

Her mother had been one of those broken-down respectabilities who cannot dig and to beg are ashamed; and who therefore, when the bad time comes, creep along the shady side of the hedge, hiding themselves and their miseries in the best way they can, coming out only under cover of darkness, and giving up life by the slow process of starvation for the sake of retaining the pride of exclusiveness and the self-respect of honour. She died just when she seemed to have solved that difficult problem of living on nothing. The last of her little store had gone, and there was no friendly prophet to bless the widow's cruse with unfailing increase. She and her daughter stood face to face with want in its blackest, bleakest aspect; and then on the cold, bare boards of a miserable cellar, the rent of which was due and could not be paid, with not a crust in the mouldy cupboard nor a spark in the rusty grate, the former governess of a baronet's daughter died, leaving her helpless child to the tender mercies of a world which has consecrated as a religious truth this axiom: "The weakest must go to the wall."

So this was how it was that Jessie had been found, hungry and footsore, resting by the wayside in her vague quest of undesignated work from unknown men. It was a child-like trust in ravens that seemed scarcely likely to be justified. And had it not been that some spirit had led John Willoughby by the hand that first of May, in all probability society would have added one more to its list of victims, and the local coroner would have sat on the body of a young female, name unknown, found dead of hunger and fatigue by the Queen's highway.

But, if hungry, Jessie was innocent; if ignorant, she was loving. She was little better than a grateful, fair-faced, docile animal; an animal that spoke some few words of intelligible English in a low, sweet, musical voice; that stood upright and clothed itself in womanly attire; that had sleek, bright, shining hair like yellowing autumn leaves in the sunshine; soft yearning eyes—the eyes of a creature whose soul was struggling to be born and could not come forth; a soft, small mouth that smiled like an opening rose when she was praised, and drooped and quivered when she was blamed; an animal that fetched and carried as it was bid, that was loving and humble in its temper, quiet and industrious in its ways; an animal that was pleasant to the eyes and useful to the hand, but that seemed to possess just so much and no more mind than if it had been a dog in human form. And indeed it was a dog in nature; only by some strange mischance of the angel who orders the affairs of earth, the dog's soul had got slipped into a human body when Jessie May was born.

Something of all this, and of the personal profit to be made thereby, Marian had seen by one of those rapid glances into the inner truth and the future working of things which sometimes are vouchsafed to us, when her father, with the dusty simple-looking beggar girl on his arm, had come into the hall when she and Ellen were paring potatoes and scraping carrots while talking of their lovers. At the first blush she had despised this new outbreak of a benevolence that reached so far and wide over humanity in the mass it had nothing left for home, as she despised all her father's doings; but a moment's quick consideration determined her to acceptance. Their father thought he had brought her and her sister a companion—a living lesson in practical democracy; she saw he had given them a slave, and that in his desire to bind their galling fetters still firmer he had put into their hands the key which would unlock them. Jessie was to be their servant, their serf; if their "sister," as the father had said, then only a sister after the pattern of Cinderella—and Cinderella in a house where no fairy godmother would come down among the ashes to turn rags into cloth of gold and create a princess out of a cinder-wench.

Nevertheless, things were equal in outward seeming. Jessie lived with the family as one of them; called the sisters by their names; received gifts of gowns and cloaks of the exact pattern and material as theirs; was spoken to by Mr. Willoughby as "my child," and frequently exhorted to forget the time when he had not been her father. His kindness to her was unbounded; and if she was never weary of showing her gratitude by hard work, he was never backward in urging her on by soft words.

In truth, she made all things better by her noiseless industry. She took the heavy end of the stick at every corner, and those whose burdens she lightened bore themselves the braver for her help. The house was cleaner and the dinners better cooked since she came. Marian's hands became finer as the coarser part of the housework dropped from them to hers; and Ellen's love of becoming millinery was more satisfied now that Jessie was at her elbow to tell her where to fasten on her bows, and how to loop up her skirts. She herself was so profoundly, calmly happy, she made a kind of mild sunshine wherever she was. She seldom spoke and never laughed; but the faithful eyes were bright and clear, and her pretty little mouth often fluttered into that childish smile which has no future and no past—the mere smile of the happy present, without thought or regret. By the time she had lived through the summer and the ripe autumn, by the time when Christmas and its vacation had come, she had niched herself so firmly in her place they could scarcely understand how they had lived without her. No one who had seen this pretty and delightful creature, whose place in the house seemed to have been hers from the beginning, and whose usefulness made a general ease and gladness that set all things free, would have thought that seven months ago she was a starving vagrant by the wayside, snatched from destruction by a mere freak of fortune and the happy chance of pleasing a strange man's sentimental fancy.

But though beloved and valued by all the rest, Ralph Rowsley was never her friend. He had set himself against her in the beginning, and his was one of those tenacious souls which pride themselves on never going back on a first impression.

"I said it from the first and I stick to it," was his favourite formula; and as he said from the first that evil would come of Jessie's adoption into the house, he stuck to it, and would not be better persuaded.

In spite of his sympathy with his sisters, Claude's visits at the Hall were rare. He made them as few as he could with decency, fewer than he ought for policy. It was a *corvée*⁵ he could not undertake for grace beyond absolute necessity; but having escaped the "Long"⁶ in the summer of this year, he felt obliged to sacrifice himself for Christmas; and accordingly he wrote to his father announcing his intended arrival on such a day, as a prince might have written to his steward. It was his way; and as he was a man, Mr. Willoughby did not resent it.

The sun was falling fast as an open trap dashed through the grand old gates that creaked on their rusty hinges, when they were flung back, in eloquent expression of the desolateness of the life within; it crashed up the tangled and neglected shrubbery drive, with the interlaced boughs hanging low above, and the fallen leaves and twigs thickly spread below; and after a few objurgations, not of the mildest kind, from both fare and driver, it stopped at the stately porch; and Claude came into the hall. Broad-leaved hat and rough grey Ulster coat, curling raven hair and the dainty silky moustache of early youth, all were covered with the snow which had fallen heavily throughout the drive. It gave him an unreal kind of air as he came in, and brought back to Jessie's mind shadowy stories of fairy princes, and strange northern gods that showed themselves as men, and the kings that came down from their thrones disguised like wayside travellers to try the temper of their subjects. He was so beautiful it seemed almost sacrilege to her that he should have suffered cold and discomfort. His way ought to

⁵ Tedious drudgery, originally fatigue duties imposed on soldiers.
⁶ The Long Vacation, in the summer months between the end of one academic year and the beginning of the next.

have been over cloth of gold strewn with roses, she thought—the sole ideas she had retained from the "Talisman"[7] she had just been reading under Ellen's superintendence; and she stood in the distant doorway looking at him as if he had been a glory suddenly revealed to her:—had she known the ground she would have said Zeus to her Semele.[8]

But born to serve as she was, and at all times ready to suppress herself and her own pleasure for the general good, her first thought, after the shock of her admiration was over, was the handmaid's thought of help. While the family greetings then, were about—the father's artificial, the son's disdainful, the sisters' exaggerated—she, still with her eyes full of that splendid presence, and her heart warmed to the same kind of worship as she had once felt when the organ played in Westminster Abbey, longing to kneel and cry and laugh, and kiss she knew not what, all at the same moment, busied herself to make things domestic fresh and comforting for him, as her share in the gladness of the moment and the honour to be paid this prince among men.

Presently she heard herself called; it was Mr. Willoughby's voice. He wanted to show his household treasure, as he called her, to his son, and to ensure their future good relations. He had always borne it on his heart as a doubt whether Claude, full of his young Oxonian's pride of caste as he was, would care to treat a ci-devant little beggar girl with respect; but if the boy was wilful, the father was adamant, and, all things considered, carried the heavier metal.

Blushing, trembling, vaguely conscious of the ordeal before her, the dog's soul in her prostrate, deprecating the harshness she dreaded and could neither resent nor resist, Jessie left her work and went into the hall to her trial.

"My third daughter," said Mr. Willoughby a little dramatically, taking her cold hand in his; while the girl stood with downcast eyes and drooping head, her face half hidden in her falling hair, not daring to look up to the prince who was to be her judge.

"Having made my sisters servants it is only logical that you should give them a servant as their equal," said Claude with hot disdain.

The pretty head drooped lower, and the poor humble soul crouched closer to the earth.

"My dear boy, you talk nonsense," answered Mr. Willoughby with admirable calmness. "I have made your sisters women such as the eternal arrangements of nature have ordained. They are women of the good old type, when sex was a recognized fact in society and feminine idleness a shame; and I am prouder of them as they are, than if they were preachers and teachers and doctors, and the Lord knows what beside, such as we read of in America. A pudding is a great truth, Claude. The world can do without female philosophers, but it cannot do without puddings."

[7] Sir Walter Scott published The Talisman in 1825.
[8] Semele (daughter of Cadmus and Harmonia) and Zeus were the parents of Dionysus. She begged Zeus to visit her in his full majesty and was killed when he did so.

"Let others instead of them learn the pudding trade!" flashed back Claude. "Money is as great a truth as cooking, and mind a greater. You can pay for the lower; why not cultivate the higher?"

"So I have done, my boy; the highest of all—natural duties. And here is the very perfection of my code," said Mr. Willoughby patting Jessie's hand; "a woman after Wordsworth's heart—nobly planned and not too good for earthly food! Accept her or not at your choice. She is to me what I say—my third daughter; and the man or woman who wishes to break bread in my house must break it with her as his equal; or not at all."

Marian, standing behind her father, made a rapid sign to her brother. Perhaps a timely recollection of that will whereby his whole future might be made or marred, had its weight; and perhaps Jessie's dog-like humility and personal loveliness, flattering his pride and pleasing his taste, unconsciously made the bitter pill somewhat easier to swallow. In any case he saw that he "had it to do;" and Claude, for all his pride and temper, was not wanting in the shrewdness and self-control which are born of a quick recognition of necessity.

"If it is your pleasure, sir, that I accept her as your daughter, I bow to your decision," he said loftily. "It is only in harmony with all the rest."

And with this he turned abruptly on his heel, and ignored his newly-presented sister as completely as if she had never been.

So matters continued for days, the attitude of each member of this strange family the same. Mr. Willoughby placid, unmoved, with a glove of silk and a hand of iron; the girls, Marian and Ellen, covertly insolent to their father or sometimes openly so, excited, restless, unsatisfactory in every direction; Jessie, the pivot on which all household things seemed to turn, the clamp by which every domestic event was kept together, docile, industrious, faithful, canine; Claude, fuming at the whole thing, but daily becoming more alive to the real value of the girl and her worth in the queer establishment called home.

"Jessie, is dinner ready?" asked Marian, one day, the third from Claude's arrival.

"Yes," said Jessie.

"Jessie, have you ironed my collars and trimmed my hat?" called Ellen, from the top of the stairs.

"Yes," said Jessie.

"Jessie, my child," breathed Mr. Willoughby from the inner room, the study, where he had been turning over papers for the last five minutes, "have you any more pamphlets to bind for me?"

"No," said Jessie.

"All here?"

"Yes, sir."

"Had you been a boy I should have had you taught bookbinding," said Mr. Willoughby with his fine air. "For a woman you have a wonderful natural aptitude for the work. See, Claude, how neatly under my directions she has bound up my fragments—a hint for you;" showing him a volume of odds and ends bound up in a home-made cover of thin wood and chintz.

"It seems to me that Jessie does everything," said Claude half satirically, and yet a little more genially than he had ever spoken of her before.

Indeed, it was the first time he had ever addressed her, even so indirectly as this.

She turned to him, and their eyes met. Her look startled him. The glad and humble gratitude that shone through those soft pleading eyes touched him as a dog's eyes touch a man. He had a strange, momentary desire to stroke her falling braids of hair as he would have pulled and played with Jet's ears. She did not seem, somehow, like a woman to him—more like a dumb uncatalogued creature of which he was absolute master, and which he might caress or tease according to his fancy—she unresisting to the one and only grateful for the other. His pride was still in arms against the degradation to which his sisters were subjected in such an association; but for himself—well! he was a man, and though a gentleman and with the gentleman's self-respect and worship of caste, still—the creature was so lovely!—and if she was a servant she did not look like one! At all events, he must accept what was offered to him; and if his father chose to order his house like a maniac, it was not in his power to prevent it. It was wonderful how much good sense came into his unspoken reasonings during the brief moment when he looked at Jessie and she looked at him; how much power those bright and faithful eyes, that sleek and shining hair, that smiling happy little mouth had to make him accept the logic of facts with dignified submission, and so save himself the useless trouble of withstanding the inevitable.

"And will you do what I want, too, Jessie?" continued Claude, half-playful, half-insolent, in his bantering.

She clasped her hands together, and her eyes grew even gladder and brighter.

"Yes," she said emphatically.

On which he laughed; the young man's superior lordly kind of laugh; but he went into dinner to-day without the usual evident, if unspoken, protest at the hardship of sitting down to table with a servant as his sister, a beggar-girl as his equal. Claude was by no means envious of either King Cophetua or Cinderella's prince.

It was the hardest winter that had been known in those parts for years. The birds died in the ice-bound woods, and the squirrels and dormice were frozen stiff and stark in their nests in the hollows and under the roots of the trees. Even the swift and heavy river had tracts of frozen places along its edges; and where the current slackened in the quieter pools there the ice grew and thickened and formed skating-rinks for the neighbourhood. But they were scarcely safe; the stream beneath was too strong, and broke them up too suddenly; and more than one accident had taken place, though none as yet fatal.

One day Claude and his sisters were out on the ice. Since Jessie's adoption the two girls had given up most of their former duties, and had taken to the use of their own time, almost like ordinary young ladies in a house where only one servant is kept. She asked nothing better. To work for them was her form of gratitude and love, as well as her personal pleasure. What, indeed, could she do with time if not employed in household work?—she, who was scarcely better educated than a child of six, and who fell asleep over even a story-book? So she stayed at home and wrought with the faithfulness by which she expressed her soul, and her "sisters" took their ease by her industry, and enjoyed pleasures which had been unknown until their father presented them with a Cinderella who should make them possible.

All Longmire was on the skating ground to-day, and among others the young lovers, Henry Marsden and Julius Stanford. And with the former and his sisters "the Earl's" daughter, Lady Margaret. She was the first lady of rank in the place, as old Marsden was the richest man; and it was in the design of both these elderly gentlemen, the Earl and the distiller, that Henry and Lady Margaret should make a match of it—the money on the one side balancing the birth on the other and making the alliance exactly even. But Henry, being at the age when material advantages count for nothing and love scores all the points, was not inclined to give up the girl he loved for the girl he ought to marry; and that day on the rink expressed his mind so plainly by his deeds that his neighbours read it as clearly as if it had been written across the black board standing out on the thin ice, marked "Dangerous."

Claude had never affected the Marsden girls; his own sisters were pre-engaged—besides, attending to one's own sisters was slow work for such a young fellow as Claude; there was not one of all assembled who took his fancy by a hair's breadth, save Lady Margaret; and she was of a certain high-bred, queenly, self-centred type that attracted him powerfully. She was practically alone too, so far as a special cavalier went; what could he do, then, but devote himself to her on the skating-ground, and give himself up to the task of winning her favour? It was a cold basis for such a fiery furnace as was laid and lighted that day; but stranger results than this have come about before from causes even more unlikely.

Claude was a good skater. In what indeed, of personal accomplishment did not that handsome youth excel? It had been his one ambition to make himself a second Admirable Crichton[9] in personal prowess of all kinds; and he had not failed in his endeavour. Being then a good skater, ambitious of distinction and fond of display, he was rash, and more than once skimmed over ice so thin that nothing but the rapidity and unbroken smoothness of his motion saved him. The pitcher, however, that goes daily to the well is sure to get broken at last; and rashness, venturing on the thin ice twice without fear, goes the third time to destruction.

So it was with Claude. Fired by Lady Margaret's kindling approval of his "style" and "daring," he skimmed this time too near; and in spite of his swiftness and his smoothness the treacherous platform broke, and Claude Willoughby was in the deep dark waters of the Mortey.

Young and strong and fearless, sure enough, was he; but what can the strength of man do against the forces of nature? The ice was thin and in no part could bear him up; each hold that he took only cut his numbing flesh and

9 James Crichton (1560–85) was distinguished as a scholar, a swordsman and a traveller. His fellow-Scot Sir Thomas Urquhart (1611?–1660?) dubbed him 'The Admirable Crichton' and the name has been used ever since for someone of outstanding abilities in many fields.

let him slip back into the water. The current below ran swiftly. It was running to the dark stretch below the Gazebo; there was no point where he could make resistance; his struggles only ended in exhaustion and defeat; and soon he began to feel that he could struggle no longer. It was bitter to die with his life still unlived; but his strength was ebbing away so fast that he soon began to think death would be sweet and restful like a soldier's sleep after battle. He was sinking, sleepy and weary; it would soon all be over; the waters were closing round him and their roar had softened to a murmur like the hum of bees, when something struck him sharply across the face and roused him just so far as to see that it was a rope, to which he clung with the one last supreme effort of instinctive despair.

Then he remembered no more, till he found himself in a strange room, with a strange face bending over him; a room he did not recognize; a face he could not remember; but that mixed itself up in his mind with a favourite setter with bright yearning eyes and long sleek ears, which had loved him, as dogs do love, without thought of self or hope of reward.

It was only Jessie; and the room he was in was the state bed-room at the Hall, which she had secretly prepared for her young prince that very day, under plea of his own needing some repairs.

There was mourning and lamentation over the danger in which the handsome heir of the house lay. Even Mr. Willoughby forgot his wide schemes of general benevolence for this occasion, and came down to the concrete acts of service needed by his sick son; and the sisters mulcted their lovers of a good half-hour's interview apiece, that they might sit about the house in the aimless way of the unhelpful when sickness is on hand, and turn their domestic talents to account by cooking in their best style messes he could not eat.

But Jessie neither cried nor sat about. She seemed to know by the dumb instinct of love what was the right thing to do, and when to do it. The cuts and bruises were washed and bound by her soft hands, the very touch of which seemed to soothe the feverish patient as not even the doctor's composing draughts soothed him. It was Jessie who noted the hours of the medicines, and gave them as punctually as the clock told the moment; Jessie, who knew exactly when to bring that little cupful of food, which was the very thing he ought to have and which was neither too much nor too little; it was Jessie who watched night after night, noiselessly, silently, showing no symptoms of fatigue when morning came, but as diligent and careful as before; Jessie who was ever in the van but carried away none of the honours; Jessie whose quiet helpfulness had come to be so much a matter of course, that no one thought of thanking her, any more than we thank the flowers for blooming or the sun for shining. And always Claude mixed up that bending face of hers with the image of his favourite setter Jet; and not even when the fever had subsided could he thoroughly disentangle his ideas, or separate completely the idea of Jessie, the human being, from that of Jet, the favourite setter.

As for herself, who can tell what she felt or thought through all these dark times? Of self indeed, she was scarcely conscious anyhow; she could not say that she was unhappy, because there was no individuality left in her. Her whole soul was fixed on the one thought, the one endeavour; "He is ill: he must be healed."

If it had been told her that he could be healed by the sacrifice of her life, she would have given that life with no thought of her own pain, with no more hesitation than she would have smoothed his pillows or held a cup of water to his parched lips. The earth held nothing that her mind could compass save that her young prince was sick unto death, and that heaven and earth should be ransacked for means whereby he might be restored; nothing too costly, no one too sacred for that supreme end; and she herself might well go with the rest! Had she been banished from his room she would have dropped out of all activity and reasonableness, and would have laid herself across his threshold, moaning. Had he died, she would have crept by night to his grave, and the morning would have found her lying there dead too. The blankness and despair of her life would have killed her, as dogs have been killed by grief. But she was kept healthy and active by the very intensity of her devotion; and it was only when her prince began to mend that she came back to the small amount of self-consciousness she usually possessed, and, feeling weary and dazed, drew herself away as sick dumb beasts do.

No one noticed her. She had worked when her work was needed, now no one saw that she flagged and gradually effaced herself. Only Mr. Willoughby watched her a little anxiously, and made her take spoonfuls of home-made nettle-tea at odd moments. But Claude who owed his life to her, seemed when not unconscious almost as if uneasy in her presence. It was as if he knew that he ought to be grateful to her, and was at odds with himself because he was not. Once indeed he did say to her, laying his hands on those long brown, loosely-fastened braids that dropped over her face when she hung it down as Jet's ears used to drop over hers, "I do believe you have saved my life, Jess."

She made no answer. Talking was never much in her line, but the happy tears rushed up into her eyes as she very softly, very humbly, took his hand in hers and kissed it.

"What a grateful little thing you are!" laughed Claude, with a certain embarrassment breaking through his high-handed superiority. For after all, Jessie was not a dumb beast and she was a woman; and Claude, in the age of woman-worship and woman-wooing, was not in the habit of having his hands kissed by one of the creatures before whom it was his pride to humble himself if only he might have the reward of their smiles.

He drew his hand hastily away; but the kiss seemed to cling somehow; and then he put on his hat and coat and strolled down to Marsden Folly, where he feigned to go for Henry Marsden and knew he should find Lady Margaret.

It was not the first time, by many, since his recovery that he had strolled down the road with the same feigned purpose and the same real end. And each time he went, the fire that had been lighted in him on that terrible day of danger burned with a more passionate fierceness—on his side; till there was not a fibre of his whole being which was not dedicated to the one sole desire, the one sole design, to win the love of a woman who loved only herself, and who but craved to receive from all what she was in no wise able to return to any.

CHAPTER III

TAKING THE AIR

FRESH air and exercise were not in Mr. Willoughby's estimate of the needs of women. House-work, if they did their duty, gave them quite enough of the latter, and the open doors and windows which they must needs pass in their day's doings supplied what of the former was necessary for health and a clear skin. He held "gadding about" in horror, as the beginning of all evil for the daughters of Eve; and looked askance even at the reasons given by his own when he called them and found them wanting, and they told him demurely they had been in the garden cutting cabbages or picking gooseberries. Convenient domestic screens, be it said, for stolen words behind friendly hedges, or letters dropped deftly into the natural pillar-boxes of decayed oak-trees.

It was Ralph's business to cut the cabbages and pick the gooseberries, he used to say severely when they told him of their doings as excuse and explanation; their's laid within doors.

But a man's will is nowhere when a woman's wits take the field; and in spite of all he could say, and of all that Ralph might bring in as the days's supply of greens or fruitage, Marian and Ellen continued to visit the kitchen garden on household errands as often as they chose, whether gooseberries were to be found there in January or not.

It was the more surprising then, and perhaps one of the strongest proofs of his affection that he could have given, that Mr. Willoughby, watching Jessie narrowly, not only gave her spoonsful of nettle-tea at odd moments, but suddenly ordered that she should "take the air." Young, strong, and unfanciful though she was, those long nights of watching and unrest had told upon her, and though she made no complaint she looked faded and out of condition. Wherefore it was that Mr. Willoughby commanded her to take the air; and Jessie obedient, went.

For all the months of her stay at Longmire Hall she had not once been beyond that neglected stretch of weeds and self-sown vegetables called by courtesy the kitchen garden: a mere waste now, though it had been in its day the pride of the country round for early growths and perfect keeping. Recreation, as has been said, was not part of the Willoughby programme, and no idle half hours fell to her lot. Consequently, when she was bidden to go out and enjoy herself this soft grey February day, she found herself in an unknown world as she turned into the wood—a world too, where there were no sign-posts to show the way or to forbid it, and where she was free to ramble at her pleasure.

She took a small, overgrown path, but one that was in places evidently used, though in others the boughs were bent down and interlaced across the walks as if no one had passed that way for centuries. Nevertheless, she followed it for a good half mile; at each step starting the shy brown beasts that were beginning to stir from their holes, or scaring from bough to bough the birds practising the first notes of their pairing-songs and already considering the best architecture for their nests. All this occupied and amused her, till suddenly the way forked and she had to make her choice which side she would take. She chose the right, and at once plunged into the famous Longmire Maze where men had wandered about before now and had died before they could find the clue to clear them.

The path became a tortuous and entangled puzzle, branching out in all directions, none leading to a definite result. Here was one way that doubled back on itself, after half an hour's walk returning to the starting point; here another, beginning smooth and broad and fair, was suddenly cut off by a belt of trees or by a deep pitfall, like a disused quarry; now one led back to the open while seeming to carry you deeper into the heart of the wood; and now another that looked as if it went straight to the Hall, ended abruptly at the river. Every hindrance that ingenuity could devise had made this Maze the most intricate of its kind; but Jessie, never pausing to think, never hesitating, never asking herself which was right, went boldly on, instinctively taking the only way that would have led her through.

At last, always climbing, she came to a small stone building of four rooms and two stories, standing half concealed in the trees.

A steep flight of steps led down to a door sunk below the level of the ground on which the building stood. Jessie ran down the steps lightly, wondering where she was and what was meant by the little house perched there on the height, so overshadowed by trees, and with such a strange meandering path to lead to it. She saw nothing but a low, strongly-barred oaken door, further secured by a huge chain fastened by a padlock. The key-hole had been stopped up, and there was not the smallest chink to let in the sunshine or to let out a sound. The smooth-built walls were unscaleable by man or beast, and the windows, if windows there were at all by which it was lighted, must be set towards the river. Altogether it was a place to prick the curiosity of the dullest, and the girl's unwonted breath of freedom seemed to have animated her into something brighter than her normal self, and to have awakened in her a sprit of girlish adventure which was by no means her usual characteristic. What was in this little house? She could see nothing on this the southern side, and to east and west were likewise only the same plain, smoothly-fashioned walls without doors or windows to give egress or ingress. Nothing to be seen but the black river below; this grim inscrutable erection; and the bare branches of the trees swaying and creaking in the fresh breeze blowing from the north.

Among these trees was one large yew, some of the boughs of which had stretched across the front of the little house where the windows were, and hung over the precipice—the black tree mirrored in the black flood. Panting, half afraid, prompted by some unfathomable instinct of discovery, Jessie climbed the yew and crept along the gnarled limb that grew so close to the front, its outer branches struck the panes at every moment with a sharp sound like a cry. Thus, lying there, stretched out like a panther along the bough, she was close against the window.

It was stanchioned fast without and grated within like the stronghold of a prison; the glass was thick with the accumulated dust and dirt of years; and the room into which she looked was dark as night. But surely her senses did not deceive her! Passing restlessly to and fro, like a wild beast pacing its den, she saw the dim outline of a creature; she could not tell what it was, whether man or beast, but a creature that sometimes moaned and sometimes growled, and then stood still as if to listen before it began that restless pacing up and down its den like a tiger in its cage. Once she thought it was a human being, for a white face was pressed up against the inner grating and she seemed to make out a pair of flaming eyes within their cavernous orbits, and long falling tresses of grey hair; she heard the grating too, shake with a sudden violence that made her start in her hiding-place; and it seemed to her as if this creature, whatever it was, had seen her and wanted to break its bars to get at her. But it was only a momentary terror. The defence-work was strong, and she knew that she was safe.

Presently, while she was watching with a horrible kind of fascination those flaming eyes, which she knew were watching her, she heard footsteps tramping through the wood; and, looking down from her hiding-place, saw old Ralph Rowsley coming up the path, carrying in one hand a tin full of what looked to her like some kind of food, and in the other a heavy bunch of keys. She saw him disappear down the steps; and then she heard him unlock the padlock, drop the clanking chain with care, unbolt the ponderous bars, and finally swing back the door, which was instantly bolted on the inside.

And as it swung, a voice, muffled and stifled truly, but a voice that froze the blood in her veins with speechless horror, it was so full of fury and despair, burst out with one sharp, sudden yell that was neither the cry of a human being nor the roar of a wild beast, but that seemed to have something of both, and that which was worst and most terrible of both.

She waited for no more, but light as a squirrel sprang to the ground, tearing her dress in her haste, and guided always by that strange instinct which stood her in stead of reason, took the true path through the Maze, and so found herself again at the point where the roads forked, and where she had taken that which had led her on to the track of a mystery of more terrible import than she could fathom.

She ran along the path opposite to that which she had taken before, with but one thought—to escape from Ralph. She had always had a strange dread of the old man who had always hated her, but this had now become a wild ungovernable fear. It was with the feeling of a hunted animal, and almost with the look and gait of one, that she scudded through the path so swiftly, so lightly, she scarcely stirred the crackling branches or the dry, crisp leaves. Finally her way led from the wood to an open meadow where sheep and cattle were grazing. She climbed the stile where the path ended, and ran for a few yards downwards, under the lee of the hedge; and then her senses failed her, and she sank into a swoon, which took her for the time from all fear and all oppression.

When she recovered the whole thing had become dark to her. Her brain, never fit to retain impressions long, had lost the recollection of all she had seen and heard in the Gazebo. Only the fact remained of a horror in which Ralph Rowsley was the chief actor, and where she was somehow implicated—at least to the extent of fear. She remembered nothing, neither of where she had been nor how she had come here. Her first thought was that she had been left here by her mother, and her first words called to the dead as if to the living. Then, by degrees, she came more fully to herself, and rubbed her eyes and looked about her.

Where was she? how had she come here? The sheep and cattle looked mild and friendly; the day was still at its height; the clouds were brooding, the wind blowing, the birds twittering, all the same as when she first went out. What had happened that she found herself, as if by enchantment, in the fields and not the house?

By slow degrees there came to her the image of Mr. Willoughby with his flowing silvery locks, his light grey eyes, and blue blouse open at the throat, bidding her paternally go out and take the air. As she remembered this, she had a sudden pang of self-reproach and fear lest she had trespassed on her patron's kindness, and stayed out longer than she ought. It was time she was at home; but which way to turn? Unknown to herself she was close to the bridge which spanned the river from the occupation-road[10] that led to Longmire Hall and the broad highway. If she kept down by the side of the hedge for a few rods further, she would come to a gate, and then her way would be clear. By chance she had turned downward when she crossed the stile and swooned; and her face being now set that way, she followed the hedgeside mechanically, and had reached the bottom of the field, when the sound of voices stopped her, and sent her crouching behind the bushes like a hare in her form.

One was the voice of Claude; the other she did not know, but it was the voice of a woman, and a young one. The two were talking earnestly together, but she did not know what they said. They spoke in a low tone and on subjects she did not understand; but as she looked through a gap in the hedge she saw what she did understand somewhat—Claude, her prince, the young god whom she worshipped with such humility of devotion, take the strange girl in his arms, press her warmly to his heart, and kiss her upturned face.

She saw no more; she knew nothing of what ailed her, only that a sharp pain struck through her heart as if she had been stabbed, and that she could scarcely breathe for the anguish she was in. Covering her eyes with her hands, she crouched closer still to the ground, longing for the power to bury herself in the earth and never see the light of day again. She did not cry nor moan nor reckon up her account anyhow; she was simply conscious of an intolerable pain, with a dumb wonder who and what had hurt her.

"My darling," then said Claude, "your promise gives me new life! If you will keep true to me, nothing can separate us. I have our future in my own hands—that future, my beloved, which will make earth a heaven!"

"I don't believe in heavens upon earth, but I shall be very glad to marry you if we have enough to live on; and I dare say we should be as happy as most people," said Lady Margaret quietly.

It was a cold response to the young man's fervour, but Lady Margaret prided herself on her common sense, and despised raptures and sentimentality as

10 A road built for the use of those occupying an area of land.

she despised sugar-plums and jelly. It was her way—a way most in harmony
with that queenly carriage, that royal kind of serene supremacy which had
first attracted Claude, and which still held him as the most beautiful grace
of the many the woman he loved possessed. It was always something to
overcome, always something to win; and Claude liked those women best who
were most difficult.

"Oh, my darling, how I love you!" he cried with a lover's self-abasement.

She smiled a gracious acceptance of his homage. She was Lady Margaret,
and it suited her.

"If I could place you on a throne and make the whole world worship
you, I would," said Claude.

"A satisfactory income would be more to the purpose at this moment,"
she answered.

"Ah, you mock me!" said Claude hastily. Then, as if he might have offended
her by his self-assertion, he added, "But laugh at me if it amuses you; I am
your slave, your dog; you may say or do with me what you like, my queen, if
only you will love me and do not desert me!"

"Shall I scold you for being so silly?" she said.

"If it will please you; anything that will make you happy," he answered,
kissing her hand. "You might kill me if it would do you any good; provided
always that you loved me!"

"And yet if we have to separate you will soon find some one to take my
place; and I yours, I suppose," said Lady Margaret, reasoning philosophically
on a remote hypothesis.

"Ah that is cruel!" he cried in real pain.

"Cruel? How can the truth be cruel? By the bye, who is that odd girl who
came down from the skies or up from the river, no one knows which, and
who nursed you so tenderly when you were ill? A victim like the rest?"

They were sitting under a cedar tree, on a bench placed there as marking
it of the Hall timber; their backs were against the bole, and they faced the
hedge and were concealed from the road.

"Jessie!" cried Claude, with a natural raising of his voice.

The poor girl's bewildered brain had caught nothing of the lovers' talk
that had been going on. All she knew now was that Claude, her prince,
called her by her name, that he wanted her, and that she must obey him.

She started up.

"Yes? You called," she said, suddenly appearing.

Lady Margaret gave a faint scream. Claude checked an oath that rose only
too readily to his lips.

"Who is this creature?" cried Lady Margaret haughtily, recovering her
self-possession and dignity with wonderful swiftness.

"How came you here, wretched creature?" said Claude angrily; to Lady
Margaret tenderly, "You need not mind her, Lady Margaret; it is only Jet.
Go home, Jessie!" he then said roughly, speaking to the girl as he would have
spoken to a dog. "What in heaven's name brought you here?"

"You called me," said Jessie, cowering close.

"Don't be a fool!—I did not call you," said Claude. "Why should I call you? What should I want with you, do you think! Go home, I say; you have no business here at all!"

Jessie drooped her head and raised her eyes from between the bright brown overhanging braids. Tears were behind rather than in them, which gave them a yet more pathetically yearning look. What had she done? Her prince had spoken to her roughly; as he had never spoken before. She had displeased him; she was to blame—she did not know how or why; only, if he was angry she must be to blame; but what was her fault?

She looked up penitent, patient, humble, asking forgiveness, suing for reinstatement. She did not justify herself so much as to say that Mr. Willoughby had sent her out to take the air. She was so utterly the slave, the creature, of the young man whom she had placed as a god before her, as to feel that even injustice was his right if he chose to be unjust. Who should withstand him? But she wanted him to forgive her before she went. She could not speak; and, indeed, what had she to say?

With the instinctive need of a mediator more in favour and more powerful than herself, she drew closer to Lady Margaret, from whom she would else have naturally shrunk, folded her hands in her childish way, and said pitifully; "I am sorry. Do you tell him so!"

"Is she all right?" asked Lady Margaret.

"No, she is half an idiot," answered Claude, angry at this interruption to his love-making—his first walk alone with his beloved. But his conscience smote him when he remembered that to this half-idiot was owing the possibility of his making love to Lady Margaret at all. So much grace, however, came to him from his shamed conscience as made him speak to her again, this time more gently.

"My good girl, I do not want you here," he said; "and you are wanted at home. They are waiting for you now, I know; so go at once and see that the kitchen fire burns well. That is more your style of thing than rambling about the fields and hedges like a maniac. There—go!"

"Then you are not angry with me!" cried Jessie, with a happy little sob. Her whole frame quivered with pleasure.

He laughed to hide his embarrassment. Her dog-like devotion embarrassed him when they were alone at home, without witnesses; before Lady Margaret, with her pride, her keen wit, and the gift of that conditional promise he had just won, it was maddening. Yet for the sake of Lady Margaret herself—now that he had had time to remember his gentlehood—he was forced to bear himself with the courage of good temper and to abjure the cowardice of brutality.

"Angry! no, you little fool!" he answered. "But I shall be if you don't go."

"Where"—she asked, looking round—"where am I?"

"Have you lost your senses? Why, where should you be but at the Hall gate!" said Claude, pointing backward with his hand; and Jessie, smiling, radiant, blissful, made a few steps onwards.

"I say!" called Claude, stopping her.

She turned round, her face irradiated with pleasure.

"Don't say up there that you have seen me," he said.

She shook her head emphatically.

"No, I will not," she answered; and went forward on her way.

"Is *that* the girl?" asked Lady Margaret disdainfully.

"Yes," answered Claude; and because he tried to speak indifferently, he had the air of wishing to conceal something; which embarrassed him all the more deeply, and roused Lady Margaret's haughty temper only the more readily.

"She is pretty," she said coldly.

"Do you think so?" answered Claude.

"Of course I do; don't you?" with an unpleasant little laugh.

"I? No, indeed! I should as soon think a doll pretty! She has neither intellect nor expression; she is a mere doll all through."

"But she nursed you well," said Lady Margaret, rasping the sore.

"Yes, like a faithful dog," was his answer.

And Lady Margaret both resented the comparison and was angry at the occasion. Though proud—who prouder?—she was not above the meanness of jealousy; and just now her whole soul was angry against Claude, the world, Jessie, and herself. Was it possible that she, Lady Margaret, had placed herself in a position where she had a cinder-wench for her rival? Granting the most absolute fidelity on his part, the very fact that a girl like Jessie should have dared to lift her eyes to the level of *her* lover's—should have presumed to worship what she honoured by her grace—annoyed and humiliated her. So that the immediate result of poor Jessie's devotion was a coolness between the young lovers which it cost Claude some trouble to destroy.

Meanwhile, Jessie flitted up the broad walk to the Hall. She had forgotten everything now but the last impression, that Claude was kind to her, and that she had been gifted with a secret to keep for him. She had been assigned her province to defend, and there was no fear of her failing her trust.

As she was going up the walk she met Ralph Rowsley shuffling towards the gate. The old dread of him that she had always had, came back on her with increased intensity. She felt her sight grow dim, her breath came short, when she saw him. It was as much as she could do to prevent herself from shrieking for help, and flying from him as from a hideous spectre. But—if he went through that gate he would see her prince, and that which he desired should be kept concealed would be betrayed. The fear of this conquered all the rest. To be faithful to her trust was the first thing she had to do—the one absolute necessity of life before which everything else must give way.

She stopped as the old man came up. Her face was as white as the face of the dead, and even Ralph's dull senses could see that she was trembling like a leaf where she stood.

"Wherever may you have been to?" he asked harshly; for it was as much a matter of surprise to him as it had been to Claude to see the quiet, home-keeping girl rambling in the grounds.

"Out!" said laconic Jessie.

"Well, a blind man could see that," he returned coarsely. "But what does 'out'"—mimicking her—"mean? What pranks have you been up to—hey, my lady? That whey-face of yours tells no good tales, I'll go bail."

He looked at her suspiciously as he came closer to her, and seized her arm in his hard gripe. Involuntarily he connected her strange presence in the grounds, her white face and visible trembling, with the unusual excitement, the anger, the fear, the incoherent mutterings, the pointings to the window of the Thing to whom he had gone on his daily duty of food and service. He laughed at himself and his suspicions a moment after. How could any one find the way through the Maze, so artfully masked as it was, so cleverly blocked at every turn?—least of all, a fool like this, with none of her five senses quite ripe?

But she was so unlike herself at this moment! Why had she stopped him? They were not on such terms as made it natural. And why did her teeth chatter as if she was half frozen? The day was fine enough, and warm for the time of year. Her eyes, too, looked wilder than ever, he thought, and her face was full of something unspoken—as if she had that to say for which she could not find words.

All this passed through his mind almost mechanically as he griped her arm, and stared with rude and insolent suspicion into her face.

For the first moment Jessie shrank at his touch, cowering from him like a beaten hound. Then she seemed to remember herself, and held herself upright and still.

"I want some potatoes," she said, with one of the most desperate efforts after intellectual creation she had ever made. The thought had come to her like inspiration; and truly, sad "sinking in poetry" as it was, in essential spirit it was an inspiration.

"'Taters?" cried Ralph; "the devil you do! And what's come o' them I brought in yesterday? If that's your way of going on the sooner the master knows of it the better. I'll have my cellar empty afore we know where we are, and not a penny's-worth will I buy, I promise you, if you don't see a skin till next summer-time. 'Taters, indeed! I'd like to 'tater you, that would I."

"Come and see if we have enough left," said Jessie, glancing back at the gate; and, with a surly oath, Ralph turned and went back with her to the house.

"Well, my child," said Mr. Willoughby kindly, when he met his favourite in the hall, "have you liked your walk?"

"I like the house better," said Jessie.

"Good domestic child! That is as it should be, and what I expected. Still, a little change cheers the spirits and beneficially affects the current of one's thoughts. Gadding is pernicious—nothing more so; but a little gentle exercise in the air is sometimes of use. And so I hope you have found it. And where have you been?"

She shook her head. "I don't know," she answered; "I lost myself."

"Let me help you. In the wood?"

"Yes," said Jessie.

"And then?"

The girl looked blank.

"The river," she then said, with an effort.

"Seen anything?"

"No," said Jessie.

Ralph looked at her, and she met his eyes. When she said "no," she told her untruth deliberately and with purpose. She had seen Claude Willoughby, but she was bound not to betray him. Now, however, when she met the old man's baleful look, the whole horror of the Gazebo came back to her as a picture, a thing she saw and lived in at the present moment. She shrieked, and flung out her arms as if to ward him off.

"Don't send me out again," she cried, rushing up to Mr. Willoughby and hiding her face against his knees as she threw herself at his feet.

"What has she seen?" asked Mr. Willoughby, turning his blanched face to the old man, while he laid his hands soothingly on her head.

"I can't tell," answered Ralph. "May be a ghost. They say one lives in the wood; and she looks scared enough for it. Such a natural as she is she ain't fit to be trusted by herself. Them fools always runs where they should not, and knows more than their betters!" he muttered angrily.

But Mr. Willoughby told him he was talking nonsense; and the old man went off in a rage, vowed to a still more bitter enmity towards the girl who had shrieked against him for fear, and warded him off with her hands as something horrible and unholy.

CHAPTER IV

DISGRACED

THINGS were beginning to look black for the young people. Henry Marsden's father was urging his son's marriage with Lady Margaret; whereof all the preliminaries were arranged save the consent of the two principals themselves, and which, when accomplished, would put the Earl in possession of a handsome sum of money and lay the coping-stone on the temple of the rich distiller's social fortune.

Henry, honestly in love with Marian and held by her in that tenacious grip which a handsome high-spirited, dark-haired woman with thin lips and a sharp nose has over a florid, fair, thick-necked and weak-willed young muscular Christian—her junior—made a clumsy but substantial resistance. Lady Margaret too, on her side—despising the man himself, disliking his family, holding those doubtful h's as moral crimes, and though not of the kind to marry poverty for love neither willing to sell herself to a plebeian however thickly lackered his yesterday's coat-of-arms might be with gold—gave her determined "No" to the Earl, and declined all further discussion on the subject.

But neither the distiller nor the nobleman accepted the refusal of the young people as a thing of consequence to the matter on hand; and continued to talk together of the marriage as an affair of which the essential circumstances were satisfactorily concluded, wanting only an insignificant formality to clinch the whole and close the account.

So there the triple love affair stood—a Gordian knot which seemed as if it was not to be undone by the cleverest fingers and the largest amount of patience extant, that must indeed be cut if it was not to hamper the free running of all the lives included. Three secret engagements; three solemn promises to marry in defiance of parental authority and the fittest kind of social arrangements; and, according to present conditions, with poverty more than probable in each of the three cases, unless fathers should prove less stern than relenting, and blessings all round should follow on universal disobedience:—at the best it was a black prospect, and a heavy price to pay for the sole reward of a love which, maybe, would not wear in any of those three cases, and a fancy that was sure not to last in one.

If the Earl had not been so keen after old Marsden's money, and if old Marsden had been content with the prizes he had already drawn out of Fortune's lucky-bag, and had not insisted on tying his son up to the aristocracy whether he liked it or no, matters might have gone on in peace and darkness for the next year or so. The young people found an unending fund of amusement in their oak-tree pillar-boxes and their stolen meetings. The false air of romance and adventure with which their "affairs" were invested, gave them additional zest; but it seemed as if the Fates had got tired of befriending them, and let that terrible Gordian knot slip to the front, where it must either be picked, cut, or submitted to as a life-long hindrance and impediment.

A council, not of war, was called; and the action determined on for Henry and Marian was flight—a runaway match, now at once, before time was a week older; else, who knows? that fair-haired, florid, and clumsy young man might be married unawares to the Earl's daughter, and Marian, like Claude, be left lamenting. It was all the fault of the fathers; why could they not leave well alone?

Example being contagious, and companionship in a doubtful plunge reassuring, Julius and Ellen decided on taking the same step. They would never have so good an opportunity; and by multiplying their disobedience each felt as if its sinfulness was shared, therefore that the punishment resulting would be lessened in proportion. Partly to make sure of a background in the day of need, and partly because they knew something of what was going on in his own life, the sisters took their brother into their confidence. It gave an air of respectability to their proceedings, which would not be without its effect when all became known; and they knew the value of fraternal sympathy and support.

But had it not been for Lady Margaret, and his passionate hopes there, when the rainbow should be caught and the rose-coloured clouds form themselves into a well-ordered human habitation, Claude would have opposed their design with all the energy of a proud man to whom *his* sisters are not as other men's sisters, but women whose smallest actions must be able to stand in the light of the sun and show no flaws within or without. He would have had no hand in their elopement, not he! He would have been more inclined to call out[11] his two intended brothers-in-law and stop their project by a bullet judiciously planted. As it was however, with his own affairs to be made so much the smoother by this little drama enacted by his sisters, he helped them with

[11] To challenge to a duel.

his countenance and advice. And the result of all those whispered conferences, those hopes and fears and tears and tremors was, that on one murky midnight at the end of February, four young people, escorted by a fifth as accessory, not principal, met at the bridge; got into a post-chaise; drove off to the nearest station; went straight up to London; and before noon the next day had got themselves made into honest men and wives, married by the law of the land and not to be unmarried again by less than the law. This was how they cut the Gordian knot which an unfriendly fate had tied for them; and when all was over, Claude came back to the Hall rather proud than otherwise of the part he had taken in the double event that had just come off.

Jessie knew nothing. Something from kindness, not to implicate so guileless a creature, not to deprive their father of so valuable a servant, and not to bring down sorrow on one who had been of so much good to them—also more for foregone despair at the uselessness of her stupidity if even they had told her—the runaways spared her the doubtful honour of their confidence. Hence, when the notes of explanation which the two girls had left pinned to their unruffled pillows were duly taken to him, and the parental philosopher's faculty of self-control was put to a ruder test than he had ever imagined possible, the poor child, against whom he turned in the first burst of his wrath, was able to say truthfully and humbly, "I saw nothing;" "I heard nothing;" "I knew nothing." And not the acutest cross-examination could elicit more.

But if she knew nothing, Claude knew all. He came back on the evening of the eventful day, and if he had not disdained the preliminary deceptions he disdained now all falsehood and subterfuge:—which would not, moreover, have advanced his cause, but would rather have damaged it the more.

When his father asked him blandly what he knew of this unhappy matter, he answered, "Everything;" his handsome head held high, his shoulders set square, and his eyes looking straight before him. Was not his own love involved in their delinquency? and for this he was prepared to do battle with any amount of parental authority, to forget that his father held the purse-strings, and even to overlook the fact that he had not finished his career at Oxford, one term of which he had moreover lost by the "ægrotat"[12] which was the result of his prowess on the ice. And until he had gone through that necessary introduction, what on earth could he do by way of shaping the rose-coloured clouds or catching the rainbow?

"And you stand there coolly, a young man six foot one in your shoes, and tell me that to my face?" said Mr. Willoughby, stepping back a few paces and looking at his son, with his picturesque head on one side, as if he was some show set up for his amusement—maybe a new specimen of man that was offering itself for philosophic inspection and accurate analysis.

"Why not, sir?" answered Claude haughtily. "Do you think that I, as a man and a gentleman, could bear to see the lives you made my sisters lead—the lives of servants, without friends, companions, pleasures, pursuits belonging to their age and condition? If you forget who we are, I cannot."

---

[12] Official recognition that the term's work was lost because of illness.

"Well spoken, my boy. Embody this in your first pleadings and you will carry the jury with you," said Mr. Willoughby with dangerous calmness. "Nevertheless, you speak like a foolish boy if a glib orator. Under my system of management your sisters were worthy women—after their own fashion; living for a purpose, doing their duty, obeying the higher law. Now what are they? The prey of two undesirable young men who have no principles of life beyond the lowest and most degraded; men who will bring them down to their own base level, and kill their souls. I say it, sir, and I mean it—kill their souls."

"They had better have their souls killed than their bodies," returned Claude irreverently. "We don't know much about the one, but we can measure the mischief done to the other. So far as I am concerned, it is a relief to me to know that my sisters are taken from their degraded life here and given to the care of men who will respect and treat them like ladies."

"They had better have their souls killed than their bodies kept in healthy subjection to the higher law? These young men are fitter caretakers of your sisters than was your father? Are these your opinions?" asked Mr. Willoughby innocently. And again he contemplated his son as a subject standing there for analysis and subsequent tabulation.

"They are," answered Claude stoutly.

"That being the case, my dear boy, I do not quite see that the eternal fitness of things is answered by your remaining longer under my roof," said Mr. Willoughby in the softest voice and smoothest manner at his command. "I believe in the soul; the soul as superior to the body; spirit before matter; and a man's household must be of his own faith. As a philosopher, setting forth a doctrine by the practice of my life, I cannot tolerate schismatics. Hence, will you oblige me by packing up your portmanteau and carrying your materialistic views to a more congenial atmosphere?"

Claude flushed to the roots of his hair. His father's words took him by surprise and found him unprepared. He had thought to play the champion of his sisters for his own future profit as well as their present defence; impressing that absurd old man belonging to them so strongly with the sense of his sins and the conviction of his iniquities, that when his own time came he would have no difficulty in bringing him round to his views respecting Lady Margaret. He had felt so certain that his father would receive this catastrophe of the elopement as the fitting punishment of his wickedness in making his daughters peel potatoes and scrape carrots, that he had forgotten to look at any other chance. He had only considered how he should best drive the nail home and bring the bitter waters of repentance with the greatest severity to those philosophic lips. When he found the tables turned so swiftly against him, he was bewildered for the first moment and violently angry for the second.

"Do you mean to say that you turn me out of the house?" he cried, snorting like a young war-horse.

"I dislike all unnecessary harshness, my dear boy," answered Mr. Willoughby blandly. "To say that your presence here is not in harmony with the eternal laws of fitness is one thing; to say, as you so coarsely put it, that you are turned out of the house, is another. It is important to have our terms precise."

"The two meet at the same point," said Claude disdainfully.

Mr. Willoughby bowed and spread out his hands, joining the finger tips together with nice adjustment.

"There we are agreed," he said. "They do meet at the same point. It is a pleasure that we need not discuss this clause."

"Then you mean what you say:—I am to go?" said Claude.

His father bowed again and separated his fingers.

"Undoubtedly, my dear boy. I can have neither pleasure nor profit in your presence here; and a man is a fool who surrounds himself with uncongenial elements. I suppose you must feel the same as myself. A son who has countenanced his sisters in their elopement with two of the least desirable young animals in the county, cannot feel at his ease in the presence of the parent he has deceived; nor can that parent feel either safety for the future or respect in the present for a son whose ideas of what is becoming to a man and a gentleman do not exclude treachery, craft, disobedience, and falsehood. I do not see that we shall get much good by further discussion;" he then added, with a gentle smile, "I have your confession of faith, you have my ultimatum; nothing remains now to be done but, as I said, pack your portmanteau and catch the seven o'clock train. If you are diligent and methodical you can do it; which will save you the inconvenience of sleeping at the local hotel, or the possible injury to your health of camping out in the woods."

What was to be done? Claude had played for a heavy stake, thrown, and lost; and all that now remained was to pay the penalty, and not to show how hard he had been hit.

"I thank you, sir, for your consideration," he said ironically to his father, who smiled blandly as was his wont, but did not answer, save by looking at his watch and saying softly; "One minute already gone. Are the beds at the Falcon aired?"

Whether the consequence of the delay might or might not be a damp bed at the Falcon, or a camping out *al fresco* by the Gazebo, Claude never stopped to inquire; but his first act when he got into his own room, the state bedroom which poor Jessie had prepared for him with such loving zeal, was to write to Lady Margaret to tell her of what had happened. It was no craven letter, be sure of that! On the contrary, it took up the position of a discarded son as if it had been some kind of distinction conferred for merit; and it insinuated all through that things would be better now with him than they had ever been. The craft of love wisely kept the means of that improvement in the background, and did not venture on too definite details; but the whole tone of the letter was so heartsome, so inspiriting, that Lady Margaret at the first caught the pleasant infection of rootless hope, and believed with Claude in the making of bricks without straw, and the ability to live like humming-birds on the honey of flowers and by the light of the sun. She came to her more sober senses in time; but for the present the intoxication was too sweet to be withstood even by her cool senses.

While Claude was writing, or rather just as he had finished, his letter to Lady Margaret, Jessie came quietly into his room. She had glided in so noiselessly he had not heard her, and only became conscious of her presence as he turned round and saw her standing by the couch folding his linen ready for packing.

She had not heard the discussion between Mr. Willoughby and his son, but she knew that mischief was about, and she instinctively guessed the form it would take. He was going away. The light was to be quenched; there would be no more day, only darkness and unending light. For all that she folded up his linen neatly and dexterously; her last feeling consecrated to his service—self-pity, active sorrow at his departure, left for the time when he should no longer want her help.

"You here, Jessie!" cried Claude, as he looked up from the table and saw her. But her spoke to her gently. In the desolation of the present moment he could not afford to reject even her humble sympathy.

"You are going away," said Jessie.

He shrugged his shoulders and laughed.

"Yes; you and the governor will have the place to yourselves," he said. "I hope you will enjoy it."

"No, I hate it!" said Jessie with energy.

He stared at the animated tone in which she spoke. It was so unlike the usual low-voiced, quiet-going girl he pleased himself by likening to his favourite Jet, that it seemed almost as if some one else was speaking.

"I hate it," she repeated, "now that they and you are gone."

"You are ungrateful; my father is kindness itself to you," said Claude, ready, with that pride of family which is not love, to take up arms for his father if he so much as fancied that any one slighted him. He himself might condemn and oppose him, but no one else should.

"Yes, he is kind; but you will be away," she repeated still folding the linen.

"I do not see what difference that can make to you," said Claude haughtily.

She lifted her eyes to him, but did not answer. Then she left the couch and her work and went over to him.

"Take me with you," she said, standing before him; her hands clasped in each other. "The place here has been full of noises to-day; full of things that move and whisper; full of blood. Take me with you. I will be your servant; you may do what you like with me. Only let me be with you!"

"You are mad!" cried Claude angrily. "Do you know that what you are saying is an unwarrantable freedom? Only that you are such an idiot, and do not half understand what you see or say, I would be very angry with you—perhaps never speak to you again!"

The tears slowly gathered to her eyes. She sighed deeply.

"I have offended you again!" she said in a weariful, hopeless way. "But I would die for you if I might!"

"Yes, yes, I know that you are a good girl; as good a girl as can be got," he returned rather more kindly. The humility, the self-abasement of her devotion, touched him; and she was beautiful, whatever he might choose to say to Lady Margaret. "If you were not so good," he continued, "you could not say such a thing to me as you have. You would know too well how it might be taken."

"It means just itself," said Jessie simply, looking at the young man plead-
ingly.

He laid his hand on her shoulder.

"My good girl, you ask an impossibility!" he said; "what, if I were to grant
it, would be your destruction."

"I should not care," interrupted Jessie.

"And make me a scoundrel," added Claude.

"Ah!" she sighed, and covered her face with her hands; then turned away and
made no farther effort.

She had laid bare her poor little timid soul, and it had been ill looked on.
Now she had nothing more to do than to help, to serve, to bear. Only when all
was ready, with her hand on the door which she was about to open for him,
she turned round and said wistfully—looking into the hard face of her prince
with her own full of the dumb yearning that gave it so much pathos—"If you
want me you will send for me, will you not?"

"Yes," he said a little impatiently. "But that is not very likely."

She drooped and shivered. Oh, why was she not strong and clever, and
so could be of use to him! But she did not speak. She opened the door,
stood aside to let him pass; and without one last look or word to her the
heir of the house strode out into the darkness of the winter night, disgraced
and discarded.

"Now you are my only child!" said Mr. Willoughby to Jessie as she came
into the Hall, bringing the philosopher's favourite cup of fragrant steaming
coffee. "You at least will not desert or disappoint me. You will never fail
me!"

"You will take the others back some day; they are you own—I am not," said
poor Jessie, trembling.

"No, good child, never! And you are my own; they are not. The children
of the spirit rank before those of the flesh; and you, my daughter of adoption,
stand nearer to me now than the discarded daughters of nature."

"They will be sorry," said Jessie. Taking her patron's hand in hers, she
knelt at his feet. "And they will be forgiven," she added, looking up into his
eyes prayerfully.

He stroked her hair fondly.

"That will depend on you, my child," he said. "Their future will hang on
you. Don't question me now. Be content to let the riddle stand unsolved for
the present. Be content to know that you are my child, that I love you, and that
I have placed my last trust in humanity in you!"

He said this just as Claude, walking down the road on the other side of
the Mortey, heard something that sounded like a suppressed wail, and saw a
dim light flicker in the windows of the Gazebo;—the "corpse light" of which
he had heard, the spectral shriek at which he had always jeered, but that now
made his breath come short, and his heart beat as he was ashamed to think a
man's heart could for superstitious fear.

CHAPTER V

IN THE PRESENCE OF DEATH

THE time passed, as all time must pass, whether with fleet feet or lagging. Nothing now stood between the philosopher and that perfect peace which is created by a desert; and his soul was so far satisfied—or ought to have been—in that he had no domestic crosses to carry. Jessie was what she had always been—incomparable in industry, unruffled in personal sweetness, supreme in household deftness. There was no need to call her in from gooseberry picking in January; to give her grave warnings of the sin lying in gadding to the garden; to preach to her on the especial value of doing her domestic duty faithfully. She was perfect in all this; and every day saw Mr. Willoughby more entirely delighted with the treasure he had picked up out of the dust, the flower he had gathered from the hedge on that bright first of May, nearly a year ago now.

But every day found poor Jessie more entirely distressed. She was grateful for her own place; none more so; but she was miserable in feeling that she had taken that of others; most of all the place of the two who, if they had been the elder sisters of Cinderella, had been elder sisters whose superiority had been accepted as a righteous ordinance, and submitted to with so much love as made submission a privilege and obedience a grace. Now that they were away in such hopeless disfavour, while she was here to receive all that ought to be theirs, she felt a usurper instead of a subject and a traitress in spite of herself.

Ralph Rowsley too, counted for something in her discomfort. The man was a surly, case-hardened old sinner, whose conscience was seared into insensibility, and whose humanity was contracted to the smallest point possible for a man to live with; but he was faithful to the family. He was over sixty years of age now, and he had been with them ever since he was a lad of seven; hired first to scare the crows from the corn. As a young man he helped the then Mr. Willoughby in his unhallowed scrapings and cleanings of the bones of small creatures; and as an old man himself he humoured the present in his craze against hired service and for garden ground delivered up to chickweed and dandelions—helping him too, in some other things which it would have been more seemly, as well as to the advantage of all the actors, if they had been ordered differently.

Naturally he had carried on his love to the children; after the manner of ancient servitors who have grown to consider the family their own, and as if they had more than the right of fee-simple in the estate. Though he grumbled at them he was proud of them, and thought them the finest set of young people going, and deserving of far better treatment than they got. He was sorry when the young ladies ran away, demeaning themselves like country wenches ashamed to face the parson; and yet who could blame them? Young people will be young people, try as hard as you will to put old heads on to their shoulders; and if their father had lived as he should have done, with a responsible set of servants and the Hall kept like a gentleman's house and not like a place fit only for pigs and heathens, this would never have happened; and they would have been married from home in veils and flowers like others of their degree. So he excused them, talking to himself while he foddered the cow and fed the chickens; and sometimes when he threaded the Maze he would say, "Poor things! poor things," quite compassionately; at odd moments of softness varying it to, "Poor lady, it's well she's not here to see it all!"

But if he delighted in the young ladies he adored Master Claude. After all, ladies or no ladies, the sisters were only women; and women according to Ralph were but poor trash at the best. But Master Claude, he was different! There was a man if you like! so high and haughty, and holding his head like a prince—so clever in fishing and shooting, and all sorts of games—one of the right sort; no danger of his wasting his youth among beasts' bones, or making systems of life that would not work when they were made and led only to messments like these!

The old man was furious when Claude was dismissed. Had he known what was going forward he would have used the influence he possessed over Mr. Willoughby—and it was influence not to be despised and never withstood—to have softened the parental decree, and have kept the young heir in his place. But perhaps it was because he knew where old Ralph was at this moment; also his probable views on the question; that Mr. Willoughby had taken time by the forelock, and banished his son in the absence of the only man who could have pleaded effectually for him.

Ralph, unable to mend matters for "his own," revenged himself on the usurper. It was no claim to his respect that Jessie was industrious, quiet, obedient, home-staying. In his eyes she was only a beggar's brat picked out of the mud and set in high places, a cinder-wench wearing the crown belonging to her betters. Besides, he resented that action of fear and repulsion. It puzzled him for the one part and offended him for the other. If it had a meaning, then the dark labour of years was undone and the dead had come to life again. And should it be suffered that a stranger like this should have found out the secret which not even the acutest had suspected? If, on the contrary, it had no meaning save personal distaste, then it was an affront for which Ralph Rowsley was only abiding his time to avenge. In any case he was biding his time, and he was not one to weary of lying in ambush. There was a dogged pertinacity of patience about the man that made lying in ambush pleasant to him. He was by nature a hunter, and he enjoyed running down his prey.

Meanwhile he made the poor girl's life a burden to her; terrifying and ill-treating her at his pleasure; she bearing all with the faithful humility that was her characteristic, making no complaint and as little remonstrance; her whole strength concentrated on the endeavour to do according to her patron's will, to make him comfortable, and to put in faithful little words of praise or pleading for the absent whenever the opportunity occurred. But if she made no complaint she none the less suffered; and under the joint conditions of fear and sorrow became so thin and worn, that not even spoonfuls of nettle tea administered every three hours could give her a colour, bring back her appetite, or as Mr. Willoughby phrased it, put a sufficiency of adipose tissue on to her osseous framework. If he could have removed Ralph and brought back the banished, the girl would have bloomed into health like a flower taken out into the sunlight from the dark; but failing these remedial measures nothing touched her; and, indeed, how should drugs benefit a spirit so oppressed and so tormented as hers?

"You think yourself fine sitting there with your borrowed plumes, like a jackdaw strutting it among the peacocks," said Ralph one evening, as he brought in the milk and found Jessie in the kitchen sewing.

This kitchen was a huge rambling old place as befitted the mansion to which it belonged; but it wanted fires and feasting, many lights, and a crowd of people to enliven its dim recesses. With a handful of sticks in the cavernous grate, one single candle on the huge oak-table, and one slender girl as its sole inmate, it looked terrifying and ghastly in its extent.

"I have done my work," said Jessie, glancing down at her dress. It had been a gown belonging to Marian, and was the first given to the girl when she came. She had worn it for her "afternoon" ever since; and she was fond of it from association. She had had it on that afternoon when Mr. Willoughby had bidden her take the air, and she had climbed the yew-tree by the Gazebo; and she had torn it when she jumped to the ground; which had been a grief to her at the time, and was still one. It was a pretty dress enough; dark blue striped in a lighter colour, and not common in those parts.

"You've done your work, have you?" answered Ralph, setting down the milk and glaring at the girl viciously. "A tramp like you ought never to have done your work. If I'd my way you'd work till you dropped and got up again. That's how I'd treat a whey-faced cuckoo-bird like you, my lady. Jessie this, and Jessie that, and Jessie everything; I'd Jessie you! 'Afore you should have turned the rightful owners out of their home, and have put yourself in their place, I'd have soon shown you the bottom bed of the Mortey, that would I; and good riddance of bad rubbish, say I."

Jessie did not answer. Never loquacious, her deadly fear of her tormentor checked even her spare speech of ordinary use. She only turned paler than usual, and trembled as she shrank back round the table as if to put a barrier between her and him. She dared not leave the kitchen; for Mr. Willoughby had certain hours in the day which he held sacred to study or meditation; and this was one of them. His daughters had been irreverent enough to say that they were hours when he simply slept; but let him use them as he might, they were taboo; and even Marian, who had braved him more than any other person had done, had found herself bound to respect them.

"Oh! you needn't slink and cringe like a dog!" said Ralph. "I'll not dirty my fingers with you, at least not yet. But as I'm a living man to-night, you'll fall into my hands at the last. I know it; and what I know always comes to pass."

"I am sorry I have offended you so much," answered Jessie with a frightened stare.

She too felt that what he said would come to pass, and that she should be his victim at the last—reserved for what fate?

"No, you have not offended *me*," said Ralph with false magnanimity. "I'd have forgiven that fast enough. A man as is a man at all—a man like me—wouldn't care much for anything a bit of a brat like you could say or do. No, it isn't me, but it's the others! What I can't forgive is that you should take the place as is not yours, that you should wear them dresses, live where you've no right, and oust the real ones from their own. It is because, as I say, you are a jackdaw among the peacocks, and a cuckoo as has ousted the true birds, that I'm your enemy, and that I've got an account to square that'll go hard and heavy against you when it's paid in. That's all I have to say, and it's plain."

"I have not ousted them!" said Jessie with something like energy. "They went, and I did not know. It was not me who sent them. They went."

"They went and they went; well, and don't I know that they went?" retorted Ralph; "but why did they go? And why didn't you go along with them? You knew what would come of it when the thing got blown. Why have you stayed here to carney the master and get his money from him, and be dressed like a lady, all in high feather and favour, when his own may be standing in London streets starving this very blessed night! I hate to see you there when I think of it!" he added with intense bitterness; "staying here on their ruin, as one may say; and as for the master, I could have done all for the master, and a sight better than you!"

"I would have gone if they had told me," said Jessie.

"I don't doubt you; with Master Claude," he sneered. "Oh! I saw the eyes you made at him, and the court you paid him. No fear! If some folks were blind others weren't! I knew your game, and marked it close enough!"

"It is false!" said Jessie, roused into sudden anger.

She scarcely knew the exact meaning of the old man's words, but she did know that he meant something evil connected with her prince, and she gave him the lie at a venture, on principle, not fact.

"So! you can wake up like any other rowdy!" cried Ralph. "I always thought there was the grain at the core. I knew you were not raked up out of the gutter for nothing, and now I've proved it. No matter. It all adds one; and the score won't run for ever!"

"You ought not to speak so of him," said Jessie.

She was defending her lord, and in her defence of him forgot her own fear.

"And you stand there and speak for him as I've carried in my arms, and given his first teaching in shooting to—you, a beggar girl from the streets, and I next thing to his father!" shouted Ralph.

"You shouldn't talk so of him," repeated Jessie still flushed and angry.

"Go on! go on!" said the old man. "It won't last for ever! I know a place where I'll put you some day—a nice little tidy house of four nice little tidy rooms, and a quiet old lady to wait on, where there'll be no fine young gentleman to make eyes to, and no young ladies to wear's dresses and make believe at sisters to them as you ain't fit to black their shoes! That's what it'll be before you're a year older, mark my words."

The bell rang. Mr Willoughby's sacred hour was over.

"Oh, yes! go after the money bags!" sneered Ralph as she was hurrying away. "If you don't feather your nest out of all this stramash,[13] it won't be for not trying!"

And with this he shuffled out of the kitchen, elated to feel that, as he expressed it, he had "given it to her well," and "spoilt her sleep for that night."

"Jessie," said Mr. Willoughby, "I am solitary without you. Bring your work here, child, and come and sit with me."

"Yes," said Jessie, trembling at the prospect of having to go back to that lonely kitchen, or perhaps tenanted with something that was worse than solitude.

It was day by day and night by night becoming a more terrible thing for her to go about that ghastly, dark, deserted house. Her imagination was wakening up into painful activity, and she peopled the dim passages and gloomy rooms with all sorts of weird shapes and horrible shadows. Wherever she turned she expected to see the wrinkled brown malicious face of Ralph, with its thatch of stubbled hair, its unshaven chin, its small ferret eyes, with that hideous scowl upon it which frightened her as much as did his words; and with him a Something, she never quite knew what, but Something the very vagueness of which was its deepest horror, Something that looked at her, and tried to get at her, and tossed its grey hair, and growled; and that would get at her some day—she knew that it would! But she showed nothing to Mr. Willoughby of either fear or reluctance, and taking up her miserable little candle went back through the long passages to the black kitchen for her work, as she was told to do; when there barring the door with trembling fingers, afraid to look behind her, and feeling that she had barred Ralph and that dreadful Something within, not without.

"I like to have you with me, my child," said the philosopher a little tremulously, after she had settled herself to her work near him; it was nothing more æsthetic than darning his woollen socks. "Your quiet presence soothes me. Your hands are always busy and your tongue is never wagging. You fulfil all my ideas of a woman—silent, humble, affectionate, industrious, obedient. What more can a man want?—and the daughter of a lady too!"

He looked at her fondly, his light grey eyes red and moist. For in truth she had replaced wholly and entirely in his affections the daughters he had lost; and he had but one hope and wish now connected with her, which he was considering how he should best carry out.

Jessie, never glib of speech, looked up at him gratefully when he spoke. If she loved the girls, and worshipped Claude, she venerated Mr. Willoughby, and held herself as much his absolute property as if she had been his slave and he her lord by law, or his daughter in a time when fathers had the right of life and death over their children. It was this unconditional submission which pleased him so much in her, and which set him thinking to-night—as so many nights before—what he could do to best mark his appreciation of her, his displeasure with his own, and yet not ruin Claude.

The upshot of these cogitations was, that the local lawyer was sent for, with a couple of witnesses; and that in their presence Mr. Willoughby made a short

[13] Noise, riot, confusion.

and decisive codicil by which he revoked every other will, and left everything he possessed absolutely and unconditionally to Jessie May Willoughby, his adopted daughter and his most dutiful child: reserving only a small pension for Ralph Rowsley, in whom, said the document, "I still place my trust as of old."

After which he said that he should rest better, and get rid of that pain about his heart that had troubled him for so long both by day and night; but chiefly at night. When he ought to be sleeping like any other wholesome creature, he would be awake counting the long hours as they droned by; thought and that gnawing pain banishing all repose, save such as embodied itself in dreams that were worse than his waking thoughts.

Had he really bought his philosophic life and adherence to abstract principles at too high a price? Perhaps, all things considered, it would have been better if he had consented to a little degradation of the ideal; if he had faced his misfortune like a man; if he had accepted social conditions as he found them, and not forced his peculiar ideas of womanly duties on the daughters of a county family, with whom the activities of ladyhood certainly do not include cooking dinners in the kitchen, or making a dwelling room of the hall to save fires and economize labour.

Now, however, if he had sinned he was suffering, and if he had guessed the great problem of worthy living wrongly, he was paying the forfeit. His health suddenly gave way. The strange inactive life he had led, and now his unspoken but ceaseless sorrow, told upon him; and he was drawing to his end. The doctor, when he was sent for, shook his head like a man who had come upon the worst; and after a brief examination told his patient bluntly enough, that his life was not worth a week's purchase, and that what he had to do in the way of settling his affairs must be done now at once. His heart was seriously diseased; and who knows when the fatal moment will come to a heart organically gone?

"Your daughters are at their husbands' homes," said the doctor by way of hint. "If you have any arrangements to make with respect to them, I am glad to know that they are handy."

"Thank you, no," said Mr. Willoughby blandly. "They have elected, and they must abide by their choice. I consider it no amelioration of their fallen condition that their husbands' fathers have received them. It is but one link the more, and the stronger, in the chain by which they have bound themselves to spiritual and moral degradation. I would rather know them poor and living for a principle than rich and without a central point of attraction to higher things."

The doctor made no answer. He was a hard-hearted, unsentimental kind of person who thought the golden calf a respectable idol enough and one that it behoved all men to worship in reason; and he had no sympathy with philosophic heroics assuming greater things than the neighbours cared for. Besides, it did not enter into his professional duties to plead for Regans and Gonerils;[14] or to convince an obstinate old man of his folly, or even of his wickedness, for the matter of that! When he had written his prescription and given his instructions his duty was at an end, and he must leave the owner of Longmire Hall to find his

---

[14] The rapacious daughters of King Lear.

own way out of the wood in which he had lost himself; "a worse maze than the one in which that poor tramp was lost!" thought the doctor, who liked straight roads and easy travelling.

Saying only, with emphasis:

"Remember what I have told you, my dear sir; with care you may live many years yet, but you are in imminent danger all the same," he took his leave, and Mr. Willoughby was left to his own reflections.

He reflected long and closely, and then he took his determination. It was to write to Claude, tell him of his illness, and summon him home without delay. If he was histrionic he was not an intentional humbug; and though he was a philosopher he was also a father, and he loved his son while he disapproved of him.

His letter found Claude in the depths. Lady Margaret had broken the spell which her lover's vague hopes had cast about her, and saw things now with the clear eyes of common sense and a young woman used to luxury and not willing to forego it. She saw that the rainbow was yet to be caught, and that rose-coloured clouds, how beautiful soever they are to look at, are but indifferent material out of which to construct a human habitation. Wherefore she had written to the young man with unalterable firmness, and had told him that, unless he had something more tangible to offer than the delightful hopes which had no foothold in fact, their dream of love must come to an end, and they must accustom themselves to the waking.

In face of such a letter as this, the young man was powerless. He was both too proud and too much in love to ask this high-born lady to descend to poverty, and mayhap to peeling potatoes and scraping carrots, after the manner of his sisters. She said that she still loved him; should always love him, though she declined to be hampered; and he did his best to find comfort in the assurance.

It was a cold comfort at the best; and he felt as if his heart was broken. He said that it was when he answered her letter; but hearts do not break easily, and Claude's was young and tough. All the same, he was miserable enough, poor boy, and turned over in his mind all manner of schemes whereby he could get that golden dross without which Lady Margaret would be lost to him for ever; not shrinking at the thought of getting it even by a crime, if he could do no better. He would not have preferred the crime, but he would not have abjured it if it would succeed and not be found out.

He was in this mood when he received his father's letter telling him of his dangerous condition, and bidding him come home at once if he would see him alive and repair the fractured structure of his fortunes.

No time was to be lost. As fast as steam and horseflesh could take him, the young man was on the road to Longmire Hall, caring less for his father than for the progress of events, and caring not at all that he should live. Claude was not a Willoughby for nothing; and if father and grandfather had used their intellects in their own way, he used his to his liking; and in his world reverence was an unknown quantity, while the desire for pleasure, for money, and to take his place among the county families according to his birth, equalled in intensity his desire to make Lady Margaret his wife; she indeed representing the culminating point, the pinnacle of his temple.

Ralph came to meet him as he drove up to the door.

"It's a sight good for sore eyes to see you here again, Master Claude!" said the old man. He was not much given to sentiment, but he felt a something unusual about his throat, and his ferret-like eyes looked watery and indistinct.

"Thanks," said Claude haughtily. "How is my father?"

"Bad; as bad as can be," answered Ralph. And with an involuntary impulse Claude looked round the place and thought, "When this is mine, then Lady Margaret!"

The old man saw his look and understood it, at least in part.

"Yes, Master Claude," he said. "It will soon all be yours, and then we shall see the old place kept as it should be, and them as has no call to be here sent to where they came from."

"I hope it will not be mine so soon as you seem to say," said Claude coldly, and passed into the Hall.

"I like it! I like it" said old Ralph, rubbing his hands when the youth had gone in. "I like to see him so proud and high! It's the good old Willoughby blood, and keeps things as they should be! And I like him to flounce and flout as he does, and me able to whisper that in his ear as should bring his head to my feet, and I with the whiphand over him for life. I wouldn't use it though—no, I wouldn't use it; but it warms me to feel I have it in my power, and that I'm master let who will be called owner!"

At the foot of the stairs stood Jessie. So little place did she hold in his memory that Claude had forgotten her in the tumult of hopes and fears which had possessed him since he had received his father's letter. When he saw her, she came before him as painfully as always does come an unpleasant fact in one's life laid aside for a time, when we are forced to take it up again.

"Well," he said coldly; "you are still here."

She looked at him with the old dumb love in her shining eyes.

"I am glad you have come," she whispered, clasping her hands. "He has been wanting to see you."

Claude laughed unpleasantly.

"If he wanted me to so much, why did he send me away?" he said.

Jessie laid her hand on his arm.

"Let bygones be," she pleaded. "Make him what you wish now. He only wants to love you; you are his own. And then, there are the others."

"You don't know him as well as I do," Claude answered bitterly. "My father never forgives."

"Yes, yes, he will forgive you," she said. "Go, and see if he will not!"

She stood aside in the old humble way to let him pass; but her words and manner had touched him. He knew that she had worked for and not against them, and though he was too proud to be grateful he was not brutal. Again, as once before, he took her hand in his and pressed it.

"You are very good, Jet!" he said, almost tenderly; "the best little girl in the world!"

The happy eyes brightened like twin stars; the pretty mouth unclosed to the old sweet smile that had been so long absent from it now; she quivered with dumb pleasure, and could scarcely repress a cry of joy; and again, her former lesson forgotten, she raised his hand to her lips and kissed it. She was his dog, his slave, his sacrifice, whom no harshness could repel, no coldness chill.

"Good Jet!" he said, and took her in his arms and kissed her; then placed her on a chair bewildered, intoxicated, almost faint with pleasure—indeed, almost in pain from its excess.

Claude sighed as he turned away. If only Lady Margaret had been like Jet—if only she had loved him as this poor faithful creature did! But no; if she had loved him in this craven way of hers, if she had been in any sense other than she was, supreme, self-controlled, haughty, superior to himself all through, he should not have worshipped her as he did. It was the best as things were, and he was glad that she was not as Jessie was. It was a transfer of humility and worship; Jessie rendering to him what he rendered to Lady Margaret, and neither worshipper repaid in kind nor in degree. And thinking all this he entered his father's room, and at the first glance saw that he had entered into the presence of death, and that before many days had come and gone he should be indeed owner of Longmire Hall.

CHAPTER VI

AT DEAD OF NIGHT

"I HAVE sent for you, Claude, because I am ill," said Mr. Willoughby, in a voice that took a slightly exaggerated tone of feebleness.

He was weak and ill sure enough, but not quite so weak, if to the full as ill, as he wished it to appear; thinking to better trade thereby on his son's natural pity. He had been careful too, to have all things in picturesque ordering, and to preserve the histrionic harmonies to the last. As he laid there in the state bed of the state room—his flowing silver hair freshly combed and smoothed—his bright blue woollen shirt making a point of colour that told well against the dull crimson of the heavy hangings—Plato and Aristophanes, and Horace and Berkeley on the bed beside him, his chosen friends and companions—truly, he looked a philosopher waiting for his end with the dignified calmness befitting his profession!

"Yes, sir, I am sorry to see you suffering," said Claude coldly in spite of himself.

He had always disliked his father's love of dramatic effect, and he could not conquer his displeasure now.

"You have given me much pain, my son," said his father. Then he paused, waiting for a sign of repentance.

Claude could only repeat his formula; "I am sorry, sir."

The philosopher caught at the words. "Are you sorry?" he said briskly for one so ill. "If so, no more need be said. All that the Supreme Being Himself demands is repentance; shall frail man want more? If you are sorry, then you acknowledge your misdeed; and if you acknowledge it, then you must confess to the righteousness of your punishment. Is not that logical?"

Claude inclined his head. He did not care to argue the point in his father's present failing state; besides, he took the words to mean the past not the future; and he was quite content that his temporary banishment should be regarded as the fitting mark of reprobation for his iniquity in helping in his sisters' disobedience.

Of course it must have been unpleasant to have the girls kick over the traces in such an uncompromising manner; and he could quite understand his father's anger—now. For, after all, he was a father, if not fit to be one; if he had his crotchets he had also his virtues; and he had certainly been always kind if queer to him, Claude;—which counted for something in the young man's estimate of things.

All these thoughts passed through him as he simply bent his head, looking at the bloodless face before him; the near presence of the death drawing closer and closer as the moments flew, influencing and softening him.

"But I have forgiven you my boy. I have made a way of escape for you from the consequences of your fault," continued Mr. Willoughby. "I am your father; you are my son; and I would not die at enmity with you, nor yet injuring you."

"Dear father! I am sure you would not," returned Claude.

"I have made my will," said Mr. Willoughby.

"Yes?" said Claude.

"Your sisters are excluded," he went on to say. "I could not reconcile it with my ideas of right to give my money to two young men, to whom, had I the power, I should have assigned lodgings in the county gaol with hard labour on the treadmill."

"Surely you judge them a little harshly, sir," said Claude. "They may not be quite up to your standard, which is a high one, but they are not so bad as that; and they treat my sisters well."

Mr Willoughby's eyes brightened up with a sudden fire.

"What you call treating well I should hold to be death and destruction," he said with feverish energy. "But that is a subject we have discussed before, I believe; we need not go over old ground. Time is passing, and I have much to say. Besides," he added petulantly, dropping his high manner and measured speech like a mask, "the doctor said I was not to excite myself."

"I am sure, sir, I should be very sorry if you did yourself harm in any conversation with me," said Claude.

He might not feel disposed to grieve inordinately for the loss of a life he held of not much good to any one; but that was different from being the proximate cause of a father's death.

"Let us go back to our point;—your sisters are excluded," said Mr. Willoughby, making a strong effort over his increasing weakness, and still retaining the artificial manner which long habit had made almost second nature to him.

Claude made a gesture of assent. He was not inclined to remonstrate. It was too late; and he could make up the deficiency and give what his father ought to have left. He rather liked the feeling of having to translate justice into generosity.

There was a long pause.

"Call Ralph and Jessie," then said Mr. Willoughby. "Both must hear what I have to say."

It did not take long to summon both; and soon the surly old serving-man and the devoted dog-like girl stood with the son of the house by the death-bed of the master.

"Come here, child," said Mr. Willoughby, holding out his hand to Jessie. "Give me your hand."

She put her hand in his.

"My boy, yours."

His son too, obeyed.

Mr. Willoughby joined them. "Claude," he said, "I have provided for you. I have left every fraction I possess to her; but you must marry her. Then it will all be yours, and more beside. There is no better girl on earth. She is all that a woman should be, and I have blessed you twice in making her your wife and my heiress."

"My wife!" cried Claude tearing away his hand. "Never!"

"Then you are a beggar!" said Mr. Willoughby, and fell back on his pillow exhausted.

Presently he opened his eyes, and surveyed the astounded group. Claude had turned away covering his face in his hands. Ralph was standing a step or two back, his clenched fists drawn up to his breast, and his eyes glaring at Jessie. Jessie herself, the cause of all this turmoil, frightened, confused, understanding nothing save that she was in some way exalted, and that Claude her prince was cast down, was looking now at the dying man whose forehead she was bathing, now at Claude, unable to help in the coil that was about them both; wishing that her good, kind patron had left her to her fate, whatever it might have been, and that she might suffer if only that beloved other should be made glad.

"Claude!" sighed the dying man feebly.

His son came back to the bedside.

"Obey your father; do as I have commanded. Take the goods offered to you by the gods, and be thankful," he said, in faint, interrupted sentences.

"Father! the task is too hard, the price too heavy!" pleaded Claude.

"Foolish boy! You prefer beggary to a wife like that; a wife without a fault—loving, obedient, humble, industrious—everything a woman should be, and the owner of all—all—all!"

"It is impossible;" groaned Claude.

"Master!" growled Ralph, "are you mad?"

"No, faithful old man; you have your portion and your work; care for *her* as you have done: I leave her still to you, poor soul! poor soul! But, Claude, listen! I have beggared you without Jessie. I did it for the best; swear that you will take her; swear it, Claude!"

"Father, I cannot!" said Claude. "It is life without anything to make it worth having!"

"Boy, you are killing me! swear!" gasped the dying man.

"Have pity on me, father! At this last moment relent and soften your terms!" The white face changed to a dull and ghastly grey.

"Too late!" he muttered. "If I have done wrong, God forgive me!"

His head sank back; his glassy eyes turned; his breathing became hard and laboured; one last struggle, one last sigh, and then there was an end of that tangled mesh of good and evil that had made John Willoughby's life.

"I did not swear!" said Claude with a strange, superstitious feeling as he closed the eyes of the dead. "And the will must be destroyed."

"Ay," muttered Ralph; "and more than the will!"

If any one had wanted to see exemplified the impotence of legal right as against human strength on the one hand, and weakness on the other, he would have seen it to its fullest extent now. In point of legal fact Jessie was the absolute owner of everything. She could have turned out Ralph, the servant of a lifetime, and Claude, the son of the dead, and have taken possession of everything. All was hers, down to the most cherished bits of household furniture; if indeed there were any such in a home that had been hated like a prison. Be that as it may, she was legally supreme; and the two standing there were nowhere.

So at least said the law. Human strength ruled it otherwise. Claude was her absolute master; Ralph her potent enemy. A frightened, ignorant girl without friends, without knowledge of her resources, and without the wish to use them had she even known them, how could she withstand these two? As well might the dove be expected to withstand the kite and the hawk, if put into a gilded cage called her own, where these others nested also. Nominally, by the terms of the will, this poor quondam beggar girl was mistress of the whole of the Willoughby wealth; practically she was Claude's slave and Ralph's victim.

They were still standing in the death-room, when Ralph, turning to Claude, said eagerly: "Are you minded to abide by it, Master Claude?"

"No," said Claude; "Jessie herself would not wish it. She has too much sense of duty—of her duty to me—to accept anything so unjust. Would you, Jet?"

"What need of asking a donnet[15] like that!" cried Ralph, impatiently. "She knows nothing of herself. You can make her say or sign what you've a mind to; but it may be a dance to a different tune if others get hold of her, and make her sign and say what *they've* a mind to. That's what you've got to provide against, Master Claude, and if I was in your shoes I'd do it effectual."

"If anything has been given to me I ought not to have, take it," said Jessie going up to Claude.

"I shall," said Claude emphatically.

He almost laughed at the idea of Jessie making an ingenuous gift of that which was hers, only as treasures are ours in a dream. Had it not been for the dead lying there he would have laughed. But he checked the bitter mirth that came only too easily, and contented himself with accepting her offer of

[15] Dialect contraction of 'do-nought', a witless, worthless person.

remuneration in a way to make her understand that it was unnecessary—as a footpad or a victorious soldier might speak to his victim minded to be generous without the need of force.

Touching the fact of despoiling her, he had neither qualms nor doubt as to the righteousness of his deed. His strongest feeling at that moment was one of self-congratulation that he had not promised to marry her; his gravest perplexity, what should he do with the girl? An oath would have been an awkward barrier to get over, though doubtless he would have surmounted it like the rest; still he was thankful to be spared the moral inconvenience of perjury, though there remained the perplexing question:—what should he do with Jessie?

He said this to Ralph, meaning no ill.

"Give her to me," answered the old man, his eyes glistening. "I can manage as she shall be well cared for, and no hindrance to you."

"No! no!" cried Jessie, shrinking nearer to Claude. "No! not to him!"

"What a foolish wench it is!" said Ralph, soothingly. "And I who has been as a father to her since she come!"

"Where would you take her?" asked Claude a little anxiously. "Though the idea of her owning the property is simple madness, I must know that she is well cared for."

"She shall be well cared for, Master Claude," answered Ralph. "I know an old lady as she will just suit; a quiet, nice old lady as wants a young maid about her that is active and willing; and Jessie will do for her first-rate. I have had the place in my eye for ever so long, and you just hand her over to me, and I'll fix her as right as a trivet!"

"Anywhere but to him," pleaded poor Jessie. "Oh! do not send me away!"

"You must go from here, and you had better go with him," answered Claude, but not unkindly. "It is impossible for you to remain with me, and to-morrow I must have the beginning of a totally new arrangement. You could not do better, Jessie, than to take the place Ralph speaks of; and you are not obliged to stay in it if you do not like it. You will not be a prisoner, child, and you can leave if it does not please you. I will take care that you are not ill-treated; only you must be obedient and reasonable, you know, else I shall not have much interest in you."

"I will leave this house to-night—go away anywhere—only do not send me with him!" again sobbed Jessie.

"Come, come, my lass, what fads are these!" said Ralph, taking her arm. Then to Claude he added' "Her wits seem to have got muddled up somehow. And no wonder with all that has been about. It was no place for a young thing like her. She wants a woman body about her. Best let me take her, Master Claude. I must go into the town for women and the like; best let me have her along with me now, before there's room for talk."

"Yes, she will be best with a woman about her; decidedly she will," said Claude. It was a new light, and helped his resolution greatly.

Frantic with terror, Jessie tore herself away from Ralph's grasp, and clung to the hand of the dead.

"Save me!" she shrieked; "save me, good master, my only friend!"

Ralph shrugged his shoulders and looked at Claude.

"Clean gone!" he said. "She ain't safe to leave. Who knows what she mayn't say and do and tell?" he added significantly.

"I think, perhaps, you had better take her to your lady," said Claude, half reluctant, half relieved. "She will be better, as you say, with a woman, and I can look after her to-morrow."

"Yes," answered Ralph gravely; "you can look after her to-morrow."

"Claude!"

Poor Jessie said no more. She had never called him by his name before, and she used it now, half-unconsciously, as a kind of spell—the last and strongest left her. She did not move from where she stood, but only turned her frightened eyes and death-white face in a kind of agony towards him. The anguish of her terror, the agony of her pleading affected him powerfully. He wished she would go quickly and quietly. It had a brutal look to force her thus and at this moment, after all that she had been to his father, and after the manner in which that father had thought to reward her; yet it must be done—she must go. If she stayed long enough to be taught her rights, things might become awkward; and Claude had no desire to see still further complicated what was already sufficiently entangled.

"My good girl, you must go," he said, going up to her and taking her hands kindly. "There are thousands of reasons why I cannot keep you here. Go, like a good Jet, with Ralph; he will take care of you to your new home."

"He will kill me," said Jessie in a hollow voice.

Both the men smiled; Ralph with a muttered, "Dear, dear! poor daft wench!" said compassionately; Claude with good-natured incredulity as at the ravings of a mad woman.

"Stuff! moonshine!" he said. "Murder you! why should he risk his neck to murder you? Besides, he never hurt any one in his life—that I can answer for."

"Nay, murder is not much in my line," said Ralph.

"You wish me to leave you; so I will; but send me away with any one but him!" pleaded Jessie, with one last despairing effort.

Claude hesitated.

"And have the story of the will known by to-morrow to all the birds in the air!" said Ralph. "Better give her to those as can make no mischief; and my old lady cannot, because," with a grin, "she's deaf and dumb."

The words decided the young man.

"I cannot have any more nonsense, Jessie," he said sternly. "Go with Ralph. You vex me by your disobedience. Do you not know that it is your duty to obey?"

Jessie gave one long look into his face. The struggle was over. That sublime patience of despair which sometimes possesses the weak and the timid, and seems to give them an heroic strength, came into her. She dropped her head.

"I will obey you," she said. "It is for your good; and I will die for you."

"Rubbish!" said Claude.

"Lord! such talk!" remonstrated Ralph, as he took both her hands in one of his and led her, his prisoner, to the door.

At the door she turned back to look once at the dead and once at the living—the man who had been as her father, and the man whom she loved with the whole strength of her innocent nature, scarcely knowing that she loved him; her prince who had given her over to the executioner. To his dying day, Claude never forgot those mournful, patient, pleading eyes. They haunted him like the eyes of a creature in its death agony, and thrilled him at the moment with a strange shiver of superstitious dread. His inner consciousness told him that he was sending her to her doom, but his intellect refused to receive the idea, and he drove it from him as a folly.

Then she passed away—the creature who had loved him best of all in the world—the creature whom his father had made rich that she might be his wife—the woman he had rejected, robbed, and had sent out into the darkness—to what? Better that she had died in the road where she was found, than to have been reserved for such a fate as this to which he had assigned her!

"It was a cruel kindness!" said Claude aloud, and looked at the face of the dead.

But a sudden something shook him; and with a half impatient "I am a fool!" muttered to himself, he left the room and went downstairs. He did not care to be alone with that white and powerless thing that had once been his father; and he had never felt the hideous dreariness and desolation of the place so oppressive as now. He was ashamed of his weakness; but he wished now that he had not sent Jessie away to-night. The presence of any living being would have been preferable to this awful stillness, broken as it was by weird sounds, strange sighs, and faint, far-off mutterings—this desolation peopled by shadowy shapes flitting to and fro, and the presence of an overwhelming horror brooding over all. How he wished he had not sent her away; and how he wished she had not looked as she did! Surely he had been precipitate. So good as she was, she would have done whatever he had wished, and he could have gained his cause by milder methods. Ah! those eyes! They seemed to follow him, reproaching him wherever he looked, and he could not free himself from the feeling of something standing menacingly behind him wherever he turned.

"God in Heaven, what is that!" he cried, as a shriek rang out clear and distinct in the midnight air; and then all was still as the grave, save for those ghostly sounds and sighs and mutterings which swarmed round the shadowy presence, and made the horror that possessed him almost more than he could live under.

Meanwhile Jessie, always held by Ralph, was passing through the wood lying in the deep blackness of the night. It was the night of the first of May, just a year and a day since she had been found by Mr. Willoughby fainting with hunger on the road, and now the end—this! The night was pitch dark; the rain was falling fast, and the feeble light of the lanthorn which the old man carried made everything seem more weird and ghostly for the distortion and blacker shadows that it threw. But Jessie neither shrank nor complained; she seemed indeed, scarcely conscious of anything whatever, or it might be that she was in part paralyzed by terror. Yet she knew it all quite well. She knew every step of the way they went, where the roads forked, and all the turnings and twistings of the master path in the Maze. Nothing came upon her with a sense of strangeness; she seemed to have lived through it all before.

As they were clearing the Maze, Ralph said in a low, hoarse whisper; "Do you know why I take you here?—because you know too much. You spied on me; I found you out, and I swore then that I'd do for you. The master's secret was mine, and I'd not give you nor any one the power of telling it. What you know you'll have to share, but you shan't be harmed. She's been kept as clean and comfortable as a lady should, and I'll do the same by you. She's above—you below; you won't clash, but you may think your life over now, for you'll never pass them doors alive—not while I'm a living man."

Still Jessie did not answer. What should she say? he was but telling her what she knew. Only when they came to the steps, and he had unbarred and unlocked the door and was leading her in, only then she shrank back and gave a shriek that was heard far and wide, startling the lonely wanderer, scaring the sleepless watcher, and striking on Claude with a sense of murder—he, the murderer, never to be freed from the stain of blood-guiltiness again. Then she was thrust in; the door was barred on the outside; and she was alone in the Gazebo. No; not alone. That awful creature was above, ceaselessly pacing backwards and forwards, now muttering incoherent words, now growling like a wild beast waiting for its food, and once or twice laughing—the most horrible sound of all!

The night wore on, and the distant church clock chimed one. Jessie sat where she had first placed herself—on a low wooden stool facing the inner door—the door which opened on to the stairs leading to the rooms above. Not a sound was to be heard, save the sullen flow of the river beneath, the hissing of the rain, and the ceaseless striking of the branches of the yew tree on the window panes. The world seemed to have died since she was brought in here, and she felt alone in the universe, cut off from all hope of help or sympathy from men—alone with that awful Thing in the chambers above.

Suddenly she heard a noise. It was the sound of a chain cautiously dropped on the floor overhead, and a chuckling laugh to follow. Then she heard the shooting of a lock, the creaking of hinges, and a stealthy step on the stairs. The step came creeping down, stair by stair, nearer—nearer—stopping every now and then as if to listen; then coming on again stealthy, cautious, creeping, but always nearer. She heard the creature's heavy breathing as the step stopped at the door; and then she heard the latch moved—and then a laugh.

The door was locked on the inside, but Ralph had taken the key with him. Again and again the latch moved softly, up and down; Jessie watching it, fascinated with terror. Then she heard something put into the lock—a scratching sound, a wrench—and the door burst open.

A tall woman, gaunt and ghastly, dressed in white; her long grey hair tossed about her face; her sinewy arms bare to her shoulder; her strong lean hands with the fingers curved and the nails hooked like the talons of a bird of prey; her hollow eyes glaring—the eyes of a maniac in whose veins was burning the passion for blood like a fever; a woman who had once been beautiful, but out of whose face now all humanity, all intellect had passed, leaving only the hideous mask of the brute-man; this was what Jessie saw as she sat motionless, waiting for her doom, struck to stone by horror.

"Ha! ha! I thought I should see you again!" laughed the maniac. "Now we are quits."

"Them branches might as well be cut," said Ralph to himself the next morning. "They whip the panes and make a stour; and now I have her safe I don't mind to torment her."

He got up into the tree as he spoke, and crawled along the limb where Jessie had lain before. His eye caught a point of colour in the fork of a jagged twig. It was the fragment of the blue striped dress torn by the girl in her descent.

"Good," he said as he thrust it into his pocket. "Now I know what I know, and I was right after all."

He was quite comforted by this piece of evidence. It soothed him somehow, and he began to lop the twigs with a lighter heart than he had before. And as he lopped them he looked into the windows of the lower room, to see how his prisoner bore herself.

"No! no! not that. As God is my judge, I never meant that!" he cried aloud. "Cursed devil! how did she break loose!"

He flung himself forward to knock at the window and startle the creature lying crouched like a wild beast on the dead body of the girl; he flung himself too far. An oath, a shriek, the sound of a breaking bough, a heavy splash in the dark waters of the sullen Mortey—and Ralph had gone to join his victim in the great world beyond.

When search was made through the premises for the missing servant, the Gazebo was included in the places ransacked. A plan of the Maze belonged to the map of the estate, and the master-path was thus easily found. Claude was with the searching party, anxious more than the rest to find the old man to learn from him where he had taken Jessie; for in truth he had placed himself in a bad position by his precipitancy, and he was eager now to have the girl restored as he had been glad to rid himself of her. The lawyer held the will, and was prepared to do battle for the rightful owner; and Claude, without her, found himself doubly ruined. If only he had not sent her away!—if he could but find Ralph!—if he had considered first of all whether the will might not be at the lawyer's, instead of, as he imagined, in his father's writing-desk!—if only he had done or remembered one or other of the many things which now occurred to him! Ah! if we could but go back on our steps when we have taken the wrong path, and begin afresh with new ground!

Thinking all this he walked through the Maze with the rest, sad, dispirited, tormented, scarcely seeing where they went till they came to the door of the so-called deserted Gazebo.

"No, this is not deserted," said one among them, noting the heavy chains and ponderous bolts and bars, all in the perfect order of careful everyday use. "There's no ghost here but a living one!:

And with that they tried the various keys they had with them; but finding none that would fit, they decided on breaking open the door. It was a long piece of business, but it was done at last; and the heavy bolts and bars and chains were broken one by one, when the massive oaken-door finally yielded. But as it opened the bravest man among them shrank back with awe and horror at what was found.

On the floor lay poor pale Jessie, dead. Still with its bony hands upon her throat, curled up like a wild beast on her breast, hungry, wolfish, crouched the maniac, Claude's mother, brought into the light of day now for the first time these twenty years.

"Yes, I did it!" she whispered. "Don't tell Ralph, but I learnt the trick of the chain and the locks, and cheated him!"

It was a fearful scandal. The country was never tired of talking of it. The maniac, the murder—the victim being the rightful owner of the estate—the dead body of old Ralph taken out of the Mortey half a mile down, with that strange wound in his head, which might have been from a fall but also might have been given by an enemy from behind and then his body flung into the river, all told against Claude, who was thus saddled with the weight of iniquities beyond what he deserved. Not even the subsequent possession of Longmire Hall, and a third share of the enormous savings made by his father, could reconcile the neighbourhood to him; and when he asked the Earl for his daughter and Lady Margaret for her hand, he was told positively by the one and coldly by the other, that families of repute do not care to connect themselves with those of a name so soiled and tarnished as his.

Left to wear through life as he best might, he every now and then reflected in his desolation on the difference there had been between the love he had despised and the love he had desired—the woman he had loved and the woman who had loved him.

"My father was right," he once said mournfully. "What I rejected was the truth, what I wanted was a sham."

But the world has no pity for life-long mourners; and when he died the people drew a long breath and said, "Thank Heaven, the last of the mad Willoughbys has gone!"

It was the sole requiem said or sung for him; the unregretted end for an unhonoured life.

Charlotte Mary Yonge

1823 – 1901

A novelist, essayist, biographer, historian and editor, Charlotte Yonge was born in Otterbourne, Winchester, where she remained for the rest of her life. She was reared in a strict religious household and educated at home by her parents who provided her with excellent instruction in modern languages, history and literature. She led a very sheltered life; she started teaching Sunday School at the age of seven years and continued for seventy-one years. Her family was shocked when in 1842 she began to write for juvenile magazines and she was allowed to continue with her writing only on condition that her father approved of her work and the profits went to good causes. When her father died, John Keble, the man who had prepared her for confirmation, assumed the responsibility for vetting her work; under his influence she became an apologist for the Oxford Movement, the High Church faction in the Church of England.

Charlotte Yonge wrote more than one-hundred-and-sixty books (most of them novels with self-sacrificing heroines) and edited a variety of religious magazines. She endeared herself to her many readers with her highly moral works but she antagonised many with her anti-feminist slant. The following is an extract from her book Womankind (Walter Smith, London, 1881 (4th edn)).

Strong-minded Women

"DOES she go in for being strong-minded? Pray don't be a strong-minded woman." What do we mean by these expressions? Generally, it may be feared that a strong-minded woman is a term for one who is either ungentle, or unwilling to be bound by the restrictions of her sex. It is a piece of modern slang, and it is unfortunate in its effect in two ways; first as disturbing respect for true feminine strength of mind, and secondly as being a compliment to those who "go in" for bravado of mind, not strength of mind.

The real article, if we may so call it, is essentially feminine. Every woman ought to be strong-minded enough not to flinch from her immediate duty, whether it be to rule a family, to rebuke a dependant, to assist at a painful operation, to announce heart-breaking tidings, even to penetrate into scenes of sin and coarseness, if she have a call to seek and save some one there, nay, to refuse to transgress the commands of conscience under the compulsion of love or fear, and to utter her testimony in season, without fear of man. Without a strong mind, a woman is nothing better than an intelligent bit of drift weed, driven hither and thither by force of circumstances, and totally dependent on her surroundings.

She will worry her husband, be over-crowed by her children and dependants; or if single, she will hang prone upon some friend and probably end by becoming a prey to her servants. Instead of raising the tone of those about her, she will sink to whatever is the level around her, and will continually realize the comparison of the broken reed to any one who leans on her.

Happily there are many whose love gives them strong hearts to bear and to do, and who, though frivolous in ordinary times, seem to change their whole nature in the time of distress or danger. The modern idea of strength of mind, however, includes something intellectual as well as something resolute.

The ideal strong-minded woman—for, like other ideals, she has probably never been found with all points of perfection at once—is supposed to have an aptitude for *all* kinds of severe studies, and to insist on pursuing them on equal terms with men. She will go anywhere and do anything with perfect coolness, trusting to an invisible armour of proof to protect her. She will also say anything to anybody, and never spare her censure or interference for the trifling consideration that it is no business of hers. Her chief dread is of prejudice, and of ancient conclusions, and she therefore thinks it weak not to read all kinds of books, especially the sceptical and the sensational, and the line she admires most in Tennyson is that in praise of "honest doubt." The popular idea of her appearance is that she is tall, grim, gaunt, and harshly strange in attire, but she is much more apt to be in the height of the fashion, and young and pretty, though sometimes she tries dressing artistically and individually, and thus manages to be most conspicuous and generally most expensive.

To men these strong-minded women, or those approaching to them, are a laughing-stock and a terror. When the strong-minded woman has the graces of freshness and beauty, they are led away by her, vote her "capital fun," and try how far she will go, but they do not respect her, they only see in her a bad imitation of themselves, and make game of her little affectations. When she has no beauty or charm, her pretensions make her merely obnoxious to them, and deprive her of that tender halo of sweet kindness and sympathy that attracts friendship and esteem.

But to please men we are told is one of the most unworthy motives imaginable to hold up to woman.

So in a degree it is, but approbation is a standard by which to judge. That which a man would not tolerate in his sister or daughter is not becoming and is unsexing.

But this is what the strong-minded woman wants. N.B.—She does not want to cease to be a woman, but she wants to make out that the woman is physically as well as mentally the superior creature, and that she should therefore be on an equality and perhaps take the lead.

To argue the case as to the physical conformation is impossible, but I would just observe that one fact which seems to me to overthrow this theory entirely is that though courtesy, fine clothes, and clearness of skin may perhaps give the woman the advantage in early youth, she is beginning to lose it when the man has only just attained his prime. The man improves as he grows older, provided he leads a good and healthy life; the woman's bloom is a much more fleeting thing.

And mentally, where has the woman ever been found who produced any great and permanent work? What woman has written an oratorio, or an epic, or built a cathedral? It is not lack of education. Women have at times been highly educated, many great men have been self-taught. The difference can only be in the mental texture.

And here comes in that which is said with some speciousness; namely, that women are capable of greater spirituality than men. It is a fine eminence that women claim, and men are ready to grant them in a semi-contemptuous, yet half-sentimental save trouble way, which views the spiritual virtues as essentially feminine.

Shame on those who have lowered the idea of religion by such teaching. Nay, they have even so read the Gospels as to fancy that the holiness of Him Who was Perfect God as well as Perfect Man, was of feminine type. They do not see the might of Him Who stood alone, sometimes confronting, sometimes leading a whole populace, winning them so that they were ready to take Him by force and make Him a King, and then stopping their manifestation at its height and sending them away, just when an ordinary leader would have been coerced by their enthusiasm. They do not see the courage that twice cleared the temple of the profane, in the teeth of all the authorities, that defied and denounced the Scribes and Pharisees on their own ground, and that went steadfastly on with Face set as a flint to the end foreseen from the beginning, The intense calmness and absence of all violence have perhaps been some excuse for those who have missed the impression of undaunted, unflinching resolution, and stern indignation against evil; but it is a miserable error, a sin in itself because it is derogatory to the honour of the Lord Who bought us, and false when it alienates from His example as if not meant for men as much as for women.

Struggle hotly and resolutely against the notion, half mawkish, half flattering, that men are not meant to be as good as women, either religiously, morally, or in the way of self-sacrifice. Both are meant to aim at perfection, and to help one another to attain it, and the man, if he chooses and seeks for grace, will attain the higher, nobler type. Woman will not do her part by him unless she really believes this and does her utmost to help him to make the most of himself, not accepting his shortcomings as masculine weakness which give occasion to show her strength and superiority.

But we are told that if we acknowledge our inferiority, and make no struggle for our rights, we induce men to despise us, and thus assist in the weight of oppression under which women groan. Let us see what this oppression amounts to. An unmarried woman is only oppressed, I suppose, by not having the franchise, and on the whole, I doubt if the lack weighs as heavily

on her as the responsibility of a vote would do. In all other matters her sense
of propriety is really her only restraint.

It is the wife who is the injured creature. She vows to obey; her
property, unless put under special restrictions, is her husband's, he can
oblige her to live with him unless he can show strong cause to the contrary,
and in case of separation, the children after seven years old are given to him
unless he have done something of which the law can take cognizance. To him
also belongs the right of appointing their guardians.

No doubt here and there the law presses hardly on individuals. No law
can be framed so that some one will not suffer under it; and till recently
there were reasons of complaint, when a worthless man could absorb his wife's
earnings. Now, however, she can secure them from him, and it is her own fault if
she do not. No law can make a woman strong against the man she loves. And thus
the marriage settlements which put a woman's capital entirely out of her own
reach or her husband's are probably much better for families than if she retained
full command over her share. Hundreds of families have thus been saved from
utter ruin where a loving wife would have given and lost all that she had.

In the charge of children in case of a separation, the utmost is
generally done to come to a just decision as to which parent is the
safest for them to be intrusted with. When the decision is committed to the
law the grievance-making books assume that it is the father who is always in
the wrong and who makes his wife's life intolerable, and then that she has to
part with her little ones at seven years old to undergo his bad example. But
there *really* are women whose violent tempers and other evil ways have made
life unbearable to the husband, who remains looking and longing for the time
when he may resume his children.

As to the father's prior power of appointing guardians, this has
sometimes been spoken of as a grievance, enabling him to indulge
spite or prejudice against the mother, but this must be so exceptional a case that
provision need hardly be made for it, and it is surely reasonable to suppose that
most men would have a wish for their children's welfare, and be able to judge
what was best for them when their own selfishness no longer clashed with the
children's interests.

As to the wives who are beaten, no law of equality would make
much difference to them. The way to prevent their miseries would be,
if possible, to raise the notions of the servant and factory-classes about marriage,
and prevent their drifting into it in the reckless godless way which may well
prevent them from being respected.

In truth our position entirely depends on what we are in ourselves,
not what we claim.

As to paths in life and education, womanhood is no obstacle to our
being as highly educated as our brains will allow.

That this should be done in close *juxtaposition* with a number of male
pupils does not, however, seem desirable, because there is a tendency
in large masses to rub off the tender home-bloom of maidenliness, which is a
more precious thing than any proficiency in knowledge.

So too with medical education for women, for which so hard a struggle has been made. An exceptional woman here and there may be so absorbed in science, so devoted to humanity, as not to be hurt by it, but promiscuous teaching could not be possible to the majority, without harm to both parties. Nor have I much faith in the effect of creating a race of lady doctors. Nurses medically instructed would be most valuable, and do much that now falls to the hands of the doctor, but in a really very serious case I doubt the capability of most women to endure the responsibility, especially where it is a matter of resolute abstinence from action. Nurses do indeed often show nerve and decision, but then they have the doctor to fall back upon, and are within prescribed limits.

The watching of a nursery of ailing children, or the daily visit to an invalid old lady, might be as usefully done by a well-instructed lady doctor as by the pet apothecary—but would the old lady think so?

No, except for certain kinds of practice, and for superior nursing, it does not seem as if enough would be gained to make it desirable to outrage feminine instincts, ay, and those of men, by the full course of scientific training.

A person engaged in hospital nursing has told us that the hardening effect of witnessing constant suffering can hardly be counteracted without special religious discipline and training; and how much greater must be the danger of mischief to mind and soul alike in the technical display of the wonderful secrets of the temple of the human body without any special safeguard. We know that medical students often do not come out unscathed from the ordeal, and can it be well to let women be exposed to it?

Such scientific instruction as can be had from books or special lectures would of course raise the character of nursing, and I believe there are ladies trained to watch some special class of illness requiring minute and skilled attention, who are sent to take charge of patients in the country.

This, and hospital nursing, or the charge of workhouse infirmaries, are real professions, as well as outlets for zeal and beneficence.

To become an upper nurse would often be an excellent plan for a lady no longer young, who has perhaps brought up her own brothers and sisters, or nephews and nieces, or has launched her children into the world. Servants are so scarce that she would be taking no one's place, and would be much happier and more valuable than moping and half starving in a wretched little lodging.

And for the younger who need support, it would be well, if they have no special talent, to try to learn to be telegraph clerks, or even dress-making, or whatever is possible in their station.

"The Year Book of Woman's Work" will point to the means of getting instruction and employment, and there is much less every year of the fear of losing caste by absolute labour.

Teaching, of course, stands higher, but nobody ought to teach who has not the power of learning or teaching. If governessing is to be a profession worth having, a certificate ought to be worked for and gained. It will open a sure command of situations either in schools or families, and if greater freedom be preferred, a course in a diocesan college for schoolmistresses will give the complete training required. The Otter College at Chichester, especially for ladies, may enable many to have happy village homes, in which perhaps to receive a widowed mother, while raising the tone of the children.

To these professions may be added those which require a special talent and training—music, art, and literature.

If a woman have musical gifts of a high order, it is plain that they are meant for the glory of God and the joy of mankind. She is bound to use them to the best advantage in these ways, not to win admiration, but to devote them, with God before all, or they become a snare.

Even choir practice and singing of hymns is often a snare, both in irreverence, conceit, and levity of demeanour. Amateur and village concerts are in like manner great delights, and often innocent ones, but needing great circumspection and instinctive modesty on the lady performers' part to keep all as it should be; and when the talent needs to be used as a means of support, the same quiet soberness and refinement must be the preservative, as in fact they are with many a professional singer and music-mistress. In fact, all depends not on what we *do*, but what we *are*.

Of art and literature I spoke in a former chapter. Neither become professions without a good deal of experience and excellence; indeed, except in the case of editors of journals, literature is generally only an addition implanted on some other means of livelihood.

The strong-minded literary woman generally writes up woman's perfections and superiority. Her world is a sort of bee-hive, all the males drones and the single sisters doing all the work. She speaks on platforms, gives lectures, and endeavours to persuade us of the wrongs we have suffered since man had the upper hand through brute force.

It is not of much use to fight the battle and contradict her. If she *does* accept the original account of the matter, she will only tell us that it was because Eve was more intellectual than Adam that she wanted to be "as gods knowing good and evil." Alas, in this at least she resembles Eve, and let us remember who it was that whispered to our first mother, and "stand fast in the liberty wherein Christ has made us free."

We have liberty to say or do anything that it is right or reasonable to say. If we do understand a matter, we are listened to on our own merits as much as men are. As Christian women of education, each one of us can take exactly the place she deserves, so long as by a foolish struggle for we know not what, we do not bring opposition and ridicule on ourselves.

To a certain degree the world will always be somewhat cruel to distinguished women. They are flattered up, told it is an honour to see them, their autographs and photographs are sought after, and they are complimented, and then the moment they are persuaded to believe themselves something remarkable, and comport themselves accordingly, they become a laughing-stock. Women are as guilty in this way as men, and it is really an additional reason for keeping in the back-ground, though after all, the discomfort and danger must have been much greater when fewer women wrote, open compliments were the fashion, and there were not such hosts of reviews to give a judgment, not in all cases fair or unbiased, but enough so to give a fair estimate of success.

Nothing but that really strong mind, which is in fact either true humility or freedom from self-consciousness, can bear a woman through these dangers of vanity.

Be strong-minded, then. With all my might I say it. Be strong-minded enough to stand up for the right, to bear pain and danger in a good cause, to aid others in time of suffering, to venture on what is called mean or degrading, to withstand a foolish fashion, to use your own judgment, to weigh the value of compliments. In all these things be strong. Be the valiant woman, but do not be strong-minded in a bad sense in discarding all the graces of humility, meekness, and submission, which are the true strength and beauty of womanhood.

Margaret Oliphant
1828 – 97

Born in Wallyford, near Edinburgh, she wrote her first novel at the age of sixteen and published her first novel (Passages in the Life of Mrs Margaret Maitland, 1849) at the age of twenty-one. When after a brief marriage (1852–59) her husband died and she was left with debts and three children to support, she turned to writing and eventually published almost one hundred novels. Dealt many sad blows in her life, Margaret Oliphant paused only briefly in her writing on the death of her daughter in 1864: she also had to overcome the grief occasioned by the death of her two sons. A prolific writer, a regular contributor to Blackwoods Magazine, she wrote stories, reviews, biographies, literary histories, translations, travel books and tales of the supernatural, as well as her novels. Throughout her working life she battled against unremitting financial pressures and family responsibilities. She formed close friendships with many other women writers of her day, including Anne Thackeray.

The following extract from The Autobiography and Letters of Mrs M. O. W. Oliphant *(Mrs Harry Coghill (ed.), William Blackwood, Edinburgh and London, 1899) gives some insight into her life and her art.*

From
The Autobiography and Letters of
Mrs M. O. W. Oliphant

WINDSOR, 1ST FEBRUARY 1885

TWENTY-ONE years have passed since I wrote what is on the opposite page.[1] I have just been reading it all with tears; sorry, very sorry for that poor soul who has lived through so much since. Twenty-one years is a little lifetime. It is curious to think that I was not very young, nearly thirty-six, at that time, and that I am not very old, nearly fifty-seven, now. Life, though it is short, is very long, and contains so much. And one does not, to one's consciousness, change as one's outward appearance and capabilities do. Doesn't Mrs Somerville say that, so far from feeling old, she was not always quite certain (up in the seventies) whether she was quite grown up! I entirely understand the feeling, though I have had enough, one would think, to make one feel old. Since the time when that most unexpected, most terrible blow overtook me in Rome—where her father had died four year before—I have had trials which, I say it with full knowledge of all the ways of mental suffering, have been harder than sorrow. I have lived a laborious life, incessant work, incessant anxiety—and yet so strange, so capricious is this human being, that I would not say I have had an unhappy life. I have said this to one or two friends who know faintly without details what I have had to go through, and astonished them. Sometimes I am miserable—always there is in me the sense that I may have active cause to be so at any moment—always the gnawing pangs of anxiety, and deep, deep dissatisfaction beyond words, and the sense of helplessness, which of itself is despair. And yet there are times when my heart jumps up in the old unreasonable way, and I am,—yes, happy—though the word seems so inappropriate—without any cause for it, with so many causes the other way. I wonder whether this is want of feeling, or mere temperament and elasticity, or if it is a special compensation—"Werena my heart licht I wad dee"[2]—Grizel Hume must have had the same.

I have been tempted to begin writing by George Eliot's life—with that curious kind of self-compassion which one cannot get clear of. I wonder if I am a little envious of her? I always avoid considering formally what my own mind is worth. I have never had any theory on the subject. I have written because it gave me pleasure, because it came natural to me, because it was

[1] The page referred to here was written in Rome at the time of her bitter grief for the loss of her daughter.
[2] If I did not have lightness of heart I would perish.

like talking or breathing, besides the big fact that it was necessary for me to work for my children. That, however, was not the first motive, so that when I laugh inquiries off and say that it is my trade, I do it only by way of eluding the question which I have neither time nor wish to enter into. Anthony Trollope's talk about the characters in his books astonished me beyond measure, and I am totally incapable of talking about anything I have ever done in that way. As he was a thoroughly sensible genuine man, I suppose he was quite sincere in what he says of them,—or was it that he was driven into a fashion of self-explanation which belongs to the time, and which I am following now though in another way? I feel that my carelessness of asserting my claim is very much against me with everybody. It is so natural to think that if the workman himself is indifferent about his work, there can't be much in it that is worth thinking about. I am not indifferent, yet I should rather like to forget it all, to wipe out all the books, to silence those compliments about my industry, &c., which I always turn off with a laugh. I suppose this is really pride, with a mixture of Scotch shyness, and a good deal of that uncomprehended, unexplainable feeling which made Mrs Carlyle[3] reply with a jibe, which meant only a whimsical impulse to take the side of opposition, and the strong Scotch sense of the absurdity of a chorus of praise, but which looks so often like detraction and bitterness, and has now definitely been accepted as such by the public in general. I don't find words to express it adequately, but I feel it strenuously in my own case. When people comment upon the number of books I have written, and I say that I am so far from being proud of that fact that I should like at least half of them forgotten, they stare—and yet it is quite true; and even here I could no more go solemnly into them, and tell why I had done this or that, than I could fly. They are my work, which I like in the doing, which is my natural way of occupying myself, though they are never so good as I meant them to be. And when I have said that, I have said all that is in me to say.

I don't quite know why I should put this all down. I suppose because George Eliot's life has, as I said above, stirred me up to an involuntary confession. How I have been handicapped in life! Should I have done better if I had been kept, like her, in a mental greenhouse and taken care of? This is one of the things it is perfectly impossible to tell. In all likelihood our minds and our circumstances are so arranged that, after all, the possible way is the way that is best; yet it is a little hard sometimes not to feel with Browning's Andrea,[4] that the men who have no wives, who have given themselves up to their art, have had an almost unfair advantage over us who have been given perhaps more than one Lucrezia to take care of. And to feel with him that perhaps in the after-life four square walls in the New Jerusalem may be given for another trial! I used to be intensely impressed in the Laurence Oliphants[5] with that curious freedom from human

[3] Jane Carlyle (1801–66), married to Thomas Carlyle, enjoyed the reputation of being one of the best letter writers in the English language.
[4] 'Andrea del Sarto' by Robert Browning, included in *Men and Women* (1855)
[5] Laurence Oliphant (1829–88), travel writer and novelist; Mrs Oliphant (no relation) published his biography in 1891.

ties which I have never known; and that they felt it possible to make up their minds to do what was best, without any sort of *arrière pensée*, without having to consider whether they could or not. Curious freedom! I have never known what it was. I have always had to think of other people, and to plan everything—for my own pleasure, it is true, very often, but always in subjection to the necessity which bound me to them. On the whole, I have had a great deal of my own way, and have insisted upon getting what I wished, but only at the cost of infinite labour, and of carrying a whole little world with me whenever I moved. I have not been able to rest, to please myself, to take the pleasures that have come in my way, but have always been forced to go on without a pause. When my poor brother's family fell upon my hands, and especially when there was question of Frank's education, I remember that I said to myself, having then perhaps a little stirring of ambition, that I must make up my mind to think no more of that, and that to bring up the boys for the service of God was better than to write a fine novel, supposing even that it was in me to do so. Alas! the work has been done; the education is over; my good Frank, my steady, good boy, is dead. It seemed rather a fine thing to make that resolution (though in reality I had no choice); but now I think that if I had taken the other way, which seemed the less noble, it might have been better for all of us. I might have done better work. I should in all probability have earned nearly as much for half the production had I done less; and I might have had the satisfaction of knowing that there was something laid up for them and for my old age; while they might have learned habits of work which now seem beyond recall. Who can tell? I did with much labour what I thought the best, and there is only a *might have been* on the other side.

In this my resolution which I did make, I was, after all, only following my instincts, it being in reality easier to me to keep on with a flowing sail, to keep my household and make a number of people comfortable, at the cost of incessant work, and an occasional great crisis of anxiety, than to live the self-restrained life which the greater artist imposes upon himself.

What casuists we are on our own behalf!—this is altogether self-defence. And I know I am giving myself the air of being *au fond* a finer sort of character than the others. I may as well take the little satisfaction to myself, for nobody will give it to me. No one even will mention me in the same breath with George Eliot. And that is just. It is a little justification to myself to think how much better off she was,—no trouble in all her life as far as appears, but the natural one of her father's death—and perhaps coolnesses with her brothers and sisters, though that is not said. And though her marriage is not one that most of us would have ventured on, still it seems to have secured her a worshipper unrivalled. I think she must have been a dull woman with a great genius distinct from herself, something like the gift of the old prophets, which they sometimes exercised with only a dim sort of perception what it meant. But this is a thing to be said only with bated breath, and perhaps further thought on the subject may change even my mind. She took herself with tremendous seriousness, that is evident, and was always on duty, never relaxing, her letters ponderous beyond description—and those to the Bray[6] party giving one the idea of a mutual improvement society for the exchange of essays.

Let me be done with this—I wonder if I will ever have time to put a few autobiographical bits down before I die. I am in very little danger of having my life written, and that is all the better in this point of view—for what could be said of me? George Eliot and George Sand make me half inclined to cry over my poor little unappreciated self—"Many love me (*i.e.*, in a sort of way), but by none am I enough beloved." These two bigger women did things which I have never felt the least temptation to do—but how very much more enjoyment they seem to have got out of their life, how much more praise and homage and honour! I would not buy their fame with these disadvantages, but I do feel very small, very obscure, beside them, rather a failure all round, never securing any strong affection, and throughout my life, though I have had all the usual experiences of woman, never impressing anybody,—what a droll little complaint!—why should I? I acknowledge frankly that there is nothing in me—a fat, little, commonplace woman, rather tongue-tied—to impress any one; and yet there is a sort of whimsical injury in it which makes me sorry for myself.

FEB. 8TH.

Here, then, for a little try at the autobiography. I ought to be doing some work, getting on a little in advance for to-morrow, which gives a special zest to doing nothing: to doing what has no need to be done—and Sunday evenings have always been a time to *fantasticare*, to do what one pleased; and I have dropped out of the letter I used to do on these occasions, having—which, by the way, is a little sad when one comes to think of it—no one to write to, of anything that is beneath the surface. Curious! I had scarcely realised it before. Now for a beginning.

I remember nothing of Wallyford, where I was born, but opened my eyes to life, so far as I remember, in the village of Lasswade, where we lived in a little house, I think, on the road to Dalkeith. I recollect the wintry road ending to my consciousness in a slight ascent with big ash-trees forming a sort of arch; underneath which I fancy was a toll-bar, the way into the world appropriately barred by that turnpike. But no, that was not the way into the world; for the world was Edinburgh, the coach for which, I am almost sure, went the other way through the village and over the bridge to the left hand, starting from somewhere close to Mr Todd the baker's shop, of which I have a faint and kind recollection. It was by that way that Frank came home on Saturday nights to spend Sunday at home, walking out from Edinburgh (about six miles) to walk in again on Monday in the dark winter mornings. I recollect nothing about the summer mornings when he set out on that walk, but remember vividly like a picture the Monday mornings in winter; the fire burning cheerfully and candles on the breakfast-table, all dark but with a subtle sense of morning, though it

6 Reference to Charles Bray, a free thinker who influenced George Eliot.

seemed a kind of dissipation to be up so long before the day. I can see myself, a small creature seated on a stool by the fire, toasting a cake of dough which was brought for me by the baker with the prematurely early rolls, which were for Frank. (This dough was the special feature of the morning to me, and I suppose I had it only on these occasions.) And my mother, who never seemed to sit down in the strange, little, warm, bright picture, but to hover about the table pouring out tea, supplying everything he wanted to her boy (how proud, how fond of him!—her eyes liquid and bright with love as she hovered about); and Frank, the dearest of companions so long—then long separated, almost alienated, brought back again at the end to my care. How bright he was then, how good always to me, how fond of his little sister!—impatient by moments, good always. And he was a kind of god to me—*my* Frank, as I always called him. I remember once weeping bitterly over a man singing in the street, a buttoned-up, shabby-genteel man, whom, on being questioned why I cried, I acknowledged I thought like my Frank. That was when he was absent, and my mother's anxiety reflected in a child's mind went, I suppose, the length of fancying that Frank too might have to sing in the street. (He would have come off very badly in that case, for he did not know one tune from another, much less could he sing a note!) How well I recollect the appearance of the man in his close-buttoned black coat, with his dismal song, and the acute anguish of the thought that Frank might have come to that for anything I knew. Frank, however, never gave very much anxiety; it was Willie, poor Willie, who was our sore and constant trouble—Willie, who lives still in Rome, as he has done for the last two- or three-and-twenty years—nearly a quarter of a century—among strangers who are kind to him, wanting nothing, I hope, yet also having outlived everything. I shrank from going to see him when I was in Italy, which was wrong; but how can I return to Rome, and how could he have come to me?—poor Willie! the handsomest, brightest of us all, with eyes that ran over with fun and laughter—and the hair which we used to say he had to poll, like Absalom,[7] so many times a-year. Alas!

What I recollect in Lasswade besides the Monday morning aforesaid is not much. I remember standing at the smithy with brother Willie, on some occasion when the big boy was very unwillingly charged to take his little sister somewhere or other,—standing in the dark, wondering at the sparks as they flew up and the dark figures of the smith and his men; and I remember playing on the road opposite the house, where there was a low wall over which the Esk and the country beyond could be seen (I think), playing with two little kittens, who were called Lord Brougham and Lord Grey. It must have been immediately after the passing of the Reform Bill, and I suppose this was why the kittens bore such names. We were all tremendously political and Radical, my mother especially and Frank. Likewise I recollect with the most vivid clearness on what must have been a warm still summer day, lying on my back in the grass, the little blue speedwells in which are very distinct before me, and looking up into the sky. The depths of it, the blueness of it, the way in which it seemed to move and fly and avoid the gaze which could not penetrate beyond that profound unfathomable

7 See II Samuel, xiv–xviii.

blue,—the bliss of lying there doing nothing, trying to look into it, growing giddy with the effort, with a sort of vague realisation of the soft swaying of the world in space! I feel the giddiness in my brain still, and the happiness, as if I had been the first discoverer of that wonderful sky. All my little recollections are like pictures to which the meaning, naturally, is put long afterwards. I did not know the world moved or anything about it, being under six at most; but I can feel the sensation of the small head trying to fix that great universe, and in the effort growing dizzy and going round.

We left Lasswade when I was six, my father's business taking him to Glasgow, to the misery of my mother, who was leaving her boys behind her. My father is a very dim figure in all that phantasmagoria. I had to be very quiet in the evenings when he was at home, not to disturb him; and he took no particular notice of me or of any of us. My mother was all in all. How she kept everything going, and comfortably going, on the small income she had to administer, I can't tell; it seems like a miracle, though of course we lived in the utmost obscurity and simplicity, she herself doing the great part of all that was done in the house. I was the child of her age—not her old age, but the sentiment was the same. She had lost three children one after another—one a girl about whom I used to make all sorts of dream-romances, to the purport that Isabella had never died at all, and was brought back in this or that miraculous way to make my mother and myself supremely happy. I was born after that period of misery, and brought back life to my mother's heart. She was of the old type of Scotch mothers, not demonstrative, not caressing, but I know now that I was a kind of idol to her from my birth. My clothes were all made by her tender hands, finer and more beautifully worked than ever child's clothes were; my under garments fine linen and trimmed with little delicate laces, to the end that there might be nothing coarse, nothing less than exquisite, about me; that I might grow up with all the delicacies of a woman's ideal child.

But she was very quick in temper notwithstanding this, and was very far from spoiling me. I was not petted nor called by sweet names. But I know now that my mere name meant everything to her. I was her Maggie—what more could mortal speech find to say? How little one realises the character or individuality of those who are most near and dear. It is with difficulty even now that I can analyse or make a character of her. She herself is there, not any type or variety of humankind. She was taller than I am, not so stout as I have grown. She had a sweet fresh complexion, and a cheek so soft that I can feel the sensation of putting mine against it still, and beautiful liquid brown eyes, full of light and fun and sorrow and anger, flashing and melting, terrible to look at sometimes when one was in disgrace. Her teeth projected, when she had teeth, but she lost and never replaced them, which did not, I think, harm her looks very much—at least, not in my consciousness. I am obliged to confess that when I remember her first she wore a brown front![8] according to the fashion of the time—which fashion she detested, and suddenly abandoning it one day, appeared with the

---

[8] A false hairpiece.

most lovely white hair, which gave a charm of harmonious colour to her beautiful complexion and brown eyes and eyebrows, but which was looked upon with consternation by her contemporaries, who thought the change wickedness. She had grown very early grey like myself, but was at this period, I should think, about forty-five. She wore always a cap with white net quilled closely round her face, and tied under her chin with white ribbons; and in winter always a white shawl; her dress cut not quite to her throat, and a very ample white net or cambric handkerchief underneath. She had read everything she could lay hands upon all her life, and was fond of quoting Pope, so that we used to call her Popish in afterdays when I knew what Popish in this sense meant.

She had entered into everything that was passing all her life with the warmest energy and animation, as was her nature; was Radical and democratic and the highest of aristocrats all in one. She had a very high idea, founded on I have never quite known what, of the importance of the Oliphant family, so that I was brought up with the sense of belonging (by her side) to an old, chivalrous, impoverished race. I have never got rid of the prejudice, though I don't think our branch of the Oliphants was much to brag of. I would not, however, do anything to dispel the delusion, if it is one, for my mother's sake, who held it stoutly and without a doubt. Her father had been a prodigal, and I fear a profligate, whose wife had not been able to bear with him (my mother would have borne anything and everything for her children's sake, to keep their home intact), and her youth had been a troubled and partially dependent one,—dependent upon relations on the one side, whom it was a relief, I suppose, to the high-spirited girl to think as much inferior in race as they were in the generosity and princeliness of nature which was hers. So far as that went she might have been a queen.

I understand the Carlyles, both he and she, by means of my mother as few people appear able to do. She had Mrs Carlyle's wonderful gift of narrative, and she possessed in perfection that dangerous facility of sarcasm and stinging speech which Sir Walter attributes to Queen Mary. Though her kindness was inexhaustible and her love boundless, yet she could drive her opponent of the moment half frantic with half-a-dozen words, and cut to the quick with a flying phrase. On the other side, there was absolutely nothing that she would not have done or endured for her own; and no appeal to her generosity was ever made in vain. She was a poor woman all her life, but her instinct was always to give. And she would have kept open house if she could have had her way, on heaven knows how little a-year. My father was in one way very different. He hated strangers; guests at his table were a bore to him. In his later days he would have nobody invited, or if guests came, retired and would not see them,—but he was not illiberal.

We lived for a long time in Liverpool, where my father had an office in the Custom-house. I don't know exactly what, except that he took affidavits—which was a joke in the house—having a special commission for that purpose. We lived for some time in the North End (no doubt a great deal changed now, and I have known nothing about it for thirty years and more), where there was a Scotch church, chiefly for the use of the engineers and their families who worked in the great foundries. One of the first things I remember here was great distress among the people, on what account I cannot tell—I must have been a girl of thirteen or so, I think. A fund was raised for their relief, of which my father was treasurer, and both my brothers were drawn in to help. This was very momentous in our family, from the fact that it was the means of bringing Frank, up to this time everything that was good except in respect to the Church, to that last and crowning excellence. He got interested about the poor, and began to come with us to church, and filled my mother's cup with happiness. Willie, always careless, always kind, ready to do anything for anybody, but who had already come by some defeat in life which I did not understand, and who was at home idle, took the charge of administering this charity, and used to go about the poor streets with a cart of coal behind him and his pockets stuffed with orders for bread and provisions of all kinds. All this I remember, I think, more through my mother's keen half anguish of happiness and pride than through my own recollection. That he had done so poorly for himself was bitter, but that he did so well for the poor was sweet; oh! and such a vindication of the bright-eyed, sweet-tempered unfortunate, who never was anybody's enemy but his own—words which were more true in his case than in most others. And then Frank was busy in the good work too, and at last a member of the Church, and all well. This is not to say that there were not domestic gusts at times.

When I was sixteen I began to have—what shall I say?—not lovers exactly, except in the singular—but one or two people about who revealed to me the fact that I too was like the girls in the poets. I recollect distinctly the first compliment, though not a compliment in the ordinary sense of the word, which gave me that bewildering happy sense of being able to touch somebody else's heart—which was half fun and infinitely amusing, yet something more. The speaker was a young Irishman, one of the young ministers that came to our little church, at that time vacant. He had joined Frank and me on a walk, and when we were passing and looking at a very pretty cottage on the slope of the hill at Everton, embowered in gardens and shrubberies, he suddenly looked at me and said, "It would be Elysium." I laughed till I cried at this speech afterwards, though at the moment demure and startled. But the little incident remains to me, as so many scenes in my early life do, like a picture suffused with a soft delightful light: the glow in the young man's eyes; the lowered tone and little speech aside; the soft thrill of meaning which was nothing and yet much. Perhaps if I were not a novelist addicted to describing such scenes, I might not remember it after—how long? Forty-one years. What a long time! I could not have been sixteen. Then came the episode of J. Y., which was very serious indeed. We were engaged on the eve of his going away. He was to go to America for three years and then return for me. He was a good, simple, pious, domestic, kind-hearted fellow, fair-haired, not good-looking, not ideal at all. He cannot have been at all clever, and I was rather. When he went away our correspondence for some time was very full; then I began to find his letters silly, and I suppose said as much. Then there were quarrels, quarrels with the Atlantic between, then explanations, and then dreadful silence. It is amusing to look back upon, but it was not at all amusing to me then. My poor little heart was broken. I remember another scene without being able to explain it: my mother and myself walking home from somewhere—I don't know where—after it was certain that there was no letter, and that all was over. I think it was a winter night and rainy, and I was leaning on her arm, and the blank of the silence, and the dark and the separation, and the cutting off of all the dreams that had grown about his name, came over me and seemed to stop my very life. My poor little heart was broken. I was just over seventeen, I think.

These were the only breaks in my early life. We lived in the most singularly secluded way. I never was at a dance till after my marriage, never went out, never saw anybody at home. Our pleasures were books of all and every kind, newspapers and magazines, which formed the staple of our conversation, as well as all our amusement. In the time of my depression and sadness my mother had a bad illness, and I was her nurse, or at least attendant. I had to sit for hours by her bedside and keep quiet. I had no liking then for needlework, a taste which developed afterwards, so I took to writing. There was no particular purpose in my beginning except this, to secure some amusement and occupation for myself while I sat by my mother's bedside. I wrote a little book in which the chief character was an angelic elder sister, unmarried, who had the charge of a family of motherless brothers and sisters, and who had a shrine of sorrow in her life in the shape of the portrait and memory of her lover who had died young. It was all very innocent and guileless, and my audience—to wit, my mother and brother Frank—were highly pleased with it. (It was published long after by W. on his own account, and very silly I think it is, poor little thing.) I think I was then about sixteen. Afterwards I wrote another very much concerned with the Church business, in which the heroine, I recollect, was a girl, who in the beginning of the story was a sort of half-witted undeveloped creature, but who ended by being one of those lofty poetical beings whom girls love. She was called, I recollect, Ibby, but why, I cannot explain. I had the satisfaction afterwards, when I came to my full growth, of burning the manuscript, which was a three-volume business. I don't think any effort was ever made to get a publisher for it.

We were living at the time in Liverpool, either in a house in Great Homer Street or in Juvenal Street—very classical in point of name but in nothing else. Probably neither of these places exists any longer—very good houses though, at least the last. I have lately described in a letter in the 'St James' Gazette' a curious experience of mine as a child while living in one of these places. It was in the time of the Anti-Corn Law[9] agitation, and I was about fourteen. There was a great deal of talk in the papers, which were full of that agitation, about a petition from women to Parliament upon that subject, with instructions to get sheets ruled for signatures, and an appeal to ladies to help in procuring them. It was just after or about the time of our great charity, and I was in the way of going thus from house to house. Accordingly I got a number of these sheets,

9 Corn was kept to a fixed price by duty on foreign grain. During the 1840s ('the hungry forties') there was agitation for repeal of the Corn Laws, especially when the potato crop failed in Ireland. Sir Robert Peel repealed the laws in 1846.

or probably Frank got them for me, and set to work. Another girl went with me, I believe, but I forget who she was. The town was all portioned out into districts under the charge of ladies appointed by the committee, but we flung ourselves upon a street, no matter where, and got our papers filled and put all the authorised agents comically out. Nobody could discover who we were. I took my sheets to the meeting of the ladies, and was much wondered at, being to the external eye a child, though to my own consciousness quite a grown-up person. The secretary of the association or committee, or whatever it was, was, I think, a Miss Hayward; at all events her Christian name was Lawrencina, which she wrote L'cina. I admired her greatly, and admired her pretty handwriting and everything about her. I myself wrote abominably, resisting up to this time all efforts to teach me better; but the circulars and notes with Miss L'cina's pretty name developed in me a warm ambition. I began to copy her writing, and mended in my own from that day. It did not come to very much, the printers would say.

I was a tremendous politician in those days.

I forget when it was that we moved to Birkenhead—not, I think, till after the extraordinary epoch of the publication of my first book. From the time above spoken of I went on writing, and somehow, I don't remember how, got into the history of Mrs Margaret Maitland. There had been some sketches from life in the story which, as I have said, I burned; but that was pure imagination. A slight reflection of my own childhood perhaps was in the child Grace, a broken bit of reflection here and there from my mother in the picture of Mrs Margaret. Willie, after many failures and after a long illness, which we were in hopes had purified him from all his defects, had gone to London to go through some studies at the London University and in the College called the English Presbyterian, to which in our warm Free Churchism we had attached ourselves. He took my MS. to Colburn, then one of the chief publishers of novels, and for some weeks nothing was heard of it, when one morning came a big blue envelope containing an agreement by which Mr Colburn pledged himself to publish my book on the half-profit system,[10] accompanied by a letter from a Mr S. W. Fullom, full of compliments as to its originality, &c. I have forgotten the terms now, but then I knew them by heart. The delight, the astonishment, the amusement of this was not to be described. First and foremost, it was the most extraordinary joke that ever was. Maggie's story! My mother laughed and cried with pride and happiness and amazement unbounded. She thought Mr S. W. Fullom a great authority and a man of genius, and augured the greatest advantage to me from his acquaintance and that of all the great literary persons about him. This wonderful event must have come most fortunately to comfort the family under new trouble; for things had again gone wrong with poor Willie—he had fallen once more into his old vice and debt and misery. He had still another term in London before he finished the course of study he was engaged in; and when the time came for his return I was sent with him to take care of him. It was almost the first time I had ever been separated from my mother. One visit of

[10] A system whereby authors received no advance payment but took half the profits (or paid half the losses) for their books.

two or three weeks to the Hasties of Fairy Knowe, which had its part too in my little development, had been my only absence from home; and how my mother made up her mind to this three months' parting I do not know, but for poor Willie's sake everything was possible. We had lodgings near Bruton Crescent in a street where our cousins, Frank and Tom Oliphant, were in the same house. We had the parlour, I remember, where I sat in the mornings when Willie was at his lectures. Afterwards he came in and I went out with him to walk. We used to walk through all the curious little passages leading, I believe, to Holborn, and full of old bookshops, which were our delight. And he took me to see the parks and various places—though not those to which I should suppose a girl from the country would be taken. The bookshops are the things I remember best. He was as good as he could be, docile and sweet-tempered and never rebellious; and I was a little dragon watching over him with remorseless anxiety. I discovered, I remember, a trifling bill which had not been included when his debts were paid, and I took my small fierce measures that it should never reach my mother's ears, nor trouble her. I ordained that for two days in the week we should give up our mid-day meal and make up at the evening one, which we called supper, for the want of it. On these days, accordingly, he did not come home, or came only to fetch me, and we went out for a long walk, sustaining ourselves with a bun until it should be time to come home to tea. He agreed to this ordinance without a murmur—my poor, good, tender-hearted, simple-minded Willie; and the little bill was paid and never known of at home.

Curiously enough, I remember little of the London sights or of any impression they made upon me. We knew scarcely anybody. Mrs Hamilton, the sister of Edward Irving's wife and a relation, took some notice of us, but she was almost the only individual I knew. And my heart was too full of my charge to think much of the cousin up-stairs with whom my fate was soon to be connected. We had known scarcely anything of each other before. We were new acquaintances, though relations. He took me, I remember, to the National Gallery, full of expectation as to the effect the pictures would have upon me. And I—was struck dumb with disappointment. I had never seen any pictures. I can't tell what I expected to see—something that never was on sea or shore. My ideal of absolute ignorance was far too high-flown, I suppose, for anything human. I was horribly disappointed, and dropped down from untold heights of imagination to a reality I could not understand. I remember, in the humiliation of my downfall, and in the sense of my cousin's astonished disappointment at my want of appreciation, fixing upon a painting—a figure of the Virgin in a Crucifixion, I think by Correggio, but I am quite vague about it—as the thing I liked best. I chose that as Wordsworth's little boy put forth the weathercock at Kilve—in despair at my own incapacity to admire. I remember also the heads of the old Jews in Leonardo's Christ in the Temple. The face of the young Redeemer with its elaborate crisped hair shocked me with a sense of profanity, but the old heads I could believe in. And that was all I got out of my first glimpse into the world of art. I cannot recollect whether it was then or after, that an equally great disillusionment in the theatre befell me. The play was "Twelfth Night," and the lovely beginning of that play—

"That strain again! it had a dying fall"

—was given by a nobody in white tights lying on a sofa and balancing a long leg
as he spoke. The disgust, the disenchantment, the fury remain in my mind now.
Once more I came tumbling down from my ideal and all my anticipations. Mrs
Charles Kean was Viola, and she was middle-aged and stout![11] I was more than
disappointed, I was angry and disgusted and cast down. What was the good of
anything if that was all that Shakespeare and the great Masters could come to?

I remember after this a day at Greenwich and Woolwich, and the sight of
the Arsenal, though why that should have made an impression on my memory,
heaven knows! I remember the pyramids of balls, and some convicts whose
appearance gave me a thrill of horror,—I think they were convicts, though why
convicts should be at Woolwich I can't tell—perhaps it was a mistake. And then Mr
Colburn kindly—I thought most kindly, and thanked him *avec effusion*—gave me
£150 for 'Margaret Maitland.' I remember walking along the street with delightful
elation, thinking that, after all, I was worth something—and not to be hustled
about. I remember, too, getting the first review of my book in the twilight of
a wintry dark afternoon, and reading it by the firelight—always half-amused at
the thought that it was *me* who was being thus discussed in the newspapers. It
was the 'Athenæum,' and it was on the whole favourable. Of course this event
preceded by a couple of months the transaction with Mr Colburn. I think the
book was in its third edition before he offered me that £150. I remember no
reviews except that one of the 'Athenæum,' nor any particular effect which my
success produced in me, except that sense of elation. I cannot think why the
book succeeded so well. When I read it over some years after, I felt nothing
but shame at its foolish little polemics and opinions. I suppose there must have
been some breath of youth and sincerity in it which touched people, and there
had been no Scotch stories for a long time. Lord Jeffrey, then an old man and very
near his end, sent me a letter of sweet praise, which filled my mother with rapture
and myself with an abashed gratitude. I was very young. Oddly enough, it has
always remained a matter of doubt with me whether the book was published
in 1849 or 1850. I thought the former; but Geraldine Macpherson,[12] whom I
met in London for the first time a day or two before it was published, declared
it to be 1850, from the fact that *that* was the year of her marriage. If a woman
remembers any date, it must be the date of her marriage![13] so I don't doubt
Geddie was right. Anyhow, if it was 1850, I was then only twenty-two, and in
some things very young for my age, as in others perhaps older than my years. I
was wonderfully little moved by the business altogether. I had a great pleasure
in writing, but the success and the three editions had no particular effect upon
my mind. For one thing, I saw very few people. We had no society. My father had
a horror of strangers, and would never see any one who came to the house, which

[11] Probably under thirty. [Orig. edn]
[12] Probably Gerardine (*sic*) Macpherson, editor of *Memoirs of Anna Jameson*, 1878.
[13] The book was published in 1849.

was a continual wet blanket to my mother's cordial, hospitable nature; but she had given up struggling long before my time, and I grew up without any idea of the pleasures and companions of youth. I did not know them, and therefore did not miss them; but I daresay this helped to make me—not indifferent, rather unconscious, of what might in other circumstances have "turned my head." My head was as steady as a rock. I had everybody to praise me except my mother and Frank, and their applause—well, it was delightful, it was everything in the world—it was life,—but it did not count. They were part of me, and I of them, and we were all in it. After a while it came to be the custom that I should every night "read what I had written" to them before I went to bed. They were very critical sometimes, and I felt while I was reading whether my little audience was with me or not, which put a good deal of excitement into the performance. But that was all the excitement I had.

I began another book called 'Caleb Field,' about the Plague in London, the very night I had finished 'Margaret Maitland.' I had been reading Defoe, and got the subject into my head. It came to one volume only, and I took a great deal of trouble about a Nonconformist minister who spoke in antitheses very carefully constructed. I don't think it attracted much notice, but I don't remember. Other matters, events even of our uneventful life, took so much more importance in life than these books—nay, it must be a kind of affectation to say that, for the writing ran through everything. But then it was also subordinate to everything, to be pushed aside for any little necessity. I had no table even to myself, much less a room to work in, but sat at the corner of the family table with my writing-book, with everything going on as if I had been making a shirt instead of writing a book. Our rooms in those days were sadly wanting in artistic arrangement. The table was in the middle of the room, the centre round which everybody sat with the candles or lamp upon it. My mother sat always at needle-work of some kind, and talked to whoever might be present, and I took my share in the conversation, going on all the same with my story, the little groups of imaginary persons, these other talks evolving themselves quite undisturbed. It would put me out now to have some one sitting at the same table talking while I worked—at least I would think it put me out, with that sort of conventionalism which grows upon one. But up to this date, 1888, I have never been shut up in a separate room, or hedged off with any observances. My study, all the study I have ever attained to, is the little second drawing-room where all the (feminine) life of the house goes on; and I don't think I have ever had two hours undisturbed (except at night, when everybody is in bed) during my whole literary life. Miss Austen, I believe, wrote in the same way, and very much for the same reason; but at her period the natural flow of life took another form. The family were half ashamed to have it known that she was not just a young lady like the others, doing her embroidery. Mine were quite pleased to magnify me, and to be proud of my work, but always with a hidden sense that it was an admirable joke, and no idea that any special facilities or retirement was necessary. My mother, I believe, would have felt her pride and rapture much checked, almost humiliated, if she had conceived that I stood in need of any artificial aids of that or any other description. That would at once have made the work unnatural to her eyes, and also to mine. I think the first time I ever secluded myself for my work was years after it had become my profession and sole dependence—when I was living after my widowhood in a relation's house, and withdrew with my book and my inkstand from the family drawing-room out of a little conscious ill-temper which made me feel guilty, notwithstanding that the retirement was so very justifiable! But I did not feel it to be so, neither did the companions from whom I withdrew.

After this period our poor Willie became a minister of the English Presbyterian Church, then invested with glory by the Free Church, its real parent, which in our fervid imagination we had by this time dressed up with all sorts of traditional splendour. It, we flattered ourselves, was the direct successor of the two thousand seceders of 1661 (was that the date?). There had been a downfall, we allowed, into Unitarianism and indifference; but this was the real, and a very respectable, tradition. Willie went to a very curious little place in the wilds of Northumberland, where my mother and I decided—with hopes strangely wild, it seems to me now, after all that had gone before—that he was at length to do well, and be as strenuous to his duty as he was gentle in temper and tender in heart. Poor Willie! It was a sort of show village with pretty flowery cottages and gardens, in a superior one of which he lived, or rather lodged, the income being very small and the position humble. It was, however, so far as my recollection goes, sufficiently like a Scotch parish to convince us that the church and parsonage were quite exotic, and the humble chapel the real religious centre of the place. A great number of the people were, I believe, Presbyterians, and the continuance of their worship and little strait ceremony undoubted from the time of the Puritans, though curiously enough the minister was known to his flock by the title of the priest. I don't in the least recollect what the place was like, yet a whiff of the rural air tinged with peat or wood, and of the roses with which the cottages were garlanded, and an impression of the subdued light through the greenish small window half veiled in flowers, remains with me,—very sweet, homely, idyllic, like something in a pathetic country story of peace overshadowed with coming trouble. There was a shadow of a ruined castle in the background, I think Norham; but all is vague,—I have not the clear memory of what I saw in my youth that many people retain. I see a little collection of pictures, but the background is all vague. The only vehicle we could get to take us to Berwick was, I recollect, a cart, carefully arranged with straw-covered sacking to make us comfortable. The man who drove it was very anxious to be engaged and taken with us as "Miss Wilson's coachman." Why mine, or why we should have taken a rustic "Jockey-to-the-fair" for a coachman, if we had wanted such an article, I don't know. I suppose there must have been some sort of compliment implied to my *beaux yeux*, or I should not have remembered this. We left Willie with thankful hearts, yet an ache of fear. Surely in that peaceful humble quiet, with those lowly sacred duties and all his goodness and kindness, he would do well! I don't remember how long it continued. So long as he kept up the closest correspondence, writing every second day and giving a full account of himself, there was an uneasy satisfaction at home. But there is always a prophetic ache in the heart when such calamity is on the way.

One day, without warning, except that his letters had begun to fail a little, my mother received an anonymous letter about him. She went off that evening, travelling all night to Edinburgh, which was the quickest way, and then to Berwick. She was very little used to travelling, and she was over sixty, which looked a great age then. I suppose the trains were slower in those days, for I know she got to Edinburgh only in the morning, and then had to go on by the other line to Berwick, and then drive six miles to the village, where she found all the evil auguries fulfilled, and poor Willie fallen again helpless into that Slough of Despond. She remained a few miserable days, and then brought him back with her, finally defeated in the battle which he was quite unfit to wage. He must have been then, I think, about thirty-three, in the prime of strength and youth; but except for a wavering and uncertain interval now and then, he never got out of the mire nor was able to support himself again. I remember the horrible moment of his coming home. Frank and I went down, I suppose, to the ferry at Birkenhead to meet the travellers. We were all very grave—not a word of reproach did any one say, but to be cheerful, to talk about nothing, was impossible. We drove up in silence to the house where we lived, asking a faint question now and then about the journey. I remember that Willie had a little dog called Brownie with him, and the relief this creature was, which did not understand being shut up in the carriage and made little jumps at the window, and had to be petted and restrained. Brownie brought a little movement, an involuntary laugh at his antics, to break the horrible silence—an angel could scarcely have done more for us. When we got home there was the settling down in idleness, the hopeless decision of any wretched possibility there might be for him. The days and weeks and months in which he smoked and read old novels and the papers, and, most horrible of all, got to content himself with that life! The anguish in all our hearts looking at him, not knowing what to do, sometimes assailed by gusts of impatience, always closing down in the hopelessness of it; the incapacity to find or suggest anything, the dreary spectacle of that content is before me, with almost as keen a sense of the misery as if it had been yesterday.

I had been in the habit of copying out carefully, quite proud of my neat MS., all my books, now becoming a recognised feature of the family life. It struck us all as a fine idea that Willie might copy them for me, and retrieve a sort of fictitious independence by getting 10 per cent upon the price of them; and I really think he felt quite comfortable on this. Of course, the sole use of the copying was the little corrections and improvements I made in going over my work again.

It was after this that my cousin Frank came upon a visit. We had seen, and yet had not seen, a great deal of each other in London during the three months I had spent there with Willie; but my mind had been preoccupied with Willie chiefly, and a little with my book. When Frank made me the extraordinary proposal for which I was totally unprepared, that we should, as he said, build up the old Drumthwacket together, my only answer was an alarmed negative, the idea never having entered my mind. But in six months or so things changed. It is not a matter into which I can enter here.

In the spring of 1851 my mother and I were in Edinburgh, and there made the acquaintance of the Wilsons, our second cousins,—George Wilson being at that time Professor of something which meant chemistry, but was not called so. His mother was an exceedingly bright, vivacious old lady, a universal devourer of books, and with that kind of scientific tendency which made her encourage her boys to form museums, and collect fossils, butterflies, &c. I forget how my mother and she got on, but I always liked her.

George Wilson was an excellent talker, full of banter and a kind of humour, full of ability, too, I believe, writing very amusing letters and talking very amusing talk, which was all the more credit to him as he was in very bad health, kept alive by the fact that he could eat, and so maintain a modicum of strength—enough to get on by. There were two daughters—Jessie and Jeanie—the younger of whom became my brother Frank's wife; and the eldest son, who was married, lived close by, and was then, I think, doing literary work for Messrs Nelson, reading for them and advising them about books. He very soon after this migrated to Canada, and became eventually President of University College, Toronto, and Sir Daniel in the end of his life.

My mother at this time renewed acquaintance with Dr Moir of Musselburgh, an old friend of hers, who had, I believe, attended me when, as a very small child, I fell into the fire, or rather against the bars of the grate, marking my arm in a way which it never recovered. This excellent man, whom everybody loved, was the Delta of 'Blackwood's Magazine,' and called everywhere by that name. He had written much gentle poetry, and one story à la Galt called 'Mansie Wauch,' neither of which were good enough for him, yet got him a certain reputation, especially some pathetic verses about children he had lost, which went to the heart of every mother who had lost children, my own mother first and foremost. He had married a very handsome stately lady, a little conventional, but with an unfailing and ready kindness which often made her mannerisms quite gracious and beautiful. There was already a handsome daughter married, though under twenty, and many other fine, tall, well-bred, handsome creatures, still in long hair and short skirts, growing up. I think I was left behind to pay a visit when my mother returned home, and then had a kind of introduction to Edinburgh literary society, in one case very important for myself. For in one expedition we made, Major Blackwood, one of the publishing firm, and brother of the editor of the 'Magazine,' was of the party; and my long connection with his family thus began. He was accompanied by a young man, a Mr Cupples, of whom, except his name, I have no recollection, but who was the author of a sea-story then, I think, going on in 'Blackwood,' called the 'Green Hand,' and who, it was hoped, would be as successful as the author of 'Tom Cringle' and the 'Cruise of the Midge,' who had been a very effective contributor twenty years before. All I remember of him was that my cousin Daniel Wilson, who was also of the party, indignantly pointed out to me the airs which this young author gave himself, "as if it was such a great thing to be a contributor to 'Blackwood'!" I am afraid I thought it was a great thing, and had not remarked the young author's airs; but Daniel was of the opposite camp. Major Blackwood, who interested me most, was a mild soldierly man, with the gentlest manners

and drooping eyelids, which softened his look, or so at least it appears to me
at the end of so many years.

I remember that one of the places we visited was Wallyford, where was
the house in which I was born, but of which I had no recollection. It must
have been a pleasant homely house, with a projecting half turret enclosing the
staircase, as in many houses in the Lothians, the passages and kitchen down-stairs
floored with red brick, and a delightful large low drawing-room above, with
five greenish windows looking out upon Arthur's Seat in the distance, and a
ghost of Edinburgh. That room charmed me greatly, and in after days I used
to think of becoming its tenant and living there, for the sake of the landscape
and the associations and that pretty old room; but before I could have carried
out such an idea, even had it been more real than a fancy, the pretty house was
pulled down, and a square, aggressive, and very commonplace new farmhouse
built in its place.

The consequence of my introduction to Major Blackwood was, that some
time in the course of the following months I sent him the manuscript of my
story 'Katie Stewart': a little romance of my mother's family, gleaned from her
recollections and descriptions. The scene of this story was chiefly laid in old
Kellie Castle, which I was not then aware was the home of our own ancestors,
from whom it had passed long before into the hands of the Erskines, Earls of
Kellie—with the daughter of which house Katie Stewart had been brought up.
She was my mother's great-aunt, and had lived to a great age. She had seen Prince
Charlie enter Edinburgh, and had told all her experiences to my mother, who
told them to me, so that I never was quite sure whether I had not been Katie
Stewart's contemporary in my own person. And this was her love-tale. I received
proofs of this story on the morning of my wedding-day, and thus my connection
with the firm of Blackwood began. They were fond of nicknames, and I was
known among them by the name of "Katie" for a long time, as I discovered lately
(1896) in some old letters. I suppose they thought me so young and simple (as
they say in these letters) that the girl's name was appropriate to me. I was not
tall ("middle height" we called it in those days), and very inexperienced,—"so
simple and yet self-possessed," I am glad to say Major Blackwood reports of me.
I was only conscious of being dreadfully *shy*.

We were married in Birkenhead on the 4th May 1852,—and the old home,
which had come to consist of such incongruous elements, was more or less
broken up. My brother Frank, discontented and wounded partly by my marriage,
partly by the determination to abandon him and follow me to London, which my
father and mother had formed, married too, hastily, but very successfully in a way
as it turned out, and so two new houses were formed out of the partial ruins of
the old. Had the circumstances been different—had they stayed in Birkenhead
and I gone alone with my husband to London—some unhappiness might have
been spared. Who can tell? There would have been other unhappiness to take
its place. They settled in a quaint little house in a place called Park Village,
old-fashioned, semi-rustic, and pretty enough, with a long strip of garden
stretching down to the edge of a deep cutting of the railway, where we used to
watch the trains passing far below. The garden was gay with flowers, quantities

of brilliant poppies of all colours I remember, which I liked for the colour and hated for the heavy ill odour of them, and the sensation as of evil flowers. Our house in Harrington Square was very near: it looked all happy enough but was not, for my husband and my mother did not get on. My father sat passive, taking no notice, with his paper, not perceiving much, I believe.

My child's birth made a momentary gleam of joy soon lost in clouds.

My mother became ailing and concealed it, and kept alive—or at least kept her last illness off by sheer stress of will until my second child was born a year and a day after the first. She was with me, but sank next day into an illness from which she never rose. She died in September 1854, suffering no attendance but mine, though she concealed from me how ill she was for a long time. I remember the first moment in which I had any real fear, speaking to the doctor with a sudden impulse, in the front of her door, all in a green shade with the waving trees, demanding his real opinion. I do not think I had any understanding of the gravity of the circumstances. He shook his head, and I knew—the idea having never entered my mind before that she was to die. I recollect going away, walking home as in a dream, not able to go to her, to look at her, from whom I had never had a secret, with this secret in my soul that must be told least of all to her; and the sensation that here was something which would not lighten after a while as all my troubles had always done, and pass away. I had never come face to face with the inevitable before. But there was no daylight here—no hope—no getting over it. Then there followed a struggle of a month or two, much suffering on her part, and a long troubled watch and nursing on mine. At the very end I remember the struggle against overwhelming sleep, after nights and days in incessant anxiety, which made me so bitterly ashamed of the limits of wretched nature. To want to sleep while she was dying seemed so unnatural and horrible. I never had come within sight of death before. And, oh me! when all was over, mingled with my grief there was—how can I say it?—something like a dreadful relief.

Within a few months after, my little Marjorie, my second child, died on the 8th February; and then with deep shame and anguish I felt what I suppose was another wretched limit of nature. My dearest mother, who had been everything to me all my life, and to whom I was everything; the companion, friend, counsellor, minstrel, story-teller, with whom I had never wanted for constant interest, entertainment, and fellowship,—did not give, when she died, a pang so deep as the loss of the little helpless baby, eight months old. I miss my mother till this moment when I am near as old as she was (sixty, 10th June 1888); I think instinctively still of asking her something, referring to her for information, and I dream constantly of being a girl with her at home. But at that moment her loss was nothing to me in comparison with the loss of my little child.

I lost another infant after that, a day old. My spirit sank completely under it. I used to go about saying to myself, "A little while and ye shall not see me," with a longing to get to the end and have all safe—for my one remaining, my eldest, my Maggie seemed as if she too must be taken out of my arms. People will say it was an animal instinct perhaps. Neither of these little ones could speak to me or exchange an idea or show love, and yet their withdrawal was like the sun going out from the sky—life remained, the daylight continued, but all was different. It seems strange to me now at this long distance—but so it was.

The glimpse of society I had during my married life in London was not of a very elevating kind; or perhaps I—with my shyness and complete unacquaintance with the ways of people who gave parties and paid incessant visits—was only unable to take any pleasure in it, or get beyond the outside petty view, and the same strange disappointment and disillusion with which the pictures and the stage had filled me, bringing down my ridiculous impossible ideal to the ground. I have tried to illustrate my youthful feelings about this several times in words. I had expected everything that was superlative,—beautiful conversation, all about books and the finest subjects, great people whose notice would be an honour, poets and painters, and all the sympathy of congenial minds, and the feast of reason and the flow of soul. But it is needless to say I found none of these things. We went "out," not very often, to parties where there was always a good deal of the literary element, but of a small kind, and where I found everything very commonplace and poor, not at all what I expected. I never did myself any justice, as a certain little lion-hunter, a Jewish patroness of the arts, who lived somewhere in the region about Harley Street, said. That is to say, I got as quickly as I could into a corner and stood there, rather wistfully wishing to know people, but not venturing to make any approach, waiting till some one should speak to me; which much exasperated my aspiring hostess, who had picked me up as a new novelist, and meant me to help to amuse her guests, which I had not the least idea how to do. I fear I must have been rather exasperating to my husband, who was more given to society than I, and tried in vain (as I can now see) to form me and make me attend to my social duties, which even in such a small matter as returning calls I was terribly neglectful of—out of sheer shyness and gaucherie, I think; for I was always glad and grateful when anybody would insist on making friends with me, as a few people did. There was an old clergyman, Mr Laing, who did, I remember, and more or less his wife—he especially. He liked me, I think, and complimented me by saying he did not like literary ladies—a sort of thing people are rather disposed to say to me. And Lance (the painter of fruits and flowers and still life), who was a wit in his way, was also a great friend of mine. He dared me to put him in a book, and I took him at his word and did so, making a very artless representation, and using some of his own stories; so that everybody recognised the sketch, which was done in mere fun and liking, and pleased him very much—the only actual bit of real life I ever took for a book. It was in 'Zaidee,' I think.

Among my literary acquaintances was the Mr Fullom who had read for old Colburn my first book, and whose acquaintance as an eminent literary man and great notability we had all thought at home it would be such a fine thing to make. He turned out a very small personage indeed, a solemn man, with a commonplace wife, people whom it was marvellous to think of as intellectual. He wrote a book called 'The Marvels of Science,' a dull piece of manufacture, for which by some wonderful chance he received a gold medal, *Für Kunst*, from the King of Hanover. I think I see him moving solemnly about the little drawing-room with this medal on his breast, and the wife following him. He soon stalked away into the unknown, and I saw him no more. I forget how I became acquainted with the S. C. Halls, who used to ask me to their parties, and who were literary people of the most prominent and conventional type, rather satisfying to the sense on the whole, as the sort of thing one expected. Mrs Hall had retired upon the laurels got by one or two Irish novels, and was surrounded by her husband with the atmosphere of admiration, which was the right thing for a "fair" writer. He took her very seriously, and she accepted the *rôle*, though without, I think, any particular setting up of her own standard. I used to think and say that she looked at me inquisitively, a little puzzled to know what kind of humbug I was, all being humbugs. Bus she was a kind woman all the same; and I never forget the sheaf of white lilies she sent us for my child's christening, for which I feel grateful still. He was certainly a humbug of the old mellifluous Irish kind—the sort of man whose specious friendliness, compliments, and "blarney" were of the most innocent kind, not calculated to deceive anybody, but always amusing. He told Irish stories capitally.

They had the most wonderful collection of people at their house, and she would stand and smile and shake hands, till one felt she must stiffen so, and had lost all consciousness who anybody was. He on his side was never tired, always insinuating, jovial, affectionate. It was at their house, I think, that we met the Howitts—Mary Howitt,[14] a mild, kind, delightful woman, who frightened me very much, I remember, by telling me of many babies whom she had lost through some defective valve in the heart, which she said was somehow connected with too much mental work on the part of the mother,—a foolish thing, I should think, yet the same thing occurred twice to myself. It alarmed and saddened me terribly—but I liked her greatly. Not so her husband, who did not please me at all. For a short time we met them everywhere in our small circle, and then they too disappeared, going abroad, I think. There was a great deal about spiritualism (so called) in the air at this time—its first development in England,—and the Howitts' eldest daughter was an art medium producing wonderful scribble-scrabbles, which it was the wonder of wonders to find her mother, so full of sense and truth, so genuine herself, full of enthusiasm about.

I remember a day at the Halls, which must have been in the summer of 1853. They had then a pretty house at Addleston, near Chertsey. My husband and I travelled down by train in company with a dark, dashing person, an American lady, whom, on arriving at the station, we found to be going to the Halls too. She and I were put into their brougham to drive there, while the gentlemen walked; and she did what she could in a patronising way to find out who I was. She thought me, I supposed, the poor little shy wife of some artist, whom the Halls were being kind to, or something of that humble kind. She turned out to be a literary person of great pretensions, calling herself Grace Greenwood, though that was not her real name,—and I was amused to find a paragraph about myself,

---

[14] Mary Howitt (1799–1888), author, editor or translator of more than 110 volumes in her own right (including children's books and the 18 volumes translated from the works of Swedish novelist, Frederika Bremer). *The Heir of West Waylan* (1847) is one of her original works, and she was joint author of many more volumes with her husband.

as "a little homely Scotchwoman," in the book which she wrote when she got back. Two incidents of this entertainment remain very clear in my memory. One was, that being placed at table beside Mr Frost, the academician, who was very deaf and very gentle and kind, I was endeavouring with many mental struggles to repeat to him something that had produced a laugh, and which his wistful look had asked to understand, when suddenly one of those hushes which sometimes come over a large company occurred, and my voice came out distinct—to my own horrified consciousness, at least—a sound of terror and shame to me. The other was, that Gavan Duffy, one of the recent Irish rebels, and my husband began to discuss, I suppose, national characteristics, or what they believed to be such, when the Irishman mentioned gravely and with some heat that the frolic and the wit usually attributed to his countrymen were a mere popular delusion, while the Scotchman with equal earnestness repudiated the caution and prudence ascribed to his race; which was whimsical enough to be remembered.

Another recollection of one of the Halls' evening parties in town at a considerably later period rises like a picture before me. They were fond of every kind of lion and wonder, great and small. Rosa Bonheur, then at the height of her reputation, was there one evening, a round-faced, good-humoured woman, with hair cut short and divided at one side like a man's, and indeed not very distinct in the matter of sex so far as dress and appearance went. There was there also a Chinese mandarin in full costume, smiling blandly upon the company, and accompanied by a missionary, who had the charge of him. By some means or other the Chinaman was made to sing what we were informed was a sentimental ballad, exceedingly touching and romantic. It was like nothing so much as the howl of a dog, one of those grave pieces of canine music which my poor old Newfoundland used to give forth when his favourite organ-grinder came into the street. (Merry's performance was the most comical thing imaginable. There was one organ among many which touched his tenderest feelings. When it appeared once a-week, he rushed to it, seated himself beside the man, listened till rapture and sentiment were wound up to the highest pitch, and then, lifting up his nose and his voice to heaven,—sang. There could be no doubt that the dear dog was giving forth all the poetry of his being in that appalling noise,—his emotion, his sentiment, his profound seriousness were indisputable, while any human being within reach was overwhelmed and helpless with laughter.) The Chinaman sang exactly like Merry, with the same effect. Rosa Bonheur, I suppose, was more civil than *nous autres*, and her efforts to restrain the uncontrollable laugh were superhuman. She almost swallowed her handkerchief in the effort to conceal it. I can see her as in a picture, the central figure, with her bushy short hair, and her handkerchief in her mouth. All my recollections are like pictures, not continuous, only a scene detached and conspicuous here and there.

Miss Muloch[15] was another of the principal figures perceptible in the somewhat dimmed panorama of that far-off life. Her friends the Lovells lived in

[15] Dinah Muloch (Craik), (1826–87), another prolific and popular novelist of the period, best known for *John Halifax, Gentleman* (1856), but unfortunately not included in this collection.

Mornington Crescent, which was close to our little house in Harrington Square, —all in a remote region near Regent's Park, upon the Hampstead Road, where it seems very strange to me we should have lived, and which, I suppose, is dreadfully shabby and out-of-the-way. Perhaps it was shabby then, one's ideas change so greatly. Miss Muloch lived in a small house in a street a little farther off even in the wilds than ours. She was a tall young woman with a slim pliant figure, and eyes that had a way of fixing the eyes of her interlocutor in a manner which did not please my shy fastidiousness. It was embarrassing, as if she meant to read the other upon whom she gazed,—a pretension which one resented. It was merely, no doubt, a fashion of what was the intense school of the time. Mrs Browning[16] did the same thing the only time I met her, and this to one quite indisposed to be read. But Dinah was always kind, enthusiastic, somewhat didactic and apt to teach, and much looked up to by her little band of young women. She too had little parties, at one of which I remember Miss Cushman, the actress, in a deep recitative, without any apparent tune in it, like the voice of a skipper at sea I thought it, giving forth Kingsley's song of "The Sands of Dee." I was rather afraid of the performer, though long afterwards she came to see me in Paris when I was in much sorrow, and her tenderness and feeling gave me the sensation of suddenly meeting a friend in the darkness, of whose existence there I had no conception. There used to be also at Miss Muloch's parties an extraordinary being in a wheeled chair, with an imperfect face (as if it had been somehow left unfinished in the making), a Mr Smedley, a terrible cripple, supposed to be kept together by some framework of springs and supports, of whom the story was told that he had determined, though the son of a rich man, to maintain himself, and make himself a reputation, and had succeeded in doing both, as the writer—of all things in the world—of sporting novels. He was the author of 'Lewis Arundel' and 'Frank Fairleigh,' both I believe athletic books, and full of feats of horsemanship and strength; which was sufficiently pathetic—though the appearance of this poor man somewhat frightened me too.

Mr Lovell, the father of one of Miss Muloch's chief friends, was the author of "The Wife's Secret," a play lately revived, and which struck me when I saw it as one of the most conventional and unreal possible, very curious to come out of that sober city man. All the guests at these little assemblies were something of the same kind. One looked at them rather as one looked at the figures in Madame Tussaud's, wondering if they were waxwork or life—wondering in the other case whether the commonplace outside might not cover a painter or a poet or something equally fine—whose ethereal qualities were all invisible to the ordinary eye.

What I liked best in the way of society was when we went out occasionally quite late in the evening, Frank and I, after he had left off work in his studio, and went to the house of another painter uninvited, unexpected, always welcome,—I with my work. Alexander Johnstone's house was the one to which we went most. I joined the wife in her little drawing-room, while he went up-stairs to the studio.

---

[16] Elizabeth Barrett Browning (1806–61), the most celebrated woman poet of her day.

(They all had the drawing-room proper of the house, the first-floor room, for their studios.) We women talked below of our subjects, as young wives and young mothers do—with a little needlework and a little gossip. The men above smoked and talked their subjects, investigating the picture of the moment, going over it with advice and criticism; no doubt giving each other their opinions of other artists and other pictures too. And then we supped, frugally, cheerfully, and if there was anything of importance in the studio the wives went up to look at it, or see what progress it had made since the last time, after supper. And then we walked home again. They paid us a return visit some days after of just the same kind. If I knew them now, which I no longer do, I would ask them to dinner, and they me, and most likely we would not enjoy it at all. But those simple evenings were very pleasant. Our whole life was upon very simple lines at this period: we dined in the middle of the day, and our little suppers were not of a kind to require elaborate preparation if another pair came in unexpectedly. It was true society in its way. Nothing of the kind seems possible now.

Christina Rossetti

1830 – 94

*C*hristina Rossetti shared the intellectual interests of her brothers, the poet *Dante Gabriel and the critic William Michael. She suffered from ill health when young and gave up attempts at working as a governess. A devout Anglican, she broke off her engagement to James Collinson – one of the Pre-Raphaelite Brotherhood, a group of artists and poets led partly by Dante Gabriel Rossetti – because he had become a Roman Catholic. She wrote prose and poetry, ranging from the devotional to the fantastic, her most famous work being the rhythmically experimental 'Goblin Market'. Some of her poetry is melancholic and there are repeated references to unhappy love and the struggle for resignation.*

The following poems are taken from The Complete Poems of Christina Rossetti *(R. W. Crump (ed.), Louisiana State University Press, 1980).*

MONNA INNOMINATA

A SONNET OF SONNETS

BEATRICE, immortalized by "altissimo poeta . . . cotanto amante"; Laura, celebrated by a great tho' an inferior bard,[1]—have alike paid the exceptional penalty of exceptional honour, and have come down to us resplendent with charms, but (at least, to my apprehension) scant of attractiveness.

These heroines of world-wide fame were preceded by a bevy of unnamed ladies "donne innominate" sung by a school of less conspicuous poets; and in that land and that period which gave simultaneous birth to Catholics, to Albigenses, and to Troubadours, one can imagine many a lady as sharing her lover's poetic aptitude, while the barrier between them might be one held sacred by both, yet not such as to render mutual love incompatible with mutual honour.

Had such a lady spoken for herself, the portrait left us might have appeared more tender, if less dignified, than any drawn even by a devoted friend. Or had the Great Poetess of our own day and nation[2] only been unhappy instead of happy, her circumstances would have invited her to bequeath to us, in lieu of the "Portuguese Sonnets," an inimitable "donna innominata" drawn not from fancy but from feeling, and worthy to occupy a niche beside Beatrice and Laura.

I

"Lo dì che han detto a' dolci amici addio."—DANTE.
"Amor, con quanto sforzo oggi mi vinci!"—PETRARCA.[3]

Come back to me, who wait and watch for you:—
    Or come not yet, for it is over then,
    And long it is before you come again,
So far between my pleasures are and few.
While, when you come not, what I do I do
    Thinking "Now when he comes," my sweetest "when:"
    For one man is my world of all the men
This wide world holds; O love, my world is you.
Howbeit, to meet you grows almost a pang
    Because the pang of parting comes so soon;

---

[1] Beatrice was celebrated by Dante (1265–1321) in the *Vita nuova* and the *Divina Commedia*; Laura was the subject of the love poetry of Petrarch (1304–74).
[2] Elizabeth Barrett Browning.
[3] These and all following translations of Dante and Petrarch were originally made by William Michael Rossetti, Christina's brother.
  The day that they have said adieu to their sweet friends. (Dante)
  Love, with how great a stress dost thou vanquish me today! (Petrarca)

My hope hangs waning, waxing, like a moon
    Between the heavenly days on which we meet:
Ah me, but where are now the songs I sang
    When life was sweet because you called them sweet?

2

"E RA già l'ora che volge il desio."—DANTE.
   "Ricorro al tempo ch'io vi vidi prima."—PETRARCA.[4]

I wish I could remember that first day,
    First hour, first moment of your meeting me,
    If bright or dim the season, it might be
Summer or Winter for aught I can say;
So unrecorded did it slip away,
    So blind was I to see and to foresee,
    So dull to mark the budding of my tree
That would not blossom yet for many a May.
If only I could recollect it, such
    A day of days! I let it come and go
    As traceless as a thaw of bygone snow;
It seemed to mean so little, meant so much;
If only now I could recall that touch,
    First touch of hand in hand—Did one but know!

3

"O OMBRE vane, fuor che ne l'aspetto!"—DANTE.
   "Immaginata guida la conduce."—PETRARCA.[5]

I dream of you to wake: would that I might
    Dream of you and not wake but slumber on;
    Nor find with dreams the dear companion gone,
As Summer ended Summer birds take flight.
In happy dreams I hold you full in sight,
    I blush again who waking look so wan;
    Brighter than sunniest day that ever shone,
In happy dreams your smile makes day of night.
Thus only in a dream we are at one,

---

[4] It was already the hour which turns back the hour. (Dante)
    I recur to the time when I first saw thee. (Petrarca)
[5] O shades, empty save in semblance! (Dante)
    An imaginary guide conducts her. (Petrarca)

Thus only in a dream we give and take
   The faith that maketh rich who take or give;
If thus to sleep is sweeter than to wake,
   To die were surely sweeter than to live,
Tho' there be nothing new beneath the sun.

4

"POCA favilla gran fiamma seconda."—DANTE.
  "Ogni altra cosa, ogni pensier va fore,
E sol ivi con voi rimansi amore."—PETRARCA.[6]

I loved you first: but afterwards your love
   Outsoaring mine, sang such a loftier song
As drowned the friendly cooings of my dove.
   Which owes the other most? my love was long,
   And yours one moment seemed to wax more strong;
I loved and guessed at you, you construed me
And loved me for what might or might not be—
   Nay, weights and measures do us both a wrong.
For verily love knows not "mine" or "thine;"
   With separate "I" and "thou" free love has done,
   For one is both and both are one in love:
Rich love knows nought of "thine that is not mine;"
   Both have the strength and both the length thereof,
Both of us, of the love which makes us one.

5

"AMOR che a nulla amato amar perdona."—DANTE.
  "Amor m'addusse in sì gioiosa spene."—PETRARCA.[7]

O my heart's heart, and you who are to me
   More than myself myself, God be with you,
   Keep you in strong obedience leal and true
To Him whose noble service setteth free,
Give you all good we see or can foresee,
   Make your joys many and your sorrows few,
   Bless you in what you bear and what you do,

[6] A small spark fosters a great flame. (Dante)
  Every other thing, every thought goes off, and love alone remains there with you. (Petrarch)
[7] Love, who exempts no loved one from loving. (Dante)
  Love led me into such joyous hope. (Petrarch)

Yea, perfect you as He would have you be.
So much for you; but what for me, dear friend?
　　To love you without stint and all I can
Today, tomorrow, world without an end;
　　　　To love you much and yet to love you more,
　　As Jordan at his flood sweeps either shore;
Since woman is the helpmeet made for man.

6

"OR puoi la quantitate
　　Comprender de l'amor che a te mi scalda."—DANTE.
"Non vo'che da tal nodo amor mi scioglia."—PETRARCA.[8]

Trust me, I have not earned your dear rebuke,
　I love, as you would have me, God the most;
　　Would lose not Him, but you, must one be lost,
Nor with Lot's wife cast back a faithless look
Unready to forego what I forsook;
　This say I, having counted up the cost,
　This, tho' I be the feeblest of God's host,
The sorriest sheep Christ shepherds with His crook.
Yet while I love my God the most, I deem
　　That I can never love you overmuch;
　　　I love Him more, so let me love you too;
　　Yea, as I apprehend it, love is such
I cannot love you if I love not Him,
　　I cannot love Him if I love not you.

7

"QUI primavera sempre ed ogni frutto."—DANTE.
　　"Ragionando con meco ed io con lui."—PETRARCA.[9]

"Love me, for I love you"—and answer me,
　"Love me, for I love you"—so shall we stand
　　As happy equals in the flowering land
Of love, that knows not a dividing sea.

[8] Now canst thou comprehend the quantity of the love which glows in me towards
thee. (Dante)
　I do not choose that love should release me from such a tie. (Petrarch)
[9] Here always spring and every fruit. (Dante)
　Conversing with me, and I with him. (Petrarch)

Love builds the house on rock and not on sand,
   Love laughs what while the winds rave desperately;
And who hath found love's citadel unmanned?
   And who hath held in bonds love's liberty?
My heart's a coward tho' my words are brave—
   We meet so seldom, yet we surely part
   So often; there's problem for your art!
      Still I find comfort in his Book, who saith,
Tho' jealousy be cruel as the grave,
   And death be strong, yet love is strong as death.

8

"COME dicesse a Dio: D'altro non calme."—DANTE.
   "Spero trovar pietà non che perdono."—PETRARCA.[10]

"I, if I perish, perish"—Esther spake:
And bride of life or death she made her fair
In all the lustre of her perfumed hair
And smiles that kindle longing but to slake.
She put on pomp of loveliness, to take
   Her husband thro' his eyes at unaware;
   She spread abroad her beauty for a snare,
Harmless as doves and subtle as a snake.
She trapped him with one mesh of silken hair,
   She vanquished him by wisdom of her wit,
      And built her people's house that it should stand:—
      If I might take my life so in my hand,
And for my love to Love put up my prayer,
   And for love's sake by Love be granted it!

9

"O dignitosa coscienza e netta!"—DANTE.
   "Spirto più acceso di virtuti ardenti."—PETRARCA.[11]

Thinking of you, and all that was, and all
   That might have been and now can never be,

---

[10] As if he were to say to God, 'I care for naught else.' (Dante)
  I hope to find pity, and not only pardon. (Petrarch)
[11] O dignified and pure conscience! (Dante)
  Spirit more lit with burning virtues. (Petrarch)

I feel your honoured excellence, and see
Myself unworthy of the happier call:
For woe is me who walk so apt to fall,
   So apt to shrink afraid, so apt to flee,
   Apt to lie down and die (ah, woe is me!)
Faithless and hopeless turning to the wall.
And yet not hopeless quite nor faithless quite,
Because not loveless; love may toil all night,
   But take at morning; wrestle till the break
      Of day, but then wield power with God and man:—
      So take I heart of grace as best I can,
Ready to spend and be spent for your sake.

10

"CON miglior corso e con migliore stella."—DANTE.
    "La vita fugge e non s'arresta un' ora."—PETRARCA.[12]

Time flies, hope flags, life plies a wearied wing;
   Death following hard on life gains ground apace;
   Faith runs with each and rears an eager face,
Outruns the rest, makes light of everything,
Spurns earth, and still finds breath to pray and sing;
   While love ahead of all uplifts his praise,
   Still asks for grace and still gives thanks for grace,
Content with all day brings and night will bring.
Life wanes; and when love folds his wings above
   Tired hope, and less we feel his conscious pulse,
      Let us go fall asleep, dear friend, in peace:
      A little while, and age and sorrow cease;
   A little while, and life reborn annuls
Loss and decay and death, and all is love.

11

"VIEN dietro a me e lascia dir le genti."—DANTE.
    "Contando i casi della vita nostra."—PETRARCA.[13]

Many in aftertimes will say of you
   "He loved her"—while of me what will they say?

[12] With better course and with better star. (Dante)
   Life flees, and stays not an hour. (Petrarch)
[13] Come after me and leave folk to talk. (Dante)
   Relating the casualties of our life. (Petrarch)

Not that I loved you more than just in play,
For fashion's sake as idle women do.
Even let them prate; who know not what we knew
  Of love and parting in exceeding pain,
  Of parting hopeless here to meet again,
Hopeless on earth, and heaven is out of view.
But by my heart of love laid bare to you,
  My love that you can make not void nor vain,
Love that foregoes you but to claim anew
    Beyond this passage of the gate of death,
  I charge you at the Judgment make it plain
  My love of you was life and not a breath.

12

"A MOR, che ne la mente mi ragiona."—DANTE.
  "Amor vien nel bel viso di costei."—PETRARCA.[14]

If there be any one can take my place
  And make you happy whom I grieve to grieve,
  Think not that I can grudge it, but believe
I do commend you to that nobler grace,
That readier wit than mine, that sweeter face;
  Yea, since your riches make me rich, conceive
  I too am crowned, while bridal crowns I weave,
And thread the bridal dance with jocund pace.
For if I did not love you, it might be
  That I should grudge you some one dear delight;
    But since the heart is yours that was mine own,
  Your pleasure is my pleasure, right my right,
Your honourable freedom makes me free,
    And you companioned I am not alone.

13

"E drizzeremo glí occhi al Primo Amore."—DANTE.
  "Ma trovo peso non da le mie braccia."—PETRARCA.[15]

If I could trust mine own self with your fate,
  Shall I not rather trust it in God's hand?

---

[14] Love, who speaks within my mind. (Dante)
  Love comes in the beautiful face of this lady. (Petrarch)
[15] And we will direct our eyes to the Primal Love. (Dante)
  But I find a burden to which my arms suffice not. (Petrarch)

Without Whose Will one lily doth not stand,
Nor sparrow fall at his appointed date;
　　Who numbereth the innumerable sand,
Who weighs the wind and water with a weight,
To Whom the world is neither small nor great,
　　Whose knowledge foreknew every plan we planned.
Searching my heart for all that touches you,
　　I find there only love and love's goodwill
Helpless to help and impotent to do,
　　　　Of understanding dull, of sight most dim;
　　　And therefore I commend you back to Him
Whose love your love's capacity can fill.

14

"E la Sua Volontade è nostra pace."—DANTE.
　　"Sol con questi pensier, con altre chiome."—PETRARCA.[16]

Youth gone, and beauty gone if ever there
　　Dwelt beauty in so poor a face as this;
　　Youth gone and beauty, what remains of bliss?
I will not bind fresh roses in my hair,
To shame a cheek at best but little fair,—
　　Leave youth his roses, who can bear a thorn,—
I will not seek for blossoms anywhere,
　　Except such common flowers as blow with corn.
Youth gone and beauty gone, what doth remain?
　　The longing of a heart pent up forlorn,
　　　A silent heart whose silence loves and longs;
　　　The silence of a heart which sang its songs
　　While youth and beauty made a summer morn,
Silence of love that cannot sing again.

[16] And His will is our peace. (Dante)
　　Only with these thoughts, with different locks. (Petrarch)

Mary Elizabeth Braddon

1837 – 1915

orn in London, Mary Elizabeth Braddon had an impoverished childhood owing to the 'unreliability' of her father; in 1840 her mother was forced to leave him and she took Mary with her. Mary began writing but it afforded insufficient support and in 1857, as Mary Seaton, she went on the stage out of financial necessity. In 1860 she turned to full-time writing again and with the publication of Lady Audley's Secret *in 1862 she became eminently successful. When she met the publisher John Maxwell (whose wife was institutionalised in Ireland) she lived with him and cared for his five children and their own six, while earning money to support the large family. In all she wrote more than seventy novels, as well as plays and some verse: she also edited several London magazines, including* Belgravia. *She was a best-selling 'sensation' novelist and one who was also witty, satirical and often irreverent.*

The following extract is taken from Vixen *(1879) and reveals something of the cutting edge in her romantic fiction.*

From

Vixen

CHAPTER XXXI
'KURZ IST DER SCHMERZ UND EWIG IST DIE FREUDE'[1]

APTAIN WINSTANLEY said no more about Lord Mallow; but Violet had to listen to much plaintive bemoaning from her mother, who could not understand how any well-brought-up young woman could refuse an Irish peer with a fine estate, and the delights of a *trousseau* made by the renowned Theodore. Upon this latter detail Mrs. Winstanley dwelt at more length than upon that minor circumstance in a marriage—the bridegroom.

[1] Pain is short; joy is eternal.

'It would have been such a pleasure to me to plan your *trousseau*, darling,' she said; 'such an occupation for my mind in these wretched winter afternoons when there is no possibility of driving or making calls. I should have attended to everything myself. Theodore's general way is to make a list of what she thinks necessary, allowing her customer to correct it; but I should not have been satisfied with that, even from Theodore, though I admit that her taste is perfect. And then, you know, she is hand in glove with Worth,[2] and that alone is a liberal education, as somebody says somewhere about something. No, dear, I would have done it all myself. I know the exact shades that suit your complexion, the dashes of colour that contrast with and light up your hair, the style that sets off your figure. Your *trousseau* should be talked about in society, and even described in the fashion magazines. And then Lord Mallow is really so very nice—and has such a charming baritone—what more can you want?'

'Only to love him, mother dearest, which I do not, and never shall. That frank loud voice of his does not stir a fibre of my heart. I like him extremely, and so I do Mr. Scobel, and Bates the groom. Lord Mallow is no more to me than either of those. Indeed, Bates is much nearer and dearer, for he loved my father.'

'My dear Violet, you have the most radical ideas. Imagine anyone putting Bates on a level with Lord Mallow!'

'I don't, mamma. I only say he is more to me than Lord Mallow could ever be.'

'Your travelling-dress,' murmured Mrs. Winstanley, her mind still dwelling on the *trousseau*; 'that affords more scope for taste than the wedding-gown. Velvet suits your style, but is too heavy for your age. A soft clinging cashmere, now, one of those delicious neutral tints that have been so fashionable lately, over an underskirt of a warmer shade in *poult de soie*, a picturesque costume that would faintly recall Lely's portraits at Hampton Court.'

'Dear mamma, what is the use of talking about dresses I am never going to require? Not for all the finery that Theodore ever made would I marry Lord Mallow, or anybody else. I am happy enough with you, and my horse, and my dog, and all the dear old things, animal and vegetable, that belong to this dear old place. I shall never leave you, or the Forest. Can you not be content to know this and let me alone?'

'You are a very wilful girl, Violet, and ridiculously blind to your own interests,' remarked Mrs. Winstanley, throwing herself back in her chair with a fretful look, 'and you put me in an absurd position. The Duchess quite congratulated me about your brilliant prospects, when we were chatting together on New Year's Eve. Anybody could see how devoted Lord Mallow was, she said, and what a splendid match it would be for you.'

'Let the Duchess marry her own daughter, and leave me alone,' cried Vixen scornfully.

This was the kind of thing she had to endure continually, during the chill winter months that followed Lord Mallow's departure. Even her old friends the

---

[2] An Englishman who became on of Paris's leading couturiers.

Scobels worried her about the Irish peer, and lamented her inability to perceive his merits. It was known throughout her particular circle that she had been idiotic enough to refuse Lord Mallow. Mrs. Winstanley had whispered the fact to all her friends, under the seal of strictest secrecy. Of all Vixen's acquaintance, Roderick Vawdrey was the only one who said no word to her about Lord Mallow; but he was much kinder to her after the Irishman's departure than he had shown himself during his visit.

Spring put on her green mantle; and when the woods were starred with primroses, and the banks lovely with heaven-hued dog-violets, everyone of any pretension to importance in the social scale began to flee from the Forest as from a loathsome place. Lord Ellangowan's train of vans and waggons set out for the railway station with their load of chests and baskets. The departure of the Israelites from Egypt was hardly a mightier business than this emigration of the Ellangowan household. The Duke and Duchess, and Lady Mabel Ashbourne, left for the Queen Anne house at Kensington, whereat the fashionable London papers broke out in paragraphs of rejoicing, and the local journals bewailed the extinction of their sun.

The London season had begun, and only the nobodies stayed in the Forest to watch the rosy sunsets glow and fade behind the yellow oaks; to see the purple of the beech-boughs change mysteriously to brightest green; and the bluebells burst into blossom in the untrodden glades and bottoms. Captain Winstanley found a small house in Mayfair, which he hired for six weeks, at a rent which he pronounced exorbitant. He sacrificed his own ideas of prudence to the gratification of his wife, who had made up her mind that she had scarcely the right to exist until she had been presented to her sovereign in her new name. But when Mrs. Winstanley ventured to suggest the Duchess of Dovedale as her sponsor on this solemn occasion, her husband sternly tabooed the notion.

'My aunt, Lady Susan Winstanley, is the proper person to present you,' he said authoritatively.

'But is she really your aunt, Conrad? You never mentioned her before we were married.'

'She is my father's third cousin by marriage; but we have always called her Aunt. She is the widow of Major-General Winstanley, who distinguished himself in the last war with Tippoo Saïb, and had a place at Court in the reign of William the Fourth.'

'She must be dreadfully old and dowdy,' sighed Mrs. Winstanley, whose only historical idea of the Sailor King's reign was as a period of short waists and beaver bonnets.

'She is not a chicken, and she does not spend eight hundred a year on her dressmaker,' retorted the Captain. 'But she is a very worthy woman, and highly respected by her friends. Why should you ask a favour of the Duchess of Dovedale?'

'Her name would look so well in the papers,' pleaded Mrs. Winstanley.

'The name of your husband's kinswoman will look much more respectable,' answered the Captain; and in this, as in most matters, he had his own way.

Lady Susan Winstanley was brought from her palatial retirement to spend a fortnight in Mayfair. She was bony, wiggy, and snuffy; wore false teeth and seedy apparel; but she was well-bred and well-informed, and Vixen got on with her much better than with the accomplished Captain. Lady Susan took to Vixen; and these two went out for early walks together in the adjacent Green Park, and perambulated the picture-galleries, before Mrs. Winstanley had braced herself up for the fatigues of a fashionable afternoon.

Sometimes they came across Mr. Vawdrey at a picture-gallery or in the Park; and at the first of these chance meetings, struck by the obvious delight with which the two young people greeted each other, Lady Susan jumped to a conclusion.

'That's your young man, I suppose, my dear,' she said bluntly, when Rorie had left them.

'O, Lady Susan!'

'It's a vulgar expression, I know, my dear, but it comes natural to me; I hear it so often from my maid. I fancied that you and that handsome young fellow must be engaged.'

'O no; we are only old friends. He is engaged to Lady Mabel Ashbourne—a very grand match.'

'That's a pity,' said Lady Susan.

'Why?'

'Well, my dear,' answered the old lady hesitatingly; 'because when one hears of a grand match, it generally means that a young man is marrying for the sake of money, and that young old friend of yours looks too good to throw himself away like that.'

'O but indeed, Lady Susan, it is not so in Rorie's case. He has plenty of money of his own!'

The important day came; and Lady Susan, Mrs. Winstanley, and Violet packed themselves and their finery into a capacious carriage, and set off for St. James's. The fair Pamela's costume was an elaborate example of Theodore's highest art; colours, design, all of the newest—a delicate harmony of half tints, an indescribable interblending of feathers, lace, and flowers. Violet was simply and elegantly dressed by the same great artist. Lady Susan wore a petticoat and train that must have been made in the time of Queen Adelaide. Yes, the faded and unknown hue of the substantial brocade, the skimpiness of the satin, the quaint devices in piping-cord and feather-stitch —must assuredly have been coeval with that good woman's famous hat and spencer.

Poor Mrs. Winstanley was horrified when she saw her husband's kinswoman attired for the ceremony, not a whit less wiggy and snuffy than usual, and with three lean ostrich feathers starting erect from her back hair, like the ladies in the proscenium boxes of Skelt's Theatre, whose gaily painted effigies were so dear to our childhood.

Poor Pamela felt inclined to shed tears. Even her confidence in the perfection of her own toilet could hardly sustain her against the horror of being presented by such a scarecrow.

The ceremony went off satisfactorily, in spite of Lady Susan's antiquated garments. Nobody laughed. Perhaps the *habitués* of St. James's were accustomed to scarecrows. Violet's fresh young beauty attracted some little notice as she waited among the crowd of *débutantes*; but, on its being ascertained that she was nobody in particular, curiosity languished and died.

Mrs. Winstanley wanted to exhibit her court-dress at the opera that evening, but her husband protested against this display as bad style. Vixen was only too glad to throw off her finery, the tulle puffings and festoonings, and floral wreaths and bouquets, which made movement difficult and sitting down almost impossible.

Those six weeks in town were chiefly devoted to gaiety. Mrs. Winstanley's Hampshire friends called on her, and followed up their calls by invitations to dinner; and at the dinners she generally met people who were on the eve of giving a garden-party, or a concert, or a dance, and who begged to be allowed to send her a card for that entertainment, spoken of modestly as a thing of no account. And then there was a hurried interchange of calls, and Violet found herself meandering about an unknown croquet-lawn, amongst unknown nobodies, under a burning sun, looking at other girls, dressed like herself in gowns *à la* Theodore, with the last thing in sleeves, and the last cut in trains, all pretending to be amused by the vapid and languid observations of the cavalier told off to them, paired like companions of the chain at Toulon, and almost as joyless.

Violet Tempest attended no less than eight private concerts during those six weeks, and heard the same new ballad, and the same latest *gavotte* in C minor, at every one of them. She was taken to pianoforte recitals in fashionable squares and streets, and heard Bach and Beethoven till her heart ached with pity for the patient labour of the performers, knowing how poorly she and the majority of mankind appreciated their efforts. She went to a few dances that were rather amusing, and waltzed to her heart's content. She rode Arion in the Row, and horse and rider were admired as perfect after their kind. Once she met Lord Mallow, riding beside Lady Mabel Ashbourne and the Duke of Dovedale. His florid cheek paled a little at the sight of her. They passed each other with a friendly bow, and this was their only meeting. Lord Mallow left cards at the house in Mayfair a week before the Winstanleys went back to Hampshire. He had been working hard at his senatorial duties, and had made some telling speeches upon the Irish land question. People talked of him as a rising politician; and whenever his name appeared in the morning papers, Mrs. Winstanley uplifted her voice at the breakfast-table, and made her wail about Violet's folly in refusing such an excellent young man.

'It would have been so nice to be able to talk about my daughter, Lady Mallow, and Castle Mallow,' said Pamela in confidence to her husband.

'No doubt, my dear,' he answered coolly; 'but when you bring up a young woman to have her own way in everything, you must take the consequences.'

'It is very ungrateful of Violet,' sighed the afflicted mother, 'after the pains I have taken to dress her prettily, ever since she was a baby. It is a very poor return for my care.'

Anne Thackeray
later Lady Ritchie
1837 – 1919

A novelist, essayist, literary critic and memoirist, Anne Thackeray was the eldest
daughter of William Thackeray, through whom she became familiar with
many of society's literary figures. She wrote eight successful impressionistic
novels which influenced her step-niece, Virginia Woolf, who drew a portrait of her
as Mrs Hilbery in Night and Day. A member of a circle of literary women (which
included Margaret Oliphant and Rhoda Broughton), she wrote perceptively about
women's literary traditions. Virginia Woolf believed that Anne Thackeray's fiction
and criticism were sadly undervalued.

The following is an extract from her book, Toilers and Spinsters and Other
Essays (Smith, Elder, London, 1874).

Heroines and Their Grandmothers[1]

Fantasio. Qui sait? Un calembour console de bien des chagrins, et jouer avec les
mots est un moyen comme un autre de jouer avec les pensées, les actions et les êtres.
Tout est calembour ici-bas, et il est ainsi difficile de comprendre le regard d'un enfant
de quatre ans, que le galimatias de trois drames modernes.

Elsbeth. Tu me fais l'effet de regarder le monde à travers un prisme tant soit peu
changeant.

Fantasio. Chacun a ses lunettes, mais personne ne sait au juste de quelle couleur
en sont les verres. Qui est ce qui pourra me dire au juste si je suis heureux ou
malheureux, bon ou mauvais, triste ou gai, bête ou spirituel?[2]

[1] This is a review-article, based on three novels: *Too Much Alone*; *City and Suburb*; *George Geith*,
by Mrs Riddell.

Mrs Riddell (Charlotte, E. L. and pseudonym F. G. Trafford): 'Mrs Riddell was born in Ireland,
at The Barn, Carrigfergus. She was the youngest daughter of Mr James Cowan, who held the post
of High Sheriff for the county of that town' (Helen Black, 1893, *Notable Women Authors of the Day*,
David Bryce & Son, Glasgow, 'Mrs Riddell' pp. 11–25). Author of more than thirty novels – the most
acclaimed of which was *George Geith of Fen Court* – she enjoyed a considerable reputation in
her day; her publisher and friend was George Bentley. The fact that there is so little biographical
information about her now is indicative of her current literary oblivion.

[2] FANTASIO: Who knows? A pun offers consolation for a good many sorrows, and playing with
words is a way of playing with thoughts, actions and people. Everything is a pun down here, and
it is just as difficult to understand the look in the eyes of a four-year-old child as all the high-flown
nonsense of three modern plays.

ELSBETH: You will make me stop looking at the world in an unchanging perspective.

FANTASIO: Everyone has their own viewpoint, but nobody knows exactly from what position
they are viewing. Who can tell me truthfully if I am happy or unhappy, good or evil, sad or gay,
stupid or intelligent?

WHY do we now-a-days write such melancholy novels? Are authoresses more miserable than they used to be a hundred years ago? Miss Austen's heroines came tripping into the room, bright-eyed, rosy-cheeked, arch, and good-humoured. Evelina and Cecilia would have thoroughly enjoyed their visits to the opera, and their expeditions to the masquerades, if it had not been for their vulgar relations. Valancourt's Emily was a little upset, to be sure, when she found herself all alone in the ghostly and mouldy castle in the south of France; but she, too, was naturally a lively girl, and on the whole showed a great deal of courage and presence of mind. Miss Edgeworth's heroines were pleasant and easily pleased; and to these may be added a blooming rose-garden of wild Irish girls, and of good-humoured and cheerful young ladies, who consented to make the devoted young hero happy at the end of the third volume, without any very intricate self-examinations; and who certainly were much more appreciated by the heroes of those days, than our modern heroines with all their workings and deep feelings and unrequited affections are now, by the noblemen and gentlemen to whom they happen to be attached.

If one could imagine the ladies of whom we have been speaking coming to life again, and witnessing all the vagaries and agonising experiences and deadly calm and irrepressible emotion of their granddaughters, the heroines of the present day, what a bewildering scene it would be! Evelina and Cecilia ought to faint with horror! Madame Duval's most shocking expressions were never so alarming as the remarks they might now hear on all sides. Elizabeth Bennett would certainly burst out laughing, Emma might lose her temper, and Fanny Price would turn scarlet and stop her little ears. Perhaps Emily of Udolpho, more accustomed than the others to the horrors of sensation, and having once faced those long and terrible passages, might be able to hold her own against such a great-granddaughter as Aurora Floyd or Lady Audley. But how would she deal with the soul-workings and heart-troubles of a Dorothea Casaubon, or of her hysterical namesake Dolly Vanborough, or of Ethel May in the 'Daisy Chain,' or Cousin Phillis, or Margaret Hale, or Jane Eyre, or Lucy Snowe, or poor noble Dinah's perplexities![3] Emily would probably prefer any amount of tortuous mysteries, winding staircases and passages, or groans and groans, and yards and yards of faded curtains, to the task of mastering these modern intricacies of feeling and reality and sentiment.

Are the former heroines women as they were, or as they were supposed to be in those days? Are the women of whom women write now, women as they are,

---

[3] Among the references to women writers and their work — apart from the references to Mrs Riddell — are the following: Fanny Burney, and her characters Madame Duval and Evelina (*Evelina*, 1778), and Cecilia (*Cecilia*, 1782); Jane Austen and her characters Elizabeth Bennett (*Pride and Prejudice*, 1813) and Emma Woodhouse (*Emma*, 1816); Ann Radcliffe and her character Emily of *The Mysteries of Udolpho* (1794); Mary Elizabeth Braddon and her characters Aurora Floyd (*Aurora Floyd*, 1868) and Lady Audley (*Lady Audley's Secret*, 1862); Charlotte Bronte and her characters Jane Eyre (*Jane Eyre*, 1840) and Lucy Snowe (*Villette*, 1853); George Eliot's Dorothea Casaubon (*Middlemarch*, 1871); Charlotte Yonge's *Daisy Chain* (1856) about the May family and their eldest daughter Margaret; Elizabeth Gaskell and her characters Phillis (*Cousin Phillis*, 1864) and Margaret Hale (*North and South*, 1855); and George Eliot's character Dinah (*Adam Bede*, 1859).

or women as they are supposed to be? Does our modern taste demand a certain sensation feeling, sensation sentiment, only because it is actually experienced?

This is a question to be answered on some other occasion; but, in the meantime, it would seem as if all the good humours and good spirits of former generations had certainly deserted our own heart-broken ladies. Instead of cheerful endurance, the very worst is made of every passing discomfort. Their laughter is forced, even their happiness is only calm content, for they cannot so readily recover from the two first volumes. They no longer smile and trip through country-dances hand-in-hand with their adorers, but waltz with heavy hearts and dizzy brains, while the hero who scorns them looks on. Open the second volume, you will see that, instead of sitting in the drawing-room or plucking roses in the bower, or looking pretty and pleasant, they are lying on their beds with agonising headaches, walking desperately along the streets they know not whither, or staring out of window in blank despair. It would be curious to ascertain in how great a degree language measures feeling. People, with the help of the penny-post and the telegraph, and the endless means of communication and of coming and going, are certainly able to care for a greater number of persons than they could have done a hundred years ago; perhaps they are also able to care more, and to be more devotedly attached, to those whom they already love; they certainly say more about it, and, perhaps, with its greater abundance and opportunity, expression may have depreciated in value. And this may possibly account for some of the difference between the reserved and measured language of a Jane Bennett or an Anne Elliot, and the tempestuous confidences of their successors.

Much that is written now is written with a certain exaggeration and an earnestness which was undreamt of in the placid days when, according to Miss Austen, a few assembly balls and morning visits, a due amount of vexation reasonably surmounted, or at most 'smiles reined in, and spirits dancing in private rapture,' a journey to Bath, an attempt at private theatricals or a thick packet of explanations hurriedly signed with the hero's initials, were the events, the emotions, the aspirations of a life-time.

They had their accomplishments, these gigot-sleeved ladies: witness Emma's very mild performances in the way of portrait taking; but as for tracking murderers, agonies of mystery, and disappointed affections, flinging themselves at gentlemen's heads, marrying two husbands at once, flashing with irrepressible emotion, or only betraying the deadly conflict going on within by a slight quiver of the pale lip—such ideas never entered their pretty little heads. They fainted a good deal, we must confess, and wrote long and tedious letters to aged clergymen residing in the country. They exclaimed 'La!' when anything surprised them, and were, we believe, dreadfully afraid of cows, notwithstanding their country connection. But they were certainly a more amiable race than their successors.

It is a fact that people do not unusually feel the same affection for phenomenons, however curious, that they do for perfectly commonplace human creatures. And yet at the same time we confess that it does seem somewhat ungrateful to complain of these living and adventurous heroines to whom, with all their vagaries, one has owed such long and happy hours of amusement and entertainment and comfort, and who have gone through so much for our edification.

Still one cannot but wonder how Miss Austen would have written if she had lived to-day instead of yesterday. It has been often said that novels might be divided into two great divisions—the objective and the subjective: almost all men's novels belong to the former; almost all women's, now-a-days, to the latter definition. Analysis of emotion instead of analysis of character, the history of feeling instead of the history of events, seems to be the method of the majority of penwomen. The novels that we have in hand to review now are examples of this mode of treatment; and the truth is, that, except in the case of the highest art and most consummate skill, there is no comparison between the interest excited by facts and general characteristics, as compared with the interest of feeling and emotion told with only the same amount of perception and ability.

Few people, for instance, could read the story of the poor lady who lived too much alone without being touched by the simple earnestness with which her sorrows are written down, although in the bare details of her life there might not be much worth recording. But this is the history of poor Mrs. Storn's feelings more than that of her life—of feelings very sad and earnest and passionate, full of struggle for right, with truth to help and untruth to bewilder her; with power and depth and reality in her struggles, which end at last in a sad sort of twilight that seems to haunt one as one shuts up the book. In 'George Geith,' of which we will speak more presently, there is the same sadness and minor key ringing all through the composition. Indeed, all this author's tunes are very melancholy—so melancholy, that it would seem almost like a defect if they were not at the same time very sweet as well as very sad. Too Much Alone is a young woman who marries a very silent, upright, and industrious chemical experimentalist. He has well-cut features, honourable feelings, a genius for discovering cheap ways of producing acids and chemicals, as well as ideas about cyanosium, which, combined with his perfect trust in and utter neglect of his wife, very nearly brings about the destruction of all their domestic happiness. She is a pale, sentimental young woman, with raven-black hair, clever, and longing for sympathy—a *femme incomprise*, it must be confessed, but certainly much more charming and pleasant and pathetic than such people usually are. Days go by, lonely alike for her, without occupation or friendship or interest; she cannot consort with the dull and vulgar people about her; she has her little son, but he is not a companion. Her husband is absorbed in his work. She has no one to talk to, nothing to do or think of. She lives all alone in the great noisy life-full city, sad and pining and wistful and weary. Here is a little sketch of her:—

'Lina was sitting, thinking about the fact that she had been married many months more than three years, and that on the especial Sunday morning in question she was just of age. It was still early; for Mr. Storn, according to the fashion of most London folks, borrowed hours from both ends of the day; and his wife was sitting there until it should be time for her to get ready and to go to church alone. Her chair was placed by the open window; and though the city was London, and the locality either the ward of Eastcheap or that of

Allhallows, Barking (I am not quite sure which), fragrant odours came wafted to her senses through the casement; for in this, as in all other things save one, Maurice had considered her nurture and her tastes, and covered the roof of the counting-house with flowers. But for the distant roll of the carriages, she might just as well have been miles away from London. . . . She was dressed in a pink morning dress, with her dark hair plainly braided upon her pale fair cheek, and she had a staid sober look upon her face, that somehow made her appear handsomer than in the days of old before she married. . . .'

This very Sunday Lina meets a dangerous fascinating man of the world, who is a friendly well-meaning creature withal, and who can understand and sympathise with her sadness and solitude only too well for her peace of mind, and for his own: again and again she appeals to her husband: 'I will find pleasure in the driest employment if you will only let me be with you, and not leave me alone.' She only asks for justice, for confidence—not the confidence of utter desertion and trust and neglect, but the daily confidence and communion, which is a necessity to some women, the permission to share in the common interests and efforts of her husband's life; to be allowed to sympathise, and to live, and to understand, instead of being left to pine away lonely, unhappy, half asleep, and utterly weary and disappointed. Unfortunately Mr. Storn thinks it is all childish nonsense, and repulses her in the most affectionate manner; poor unhappy Lina behaves as well as ever she can, and devotes herself to her little boy, only her hair grows blacker, and her face turns paler and paler, day by day; she is very good and struggles to be contented, and will not allow herself to think too much of Herbert Clyne, and so things go on in the old way for a long, long time; and we turn page after page, feeling that each one may bring some terrible catastrophe. At last a crisis comes—troubles thicken—Maurice Storn is always away when he is most wanted; little Geordie, the son, gets hold of some of his father's chemicals, which have cost Lina already so much happiness and confidence, and the poor little boy poisons himself with something sweet out of a little bottle. All the description which follows is very powerfully and pathetically told—Maurice Storn's silence and misery, Lina's desperation and sudden change of feeling. After all her long struggles and efforts she suddenly breaks down, all her courage leaves her, and her desperate longings for right and clinging to truth.

'She said in her soul, "I have lost the power either to bear or to resist. I have tried to face my misfortune and I feel I am incapable of doing it . . . why should I struggle or fear any more? I know the worst that life can bring me; I have buried my heart and my hopes with my boy. Why should I strive or struggle any more?" And Lina had got to such a pass that she forgot to answer to herself, Because it is right—Right and wrong, she had lost sight of them both.'

Poor Mrs. Storn is unconscious that already people are beginning to talk of her, first one and then another. Nobody seems very bad. Everybody is going wrong. Maurice abstracted over his work, Lina in a frenzy of wretchedness; home-fires are extinct, outside the cold winds blow, and the snow lies half melted on the ground. The man of the world is waiting in the cold, very miserable too—waiting for Lina, who has almost made up her mind now; their best impulses and chances seem failing them; all about there seems to be only pain, and night, and trouble, and sorrow for every one. But at last, when the night is blackest, the morning dawns, and Lina is saved.

Everything is then satisfactorily arranged, and Maurice is ruined, and Lina's old affection for him returns. The man of the world is also ruined, and determines to emigrate to some distant colony. Mr. and Mrs. Storn retire to an old-fashioned gabled house at Enfield, where they have no secrets from each other; and it is here that her husband one day tells Lina that he has brought an old friend to say good-bye to her, and then poor Herbert Clyne, the late man of the world, comes across the lawn, and says farewell for ever to both his friends in a very pathetic and touching scene.

Lina Storn is finally disposed of in 'Too Much Alone;' but Maurice Storn reappears in disguise, and under various assumed names, in almost all the author's subsequent novels. We are not sorry to meet him over and over again; for although we have never yet been able to realise this stern-cut personage as satisfactorily as we should have liked to do, yet we must confess to a partiality for him, and a respect for his astounding powers of application. Whether he turns his attention to chemistry, to engineering, to figures, to theology, the amount of business he gets through is almost bewildering. At the same time something invariably goes wrong, over which he has no control, notwithstanding all his industry and ability; and he has to acknowledge the weakness of humanity, and the insufficiency of the sternest determination, to order and arrange the events of life to its own will and fancy. To the woman or women depending upon him he is invariably kind, provokingly reserved, and faithfully devoted. He is of good family and extremely proud, and he is obliged for various reasons to live in the city. All through the stories one seems to hear a suggestive accompanying roll of cart-wheels and carriages. Poor Lina's loneliness seems all the more lonely for the contrast of the busy movement all round about her own silent, sad life. 'At first it seemed to give a sort of stimulus to her own existence, hearing the carts roll by, the cabs rattle past, the shout and hum of human voices break on her ear almost before she was awake of a morning. . . . But wear takes the gloss off all things, even off the sensation of being perplexed and amused by the whirl of life.'

In 'City and Suburb,' this din of London life, and the way in which city people live and strive, is capitally described; the heroine is no less a person than a Lady Mayoress, a certain Ruby Ruthven, a beauty, capricious and wayward and impetuous, and she is perhaps one of the best of Mrs. Riddell's creations. For old friendship's sake, we cannot help giving the preference to 'Too Much Alone;' but 'City and Suburb' is in many respects an advance upon it, and 'George Geith' is in its way better than either.

It seems strange as one thinks of it that before these books came out no one except Mr. Dickens had ever thought of writing about city life; there is certainly an interest and a charm about old London, its crowded busy streets, its ancient churches and buildings, and narrow lanes and passages with quaint names, of which we dwellers in the stucco suburbs have no conception. There is the river with its wondrous freight, and the busy docks, where stores of strange goods are lying, that bewilder one as one gazes. Vast horizons of barrels waiting to be carted, forests of cinnamon-trees and spices, of canes, of ivory, thousands and thousands of great elephant tusks, sorted and stored away, workmen, sailors of every country, a great unknown strange life and bustle. Or if you roam from the busy highway, you find silence, solitude, grass growing between the stones, old courts, iron gateways, ancient squares where the sunshine gathers quietly, a glint of the past, as it were, a feeling of what has been, and what still lingers among the old worn stones and bricks, and traditions of the city. Even the Mansion House, with its kindly old customs and welcome and hospitality, has a charm and romance of its own, that is quite indescribable, from the golden postilion standing behind the Lord Mayor's high chair of state, to the heavy little mutton-pies, which are the same as they were hundreds and hundreds of years ago. All this queer sentiment belonging to old London, and the author feels and describes with great cleverness and appreciation.

'George Geith'[4] is the latest and the most popular of Mrs. Riddell's novels, and it deserves its popularity. It is the history of the man whose name it bears—a man 'to work so long as he has a breath left to draw, who would die in his harness rather than give up, who would fight against opposing circumstances whilst he had a drop of blood in his veins, whose greatest virtues are untiring industry and indomitable courage, and who is worth half-a-dozen ordinary men, if only because of his iron frame and unconquerable spirit.' Here is a description of the place in which he lived, on the second floor of the house which stands next but one to the old gateway on the Fenchurch Street side:-

'If quietness was what he wanted, he had it; except in the summer evenings when the children of the Fenchurch Street housekeepers brought their marbles through the passage, and fought over them on the pavement in front of the office-door, there was little noise of life in the old churchyard. The sparrows in the trees or the foot-fall of some one entering or quitting the court alone disturbed the silence. The roar of Fenchurch Street on the one side, and of Leadenhall Street on the other, sounded in Fen Court but as a distant murmur; and to a man whose life was spent among figures, and who wanted to devote his undivided attention to his work, this silence was a blessing not to be properly estimated save by those who have passed through that maddening ordeal which precedes being able to abstract the mind from external influence.... For the historical recollections associated with the locality he had chosen George Geith did not care a rush.'

George Geith lives with his figures, 'climbing Alps on Alps of them with silent patience, great mountains of arithmetic with gold lying on their summits for him to grasp;' he works for eighteen hours a day. People come up his stairs to ask for his help—

'Bankrupts, men who were good enough, men who were doubtful, and men who were (speaking commercially) bad, had all alike occasion to seek the accountant's advice and assistance; retailers, who kept clerks for their sold books, but not for their bought; wholesale dealers, who did not want to let their clerks see their books at all; shrewd men of business, who yet could not balance

4 Written in 1865.

a ledger; ill-educated traders, who, though they could make money, would have been ashamed to show their ill-written and worse-spelled journals to a stranger; unhappy wretches, shivering on the brink of insolvency; creditors, who did not think much of the cooking of some dishonest debtors' accounts;—all these came and sat in George Geith's office, and waited their turn to see him.'

And among these comes a country gentleman, a M. Molazane, who is on the brink of ruin, and who has three daughters at home at the Dower House, near Wattisbridge.

There is a secret in George Geith's life and a reason for which he toils; and although early in the story he makes a discovery which relieves him from part of his anxiety and need for money, he still works on from habit, and one day he receives a letter from this M. Molozane, begging him to come to his assistance, and stating that he is ill and cannot come to town. George thinks he would like a breath of country air, and determines to go. The description of Wattisbridge and the road thither is delightful; lambs, cool grass, shaded ponds and cattle, trailing branches, brambles, roses, here a house, there a farm-yard, gently sloping hills crowned with clumps of trees, distant purple haze, a calm blue sky and fleecy clouds, and close at hand a grassy glade with cathedral branches, a young lady, a black retriever and a white poodle, all of which George Geith notices as he walks along the path, 'through the glade, under the shadow of the arching trees, straight as he can go to meet his destiny.'

Beryl Molozane, with the dear sweet kindly brown eyes, that seemed to be always laughing and loving, is as charming a destiny as any hero could wish to meet upon a summer's day, as she stands with the sunshine streaming on her nut-brown, red golden hair. She should indeed be capable of converting the most rabid of reviewers to the modern ideal of what a heroine should be, with her April moods and her tenderness and laughter, her frankness, her cleverness, her gay innocent chatter, her outspoken youth and brightness. It is she who manages for the whole household, who works for her father, who protects her younger sister, who schemes and plans, and thinks, and loves for all. No wonder that George loses his heart to her; even in the very beginning we are told, when he first sees her, that he would have

'Taken the sunshine out of his own life to save the clouds from darkening down on hers. He would have left her dear face to smile on still, the guileless heart to throb calmly. He would have left his day without a noon to prevent night from closing over hers. He would have known that it was possible for him to love so well that he should become unselfish. . . .'

One cannot help wondering that the author could have had the heart to treat poor pretty Beryl so harshly, when her very creation, the stern and selfish George himself, would have suffered any pain to spare her if it were possible.

It is not our object here to tell a story at length, which is interesting enough to be read for itself, and touching enough to be remembered long after the last of the three volumes is closed. To be remembered, but so sadly, that one cannot but ask oneself for what reason are such stories written. Are they written to cheer one in dull hours, to soothe, to interest, and to distract from weary thoughts, from which it is at times a blessing to escape? or is it to make one sad with sorrows which never happened, but which are told with so much truth and pathos that they almost seem for a minute as if they were one's own? Is it to fill one's eyes with tears for griefs which might be, but which have not been, and for troubles that are not, except in a fancy, for the sad, sad fate of a sweet and tender woman, who might have been made happy to gladden all who were interested in her story?

A lady putting down this book the other day, suddenly burst into tears, and said, 'Why did they give me this to read?' Why, indeed! Beryl might have been more happy, and no one need have been the worse. She and her George might have been made comfortable together for a little while, and we might have learnt to know her all the same. Does sorrow come like this, in wave upon wave, through long sad years, without one gleam of light to play upon the waters? Sunshine *is* sunshine, and warms and vivifies, and brightens, though the clouds are coming too, sooner or later; but in nature no warning voices spoil the happiest hours of our lives by useless threats and terrifying hints of what the future may bring forth. Happiness remembered, is happiness always; but where would past happiness be if there was some one always standing by, as in this book, to point with a sigh to future troubles long before they come, and to sadden and spoil all the pleasant spring-time and all the sport and youth by dreary forebodings of old age, of autumn, and winter snow, and bitter winds that have not yet begun to blow? 'So smile the heavens upon that holy act,' says the Friar, 'that after sorrow chide us not.' 'Amen, amen,' says Romeo; 'but come what sorrow can, it cannot countervail the exchange of joy that one short minute gives me in her sight.' And we wish that George Geith had been more of Romeo's way of thinking.

A tragic ending is very touching at the time, and moves many a sympathy; but in prose—for poetry is to be criticised from a different standard—who ever reads a melancholy story over and over and over as some stories are read? The more touchingly and earnestly the tale is told, the less disposed one is to revert to it; and the more deeply one feels for the fictitious friends whom one cannot help loving at times, almost as if they were real ones; the less heart one has to listen to the history of their pains and fears and sufferings—knowing, as one does, that there is only sorrow in store for them, no relief coming, no help anywhere, no salvation at hand. My father used to say that a bad ending to a book was a great mistake; that he never would make one of his own finish badly. What was the use of it? Nobody ever cared to read a book a second time when it ended unhappily.

There is a great excuse in the case of the writer of 'George Geith,' who possesses in no common degree sad powers of pathos. Take for instance the parting between George and Beryl. She says that it is no use talking about what is past and gone; that they must part, and he knows it.

'Then for a moment George misunderstood her. The agony of her own heart, the intense bitterness of the draught she was called upon to drink, the awful hopelessness of her case, and the terrible longing she felt to be permitted to live and love once more, sharpened her voice and gave it a tone she never intended.

'"Have you grown to doubt me?" he asked. "Do you not know I would marry you to-morrow if I could? Do you think that throughout all the years to come, be they many or be they few, I could change to you? Oh, Beryl! do you not believe that through time and through eternity I shall love you and none other?"

"'I do not doubt; I believe," and her tears fell faster and her sobs become more uncontrollable. . . . .

'What was she to him at that moment? More than wife; more than all the earth; more than heaven; more than life. She was something more, far more, than any poor words we know can express. What he felt for her was beyond love; the future he saw stretching away for himself without her, without a hope of her, was in its blank weariness so terrible as to be beyond despair. Had the soul been taken out of his body, life could not have been more valueless. Take away the belief of immortality, and what has mortality left to live for?

'At the moment George Geith knew, in a stupid, dull kind of way, that to him Beryl had been an earthly immortality; that to have her again for his own, had been the one hope of his weary life, which had made the days and the hours endurable unto him.

'Oh! woe for the great waste of love which there is in this world below; to think how it is filling some hearts to bursting, whilst others are starving for the lack thereof; to think how those who may never be man and wife, those who are about to be parted by death, those whose love can never be anything but a sorrow and trial, merge their own identity in that of one another, whilst the lawful heads of respectable households wrangle and quarrel, and honest widows order their mourning with decorous resignation, and disconsolate husbands look out for second wives!

'Why is it that the ewe-lamb is always that selected for sacrifice? Why is it that the creature upon which man sets his heart shall be the one snatched from him? Why is it that the thing we prize perishes? That as the flower fades and the grass withereth, so the object of man's love, the delight of his eyes and the desire of his soul, passeth away to leave him desolate?

'On George Geith the blow fell with such force that he groped darkly about, trying to grasp his trouble; trying to meet some tangible foe with whom to grapple. Life without Beryl; days without sun; winter without a hope of summer; nights that could never know a dawn. My reader, have patience, have patience with the despairing grief of this strong man, who had at length met with a sorrow that crushed him.

'Have patience whilst I try to tell of the end that came to his business and to his pleasure; to the years he had spent in toil; to the hours in which he had tasted enjoyment! To the struggles there had come success; to the hopes fruition; but with success and with fruition there had come likewise death.

'Everything for him was ended in existence. Living, he was as one dead. Wealth could not console him; success could not comfort him; for him, for this hard, fierce worker, for the man who had so longed for rest, for physical repose, for domestic pleasures, the flowers were to have no more perfume, home no more happiness; the earth no more loveliness. The first spring blossoms, the summer glory on the trees and fields, the fruits and flowers, and thousand tinted leaves of autumn, and the snows and frosts of winter, were never to touch his heart, nor stir his senses in the future.

'Never the home he pictured might be his, never, ah, never! He had built his dream-house on the sands, and, behold, the winds blew and the waves beat, and he saw it all disappear, leaving nought but dust and ashes, but death and despair! Madly he fought with his sorrow, as though it were a living thing that he could grasp and conquer; he turned on it constantly, and strove to trample it down.'

No comment is needed to point out the power and pathos of this long extract. The early story of George Geith is in many respects the same as the story of Warrington in 'Pendennis,'[5] but the end is far more sad and disastrous, and, as it has been shown, pretty bright Beryl dies of her cruel tortures, and it is, in truth, difficult to forgive the author for putting her through so much unnecessary pain and misery.

One peculiarity which strikes us in all these books is, that the feelings are stronger and more vividly alive than the people who are made to experience them. Even Beryl herself is more like a sweet and tender idea of a woman than a living woman with substance and stuff, and bone and flesh, though her passion and devotion are all before us as we read, and seem so alive and so true, that they touch us and master us by their intensity and vividness.

The sympathy between the writer and the reader of a book is a very subtle and strange one, and there is something curious in the necessity for expression on both sides: the writer pouring out the experience and feelings of years, and the reader, relieved and strengthened in certain moods to find that others have experienced and can speak of certain feelings, have passed through phases with which he himself is acquainted. The imaginary Public is a most sympathising friend; he will listen to the author's sad story; he does not interrupt or rebuff him, or weary with impatient platitudes, until he has had his say and uttered all that was within him. The author perhaps writes on good and ill, successes, hopes, disappointments, or happier memories, of unexpected reprieves, of unhoped-for good fortunes, of old friendships, long-tried love, faithful sympathies enduring to the end. All this, not in the words and descriptions of the events which really happened, but in a language of which he or she alone holds the key, or of which, perhaps, the full significance is scarcely known even to the writer. Only in the great unknown world which he addresses there surely is the kindred spirit somewhere, the kind heart, the friend of friends who will understand him. Novel-writing must be like tears to some women, the vent and the relief of many a chafing spirit. People say, Why are so many novels written? and the answer is, Because there are so many people feeling, thinking, and enduring, and longing to give voice and expression to the silence of the life in the midst of which they are struggling. The necessity for expression is a great law of nature, one for which there is surely some good and wise reason, as there must be for that natural desire for sympathy which is common to so many. There seems to be something wrong and incomplete in those natures which do not need it, something inhuman in those who are incapable of understanding the mystical

---

[5] In William Thackeray's *The History of Pendennis* (1848–50), George Warrington starts Pendennis on a literary career.

and tender bond by which all humanity is joined and bound together. A bond of common pain and pleasure, of common fear and hope, and love, and weakness.

Poets tell us that not only human creatures, but the whole universe, is thrilling with sympathy and expression, speaking, entreating, uttering, in plaints or praise, or in a wonder of love and admiration. What do the sounds of a bright spring day mean? Cocks crow in the farmyards and valleys below; high up in the clear heavens the lark is pouring out its sweet passionate thrills; shriller and sweeter, and more complete as the tiny speck soars higher and higher still, 'flow the profuse strains of unpremeditated art.' The sheep baa and browse, and shake their meek heads; children shout for the very pleasure of making a sound in the sunshine. Nature is bursting with new green, brightening, changing into a thousand lovely shades. Seas washing and sparkling against the shores, streaks of faint light gleam in distant horizons, soft winds are blowing about the landscape; what is all this but an appeal for sympathy, a great natural expression of emotion?

And perhaps, after all, the real secret of our complaint against modern heroines is not so much that they are natural and speak out what is in them, and tell us of deeper and more passionate feeling than ever stirred the even tenour of their grandmothers' narratives, but that they are morbid, constantly occupied with themselves, one-sided, and ungrateful for the wonders and blessings of a world which is not less beautiful now than it was a hundred years ago, where perhaps there is a less amount of pain than at the time when Miss Austen and Miss Ferrier[6] said their say.

Jane Austen's own story was more sad and more pathetic than that of many and many of the heroines whom we have been passing in review and complaining of, and who complain to us so loudly; but in her, knowledge of good and evil, and of sorrow and anxiety and disappointment, evinced itself, not in impotent railings against the world and impatient paragraphs and monotonous complaints, but in a delicate sympathy with the smallest events of life, a charming appreciation of its common aspects, a playful wisdom and kindly humour, which charm us to this day.

Many of the heroines of to-day are dear and tried old friends, and would be sorely missed out of our lives, and leave irreparable blanks on our bookshelves; numbers of them are married and happily settled down in various country-houses and parsonages in England and Wales; but for the sake of their children who are growing up round about them, and who will be the heroes and heroines of the next generation or two, we would appeal to their own sense of what is right and judicious, and ask them if they would not desire to see their daughters brought up in a simpler, less spasmodic, less introspective state of mind than they themselves have been? Are they not sometimes haunted by the consciousness that their own experiences may have suggested a strained and affected view of life to some of their younger readers, instead of encouraging them to cheerfulness, to content, to a moderate estimate of their own infallibility, a charity for others, and a not too absorbing contemplation of themselves,

---

[6] Susan Ferrier (1782–1854), friend of Walter Scott and highly esteemed Scottish novelist who wrote *Marriage* (1818), *The Inheritance* (1824) and *Destiny* (1831).

their own virtues and shortcomings? 'Avant tout, le temps est *poseur*,' says George Sand, 'et toi qui fais la guerre à ce travers, tu en es pénétré de la tête aux pieds.'[7]

Mrs Humphry Ward

(MARY AUGUSTA WARD)

1851 – 1920

B*orn in Tasmania, Australia, she was a member of the Arnold family; in 1865, the family moved to Oxford where she met her future husband whom she married in 1872, and thereafter wrote as Mrs Humphry Ward.* *When her husband was appointed to the staff of* The Times *the couple moved to London in 1887. Her concern with the theory and practice of Christianity prompted the beginning of her literary career. An article she wrote for the* Dictionary of Christian Biography *led to her first novel,* Miss Bretherton *(1884), and her most famous work,* Robert Elsmere *(1888), along with almost thirty other works of fiction.*

Her reputation was secured with Robert Elsmere *which was hailed as a remarkable achievement by the literary periodicals of the day; it was quoted in pulpits, denounced by Marie Corelli, discussed by William Gladstone and translated into dozens of languages. So great was her prestige and popularity she was frequently accorded parity with George Eliot. While supportive of reforms for women (including those that related to education) Mary Augusta Ward was an opponent of women's suffrage.*

The following extract from A Writer's Recollections *(Collins, London, 1918) outlines her approach to her novel,* Robert Elsmere.

7 Above all, time is a poseur and you who oppose it are yourself suffused by it.

From

A *Writer's Recollections*

CHAPTER XII

THE PUBLICATION OF 'ROBERT ELSMERE'

I T was in 1885, after the completion of the Amiel translation, that I began 'Robert Elsmere,' drawing the opening scenes from that expedition to Long Sleddale[1] in the spring of that year which I have already mentioned. The book took me three years—nearly—to write. Again and again I found myself dreaming that the end was near, and publication only a month or two away; only to sink back on the dismal conviction that the second, or the first, or the third volume—or some portion of each—must be rewritten, if I was to satisfy myself at all. I actually wrote the last words of the last chapter in March 1887, and came out afterwards, from my tiny writing-room at the end of the drawing-room, shaken with tears, and wondering as I sat alone on the floor, by the fire, in the front room, what life would be like now that the book was done! But it was nearly a year after that before it came out, a year of incessant hard work, of endless re-writing, and much nervous exhaustion. For all the work was saddened and made difficult by the fact that my mother's long illness was nearing its end, and that I was torn incessantly between the claim of the book, and the desire to be with her whenever I could possibly be spared from my home and children. Whenever there was a temporary improvement in her state, I would go down to Borough[2] alone to work feverishly at revision, only to be drawn back to her side before long by worse news. And all the time London life went on as usual, and the strain at times was great.

The difficulty of finishing the book arose first of all from its length. I well remember the depressed countenance of Mr. George Smith—who was to be to me through fourteen years afterwards the kindest of publishers and friends—when I called one day in Waterloo Place, bearing a basketful of type-written sheets. 'I am afraid you have brought us a perfectly unmanageable book!' he said; and I could only mournfully agree that so it was. It was far too long, and my heart sank at the thought of all there was still to do. But how patient Mr. Smith was over it!—and how generous in the matter of unlimited fresh proofs and endless corrections. I am certain that he had no belief in the book's success; and yet on the ground of his interest in 'Miss Bretherton' he had made liberal terms with me, and all through the long incubation he was always indulgent and sympathetic.

The root difficulty was of course the dealing with such a subject in a novel at all. Yet I was determined to deal with it so, in order to reach the public. There

---

[1] Lake District valley, north of Kendal (formerly Westmorland, now Cumbria).
[2] District of London, south of London Bridge.

were great precedents—Froude's 'Nemesis of Faith,' Newman's 'Loss and Gain,' Kingsley's 'Alton Locke,'[3]—for the novel of religious or social propaganda. And it seemed to me that the novel was capable of holding and shaping real experience of any kind, as it affects the lives of men and women. It is the most elastic, the most adaptable of forms. No one has a right to set limits to its range. There is only one final test. Does it interest?—does it appeal? Personally, I should add another. Does it make in the long run for *beauty*? Beauty taken in the largest and most generous sense, and especially as including discord, the harsh and jangled notes which enrich the rest—but still Beauty—as Tolstoy was a master of it.

But at any rate, no one will deny that *interest* is the crucial matter.

> There are five and twenty ways
> Of constructing tribal lays—
> And every single one of them is right![4]

—always supposing that the way chosen quickens the breath and stirs the heart of those who listen. But when the subject chosen has two aspects, the one intellectual and logical, the other poetic and emotional, the difficulty of holding the balance between them so that neither overpowers the other, and interest is maintained, is admittedly great.

I wanted to show how a man of sensitive and noble character, born for religion, comes to throw off the orthodoxies of his day and moment, and to go out into the wilderness where all is experiment, and spiritual life begins again. And with him I wished to contrast a type no less fine of the traditional and guided mind—and to imagine the clash of two such tendencies of thought, as it might affect all practical life, and especially the life of two people who loved each other.

Here then—to begin with—were Robert and Catherine. Yes—but Robert must be made intellectually intelligible. Closely looked at, all novel-writing is a sort of shorthand. Even the most simple and broadly human situation cannot really be told in full. Each reader in following it unconsciously supplies a vast amount himself. A great deal of the effect is owing to things quite out of the picture given—things in the reader's own mind, first and foremost. The writer is playing on common experience; and mere suggestion is often far more effective than analysis. Take the paragraph in Turguénieff's[5] 'Lisa'—it was pointed out to me by Henry James—where Lavretsky on the point of marriage, after much suffering, with the innocent and noble girl whom he adores, suddenly hears that his intolerable first wife whom he had long believed dead is alive. Turguénieff, instead of setting out the situation in detail, throws himself on the reader. 'It was dark. Lavretsky went into the garden, and walked up and down there till dawn.'

That is all. And it is enough. The reader who is not capable of sharing that night walk with Lavretsky, and entering into his thoughts, has read the novel to

---

[3] Froude and (Cardinal) Newman were Roman Catholic apologists; [see note 9 p. 000] Charles Kingsley's *Alton Locke* (1856) reflects his (Protestant) 'Christian Socialism'.
[4] Rudyard Kipling in *The Naulahka* (Macmillan, London, 1893).
[5] i.e. Turgenev.

no purpose. He would not understand, though Lavretsky or his creator were to spend pages on explaining.

But in my case, what provoked the human and emotional crisis—what produced the *story*—was an intellectual process. Now the difficulty here in using suggestion—which is the master tool of the novelist—is much greater than in the case of ordinary experience. For the conscious use of the intellect on the accumulated data of life—through history and philosophy—is not ordinary experience. In its more advanced forms, it only applies to a small minority of the human race.

Still, in every generation, while a minority is making or taking part in the intellectual process itself, there is an atmosphere, a diffusion, produced around them, which affects many many thousands who have but little share—but little *conscious* share, at any rate— in the actual process.

Here then is the opening for suggestion—in connection with the various forms of imagination which enter into Literature; with poetry, and fiction, which, as Goethe saw, is really a form of poetry. And a quite legitimate opening. For to use it is to quicken the intellectual process itself, and to induce a larger number of minds to take part in it.

The problem then, in intellectual poetry or fiction, is so to suggest the argument, that both the expert and the popular consciousness may feel its force. And to do this without overstepping the bounds of poetry or fiction; without turning either into mere ratiocination, and so losing the 'simple, sensuous, passionate' element which is their true life.

It was this problem which made 'Robert Elsmere' take three years to write instead of one. Mr. Gladstone complained in his famous review of it that a majestic system which had taken centuries to elaborate, and gathered into itself the wisest brains of the ages had gone down in a few weeks or months before the onslaught of the Squire's arguments; and that if the Squire's arguments were few the orthodox arguments were fewer! The answer to the first part of the charge is that the well-taught schoolboy of to-day is necessarily wiser in a hundred respects than Sophocles or Plato, since he represents not himself, but the brainwork of a hundred generations since those great men lived. And as to the second, if Mr. Gladstone had seen the first redactions of the book—only if he had, I fear he would never have read it!—he would hardly have complained of lack of argument on either side, whatever he might have thought of its quality. Again and again I went on writing for hours, satisfying the logical sense in one's self, trying to put the arguments on both sides as fairly as possible, only to feel despairingly at the end that it must all come out. It might be decent controversy; but life, feeling, charm, *humanity* had gone out of it; it had ceased therefore to be 'making,' to be literature.

So that in the long run there was no other method possible than suggestion—and, of course *selection*!—as with all the rest of one's material. That being understood, what one had to aim at was so to use suggestion as to touch the two zones of thought—that of the scholar, and that of what one may call the educated populace; who without being scholars, were yet aware, more or less clearly, of what the scholars were doing. It is from these last that 'atmosphere' and 'diffusion' come; the atmosphere and diffusion which alone make wide penetration for a book illustrating an intellectual motive possible. I had to learn that, having read a great deal, I must as far as possible wipe out the traces of reading. All that could be done was to leave a few sign-posts as firmly planted as one could, so as to recall the real journey to those who already knew it, and for the rest, to trust to the floating interest and passion surrounding a great controversy—the *second* religious battle of the nineteenth century—with which it had seemed to me both in Oxford and in London that the intellectual air was charged.

I grew very weary in the course of the long effort, and often very despairing. But there were omens of hope now and then; first, a letter from my dear eldest brother, the late W. T. Arnold, who died in 1904, leaving a record as journalist and scholar which has been admirably told by his intimate friend and colleague, Mr.—now Captain—C. E. Montague. He and I had shared many intellectual interests connected with the history of the Empire. His monograph on 'Roman Provincial Administration,' first written as an Arnold Essay, still holds the field; and in the realm of pure literature, his one-volume edition of Keats is there to show his eagerness for beauty and his love of English verse. I sent him the first volume in proof, about a year before the book came out, and awaited his verdict with much anxiety. It came one May day in 1889. I happened to be very tired and depressed at the moment, and I remember sitting alone for a little while with the letter in my hand, without courage to open it. Then at last I opened it.

> Warm congratulation—Admirable!—Full of character and colour. . . . 'Miss Breth-erton' was an intellectual exercise. This is quite a different affair, and has interested and touched me deeply, as I feel sure it will all the world. The biggest thing that—with a few other things of the same kind—has been done for years.

Well!—that was enough to go on with, to carry me through the last wrestle with proofs and revision. But by the following November, nervous fatigue made me put work aside for a few weeks, and we went abroad for rest, only to be abruptly summoned home by my mother's state. Thenceforward I lived a double life—the one overshadowed by my mother's approaching death, the other amid the agitation of the book's appearance, and all the incidents of its rapid success.

I have already told the story in the Introduction to the Library Edition of 'Robert Elsmere,' and I will only run through it here, as rapidly as possible, with a few fresh incidents and quotations. There was never any doubt at all of the book's fate, and I may repeat again that before Mr. Gladstone's review of it the three volumes were already in a third edition, the rush at all the libraries was in full course, and Matthew Arnold—so gay and kind, in those March weeks before his own sudden death!—had clearly foreseen the rising boom. 'I shall take it with me to Bristol next week and get through it there, I hope [but he didn't achieve it!]. It is one of my regrets not to have known the Green of your dedication.' And a week or two later he wrote an amusing letter to his sister describing a country-house party at beautiful Wilton, Lord Pembroke's home near Salisbury, and the various stages in the book reached by the members of the party, including Mr. Goschen, who were all reading it, and all talking of it. I never, however, had any criticism of it from him, except of the first volume, which he liked. I doubt very much whether the second and third volumes would have appealed to him. My uncle was a Modernist long before the time. In 'Literature and Dogma,' he threw out in detail much of the argument suggested in 'Robert Elsmere,' but to the end of his life he was a contented member of the Anglican Church, so far as attendances at her services was concerned, and belief in her mission of 'edification' to the English people. He had little sympathy with people who 'went out.' Like Mr. Jowett, he would have liked to see the Church slowly reformed and 'modernised' from within. So that with the main theme of my book—that a priest who doubts must depart—he could never have had full sympathy. And in the course of years—as I showed in a later novel written twenty-four years after 'Robert Elsmere'—I feel that I have very much come to agree with him! These great national structures that we call churches are too precious for iconoclast handling, if any other method is possible. The strong assertion of individual liberty within them, as opposed to the attempt to break them down from without:—that seems to me now the hopeful course. A few more heresy trials like those which sprang out of 'Essay and Reviews,' or the persecution of Bishop Colenso, would let in fresh life and healing nowadays, as did those old stirrings of the waters. The first Modernist bishop who stays in his place, forms a Modernist chapter and diocese around him, and fights the fight where he stands, will do more for liberty and faith in the Church, I now sadly believe, than those scores of brave 'forgotten dead' who have gone out of her for conscience' sake, all these years.

But to return to the book. All through March the tide of success was rapidly rising; and when I was able to think of it, I was naturally carried away by the excitement and astonishment of it. But with the later days of March a veil dropped between me and the book. My mother's suffering and storm-beaten life was coming rapidly to its close, and I could think of nothing else. In an interval of slight improvement, indeed, when it seemed as though she might rally for a time, I heard Mr. Gladstone's name quoted for the first time in connection with the book. It will be remembered that he was then out of office, having been overthrown on the Home Rule Question in '86,[6] and he happened to be staying for an Easter visit with the Warden of Keble, and Mrs. Talbot, who was his niece by marriage. I was with my mother about a mile away, and Mrs. Talbot, who came to ask for news of her, reported to me that Mr. Gladstone was deep in the book. He was reading it pencil in hand, marking all the passages he disliked or quarrelled with, with the Italian '*Ma!*'—and those he approved of with mysterious signs which she who followed him through the volumes could not always decipher. Mr. Knowles, she reported, the busy editor of the *Nineteenth Century*, was trying to persuade the great man to review it. But 'Mr. G.' had not made up his mind.

[6] In 1886 Gladstone, then Prime Minister, fought a General Election on the question of Home Rule for Ireland (which he supported) and was defeated.

Then all was shut out again. Through many days my mother asked constantly for news of the book, and smiled with a flicker of her old brightness, when anything pleased her in a letter or review. But finally there came long hours when to think or speak of it seemed sacrilege. And on April 7 she died.

The day after her death, I saw Mr. Gladstone at Keble. We talked for a couple of hours and then when I rose to go, he asked if I would come again on the following morning before he went back to town. I had been deeply interested and touched, and I went again for another long visit. My account, written down at the time, of the first day's talk, has been printed as an appendix to the Library Edition of the book. Of the second conversation, which was the more interesting of the two since we came to much closer quarters in it, my only record is the following letter to my husband:

> I have certainly had a wonderful experience last night and this morning! Last night two hours' talk with Gladstone, this morning, again, an hour and a half's strenuous argument; during which the great man got quite white sometimes and tremulous with interest and excitement. . . . The talk this morning was a battle royal over the book and Christian evidences. He was *very* charming personally, though at times he looked stern and angry and white to a degree, so that I wondered sometimes how I had the courage to go on—the drawn brows were so formidable! There was one moment when he talked of 'trumpery objections,' in his most House of Commons manner. It was as I thought. The new lines of criticism are not familiar to him, and they really press him hard. He meets them out of Bishop Butler,[7] and things analogous. But there is a sense, I think, that question and answer don't fit, and with it ever increasing interest and—sometimes—irritation. His own autobiographical reminiscences were wonderfully interesting, and his repetition of the 42nd psalm—'Like as the hart desireth the water-brooks'—*grand*!
>
> He said that he had never read any book on the hostile side written in such a spirit of 'generous appreciation' of the Christian side.

Yes—those were hours to which I shall always look back with gratitude and emotion. Wonderful old man! I see him still standing, as I took leave of him, one hand leaning on the table beside him, his lined, pallid face and eagle eyes, framed in his noble white hair, shining amid the dusk of the room. 'There are still two things left for me to do!' he said, finally, in answer to some remark of mine.—'One is to carry Home Rule—the other is to prove the intimate connection between the Hebrew and Olympian revelations!'[8]

Could any remark have been more characteristic of that double life of his—the life of the politician, and the life of the student—which kept him fresh and eager to the end of his days? Characteristic too of the amateurish element in all his historical and literary thinking. In dealing 'with early Greek mythology, genealogy and religion,' says his old friend Lord Bryce, Mr. Gladstone's theories

---

[7] Joseph Butler, Bishop of Durham (1692–1752), Anglican theologian who asserted Christian revelation against the Deist notion of natural virtue.
[8] The Judaeo-Christian and the Ancient Greek religions.

'have been condemned by the unanimous voice of scholars as fantastic.' Like his great contemporary, Newman,[9]—on whom a good deal of our conversation turned—he had no critical sense of evidence; and when he was writing on 'The Impregnable Rock of Scripture' Lord Acton, who was staying at Hawarden at the time, ran after him in vain, with Welhausen[10] or Kuenen[11] under his arm, if haply he might persuade his host to read them.

But it was not for that he was born; and those who look back to the mighty work he did for his country in the forty years preceding the Home Rule split, can only thank the Powers 'that hold the broad Heaven' for the part which the passion of his Christian faith, the eagerness of his love for letters—for the Homer and the Dante he knew by heart—played in refreshing and sustaining so great a soul. I remember returning, shaken and uplifted, through the April air, to the house where my mother lay in death; and among my old papers lies a torn fragment of a letter thirty years old, which I began to write to Mr. Gladstone a few days later, and was too shy to send.

> This morning [says the letter, written from Fox How, on the day of my mother's funeral] we laid my dear Mother to rest in her grave among the mountains, and this afternoon I am free to think a little over what has befallen me personally and separately during this past week. It is not that I wish to continue our argument—quite the contrary. As I walked home from Keble on Monday morning, I felt it a hard fate that I should have been arguing, rather than listening.... Argument perhaps was inevitable, but none the less I felt afterwards as though there were something incongruous and unfitting in it. In a serious discussion it seemed to me right to say plainly what I felt and believed; but if in doing so, I have given pain; or expressed myself on any point with a too great trenchancy and confidence, please believe that I regret it very sincerely. I shall always remember our talks. If consciousness lasts 'beyond these voices'—my inmost hope as well as yours—we shall know of all these things. Till then I cherish the belief that we are not so far apart as we seem.

But there the letter abruptly ended, and was never sent. I probably shrank from the added emotion of sending it, and I found it again the other day in a packet that had not been looked at for many years. I print it now as evidence of the effect that Mr. Gladstone's personality could produce on one forty years younger than himself, and in sharp rebellion at that time against his opinions and influence in two main fields—religion and politics.

Four days later, Monday, April 16, my husband came into my room with the face of one bringing ill tidings. 'Matthew Arnold is dead!' My uncle, as many will remember, had fallen suddenly in a Liverpool street while walking with his wife to meet his daughter expected that day from America, and without

[9] John Henry Newman (1801–90), eminent Anglican convert to Roman Catholicism, and later Cardinal; author of *The Dream of Gerontius* (1866), *Essay in aid of a Grammar of Assent* (1870), *The Idea of a University* (1873), etc.
[10] Welhausen, Julius; Biblical scholar 1844–1918.
[11] Abraham Kuenen (1828–91), Dutch theologian.

a sound or movement had passed away. The heart disease which killed so many of his family was his fate also. A merciful one it always seemed to me, which took him thus suddenly and without pain from the life in which he had played so fruitful and blameless a part. That word 'blameless' has always seemed to me particularly fit to him. And the quality to which it points, was what made his humour so sharp-tipped and so harmless. He had no hidden interest to serve—no malice—not a touch, not a trace of cruelty—so that men allowed him to jest about their most sacred idols and superstitions and bore him no grudge. . .

. . . It was on the way home from Laleham after my uncle's burial there, that Mr. George Smith gave me fresh and astonishing news of 'Robert Elsmere's' success. The circulating libraries were being fretted to death for copies, and the whirlwind of talk was constantly rising. A little later in the same month of April, if I remember right, I was going from Waterloo to Godalming and Borough Farm, when, just as the train was starting, a lady rushed along the platform waving a book aloft and signalling to another lady who was evidently waiting to see her off. 'I've got it—I've got it!' she said triumphantly. 'Get in, Ma'am—get in!' said the porter, bundling her into the compartment where I sat alone. Then she hung out of the window breathlessly talking. 'They told me no chance for weeks—not the slightest! Then—just as I was standing at the counter, who should come up, but somebody bringing back the first volume. Of course it was promised to somebody else—but as I was *there*, I laid hands on it, and here it is!' The train went off, my companion plunged into her book, and I watched her as she turned the pages of the familiar green volume. We were quite alone. I had half a mind to say something revealing; but on the whole it was more amusing to sit still!

And meanwhile letters poured in.

'I try to write upon you,' wrote Mr. Gladstone,—'wholly despair of satisfying myself—cannot quite tell whether to persevere or desist.' Mr. Pater let me know that he was writing on it for the *Guardian*. 'It is a *chef d'œuvre* after its kind, and justifies the care you have devoted to it.' 'I see,' said Andrew Lang on April 30, 'that R. E. is running into as many editions as "The Rights of Man" by Tom Paine. . . . You know he is not *my* sort (at least unless you have a ghost, a murder, a duel and some savages).' Burne Jones wrote with the fun and sweetness that made his letters a delight:—

Not one least bitter word in it!—threading your way through intricacies of parsons so finely and justly. . . . As each new one came on the scene, I wondered if you would fall upon him and rend him—but you never do. . . . Certainly I never thought I should devour a book about parsons—my desires lying towards—'time upon once there was a dreadful pirate'—but I am back again five and thirty years and feeling softened and subdued with memories you have wakened up so piercingly—and I wanted to tell you this.

And in the same packet lie letters from the honoured and beloved Edward Talbot, now Bishop of Winchester, Stopford Brooke—the Master of Balliol—Lord

Justice Bowen—Professor Huxley—and so many, many more. Best of all, Henry James! His two long letters I have already printed, naturally with his full leave and blessing, in the Library Edition of the novel. Not his the grudging and fault-finding temper that besets the lesser man when he comes to write of his contemporaries! Full of generous honour for what he thought good and honest work, however faulty, his praise kindled,—and his blame no less. He appreciated so fully *your* way of doing it; and his suggestion, alongside, of what would have been *his* way of doing it, was so stimulating—touched one with so light a Socratic sting, and set a hundred thoughts on the alert. Of this delightful critical art of his his letters to myself over many years are one long illustration.

And now—'There is none like him—none!' The honied lips are silent, and the helping hand at rest.

With May appeared Mr. Gladstone's review—'the refined criticism of Robert Elsmere'—'typical of his strong points,' as Lord Bryce describes it:—certainly one of the best things he ever wrote. I had no sooner read it than, after admiring it, I felt it must be answered. But it was desirable to take time to think how best to do it. At the moment my one desire was for rest and escape. At the beginning of June we took our two eldest children, aged eleven and thirteen, to Switzerland for the first time. Oh! the delight of Glion!—with its hay-fields thick with miraculous spring flowers, the 'peak of Jaman delicately tall,' and that gorgeous pile of the Dent du Midi, bearing up the June heaven, to the east!—the joy of seeing the children's pleasure, and the relief of the mere physical rebound in the Swiss air, after the long months of strain and sorrow. My son—a slip of a person in knicker-bockers—walked over the Simplon as though Alps were only made to be climbed by boys of eleven; and the Defile of Gondo, Domo d'Ossola, and beautiful Maggiore:—they were all new and heavenly to each member of the party. Every year now there was growing on me the spell of Italy, the historic, the Saturnian land; and short as this wandering was, I remember, after it was over, and we turned homeward across the St. Gothard, leaving Italy behind us, a new sense as of a hidden treasure in life—of something sweet and inexhaustible always waiting for one's return; like a child's cake in a cupboard, or the gold and silver hoard of Odysseus, that Athene helped him to hide in the Ithacan cave.

Then one day towards the end of June or the beginning of July, my husband put down beside me a great brown paper package which the post had just brought. 'There's America beginning!' he said, and we turned over the contents of the parcel in bewilderment. A kind American friend had made a collection for me of the reviews, sermons and pamphlets that had been published so far about the book in the States, the correspondences, the odds and ends of all kinds, grave and gay. Every mail, moreover, began to bring me American letters from all parts of the States. 'No book since "Uncle Tom's Cabin" has had so sudden and wide a diffusion among all classes of readers,'—wrote an American man of letters—'and I believe that no other book of equal seriousness ever had so quick a hearing. I have seen it in the hands of nursery-maids and of shop-girls behind the counters; of frivolous young women who read every novel that is talked about; of business men, professors, and students. . . . The proprietors of those large shops where anything—from a pin to a piano—can be bought, vie with each other in selling the cheapest edition. One pirate put his price even so low as four cents—two pence!' (Those, it will be remembered, were the days before Anglo-American copyright.)

Oliver Wendell Holmes, to whom I was personally a stranger, wrote to me just such a letter as one might have dreamed of from the 'Autocrat':—'One of my elderly friends of long ago, called a story of mine you may possibly have heard of—"Elsie Venner"—"a medicated novel," and such she said she was not in the habit of reading. I liked her expression; it titillated more than it tingled. "Robert Elsmere" I suppose we should all agree is "a medicated novel." But it is, I think, beyond question, the most effective and popular novel we have had since "Uncle Tom's Cabin."'

A man of science, apparently an agnostic, wrote severely—'I regret the popularity of "Robert Elsmere" in this country. Our western people are like sheep in such matters. They will not see that the book was written for a people with a State Church on its hands, so that a gross exaggeration of the importance of religion was necessary. It will revive interest in theology and retard the progress of rationalism.'

Another student and thinker from one of the Universities of the West, after a brilliant criticism of the novel, written about a year after its publication, winds up—'The book, here, has entered into the evolution of a nation.'

Goldwin Smith—my father's and uncle's early friend—wrote me from Canada:

The Grange, Toronto, Oct. 31, 1888.

MY DEAR MRS. WARD,—You may be amused by seeing what a stir you are making even in this sequestered nook of the theological world, and by learning that the antidote to you is 'Ben Hur.' I am afraid, if it were so, I should prefer the poison to the antidote.

The state of opinion on this Continent is, I fancy, pretty much that to which Robert Elsmere would bring us—Theism, with Christ as a model of character, but without real belief in the miraculous part of Christianity. Churches are still being everywhere built, money is freely subscribed, young men are pressing into the clerical profession, and religion shows every sign of vitality. I cannot help suspecting however that a change is not far off. If it comes, it will come with a vengeance; for over the intellectual dead level of this democracy opinion courses like the tide running in over a flat.

As the end of life draws near I feel like the Scotchman who, being on his deathbed when the trial of O'Connell was going on, desired his Minister to pray for him that he might just live to see what came of O'Connell. A wonderful period of transition in all things however has begun, and I should like very much to see the result. However it is too likely that very rough times may be coming and that one will be just as well out of the way.

Yours most truly,
GOLDWIN SMITH.

Exactly twenty years from the date of this letter, I was in Toronto for the first time, and paid my homage to the veteran fighter, who, living as he did amid a younger generation hotly resenting his separatist and anti-Imperial views, and his contempt for their own ideal of an equal and permanent union of free states under the British flag, was yet generously honoured throughout the Dominion for his services to literature and education. He had been my father's friend at Oxford—where he succeeded to Arthur Stanley's tutorship at University College—and in Dublin. And when I first began to live in Oxford he was still Regius Professor, inhabiting a house very near that of my parents, which was well known to me afterwards through many years as the house of the Max Müllers. I can remember the catastrophe it seemed to all his Oxford friends, when he deserted England for America, despairing of the republic, as my father also, for a while in his youth, had despaired, and sick of what seemed to him the forces of reaction in English life. I was eighteen when 'Endymion' came out, with Dizzy's absurd attack on the 'sedentary' professor who was also a 'social parasite.' It would be difficult to find two words in the English language more wholly and ludicrously inappropriate to Goldwin Smith; and the furious letter to the *Times* in which he denounced 'the stingless insults of a coward' might well have been left unwritten. But I was living then among Oxford Liberals, and under the shadow of Goldwin Smith's great reputation as historian and pamphleteer, and I can see myself listening with an angry and sympathetic thrill to my father as he read the letter aloud. Then came the intervening years, in which one learnt to look on Goldwin Smith as *par excellence* the great man 'gone wrong,' on that vital question, above all, of a sane Imperialism. It was difficult after a time to keep patience with the Englishman whose most passionate desire seemed to be to break up the Empire, to incorporate Canada in the United States, to relieve us of India, that 'splendid curse,' to detach from us Australia and South Africa, and thereby to wreck for ever that vision of a banded commonwealth of free nations which for innumerable minds at home was fast becoming the romance of English politics.

So it was that I went with some shrinking, yet still under the glamour of the old Oxford loyalty, to pay my visit at the Grange in 1908, walking thither from the house of one of the staunchest Imperialists in Canada, where I had been lunching. 'You are going to see Mr. Goldwin Smith?' my host had said. 'I have not crossed his threshold for twenty years. I abhor his political views. All the same we are proud of him in Canada!' When I entered the drawing-room, which was rather dark though it was a late May afternoon, there rose slowly from its chair beside a bright fire, a figure I shall never forget. I had a fairly clear remembrance of Goldwin Smith in his earlier days. This was like his phantom, or, if one may say so, without disrespect—his mummy. Shrivelled and spare, yet erect as ever, the iron-grey hair, closely-shaven beard, dark complexion, and black eyes still formidably alive, made on me an impression at once of extreme age, and unabated will. A prophet!—still delivering his message, but well aware that it found but few listeners in a degenerate world. He began immediately to talk politics, denouncing English Imperialism whether in some sort—of the Catholic reaction in France, began a negotiation with me for the appearance of a French translation of the whole or part of the book in his *Revue*. 'But how'—I asked him (we were sitting in his editor's sanctum, in the old house of the Rue de l'Université)—'could it possibly suit you, or the *Revue*, to do anything of the kind? And *now*—after fifteen years?'

But according to him, the case was simple. When the book first appeared, the public of the *Revue* could not have felt any interest in it. France is a logical country—a country of clear-cut solutions. And at that time either one was a Catholic—or a free thinker. And if one was a Catholic, one accepted from the Church—say, the date of the book of Daniel, as well as everything else. Renan[12] indeed left the Church thirty years earlier because he came to see with certainty that the book of Daniel was written under Antiochus Epiphanes, and not when his teachers at St. Sulpice said it was written. But while the secular world listened and applauded, the literary argument against dogma made very little impression on the general Catholic world for many years.

> 'But now,' said M. Brunetière, 'everything is different. Modernism has arisen. It is penetrating the Seminaries. People begin to talk of it in the streets. And 'Robert Elsmere' is a study in Modernism—or at any rate it has so many affinities with Modernism; that *now*—the French public would be interested.'

The length of the book, however, could not be got over, and the plan fell through. But I came away from my talk with a remarkable man, not a little stirred. For it had seemed to show that with all its many faults—and who knew them better than I?—my book had yet possessed a certain representative and pioneering force; and that, to some extent at least, the generation in which it appeared had spoken through it.

[12] Joseph Ernest Renan (1823–92), French religious historian, disapproved of by the Church for his analytical criticism of Biblical texts.

Somerville and Ross

EDITH SOMERVILLE
1858 – 1946

and

VIOLET MARTIN
– 'MARTIN ROSS'
1862 – 1915

*T*ogether these two women formed a highly successful literary partnership, and were best known for their Irish fictions. Edith Somerville was born in Corfu where her soldier father was stationed; in 1859 the family returned to County Cork and Edith was educated at Alexandra College, Dublin, and later studied art in London, Paris and Dusseldorf. She was a passionate foxhunter and later in her life was one of the first women to become a Master of Foxhounds. In 1886 she met her cousin, Violet Martin: an intense friendship and a joint literary life followed. Violet Martin was born in Galway, the youngest of eleven children, and she too was educated at Alexandra College, and was a keen horsewoman. Both were also ardent feminists.

Their first book together – An Irish Cousin – was published in 1889; fourteen more titles followed, including the highly successful Experiences of an Irish R.M. (1899), before Violet's death in 1915. Edith was adamant that their partnership was not destroyed by death and she went on to write ten more titles for which she claimed 'joint authorship'.

The following short story from All on the Irish Shore; Irish Sketches (Longmans Green, London, New York and Bombay, 1903) reveals their characteristic tone and humour.

Fanny Fitz's Gamble

"*W*HERE'S Fanny Fitz?" said Captain Spicer to his wife.

They were leaning over the sea-wall in front of a little fishing hotel in Connemara, idling away the interval usually vouchsafed by the Irish car-driver between the hour at which he is ordered to be ready and that at which he appears. It was a misty morning in early June, the time of all times for Connemara, did the tourist only know it. The mountains towered green and grey above the palely shining sea in which they stood; the air was full of the sound of streams and the scent of wild flowers; the thin mist had in it something of the dazzle of the sunlight that was close behind it. Little Mrs. Spicer pulled down her veil: even after a fortnight's fly-fishing she still retained some regard for her complexion.

"She says she can't come," she responded; "she has letters to write or something—and this is our last day!"

Mrs. Spicer evidently found the fact provoking.

"On this information the favourite receded to 1," remarked Captain Spicer. "I think you may as well chuck it, my dear."

"I should like to beat them both!" said his wife, flinging a pebble into the rising tide that was very softly mouthing the seaweedy rocks below them.

"Well, here's Rupert; you can begin on him."

"Nothing would give me greater pleasure!" said Rupert's sister vindictively. "A great teasing, squabbling baby! Oh, how I hate fools! and they are *both* fools!—Oh, there you are, Rupert," a well-simulated blandness invading her voice; "and what's Fanny Fitz doing?"

"She's trying to do a Mayo man over a horse-deal," replied Mr. Rupert Gunning.

"A horse-deal!" repeated Mrs. Spicer incredulously. "Fanny buying a horse! Oh, impossible!"

"Well, I don't know about that," said Mr. Gunning, "she's trying pretty hard. I gave her my opinion——"

"I'll take my oath you did," observed Captain Spicer.

"——And as she didn't seem to want it, I came away," continued Mr. Gunning imperturbably. "Be calm, Maudie; it takes two days and two nights to buy a horse in these parts; you'll be home in plenty of time to interfere, and here's the car. Don't waste the morning."

"I never know if you're speaking the truth or no," complained Mrs. Spicer; nevertheless, she scrambled on to the car without delay. She and her brother had at least one point in common—the fanatic enthusiasm of the angler.

In the meantime, Miss Fanny Fitzroy's negotiations were proceeding in the hotel yard. Fanny herself was standing in a stable doorway, with her hands in the pockets of her bicycle skirt. She had no hat on, and the mild breeze blew her hair about; it was light brown, with a brightness in it; her eyes also were light brown, with gleams in them like the shallow places in a Connemara trout stream. At this moment they were scanning with approval, tempered by anxiety, the muddy legs of a lean and lengthy grey filly, who was fearfully returning her gaze from between the strands of a touzled forelock. The owner of the filly, a small man, with a face like a serious elderly monkey, stood at her head in a silence that was the outcome partly of stupidity, partly of caution, and partly of lack of English speech. The conduct of the matter was in the hands of a friend, a tall young man with a black beard, nimble of tongue and gesture, profuse in courtesies.

"Well, indeed, yes, your ladyship," he was saying glibly, "the breed of horses is greatly improving in these parts, and them hackney horses——"

"Oh," interrupted Miss Fitzroy hastily, "I won't have her if she's a hackney."

The eyes of the owner sought those of the friend in a gaze that clearly indicated the question.

"What'll ye say to her now?"

The position of the vendors was becoming a little complicated. They had come over through the mountains, from the borders of Mayo, to sell the filly to the hotel-keeper for posting, and were primed to the lips with the tale of her hackney lineage. The hotel-keeper had unconditionally refused to trade, and here, when a heaven-sent alternative was delivered into their hands, they found themselves hampered by the coils of a cast-off lie. No shade, however, of hesitancy appeared on the open countenance of the friend. He approached Miss Fitzroy with a mincing step, a deprecating wave of the hand, and a deeply respectful ogle. He was going to adopt the desperate resource of telling the truth, but to tell the truth profitably was a part that required rather more playing than any other.

"Well, your honour's ladyship," he began, with a glance at the hotel ostler, who was standing near cleaning a bit in industrious and sarcastic silence, "it is a fact, no doubt, that I mentioned here this morning that this young mare was of the Government hackney stock. But, according as I understand from this poor man that owns her, he bought her in a small fair over the Tuam side, and the man that sold her could take his oath she was by the Grey Dawn—sure you'd know it out of her colour."

"Why didn't you say so before?" asked Miss Fitzroy, bending her straight brows in righteous severity.

"Well, that's true indeed, your ladyship; but afther all—I declare a man couldn't hardly live without he'd tell a lie sometimes!"

Fanny Fitz stooped, rather hurriedly, and entered upon a renewed examination of the filly's legs. Even Rupert Gunning, after his brief and unsympathetic survey, had said she had good legs; in fact, he had only been able to crab her for the length of her back, and he, as Fanny Fitz reflected with a heat that took no heed of metaphor, was the greatest crabber that ever croaked.

"What are you asking for her?" she demanded with a sudden access of decision.

There was a pause. The owner of the filly and his friend withdrew a step or two and conferred together in Irish at lightning speed. The filly held up her head and regarded her surroundings with guileless wonderment. Fanny Fitz made a mental dive into her bankbook, and arrived at the varied conclusions that she was £30 to the good, that on that sum she had to weather out the summer and autumn, besides pacifying various cormorants (thus she designated her long-suffering tradespeople), and that every one had told her that if she only kept her eyes open in Connemara she might be able to buy something cheap and make a pot of money on it.

"This poor honest man," said the friend, returning to the charge, "says he couldn't part her without he'd get twenty-eight pounds for her; and, thank God, it's little your ladyship would think of giving that!"

Fanny Fitz's face fell.

"Twenty-eight pounds!" she echoed. "Oh, that's ridiculous!"

The friend turned to the owner, and, with a majestic wave of the hand, signalled to him to retire. The owner, without a change of expression, coiled up the rope halter and started slowly and implacably for the gate; the friend took off his hat with wounded dignity. Every gesture implied that the whole transaction was buried in an irrevocable past.

Fanny Fitz's eyes followed the party as they silently left the yard, the filly stalking dutifully with a long and springy step beside her master. It was a moment full of bitterness, and of a quite irrational indignation against Rupert Gunning.

"I beg your pardon, miss," said the ostler, at her elbow, "would ye be willing to give twenty pounds for the mare, and he to give back a pound luckpenny?"

"I would!" said the impulsive Fanny Fitz, after the manner of her nation.

When the fishing party returned that afternoon Miss Fitzroy met them at the hall door.

"Well, my dear," she said airily to Mrs. Spicer, "what sort of sport have you had? I've enjoyed myself immensely. I've bought a horse!"

Mrs. Spicer sat, paralysed, on the seat of the outside car, disregarding her brother's outstretched hands.

"Fanny!" she exclaimed, in tones fraught with knowledge of her friend's resources and liabilities.

"Yes, I have!" went on Fanny Fitz, undaunted. "Mr. Gunning saw her. He said she was a long-backed brute. Didn't you, Mr. Gunning?"

Rupert Gunning lifted his small sister bodily off the car. He was a tall sallow man, with a big nose and a small, much-bitten, fair moustache.

"Yes, I believe I did," he said shortly.

Mrs. Spicer's blue eyes grew round with consternation.

"Then you really have bought the thing!" she cried. "Oh, Fanny, you idiot! And what on earth are you going to do with it?"

"It can sleep on the foot of my bed to-night," returned Fanny Fitz, "and I'll ride it into Galway to-morrow! Mr. Gunning, you can ride half-way if you like!"

But Mr. Gunning had already gone into the hotel with his rod and fishing basket. He had a gift, that he rarely lost a chance of exercising, of provoking Fanny Fitz to wrath, and the fact that he now declined her challenge may or may not be accounted for by the gloom consequent upon an empty fishing basket.

Next morning the various hangers-on in the hotel yard were provided with occupation and entertainment of the most satiating description. Fanny Fitz's new purchase was being despatched to the nearest railway station, some fourteen miles off. It had been arranged that the ostler was to drive her there in one of the hotel cars, which should then return with a horse that was coming from Galway for the hotel owner; nothing could have fitted in better. Unfortunately the only part of the arrangement that refused to fit in was the filly. Even while Fanny Fitz was finishing her toilet, high-pitched howls of objurgation were rising, alarmingly, from the stable-yard, and on reaching the scene of action she was confronted by the spectacle of the ostler being hurtled across the yard by the filly, to whose head he was clinging, while two helpers upheld the shafts of the outside car from which she had fled. All were shouting directions and warnings at the tops of their voices, the hotel dog was barking, the filly alone was silent, but her opinions were unmistakable.

A waiter in shirt-sleeves was leaning comfortably out of a window, watching the fray and offering airy suggestion and comment.

"It's what I'm telling them, miss," he said easily, including Fanny Fitz in the conversation; "if they get that one into Recess to-night it'll not be under a side-car."

"But the man I bought her from," said Fanny Fitz, lamentably addressing the company, "told me that he drove his mother to chapel with her last Sunday."

"Musha then, may the divil sweep hell with him and burn the broom afther!" panted the ostler in bitter wrath, as he slewed the filly to a standstill. "I wish himself and his mother was behind her when I went putting the crupper on her! B'leeve me, they'd drop their chat!"

"Sure I knew that young Geogheghan back in Westport," remarked the waiter, "and all the good there is about him was a little handy talk. Take the harness off her, Mick, and throw a saddle on her. It's little I'd think meself of canthering her into Recess!"

"How handy ye are yerself with your talk!" retorted the ostler; "it's canthering round the table ye'll be doing, and it's what'll suit ye betther!"

Fanny Fitz began to laugh. "He might ride the saddle of mutton!" she said, with a levity that, under the circumstances, did her credit. "You'd better take the harness off, and you'll have to get her to Recess for me somehow."

The ostler took no notice of this suggestion; he was repeating to himself: "Ride the saddle o' mutton! By dam, I never heard the like o' that! Ride the saddle o' mutton——!" He suddenly gave a yell of laughing, and in the next moment the startled filly dragged the reins from his hand with a tremendous plunge, and in half a dozen bounds was out of the yard gate and clattering down the road.

There was an instant of petrifaction. "Diddlety—iddlety—idlety!" chanted the waiter with faraway sweetness.

Fanny Fitz and the ostler were outside the gate simultaneously: the filly was already rounding the first turn of the road; two strides more, and she was gone as though she had never been, and "Oh, my nineteens pounds!" thought poor Fanny Fitz.

As the ostler was wont to say in subsequent repetitions of the story: "Thanks be to God, the reins was rotten!" But for this it is highly probable that Miss Fitzroy's speculation would have collapsed abruptly with broken knees, possibly with a broken neck. Having galloped into them in the course of the first hundred yards, they fell from her as the green withes fell from Samson, one long streamer alone remaining to lash her flanks as she fled. Some five miles from the hotel she met a wedding, and therewith leaped the bog-drain by the side of the road and "took to the mountains," as the bridegroom poetically described it to Fanny Fitz, who, with the ostler, was pursuing the fugitive on an outside car.

"If that's the way," said the ostler, "ye mightn't get her again before the winther."

Fanny Fitz left the matter, together with a further instalment of the thirty pounds, in the hands of the sergeant of police, and went home, and, improbable as it may appear, in the course of something less than ten days she received an invoice from the local railway station, Enniscar, briefly stating: "1 horse arrd. Please remove."

Many people, most of her friends indeed, were quite unaware that Fanny Fitz possessed a home. Beyond the fact that it supplied her with a permanent address, and a place at which she was able periodically to deposit consignments of half-worn-out clothes, Fanny herself was not prone to rate the privilege very highly. Possibly, two very elderly maiden step-aunts are discouraging to the homing instinct; the fact remained that as long as the youngest Miss Fitzroy possessed the wherewithal to tip a housemaid she was but rarely seen within the decorous precincts of Craffroe Lodge.

Let it not for a moment be imagined that the Connemara filly was to become a member of this household. Even Fanny Fitz, with all her optimism, knew better than to expect that William O'Loughlin, who divided his attentions between the ancient cob and the garden, and ruled the elder Misses Fitzroy with a rod of iron, would undertake the education of anything more skittish than early potatoes. It was to the stable, or rather cow-house, of one Johnny Connolly, that the new purchase was ultimately conveyed, and it was thither that Fanny Fitz, with apples in one pocket and sugar in the other, conducted her ally, Mr. Freddy Alexander, the master of the Craffroe Hounds. Fanny Fitz's friendship with Freddy was one of long standing, and was soundly based on the fact that when she had been eighteen he had been fourteen; and though it may be admitted that this is a discrepancy that somewhat fades with time, even Freddy's mother acquitted Fanny Fitz of any ulterior motive; and Freddy was an only son.

"She was very rejected last night afther she coming in," said Johnny Connolly, manipulating as he spoke the length of rusty chain and bit of stick that fastened the door. "I think it was lonesome she was on the thrain."

Fanny Fitz and Mr. Alexander peered into the dark and vasty interior of the cow-house; from a remote corner they heard a heavy breath and the jingle of a training bit, but they saw nothing.

"I have the cavesson and all on her ready for ye, and I was thinking we'd take her south into Mr. Gunning's land. His finces is very good," continued Johnny, going cautiously in; "wait till I pull her out."

Johnny Connolly was a horse trainer who did a little farming, or a farmer who did a little horse training, and his management of young horses followed no known rules, and indeed knew none, but it was generally successful. He fed them by rule of thumb; he herded them in hustling, squabbling parties in pitch-dark sheds; he ploughed them at eighteen months; he beat them with a stick like dogs when they transgressed, and like dogs they loved him. He had what gardeners call "a lucky hand" with them, and they throve with him, and he had, moreover, that gift of winning their wayward hearts that comes neither by cultivation nor by knowledge, but is innate and unconscious. Already, after two days, he and the Connemara filly understood each other; she sniffed distantly and with profound suspicion at Fanny and her offerings, and entirely declined to permit Mr. Alexander to estimate her height on the questionable assumption that the point of his chin represented 15·2, but she allowed Johnny to tighten or slacken every buckle in her new and unfamiliar costume without protest.

"I think she'll make a ripping good mare," said the enthusiastic Freddy, as he and Fanny Fitz followed her out of the yard; "I don't care what Rupert Gunning says, she's any amount of quality, and I bet you'll do well over her."

"She'll make a real nice fashionable mare," remarked Johnny, opening the gate of a field and leading the filly in, "and she's a sweet galloper, but she's very frightful in herself. Faith, I thought she'd run up the wall from me the first time I went to feed her! Ah ha! none o' yer thricks!" as the filly, becoming enjoyably aware of the large space of grass round her, let fling a kick of malevolent exuberance at the two fox-terriers who were trotting decorously in her rear.

It was soon found that, in the matter of "stone gaps," the A B C of Irish jumping, Connemara had taught the grey filly all there was to learn.

"Begor, Miss Fanny, she's as crabbed as a mule!" said her teacher approvingly. "D'ye mind the way she soaks the hind legs up into her! We'll give her a bank now."

At the bank, however, the trouble began. Despite the ministrations of Mr. Alexander and a long whip, despite the precept and example of Mr. Connolly, who performed prodigies of activity in running his pupil in at the bank and leaping on to it himself the filly time after time either ran her chest against it or swerved from it at the last instant with a vigour that plucked her preceptor from off it and scattered Fanny Fitz and the fox-terriers like leaves before the wind. These latter were divided between sycophantic and shrieking indignation with the filly for declining to jump, and a most wary attention to the sphere of influence of the whip. They were a mother and daughter, as conceited, as craven, and as wholly attractive as only the judiciously spoiled ladies of their race can be. Their hearts were divided between Fanny Fitz and the cook, the rest of them appertained to the Misses Harriet and Rachael Fitzroy, whom they regarded with toleration tinged with boredom.

"I tell ye now, Masther Freddy, 'tis no good for us to be goin' on sourin' the mare this way. 'Tis what the fince is too steep for her. Maybe she never seen the like in that backward counthry she came from. We'll give her the bank below with the ditch in front of it. 'Tisn't very big at all, and she'll be bound to lep with the sup of wather that's in it."

Thus Johnny Connolly, wiping a very heated brow.

The bank below was a broad and solid structure, well padded with grass and bracken, and it had a sufficiently obvious ditch, of some three feet wide, on the nearer side. The grand effort was duly prepared for. The bank was solemnly exhibited to the filly; the dogs, who had with unerring instinct seated themselves on its most jumpable portion, were scattered with one threat of the whip to the horizon. Fanny tore away the last bit of bracken that might prove a discouragement, and Johnny issued his final order.

"Come inside me with the whip, sir, and give her one good belt at the last."

No one knows exactly how it happened. There was a rush, a scramble, a backward sliding, a great deal of shouting, and the Connemara filly was couched in the narrow ditch at right angles to the fence, with the water oozing up through the weeds round her, like a wild duck on its nest; and at this moment Mr. Rupert Gunning appeared suddenly on the top of the bank and inspected the scene with an amusement that he made little attempt to conceal.

It took half an hour, and ropes, and a number of Rupert Gunning's haymakers, to get Fanny Fitz's speculation on to its legs again, and Mr. Gunning's comments during the process successfully sapped Fanny Fitz's control of her usually equable temper.

"He's a beast!" she said wrathfully to Freddy, as the party moved soberly homewards in the burning June afternoon, with the horseflies clustering round them, and the smell of new-mown grass wafting to them from where, a field or two away, came the rattle of Rupert Gunning's mowing-machine. "A crabbing beast! It was just like my luck that he should come up at that moment and have the supreme joy of seeing Gamble—" Gamble was the filly's rarely-used name—"wallowing in the ditch! That's the second time he's scored off me. I *pity* poor little Maudie Spicer for having such a brother!"

In spite of this discouraging *début*, the filly's education went on and prospered. She marched discreetly along the roads in long reins; she champed detested mouthfuls of rusty mouthing bit in the process described by Johnny Connolly as "getting her neck broke"; she trotted for treadmill half-hours in the lunge; and during and in spite of all these penances, she fattened up and thickened out until that great authority, Mr. Alexander, pronounced it would be a sin not to send her up to the Dublin Horse Show, as she was just the mare to catch an English dealer's eye.

"But sure ye wouldn't sell her, miss?" said her faithful nurse, "and Masther Freddy afther starting the hounds and all!"

Fanny Fitz scratched the filly softly under the jawbone, and thought of the document in her pocket—long, and blue, and inscribed with the too familiar notice in red ink: "An early settlement will oblige".

"I must, Johnny," she said, "worse luck!"

"Well, indeed, that's too bad, miss," said Johnny comprehendingly. "There was a mare I had one time, and I sold her before I went to America. God knows, afther she went from me, whenever I'd look at her winkers hanging on the wall I'd have to cry. I never seen a sight of her till three years afther that, afther I coming home. I was coming out o' the fair at Enniscar, an' I was talking to a man an' we coming down Dangan Hill, and what was in it but herself coming up in a cart! "An' I didn't look at her, good nor bad, nor know her, but sorra bit but she knew me talking, an' she turned in to me with the cart! 'Ho, ho ho!' says she, and she stuck her nose into me like she'd be kissing me. Be dam, but I had to cry. An' the world wouldn't stir her out o' that till I'd lead her on meself. As for cow nor dog nor any other thing, there's nothing would rise your heart like a horse!"

••••••••••

It was early in July, a hot and sunny morning, and Fanny Fitz, seated on the flawless grassplot in front of Craffroe Lodge hall-door, was engaged in washing the dogs. The mother, who had been the first victim, was morosely licking herself, shuddering effectively, and coldly ignoring her oppressor's apologies. The daughter, trembling in every limb, was standing knee-deep in the bath; one paw, placed on its rim, was ready for flight if flight became practicable; her tail, rigid with anguish would have hummed like a violin-string if it were touched. Fanny, with her shirtsleeves rolled up to her elbows, scrubbed in the soap. A clipped fuchsia hedge, the pride of William O'Loughlin's heart, screened the little lawn and garden from the high road.

"Good morning, Miss Fanny," said a voice over the hedge.

Fanny Fitz raised a flushed face and wiped a fleck of Naldyre off her nose with her arm.

"I've just been looking at your mare," went on the voice.

"Well, I hope you liked her!" said Fanny Fitz defiantly, for the voice was the voice of Rupert Gunning, and there was that in it that in this connection acted on Miss Fitsroy as a slogan.

"Well, 'like' is a strong word, you know!" said Mr. Gunning, moving on and standing with his arms on the top of the white gate and meeting Fanny's glance with provoking eyes. Then, as an after-thought, "Do you think you give her enough to eat?"

"She gets a feed of oats every Sunday, and strong tea and thistles through the week," replied Fanny Fitz in furious sarcasm.

"Yes, that's what she looks like," said Rupert Gunning thoughtfully. "Connolly tells me you want to send her to the show—Barnum's, I suppose—as the skeleton dude?"

"I believe you want to buy her yourself," retorted Fanny, with a vicious dab of the soap in the daughter's eye.

"Yes, she's just about up to my weight, isn't she? By-the-bye, you haven't had her backed yet, I believe?"

"I am going to try her to-day!" said Fanny with sudden resolve.

"Ride her yourself!" said Mr. Gunning, his eyebrows going up into the roots of his hair.

"Yes!" said Fanny, with calm as icy as a sudden burst of struggles on the part of the daughter would admit of.

Rupert Gunning hesitated; then he said, "Well, she ought to carry a side-saddle well. Decent shoulders, and a nice long——" Perhaps he caught Fanny Fitz's eye; at all events, he left the commendation unfinished, and went on, "I should like to look in and see the performance, if I may? I suppose you wouldn't let me try her first? No?"

He walked on.

"Puppy, *will* you stay quiet!" said Fanny Fitz very crossly. She even slapped the daughter's soap-sud muffled person, for no reason that the daughter could see.

"Begorra, miss, I dunno," said Johnny Connolly dubiously when the suggestion that the filly should be ridden there and then was made to him a few minutes later; "wouldn't ye wait till I put her a few turns under the cart, or maybe threw a sack o' oats on her back?"

But Fanny would brook no delay. Her saddle was in the harness-room: William O'Loughlin could help to put it on; she would try the filly at once.

Miss Fitzroy's riding was of the sort that makes up in pluck what it wants in knowledge. She stuck on by sheer force of character; that she sat fairly straight, and let a horse's head alone were gifts of Providence of which she was wholly unconscious. Riding, in her opinion, was just getting on to a saddle and staying there, and making the thing under it go as fast as possible. She had always ridden other people's horses, and had ridden them so straight, and looked so pretty, that—other people in this connection being usually men—such trifles as riding out a hard run minus both fore shoes, or watering her mount generously during a check, were endured with a forbearance not frequent in horse owners. Hunting people, however, do not generally mount their friends, no matter how attractive, on young and valuable horses. Fanny Fitz's riding had been matured on well-seasoned screws, and she sallied forth to the subjugation of the Connemara filly with a self-confidence formed on experience only of the old, and the kind, and the cunning.

The filly trembled and sidled away from the garden-seat up to which Johnny Connolly had manœuvred her. Johnny's supreme familiarity with young horses had brought him to the same point of recklessness that Fanny had arrived at from the opposite extreme, but some lingering remnant of prudence had induced him to put on the cavesson headstall, with the long rope attached to it, over the filly's bridle. The latter bore with surprising nerve Fanny's depositing of herself in the saddle.

"I'll keep a holt o' the rope, Miss Fanny," said Johnny, assiduously fondling his pupil; "it might be she'd be strange in herself for the first offer. I'll lead her on a small piece. Come on, gerr'l! Come on now!"

The pupil, thus adjured, made a hesitating movement, and Fanny settled herself down into the saddle. It was the shifting of the weight that seemed to bring home to the grey filly the true facts of the case, and with the discovery she shot straight up into the air as if she had been fired from a mortar. The rope whistled through Johnny Connolly's fingers, and the point of the filly's shoulder laid him out on the ground with the precision of a prize-fighter.

"I felt, my dear," as Fanny Fitz remarked in a letter to a friend, "as if I were in something between an earthquake and a bad dream and a churn. I just *clamped* my legs round the crutches, and she whirled the rest of me round her like the lash of a whip. In one of her flights she nearly went in at the hall door, and I was aware of William O'Loughlin's snow-white face somewhere behind the geraniums in the porch. I think I was clean out of the saddle then. I remember looking up at my knees, and my left foot was nearly on the ground. Then she gave another flourish, and swung me up on top again. I was hanging on to the reins hard; in fact, I think they must have pulled me back on to the saddle, as I *know* at one time I was sitting in a bunch on the stirrup! Then I heard most heart-rending yells from the poor old Aunts: 'Oh, the begonias! O Fanny, get off the grass!' and then, suddenly, the filly and I were perfectly still, and the house and the trees were spinning round me, black, edged with green and yellow dazzles. Then I discovered that some one had got hold of the cavesson rope and had hauled us in, as if we were salmon; Johnny had grabbed me by the left leg, and was trying to drag me off the filly's back; William O'Loughlin had broken two pots of geraniums, and was praying loudly among the fragments; and Aunt Harriet and Aunt Rachel, who don't to this hour realise that anything unusual had happened, were reproachfully collecting the trampled remnants of the begonias."

It was, perhaps unworthy on Fanny Fitz's part to conceal the painful fact that it was that distinguished fisherman, Mr. Rupert Gunning, who had landed her and the Connemara filly. Freddy Alexander, however, heard the story in its integrity, and commented on it with his usual candour. "I don't know which was the bigger fool, you or Johnny," he said; "I think you ought to be jolly grateful to old Rupert!"

"Well, I'm not" returned Fanny Fitz.

After this episode the training of the filly proceeded with more system and with entire success. Her nerves having been steadied by an hour in the lunge with a sack of oats strapped, Mazeppalike, on to her back, she was mounted without difficulty, and was thereafter ridden daily. By the time Fanny's muscles and joints had recovered from their first attempt at rough-riding, the filly was taking her place as a reasonable member of society, and her nerves, which had been as much *en évidence* as her bones, were, like the latter, finding their proper level, and becoming clothed with tranquillity and fat. The Dublin Horse Show drew near, and, abetted by Mr. Alexander, Fanny Fitz filled the entry forms and drew the necessary cheque, and then fell back in her chair and gazed at the attentive dogs with fateful eyes.

"Dogs!" she said, "if I don't sell the filly I am done for!"

The mother scratched languidly behind her ear till she yawned musically, but said nothing. The daughter, who was an enthusiast, gave a sudden bound on to Miss Fitzroy's lap, and thus it was that the cheque was countersigned with two blots and a paw mark.

None the less, the bank honoured it, being a kind bank, and not desirous to emphasise too abruptly the fact that Fanny Fitz was overdrawn.

In spite of, or rather, perhaps, in consequence of this fact, it would have been hard to find a smarter and more prosperous-looking young woman than the owner of No. 548, as she signed her name at the season-ticket turnstile and entered the wide soft aisles of the cathedral of horses at Ballsbridge. It was the first day of the show, and in token of Fanny Fitz's enthusiasm be it recorded, it was little more than 9.30 A.M. Fanny knew the show well, but hitherto only in its more worldly and social aspects. Never before had she been of the elect who have a horse "up," and as she hurried along, attended by Captain Spicer, at whose house she was staying, and Mr. Alexander, she felt magnificently conscious of the importance of the position.

The filly had preceded her from Craffroe by a couple of days, under the charge of Patsey Crimmeen, lent by Freddy for the occasion.

"I don't expect a prize, you know," Fanny had said loftily to Mr. Gunning, "but she has improved so tremendously, every one says she ought to be an easy mare to sell."

The sun came filtering through the high roof down on to the long rows of stalls, striking electric sparks out of the stirrup-irons and bits, and adding a fresh gloss to the polish that the grooms were giving to their charges. The judging had begun in several of the rings, and every now and then a glittering exemplification of all that horse and groom could be would come with soft thunder up the tan behind Fanny and her squires.

"We've come up through the heavy weights," said Captain Spicer; "the twelve-stone horses will look like rats——" He stopped.

They had arrived at the section in which figured "No. 548. Miss F. Fitzroy's 'Gamble,' grey mare; 4 years, by Grey Dawn," and opposite them was stall No. 548. In it stood the Connemara filly, or rather something that might have been her astral body. A more spectral, deplorable object could hardly be imagined. Her hind quarters had fallen in, her hips were standing out; her ribs were like the bars of a grate; her head, hung low before her, was turned so that one frightened eye scanned the passers-by, and she propped her fragile form against the partition of her stall, as though she were too weak to stand up.

To say that Fanny Fitz's face fell is to put it mildly. As she described it to Mrs. Spicer, it fell till it was about an inch wide and five miles long. Captain Spicer was speechless. Freddy alone was equal to demanding of Patsey Crimmeen what had happened to the mare.

"Begor, Masther Freddy, it's a wonder she's alive at all!" replied Patsey, who was now perceived to be looking but little better than the filly. "She was middlin' quiet in the thrain, though she went to lep out o' the box with the first screech the engine give, but I quietened her some way, and it wasn't till we got into the sthreets here that she went mad altogether. Faith, I thought she was into the river with me three times! 'Twas hardly I got her down the quays; and the first o' thim alecthric thrams she seen! Look at me hands, sir! She had me swingin' on the rope the way ye'd swing a flail. I tell you, Masther Freddy, them was the ecstasies!"

Patsey paused and gazed with a gloomy pride into the stricken faces of his audience.

"An' as for her food," he resumed, "she didn't use a bit, hay, nor oats, nor bran, bad nor good, since she left Johnny Connolly's. No, nor drink. The divil dang the bit she put in her mouth for two days, first and last. Why wouldn't she eat is it, miss? From the fright sure! She'll do nothing, only standing that way, and bushtin' out sweatin', and watching out all the time the way I wouldn't lave her. I declare to God I'm heart-scalded with her!"

At this harrowing juncture came the order to No. 548 to go forth to Ring 3 to be judged, and further details were reserved. But Fanny Fitz had heard enough.

"Captain Spicer," she said, as the party paced in deepest depression towards Ring 3, "if I hadn't on a new veil I should cry!"

"Well, I haven't," replied Captain Spicer; "shall I do it for you? Upon my soul, I think the occasion demands it!"

"I just want to know one thing," continued Miss Fitzroy. "When does your brother-in-law arrive?"

"Not till to-night."

"That's the only nice thing I've heard to-day," sighed Fanny Fitz.

The judging went no better for the grey filly than might have been expected, even though she cheered up a little in the ring, and found herself equal to an invalidish but well-aimed kick at a fellow-competitor. She was ushered forth with the second batch of the rejected, her spirits sank to their former level, and Fanny's accompanied them.

Perhaps the most trying feature of the affair was the reproving sympathy of her friends, a sympathy that was apt to break down into almost irrepressible laughter at the sight of the broken-down skeleton of whose prowess poor Fanny Fitz had so incautiously boasted.

"Y' know, my dear child," said one elderly M.F.H., "you had no business to send up an animal without the condition of a wire fence to the Dublin Show. Look at my horses! Fat as butter, every one of 'em!"

"So was mine, but it all melted away in the train," protested Fanny Fitz in vain. Those of her friends who had only seen the mare in the catalogue sent dealers to buy her, and those who had seen her in the flesh—or what was left of it—sent amateurs; but all, dealers and the greenest of amateurs alike, entirely declined to think of buying her.

The weather was perfect; every one declared there never was a better show, and Fanny Fitz, in her newest and least-paid-for clothes, looked brilliantly successful, and declared to Mr. Rupert Gunning that nothing made a show so interesting as having something up for it. She even encouraged him to his accustomed jibes at her Connemara speculation, and personally conducted him to stall No. 548, and made merry over its melancholy occupant in a way that scandalised Patsey, and convinced Mrs. Spicer that Fanny's pocket was even harder hit than she had feared.

On the second day, however, things looked a little more hopeful.

"She ate her grub last night and this morning middlin' well, miss," said Patsey, "and"—here he looked round stealthily and began to whisper—"when I had her in the ring, exercisin', this morning, there was one that called me in to the rails; like a dealer he was. 'Hi! grey mare!' says he. I went in. 'What's your price?' says he. 'Sixty guineas, sir,' says I. 'Begin at the shillings and leave out the pounds!' says he. He went away then, but I think he's not done with me."

"I'm sure the ring is our best chance, Patsey," said Fanny, her voice thrilling with the ardour of conspiracy and of reawakened hope. "She doesn't look so thin when she's moving. I'll go and stand by the rails, and I'll call you in now and then just to make people look at her!"

"Sure I had Masther Freddy doing that to me yestherday," said Patsey; but hope dies hard in an Irishman, and he saddled up with all speed.

For two long burning hours did the Connemara filly circle in Ring 3, and during all that time not once did her owner's ears hear the longed-for summons, "Hi! grey mare!" It seemed to her that every other horse in the ring was called in to the rails, "and she doesn't look so very thin today!" said Fanny indignantly to Captain Spicer, who, with Mr. Gunning, had come to take her away for lunch.

"Oh, you'll see, you'll sell her on the last day; she's getting fitter every minute," responded Captain Spicer. "What would you take for her?"

"I'm asking sixty," said Fanny dubiously. "What would *you* take for her, Mr. Gunning—on the last day, you know?"

"I'd take a ticket for her," said Rupert Gunning, "back to Craffroe—if you haven't a return."

The second and third days crawled by unmarked by any incident of cheer, but on the morning of the fourth, when Fanny arrived at the stall, she found Patsey had already gone out to exercise. She hurried to the ring and signalled to him to come to her.

"There's a fella' afther her, miss!" said Patsey, bending very low and whispering at close and tobacco-scented range. "He came last night to buy her; a jock he was, from the Curragh, and he said for me to be in the ring this morning. He's not come yet. He had a straw hat on him."

Fanny sat down under the trees and waited for the jockey in the straw hat. All around were preoccupied knots of bargainers, of owners making their final arrangements, of would-be-buyers hurrying from ring to ring in search of the paragon that they had now so little time to find. But the man from the Curragh came not. Fanny sent the mare in, and sat on under the trees, sunk in depression. It seemed to her she was the only person in the show who had nothing to do, who was not clinking handfuls of money, or smoothing out banknotes, or folding up cheques and interring them in fat and greasy pocket-books. She had never known this aspect of the Horse Show before, and—so much is in the point of view—it seemed to her sordid and detestable. Prize-winners with their coloured rosettes were swaggering about everywhere. Every horse in the show seemed to have got a prize except hers, thought Fanny. And not a man in a straw hat came near Ring 3.

She went home to lunch, dead tired. The others were going to see the polo in the park.

"I must go back and sell the mare," said Fanny valiantly, "or else take that ticket to Craffroe, Mr. Gunning!"

"Well, we'll come down and pick you up there after the first match, you poor, miserable thing," said Mrs. Spicer, "and I hope you'll find that beast of a horse dead when you get there! You look half dead yourself!"

How sick Fanny was of signing her name at the turnstile! The pen was atrocious every time. How tired her feet were! How sick she was of the whole thing, and how incredibly big a fool she had been! She was almost too tired to know what she was doing, and she had actually walked past stall No. 548 without noticing it, when she heard Patsey's voice calling her.

"Miss Fanny! Miss Fanny! I have her sold! The mare's sold, miss! See here! I have the money in me pocket!"

The colour flooded Fanny Fitz's face. She stared at Patsey with eyes that more than ever suggested the Connemara trout-stream with the sun playing in it; so bright were they, so changing, and so wet. So at least thought a man, much addicted to fishing, who was regarding the scene from a little way off.

"He was a dealer, miss," went on Patsey; "a Dublin fella'. Sixty-three sovereigns I asked him, and he offered me fifty-five, and a man that was there said we should shplit the differ, and in the latther end he gave me the sixty pounds. He wasn't very stiff at all. I'm thinking he wasn't buying for himself."

The man who had noticed Fanny Fitz's eyes moved away unostentatiously. He had seen in them as much as he wanted; for that time at least.

May Sinclair

1863? – 1946

There is some uncertainty over her birth date and little is known of her early life except that she had no formal education until her eighteenth year when she became the protegée of Dorothea Bealé, the pioneering Headmistress of Cheltenham Ladies' College: under her influence, May Sinclair began to read the classics and to write first poetry, then fiction. Her first novel, Audrey Craven (1896) was well received by critics who recognized her talent. She was amongst the first writers to explore and develop the 'stream of consciousness' technique. Divine Fire (1904), The Creators (1910) and The Three Sisters (1915) consolidated her literary reputation.

A staunch supporter of women's rights, as her novels often show, she worked with other women writers (including Cicely Hamilton and Violet Hunt) in the interest of 'The Cause'; during the last years of her life she suffered from Parkinson's Disease and while an invalid she became interested in psychic phenomena.

The following extract consists of the opening chapters of The Three Sisters (Hutchinson, London, 1915 (4th edn)).

From

The Three Sisters

I

NORTH of east, in the bottom, where the road drops from the High Moor, is the village of Garth in Garthdale.

It crouches there with a crook of the dale behind and before it, between half-shut doors of the west and south. Under the mystery and terror of its solitude it crouches, like a beaten thing, cowering from its topmost roof to the bowed back of its stone bridge.

It is the last village up Garthdale; a handful of grey houses, old and small and humble. The high road casts them off, and they turn their backs to it in their fear and huddle together, humbly, down by the beck. Their stone roofs and walls are naked and blackened by wind and rain as if fire had passed over them.

They have the silence, the darkness and the secrecy of all ultimate habitations.

North, where the high road begins to rise again, the Vicarage stands all alone. It turns its face towards the village, old and grey and humble as any house there, and looks on the road sideways, through the small shy window of its gable-end. It has a strip of garden in front and on its farther side and a strip of orchard at the back. The garden slopes down to the churchyard, and a lane leading to the pastures, runs between.

And all these things of stone—the village, the Vicarage, the church, the churchyard and the gravestones of the dead—are alike naked and black, blackened as if fire had passed over them. And in their greyness and their desolation they are one with each other, and with the network of low walls that links them to the last solitary farm on the High Moor. And on the breast of the earth they show, one moment, solid as if hewn out of her heart, and another, slender and wind-blown as a tangle of grey thread on her green gown.

II

THROUGH four of its five front windows the house gave back darkness to the dark. One, on the ground-floor, showed a golden oblong, skirted with watery grey where the lamplight thinned the solid blackness of the wall.

The three sisters, Mary, Gwendolen and Alice, daughters of James Cartaret, the Vicar of Garth, were sitting there in the dining-room behind the yellow blind, doing nothing. In their supine, motionless attitudes they seemed to be waiting for something to happen, to happen so soon that, if there had been anything to do, it was not worth their while doing it.

All three were alike in the small, broad faces that brooded, half sullen and half sad; in the wide eyes that watched vaguely; in the little tender noses, and in the mouths, tender and sullen too; in the arch and sweep of the upper lips, the delicate fullness of the lower; in the way of the thick hair, parted and turned back over the brows in two wide and shallow waves.

Mary, the eldest, sat in a low chair by the fireside. Her hands were clasped loosely on the black woollen socks she had ceased to darn.

She was staring into the fire with her grey eyes, the thick grey eyes that never let you know what she was thinking. The firelight woke the flame in her reddish-tawny hair. The red of her lips was turned back and crushed against the white. Mary was shorter than her sisters, but she was the one that had the colour. And with it she had a stillness that was not theirs. Mary's face brooded more deeply than their faces, but it was untroubled in its brooding.

She had learned to darn socks for her own amusement on her eleventh birthday, and she was twenty-seven now.

Alice, the youngest girl (she was twenty-three) lay stretched out on the sofa.

She departed in no way from her sister's type, but that her body was slender and small boned, that her face was lightly finished, that her grey eyes were clear and her lips pale against the honey-white of her face, and that her hair was colourless as dust except where the edge of the wave showed a dull gold.

Alice had spent the whole evening lying on the sofa. And now she raised her arms and bent them, pressing the backs of her hands against her eyes. And now she lowered them and lifted one sleeve of her thin blouse, and turned up the milk-white under surface of her arm, and lay staring at it and feeling its smooth texture with her fingers.

Gwendolen, the second sister, sat leaning over the table, with her arms flung out on it as they had tossed from her the book she had been reading.

She was the tallest and the darkest of the three. Her face followed the type obscurely, and vividly and emphatically it left it. There was dusk in her honey-whiteness and dark blue in the grey of her eyes. The bridge of her nose and the arch of her upper lip were higher, lifted, as it were, in a decided and defiant manner of their own. About Gwenda there was something alert and impatient. Her very supineness was alive. It had distinction, the savage grace of a creature utterly abandoned to a sane fatigue.

Gwenda had gone fifteen miles over the moors that evening. She had run and walked and run again in the riotous energy of her youth.

Now she was too tired to read.

Gwenda was the first to speak.

"Is it ten yet?"

"No." Mary smiled, but the word shuddered in her throat like a weary moan.

"How long?"

"Forty-three minutes."

"Oh Lord!" Gwenda laughed the laugh of brave nerves tortured.

From her sofa beyond the table Alice sighed.

At ten o'clock Essy Gale, the maid-servant, would come in from the kitchen and the Vicar from the inner room. And Essy would put the Bible and Prayer-book on the table, and the Vicar would read Prayers.

That was all they were waiting for. It was all that could happen. It happened every night at ten o'clock.

III

ALICE spoke next.
"What day of the month is it?"

"The thirtieth," Mary answered.

"Then we've been here exactly five months to-day."

"That's nothing," said Mary, "to the months and years we shall be here."

"I can't think what possessed Papa to come and bury us all in this rotten place."

"Can't you?" Mary's eyes turned from their brooding. Her voice was very quiet, barely perceptible the significant stress.

"Oh, if you mean it's *me* he wants to bury—— You needn't rub that in."

"I'm not rubbing it in."

"You are. You're rubbing it in every time you look like that. That's the beastly part of it. Supposing he does want to get back on me, why should he go and punish you two?"

"If he thinks he's punishing me he's sold," said Gwenda.

"He couldn't have stuck you in a rottener hole."

Gwenda raised her head.

"A hole? Why, there's no end to it. You can go for miles and miles without meeting anybody, unless some darling mountain sheep gets up and looks at you. It's—it's a divine place, Ally."

"Wait till you've been another five months in it. You'll be as sick as I am."

"I don't think so. You haven't seen the moon get up over Greffington Edge. If you had—if you knew what this place was like, you wouldn't lie there grizzling. You wouldn't talk about punishing. You'd wonder what you'd done to be allowed to look at it—to live in it a day. Of course, I'm not going to let on to Papa that I'm in love with it."

Mary smiled again.

"It's all very well for you," she said. "As long as you've got a moor to walk on *you're* all right."

"Yes. I'm all right," Gwenda said.

Her head had sunk again and rested in the hollow of her arms. Her voice, muffled in her sleeve, came soft and thick. It died for drowsiness.

In the extreme immobility and stillness of the three, the still house stirred and became audible to them, as if it breathed. They heard the delicate fall of the ashes on the hearth, and the flame of the lamp jerking as the oil sputtered in the burnt wick. Their nerves shook to the creeping, crackling sounds that came from the wainscot, infinitely minute. A tongue of fire shot hissing from the coal. It seemed to them a violent and terrifying thing. The breath of the house passed over them in thick smells of earth and must, as the fire's heat sucked at its damp.

The church clock struck the half-hour. Once, twice: two dolorous notes that beat on the still house and died.

Somewhere out at the back a door opened and shut, and it was as if the house drew in its breath at the shock of the sound.

Presently a tremor crept through Gwenda's young body as her heart shook it.

She rose and went to the window.

IV

SHE was slow and rapt in her going, like one walking in her sleep, moved by some impulse profounder than her sleep.

She pulled up the blind. The darkness was up against the house, thick and close to the pane. She threw open the window, and the night entered palpably like slow water, black and sweet and cool.

From the unseen road came the noise of wheels and of a horse that in trotting clanked for ever one shoe against another.

It was young Rowcliffe, the new doctor, driving over from Morthe to Upthorne on the Moor, where John Greatorex lay dying.

The pale light of his lamps swept over the low garden wall.

Suddenly the four hoofs screamed, grinding together in the slide of their halt. The doctor had jerked his horse up by the Vicarage gate.

The door at the back opened and shut again, suddenly, sharply, as if in fear.

A voice swung out like a mournful bell into the night. A dalesman's voice—such a voice as the lonely land fashions sometimes for its own delight, drawling and tender, hushed by the hills and charged with the infinite, mysterious sadness of their beauty.

It belonged to young Greatorex and it came from the doorway of the Vicarage yard.

"That yo, Dr. Rawcliffe? I wuss joost gawn oop t'road t'see ef yo wuss coomin'."

"Of course I was coming."

The new doctor was short and stern with young Greatorex.

The two voices, the soft and the stern, spoke together for a moment, low, inaudible. Then young Greatorex's voice was heard again, and in its softness there was the furtive note of shame.

"I joost looked in to Vicarage to leave woord with Paason."

The noise of the wheels and hoofs began again, the iron shoes clanked together and struck out the rhythm that the sisters knew.

And with the first beat of it, and with the sound of the two voices in the road, life, secret and silent, stirred in their blood and nerves. It quivered like a hunting thing held on the leash.

V

Their stillness, their immobility were now intense. And not one spoke a word to the other.

All three of them were thinking.

Mary thought: "Wednesday is his day. On Wednesday I will go into the village and see all my sick people. Then I shall see him. And he will see me. He will see that I am kind and sweet and womanly." She thought: "That is the sort of woman that a man wants." But she did not know what she was thinking.

Gwenda thought: "I will go out on to the moor again. I don't care if I *am* late for Prayers. He will see me when he drives back and he will wonder who is that wild, strong girl who walks by herself on the moor at night and isn't afraid. He has seen me three times, and every time he has looked at me as if he wondered. In five minutes I shall go." She thought (for she knew what she was thinking): "I shall do nothing of the sort. I don't care whether he sees me or not. I don't care if I never see him again. I don't care."

Alice thought: "I will make myself ill—so ill that they'll *have* to send for him. I shall see him that way."

VI

ALICE sat up. She was thinking another thought. "If Mr. Greatorex is dead, Dr. Rowcliffe won't stay long at Upthorne. He will come back soon. And he will have to call and leave word. He will come in and I shall see him."

But if Mr. Greatorex was not dead? If Mr. Greatorex were a long time over his dying? Then he might be kept at Upthorne, perhaps till midnight, perhaps till morning. Then, even if he called to leave word, she would not see him. When she looked deep she found herself wondering how long Mr. Greatorex would be over his dying. If she had looked a little deeper she would have found herself hoping that Mr. Greatorex was already dead.

If Mr. Greatorex was dead before he got to Upthorne, he would come very soon, perhaps before prayer-time.

And he would be shown into the drawing-room.

Would he? Would Essy have the sense? No. Not unless the lamp was lit there. Essy would not show him into a dark room. And Essy was stupid. She might have *no* sense. She might take him straight into the study and Papa would keep him there. Trust Papa.

Alice got up from her sofa and left the room, moving with her weary grace and a little air of boredom and of unconcern. She was always most unconcerned when she was most intent.

Outside, in the passage, she stood a moment, listening. All the ways of the house gave upon the passage in a space so narrow that by stretching out one arm she could have touched both walls.

With a door open anywhere the passage became a gully for the north wind. Now, with all doors shut it was as if the breath of the house was being squeezed out there, between closing walls. The passage, instead of dividing the house, drew it together tight. And this tightness was intolerable to Alice.

She hated it. She hated the whole house. It was so built that there was not a corner in it where you could get away from Papa. His study had one door opening into the passage and one into the dining-room. The window where he sat raked the garden on the far side. The window of his bedroom raked the front; its door commanded the stairhead. He was aware of everything you did, of everything you did not do. He could hear you in the dining-room; he could hear you overhead; he could hear you going up and down stairs. He could positively hear you breathe, and he always knew whether you were in bed or not. She drew in her breath lest he should hear it now.

At the far end of the passage, on the wall-space between the staircase and the kitchen door, raised on a small bracket, a small tin lamp showed a thrifty flame. Under it, on a mahogany table-flap, was a row of bedroom candlesticks with their matchboxes.

Her progress to the table-flap was stealthy. She exalted this business of lighting the drawing-room lamp to a desperate, perilous adventure. The stone floor deadened her footsteps as she went.

Her pale eyes, half sullen, half afraid, slewed round to the door of the study on her right. With a noiseless hand she secured her matches and her candle. With noiseless feet she slid into the darkness of the drawing-room. She dared not light her candle out there in the passage. For the Vicar was full of gloom and of suspicion in the half-hour before prayer-time, and at the spurt of the match he might come out blustering, and insist on knowing what she was doing and where she was going; whereas presently he would know, and he might be quiet as long as he was satisfied that she was not shirking Prayers.

Stealthily, with her air of desperate adventure, she lit the drawing-room lamp. She shook out the puffs and frills of its yellow paper shade. Under its gaudy skirts the light was cruel to the cramped and shabby room, to the huddled furniture, to the tarnished gilt, the perishing tones of grey and amber.

Alice set the lamp on the top of the cottage piano that stood slantwise in a side window beyond the fireplace. She had pulled back the muslin curtains and opened both windows wide, so that the room was now bared to the south and west. Then, with the abrupt and passionate gesture of desire deferred, she sat down at the little worn-out Erard and began to play.

Sitting there, with the open window behind her, she could be seen, and she knew that she could be seen, from over the wall by anybody driving past in a high dog-cart.

And she played. She played the Chopin 'Grande Polonaise,' or as much of it as her fingers, tempestuous and inexpert, could clutch and reach. She played, neither with her hands nor with her brain, but with her temperament, febrile and frustrate, seeking its outlet in exultant and violent sound. She fell upon the Erard like some fierce and hungry thing, tearing from the forlorn, humble instrument a strange and savage food. She played—with incredible omissions, discords and distortions, but she played. She flung out her music through the windows into the night as a signal and an appeal. She played (on the little worn-out Erard) in ecstasy and expectation, as if something momentous hung upon her playing. There was joy and triumph and splendour in the 'Grande Polonaise'; she felt them in her heart and nerves as a delicate, dangerous tremor, the almost intolerable oncoming of splendour, of triumph and of joy.

And as she played the excitement gathered; it swung in more and more vehement vibrations; it went warm and flooding through her brain like wine. All the life of her bloodless body swam there, poised and thinned, but urgent, aspiring to some great climax of the soul.

VII

THE whole house was full of the Chopin 'Grande Polonaise.'
    It raged there like a demon. Tortured out of all knowledge, the 'Grande Polonaise' screamed and writhed in its agony. It writhed through the window, seeking its natural attenuation in the open air. It writhed through the shut house and was beaten back, pitilessly, by the roof and walls. To let it loose thus was Alice's defiance of the house and her revenge.

Mary and Gwenda heard it in the dining-room, and set their mouths and braced themselves to bear it. The Vicar, in his study behind the dining-room, heard it and scowled. Essy, the maid-servant, heard it—she heard it worse than anybody—in her kitchen on the other side of the wall. Now and then, when the Polonaise screamed louder, Mary drew a hissing breath of pain through her locked teeth, and Gwenda grinned. Not that to Gwenda there was anything funny in the writhing and screaming of the 'Grande Polonaise.' It was that she alone appreciated its vindictive quality; she admired the completeness, the audacity of Alice's revenge.

But Essy in her kitchen made no effort to stand up to the 'Grande Polonaise.' When it began she sat down and laid her arms on the kitchen table, and her head, muffled in her apron, on her arms, and cried. She could not have told you what the Polonaise was like or what it did to her; all that she could have said was that it went through and through her. She did not know—Essy did not—what had come over her; for whatever noise Miss Alice made, she had not taken any notice, not at first. It was in the last three weeks that the Polonaise had found her out, and had begun to go through and through her, till it was more than she could bear. But Essy, crying into her apron, would not have lifted a finger to stop Miss Alice.

"Poor laass," Essy said to herself; "she looves to plaay. And Vicar, he'll not hold out mooch longer. He'll put foot down 'fore she gets trow."

Through the screaming of the Polonaise Essy listened for the opening of the study door.

VIII

THE study door did not open all at once.

"Wisdom and patience, wisdom and patience—" the Vicar kept on muttering as he scowled. Those were his watchwords in his dealings with his womenkind.

The Vicar was making a prodigious effort to maintain what seemed to him his god-like serenity. He was unaware that he was trying to control at one and the same time his temper and his temperament.

He was a man of middle height and squarish build, dark, pale-skinned and blue-eyed like his daughter Gwendolen. The Vicar's body stretched tight the seams of his black coat, and kept up, at fifty-seven, a false show of muscular energy. The Vicar's face had a subtle quality of deception. The austere nose, the lean cheek-bones, the square-cut moustache and close-clipped, pointed beard (black, slightly grizzled), made it appear, at a little distance, the face of an ascetic. It approached, and the blue of the eyes, and the black of their dilated pupils, the stare of the nostrils and the half hidden lines of the mouth revealed its profound and secret sensuality.

The interior that contained him was no less deceptive. Its book-lined walls advertised him as the scholarly recluse that he was not. He had had an eye to this effect. He had placed in prominent positions the books that he had inherited from his father, who had been a schoolmaster. You were caught at the very door by the thick red line of the Tudor Classics; by the eleven volumes of the Bekker's Plato, with Notes, bound in russia leather, side by side with Jowett's Translations, in cloth; by Sophocles and Dean Plumptre, the "Odyssey" and Butcher and Lang; By Æschylus and Robert Browning. The Vicar had carried the illusion of scholarship so far as to hide his Aristophanes behind a little curtain, as if it contained for him an iniquitous temptation. Of his own accord and with a deliberate intention to deceive, he had added the Early Fathers, Tillotson's "Sermons" and Farrar's "Life of Christ."

On another shelf, rather less conspicuous, were some bound volumes of the *Record*, with the novels of Mrs. Henry Wood and Miss Marie Corelli. On the ledge of his bureau *Blackwood's Magazine*, uncut, lay ready to his hand. The *Spectator*, in process of skimming, was on his knees. The *Standard*, fairly gutted, was on the floor. There was no room for it anywhere else.

For the Vicar's study was much too small for him. Sitting there, in an arm-chair and with his legs in the fender, he looked as if he had taken flight before the awful invasion of his furniture. His bookcases hemmed him in on three sides. His roll-top desk, advancing on him from the window, had driven and squeezed him into the arm-chair. His bureau, armed to the teeth, leaning from its ambush in the recess of the fireplace, threatened both the retreat and the left flank movement of the chair. The Vicar was neither tall nor powerful, but his study made him look like a giant imprisoned in a cell.

The room was full of the smell of tobacco, of a smouldering coal fire, of old worn leather and damp walls, and of the heavy, virile odour of the Vicar.

A brown felt carpet and thick serge curtains shut out the draught of the north-east window.

On a September evening, the Vicar was snug enough in his cell; and before the 'Grande Polonaise' had burst in upon him, he had been at peace with God and man.

But when he heard those first exultant, challenging bars, he scowled inimically.

Not that he acknowledged them as a challenge. He was inclined rather to the manly course of ignoring the 'Grande Polonaise' altogether. And not for a moment would he have admitted that there had been anything in his behaviour that could be challenged or defied, least of all by his daughter Alice. To himself in his study Mr. Cartaret appeared as the image of righteousness established in an impregnable place. Whereas his daughter Alice was not at all in a position to challenge and defy.

She had made a fool of herself.

She knew it; he knew it; everybody knew it in the parish they had left five months ago. It had been the talk of the little southern seaside town. He thanked God that nobody knew it, or was ever likely to know it here.

For Alice's folly was not any ordinary folly. It was the kind that made the parish which was so aware of it uninhabitable to a sensitive Vicar.

He reflected that she would be clever if she made a fool of herself here. By his decisive action in removing her from that southern seaside town he had saved her from continuing her work. In order to do it he had ruined his prospects. He had thrown up a good living for a poor one; a living that might (but for Alice it certainly would) have led to preferment for a living that could lead to nothing at all; a living where he could make himself felt for a living where there was nobody to feel him.

And having done it he was profoundly sorry for himself.

So far as Mr. Cartaret could see, there had been nothing else to do. If it had all to be done over again, he told himself that he would do it.

But there Mr. Cartaret was wrong. He could not have done it or anything like it twice. It was one of those deeds, supremely sacrificial, that strain a man's moral energies to breaking-point and render him incapable of further sacrifice; if, indeed, it did not render further sacrifice superfluous. Mr. Cartaret honestly felt that even an exacting deity could require no more of him.

And it was not the first time either, nor his daughter Alice the first woman who had come between the Vicar and his prospects. Looking back, he saw himself driven from pillar to post, from parish to parish, by the folly or incompetence of his womenkind.

Strictly speaking, it was his first wife, Mary Gwendolen, the one the children called Mother, who had begun it. She had made his first parish unendurable to him by dying in it. This she had done when Alice was born, thereby making Alice unendurable to him too. Poor Mamie! He always thought of her as having, inscrutably, failed him.

All three of them had failed him.

His second wife, Frances, the one the children called Mamma (the Vicar had made himself believe that he had married her solely on their account), had turned into a nervous invalid on his hands before she died of that obscure internal trouble which he had so wisely and patiently ignored.

His third wife, Robina (the one they called Mummy) had run away from him in the fifth year of their marriage. When she implored him to divorce her, he said that whatever her conduct had been, that course was impossible to him as a Churchman, as she well knew; but that he forgave her. He had made himself believe it.

And all the time he was aware, without admitting it, that if the thing came into court, Robina's evidence might be a little damaging to the appearances of wisdom and patience, of austerity and dignity which he had preserved so well. He had had an unacknowledged vision of Robina standing in the witness-box, very small and shy, with her eyes fluttering while she explained to the gentlemen of the jury that she ran away from her husband because she was afraid of him. He could hear the question: "Why were you afraid?" and Robina's answer. But at that point he always reminded himself that it was as a Churchman that he objected to divorce.

For his profession had committed him to a pose. He had posed for more than thirty years to his parish, to his three wives, to his three children and to himself, till he had become unconscious of his real thoughts, his real motives, his real likings and dislikings. So that when he told himself that it would have been better if his third wife had died, he thought he meant that it would have been better for her and for his opinion of her, whereas what he really did mean was that it would have been better for himself.

For if Robina had died he could have married again. As it was, her infidelity condemned him to a celibacy for which, as she knew, he was utterly unsuited.

Therefore he thought of her as a cruel and unscrupulous woman. And when he thought of her he became more sorry for himself than ever.

Now, oddly enough, the 'Grande Polonaise' had set Mr. Cartaret thinking of Robina. It was not that Robina had ever played it. Robina did not play. It was not the discords introduced into it by Alice, though Robina had been a thing of discords. It was that something in him, obscurely but intimately associated with Robina, responded to that sensual and infernal tremor that Alice was wringing out of the Polonaise. So that, without clearly knowing why it was abominable, Mr. Cartaret said to himself that the tune Alice was playing was an abominable tune and must be stopped at once.

He went into the drawing-room to stop it.

And Essy, in the kitchen, raised her head and dried her eyes on her apron.

"If you must make a noise," said Mr. Cartaret, "be good enough to make one that is less—disturbing."

He stood in the doorway staring at his daughter Alice.

Her excitement had missed by a hair's-breadth the spiritual climax. It had held itself in for one unspeakable moment, then surged, crowding the courses of her nerves. Beaten back by the frenzy of the Polonaise, it made a violent return; it rose, quivering, at her eyelids and her mouth; it broke, and with a shudder of all her body spilt itself and fell.

The Vicar stared. He opened his mouth to say something, and said nothing; finally, he went out, muttering.

"Wisdom and patience. Wisdom and patience."

It was a prayer.

Alice trailed to the window and leaned out, listening for the sound of hoofs and wheels. Nothing there but the darkness and stillness of the moors. She trailed back to the Erard and began to play again.

This time it was Beethoven, the 'Pathetic Sonata.'

IX

MR. Cartaret sat in his study, manfully enduring the 'Pathetic Sonata.' He was no musician, and he did not certainly know when Alice went wrong; therefore, except that it had some nasty loud moments, he could not honestly say that the First Movement was disturbing. Besides, he had scored. He had made Alice change her tune.

Wisdom and patience required that he should be satisfied, so far. And being satisfied, in the sense that he no longer had a grievance, meant that he was very badly bored.

He began to fidget. He took his legs out of the fender and put them back again. He shifted his weight from one leg to the other, but without relief. He turned over his *Spectator* to see what it had to say about the Deceased Wife's Sister Bill, and found that he was not interested in what it had to say. He looked at his watch and compared it with the clock in the faint hope that the clock might be behindhand.

The watch and clock both agreed that it was not a minute later than fifteen minutes to ten. A whole quarter of an hour before prayer-time.

There was nothing but prayer-time to look forward to.

He began to fidget again. He filled his pipe and thought about smoking it. Then he rang the bell for his glass of water.

After more delay than was at all necessary, Essy appeared, bringing the glass of water on a plate.

She came in, soft-footed, almost furtive, she who used to enter so suddenly and unabashed. She put the plate down on the roll-top desk and turned softly, furtively away.

The Vicar looked up. His eyes were large and blue as suspicion drew in the black of their pupils.

"Put it down here," he said, and he indicated the ledge of the bureau.

Essy stood still and stared like a half-wild creature in doubt as to its way. She decided to make for the bureau by rounding the roll-top desk on the far side, thus approaching her master from behind.

"What are you doing?" said the Vicar. "I said, Put it down here."

Essy turned again and came forward, tilting the plate a little in her
nervousness. The large blue eyes, the stern voice fascinated her, frightened
her.

The Vicar looked at her steadily, remorselessly, as she came.

Essy's lowered eyelids had kept the stain of her tears. Her thick brown
hair was loose and rumpled under her white cap. But she had put on a
clean, starched apron. It stood out stiffly, billowing, from her waist. Essy had
not always been so careless about her hair or so fastidious as to her aprons.
There was a little strained droop at the corners of her tender mouth, as if
they had been tied with string. Her dark eyes still kept their young largeness
and their light, but they looked as if they had been drawn tight with string at
their corners too.

All these signs the Vicar noted as he stared. And he hated Essy. He hated
her for what he saw in her, and for her buxom comeliness, and for the
softness of her youth.

"Did I hear young Greatorex round at the back door this evening?" he said.

Essy started, slanting her plate a little more.

"I doan knaw ef I knaw, sir."

"Either you know or you don't know," said the Vicar.

"I doan knaw, I'm sure, sir," said Essy.

The Vicar was holding out his hand for his glass of water, and Essy pushed
the plate towards him, so blindly and at such a perilous slant that the glass
slid and toppled over and broke itself against the Vicar's chair.

Essy gave a little frightened cry.

"Clever girl. She did that on purpose," said the Vicar to himself.

Essy was on her knees beside him, picking up the bits of glass and
gathering them in her apron. She was murmuring: "I'll mop it oop. I'll
mop it oop."

"That'll do," he said roughly. "That'll do, I tell you. You can go."

Essy tried to go. But it was as if her knees had weights on them that
fixed her to the floor. Holding up her apron with one hand, she clutched
the arm of her master's chair with the other and dragged herself to her feet.

"I'll mop it oop," she repeated, shamefast.

"I told you to go," said the Vicar.

"S'll I fetch yo anoother glaass?" she whispered. Her voice was hoarse with
the spasm in her throat.

"No," said the Vicar.

Essy slunk back into her kitchen with terror in her heart.

Elizabeth Robins

1873 – 1957

B orn in Louisville, Kentucky, she grew up in Gainsville, Ohio; the Putnam
Female Seminary was responsible for the formal education she received
and launched her on her multi-faceted career as actress, writer and
feminist activist. Sent to Vassar to study medicine, she ran away and went on
the stage; after a brief and distressing marriage she renounced domestic duties
and journeyed to London where she soon established herself as a leading actress
and introduced reforms to the theatre. A founding member, sometime editor,
and regular contributor to the women's political periodical, Time and Tide,
and an active participant in the Actresses' Franchise League, Elizabeth Robins
devoted her life and her art to improving the conditions of women. She wrote
short stories, novels, plays, feminist treatises and literary criticism – and a steady
stream of articles defending the British suffragettes and their methods for wide
circulation in North America; her play Votes for Women (1907) was a box office
success and her feminist protest, Ancilla's Share (1924) remains relevant today;
her novel, The Convert (1907), which was based on her recordings of many of
the actual speeches of Christabel Pankhurst, is a remarkable documentary of
this exciting period of women's history.

The following short story was originally published in 1908.

Under His Roof

A STORY OF MILITANT SUFFRAGE

T HE two women had never supposed they would meet again. They had not only
that bitter quarrel like a drawn sword between them. They had a memory of
baseness each had evoked in each—a memory which neither was base enough
to be able to recall without wincing.

September had come round again. The thing had happened in September.
The memory of it came alive each year, borne on that influence—less
a depressant than a stimulus—the high, fine melancholy of the first days
of autumn.

The old pain, overlaid by so much happiness, thrust its pale face above
the surface of existence, much as the autumn crocus surprised one in some
forgotten corner of the smooth immaculate lawn. The long-ended conflict had

not for years been so fresh in Esther Bonham's mind as in this hour. Her own victory. Miranda's defeat.

She stood in the after-sunset light, herself and the long white room steeped in the changing radiance. As she put last touches to a bowl of flowers, her inveterate romanticism saw herself as fulfilling the terms of a gracious picture. In her creamy country clothes, shining in that transient brightness, she looked for the moment almost as young as when she had come to Shipbroads, a bride, ten years before.

But Miranda——

She kept glancing through the window towards the drive, as she gathered up the petals of the dear, late-flowering, roses—so exquisite and with so little vigour of bloom. They droop, they drop in an hour. They fall at a touch. At this last moment, when the guest was due, Esther had found ravages she must repair. There must be nothing that was not perfect about this perfect house, the first time Miranda should sleep under Shipbroad's roof. For Miranda must be made to stay. Esther had made up her mind about that, as she bent over the roses, warmed, like them, by a belated generosity.

She contrasted her fate with Miranda's. Miranda for twelve years had always, at every crisis, 'got the worst of it'. Life had bruised and battered her and flung her aside. She had failed everywhere. Her very advantages had helped in her undoing. She had been too pretty and too well-loved at home to be allowed to go away and paint. At twenty-four she had lost the father who adored her. On Sir James's death his daughter had dropped from a brilliant, luxurious life to one of petty poverty. Almost in the same hour she had heard that Esther was engaged to the man both women loved.

Miranda was thirty-six now. No older after all than the mistress of Shipbroads herself, who had her days of looking twenty-five. But to be thirty-six in the country is to be young still. To be thirty-six in London, in ill-health and low spirits, is to be middle-aged.

Miranda had never been strong: not even in her shielded youth. These twelve years, since the quarrel, no wonder they had left her what her cousin's letter said: 'A frail ghost of a woman, battling with a mortal malady.' What need for her to go out of her way to seek another enemy in the rough places of the world? Above all why, now that her half-brother had died and she was a woman of means, why should she (as the unnerving rumour whispered) be planning to throw away her last chance of happiness! Perhaps throw away her life.

How Miranda's desperate resolution had been reached, Esther could see clearer on this golden and scented evening. Miranda had no such haven as Shipbroads. A woman of fastidious tastes needed a proper setting. Few could hope for a Shipbroads. But half a mile across the meadow was a more ambitious, if less romantic, house with terraced gardens. Life in the country!—oh, Esther had her scheme for the rescue of that old enemy, old friend, from the horror that hung over her.

She walked up and down the room. How strange that they should meet here. Here where he had lived. Where he had read and written. Where he had smoked in front of winter fires. Where he had praised the roses for the last time two

summers ago; where, so calmly, one evening he had died. His chair. She bent
over it. The place had always been full of him. But never since his going had
the sense of his presence been so insistent as it was to-night. To this house of
his that he had loved as though it had been alive and human, under this roof
where Miranda had hoped to live beside him, she was coming on what was like
to be the last night she would need a roof, or any human friending.

Unless Esther's plan should succeed.

It must succeed. Esther had written her: "I have a great wish to see you. Could
you bear to come?" And Miranda had written back: "I will come gladly. All that
old misery was long, long ago burnt out of me and even the ashes scattered."

That was the kind of thing a person of any pride would say. The encounter
would not be easy for either of them. Better to go out and meet her at the
gate. Esther had noticed, in the way of the sensitive, how, in the open, passions
are calmed and manners simpler. As pettiness attitudinises and ill-will thrives
indoors, so embarrassments fall away in fields and gardens. That old quarrel
between the two women had about it something large and elemental. Its very
ghost would walk with a less furtive mien with only the roof of heaven above.

The barking of dogs. There she was!—coming across the meadow. So she
had sent the carriage away. She was stopping now to speak to the dogs.
Esther's first thought—she keeps her little school-girl figure. She's not altered
as I expected—turned, on coming nearer, to: She's changed beyond anything
I ever dreamed. This pale slip of a woman had never walked with so sure a
step in the days of her cherished youth. The edge of Esther's sympathy dulled
before that advance. The look in the face, too. Was that brightness a blind? Or
an effect of sheer excitement in view of the double ordeal?—finding herself at
Hugh's gate at last, and remembering—to-morrow.

Yet there was nothing fevered in the small face. The pointed chin lifted
a little. Quiet eyes on the steep-pitched roof—the famous roof of slabs of
Horsham stone. Where it wasn't mossed and lichen-grown it showed grey, and
rippled like sea sand, salt-encrusted.

"What a roof! I never saw roof like that," she said—just like any other visitor,
seeing for the first time the great feature of the house.

That they met so without embarrassment—that was yet another kindness
Esther owed those sheltering stones.

"You lie so hidden in your hollow, the wonder is I found you."

"Yes," Esther answered, "coming across the fields one sees nothing but
the roof."

And Miranda agreed: "It seems to sit on the ground like a group of grey stone
tents." She stood there looking up. "The roof was too massive for the walls," she
said (tact had never been poor Miranda's forte). "It dwarfs the house."

Was she trying to show Esther that she had no more envy of all that was
implied in the privilege of calling that roof one's own?

In any case, a blessed refuge in the difficult first moments, this idle talk
on some safe theme. And what so safe as Shipbroads' roof! It was the very type
and sign of safety. No such roof, Miranda was told, could cover any house less
than centuries old. There were no more such slabs of glorious rippled stone.

And even if more were found, no builder of these days could lavish oak on the Shipbroads' scale, to bear the tons on tons' weight of a roof like this. Miranda need only look at the older wing where the timbers showed—framing panels of weathered brick—and the great corner joists, grooved and gullied by action of frost and sun, yet more enduring than iron, which would rust; tougher than steel which might corrode; outlasting stone which scaled and crumbled. The two walked round the house. Did Miranda see the roses and the cypresses? She said "yes" and "yes," but her eyes seemed intent on some other, far-off beauty. Esther stopped her by the outer wall of the stone ingle that bore on its shoulders the tall chimney. Everyone admired that chimney. Miranda's face was lifted too, obedient, absent. She seemed to feel something was expected of her. Her eyes explored the fissure that zig-zagged like a streak of harmless lightning down the pink and orange of lichened brick:—"Is that crack old?" she asked inconsequently.

"Yes," Esther answered, "very old. This part is Elizabethan," she said with pride.

In some curious way an Elizabethan chimney seemed suddenly a less satisfying thing. On the hostess fell that old sense of vague, undefined disadvantage that she had so often felt in Miranda's presence. Miranda who had lost at every point. Miranda who was so broken and spent that she was ready to fling away what was left of life.

How calm she was. No one who didn't know would ever suspect.

She was made to notice the depth of the eaves. The walls were really higher than they looked—

Miranda shook her head in the old wilful way. "Your roof makes one think of a little man swaggering in a big man's hat. It comes down over his ears. It fairly extinguishes him."

"It doesn't extinguish Shipbroads!" Esther said. "Come in and see." It was less an invitation than a challenge.

They went through stone passages white-walled, and crossed by oak beams, proudly bared now—"all plastered over, when—" on the brink of utterance of that name Esther stopped herself, like a runner checked at the edge of a cliff.

"When Hugh first came?" Miranda said. "Yes, I remember hearing that."

That the nervousness and shrinking seemed to be all Esther's, did not quiet her nerves. The first rush of protecting gentleness that had gone out in welcome to her guest, moment by moment it gave way to the old gêne and sense of rivalry. Never otherwise could Esther have yielded to the temptation to vaunt her prize. Shipbroads—outward and visible sign of that old conquest. Surely Miranda must see for herself the greater beauties. Esther could affect a certain lightness: "This is Red Riding Hood's door. Pull the bobbin and the latch flies up."

But as Miranda went from room to room she gave no sign of fastening hungrily on the quaintness and the beauty that one might think (considering all) would mean more to her than to any other. The unseeing brightness of her eyes seemed to rest on these things without reporting them to her brain. Still she followed her guide with tranquil, unmoved face. Wait till they should reach that upper chamber—but not yet. That should come last when the light was greyer. When they couldn't see each other's eyes too clearly.

Up and down, from room to room, on different levels. In a dim passage Miranda tripped at an inequality.

"Oh, I ought to have warned you. These floors are full of pitfalls." Esther said it, fatuously, as in contempt for the spirit level and the stranger foot.

"How quickly the light goes here," the visitor said.

She was told, "It is always dark up here long before it's dark down stairs. The overhanging eaves shut out the light."

When they came to what Esther called the Captain's Cabin, they stood in dusk under the heavy transverse beam of a raftered ceiling, dark with age. A maid went by with candles. Esther took one, saying some people were so barbaric as to tell her she ought to put in electric light. "Imagine electric light at Shipbroads!" She lifted the candle high. "You see that wainscot with the little panelled door and the linen pattern above. Well," a thrill came into her voice, "I've found out something lately about all this oak—"

Miranda wasn't listening. She stood, half turned away, staring down at the corner. "What's this?" she said.

A heap of something brown flung against the corner joist that came up from the foundation, through the floor, and through the ceiling to the roof. The dark-coloured hillock showed on the white matting with that something unpleasant in any unverified thing that gets into a well-kept house. Was it merely earth? and if so how had it come there? Something the dogs had brought indoors? Esther sniffed the air, arriving at no better knowledge.

"Dust," Miranda said. Then leaning down: "It's like a heap of grated chocolate." She put out her hand.

"Don't touch it!" Esther drew her away. "I'll send a servant." Hastily she opened the next door. "You haven't been in here yet."

The light of the single candle seemed lost in this room. A ceiling as high as that in the Captain's Cabin was low—and showing an open-timbered roof.

An effect of amplitude and peace.

They stood there saying nothing.

In the silence, a little noise—like a fairy saw.

"This used to be the lowest room in the house."

"I remember," Miranda said, as though she had lived here in old days. In a sense she had.

Esther remembered too: Miranda convalescent in a long chair on the lawn at Ardingly Manor. Her girl friend beside her. Not obtrusively more devoted after Hugh's appearance on the scene, yet showing an uncanny skill in hitting on the times when he was there—a casual-seeming, unfailing presence. The silent duel between the two girls. Hugh, all-unconscious—absorbed in Miranda. His nearest approach to realizing the pretty friend from the Rectory had been that day he invoked Esther's aid to get Sir James away—to help the lover to an hour alone with Miranda. Esther's anguish of acquiescence. The return to those two radiant ones.

That was the first day Esther heard of Shipbroads—all its merits summed in being the house Miranda would love. Hugh beside her. His bright head bent over her drawing book. "This is the gate . . . You come up the path. This is how it looks." He exaggerated the roof. Yet Miranda never found a fault in it then. He made diagrams of each floor. No room but Miranda knew. They discussed changes, for the most part reversions to an older order, as in this room where two windows had been bricked up from the times of the window tax. He had opened them east and south. And still he was afraid—Miranda had been so spoilt. "Spoilt?" Yes by sleeping in the garden. She had got the better of her illness so. Her room at Shipbroads might seem too low for eyes that had looked all Summer on the stars. But in every other way that room was the room, he said, for Miranda's dreams.

Then the day he cut across the fields and came running up the garden. Esther could see that look of his shining still—his hat in his hand, his head held high. The tall figure borne along with a resilient lightness, more boy than man, in the moment of action and of gladness at nearing the goal. The goal, a smiling welcome in the sun—smiling at the vigorous on-coming beauty that was hers—smiling, till she caught Esther's eye. Esther drew her breath against that edge of pain again—the agony of self-betrayal. She had not suffered herself to leave them instantly. Too much like being shown the door, and meekly going. She had stayed while Hugh, flushed, bright-eyed, triumphed over the low ceiling. More space above it than in the room below! "I'm having the whole blessed thing out!" Through a trap-door he had climbed into the attic. The dust of ages, "Cobwebs in festoons like Spanish moss. A roof magnificently timbered. I am throwing all that upper space into your room, Miranda." His laughing parody of the builder: "'Couldn't be done, sir! The tons on tons weight of stone couldn't be sustained, sir, if those cross timbers, flooring the attic, sir, were lifted.'" Modern builders, men of no imagination. Hugh dismissed them gleefully. "They don't know how solidly the old fellow's built." More diagrams. "Like this at present." When Miranda came she would find it so, and so. Oh very clearly Miranda had seen this room with her mind's eye, and known it for the Bridal chamber. So it had been. For another bride.

"What is that?" Miranda asked.

"What?"

"That sound."

"I don't hear anything. Some people don't like this room," Esther went on. "They'd as soon sleep in a College Hall, they say. *I* don't mind it." So she masked a pride of possession scarcely decent. But great as the space was, those presences filled it ... they were crowding Esther out. Again that sense of having to assert herself against Miranda. The need seized her to emphasize her place here; to show that she had set her mark on this particular room.

"I've improved it, I think, just lately." She lifted the candle to the central beam. "You see those two deep notches? And here, at the end, the auger-holes and mortices? They tell a wonderful story." Esther's sailor brother had read these marks as though they had been chapters out of one of his naval histories. "This oak has been in strange places! It's gone about the world, ploughing its way thought salt water. It's been warped in hotter suns than any England knows. That long split—perhaps that came of charging into icebergs in the dark. It has seen the great storms. Perhaps battles too. That stain . . . who knows . . .? It's all *old ship's wood*."

Miranda's eyes shone. "So far inland?"

"Far enough now. But not so far in old days. The estuary of our little river was a navigable channel once. The Roman galleys used to come as far up as the Castle." Esther pointed to the central support. "That battered old king post may have gone out to meet the Armada! And then one of these modern builders comes and overlays all that history with his pettifogging blocks and braces!"

Every one of those queer-shaped holes had been filled in when Esther came here—"filled with new oak stained dark to match the old." An outrage. Worse than a Russian censor's blacking out the finest pages of a contraband book.

"There it is again!" Miranda said. They listened

"Oh, you mean the rats. I'm so used to them I don't hear them any more. The builder who raised the ceiling stuck in a great new beam—a smooth machine-made thing—the whole length of the room under that old cross-beam. An intolerable eyesore. It couldn't help being so staring new, poor thing! You can't get hand-hewn oak any more. But the new beam wasn't even chamfered. Edges sharp as a hatchet. I had it out two years ago. No pompous big-wig builders meddling. Our little local people got that, and all the other new bits, out. The relief when they'd finished."

A faint filing filled the pause.

"Your 'little people' don't seem quite to have finished yet."

"You mean—the rats?" She laughed. "In all old houses—." Her eyes swept her handiwork. "Not an inch of oak in the place now less than centuries old."

"Wrecked ships!" Miranda said.

"Ships come home." Characteristically Esther evaded the grimmer implication.

"Ships are not like men and women," persisted the other. "A ship that's sea-worthy goes again to sea."

She was jealous! She must pick flaws! "Experts say: 'A perfect piece of old England!'"

They had stood for that instant in a silence unbroken by any human accent. But sound there was. Slight, surreptitious. The mean scratching and gnawing of vermin. The mistress of Shipbroads blew the final blast of triumph. "There's not a false note in the whole house now."

Again that slow insistent grate, grate—gnawing, filing. Following hard on the woman's boast, there was a hint of obscure insult in the small insolence of vermin. Their very pettiness penetrated Esther's inflated satisfaction like a pointed tooth. She dropped her eyes to the little schoolgirl figure going to and fro under the banded shadow. A wave of pity broke over Esther. Poor storm-tossed Miranda—facing that tornado in Parliament Square to-morrow. No. No. On a flood of shame at her own meanness, Esther was lifted out of "the shallows and the miseries" of rivalry. She set the candle down and drew Miranda to the window. They looked out at the tall cypress spreading voluminous Victorian skirts, untarnished by the autumn. Yet all the air was full of the scent of fallen leaves. Pungent, tonic, penetrating—the quintessence of the Fall came flooding through the window.

Miranda breathed it in. "How good!" she said. She leaned out till she caught the glitter of silver. The moon had risen as high as the upper reaches of the cypress—caught there like a crescent in a woman's loosened hair.

Miranda called to mind that dear inconsequent saying of Mrs. Browning's, "The best place in the house is the leaning out of the window." "Not but what the house is beautiful," she said, quick to recall a possible slight. "Beautiful beyond saying."

"You feel that?" Esther asked eagerly.

"I feel it is part of the fields, and part of the woods. That shows it's a nice house," she answered in her unemotional way.

They leaned together over the low sill.

"Miranda, I didn't ask you to come for nothing. I wanted you to see and feel this beauty. I wanted so much to show you how good it is to live away from cities, in a house you can love. It's such a waste of the beauty there is in the world, for people like you not to ... not to cherish it. One mustn't wait till one is too old. A house has to grow as well as a garden. Three hundred years weren't enough here. I was ten years making it fit."—(she saved herself from "us")—"making it fit me. And, Miranda, I've found a house for you!"

"For me!" A house would seem to be as little needed by this creature as a cavern or a mountain peak.

"Yes, I want you to stay to-night, and let me drive you there to-morrow."

"I mustn't do that," she said.

"Why not?"

"I have to be in London to-morrow."

Esther couldn't face the issue yet. She talked on, with a feverish enthusiasm, about the possibilities of this other old house she'd found, about the need of every woman for a house of her own. Without it, a woman was like a picture without a frame—without a wall to hang upon. She sang the joy of gardens. The need to make some corner of earth smile—to make some spot perfect before you die.

"That's my ambition, too," said the other. "Only I am less modest than you. I want, not only here and there a corner. I want all the beautiful earth to smile."

"We can't re-make the world."

"We must. We can." In the pause again, with pygmy saw and file—that ghostly carpentering. Miranda turned to listen. Then suddenly, "Let us go back, into the room where that strange stuff lies in the corner."

"Why? We ... don't know what it is——."

"That's a reason for finding out," Miranda laughed. "I believe you're afraid of it."

Of course Esther wasn't afraid. "Only it looks—horrid."

They took the candle in. Miranda stooped, thrust down her hand and sifted stuff rained out between her fingers. "I thought so. It's sawdust. Your 'little local people' have gnawed a new passage."

"But all that! Where in the world does it come from?" While they looked the dressing-bell rang.

The slight chill in the air since sunset was not enough to account for the wood fire burning in the ingle of the dining-room, Esther acknowledged that as they sat down. "Pure vanity," she said, smiling. "The old fireplace looks so nice lit up."

The rather silent meal was nearly finished, and Esther had told the servant he might go. The door closed behind him, and the two women looked down a little self-consciously into their plates. Suddenly they were facing each other with wide scared eyes. A report had rung out like a gun-shot in a cavern. Then, among the troop of secondary concussions—plunging, colliding echoes—came a full-throated roar out of the great chimney. The thunder of it seemed to make its progress down a stair, rattling, crashing, uttering fresh explosions, step by step, till it met the final shock of impact with the earth. Not to end there. It wrestled as with an enemy. It escaped. It burrowed—running along under the house. It kept muttering a subterranean anger down there. Over the ingle end of the room had fallen a rain of broken brick, pieces of mortar, dust and soot and grit. Where the sparks of a fire had risen, the evening air was blowing in. The back of the ingle showed a mouth of blackness gaping on the night.

The old chimney had fallen.

••••••••••

Outside, dogs were barking and servants were running about unmindful of usual duties, usual deferences. Men shouted excitedly as they came running up from the stables with a lantern and a carriage lamp. The moonlight showed clearly enough the amorphous ruin of what had stood and served so long. But the sight of the wrecked chimney had no such power to set nerves jangling as the long thunder of the fall.

The effect of some sharp physical jar is often to shatter hesitations, and to break through barriers that seemed built to outface death. Through the fierce cudgelling of the senses, instead of shrinking and submission, comes a strange and alien freedom. Locked doors open silently, and for one memorable hour the most trammelled soul stands free.

As the two stood there they took hands. Who made the motion first, neither knew. They leaned close. They talked in whispers.

"Come away," Miranda said. "Nothing can be done until to-morrow."

To-morrow! The word made a breach in Esther's thought wider than the gaping blackness that had been the Ingle Nook.

"Miranda, I've *heard*."

"Heard—?"

"What you want to do to-morrow. Listen," she crushed the thin hand. "I've waked each morning since I knew, with a sense of disaster. What I've thought —what is it, dreadful, that's hanging over me? Then, when I was fully awake, I knew. You—*won't* do it. You'll stay here to-night and to-morrow."

"No," Miranda said, "I have to go."

Esther caught her breath in a sob. "Your father—you used to care for your father. What would he have thought?"

"I hope he would have understood."

"You *know* he would have gone mad at the idea. He would have done anything rather than see you ... He would have shut you up—Miranda, he would rather have seen you dead."

"In many a war families have been divided."

"War! A sickening struggle in the streets. You pushed and dragged. Bruised, flung about. Oh, I've read about these raids."

"And you haven't minded before? You've sat here safe and happy?"

"What could I do? What can *you* do?" Esther held the thin hand tighter. "A little slight creature, a wind would blow away."

She used to be delicate, she admitted. Not now. That was one of the many miracles. The new need for strength had cured her of her ills.

"Has it cured *all* the old pain?" the other woman cried. "Has it cured remembering?"

"Cured or set aside," Miranda answered. "I have better things to think of now." Then she told what. How the Vision Splendid (a world lifted out of the mire of ages) had shone through all the gloom and mists, and saved her from despair.

A beautiful dream! Esther could understand that. But the hideous reality! "Oh, I've been hearing—in these sickening encounters more than one, you know it's true, more than one has been horribly injured. *Kicked*—."

"Two women have died," Miranda said.

"And for what!" the other burst out. "If it's coming, this change—it will come."

"Do you know why it will come? Because those two were ready to show the way. And because others are ready to follow."

"Not you—not you! Oh, my dear, I think of you when you were little." Esther was crying. "All that care and worship. To end like this. You. You of all women on the earth." When, before, she had spoken of Sir James, her heart kept saying Hugh. And now her tongue was shaping the name that had divided them. "Hugh," she whispered, "what would Hugh have said?"

Miranda put out her hand to ward the question off. And then: "He was the most chivalrous man I ever knew." She seemed to think the question answered.

The other drew a quick breath. "Miranda, it seems you've got to know."

Something in Esther's face made the other woman drop her eyes. "Believe me—it doesn't matter. Not now."

"Oh, that shows!"

"Hush! It's all done with."

"Only because it hurt you beyond bearing."

"No. Because I see life is a finer thing than anyone ever told me."

"That's the sort of empty generality people fly to when the particular good has failed them. I never thought I'd find myself telling you. But I *can't* let you go through with this ghastly plan of yours." Her voice went down. "You won't dare to take into that kind of struggle the woman Hugh loved."

Again that motion setting aside, soothing.

"Oh, you've got to know. He never cared for me as he cared for you. That was my punishment. For not playing fair. I made him think—Oh, Miranda. I lied and lied and lied."

The small figure shrank for the first time. "*My* hands weren't clean either. I don't like remembering how badly we behaved to each other."

"We must remember this once."

"Why? After all women used to think all was fair in love and war."

"Love! You call it love! Well, you've got to know. Love *did* come. But after. I'd have married anybody."

"*Don't!*"

"You despise me for that?"

"It's so much worse," Miranda said, "than anything that can happen to us to-morrow."

Esther winced sharply. The speech had cut her like a whip lash. "Oh, it's all very well for you!—*you* weren't a poor parson's daughter, one of six scrambling after husbands! *You* hadn't been made to feel, since you were twelve, that the only refuge from the misery of governessing was to get some man to marry you. You weren't afraid of hardship, afraid of poverty, afraid of loneliness—afraid of life. Deathly, deathly afraid." Her voice broke. "If you'd been looking out all your youth for shelter—" she fell into a passion of weeping. "No. You had everything. That was how I made it seem right. And my wickedness prospered so!" She hung for a moment to her first realization of the strangeness of the years behind. "I don't know what I'm made of. For I've been happy here."

"No one," said Miranda gently, "could be with Hugh and not be happy."

The other struggled to regain a footing on some coign of justification. "After all what was a good marriage for me, would have been a come down for you."

Miranda shook her head: "We were both right so far. To have his love was to have the best that love can bring."

How she said that! "So . . . they haven't made you forget him, then?"

"*Forget?*"

Never till she died should Esther, in her turn, forget the accent of that word. "I'd like you to believe," she said, "I didn't realise how much you cared, till—"

"Till I turned against you so venomously. Oh, that was a muddy bit of road!"

"But now" Esther looked at her with miserable eyes. "Now, I've found shelter. And you are out in the storm." But it wasn't Miranda who shivered. "Let us get our cloaks," said Esther. They put them on in the hall. "You don't need your hat." But Miranda kept it in her hand. They walked in silence round the house. A group of men still stood about the heap of ruin. Esther felt herself drawn away. The two went silently out at the gate and across the field. The moonlight lay white on the close-cropped grass.

Near the far gate Esther stopped and looked round at Shipbroads. "We'll go back now."

Miranda seemed to hesitate. But there was no yielding in her face. Only a new tenderness. "I wouldn't leave you to-night," she said, "for anything but this." She rode over Esther's protest of "too late to order the carriage—." "The people of the Inn will have one waiting at the end of the lane." Miranda opened the gate with Esther following hard—"I shall catch the 10.15."

"I can't let you go!" Esther clung to her. "Listen. The woman he loved *must not* go out to meet that horror!"

"Some of us must meet it. We shall drive it before us to-morrow!" The sharp face shone like a sword.

"—you'll drag in the dust the dignity that was dear to Hugh!"

"Try to understand. I never knew what dignity was till I learned it in this service."

"—to stand in the street and be hooted at—! The struggle. The fighting—."

The low voice breaking in was stern to hardness. "You and I, Esther, didn't shrink from a struggle of a meaner sort."

"Say what you like about me. *He* played fair. For his sake, stay awhile, under his roof. You belong here," Esther said brokenly. "The old house is a shrine. Everything in it and about it that was dear to him—I've tended and cherished them, everyone. But I know he meant them all for you. Be generous. Come back. Think it's Hugh who's asking you."

"You live too much in the past, here," said the other gently. "You don't see there's a glorious present waiting a little way down the road."

"*Don't* look down the road." She turned to go back. One hand held the gate open. "Think that just over the meadow Hugh is waiting."

"I didn't find him there." She turned suddenly. "Shall I tell you where I found him? Out in the thick of the strife."

"*Hugh!*" The heavy gate slipped out of Esther's hold. It clanged between them. "Hugh!"

"I can only tell you he has never been so near me since—we parted, as he has been these last two years. Whenever my weakness needs him I feel him at my side. I hope you are not hurt to have me say that?"

The other woman stood in tears. "I seem to see you," she whispered, "as you'll be to-morrow. A bit of human drift in the storm. I see the police riding you down."

"I don't think I shall be ridden down."

"You imagine you can prevent it!"

"The horses are good creatures. I understand horses."

"What good is that when angry men are riding them?"

"I shall take the horses by their bridles."

"You don't think *that* will stop the men."

"The men are human."

"I've heard that even good men, in crowds, aren't quite human. Besides —there are the loafers—the hooligans."

"Even they are men. It is partly for their sake we go. Besides it wouldn't matter, now, if they were wild beasts. We must go out to meet—whatever comes."

"Good-bye then. I shall never see you again. Oh I was so sure if you knew he loved you, *that* would save you! I was ready—I *am* ready if, for Hugh's sake, you'll do what I ask, for I'll do anything, *anything* for you."

The white face leaned over the gate. "Why not come with me?" Miranda said.

"With you!"

"If we stood side by side to-morrow we should wipe out that old dishonour."

Esther had fallen back. A good yard lay between her and the dividing gate. "You know," she said, with forced quietness, "it isn't in me. You might as well ask that rabbit scuttling to its burrow. Oh yes, I'm very like the rabbit." Her eyes turned home. The gate had swung open again. Close to Esther's shrinking Miranda's face was shining with a light greater than the moon can give.

"Yes, why not? Come with Hugh and me." She stood there, with that terrible brightness in her face, holding out her hand and saying "Come."

For one instant the other stood staring, fascinated. Dizziness made her seem to waver. The faint forward motion was checked and turned. The dilated eyes scoured the field of vision. Shipbroads swam in view. In its shadow-filled hollow the steep-pitched roof showed in the moonlight paler than by day. A flood of gratitude for the safety waiting there broke over the woman. She heard the carriage in the lane. She never so much as looked back. She ran across the meadow with hands out-stretched like a fugitive praying shelter.

•••••••••••

In bed that night, with curtains back and windows wide as always, she stared up at the rafters.

"Kind. kind," she said. And: "*Keep me safe.*"

The little carpenters were sawing and filing when she fell asleep.

No dreams, but in the middle of the night she woke again to that sense of immense disaster. What was it? It had come with a vague unnerving noise . . . a noise that echoed still. Oh yes, the chimney had fallen. Miranda had fallen. Trampled under iron hooves. Would to God Miranda had stayed here in safety, under the roof Hugh meant should shelter her.

But what was the matter with the roof? The woman lying under the rafters caught her breath. Was it some trick of moonlight that made the timbers look askew? The ceiling sagged like the ceiling of one's cabin in a gale. Again that mysterious noise. A grating, a harsh sliding. The woman lay as still as the mice and rats. She had no illusion of being the victim of a nightmare. She knew herself awake in every sense and quick in every nerve. She saw the king-post sway like a drunken man. An oaken buttress shot out. It fell crashing to the floor.

The tons on tons' weight settled slowly down.

A glimpse of stars—a blow—a blackness.

Charlotte Mew

1869 – 1928

Charlotte Mew was born in London, the eldest child of an architect father; she was deeply devoted to her mother and sister. She attended Lucy Harrison's School for Girls and lectures at University College London. Her first publication was a short story in The Yellow Book *and this was followed by stories and poems in* The Egoist, The Englishwoman, The Nation *and* Temple Bar. *A close friend of May Sinclair's, her literary reputation rests primarily on her verse published in two volumes –* The Farmer's Bride *(1916) and* The Rambling Sailor *(1929). Her work admired by many fellow-poets, including Thomas Hardy and Siegfried Sassoon, and she was granted a Civil List Pension in 1923. She was deeply upset by the death of her mother in 1923 and her sister in 1927, and in 1928 she committed suicide.*

The following poems are selected from Charlotte Mew: Collected Poems and Prose *(Val Warner (ed.), Virago, London, 1982). The first two were originally published in 1916, the last in 1929.*

The Farmer's Bride

To ———
He asked life of thee and thou gavest him a long life:
   even for ever and ever.

THREE Summers since I chose a maid,
   Too young maybe—but more's to do
At harvest-time than bide and woo.
   When us was wed she turned afraid
Of love and me and all things human;
Like the shut of a winter's day.
Her smile went out, and 'twasn't a woman—
   More like a little frightened fay.
   One night, in the Fall, she runned away.

"Out 'mong the sheep, her be," they said,
'Should properly have been abed;
But sure enough she wasn't there
Lying awake with her wide brown stare.

So over seven-acre field and up-along across the down
   We chased her, flying like a hare
Before our lanterns. To Church-Town
    All in a shiver and a scare
We caught her, fetched her home at last
    And turned the key upon her, fast.

She does the work about the house
As well as most, but like a mouse:
   Happy enough to chat and play
   With birds and rabbits and such as they,
   So long as men-folk keep away.
"Not near, not near!" her eyes beseech
When one of us comes within reach.
   The women say that beasts in stall
   Look round like children at her call.
   I've hardly heard her speak at all.

Shy as a leveret, swift as he,
Straight and slight as a young larch tree,
Sweet as the first wild violets, she,
To her wild self. But what to me?

The short days shorten and the oaks are brown,
   The blue smoke rises to the low grey sky,
One leaf in the still air falls slowly down,
   A magpie's spotted feathers lie
On the black earth spread white with rime,
The berries redden up to Christmas-time.
   What's Christmas-time without there be
   Some other in the house than we!

   She sleeps up in the attic there
   Alone, poor maid. 'Tis but a stair
Betwixt us. Oh! my God! the down,
The soft young down of her, the brown,
The brown of her—her eyes, her hair, her hair!

Beside the Bed

SOMEONE has shut the shining eyes, straightened and folded
  The wandering hands quietly covering the unquiet breast:
So, smoothed and silenced you lie, like a child, not again to be questioned
          or scolded;
  But, for you, not one of us believes that this is rest.

Not so to close the windows down can cloud and deaden
    The blue beyond: or to screen the wavering flame subdue its breath:
Why, if I lay my cheek to your cheek, your grey lips, like dawn, would
                quiver and redden,
    Breaking into the old, odd smile at this fraud of death.

Because all night you have not turned to us or spoken
    It is time for you to wake; your dreams were never very deep:
I, for one, have seen the thin, bright, twisted threads of them dimmed
                suddenly and broken,
    This is only a most piteous pretence of sleep!

My Heart is Lame

M Y heart is lame with running after yours so fast
      Such a long way,
Shall we walk slowly home, looking at all the things we passed
      Perhaps to-day?

Home down the quiet evening roads under the quiet skies,
      Not saying much,
You for a moment giving me your eyes
      When you could bear my touch.

But not to-morrow. This has taken all my breath;
      Then, though you look the same,
There may be something lovelier in Love's face in death
As your heart sees it, running back the way we came;
      My heart is lame.

Cicely Hamilton
1872 – 1952

B*orn Cicely Mary Hammill, and of a relatively poor family, she earned her living as a teacher before turning to the stage and to a writing life as a playwright, novelist and travel journalist. Most of her writing reflects her strong feminist views and her book* Marriage as a Trade *(1909) was a bitter denunciation of the way women were required to trade their bodies in return for board and lodging. A staunch supporter of improved employment opportunities for women, she was not averse to stating her case (albeit often in humorous form) in her many works of fiction. In the theatrical world she established her reputation with* Diana of Dobsons *(1908); she wrote about twenty plays in all, including two suffrage ones.*

How the Vote Was Won *began as a pamphlet, illustrated by C. Hedley Charlton and published in 1908 by the Women Writers' Suffrage League: it was so successful that Cicely Hamilton resolved to turn it into a play and Christopher St John (Christabel Marshall) assisted her in this endeavour. It was first performed at The Royalty Theatre, London, in April 1909 – and went on to become a great success.*

How the Vote Was Won *is taken from* How the Vote Was Won and Other Suffrage Plays *(Dale Spender and Carole Hayman (eds), Methuen, London, 1985).*

How the Vote Was Won

S**CENE**: *Sitting-room in* HORACE COLE'S *house at Brixton. The room is cheaply furnished in a genteel style. The window looks out on a row of little houses, all of the Cole pattern. The door (centre) leads into a narrow passage communicating at once with the front door. The fireplace (left) has a fancy mantel border, and over it is an overmantel, decorated with many photographs, and cheap ornaments. The sideboard (right), a small bookcase (right), a table (left centre up stage), and a comfortable armchair (centre by table), are the chief articles of furniture. The whole effect is modest, and quite unpleasing.*

Time: *Late afternoon on a spring day in any year in the future.*

When curtain rises, MRS HORACE COLE *is sitting in the comfortable armchair (centre) putting a button on to her husband's coat. She is a pretty, fluffy little woman who could never be bad-tempered, but might be fretful. At this minute she is smiling indulgently, and rather irritatingly, at her sister* WINIFRED, *who is sitting by the fire (left) when the curtain rises, but gets up almost immediately to leave.* WINIFRED *is a tall and distinguished looking young woman with a cheerful, capable manner and an emphatic diction which betrays the public speaker. She wears the colours of the* NWSPU.

WINIFRED: Well, good-bye, Ethel. It's a pity you won't believe me. I wanted to let you and Horace down gently, or I shouldn't be here.

ETHEL: But you're always prophesying these dreadful things, Winnie, and nothing ever happens. Do you remember the day when you tried to invade the House of Commons from submarine boats? Oh, Horace did laugh when he saw in the papers that you had all been landed on the Hovis wharf by mistake! 'By accident, on purpose!' Horace said. He couldn't stop laughing all the evening. 'What price your sister, Winifred?' he said. 'She asked for a vote, and they gave her bread.' He kept on – you can't think how funny he was about it!

WINIFRED: Oh, but I can! I know my dear brother-in-law's sense of humour is his strong point. Well, we must hope it will bear the strain that is going to be put on it today. Of course, when his female relations invade his house – all with the same story, 'I've come to be supported' – he may think it excruciatingly funny. One never knows.

ETHEL: Winnie, you're teasing me. They would never do such a thing. They must know we have only one spare bedroom, and that's to be for a paying guest when we can afford to furnish it.

WINIFRED: The servants' bedroom will be empty. Don't forget that all the domestic servants have joined the League and are going to strike, too.

ETHEL: Not ours, Winnie. Martha is simply devoted to me, and poor little Lily *couldn't* leave. She has no home to go to. She would have to go to the workhouse.

WINIFRED: Exactly where she will go. All those women who have no male relatives, or are refused help by those they have, have instructions to go to the relieving officer. The number of female paupers who will pour through the workhouse gates tonight all over England will frighten the Guardians into blue fits.

ETHEL: Horace says you'll never *frighten* the Government into giving you the vote. He says every broken window is a fresh nail in the coffin of women's suffrage. It's quite true. Englishmen can't be bullied.

WINIFRED: No, but they can *bully*. It's your husband, your dear Horace, and a million other dear Horaces who are going to do the bullying and frightening this time. The women are going to stay quiet, at home. By tomorrow, perhaps before, Horace will be marching to Westminster shouting out 'Votes for Women!'

ETHEL: Winnie, how absurd you are! You know how often you've tried to convert Horace and failed. Is it likely that he will become a Suffragette just because–

WINIFRED: Just because–? Go on, Ethel.

ETHEL: Well, you know – all this you've been telling me about his relations coming here and asking him to support them. Of course, I don't believe it. Agatha, for instance, would never dream of giving up her situation. But if they did come Horace would just tell them he *couldn't* keep them. How could he on £4 a week?

WINIFRED: How could he? That's the point! He couldn't, of course. That's why he'll want to get rid of them at any cost – even the cost of letting women have the vote. That's why he and the majority of men in this country shouldn't for years have kept alive the foolish superstition that all women are supported by men. For years we have told them it was a delusion, but they could not take our arguments seriously. Their method of answering us was exactly that of the little boy in the street who cries 'Yah – Suffragette!' or 'Where's your "'ammer"?' when he sees my badge.

ETHEL: I always wish you wouldn't wear it when you come here . . . Horace does so dislike it. He thinks it unwomanly.

WINIFRED: Oh! does he? Tomorrow he may want to borrow it – when he and the others have had their object-lesson. They wouldn't listen to argument . . . so we had to expose their pious fraud about woman's place in the world in a very practical and sensible way. At this very minute working women of every grade in every part of England are ceasing work, and going to demand support and the necessities of life from their nearest male relatives, however distant the nearest relative may be. I hope, for your sake, Ethel, that Horace's relatives aren't an exacting lot!

ETHEL: There wasn't a word about it in the *Daily Mail* this morning.

WINIFRED: Never mind. The evening papers will make up for that.

ETHEL: What male relative are you going to, Winnie? Uncle Joseph?

WINIFRED: Oh, I'm in the fighting line, as usual, so our dear uncle will be spared. My work is with the great army of women who have no male belongings of any kind! I shall be busy till midnight marshalling them to the workhouse . . . This is perhaps the most important part of the strike. By this we shall hit men as ratepayers even when they have escaped us as relatives! Every man, either in a public capacity or a private one, will find himself face to face with the appalling problem of maintaining millions of women in idleness. Do you think the men will take up the burden? Not they! (*Looks at her watch.*) Good heavens! The strike began ages ago. I must be off. I've wasted too much time here already.

ETHEL (*looking at the clock*): I had no idea it was so late. I must see about Horace's tea. He may be home any minute. (*Rings the bell, left.*)

WINIFRED: Poor Horace!

ETHEL (*annoyed*): Why 'poor Horace'? I don't think he has anything to complain of. (*Rings again.*)

WINIFRED: At this minute I feel some pity for all men.

ETHEL: What can have happened to Martha?

WINIFRED: She's gone, my dear, that's all.

ETHEL: Gone! Nonsense. She's been with me ever since I was married, and I pay her very good wages.

Enter LILY, *a shabby little maid-of-all-work, dressed for walking, the chief effort of the toilette being a very cheap and very smart hat.*

ETHEL: Where's Martha, Lily?

LILY: She's left, m'm.

ETHEL: Left! She never gave me notice.

LILY: No, m'm, we wasn't to give no notice, but at three o'clock we was to quit.

ETHEL: But why? Don't be a silly little girl. And you mustn't come in here in your hat.

LILY: I was just goin' when you rang. That's what I've got me 'at on for.

ETHEL: Going! Where? It's not your afternoon out.

LILY: I'm going' back to the Union. There's dozens of others goin' with me.

ETHEL: But why –?

LILY: Miss Christabel – she told us. She says to us: 'Now look 'ere, all of yer – you who've got no men to go to on Thursday – yer've got to go to the Union, she says: 'and the one who 'angs back' – and she looked at me she did – 'may be the person 'oo the 'ole strain of the movement is restin' on, the traitor 'oo's sailin' under the 'ostile flag,' she says: and I says, 'That won't be me – not much!'

During this speech WINIFRED *puts on a sandwich board which bears the inscription: 'This way to the Workhouse.'*

WINIFRED: Well, Ethel, are you beginning to believe?

ETHEL: Oh, I think it's very unkind – very wicked. How am I to get Horace anything to eat with no servants?

WINIFRED: Cheer up, my dear. Horace and the others can end the strike when they choose. But they're going to have a jolly bad time first. Goodbye. (*Exit* WINNIE, *singing the 'Marseillaise.'*)

LILY: Wait a bit, Miss. I'm comin' with yer. (*Sings the 'Marseillaise' too.*)

ETHEL: No, no. Oh, Lily, please don't go, or at any rate bring up the kettle first, and the chops, and the frying pan. Please! Then I think I can manage.

LILY (*coming back into the room and speaking impressively*): There's no ill-feeling. It's an objick-lesson – that's all.

Exit LILY. ETHEL *begins to cry weakly; then lays the table; gets bread, cruet, tea, cups, etc. from the cupboard, right.* LILY *re-enters with a frying pan, a kettle, and two raw chops.*

LILY: 'Ere you are – it's the best I can do. You see, mum, I've got to be recognised by the State. I don't think I'm a criminal nor a lunatic, and I oughtn't to be treated as sich.

ETHEL: You poor little simpleton. Do you suppose that, even if this absurd plan succeeds, *you* will get the vote?

LILY: I may – you never know your luck; but that's not why I'm giving up work. It's so as I shan't stop them as ought to 'ave it. The 'ole strain's on me, and I'm goin' to the Union – so goodbye, mum. (*Exit* LILY.)

ETHEL: And I've always been kind to you! Oh, you little brute! What *will* Horace say? (*Looking out of the window.*) It can't be true. Everything looks the same as usual. (HORACE'S *voice outside*)

HORACE: We must have at least sixteen more Dreadnoughts this year. (WILLIAMS' *voice outside*)

WILLIAMS: You can't get 'em, old chap, unless you expect the blooming colonies to pay for 'em.

ETHEL: Ah, here is Horace, and Gerald Williams with him. Oh, I hope Horace hasn't asked him to tea! (*She powders her nose at the glass, then pretends to be busy with the kettle.*)

Enter HORACE COLE – *an English master in his own house* – *and* GERALD WILLIAMS, *a smug young man stiff with self-consciousness.*

ETHEL: You're back early, aren't you, Horry? How do you do, Mr Williams?

GERALD WILLIAMS: How do you do, Mrs Cole. I've just dropped in to fetch a book your husband's promised to lend me.

HORACE *rummages in book-shelves.*

ETHEL: Had a good day, Horry?

HORACE: Oh, much as usual. Ah, here it is (*Reading out the title:*) 'Where's the Wash-tub now?' with a preface by Lord Curzon of Kedleston, published by the Men's League for Opposing Women's Suffrage. If that doesn't settle your missus, nothing will.

ETHEL: Is Mrs Williams a Suffragette?

GERALD: Rather, and whenever I say anything, all she can answer is, 'You know nothing about it.' I call that illogical. Thank you, old man. I'll read it to her after tea. So long. Goodbye, Mrs Cole.

ETHEL: Did Mrs Williams tell you anything this morning ... before you went to the City?

GERALD: About Votes for Women, do you mean? Oh, no. Not allowed at breakfast. In fact, not allowed at all. I tried to stop her going to these meetings where they fill the women's heads with all sorts of rubbish, and she said she'd give 'em up if I'd give up footer matches on Saturday afternoons; so we agreed to disagree. See you tomorrow, old chap. Goodbye, Mrs Cole.

Exit GERALD WILLIAMS

HORACE: You might have asked him to stop to tea. You made him very welcome – I don't think.

ETHEL: I'm sorry; but I don't think he would have stayed if I *had* asked him.

HORACE: Very likely not, but you should always be hospitable. Tea ready?

ETHEL: Not quite, dear. It will be in a minute.

HORACE: What on earth is all this!

ETHEL: Oh, nothing. I thought I would cook your chop for you up here today – Just for fun.

HORACE: I really think, Ethel, that as long as we can afford a servant, it's rather unnecessary.

ETHEL: You know you're always complaining of Martha's cooking. I thought you would like me to try.

HORACE: My dear child! It's very nice of you. But why not cook in the kitchen? Raw meat in the drawing room! Do you want to turn me into a poor miserable vegetarian?

ETHEL: Oh, Horry, don't!

She puts her arms round his neck and sobs. The chop at the end of the toasting fork in her hand dangles in his face.

HORACE: What on earth's the matter? Ethel, dear, don't be hysterical. If you knew what it was to come home fagged to death and be worried like this ... I'll ring for Martha and tell her to take away those beastly chops. They're getting on my nerves.

ETHEL: Martha's gone.

HORACE: When? Why? Did you have a row? I suppose you had to give her a month's wages. I can't afford that sort if thing, you know.

ETHEL (*soothing*): It's not you who afford it, anyhow. Don't I pay Martha out of my own money?

HORACE: Do you call it ladylike to throw that in my face . . .

ETHEL (*incoherently*): I'm not throwing it in your face . . . but as it happens I didn't pay her anything. She went off without a word . . . and Lily's gone, too. (*She puts her head down on the table and cries.*)

HORACE: Well, that's a good riddance. I'm sick of her dirty face and slovenly ways. If she ever does clean my boots, she makes them look worse than when I took them off. We must get a char-woman.

ETHEL: We shan't be able to. Isn't it in the papers?

HORACE: What *are* you talking about?

ETHEL: Winifred said it would be in the evening papers.

HORACE: Winifred! She's been here, has she? That accounts for everything. How that woman comes to be your sister I can't imagine. Of course, she's mixed up with this wild-cat scheme.

ETHEL: Then you know about it!

HORACE: Oh. I saw something about 'Suffragettes on Strike' on the posters on my way home. Who cares if they do strike? They're no use to anyone. Look at Winifred. What does she ever do except go round making speeches, and kicking up a row outside the House of Commons until she forces the police to arrest her. Then she goes to prison and poses as a martyr. Martyr! We all know she could go home at once if she would promise the magistrate to behave herself. What they ought to do is to try all these hysterical women privately and sentence them to be ducked – privately. Then they'd soon give up advertising themselves.

ETHEL: Winnie has a splendid answer to that, but I forget what it is. Oh, Horry, was there anything on the posters about the nearest male relative?

HORACE: Ethel, my dear, you haven't gone dotty, have you? When you have quite done with my chair, I – (*He helps her out of the chair and sits down.*) Thank you.

ETHEL: Winnie said that not only are all the working women going to strike, but they are going to make their nearest male relatives support them.

HORACE: Rot!

ETHEL: I thought how dreadful it would be if Agatha came, or that cousin of yours on the stage whom you won't let me know, or your Aunt Lizzie! Martha and Lily have gone to *their* male relatives at least, Lily's gone to the workhouse – it's all the same thing. Why shouldn't it be true? Oh, look, Horace, there's a cab – with luggage. Oh, what shall we do?

HORACE: Don't fuss! It's stopping next door, not here at all.

ETHEL: No, no; it's here. (*She rushes out.*)

HORACE (*calling after her*): Come back! You can't open the door yourself. It will look as if we didn't keep a servant.

Re-enter ETHEL *followed after a few seconds by* AGATHA. AGATHA *is a weary-looking woman of about thirty-five. She wears the National Union colours, and is dowdily dressed.*

ETHEL: It *is* Agatha – and such a big box. Where *can* we put it?

AGATHA (*mildly*): How do you do, Horace. (*Kisses him.*) Dear Ethel! (*Kisses her.*) You're not looking so well as usual. Would you mind paying the cabman two shillings, Horace, and helping him with my box? It's rather heavy, but then it contains all my worldly belongings.

HORACE: Agatha – you haven't lost your situation! You haven't left the Lewises?

AGATHA: Yes, Horace; I left at three o'clock.

HORACE: My dear Agatha – I'm extremely sorry – but we can't put you up here.

AGATHA: Hadn't you better pay the cab? Two shillings so soon becomes two-and-six. (*Exit* HORACE.) I am afraid my brother doesn't realise that I have some claim on him.

ETHEL: We thought you were so happy with the Lewises.

AGATHA: So were the slaves in America when they had kind masters. They didn't want to be free.

ETHEL: Horace said you always had late dinner with them when they had no company.

AGATHA: Oh, I have no complaint against my late employers. In fact, I was sorry to inconvenience them by leaving so suddenly. But I had a higher duty to perform than my duty to them.

ETHEL: I don't know what to do. It will worry Horace dreadfully.

Re-enter HORACE.

HORACE: The cab *was* two-and-six, and I had to give a man twopence to help me in with that Noah's ark. Now, Agatha, what does this mean? Surely in your position it was very unwise to leave the Lewises. You can't stay here. We must make some arrangement.

AGATHA: Any arrangement you like, dear, provided you support me.

HORACE: I support you!

AGATHA: As my nearest male relative, I think you are obliged to do so. If you refuse, I must go to the workhouse.

HORACE: But why can't you support yourself? You've done it for years.

AGATHA: Yes - ever since I was eighteen. Now I am going to give up work, until my work is recognised. Either my proper place is the home – the home provided for me by some dear father, brother, husband, cousin, or uncle – or I am a self-supporting member of the State, who ought not to be shut out from the rights of citizenship.

HORACE: All this sounds as if you had become a Suffragette! Oh, Agatha, I always thought you were a lady.

AGATHA: Yes, I *was* a lady – such a lady that at eighteen I was thrown upon the world, penniless, with no training whatever which fitted me to earn my own living. When women become citizens I believe that daughters will be given the same chance as sons, and such a life as mine will be impossible.

HORACE: Women are so illogical. What on earth has all this to do with your planting yourself on me in this inconsiderate way? You put me in a most unpleasant position. You must see, Agatha, that I haven't the means to support a sister as well as a wife. Couldn't you go to some friends until you find another situation?

AGATHA: No, Horace. I'm going to stay with you.

HORACE (*changing his tone, and turning nasty*): Oh, indeed! And for how long – if I may ask?

AGATHA: Until a Bill for the removal of the sex disability is passed.

HORACE (*impotently angry*): Nonsense. I can't keep you, and I won't. I have always tried to do my duty by you. I think hardly a week passes that I don't write to you. But now that you have deliberately thrown up an excellent situation as a governess, and come here and threatened me – yes, threatened me – I think it's time to say that, sister or no sister, I intend to be master in my own house!

Enter MOLLY, *a good-looking young girl of about twenty. She is dressed in well-cut, tailor-made clothes, wears a neat little hat, and carries some golf-clubs and a few books.*

MOLLY: How are you, Uncle Horace? Is that Aunt Aggie? How d'ye do? I haven't seen you since I was a kid.

HORACE: Well, what have you come for?

MOLLY: There's a charming welcome to give your only niece!

HORACE: You know perfectly well, Molly, that I disapprove of you in every way. I hear – I have never read it, of course – but I hear that you have written a most scandalous book. You live in lodgings by yourself, when if you chose you could afford some really nice and refined boarding-house. You have most undesirable acquaintances, and altogether –

MOLLY: Cheer up, Uncle. Now's your chance of reforming me. I've come to live with you. You can support me and improve me at the same time.

HORACE: I never heard such impertinence. I have always understood from you that you earn more than I do.

MOLLY: Ah, yes; but you never *liked* my writing for money, did you? You called me 'sexless' once because I said that as long as I could support myself I didn't feel an irresistible temptation to marry that awful little bounder Weekes.

ETHEL: Reginald Weekes! How can you call him a bounder! He was at Oxford.

MOLLY: Hullo, Auntie Ethel! I didn't notice you. You'll be glad to hear I haven't brought much luggage – only a night-gown and some golf clubs.

HORACE: I suppose this is a joke!

MOLLY: Well, of course, that's one way of looking at it. I'm not going to support myself any longer. I'm going to be a perfect lady, and depend on my Uncle Horace – my nearest male relative – for the necessities of life. (*A motor horn is heard outside.*) Aren't you glad that I am not going to write another scandalous book, or live in lodgings by myself?

ETHEL (*at the window*): Horace! Horace! There's someone getting out of a motor – a grand motor. Who can it be? And there's no one to answer the door.

MOLLY: That doesn't matter. I found it open, and left it open to save trouble.

ETHEL: She's got luggage, too! The chauffeur is bringing in a dressing-case.

HORACE: I'll turn her into the street – and the dressing-case, too.

He goes fussily to the door, and meets MADAME CHRISTINE *on the threshold. The lady is dressed smartly and tastefully. Age about forty, manners elegant, smile charming, speech resolute. She carries a jewel-case, and consults a legal document during her first remarks.*

MADAME CHRISTINE: You are Mr Cole?

HORACE: No! Certainly not! (*Wavering.*) At least, I was this morning, but –

MADAME CHRISTINE: Horace Cole, son of John Hay Cole, formerly of Streatham, where he carried on the business of a –

A motor horn sounds outside.

HORACE: I beg your pardon, but my late father's business has really nothing to do with this matter, and to a professional man it's rather trying to have these things raked up against him. Excuse me, but do you want your motor to go?

MADAME CHRISTINE: It's not my motor any longer; and – yes, I do want it to go, for I may be staying here some time. I think you had one sister, Agatha, and one brother, Samuel, now dead. Samuel was much older than you –

AGATHA: Why don't you answer, Horace? Yes, that's perfectly correct. I am Agatha.

MADAME CHRISTINE: Oh, are you? How d'ye do?

MOLLY: And Samuel Cole was my father.

MADAME CHRISTINE: I'm very glad to meet you. I didn't know I had such charming relations. Well, Mr Cole, my father was John Hay Cole's first cousin; so you, I think, are my second cousin, and my nearest male relative.

HORACE: (*distractedly*): If anyone calls me that again I shall go mad.

MADAME CHRISTINE: I am afraid you aren't quite pleased with the relationship!

HORACE: You must excuse me – but I don't consider a second cousin a relation. A second cousin is a – well –

MADAME CHRISTINE: Oh, it answers the purpose. I suddenly find myself destitute, and I want you to support me. I am sure you would not like a Cole to go to the workhouse.

HORACE: I don't care a damn where any of you go.

ETHEL (*shocked*): Horry! How can you!

MADAME CHRISTINE: That's frank, at any rate; but I am sure, Cousin Horace, that in spite of your manners, your heart's in the right place. You won't refuse me board and lodging, until Parliament makes it possible for me to resume my work?

HORACE: My dear madam, do you realise that my salary is £3.10s. a week – and that my house will hardly hold your luggage, much less you?

MADAME CHRISTINE: Then you must agitate. Your female relatives have supported themselves up till now, and asked nothing from you. I myself, dear cousin, was, until this morning, running a profitable dressmaking business in Hanover Square. In my public capacity I am Madame Christine.

MOLLY: I know! You make sweet gowns, but I've never been able to afford you.

HORACE: And do you think, Madame Christine –

MADAME CHRISTINE: Cousin Susan, please.

HORACE: Do you think that you are justified in coming to a poor clerk, and asking him to support you – you, who could probably turn over my yearly income in a single week! Didn't you come here in your own motor?

MADAME CHRISTINE: At three o'clock that motor became the property of the Women's Social and Political Union. All the rest of my property and all available cash have been divided equally between the National Union and the Women's Freedom League. Money is the sinews of war, you know.

HORACE: Do you mean to tell me that you've given all your money to the Suffragettes! It's a pity you haven't a husband. He'd very soon put an end to such folly.

MADAME CHRISTINE: I had a husband once. He liked me to do foolish things – for instance, to support him. After that unfortunate experience, Cousin Horace, you may imagine how glad I am to find a man who really is a man, and will support me instead. By the way, I should *so* much like some tea. Is the kettle boiling?

ETHEL (*feebly*): There aren't enough cups! Oh, what *shall* I do?

HORACE: Never mind, Ethel; I shan't want any. I am going to dine in town, and go to the theatre. I shall hope to find you all gone when I come back. If not, I shall send for the police.

Enter MAUDIE SPARK, *a young woman with an aggressively cheerful manner, a voice raucous from much bellowing of music-hall songs, a hat of huge size, and a heart of gold.*

MAUDIE: 'Ullo! 'Ullo! Who's talking about the police? Not my dear cousin Horry?

HORACE: How dare you come here?

MAUDIE: Necessity, old dear. If I could have found a livelier male relative you may bet I'd have gone to him! But you, Horace, are the only first cousin of this poor orphan. What are you in such a hurry for?

HORACE: Let me pass! I'm going to the theatre.

MAUDIE: Silly jay! the theatres are all closed – and the halls, too. The actresses have gone on strike – resting indefinitely. I've done my little bit towards that. They won't get any more work out of Maudie Spark, Queen of Comediennes, until the women have got the vote. Ladies and fellow-relatives, you'll be pleased to hear the strike's going fine. The big drapers can't open tomorrow. One man can't fill the place of fifteen ladies at once, you see. The duchesses are out in the streets begging people to come in and wash their kids. The City men are trying to get taxi men in to do their typewriting. Every man, like Horry here, has his house full of females. Most of 'em thought, like Horry, that they'd go to the theatre to escape. But there's not a blessed theatre to go to! Oh, what a song it'll make. 'A woman's place is the home – I don't think, I don't think, I don't think.'

HORACE: Even if this is not a plot against me personally, even if there are other women in London at this minute disgracing their sex –

MAUDIE: Here, stop it – come off it! If it comes to that, what are *you* doing – threatening your womankind with the police and the workhouse.

HORACE: I was not addressing myself to you.

AGATHA: Why not, Horace? She's your cousin. She needs your protection just as much as we do.

HORACE: I regard that woman as the skeleton in the cupboard of a respectable family; but that's neither here nor there. I address myself to the more ladylike portion of this gathering, and I say that whatever is going on the men will know what to do, and will do it with dignity and firmness. (*The impressiveness of this statement is marred by the fact that* HORACE'S *hand, in emphasising it, comes down heavily on the loaf of bread on the table.*) A few exhibitions of this kind won't frighten them.

MAUDIE: Oh, won't it! I like that! They're being so firm and so dignified that they's running down to the House of Commons like lunatics, and blackguarding the Government for not having given us the vote before! (*Shouts outside of newsboys in the distance.*)

MOLLY: Splendid! Have they begun already?

MADAME CHRISTINE: Get a paper, Cousin Horace. I know some men will never believe anything till they see it in the paper.

ETHEL: The boys are shouting out something now. Listen.

Shouts outside: 'Extry special. Great strike of women. Women's strike. Theatres closed. Extry special edition. "Star!" "News!" 6.30 edition'.

MOLLY: You see. Since this morning Suffragettes have become women!

ETHEL (*at window*): Here, boy, paper! *Cries go on: 'Extra special "Star". Men petition the Government. Votes for Women. Extry special.'*
Oh, heavens, here's Aunt Lizzie!

As ETHEL *pronounces the name* HORACE *dives under the table. Enter* AUNT LIZZIE *leading a fat spaniel and carrying a bird cage with a parrot in it.* MISS ELIZABETH WILKINS *is a comfortable, middle-aged body of a type well known to those who live in the less fashionable quarter of Bloomsbury. She looks as if she kept lodgers, and her looks do not belie her. She is not very well educated, but has a good deal of native intelligence. Her features are homely, and her clothes about thirty years behind the times.*

AUNT LIZZIE: Well, dears, all here? That's right. Where's Horace? Out? Just as well; we can talk more freely. I'm sorry I'm late, but animals do so hate a move. It took a long time to make them understand the strike. But I think they will be very comfortable here. You love dogs, don't you, Ethel?

ETHEL: Not Ponto. He always growls at me.

AUNT LIZZIE: Clever dog! he knows you don't sympathise with the cause.

ETHEL: But I do, Aunt; only I have always said that as I was happily married I thought it had very little to do with me.

AUNT LIZZIE: You've changed your mind about that today, I should think! What a day it's been! We never expected everything would go so smoothly. They say the Bill's to be rushed through at once. No more deceitful promises, no more dishonest 'facilities'; deeds, not words, at last! Seen the papers? The Press are not boycotting us today, my dears. (MADAME CHRISTINE, MOLLY, *and* MAUDIE *each take a paper.*) The boy who sold them to me put the money back into Ponto's collecting box. That dog must have made five pounds for the cause since this morning.

HORACE (*puts his head out*): 'Liar!'

MOLLY: Oh, do listen to this. It's too splendid! (*Reading from the paper*) 'Women's Strike. – Latest: Messrs Lyons and Co. announce that by special arrangement with the War Office the places of their defaulting waitresses will be filled by the non-commissioned officers and men of the 2nd Battalion Coldstream Guards. Business will therefore be carried on as usual.'

MADAME CHRISTINE: What do you think of this? (*Reading*) 'Latest Intelligence. – It is understood that the Naval Volunteers have been approached by the authorities with the object of inducing them to act as charwomen to the House of Commons.'

AUNT LIZZIE (*to* ETHEL): Well, my dear! What have you got there? Read what the *Star* says.

ETHEL (*tremulously reading*): 'The queue of women waiting for admission to Westminster Workhouse is already a mile and a half in length. As the entire police force are occupied in dealing with the men's processions, Lord Haldane has been approached with a view to ascertaining if the Territorials can be sworn in as special constables.'

MAUDIE (*laughing*): This is a little bit of all right. (*Reading*) 'Our special representative, on calling upon the Prime Minister with the object of ascertaining his views on the situation, was informed that the Right Honourable gentleman was unable to receive him, as with the assistance of the boot-boy and a Foreign Office messenger, he was actively engaged in making his bed.'

AUNT LIZZIE: Always unwilling to receive people, you see! Well, he must be feeling sorry now that he never received us. Everyone's putting the blame on him. It's extraordinary how many men – and newspapers, too – have suddenly found out that they have always been in favour of woman's suffrage! That's the sensible attitude, of course. It would be humiliating for them to confess that it was not until we held a pistol to their heads that they changed their minds. Well, at this minute I would rather be the man who has been our ally all along than the one who has been our enemy. It's not the popular thing to be an 'anti' any more. Any man who tries to oppose us today is likely to be slung up to the nearest lamp post.

ETHEL (*rushing wildly to the table*): Oh, Horry! My Horry!

HORACE *comes out from under the table.*

AUNT LIZZIE: Why, bless the boy, what are you doing there?

HORACE: Oh, nothing. I merely thought I might be less in the way here, that's all.

AUNT LIZZIE: You didn't hide when I came in, by any chance!

HORACE: I hide from you! Aren't you always welcome in this house?

AUNT LIZZIE: Well, I haven't noticed it particularly; and I'm not calling today, you understand, I've come to stay.

HORACE, *dashed and beaten, begins to walk up and down the room, and consults* ETHEL. Well, well! I won't deny it was a wrench to leave 118a, Upper Montagu Place, where I've done my best for boarders, old and young, gents and ladies, for twenty-five years – and no complaints! A home from home, they always call it. All my ladies had left before I started out, on the same business as ourselves – but what those poor boys will do for their dinner tonight I don't know. They're a helpless lot! Well, it's all over; I've given up my boarding-house, and I depend on you, Horace, to keep me until I am admitted to citizenship. It may take a long time.

HORACE: It must *not* take a long time! I shan't allow it. It shall be done at once. Well, you needn't all look so surprised. I know I've been against it, but I didn't realise things. I thought only a few hooligan window-smashers wanted the vote; but when I find that *you* – Aunt – Fancy a woman of your firmness of character, one who has always been so careful with her money, being declared incapable of voting! The thing is absurd.

MAUDIE: Bravo! Our Horry's waking up.

HORACE (*looking at her scornfully*): If there are a few women here and there who *are* incapable – I mention no names, mind – it doesn't affect the position. What's going to be done? Who's going to do it? If this rotten Government think we're going to maintain millions of women in idleness just because they don't like the idea of my Aunt Lizzie making a scratch on a bit of paper and shoving it into a ballot-box once every five years, this Government have reckoned without the men – (*General cheering.*) I'll show 'em what I've got a vote for! What do they expect? You can't all marry. There aren't enough men to go round, and if you're earning your own living and paying taxes you ought to have a say; it's only fair. (*General cheering and a specially emphatic* 'Hear, hear' *from* MADAME CHRISTINE.) The Government are narrow-minded idiots!

MADAME CHRISTINE: Hear, hear!

HORACE: They talk as if all the women ought to stay at home washing and ironing. Well, before a woman has a wash-tub, she must have a home to put it in, mustn't she? And who's going to give it her? I'd like them to tell me that. Do they expect *me* to do it?

AGATHA: Yes, dear.

HORACE: I say if she can do it herself and keep herself, so much the better for everyone. Anyhow, who are the Government? They're only representing *me*, and being paid thousands a year by *me* for carrying out *my* wishes.

MOLLY: Oh, er – what ho!

HORACE (*turns on her angrily*): I like a woman to be a woman – that's the way I was brought up; but if she insists on having a vote – and apparently she does.

ALL: She does! she does!

HORACE: – I don't see why she shouldn't have it. Many a woman came in here at the last election and tried to wheedle me into voting for her particular candidate. If she has time to do that – and I never heard the member say then that she ought to be at home washing and ironing the baby – I don't see why she hasn't time to vote. It's never taken up much of *my* time, or interfered with *my* work. I've only voted once in my life – but that's neither here nor there. I know what the vote does for me. It gives me a status; that's what you women want – a status.

ALL: Yes, yes, a status.

HORACE: I might even call it a *locus standi*. If I go now and tell these rotten Cabinet Ministers what I think of them, it's my *locus standi*–

MAUDIE: That's a good word.

HORACE: – that will force them to listen to me. Oh, I know. And, by gum! I'll give them a bit of my mind. They shall hear a few home truths for once. 'Gentlemen,' I shall say – well, that won't be true of all of them to start with, but one must give 'em the benefit of the doubt – 'gentlemen, the men of England are sick and tired of your policy. Who's driven the women of England into this? *You* – (*he turns round on* ETHEL, *who jumps violently.*) – because you were too stupid to know that they meant business – because you couldn't read the writing on the wall.' (*Hear, hear*) It may be nothing to you, gentlemen, that every industry in this country is paralysed and every Englishman's home turned into a howling wilderness –

MOLLY: Draw it mild, Uncle.

HORACE: A howling wilderness, I repeat – by your refusal to see what's as plain as the nose on your face; but I would have you know, gentlemen, that it *is* something to us. We aren't slaves. We never will be slaves –

AGATHA: Never, never!

HORACE: And we insist on reform. Gentlemen, conditions have changed, and women have to work. Don't men encourage them to work, *invite* them to work?

AGATHA: *Make* them work.

HORACE: And women are placed in the battle of life on the same terms as we are, short of one thing, the *locus standi* of a vote.

MAUDIE: Good old *locus standi!*

HORACE: If you aren't going to give it them, gentlemen, and if they won't go back to their occupations without it, we ask you how they're going to live? Who's going to support them? Perhaps you're thinking of giving them all old age pensions and asking the country to pay the piper! The country will see you damned first, if, gentlemen, you'll pardon the expression. It's dawning upon us all that the women would never have taken such a step as this if they hadn't been the victims of a gross injustice.

ALL: Never.

HORACE: Why shouldn't they have a voice in the laws which regulate the price of food and clothes? Don't they pay for their food and clothes?

MAUDIE: Paid for mine since the age of six.

HORACE: Why shouldn't they have a voice in the rate of wages and the hours of labour in certain industries? Aren't they working at those industries? If you had a particle of common sense or decent feeling, gentlemen –

Enter GERALD WILLIAMS *like a souvenir of Mafeking night. He shouts incoherently and in a hoarse voice. He is utterly transformed from the meek, smug being of an hour before. He is wearing several ribbons and badges and carries a banner bearing this inscription: 'The men of Brixton demand votes for women this evening.'*

WILLIAMS: Cole, Cole! Come on! Come on! You'll be late. The procession's forming up at the town hall. There's no time to lose. What are you slacking here for? Perhaps this isn't good enough for you. I've got twelve of them in my drawing-room. We shall be late for the procession if we don't start at once. Hurry up! Come on! Votes for Women! Where's your banner? Where's your badge? Down with the Government! Rule Britannia! Votes for Women! D'you want to support a dozen women for the rest of your life, or don't you? . . . Every man in Brixton is going to Westminster. Borrow a ribbon and come along. Hurry up, now! Hooray! (*Rushes madly out crying* 'Votes for Women! Rule Britannia; Women never, never shall be slaves! Votes for Women!)

All the women who are wearing ribbons decorate HORACE.

ETHEL: My hero! (*She throws her arms round him.*)

HORACE: You may depend on me – all of you – to see justice done. When you want a thing done, get a man to do it! Votes for Women!

AGATHA *gives him a flag which he waves triumphantly.*

Curtain tableau: HORACE *marching majestically out of the door, with the women cheering him enthusiastically.*

Dorothy Richardson

1873 – 1957

D orothy Richardson was the third of four daughters. Her father went bankrupt when she was twenty and her mother committed suicide shortly afterwards. She became a governess, a dental assistant and a secretary and later a journalist in London, where she met the married author H. G. Wells. Wells encouraged her to write and in 1915 appeared Pointed Roofs, the first of a series of autobiographical novels collectively entitled Pilgrimage, the last volume of which was published posthumously in 1967. A pioneer in the 'stream-of-consciousness' technique which aimed to capture the flow of individual consciousness, she was described by her friend Virginia Woolf as the inventor of the feminine sentence.

The following short story, 'Ordeal', is taken from Window (1 October 1930 edition).

Ordeal

W HEN the taxi stopped, Agatha jumped out and gave the man money, evidently held ready in her hand all the way, and probably too much, to avoid a halt.

And when the lady-in-charge of the office asked if she were to send any telegrams, Agatha lost her head and stumbled over the address. Fan saw clearly then into her mind, the images it had held while she had talked so glibly in the cab.

In the hall she was even more un-nerving. Really, it was hopeless of her, just before her farewell hug, to let her eyes stray and find a nurse happening to pass, and recoil. Result of her recent too strenuous mental exercise. Truly it was a blessing she was not coming upstairs. . . .

Before Fan could recover from the spectacle of Agatha departing, to suffer all that her simple imagination and her inarticulateness in combination could force upon her, the lady-in-charge caught her with a remark to which she responded almost in Agatha's own manner; rushing wastefully outside herself into an obedient caricature of the speaker: in this case brusque and preoccupied, the fashion of one with mind alert and eyes all round the head. And was obliged, since the maid appearing at her side to take her suit-case had been a witness, to keep to this manner when she stepped out of the lift almost into the arms of a tall sister behind whom was waiting a short nurse.

She felt herself a guest being passed from hand to hand without release —being entertained. And indeed, for a moment, by each fresh face and fresh immediately revealed personality she *was* entertained. But she could not flatter herself into believing that these entertaining officials were themselves entertained. For them each visible hair of her head did not, as did theirs for her, stand out, a single separate mystery. If they felt anything at all it was relief, in finding that number seven had at her disposal as much manner as they. Their planned continuous engagement of her attention was very "psychological"—horribly wise, feminine. It had created for her a miniature past in this house, and when presently she was shut up alone in her room, undressing, she did not feel a stranger there. The room had stated itself while she was talking with the sister and nurse, and was now a known room. It seemed long ago that Agatha had gone away through the hall.

She had thought in advance that her sense of personal life must cease when she entered the door of the nursing home. But instead it was intensified, as if, brought up against a barrier from behind which no certain future poured into it, her life flowed back upon itself, embarrassing her with its vivid palpitation. Her known self, arrested thus, was making all its statements at once. The most welcome was its cheerfulness, inexplicable and as little expected as the wise-seeming state of composure that had risen unsummoned during the last two days, like a veil between herself and her knowledge of her lack of courage. That was negative, acceptance of the inevitable. But there was nothing negative in this deep, good cheer that made her smile as she hung up her garments in a wardrobe, perhaps for the last time. It was not stoicism. It might be unconscious organic certainty of getting through. In her conscious mind was no certainty but that of the life-risk. Perhaps that itself was the invigorating factor. Whatever its cause, this present intensity of being made the possible future look like a shallow expanse; something very easy to sacrifice if she considered only herself. And those others out in life seemed now to call for solicitude only because they did not know how strange was the being in which they were immersed.

Very carefully she arranged her hair, firmly putting in extra pins, being back while she did so within the final moments of arranging herself for parties in her girlhood. And all the time the lugubrious thoughts and anticipations belonging to the occasion, and so fertile in her mind a week ago, seemed hovering in the background seeking in vain for space to intervene.

The short nurse brought the cup of thin soup that was breakfast and lunch, left hurriedly promising to come back in a moment, and came, with her already so well-known way of opening the door—a quiet, wide flourish that showed the whole of her at once, arm outstretched by hand holding door-knob.

They were all trained of course, Fan reflected, not to sneak into rooms: "Open the door wide, *so*, come in through the centre of the doorway and face at once *towards* the patient, close the door quietly behind you and advance, making a cheerful remark."

"Well? How are we?" the nurse had said, and paused in the middle of the room as if offering herself only as a momentary spectacle.

"Quite happy for the present. Are you going to stay with me for a bit?"

"I can't," she said, "I've got to attend to number eight," and perceived the tray and came forward to take it. "You've got to sleep now, till I come for you at five." This, then, was farewell to humanity on this side of the barrier. Fan asked leave to smoke—a single cigarette. While giving permission the nurse got herself to the door and away, as if hurriedly, as if driven, and in a moment Fan heard her voice asking cheerful questions in the next room. The replies came in a moaning monotone.

There was chattering in an open-doored room near by. Dining-room, common-room of nurses on duty on this floor of the great house where they earned their livings amidst pain and death. Whirring of the lift. Footsteps. Gushing of water into a basin. Swift rinsing, more gushing of water.

The sounds brought vivid images that ought, she felt, to be shocking, and rousing her to resist their suggestive power. But they passed through her mind without attaining her. Between them and the centre of her attention was something that had been waiting within the quietude of the room for its moment. Approaching now, as she sat back against the raised pillows and set down her book, with the note for Tom sticking out of it like a book-marker, on the table at her side with cigarette case and matches. These doings seemed the preliminaries to an interview.

A week ago, this moment of being left alone to wait for the summons had drawn her forward into itself and kept her there. She recalled the shock of finding the life all about her no longer her concern, the cold dry horror of the prospect of getting through the days and playing her part. And how at times with an effort she had forced herself out of her trance, dropped her own cancelled life, and felt each life about her, sharply, disinterestedly, seeing each one in its singleness to be equally significant; been aware of a strange, sure wisdom within her that seemed capable of administering the affairs of everyone she knew, guiding each life without offence. Had realised at one moment with an overwhelming clarity how it is that the character of an individual operates more securely, upon those who have known him, after he is dead. But for the last two days she had longed for this moment and the relief it would bring.

It was like being in great open spaces, in solitude. She rejoiced that she had decided not to tell Tom. This strange, familiar intimation all about her owed the power that was about to overwhelm her to her undivided solitude. Agatha, going, had gone utterly. If Tom had known, his suffering presence would have been in the room with her. She was severed even from Tom. With a deep, blissful sigh she felt all the tensions of her life relax. She was back again in the freedom of her own identity, in pre-marriage freedom, in more than childhood's freedom, with all the strength of her maturity to savour its joy. In bright daylight the afternoon lay before her, endless—*the first holiday of her adult life.* . . .

Laughing softly and luxuriously, beside herself with the joy of complete return, she looked gratefully about at the features of the ugly, barely furnished room and lit the permitted cigarette. The act of smoking threw her back to the minute before last. It was occupation, distraction, waste of priceless opportunity, of time. No, of something that was more than time! It was cutting her off from her

deep life. It was unnecessary, because now she was back in her pre-smoking state
of existence, and it had brought her to the present surface of life, away from the
state of being into which she had just plunged. She crushed the burning end upon
the match-box. The edge of that first blissful expansion was blunted, but the fruit
of its moments lay in her thoughts and in her refreshed, delighted limbs, and
in her recognition of the way the hint of tobacco smoke upon the air enhanced
the familiar, remembered, surrounding freshness that was like that of a dewy
garden in the early morning. All about her, emanating from her relaxed mind,
was all the garden and countryside beauty she had ever known, its concentrated
essence, so that what she saw was not any single distinct scene, but a hovering
and mingling of them all—their visible spirit which was one with her own.

If this blissful state were the gift of the holiday from responsibility and
from the tension of human relationships that only the chance of death had
had the power to give her, then perhaps the perfect certainty of death must always
bring it at the last? Perhaps people who were engaged in doing their dying were
enjoying, behind even the most awful of the outward appearances, at the end of
the exciting, absorbing struggle that prevented them from communicating their
thoughts, the sense of being in its perfect fullness. . . .

• • • • • • • • • •

She put down the book to question, as if it were a person with her in the
room, the fact that she had forgotten, in the intensity of her absorption in
Green Mansions, what lay ahead. The experience had been a fresh voyage of
discovery into unchanged, underlying, timeless reality.

But with the book lying there closed, the sense of passing time came back.
Her watch said half-past four. In half an hour. . . .

The door opened upon the sister almost ostentatiously displaying a hypoder-
mic syringe. What hospital trick was this, sprung without warning?

"Your nurse is in the theatre, so I've come for this little job."

"What little job? What's the mystery in the syringe?"

"No mystery," smiled the sister, slipping the jacket from Fan's arm. "We
always give this before the theatre."

"Theatre, theatre, theatre," absurd unsuitable word for the reality now near
at hand and to remain, excluding all else for half an hour—an eternity—after
the sister had gone.

"It prevents bleeding," said the steady, lying voice below eyes that looked
serenely through the window as the syringe pricked home.

"I'd have gone quietly," said Fan resentfully.

"I daresay you would. But now you'll be happy for a quarter of an hour
before the nurse comes." She spoke sternly, but finished with a smile; . . . the
gleeful smile of one who outwits a naughty child. Brush, between two women.
Managers? All women are managers. That's why they daren't give in to each
other. That's why. . . . The nurse had gone. A quarter of an hour. Watch slow.
This was some kind of drug. Stupefier. *Very* psychological. But that's why, I was
saying. . . . Thoughts would not come.

Her effort to call up a picture of the theatre brought only a confused sliding together of images in a mind that could not hold them. Oh, *very* psychological. Perhaps they were wise. She could not decide. Would have liked to go down in full possession of all her senses, yet was grateful for this not unpleasant numbness.

With the nurse at her side she was walking down a shallow flight of stairs. Towards death ... life? At the bottom of the stairs was another nurse, who greeted her as she passed, and whose greeting she returned. A turning to the left, another nurse in the offing, standing like a sentry at an open door, who also said "Good afternoon" and had to be answered. This was the theatre. Not yet quite. A corridor leading to the theatre's arched doorway, but giving no vista. The nurse was behind now. She was going forward alone, quite clear-headed and very matter of fact, not needing this careful passing from hand to hand. ... In the doorway she was greeted by yet another nurse standing away to the right, leading her on with her dreadful "Good afternoon." Oh, *too* psychological. Farcical. She was round the bend. Here it was, the lofty room, the white-clad forms, high windows open, no smell of anaesthetic or of disinfectant. Trees beyond the window.

Which still she could see as she lay—belonging completing.

"Breathe quite naturally, Mrs Peele."

Fresh and powerful came the volatile essences, playing in the air before her nostrils like a fountain. Her heart answered, her blood answered; but not herself. Desperately and quite independently her threatened heart fought against this power that was bearing her down. She raised her hands to still it.

"Clasp your hands."

All of herself was in her clasped hands, beating, throbbing. Less, and less, and ... less. ...

Rose Macaulay

1881 – 1958

A novelist, essayist and travel writer, Rose Macaulay was born in England, and lived in Italy from 1887 to 1894, when the family moved to Oxford. In 1900 she entered Somerville College, and started to write; her first *novel,* Abbots Vernay *(which had an Italian setting), was published in 1906. A subtle satirist, she went on to write a steady stream of fiction and non-fiction, including the novels* Potterism *(1920),* They Were Defeated *(1932),* The World My Wilderness *(1950) and* The Towers of Trebizond *(1956).* Pleasures of Ruins *(1953) is among the best known of her non-fiction work.*

The following chapter from her novel, Told by an Idiot *(first published in 1923 and reprinted by Virago, London, 1983), reveals her satirical touch and something of her concern with matters of religious conviction.*

From

Told by an Idiot

I

A FAMILY AT HOME

ONE evening, shortly before Christmas, in the days when our forefathers, being young, possessed the earth,—in brief, in the year 1879,—Mrs. Garden came briskly into the drawing-room from Mr. Garden's study and said in her crisp, even voice to her six children, "Well, my dears, I have to tell you something. Poor papa has lost his faith again."

Poor papa had very often lost his faith during the fifty years of his life. Sometimes he became, from being an Anglican clergyman, a Unitarian minister, sometimes a Roman Catholic layman (he was, by nature, habit and heredity, a priest or minister of religion, but the Roman Catholic church makes trouble about wives and children), sometimes some strange kind of dissenter, sometimes a plain agnostic, who believed that there lived more faith in honest doubt than in half the creeds (and as to this he should know, for on quite half the creeds he was by now an expert). On his last return to Anglicanism, he had accepted a country living.

Victoria, the eldest of the six children, named less for the then regnant queen than for papa's temporary victory over unbelief in the year of her birth, 1856, spoke sharply. She was twenty-three, and very pretty, and saw no reason why papa should be allowed so many more faiths and losses of faith in his career than the papas of others.

"*Really,* mamma ... it is too bad of papa. I knew it was coming; I said so, didn't I, Maurice? His sermons have been so funny lately, and he's been reading Comte all day in his study instead of going out visiting, and getting all kinds of horrid pamphlets from the Rationalist Press Association, and poring over an article in the *Examiner* about 'A Clergyman's Doubts.' And I suppose St. Thomas's Day has brought it to a head." (Victoria was High Church, so knew all about saints' days.) "And now we shall have to leave the vicarage, just when we've made friends with all sorts of nice people with tennis courts and ball-rooms. Papa *should* be more careful, and it *is* too bad."

Maurice, the second child (named for Frederick Denison) who was at Cambride, and a firm rationalist, having fought and lost the battle of belief while a freshman, inquired, cynically, but not undutifully, and with more patience than his sister, "What is he going to be this time?"

"An Ethicist," said Mrs. Garden, in her clear, non-committal voice. "We are joining the Ethical Society."

"Whatever's that?" Vicky crossly asked.

"It has no creeds but only conduct" ... ("And I," Vicky interpolated, "have no conduct but only creeds.") ... "and a chapel in South Place, Finsbury Pavement, and a magazine which sometimes has a poem by Robert Browning. It published that one about a man who strangled a girl he was fond of with her own hair on a wet evening. I don't know why he thought it specially suitable for the Ethical Society Magazine. ... They meet for worship on Sundays."

"Worship of what, mamma?"

"Nobility of character, dear. They sing ethical hymns about it."

Vicky gave a little scream.

Mrs. Garden looked at Stanley, her third daughter (named less for the explorer than for the Dean, whom Mr. Garden had always greatly admired) and found, as she had expected, Stanley's solemn blue eyes burning on hers. Stanley was, in fancy, in the South Place Ethical Chapel already, singing the ethical hymns ...

> "Fall, fall, ye ancient litanies and creeds!
>   Not prayers nor curses deep
>   The power can longer keep
> That once ye kept by filling human needs.
>
> Fall, fall, ye mighty temples to the ground!
>   Not in their sculptured rise
>   Is the real exercise
> Of human nature's brightest power found.
>
> 'Tis in the lofty hope, the daily toil,
>   'Tis in the gifted line,
>   In each far thought divine,
> That brings down heaven to light our common soil.
>
> 'Tis in the great, the lovely and the true,
>   'Tis in the generous thought
>   Of all that man has wrought,
> Of all that yet remains for man to do."

Stanley had read this and other hymns in a little book her papa had.

"Then I suppose," said Rome, the second daughter, who knew of old that papa must always live near a place of worship dedicated to his creed of the moment, "then I suppose we are moving to Finsbury Pavement." Rome had been named less for the city than for the church, of which papa had been a member at the time of her birth, twenty years ago; and, after all, if Florence, why not Rome? Rome looked clever. She had a white, thin face, and vivid blue-green eyes, like the sea beneath rocks; and she thought it very original of papa to believe so much and so often. Her own mind was sceptical.

Vicky's brow smoothed. Moving to London. There was something in that. Though, of course, it mustn't be Finsbury Pavement; she would see to that.

Irving, the youngest but one (named less for the actor than to commemorate the brief period when papa had been an Irvingite, and had believed in twelve living apostles who must all die and then would come the Last Day), said, "Golly, what a lark!" Irving was sixteen, and was all for a move, all for change, of residence, if not of creed. He was an opportunist and a realist, and made the best of the vagaries of circumstance. He was destined to do well in life. He was not, like Maurice, sicklied o'er with the pale cast of thought, nor, like Vicky, caught in the mesh of each passing fashion, nor, like Stanley, an ardent hunter of the Idea, nor, like Rome, a critic. He was more like (only he had more enterprise and initiative) his younger sister, Una, a very calm and jolly schoolgirl, named less for her who braved the dragon than for the One Person in whom papa had believed at the time of her birth (One Person not in the Trinitarian, but in the Unitarian, sense).

"Three hundred a year less," remarked Rome, from the couch whereon she lay (for her back was often tired) and looked ironically at Vicky, to see how she liked the thought of that.

Vicky's smooth cheek flushed. She had forgotten about money.

"Oh *really* . . . Oh, I do think papa is too bad. Mamma, *must* he lose it just this winter—his faith, I mean? Can't he wait till next?"

Mamma's faint (was it also ironic, or merely patient?) movement of the eyebrows meant that it was too late: papa's faith was already lost.

"By next winter he may have found it again," Rome suggested.

"Well, even if so," said Vicky, "who's going to go on giving him livings every time? . . . Oh, yes, mamma, I know all the bishops love him, but there *is* a limit to the patience of bishops. . . . Does the Ethical Society have clergymen or anything?"

"I believe they have elders. Papa may become an elder."

"*That's* no use. Elders aren't paid. Don't you remember when he was a Quaker elder, when we were all little? I'm sure it's not a paid job. We shall be loathsomely poor again, and have to live without any fun or pretty things. And I dare say it's low class, too. Papa never bothers about that, of course. He'd follow General Booth into the Army, if he thought he had a call."

"I trust that I should, Vicky."

Papa had entered the room, and stood looking on them all, with his beautiful, distinguished, melancholy face (framed in small side whiskers), and his deep blue eyes like Stanley's. Vicky's ill-humour melted away, because papa was so gentle and so beautiful and so kind. And, after all, London was London, even with only four hundred a year.

"Mamma has told you our news, I see," said papa, in his sweet, mellow voice. He looked and spoke like a papa out of Charlotte M. Yonge, though his conduct with regard to the Anglican church was so different.

"Yes, Aubrey, I've told them," said mamma.

"I hope you won't mind, papa," said Vicky saucily, "if *I* go to church at St. Albans, Holborn. *I'm* a ritualist, not an ethicist."

"Indeed, Vicky, I should be very sorry if you did not all follow your own lights, wherever they lead you."

Papa's broad-mindedness amounted to a disease, Vicky sometimes thought. A queer kind of clergyman he was. What would Father Stanton and Father Mackonichie of St. Albans think of him? Father Mackonichie, who was habitually flung into jail because he would face east when told to face north—as important as all that, he felt it.

"Well, my darlings," papa went on in his nice voice, "I must apologise to you all for this—this disturbance of your lives and mine. I would have spared it you if I could. But I have been over and over the ground, and I see no other way compatible with intellectual honesty. Honesty must come first. . . . Your mother and I are agreed."

Of course; they always were. From Anglicanism to Roman Catholicism, from Catholicism to Quakerism, from Quakerism to Unitarianism, Positivism, Baptistism (yes, they had once sunk, to Vicky's shame, as low as that in the social scale, owing chiefly to the influence of Charles Spurgeon), and back to Anglicanism again—through everything, mamma, silent, resigned and possibly ironic, had followed papa. And little Stanley had seen the idea behind all papa's religions and tumbled headlong after him, and Maurice had grimly decided that it was safer to abjure all creeds, and Rome had critically looked on, with her faint, amused smile and her single eyeglass, and Irving and Una had been led, heedless and incurious, to each of papa's places of worship in turn, but had understood none of them. They had not the religious temperament. Nor had Vicky, who attended her ritualistic churches from aesthetic fancy and a flair for being in the fashion, for seeing and hearing some new thing. *She* didn't care which way priests faced, though she did enjoy incense. Vicky was a gay soul, and preferred dances and lawn tennis and young men to religion. Stanley, too, was gay—as merry as a grig, papa called her—but she had a burning ardour of mind and temper that made the world for her a place of exciting experiments. She now thought it worthy and honourable to be poor, for she had been reading William Morris and Ruskin and Socialism, as intelligent young women did in those days, and was all for handicrafts and the one-man job. She was eighteen, and had had her first term at Somerville College, Oxford, which had just been founded and had twelve members.

Irving, always practical, said, "When are we going to move? And where to?"

"In February," said mamma. "Probably we shall live in Bloomsbury. We have heard of a house there."

"Bloomsbury," said Vicky. "That's not so bad."

Sitting down at the piano, she began softly to play and sing.

Papa sat by the fire, his thin hand on mamma's, his thoughtful face pale and uplifted, as if he had made the Great Sacrifice once more, as indeed he had. Stanley sat on a cushion at his feet, and leant her dark head against his knee. She was a small, sturdy girl, and she wore a frock of blue, hand-embroidered cloth, plain and tight over the shoulders and breast, high-necked, with white ruching at the throat, and below the waist straighter than was the fashion, because Mr. Morris said that ripples and flounces wasted material and ruined line. Vicky, sinuous and green, rippled to the knees like running water. Irving sat on a Morris-chintz chair, reading *The Moonstone*; Maurice on a Liberty cretonne sofa, reading a leader in yesterday's *Observer*.

"It is, unfortunately, impossible to conceal from ourselves that the condition of Ireland, never perceptibly improved by the announcement of the projected remedy for her distress and discontents, has for some weeks gone steadily from bad to worse. The state of things which exists there is, for all practical purposes, indistinguishable from civil war. The insurrectionary forces arrayed against law and order are not, indeed, drilled and disciplined bodies; but what they lack in this respect they make up for in numbers and in recklessness."

Such was the sad state of Ireland in December, 1879, as sometimes before, as sometimes since. Or, anyhow, such was its state according to the *Observer*, a paper with which Maurice seldom, and Stanley never, agreed. Stanley put her faith in Mr. Gladstone, and Maurice in no politicians, though he appreciated Dizzy as a personality. Papa had always voted Liberal and Gladstone, but thought that the latter lacked religious tolerance.

Maurice turned to another leader, which began, "In these troubled times . . ." And certainly they *were* troubled, as times very nearly always, perhaps quite always, are. The *Observer* told news of the Basuto war, the Russian danger in Afghanistan, Land League troubles, danger of war with Spain, trouble in Egypt, trouble in Bulgaria, trouble in Midlothian (where Mr. Gladstone was speaking against the government), trouble of all sorts, everywhere. What a world! Stanley, an assiduous student of it, sometimes almost gave it up in despair; but never quite, for she always thought of something one ought to do, or join, or help, which might avert shipwreck. Just now it was handicrafts, and the restoration of beauty to rich and poor.

Virginia Woolf

1882 – 1941

Virginia Woolf was the daughter of Sir Leslie Stephen, a famous Victorian man of letters, and his second wife Julie Duckworth. After her father's death in 1904, she and her brothers and sisters formed the centre of the Bloomsbury Group of avant-garde writers, critics and artists. She married Leonard Woolf in 1912 and with him founded the Hogarth Press. She had already begun writing fiction, experimenting with indirect narrative and fluid, impressionistic presentation of consciousness. Her innovative technique found its most complete expression in her major novels Mrs Dalloway *(1925),* To the Lighthouse *(1927) and* The Waves *(1931). Woolf suffered from bouts of mental ill health, in the last of which she drowned herself near her home in Sussex.*

The following extract is taken from A Room of One's Own *(1928; Granada, London, 1981). In the preceding chapter she has asked why there are so few women writers in the Elizabethan period. She concludes that women then had a grievance and that they had not the security of a Shakespeare. 'If ever a human being got his work expressed completely, it was Shakespeare,' she declares, 'If ever a mind was incandescent, unimpeded, I thought, turning again to the book case, it was Shakespeare's mind.'*

From

A Room of One's Own

4

THAT one would find any woman in that state of mind in the sixteenth century was obviously impossible. One has only to think of the Elizabethan tombstones with all those children kneeling with clasped hands; and their early deaths; and to see their houses with their dark, cramped rooms, to realize that no woman could have written poetry then. What one would expect to find would be that rather later perhaps some great lady would take advantage of her comparative freedom and comfort to publish something with her name to it and risk being thought a monster. Men, of course, are not snobs, I continued, carefully eschewing 'the arrant feminism' of Miss Rebecca West;[1] but they appreciate with

[1] See the entry 'Rebecca West', this volume, pp. 763–84.

sympathy for the most part the efforts of a countess to write verse. One would expect to find a lady of title meeting with far greater encouragement than an unknown Miss Austen or a Miss Brontë at that time would have met with. But one would also expect to find that her mind was disturbed by alien emotions like fear and hatred and that her poems showed traces of that disturbance. Here is Lady Winchilsea,[2] for example, I thought, taking down her poems. She was born in the year 1661; she was noble both by birth and by marriage; she was childless; she wrote poetry, and one has only to open her poetry to find her bursting out in indignation against the position of women:

> How we are fallen! fallen by mistaken rules,
> And Education's more than Nature's fools;
> Debarred from all improvements of the mind,
> And to be dull, expected and designed;
> And if someone would soar above the rest,
> With warmer fancy, and ambition pressed,
> So strong the opposing faction still appears,
> The hopes to thrive can ne'er outweigh the fears.

Clearly her mind has by no means 'consumed all impediments and become incandescent'. On the contrary, it is harassed and distracted with hates and grievances. The human race is split up for her into two parties. Men are the 'opposing faction'; men are hated and feared, because they have the power to bar her way to what she wants to do – which is to write.

> Alas! a woman that attempts the pen,
> Such a presumptuous creature is esteemed,
> The fault can by no virtue be redeemed.
> They tell us we mistake our sex and way;
> Good breeding, fashion, dancing, dressing, play,
> Are the accomplishments we should desire;
> To write, or read, or think, or to enquire,
> Would cloud our beauty, and exhaust our time,
> And interrupt the conquests of our prime,
> Whilst the dull manage of a servile house
> Is held by some our utmost art and use.

Indeed she has to encourage herself to write by supposing that what she writes will never be published; to soothe herself with the sad chant:

> To some few friends, and to thy sorrows sing,
> For groves of laurel thou wert never meant;
> Be dark enough thy shades, and be thou there content.

[2] See the entry Anne Finch, 'Countess of Winchilsea', this volume, pp. 154–8.

Yet it is clear that could she have freed her mind from hate and fear and not heaped it with bitterness and resentment, the fire was hot within her. Now and again words issue of pure poetry:

> Nor will in fading silks compose,
> Faintly the inimitable rose.

—they are rightly praised by Mr Murry,[3] and Pope, it is thought, remembered and appropriated those others:

> Now the jonquille o'ercomes the feeble brain;
> We faint beneath the aromatic pain.

It was a thousand pities that the woman who could write like that, whose mind was tuned to nature and reflection, should have been forced to anger and bitterness. But how could she have helped herself? I asked, imagining the sneers and the laughter, the adulation of the toadies, the scepticism of the professional poet. She must have shut herself up in a room in the country to write, and been torn asunder by bitterness and scruples perhaps, though her husband was of the kindest, and their married life perfection. She 'must have', I say, because when one comes to seek out the facts about Lady Winchilsea, one finds, as usual, that almost nothing is known about her. She suffered terribly from melancholy, which we can explain at least to some extent when we find her telling us how in the grip of it she would imagine:

> My lines decried, and my employment thought
> An useless folly or presumptuous fault:

The employment, which was thus censured, was, as far as one can see, the harmless one of rambling about the fields and dreaming:

> My hand delights to trace unusual things,
> And deviates from the known and common way,
> Nor will in fading silks compose,
> Faintly the inimitable rose.

Naturally, if that was her habit and that was her delight, she could only expect to be laughed at; and, accordingly, Pope or Gay[4] is said to have satirized her 'as a blue-stocking with an itch for scribbling'. Also it is thought that she offended Gay by laughing at him. She said that his *Trivia* showed that 'he was more proper to walk before a chair than to ride in one'. But this is all 'dubious gossip' and, says

[3] John Middleton Murry (1889–1957), husband of Katherine Mansfield, and editor of *The Athenaeum* from 1919–21 and founder of *The Adelphi* in 1923.
[4] John Gay (1685–1732), satirist and dramatist, author of *The Beggar's Opera* (1728) and *Trivia* (also referred to here) in 1716.

Mr Murry, 'uninteresting'. But there I do not agree with him, for I should have liked to have had more even of dubious gossip so that I might have found out or made up some image of this melancholy lady, who loved wandering in the fields and thinking about unusual things and scorned, so rashly, so unwisely, 'the dull manage of a servile house'. But she became diffuse, Mr Murry says. Her gift is all grown about with weeds and bound with briars. It had no chance of showing itself for the fine distinguished gift it was. And so, putting her back on the shelf, I turned to the other great lady, the Duchess whom Lamb loved, hare-brained, fantastical Margaret of Newcastle,[5] her elder, but her contemporary. They were very different, but alike in this that both were noble and both childless, and both were married to the best of husbands. In both burnt the same passion for poetry and both are disfigured and deformed by the same causes. Open the Duchess and one finds the same outburst of rage, 'Women live like Bats or Owls, labour like Beasts, and die like Worms. . . .' Margaret too might have been a poet; in our day all that activity would have turned a wheel of some sort. As it was, what could bind, tame or civilize for human use that wild, generous, untutored intelligence? It poured itself out, higgledy-piggledy, in torrents of rhyme and prose, poetry and philosophy which stand congealed in quartos and folios that nobody ever reads. She should have had a microscope put in her hand. She should have been taught to look at the stars and reason scientifically. Her wits were turned with solitude and freedom. No one checked her. No one taught her. The professors fawned on her. At Court they jeered at her. Sir Egerton Brydges complained of her coarseness – 'as flowing from a female of high rank brought up in the Courts'. She shut herself up at Welbeck alone.

What a vision of loneliness and riot the thought of Margaret Cavendish brings to mind! as if some giant cucumber had spread itself over all the roses and carnations in the garden and choked them to death. What a waste that the woman who wrote 'the best bred women are those whose minds are civilest' should have frittered her time away scribbling nonsense and plunging ever deeper into obscurity and folly till the people crowded round her coach when she issued out. Evidently the crazy Duchess became a bogey to frighten clever girls with. Here, I remembered, putting away the Duchess and opening Dorothy Osborne's letters, is Dorothy writing to Temple[6] about the Duchess's new book. 'Sure the poore woman is a little distracted, shee could never bee soe rediculous else as to venture at writeing book's and in verse too, if I should not sleep this fortnight I should not come to that.'

And so, since no woman of sense and modesty could write books, Dorothy, who was sensitive and melancholy, the very opposite of the Duchess in temper, wrote nothing. Letters did not count. A woman might write letters while she was sitting by her father's sick-bed. She could write them by the fire whilst the men talked without disturbing them. The strange thing is, I thought, turning over the

[5] Margaret Cavendish, Duchess of Newcastle, was written of with sympathy and admiration by Charles Lamb. See also pp. 16–28 of this volume.
[6] Dorothy Osborne (1627–75) married William Temple in 1654; in the period prior to their marriage she kept up a regular correspondence with her lover. The letters were first published as an Appendix in T. P. Courtenay's *Life of William Temple* in 1836.

pages of Dorothy's letters, what a gift that untaught and solitary girl had for the framing of a sentence, for the fashioning of a scene. Listen to her running on:

'After dinner wee sitt and talk till Mr B. com's in question and then I am gon. the heat of the day is spent in reading or working and about sixe or seven a Clock, I walke out into a Common that lyes hard by the house where a great many young wenches keep Sheep and Cow's and sitt in the shades singing of Ballads; I goe to them and compare their voyces and Beauty's to some Ancient Shepherdesses that I have read of and finde a vaste difference there, but trust mee I think these are as innocent as those could bee. I talke to them, and finde they want nothing to make them the happiest People in the world, but the knoledge that they are soe. most commonly when we are in the middest of our discourse one looks aboute her and spyes her Cow's goeing into the Corne and then away they all run, as if they had wing's at theire heels. I that am not soe nimble stay behinde, and when I see them driveing home theire Cattle I think tis time for mee to retyre too. when I have supped I goe into the Garden and soe to the syde of a small River that runs by it where I sitt downe and wish you with mee. . . .'

One could have sworn that she had the makings of a writer in her. But 'if I should not sleep this fortnight I should not come to that' – one can measure the opposition that was in the air to a woman writing when one finds that even a woman with a great turn for writing has brought herself to believe that to write a book was to be ridiculous, even to show oneself distracted. And so we come, I continued, replacing the single short volume of Dorothy Osborne's letters upon the shelf, to Mrs Behn.[7]

And with Mrs Behn we turn a very important corner on the road. We leave behind, shut up in their parks among their folios, those solitary great ladies who wrote without audience or criticism, for their own delight alone. We come to town and rub shoulders with ordinary people in the streets. Mrs Behn was a middle-class woman with all the plebian virtues of humour, vitality and courage; a woman forced by the death of her husband and some unfortunate adventures of her own to make her living by her wits. She had to work on equal terms with men. She made, by working very hard, enough to live on. The importance of that fact outweighs anything that she actually wrote, even the splendid 'A Thousand Martyrs I have made', or 'Love in Fantastic Triumph sat', for here begins the freedom of the mind, or rather the possibility that in the course of time the mind will be free to write what it likes. For now that Aphra Behn had done it, girls could go to their parents and say, You need not give me an allowance; I can make money by my pen. Of course the answer for many years to come was, Yes, by living the life of Aphra Behn! Death would be better! and the door was slammed faster than ever. That profoundly interesting subject, the value that men set upon women's chastity and its effect upon their education, here suggests itself for discussion, and might provide an interesting book if any student at Girton or Newnham cared to go into the matter. Lady Dudley, sitting in diamonds among the midges of a Scottish moor, might serve for frontispiece. Lord Dudley, *The Times* said when Lady Dudley died the other day, 'a man of

7 See Aphra Behn, this volume, pp. 32–154.

cultivated taste and many accomplishments, was benevolent and bountiful, but whimsically despotic. He insisted upon his wife's wearing full dress, even at the remotest shooting-lodge in the Highlands; he loaded her with gorgeous jewels', and so on, 'he gave her everything – always excepting any measure of responsibility'. Then Lord Dudley had a stroke and she nursed him and ruled his estates with supreme competence for ever after. That whimsical despotism was in the nineteenth century too.

But to return. Aphra Behn proved that money could be made by writing at the sacrifice, perhaps, of certain agreeable qualities; and so by degrees writing became not merely a sign of folly and a distracted mind, but was of practical importance. A husband might die, or some disaster overtake the family. Hundreds of women began as the eighteenth century drew on to add to their pin money, or to come to the rescue of their families by making translations or writing the innumerable bad novels which have ceased to be recorded even in text-books, but are to be picked up in the fourpenny boxes in the Charing Cross Road. The extreme activity of mind which showed itself in the later eighteenth century among women – the talking, and the meeting, the writing of essays on Shakespeare, the translating of the classics – was founded on the solid fact that women could make money by writing. Money dignifies what is frivolous if unpaid for. It might still be well to sneer at 'blue stockings with an itch for scribbling', but it could not be denied that they could put money in their purses. Thus, towards the end of the eighteenth century a change came about which, if I were rewriting history, I should describe more fully and think of greater importance than the Crusades or the Wars of the Roses. The middle-class woman began to write. For if *Pride and Prejudice* matters, and *Middlemarch* and *Villette* and *Wuthering Heights* matter, then it matters far more than I can prove in an hour's discourse that women generally, and not merely the lonely aristocrat shut up in her country house among her folios and her flatterers, took to writing. Without those forerunners, Jane Austen and the Brontës and George Eliot could no more have written than Shakespeare could have written without Marlowe, or Marlowe without Chaucer, or Chaucer without those forgotten poets who paved the ways and tamed the natural savagery of the tongue. For masterpieces are not single and solitary births; they are the outcome of many years of thinking in common, of thinking by the body of the people, so that the experience of the mass is behind the single voice. Jane Austen should have laid a wreath upon the grave of Fanny Burney, and George Eliot done homage to the robust shade of Eliza Carter – the valiant old woman who tied a bell to her bedstead in order that she might wake early and learn Greek. All women together ought to let flowers fall upon the tomb of Aphra Behn, which is, most scandalously but rather appropriately, in Westminster Abbey, for it was she who earned them the right to speak their minds. It is she – shady and amorous as she was – who makes it not quite fantastic for me to say to you to-night: Earn five hundred a year by your wits.

Here, then, one had reached the early nineteenth century. And here, for the first time, I found several shelves given up entirely to the works of women. But why, I could not help asking, as I ran my eyes over them, were they, with very few exceptions, all novels? The original impulse was to poetry. The 'supreme head of song' was a poetess. Both in France and in England the women poets precede the women novelists. Moreover, I thought, looking at the four famous names, what had George Eliot in common with Emily Brontë? Did not Charlotte Brontë fail entirely to understand Jane Austen? Save for the possibly relevant fact that not one of them had a child, four more incongruous characters could not have met together in a room – so much so that it is tempting to invent a meeting and a dialogue between them. Yet by some strange force they were all compelled when they wrote, to write novels. Had it something to do with being born of the middle class, I asked; and with the fact, which Miss Emily Davies[8] a little later was so strikingly to demonstrate, that the middle-class family in the early nineteenth century was possessed only of a single sitting-room between them? If a woman wrote, she would have to write in the common sitting-room. And, as Miss Nightingale was so vehemently to complain, – 'women never have an half hour . . . that they can call their own' – she was always interrupted.[9] Still it would be easier to write prose and fiction there than to write poetry or a play. Less concentration is required. Jane Austen wrote like that to the end of her days. 'How she was able to effect all this', her nephew writes in his Memoir, 'is surprising, for she had no separate study to repair to, and most of the work must have been done in the general sitting-room, subject to all kinds of casual interruptions. She was careful that her occupation should not be suspected by servants or visitors or any persons beyond her own family party.'[10] Jane Austen hid her manuscripts or covered them with a piece of blotting-paper. Then, again, all the literary training that a woman had in the early nineteenth century was training in the observation of character, in the analysis of emotion. Her sensibility had been educated for centuries by the influences of the common sitting-room. People's feelings were impressed on her; personal relations were always before her eyes. Therefore, when the middle-class woman took to writing, she naturally wrote novels, even though, as seems evident enough, two of the four famous women here named were not by nature novelists. Emily Brontë should have written poetic plays; the overflow of George Eliot's capacious mind should have spread itself, when the creative impulse was spent, upon history or biography. They wrote novels, however; one may even go further, I said, taking *Pride and Prejudice* from the shelf, and say that they wrote good novels. Without boasting or giving pain to the opposite sex, one may say that *Pride and Prejudice* is a good book. At any rate, one would not have been ashamed to have been caught in the act of writing *Pride and Prejudice*. Yet Jane Austen was glad that a hinge creaked, so that she might hide her manuscript before anyone came in. To Jane Austen there was something discreditable in writing *Pride and Prejudice*. And, I wondered, would *Pride and Prejudice* have been a

[8] Emily Davis, 'Home and the Higher Education' (1878) in Dale Spender, ed., 1987, *The Education Papers*, Routledge, London, pp. 111–12.
[9] Florence Nightingale, 'Cassandra' in Ray Strachey, *The Cause: A Short History of the Women's Movement in Great Britain* (first published, George Bell & Sons, London, 1928; reprinted by Virago, London, 1978), Appendix, pp. 395–418.
[10] *Memoir of Jane Austen*, by her nephew, James Edward Austen-Leigh.

better novel if Jane Austen had not thought it necessary to hide her manuscript
from visitors? I read a page or two to see; but I could not find any signs that
her circumstances had harmed her work in the slightest. That, perhaps, was the
chief miracle about it. Here was a woman about the year 1800 writing without
hate, without bitterness, without fear, without protest, without preaching. That
was how Shakespeare wrote, I thought, looking at *Anthony and Cleopatra*; and
when people compare Shakespeare and Jane Austen, they may mean that the
minds of both had consumed all impediments; and for that reason we do not
know Jane Austen and we do not know Shakespeare, and for that reason Jane
Austen pervades every word that she wrote, and so does Shakespeare. If Jane
Austen suffered in any way from her circumstances it was in the narrowness
of life that was imposed upon her. It was impossible for a woman to go about
alone. She never travelled; she never drove through London in an omnibus or
had luncheon in a shop by herself. But perhaps it was the nature of Jane
Austen not to want what she had not. Her gift and her circumstances matched
each other completely. But I doubt whether that was true of Charlotte Brontë,
I said, opening *Jane Eyre* and laying it beside *Pride and Prejudice*.

I opened it at Chapter Twelve and my eye was caught by the phrase
'Anybody may blame me who likes'. What were they blaming Charlotte Brontë
for? I wondered. And I read how Jane Eyre used to go up on to the roof when
Mrs Fairfax was making jellies and looked over the fields at the distant view.
And then she longed – and it was for this that they blamed her – that

'then I longed for a power of vision which might overpass that limit; which might
reach the busy world, towns, regions full of life I had heard of but never seen: that
then I desired more of practical experience than I possessed; more of intercourse
with my kind, of acquaintance with variety of character than was here within my
reach. I valued what was good in Mrs Fairfax, and what was good in Adèle; but I
believed in the existence of other and more vivid kinds of goodness, and what I
believed in I wished to behold.

'Who blames me? Many, no doubt, and I shall be called discontented. I could not
help it: the restlessness was in my nature; it agitated me to pain sometimes. . . .

'It is vain to say human beings ought to be satisfied with tranquillity: they must
have action; and they will make it if they cannot find it. Millions are condemned
to a stiller doom than mine, and millions are in silent revolt against their lot.
Nobody knows how many rebellions ferment in the masses of life which people
earth. Women are supposed to be very calm generally: but women feel just as
men feel; they need exercise for their faculties and a field for their efforts as
much as their brothers do; they suffer from too rigid a restraint, too absolute a
stagnation, precisely as men would suffer; and it is narrow-minded in their more
privileged fellow-creatures to say that they ought to confine themselves to making
puddings and knitting stockings, to playing on the piano and embroidering bags.
It is thoughtless to condemn them, or laugh at them, if they seek to do more or
learn more than custom has pronounced necessary for their sex.

'When thus alone I not unfrequently heard Grace Poole's laugh. . . .'

That is an awkward break, I thought. It is upsetting to come upon Grace Poole
all of a sudden. The continuity is disturbed. One might say, I continued, laying

the book down beside *Pride and Prejudice*, that the woman who wrote those pages had more genius in her than Jane Austen; but if one reads them over and marks that jerk in them, that indignation, one sees that she will never get her genius expressed whole and entire. Her books will be deformed and twisted. She will write in a rage where she should write calmly. She will write foolishly where she should write wisely. She will write of herself where she should write of her characters. She is at war with her lot. How could she help but die young, cramped and thwarted?

One could not but play for a moment with the thought of what might have happened if Charlotte Brontë had possessed say three hundred a year – but the foolish woman sold the copyright of her novels outright for fifteen hundred pounds; had somehow possessed more knowledge of the busy world, and towns and regions full of life; more practical experience, and intercourse with her kind and acquaintance with a variety of character. In those words she puts her finger exactly not only upon her own defects as a novelist but upon those of her sex at that time. She knew, no one better, how enormously her genius would have profited if it had not spent itself in solitary visions over distant fields; if experience and intercourse and travel had been granted her. But they were not granted; they were withheld; and we must accept the fact that all those good novels, *Villette, Emma, Wuthering Heights, Middlemarch*, were written by women without more experience of life than could enter the house of a respectable clergyman; written too in the common sitting-room of that respectable house and by women so poor that they could not afford to buy more than a few quires of paper at a time upon which to write *Wuthering Heights* or *Jane Eyre*. One of them, it is true, George Eliot, escaped after much tribulation, but only to a secluded villa in St John's Wood. And there she settled down in the shadow of the world's disapproval. 'I wish it to be understood', she wrote, 'that I should never invite anyone to come and see me who did not ask for the invitation'; for was she not living in sin with a married man and might not the sight of her damage the chastity of Mrs Smith or whoever it might be that chanced to call? One must submit to the social convention, and be 'cut off from what is called the world'. At the same time, on the other side of Europe, there was a young man living freely with this gypsy or with that great lady; going to the wars; picking up unhindered and uncensored all that varied experience of human life which served him so splendidly later when he came to write his books. Had Tolstoi lived at the Priory in seclusion with a married lady 'cut off from what is called the world', however edifying the moral lesson, he could scarcely, I thought, have written *War and Peace*.

But one could perhaps go a little deeper into the question of novel-writing and the effect of sex upon the novelist. If one shuts one's eyes and thinks of the novel as a whole, it would seem to be a creation owning a certain looking-glass likeness to life, though of course with simplifications and distortions innumerable. At any rate, it is a structure leaving a shape on the mind's eye, built now in squares, now pagoda shaped, now throwing out wings and arcades, now solidly compact and domed like the Cathedral of Saint Sofia at Constantinople. This shape, I thought, thinking back over certain famous novels, starts in one the kind of emotion that is appropriate to it. But that emotion at once blends itself with others, for the 'shape' is not made by the relation of stone to stone, but by the relation of human being to human being. Thus a novel starts in us all sorts of antagonistic and opposed emotions. Life conflicts with something that is not life. Hence the difficulty of coming to any agreement about novels, and the immense sway that our private prejudices have upon us. On the one hand, we feel You – John the hero – must live, or I shall be in the depths of despair. On the other, we feel, Alas, John, you must die, because the shape of the book requires it. Life conflicts with something that is not life. Then since life it is in part, we judge it as life. James is the sort of man I most detest, one says. Or, This is a farrago of absurdity, I could never feel anything of the sort myself. The whole structure, it is obvious, thinking back on any famous novel, is one of infinite complexity, because it is thus made up of so many different judgements, of so many different kinds of emotion. The wonder is that any book so composed holds together for more than a year or two, or can possibly mean to the English reader what it means for the Russian or the Chinese. But they do hold together occasionally very remarkably. And what holds them together in these rare instances of survival (I was thinking of *War and Peace*) is something that one calls integrity, though it has nothing to do with paying one's bills or behaving honourably in an emergency. What one means by integrity, in the case of the novelist, is the conviction that he gives one that this is the truth. Yes, one feels, I should never have thought that this could be so; I have never known people behaving like that. But you have convinced me that so it is, so it happens. One holds every phrase, every scene to the light as one reads – for Nature seems, very oddly, to have provided us with an inner light by which to judge of the novelist's integrity or disintegrity. Or perhaps it is rather that Nature, in her most irrational mood, has traced in invisible ink on the walls of the mind a premonition which these great artists confirm; a sketch which only needs to be held to the fire of genius to become visible. When one so exposes it and sees it come to life one exclaims in rapture, But this is what I have always felt and known and desired! And one boils over with excitement, and, shutting the book even with a kind of reverence as if it were something very precious, a stand-by to return to as long as one lives, one puts it back on the shelf, I said, taking *War and Peace* and putting it back in its place. If, on the other hand, these poor sentences that one takes and tests rouse first a quick and eager response with their bright colouring and their dashing gestures but there they stop: something seems to check them in their development: or if they bring to light only a faint scribble in that corner and a blot over there, and nothing appears whole and entire, then one heaves a sigh of disappointment and says. Another failure. This novel has come to grief somewhere.

And for the most part, of course, novels do come to grief somewhere. The imagination falters under the enormous strain. The insight is confused; it can no longer distinguish between the true and the false, it has no longer the strength to go on with the vast labour that calls at every moment for the use of so many different faculties. But how would all this be affected by the sex of the novelist, I wondered, looking at *Jane Eyre* and the others. Would the fact of her sex in any way interfere with the integrity of a woman novelist – that integrity which I take to be the backbone of the writer? Now, in the passages I have quoted from *Jane Eyre*, it is clear that anger was tampering with the integrity of Charlotte Brontë the novelist. She left her story, to which her entire devotion was due, to attend to some personal grievance. She remembered that she had been starved of her proper due of experience – she had been made to stagnate in a parsonage mending stockings when she wanted to wander free over the world. Her imagination swerved from indignation and we feel it swerve. But there were many more influences than anger tugging at her imagination and deflecting it from its path. Ignorance, for instance. The portrait of Rochester is drawn in the dark. We feel the influence of fear in it; just as we constantly feel an acidity which is the result of oppression, a buried suffering smouldering beneath her passion, a rancour which contracts those books, splendid as they are, with a spasm of pain.

And since a novel has this correspondence to real life, its values are to some extent those of real life. But it is obvious that the values of women differ very often from the values which have been made by the other sex; naturally, this is so. Yet it is the masculine values that prevail. Speaking crudely, football and sport are 'important'; the worship of fashion, the buying of clothes 'trivial'. And these values are inevitably transferred from life to fiction. This is an important book, the critic assumes, because it deals with war. This is an insignificant book because it deals with the feelings of women in a drawing-room. A scene in a battlefield is more important than a scene in a shop – everywhere and much more subtly the difference of value persists. The whole structure, therefore, of the early nineteenth-century novel was raised, if one was a woman, by a mind which was slightly pulled from the straight, and made to alter its clear vision in deference to external authority. One has only to skim those old forgotten novels and listen to the tone of voice in which they are written to divine that the writer was meeting criticism; she was saying this by way of aggression, or that by way of conciliation. She was admitting that she was 'only a woman', or protesting that she was 'as good as a man'. She met that criticism as her temperament dictated, with docility and diffidence, or with anger and emphasis. It does not matter which it was; she was thinking of something other than the thing itself. Down comes her book upon our heads. There was a flaw in the centre of it. And I thought of all the women's novels that lie scattered, like small pock-marked apples in an orchard, about the second-hand book shops of London. It was the flaw in the centre that had rotted them. She had altered her values in deference to the opinion of others.

But how impossible it must have been for them not to budge either to the right or to the left. What genius, what integrity it must have required in face of all that criticism, in the midst of that purely patriarchal society, to hold fast to the thing as they saw it without shrinking. Only Jane Austen did it and Emily Brontë. It is another feather, perhaps the finest, in their caps. They wrote as women write, not as men write. Of all the thousand women who wrote novels then, they alone entirely ignored the perpetual admonitions of the eternal pedagogue – write this, think that. They alone were deaf to that persistent voice, now grumbling, now patronizing, now domineering, now grieved, now shocked, now angry, now avuncular, that voice which cannot let women alone, but must be at them like some too-conscientious governess, adjuring them, like Sir Egerton Brydges, to be refined; dragging even into the criticism of poetry criticism of sex;[11] admonishing them, if they would be good and win, as I suppose, some shiny prize, to keep within certain limits which the gentleman in question thinks suitable – '... female novelists should only aspire to excellence by courageously acknowledging the limitations of their sex'.[12] That puts the matter in a nutshell, and when I tell you, rather to your surprise, that this sentence was written not in August 1828 but in August 1928, you will agree, I think, that however delightful it is to us now, it represents a vast body of opinion – I am not going to stir those old pools; I take only what chance has floated to my feet – that was far more vigorous and far more vocal a century ago. It would have needed a very stalwart young woman in 1828 to disregard all those snubs and chidings and promises of prizes. One must have been something of a firebrand to say to oneself, Oh, but they can't buy literature too. Literature is open to everybody. I refuse to allow you, Beadle though you are, to turn me off the grass. Lock up your libraries if you like; but there is no gate, no lock, no bolt that you can set upon the freedom of my mind.

But whatever effect discouragement and criticism had upon their writing – and I believe that they had a very great effect – that was unimportant compared with the other difficulty which faced them (I was still considering those early nineteenth-century novelists) when they came to set their thoughts on paper – that is that they had no tradition behind them, or one so short and partial that it was of little help. For we think back through our mothers if we are women. It is useless to go to the great men writers for help, however much one may go to them for pleasure. Lamb, Browne, Thackeray, Newman, Sterne, Dickens, De Quincey – whoever it may be – never helped a woman yet, though she may have learnt a few tricks of them and adapted them to her use. The weight, the pace, the stride of a man's mind are too unlike her own for her to lift anything substantial from him successfully. The ape is too distant to be sedulous. Perhaps the first thing she would find, setting pen to paper, was that there was no common sentence ready for her use. All the great novelists like Thackeray and Dickens and Balzac have written a natural prose, swift but not slovenly, expressive but not precious, taking their own tint without ceasing to be common property. They have based it on the sentence that was current at the time. The sentence that was current at the beginning of the nineteenth century ran something like this perhaps: 'The grandeur of their works was an argument with them, not to stop short, but to proceed. They could have no higher excitement or

[11] '[She] has a metaphysical purpose, and that is a dangerous obsession, especially with a woman, for women rarely possess men's healthy love of rhetoric. It is a strange lack in the sex which is in other things more primitive and more materialistic.' – *New Criterion*, June 1928.
[12] 'If, like the reporter, you believe that female novelists should only aspire to excellence by courageously acknowledging the limitations of their sex (Jane Austen [has] demonstrated how gracefully this gesture can be accomplished ...).' – *Life and Letters*, August 1928.

satisfaction than in the exercise of their art and endless generations of truth and beauty. Success prompts to exertion; and habit facilitates success.' That is a man's sentence; behind it one can see Johnson, Gibbon and the rest. It was a sentence that was unsuited for a woman's use. Charlotte Brontë, with all her splendid gift for prose, stumbled and fell with that clumsy weapon in her hands. George Eliot committed atrocities with it that beggar description. Jane Austen looked at it and laughed at it and devised a perfectly natural, shapely sentence proper for her own use and never departed from it. Thus, with less genius for writing than Charlotte Brontë, she got infinitely more said. Indeed, since freedom and fullness of expression are of the essence of the art, such a lack of tradition, such a scarcity and inadequacy of tools, must have told enormously upon the writing of women. Moreover, a book is not made of sentences laid end to end, but of sentences built, if an image helps, into arcades or domes. And this shape too has been made by men out of their own needs for their own uses. There is no reason to think that the form of the epic or of the poetic play suit a woman any more than the sentence suits her. But all the older forms of literature were hardened and set by the time she became a writer. The novel alone was young enough to be soft in her hands – another reason, perhaps, why she wrote novels. Yet who shall say that even now 'the novel' (I give it inverted commas to mark my sense of the words' inadequacy), who shall say that even this most pliable of all forms is rightly shaped for her use? No doubt we shall find her knocking that into shape for herself when she has the free use of her limbs, and providing some new vehicle, not necessarily in verse, for the poetry in her. For it is the poetry that is still denied outlet. And I went on to ponder how a woman nowadays would write a poetic tragedy in five acts. Would she use verse? – would she not use prose rather?

But these are difficult questions which lie in the twilight of the future. I must leave them, if only because they stimulate me to wander from my subject into trackless forests where I shall be lost and, very likely, devoured by wild beasts. I do not want, and I am sure that you do not want me, to broach that very dismal subject, the future of fiction, so that I will only pause here one moment to draw your attention to the great part which must be played in that future so far as women are concerned by physical conditions. The book has somehow to be adapted to the body, and at a venture one would say that women's books should be shorter, more concentrated, than those of men, and framed so that they do not need long hours of steady and uninterrupted work. For interruptions there will always be. Again, the nerves that feed the brain would seem to differ in men and women, and if you are going to make them work their best and hardest, you must find out what treatment suits them – whether these hours of lectures, for instance, which the monks devised, presumably, hundreds of years ago, suit them – what alternations of work and rest they need, interpreting rest not as doing nothing but as doing something but something that is different; and what should that difference be? All this should be discussed and discovered; all this is part of the question of women and fiction. And yet, I continued, approaching the bookcase again, where shall I find that elaborate study of the psychology of women by a woman? If through their incapacity to play football women are not going to be allowed to practise medicine–

Happily my thoughts were now given another turn.

Radclyffe Hall
1880 – 1943

Radclyffe Hall, born in Bournemouth into an upper middle-class family of an American mother and an English father, was raised in an almost entirely female household. She produced volumes of poetry and songs before the First World War but turned to prose writing under the inspiration of her first serious lover, Mabel Batten (known as 'Ladye'). In time this relationship was eroded by Ladye's invalid state following a car accident and during the last few months of Ladye's life Radclyffe Hall took another lover, Una Troubridge, the separated wife of an admiral. With the exception of one novel, all her future books were dedicated to 'Our Three Selves': Una, Ladye and Radclyffe Hall. She wanted to produce a book that would change people's attitudes to 'inversion' but she waited until she had made a reputation as a novelist before publishing the openly homoerotic The Well of Loneliness *in 1928. The book was met with hysteria and immediately prosecuted both in Britain and the US; it made its way back into circulation in Britain in the late 1940s.*

Radclyffe Hall also wrote short stories, collected in the volume Miss Ogilvy Finds Herself *(Heinemann, London, 1934); they include 'Fräulein Schwartz', which is reprinted here.*

Fräulein Schwartz

I

MRS Raymond preferred that her boarding-house should be known as a private family hotel, thus: 'Raymond's Private Hotel' had been painted in brown on the peeling Corinthian columns, and again above the shabby front door in gilt letters across the fanlight. The house stood in a street that had seen better days; it was one of those endless Pimlico streets that meander dully towards the river. All its houses were fashioned precisely alike: tall fronts, sash windows, damp areas; moreover, they were large but without dignity, and solid while conveying no sense of comfort.

Mrs. Raymond was the childless widow of a merchant who had had the misfortune to speculate in rubber; of that rash speculation nothing now remained but a starved rubber plant in the dining-room window. However, being a hard-headed woman and blessed by a lack of imagination, she had promptly opened a boarding-house which pretended to offer every home comfort.

'A home from home,' Mrs. Raymond would say, 'that's what I aim at – a home from home.' And since it was cheap as such places went, her clients preferred not to contradict her.

Like every experienced landlady, Mrs. Raymond had a very marked preference in boarders. She much preferred youthful and unattached men because, as a rule, they were docile and timid. At this time she had three such young men in her house: Mr. Pitt, Mr. Narayan Dutt and Mr. Winter.

Mr. Pitt belonged to the Y.M.C.A. He was secretary of some local branch, and he made a hobby of physical training. Mr. Pitt spent much time running round Richmond Park in modest duck shorts and a drenched cotton singlet. When he ran his hands sawed the air helplessly, his chest heaved and his eyes bulged behind his glasses. Mr. Narayan Dutt, who hailed from Bengal, was an earnest and a diligent medical student; he affected amazingly tight grey clothes and soft boots of a very unusual yellow. Mr. Winter worked in a city office; his prospects were poor and so was his health – he suffered from chronic nervous dyspepsia.

Apart from a few occasional boarders, there were four other 'regulars,' as they were called: Colonel Armstrong, of doubtful antecedents – he was said to be late of the Volunteers – two spinster sisters, the Misses Trevelyan, whose father had been a naval paymaster and who therefore despised the ambiguous Colonel, and an elderly person, by name Fräulein Schwartz, who gave German lessons at a couple of schools and eked out a living with private pupils.

Fräulein Schwartz was little and round and fifty, with neat greying hair and a very high bosom. She frequently sighed, and whenever this happened the plaid silk of her blouse creaked in sympathy – like many a German of her generation she displayed a mysterious preference for tartan. Gentle, and bewildered by life was Fräulein Schwartz; she had never been able to make up her mind about anything since the days of her childhood, and yet she had had to face grave decisions. She was incomplete, part of a philippine,[1] the major portion of which was missing.

Her father had been a most learned professor – that is, learned in all save the getting of money. They had lived in a pleasant suburb of Dresden not far from the bridge called 'Der Blaue Wunder.' As a child she had frequently stood

---

[1] A double-kernelled hazel nut, but also a German social game involving two participants.

on that bridge and gazed down at the Elbe, feeling rather afraid, gripping her father's protective hand, so impressed had she been by the depth of the water. After his death, when she was past thirty, she had dutifully wished to support her mother by teaching English, God save the mark! She had failed, which was not in the least surprising, for among those problems that had always bewildered her most might be counted the English language. But indeed she had tried a number of things for nine years, until she had lost her mother: fine needlework; knitting thick, gaudy stockings for the muscular legs of those who climbed mountains; even serving in a shop had Fräulein Schwartz tried, but not one of her ventures had been successful. Yet now here she was giving German lessons in London, and actually making a living.

Fräulein Schwartz was the friend of all the world, a fact which naturally made her feel lonely, since the world had no time for Fräulein Schwartz, nor had it expressed the least wish for her friendship. She loved children and after them animals; but children had never found her amusing. Stray dogs liked her, and sparrows would feed from her hand – but this only if the weather were frosty. Her true romance never having been born, she must cherish the memory of her parents, of her childhood, of her distant Fatherland; her large Bible resembled a photograph album. And let no one presume to despise Fräulein Schwartz if her links with the past were connected with eating. Why not? The bread that is broken in love, in guileless enjoyment and simplicity, may sometimes become as manna from Heaven. And although her mouth watered a little, it is true – she suffered long years of boarding-house cooking – her eyes watered still more for the innocent days that were gone past all earthly hope of recalling.

Zwieback and a glass of fine, creamy milk ... a spring morning in a tidy suburban garden; the witch-ball supported on stiff iron legs, a large luminous sphere reflecting the world, itself as immense as the world in proportions. Two earthenware dwarfs with curly grey beards; friendly, affable dwarfs clasping circular bellies: 'Liebchen,[2] do not make all those crumbs on the cloth; eat more carefully. What will the little men say? They are surely much grieved by untidy children!'

Apfelkuchen, always sweeter than sweet and tasting of the good, honest smell of ripe apples ... the confectioner's shop in the Prager Strasse to which she had been taken on her sixth birthday. A smiling young salesman behind the counter. who, when he had learned of the great occasion, had actually called her: 'Gnädiges Fräulein.'[3]

Schinkenbrot, crisp rolls stuffed with tender pink ham ... picnics to Bastei with her parents in summer. The stout little steam-boat, so busy, so willing. The songs they would sing steaming home in the evening: 'Lorelei,' because they were on the river, and sad old folk-songs because happy people will not infrequently sing about sadness.

Pumpernickel, the delectable sticky black bread ... her mother cutting it into thin slices. Her mother's spreading and matronly hips, so reassuring

2 Dearest.
3 Madam.

beneath the check apron: 'Nein, Liebchen, you must wait for your Pumpernickel.'

Wiener Schnitzel, fried slices of juicy veal; a dish well beloved of her learned father. The dining-room of their suburban home ... a tiled stove of such aggressive dimensions that it all but ousted the dining-table. Her father, big, bearded and very blue-eyed, a kind of paternal and ageing Siegmund, bending over his plate of Wiener Schnitzel.

The hot spiced wine of All Hallowes E'en, and the childish games that would follow after. Flushed cheeks – that hot spiced wine was so strong – and a great deal of mirth when she and her friends must evoke ancient spells, each to get her a husband. Her father and mother holding hands, grown young again thanks to the hot spiced wine. They had been middle-aged just as she was now, and how strange that seemed – the kind father and mother.

And those little brown loaves of marzipan that invariably made their appearance at Christmas. Ach, du liebe Zeit,[4] Christmas! The old market-place as fragrant and green as a miniature forest. Rich and poor alike buying Christmas trees and driving away with them then and there in old country carts or fine equipages. Snow and sunshine; the lake in the park frozen over, the band playing a waltz, the curvings and swayings of endless rosy-cheeked, bright-eyed skaters. Little ice sleighs, fashioned like gaudy birds. That fine pair of new skates with the curling fronts – what a lot they had cost. Ach, du liebe Zeit! she had surely possessed the most generous parents. Christmas day with its careful family presents; so much love had gone into each one with the making. Christmas night and the tree lighted up in the window just in case some poor creature outside should feel lonely: 'Töchterchen,[5] raise the blind before we light up – ja, so! Töchterchen, we should always remember the sad people who cannot have Christmas trees ...'

Remember! Fräulein Schwartz could hardly forget since now she herself was one of those people. Sentimental? Perhaps. But then Fräulein Schwartz had always been incurably sentimental.

2

WHETHER it was Providence who sent her a present, or Chance, is a very difficult question; but the fact remains that returning from a walk one Christmas Eve, Fräulein Schwartz found a kitten on the doorstep of Raymond's Private Hotel. It mewed; it looked at her with anxious blue eyes; it had draggled grey fur and a very pink nose; it was young, it was starving, and it needed protection.

Fräulein Schwartz's defrauded maternal heart leapt up at this sight: 'Armer Kerl!'[6] she exclaimed. Then she gathered the kitten into her arms and proceeded to warm it under her jacket.

[4] Oh, happy time.
[5] Little daughter.
[6] Poor fellow!

'You can't bring that thing in', Mrs. Raymond said firmly; 'I won't have a kitten messing up all my carpets.'

'Vhat you zay?' enquired Fräulein Schwartz. 'But he starve, he is young and he also needs me.'

'You can't bring him in,' Mrs. Raymond repeated, 'it's a rule of this hotel not to take people's pets.'

'Dat is rubbish!' said Fräulein Schwartz, equally firm. And then: 'I inzist dat I bring him in.' And her pale Teuton eyes were so bright and so fierce, and her thick Teuton voice was so pregnant with battle that Mrs. Raymond was completely nonplussed for a moment, and that moment gave her boarder the victory. 'I go buy him a tray and some nice zoft sand; he be clean, you vill see', coaxed Fräulein Schwartz; for the beast's sake now bent on conciliation.

So the kitten was carried upstairs to her bedroom and was fed and caressed and generally tended. And its name, from that evening on, was Karl Heinrich, in memory of a very learned professor: 'For,' said Fräulein Schwartz, as she combed its thin fur, 'der liebe Vater vould never object, and you haf his blue eyes – so clear and so childish. Jawohl,[7] I vill certainly giff you his name.' Then feeling a little doubtful she warned: 'But remember, dat name is a ferry great honour!'

This had been between five and six months ago, and now Karl Heinrich was growing up daily. He had changed his milk teeth, and had visited the vet. for the purpose of sacrificing his manhood. He had learned that all carpets demanded respect and that Mrs. Raymond would see that they got it. He had learned that sparrows were hatched to be fed and not necessarily to be eaten; whereas mice, could one catch them, were considered fair game – though Fräulein Schwartz never praised him for mousing. He was learning that Alice the parlourmaid, was one of those incomprehensible people who feel sick when a cat strolls into the room, and who consequently abhor the whole species. There was so much to learn with first this, then that, and yet life seemed wonderfully good to Karl Heinrich.

As for Fräulein Schwartz, it was really surprising what a difference his advent had brought about in her. She felt so much less lonely now at the thought that when she got home from work he would be waiting; that his food must be given, his coat brushed and combed, his ears looked to in case he be threatened with canker, his blue eyes watched for conjunctivitis, his temperature taken at least once a week, because being young he might get distemper – love, and a handbook on how to rear cats, had made her as crafty as any vet. Thus it must be conceded that Providence or Chance had been right in this choice of a Christmas present. For Fräulein Schwartz whose heart was so burdened with that large overload of maternal affection, Fräulein Schwartz the unwanted friend of all the world, was now wanted at last by a living creature. While Karl Heinrich, although, of course, as a cat who could trace his descent from a deity of Egypt, he could not quite sink to the level of a dog with lickings and wooffings and foolish tail-waggings; although he must stalk in the opposite direction, head in air, tail erect, when his owner called him – this just as a matter of etiquette – Karl

7 Yes indeed.

Heinrich had grown to adore that owner, and his purr when he rubbed his sleek length against her skirt would be vibrant and long with controlled emotion.

'Ach, du viel geliebtes Ding[8] . . .,' she must frequently murmur, kneeling down to stroke his grey comeliness. 'Ach, du mein Schatz',[9] and other fond words she must speak to the cat in her guttural German.

And whether it was purely imagination – the imagination of a Fräulein Schwartz who was only too anxious to find compensations – or whether, as she sometimes assured Mr. Winter, Karl Heinrich did really struggle to respond, making queer and very uncatlike sounds while blinking his eyes as though from great effort; whether all this was true mattered not in the least, since it gave such deep pleasure and consolation.

3

BETWEEN Alan Winter and Fräulein Schwartz there existed a kind of companionable liking. They met very seldom except at meals, but when they did meet they always felt friendly. He pitied her and she pitied him.

He would think: 'It's hard lines to be growing old and to have no real home – only this putrid place. I wonder what will happen when she's really old; her sort never manage to save much money.'

And she would be thinking how tired he looked, and how young he was to be so quiet and staid, and would long to teach him the student songs that she had been taught by her learned father, and would long to see him drink pints of beer, good iced beer – this in spite of his chronic dyspepsia. And though neither expressed sympathy for the other, since both of them were extremely shy people, yet they sometimes stopped if they passed on the stairs, stopped to talk for a little about Karl Heinrich. And Alan bought a ball on elastic which Karl Heinrich could make swing backwards and forwards, striking it deftly with soft, padded paws – a game that he found to be very amusing. And Fräulein Schwartz bought a bottle of tablets which the chemist assured her would cure indigestion, and she gave them to Alan who threw them away, but who, nevertheless, lied manfully when she asked him if he were not feeling better.

Thus the days drifted by. Fräulein Schwartz taught German and Alan Winter slaved at his office; Mr. Pitt ran round and round Richmond Park, and Mr. Narayan Dutt went to lectures; and the Colonel was distant to the Misses Trevelyan, and the Misses Trevelyan were cold to the Colonel, and Mrs. Raymond played bridge with her guests every evening, but methodically underfed them, and no one believed that a war would come, despite ominous hints that appeared in the Press.

'The world is now governed by high finance, the financiers would never permit such a thing', said Mrs. Raymond complacently . . . a view that was shared by even the Colonel.

---

[8] Oh, you adorable thing.
[9] Oh, my treasure.

4

THE night after England's declaration of war[10] Alan Winter returned from the City dead-beat. His head ached and he had a dull pain in his chest. All day the office had been in confusion, all day he had struggled to grasp the fact that this war, which seemed like an evil dream, might become for him a reality.

'But I cannot go out there and kill', ran his thoughts. And then: 'Is it that, or am I a coward? Am I really afraid of being killed?' A question to which he had found no answer.

Raymond's Private Hotel was blazing with lights. He could hear the sound of excited voices as he vainly tried to escape to his room: 'Is that you, Mr. Winter?' called Mrs. Raymond. 'We've been waiting up for you. Well, what's the news? Come and tell us what they say in the City.'

Amazing the futilities that worried these people, he could scarcely credit his ears as he listened: what was likely to happen to trustee stocks, to consols and other gilt-edged investments? What was meant by national bankruptcy – did the City think it was likely to happen? And the income-tax; what did the City think?

Alan shrugged his thin shoulders, hating them all. 'I can't tell you because I don't know', he snapped.

Colonel Armstrong eyed him malevolently: 'This,' said the Colonel, puffing out his chest, 'this, in my opinion, is Armageddon!'

And then it began. They argued, they disputed, they grew bitter towards the Kaiser and each other. Quiet people, hurled violently out of their ruts, their nerves had been jarred and their tempers suffered. It was natural enough, the whole thing was so strange – so terrifyingly sudden and strange; for the moment they buzzed like angry flies who were caught in the grip of some monstrous spider. Given time they would find their dignity again, but just for the moment they lost their tempers. Colonel Armstrong resented the Misses Trevelyan's irritating allusions to the senior service. The Misses Trevelyan retaliated by asking impertinent, personal questions. Mr. Pitt of the Y.M.C.A. called for vengeance upon every head wearing a Prussian helmet. Mr. Narayan Dutt smiled enigmatically and remarked that such sentiments did not sound Christian; while Mrs. Raymond, tired out and much worried, inveighed hotly against the food profiteers, declaring that she might have to put up her prices.

Some recent arrivals, a young couple from Norfolk, brought a stock of the most disconcerting rumours. The Germans had perfected Napoleon's idea and built rafts – they might shortly be landing at Dover; residents had been warned and were leaving the town which would be defended by an army of Russians. Food would soon become scarce; they might have to eat rats as the starving had done in the Siege of Paris – Mrs. Wilson knew for a positive fact that the Government was going to commandeer chickens. Queer people had been met with all over the Broads, two such persons were drifting about in a wherry; spies of course, all England was riddled with spies and the police doing less than nothing about it. The Germans had bottled innumerable germs, anthrax and cholera germs among

10 The First World War.

others, and these they would scatter in buses and tubes, spreading infection throughout the whole country. The navy was bristling with enemies, some of whom were flaunting their German names – Prince Louis of Battenberg, for instance; it was common knowledge that he would be shot, or at least arrested and put in the Tower – Mrs. Wilson hoped it would be in a dungeon. Spies were everywhere, not a corner was safe; why, the great wireless station quite near Llandudno had been run by a German man for years; he called himself Smith, but was really Schmidt. Mrs. Wilson's uncle lived down in those parts and had long had his eye on this dangerous fellow. But the real peril lay much less in the men than in the vast, secret army of women; female spies masquerading as ladies' maids, private secretaries, and even as teachers. They had wormed their way into important houses where, of course, they had overheard conversations. And not to be outdone, Colonel Armstrong, Mrs. Raymond, the Misses Trevelyan and Mr. Pitt, must produce even more startling contributions, so that to hear them was to feel little doubt regarding the ultimate fate of the Empire.

Then Mr. Pitt of the Y.M.C.A. stood forth as the champion of civilization; and his strong duplex spectacles catching the light, seemed to glow with the flames of his righteous wrath as he spoke of the brutal invasion of Belgium; of the broken treaty, the iron heel, the will to destroy a defenceless nation; of the Kaiser puffed up with arrogance like the blasphemous Beast of Revelation. Merciless they had been, those invading hordes, yes, and well prepared for their devilish work:

'God pity the women and children,' said he; 'this sort of thing isn't civilized. They'll stop at nothing, you mark my words. I'd like to exterminate the whole brood, yes, I would; they don't deserve anything else. What they need is total extermination!'

He was kind and extremely placid by nature, and on the whole quite a passable Christian. He had never handled a rifle in his life or done bodily ill to a living creature. He had certainly run round and round Richmond Park in a harmless desire for physical fitness, but prize-fights had always made him feel sick – he had said many times that they were degrading. But tonight something potent had gone to his head, something that was in the very air he was breathing, so that he demanded an eye for an eye, forgetting the crucified God of his Gospels. And although he did pity the women and children and sincerely believe in his own good intentions, although, Heaven knew, there was reason enough to cry out against this thing that had happened, Mr. Pitt was not solely stirred by the wrongs and the agonies of an invaded Belgium. For side by side with his genuine pity and his quite justifiable indignation, lurked an instinct that was very unregenerate and old – mild Mr. Pitt of the Y.M.C.A. was seeing red, as a long time ago some hairy-armed cave-man had done before him.

Alan said abruptly: 'I'm going upstairs.'

His head was now aching beyond endurance. He was weary unto death of Mr. Pitt, of the Wilsons, of the Colonel, of them all, for that matter. He wanted to put the war out of his mind, if only for a few blessed hours during sleep. Without saying good-night he turned and left them.

And away in a corner of the drawing-room, alone, stupefied, for the moment forgotten; half convinced that her country had committed a crime, and yet yearning painfully over that country; credulous one minute, incredulous the next, as she clung to the memory of her parents, of the Germany that she had once known – diligent, placid, child-loving and simple; a land of fairy tales, Christmas trees, and artless toys fashioned for little children – away in a corner of the drawing-room sat Fräulein Schwartz, weeping large childish tears which dripped on to her tartan silk blouse unheeded.

5

ENGLAND settled in to the grim stride of war. The Empire had swayed but had quickly recovered. Food rose sharply in price but nobody starved. A moratorium strengthened the banks which, despite Colonel Armstrong's fears, remained solvent; although after a time little, mean paper notes were to take the place of their weighty gold sovereigns.

Fellow clerks at Alan's office enlisted and their posts were soon filled by adventurous women, all anxious to do their bit for their country, all anxious to learn, yet impatient of learning. But Alan, the victim of his treacherous nerves, of his body that had failed him ever since childhood, of his horror of blood and of violent deeds, above all of his vivid imagination, Alan held back and did not respond to the loud bugle call of Kitchener's army.

Mr. Pitt of the Y.M.C.A. was in khaki. He had twice been refused on account of bad eyesight, but had managed to get himself taken at last, and this was immediately made the excuse for a very unworthy campaign of baiting. Alan was a handy and obvious butt, sitting all day on a stool in safety. The Misses Trevelyan cut him dead when they met; Colonel Armstrong – himself much too old to serve – made frequent and barbed patriotic allusions. Even Mrs. Raymond, try though she might to remember that Alan paid his bills promptly, that he seldom if ever complained of the food, the economy in fires or the tepid bath water, even Mrs. Raymond now viewed him askance, and if she addressed him at all did so coldly.

It was true that he was not the only blot, there was Fräulein Schwartz to whom nobody spoke except Alan, who felt very pitiful of her. There was also Mr. Narayan Dutt of Bengal – he had suddenly decided to leave the hotel, which the Misses Trevelyan thought highly suspicious. But then, as young Mrs. Wilson remarked with more force than refinement: 'He's a yellow-belly!' Mr. Wilson was being drilled down in Cornwall where his wife was daily expecting to join him. It was not very pleasant, indeed, quite the reverse, but Alan would not let his thoughts dwell on these people; after all, he was fighting on the business front, and England's motto was: 'Business as usual!'

But if Alan's position was not very pleasant, Fräulein Schwartz's position was becoming desperate, for who in their senses would wish to learn German? Moreover, her very presence in the house was looked upon as a potential danger. Mrs. Raymond had already asked her to leave, but Fräulein Schwartz had protested with tears that, alas, she could find nowhere else to go. For Fräulein Schwartz had but to open her mouth to arouse an immediate antagonism. One woman had banged the door in her face: 'No, I 'aven't a room for the likes of you! Why don't yer go 'ome and stay with the Kaiser?' Yet cheap lodgings were an urgent necessity, since now she must live on her meagre savings.

Poor, ageing, inadequate Fräulein Schwartz, so anxious to be the friend of all the world yet so tactless in her methods of setting about it; for what must she suddenly try to do but perform little acts of unwelcome kindness, and this at a time when war-racked nerves would naturally lead to the worst interpretations. Mrs. Wilson was convinced that she was a spy, hence those crafty offers to help with the housework; she wanted, of course, to get the run of the place, hoping to unearth some information. Mrs. Wilson threatened to go to the police and was only dissuaded by Mrs. Raymond who declared that this might ruin her hotel, especially if it got into the papers. In the end Mrs. Wilson bought a miniature safe so that she could lock up her husband's letters.

Poor, ageing, inadequate Fräulein Schwartz; a more positive woman would have packed her trunks and tried to return to her native land. But the thought of that long and difficult journey, of passports, of frightening official delays punctuated by even more frightening questions, of a dwindling purse, and God knew what expense to be faced before she at last reached her country, had completely deprived her of her small stock of will, and so she had stayed on from week to week, innocent, blundering, bewildered and helpless.

Oh, but she was being crushed on the wheel, the fate of all those who are too tender-hearted. War, to her, seemed a great and most pitiful sin, even as it had to her learned father. It was said that her people did terrible things; it was also said that the English would starve them, two wrongs which could surely not make a right, and which left her more bewildered than ever. Each morning she prayed with great earnestness that God would bring peace to the warring nations; but at times God appeared to be very far off, so that she must seek a more present help in trouble. Getting up from her knees she would look at Karl Heinrich; then taking him on to her lap she would talk, for like most of her nation she dearly loved talking – indeed, she had suffered far more than they knew from the silence imposed by her fellow-boarders. And to all those deep problems which vexed her soul, Karl Heinrich would listen with infinite patience, though every recital would end much the same way: 'Aber, vhat has gone wrong mit de vorld, Karl Heinrich?'

Karl Heinrich would find himself at a loss, since not even the wisdom of Ancient Egypt, as he very well knew, could have answered that question. And so he would start to sway his sleek tail, conscious of a disagreeable sensation in the region of the fur along his spine, for cats hate to be placed at a disadvantage. Then all that frustrated love of long years, all that urge to serve, all that urge to succour, all that will to protect the helpless of the earth, would Fräulein Schwartz pour out on her rescue. And since those whom we speak of as lesser creatures have their own quiet ways of divining our emotions, Karl Heinrich would cease from swaying his tail and would try to sit very still on her lap, so fearful was he of hurting her feelings.

Passing the door on her way downstairs, the parlourmaid, Alice, would pause to listen. And that low guttural voice would fill her with rage; with a senseless rage that made her feel giddy, so that now Karl Heinrich must suffer as well – they must suffer together, he and his mistress. Not that he was a German. He could prove that his father who frequented the backyards of Pimlico, had been born in a coal-cellar here in London. He could prove that his mother who lived five doors away had come into the world *via* a cupboard in Chelsea; all the same he must suffer from the girl's hostile eyes that made him feel intensely uneasy. Then again, she refused to bring up his food, declaring that the cook would no longer prepare it; and once she had given him a surreptitious kick, an outrage which he bore with philosophy, reflecting that Alice did not like cats – it seemed a just possible explanation.

Fräulein Schwartz must go out and buy milk in a can from the dairy and a loaf of stale bread from the baker; and on this meagre diet Karl Heinrich must live, since no scraps were available from the kitchen. But one day, although money was growing so scarce, Fräulein Schwartz bought Karl Heinrich a fine red collar; and she scratched his name on the plate with a pin – she had feared that the shop might refuse to engrave it. Gentle she was, and bewildered by life, yet this collar was in the nature of a challenge.

'Can't abide the beast,' Alice confided to the cook, 'and 'im belonging to that German woman. Ought to kick the pair of 'em out of the 'ouse. *And* 'is name! If she 'asn't gone and scratched it on 'is collar. The impudence of it, but then that's 'er! Any'ow the beast turns me sick at me stomach.'

Ah, yes, Alice was very bitter these days; a little queer too and inclined to be spiteful, for her wide muslin apron hid more than her skirt. Much clasping in a thicket on Hampstead Heath had resulted in what she hid under her apron.

He had said: 'Oh, come on! Ain't I goin' to the front? Ain't I one of the 'eroes wot's about to protect yer? 'Course I'll marry yer when I gets 'ome on leave. But, Gawd, don't go keepin' me 'anging' about . . .' And one or two other things he had said; it had not been at all a romantic seduction. So possibly Alice was less to blame for her queerness than was 'Erb, and what he had called in his moments of spiritual insight: 'Nature.'

6

INCREDIBLE of course that Fräulein Schwartz should have suddenly longed for her fellow-boarders, yet so it was, and the evening arrived when she could not endure coventry any longer; when tucking Karl Heinrich under her arm, she went down to the gloomy drawing-room and, much daring, broke into the conversation. Alan Winter, who had not as yet gone upstairs, was filled with a sense of impending disaster. What a moment to select, the poor tactless old fool! Hadn't she looked at the evening papers? They would think she had come to gloat over the news. And why bring the cat? His name was enough – a nice beast, but such an unfortunate name! Fräulein Schwartz had not seen any papers for days, indeed, she now frequently feared to see them.

She was trembling, already regretting her impulse, already regretting that she had brought Karl Heinrich. He would not sit still, he wanted to play and the chair had some very alluring buttons.

'Sieh' mal,[11] dat is naughty – you must be a goot boy. Do not do it! Be quiet a little, Karl Heinrich.'

She smiled awkwardly, glancing from face to face as a mother might do, half apologetic, half expecting a tolerant answering smile. But none came. Those animal-loving English could not find it in them to love Karl Heinrich – not just then, with the terrible lists of killed, of wounded and, more terrible still, of missing. Death and bereavement were everywhere now; no one in that room was nearly affected, yet bereavement had entered into the house. There had been a great noise of sobbing in the kitchen and the housemaid had had to serve the dinner that night. The girl had explained that some very sad news had reached Alice, hence those sounds of sobbing in the kitchen. And this German woman sat and played with her cat! It was true that she had not come down to dinner, that her room being at the top of the house she could not have heard what went on in the basement, nevertheless, she should have more shame; her presence was little short of an insult. No, they could not smile at the playful Karl Heinrich.

And he ought to have known better. He, so wise a cat, was being nearly as tactless as his mistress. What imp had got under his glossy grey fur and made him behave like a wilful kitten? Fräulein Schwartz's round forehead began to shine as she sweated with worry and mortification. And she talked, how she talked! It was almost as though her long enforced silence had left her bursting, so that now she must let loose a torrent of words. Alan thought as he listened that never before had he heard Fräulein Schwartz being quite so foolish or speaking in such abominable English.

'If only I could manage to stop her', he thought, glancing anxiously at their fellow-boarders.

They were doing their best. They were honestly trying to control their tongues and stifle their feelings; trying to answer her naturally, as though they were quite at their ease in her presence; trying in their unimaginative way to do the right thing, the dignified thing, on what to them was an odious occasion. But her thick Teuton voice jarred their every nerve, while her round Teuton face in their midst seemed an outrage when they thought of those wounded, missing, and dead. Quite suddenly they could not endure it and must start to castigate Fräulein Schwartz as if by so doing they struck at her country.

And now into the eyes of those quiet, dull people, crept a look that was unexpectedly cruel; the look of the hunter who corners his prey, watchful, alert with a sense of power – the power over life in the act of killing; while into Fräulein Schwartz's pale eyes came the puzzled, protesting look of the hunted. Then Fräulein Schwartz plunged, committing a blunder more grotesque than any that had gone before it. In her genuine will towards peace on earth, in her genuine conviction that all men are brothers, in her genuine distress at the miseries of war, she must try to make everyone there understand that she

[11] Look here.

not only asked for, but offered friendship. But they did not understand; they mistook it for shame, since, alas, in this world it is seldom wise to show the cross hilt instead of the sword blade.

'Dere is someting I vant to zay,' she was stammering, 'it is dis. Mein Vater vas against all vars; he belonged to de Socialdemokraten, de people's party, de party for peace. He thought var vas a great und most pitiful zin . . . ach, ja, and I feel as did my dear Vater. But ve here, ve hafe not made de var, nicht wahr?[12] It is not ve here who hafe vished to make it. I am Cherman and derefore I lofe my land; you are English and derefore you lofe dis England; and I tink dat ve all hafe zo much lofe in our hearts dat ve cannot help ourselves lofing one another . . .' She paused, gasping a little, but only for a moment, for now she was carried away by her creed. She was holding up the cross hilt of the sword and was strangely elated by what she was doing, so that her voice when next she spoke held in it the triumphant ring of the martyr: 'Because of my country I hafe wept many nights. It is said dat our zoldiers hafe killed little children – I do not know. It is alzo said dat your English navy is going to starve us; you cannot starve only vomen and men, and derefore you alzo vill kill little children – I do not know. I know only dis, dat ve all should unite to stop zo much zuffering. Ach, listen! I feel dat de spirit of my Vater is in me here', and she struck her plump breast, 'dat my Vater vants me to say dese tings; dat my Vater zays he implores you to listen. He zays dat in our dear countries tonight, dere are many goot people who feel as ve do, and dat if dey could dey vould stretch out dere hands and vould zay: "Wir sind ja alle Brüder und Schwestern."'[13] Fräulein Schwartz stopped speaking; the light died from her eyes leaving them dull and curiously vacant.

Then a dreadful thing happened. Mrs. Wilson laughed shrilly; she laughed peal upon peal, for she could not help it, was indeed scarcely conscious of what she did – she was very near an hysterical breakdown. Fräulein Schwartz's face became ashen, and from one of those dimly lit chasms of the mind in which lurk abhorrent and forbidden thoughts that engender great hatreds and great disasters; in which lurk all the age-old cruelties that have stood to the races for self-preservation; in which lurk the hot angers of humbleness scorned, and the blinding resentments that urge to vengeance; from one of those dimly lit chasms of the mind there rushed up a mighty force fully armed, and it gripped Fräulein Schwartz and possessed her entirely, so that she who had been the friend of all the world was now shaken by gusts of primitive fury.

'Ach, accursed English, you vhat laugh at de dead; you who hafe not de heart vhat can feel compassion! May be it is lies vhat you zay of our men – yes – I tink it is you vhat kill vomen and children. I tell you all vhat my Vater vould hafe me, und you laugh, und you laugh at my dear dead Vater! But may be you laugh less one of dese days vhen our Uhlans[14] ride through de streets of your London. May be you laugh much less vhen our ships blow up all of your cruel child-murdering navy. Gott! I tink ve vas right to make zuch a var; now I pray

[12] Isn't that so?
[13] We are all brothers and sisters.
[14] Lancers.

to Gott alvays dat He give us de victory!' And gathering Karl Heinrich into her arms she fled, while they sat stupefied and dumbfounded.

But someone was watching as she lumbered upstairs, clasping the cat to her heaving bosom. Alice stood aside to allow her to pass – she had heard that impassioned, tempestuous outburst.

'So,' she muttered, 'so you 'opes as your bloody Germans is comin' to ride through the streets of London; the devils as 'ave made my baby a bastard and me nothing but an 'ore all the rest of me days. So that's what you 'opes, you foul German bitch. Well, I'll teach yer; so now you can go on 'opin'!' And Alice shook her trembling fist in the air, half demented by the thought of her coming child, the bitter fruit of a brutal deflowering.

7

THE next afternoon being Saturday, Alan Winter returned from the office early. It struck him that the parlour-maid looked rather queer when she opened the door, but the thought soon passed. Alice, as he knew, had received bad news which would doubtless account for her strained expression.

Then stumbling downstairs came Fräulein Schwartz, her eyes red, her grey hair grotesquely dishevelled; and she clung to his sleeve, peering up at his face as though not very certain of her reception. But for all that she clung with tenacity.

'Gott sei Dank it is you and not one of de others . . .' she panted. And then: 'Come quick up to Karl Heinrich!'

He stared at her, wondering if she had gone mad: 'Karl Heinrich!' he repeated stupidly. He was tired, and his head was still heavy with figures.

She nodded: 'Ach, Gott, he is terribly ill. If you vil not help me because I am Cherman, den help him, for he surely haf done notting wrong.'

Alan thought: 'And neither have you, you poor soul,' Aloud he said: 'I'll come up and see him.'

They climbed the interminable stairs side by side, and as they did so she tried to explain how it was that Karl Heinrich had been brought so low; tried hard to keep calm and tell Alan the symptoms. It seemed that she had gone out to look for a room, and that on her return she had found him in convulsions.

'I do not know much, but I run to my book on de cat, und I tink it vere surely convulsions. . . . And vhen I look round he hafe been very sick . . . ach, but sick, sick, sick hafe he been in my absence. Und vhen de convulsions vas past come de pain, de 'orrible pain. . . . Ach, my poor Karl Heinrich! Und now dere hafe come de very great weakness. And I cannot understand; I myself buy his milch, und his bread I also buy from de baker, und no meat hafe he eaten for many days; und vhen I leave him to go hunt a room, he was vell as never before hafe I seen him. Herr Gott! Vhat has happened? Vhat can hafe befallen?'

Alan tried to soothe her as best he could, but he felt a queer sinking in the pit of his stomach and a sudden tightening across his chest: 'Don't be frightened, it can't be serious,' he soothed, 'not if the cat was so fit when you left him . . .'

They had reached the top landing, he gasping for breath. The next moment she was pushing him into her bedroom. It was small and squalid, a despicable room, a disgrace to the house and to Mrs. Raymond. He had never been in it until that moment, and he saw it for the unhappy thing that it was, the sole refuge of a derelict human being. He supposed that there must be many such rooms in all cities, and many such derelict beings. Then his thoughts stopped abruptly – he had seen Karl Heinrich.

She had dragged the meagre pillow from her bed and had laid him upon it, just under the window. The beast seemed to have shrunk to half his size, and that was so queer – rather horrible even. And his glossy grey coat was now matted and dull. Some milk had stiffened the fur on his chest, spilt there when she had endeavoured to feed him. His whole body looked pitifully soiled but resigned, and Alan could feel its profound desolation. For seeing him thus, was to know that Karl Heinrich realized in some dim way that he was dying, and that he had not yet made friends with death – perhaps because he was still so young and had been very full of the joy of living.

Then Fräulein Schwartz sank on to her knees, not in prayer to God, but in love for His creature, and she slipped her arms under Karl Heinrich and rocked him as though she were rocking an ailing baby; and she murmured soft and consoling words, as though she herself were indeed a mother:

'Kleines Wörmchen,[15] do not doubt und do not feel frightened. ... Gott is kind, and all vill be vell, Karl Heinrich. He lofes you, for you are His little grey cat – tink of it dat vay, for Gott He made you. And I vill not leave you never, ach, nein, zo dat you shall not feel frightened und lonely. Can you hear me? Do you know I am mit you, Karl Heinrich? Ja, I tink dat you do, und dat it consoles you. Hafe great hope and fear notting at all, mein Schatz.[16] ... Zee, I shall alvays be very close,' She appeared to have forgotten Alan Winter.

'Look here, I'm going for a vet', he said gruffly.

8

WHEN he returned with the vet in half an hour, Fräulein Schwartz was sitting on the floor by the pillow. She was stroking Karl Heinrich methodically, and still talking – only now she was talking in German. For her mind had slipped back over many years to her mother and the days of her own young childhood, so that she was using little tricks of speech, half playful, half grave, and wholly consoling; so that she was telling of gnomes, but kind gnomes, and of other such folk who were all very kind; trying to lure Karl Heinrich away from the realms of pain into those of enchantment.

'Is she a German then?' whispered the vet.

[15] Dear little mite.
[16] My darling.

Alan nodded: 'She is, but the poor beast isn't.'

The man flushed: 'I'm a healer, not an Empire!' he said sharply.

Turning, he went to Fräulein Schwartz: 'This gentleman has brought me to look at your cat. Do you mind if I make an examination? He's told me the symptoms. . . . I'm afraid they're pretty grave.'

Fräulein Schwartz got clumsily on to her feet and motioned to the vet to take her place. She gave him a searching look but said nothing. With gentle deftness he set about his task; lifting the eyelids, opening the mouth, pressing his ear to the beast's shrunken side, and listening again and again for the heartbeats. But Karl Heinrich was already a long way away; he had gone to the country that needs no frontiers, and where wars and the rumours of wars are forgotten.

The man shook his head: 'I'm too late,' he told them, 'but in any case I don't think I could have saved him. In my opinion this cat's been poisoned.'

'Poisoned? Oh, no, that's impossible! Who on earth would have done such a thing?' exclaimed Alan.

But Fräulein Schwartz spoke in an odd, hushed voice: 'If dat is de truth, den for me has he suffered, and for my nation, und for all de nations vhat zo cruelly go out to hurt vone another. Karl Heinrich vas only a little grey cat vhat I rescue vhen he was cold and starving; but now Karl Heinrich is very much more, he is zomething enormous und terrible: a reproach before Gott who vill not forget de zufferings of poor dumb beasts und of children. I hafe maybe lost him for a little vhile, ja. I hafe lent him to Gott, but only for a little; because Gott, who hates var, vill give him me back. He vill say: "Karl Heinrich hafe told Me about it; all de pain und de fear und de doubts vhat he felt before you come home in de end und find him. zo dat now he shall go again vhere he vould be, und dat is mit you – I gife back your Karl Heinrich."'

The vet glanced at Alan uneasily: 'I'd like to make an autopsy', he murmured.

But Alan shook his head: 'Don't suggest it – no good – she's half crazy with grief, it would only distress her.'

'But she can't keep him here. I could take the body . . .'

Fräulein Schwartz swung round: 'Vhat is dat you are zaying? Aber nein; I vill bury him myzelf.'

'Well – I'm sorry I couldn't save him, Fräulein.' The vet looked at his watch; there was nothing he could do, and moreover he had another appointment.

'If you'll come downstairs, I'll attend to your fee', muttered Alan, and he almost ran from the room, conscious only of a wild desire to escape from the blemished beast and the grief-stricken woman.

Alone with her dead, Fräulein Schwartz spoke to God, and she told Him quite quietly about this great sorrow, and about the troubles that had gone before – her loneliness, her fears, her inadequacy, and the feeling that life had denied her fulfilment. She told Him of the wish she had always cherished to befriend the whole world, to be one great heart into which the whole world could creep for protection, and of how she had found that nobody came, that nobody wanted her heart but Karl Heinrich, who had thus in some strange way become the whole world, which was surely God's compassionate dispensation.

Then she asked His forgiveness for all her transgressions; for her anger upon the previous evening and for all those terrible things she had said – none of which she had really meant, she assured Him. And for what she would now do she asked it also if, indeed, according to His wisdom it were sinful, which she could not believe since none other than He had sent her this very great love for Karl Heinrich.

'And I promise dat I vould not leave him, ach, nein, because he is only zo helpless a ding vhat I care for zince he vas a tiny kitten. Und he might feel strange, even mit You, mein Vater im Himmel, though I tell him of all Your kindness . . .'

For some reason she was praying in English, in the thick Teuton English that made people angry, that indeed, had nearly cost her her home – but perhaps God did not notice her accent. In any case she drew much comfort from her prayer and much courage; both excellent reasons for praying.

Presently, she was setting her bedroom in order, so that when they went in they should find it tidy; and this done she got money out of her trunk and left it on the table for Mrs. Raymond.

'Zo! Und now I owe nobody notting,' she murmured, 'I am glad, for had it been otherwise, they vould all hafe zaid dat I paid not my rent because I vas vhat dey call: "A damn Cherman."' And she actually smiled a little to herself, not unkindly, but rather with a vague toleration.

Finally, she pinned on her shabby black hat, then she slipped her arms into an old tweed ulster – it was simple, almost too big she remembered, and thus it could easily shelter them both. Lifting the stiffening body of the cat, she buttoned it gently under the ulster.

Poor, ageing, inadequate Fräulein Schwartz; even at this stupendous moment when for once in her life she had made up her mind, when for once she was filled with a great resolve, even now she must walk lop-sided through the streets, looking as though some abominable growth had laid its distorting hand upon her; indeed, more than one person turned to stare at the odd little woman who walked so quickly. Quickly, yes, for she had a long way to go before she would come to that quiet place where the trees bent forward over the river; where the river was dark and brooding with peace. By the time she had reached it she would be very tired and glad of her sleep, for the night would have fallen. Karl Heinrich was already fast asleep – she could feel him lying against her bosom.

Edith Sitwell

1887 – 1964

E dith Sitwell was born into the affluent family of Sir George and Lady Sitwell in Derbyshire. Educated at home she felt disapproval because of her unfashionable looks and intellectual interests. Through her governess, with whom she later lived, she became fascinated with French Symbolist poetry and in 1915 published her own first volume of poems. Over the next years she wrote several other volumes, edited collections of new poetry, and became friends with many of the leading literary figures of her day, such as Aldous Huxley, Virginia Woolf and T.S. Eliot. In the early 1920s she was notorious for theatrically performing her rhythmical poems to music. In the 1930s, needing money, she wrote several prose works and some journalism. Deeply moved by the Second World War, she expressed her horror in a succession of pacifist poems including one describing the nuclear bombing of Hiroshima. In 1955 she became a Roman Catholic and her later poetry reflects her religious faith.

The following poems have been taken from Edith Sitwell: Fire of the Mind (Elizabeth Salter and Allanah Harper (eds), Michael Joseph, London, 1976).

From

The Sleeping Beauty

CANTO 12

The Princess:

'U PON the infinite shore by the sea
The lovely ladies are walking like birds,
Their gowns have the beauty, the feathery
Grace of a bird's soft raiment; remote
Is their grace and their distinction—they float
And peck at their deep and honeyed words
As though they were honeyed fruits; and this

Is ever their life, between sleep and bliss,
Though they are winged for enchanted flight,
They yet remain ever upon the shore
Of Eternity, seeking for nothing more,
Until the cold airs dull their beauty
And the snows of winter load those dazzling
Wings, and no bird-throat can sing!'

The Governante:

'LOOK not on the infinite wave,
Dream not of the siren cave,
Nor hear the cold wind in the tree
Sigh of worlds we cannot see.'

From

The Sleeping Beauty

CANTO 20

THE mauve summer rain
Is falling again—
It soaks through the eaves
And the ladies' sleeves—
It soaks through the leaves

That like silver fish fall
In the fountains, recall
Afternoons when I
Was a child small and shy
In the palace . . . Fish lie

On the grass with lives darkling.
Our laughter falls sparkling
As the mauve raindrops bright
When they fall through the light
With the briefest delight.

The pavilions float
On the lake like a boat . . .
Mauve rains from trees fall
Like wistaria flowers . . . all

My life is like this
And drifts into nothingness!

The strange ladies sigh
'The autumn is nigh' . . .
The King bows and mutters . . .
His eyelids seem shutters
Of a palace pavilion
Deserted a million

Echoing years ago.
Oh, but the rain falls slow.

Aubade

JANE, Jane,
Tall as a crane,
The morning light creaks down again;

Comb your cockscomb-ragged hair,
Jane, Jane, come down the stair.

Each dull blunt wooden stalactite
Of rain creaks, hardened by the light,

Sounding like an overtone
From some lonely world unknown.

But the creaking empty light
Will never harden into sight,

Will never penetrate your brain
With overtones like the blunt rain.

The light would show (if it could harden)
Eternities of kitchen garden,

Cockscomb flowers that none will pluck,
And wooden flowers that 'gin to cluck.

In the kitchen you must light
Flames as staring, red and white,

As carrots or as turnips, shining
Where the cold dawn light lies whining.

Cockscomb hair on the cold wind
Hangs limp, turns the milk's weak mind . . .

Jane, Jane,
Tall as a crane,
The morning light creaks down again!

Said King Pompey

SAID King Pompey, the emperor's ape,
Shuddering black in his temporal cape
Of dust, 'The dust is everything—
The heart to love and the voice to sing,
Indianapolis
And the Acropolis,
Also the hairy sky that we
Take for a coverlet comfortably.'
Said the Bishop,
Eating his ketchup:
'There still remains Eternity
Swelling the diocese,
That elephantiasis,
The flunkeyed and trumpeting sea.'

Waltz

DAISY and Lily,
Lazy and silly,
Walk by the shore of the wan grassy sea,—
Talking once more 'neath a swan-bosomed tree.
Rose castles,
Tourelles,[1]
Those bustles
Where swells
Each foam-bell of ermine,
They roam and determine
What fashions have been and what fashions will be,—
What tartan leaves born,
What crinolines worn.
By Queen Thetis,[2]
Pelisses

[1] Turrets.
[2] One of the Nereids who married King Peleus.

Of tarlatine[3] blue,
Like the thin plaided leaves that the castle crags grew;
Or velours d'Afrande:
On the water-gods' land
Her hair seemed gold trees on the honey-cell sand
When the thickest gold spangles, on deep water seen,
Were like twanging guitar and like cold mandoline,
And the nymphs of great caves,
With hair like gold waves
Of Venus, wore tarlatine.
Louise and Charlottine
(Boreas'[4] daughters)
And the nymphs of deep waters,
The nymph Taglioni, Grisi the ondine,[5]
Wear plaided Victoria and thin Clementine[6]
Like the crinolined waterfalls;
Wood-nymphs wear bonnets, shawls;
Elegant parasols
Floating were seen.
The Amazons wear balzarine of jonquille[7]
Beside the blond lace of a deep-falling rill;
Through glades like a nun
They run from and shun
The enormous and gold-rayed rustling sun;
And the nymphs of the fountains
Descend from the mountains
Like elegant willows
On their deep barouche pillows,
In cashmere Alvandar, barège[8] Isabelle,
Like bells of bright water from clearest wood-well.
Our élégantes favouring bonnets of blond,
The stars in their apiaries,
Sylphs in their aviaries,
Seeing them, spangle these, and the sylphs fond
From their aviaries fanned
With each long fluid hand
The manteaux espagnoles,
Mimic the waterfalls
Over the long and the light summer land.

· · · · · · · · · ·

[3] A kind of open muslin.
[4] North wind.
[5] Maria Taglioni (1804–84) was an Italian ballet dancer; Giulia Grisi (1811–69) was an Italian opera singer; an ondine is a female water-sprite.
[6] Kinds of fabric.
[7] Amazons are legendary female warriors; balzarine is a thin material.
[8] Gauze-like silky dress fabric.

So Daisy and Lily,
Lazy and silly,
Walk by the shore of the wan grassy sea,
Talking once more 'neath a swan-bosomed tree.
Rose castles,
Tourelles,
Those bustles!
Mourelles
Of the shade in their train follow.
Ladies, how vain,—hollow,—
Gone is the sweet swallow,—
Gone, Philomel![9]

Song

WE are the darkness in the heat of the day,
    The rootless flowers in the air, the coolness: we are the water
Lying upon the leaves before Death, our sun,
And its vast heat has drunken us ... Beauty's daughter,
The heart of the rose, and we are one.

We are the summer's children, the breath of evening, the days
When all may be hoped for,—we are the unreturning
Smile of the lost one, seen through the summer leaves—
That sun and its false light scorning.

Green Song

TO DAVID HORNER

AFTER the long and portentous eclipse of the patient sun
    The sudden spring began
With the bird-sounds of Doom in the egg, and Fate in the bud that is
    flushed with the world's fever—
But those bird-songs have trivial voices and sound not like thunder,
And the sound when the bud bursts is no more the sound of the
    worlds that are breaking.—

---

[9] Philomela and Procne were sisters who were turned into a nightingale and a swallow.

But the youth of the world, the lovers, said, 'It is Spring!
And we who were black with the winter's shade, and old,
See the emeralds are awake upon the branches
And grasses, bird-blood leaps within our veins
And is changed to emeralds like the sap in the grasses.
The beast-philosopher hiding in the orchards,
Who had grown silent from the world's long cold,
Will tell us the secret of how Spring began
In the young world before the Fall of Man.
For you are the young spring earth
And I, O Love, your dark and lowering heaven.'

But an envious ghost in the spring world
Sang to them a shrunken song
Of the world's right and wrong—
Whispered to them through the leaves, 'I wear
The world's cold for a coat of mail
Over my body bare—
I have no heart to shield my bone
But with the world's cold am alone—
And soon your heart, too, will be gone—
My day's darling.'

The naked Knight in the coat of mail
Shrieked like a bird that flies through the leaves—
The dark bird proud as the Prince of the Air—
'I am the world's last love . . . Beware—

Young girl, you press your lips to lips
That are already cold—
For even the bright earthly dress
Shall prove, at last, unfaithfulness.

His country's love will steal his heart—
To you it will turn cold
When foreign earth lies on the breast
Where your young heart was wont to rest
Like leaves upon young leaves, when warm was the green spray,
And warm was the heart of youth, my day's darling.

And if that ghost return to you—
(The dead disguised as a living man)
Then I will come like Poverty
And wear your face, and give your kiss,
And shrink the world and that sun, the heart,
Down to a penny's span:

For there is a sound you heard in youth,
A flower whose light is lost—

There is a faith and a delight—
They lie at last beneath my frost
When I am come like Time that all men, faiths, loves, suns defeat,
My frost despoils the day's young darling.

For the young heart like the spring wind grows cold
And the dust, the shining racer, is overtaking
The laughing young people who are running like fillies,
The golden ladies and the ragpickers,
And the foolish companions of spring, the wild wood lilies.'
But the youth of the world said, 'Give me your golden hand
That is but earth, yet it holds the lands of heaven;
And you are the sound of the growth of spring in the heart's deep
    core,
The hawthorn-blossoming boughs of the stars and the young
    orchards' emerald lore.'

And hearing that, the poor ghost fled like the winter rain—
Sank into greenish dust like the fallen moon
Or the sweet green dust of the lime-flowers that will be blossoming
    soon.
And spring grew warm again—

No more the accusing light, revealing the rankness of Nature,
All motives and desires and lack of desire
In the human heart; but loving all life, it comes to bless
Immortal things in their poor earthly dress—
The blind of life beneath the frost of their great winter,
And those for whom the winter breaks in flower
And summer grows from a long-shadowed kiss.
And Love is the vernal equinox in the veins
When the sun crosses the marrow and pith of the heart
Among the viridian smells, the green rejoicing.
All names, sounds, faiths, delights, and duties lost
Return to the hearts of men, those households of high heaven.
And voices speak in the woods as from a nest
Of leaves—they sing of rest,
And love, and toil, the rhythms of their lives,
Singing how winter's dark was overcome,
And making plans for tomorrow as though yesterday
Had never been, nor the lonely ghost's old sorrow,
And Time seemed but the beat of heart to heart,
And Death the pain of earth turning to spring again
When lovers meet after the winter rain.
And when we are gone, they will see in the great mornings
Born of our lives, some memory of us, the golden stalk

Of the young, long-petalled flower of the sun in the pale air
Among the dew ... Are we not all of the same substance,
Men, planets, and earth, born from the heart of darkness,
Returning to darkness, the consoling mother,
For the short winter sleep—O my calyx of the flower of the world,
    you the spirit
Moving upon the waters, the light on the breast of the dove.

Rebecca West
1892 – 1983

'*R*ebecca West' was the name adopted by Cecily Isabel Fairfield (taken
    from Ibsen's heroine in Rosmersholm) after an early and brief career
    upon the stage. Moving from Edinburgh to London, she became a
feminist and a journalist and from 1911 wrote for The Freewoman, The New
Freewoman and the Clarion. Her outrageous and witty journalism attracted
wide attention and much respect. In 1918 she published her first novel, The
Return of the Soldier: this was followed by The Judge (1922), The Strange
Necessity (1928), Harriet Hume (1929) and The Thinking Reed (1936), and
these established her reputation as an important writer of fiction. The next phase
of her career focused more on non-fiction, with her two volume study of the
Yugoslav nation – Black Lamb and Grey Falcon – appearing in 1941 and The
Meaning of Treason (in part her analysis of the Nuremberg Trials on which she
reported) in 1949. She returned to fiction in 1956 with The Fountain Overflows
and then The Birds Fall Down (1966). Three novels were published posthumously:
This Real Night (Macmillan, 1985), Cousin Rosamund (Macmillan, 1985) and
Sunflower (Virago, 1986).
    The following short story, taken from Rebecca West: A Celebration
(Macmillan, London, 1977).

Parthenope[1]

MY Uncle Arthur had red hair that lay close to his head in flat, circular curls,
and a pointed red beard, and his blue-green eyes were at once penetrating
and bemused. He was the object of mingled derision and respect in our family.

[1] In mythology, Parthenope was one of the sirens: daughter of Stymphalus.

He was a civil servant who had early attracted attention by his brilliance; but the chief of his department, like so many English civil servants, was an author in his spare time, and when he published a history of European literature, my uncle reviewed it in the leading weekly of the day, pointing out that large as was the number of works in the less familiar languages that his chief supposed to be written in prose, though in fact they were written in verse, it was not so large as the number of such works that he supposed to be written in verse, though in fact they were written in prose. He wrote without malice, simply thinking his chief would be glad to know. My uncle never connected this review with his subsequent failure to gain a promotion that had seemed certain, or to have the day as snug as civil servants usually had it in the nineteenth century. But in the course of time his chief died, and my uncle rose to be an important official. However, he did a Cabinet Minister much the same service he had rendered his chief, and he never received the title that normally went with his post.

So he seesawed through life, and I liked his company very much when he was an old man and I was a young girl, for it was full of surprises. When I asked him a question, I never knew if his answer would show that he knew far less than I did or far more; and though he was really quite old, for he was my father's elder by many years, he often made discoveries such as a schoolchild might make, and shared them with an enthusiasm as little adult. One day he gave me no peace till I had come with him to see the brightest field of buttercups he had ever found near London; it lay, solid gold, beside the great Jacobean mansion Ham House, by the river Thames. After we had admired it he took me to nearby Petersham Church, to see another treasure, the tomb of Captain Vancouver, who gave his name to the island; my uncle liked this tomb because he had spent some years of his boyhood in Canada and had been to Vancouver Island when it was hardly inhabited. Then we had tea in an inn garden and it happened that the girl who waited on us was called away by the landlord as she set the china on the table. His voice came from the kitchen: "Parthenope! Parthenope!" My uncle started, for no very good reason that I could see. There had been a time when many ships in the British Navy were called after characters in Greek history and mythology, male and female, and therefore many sailors' daughters had been given the names of nymphs and goddesses and Homeric princesses and heroines of Greek tragedy. The only strange thing was that it was a long time since British ships had been christened so poetically, and most of the women who had acquired these classical names by this secondary interest were by now old or middle-aged, while our little waitress was very young. She had, as she told us when she came back, been called after a grandmother. But my uncle was plainly shaken by hearing those four syllables suddenly borne on the afternoon air. His thin hand plucked at the edge of the tablecloth, he cast down his eyes, his head began to nod and shake. He asked me if he had ever told me the story of the Admiral and his seven daughters, in a tone that suggested that he knew he had not and was still trying to make up his mind whether he wanted to tell it now. Indeed, he told me very little that day, though I was to hear the whole of it before he died.

The story began at the house of my grandmother's sister, Alice Darrell, and it could hardly have happened anywhere else. When her husband, an officer in the Indian Army, died of fever, her father-in-law had given her a house that he had recently and reluctantly inherited and could not sell because it was part of an entailed estate. He apologized for the gift, pleading justly that he could not afford to buy her another, and she accepted it bravely. But the house lay in a district that would strain anybody's bravery. To reach it, one travelled about eight miles out of London along the main Hammersmith Road, the dullest of highways, and then turned left and found something worse. For some forgotten reason, there had sprung up at this point a Hogarthian slum, as bad as anything in the East End, which turned into a brawling hell every Saturday night. Beyond this web of filthy hovels lay flatlands covered by orchards and farmlands and market gardens, among which there had been set down three or four large houses. There was nothing to recommend the site. The Thames was not far distant, and it was comprehensible enough that along its bank there had been built a line of fine houses. But at Alice Darrell's there was no view of the river, though it lay near enough to shroud the region in mist during the winter months. It was true that the gardens had an alluvial fertility, but even they did not give the pleasure they should have done, for the slum dwellers carried out periodical raids on the strawberry beds and raspberry canes and orchards.

These stranded houses had been built in Regency times and were beautiful, though disconcerting, because there was no reason why they should be there, and they were so oddly placed in relation to each other. They all opened off the same narrow road, and Aunt Alice's house, Currivel Lodge, which was the smallest of them, lay at the end of a drive, and there faced sideways, so that its upper windows looked straight down on the garden of the much bigger house beside it, as that had been built nearer the road. This meant that my grandaunt could not sit on the pretty balcony outside her bedroom window without seeming to spy on her neighbours, so she never used it. But when my Uncle Arthur went to stay with her as a little boy, which was about a hundred years ago, nothing delighted him more than to shut himself in his bedroom and kneel on his window and do what his Aunt Alice could not bear to be suspected of doing.

Currivel Lodge should have been a dreary place for the child. There was nowhere to walk and nowhere to ride. There was no village where one could watch the blacksmith at his forge and the carpenter at his bench. In those days, nobody rowed on the Thames anywhere but at Oxford, unless they were watermen earning their living. There was little visiting, for it took a good hour to an hour and a half to drive to London, and my needy grandaunt's horses were old crocks. Her children were all older than little Arthur. But he enjoyed his visit simply because of the hours he spent on that window seat. I know the setting of the scene on which he looked, since I often stayed in that house many years later; for of course my grandaunt's family never left it. When the entail came to an end and the property could have been sold, there were the Zulu Wars, and South African War, the First World War, and all meant that the occupants were too busy or too troubled to move; and they were still living there when the house was swept away in a town-planning scheme during the twenties. What Arthur in his day and I in mine looked down on was a croquet lawn framed by trees, very tall trees—so tall and strong, my uncle said with approval, that though one could not see the river, one knew that there must be one not far away. Born and reared in one of the wettest parts of Ireland, he regarded dry weather and a dry soil as the rest of us regard dry bread.

To the left of his lawn, seen through foliage, was a stone terrace overgrown with crimson and white roses. Behind the terrace rose the mellow red rectangle of a handsome Regency house with a green copper cupola rising from its roof. What my uncle saw there that was not there for me to see was a spectacle that gave him the same sort of enjoyment I was to get from the ballet "Les Sylphides." When the weather was fine, it often happened that there would come down the broad stone steps of the terrace a number of princesses out of a fairy tale, each dressed in a different pale but bright colour. Sometimes there were as few as four of these princesses; occasionally there were as many as seven. Among the colours that my uncle thought he remembered them wearing were hyacinth blue, the green of the leaves of lilies of the valley, a silvery lilac that was almost grey, a transparent red that was like one's hand when one holds it up to a strong light, primrose yellow, a watery jade green, and a gentle orange. The dresses were made of muslin, and billowed in loops and swinging circles as their wearers' little feet carried them about in what was neither a dance nor the everyday motion of ordinary people. It was as if these lovely creatures were all parts of a brave and sensitive and melancholy being, and were at once confiding in each other about their griefs, which were their common grief, and giving each other reassurance.

Some carried croquet mallets and went on to the lawn and started to play, while the others sat down on benches to watch them. But sooner or later the players would pause and forget to make the next stroke, move toward each other and stand in a group, resting their mallets on the ground, and presently forget them and let them fall, as the spectators rose from their seats to join them in their exchange of confidences. Though they appeared in the garden as often as three times a week, they always seemed to have as much to say to one another as if they met but once a year; and they were always grave as they talked. There was a wildness about them, it was impossible to tell what they would do next, one might suddenly break away from the others and waltz round the lawn in the almost visible arms of an invisible partner; but when they talked, they showed restraint, they did not weep, though what they said was so plainly sad, and they rarely laughed. What was true of one of them was true of all, for there seemed very little difference between them. All were golden-headed. The only one who could be told apart was the wearer of the lilac-grey dress. She was taller than the rest, and often stood aloof while they clustered together and swayed and spoke. Sometimes a woman in a black gown came down from the terrace and talked to this separate one.

The girls in the coloured dresses were the seven daughters of the Admiral who owned the house. My uncle saw him once, when he called on Alice Darrell to discuss with her arrangements for repairing the wall between their properties: a tall and handsome man with iron-grey hair, a probing, defensive gaze, and a mouth so sternly compressed that it was a straight line across his face. The call would never have been made had there not been business to discuss. The Admiral would have no social relations with his neighbours; nobody had ever been invited to his house. Nor, had such an invitation been sent, would Aunt Alice have accepted it, for she thought he treated his daughters abominably. She could not help smiling when she told her nephew their names, for they came straight off the Navy List: Andromeda, Cassandra, Clytie, Hera, Parthenope, Arethusa, and Persephone. But that was the only time she smiled when she spoke of them, for she thought they had been treated with actual cruelty, though not in the way that might have been supposed. They were not immured in this lonely house by a father who wanted to keep them to himself; their case was the very opposite.

The Admiral's daughters were, in effect, motherless. By Aunt Alice my Uncle Arthur was told that the Admiral's wife was an invalid and had to live in a mild climate in the West of England, but from the servants he learned that she was mad. Without a wife to soften him, the Admiral dealt with his daughters summarily by sending each of them, as she passed her seventeenth birthday, to be guided through the London season by his only sister, a wealthy woman with a house in Berkeley Square, and by giving each to the first man of reasonably respectable character who made her an offer of marriage. He would permit no delay, though his daughters, who had inheritances from a wealthy grandfather, as well as their beauty, would obviously have many suitors. These precipitate marriages were always against the brides' inclinations, for they had, strangely enough, no desire but to go on living in their lonely home.

"They are," Aunt Alice told her nephew, hesitating and looking troubled, "oddly young for their ages. I know they are not old, and that they have lived a great deal alone, since their mother cannot be with them. But they are really very young for what they are." They had yielded, it was said, only to the most brutal pressure exercised by their father. It astonished my uncle that all this was spoken of as something that had happened in the past. They did not look like grown-up ladies as they wandered in the garden, yet all but two were wives, and those two were betrothed, and some of them were already mothers. Parthenope, the one with most character, the one who had charge of the house in her father's absence, had married a North Country landowner who was reputed to be a millionaire. It was a pity that he was twice her age and had, by a dead wife, a son almost as old as she was, but a fortune is a great comfort; and none of her sisters was without some measure of that same kind of consolation. Nevertheless, their discontent could be measured by the frequency with which they returned to the house of their childhood.

The first time my uncle visited Currivel Lodge, the Admiral's seven daughters were only a spectacle for his distant enjoyment. But one day during his second visit, a year later, his aunt asked him to deliver a note for Miss Parthenope at the house next door. Another section of the wall between the properties was in need of buttresses, and the builder had to have his orders. My uncle went up to his bedroom and smoothed his hair and washed his face, a thing he had never done before between morning and night of his own accord, and when he got to the Admiral's house, he told the butler, falsely but without a tremor, that he had been told to give the note into Miss Parthenope's own hands. It did not matter to him that the butler looked annoyed at hearing this: too much was at stake. He followed the butler's offended back through several rooms full of fine furniture, which were very much like the rooms to which he was accustomed, but had a sleepy air, as if the windows were closed, though they were not. In one there were some dolls thrown down on the floor, though he had never heard that there were any children living in the house. In the last room, which opened on the stone terrace and its white and crimson roses, a women in a black dress with a suggestion of a uniform about it was sitting at an embroidery frame. She stared at him as if he presented a greater problem than schoolboys usually do, and he recognized her as the dark figure he had seen talking with the tallest of the daughters in the garden.

She took the letter from him, and he saw that the opportunity he had seized was slipping out of his grasp, so he pretended to be younger and simpler than he was, and put on the Irish brogue, which he never used at home except when he was talking to the servants or the people on the farms, but which he had found charmed the English. "May I not go out into the garden and see the young ladies?" he asked. "I have watched them from my window, and they look so pretty."

It worked. The woman smiled and said. "You're from Ireland, aren't you?" and before he could answer she exclaimed, as if defying prohibitions of which she had long been weary, "What is the harm? Yes, go out and give the note to Miss Parthenope yourself. You will know her—she is wearing grey and is the tallest." When he got out on the terrace, he saw that all seven of the Admiral's daughters were on the lawn, and his heart was like a turning windmill as he went down the stone steps. Then one of the croquet players caught sight of him—the one who was wearing a red dress, just nearer flame colour than flesh. She dropped her mallet and cried, "Oh, look, a little boy! A little red-haired boy!" and danced toward him, sometimes pausing and twirling right round, so that her skirts billowed out round her. Other voices took up the cry, and, cooing like pigeons, the croquet players closed in on him in a circle of unbelievable beauty. It was their complexions that he remembered in later life as the marvel that made them, among all the women he was ever to see, the nonpareils. Light lay on their skin as it lies on the petals of flowers, but it promised that it would never fade, that it would last forever, like the pearl. Yet even while he remarked their loveliness and was awed by it, he was disconcerted. They came so close, and it seemed as if they might do more than look at him and speak to him. It was as if a flock of birds had come down on him, and were fluttering and pecking about him; and they asked so many questions, in voices that chirped indefatigably and were sharper than the human note. "Who are you?" "You are Mrs Darrell's nephew?" "Her brother's child or her sister's?" "How old are you?" "What is your name?" "Why is your middle name Greatorex?" "Oh, what lovely hair he has—true Titian! And those round curls like coins!" "Have you sisters?" "Have they hair like yours?" Their little hands darted out and touched his hands, his cheeks, his shoulders, briefly but not pleasantly. His flesh rose in goose pimples, as it did when a moth's wing brushed his face as he lay in bed in the dark. And while their feathery restlessness poked and cheeped at him, they looked at him with eyes almost as fixed as if they were blind and could not see him at all. Their eyes were immense and very bright and shaded by lashes longer than he had ever seen; but they were so light a grey that they were as colourless as clear water running over a bed of pebbles. He was glad when the woman in the black dress called from the terrace. "Leave the boy alone!" He did not like anything about the Admiral's daughters, now he saw them at close range. Even their dresses, which had looked beautiful from a distance, repelled him. If a lady had been sitting to a portrait painter in the character of a wood nymph, she might have worn such draperies, but it was foolish to wear them in a garden, when there was nobody to see them. "Leave the boy alone!" the woman in black called again. "He has come with a letter for Parthenope."

She had not been one of the circle. Now that the others fell back, my uncle saw her standing a little way off, biting her lip and knitting her brows, as if the scene disturbed her. There were other differences, beyond her height, that distinguished her from her sisters. While they were all that was most feminine, with tiny waists and hands, and feet, she might have been a handsome and athletic boy dressed in woman's clothes for a school play. Only, of course, one knew quite well that she was not a boy. She stood erect, her arms hanging by her sides, smoothing back the muslin billows of her skirt, as if they were foolishness she would be glad to put behind her; and indeed, she would have looked better in Greek dress. Like her sisters, she had golden hair, but hers was a whiter gold. As my uncle and she went toward each other, she smiled, and he was glad to see that her eyes were a darker grey than her sisters', and were quick and glancing. He told her who he was, speaking honestly, not putting on a brogue to win her, and she smiled and held out her hand. It took her a little time to read the letter, and she frowned over it and held her forefinger to her lips, and bade him tell his aunt that she would send over an answer later in the day, after she had consulted her gardeners, and then she asked him if he would care to come into the house and drink some raspberry vinegar. As she led him across the lawn to the terrace, walking with long strides, he saw that her sisters were clustered in a group, staring up at a gutter high on the house, where a rook had perched, as if the bird were a great marvel. "Should I say good-bye to the ladies?" he asked nervously, and Parthenope answered, "No, they have forgotten you already." However, one had not. The sister who wore the light-red dress ran after him, crying, "Come back soon, little boy. Nobody ever comes into this garden except to steal our strawberries."

Parthenope took him through the silent house, pausing in the room where the dolls lay on the floor to lift them up and shut them in a drawer, and they came to a dining room, lined with pictures of great ships at war with stormy seas. There was no raspberry vinegar on the top of the sideboard—only decanters wearing labels marked with the names of adult drinks he was allowed only at Christmas and on his birthday, and then but one glass, and he always chose claret. So they opened the cupboard below, and sat down together on the carpet and peered into the darkness while he told her that he did not really want any but if it had gone astray he would be pleased to help her find it. But when the decanter turned up at the very back of the shelf (and they agreed that that was what always happened when one lost anything, and that there was no doubt that objects can move), they both had a glass, talking meanwhile of what they liked to eat and drink. Like him, she hated boiled mutton, and she, too, liked goose better than turkey. When he had finished and the talk had slowed down, he rose and put his glass on the sideboard, and offered her a hand to help her up from the floor, but she did not need it; and he gave a last look round the room, so that he would not forget it. He asked her, "Why is your chandelier tied up in a canvas bag? At home that only happens when the family is away." She answered, "Our family is away," speaking so grimly that he said, "I did not mean to ask a rude question." She told him. "You have not asked a rude question. What I meant was that all but two of us have our own homes, and those two will be leaving here soon." It would not have been right to say that she spoke sadly. But her tone was empty of all it had held when they had talked about how much better chicken tastes when you eat it with your fingers when you are out shooting. He remembered all the sad things he had heard his aunt say about her family, the sadder things he had heard from the servants. He said, "Why don't you come back with me and have tea with my aunt?" She said, smiling, "She has not asked me." And he said, "Never think of that. We are not proper English, you know; we are from Ireland, and friends come in any time." But she thanked him, sighing, so that he knew she would really have liked to come, and said that she must go back to her sisters. As the butler held the front door open for my uncle, she gave him a friendly slap across the shoulders, as an older boy might have done.

After that, my uncle never watched the Admiral's daughters again. If a glance told him that they were in the garden, he turned his back on the window. He had not liked those staring eyes that were colourless as water, and it troubled him that though some of them had children, none had said, "I have a boy, too, but he is much younger than you," for mothers always said that. He remembered Parthenope so well that he could summon her to his mind when he wished, and he could not bear to see her with these women who made him feel uneasy, because he was sure that he and she felt alike, and therefore she must be in a perpetual state of unease. So when, the very day before he was to go back to Ireland, he looked out of his bedroom window and saw her alone on the lawn, he threw up the sash and called to her; but she did not hear him.

She was absorbed in playing a game by herself, a game that he knew well. She was throwing a ball high into the air, then letting her arms drop by her sides, and waiting to the last, the very last moment, before stretching out a hand to catch it. It was a strange thing for a grown-up lady to be doing, but it did not distress him like the play-ground gambolling and chattering of her sisters. They had been like children as grownups like to think of them, silly and meaningless and mischievous. But she was being a child as children really are, sobered by all they have to put up with and glad to forget it in play. There was currently some danger that his own father was going to get a post in some foreign place and that the whole family would have to leave County Kerry for years and years; and when he and his brothers and sisters thought of this, they would go and, each one apart, would play this very same game that Parthenope was playing.

He did not want to raise his voice in a shout, in case he was overheard by his aunt or his mother. They would not understand that although Parthenope and he had met only once, they knew each other quite well. He got up from the window seat and went out of his room and down through the house and out into the garden. There was a ladder in the coach house, and he dragged it to the right part of the wall and propped it up and stopped it with stones, and climbed to the top and called "Miss Parthenope!" When she saw him, she smiled and waved at him as if she really were glad to see him again.

"Where are your sisters?" he asked cautiously.

"They have all gone away. I am going home tomorrow."

"So am I."

"Are you glad?"

"Papa will be there," he said, "and my brothers and sisters, and Garrity the groom, and my pony."

She asked him the names of his brothers and sisters, and how old they were, and where his home was; and he told her all these things and told her, too, that his father was always being sent all over the world, and that of late he and his brothers and sisters had heard talk that someday, and it might be soon, he would be sent to some foreign place for so long that they would have to go with him, and they didn't want this to happen; for though they loved him and wanted to be near him, they loved County Kerry, too. At that, she stopped smiling and nodded her head, as if to say she knew how he must feel. "But perhaps it won't happen," he said, "and then you must come and stay with us for the hunting."

He thought of her in a riding habit, and at that he noticed that she was wearing a dress such as his own mother might have worn—a dress of grey cloth, with a tight bodice and a stiffened skirt, ornamented with braid. He said, "How funny to see you dressed like other ladies. Don't you usually wear that lilac-grey muslin dress?"

She shook her head. "No. My sisters and I only wear those muslin dresses when we are together here. My sisters like them."

"Don't you?" he said, for her tone had gone blank again.

"No," she answered, "not at all."

He was glad to hear it, but it seemed horribly unfair that she should have to wear clothes she did not like, just because her sisters did; nothing of the sort happened in his own family. "Then don't wear them!" he said passionately. "You mustn't wear them! Not if you don't like them!"

"You're making your ladder wobble," she said, laughing at him, "and if you fall down, I can't climb over the wall and pick you up." She started across the lawn toward the house.

"Garrity says that you're lost if you let yourself be put upon," he cried after her, his brogue coming back to him, but honestly, because he spoke to Garrity as Garrity spoke to him. He would have liked to have the power to make her do what she ought to do, and save her from all this foolishness.

"Good-bye, good-bye," she called across the growing distance. "Be a good boy, and come back to see us next year."

"You will be here for sure?" he asked eagerly.

"Oh, yes," she promised. "We will always be back here for some time in the summer. My sisters would rather be here than anywhere in the world."

"But do you like it yourself?" he asked angrily.

It was no use. She had run up the steps to the terrace.

My uncle did not come back the next year, because his fears were realized and his father was appointed to a post in Canada. But from his aunt's letters to his mother he learned that even if he had returned to Currivel Lodge, he would not have seen Parthenope, for the Admiral sold the house later that year, as soon as his two remaining daughters went to the altar, which they did with even greater reluctance than their elder sisters. Alice Darrell's maid happened to be at the window one winter day and saw the two of them walking up and down the lawn, dressed in those strange, bright muslin gowns and wearing no mantles, though the river mist was thick, while they wept and wrung their hands. Aunt Alice felt that even if the Admiral had felt obliged to bundle all his daughters into matrimony, he should at least not have sold the house, which was the one place where they could meet and have a little nursery happiness again.

In the course of time, Uncle Arthur came back to Ireland, and went to Trinity College, Dublin, and passed into the English Civil Service, and was sent to London. The first time he went back to Currivel Lodge, he stood at his bedroom window and stared out at the croquet lawn of the house next door, and it looked very much like other croquet lawns. Under the trees two men and two women were sitting round a tea table, all of them presenting the kind of appearance, more common then than now, that suggests that nothing untoward happens to the human race. It occurred to him that perhaps his boyish imagination had made a story out of nothing, but Aunt Alice gave him back his version intact. The Admiral had really hectored his daughters into early and undesired marriages, with the most brutal disregard for their feelings, and the daughters had really been very strange girls, given to running about the garden in a sort of fancy dress and behaving like children—all except Parthenope, who was quite remarkable. She had made her mark in society since then. Well, so they all had, in a way. Their photographs were always in the papers, at one time, and no wonder, they were so very pretty. But that seemed over now, and, indeed, they must all be out of their twenties by now, even the youngest. Parthenope's triumphs, however, had been more durable. It was said that Queen Victoria greatly approved of her, and she was often at Court.

My uncle always thought of Parthenope when he was dressing for any of the grander parties to which he was invited, and he soon found his way to the opera and ascertained which was her box, but she was never at the parties, and, unless she had changed out of all recognition, never in her box at Covent Garden, either. My uncle did not wish to approach her, for he was a poor young man, far below her grandeur, and they belonged to different generations; at the least, she was twelve years older than he was. But he would have liked to see her again. Soon, however, he received an intimation that that would not be possible. One morning at breakfast he unfolded his newspaper and folded it again almost immediately, having read a single paragraph, which told him that Parthenope had met a violent death.

He had failed to meet her at parties and to see her in her opera box because she had been spending the winter abroad, taking care of two of her sisters who had both been the victims of prolonged illness. Originally, they had settled at Nice, but had found it too urban, and had moved to a hotel at Grasse, where they spent some weeks. Then a friend had found them a pleasant villa at Hyéres, and the party had started off from Grasse in two carriages. Parthenope and her sisters and a lady's maid had travelled in the first, and another maid and a courier had followed in the second. The second carriage had dropped far behind. Afterwards, the coachman remembered that he had been oddly delayed in leaving the inn where they had stopped for a midday meal; he had been told that a man was looking for him with a letter for his employers, and failing to find him had gone to a house some way down the village street. The coachman sought him but there was nobody there; and on his return to his horses he discovered that a harness strap was broken, and he had to mend it before they could resume their journey. After a sharp turn in the road, he had found himself driving into a felled tree trunk, and when the courier and the maid and the coachman got out, they could see no sign of the first carriage. It was found some hours later, abandoned on a cart track running through a wood to a river. There was no trace of any of its occupants. Later that same day the maid crawled up to a farmhouse door. Before she collapsed she was able to tell the story of an attack by masked men, who had, she thought, killed the three sisters outright because they refused to tell in which trunk their jewel cases were packed. She had escaped during the struggle, and while she was running away through the woods, she had heard terrible prolonged screaming from the riverbank. As the river was in flood, there was no hope of recovering the bodies.

After my uncle had read all the accounts of the crime that appeared in the newspapers, and had listened to all he could hear from gossiping friends, there hung, framed on the wall of his mind, a romantic picture of a highway robbery, in the style of Salvator Rosa, with coal-black shadows and highlights white on hands lifted in imploration, and he felt no emotion whatsoever. When he had opened *The Times* at breakfast, his heart had stopped. But now he felt as if he had been stopped before an outmoded and conventional picture in a private gallery by a host who valued it too highly.

A year or so later, Alice Darrell mentioned to him an odd story she had heard. It appeared that Parthenope had been carrying a great deal more jewelry than would seem necessary for a woman travelling quietly with two invalid sisters. To be sure, she had not taken all the jewelry she possessed, but she had taken enough for the value to be estimated at fifty thousand pounds; and of this not a penny could be recovered, for it was uninsured. Her husband had left the matter for her to handle, because she had sold some old jewelry and had bought some to replace it just about the time that the policy should have been renewed, but she had failed to write the necessary letter to her lawyers till the very night before the journey to Hyéres, and it was found, unposted, at the hotel in Grasse.

"Parthenope!" my uncle said. "Let an insurance policy lapse! Parthenope! I'll not believe it."

"That's just what I said," Alice Darrell exclaimed. "Any of the others, but not Parthenope. She had her hand on everything. Yet, of course, she may have changed. They are a queer family. There was the other one, you know—the one who disappeared. That was after the accident."

It seemed that another sister—Hera, Aunt Alice thought it was—had also suffered ill health, and had gone to France with a nurse, and one day her cloak and bonnet were found on the bank of a river.

"I wish that things turned out better," Aunt Alice remarked sadly. "They do sometimes, but not often enough."

This was the only criticism of life he had ever heard her utter, though she had had a sad life, constantly losing the people she loved, to tropical diseases or to wars against obscure tribes that lacked even the interest of enmity. What she uttered now made him realize that she had indeed thought Parthenope remarkable, and he said, smiling, "Why, we are making ourselves quite miserable about her, though all we know for sure is that she let an insurance policy lapse."

He did not hear of the Admiral's daughters again until after a long space of time, during which he had many other things to think about: his career, which was alternatively advanced by his brilliance and retarded by his abstracted candour; a long affair with a married woman older than himself, some others that were briefer; and his marriage, which, like his career, and for much the same reason, was neither a success nor a failure. One day when he was reading the papers at his club, he heard two men speaking of a friend who was distressed about his mother, whose behaviour had been strange since she had been left a widow. She had rejected the dower house and gone off to the Continent to travel by herself, and now refused to come back to see her family or to meet them abroad. The mother had an old Greek name, and so had a sister, who had got herself murdered for her jewels in the South of France. My uncle went on staring at his newspaper, but it was as if a door in his mind were swinging backward and forward on a broken hinge.

Many years later, when Aunt Alice was dead and my uncle was a middle-aged man, with children who were no longer children, he broke his journey home from a conference in Spain at a certain town in the southwest of France, for no other reason than that its name had always charmed him. But it proved to be a dull place, and as he sat down to breakfast at a café in the large and featureless station square, it occurred to him to ask the waiter if there were not some smaller and pleasanter place in the neighbourhood where he could spend the rest of the day and night. The waiter said that if Monsieur would take the horse-bus that started from the other side of the square in half an hour, it would take him to the village where he, the waiter, was born, and there he would find a good inn and a church that people came all the way from Paris to see. My uncle took his advice; and because his night had been wakeful, he fell asleep almost as soon as the bus started. He woke suddenly to find that the journey had ended and he was in a village which was all that he had hoped it would be.

A broad, deliberate river, winding among low wooded hills, spread its blessings at this point through a circular patch of plain, a couple of miles or so across, which was studded with farmhouses, each standing beside its deep green orchard. In the centre of this circle was a village that was no more than one long street, which looked very clean. The houses were built of stone that had been washed by the hill rains, and beside the road a brook flowed over a paved bed. There were bursts of red valerian growing from the cracks in the walls and in the yard-long bridges that crossed the brook. The street ended in a little square, where the church and the inn looked across cobblestones, shaded by pollarded limes, at the *mairie* and the post office. At the inn, my uncle took a room and slept for an hour or two in a bed smelling of the herbs with which the sheets had been washed. Then, as it was past noon, he went down to lunch, and ate some potato soup, a trout, some wood strawberries, and a slice of cheese. Afterwards, he asked the landlord how soon the church would be open, and was told that he could open it himself when he chose. The priest and his housekeeper were away until vespers, and had left the church keys at the inn.

When he went to the church, it was a long time before he unlocked the door, for there was a beautiful tympanum in the porch, representing the Last Judgement. It was clear-cut in more than one sense. There was no doubt who was saved and who was damned: there was a beatific smile on the faces of those walking in Paradise, which made it seem as if just there a shaft of sunlight had struck the dark stone. Also the edges of the carving, though the centuries had rubbed them down, showed a definition more positive than mere sharpness. Often my uncle played games when he was alone, and now he climbed on a wooden stool which was in the porch, and shut his eyes and felt the faces of the blessed, and pretended that he had been blind for a long time, and that the smiles of the blessed were striking into his darkness through his fingertips.

When he went into the church, he found, behind an oaken door, the steps that led to the top of the tower. He climbed up through darkness that was transfixed every few steps by thin shafts of light, dancing with dust, coming through the eyelet windows, and he found that though the tower was not very high, it gave a fine view of an amphitheatre of hills, green on their lower slopes with chestnut groves, banded higher with fir woods and bare turf, and crowned with shining rock. He marked some likely paths on the nearest hills, and then dropped his eyes to the village below, and looked down into the oblong garden of a house that seemed larger than the rest. At the farther end was the usual, pedantically neat French vegetable garden; then there was a screen of espaliered fruit trees; then there was a lawn framed in trees so tall and strong that it could have been guessed from them alone that not far away there was a river. The lawn was set with croquet hoops, and about them were wandering four figures in bright dresses—one hyacinth blue, one primrose yellow, one jade green, one clear light red. They all had croquet mallets in their hands, but they had turned from the game, and as my uncle watched them they drew together, resting their mallets on the ground. Some distance away, a woman in black, taller than the others, stood watching them.

When one of the croquet players let her mallet fall on the grass, and used her free hands in a fluttering gesture, my uncle left the top of the tower and went down through the darkness and shafts of light and locked the church door behind him. In the corner of the square he found what might have been the château of the village—one of those square and solid dwellings, noble out of proportion to their size, which many provincial French architects achieved in the seventeenth century. My uncle went through an iron gateway into a paved garden and found that the broad door of the house was open. He walked into the vestibule and paused, looking up the curved staircase. The pictures were as old as the house, and two had been framed to fit the recessed panels in which they hung. The place must have been bought as it stood. On the threshold of the corridor beyond, he paused again, for it smelled of damp stone, as all the back parts of his father's house in County Kerry did, at any time of the year but high summer. It struck him as a piece of good fortune for which he had never before been sufficiently grateful that he could go back to that house any time he pleased; he would be there again in a few weeks' time. He passed the open door of a kitchen, where two women were rattling dishes and pans and singing softly, and came to a closed door, which he stared at for a second before he turned the handle.

He found himself in a salon that ran across the whole breadth of the house, with three French windows opening on a stone terrace overlooking the garden. As he crossed it to the steps that led down to the lawn, he came close to a bird cage on a pole, and the scarlet parrot inside broke into screams. All the women on the lawn turned and saw him, and the tall woman in black called, "*Que voulez-vous, Monsieur?*" She had put her hand to her heart, and he was eager to reassure her, but could not think how, across that distance, to explain why he had come. So he continued to walk toward her, but could not reach her because the four others suddenly scampered toward him, crying "Go away! Go away!" Their arms flapped like bats' wings, and their voices were cracked, but, under their white hair, their faces were unlined and their eyes were colourless as water. "Go away!" shrilled the one in light red. "We know you have come to steal our strawberries. Why may we not keep our own strawberries?" But the figure in black had come forward with long strides, and told them to go on with their game, and asked again, "*Que voulez-vous, Monsieur?*"

Her hair was grey now, and her mouth so sternly compressed that it was a straight line across her face. She reminded my uncle of a particular man—her father, the Admiral—but she was not like a man, she was still a handsome and athletic boy, though a frost had fallen on him; and still it was strange that she should look like a boy, since she was also not male at all. My uncle found that now he was face to face with her, it was just as difficult to explain to her why he had come. He said, "I came to this village by chance this morning, and after

I had luncheon at the inn I went to the top of the church tower, and looked down on this garden, and recognized you all. I came to tell you that if there is anything I can do for you I will do it. I am a civil servant who has quite a respectable career, and so I can hope that I might be efficient enough to help you, if you need it."

"That is very kind," she said, and paused, and it was as if she were holding a shell to her ear and listening to the voice of a distant sea. "Very kind," she repeated. "But who are you?"

"I am the nephew of your neighbour, Mrs Darrell," said my uncle. "I brought you a letter from her, many years ago, when you were all in your garden."

Her smile broke slowly. "I remember you," she said. "You were a fatherly little boy. You gave me good advice from the top of a ladder. Why should you have found me here, I wonder? It can't be that, after all, there is some meaning in the things that happen. You had better come into the house and drink some of the cherry brandy we make here. I will get the cook to come out and watch them. I never leave them alone now."

While she went to the kitchen, my uncle sat in the salon and noted that, for all its fine furniture and all its space and light, there was a feeling that the place was dusty, the same feeling that he had noticed in the Admiral's house long ago. It is the dust of another world, he thought with horror, and the housemaids of this world are helpless against it. It settles wherever these women live, and Parthenope must live with them.

When she came back, she was carrying a tray with a slender decanter and very tiny glasses. They sat sipping the cherry brandy in silence until she said, "I did nothing wrong." He looked at her in astonishment. Of course she had done nothing wrong. Wrong was what she did not do. But she continued gravely. "When we all die, it will be found that the sum I got for the jewelry is intact. My stepson will not be a penny the worse off. Indeed, he is better off, for my husband has had my small inheritance long before it would have come to him if I had not done this."

"I knew you would have done it honestly," said my uncle. He hesitated. "This is very strange. You see, I knew things about you which I had no reason to know. I knew you had not been murdered."

Then my uncle had to think carefully. They were united by eternal bonds, but hardly knew each other, which was the reverse of what usually happened to men and women. But they might lapse into being strangers and nothing else if he showed disrespect to the faith by which she lived. He said only, "Also I knew that what you were doing in looking after your family was terrible."

She answered, "Yes. How good it is to hear somebody say that it is terrible, and to be able to answer that it is. But I had to do it. I had to get my sisters away from their husbands. They were ashamed of them. They locked them up in the care of strangers. I saw their bruises." My uncle caught his breath. "Oh," she said, desperately just, "the people who looked after them did not mean to be cruel. But they were strangers; they did not know the way to handle my sisters. And their husbands were not bad men, either. And even if they had been, I could not say a word against them, for they were cheated; my father cheated them.

They were never told the truth about my mother. About my mother and half her family." She raised her little glass of cherry brandy to her lips and nodded, to intimate that that was all she had to say, but words rushed out and she brought her glass down to her lap. "I am not telling the truth. Their husbands cheated, too.... No, I am wrong. They did not cheat. But they failed to keep their bond. Still, there is no use talking about that."

"What bond did your sisters' husbands not keep?" my uncle asked.

"They married my sisters because they were beautiful, and laughed easily, and could not understand figures. They might have considered that women who laugh easily might scream easily, and that if figures meant nothing to them, words might mean nothing, either, and that if figures and words meant nothing to them, thoughts and feelings might mean nothing, too. But these men had the impudence to feel a horror of my sisters."

She rose, trembling, and told him that he must have a sweet biscuit with his cherry brandy, and that she would get him some; they were in a cupboard in the corner of the room. Over her shoulder, she cried, "I cannot imagine you marrying a woman who was horrible because she was horrible, and then turning against her because she was horrible." She went on setting some wafers out on a plate, and he stared at the back of her head, unable to imagine what was inside it, saying to himself, "She realizes that they are horrible; there is no mitigation of her state."

When she sat down again, she said, "But it was my father's fault."

"What was your father's fault?" he asked gently, when she did not go on.

"Why, he should not have made us marry; he should not have sold our house. My sisters were happy there, and all they asked was to be allowed to go on living there, like children."

"Your father wanted his daughters to marry so that they would have someone to look after them when he was dead," my uncle told her.

"I could have looked after them."

"Come now," said my uncle, "you are not being fair. You are the same sort of person as your father. And you know quite well that if you were a man you would regard all women as incapable. You see, men of the better kind want to protect the women they love, and there is so much stupidity in the male nature and the circumstances of life are generally so confused that they end up thinking they must look after women because women cannot look after themselves. It is only very seldom that a man meets a woman so strong and wise that he cannot doubt her strength and wisdom, and realizes that his desire to protect her is really the same as his desire to gather her into his arms and partake of her glory."

Moving slowly and precisely, he took out his cardcase and was about to give her one of his cards when a thought struck him. She must have the name of his family's house in County Kerry as well as his London address, and know that he went there at Christmas and at Easter, and in the summer, too. She would be able to find him whenever she wanted him, since such bootblack service was all he could render her.

She read the card and said in an astonished whisper. "Oh, how kind, how kind." Then she rose and put it in a drawer in a *secrétaire*, which she locked with a key she took from a bag swinging from the belt of her hateful black gown. "I have to lock up everything," she said, wearily. "They mean no harm, but sometimes they get at papers and tear them up."

"What I have written on that card is for an emergency," said my uncle. "But what is there I can do now? I do not like the thought of you sitting here in exile, among things that mean nothing to you. Can I not send you out something English—a piece of furniture, a picture, some china or glass? If I were in your place, I would long for something that reminded me of the houses where I had spent my childhood."

"If you were in my place, you would not," she said. "You are very kind, but the thing that has happened to my family makes me not at all anxious to remember my childhood. We were all such pretty children. Everybody always spoke as if we were bound to be happy. And in those days nobody was frightened of Mamma—they only laughed at her, because she was such a goose. Then one thing followed another, and it became quite certain about Mamma, and then it became quite certain about the others; and now I cannot bear to think of the good times that went before. It is as if someone had known and was mocking us. But you may believe that it is wonderful for me to know that there is someone I can call on at any time. You see, I had supports, which are being taken away from me. You really have no idea how I got my sisters out here?"

My uncle shook his head. "I only read what was in the newspapers and knew it was not true."

"But you must have guessed I had helpers," she said. "There was the highway robbery to be arranged. All that was done by somebody who was English but had many connections in France, a man who was very fond of Arethusa. Arethusa is the one who spoke to you in the garden; she always wears red. This man was not like her husband; when she got worse and worse, he felt no horror for her, only pity. He has always been behind me, but he was far older than we were, and he died three years ago; and since then his lawyer in Paris has been a good friend, but now he is old, too, and I must expect him to go soon. I have made all arrangements for what is to happen to my sisters after my death. They will go to a convent near here, where the nuns are really kind, and we are preparing them for it. One or other of the nuns comes here every day to see my sisters, so that they will never have to be frightened by strange faces; and I think that if my sisters go on getting worse at the same rate as at present, they will by then believe the nuns when they say that I have been obliged to go away and will come back presently. But till that time comes, I will be very glad to have someone I can ask for advice. I can see that you are to be trusted. You are like the man who loved Arethusa. My poor Arethusa! Sometimes I think," she said absently, "that she might have been all right if it had been that man whom she had married. But no," she cried, shaking herself awake, "none of us should have married, not even me."

"Why should you not have married? asked my uncle. "That the others should not I understand. But why not you? There is nothing wrong with you."

"Is there not?" she asked. "To leave my family and my home, to stage a sham highway robbery, and later to plot and lie, and lie and plot, in order to get my mad sisters to a garden I had once noted, in my travels, as something like the garden taken from them when they were young. There is an extravagance in the means my sanity took to rescue their madness that makes the one uncommonly like the other."

"You must not think that," my uncle told her. "Your strange life forced strangeness on your actions, but you are not strange. You were moved by love, you had seen their bruises."

"Yes, I had seen their bruises," she agreed. "But," she added, hesitantly, "you are so kind that I must be honest with you. It was not only for the love of my sisters that I arranged this flight. It is also true that I could not bear my life. I was not wholly unselfish. You do not know what it is like to be a character in a tragedy. Something has happened which can only be explained by supposing that God hates you with merciless hatred, and nobody will admit it. The people nearest you stand round you saying that you must ignore this extraordinary event, you must—what were the words I was always hearing?—'keep your sense of proportion,' 'not brood on things.' They do not understand that they are asking you to deny your experiences, which is to pretend that you do not exist and never have existed. And as for the people who do not love you, they laugh. Our tragedy was so ridiculous that the laughter was quite loud. There were all sorts of really funny stories about the things my mother and sisters did before they were shut up. That is another terrible thing about being a character in a tragedy; at the same time you become a character in a farce. Do not deceive yourself," she said, looking at him kindly and sadly. "I am not a classical heroine, I am not Iphigenia or Electra or Alcestis, I am the absurd Parthenope.[2] There is no dignity in my life. For one thing, too much has happened to me. One calamity evokes sympathy; when two calamities call for it, some still comes, but less. Three calamities are felt to be too many, and when four are reported, or five, the thing is ludicrous. God has only to strike one again and again for one to become a clown. There is nothing about me which is not comical. Even my flight with my sisters has become a joke." She sipped at her glass. "My sisters' husbands and their families must by now have found out where we are. I do not think my husband ever did, or he would have come to see me. But there are many little indications that the others know, and keep their knowledge secret, rather than let loose so monstrous a scandal."

"You say your husband would have come to see you?" asked my uncle, wanting to make sure. "But that must mean he loved you."

At last the tears stood in her eyes. She said, her voice breaking, "Oh, things might have gone very well with my husband and myself, if love had been possible for me. But of course it never was."

"How wrong you are," said my uncle. "There could be nothing better for any man than to have you as his wife. If you did not know that, your husband should have made you understand it."

[2] Iphigenia and Electra, both daughters of Agammenon and Clytemnestra; Alcestis, daughter of Pelias and Anaxibia, and wife of Admetus; all are characters in Greek dramas of familial and state power.

"No, no," she said. "The fault was not in my husband or myself. It was in love, which cannot do all that is claimed for it. Oh, I can see that it can work miracles, some miracles, but not all the miracles that are required before life can be tolerable. Listen: I love my sisters, but I dare not love them thoroughly. To love them as much as one can love would be to go to the edge of an abyss and lean over the edge, farther and farther, till one was bound to lose one's balance and fall into the blackness of that other world where they live. That is why I never dared let my husband love me fully. I was so much afraid that I might be an abyss, and if he understood me, if we lived in each other, he would be drawn down into my darkness."

"But there is no darkness in you," said my uncle, "you are not an abyss, you are the solid rock."

"Why do you think so well of me?" she wondered. "Of course, you are right to some extent—I am not the deep abyss I might be. But how could I be sure of that when I was young? Every night when I lay down in bed I examined my day for signs of folly. If I had lost my temper, if I had felt more joy than was reasonable, I was like one of a tuberculous family who has just heard herself cough. Only the years that had not then passed made me sure that I was unlike my sisters, and until I knew, I had to hold myself back. I could not let the fine man who was my husband be tempted into my father's fault."

"What was your father's fault?" asked my uncle, for the second time since he had entered that room.

Again her disapproval was absolute, her eyes were like steel. But this time she answered at once, without a moment's hesitation: "Why, he should not have loved my mother."

"But you are talking like a child!" he exclaimed. "You cannot blame anyone for loving anyone."

"Did you ever see him?" she asked, her eyes blank because they were filled with a distant sight. "Yes? You must have been only a boy, but surely you say that he was remarkable. And he had a mind, he was a mathematician, he wrote a book on navigation that was thought brilliant; they asked him to lecture to the Royal Society. And one would have thought from his face that he was a giant of goodness and strength. How could such a man love such a woman as my mother? It was quite mad, the way he made us marry. How could he lean over the abyss of her mind and let himself be drawn down into that darkness?"

"Do not let your voice sink to a whisper like that," my uncle begged her. "It—it—"

"It frightens you," she supplied.

"But have you," he pressed her, "no feeling for your mother?"

"On yes," she said, her voice breaking. "I loved my mother very much. But when she went down into the darkness, I had to say good-bye to her or I could not have looked after my sisters." It seemed as if she was going to weep, but she clung to her harshness and asked again, "How could my father love such a woman?"

My uncle got up and knelt in front of her chair and took her trembling hands in his. "There is no answer, so do not ask the question."

"I must ask it," she said. "Surely it is blasphemy to admit that one can ask questions to which there are no answers. I must ask why my father leaned over the abyss of my mother's mind and threw himself into it, and dragged down victim after victim with him—not only dragging them down but manufacturing them for that sole purpose, calling them out of nothingness simply so that they could fall and fall. How could he do it? If there is not an answer—"

He put his hand over her lips. "He cannot have known that she was mad when he begot his children."

Her passion had spent itself in her question. She faintly smiled as she said, "No, but I never liked the excuse that he and my sisters' husbands made for themselves. They all said that at first they had simply thought their wives were rather silly. I could not have loved someone whom I thought rather silly. Could you?"

"It is not what I have done," said my uncle. "May I have some more cherry brandy?"

"I am so glad you like it," she said, suddenly happy. "But you have given me the wrong glass to fill. This is mine."

"I knew that," he told her. "I wanted to drink from your glass."

"I would like to drink from yours," she said, and for a little time they were silent. "Tell me," she asked meekly, as if now she had put herself in his hands, "do you think it has been wrong for me to talk about what has happened to me? When I was at home they always said it was bad to brood over it."

"What nonsense," said my uncle. "I am sure that it was one of the major misfortunes of Phèdre and Bérénice that they were unable to read Racine's clear-headed discussions of their miseries."[3]

"You are right," said Parthenope. "Oh, how kind Racine was to tragic people! He would not allow for a moment that they were comic. People at those courts must have giggled behind their hands at poor Bérénice, at poor Phèdre. But he ignored them. You are kind like Racine." There was a tapping on the glass of the French window, and her face went grey. "What has happened now? Oh, what has happened now?" she murmured to herself. It was the cook who had tapped, and she was looking grave.

Parthenope went out and spoke with her for a minute, and then came back, and again the tears were standing in her eyes. "I thought I might ask you to stay all day with me," she said. "I thought we might dine together. But my sisters cannot bear it that there is a stranger here. They are hiding in the raspberry canes, and you must have heard them screaming. Part of that noise comes from the parrot, but part from them. It sometimes takes hours to get them quiet. I cannot help it; you must go."

He took both her hands and pressed them against his throat, and felt it swell as she muttered, "Good-bye."

But as he was going through the paved garden to the gateway he heard her call "Stop! Stop!" and she was just behind him, her skirts lifted over her ankles so that she could take her long strides. "The strangest thing," she said, laughing.

[3] The French dramatist Jean Racine wrote *Phèdre* (1677) and *Bérénice* (1670)

"I have not told you the name by which I am known here." She spelled it out to him as he wrote it down in his diary, and turned back toward the house, exclaiming, "What a thing to forget!" But then she swung back again, suddenly pale, and said, "But do not write to me. I am only giving you the name so that if I send you a message you will be able to answer it. But do not write to me."

"Why not?" he asked indignantly. "Why not?"

"You must not be involved in my life," she said. "There is a force outside the world that hates me and all my family. If you wrote to me too often it might hate you, too."

"I would risk that," he said, but she cried, covering her eyes, "No, no, by being courageous you are threatening my last crumb of happiness. If you stay a stranger, I may be allowed to keep what I have of you. So do as I say."

He made a resigned gesture, and they parted once more. But as she got to her door, he called to her to stop and hurried back. "I will not send you anything that will remind you of your home," he said, "but may I not send you a present from time to time—some stupid little thing that will not mean much but might amuse you for a minute or two?"

She hesitated but in the end nodded. "A little present, a very little present," she conceded. "And not too often." She smiled like the saved in the sculpture in the church, and slowly closed the door on him.

But when he was out in the square and walking toward the inn, he heard her voice crying again, "Stop! Stop!" This time she came quite close to him and said, as if she were a child ashamed to admit to a fault, "There is another thing that I would like to ask of you. You said that I might write to you if I wanted anything, and I know that you meant business things—the sort of advice men give women. But I wonder if your kindness goes beyond that; you are so very kind. I know all about most dreadful things in life, but I know nothing about death. Usually I think I will not mind leaving this world, but just now and then, if I wake up in the night, particularly in winter, when it is very cold, I am afraid that I may be frightened when I die."

"I fear that, too, sometimes," he said.

"It seems a pity, too, to leave this world, in spite of the dreadful things that happen in it," she went on. "There are things that nothing can spoil—the spring and the summer and the autumn."

"And, indeed, the winter, too," he said.

"Yes, the winter, too," she said and looked up at the amphitheatre of hills round the village. "You cannot think how beautiful it is here when the snow has fallen. But, of course, death may be just what one has been waiting for; it may explain everything. But still, I may be frightened when it comes. So if I do not die suddenly, if I have warning of my death, would it be a great trouble for you to come and be with me for a little?"

"As I would like to be with you always, I would certainly want to be with you then," he said. "And if I have notice of my death and you are free to travel, I will ask you to come to me."

My uncle found that he did not want to go back to the inn just then, and he followed a road leading up to the foothills. There he climbed one of the paths he had remarked from the top of the church tower, and which he got to the bare rock, he sat down and looked at the village beneath him till the twilight fell. On his return to London, he painted a water-colour of the view of the valley as he recollected it, and pasted it in a book, which he kept by his bedside. From time to time, some object in the window of an antique shop or a jeweller's would bring Parthenope to his mind, and he would send it to her. The one that pleased him as most fitting was a gold ring in the form of two leaves, which was perhaps Saxon. She acknowledged these presents in brief letters; and it delighted him that often her solemn purpose of brevity broke down and she added an unnecessary sentence or two, telling him of something that had brightened her day—of a strayed fawn she had found in her garden, or a prodigious crop of cherries, which had made her trees quite red. But after some years these letters stopped. When he took into account how old she was, and by how many years she had been the elder, he realized that probably she had died. He told himself that at least she had enjoyed the mercy of sudden death, and presently ceased to think of her. It was as if the memory of her were too large to fit inside his head; he felt actual physical pain when he tried to recollect her. This was the time when such things as the finest buttercup field near London and the tomb of Captain Vancouver seemed to be all that mattered to him. But from the day when he heard the girl at the inn called by the name of his Parthenope, he again found it easy to think of her; and he told me about her very often during the five years that passed before his death.

Vera Brittain
· 1893 – 1970

A novelist, polemicist, poet, biographer and journalist, Vera Brittain was raised in relative comfort in Buxton, in the North of England. She defied family convention and in 1914 took up an exhibition at Somerville

College, Oxford; but her life and her studies were rudely interrupted by the war, during which she served as a V.A.D. in Malta and France. Returning to Oxford after the war, she became a close companion of Winifred Holtby and, on Holtby's early death, published Testament of Friendship (1940) in commemoration of her friend. A pacifist and a feminist, Vera Brittain wrote numerous articles and books on women's position in society, including Women's Work in Modern England (1928) and Lady into Woman (1953). The author of much journalism (the Manchester Guardian and Time and Tide), she wrote twenty-nine volumes in all; her impressive list includes Testament of Youth (published in 1933 and containing an account of her struggle for education, her adoption of feminism and her experience of the war) and Testament of Experience (1957).

The following extract is taken from Testament of Youth (Victor Gollancz, London, 1933) and reveals the author's increasing discomfort with her hard won and privileged existence at Oxford while the country is at war.

From

Testament of Youth

CHAPTER III
OXFORD VERSUS WAR

AUGUST, 1914

GOD said: "Men have forgotten Me;
The souls that sleep shall wake again,
And blinded eyes be taught to see."

So, since redemption comes through pain,
He smote the earth with chastening rod,
And brought destruction's lurid reign;

But where His desolation trod,
The people in their agony
Despairing cried: "There is no God!"
V. B. 1914.
From Verses of a V.A.D.[1]

I

MY diary for August 3rd, 1914, contains a most incongruous mixture of war and tennis.

---

[1] A member of the Voluntary Aid Detachment, men and especially women, trained in first aid and nursing, who served with the armed forces during the First World War.

The day was Bank Holiday, and a tennis tournament had been arranged at the Buxton Club. I had promised to play with my discouraged but still faithful suitor, and did not in the least want to forgo the amusement that I knew this partnership would afford me—particularly as the events reported in the newspapers seemed too incredible to be taken quite seriously.

"I do not know," I wrote in my diary, "how we all managed to play tennis so calmly and take quite an interest in the result. I suppose it is because we all know so little of the real meaning of war that we are so indifferent. B.[2] and I had to owe 30. It was good handicapping as we had a very close game with everybody."

In spite of my vague memories of the South African campaigns, Spion Kop[3] and Magersfontein[4] were hardly more real to me than the battles between giants and mortals in the Andrew Lang fairy-books[5] that I began to read soon afterwards. My father had taken Edward[6] and myself round Macclesfield in a cab on Mafeking Night,[7] and I had a confused recollection of fireworks and bonfires and excited shouting which were never clearly distinguished in my mind from the celebrations for Edward the Seventh's postponed coronation.

Throughout July, and especially after the failure of the Home Rule Conference and the agitation over the Dublin shooting, there had been prayers in all the churches for salvation from the danger of civil war in Ireland, and to those of us who, wrapped up in our careers or our games or our love-affairs, had paid no attention to the newspapers, the direction from which the storm was rolling was quite unexpected. At St. Monica's, Miss Heath Jones, with the accurate foresight of the vigilant, had endeavoured to prepare our sceptical minds for disasters that she believed to be very near; I remembered her gravity in 1911 at the time of the Agadir crisis, and the determination with which, when she and my aunt were visiting Buxton a year or two earlier, she had made me accompany her to the local theatre to see a play that I had thought crude and ridiculous, called *An Englishman's Home*. At school we had treated her obsession with the idea of a European War as one of those adult preoccupations to which the young feel so superior. "She's got her old German mania again," we said.

[2] An admirer. B. proposed marriage to Vera Brittain but she turned him down.
[3] During the Boer War Spion Kop was taken by Britain in January 1900, but proved too costly to hold.
[4] The Battle of Magersfontein, 11 December 1899, occurred during the 'Black Week' at the start of the Boer War, and was led by Lord Methuen. It involved heavy British losses, including the death of General Wauchope.
[5] Andrew Lang (1844–1912); poet, essayist and folklorist, best remembered for his compilation of fairy stories which helped revive interest in the genre.
[6] Edward Harold Brittain (1895–1918), Vera Brittain's brother. Although a talented musician, when the war began he insisted on fighting and obtained the reluctant agreement of his father. Badly injured in 1915, he was awarded the Military Cross. He returned to fight in Italy and was killed on 15 July 1918.
[7] This celebrated an event in the Boer War (1899–1902) between Britain and the Dutch Boer Republic in South Africa. During this war the town of Mafeking was heroically held by Colonel Baden-Powell, until its relief by British forces in February 1900.

But when I arrived home warm and excited from the amusing stimulus of the tournament, the War was brought nearer than it had yet been by the unexpected appearance of Edward—whom I had supposed to be at Aldershot[8]—still wearing his O.T.C.[9] uniform.

The previous midnight, he told me, they had had orders from the War Office to disband and vanish as quickly as possible; the cooks and military apparatus were required for purposes more urgent than schoolboy manoeuvres. He had made his way home between southern trains congested and disorganised by troops hastening to join their regiments, leaving a few seniors—such as Roland[10]—to clear up the camp.

A sudden chill momentarily banished my self-satisfaction as I saw him looking so handsome and fit and efficient; that brief misgiving was my first realisation that a war of the size which was said to be impending was unlikely to remain excitingly but securely confined to the columns of newspapers. So I made myself face what seemed the worst that could possibly happen to us.

"I was glad to see him back," I wrote of Edward that evening, "though if matters become extreme it is not impossible that he being a member of the O.T.C. may be called up for home defence."

After that events moved, even in Buxton, very quickly. The German cousins of some local acquaintances left the town in a panic. My parents rushed over in the car to familiar shops in Macclesfield and Leek, where they laid in stores of cheese, bacon and butter under the generally shared impression that by next week we might all be besieged by the Germans. Wild rumours circulated from mouth to mouth; they were more plentiful than the newspapers, over which a free fight broke out on the station platform every time a batch came by train from London or Manchester. Our elderly cook, who had three Reservist sons, dissolved into continuous tears and was too much upset to prepare the meals with her usual competence; her young daughter-in-law, who had had a baby only the previous Friday, became hysterical and had to be forcibly restrained from getting up and following her husband to the station. One or two Buxton girls were hurriedly married to officers summoned to unknown destinations. Pandemonium swept over the town. Holiday trippers wrestled with one another for the *Daily Mail*; habitually quiet and respectable citizens struggled like wolves for the provisions in the food-shops, and vented upon the distracted assistants their dismay at learning that all prices had suddenly gone up.

My diary for those few days reflects *The Times* in its most pontifical mood. "Germany has broken treaty after treaty, and disregarded every honourable tie with other nations.... Germany has destroyed the tottering hopes of peace.... The great fear is that our bungling Government will declare England's neutrality....

8 Military base.
9 Officer's Training Corps.
10 Roland A. Leighton (1895–1915); Vera Brittain's first love. He attended Uppingham School with Edward, and was a star pupil. He first met Vera Brittain when staying with the Brittain family at Easter 1914. Like Edward, he fought in the First World War, and was killed in Louvencourt on 23 December 1915.

If we at this critical juncture refuse to help our friend France, we should be guilty of the grossest treachery."

I prefer to think that my real sentiments were more truly represented by an entry written nearly a month later after the fabulously optimistic reports of the Battle of Le Cateau. I had been over to Newcastle-under-Lyme to visit the family dentist, and afterwards sat for an hour in a tree-shadowed walk called The Brampton and meditated on the War. It was one of those shimmering autumn days when every leaf and flower seems to scintillate with light, and I found it "very hard to believe that not far away men were being slain ruthlessly, and their poor disfigured bodies heaped together and crowded in ghastly indiscrimination into quickly provided common graves as though they were nameless vermin.... It is impossible," I concluded, "to find any satisfaction in the thought of 25,000 slaughtered Germans, left to mutilation and decay; the destruction of men as though beasts, whether they be English, French, German or anything else, seems a crime to the whole march of civilisation."

Only that day I had heard from my dentist that a hundred thousand Russians had been landed in England; "a whole trainful of them," I reported, "is said to have passed through Stoke, so that is why the Staffordshire people are so wise." But when I returned to Buxton I learnt that a similar contingent had been seen in Manchester, and for a few days the astonishing ubiquitousness of the invisible Russians formed a topic of absorbing interest at every tea-table throughout the country.

By the time, however, that we started believing in Russians, England had become almost accustomed to the War. On the night that the British ultimatum to Germany expired, I went up to Higher Buxton for a meeting of the University Extension Committee,[11] to which I had recently been elected; we took only a moment to decide to do nothing until the never very ardent local zest for learning re-emerged from its total eclipse by the European deluge, so I spent the rest of the evening in wandering round the town. I read, with a feeling that I had been transported back into an uglier century, the mobilisation order on the door of the Town Hall; I joined the excited little group round the Post Office to watch a number of local worthies who had suddenly donned their Territorial uniforms and were driving importantly about in motor-cars with their wives or their chauffeurs at the wheel. Later, on my way home, I found the Pavilion Gardens deserted, and a depressed and very much diminished band playing lugubriously to rows of empty chairs.

My feet ached, and my head whirled dizzily from the vain endeavour to take in what was happening. To me and my contemporaries, with our cheerful confidence in the benignity of fate, War was something remote, unimaginable, its monstrous destructions and distresses safely shut up, like the Black Death and the Great Fire, between the covers of history books. In spite of the efforts of Miss

[11] The two aims of the University Extension Committee were: 1. To extend university education to women (Vera Brittain's involvement with the Committee gave her the confidence to apply to Oxford. She also lectured for the Committee before going to university.) 2. As an adult education movement, it aimed to bridge the divide between academia and politics.

Heath Jones and other intelligent teachers, "current events" had remained for us unimportant precisely because they were national; they represented something that must be followed in the newspapers but would never, conceivably, have to be lived. What really mattered were not these public affairs, but the absorbing incidents of our own private lives—and now, suddenly, the one had impinged upon the other, and public events and private lives had become inseparable.... Uneasily I recalled a passage from *Daniel Deronda* that I had read in comfortable detachment the year before:

> "There comes a terrible moment to many souls when the great movement of the world, the larger destinies of mankind, which have lain aloof in newspapers and other neglected reading, enter like an earthquake into their own lives—when the slow urgency of growing generations turns into the trend of an invading army or the dire clash of civil war.... Then it is that the submission of the soul to the Highest is tested and ... life looks out from the scene of human struggle with the awful face of duty."

Edward, whose risks, whatever happened, were likely to be greater than mine, took the whole situation more calmly, as he always took everything. On that evening of August 4th he had gone serenely to the local Hippodrome with a Buxton friend, Maurice Ellinger, who had been with him at school. Maurice was a cousin of the musical comedy actress, Desirée Ellinger, who in those days often stayed in Buxton, a tiny dark doll of a girl about my own age. Her real name was Dorothy; she seemed very childish and often came to our house to sing, in the lovely young voice which she then intended for Grand Opera, Elizabeth's Prayer from *Tannhäuser* or the Jewel Song from *Faust* to my capricious accompaniment.

Already the two boys were discussing, though quite vaguely, the possibilities of enlisting. When they returned from the Hippodrome they brought back a "Late Special" which told us that no answer had been received from Germany, and Edward related, with much amusement, how he had seen a German waiter thrown over the wall of the Palace Hotel.

For the next few weeks we all suffered from the epidemic of wandering about that had seized everyone in the town. After the tearing-up of the "scrap of paper," the *Daily Mail* had a heart-ravishing leader called "The Agony of Belgium" which made us feel guilty and miserable. At home the atmosphere was electric with family rows, owing to Edward's expressed wish to "do something." The suggestions put forward with such authoritarian impressiveness by the Headmaster of Uppingham and the O.T.C. organisers had already served their purpose in the national exploitation of youth by its elders; the "Three Musketeers," like so many others, were not only willing but anxious to risk their lives in order to save the face of a Foreign Secretary who had committed his country to an armed policy without consulting it beforehand.

My father vehemently forbade Edward, who was still under military age, to join anything whatsoever. Having himself escaped immersion in the public-school tradition, which stood for militaristic heroism unimpaired by the damping exercise of reason, he withheld his permission for any kind of military training, and ended by taking Edward daily to the mills to divert his mind from the War. Needless to say, these uncongenial expeditions entirely failed of their desired effect, and constant explosions—to which, having inherited so many of my father's characteristics, I seemed only to add by my presence—made our house quite intolerable. A new one boiled up after each of Edward's tentative efforts at defiance, and these were numerous, for his enforced subservience seemed to him synonymous with everlasting disgrace. One vague application for a commission which he sent to a Notts and Derby regiment actually was forwarded to the War Office—"from which," I related with ingenuous optimism, "we are expecting to hear every post."

When my father discovered this exercise of initiative, his wrath and anxiety reached the point of effervescence. Work of any kind was quite impossible in the midst of so much chaos and apprehension, and letters to Edward from Roland, describing his endeavours to get a commission in a Norfolk regiment, did nothing to ease the perpetual tension. Even after the result of my Oxford Senior came through, I abandoned in despair the Greek textbooks that Roland had lent me. I even took to knitting for the soldiers, though only for a very short time; utterly incompetent at all forms of needlework, I found the simplest bed-socks and sleeping-helmets altogether beyond me. "Oh, how I wish I could wake up in the morning," concludes one typical day's entry describing these commotions, "to find this terrible war the dream it seems to me to be!"

2

FEW of humanity's characteristics are more disconcerting than its ability to reduce world-events to its own level, wherever this may happen to lie. By the end of August, when Liège and Namur had fallen, and the the misfortunes of the British Army were extending into the Retreat from Mons, the ladies of the Buxton élite had already set to work to provincialise the War.

At the First Aid and Home Nursing classes they cluttered about the presiding doctor like hens round a barnyard cock, and one or two representatives of "the set," who never learnt any of the bandages correctly themselves, went about showing everybody else how to do them. In order to have something to take me away from the stormy atmosphere at home, I went in for and passed both of these elementary examinations, at which stout "patients," sitting on the floor with flushed and worried faces, were treated for various catastrophies by palpitating and still stouter "nurses."

An hotel in the main street, Spring Gardens, was turned into a Red Cross Supply Depôt, where "helpers" went to listen to the gossip that would otherwise have been carried on more privately over tea-tables. They wasted so much material in the amateur cutting-out of monstrous shirts and pyjamas, that in the end a humble local dressmaker whom my mother employed for our summer cottons had to be called in to do the real work, while the polite female society of Buxton stalked up and down the hotel rooms, rolled a few bandages, and talked about the inspiration of helping one's country to win the War. One or two would-be leaders of fashion paraded continually through the town in new Red Cross uniforms. Dressed in their most elaborate lace underclothing, they offered themselves as patients to would-be bandagers and bed-makers, and one of them disliked me intensely because, in a zestful burst of vigour, I crumpled the long frills of her knickers by tucking them firmly into the bed.

Already my link with Oxford had given me the ability to regard local scrambles and squabbles over the Home Nursing classes, and the Supply Depôt, and the newly-opened Red Cross convalescent hospital, with an amused detachment of which I had not been capable so long as Buxton had seemed to me a Nazareth whence no good thing and no worth-while person was ever likely to emerge. This sense of release from the strain of the first shattering weeks increased considerably after I had received another letter from Roland, who wrote that his application for a commission had been refused on account of imperfect eyesight—a defect which his youthful vanity had hitherto concealed from me. He had tried in vain the infantry, the artillery, and the Army Service Corps, and though he was still endeavouring to get the objection to his eyesight removed, the possibility that he would be at Oxford with me after all came once more into the foreground.

"Come what may," he told me in sudden enthusiasm after hearing that I was safely through my Oxford Senior, "I *will* go now. And I look forward to facing a hedge of chaperons and Principals with perfect equanimity if I may be allowed to see something of you on the other side."

My heart rejoiced absurdly, but I made one of my spasmodic resolutions to be sceptical.

"I don't think I am ever likely to marry as I am too hard to please... " I informed my diary after going to one of the numerous local weddings that followed the outbreak of War. "I would be satisfied with nothing less than a mutually comprehensive loving companionship. I could not endure to be constantly propitiating any man, or to have a large range of subjects on which it was quite impossible to talk to him."

In the early autumn, Edward and I went to stay for a week at St. Monica's, for I wanted to buy some new clothes in London—where the numerous flags fluttering above the river made me childishly pleased that we had so many Allies—and Edward, after what seemed like an eternity of perturbation but was really only a few weeks after the outbreak of War, had at last been given reluctant permission by my father to apply to the Senior O.T.C. at Oxford for training as an officer.

It was a very bright, clear September in which the British and French Armies won their decisive victories on the Marne and the Aisne. "ALLIES ADVANCING!" triumphantly announced the placards which told us that Paris had been saved, but though the news sent a shudder of relief through London, the air was thicker than ever with dramatic and improbable rumours. Stories of atrocities mingled with assertions that in ten days' time the Austrian Emperor would be suing for peace and in fourteen the Kaiser fleeing from his people. Edward, while waiting vainly for news from Oxford, composed a violin ballade;

he and I were plunged into gloom by a fresh though inaccurate rumour that
Fritz Kreisler, his favourite violinist, had been killed on the Austrian front, but
his anxiety lasted longer than mine, for I found St. Monica's garden a most peaceful
and appropriate place in which to soliloquise about Roland. He was, I told myself,
"a unique experience in my existence; I never think definitely of him as man
or boy, as older or younger, taller or shorter than I am, but always of him as a
mind in tune with mine, in which many of the notes are quite different from
mine but are all in the same key."

Whether it was really true at that time that Roland represented to me
only a congenial mind, I cannot now determine. If it was, it did not remain
so for very much longer. One afternoon during a game of golf when we had
returned to Buxton, Edward and I discovered a fairy ring; I stood in it, and
quite suddenly found myself wishing that Roland and I might become lovers,
and marry. Edward asked me to tell him my wish. I replied: "I'll tell you if you
ask me again in five years' time, for by then the wish will have come true or be
about to come true, or it will never come true at all."

Although we had examined, only a day or two before, some Press
photographs of the damage done by the German bombardment of Rheims,
we still talked as though our lifelong security had not been annihilated and
time would go on always for those whom we loved. And it was just then
that Roland wrote that he had, after all, some chance of a commission in a
Norfolk regiment.

"Anyhow," he told me, "I don't think in the circumstances I could easily
bring myself to endure a secluded life of scholastic vegetation. It would seem
a somewhat cowardly shirking of my obvious duty.... I feel that I am meant to take
active part in this War. It is to me a very fascinating thing—something, if often
horrible, yet very ennobling and very beautiful, something whose elemental
reality raises it above the reach of all cold theorising. You will call me a militarist.
You may be right."

"Scholastic vegetation," hurt just a little; it seemed so definitely to put
me outside everything that now counted in life, as well as outside his
own interests, and his own career. I felt it altogether contrary to his professed
feminism—but then, so was the War; its effect on the women's cause was
quite dismaying.

"Women get all the dreariness of war, and none of its exhilaration," I
wrote in reply. "This, which you say is the only thing that counts at present,
is the one field in which women have made no progress—perhaps never will
(though Olive Schreiner[12] thinks differently). I sometimes feel that work at
Oxford, which will only bear fruit in the future and lacks the stimulus of direct
connection with the War, will require a restraint I am scarcely capable of. It is
strange how what we both so worked for should now seem worth so little."

Obviously I was suffering, like so many women in 1914, from an inferiority
complex. I did not know that only a week or two before his letter, he had

---

[12] Olive Schreiner (1855–1920); novelist and polemicist, a pioneer feminist, whose best
known novel, *The Story of an African Farm*, appeared in 1883.

written one of his curiously prophetic poems, "I walk alone," which certainly did not suggest that I and my work no longer counted. It bears, I think, only one interpretation—that he visualised me as having fulfilled those ambitions of which we were always talking and writing, but pictured himself as dead.

Actually, he went to Norwich about a fortnight later and was gazetted to the Norfolks shortly afterwards. But at the beginning of October, when I was getting ready to go to Somerville, neither Edward nor Roland nor Victor, who lived at Hove and had periodically tackled various battalions of the Royal Sussex Regiment, seemed much nearer commissions than they had been in August. Though all three had definitely decided not to go up to their various colleges, the prospect, which at moments had come near, of the War affecting me personally, seemed once again to become quite remote.

3

S O I went up to Oxford, and tried to forget the War. At first, though Edward should have gone up the day that I did and Roland the day after, I succeeded pretty well.

"This is an important step I am taking, the biggest since I left school, perhaps the biggest I have ever taken," I reflected with the consoling priggishness that then sustained me through the initial stages of every new experience: "But it does not do to dwell overmuch on the responsibilities such a decision as I made a year ago will now begin to involve, but rather to take them up as they come, and throughout them all remain true to myself and my ideals."

As soon as I arrived at Somerville, I was dismayed to learn that I had to take Responsions Greek in December and Pass Moderations the following June,[13] instead of embarking, as I had fondly imagined, straight away upon English. The unwelcome discovery was made the more bitter by the fact that my Classical tutor obviously attributed my lack of Greek to laziness, instead of to a complete inability to understand why the Principal, after learning the result of my Oxford Senior, had advised me to study it.

"Oh, how many better ways I might have chosen to get into Oxford than the ones I did in my ignorance choose!" I lamented to my diary; "How much better prepared I might easily have been!"

But my perturbation quickly evaporated as soon as I emerged from the first confusion of newness, and drifted into the company of Norah H., a first-year student from Winchester, who had come up to college chiefly because she was bored by the Cathedral set. Our mutual detestation of small-town snobberies made us friends for the time being, and together we observed and discussed the more interesting personalities of the different Years.

"There are," I observed, "two classes of second- and third-year people, (1) those who thoroughly examine every atom of you, (2) those who do not look

[13] The first of three examinations which must be passed by candidates for the BA Degree at Oxford.

at you at all; and appear perfectly oblivious of your presence even if you get in their way. Of the two I prefer the former."

Several potentially interesting young women were then in their last year at Somerville. They included Charis Ursula Barnett, now Mrs. Sidney Frankenburg and the author of numerous books and articles on birth-control and the rearing of children; Margaret Chubb, who soon afterwards became Mrs. Geoffrey Pyke and is now Secretary of the National Birth Control Association; Muriel Jaegar, subsequently the writer of several intelligent novels; Jeannie Petrie, daughter of the celebrated Egyptologist, and Dorothy L. Sayers, who dominated her group at college, and does so still by the fame of her vigorous detective stories.

I took an immediate liking to Dorothy Sayers, who was affable to freshers and belonged to the "examine-every-atom-of-you" type. A bouncing, exuberant young female who always seemed to be preparing for tea-parties, she could be seen at almost any hour of the day or night scuttling about the top floor of the new Maitland building with a kettle in her hand and a little checked apron fastened over her skirt. She belonged to the Bach Choir, which I too had joined, and her unconcealed passion for Sir Hugh—then Doctor—Allen was a standing joke in college. During the practices of the Verdi Requiem, which we were preparing to sing in the Easter term, she sat among the mezzo-contraltos and gazed at him with wide, adoring eyes as though she were in church worshipping her only God. But a realistic sense of humour always saved her from becoming ridiculous, and at the Going-Down Play given by her Year the following summer, she caricatured her idol with triumphant accuracy and zest.

Against one of these Third-Years, a plain, mature-looking girl with penetrating eyes, who wore high-collared blouses and knew how to put freshers in their places, I conceived the strong prejudice natural to the snubbed after meeting her at a tea-party to which I had been invited by a friendly senior. Ten minutes after the introduction, she suddenly turned to me and inquired witheringly: "*What* is your name? I wasn't paying any attention when it was told me." Infatuated still by the glamour of Oxford, I did not remark as I might have done how closely the manners of Third-Years to First-Years resembled those of the Buxton élite to persons outside "the set." But I noted in my diary that evening that the Principal was "not nearly so condescending as one or two of the third-year people."

I soon found that a far more persistent and disturbing centre of interest than any third-year student was Agnes Elizabeth Murray, Professor Gilbert Murray's[14] beautiful daughter, whose presence relegated her second-year contemporaries to impersonal mediocrity. Wildly brilliant and fiercely in love with life, she did not in the least suggest her mournful fate of early death. At college she had not yet acquired the lovely elegance which for a short time after the War caused her to shine like a bright meteor amid the constellation of humbler stars at the League of Nations Union. Her eccentric clothes were untidy, and her straight black hair was often unkempt, but she strode like a young goddess through the Somerville students and condescended to notice very few of them outside a small group which included her devoted friend, Phyllis Siepmann. They were

[14] Gilbert Murray (1866–1957); perhaps the most brilliant Greek scholar and translator of his generation in Britain.

a tragically predestined couple, for Phyllis died before Elizabeth, in 1920—as the result, I believe, of an illness due to war-work.

Norah and I blinked our eyes with proper reverence at these radiant lights, but we discussed with less respectful frankness the members of our own first year, and particularly a trio which later co-opted me as a fourth—an English scholar whom we all knew as "E. F.," Marjorie B., afterwards a teacher, and Theresa S., a fair, gay, half-Belgian girl, who developed into my one real friend amongst these 1914 contemporaries. "E. F." was subsequently to fulfil in appropriate fashion her early promise, for she became a don at a famous women's college and a distinguished authority on Marlowe, but, like many other successful academics, she was the source in her student days of a good deal of secret amusement.

A slight girl with fine, clear-cut features, smooth dark hair and dreamy, humourless eyes, she bore a strong resemblance to Gwen Ffrangçon-Davies, the actress, and went about the corridors with an expression of earnest pursuit. Her attitude towards Marlowe was mystical, and though she never quite reached the point of putting it into words, we suspected her of a private belief in herself as his reincarnation. A more incongruous embodiment of that roystering taverner it would be difficult to imagine, for "E. F." then possessed a soft, precise voice and a deferential manner to conspicuous seniors. Her special goddesses belonged to an eclectic group known as M.A.S. (Mutual Admiration Society), the members of which had made a corner in literary aspirations. They took themselves very seriously, and apparently do so still, for only a year or two ago one of them wrote to me to protest that in a popular article on Somerville novelists I had underestimated their subsequent achievements.

4

IN spite of the prosaic demands of Greek verbs and the tedium of ploughing with a "crib" through the *Alkestis* of Euripides almost before I knew the Greek alphabet, I spent my first few weeks at Somerville in a state of exhilaration, "half-delightful, half-disturbing, wholly exciting." I had never known anything so consistently stimulating as that urgent, hectic atmosphere, in which a number of highly strung young women became more neurotic and *exaltées* than ever through over-work and insufficient sleep.

Like the half dozen freshers with whom I consorted, I rarely went to bed before 2 a.m. through the whole of that term. Having hitherto been thrown for speculative companionship chiefly upon my own society, I found cocoa-parties and discussions on religion, genius, dons and Third-Years far too enthralling to be abandoned merely for the sake of a good night's rest. After years of regular ten-o'clock bedtime in Buxton, the short nights told on me very quickly, but I never dreamed of attributing my excitement to fatigue.

Early in the term, with a heart swelling with pride, I learnt from Norah that I was considered one of the "lions" of my year. This information inspired me with a pleasant sense of mental and moral superiority, of which I was particularly aware at a certain tea-party where, as I recorded in my diary, "we talked religion most of the time. Miss G. and Miss P. were there too—two simple souls who evidently had not thought much for themselves, and who cannot—yet, at any rate—stand alone, or ever conceive the idea of doing so.

"It is so vastly different from me, who think one has no right to have great and intimate friends unless one can stand alone first," I reflected with satisfaction. "The time may come—in fact does come to everyone—when we have to decide something important on our own, be responsible perhaps not only for our own lives and fortunes, but those of other people. And if when the momentous decision must be made by us alone, if we have been accustomed to depend on others, to refer all resolutions to others, and never to be sufficient unto themselves—what then? We may fall," I concluded tragically, "never more to rise."

My elated consciousness of growing prominence soon drove me vigorously into action. I joined the Oxford Society for Woman Suffrage; I joined the Bach Choir; I joined the War and Peace Society; I reviewed *Sinister Street* for the women's intercollegiate magazine, the *Fritillary*; I did not, despite much persuasion, join the Christian Union. For the choir, Dr. Allen, who enjoyed living up to his Oxford reputation of *enfant-terrible* eccentricity, tested my voice and asked me if I thought I had a good one. When I replied that I imagined I was a soprano though I really wanted to sing alto, he remarked: "I see. You're one of those cantankerous people. I suppose if you'd been an alto you'd have wanted to sing soprano."

To the War and Peace Society I paid my two-and-sixpenny subscription "chiefly to see Gilbert Murray. He was not at all like what I expected but the impression was not at all disappointing. He is a tall, slight man, not at all past middle age, with brown hair scarcely grey anywhere, and a curious shaped head just going bald. He has a rather penetrating but very kindly glance and wears spectacles, and also has an unassuming undidactic way of talking which appealed to me very much, especially as it was unexpected. His daughter hardly gives the impression of having anything unpretentious about her."

It was all so thrilling that for the time being the neglected War, with its Siege of Antwerp, its First Battle of Ypres and the *Sydney's* prolonged pursuit of the *Emden*, seemed quite out of the picture. Although Roland had now become a Territorial second-lieutenant, and Edward had appeared in Oxford only a week later than myself in order to begin his O.T.C. training under the auspices of New College, I wondered why I had ever been so much concerned about the troubles of Europe. After all, I told myself, they could never really touch me very closely, whereas the activities of college did and must. Somerville seemed at the moment so enormously important that I endeavoured to cheer Roland's spiritual isolation among the subalterns at Norwich by telling him—of course from a very lofty standpoint—all that I thought about it.

"I like it very well indeed," I informed him, "but I am never likely to fall into the typical college woman's blind infatuation with everybody and everything, or to think this place the only place, or these ideas the only ideas. It is an immense advantage to have been at home for a while and have seen other points of view besides this one. At present I am almost equally aware of its limitations and its advantages. It is a delightful change to me to be in surroundings where work is expected of you, instead of where you are thought a fool for wanting to do it, and of course the whole atmosphere of Oxford is ideal if you want to study or think or prepare to be. The last 'if' however points to one of the limitations here, as already I have come across several people who seem to regard their residence here as an end in itself, instead of a mere preparation for better and wider things in the future."

In the intervals snatched from cocoa, Greek and religion, I saw something of Edward. On account of the strict chaperonage regulations of those days (always disrespectfully referred to as "chap. rules") I was not allowed to go to his rooms in Oriel Street lest I should encounter the seductive gaze of some other undergraduate, but I met him in cafés and at the practices of the Bach Choir and Orchestra, for which Dr. Allen had chosen him to be a first violin. If ever he dropped in unexpectedly to tea with me at Somerville, I was obliged hastily to eject any friends who might be sitting in my room, for fear his tabooed sex might contaminate their girlish integrity.

Towards the end of November he was gazetted to the 11th Sherwood Foresters, and the next day he left Oxford for Sandgate. With his tall figure, his long beautiful hands, and the dark arched eyebrows which almost met above his half-sad, half-amused eyes, he looked so handsome in his new second-lieutenant's uniform that the fear which I had felt when he returned from Aldershot on the eve of the War suddenly clutched me again. Reluctantly I said good-bye to him in the Woodstock Road at the entrance to Little Clarendon Street, almost opposite the place where the Oxford War Memorial was to be erected ten years afterwards "In memory of those who fought and those who fell."

I often thought of him in camp as the November rain deluged the city and churned the Oxfordshire roads into mud, and once again the War crept forward a little from its retreat in the back of my mind. One student in my Year had a brother who was actually at the front; I contemplated her with awe and discomfort, and carefully avoided her for the rest of the term.

Sylvia Townsend Warner

1893 – 1978

orn in Harrow, she was early interested in music and was for ten years one of the editors of Tudor Church Music. *Poet and fiction writer, her first volume of verse,* The Espalier, *was published in 1925; her literary reputation was consolidated with the novels* Lolly Willowes *(1926),* Mr Fortune's Maggot *(1927), and* The True Heart *(1928). She was also acclaimed as a short story writer in Britain and the United States. In all, she published seven novels, three volumes of poetry, a volume of essays, a biography, and eight volumes of short stories. In 1933,* Whether a Dove or a Seagull *appeared; a volume of verse, it was a literary partnership undertaken with her lover Valentine Ackland, with whom she lived for many years in Dorset.*

Exploratory and innovative in style and content (her novels encompass tales of the supernatural and a version of the Cupid and Psyche story), she gained a recognised place in literary circles. The following short story is taken from The Innocent and the Guilty *(Chatto and Windus, London, 1971).*

But at the Stroke of Midnight

SHE was last seen by Mrs. Barker, the charwoman. At ten minutes to eleven (Mrs. Ridpath was always punctual, you could set your watch by her) she came into the kitchen, put on the electric kettle, got out the coffee-pot, the milk, the sugar, the two pink cups and saucers, the spoons, the coffee canister. She took the raisin cake out of the cake tin, cut two good slices, laid them on the pink plates that went with the two cups, though not a match. The kettle boiled, the coffee was made. At the hour precisely the two women sat down to their elevenses. It was all just as usual. If there had been anything not just as usual with Mrs. Ridpath, Mrs. Barker would certainly have noticed it. Such a thing would be quite out of the common; it would force itself on your notice. Mrs. Ridpath was never much of a talker, though an easy lady to talk to. She asked after Mrs. Barker's Diane and David. She remarked that people in the country would soon be hearing the first cuckoo. Mrs. Barker said she understood that the Council were poisoning the poor pigeons again, and together they agreed that London was no longer what it was. Mrs. Barker could remember when Pimlico was a pleasure to live in—and look at it now, nothing but barracks and supermarkets where they treated you with no more consideration than if you were a packet of lentils yourself. And at eleven-fifteen she said she must be getting on with her work. Later, while she was polishing the bath, she saw Mrs. Ridpath come out of the bedroom and go to the front door. She was wearing her gray and had a scarf over her head. Mrs. Barker advised her to put on a mac, for it looked like rain. Mrs. Ridpath did so, picked up her handbag, and went out. Mrs. Barker heard the lift come up and go down, and that was the last she knew. It was Saturday, the day when she was paid her week's money, and she hung about a bit. But Mrs. Ridpath didn't come back, and at a quarter past one she left. Her credit was good, thank God! She could manage her weekend shopping all right, and Mrs. Ridpath would pay her on Monday.

On Monday she let herself in. The flat was empty. The Aga Cooker was stone-cold, the kitchen was all anyhow; the milk bottles hadn't been rinsed, let alone put out. The telephone rang, and it was Mr. Ridpath, saying that Mrs. Ridpath was away for the weekend.

By then, Aston Ridpath was so determined that this must be so that when Mrs. Barker answered him he waited for a moment, allowing time for her to say that Mrs. Ridpath had just come in.

For naturally, when he got home from his office on Saturday (the alternate Saturday when he worked during the afternoon), he expected to find Lucy in the flat, probably in the kitchen. There was no Lucy. There was no smell of cooking. In the refrigerator there was a ham loaf, some potato salad, and the remains of the apple mousse they had had on Friday. It was unlike Lucy not to be there. He turned on the wireless for the six o'clock news and sat down to wait. By degrees an uneasiness and then a slight sense of guilt stole into his mind. Had Lucy told him she would not be back till after six? He had had a busy day; it might well have slipped his memory. It was even possible that she had told him and that he had not attended. It was easy not to attend to Lucy. She had a soft voice, and a habit of speaking as if she did not expect to be attended to. Probably she had told him she was going out to tea, or something of that sort. She sometimes went to picture galleries. But surely, if she had told him she would not be back in time to get dinner, he would have noticed it? By eight o'clock it became obvious that she must have told him she would not be back in time for dinner. No doubt she had told him about the ham loaf, too. She was thoughtful about such matters—which was one reason why her conversation was so seldom arresting. It would not do to seem inattentive, so he would eat and if there was time before she got back, he would also wash up.

He ate. He washed up. He hung the dishcloth on the rail. In some ways he was a born bachelor.

The telephone rang. As he expected, it was Golding, who had said he might come round that evening with the stamp album he had inherited from an uncle who had gone in for philately. He didn't know if there was anything in it worth having; Ridpath would know. Golding was one of those calm, tractable bores who appear to have been left over from ampler days. Every Sunday he walked from Earls Court to St. Paul's to attend matins. Now he arrived carrying a large brown paper parcel and a bunch of violets. "Lucy's out," said Aston, seeing Golding look round for somewhere to dispose of the flowers. "She's gone out to dinner. Have a whisky?"

"Well, yes. That would be very pleasant."

The album turned out to be unexpectedly interesting. It was after eleven when Golding began to wrap it up. His eye fell on the violets.

"I don't suppose I shall see Mrs. Ridpath. I think you said she was dining out."

"She's dining with some friends."

"Rather a long dinner," said Golding.

"You know what women are like when they get together," said Aston. "Talk, talk, talk."

Golding said sympathetically, "Well, I like talking, too."

Golding was gone. As Aston picked up his violets, which would have to put into some sort of vase, he realised with painful actuality that if Lucy wasn't back by midnight he would have to do something about it—ring up hospitals, ring up the police. It would be necessary to describe her. When one has been happily married to a woman for nearly twenty-five years it is too much to be expected to describe her. Tall. Thin. Knock-kneed. Walks with a stoop. Brown eyes, brown hair—probably safer to say grizzled. Wearing— How the hell was he to know what Lucy would be wearing if she had gone out to dinner? If he were to say what occurred to him, it would be tweeds.

Suppose she had not gone out to dinner? Suppose—for fiction is after all based on real life—suppose she had gone off, leaving that traditional note on her pincushion? If she had a pincushion. He walked into their bedroom. There was a pincushion, a very old and wilted one, but there was no note on it. He could see no note anywhere. There were some letters on her desk. He read them. They were from shops, or from friends, recounting what the friends had been doing.

If only he had listened! If only she had not got into this unfortunate trick of mumbling! For she would certainly have told him whom she was going out to. "Aston, I'm having dinner ..." It seemed as if he could almost recapture the words. "Aston, I'm going ..." Could she have continued, "away for the weekend"? For that would explain everything. It was perfectly possible. There were all those friends who wrote to her about flying in Hovercrafts to the Isle of Wight, visiting Leningrad, coming back from cruises to the West Indies. Why shouldn't she be spending the weekend with one or other of these Sibyls or Sophies? It was April, a season when it is natural to spend weekends in the country—if you like that sort of thing. Only a few weeks ago he had remarked that she was looking tired and would be the better for country air. An invitation had come; mindful of his encouragement she had accepted. He could now almost swear he had heard the words "Aston, I am going away for the weekend." No doubt she had also told him where. He had failed to remember it, but one cannot remember everything.

He ate some biscuits, went to bed with a clear conscience, and was asleep in five minutes.

In the morning his first conscious thought was that Lucy was away for the weekend. The conviction was so strong that presently he was able to imagine her being brought breakfast in bed—brown-bread toast, honey,

piping-hot coffee; he could positively see the tray. There she would lie, listening
to the birds. If it had not been for that unlucky moment of inattention, he
would have been able to construct some approximation of the surrounding
landscape. London is surrounded by the Home Counties. Somewhere in the
Home Counties—for if she had told him she was going to Yorkshire or Cape
Wrath he would surely have registered the fact—Lucy was having breakfast in
bed. He was glad of it. It would do her good. Thinking affectionately of Lucy,
he lay in bed for some while longer, then got up and made his breakfast. The
bacon took a long time to cook. He had omitted to riddle the stove overnight;
the fire had choked and was almost out. He looked about conscientiously to
see if Lucy had left any food he ought to heat up. He did not want to be found
with any kind provisions uneaten. When Lucy went to visit her cousin Aurelia
in Suffolk, she always left, he remembered, quantities of soup. This time she had
left nothing. No doubt she had said, at that moment when he wasn't attending,
that he had better eat out.

Accordingly, Aston ate out. His mind was at rest. Wherever Lucy might
be, she could not be with Aurelia and would return from wherever it
might have been his own normal Lucy. During those Suffolk absences all he
could be sure of was that Aurelia was leading Lucy, whether up a windmill or
to Paris, by the nose, and that what he received back would be Aurelia's Lucy;
talking in Aurelia's voice, asserting Aurelia's opinions, aping Aurelia's flightiness,
flushed, overexcited, and giggling like a schoolgirl. Thoroughly unsettled, in
short, and needing several days to become herself again. Family affection is
all very well, but it was absurd that visits to a country cousin—a withererd
virgin and impecunious at that—should be so intoxicating that Lucy returned
from them as from an assignation, and acknowledged them as such by leaving
him with such quantities of soup. Even when she went to Aurelia's funeral she
provided it; and came home saying in Aurelia's voice that cremations would be
all right if they weren't so respectful. But now there was no soup and his mind
continued to be at rest till he was in the bathroom brushing his teeth before
going to bed and noticed Lucy's sponge. It was a new sponge; he had given
it to her for Christmas. There was no excuse for leaving it behind. Apparently
she had not taken anything—not her hand lotion, not her dusting powder.
Examining Lucy's dressing table, he saw that she had taken nothing from that
either. In a moment of blind panic he fell on his knees and looked for her
body under the bed.

This was probably due to Wordsworth's tiresome trick of staying about
in one's memory. If Lucy had been christened Angelina, he would not
have been under the same compulsion to suppose she was dead. Lucy (his
Lucy) kept Wordsworth beside her bed. He looked up the poem and found
that on this occasion Wordsworth was mistaken, though in the following lyrics
he had lost her and it made a great difference to him. Then he remembered
that Samuel Butler had wickedly put it about that Wordsworth, aided by Southey
and Coleridge, had murdered Lucy. This meant returning to the sitting room
for Butler. Half an hour with Butler recalled him to reason. Lucy must have
forgotten to pack her sponge and had bought a new hairbrush.

But the sponge and the hairbrush had shaken him. He did not sleep so well that night, and when he got up to a cold, companionless Monday morning the reality of Lucy's absence was stronger than the ideality of her breakfast tray floating somewhere in the Home Counties, and he hoped very much she would soon be back—by which time Mrs. Barker would have put things straight, so that there would be nothing to impede him from saying, "And now tell me all about it." For that was the form of words he had decided on.

When he came back that evening everything had been put straight. But still there was no Lucy.

Anxiety hardens the heart. Addressing the absent Lucy, Aston said, "I shall ring up Vere." Vere was his sister—a successful widow. He did not like her very much and Lucy did not like her at all. She lived in Hampstead. He rang up Vere, who cut short his explanations by saying she would come at once and grapple.

She came with a suitcase and again cut short his explanations.

"I suppose you have told the police."

"Told the police, Vere? Why the hell should I tell the police? It's no business of theirs. Nothing would induce me to tell the police."

"If Lucy doesn't reappear and you haven't told the police, you'll probably be suspected of murder."

As Aurelia walked toward the Tate Gallery she noticed that she was wearing a wedding ring. Her first impulse—for she was a flighty creature—was to drop it into a pillar-box. Then some streak of latent prudence persuaded her that it would be more practical to sell it. She pulled it off—it was too large for her and revolved easily on her finger—and dropped it into her bag. She remembered that there had been a second-hand jewellery shop a little farther along. She had sometimes looked in through its wire-meshed windows at coral earrings and mosaic brooches of the Colosseum, St. Peter's, and other large celebrities. Once, long ago, she had bought herself an unset moss agate there. It was only a simulacrum of moss, but the best that then presented itself. The shop was still in its old place. She went in and presented the ring. The jeweller looked with compassion at the sad middle-aged woman in a mackintosh with a wisp of graying hair plastered to her forehead by the rain. To judge by the ring, she must have known better days. It was both broad and heavy, and he could give her a good sum for it. "I'm afraid I must ask for the name," he said. "It's a formality."

"Aurelia Lefanu, Shilling Street, Lavenham." She smiled as she gave the address.

Well, at any rate, the poor thing loved her home.

The same unaccountable streak of prudence now told Aurelia she must do some shopping. Stockings, for instance. It was raining harder, and her feet felt wet already. One need suggested another, and impressed by her own efficiency she bought some underclothes. Finally, as it was now raining extremely hard and she had collected several paper parcels, she bought a tartan grip. The Tate would be full of people who had gone in to shelter from the rain; but they wouldn't be looking at the Turners. Joseph Mallord William Turner, staring from under his sooty chimney-pot hat, sucking in colour as if from a fruit, making and remaking his world like some unendingly ambitious Jehovah and, like a Jehovah, peopling it with rather unsuccessful specimens of the human race, was hers and hers alone for the next hour. When she left the gallery, Joseph Mallord William Turner had got there before her. The rain had stopped. A glittering light thrust from beneath the arch of cloud and painted the river with slashing strokes of primrose and violet. The tide was at the full, and a procession of Thames shipping rode on it in blackness and majesty.

"Oh!"

In her excitement she seized the elbow of the man beside her; for he too was looking, he too, no doubt, was transfixed. Touched by her extreme emotion and her extreme wetness, he said, "I'm hoping to catch a taxi. Can I give you a lift? It's going to pelt again in a moment, you know.

"I've forgotten to take out my bag. Could you wait an instant?"

Seeing its cheapness—indeed, he could read the price, for the tag was still hanging from it—he supposed she was some perpetual student who would be much the better for a good square tea. She had a pretty voice.

The light grew dazzling. In another minute a heavier rain would descent; if he could not secure the taxi that had just drawn up to discharge its passenger, there would be no hope of another. He hauled her down the steps, signalling with her tartan bag, and pushed her in.

"Where can I take you?"

"Where? ... I really don't know. Where would be suitable?" And gazing out of the window at the last defiance of the light, she murmured, "'Whither will I not go with gentle Ithamore?'"

He gave his own address to the driver. The taxi drove off.

Turning to him, she said, "Marlowe, not me, I'm afraid it may have sounded rather forward."

"I've never been called Ithamore in all my life. It's a pretty name. What's yours?"

"Mine's a pretty name, too. Aurelia."

So it was in London that she breakfasted in bed, that Sunday morning, wearing white silk pyjamas with black froggings—for however cleverly one goes shopping one cannot remember everything, and she had forgotten to buy a nightdress. In all his life he had never been called Ithamore. In all his life he had never met anything like Aurelia. She was middle-aged, plain, badly kept, untravelled—and she had the aplomb of a *poule de luxe*. Till quite recently she must have worn a wedding ring, for the dent was on her finger; but she bore no other mark of matrimony. She knew how to look at pictures, and from her ease in nakedness he might have supposed her a model—but her movements never set into a pose. He could only account for her by supposing she had escaped from a lunatic asylum.

She must be saved from any more of that. He must get out of England as soon as possible. This would involve getting him out of England, too, which would be inconvenient for Jerome and Marmor, Art Publishers, but the firm could survive his absence for a few weeks. It would not be longer than that. Once settled at Saint-Rémy de Provence, with Laure and Dominique to keep an eye on her, and with a polite subsidy, she would do very well for herself—set up an easel, maybe; study astronomy. She would feel no need for him. It was he who would feel need, be consumed with an expert's curiosity.

She had spoken of how Cézanne painted trees in slats, so he drove her through the beechwoods round Stokenchurch and along a canal to a hotel that concealed its very good cooking behind a rustic Edwardian face. Here she said she was tired of eating cooked food, she would prefer fruit. She was as frank as a nymph about it, or a kinkajou. This frankness was part of her savour. It touched him because it was so totally devoid of calculation or self-consciousness. It would have been remarkable even in a very young girl; in a middle-aged woman showing such marks of wear and tear it was resplendent. It was touching, too, though rather difficult to take, that she should be so unappreciative of his tact. He had led her to a prospect of Provence; he had intimated that he sometimes went there himself; that he might have to go there quite soon; that he hoped it might be almost immediately, in order to catch the nightingales and the wisteria. . . .

"Will you take me, too?" she inquired. To keep his feet on the ground, he asked if she had a passport.

On Monday morning he rang up Jerome and Marmor to say he had a cold and would not be coming in for a few days; and would Miss Simpson bring him a passport-application form, please. The form was brought. He left Aurelia to fill it in while he went to his bank. As this was a first application, someone would have to vouch for her, and he would ask Dawkins to do it. Dawkins was closeted with a customer. He had to wait. When he got at him, Dawkins was so concerned to show that the slight illegality of vouching for someone he had never set eyes on meant nothing to him that he launched into conversation and told funny stories about Treasury officials for the next fifteen minutes.

"Aurelia! I'm sorry to have left you for so long.... Aurelia?"

Standing in the emptied room he continued to say, "Aurelia." The application form lay on the table. With a feeling of indecency, he read it. "AURELIA LEFANU. Born: Burford, Oxon. 11th May 1923 Height: 5 ft. 10. Eyes: Brown. Hair: Gray." The neat printing persisted without a waver. But at the Signature of Applicant something must have happened. She had begun to write—it seemed to be a name beginning with "L"—and had violently, scrawlingly erased it.

She had packed her miserable few belongings and was gone. For several weeks he haunted the Tate Gallery and waited to read an unimportant paragraph saying that the body of a woman, aged about forty-five, had been recovered from the Thames.

"If you haven't told the police—" The thought of being suspected of murdering Lucy left Aston speechless. The aspersion was outrageous; the notion was ridiculous. Twenty years and more had passed since they were on murdering terms. But the police were capable of believing anything, and Vere's anxiety to establish his innocence was already a rope round his neck. Vere was at the telephone, saying that Mr. Ridpath wished to see an officer immediately. There appeared to be some demurring at the other end, but she overcame it. While they waited, she filled in the time by cross-examining him. When did Lucy tell him she was going away for the weekend? How did she look when telling him? If he wasn't quite sure that she had done so, what made him think she had? Had she been away for other weekends? Had he noticed any change in her? Was she restless at night? Flushed? Hysterical? Had her speech thickened? If not, why did he say she mumbled? Had he looked in all her drawers? Her wardrobe? The wastepaper baskets? Why not? Had she drawn out money from her post-office savings? Had she been growing morbid? Had she been buying cosmetics, new clothes, neglecting the house, reading poetry, losing her temper? Why hadn't he noticed any of this? Were they growing apart? Did she talk in her sleep? Why did she never come to Hampstead? And why had he waited till Monday evening before saying a word of all this?

When the police officer came, she transferred the cross-examination to him. He was a large, calm man in need of sleep, and resolutely addressed himself to Aston. Aston began to feel better.

"And you were the last person to see Mrs. Ridpath?"

Interrupting Vere's florid confirmation, Aston had the pleasure of saying "No," and the further pleasure of saving her face. "My sister had forgotten about our charwoman. Mrs. Barker must have seen her after I did. She came up in the lift just as I was leaving for work."

The police officer made a note of Mrs. Barker and went away, saying that every endeavour would be made. "But if the lady should be suffering from a loss of memory, it may not be so easy to find her."

"Why?" said Vere. "I should have thought—"

"When persons lose their memory, in a manner of speaking they lose themselves. They aren't themselves. It would surprise you have unrecognizable they become."

When he had gone, Vere exclaimed, "Stuff and nonsense! I'm sure I could recognize Lucy a mile off. And she hasn't much to be recognized by, except her stoop."

Bereft of male companionship, Aston sat down with his head in his hands. Vere began to unpack.

She was in the kitchen, routing through the store-cupboard, when Mrs. Barker arrived on Tuesday morning. She said, "Well, I suppose you know about Mrs. Ridpath?"

Mrs. Barker put down her bag, took off her hat and coat, opened the bag, drew out an apron and tied it on. Then, folding her hands on her stomach, she replied, "No, Madam. Not that I know of." Her heart sank; but a strong dislike is a strong support.

"Well, she's gone. And Mr. Ridpath has put it in the hands of the police."

"Indeed, Madam."

"Not that that will be much use. You know what the police are like."

"No, Madam. I have had no dealings with them."

"They bungle everything. Now, why three packets of prunes? It does seem extraordinary. She was the last person in the world one would expect to do anything unexpected. Did she ever talk to you about going away? By herself, I mean?"

"No, Madam. Never."

Mrs. Barker had no doubt as to where Lucy had gone. She had gone to the South of France—to a pale landscape full of cemetery trees, as in the picture postcard, not sent by anyone, which she kept stuck in her dressing glass and said was the South of France. Remarking that she must get on with her work, Mrs. Barker went smoothly to the bedroom, removed the postcard, and tucked it into her bosom.

Loath as she was to admit that her sister-in-law could have a lover, Vere was sure that she had eloped. (Men are so helpless, their feelings so easily played on.) She was sure that Lucy's detestable charwoman knew her whereabouts and had been heavily bribed. A joint elevenses was when she'd catch the woman and trip her into the truth.

This was forestalled by Mrs. Barker bringing her a tray for one at ten-fifty, remarking that Madam might be glad of it, seeing how busy she was with her writing: and quitting the room with an aggressively hushed tread. Vere believed in leaving no stone unturned. Though she was sure that Lucy had eloped, this didn't seem to have occurred to Aston yet. A series of confidential letters to Lucy's friends might produce evidence that would çalm his mind. Not one of the tiresome women had signed with more than a given name, so the envelopes would have to be directed to "Sibyl," "Sophie," "Peg," and "Lalla;" but a "Dear Madam" would redress that. The rest would be easy: a preliminary announcement that she was Aston's sister and was writing to say that Lucy had left home for no apparent reason since she and Aston had always seemed such a happy couple; and that if Lalla, Peg, Sophie, or Sibyl could throw any light on this, of course in strictest confidence, it would be an inexpressible relief. More she would not say; she did not want to prejudice anyone against Lucy.

All this took time. The friends might know each other and get together; it would not do if her letters to them were identical. It would suggest a circular. Her four letters done—for she did not propose to write to people like the linendraper in Northern Ireland who regretted he could no longer supply huckaback roller towels—she would get to work on Mrs. Barker; differently, this time, and appealing to her feelings.

It was in vain. However, she managed to get the woman's address from her, so she rang up the police station and stated her conviction that Mrs. Barker knew what she wouldn't say and should be questioned and, if need be, watched. As Vere was one of those people who are obeyed—on the fallacious hypothesis that it tends to keep them quiet—an inspector called that afternoon on Mrs. Barker. He could not have been pleasanter, but the harm had been done; everybody in the street would know she had been visited by the police. Both the children knew it when they got in—David from school, Diane from her job at the fruiterer's. "Mum! Whatever's happened?" "Mum! Is anything wrong?"

The sight of them turned the sword in her heart. But she did not waver. Go back to those Ridpaths she would not, nor demean herself by asking for the money she owed, though it might mean that the payments on David's bicycle and the triple mirror in Diane's bedroom could not be kept up. Pinch, pawn, go on the street or the Public Assistance—but grovel for her lawful money to that two-faced crocodile who set the police on her she would not. She drew on her savings; and comforted herself with the thought of the two-faced crocodile down on her knees and doing her own scrubbing. The picture was visionary. Vere was on a committee—among other committees—of a Training Home for Endangered Girls, and whistled up an endangered mental deficient in no time.

"Now, now." Aurelia adjured herself, gathering her belongings together. "Now, now. Quickly does it. Don't lose your head." Going down in the lift she was accompanied by the man in Dante—the decapitated man who held his head in front of him like a lantern and said through its lips, "Woe's me." But fortunately he got stuck in the swing door. She was alone in the street and knew that she must find a bus. A taxi would not do, it must be a bus; for a bus asks you nothing, it substitutes its speed and direction for yours, it takes you away from your private life. You sit in it, released, unknown, an anonymous destiny, and look out of the window or read the advertisements. A bus that had gone by at speed slowed as a van came out of a side street. She ran, caught up with it just as it moved again, clambered in, and sat down next to a stout man who said to her, "You had to run for it, my girl." She smiled, too breathless to speak. Her smile betrayed her. He saw she was not so young as he took her for. She spent the day travelling about London in buses, with a bun now and then to keep her strength up. In the evening she attended a free lecture on town and country planning, given under the auspices of the London County Council. This was in Clerkenwell. During the lecture she noticed that her hands had left off shaking and that for a second time she had yawned quite naturally. Whatever it had been she had so desperately escaped from, she had escaped it. Like the lecture, she was free. It had been rather an expensive day. She atoned for this by walking to King's Cross and spending the night in the ladies' waiting room. It was warm, lofty, impartial—preferable, really, to any bedroom. The dutiful trains arrived and departed—demonstrations of a world in which all was controlled and orderly and would get on very nicely without her. Tomorrow she would go to some quiet place—Highgate Cemetery would do admirably—and decide where to go next.

It was in Highgate Cemetery, studying a headstone which said "I will dwell in the house of the Lord for ever," that Aurelia remembered hostels. The lecturer in Clerkenwell had enlarged on youth hostels. But there were middle-aged hostels, too—quiet establishments, scenes of unlicensed sobriety; and as youth hostels are scattered in wild landscapes for the active who enjoyed rock-climbing and rambling (he had dwelt on rambling and the provision of ramblers' routes), middle-aged hostels are clustered round devotional landmarks for the sedentary who enjoyed going to compline. She had enough money to dwell in a middle-aged hostel for a week. A week was quite far enough to plan for. Probably the best person to consult would be a clergyman. There was bound to be a funeral before long. She would hang on its outskirts and buttonhole the man afterward. "Excuse me," she would begin. "I am a stranger...."

"Excuse me," she began, laying hold of him by the surplice. He had a sad, unappreciated face. "I am a stranger."

Thinking about her afterward—and she was to haunt his mind for the rest of his life—Lancelot Fogg acknowledged a saving mercy. His Maker, whom he had come to despair of, an ear that never heard, a name that he was incessantly obliged to take in vain, had done a marvel and shown him a spiritual woman. His life was full of women: good women, pious women, energetic, forceful women, blighted women, women abounding in good works, women learned in liturgies, women with tragedies, scruples, fallen arches—not to mention women he was compelled to classify as bad women: bullies, slanderers, backbiters, schemers, organizers, women abounding in wrath; there were even a few kind women. But never a spiritual woman till now. So tall and so thin, so innocently frank, it was as if she had come down from the west front of Chartres into a world where she was a stranger.

There was nothing remarkable in what she had to say. She wanted to find a hostel somewhere away from London—but not far, because of paying for the ticket—where she could be quiet and go to compline and do some washing. He understood about washing, for being poor he sometimes tried to do his own. But her spirituality shone through her words; it was as if a lily were speaking of cleanliness. Spirituality shone even more clearly through her silences. While he was searching his mind for addresses, she looked at him with tranquil interest, unconcerned trust, as though she had never in her life known care or frustration—whereas from the lines in her face it was obvious she had known both. She was so exceedingly tranquil and trustful, in fact, that she gave an impression of impermanence—as if at any moment some bidding might twitch her away. Non-attachment, he remembered, was the word. The spiritual become non-attached.

"Would Bedfordshire be too far?"

"I don't think so. I should only be there a week."

He had remembered one of the women in his life who had been kind and who now kept a guest-house near a Benedictine monastery. He gave her the address. She thanked him and was gone. So was the funeral party. The grave was being filled in with increasing briskness. That afternoon, he must preside at the quarterly meeting of St. Agatha's Guild.

The mistake, thought Aurelia, had been to dwell on compline. Doing so she had given a false impression of herself. The recommended Miss Larke of St. Hilda's Guest-house had no sooner let her in than she was exclaiming. "Just in time, just in time! Reverend Fogg rang up to say you were coming—the silly man forgot to mention your name, but you are the lady he met, aren't you?—and that you would be going to compline. I'm afraid we've finished supper. But I'll keep some soup hot for you for when you get back. And here is Mrs. Bouverie who will show you the way. She's waited on purpose."

"How do you do? How kind of you. My name is Lefanu. Is the abbey far away?"

"If we start now we'll make it," said Mrs. Bouverie.

They started. Mrs. Bouverie was short and stout and she had a short stout manner of speech. Presently she inquired, "R.C. or A.C.?"

Aurelia was at a loss. The question suggested electricity or taps.

"Roman or Anglo?"

Aurelia replied, "Anglo." It seemed safer, though it was difficult to be sure in the dark.

"Mrs. or Miss?"

Aurelia replied, "Miss."

She had felt so sure that she would be fed on arrival that this day, too, she had relied on buns, resisting those jellied eels which looked so interesting in the narrow street that twisted down to the river—for instead of going straight to the guest-house she had spent an hour or so exploring the town to see if she'd like it. She did like it. But she had never eaten jellied eels.

She had never been to compline, either. This made it impossible to guess how long it would go on, or exactly what was going on, except that people were invisibly singing or reciting in leisured tones. If she had not been so hungry, Aurelia decided, she could have understood why compline should exercise this charm on people. There was a total lack of obligation about it which was very agreeable. And when it had mysteriously become over, and they were walking back, and Mrs. Bouverie remarked how beautifully it ended a day, didn't it, Aurelia agreed—while looking forward to the soup. The soup was lentil. It was hot and thick, and she felt her being fasten on it. The room was full of chairs, the chairs were full of people, the television was on. She sat clasping the mug where the soup had been. But it wilted in her grasp. She knew that at all costs she must not faint. "Smelling salts!" she exclaimed. A flask of vinegar was pressed to her nose, her head was bowed between her knees. When she had been taken off to be put to bed with a hot-water bottle, Mrs. Bouverie announced, "She's Anglo."

"Naturally. They are always so absurdly emotional," said a lady who was Roman.

Miss Larke returned, reporting that the poor thing was touchingly grateful and had forgotten to bring a nightdress.

In the morning Aurelia woke hungry but without a vestige of gratitude. The sun shone, a thrush was singing in the garden, it was a perfect drying day.

Aurelia, the replacement of Lucy, was a nova—a new appearance in the firmament, the explosion of an ageing star. A nova is seen where no star was and is seen as a portent, a promise of what is variously desired: a victory, a pestilence, the birth of a hero, a rise in the price of corn. To the man never before called Ithamore she was at last an object of art he could not account for. To Lancelot Fogg she was at last a spiritual woman. To the denizens of St. Hilda's guest-house she was something new to talk about—arresting but harmless. At least, she was harmless till the evening she brought in that wretched tomcat and insisted on keeping it as a pet. If Lancelot Fogg had not recommended her so fervently, Aurelia with that misnamed pet of hers would have been directed to lodgings elsewhere. It was bad enough to adopt a most unhealthy-looking tomcat, but to call the animal Lucy made it so much worse; it seemed a deliberate flout, a device to call attention to the creature's already too obvious sex.

"But why Lucy, Miss Lefanu? Surely it's inappropriate?"

"It's a family name," she replied.

Lucy developed on Aurelia's fourth evening at the guest-house. She was again accompanying Mrs. Bouverie to compline when a distant braying caught her ear. Looking in the direction of the braying, she saw a livid glow and exclaimed, "A circus!"

"It's that dreadful fair," Mrs. Bouverie replied. "As I was telling you, my brother-in-law who had that delightful place in Hampshire, not far from Basingstoke, such rhododendrons! I've never seen such a blaze of colour as when they were out...."

When she had seen Mrs. Bouverie safely down on her knees, Aurelia stole away and went off to find the fair. Fairs, of course, are not what they used to be, but they are still what they are, and Aurelia enjoyed herself a great deal till two haunted young men in frock coats and ringlets attached themselves to her, saying at intervals, "Spare us a reefer, beautiful. Have a heart." For they, too, had seen her as a nova. At last she managed to give them the slip and hurried away through the loud entrails of a Lunar Flight. This brought her to the outskirts of the fair, and it was there she saw the cat lying on the muddied grass under the bonnet of a lorry. Its eyes were shut, its ears laid back. It had gone under the lorry for warmth, and was paying the price.

When she came back with a hot dog, it had re-arranged itself. In its new attitude she could see how thin it was and how despairingly shabby. She knelt down and addressed it from a distance. It heard her, for it turned its head away. The smell of the hot dog was more persuasive. It began to thresh its tail. "You'll eat when I'm gone," she said, with fellow-feeling, and scattered bits of hot dog under the bonnet and began to walk away—knowing that its precarious balance between mistrust and self-preservation could be over-set by a glance. She had left the fairground and was turning into a street full of warehouses when she saw that the cat, limping and cringing, was following her. She stopped, and it came on till it was beside her. Then it sat down and raised its face toward her. Its expression was completely mute—and familiar. The cat was exactly like her cousin Lucy.

When she picked it up it relaxed in her arms, rubbed its head against her shoulder, and purred. The cat took it absolutely for granted that it should be carried off by a deity. Still throned in her arms, it blinked serenely at the mortals in the guest-house, sure that they soon would be disposed of.

There were a great many things to be done for Lucy. His suppurating paw had to be dressed, his ears had to be cleaned and his coat brushed, food had to be bought for him, and four times a day he had to be exercised in the garden. In the intervals of this, his fleas had to be dealt with. Using a fine tooth comb she searched them out, pounced on them, dropped them in a bowl of soapy water, resumed the search. It was a dreamlike occupation: it put her in touch with the infinite. Twenty. Thirty. Forty-seven. Fifty-two. From time to time she looked sharply at the bowl of soapy water and pushed back any wretches that had struggled to the rim.

The total of fleas went up in bounds. The money in her purse decreased. Even using the utmost economy, stealing whenever she conveniently could, having sardines put down to Miss Larke, she would not be left with enough to pay for a second week at the guest-house. Lucy's paw healed slowly; It would be some while yet before he could provide for himself. She noticed that Lucy's paw was increasingly asked about; that suggestions for his welfare multiplied.

"I wonder why you don't put an advertisement in the local paper, saying 'Found.' All this time his real owners may be hunting for him, longing to get him back."

Aurelia looked deeply at the speaker. It might be worth trying. There is no harm in blackmail, since no one is obliged to give in to it. On the other hand, it is no good unless they do.

She composed two letters: "Unless you send me fifty pounds in notes, I shan't be able to come back." "Unless you send me fifty pounds in notes, I shall be forced to return."

Combing out fleas to a new rhythm of "he loves me, he loves me not," she weighed these alternatives. The second would probably have the stronger appeal to Aston's heart. Poor Aston, she had defrauded him too long of the calm expansion of widowerhood. But the stomach is a practical organ; the first alternative might be the more compelling. She did not, of course, mean to return, in either case. Since her adoption of Lucy, she had become so unshakably Aurelia that she could contemplate being Lucy, too, so far as being Lucy would further Aurelia's designs. But Lucy, the former Lucy, must be Aurelia's property. There must be no little escapades into identity, no endorsing of cheques, no more slidings into Lucy Ridpath. That was why the money must come in notes. Even so, who was it to be addressed to?

It was time for Lucy to scratch in the garden. For the first time, he tried to scratch with both hind legs. Everything became easy. Whichever the chosen form of the letter demanding money with menaces, Aurelia, signing with a capital L., would ask for the money to be directed to Miss Lefanu, *poste restante*. Lucy had been Lefanu when Aston married her. He could not have forgotten this; it might even touch his heart and dispose him to add another five pounds. All that remained was to decide which letter to send, and to post it from Bedford, which was nearby and non-committal. The envelope had been posted before she realized that both letters were enclosed.

"Lucy's handwriting," said Aston. "She's alive. What an infinite relief!"

"I never supposed she wasn't," said Vere. "Still, if it's a relief to you to see her handwriting—it doesn't seem such a niggle as usual, but that's her 'L'—I'm sure I'm glad"

"But Vere, on Monday evening, on *Monday evening*, you said I must ring up the police or I should be suspected of murdering her."

"So you would have been. They always jump to conclusions. Well, what does Lucy say?"

The letters had been folded up together. The first alternative was uppermost.

"She seems to have got into some sort of trouble. She says she can't come home unless I send her fifty pounds."

"Fifty pounds? Where is she, then. California?"

"The postmark is Bedford. She's gone back to her maiden name."

"Fifty pounds to get back from Bedford. Fifty pounds! She must have got herself mixed up in something pretty fishy. Yes. I heard only the other day that Bedford is an absolute hotbed of the drug traffic. That's what she wants the money for. Poor silly Lucy, she'd be wax in their hands. Aston! You'll have to think very carefully, apart from this absurd demand for money, about having her back. If she were here alone all day with no one to keep an eye on her—What does she say on the second sheet?"

"Is there a second sheet? I hadn't noticed. She says—Vere, I can't make this out. She says, 'Unless you send me fifty pounds in notes I shall be forced to return.'"

"Nonsense, Aston! You're misreading it. She just made a fair copy and then put them both in."

"But Vere, she says unless I send her the money she will be forced to return."

"She must be raving. Why on earth should she expect you to pay her to keep away? Let me see."

After a pause, she said, "My poor Aston."

Her voice was heavy with commiseration. It fell on Aston like a wet sponge. His brief guilty dazzle of relief (for as long as Lucy wasn't dead he really didn't want to live with her again; what he wanted was manly solitude, and he had already taken the first steps toward getting shot of Vere) sizzled out.

"Poor Lucy! I must send her something, I suppose."

"Yes, you ought to. But not too much. Ten pounds would be ample. What's Bedford? No way at all."

When Aurelia called at the post office, the clerk handed her two letters. She opened Aston's first.

Dear Lucy,
I will not try to persuade you. The heart has its reasons. But if a time ever comes when you want to come back, remember there will always be a door on the latch and a light in the window.
I will say nothing of the anxiety your leaving without a word has caused me.

—Aston

Four five-pound notes were enclosed.

The other letter was from Vere. It ran:

Aston is now recovering. I will thankfully pay you to keep away.

This letter was accompanied by ten ten-pounds notes.

Aurelia bought Lucy some tinned salmon and a handsome travelling basket. But for the greater part of that afternoon's journey, Lucy sat erect on her knee looking out of the window and held like a diviner's twig by his two front legs. She relied on Lucy to know at a snuff which station to get out at, just as he had known how to succeed in blackmailing—for while she was debating which of the two letters to send he had leaped onto the table, laid his head on her hand, and rolled with such ardour and abandonment that she forgot all else, so that both letters went off in the one envelope. Relying on Lucy, she had chosen a stopping train. It joggled through a green unemphatic landscape with many willow trees and an occasional broached spire. Lucy remained unmoved. She began to wonder if his tastes ran to the romantic, if high mountains were to him a feeling—in which case she had brought him to quite the wrong part of England. In the opposite corner sat a man with leather patches on his elbows, paying them no attention. Then at a station called Peckover Junction two ladies got in, and resumed (they were travelling together) a conversation about their grandchildren. From their grandchildren they turned to the ruin of the countryside—new towns, overspill, and holiday camps.

"Look at those caravans! They've got here, now."

"Don't speak to me of caravans," said the other lady.

Disregarding this, the first lady asked if there were as many as ever.

"More! Such hideosities at poor Betcombe . . . and the children! Swarming everywhere. I shall never find a tenant now. Besides, all these new people have such grand ideas. They must have this, they must have that. They don't appreciate the past. For me, that's its charm. If it weren't for the caravans, I'd be at Betcombe still, glorying in my beams and my pump. Do you know, it was eighteenth century, my pump?"

"Would you like me as a tenant?" said Aurelia. "I can't give you any references just now, but I'd pay ten shillings a week. No, darling!" This last remark was addressed to Lucy, who had driven his claws into her thigh.

"Ten shillings a week—for my lovely little cottage?"

"A pound a week."

"Really, this is so sudden, so unusual. No references . . . and I suppose you'd be bringing that cat. I'm a bird-lover. No, I'm afraid it's out of the question. Come, Mary, we get out here."

For the train was coming to a halt. Both ladies gathered their belongings and got out. From the window Aurelia saw them get in again, a few carriages farther up.

"You're well out of that," observed the man with leather patches. "I know her place. It's a hovel. No room to swing a cat in, begging your cat's pardon."

Lucy rounded himself like a poultice above his scratch. Aurelia said she expected she had been silly. The train went on. An atmosphere of acquaintance established itself. Presently the man asked if she had any particular place in mind.

"No. Not exactly. I'm a stranger."

"Because I happen to know of something that might suit you—if you don't object to it being a bit out of the way. It's a bungalow, and it's modern. If you're agreeable, I'll take you to see it."

It was impossible not to be agreeable, because he was so plainly a shy man and surprised at finding himself intervening. So when he got out she got out with him, and he took her to a Railway Arms where she and Lucy would be comfortable, and said he would call for her at ten the next morning.

He was exactly punctual. When she had assured him how comfortable she and Lucy had been, there seemed to be nothing more to say. Fortunately, he was one of those drivers who give their whole mind to driving. They drove in his van. It was lettered "George Bastable, Builder and Plumber," and among the things in the back was a bathtub wrapped in cellophane. They drove eastward, through the same uneventful landscape. He turned the van into a track that ran uphill—only slightly uphill, but in that flat landscape it seemed considerable. "There it is."

A spinney of mixed trees ran along the top of the ridge. Smoke was rising through the boughs. So she would have a neighbour. She had not reckoned on that.

But the smoke was rising from the chimney of a bungalow, and there was no other building there.

He must have got up very early, for the fire was well established, the room was warm and felt inhabited. The kitchen floor was newly washed and a newspaper path was spread across it.

"You'd find it comfortable," he said.

"Oh, yes," she said, looking at the two massive armchairs that faced each other across a hideous hearth mat.

"It hasn't been lived in for three years, though I come out from time to time to give a look to it. But no damp anywhere—that'll show how sound it is."

"No. It feels wonderfully dry," she said, looking at a flight of blue pottery birds on the wall.

Lucy was shaking his basket.

"May I let your cat out? He'd like a run, and I daresay he'd pick up a breakfast, bird's-nesting."

Before she could answer, he had unfastened the lid and Lucy had bounded over the threshold. How was she to answer this man who had taken so much trouble and was so proud of his bungalow?

"Did you build it yourself?"

"I did. That's why I know it's a good one. I built it for my young lady. When I saw you in the train, you put me in mind of her, somehow. So when you said you wanted somewhere to live—" He stared at her, standing politely at a distance trying to recapture the appearance of his nova in this half-hearted lady, no longer young.

The house had stood empty for three years. She had died. Poor Mr. Bastable! Aurelia's face assumed the right expression.

"She left," he said.

"How *could* she?" exclaimed Aurelia.

This time, there was no need to put on the right expression. She was wholeheartedly shocked at the behaviour of Mr. Bastable's young lady—and if the young lady had come in just then she would have boxed the ungrateful minx's ears. Instead, it was Lucy who trotted in, looking smug, with fragments of egg-shell plastered to his chops, sat down in front of the fire, and began cleaning himself. Mr. Bastable remarked that Lucy had found a robin's nest. He was grateful for Aurelia's indignation but shy of saying so. He suspected he had gone too far. Somewhat to his surprise he learned that Aurelia would like to move into his lovely bungalow immediately. He drove her to the village to do her shopping, came back to show her where the coal was kept, gave her the key. Watching him drive away she suddenly became aware of the landscape she would be taking for granted. It sparkled with crisscrossing drains and ditches; a river wound through it. A herd of caravans was peacefully grazing in the distance.

Happiness is an immunity. In a matter of days Aurelia was unaffected by the flight of blue pottery birds, sat in armchairs so massive she could not move them and felt no wish to move them, slept deliciously between pink nylon sheets. With immunity she watched Lucy sharpening his claws on the massive armchairs. She had a naturally happy disposition and preferred to live in the present. Happiness immunized her from the past—for why look back for what has slipped from one's possession?—and from the future, which may never even be possessed. Perhaps never in the past, perhaps never in the future, had she been, could she be, so happy as she was now. The cuckoo woke her; she fell asleep to Lucy's purr. In the mornings he had usually left a dent beside her and gone out for his sunrising. Whatever one may say about bungalows, they are ideal for cats. She hunted his fleas on Sundays, and Thursdays. He was now so strong and splendid that for the rest of the week he could perfectly well deal with them himself. She lived with carefree economy, seldom using more than a single plate, drinking water to save rinsing the teapot, and as far as possible eating raw foods, which entailed the minimum of washing up. Every Saturday she bought seven new-laid eggs, hard-boiled them, and spaced them out during the week—a trick she had learned from Vasari's *Lives of the Artists*. It was not an adequate diet for anyone leading an active life, but her life was calculatedly inactive—as though she were convalescing from some forgotten illness.

On Saturday evenings Mr. Bastable called to collect the rent and to see if anything needed doing—a nail knocked in or a tap tighened up. He always brought some sort of present: a couple of pigeons, the first tomatoes from his greenhouse, breakfast radishes. As the summer deepened, the presents enlarged into basketloads of green peas, bunches of roses, strawberries, sleek dessert gooseberries. But as the summer deepened and in spite of all the presents and economies Aurelia's wealth of one hundred and twenty pounds lessened, and she knew she must turn her mind to doing something about this. She could not dig; there was no one but Mr. Bastable to beg from. The times were gone when one could take in plain sewing. Surveying the landscape she had come to take for granted, she saw the caravans in a new light—no longer peacefully grazing but fermenting with ambitions and cultural unrest.

By now they must have bought all the picture postcards at the shop. She had always wanted to paint. For all she knew, she might turn out to be quite good at it. Willows would be easy—think of all the artists who painted them. By now the caravaners must be tired of looking at real willows and would welcome a change to representational art. She took the bus to Wisbech, found an arts-and-crafts shop, bought paper, brushes, gouache paints, and a small easel. That same evening she did two pictures of willows—one tranquil, one storm-tossed. Three days later, she sat up the easel on the outskirts of the caravan site and began a caravan from life. It was harder than willows—there were no precursors to inspire her—but when she had complied with a few suggestions from the caravan's owner she made her sale and received two further commissions. By the beginning of August she was rich enough to go on to oils—which was more fun and on the whole easier. It was remarkable how easily she painted, and with what assurance. The demand was chiefly for caravans. She varied them, as Monet varied his haystacks. Caravan with buckets. Caravan with sunset. Pink Caravan. One patron wanted a group of cows—though his children were cold toward them. She evaded portraits, but yielded to a request for an abstract. This was the only commission that really taxed her. Do as she might, it kept on coming out like a draper's window display. But she mastered it in the end, and signed it A. Lefanu like the rest.

By the end of September she had made enough to keep her in idleness till Christmas—when she would have thought of something else.

Winter would bring a new variety of happiness—slower, more conscious, and with more strategy in it. The gales of the equinox blowing across the flats struck at the spinney along the ridge, blew down one tree, and shook deadwood out of others. Here was an honest occupation. She set herself to build up a store of fuel against the winter. It was heavy work dragging the larger branches over the rough ground clogged with brambles and tall grass, but Lucy lightened it by flirting round her as she worked, darting after the tail of the branches, ambushing them and leaping on them as they rustled by. She was collecting fuel, Lucy was growing a thick new coat; both of them were preparing their defences against the wintry months ahead. Mr. Bastable said that by all the signs it would be a hard winter, preceded by much rain and wind. He advised her to get her wood in before the rain fell and made the ground too soggy to shift it. If she manages the first winter, he thought, she will settle. Though she was an ungrateful tenant, or at any rate an inattentive receiver, he wanted her to settle; it delighted him to see her making these preparations. Later on, he would complete them by chopping the heavier pieces into nice little logs. Taking Mr. Bastable's advice, Aurelia decided to get the wood in, working on till the dusk was scythed by the headlights of passing cars, till Lucy vanished into a different existence of being a thing audible—a sudden plop or a scuffling. She never had to call him when she went indoors. By the time she was on the threshold he was there, rubbing against her, raising his feet in a ritual exaggeration. He was orderly in his ways, a timekeeper. He took himself in and out, but rarely strayed. When she came back from selling those unprincipled canvases, he was always waiting about for her, curled up on the lid of the water butt, drowsing under the elder, sitting primly on the sill of the window left open for him. He was happy enough out of her sight, but he liked to have her within his.

So she told herself, later on, that foggy, motionless November evening when he had not come in at his usual time. She had kindled a fire, not that it was cold—indeed, it was oddly warm and fusty; but the fog made it cheerless. It was a night to pull the curtains closer, listen to the snap and crackle of a brief fire, go early to bed. She had left the curtains unclosed, however. If Lucy saw that a fire had been kindled, he would be drawn from whatever busied him. He was a very chimney-corner cat, although he was a tom. Twice the brief fire died down, twice she made it up again. She went to the door, peered uselessly into the fog, called him. It was frightening to call into that silent, immediate obscurity.

"Lucy. Lucy."

She waited. No Lucy. She must resign herself to it. Tonight Lucy was engaged in being a tom. As she stood there, resigning herself to it and straining her ears, she felt the damp of the foggy air pricked with a fine drizzling rain. A minute later, the rain was falling steadily; not hard but steadily. She had not the courage to go on calling. The pitch of her voice had frightened her; it sounded so anxious. She went indoors and sat down to wait. On a different night she would have left the window open and gone to bed, and in the morning Lucy would have been there, too, and in her sleep her arm would have gone out and round him.

With the rain, it had become colder. She added coal to the fire. It blazed up but did not warm her. She counted the blue pottery birds and listened. She listened for so long that finally she became incapable of listening, and when there was a sound which was not the interminable close patter of rain she did not hear it, only knew that she had heard something. A dragging sound ... the sound of something being dragged along the path to the door. It had ceased. It began again. Ceased.

When she snatched the door open, she could see nothing but the rain, a curtain of flashing arrows lit by her lighted room. A noise directed her—a tremulous yowl. He struck at her feebly when she stooped to pick him up, then dragged himself on into the light of the doorway. She fell on her knees. This sodden shapeless thing was Lucy. He looked at her with one eye; the other sagged on his cheek. His jaw dangled. One side of his head had been smashed in; his front leg was broken. When she touched him he shrank from her hand and yowled beseechingly. Slowly, distortedly, he hitched himself over the threshold, across the room, tried to sit up before the fire, fell over, and lay twitching and gasping for breath. When at last she dared touch him, his racing heartbeats were like a machine fastened in him. She talked to him and stroked his uninjured paw. He did not shrink from her now, and perhaps her voice lulled him as the plumpness of his muscular soft paw lulled her, for he relaxed and curled his tail round his flank as though he were preparing to fall asleep. Long after he seemed to be dead, the implacable machine beat on. Then it faltered, stumbled, began again at a slower rate, fluttered. A leaden tint suffused his eye and his lolling tongue. His breathing stopped. He flattened. It was inconceivable that he could ever have been loved, handsome, alive.

"Lucy!"

The cry broke from her. It unloosed another.

"Aurelia!"

She could not call back the one or the other. She was Lucy Ridpath, looking at a dead cat who had never known her.

The agony of dislocation was prosaic. She endured it because it was there. It admitted no hope, so she endured it without the support of resentment.

The rain had gone on all the time and was still going on.

Lucy Ridpath's mackintosh was hanging in the closet, ready to meet it. Mrs. Barker had advised her to put it on and she had done so. Tomorrow she would put it on again when she went out to dig a hole in the sodden ground for the cat's burial. It is proper to bury the dead; it is a mark of respect. Lucy would bury Lucy, and then there would be one Lucy left over.

She sat in the lighted room long after the light of day came into it. Then she put on the mackintosh and took up the body and carried it out. The air was full of a strange roar and tumult, a hollow booming that came from everywhere at once. The level landscape was gone. The hollow booming rose from a vast expanse and confusion of floodwater. Swirling, jostling, traversed with darker streaks, splintering into flashes of light where it contested with an obstacle, it drove toward the river. Small rivulets were flowing down from the ridge to join it, the track to the road was a running stream. In all that water there must be somewhere a place to drown.

With both hands holding the cat clasped to her bosom, she walked slowly down the track. When she came to the road, the water was halfway to her knees. A little farther along the road there was a footbridge over the roadside ditch. It was under water but the handrail showed. She waded across it. The water rose to her knees. With the next few steps she was in water up to her thighs. It leaned its ice-cold indifferent weight against her. When a twig was carried bobbing past her, she felt a wild impulse to clutch it. But her arms were closed about the cat's body, and she pressed it more closely to her and staggered on. All sense of direction was gone; sometimes she saw light, sometimes she saw darkness. The hollow booming hung in the air. Below it was an incessant hissing and seething. The ground rose under her feet; the level of water had fallen to her knees. Tricked and impatient, she waded faster, took longer strides. The last stride plunged her forward. She was out of her depth, face down in the channel of a stream. She rose to the surface. The current bowed her, arched itself above her, swept her onward, cracked her skull against the concrete buttress of a revetment, whirled the cat out of her grasp.

Naomi Mitchison

1897 –

A novelist, short story writer and poet, Naomi Mitchison was born in
Edinburgh, the daughter of Kathleen Trotter and John Scott Haldane, and
enjoyed a good education at The Dragon School in Oxford; she married
the barrister and Labour politician G.R. Mitchison in 1916. The author of almost
eighty books, Naomi Mitchison's writing career was launched with the novel
The Conquered (1923), and her reputation as the author of serious historical
fiction was securely established with the publication in 1931 of The Corn King
and the Spring Queen. Her preoccupation with classical subjects gave way over
the years to a concern with more contemporary politics, and her interest in the
developing world and issues of social justice is reflected in Not by Bread Alone
(1983) and her short stories, Images of Africa (1981).

The following short story is taken from The Delicate Fire: Short Stories
and Poems (Jonathan Cape, London, 1933).

The Poor Relation and the Secretary

UNTIL they were a mile outside Rome, Claudia kept the curtains of the litter
drawn. She did not like crowds and was bad at answering back if someone was
rude. Those always seems to be the moments the bearers chose to go slowest.
Naturally she had been given the oldest and slowest bearers, but she did not
expect anything else; she was lucky to have that. In the half light of the jolting litter,
she looked through her tablets, considering the long list of things she was to do
when she got to the country house. Which room Lady Quintilia was to have, and
which Lady Rufa, and all the rest of them; what curtains were to go where; what
provisions she was to get in; which of the country slaves were to be told to do
what; she was to see that the fountains were started—no, Phillos could do that,
it was a man's job — and have the aviary cleaned up and if necessary re-stocked;
the garden was to look nice for the guests. And so on and so forth. She thought she
could manage it all, though she had not been given much time. They wouldn't
for instance notice about the aviary for days! But she was a competent person,
as they all said. If one was a poor relation whose parents had been Unfortunate
— as one always said — during the Civil Wars, it was as well to be competent.
Or beautiful. But she was not that. And the family standard was particularly high.

Was there not the exquisite Lady Norbana whom the Emperor himself — well, better not mention it perhaps, considering she was to be married next month. Some conventions are better kept up.

Once out on the road beyond the houses, she drew the curtains a little. Phillos, the secretary, was walking level with her. The baggage mules were behind. She looked out across acres of green vineyard, not very interesting, but still, the country would be pleasant after all these months in town. Phillos looked up and smiled a little, but said nothing; it was not his place to speak first. He seemed to be walking rather lame. She asked him if he would see to the fountains, and he said yes, but would she give him authority? The country slaves never saw any reason why they should do what he said. 'It's bad enough with the bailiff,' he said, 'but at any rate they know I'm there to do accounts. Still, he makes it as difficult as possible.'

Claudia leaned over the edge of the litter and laughed. He's a horrid man!' she said, 'but I don't mind dealing with him if there's any special difficulty, Phillos. He remembers father, so he's still got a little respect for me!'

'Thank you, Miss Claudia,' said Phillos gratefully, 'I think I may want a little help. It was bad enough last time. I can't work when he stands over me and grins.'

A flock of sheep went by just then, raising a cloud of dust. She drew her curtains against it. The bearers swore and jolted worse than ever. She shut her eyes for a few minutes; she was sorry for her cousins' secretary. A dog's life, being a slave, if you had any kind of perceptions and fine feelings. She wondered if they were going to free him. Perhaps later on, when he was middle-aged; then he would stay on with them. Probably he was saving up to buy his freedom now, but it would mean a good deal of money, more than he was likely to have for a long time. Middle age. A grim business to grow old with no home of your own, no one to look after you or be kind to you. One would go on being competent up to middle age. But what about later on? When all the young cousins were married off, like Norbana, before or after the Emperor — well, well, she mustn't be catty about it! But it must be wonderful to have men wanting you like that. Anyone wanting you for anything except — well, competence. Somebody wanting you just to be kind to them.

When she drew the curtains again, the hills were in sight. She cried out with pleasure: 'Aren't they lovely, Phillos! So cool and big and shadowy! It makes one think one's a child again.'

He looked at them unenthusiastically. Abruptly he said: 'I'd like some day to see the Greek hills. My mother used to tell me about them. Much higher than these and more beautiful shapes. But I don't suppose I ever shall.'

She hardly knew what to say to that. It was such an odd outburst, from Phillos of all people, whom one never remembered was a Greek at all! Then she noticed he was really walking very lame. 'What's the matter?' she said, 'Have you cut yourself?'

'No,' he said. 'It's only my knee, Miss Claudia. It goes like that after a few miles.'

'Does it hurt?'

'Not very much,' he said, 'thank you all the same for asking.'

She was rather distressed, though; the man looked whiteish, like someone in pain. 'You'd better get up into the litter for a mile or two; that'll ease it.' She called down to the bearers to halt. 'Get in at the other end; it'll take you easily.'

Phillos protested, and so, more loudly, did the litter bearers, one of whom produced a sore shoulder.

'Nonsense,' said Claudia. 'Am I the mistress here, or not? No, you are merely being lazy! Change to the other pole. Men that can't carry a litter are only fit for field work — shall I tell Lady Quintilia that? Pretty it would be for your mistress's secretary to be lamed just because you are a set of good-for-nothing dogs! Up you get, Phillos.' The litter jolted sullenly on again. 'I've got *that* much authority,' she said, satisfied. 'Now, Phillos, what about this knee? What's wrong with it? Why haven't I known before?'

'It's an old blow,' he said. 'Really Miss Claudia, you shouldn't have bothered! It's only the body. The stupid, unimportant body.'

'Don't go trying any of your stoicism on me!' said Claudia. 'I've read all the books. A pack of nonsense. One can't get away from the body. When was it done?'

'Some time ago,' he said, 'my last place. One *must* have some philosophy, and that's the only one for slaves.'

'If I were you,' said Claudia, 'I should have a nice exciting mystery religion. However, I can't talk, I haven't got one myself! What about these Christians one's beginning to hear about? — wouldn't that be comforting?'

'A lot of dirty Jews!'

'Well, very likely. They're all much alike, I dare say. Or there's Isis. I've got a certain feeling for Isis myself. If one were the kind of person who liked religions. — But about this knee, did someone hit you?'

'Yes, Miss Claudia. My master. I suppose I'd been stupid. But he did know where to get one. My knee swelled and I was lame for a long time. Now it only gets me when I'm tired.'

He put both hands down on his knee, pressing over it; he had broad, clean hands, each finger separately tensed. The other leg was curled under him and he sat rather upright, so as not to take up too much room. She reached over and handled the knee-cap herself; it was rather swollen. She was used to dealing with sick slaves — it was part of her job. But he leant back away from her, half shutting his eyes, as though abstracting himself, leaving nothing with her but the knee. His legs were very dusty from the road, but not stickily engrained like some of the slave skins she had to handle.

When they got to the villa, she became immersed in jobs, and was startled to find it was supper-time when they came to tell her. She had rather enjoyed being busy and competent and talking to a lot of people; she wanted to go on talking. 'Tell the secretary he is to have his supper with me,' she said, 'I've a lot to talk over with him.' Phillos came in shyly, bringing in his tray, which looked rather unappetising. 'This is very kind of you, Miss Claudia,' he said. 'Nonsense!' she said, rather surprised, because she had really had no idea of being kind, and told them sharply to bring him up the remains of the bird she was having. She told him all the things she had been doing and the obstacles which she had been successfully overcoming. He had started on the estate accounts, but was a little depressed about them. His knee seemed to have settled down again, and he didn't take her suggestion of a hot poultice. After a time they drifted into a rather pleasant philosophical discussion, seasoned with quotations. At dusk they wished each other good night and separated.

Claudia was enjoying herself. She liked having this large house to herself before the others arrived. She went through all the rooms with a lamp, talking to herself, welcoming or speeding imaginary guests, not quite daring to go the whole way and make herself husband or children. She wished the others weren't coming to-morrow to shatter her images against their own brilliant reality.

The next morning she got up early and went on putting things to order; she found Phillos had got the fountains to work, which reminded her to go and tackle the bailiff for him. The man was, as usual, being extremely rude and obstructive about his accounts, but caved in to her at once, with reminiscences of her father. They walked out of the room together and as he passed the secretary crouched over his desk and the rows of semi-legible figures, he tweaked his ear rather hard. Phillos said nothing, only frowned more deeply, and Claudia said nothing either, but it annoyed her. 'That impudent little Greek!' said the bailiff, 'I can't stand the fellow. Why Lady Quintilia has a man like that! Ah, your father, now, he always stuck to his own people and didn't get cheated out of a quarter so much.' But Claudia preferred to discuss with him the rapid bedding out of damask roses and blue daisies to fill up the gaps in the garden.

She put flowers in the rooms, changed her dress and prepared to receive the cousins, but instead got a messenger on mule-back with a letter to say that they weren't coming till the next day, after all. A party had materialized. They did hope she wasn't too bored! She sent the messenger in for a drink, and stood for a moment with the letter in her hand. No, she wasn't bored! She could have her own shadow party again to-night. And this afternoon? She would go out into the hills where she and her cousins had played hide-and-seek and teased the shepherds — a long time ago, when they were all equals, more or less. A long time ago, under old Emperor Claudius, before the worst of the Troubles. She picked up her cloak and started out through the garden, but she walked slower and slower and at last came to a stop. She had discovered that she was rather frightened of going by herself into the hills now. So many evil things had happened since those days; she couldn't go all alone and be play-haunted by herself fifteen years ago! She ran back suddenly to the house and into the old library where the secretary was still in the thick of accounts. 'They are not arriving till to-morrow,' she said, 'and I am going to walk in the hills. Escort me, please. There are dogs.' Obediently Phillos put his lists to one side and got up. They went through the garden and out into the hills. She found she remembered the paths wonderfully well. She was not frightened now.

Phillos followed a couple of paces behind, as was proper. Suddenly she wondered if it was bad for his knee, and turned sharply to look, at a cross-ways between hill pasture and olives. He did not seem to be walking lame, and he had his hands full of flowers, the dry, long-stemmed summery things from the sides of the paths and cracks in the walls, coloured daisies and thin red and purple spikes. As she looked at them, his fingers closed on them with whitening knuckles. She smiled: 'We'll go down through the fields here; there used to be a stream. You'll find more.'

It was a beautiful pasture, with oaks and a few great rocks, not yet cropped dry. Half-way down she stopped in a patch of shade under one of the trees and lay down on the grass. Her hands fingered about among the warm grass blades, just as they had done fifteen years ago. The smell of wild dust and leaves was the same. Phillos stood in the edge of the shade, rubbing the bunch of pretty colours against his face. She beckoned him to come farther under the tree and sit down. He stretched out his knee a little stiffly among the grasses; she felt suddenly rather guilty and spoke friendlily to him about the country, and poked a cricket to jump towards his hand. He rolled over on to his face, his head turned away from her, and lay breathing in the summer out of the hillside. After a time she became aware, more by his silence than by any noise, that he was crying. He had probably strained the knee after all. She wondered how it had been damaged. The idiocy of some masters, spoiling a valuable possession, changing the thing from useful to less useful, the man from friend to enemy! Even women were sometimes both fools and cruel with their slaves, but at least they didn't, on the whole, do things to them when they were drunk!

She reached over and patted his head, which twitched and withdrew itself like a snail's eye. 'My poor Phillos!' she said, 'is it hurting so much?' A kind of negative movement appeared in the body. 'Was it the bailiff then?' she asked, 'you shouldn't take any notice of him. He's an uneducated man, honest, rough. He doesn't understand you're a person, at all.' Phillos answered with something quite inaudible, but that had the effect of a child's unhappiness. She moved nearer and put her hand on his head. For a moment it quivered, too; then lay passive under her fingers like a tame beast. 'Poor thing!' she said, rubbing into the base of the hair and then down onto the forehead, a new surface, warmer and softer. It amused her to go on. Suddenly she remembered coming here before with a puppy the children had, and stroking it as it lay on the grass, panting after play; that was the touch that had come back into her fingers. They felt on, checking at a line of eyebrow, and stroked it to the corner of the eye; the skin stayed curiously still — she thought he must be holding his breath. Then at the corner of the eye they came on something fresh, the wet of tears, checking the finger tips with something new and unlike the puppy that had grown up into a big hound and died years and years ago. Something human.

'What is it?' she said, 'has someone been unkind to you? Tell me, Phillos.' And again: 'You'd better tell me. Probably I can put it right.' He was one of her cousin's most valuable slaves; she mustn't let him be damaged. A hand came up over the face and covered hers, pulling at it a little. For a moment she almost lost her balance, leaning over, but then recovered it. She felt his lips against the inside of her fingers: very odd, a man's lips scarcely kissing, just touching in some very pathetic way, as the dog had dropped his muzzle into one's hand fifteen years ago. It was more dignified to let it be, not to withdraw it hurriedly. An uncomfortable position, all the same. The tension on her arm spread from wrist to shoulder. 'Now, Phillos,' she said, 'that'll do. Sit up and tell me what you're crying about.'

He obeyed almost at once, let go her hand and sat up. He must have lain with the flowers under his chin, for there were squashed petals and leaves on his neck still. 'I'm sorry, Miss Claudia,' he said, 'but I don't often have time off in the country. It gets one somehow.'

'Sure it's not your knee?' she said. He shook his head, even smiling. 'Or the bailiff?'

'No, no! At least, hardly. But I only save up so slowly.'

'Save up — ? To buy your freedom?' He nodded. 'What would you do if you were free?'

It seemed a difficult question to answer. At last he said: 'I'd stop being so lonely.'

'But are you?' she asked, surprised. 'In a big household like this? Surely you've got plenty of friends?'

'No,' he said.

And she considered that, after all, he hadn't much in common with most of them — always looked out of it at the slaves' festival, the Saturnalia, when there were games and little presents, and she went round, encouraging them to laugh and sing and do things all together and be jolly. She had found him reading a book once that day, in a corner of the big library, hunched up between two chests of book rolls; she remembered how she had packed him out, cheerfully but firmly, and partnered him with one of the Lady Rufa's maids for a singing game.

'What would you do?' she repeated.

He said: 'You'll think it silly, Miss Claudia.' Then: 'Well, I've got one friend, a Greek like me. He keeps a book shop by the new baths. You know it, perhaps. Meno's. He told me if I ever got free he'd give me a regular job there, copying or dictating or selling. There would be several of us working at it together. I'd like that. And perhaps some day to see Greece.'

'Yes,' she said, 'it seems very sensible. Not terribly exciting perhaps. I'm sorry you feel so lonely, Phillos. We must see what can be done about it.'

'Oh, don't bother, Miss Claudia,' he said, 'mostly I haven't time to bother myself. It was being out here. It's very beautiful country. Is this really your home, Miss Claudia? It must be fine for you, coming back, and then to-morrow the others will come, too, and you'll be all together. You ladies will come out here, I suppose, to this very field, and laugh and talk and remember times you've shared.'

'I doubt it,' said Claudia, dryly, and laughed a little. 'No. You've got it wrong, Phillos. The others have got now: the present, all bright and sparkling and jolly. And this hill, this stupid hill is only then: the dull, unimportant past. So I'm alone on it.'

'Are you?' he said, looking directly at her, for almost the first time, 'but you're never lonely, Miss Claudia?'

She prepared to smile at this ridiculousness, but the smell of turf came up at her, making her act blindly and childishly. 'You stupid!' she said, and beat on it with her fists. 'Why did you think I made you come with me?'

He stared at her for nearly a minute, then dropped his eyes and began picking out the least squashed flowers. She watched his hands doing it and tried to forget what she had said. She saw them making a wreath, pretty and mixed and funny, a child's crown. He offered it uncertainly, but she bent her head for it, in some way glad to hide her face. 'Now,' she ordered, 'you get me some.' He jumped up and went quickly from patch to patch, moving in the sun mostly; she had never seen him moving so easily before. She put her hands up over her own cheeks; they were hot; she felt the corner of her mouth twitching and smiling and tried to compose herself to gravity — what was there to smile at? Her cousins' slave secretary doing what he was told? Because he was a slave, not because she was a woman. Obviously he was not regarding her in that light. Stupid to suppose he might be. And dangerous impudence if he did! But what would be happening if she had a face and figure like Norbana's? — well, she wouldn't be sitting on a dry bank miles from Rome staring at a slave coming back with flowers — common, wild flowers — and thinking he needed a new pair of sandals!

He stood in front of her and dropped them into her lap; she began naming them to him — he did not know their country names. She stopped thinking about Norbana and what it would be like, and fell to threading the flowers together on a long grass. Her wreath was much better than his, thick and close and competently made so that it didn't come to pieces and hang over the left ear as the one on her own head was doing already! He knelt apologetically, to put it right, touching her hair; her head stayed tremulously still, determined not to slant itself towards a slave's hands. She put the last touches to her own wreath, admiring it as it dangled from her hand. He admired it, too, but from a distance, obviously refusing to consider in his own mind what she meant to do with it. 'Here, Phillos!' she said, 'take it, you stupid creature!' Even so, he did not dare duck his head for her to crown him, but took it in his hands and put it on himself. She jumped up. 'You've got it quite crooked. Now, stand still, I'll do it.' It was possible to retain an air of complete mastery still.

She put it straight. He had the right shaped head for it, as she had known, squarish, with hair that stood up springily under the leaves. The shadow of it seemed to brighten his eyes, too. He reached out, gently, hesitatingly, and took her hand and swung if for a moment in the sweet air between them. She asked him what books his friend published — poetry, history, astronomy, cookery books? He began very eagerly to tell her, and about the excitement of a new book, the polished tops of the rolls, the ruled lines in scarlet, bright and shiny, the thrill of who would come the first day to buy, reading it oneself and getting the points clear in one's head for customers who asked! And then the copying of books, poetry especially, getting the feel of a new metre — some phrase that jumped out at one like a jewel! And fresh editions of the old: philosophy, mathematics. They talked about it all the way back, walking side by side along the hill paths this time.

The cousins came and everything went according to plan. And then, towards the end of their stay, something really awkward and annoying happened. Lady Norbana lost her sapphire brooch. The whole of the villa was turned upside down. Claudia worried about it dreadfully, feeling that its loss was a reflection of her own competence. As, indeed, it was in some odd way made out to be. She began to suspect any and all the slaves, had them up, questioned them, bullied them, searched their bedding. All no good. And then suddenly she found it herself in the box edging of a flower bed.

She picked it up and looked at it angrily for having given her so much trouble. It stared back out of her palm in the odd, calm way that round polished stones have; it had been there all the time, waiting, in no hurry. She liked handling jewels; it did not happen often. She tried it on herself, pinning it first on the shoulder of her mantle, then at the cross-over of her dress. Lady Norbana, her cousin, was already ceasing to fuss about it. A jeweller had come that morning from town, sent by her betrothed with an assortment of even more beautiful brooches for her to choose from; the only difficulty lay in the decision! Would she, after all, be so very glad to get this sapphire back?

What was it worth, Claudia wondered? The price of one of the rose terraces. The price of a painted summer-house. The price of a skilled slave. Some people would give their ears for it. She jumped it up and down in the palm of her hand. The price of a skilled slave. Supposing a slave had found it and not told, but sold it in Rome — at one of the little jewellers in the Suburra. Who would have been any the worse? Not really Lady Norbana with her new one which was going to be the envy of all her friends! Perhaps the slave himself would be hurt: by the doing of something wrong and concealment of it. Wrong? Against the laws. The laws are there to defend property, to defend the owners, the innocent owners, the stupid owners, the careless owners who would just as soon have something else if they could get it! Supposing the slave who had found it and sold it used the money, not slavishly for mean little pleasures and gratifications of the body, but to buy his freedom and be a free man among his friends? Yes, Claudia pinned her cousin's sapphire brooch into her own dress under the belt, and went back to the house. Then she locked it in a box with her few valuable possessions and managed to forget about it quite successfully almost all the time. Norbana's taste had changed. She was tired of large, plain stones. She preferred them engraved; there was an amethyst with a winged cupid dancing and carrying torches — when you held it up to the light it seemed to waver with a translucent life and gaiety of its own: a piece of Alexandrian work. That was the final choice.

When the cousins were all there, Claudia had very little time to herself. There was a constant bustle and laughter and things to be arranged, or cleared up after they had been disarranged. On a quiet day, they wanted her usually to read aloud to them while they embroidered, all sitting under a holm oak by one of the fountains. She had a good voice with plenty of expression; she brought out the points. And there were so many books coming out now! Lady Quintilia had a taste for philosophy and the vaguer mathematics, but the others preferred poetry or poetic romances.

Phillos was busy, too. Between doing accounts and writing business letters he had to copy out their grandfather's memoirs of campaigning and politics in the early years of the Empire, occasionally expanding or annotating when they seemed too obscure. He was getting on with it steadily, but there was plenty left. Every evening he had to bring out what he had copied that day to Lady Quintilia and read it aloud to her. Usually Claudia was there, too, and the others pretended to be interested sufficiently to come in from time to time and comment wittily. Occasionally Quintilia made corrections in the manuscript, which had then to be recopied. Claudia gave Phillos most of his orders, and there might be a few minutes' conversation, all very much as it should be, diffident from him and assured from her. He did not look at her directly during their interviews, but kept his eyes down on his tablets; and she would have been ashamed to do her hair more carefully or wear her new fringed mantle just to talk to the secretary! They were going back to Rome in a week.

Sometimes she regretted that she had seen no more of the hills. But it had not seemed possible. There had been occasional tours of the estate on mule-back, mostly by Lady Quintilia and herself, and one or two excursions to the lake by the whole party. But after all, why be uncomfortable? Hill paths are rough and dusty and tear one's best dress, and the garden was always expectant and delicious — the damask roses really the greatest success! — and one could keep in the shade, and send back to the house for anything one had forgotten, and feed the gold fish and tame swans, and everything was just so, and one felt deep in oneself that one had power over it. The garden with the fountains was man-made and docile and friendly like a beautiful riding-horse, but the hills were wild and separate from man, enemies, dark wild bulls with tossing crests like horns! Why try to get companionship out of such alien forms?

A few days after they got back, when the household was all settled in again, Claudia unlocked her box, took out the brooch, and went with it to the little shop in the Suburra which she had decided on. She wore a solid brown cloak and walked quickly; no one spoke to her. While the jeweller handled and weighed the brooch, she sat on a stool beside his table, looking with quite a real interest at the specimens of his craftsmanship. She knew from Norbana about what the jewel was worth, but did not suppose she would get that. The first offer, of course, was ridiculously low, but she had always found bargaining quite pleasant and easy when it was a business matter: she had been the one to settle most of the estate business three years ago when Lady Quintilia had been so upset over the Troubles. The thing settled itself between her and the jeweller to their mutual satisfaction. She counted the money and put it into the purse she had brought with her.

On the way back she suppressed firmly all kinds of unpleasant images. The brooch recognized: the jeweller questioned: herself described. Nonsense. If she denied it completely — and they would hardly even have the face to accuse her! — it was her word against the jeweller's. There was nothing to be anxious about. The difficult part was over.

She sent for Phillos and gave him instructions about some letters he was to write. Then she said: 'You still want to go and shop-keep with your book-seller friends?'

'Yes, Miss Claudia,' he said, 'but there's not much chance of it yet.'

'How much have you saved so far?'

He told her, rather dully; it was all in the remote future and he was getting older every day; and they were back in Rome where he couldn't even look out over his desk at sunlight on blue daisies. 'Another six or seven years, if I'm lucky.'

'I think we can do better than that,' she said, and slid the money out of her purse on to the table.

He stared at it and then at her, straight into her face this time. 'Do you mean — you'll lend it to me, Miss Claudia?'

'No,' she said, 'it would take you too long to pay me back. I'm giving it to you.' He did not answer at all, only his eyes went back to the money and stared and stared; his hands began to shake and then his body; he shut his eyes. 'Don't be stupid!' she said sharply, 'it won't be as nice as you think, being free!'

'But why are you doing this,' he said, 'why, why? What do you get for it?' 'It's only some money that — came to me — lately,' she said, 'a windfall. I don't need it. I gathered that you did.'

Then he slid suddenly down to his knees and took her hands and began kissing them. She disentangled one and laid it on his head; it was odd how she remembered the feel of his hair. This way, he could not look up suddenly and see her face. She could let it wear any expression it chose. She could let her other hand soak for a minute in these kisses, which were, rightly and properly, nothing but gratitude. Gratitude. A pretty emotion as between lady and slave. Kisses not of the lips and senses but of the whole mind and body. Looking down at him, it seemed to her that they were being shaken out from under his shoulders, from the heart itself. And all for Norbana's brooch! Her cousin's brooch and her own presence of mind: no one any the worse. Presence of mind and absence of fear: a slave's emotion. Phillos would have been too frightened to do it himself—even though he might think he was a Stoic!

The cousins would need to get a new secretary now. If she had not acted as she had, Phillos would still be their secretary for years and years, never go off to his book-shop and his Greek friends. She would still be seeing him every day, having that few minutes' talk. Not that it mattered. She would train the new secretary to take her orders just as quickly. Perhaps it would be better if they got a Latin of some kind, rather than a Greek. Better with the bailiff and the estate people. It would be the new secretary who would stay for years and years: till she was old herself. Well, well, why think about unpleasant subjects?

'That'll do, Phillos!' she said cheerfully. Her right hand pulled itself away from his lips, her left hand from his hair. They would never stay like that again. 'Now,' she said, 'we'll count the money. You must go to Lady Quintilia this evening and tell her you have the price. I think I would rather you did not say it had anything to do with me, Phillos. We'll get the Quaestor in to-morrow and free you. The next time I'm buying a book I shall certainly come to your book-shop. And I hope you will make a great success of it!'

Antonia White

1899 – 1979

*N*ovelist and translator, she was educated at the Convent of the Sacred Heart, Roehampton, and at St Paul's School for Girls. Her convent childhood is reflected in much of her writing, being the major focus of her first novel Frost in May – which was begun when she was sixteen and completed when she was thirty-three (an incident which Antonia White sometimes used critically against herself as an indication of her work pace). A great deal of her writing was autobiographical, with three novels, The Lost Traveller *(1950),* The Sugar House *(1952) and* Beyond the Glass *(1954) each encompassing various periods in her life, including that of her experience of confinement in a mental institution. She also translated many of the novels of Colette.*

The following short story is taken from Strangers *(first published in 1954 and reprinted by Virago, London, 1981, 1984), a striking example of her portrayal of a woman's madness.*

The House of Clouds

THE night before, Helen had tried to drown herself. She did not know why, for she had been perfectly happy. The four of them, she and Robert and Dorothy and Louis, had been getting supper. Louis had been carrying on one of his interminable religious arguments, and she remembered trying to explain to him the difference between the Virgin Birth and Immaculate Conception as she carried plates out of the kitchen. And then, suddenly, she had felt extraordinarily tired and had gone out into the little damp courtyard and out through the gate into the passage that led to the Thames. She wasn't very clear what happened next. She remembered that Robert had carried her back to Dorothy's room and had laid her on the bed and knelt beside her for a long time while neither of them spoke. And then they had gone back into the comfortable noise and warmth of Louis's studio next door, and the others had gone on getting supper exactly as if nothing had happened. Helen had sat by the fire, feeling a little sleepy and remote, but amazingly happy. She had not wanted any supper, only a little bread and salt. She was insistent about the salt, because salt keeps away evil spirits, and they had given it to her quietly without any fuss. They were gentle with her, almost reverent. She felt they understood that something wonderful was going to happen to her. She would let no one touch her, not Robert even. It was as if she were being charged with some force, fiery and beautiful, but so dangerous that a touch would explode it.

She did not remember how she got home. But today had been quite normal, till at dinner-time this strong impulse had come over her that she must go to Dorothy's and here, after walking for miles in the fog, she was. She was lying in Dorothy's bed. There was a fire in the room, but it could not warm her. She kept getting up and wandering over to the door and looking out into the foggy courtyard. Over and over again, gently and patiently, as if she were a child, Dorothy had put her back to bed again. But she could not sleep. Sometimes she was in sharp pain; sometimes she was happy. She could hear herself singing over and over again, like an incantation:

> O Deus, ego amo te
> Nec amo te ut salves me
> Nec quia non amantes te
> Aeterno punis igne.[1]

The priest who had married her appeared by her bed. She thought he was his own ghost come to give her the last sacraments and that he had died at that very moment in India. He twisted his rosary round her wrist. A doctor came too; the Irish doctor she hated. He tried to give her an injection, but she fought him wildly. She had promised someone (was it Robert?) that she would not let them give her drugs. Drugs would spoil the sharpness of this amazing experience that was just going to break into flower. But, in spite of her fighting, she felt the prick of the needle in her arm, and sobbing and struggling still, she felt the thick wave of the drug go over her. Was it morphia? Morphia, a word she loved to say, lengthening the first syllable that sounded like the note of a horn. 'Morphia, mo-orphia, put an "M" on my forehead,' she moaned in a man's voice.

Morning came. She felt sick and mortally tired. The doctor was there still; her father, in a brown habit, like a monk, sat talking to him. Her father came over to the bed to kiss her, but a real physical dislike of him choked her, and she pushed him away. She knew, without hearing, what he and the doctor had been talking about. They were going to take her away to use her as an experiment. Something about the war. She was willing to go; but when they lifted her out of bed she cried desperately, over and over again, for Robert.

She was in a cab, with her head on a nurse's shoulder. Her father and two other men were there. It seemed odd to be driving through South Kensington streets in broad daylight, dressed only in one of Dorothy's nightgowns and an old army overcoat of Robert's. They came to a tall house. Someone, Louis, perhaps, carried her up flights and flights of steps. Now she was in a perfectly ordinary bedroom. An old nurse with a face she liked sat by the fire; a young one, very pink and white and self-conscious, stood near her. Helen wandered over to the

---

[1] Oh God, I love you, but I do not love you in order that you might save me, nor because you punish those who do not love you with eternal fire.

window and looked out. There went a red bus, normal and reassuring. Suddenly the young nurse was at her elbow, leading her away from the window.

'I shouldn't look out of the window if I were you, dear,' she said in a soft hateful voice. 'It's so ugly.' Helen let herself be led away. She was puzzled and frightened; she wanted to explain something; but she was tired and muddled; she could not speak. Presently she was in bed, alone but for the old nurse. The rosary was still on her wrist. She felt that her parents were downstairs, praying for her. Her throat was dry; a fearful weariness weighed her down. She was in her last agony. She must pray. As if the old nurse understood, she began the 'Our Father' and 'Hail Mary'. Helen answered. Decade after decade they recited in a mechanical rhythm. There were cold beads on Helen's forehead, and all her limbs felt bruised. Her strength was going out of her in holy words. She was fighting the overpowering sleepiness that she knew was death. 'Holy Mary, Mother of God,' she forced out in beat after beat of sheer will-power. She lapsed at last. She was dead, but unable to leave the flesh. She waited, light, happy, disembodied.

Now she was a small child again and the nurse was the old Nanny at the house in Worcestershire. She lay very peacefully watching the nurse at her knitting under the green lamp. Pleasant thoughts went through her head of the red-walled kitchen garden, of the frost on the rosemary tufts, of the firelight dancing in the wintry panes before the curtains were drawn. Life would begin again here, a new life perfected day by day through a new childhood, safe and warm and orderly as this old house that smelt of pines and bees-wax. But the nightmares soon began. She was alone in a crypt watching by the coffin of a dead girl, an idiot who had died at school and who lay in a glass-topped coffin in her First Communion dress, with a gilt paper crown on her head. Helen woke up and screamed.

Another nurse was sitting by the green lamp.

'You must be quiet, dear,' said the nurse.

There were whispers and footsteps outside.

'I hear she is wonderful,' said a woman's voice.

'Yes,' said another, 'but all the conditions must be right, or it will be dangerous for her.'

'How?'

'You must all dress as nurses,' said the second voice, 'then she thinks she is in a hospital. She lives through it again, or rather, they do.'

'Who . . . the sons?'

'Yes. The House of Clouds is full of them.'

One by one, women wearing nurses' veils and aprons tiptoed in and sat beside her bed. She knew quite well that they were not nurses; she even recognized faces she had seen in picture papers. These were rich women whose sons had been killed, years ago, in the war. And each time a woman came in, Helen went through a new agony. She became the dead boy. She spoke with his voice. She felt the pain of amputated limbs, of blinded eyes. She coughed up blood from lungs torn to rags by shrapnel. Over and over again, in trenches, in field hospital, in German camps, she died a lingering death. Between the

bouts of torture, the mothers, in their nurses' veils, would kiss her hands and
sob out their gratitude.

'She must never speak of the House of Clouds,' one said to another.

And the other answered:

'She will forget when she wakes up. She is going to marry a soldier.'

Months, perhaps years, later, she woke up in a small bare cell. The walls
were whitewashed and dirty and she was lying on a mattress on the floor,
without sheets, with only rough, red-striped blankets over her. She was wearing
a linen gown, like an old-fashioned nightshirt, and she was bitterly cold. In
front of her was the blank yellow face of a heavy door without a handle of
any kind. Going over to the door, she tried frantically to push it open. It was
locked. She began to call out in panic and to beat on the door till her hands
were red and swollen. She had forgotten her name. She did not know whether
she were very young or very old; a man or a woman. Had she died that night
in Dorothy's studio? She could remember Dorothy and Robert, yet she knew
that her memory of them was not quite right. Was this place a prison? If only,
only her name would come back to her.

Suddenly the door opened. A young nurse was there, a nurse with a new
face. As suddenly as the door had opened, Helen's own identity flashed up
again. She called wildly, 'I know who I am. I'm Helen Ryder. You must ring up
my father and tell him I'm here. I must have lost my memory. The number
is Western 2159.'

The nurse did not answer, but she began to laugh. Slowly, mockingly,
inch by inch, though Helen tried with all her strength to keep it open, she
closed the door.

The darkness and the nightmare came back. She lost herself again; this time
completely. For years she was not even a human being; she was a horse. Ridden
almost to death, beaten till she fell, she lay at last on the straw in her stable and
waited for death. They buried her as she lay on her side, with outstretched head
and legs. A child came and sowed turquoises round the outline of her body in
the ground, and she rose up again as a horse of magic with a golden mane, and
galloped across the sky. Again she woke on the mattress in her cell. She looked
and saw that she had human hands and feet again, but she knew that she was
still a horse. Nurses came and dragged her, one on each side, to an enormous
room filled with baths. They dipped her into bath after bath of boiling water.
Each bath was smaller than the last, with gold taps that came off in her hands
when she tried to clutch them. There was something slightly wrong about
everything in this strange bathroom. All the mugs were chipped. The chairs had
only three legs. There were plates lying about with letters round the brim, but
the letters never read the same twice running. The nurses looked like human
beings, but Helen knew quite well that they were wax dolls stuffed with hay.

They could torture her for all that. After the hot baths, they ducked her,
spluttering and choking, into an ice-cold one. A nurse took a bucket of cold
water and splashed it over her, drenching her hair and half-blinding her. She
screamed, and nurses, dozens of them, crowded round the bath to laugh at
her. 'Oh, Nelly, you naughty, naughty girl,' they giggled. They took her out and

dried her and rubbed something on her eyes and nostrils that stung like fire. She had human limbs, but she was not human; she was a horse or a stag being prepared for the hunt. On the wall was a looking-glass, dim with steam.

'Look, Nelly, look who's there,' said the nurses.

She looked and saw a face in the glass, the face of a fairy horse or stag, sometimes with antlers, sometimes with a wild, golden mane, but always with the same dark, stony eyes and nostrils red as blood. She threw up her head and neighed and made a dash for the door. The nurses caught and dragged her along a passage. The passage was like a long room; it had a shiny wooden floor with double iron tracks in it like the tracks of a model railway. The nurses held her painfully by the armpits so that her feet only brushed the floor. The passage was like a musty old museum. There were wax flowers under cases and engravings of Queen Victoria and Balmoral. Suddenly the nurses opened a door in the wall, and there was her cell again. They threw her down on the mattress and went out, locking the door.

She went to sleep. She had a long nightmare about a girl who was lost in the dungeons under an old house on her wedding-day. Just as she was, in her white dress and wreath and veil, she fell into a trance and slept for thirty years. She woke up, thinking she had slept only a few hours, and found her way back to the house, and remembering her wedding, hurried to the chapel. There were lights and flowers and a young man standing at the altar. But as she walked up the aisle, people pushed her back, and she saw another bride going up before her. Up in her own room, she looked in the glass to see an old woman in a dirty satin dress with a dusty wreath on her head. And somehow, Helen herself was the girl who had slept thirty years, and they had shut her up here in the cell without a looking-glass so that she should not know how old she had grown.

And then again she was Robert, endlessly climbing up the steps of a dark tower by the sea, knowing that she herself was imprisoned at the top. She came out of this dream suddenly to find herself being tortured as a human being. She was lying on her back with two nurses holding her down. A young man with a signet ring on his finger was bending over her, holding a funnel with a long tube attached. He forced the tube down her nose and began to pour some liquid down her throat. There was a searing pain at the back of her nose; she choked and struggled, but they held her down ruthlessly. At last the man drew out the tube and dropped it coiling in a basin. The nurses released her, and all three went out and shut the door.

This horror came at intervals for days. She grew to dread the opening of the door, which was nearly always followed by the procession of nurses and the man with the basin and the funnel. Gradually she became a little more aware of her surroundings. She was no longer lying on the floor, but in a sort of wooden manger clamped to the ground in the middle of a cell. Now she had not even a blanket, only a kind of stiff canvas apron, like a piece of sail-cloth, stretched over her. And she was wearing, not a shirt, but a curious enveloping garment, very stiff and rough, that encased her legs and feet and came down over her hands. It had a leather collar, like an animal's, and a belt with a metal ring. Between the visitations of the funnel she dozed and dreamt. Or she would lie quietly, quite happy to watch, hour after hour, the play of pearly colours on the piece of sail-cloth. Her name had irrevocably gone, but whole piece of her past life, people, episodes, poems, remained embedded in her mind. She could remember the whole of 'The Mistress of Vision' and say it over to herself as she lay there. But if a word had gone, she could not suggest another to fill the gap, unless it was one of those odd, meaningless words that she found herself making up now and then.

One night there was a thunderstorm. She was frightened. The manger had become a little raft; when she put out her hand she could feel waves lapping right up to the brim. She had always been afraid of water in the dark. Now she began to pray. The door opened and a nurse, with a red face and pale hair and lashes, peered round the door, and called to her:

'Rosa Mystica.'

Helen called back:

'Turris Davidica.'

'Turris Eburnea,' called the nurse.

'Domus Aurea,' cried Helen.[2]

And so, turn by turn, they recited the whole of the Litany of Our Lady.

One day she discovered that, by standing up in the manger, she could see through a high window, covered with close wire-netting, out into a garden. This discovery gave her great pleasure. In the garden women and nurses were walking; they did not look like real people, but oddly thin and bright, like figures cut out of coloured paper. And she could see birds flying across the sky, not real birds, but bird-shaped kites, lined with strips of white metal that flew on wires. Only the clouds had thickness and depth and looked as clouds had looked in the other world. The clouds spoke to her sometimes. They wrote messages in white smoke on the blue. They would take shape after shape to amuse her, shapes of swans, of feathers, of charming ladies with fluffy white muffs and toques, of soldiers in white busbies.

Once the door of her cell opened and there appeared, not a nurse, but a woman with short, frizzy hair, who wore a purple jumper, a tweed skirt, and a great many amber beads. Helen at once decided that this woman's name was Stella. She had a friendly, silly face, and an upper lip covered with dark brown.

'I've brought you a pencil,' she announced suddenly. 'I think you're so sweet. I've seen you from the garden, often. Shall we be friends?'

But before Helen could answer, the woman threw up her head, giggled, shot Helen an odd, sly look, and disappeared. With a sudden, sharp, quite normal horror, Helen thought, 'She's mad.'

She thought of the faces she had seen in the garden, with that same sly, shallow look. There must be other people in the place, then. For the first time, she was grateful for the locked door. She had a horror of mad people, of madness. Her own private horror had always been that she would go mad.

---

[2] 'Mystical Rose, Tower of David, Tower of Ivory, House of Gold' – part of the Litany of the Blessed Virgin.

She was feeling quiet and reasonable that day. Her name had not come back to her, but she could piece together some shreds of herself. She recognized her hands; they were thinner and the nails were broken, but they were the hands she had had in the life with Dorothy and Robert and the others. She recognized a birthmark on her arm. She felt light and tired, as if she had recovered from a long illness, but sufficiently interested to ask the nurse who came in:

'What is this place?'

The nurse, who was young and pretty, with coppery hair and green eyes, looked at Helen with pity and contempt. She was kindly, with the ineffable stupid kindliness of nurses.

'I'm not supposed to tell you anything, you know.'

'I won't give you away,' promised Helen.

'What is it?'

'Well! it's a hospital, if you must know.'

'But what *kind* of a hospital?'

'Ah, that'd be telling.'

'What *kind* of a hospital?' persisted Helen.

'A hospital for girls who ask too many questions and have to give their brains a rest. Now go to sleep.'

She shook a playful finger and retreated.

It was difficult to know when the episode of the rubber room took place. Time and place were very uncertain, apt to remain stationary for months, and then to dissolve and fly in the most bewildering way. Sometimes it would take her a whole day to lift a spoon to her mouth; at other times she would live at such a pace that she could see the leaves of the ivy on the garden wall positively opening and growing before her eyes. The only thing she was sure of was that the rubber room came after she had been changed into a salmon and shut up in a little dry, waterless room behind a waterfall. She lay wriggling and gasping, scraping her scales on the stone floor, maddened by the water pouring just beyond the bars that she could not get through. Perhaps she died as a salmon as she had died as a horse, for the next thing she remembered was waking in a small, six-sided room whose walls were all thick bulging panels of grey rubber. The door was rubber-padded too, with a small red window, shaped like an eye, deeply embedded in it. She was lying on the floor, and through the red, a face, stained red too, was watching her and laughing.

She knew without being told, that the rubber room was a compartment in a sinking ship, near the boiler room, which would burst at any minute and scald her to death. Somehow she must get out. She flung herself wildly against the rubber walls as if she could beat her way out by sheer force. The air was getting hotter. The rubber walls were already warm to touch. She was choking, suffocating: in a second her lungs would burst. At last the door opened. They were coming to rescue her. But it was only the procession of nurses and the funnel once more.

The fantasies were not always horrible. Once she was in a cell that was dusty and friendly, like an attic. There were spider-webs and an old ship's lamp on the ceiling. In the lamp was a face like a fox's mask, grinning down at her. She was sitting on a heap of straw, a child of eleven or so, with hair the colour of straw, and an old blue pinafore. Her name was Veronica. With crossed legs and folded arms she sat there patiently making a spell to bring her brother Nicholas safe home. He was flying back to her in a white aeroplane and with a green propeller. She could see his face quite clearly as he sat between the wings. He wore a fur cap like a cossack's and a square green ring on his little finger. Enemies had put Veronica in prison, but Nicholas would come to rescue her as he had always come before. She and Nicholas loved each other with a love far deeper and more subtle than any love between husband and wife. She knew at once if he were in pain or danger, even if he were a thousand miles away.

Nicholas came to her window and carried her away. They flew to Russia, and landed on a plain covered with snow. Then they drove for miles in a sledge until they came to a dark pine forest. They walked through the forest, hand in hand, Veronica held close in Nicholas's great fur cape. But at last she was tired, dazed by the silence and the endless trees, all exactly alike. She wanted to sit down in the snow, to sleep.

Nicholas shook her: 'Never go to sleep in the snow, Ronnie, or you will die.'

But she was too tired to listen, and she lay down in the snow that was soft and strangely warm, and fell into an exquisite dreamy torpor. And perhaps she did die in the snow as Nicholas had said, for the next thing she knew was that she was up in the clouds, following a beautiful Indian woman who sailed before her, and sifting snow down on the world through the holes in her pinafore.

Whenever things became too intolerable, the Indian woman would come with her three dark, beautiful sons, and comfort her. She would draw her sweet-smelling yellow veil over Helen and sing her songs that were like lullabies. Helen could never remember the songs, but she could often feel the Indian woman near, when she could not see her, and smell her sweet, musky scent.

She had a strange fantasy that she was Lord of the World. Whatever she ordered came about at once. The walls of the garden outside turned to blue ice that did not melt in the sun. All the doors of the house flew open and the passages were filled with children dressed in white and as lovely as dreams. She called up storms; she drove ships out of their courses; she held the whole world in a spell. Only herself she could not command. When the day came to an end she was tired out, but she could not sleep. She had forgotten the charm, or never known it, and there was no one powerful enough to say to her, 'Sleep.'

She raved, she prayed, but no sleep came. At last three women appeared.

'You cannot sleep unless you die,' they said.

She assented gladly. The took her to a beach and fettered her down on some stones, just under the bows of a huge ship that was about to be launched. One of the three gave a signal. Nothing could stop it now. On it came, grinding the pebbles to dust, deafening her with noise. It passed, slowly, right over her body. She felt every bone crack; felt the intolerable weight on her shoulders, felt her skull split like a shell. But she could sleep now. She was free from the intolerable burden of having to will.

After this she was born and re-born with incredible swiftness as a woman, as an imp, as a dog, and finally as a flower. She was some nameless, tiny bell, growing in a stream, with a stalk as fine as hair and a human voice. The water flowing through her flower throat made her sing all day a little monotonous song, 'Kulallah, Kulallah.' This happy flower-life did not last long. Soon there came a day when the place was filled with nurses who called her 'Helen'. She did not recognize the name as her own, but she began to answer it mechanically as a dog answers a familiar sound.

She began to put on ordinary clothes, clumsily and with difficulty, as if she had only just learned how, and to be taken for walks in a dreary yard; an asphalt-paved square with one sooty plane-tree and a broken bench in the middle. Wearily she would trail round and round between two nurses who polished their nails incessantly as they walked and talked about the dances they had been to. She began to recognize some of her companions in the yard. There was the woman with the beads, the Vitriol woman, and the terrible Caliban girl. The Caliban girl was called Micky. She was tall and rather handsome, but Helen never thought of her except as an animal or a monster, and was horrified when Micky tried to utter human words. Her face was half-beautiful, half-unspeakable, with Medusa curls and great eyes that looked as if they were carved out of green stone. Two long, yellow teeth, like tiger's fangs, grew right down over her lip. She had a queer passion for Helen, who hated and feared her. Whenever she could, Micky would break away from her nurses and try to fondle Helen. She would stroke her hair, muttering, 'Pretty, pretty,' with her deformed mouth. Micky's breath on her cheek was hot and sour like an animal's, her black hair was rough as wire. The reality of Micky was worse than any nightmare; she was shameful, obscene.

The Vitriol woman was far more horrible to look at, but far less repulsive. Helen had heard the nurses whispering how the woman's husband had thrown acid at her. Her face was one raw, red, shining burn, without lid or brow, almost without lips. She always wore a neat black hat and a neat, common blue coat with a fur collar. Everyone she met she addressed with the same agonized question: 'Have you see Fred? Where's Fred? Take me to Fred!'

On one of the dirty walls someone had chalked up:

'Baby.'

'Blood.'

'Murder.'

And no one had bothered to wipe it out.

The yard was a horror that seemed to have no place in the world, yet from beyond the walls would come pleasant ordinary noises of motors passing, and people walking and bells ringing. Above the walls, Helen could see a rather beautiful, slender dome, pearl-coloured against the sky, and tipped with a gilt spear. It reminded her of some building she knew very well but whose name, like her own, she had forgotten.

One day, she was left almost alone in the yard. Sitting on the broken bench by the plane-tree was a young girl, weeping. Helen went up to her. She had a gentle, bewildered face; with loose, soft plaits falling round it. Helen went and sat by her and drew the girl's head on to her own shoulder. It seemed years since she had touched another person with affection. The girl nestled against her. Her neck was greenish-white, like privet; when Helen touched it curiously, its warmth and softness were so lovely that tears came into her eyes. The girl was so gentle and defenceless, like some small, confiding animal, that Helen felt a sudden love for her run through all her veins. There was a faint country smell about her hair, like clover.

'I love you,' murmured Helen, hardly knowing what she said.

But suddenly a flock of giggling nurses were upon them with a chatter of:

'Look at this, will you?' and,

'Break away there.'

She never saw the country girl again.

And so day after day went past, punctuated by dreary meals and drearier walks. She lived through each only because she knew that sooner or later Robert must come to fetch her away, and this hope carried her through each night. There were messages from him sometimes, half-glimpsed in the flight of birds, in the sound of a horn beyond the walls, in the fine lines ruled on a blade of grass. But he himself never came, and at last there came a day when she ceased to look for him. She gave up. She accepted everything. She was no longer Helen or Veronica, no longer even a fairy horse. She had become an Inmate.

Stevie Smith

1902 – 71

S *tevie Smith was brought up by her mother and later her aunt in Palmers Green in North London where she continued to live with her aunt during her adult years. The area became the setting for much of her fiction and poetry. For thirty years of her life she worked as a secretary for magazine publishers while writing her own poetry, fiction and reviews. Much of her work appears whimsical or comically simple, using nursery rhyme rhythms, comic drawings and inconsequential happenings, but it manages to unsettle conventional interpretations of Christian doctrine and canonical literature and conventional expectations of the treatment of such serious subjects as death and war. Smith was tireless in deflating affectation and pomposity wherever she discovered it in militarists, imperialists or pacifists.*

The following short story and poems have been taken from Me Again: Uncollected Writings of Stevie Smith *(Jack Barbera and William McBrien (eds), Virago, London, 1981).*

Surrounded by Children

UNDER the shadow of the trees in Hyde Park the mothers are nursing the babies, and in the long grass of Kensington Gardens and on the banks of the Serpentine the sisters are caring for the brothers, under the trees the aunt walks. What is the aunt doing, under the trees walking? She is thinking of the young man who has the ice-cream vendor's cart; the cart of the ice-cream vendor is upon the road, he is peddling briskly away from the walking aunt.

The brothers of the sisters and the babies of the mothers have no care at all; theirs is a careless fate, to be pampered and cared for, no matter if there is no money the brothers will have the sisters to jump around after them, the babies will have the mothers to nurse them, the aunt will have the pleasure of sweet dreams under the tree and the ice-cream vendor will have his escape upon the saddle of his bicycle cart.

It is a pleasant English summer's day in the Gardens and in the Park. The brother of the sister has an ice-cream which he is eating, it is plastered upon his mouth, it is all over his whole face; he relishes the ice-cream. The sister anxiously combs back from her brow with long soiled finger the lank lock; she is worried to keep at the same time an eye upon the eater of the ice-cream and upon the younger brother who will paddle in the Serpentine, nobody shall say him no.

The little brothers and sisters who are the children of rich parents play also in the Park, but their play is watched by ferocious nannas. The children are fat and pink-cheeked but listless rather at their pleasures; their voices are the high-class English voices, the baby accents of the ruling classes, the clichés too, already they are there, a little affected is it not? and sad, too, that already the children are so self-aware almost already at a caricature of themselves—'we are having fun.' 'Did you enjoy your walk in the Park?' says Mama upon the child's return. 'Why, yes, it was fun you know, just rather fun. Did we enjoy the walk Priscilla?' Priscilla sneers with tight lips above baby teeth. 'Why yes, I suppose so, it was fun, rather fun.'

Towards both these groups of children is now coming a famously ugly old girl, she has wisps of grey hair carelessly dyed that is rioting out from under her queer hat, as she walks, she mutters to herself. Very different is the walking dream of the old girl from the walking dream of the love of the ice-cream vendor. Ah, upon the old girl is no eligible imagination for the nurture of love-life of entertainment value. As she walks she talks, and also her hands that are delicate and long, like delicate long birds' claws, clasp the air about her. She fetches up to a standstill beneath the rich chestnut tree; in the shadow of the tree is reposed a grand pram for a rich child. The pram is empty but the covers are turned back. How invitingly securely rich is the interior of this equipage that is for a grand infant of immensely rich parentage, how inviting indeed the interior where the covers lie backwards upon the pram beneath the green tree!

The famously ugly old girl is transfixed by this seducing vision of an open and deserted perambulator, she will get into it, come what may that is what she will do, that is her thought. Her hands now stretch upward to remove the queer hat to fling it down upon the grass, the toque lies at her feet. Tearing apart the lapels of her tightly buttoned coat she will not wait, the flimsy bombazine tears, the coat if off; with one hand she props herself against the dear perambulator, kicks shoe from shoe, stands stockingfoot.

But now the children gather round, close in upon her fast, for what is going on here? The children of the rich parents and the children of the poor parents are now united in a childish laughter, the sisters of the brothers have forgotten their care, the nephews and nieces of the aunt are here, the rich children have escaped their nannas, laughing and staring they close in upon the poor old girl, they join hands and laugh.

'Ah,' cries the sad beldame, transfixed in grotesque crucifixion upon the perambulator, stabbing at herself with a hatpin of the old fashion so that a little antique blood may fall upon the frilly pillow of the immaculate vehicle, 'what fate is this, what nightmare more *agaçant* so to lie and so to die, in great pain, surrounded by children.'

1939

Rise From Your Bed of Languor

R ISE from your bed of languor
Rise from your bed of dismay
Your friends will not come tomorrow
As they did not come today

You must rely on yourself, they said,
You must rely on yourself,

Oh but I find this pill so bitter said the poor man
As he took it from the shelf

Crying, O sweet Death come to me
Come to me for company,
Sweet Death it is only you I can
Constrain for company.

My Muse Sits Forlorn

MY Muse sits forlorn
She wishes she had not been born
She sits in the cold
No word she says is ever told.

God the Eater

THERE is a god in whom I do not believe
Yet to this god my love stretches,
This god whom I do not believe in is
My whole life, my life and I am his.

Everything that I have of pleasure and pain
(Of pain, of bitter pain and men's contempt)
I give this god for him to feed upon
As he is my whole life and I am his.

When I am dead I hope that he will eat
Everything I have been and have not been
And crunch and feed upon it and grow fat
Eating my life all up as it is his.

A Dream of Comparison

After Reading Book Ten of 'Paradise Lost'

TWO ladies walked on the soft green grass
On the bank of a river by the sea

And one was Mary and the other Eve
And they talked philosophically.

'Oh to be Nothing' said Eve, 'oh for a
Cessation of consciousness
With no more impressions beating in
Of various experiences.'

'How can Something envisage Nothing?' said Mary,
'Where's your philosophy gone?'
'Storm back through the gates of Birth,' cried Eve.
'Where were you before you were born?'

Mary laughed: 'I love Life,
I would fight to the death for it,
That's a feeling you say? I will find
A reason for it.'

They walked by the estuary,
Eve and the Virgin Mary,
And they talked until nightfall,
But the difference between them was radical.

I Forgive You

I FORGIVE you, Maria,
  Things can never be the same,
But I forgive you, Maria,
Though I think you were to blame.
I forgive you, Maria,
I can never forget,
But I forgive you, Maria,
Kindly remember that.

None of the Other Birds

NONE of the other birds seem to like it
  It sits alone on the corner edge of the outhouse gutter
They do not even dislike it
Enough to bite it
So it sits alone unbitten
It is always alone.

The Holiday

THE time is passing now
And will come soon
When you will be able
To go home.

The malice and the misunderstanding
The loneliness and pain
Need not in this case, if you are careful,
Come again.

Say goodbye to the holiday, then,
To the peace you did not know,
And to the friends who had power over you,
Say goodbye and go.

Elizabeth Taylor
1912 – 75

Born Elizabeth Coles, she was educated at the Abbey School, Reading, and then worked as a tutor and librarian until her marriage in 1936. Her first novel, At Mrs Lippincote's (1945) was followed by ten more works of extended fiction; among them Palladian (1946), A Wreath of Roses (1949), A Game of Hide-and-Seek (1951), The Sleeping Beauty (1953), Angel (1957) and Mrs Palfrey at the Claremont (1971). Her short stories also enjoyed considerable acclaim; they appeared in numerous magazines (New Yorker, Harper's, Vogue etc.) as well as in four volumes – Hester Lilly and Other Stories (1954), The Blush and Other Stories (1958), A Dedicated Man and Other Stories (1965) and Devastating Boys (1972). Her shrewd observations and moving portrayals of *human vulnerability helped to establish her reputation as one of the notable British women writers of the twentieth century.*

The following two short stories, are taken from Hester Lilly and Other Stories *(Peter Davies, London, 1954).*

'Taking Mother Out'

"GIVE the credit where it is due," Mrs Crouch said, smiling at her son. We had, of course, been marvelling at her youthfulness. Every gesture she made, even the most simple, seemed calculated to defy old age. She constantly drew our attention to her eighty years, referred to herself as an old fogey; insisted on this when we were obliged to demur. And then insisted on insisting. We offered her a drink. She became husky, Marie Lloydish, a little *broad*.[1] Her glass of gin she turned into a music-hall act. A further little speech was made over a cigarette, my brother waiting with his lighter flaring ready, she launched off into an explanation about herself: how she liked a bit of fun, liked young people, was as old as she felt, merely.

I glanced at her son; but not as if he were anything within my, or anybody's, reach. He was flashy, cynical, one of those men who knows about everything; makes sinister implications of rumours in the City, panic in the Cabinet; hints at inside information; has seen everything, seen through everything; known everybody, loved nobody; bought everything, at a special price; and sold it again, at a great profit. His mother admired him of all her children the most. She displayed him, was indebted to him, gave credit to him, as she was doing now.

He looked in her direction and smiled, a little bored with the elderly bird-watcher, who had sat down beside him to describe without pause his day on the marshes. He was right to be bored by the bird-watcher—a relation of ours, who menaced our every summer.

The evening light enhances those marshes. We sipped our drinks, narrowed our eyes, gazing down over the green flatness where masts in the middle of a field seemed to indicate the estuary. Little silences fell over us from time to time. The gentle vista before us, the gradual cadences, the close-cropped grass tufted with rough weeds which the slow-moving sheep had left, untidy little sheets of water, far off the glitter of the sea—all of this held our attention, even from one another, for English people love a view. Only the bird-watcher droned on.

Mrs Crouch twirled her glass, brushed at her skirt, examined her rings, wondering, I guessed, what the Spotted Crake had to do with her and how remarkably she carried her age. She decided to begin a counter-conversation and turned to my brother, raising her voice, for she was a little deaf and usually shouted.

[1] Marie Lloyd (1870–1922), successful music hall singer with distinctive delivery and voice.

"I hope, my dear, you won't think I tie Roy to my apron-strings. As a matter of fact, I am always saying to him, Roy, I say, you ought to be taking out a beautiful young blonde instead of your old mother. But he won't have it. Of course, I love my little outings, going out and meeting young people. When I'm asked how it is I carry my age so well, I say it's being with young people, and most of all being with Roy. He won't *let* me settle down. Come along, Mother, he says, let's go off on a binge." She savoured this word, chuckling. My brother fidgeted gloomily with his wrist-watch. Roy Crouch fidgeted with his, too.

"No," said the bird-watcher, as if contradicting himself, "not a common sight, but a remarkable one, the male bird sitting on the nest. No mistaking that, even at a distance, through field-glasses. The female is smaller and duller."

"Quite," said Roy nastily.

"I've had a full life," his mother was saying. My brother swallowed and glanced out across the salt-marshes.

"Did you ever see a Richard's Pipit?" Roy suddenly asked.

"No," said the bird-watcher shortly. "Did you?"

"Yes."

The bird-watcher turned right round in his chair and stared at him. He could not call him a liar, but he said: "Then you were very fortunate, sir. May I enquire where?"

"In Norfolk," Roy said carelessly.

"Very fortunate," the bird-watcher repeated, still glaring.

"I think that's why Roy likes to take me out, because I enjoy myself."

"I expect so," my brother agreed.

I refilled glasses. The bird-watcher recovered. He began to talk of the Water-Rail, how he had lain in a bed of reeds and counted seven pairs that morning. A wonderful sight. Perhaps not Richard's Pipits, you bounder, he seemed to imply. But a wonderful sight all the same.

"Talking of wonderful sights," said Roy, getting into his stride, "I was staying near the Severn Estuary in the spring and saw a very unusual thing—rather a romantic sight . . ." He laughed apologetically. "I happened to look out of my bedroom window one night when it was quite dark and I could see something moving down in the water-meadows, something rippling"—he rippled his fingers, to show us. "Something that shimmered"—his hand shimmered. "I stood very still and watched, hardly able to believe my eyes, but at last I realised what it was." He looked at the bird-watcher and at me. My brother was out of this conversation.

"But I really don't think," Mrs Crouch was telling him, "that the new tunes are half so jolly as the old . . ."

"And what do you think it was?" Roy asked us.

We did not know.

We did not know, we said.

"Eels," he said impressively, "young eels, or rather, I should say 'elvers'," he corrected himself. "I shall never forget that sight. It was ghostly, unreal. In a silver flood, they rippled through the grass in the moonlight, through a little stream and then on up the slope . . . beautiful. They come up from the sea, you know. Every spring. I've heard people say they *couldn't* travel across land, but there it was, I saw with my own eyes."

My brother was nearly asleep. Mrs Crouch said suddenly, testily, "What are you all nodding your heads so solemnly about?"

"Eels," I said lightly.

"Eels? Oh, eels! Why, only last night some friends of ours, a Mr and Mrs Sibley, were telling us about an experience they had when they were staying near the Severn Estuary. They were going to bed one night and Mr Sibley happened to look out of the window, and he suddenly called out to Mrs Sibley, 'Just come and look at this,' he said. 'There's something moving down there on the grass,' and Mrs Sibley said, 'Frank, do you know what I think those are? I do believe they're eels, young eels'—I forget the name she gave to them. What was that word, Roy?"

"No one has a drink," I cried, running frantically from one glass to another. The bird-watcher looked gravely, peacefully, at the view.

"Thank you, dear," said Mrs Crouch. "I am not at all sure that I haven't had too much already. What *was* that word, Roy? I have it at the tip of my tongue."

"Elvers," he muttered, and took a great swallow at his gin. He looked dejected worn, as old as his mother almost. They might have been husband and wife.

Nods and Becks and Wreathèd Smiles

"**I** WAS *hours* with Jennifer," Mrs Miller said, and she lifted the lump of sugar out of her coffee to see how much of it had melted. "I went in at ten o'clock at night, and she didn't arrive until after tea the next day."

Mrs Graham, not really attending, had a sudden vision of Jennifer, quite grown up, stepping out of a cab with all her luggage, just as it was getting dark. Such pictures were constantly insinuating themselves into her mind, were sharply visual, more actual than this scene in the teashop in the High Street among her friends, from whose conversation she often retracted painfully, to whose behaviour she usually reacted absurdly.

"... and dares to tell me there are no such things as labour pains," Mrs Miller was saying. "'It's all psychology,' he said, and I said, 'So are too many things nowadays.'"

Mrs Howard said, "He told me just to relax. Well, I relaxed like mad and I still had to have seven stitches."

Her voice had risen in her indignation, and Mrs Miller gave a little sideways warning glance at a man at the corner table, who had turned up his coat collar and was rustling his newspaper.

"Well, it was certainly the worst experience I ever had," Mrs Howard said emphatically. "I hope never to go through—"

"I thought neuralgia was worse," Mrs Graham forgot herself enough to say.

At first, they were too surprised to speak. After all, *men* could have neuralgia. Then Mrs Miller gave her own special little laugh. It was light as thistledown. It meant that Mrs Graham only said that to be different, probably because she was a vegetarian. And was always so superior, so *right* about everything—had said that there wouldn't be a war at the time of Munich, when they were sitting in this very café surrounded by the dried fruit and the tinned food they had been so frantically buying, and the next year, when they *hadn't* bought the fruit, she *had*.

"My God, Dolly! What *have* you done?" Mrs Miller suddenly exclaimed.

Groping tragically before her, like Oedipus going into exile, Mrs Fisher came stumbling toward them, a bandage over one eye, her hat crooked.

They all scraped their chairs back, making room for her.

"Conjunctivitis," she said faintly.

"You poor darling! Is it infectious?" Mrs Howard asked all in one breath.

"It's the same as pinkeye," Mrs Miller said.

"In a more virulent form," Dolly Fisher added. "Coffee," she said to the waitress. "Nothing to eat. What's that you've got, Laura?"

"A scone, dear," Mrs Miller said.

"I thought you'd given it up."

"Oh, I did—for at least three weeks. It didn't do any good."

"A scone and butter," Dolly Fisher said to the waitress when she brought the coffee.

"Wherever did you *pick that* up?" Mrs Miller went on, and her voice made the affliction sound very sordid indeed.

"I've been run down," Dolly said.

"You don't get it from being run down. You pick it up." Mrs Miller spread margarine over half a scone and popped it into her mouth.

* * *

"Oh, I'm late!" said Mrs Liddell. She put down her empty shopping basket and pulled up a chair. "I haven't started yet. I wonder is there any fish about?"

"There *was* some halibut," Mrs Miller said. "I went for mine as soon as I'd taken Arthur to the station."

"Oh, dear! Wasn't there anything else?"

"I seem to remember some sprats."

"But, Dolly, dear! What *have* you done?"

"She's picked up pinkeye from somewhere," Mrs Howard said. From somewhere not very nice, she implied.

Oedipus sat munching her scone. "It's the worst pain I think I ever had," she said defiantly.

The man at the corner table stood up hastily and called for his bill.

"Now what are you hiding from us?" Mrs Miller asked Mrs Liddell, who blushed and said, "Oh, of course, none of you've seen it. Hughie gave it to me."

She had been hiding nothing but had turned her hand a great deal in the light and now laid it in the middle of the table, as if she were pooling it.

"What a lovely ring!" they cried.

"For my birthday." She drew it off and let it lie in the palm of her hand.

"Oh, do let me!" Mrs Miller begged. "If my poor old hands aren't too fat." The ring was, after all, rather loose on her.

"It's so unusual!" Mrs Howard said, "I wonder where on earth he got it."

"It really has character," Mrs Miller announced, after long consideration and turning her hand this way and that to catch the light. "Yes, it really has. And it's *your* ring." She passed it back to Mrs Liddell. "Clever Hughie!"

"That will be the day," Oedipus said, "when Sidney gives me a ring for *my* birthday."

"It's a very old ring, he said," Mrs Liddell began.

"What of it?" Mrs Miller said generously. "You will often get far better value with second-hand things."

"Last year, he gave me a set of saucepans we had to have anyhow."

"Cheer up, Dolly, we're all in the same boat. None of *our* husbands gives us rings."

"I shall have to go," Mrs Liddell said, finishing her coffee quickly. She had had her little triumph and now must hurry with it to the fishmonger's.

"I must come, too," said Oedipus. They left together, and Dolly went off down the High Street toward the hills of Cithaeron.

"Well!" Mrs Miller said. "Fancy Hughie!" She gave her famous laugh.

They looked at one another.

"It was a very beautiful ring," said Mrs Graham, who always liked to be different.

Mrs Miller put down her cup. "I wouldn't have it as a gift," she said. "Personally."

Muriel Spark

1918 –

A novelist, short story writer, biographer, poet and author of literary criticism, Muriel Spark was born in Edinburgh (of Scottish-Jewish descent although she later converted to Roman Catholicism). She spent some time *in Central Africa before returning to an appointment at the British Foreign Office at the time of the Second World War. She started her literary career as an editor and biographer and after winning* The Observer *short story prize in 1951 she wrote a steady stream of highly acclaimed and distinctive fiction. The* Comforter *(1957) was her first novel and among her many publications are* The Ballad of Peckham Rye *(1960), a startling tale of the underworld;* The Prime of Miss Jean Brodie *(1961), a discomforting study of an Edinburgh school mistress and her select pupils;* The Girls of Slender Means *(1963); and* The Driver's Seat *(1970) – about a woman obsessed by death;* The Abbess of Crewe *(1974) is a satirical study of matters clerical and political; and* Loitering With Intent *(1981) represents her interest in the complexity of biography and autobiography. In 1967* Collected Poems *and* Collected Plays *were published.*

The following short story is taken from Voices at Play *(Macmillan, London, 1961).*

The Dark Glasses

COMING to the edge of the lake we paused to look at our reflections in the water. It was then I recognised her from the past, her face looking up from the lake. She had not stopped talking.

I put on my dark glasses to shield my eyes from the sun and conceal my recognition from her eyes.

'Am I boring you?' she said.

'No, not a bit, Dr. Gray.'

'Sure?'

It is discouraging to put on sun glasses in the middle of someone's intimate story. But they were necessary, now that I had recognised her, and was excited, and could only honourably hear what she had to say from a point of concealment.

'Must you wear those glasses?'

'Well, yes. The glare.'

'The wearing of dark glasses,' she said, 'is a modern psychological phenomenon. It signifies the trend towards impersonalisation, the weapon of the modern Inquisitor, it—'

'There's a lot in what you say.' But I did not remove my glasses, for I had not asked for her company in the first place, and there is a limit to what one can listen to with the naked eye.

We walked round the new concrete verge of the old lake, and she continued the story of how she was led to give up general medical practice and take up psychology; and I looked at her as she spoke through my dark glasses, and because of the softening effect these have upon things I saw her again as I had seen her looking up from the lake, and again as in my childhood.

At the end of the 'thirties Leesden End was an L-shaped town. Our house
stood near the top of the L. At the other extreme was the market. Mr.
Simmonds, the oculist, had his shop on the horizontal leg, and he lived there
above the shop with his mother and sister. All the other shops in the row were
attached to each other, but Mr. Simmonds' stood apart, like a real house, with a
lane on either side.

I was sent to have my eyes tested. He took me into the darkened interior
and said, 'Sit down, dear.' He put his arm round my shoulder. His forefinger
moved up and down on my neck. I was thirteen and didn't like to be rude to
him. Dorothy Simmonds, his sister, came downstairs just then; she came upon
us silently and dressed in a white overall. Before she had crossed the room to
switch on a dim light Mr. Simmonds removed his arm from my shoulder with
such a jerk that I knew for certain he had not placed it there in innocence.

I had seen Miss Simmonds once before, at a garden fête, where she stood
on a platform in a big hat and blue dress, and sang 'Sometimes between long
shadows on the grass', while I picked up windfall apples, all of which seemed
to be rotten. Now in her white overall she turned and gave me a hostile look,
as if I had been seducing her brother. I felt sexually in the wrong, and started
looking round the dark room with a wide-eyed air.

'Can you read?' said Mr. Simmonds.

I stopped looking round. I said, 'Read what?'– for I had been told I would
be asked to read row after row of letters. The card which hung beneath the
dim light showed pictures of trains and animals.

'Because if you can't read we have pictures for illiterates.'

This was Mr. Simmonds' joke. I giggled. His sister smiled and dabbed her
right eye with her handkerchief. She had been to London for an operation
on her right eye.

I recall reading the letters correctly down to the last few lines, which
were too small. I recall Mr. Simmonds squeezing my arm as I left the shop,
turning his sandy freckled face in a backward glance to see for certain that his
sister was not watching.

My grandmother said, 'Did you see—'

'– Mr. Simmonds' sister?' said my aunt.

'Yes, she was there all the time,' I said, to make it definite.

My grandmother said, 'They say she's going—'

'– blind in one eye,' said my aunt.

'And with the mother bedridden upstairs—' my grandmother said.

'– she must be a saint,' said my aunt.

Presently – it may have been within a few days or a few weeks – my reading
glasses arrived, and I wore them whenever I remembered to do so.

I broke the glasses by sitting on them during my school holidays two
years later.

My grandmother said, after she had sighed, 'It's time you had your
eyes tested—'

'– eyes tested in any case,' said my aunt when she had sighed.

I washed my hair the night before and put a wave in it. Next morning at eleven I walked down to Mr. Simmonds' with one of my grandmother's long hat-pins in my blazer pocket. The shop front had been done up, with gold lettering on the glass door; Basil Simmonds, Optician, followed by a string of letters which, so far as I remember, were F.B.O.A., A.I.C., and others.

'You're quite the young lady, Joan,' he said, looking at my new breasts.

I smiled and put my hand in my blazer pocket.

He was smaller than he had been two years ago. I thought he must be about fifty or thirty. His face was more freckled than ever and his eyes were flat blue as from a box of paints. Miss Simmonds appeared silently in her soft slippers. 'You're quite the young lady, Joan,' she said from behind her green glasses, for her right eye had now gone blind and the other was said to be troubling her.

We went into the examination room. She glided past me and switched on the dim light above the letter card. I began to read out the letters while Basil Simmonds stood with folded hands. Someone came into the front shop. Miss Simmonds slid off to see who it was and her brother tickled my neck. I read on. He drew me towards him. I put my hand into my blazer pocket. He said, 'Oh!' and sprang away as the the hat-pin struck through my blazer and into his thigh.

Miss Simmonds appeared in the doorway in her avenging white overall. Her brother, who had been rubbing his thigh in a puzzled way, pretended to be dusting a mark off the front of his trousers.

'What's wrong? Why did you shout?' she said.

'No, I didn't shout.'

She looked at me, then returned to attend to the person in the shop, leaving the intervening door wide open. She was back again almost immediately. My examination was soon over. Mr. Simmonds saw me out at the front door and gave me a pleading unhappy look. I felt like a traitor and I considered him horrible.

For the rest of the holidays I thought of him as 'Basil', and by asking questions and taking more interest than usual in the conversation around me I formed an idea of his private life.'Dorothy,' I speculated, 'and Basil.' I let my mind dwell on them until I saw a picture of the rooms above the shop. I hung round at tea-time and, in order to bring the conversation round to Dorothy and Basil, told our visitors I had been to get my eyes tested.

'The mother bedridden all these years and worth a fortune. But what good is it to her?'

'What chance is there for Miss Simmonds now, with that eye?'

'She'll get the money. He will get the bare legal minimum only.'

'No, they say he's to get everything. In trust.'

'I believe Mrs. Simmonds has left everything to her daughter.'

My grandmother said, 'She should divide her fortune—'

'– equally between them,' said my aunt. 'Fair's fair.'

I invented for myself a recurrent scene in which brother and sister emerged from their mother's room and, on the narrow landing, allowed their gaze to meet in unspoken combat over their inheritance. Basil's flat-coloured eyes did not themselves hold any expression, but by the forward thrust of his red neck he indicated his meaning; Dorothy made herself plain by means of a corkscrew twist of the head – round and up – and the glitter of her one good eye through the green glasses.

I was sent for to try on my new reading glasses. I had the hat-pin with me. I was friendly to Basil while I tested the new glasses in the front shop. He seemed to want to put a hand on my shoulder, hovered, but was afraid. Dorothy came downstairs and appeared before us just as his hand wavered. He protracted the wavering gesture into one which adjusted the stem of my glasses above my ear.

'Auntie says to try them properly,' I said, 'while I'm about it.' This gave me an opportunity to have a look round the front premises.

'You'll only want them for your studies,' Basil said.

'Oh, I sometimes need glasses even when I'm not reading,' I said. I was looking through a door into a small inner office, darkened by a tree outside in the lane. The office contained a dumpy green safe, an old typewriter on a table, and a desk in the window with a ledger on it. Other ledgers were placed—

'Nonsense,' Dorothy was saying. 'A healthy girl like you – you hardly need glasses at all. For reading, to save your eyes, perhaps *yes*. But when you're not reading . . .'

I said, 'Grandmother said to enquire after your mother.'

'She's failing,' she said.

I took to giving Basil a charming smile when I passed him in the street on the way to the shops. This was very frequently. And on these occasions he would be standing at his shop door awaiting my return; then I would snub him. I wondered how often he was prepared to be won and rejected within the same ten minutes.

I took walks before supper round the back lanes, ambling right round the Simmonds' house, thinking of what was going on inside. One dusky time it started to rain heavily, and I found I could reasonably take shelter under the tree which grew quite close to the grimy window of the inner office. I could just see over the ledge and make out a shape of a person sitting at the desk. Soon, I thought, the shape will have to put on the light.

After five minutes' long waiting time the shape arose and switched on the light by the door. It was Basil, suddenly looking pink-haired. As he returned to the desk he stooped and took from the safe a sheaf of papers held in the teeth of a large clip. I knew he was going to select one sheet of paper from the sheaf, and that this one document would be the exciting, important one. It was like reading a familiar book: one knew what was coming, but couldn't bear to miss a word. He did extract one long sheet of paper, and hold it up. It was typewritten with a paragraph in handwriting at the bottom on the side visible from the window. He laid it side by side with another sheet of paper which was lying on the desk. I pressed close up to the window, intending to wave and smile if I was seen, and to call out that I was sheltering from the rain which was now coming down in thumps. But he kept his eyes on the two sheets of paper. There were other papers lying about the desk; I could not see what was on them. But I was quite convinced that he had been practising handwriting on them, and that he was in the process of forging his mother's will.

Then he took up the pen. I can still smell the rain and hear it thundering about me, and feel it dripping on my head from the bough overhanging above me. He raised his eyes and looked out at the rain. It seemed his eyes rested on me, at my station between the tree and the window. I kept still and close to the tree like a hunted piece of nature, willing myself to be the colour of bark and leaves and rain. Then I realised how much more clearly I could see him than he me, for it was growing dark.

He pulled a sheet of blotting paper towards him. He dipped his pen in the ink and started writing on the bottom of the sheet of paper before him, comparing it from time to time with the one he had taken out of the safe. I was not surprised, but I was thrilled, when the door behind slowly opened. It was like seeing the film of the book. Dorothy advanced on her creeping feet, and he did not hear, but formed the words he was writing, on and on. The rain pelted down regardless. She was looking crookedly, through her green glasses with her one eye, over his shoulder at the paper.

'What are you doing?' she said.

He jumped up and pulled the blotting paper over his work. Her one eye through her green glasses glinted upon him, though I did not actually see it do so, but saw only the dark green glass focused with a squint on to his face.

'I'm making up the accounts,' he said, standing with his back to the desk, concealing the papers. I saw his hand reach back and tremble among them.

I shivered in my soaking wet clothes. Dorothy looked with her eye at the window. I slid sideways to avoid her and ran all the way home.

Next morning I said, 'I've tried to read with these glasses. It's all a blur. I suppose I'll *have* to take them back?'

'Didn't you notice anything wrong when you tried—'

'– tried them on in the shop?'

'No. But the shop's so dark. *Must* I take them back?'

I took them into Mr. Simmonds early that afternoon.

'I tried to read with them this morning, but it's all a blur.' It was true that I had smeared them with cold cream first.

Dorothy was beside us in no time. She peered one-eyed at the glasses, then at me.

'Are you constipated?' she said.

I maintained silence. But I felt she was seeing everything through her green glasses.

'Put them on,' Dorothy said.

'Try them on.' said Basil.

They were ganged up together. Everything was going wrong, for I had come here to see how matters stood between them after the affair of the will.

Basil gave me something to read. 'It's all right now,' I said, 'but it was all a blur when I tried to read this morning.'

'Better take a dose,' Dorothy said.

I wanted to get out of the shop with my glasses as quickly as possible, but the brother said, 'I'd better test your eyes again while you're here just to make sure.'

He seemed quite normal. I followed him into the dark interior. Dorothy switched on the light. They both seemed normal. The scene in the little office last night began to lose its conviction. As I read out the letters on the card in front of me I was thinking of Basil as 'Mr. Simmonds' and Dorothy as 'Miss Simmonds', and feared their authority, and was in the wrong.

'That seems to be all right,' Mr. Simmonds said. 'But wait a moment.' He produced some coloured slides with lettering on them.

Miss Simmonds gave me what appeared to be a triumphant one-eyed leer, and as one who washes her hands of a person, started to climb the stairs. Plainly, she knew I had lost my attraction for her brother.

But before she turned the bend in the stairs she stopped and came down again. She went to a row of shelves and shifted some bottles. I read on. She interrupted:

'My eye-drops, Basil. I made them up this morning. Where are they?'

Mr. Simmonds was suddenly watching her as if something inconceivable was happening.

'Wait, Dorothy. Wait till I've tested the girl's eyes.'

She had lifted down a small brown bottle. 'I want my eye-drops. I wish you wouldn't displace—Are these they?'

I noted her correct phrase, 'Are these they?' and it seemed just over the border of correctness. Perhaps after all, this brother and sister were strange, vicious, in the wrong.

She had raised the bottle and was reading the label with her one good eye. 'Yes, this is mine. It has my name on it,' she said.

Dark Basil, dark Dorothy. There was something wrong after all. She walked upstairs with her bottle of eye-drops. The brother put his hand on my elbow and heaved me to my feet, forgetting his coloured slides.

'There's nothing wrong with your eyes. Off you go.' He pushed me into the front shop. His flat eyes were wide open as he handed me my glasses. He pointed to the door. 'I'm a busy man,' he said.

From upstairs came a long scream. Basil jerked open the door for me, but I did not move. Then Dorothy, upstairs, screamed and screamed and screamed. Basil put his hands to his head, covering his eyes. Dorothy appeared on the bend of the stairs, screaming, doubled-up, with both hands covering her good eye.

I started screaming when I got home, and was given a sedative. By evening everyone knew that Miss Simmonds had put the wrong drops in her eyes.

'Will she go blind in that eye, too?' people said.

'The doctor says there's hope.'

'There will be an inquiry.'

'She was going blind in that eye in any case,' they said.

'Ah, but the pain . . .'

'Whose mistake, hers or his?'

'Joan was there at the time. Joan heard the screams. We had to give her a sedative to calm—'
'– calm her down.'
'But who made the mistake?'
'She usually makes up the eye-drops herself. She's got a dispenser's—'
'– dispenser's certificate, you know.'
'Her name was on the bottle, Joan says.'
'Who wrote the name on the bottle? That's the question. They'll find out from the handwriting. If it was Mr. Simmonds he'll be disqualified.'
'She always wrote the names on the bottles. She'll be put off the dispensers' roll, poor thing.'
'They'll lose their licence.'
'I got eye-drops from them myself only three weeks ago. If I'd have known what I know now, I'd never have—'
'The doctor says they can't find the bottle, it's got lost.'
'No, the sergeant says definitely they've got the bottle. The handwriting is hers. She must have made up the drops herself, poor thing.'
'Deadly nightshade, same thing.'
'Stuff called atropine. Belladonna. Deadly nightshade.'
'It should have been stuff called eserine. That's what she usually had, the doctor says.'
'Dr. *Gray* says?'
'Yes, Dr. Gray.'
'Dr. Gray says if you switch from eserine to atropine—'
It was put down to an accident. There was a strong hope that Miss Simmonds' one eye would survive. It was she who had made up the prescription. She refused to discuss it.
I said, 'The bottle may have been tampered with, have you thought of that?'
'Joan's been reading books.'
The last week of my holidays old Mrs. Simmonds died above the shop and left all her fortune to her daughter. At the same time I got tonsilitis and could not return to school.
I was attended by our woman doctor, the widow of the town's former doctor who had quite recently died. This was the first time I had seen Dr. Gray, although I had known the other Dr. Gray, her husband, whom I missed. The new Dr. Gray was a sharp-faced athletic woman. She was said to be young. She came to visit me every day for a week. After consideration I decided she was normal and in the right, though dull.
Through the feverish part of my illness I saw Basil at the desk through the window and I heard Dorothy scream. While I was convalescent I went for walks, and always returned by the lane beside the Simmonds' house. There had been no bickering over the mother's will. Everyone said the eye-drop affair was a terrible accident. Miss Simmonds had retired and was said to be going rather dotty.
I saw Dr. Gray leaving the Simmonds' at six o'clock one evening. She must have been calling on poor Miss Simmonds. She noticed me at once as I emerged from the lane.

'Don't loiter about, Joan. It's getting chilly.'

The next morning I saw a light in the office window. I stood under the tree and looked. Dr. Gray sat upon the desk with her back to me, quite close. Mr. Simmonds sat in his chair talking to her, tilting back his chair. A bottle of sherry stood on the table. They each had a glass half-filled with sherry. Dr. Gray swung her legs, she was in the wrong, sexy, like our morning help who sat on the kitchen table swinging her legs.

But then she spoke. 'It will take time,' she said. 'A very difficult patient, of course.'

Basil nodded. Dr. Gray swung her legs, and looked professional. She was in the right, she looked like our games mistress who sometimes sat on a desk swinging her legs.

Before I returned to school I saw Basil one morning at his shop door. 'Reading glasses all right now?' he said.

'Oh yes, thank you.'

'There's nothing wrong with your sight. Don't let your imagination run away with you.'

I walked on, certain that he had known my guilty suspicions all along.

'I took up psychology during the war. Up till then I was in general practice.'

I had come to the summer school to lecture on history and she on psychology. Psychiatrists are very often ready to talk to strangers about their inmost lives. This is probably because they spend so much time hearing out their patients. I did not recognise Dr. Gray, except as a type, when I had attended her first lecture on 'the psychic manifestations of sex'. She spoke of child-poltergeists, and I was bored, and took refuge in observing the curious language of her profession. I noticed the word 'arousement'. 'Adolescents in a state of sexual arousement,' she said, 'may become possessed of almost psychic insight.'

After lunch, since the Eng. Lit. people had gone off to play tennis, she tacked on to me and we walked to the lake across the lawns, past the rhododendrons. This lake had once been the scene of a love-mad duchess's death.

'. . . during the war. Before that I was in general practice. It's strange,' she said, 'how I came to take up psychology. My second husband had a breakdown and was under a psychiatrist. Of course, he's incurable, but I decided . . . It's strange, but that's how I came to take it up. It saved *my* reason. My husband is still in a home. His sister, of course, became quite incurable. *He* has his lucid moments. I did not realise it, of course, when I married, but there was what I'd now call an oedipus-transference on his part, and . . .'

How tedious I found these phrases! We had come to the lake. I stooped over it and myself looked back at myself through the dark water. I looked at Dr. Gray's reflection and recognised her. I put on my dark glasses, then.

'Am I boring you?' she said.

'No, carry on.'

'Must you wear those glasses? . . . it is a modern psychological phenomenon . . . the trend towards impersonalisation . . . the modern Inquisitor.'

For a while, she watched her own footsteps as we walked round the lake. Then she continued her story. '... an optician. His sister was blind – *going* blind when I first attended her. Only the one eye was affected. Then there was an accident, one of those *psychological* accidents. She was a trained dispenser, but she mixed herself the wrong eye-drops. Now it's very difficult to make a mistake like that, normally. But subconsciously she wanted to, she *wanted* to. But she wasn't normal, she was not normal.'

'I'm not saying she was,' I said.

'What did you say?'

'I'm sure she wasn't a normal person,' I said, 'if you say so.'

'It can all be explained psychologically, as we've tried to show to my husband. We've told him and told him, and given him every sort of treatment – shock, insulin, everything. And after all, the stuff didn't have any effect on his sister immediately, and when she did go blind it was caused by acute glaucoma. She would probably have lost her sight in any case. Well, she went off her head completely and accused her brother of having put the wrong drug in the bottle deliberately. This is the interesting part from the psychological point of view – she said she had seen something that he didn't want her to see, something disreputable. She said he wanted to blind the eye that saw it. She said ...'

We were walking round the lake for the second time. When we came to the spot where I had seen her face reflected I stopped and looked over the water.

'I'm boring you.'

'No, no.'

'I wish you would take off those glasses.'

I took them off for a moment. I rather liked her for her innocence in not recognising me, though she looked hard and said, 'There's a subconscious reason why you wear them.'

'Dark glasses hide dark thoughts,' I said.

'Is that a saying?'

'Not that I've heard. But it is one now.'

She looked at me anew. But she didn't recognise me. These fishers of the mind have no eye for outward things. Instead, she was 'recognising' my mind: I daresay I came under some category of hers.

I had my glasses on again, and was walking on.

'How did your husband react to his sister's accusations?' I said.

'He was remarkably kind.'

'Kind?'

'Oh, yes, in the circumstances. Because she started up a lot of gossip in the neighbourhood. It was only a small town. It was a long time before I could persuade him to send her to a home for the blind where she could be looked after. There was a terrible bond between them. Unconscious incest.'

'Didn't you know that when you married him? I should have thought it would have been obvious.'

She looked at me again. 'I had not studied psychology at that time,' she said.

I thought, neither had I.

We were silent for the third turn about the lake. Then she said, 'Well, I was telling you how I came to study psychology and practise it. My husband had this breakdown after his sister went away. He had delusions. He kept imagining he saw eyes looking at him everywhere. He still sees them from time to time. But *eyes*, you see. That's significant. Unconsciously he felt he had blinded his sister. Because unconsciously he wanted to do so. He keeps confessing that he did so.'

'And attempted to forge the will?' I said.

She stopped. 'What are you saying?'

'Does he admit that he tried to forge his mother's will?'

'I haven't mentioned anything about a will.'

'Oh, I thought you had.'

'But, in fact, that was his sister's accusation. What made you say that? How did you know?'

'I must be psychic,' I said.

She took my arm. I had become a most endearing case history.

'You must be psychic indeed,' she said. 'You must tell me more about yourself. Well, that's the story of my taking up my present profession. When my husband started having these delusions and making these confessions I felt I had to understand the workings of the mind. And I began to study them. It has been fruitful. It has saved my own reason.'

'Did it ever occur to you that the sister's story might be true?' I said. 'Especially as he admits it.'

She took away her arm and said. 'Yes, I considered the possibility. I must admit I considered it well.'

She saw me watching her face. She looked as if she were pleading some personal excuse.

'Oh do,' she said, 'please take off those glasses.'

'Why don't you believe his own confession?'

'I'm a psychiatrist and we seldom believe confessions.' She looked at her watch as if to suggest I had started the whole conversation and was boring her.

I said, 'He might have stopped seeing eyes if you'd taken him at his word.'

She shouted, 'What are you saying? What are you thinking of? He wanted to give a statement to the police, do you realise ...'

'You know he's guilty,' I said.

'As his wife,' she said, 'I know he's guilty. But as a psychiatrist I must regard him as innocent. That's why I took up the subject.' She suddenly turned angry and shouted, 'You damned inquisitor, I've met your type before.

I could hardly believe she was shouting, who previously had been so calm. 'Oh, it's not my business,' I said, and took off my glasses to show willing.

I think it was then she recognised me.

Doris Lessing

1919 –

D oris Lessing was born in Persia and raised on a poor homestead in Southern Rhodesia where her mother constantly longed for the London she had left. She became a secretary, married twice, had three children and, during the Second World War, joined various Left-wing groups. She came to London in 1949 and her first novel, The Grass is Singing, was published the year after. She has continued to live and write in London, remaining politically active and treating social and political issues in her novels and short stories. Her most famous work is probably The Golden Notebook (1962) which was praised for its early investigation of feminist issues and for its depiction of women's consciousness entrapped in the past.

The following short story has been taken from Doris Lessing: Collected Stories, Vol. II (Panther, London 1979).

An Old Woman and Her Cat

H ER name was Hetty, and she was born with the twentieth century. She was seventy when she died of cold and malnutrition. She had been alone for a long time, since her husband had died of pneumonia in a bad winter soon after the Second World War. He had not been more than middle-aged. Her four children were now middle-aged, with grown children. Of these descendants one daughter sent her Christmas cards, but otherwise she did not exist for them. For they were all respectable people, with homes and good jobs and cars. And Hetty was not respectable. She had always been a bit strange, these people said, when mentioning her at all.

When Fred Pennefather, her husband, was alive, and the children just growing up, they all lived much too close and uncomfortable in a Council flat in that part of London which is like an estuary, with tides of people flooding in and out: they were not half a mile from the great stations of Euston, St Pancras and King's Cross. The blocks of flats were pioneers in that area, standing up grim, grey, hideous, among many acres of little houses and gardens, all soon to be demolished so that they could be replaced by more tall grey blocks. The Pennefathers were good tenants, paying their rent, keeping out of debt; he was a building worker, 'steady', and proud of it. There was no evidence then of Hetty's future dislocation from the normal, unless it was that she very often slipped down for an hour or so to the platforms where the locomotives drew in and ground out again. She liked the smell of it all, she said. She liked to see people moving about, 'coming and going from all those foreign places'. She meant Scotland, Ireland, the North of England. These visits into the din, the smoke, the massed swirling people, were for her a drug, like other people's drinking or gambling. Her husband teased her, calling her a gipsy. She was in fact part-gipsy, for her mother had been one, but had chosen to leave her people and marry a man who lived in a house. Fred Pennefather liked his wife for being different from the run of the women he knew, and had married her because of it; but her children were fearful that her gipsy blood might show itself in worse ways than haunting railway stations. She was a tall woman with a lot of glossy black hair, a skin that tanned easily, and dark strong eyes. She wore bright colours, and enjoyed quick tempers and sudden reconciliations. In her prime she attracted attention, was proud and handsome. All this made it inevitable that the people in those streets should refer to her as 'that gipsy woman'. When she heard them, she shouted back that she was none the worse for that.

After her husband died and the children married and left, the Council moved her to a small flat in the same building. She got a job selling food in a local store, but found it boring. There seem to be traditional occupations for middle-aged women living alone, the busy and responsible part of their lives being over. Drink. Gambling. Looking for another husband. A wistful affair or two. That's about it. Hetty went through a period of, as it were, testing out all these, like hobbies, but tired of them. While still earning her small wage as a saleswoman, she began a trade in buying and selling second-hand clothes. She did not have a shop of her own, but bought or begged clothes from householders, and sold these to stalls and the second-hand shops. She adored doing this. It was a passion. She gave up her respectable job and forgot all about her love of trains and travellers. Her room was always full of bright bits of cloth, a dress that had a pattern she fancied and did not want to sell, strips of beading, old furs, embroidery, lace. There were street traders among the people in the flats, but there was something in the way Hetty went about it that lost her friends. Neighbours of twenty or thirty years' standing said she had gone queer, and wished to know her no longer. But she did not mind. She was enjoying herself too much, particularly the moving about the streets with her old perambulator, in which she crammed what she was buying or selling. She liked the gossiping, the bargaining, the wheedling from householders. It was this last which – and she knew this quite well of course – the neighbours objected to. It was the thin edge of the wedge. It was begging. Decent people did not beg. She was no longer decent.

Lonely in her tiny flat, she was there as little as possible, always preferring the lively streets. But she had after all to spend some time in her room, and one day she saw a kitten lost and trembling in a dirty corner, and brought it home to the block of flats. She was on a fifth floor. While the kitten was growing into a large strong tom, he ranged about that conglomeration of staircases and lifts and many dozens of flats, as if the building were a town. Pets were not actively persecuted by the authorities, only forbidden and then tolerated. Hetty's life from the coming of the cat became more sociable, for the beast was always making friends with somebody in the cliff that was the block of flats across the court, or not coming home for nights at a time so that she had to go and look for him and knock on doors and ask, or returning home kicked and limping, or bleeding after a fight with his kind. She made scenes with the kickers, or the owners of the enemy cats, exchanged cat lore with cat-lovers, was always having to bandage and nurse her poor Tibby. The cat was soon a scarred warrior with fleas, a torn ear, and a ragged·look to him. He was a multicoloured cat and his eyes were small and yellow. He was a long way down the scale from the delicately coloured, elegantly shaped pedigree cats. But he was independent, and often caught himself pigeons when he could no longer stand the tinned cat food, or the bread and packet gravy Hetty fed him, and he purred and nestled when she grabbed him to her bosom at those times she suffered loneliness. This happened less and less. Once she had realized that her children were hoping that she would leave them alone because the old rag-trader was an embarrassment to them, she accepted it, and a bitterness that always had wild humour in it welled up only at times like Christmas. She sang or chanted to the cat: 'You nasty old beast, filthy old cat, nobody wants you, do they Tibby, no, you're just an ally tom, just an old stealing cat, hey Tibs, Tibs, Tibs.'

The building teemed with cats. There were even a couple of dogs. They all fought up and down the grey cement corridors. There were sometimes dog and cat messes which someone had to clear up, but which might be left for days and weeks as part of neighbourly wars and feuds. There were many complaints. Finally an official came from the Council to say that the ruling about keeping animals was going to be enforced. Hetty, like the others, would have to have her cat destroyed. This crisis coincided with a time of bad luck for her. She had had flu' had not been able to earn money; had found it hard to get out for her pension; had run into debt. She owed a lot of back rent, too. A television set she had hired and was not paying for attracted the visits of a television representative. The neighbours were gossiping that Hetty had 'gone savage'. This was because the cat had brought up the stairs and along the passageways a pigeon he had caught, shedding feathers and blood all the way; a woman coming in to complain found Hetty plucking the pigeon to stew it, as she had done with others, sharing the meal with Tibby.

'You're filthy,' she would say to him, setting the stew down to cool in his dish. 'Filthy old thing. Eating that dirty old pigeon. What do you think you are, a wild cat? Decent cats don't eat dirty birds. Only those old gipsies eat wild birds.'

One night she begged help from a neighbour who had a car, and put into the car herself, the television set, the cat, bundles of clothes, and the pram. She was driven across London to a room in a street that was a slum because it was waiting to be done up. The neighbour made a second trip to bring her bed and her mattress, which were tied to the roof of the car, a chest of drawers, an old trunk, saucepans. It was in this way that she left the street in which she had lived for thirty years, nearly half her life.

She set up house again in one room. She was frightened to go near 'them' to re-establish pension rights and her identity, because of the arrears of rent she had left behind, and because of the stolen television set. She started trading again, and the little room was soon spread, like her last, with a rainbow of colours and textures and lace and sequins. She cooked on a single gas ring and washed in the sink. There was no hot water unless it was boiled in saucepans. There were several old ladies and a family of five children in the house, which was condemned.

She was in the ground-floor back, with a window which opened on to a derelict garden, and her cat was happy in a hunting ground that was a mile around this house where his mistress was so splendidly living. A canal ran close by, and in the dirty city-water were islands which a cat could reach by leaping from moored boat to boat. On the islands were rats and birds. There were pavements full of fat London pigeons. The cat was a fine hunter. He soon had his place in the hierarchies of the local cat population and did not have to fight much to keep it. He was a strong male cat, and fathered many litters of kittens.

In the place Hetty and he lived five happy years. She was trading well, for there were rich people close by to shed what the poor needed to buy cheaply. She was not lonely for she made a quarrelling but satisfying friendship with a woman on the top floor, a widow like herself who did not see her children either. Hetty was sharp with the five children, complaining about their noise and mess, but she slipped them bits of money and sweets after telling their mother that 'she was a fool to put herself out for them, because they wouldn't appreciate it.' She was living well, even without her pension. She sold the television set and gave herself and her friend upstairs some day-trips to the coast, and bought a small radio. She never read books or magazines. The truth was that she could not write or read, or only so badly it was no pleasure to her. Her cat was all reward and no cost, for he fed himself, and continued to bring in pigeons for her to cook and eat, for which in return he claimed milk.

'Greedy Tibby, you greedy *thing*, don't think I don't know, oh yes I do, you'll get sick eating those old pigeons, I do keep telling you that, don't I?'

At last the street was being done up. No longer a uniform, long, disgraceful slum, houses were being bought by the middle-class people. While this meant more good warm clothes for trading – or begging, for she still could not resist the attraction of getting something for nothing by the use of her plaintive inventive tongue, her still flashing handsome eyes – Hetty knew, like her neighbours, that soon this house with its cargo of poor people would be bought for improvement.

In the week Hetty was seventy years old came the notice that was the end of this little community. They had four weeks to find somewhere else to live.

Usually, the shortage of housing being what it is in London – and everywhere else in the world, of course – these people would have had to scatter, fending for themselves. But the fate of this particular street was attracting attention, because a municipal election was pending. Homelessness among the poor was finding a focus in this street which was a perfect symbol of the whole area, and indeed the whole city, half of it being fine, coverted, tasteful houses, full of people who spent a lot of money, and half being dying houses tenanted by people like Hetty.

As a result of speeches by councillors and churchmen, local authorities found themselves unable to ignore the victims of this redevelopment. The people in the house Hetty was in were visited by a team consisting of an unemployment officer, a social worker and a rehousing officer. Hetty, a strong gaunt old woman wearing a scarlet wool suit she had found among her cast-offs that week, a black knitted tea-cosy on her head, and black-buttoned Edwardian boots too big for her, so that she had to shuffle, invited them into her room. But although all were well used to the extremes of poverty, none wished to enter the place, but stood in the doorway and made her this offer: that she should be aided to get her pension – why had she not claimed it long ago? – and that she, together with the four other old ladies in the houses should move to a Home run by the Council out in the northern suburbs. All these women were used to, and enjoyed, lively London, and while they had no alternative but to agree, they fell into a saddened and sullen state. Hetty agreed too. The last two winters had set her bones aching badly, and a cough was never far away. And while perhaps she was more of an urban soul even than the others, since she had walked up and down so many streets with her old permabulator loaded with rags and laces, and since she knew so intimately London's texture and taste, she minded least of all the idea of a new home 'among green fields'. There were, in fact, no fields near the promised Home, but for some reason all the old ladies had chosen to bring out this old song of a phrase, as if it belonged to their situation, that of old women not far off death. 'It will be nice to be near green fields again,' they said to each other over cups of tea.

The housing officer came to make final arrangements. Hetty Pennefather was to move with the others in two weeks' time. The young man, sitting on the very edge of the only chair in the crammed room, because it was greasy and he suspected it had fleas or worse in it, breathed as lightly as he could because of the appalling stink: there was a lavatory in the house, but it had been out of order for three days, and it was just the other side of a thin wall. The whole house smelled.

The young man, who knew only too well the extent of the misery due to lack of housing, who knew how many old people abandoned by their children did not get the offer to spend their days being looked after by the authorities, could not help feeling that this wreck of a human being could count herself lucky to get a place in his Home, even if it was – and he knew and deplored the fact – an institution in which the old were treated like naughty and dim-witted children until they had the good fortune to die.

But just as he was telling Hetty that a van would be coming to take her effects and those of the other four old ladies, and that she need not take anything more with her than her clothes 'and perhaps a few photographs', he saw what he had thought was a heap of multicoloured rags get up and put its ragged gingery-black paws on the old woman's skirt. Which today was a cretonne curtain covered with pink and red roses that Hetty had pinned around her because she liked the pattern.

'You can't take that cat with you,' he said automatically. It was something he had to say often, and knowing what misery the statement caused, he usually softened it down. But he had been taken by surprise.

Tibby now looked like a mass of old wool that has been matting together in dust and rain. One eye was permanently half-closed, because a muscle had been ripped in a fight. One ear was vestigial. And down a flank was a hairless slope with a thick scar on it. A cat-hating man had treated Tibby as he treated all cats, to a pellet from his airgun. The resulting wound had taken two years to heal. And Tibby smelled.

No worse, however, than his mistress, who sat stiffly still, bright-eyed with suspicion, hostile, watching the well-brushed tidy young man from the Council.

'How old is that beast?'

'Ten years, no, only eight years, he's a young cat about five years old,' said Hetty, desperate.

'It looks as if you'd do him a favour to put him out of his misery,' said the young man.

When the official left, Hetty had agreed to everything. She was the only one of the old women with a cat. The others had budgerigars or nothing. Budgies were allowed in the Home.

She made her plans, confided in the others, and when the van came for them and their clothes and photographs and budgies, she was not there, and they told lies for her. 'Oh, we don't know where she can have gone, dear,' the old women repeated again and again to the indifferent van-driver. 'She was here last night, but she did say something about going to her daughter in Manchester.' And off they went to die in the Home.

Hetty knew that when houses have been emptied for re-development they may stay empty for months, even years. She intended to go on living in this one until the builders moved in.

It was a warm autumn. For the first time in her life she lived like a gipsy forbears, and did not go to bed in a room in a house like respectable people. She spent several nights, with Tibby, sitting crouched in a doorway of an empty house two doors from her own. She knew exactly when the police would come around, and where to hide herself in the bushes of the overgrown shrubby garden.

As she had expected, nothing happened in the house, and she moved back in. She smashed a back window-pane so that Tibby could move in and out without her having to unlock the front door for him, and without leaving a window suspiciously open. She moved to the top back room and left it every morning early, to spend the day in the streets with her pram and her rags. At night she kept a candle glimmering low down on the floor. The lavatory was still out of order, so she used a pail on the first floor instead, and secretly emptied it at night into the canal which in the day was full of pleasure boats and people fishing.

Tibby brought her several pigeons during that time.

'Oh, you are a clever puss, Tibby, Tibby! Oh, you're clever, you are. You know how things are, don't you, you know how to get around and about.'

The weather turned very cold; Christmas came and went. Hetty's cough came back, and she spent most of her time under piles of blankets and old clothes, dozing. At night she watched the shadows of the candle flame on floor and ceiling – the window-frames fitted badly, and there was a draught. Twice tramps spent the night in the bottom of the house and she heard them being moved on by the police. She had to go down to make sure the police had not blocked up the broken window the cat used, but they had not. A blackbird had flown in and had battered itself to death trying to get out. She plucked it, and roasted it over a fire made with bits of floorboard in a baking-pan: the gas of course had been cut off. She had never eaten very much, and was not frightened that some dry bread and a bit of cheese was all that she had eaten during her sojourn under the heap of clothes. She was cold, but did not think about that much. Outside there was slushy brown snow everywhere. She went back to her nest, thinking that soon the cold spell would be over and she could get back to her trading. Tibby sometimes got into the pile with her, and she clutched the warmth of him to her. 'Oh, you clever cat, you clever old thing, looking after yourself, aren't you? That's right, my ducky, that's right, my lovely.'

And then, just as she was moving about again, with snow gone off the ground for a time but winter only just begun, in January, she saw a builder's van draw up outside, a couple of men unloading their gear. They did not come into the house: they were to start work next day. By then Hetty, her cat, her pram piled with clothes and her two blankets, were gone. She also took a box of matches, a candle, an old saucepan and a fork and spoon, a tin-opener and a rat-trap. She had a horror of rats.

About two miles way, among the homes and gardens of amiable Hampstead, where live so many of the rich, the intelligent and the famous, stood three empty, very large houses. She had seen them on an occasion, a couple of years before, when she had taken a bus. This was a rare thing for her, because of the remarks and curious looks provoked by her mad clothes, and by her being able to appear at the same time such a tough battling old thing, and a naughty child. For the older she got, this disreputable tramp, the more there strengthened in her a quality of fierce, demanding childishness. It was all too much of a mixture; she was uncomfortable to have near.

She was afraid that 'they' might have rebuilt the houses, but there they still stood, too tumbledown and dangerous to be of much use to tramps, let alone the armies of London's homeless. There was no glass left anywhere. The flooring at ground level was mostly gone, leaving small platforms and juts of planking over basements full of water. The ceilings were crumbling. The roofs were going. The houses were like bombed buildings.

But in the cold dark of a late afternoon she pulled the pram up the broken stairs and moved cautiously around the frail boards of a second-floor room that had a great hole in it right down to the bottom of the house. Looking into it was like looking into a well. She held a candle to examine the state of the walls, here more or less whole, and saw that rain and wind blowing in from the window would leave one corner dry. Here she made her home. A sycamore tree screened the gaping window from the main road twenty yards away. Tibby, who was cramped after making the journey under the clothes piled in the pram, bounded down and out and vanished into neglected undergrowth to catch his supper. He returned fed and pleased, and seemed happy to stay clutched in her hard thin old arms. She had come to watch for his return after hunting trips, because the warm purring bundle of bones and fur did seem to allay, for a while, the permanent ache of cold in her bones.

Next day she sold her Edwardian boots for a few shillings – they were fashionable again – and bought a loaf and some bacon scraps. In a corner of the ruins well away from the one she had made her own, she pulled up some floorboards, built a fire, and toasted bread and the bacon scraps. Tibby had brought in a pigeon, and she roasted that, but not very efficiently. She was afraid of the fire catching and the whole mass going up in flames; she was afraid too, of the smoke showing and attracting the police. She had to keep damping down the fire, and so the bird was bloody and unappetizing and in the end Tibby got most of it. She felt confused, and discouraged, but thought it was because of the long stretch of winter still ahead of her before spring could come. In fact, she was ill. She made a couple of attempts to trade and earn money to feed herself before she acknowledged she was ill. She knew she was not yet dangerously ill, for she had been that in her life, and would have been able to recognize the cold listless indifference of a real last-ditch illness. But all her bones ached, and her head ached, and she coughed more than she ever had. Yet she still did not think of herself as suffering particularly from the cold, even in that sleety January weather. She had never, in all her life, lived in a properly heated place, had never known a really warm home, not even when she lived in the Council flats. Those flats had electric fires, and the family had never used them, for the sake of economy, except in very bad spells of cold. They piled clothes on to themselves, or went to bed early. But she did know that to keep herself from dying now she could not treat the cold with her usual indifference. She knew she must eat. In the comparatively dry corner of the windy room, away from the gaping window through which snow and sleet were drifting, she made another nest – her last. She had found a piece of polythene sheeting in the rubble, and she laid that down first, so that the damp would not strike up. Then she spread her two blankets over that. Over them were heaped the mass of old clothes. She wished she had another piece of polythene to put on top, but she used sheets of newspaper instead. She heaved herself into the middle of this, with a loaf of bread near to her hand. She dozed, and waited, and nibbled bits of bread, and watched the snow drifting softly in. Tibby sat close to the old blue face that poked out of the pile and put up a paw to touch it. He miaowed and was restless, and then went out into the frosty morning and brought in a pigeon. This the cat put, still struggling and fluttering a little, close to the old woman. But she was afraid to get out of the pile in which the heat was being made and kept with such difficulty. She really could not climb out long enough to pull up more splinters of plank from the floors, to make a fire, to pluck the pigeon, to roast it. She put out a cold hand to stroke the cat.

'Tibby, you old thing, you brought it for me, then, did you? You did, did you? Come here, come in here...' But he did not want to get in with her. He miaowed again, pushed the bird closer to her. It was now limp and dead.

'You have it, then. You eat it. I'm not hungry, thank you, Tibby.'

But the carcass did not interest him. He had eaten a pigeon before bringing this one up to Hetty. He fed himself well. In spite of his matted fur, and his scars and his half-closed yellow eye, he was a strong, healthy cat.

At about four the next morning there were steps and voices downstairs. Hetty shot out of the pile and crouched behind a fallen heap of plaster and beams, now covered with snow, at the end of the room near the window. She could see through the hole in the floorboards down to the first floor, which had collapsed entirely, and through it to the ground floor. She saw a man in a thick overcoat and muffler and leather gloves holding a strong torch to illuminate a thin bundle of clothes lying on the floor. She saw that this bundle was a sleeping man or woman. She was afraid because she had not been aware of this other tenant of the ruin. Had he, or she, heard her talking to the cat? And where was the cat? If he wasn't careful he could be caught, and that would be the end of him! The man with a torch went off and came back with a second man. In the thick dark far below Hetty, was a small cave of strong light, which was the torchlight. In this space of light two men bent to lift the bundle, which was the corpse of a man or a woman like Hetty. They carried it across the danger-traps of fallen and rotting boards that made gangplanks over the water-filled basement. One man was holding the torch in the hand that supported the dead person's feet, and the light jogged and lurched over trees and grasses: the corpse was being taken through the shrubberies to a car.

There are men in London who, between the hours of two and five in the morning, when the real citizens are asleep, who should not be disturbed by such unpleasantness as the corpses of the poor, make the rounds of all the empty, rotting houses they know about, to collect the dead, and to warn the living that they ought not to be there at all, inviting them to one of the official Homes or lodgings for the homeless.

Hetty was too frightened to get back into her warm heap. She sat with the blankets pulled around her, and looked through gaps in the fabric of the house, making out shapes and boundaries and holes and puddles and mounds of rubble, as her eyes, like her cat's, became accustomed to the dark.

She heard scuffling sounds and they were rats. She had meant to set the trap, but the thought of her friend Tibby, who might catch his paw, had stopped her. She sat up until the morning light came in grey and cold, after nine. Now she did know herself to be very ill and in danger, for she had lost all the warmth she had huddled into her bones under the rags. She shivered violently. She was shaking herself apart with shivering. In between spasms she drooped limp and exhausted. Through the ceiling above her – but it was not a ceiling, only a cobweb of slats and planks – she could see into a dark cave which had been a garret, and through the roof above that, the grey sky, teeming with incipient rain. The cat came back from where he had been hiding, and sat crouched on her knees, keeping her stomach warm, while she thought out her position. These were her last clear thoughts. She told herself that she would not last out until spring unless she allowed 'them' to find her, and take her to hospital. After that, she would be taken to a Home.

But what would happen to Tibby, her poor cat? She rubbed the old beast's scruffy head with the ball of her thumb and muttered: 'Tibby, Tibby, they won't get you, no, you'll be all right, yes, I'll look after you.'

Towards midday, the sun oozed yellow through miles of greasy grey cloud, and she staggered down the rotting stairs, to the shops. Even in those London Streets, where the extraordinary had become usual, people turned to stare at a tall gaunt woman, with a white face that had flaming red patches on it, and blue compressed lips, and restless black eyes. She wore a tightly buttoned man's overcoat, torn brown woollen mittens, and an old fur hood. She pushed a pram loaded with old dresses and scraps of embroidery and torn jerseys and shoes, all stirred into a tight tangle, and she kept pushing this pram up against people as they stood in queues, or gossiped, or stared into windows, and she muttered: 'Give me your old clothes, darling, give me your old pretties, give Hetty something, poor Hetty's hungry.' A woman gave her a handful of small change, and Hetty bought a roll filled with tomato and lettuce. She did not dare go into a café, for even in her confused state she knew she would offend, and would probably be asked to leave. But she begged a cup of tea at a street stall, and when the hot sweet liquid flooded through her she felt she might survive the winter. She bought a carton of milk and pushed the pram back through the slushy snowy street to the ruins.

Tibby was not there. She urinated down through the hole in the boards, muttering, 'A nuisance, that old tea,' and wrapped herself in a blanket and waited for the dark to come.

Tibby came in later. He had blood on his foreleg. She had heard scuffling and she knew that he had fought a rat, or several, and had been bitten. She poured the milk into the tilted saucepan and Tibby drank it all.

She spent the night with the animal held against her chilly bosom. They did not sleep, but dozed off and on. Tibby would normally be hunting, the night was his time, but he had stayed with the old woman now for three nights.

Early next morning they again heard the corpse-removers among the rubble on the ground floor, and saw the beams of the torch moving on wet walls and collapsed beams. For a moment the torchlight was almost straight on Hetty, but no one came up: who could believe that a person could be desperate enough to climb those dangerous stairs, to trust those crumbling splintery floors, and in the middle of winter?

Hetty had now stopped thinking of herself as ill, of the degrees of her illness, of her danger – of the impossibility of her surviving. She had cancelled out in her mind the presence of winter and its lethal weather, and it was as if spring were nearly here. She knew that if it had been spring when she had had to leave the other house, she and the cat could have lived here for months and months, quite safely and comfortable. Because it seemed to her an impossible and even a silly thing that her life, or, rather, her death, could depend on something so arbitrary as builders starting work on a house in January rather than in April, she could not believe it: the fact would not stay in her mind. The day before she had been quite clear-headed. But today her thoughts were cloudy, and she talked and laughed aloud. Once she scrambled up and rummaged in her rags for an old Christmas card she had got four years before from her good daughter. In a hard harsh angry grumbling voice she said to her four children that she needed a room of her own now that she was getting on. 'I've been a good mother to you,' she shouted to them before invisible witness – former neighbours, welfare workers, a doctor. 'I never let you want for anything, never! When you were little you always had the best of everything! You can ask anybody, go on, ask them then!'

She was restless and made such a noise that Tibby left her and bounded on to the pram and crouched watching her. He was limping, and his foreleg was rusty with blood. The rat had bitten deep. When the daylight came, he left Hetty in a kind of a sleep, and went down into the garden where he saw a pigeon feeding on the edge of the pavement. The cat pounced on the bird, dragged it into the bushes, and ate it all, without taking it up to his mistress. After he had finished eating, he stayed hidden, watching the passing people. He stared at them intently with his blazing yellow eye, as if he were thinking, or planning. He did not go into the old ruin and up the crumbling wet stairs until late – it was as if he knew it was not worth while going at all.

He found Hetty, apparently asleep, wrapped loosely in a blanket, propped sitting in a corner. Her head had fallen on her chest, and her quantities of white hair had escaped from a scarlet woollen cap, and concealed a face that was flushed a deceptive pink – the flush of coma from cold. She was not yet dead, but she died that night. The rats came up the walls and along the planks and the cat fled down and away from them, limping still, into the bushes.

Hetty was not found for a couple of weeks. The weather changed to warm, and the man whose job it was to look for corpses was led up the dangerous stairs by the smell. There was something left of her, but not much.

As for the cat, he lingered for two or three days in the thick shrubberies, watching the passing people and beyond them, the thundering traffic of the main road. Once a couple stopped to talk on the pavement, and the cat, seeing two pairs of legs, moved out and rubbed himself against one of the legs. A hand came down and he was stroked and patted for a little. Then the people went away.

The cat saw he would not find another home, and he moved off, nosing and feeling his way from one garden to another, through empty houses finally into an old churchyard. This graveyard already had a couple of stray cats in it, and he joined them. It was the beginning of a community of stray cats going wild. They killed birds, and the field mice that lived among the grasses, and they drank from puddles. Before winter had ended the cats had had a hard time of it from thirst, during the two long spells when the ground froze and there was snow and no puddles and the birds were hard to catch because the cats were so easy to see against the clean white. But on the whole they managed quite well. One of the cats was a female, and soon there were a swarm of wild cats, as wild as if they did not live in the middle of a city surrounded by streets and houses. This was just one of half a dozen communities of wild cats living in that square mile of London.

Then an official came to trap the cats and take them away. Some of them escaped, hiding till it was safe to come back again. But Tibby was caught. Not only was he getting old and stiff – he still limped from the rat's bite – but he was friendly, and did not run away from the man, who had only to pick him up in his arms.

'Your're an old soldier, aren't you?' said the man. 'A real tough one, a real old tramp.'

It is possible that the cat even thought that he might be finding another human friend and a home.

But it was not so. The haul of wild cats that week numbered hundreds, and while if Tibby had been younger a home might have been found for him, since he was amiable, and wished to be liked by the human race, he was really too old, and smelly and battered. So they gave him an injection and, as we say, 'put him to sleep'.

Fay Weldon
1933 –

Fiction writer, dramatist and television screen writer, she was born in Worcester and attended the University of St Andrews. One of the best known of contemporary British writers, her tragi-comic treatment of women's predicament has been influential in popular as well as literary circles. Her early fiction (The Fat Woman's Joke, 1967; Down Among the Women, 1971; Female Friends 1975) represents some of the concerns of the women's movement, while her later fiction (The Life and Adventures of a She-Devil, 1984, The Leader of the Band, 1988) takes on slightly more fantastic proportions. Politics in the widest sense is a preoccupation in much of her writing with The Shrapnel Academy reflecting her critique of violence and war.

The following short story first appeared in The Observer (7 August 1988).

IND AFF – or Out of Love in Sarajevo

THIS is a sad story. It has to be. It rained in Sarajevo, and we expected fine weather. The rain filled up Sarajevo's pride, two footprints set into a pavement, which mark the spot where the young assassin Princip stood to shoot the Archduke Ferdinand and his wife. (Don't forget his wife: everyone forgets his wife, the Archduchess.) That was in the summer of 1914. Sarajevo is a pretty town, Balkan style, mountain rimmed. A broad, swift, shallow river runs through its centre, carrying the mountain snows away, arched by many bridges. The one nearest the two footprints has been named The Princip Bridge. The young man is a hero in these parts. Not only does he bring in the tourists – look, look, the spot, the very spot! – but by his action, as everyone knows, he lit the spark which fired the timber which caused World War I which crumbled the Austro-Hungarian Empire, the crumbling of which made modern Yugoslavia possible. Forty million dead (or was it thirty?) but who cares? So long as he loved his country.

The river, they say, can run so shallow in the summer it's known derisively as 'the wet road'. Today, from what I could see through the sheets of falling rain, it seemed full enough. Yugoslavian streets are always busy – no one stays home if they can help it (thus can an indecent shortage of housing space create a sociable nation) and it seemed that as if by common consent a shield of bobbing umbrellas had been erected two metres high to keep the rain off the streets. It just hadn't worked around Princip's corner.

'Come all this way,' said Peter, who was a Professor of Classical History, 'and you can't even see the footprints properly, just two undistinguished puddles.' Ah, but I loved him. I shivered for his disappointment. He was supervising my thesis on varying concepts of morality and duty in the early Greek States as evidenced in their poetry and drama. I was dependent upon him for my academic future. He said I had a good mind but not a first class mind, and somehow I didn't take it as an insult. I had a feeling first class minds weren't all that good in bed.

Sarajevo is in Bosnia, in the centre of Yugoslavia, that grouping of unlikely states, that distillation of languages into the phonetic reasonableness of Serbo-Croat. We'd sheltered from the rain in an ancient mosque in Serbian Belgrade: done the same in a monastery in Croatia: now we spent a wet couple of days in Sarajevo beneath other people's umbrellas. We planned to go on to Montenegro, on the coast, where the fish and the artists come from, to swim and lie in the sun, and recover from the exhaustion caused by the sexual and moral torments of the last year. It couldn't possibly go on raining for ever. Could it? Satellite pictures showed black cloud swishing gently all over Europe, over the Balkans, into Asia – practically all the way from Moscow to London, in fact. It wasn't that Peter and myself were being singled out. No. It was raining on his wife, too, back in Cambridge.

Peter was trying to decide, as he had been for the past year, between his wife and myself as his permanent life partner. To this end we had gone away, off the beaten track, for a holiday: if not with his wife's blessing, at least with her knowledge. Were we really, truly suited? We had to be sure, you see, that this was more than just any old professor-student romance: that it was the Real Thing, because the longer the indecision went on the longer Mrs Piper would be left dangling in uncertainty and distress. They had been married for twenty-four years; They'd stopped loving each other a long time ago, of course – but there would be a fearful personal and practical upheaval entailed if he decided to leave permanently and shack up, as he put it, with me. Which I certainly wanted him to do. I loved him. And so far I was winning hands down. It didn't seem much of a contest at all, in fact. I'd been cool and thin and informed on the seat next to him in a Zagreb theatre. (Mrs Piper was sweaty and only liked telly), was now eager and anxious for social and political instruction in Sarajevo (Mrs Piper spat in the face of knowledge, he'd once told me) and planned to be lissom (and I thought topless but I hadn't quite decided: this might be the area where the age difference showed) while I splashed and shrieked like a bathing belle in the shallows of the Croatian coast. (Mrs Piper was a swimming coach: I imagined she smelt permanently of chlorine)

In fact so far as I could see it was no contest at all between his wife and myself. But Peter liked to luxuriate in guilt and indecision. And I loved him with an inordinate affection.

Princip's prints are a metre apart, placed as a modern cop on a training shoot-out would place his feet – the left in front at a slight outward angle, the right behind, facing forward. There seemed great energy focused here. Both hands on the gun, run, stop, plant the feet, aim, fire! I could see the footprints well enough, in spite of Peter's complaint. They were clear enough to me.

We went to a restaurant for lunch, since it was too wet to do what we loved to do: that is, buy bread, cheese, sausage, wine and go off somewhere in our hired car, into the woods or the hills, and picnic and make love. It was a private restaurant – Yugoslavia went over to a mixed capitalist-communist economy years back, so you get either the best or worst of both system, depending on your mood – that is to say, we knew we would pay more but be given a choice. We chose the wild boar.

'Probably ordinary pork soaked in red cabbage water to darken it,' said Peter. He was not in a good mood.

Cucumber salad was served first.

'Everything in this country comes with cucumber salad,' complained Peter. I noticed I had become used to his complaining. I supposed that when you had been married a little you simply wouldn't hear it. He was 46 and I was 25. 'They grow a lot of cucumber,' I said.

'If they can grow cucumbers,' Peter then asked, 'why can't they grow mange-tout?' It seemed a why-can't-they-eat-cake sort of argument to me, but not knowing enough about horticulture not to be outflanked if I debated the point, I moved the subject on to safer ground.

'I suppose Princip's action couldn't really have started World War I,' I remarked. 'Otherwise, what a thing to have on your conscience! One little shot and the deaths of thirty million.'

'Forty,' he corrected me. Though how they reckon these things and get them right I can't imagine. 'Of course he didn't start the war. That's just a simple tale to keep the children quiet. It takes more than an assassination to start a war. What happened was that the build-up of political and economic tensions in the Balkans was such that it had to find some release.'

'So it was merely the shot that lit the spark that fired the timber that started the war, etcetera?'

Quite,' he said. 'World War I would have had to have started sooner or later.'

'A bit later or a bit sooner,' I said, 'might have made the difference of a million or so: if it was you on the battlefield in the mud and the rain you'd notice: exactly when they fired the starting-pistol: exactly when they blew the final whistle. Is that what they do when a war ends: blow a whistle? So that everyone just comes in from the trenches?'

But he wasn't listening. He was parting the flesh of the soft collapsed orangey red pepper which sat in the middle of his cucumber salad; he was carefully extracting the pips. He didn't like eating pepper pips. His Nan had once told him they could never be digested, would stick inside and do terrible damage. I loved him for his vulnerability, the bit of him that was forever little boy: I loved him for his dexterity and patience with his knife and fork. I'd finished my salad yonks ago, pips and all. I was hungry. I wanted my wild boar.

Peter might be 46 but he was six foot two and grizzled and muscled with it, in a dark-eyes, intelligent, broad jawed kind of way. I adored him. I loved to be seen with him. 'Muscular academic, not weedy academic' as my younger sister Clare once said. 'Muscular academic is just a generally superior human being: everything works well from the brain to the toes. Weedy academic is when there isn't enough vital energy in the person, and the brain drains all the strength from the other parts.' Well, Clare should know. Clare is only 23, but of the superior human variety kind herself, vividly pretty, bright and competent – somewhere behind a heavy curtain of vibrant red hair, which she only parts for effect. She had her first degree at 20. Now she's married to a Harvard Professor of Economics seconded to the United Nations. She can even cook. I gave up competing yonks ago. Though she too is capable of self-deception. I would say her husband was definitely of the weedy academic rather than the muscular academic type. And they have to live in Brussels.

The Archduke's chauffeur had lost his way, and was parked on the corner trying to recover his nerve when Princip came running out of a cafe, planted his feet, aimed and fired. Princip was 17 – too young to hang. But they sent him to prison for life and, since he had TB to begin with, he only lasted three years. He died in 1917, in a Swiss prison. Or perhaps it was more than TB: perhaps they gave him a hard time, not learning till later, when the Austro-Hungarian Empire collapsed, that he was a hero. Poor Princip, too young to die – like so many other millions. Dying for love of a country.

'I love you,' I said to Peter, my living man, progenitor already of three children by his chlorinated, swimming coach wife.

'How much do you love me?'

'Inordinately! I love you with inordinate affection.'

It was a joke between us. Ind Aff!

'Inordinate affection is a sin,' he'd told me. 'According to the Wesleyans. John Wesley himself worried about it to such a degree he ended up abbreviating it in his diaries. Ind. Aff. He maintained that what he felt for young Sophie, the 18-year-old in his congregation, was not Ind Aff, which bears the spirit away from God towards the flesh: he insisted that what he felt was a pure and spiritual, if passionate, concern for her soul.'

Peter said now, as we waited for our wild boar, and he picked over his pepper, 'Your ind aff is my wife's sorrow, that's the trouble.' He wanted, I knew, one of the long half-wrangles, half soul-sharings that we could keep going for hours, and led to piercing pains in the heart which could only be made better in bed. But our bedroom at the Hotel Europa was small and dark and looked out into the well of the building – a punishment room if ever there was one. (Reception staff did sometimes take against us.) When Peter had tried to change it in his quasi Serbo-Croat, they'd shrugged their Bosnian shoulders and pretended not to understand, so we'd decided to put up with it. I did not fancy pushing hard single beds together – it seemed easier not to have the pain in the heart in the first place.

'Look,' I said, 'this holiday is supposed to be just the two of us, not Mrs Piper as well. Shall we talk about something else?'

Do not think that the Archduke's chauffeur was merely careless, an inefficient chauffeur, when he took the wrong turning. He was, I imagine, in a state of shock, fright and confusion. There had been two previous attempts on the Archduke's life since the cavalcade had entered town. The first was a bomb which got the car in front and killed its driver. The second was a shot fired by none other than young Princip, which had missed. Princip had vanished into the crowd and gone to sit down in a corner cafe and ordered coffee to calm his nerves. I expect his hand trembled at the best of times – he did have TB. (Not the best choice of assassin, but no doubt those who arrange these things have to make do with what they can get.) The Archduke's chauffeur panicked, took the wrong road, realised what he'd done, and stopped to await rescue and instructions just outside the cafe where Princip sat drinking his coffee.

'What shall we talk about?' asked Peter, in even less of a good mood.

'The collapse of the Austro-Hungarian Empire?' I suggested.

'How does an Empire collapse? Is there no money to pay the military or the police, so everyone goes home? Or what?' He liked to be asked questions.

'The Hungro-Austrarian Empire,' said Peter to me, 'didn't so much collapse as fail to exist any more. War destroys social organisations. The same thing happened after World War II. There being no organising bodies left between Moscow and London – and for London read Washington, then as now – it was left to these two to put in their own puppet governments. Yalta, 1944. It's taken the best part of forty-five years for nations of West and East Europe to remember who they are.'

'Austro-Hungarian,' I said, 'not Hungro-Austrarian.'

'I didn't say Hungro-Austrarian,' he said.

'You did,' I said.

'Didn't ,' he said. 'What the hell are they doing about our wild boar? Are they out in the hills shooting it?'

My sister Clare had been surprisingly understanding about Peter. When I worried about him being older, she pooh-poohed it; when I worried about him being married, she said 'just go for it, sister. If you can unhinge a marriage, it's ripe for unhingeing, it would happen sooner or later; it might as well be you. See a catch, go ahead and catch! Go for it!'

Princip saw the Archduke's car parked outside, and went for it. Second chances are rare in life: they must be responded to. Except perhaps his second chance was missing in the first place? Should he not have taken his cue from fate, and just sat and finished his coffee, and gone home to his mother? But what's a man to do when he loves his country? Fate delivered the Archduke into his hands: how could he resist it? A parked car, a uniformed and medalled chest, the persecutor of his country – how could Princip not, believing God to be on his side, but see this as His intervention, push his coffee aside and leap to his feet?

Two waiters stood idly by and watched us waiting for our wild boar. One was young and handsome in a mountainous Bosnian way – flashing eyes, hooked nose, luxuriant black hair, sensuous mouth. He was about my age. He smiled. His teeth were even and white. I smiled back, and instead of the pain in the heart I'd become accustomed to as an erotic sensation, now felt, quite violently, an associated yet different pang which got my lower stomach. The true, the real pain of Ind Aff!

'Fancy him?' asked Peter.

'No,' I said. 'I just thought if I smiled the wild boar might come quicker.'

The other waiter was older and gentler: his eyes were soft and kind. I thought he looked at me reproachfully. I could see why. In a world which for once, after centuries of savagery, was finally full of young men, unslaughtered, what was I doing with this man with thinning hair.

'What are you thinking of?' Professor Piper asked me. He liked to be in my head.

'How much I love you,' I said automatically, and was finally aware how much I lied. 'And about the Archduke's Assassination,' I went on, to cover the kind of tremble in my head as I came to my senses, 'and let's not forget his wife, she died too – how can you say World War I would have happened anyway. If Princip hadn't shot the Archduke something else, some undisclosed, unsuspected variable, might have come along and defused the whole political/military situation, and neither World War I and II ever happened. We'll just never know, will we?'

I had my passport and my travellers' cheques with me. (Peter felt it was less confusing if we each paid our own way.) I stood up, and took my raincoat from the peg.

'Where are you going?' he asked, startled.

'Home,' I said. I kissed the top of his head, where it was balding. It smelt gently of chlorine, which may have come from thinking about his wife so much, but might merely have been that he'd taken a shower that morning. ('The water all over Yugoslavia, though safe to drink, is unusually highly chlorinated': Guide Book.) As I left to catch a taxi to the airport the younger of the two waiters emerged from the kitchen with two piled plates of roasted wild boar, potatoes duchesse, and stewed peppers. ('Yugoslavian diet is unusually rich in proteins and fats': Guide Book.) I could tell from the glisten of oil that the food was no longer hot, and I was not tempted to stay, hungry though I was. Thus fate – or was it Bosnian wilfulness? – confirmed the wisdom of my intent.

And that was how I fell out of love with my professor, in Sarajevo, a city to which I am grateful to this day, though I never got to see much of it, because of the rain.

It was a silly sad thing to do, in the first place, to confuse mere passing academic ambition with love: to try and outdo my sister Clare. (Professor Piper was spiteful, as it happened, and did his best to have my thesis refused, but I went to appeal, which he never thought I'd dare, and won. I had a first class mind after all.) A silly sad episode, which I regret. As silly and sad as Princip, poor young man, with his feverish mind, his bright tubercular cheeks, and his inordinate affection for his country, pushing aside his cup of coffee, leaping to his feet, taking his gun in both hands, planting his feet, aiming and firing – one, two, three shots and starting World War I. The first one missed, the second got the wife (never forget the wife) and the third got the Archduke and a whole generation, and their children, and their children's children, and on and on for ever. If he'd just hung on a bit, there in Sarajevo, that August day, he might have come to his senses. People do, sometimes quite quickly.

Caryl Churchill
1938 –

Born in London, Caryl Churchill was educated at Lady Margaret Hall, Oxford. Her work is radical and predominantly feminist. The author of radio and television plays, she enjoys a reputation as one of the leading contemporary British writers for the stage. Among those plays that were launched at the Royal Court Theatre, are Owners (1972), Objections to Sex and Violence (1975), Light Shining in Buckinghamshire (1976), Cloud Nine

(1979), Top Girls *(1982) and* Serious Money *(1986). Her play* Fen, *which won the Susan Smith Blackburn Prize was staged at the Royal Court in 1983 and also at the Public Theatre, New York.*

The following play, Three More Sleepless Nights, *is published here for the first time.*

Three More Sleepless Nights

Cast

MARGARET
FRANK
PETE
DAWN

There are three scenes which happen in different rooms but the set is the same all through, a double bed.

Throughout the first scene more than one person speaks at the same time. The point at which a second person speaks is indicated by / in the other person's speech.

1 Margaret and Frank

MARGARET:	FRANK:
Night after night you're round there, don't bother lying, night after night, you can clear out round and live there, I don't care.	
Night after night / coming home pissed, what am I for, clean up your mess? Times I've cleaned your sick off the floor, you was sick on the Christmas presents Christmas eve, time you shat yourself / tell her that she'd like that, clean up your shit. Give her something to think about. She thinks the sun shines out of your arse,	Shut it.
	Shut it.

I could tell her different,
ten years / of you, let her
try ten years, she don't know
half, spruce yourself up with
aftershave me mum give you
Christmas, she don't know who
you are, thinks you walked
out the telly, that's what
you fancy, someone don't know
nothing about you. You can
come over big, talk big, big
spender, Mr Big, Mr Big Pig
coming home night after night /
pissed out of your mind, what
mind you got to be pissed out
of?

Ask Charlie.

Charlie'd say anything.

Ask her shall I?

Go round there shall I, ask her,
silly cow, she'd tell me too,
all smiles, tears in her eyes,
can't we be friends, can we fuck,
must have been desperate to be
friends with her. Anyone with a
pram and a cup of tea, / can't think
what you see in her, her hair's
growing out too, looks dreadful,
looks cheap, she's cheap. Word my
mum was fond of, cheap. See the
point of it now, cheap. She don't

Shut up will you. Five minutes
peace, come through my own
front door you start rucking,
what sort of home's that?
Any wonder I don't come home,
minute I come in you start, any
wonder, Christ.

Shut up will you. I've not
been there. I've not been to
see her two weeks now. I've not
been round there two weeks,
I told you I was stopping seeing
her. She come up the garage
dinnertime. I says no, I told
Margaret I'm not seeing you.
And it's true I'm not seeing
her, ask anyone, ask Charlie.
I been up the pub that's all /
I suppose I'm not let go up
the pub now is it, sorry mates
my wife won't let me. I been
up the pub, I been to Charlie's
for a few pints after, ask
Charlie / ask anyone, my wife's
just checking up on me, she
don't believe a word I say.
Don't believe a word I say
do you? / What sort of marriage,
what sort of wife are you? /
What sort of marriage? What's
left? What do I bother for?
What I give her up for?

Might as well still see her, might
as well, Go round there
now, Your fault, you drive me,
you drive me round
there, don't believe a word,
what's the point, you think I'm

look younger than me, she's five
years, what you must think of me
if you fancy that. Try to look
after myself / don't look bad,
could have been a model, could
have been a hairdresser, could
have been a shorthand typist
easy the grades I had in commerce,
I had good speeds, could have
been a temp made a fortune by
now, secretary to an executive /
gave it up to be a wife to you,
could have took the pill gone
raving, could have had blokes
wouldn't look at her, cheap she
is, hair growing out, stupid
cow, can't type even, can't read,
what you must think of me if
you fancy that. Puts you in
your place, what you must be like,
must be desperate, feeling your
age a bit, take what's on offer,
last chance, think what other
blokes she's had / can't hold
jobs, weirdos, that's where
you're heading, weirdos and
winos, that's about it with
her, all she can get. There was
one looked like a goldfish
couldn't shut his mouth,
come in handy I suppose with
the kissing, surprised you
can shut yours / all the time
you spend round there, want
to watch out you don't end
up looking like a goldfish.
I do not fancy Charlie / so
don't start that. I quite like
him, he's your friend. / You're
the one he tells lies for.
Your friend. I don't like him. /
like that, I quite like him. /

I don't get nothing.

I don't try. I don't know what

having it off, come in the door
start rucking, might as well
enjoy it.
I go round there now you know
whose fault it is, What sort
of marriage is this? What sort
of wife are you? Come in my own
front door.

Yeah yeah yeah yeah yeah.

You fancy Charlie.

You fancy Charlie.

You like him don't you?

We all know whose friend he is,
you like him don't you?
You fancy him.
You quite like him, you quite
like what you get, you quite
like it, / you like it.
You don't get nothing. Not for
want of trying. / Not for want of

you're talking about.

I don't want Charlie, I'm
not interested, I love you.

I don't / dislike him / but that
don't mean I fancy him.
He's not said nothing.

He's not said he dislikes me.

He hasn't said he likes me
either.

He don't.

Nothing to get on with.

How do you know what he thinks?

I don't know what he thinks.

Don't be stupid.

No it wouldn't.

He's just a friend. He's your
friend.

I don't want to move out, I
love you, why don't you

trying is it. No you don't try,
too good aren't you, fancy yourself
he's not pulled that easy, you've
no style, no class / he's got them
queuing up, Charlie.
And you like him.
And he don't / dislike you. Eh? Has
he said that? He don't dislike you?
He don't dislike you.
That's a lie, never stops
talking to you / every time I
take you up the pub.
I'm sure he hasn't said he dislikes
you / no, he wouldn't.

Hasn't said he likes you? My heart
bleeds. I'm very sorry he hasn't
said he likes you. You'll have to
make do with him touching you up. /
You're wasting your time, seems to
me. Don't know why you don't get on
with it / instead of making me hang
about. Nothing to get on with? He
thinks there is / oh yes he does.
Oh it's only you knows what he
thinks is it? / What does he think?
I should ask him. Phone him up.
Ask him. / Go on, phone him up,
ask him. He might say no he don't
fancy you, that would hurt your
feelings / that would be a shock.
Charlie not fancy you. I don't see
why not, it would hurt my feelings
if it was me, you en got no feeling
that's your trouble, think you're
wonderful, don't care what nobody
thinks of you. Just as well / way
your skin's going, nobody's going
to want to know. You're putting on
weight too. You be friendly, I'm
not bothered, you be friendly,
you take him to the pictures. Don't
you stop for me, I'm not bothered.
I'd move out if I was you, go on /
why don't you move out leave me in
peace, come in my own front door

listen to me, what you doing
to us, what's it for?

Night after night you come
home pissed, I've had enough
of you. Serve you right if
I did fancy Charlie, what if
I did, what about you and her.
Round there every night. I
know you are whatever you say.

Where were you then, upstairs
with her, that's where you were,
Christmas party, who was sick
on the presents?

Take her with a different prick
do you?

All right is it?
I don't understand, I don't want
to understand.

Piss off round there then
and I hope it's something special
and I hope you get a hot dinner
with it and your socks washed –

start rucking. You want it both
ways don't you me and him, well I'm
not playing that little game.
Like him do you, I like him, bet
he's got a big one eh? Gets big for
you eh? You'd like that wouldn't
you? Get all wet thinking of him eh?
Think of him in bed do you? / Lying
there thinking of him then give me
a rucking. Thinking of him were you?
Think of him when you're with me?
Pretend it's him do you? Eh?
Wasting your time there because
Charlie wouldn't touch you if
you was the last woman. He's
said that to me, he's said that
only that time he was drunk
last Christmas, you couldn't
keep your hands off him at the
party, I was ashamed to know
where to look in front of my
friends / if Charlie wasn't my
mate I'd break his neck, he knows
that, he apologised to me. He
didn't know what he was doing,
could have been his grandmother
under the mistletoe if she come
at him the way you did, I didn't
know where to look, showing me
up in front of my friends. At
least what I do I do decent. I don't
shame nobody, I take her different
places than what I take you /
don't go the same pub, nothing,
nobody knows, I don't flirt like
you do, it's all right between
me and her, it's not flirting,
it's something special you wouldn't
understand / go in her door
don't get this / don't get rucking,
get some peace after a day's work.
Talk about cheap, you're cheap, /
anyone you can rub up against
at a party, nobody's interested
are they, that's the trouble.
You don't want me – that's what it

CHILD off: Mummy.

is you don't want me, you'd
have anyone else you could get.
You don't want me, you can't get

                Mummy.
Shut up, shush, wait.

nobody else / that's all it is
/ you don't want me.

Silence

Go on then go and see him, don't
mind me, everyone's more important
It'll go off, sh.

than me, / just has to call out,
drop everything.

Silence

I don't want a row. / Put out the
light.
'Course I've set the clock.

I don't want a row. I want a
good night's sleep before tomorrow.
Set the clock have you? / Didn't
go off this morning.

That was yesterday. It went off
all right this morning, / you
didn't wake up that's all.

Whichever day it was. Set it
properly have you?

Frank puts out the light

You don't enjoy it with me. You don't
want me that's what it is. You don't
Oh God.

enjoy it with me, you said that, /
I remember every word you say, you
said that. Don't deny it. You said it, /
I said it once, I said I didn't
enjoy it that time, I didn't
say I don't enjoy it

can't get out of it now. No man wants
a woman don't want him, stands to
only human, Christ you think I'm
a fucking machine, you got a
washing machine, drying machine,

Didn't enjoy it that time,
my God you was drunk, you
just been with her, you said
she was better than me, she
moved about more, what am I
supposed to do? I'd had a day
and a half with the kids, Johnny
had tonsillitis / you never come
machine, / I'm not your fucking fuck
machine.

home till late, you said you'd
be in, I'd cooked spaghetti
and you never come home, Johnny

You're talking about a year ago.

wouldn't stay in bed till I
hit him, not move about. I'm
surprised I was conscious, move
about more, hell, what does
she do, do it in a track suit
does she? / go jogging, do it
while she's jogging?

I'm not going in for this
competition, I don't care who's
winning your little prize
because I'm not going in for
it. I don't have to compete
because I'm your wife, you're
already mine, I won already,
some prize / I'm not competing.
Why should I have to pull
my stomach in for you, is my
hair all right, you're who I
live with, I'm not going in for
it, I'm not putting makeup on
in bed. / If she's
what you want, if that's the
sort of person you are, my
mistake I ever married you.
You've always had a hard day. /
You think I don't have a hard
day? Lift wasn't working again
for three hours, I put off
going to the shops then I had
to go or they'd have shut.
There was no bread left. I
carried the whole lot up the
stairs and the bag broke / the
eggs fell out, there's no eggs
for breakfast you can do without.
Thirty two p. the eggs, you've
had your eggs in beer, you've
had your kids' dinners and your
kids' new shoes and your kid's
school journey he can't go on
because that would be a luxury /
he don't need it like you need
six pints.
Get a job myself, get a

Look I don't think she's better
than you, why am I still with you.
I think you're the greatest that's
why I stopped seeing her, you're
better than she is / I stopped, I
give her up, you don't believe me
what's the point. I might as well
go and see her again, I'll go
tomorrow night. Don't expect me
home because I won't be home
tomorrow night.
[Frank puts the light on.] Is there
anything to drink?

I've had a hard day.

Yes I always have a hard day
and who's it for? Come back to this
any wonder I don't come home? Who
has the money off me eh? Who has
the money?

It's your job. I don't moan,
I get on with it, what's wrong
with this country nothing but
moans, country of old women.

Who earns it? Who earns it? Sooner
I'm dead, then you'll see who
earns the money, see what's what,
see what it's like / managing on

job up the school, school
helper, could get that now /
think I will, you can't support
your family by yourself /
better go out to work and help
myself, enough of your talk.

your own.
What you get for that? Nothing.

Don't tell me I don't support
my family, don't you say that.
If my dad heard you say that,
what he'd do if my mum said
that, don't you say I don't support
my family. Who has the money off me.
If you can't make it last that's
your lookout, you buy the wrong
stuff / you buy frozen food, my
mum never let us go hungry. You're
no good in the house, rotten
housekeeper, you buy rubbish.
If I give her money, if I lend
her money it's my money to lend.
She's a woman on her own bringing up
a child, I'd expect to hear more
human sympathy from you / always
on about feelings. You got no
feelings for other people, only
got feelings for yourself.

You give her money.

Not enough money for the
school journey, he could have
gone to the sea and you give
her money, your own kid, showing
him up in front of his mates,
your own kid and you give the
money to her, give her the whole
lot I should, give her the
housekeeping and let her cook
your dinner / frozen food, you'll
be lucky if she can see out past
her eyelashes to cook a fishfinger.

You got no feelings, I don't want
to talk to you. I don't want to
listen. I don't like you.

Silence

I'm not very happy. Are you
happy?

No.

My fault is it?

I'm not saying it's your fault /
but
Come on, I don't want a row.

But.

Who's starting a row?

I can't even talk to you without
you shouting at me / because
you're too pissed / to have

Who's shouting
Who's pissed?

a proper talk.

I'm not for one. I don't get
to go out / it's you goes out.

Drink at home by myself, no
thank you, old lady with a
gin bottle.

I do have feelings, you wouldn't
know, you're never here, you
don't know nothing about me,
night after night round with
her or up the pub or out with
Charlie wherever you are it's
not here that's all I know, what
am I doing sitting here waiting
for you night after night, never
here when you're needed like the
time I had the miscarriage
where were you? You knew I'd
started and you went to the pub
and you went to Charlie's / you're
here for the fun but that's all,
here for the beer, you did know
what was happening, you're a liar.
You always was a liar, you stopped
out on purpose / you knew, you
did know, could have died all
you cared, I don't care if it's
ten years ago I'll never forgive you /
and every time you go out now I'm
not surprised, I think yeh yeh
that's him, off he goes, selfish
bugger / what do you expect, what
are you surprised for, haven't you
learnt yet that's what he's like,
think he loves you stupid / course
he don't. Why don't you go and live
with her, she's got a nice place.
Don't stay with me just to keep
yourself in beer, go and live
with her, / see how you like it.

Eh, who's pissed?

You want a drink? Do I stop
you having a drink? You can buy
drink in the supermarket, is it
my fault you don't enjoy yourself /
you make yourself a martyr, if I
take you down the pub you don't
enjoy it or you start chatting up
Charlie don't you, think I'm stupid,
blame me for everything, go on
blame me, that's what I'm for /
come home at night so you've got
someone to moan at.

Didn't know what was happening
did I.

This is five years ago, do us a
favour, this is five years ago.

You don't want me, you don't want
me

If I could afford it, I'd leave you.
If I could get a place.

If it wasn't for the money and the kids.

Don't want to live with her. I don't

I knew you was.
I'd like to put a brick through
her window. I'd like to go round
with a gun / and she opens the
door and I shoot her in the stomach.
If it wasn't for the kids I'd
get a gun. I'd like to see her
bleed. / I'd like to stamp on her
face. She's not that pretty. /
What you must think of me.

even like her, don't know why I
keep seeing her. I was round there
tonight / is it any wonder? First
time for a week, / I don't know.

Stop talking stupid.

Shut it. Shut it.
It's not her.
It's not you.

2 Pete and Dawn

Lying on the bed.
Long silence.
Pete asks Dawn if she's all right:

PETE: Uyuh?
DAWN: Mmm.
PETE: Ah.

Dawn moans:

DAWN: Ohhhhh.

Short silence.
Pete asks how Dawn is:

PETE: Mm?
           Mmm?
DAWN: Uh.

Long silence.
Pete puts out the light. He asks if it was all right to put out the light:

PETE: Uh?

Silence.
Dawn moans:

DAWN: Ohhhhh.

Silence.
Pete is comfortable:

PETE: Ah.

Long silence.
Dawn wakes with a start:

DAWN: Oh.
PETE: Huh?
DAWN: Ohhhhh.
PETE: Mmmm?

Long silence.
Dawn moans, Pete acknowledges,
Dawn is fed up with the night, Pete sees
where things have got to:

DAWN: Ohhhhh.
PETE: Mmm.
DAWN: Ugh.
PETE: Uh huh.

Short silence.

PETE: The plot of Alien is very simple. You have a group of people and
           something nasty and one by one the nasty picks them off. If you're
           not going to see it I'll tell you the story. Mm?
DAWN: Mm.
PETE: There's these people in a spaceship right and it's not like Startek
           because the women wear dungarees and do proper work and there's
           a black guy and they talk about their wages. So they get a signal there's
           something alive out in space and it's one of their rules they have to
           investigate anything that might be alive, so they go to see what it is
           right and a couple of them go poking about in this planet and it's like
           a weird giant fossil and they find some kind of eggs, and go poking
           about, and then there's a horrible jump and this thing gets onto John
           Hurt's face. They let him back in the ship and this horrible thing's
           all over his face and how can they get if off, that's quite unpleasant.
           Then it gets off itself and disappears and he gets better. And then
           there's the horrible bit everyone knows about where he's eating his
           dinner and it comes bursting out of his stomach and there's blood
           everywhere and it looks like a prick with teeth, a real little monster,
           but it's worse in the stills than in the movie because it goes so fast
           you hardly ever see it. That's quite good, I like that, when you think
           they might have shown it you all the time and they don't.

Dawn puts the light on, Pete protests:

PETE: Errr.
DAWN: I feel completely unreal.

Silence.
Dawn gets up.

PETE: Uh?

Silence.

PETE: I like movies where nothing much happens. Long movies, you can
          just sit there and look at them. The Tree of Wooden Clogs is a long
          movie. I wished they didn't have an interval.

Long silence.

DAWN: I don't know if I'm unreal or everything else, but something is.
PETE: Uh huh.

Silence.
Pete gets a book and reads.
Dawn dials a number on the phone, there's no reply.

DAWN: I think I'm dead.

Silence.

PETE: We could have something to eat.

Silence.
Pete goes on reading.
He asks if she wants something to eat:

PETE: Mm?
DAWN: Mm.

Pete goes out.
Dawn gets dressed, beautifully, in a dress.
She sits on the bed.
Pete comes back with tray of food including loaf, knife.

PETE: Ooh?
DAWN: I thought I might go out.
PETE: It is three in the morning.

DAWN: Ah.
PETE: Don't let me stop you.
DAWN: Right.

Pete eats. Dawn doesn't eat much.

PETE: Then there's this creature you see loose in the spaceship and it
          might take any shape and it might get any one of them any time,
          and of course it does. There's a lot of creeping about in the dark
          looking for it and wondering when it's going to pounce and what
          it's going to look like. If you're looking forward to being frightened
          you can be frightened but a friend of mine went to sleep because
          it was so dark.

Silence.
Pete eats. Dawn gets undressed.
Pete asks if she wants any more food, she says no, he is pleased to eat it:

PETE: Uh?
DAWN: Uhuh.
PETE: Mmm.

Silence.

DAWN: I'm frightened.

Silence.

PETE: You'd think from those German movies that Germans were always
          sitting about not doing much and staring into space and then
          whenever you meet Germans they're not like that at all, they're very
          adult. I suppose the movies seem quite different there.

Silence.

PETE: I'm thinking of The Left-handed Woman. The Goalkeeper's Fear
          of the Penalty. The American Friend. No, there's more rushing
          about in the American Friend. I won't tell you the plot, it's quite
          confusing.

Silence.

DAWN: I'm frightened.

Silence.
Pete finishes eating.

PETE: The most frightening bit of Alien for me was when one of the crew
          turns out to be a robot and his head comes off.

Silence.
Pete asks Dawn if she's all right:

PETE: Uyuh?

Pete puts some music on and goes to bed.
Dawn phones again, again no reply.

PETE: I haven't seen my brother for two years.
          I haven't seen my mother for five years.
          I haven't seen my father for ten years.

Silence. Music.

Redupers, that's another German movie. It's short for the All round reduced
personality. Did I see it with you?

Silence. Music.
Dawn plays with the knife.

DAWN: There's a voice in my head. No there's not a voice in my head, come
          on, I keep saying to myself in my head, I want to be dead, I want to
          be dead, and I don't think it's true.

Silence. Music.

PETE: So eventually there's no one left except this girl and she runs away
          up and down the spaceship a whole lot of times. And she gets away
          in a little escape space ship and thinks she's safe and of course the
          thing's in there with her. And she's getting undressed, which I thought
          was a bit unnecessary but I suppose it makes her more vulnerable
          is the idea, and in the end she gets the door open and it's sucked
          out into space. So she gets a good night's sleep which is more than
          I can say for some people.

Dawn takes the knife and gets into bed.
Pete is getting sleepy. He's glad she has come to bed. He asks if she's all right,
she says yes. He settles down more comfortably:

PETE: Mmmm. Mmm?
DAWN: Mm.

PETE: Ahhhhh.

Long silence. Music.
They are lying back to back.
Under the sheet Dawn cuts her wrist.
Pete stirs.

DAWN: Ah –
PETE: Uh?

Silence.
Blood begins to come through the sheet.
The music ends.
Pete reaches out and puts out the light without seeing.

3 *Margaret and Pete*

MARGARET: I was so insecure, that was part of it.
PETE: You had no life of your own.
MARGARET: I was just his wife. I wasn't a person.
PETE: You can't blame him though I mean.
MARGARET: I don't. I don't any more. I'm sorry for him.
PETE: Yes I'm sorry for him.
MARGARET: He's still drinking. He hasn't changed.
PETE: You're the one who's changed.
MARGARET: I've changed. I was just his wife before. I had no life.
PETE: You can't blame him. It's what you learn to be like.
MARGARET: It's what you learn but you can change yourself. I've changed
             myself.
PETE: I'm not saying a man can't change.
MARGARET: You've changed, you say you've changed.
PETE: I have yes but I can see as a man what the problem is for him.
MARGARET: You're not like a man in some ways, not like what I think of a
             man when I think what's wrong with men.
PETE: I'm still a man. I've just changed.
MARGARET: We've both changed.
PETE: Yes.
MARGARET: It was getting the job made the difference. If I'd met you before
             I got the job I'd have got in a panic. I'd have thought is he going
             to marry me or what, is he going to be a father to my children, I
             couldn't just be happy. When I decided to go for being a nursery
             assistant and get some training, that was amazing for me to think
             I could get trained and do something.

PETE:	You can't though can you.
MARGARET:	No I can't but that's the cuts.
PETE:	At least you know what you want to do.
MARGARET:	That's it. I've got some idea of myself. I used not to be a person.
PETE:	I think you're wonderful.
MARGARET:	When I saw him last week it was like seeing a ghost. It's better when the kids go round to him and I don't see him. It makes me feel like a ghost myself. It used to be so horrible you can feel it in the air when you meet. I don't want to be like that any more. You wouldn't have liked me.
PETE:	I would, I would have known.
MARGARET:	I was horrible.
PETE:	You were very insecure.
MARGARET:	I had no life of my own, I was just his wife.
PETE:	I was horrible. I could hardly speak. I couldn't talk to Dawn. You and I just lie here and talk but I'd got with Dawn so I didn't know what to say to her. And she couldn't talk. It was me killing her. If we'd stayed together she'd be dead by now. She'd have done it in the end so it worked, she'd be dead. I was doing that.
MARGARET:	She was putting a lot of pressure on you.
PETE:	She was asking for help.
MARGARET:	You couldn't put the world right for her.
PETE:	I could have talked. I was out of touch with my feelings.
MARGARET:	You're not now.
PETE:	No, I'm different now and she's different. If I run into her now she's fine, chats away, we chat away perfectly all right. I didn't want her depending on me like that, I couldn't put the world right for her. I couldn't take the pressure. I hated London, I hated what it was doing to the kids I taught, I could hardly walk down the street let alone sort her out, I couldn't take it.
MARGARET:	You needed someone less dependent.
PETE:	It was a very destructive relationship.
MARGARET:	You were out of touch with your feelings.
PETE:	I dream about her with that sheet covered in blood.
MARGARET:	We talk about them a lot.
PETE:	Of course we do.
MARGARET:	We say the same things over and over.
PETE:	I suppose we're bound to for a bit.
MARGARET:	Of course we are.
PETE:	We have learnt.

Silence.

MARGARET:	If I can't get the nursery training I'll have to do something.
PETE:	Of course you will.

MARGARET: You say of course I will but it's not that easy, I can't even be a
            helper now they've cut the helpers. I don't want to be at home
            all the time, I'm a bit frightened of that. And I need money.
PETE: You don't have to make a martyr of yourself with the housework.
MARGARET: I don't make a martyr.
PETE: No.
MARGARET: It just makes sense if I'm the one who's here and you're at work.
PETE: I can't help it. I cook.
MARGARET: Of course you do and the kids are mine, the mess is mine.
PETE: Don't worry so much about money. I'm earning money.
MARGARET: That's your money.
PETE: I want to go to sleep.
MARGARET: Are you unhappy?
PETE: I'm tired.

Light out. Silence.

PETE: The microchip can do a billion thought processes in a second.
MARGARET: You can't get a speck of dust on it.
PETE: When I'm out of work too I'll clean the floor.
MARGARET: You can do it Saturday.

Silence.

MARGARET: When did you last see Dawn?
PETE: Last week sometime.
MARGARET: Which day?
PETE: Wednesday, Tuesday.
MARGARET: Where was it?
PETE: She was in the pub dinnertime.
MARGARET: Don't you have to be at school at dinnertime?
PETE: No.
MARGARET: I thought you did special football dinnerplay.

Silence.

PETE: You see Frank more than I see Dawn.
MARGARET: I don't see Frank.

Silence

MARGARET: Everyone's going to have to have hobbies.
PETE: Everyone's going to be on the dole.
MARGARET: It's the future, you have to go forward.
PETE: Who's going to make money out of it?
MARGARET: Think of robots. Don't you like the thought of robots?
PETE: You're very wide awake.

MARGARET: Sorry.
PETE: Sorry but I do have to get up in the morning.

Long silence.

PETE: I'm very wide awake now.
MARGARET: Uh?
PETE: Sorry.
MARGARET: What?
PETE: Sh.
MARGARET: Mm.
MARGARET: Are you asleep?
PETE: No.
MARGARET: What's the matter?
PETE: I'm worrying.
MARGARET: What about?
PETE: Fascists.
MARGARET: What?

Silence.

MARGARET: Is it us?
PETE: What?
MARGARET: You keep being unhappy.
PETE: What makes you think it's us?
MARGARET: You used to be happy.
PETE: I'm happy about us.
MARGARET: Then what's the matter?

Silence.

MARGARET: What is it?
PETE: I don't know.
MARGARET: What sort of thing?

Silence.

MARGARET: It's not surprising I think it's us. If you keep being unhappy and won't tell me. I can't help thinking when I'm on my own. I know I'll be better when I get a job. I don't like being on my own and I know your meetings are important but I get frightened in the evening when the kids are asleep, I think what have I done? You don't like me talking like this, I can't help it, I've no one else to talk to, sometimes I don't talk to anyone all day, I can't help it if I'm frightened.

PETE: I'm going to put the light on.

Pete puts the light on.

MARGARET: I don't want to say this but I worry about Dawn. You keep seeing
               her, you say you run into her, what you keep running into her
               for? If you're seeing her why not say so, I don't mind, I'm just
               afraid you might go back to her. I don't mind nothing if you tell
               me, it's when you don't tell me I think you're hiding something, I
               think you're seeing her and not telling me, is that true? I don't like
               lies, I never did like lies, I know I'm insecure and why shouldn't
               you see her, sleep with her if you want to, you're perfectly free,
               we're not married, I don't want to be married, never again, I
               don't want me and Frank, I wasn't a person, and you and Dawn,
               I don't want that, so what are you doing? Night after night out at
               meetings, I know they're important, I get frightened, what have
               I done, I left him for you, what have I done to the kids, what's
               happening, and are you always at a meeting or do you see Dawn,
               is that stupid? I want to make you happy and I can't and I get
               frightened and you've got to tell me everything. I don't want to
               be like this, you've got to help me, please say something.

Long silence.

PETE: I don't know what to say.
MARGARET: No.
PETE: I'm not doing this deliberately. I've stopped being like this.
MARGARET: Yes.
PETE: Are you definitely not going to see Apocalypse Now?
MARGARET: I don't like war films.
PETE: There's this guy who's already a war veteran and he's back in
               Vietnam, he's a wreck but he can't keep away from it, and he's
               given a mission to go up the river and find this colonel who's
               gone mad and kill him, right.
MARGARET: Right.
PETE: So he goes on a boat up the river to find him. And the main
               thing is these amazing set pieces of destruction, it starts with a
               sort of still grey shot of the jungle and it bursts into flames and
               the whole thing looks stunning, planes coming over and things
               exploding, there's music. So he's going up the river on this boat
               to find the mad colonel and kill him, or maybe not kill him, he's
               sort of attracted by him and we are of course because we know
               it's Marlon Brando. And on the way the Americans are killing
               everybody and there's a mad officer who gets his soldiers to go
               surfing and on the boat they kill a girl and rescue a puppy and
               the black kid on the boat gets killed and it's a real nightmare
               and he goes on up the river to find the colonel.

Margaret Drabble

1939–

A novelist, short story writer, literary critic and editor, Margaret Drabble was born in Sheffield and educated at a Quaker boarding school in York and at Newnham College, Cambridge, where she took a double first in English. Her fiction has been influential in contemporary feminism where her realistic exposés of women's experience have earned her a reputation as the chronicler of her time. Among her novels are The Summer Birdcage (1963), The Garrick Year (1964), The Millstone (1966), Jerusalem the Golden (1967), The Waterfall (1969), The Realms of Gold (1975), The Ice Age (1977), The Middle Ground (1980) and The Radiant Way (1987). She has also written a biography of Arnold Bennett (1974) and edited the Oxford Companion to English Literature (1985).

The following short story, 'The Reunion' is taken from Women Writing (Denys Val Baker (ed.), Sidgwick & Jackson, London, 1980).

The Reunion

THERE must have been a moment at which she decided to go down the street and round the corner and into the café. She knew that: for she knew that at one point she was walking quite idly, quite innocently, with no recollection or association in her head but the dimmest faintest palest shadow of long long past knowledge, and that within ten yards perhaps of innocence, the distance of two frontages of those ancient crumbling small tall buildings, now so uniformly shoddy warehouse, she had made up her mind that she would go and have her lunch there, in that place where they had always had their lunch together. Or no, she said to herself, not even always (excusing herself, apologetic, already diminishing any possible significance of her act), they had not had their lunch there always, they had had it there merely occasionally, once a fortnight or so over that long and lovely year, and the first time that they had gone there had had no significance at all, for it was simply that, being in such an area they did not know well, they had had lunch in the only place that they could find. And they had liked it there, and so they had gone back, because it was the kind of place where nobody would ever see them, where nobody that either of them knew would

ever go, and yet at the same time not impossibly inconvenient, not so very far
from Holborn, where they both had good reason from time to time to be. They
had felt safe there, as safe as they could ever feel, yet at the same time aware that
they had not allowed themselves to be driven into grotesque precautions. They
had found it themselves so much by chance, and they did not think that anyone
they knew could chance to walk that way.

And now, after so long, after a three year gap, she had found herself
there and almost as it were upon the threshold, and at lunch time too. She
was hungry. There is nothing more to it than that, she said to herself, as she
found herself walking so instinctively towards it: I happened to be near, and
wanting my lunch, and the fact that I wanted my lunch merely reminded me
of this place, and that I did curiously enough know it was here, and moreover
that there is nowhere else possible within a five minutes walk. She had done
enough walking she thought: she had never liked walking: it had been enough
of a walk, from Old Street tube station to the place where they had made her new
tooth. She ran her tongue over her new front tooth, reassuringly, and was slightly
ashamed by the immense relief that she felt at being once more presentable,
no longer disfigured by that humiliating gap: being beautiful, she had always
made much of caring little for her beauty, and was always profoundly disturbed
by the accidents which from time to time brought her faced to face with her
own vanity – by the inconvenient pimple, by the unperceived smudge on the
cheek, by the heavy cold. And that lost tooth had been something of a test
case, ever since she had had it knocked out, while still at school. Her dentist
had made for her the most elaborate and delicate bridge, so that not even she
herself would ever have to endure the sight of herself toothless, but the night
before last she had fallen downstairs after a party and broken it. She had rung
up her dentist in the morning, and made a dreadful fuss, and a special visit,
and he had promised her a temporary plate to last her until he had made her
a new elaborate and delicate bridge: and when he had told her the name of
the place that she should go to collect the plate, she had noticed in herself a
small, hardly noticeable flicker of recollection. He went on explaining to her,
obliging yet irritable, 'You've got that then, Mrs Harvey, 82 St Luke's Street? You go
to Old Street station, then turn right . . .' and she heard herself saying, 'Oh yes, St
Luke's Street, that's just off Tunstall Square'. As though anybody might be expected
to know about Tunstall Square. And he had agreed, without surprise, about its
proximity to Tunstall Square, and then had continued to explain to her about the
fact that he was doing her a special favour, and that she should suitably express
her gratitude to the man at the works, in view of the shortness of the notice:
and she had duly expressed it to the man at the works when he had handed
her, ten minutes ago, her tooth, all wrapped up somewhat brutally she thought
in a brown paper bag. She had been effusive, in her gratitude, and the man had
looked at her blankly and said oh that was quite all right, no trouble at all.

And then she had come out, and walked along this street. And as she
paused at the café door, she knew that she had been thinking of him and
of that other year all the time, that she could not very well have avoided the
thought of him, amongst so much familiar scenery. There they had sat in the

car, and kissed and endlessly discussed the impossibility of kissing: there they had stood by that lamp-post, transfixed, unable to move. The pavement seemed still to bear the marks of their feet. And yet it was all so long ago, so thoroughly slaughtered and decayed. She did not care at all: it was two years since she had cared, more than two years since she had suffered, since she suffered more for the loss of him than for the old tedium of her life, and the other anxieties, which had existed before him, and which would exist forever, because they were what she was made of. Inadequacy, loneliness, panic, vanity, decay. These words she said to herself, because words consoled her.

Though she was not unhappy. She was content, she was occupied, she had got her tooth back, everything was under control, the evening would be fine, now that the horror and strain of pretending not to mind that one had a tooth missing had been so successfully averted. She had even quite enjoyed going to that odd place where they made teeth: it was the kind of place that she enjoyed seeing, and she would even be able to tell people about her panic about her tooth, now that the real panic was truly over. And perhaps in a way it made her almost happy, even a little happier than usual, to be back in this place, to find how thoroughly dead it all was, how most efficiently she had died. She saw no ghosts of him here: for a year after their parting she had seen him on every street corner, in every passing car, in shapes of head and hand and forms of movement, but now he was nowhere any more, not even here. For as long as she had imagined that she saw him, she had imagined that he had remembered: that those false ghosts had been in some way the projected shadows of his love: but now she knew that surely that had both forgotten. Remembering him, she thought that this was what she knew.

She pushed open the door and went in. It looked the same. Nothing had changed. She realized that she had been imagining that it must look different, had been preparing herself for heaven knows what ugly transformations and redecorations, but it looked the same. The sameness of it made her pause, took her breath away, though even as she stood there she said to herself, how foolish to imagine it takes my breath away, for I am breathing quite regularly, quite normally. It is simply that I have become, for an instant, aware of the fact that I am breathing.

She went to the side of the room that they had always favoured, the wall side, away from the door and the window, and sat on the corner table, where they had always sat when they could with her back to the door. She sat there, and looked down at the red veined Formica table top, with its cluster of salt pot, pepper pot, mustard pot, sauce bottle, and ash tray: the salt pot was of thick-ribbed Perspex, and she remember the exact common mounting scallops of its edges. She took it in her hand, and felt it. She did not often now lunch in places where such objects might be found. Then she looked up at the dark yellow ceiling, with its curiously useless trellis work hung with plastic lemons and bananas: and then at the wall, the wall papered as before in a strange delicate dirty flowered print, with paper badly cut, and joining badly at the seams, and broken up by protruding obsolescent functionless bits of woodwork, dating from former decorative schemes. On the wall hung the only thing that was different.

It was a calendar, a gift from a garage, and the picture showed an Alpine hut in snowy mountains, for all that the month was May. In their day, the calendar had been one donated by a fruit juice firm, and they had seen it through three seasons; she recalled the anguish with which she had seen its leaves turn, more relentless even than those leaves falling so dreadfully and ominously from more natural trees, and she recalled the appalling photograph of their parting, which had portrayed an autumn evening in a country garden, with an old couple sitting by their creeper-covered door. They had both been insatiable, merciless deliverers of ultimatums, the one upon the other. And she had selected in her own soul this month, and one day of this month – the twenty-third, she knew it even now, the twenty-third – for her final, last, unalterable decision, and she had watched it come up upon them; she had sat at this table, or perhaps after all not at this one but at the one next to it, and she had said, 'Look, that's it, on the twenty-third, that's it, and I mean it this time.' She wondered if he had known that she had meant it: whether an indefinable resolution in her, so small that she did not herself trust it, had somehow communicated itself to him, so that he had known that for this one last time it was for real. Because he had taken her at her word. It was the first time that she had not relented, nor he persisted; each other time he had left her forever, a phone call had been enough to regain him, and each time she had left him, she had sat by the telephone biting her nails and waiting for it to ring. But this time he did not ring, and after a couple of days she ceased to leave the receiver off when nobody was looking. She said to herself from time to time, perhaps in those two days he rang, and rang repeatedly, rang every hour and found me perpetually engaged, and knew what I had done, and knew that at last I meant what I had said: but she knew that she would never never know, and that for her it was all the same if he once rung, or twenty times, or never even tried. It had happened, after so many false attempts, it had finally happened; preparations for death had been in a way like death itself, and she supposed that was why they must so incessantly have made them, more merciful to each other than they knew, for the experience of losing him, so often endured in imagination had solidified from imagination into reality so slowly, with such obdurate slow accretions, that there was no point at which she said, Look, it is done and done for good. There had always seemed a point at which it might be undone. But not now, not now. She looked at the snowy hut upon the wall, at the icy mountains and the frozen glaciers, and she thought, Ah well, there was a point at which I feared we did not have it in us to part. And a kind of admiration for her past self possessed her, a respect for a woman who had been so thoroughly capable of so sizeable a renunciation.

The menu, when it was brought to her, had not altered much. She was glad of this, for without her glasses she doubted whether she would have made much of its faded violet overduplicated manuscript. Though she never knew why she bothered to read menus, for she always with unfailing regularity wherever she was ate the same lunch: she always had cheese omelette and chips. So she ordered her meal, and then sat back to wait. Usually, whenever left alone in a public place, she would read, and through habit she propped her book up against the sauce bottle and rested her eyes upon it, but she did not look at the words. Nor was she dwelling entirely upon the past, for a certain pleasurable anxiety about her evening's engagement was stealing most of her attention, and she found herself wondering whether she had adequately prepared her piece, and whether David Rathbone would offer to drive her home, and whether her hair would look all right, for the last time she had been on the television there had been a girl in the make-up place who had messed it about dreadfully, and cut bits off her fringe, and generally made her look like some quite other kind of person. And most of all, she wondered if she ought to wear her grey skirt. She was really worried about the grey skirt question: all the anxiety that had previously attached itself to the importance of getting her tooth in time had now transferred itself to the skirt, for although she liked it very much she was not at all sure that it was not just a very very little bit tight. If it wasn't, then it was perfect, for it was the kind of thing that she always looked marvellous in: but just supposing that it was? There was nobody in the whole world who could tell her, who could decide for her this delicate point: she had even asked her husband about it, the night before, and he had looked at it and nodded his head and said it looked lovely, and she knew exactly how much and how little that meant. There was nobody but herself with the finesse, with the information to decide such a point, and she could not decide; and she was just saying to herself, the very fact that I'm *worrying* about it must mean that it must be too tight after all, or the thought of its being too tight wouldn't have crossed my mind, would it? when she saw him.

What was really most shocking about it was the way that they noticed each other at exactly the same moment, simultaneously, without a chance of turning away or in any way managing the shock. They were both such managers, but this time they had not a chance. Their eyes met, and they both jerked, beyond hope of dissimulation.

'Oh Christ,' he said, after a second or two, and stood there and went on looking at her.

And she felt at such a loss, sitting there with her book propped up against the tomato ketchup, and her head full of skirts and false teeth, and she said, hurriedly, throwing away what might after all to such as her have been really quite a moment, 'Oh Lord, oh well, since you're there, do sit down, I mean you might as well sit down!' and she moved up the small two-seater bench, pushing her bag along, losing a shoe, for she had kicked them off under the table, inelegantly dragging her jacket out of his way, closing up her book with a rapid snap, averting her eyes, confused, deprecating unable to look.

And he sat down by her, and then said quite suddenly and intimately, as though perfectly at home with her after so many years of silence, as though perfectly confident that she would share whatever he might have to think or say.

'Oh Lord, my darling, what a dreadful dreadful surprise, I don't think I shall ever ever recover.'

'Oh, I don't know,' she said, as though she too had discovered exactly where she was. 'Oh, I don't know. One gets over these things quite quickly. I feel better already, don't you?'

'Why, yes, I suppose I do,' he said. 'I feel better now I'm sitting down, thought I was going to faint, standing there and looking at you.'

'Well,' she said, 'it wasn't quite a fair test of me, was it, because after all I was sitting down already. I mean, nobody ever fainted sitting down, surely?'

'Oh, I'm sure it has been done,' he said. 'If you'd fainted, I'd have had to put your head between your knees. And God knows how we'd have managed that at one of these tables. I'd forgotten how cramped it all was. But we used to like that, I suppose, didn't we?'

'Yes, I suppose we did,' she said.

'Even though you didn't faint,' he said, 'didn't you feel some sort of slight tremor? Surely you must have done?'

'It's hard to tell,' she said, 'when one's sitting down. It isn't a fair test. Even of tremors.'

'No,' he said, 'no.'

Then they were silent for a moment or two, and then she said, very precisely and carefully, offering her first generous signal of intended retreat,

'I suppose that what *is* odd, really, is that we haven't come across one another before?'

'Oh, I don't know,' he said, with equal, disappointing neutrality. 'Where would we have met? It's not as though we ever belonged to what you might call the same world.'

'No,' she said, 'no, I suppose not.'

'Have you ever been back here before?' he asked.

'No, never,' she said. 'Have you?'

'Yes,' he said. 'Yes, I have. And if you had been back, you might have seen me. I looked for you.'

'You're lying,' she said quickly, elated, looking at him for the first time since he had sat down by her, and them looking away quickly, horrified by the dangerous and appalling proximity of his head, but keeping nevertheless her nerve, being more or less sure that he was in fact lying.

'No, I'm not,' he said. 'I came here, and looked for you. I was sure that you would come.'

'It's a safe lie,' she said, 'like all your lies. A lie I could never catch you out in. Unless I really had been here, looking for you, and simply hadn't wanted to admit it.'

'And even then,' he said, 'we might merely have missed each other.'

'Yes,' she conceded.

'But,' he said with conviction, 'you weren't here at all. I know you weren't here. I was here, I came, but you didn't. You were faithless, weren't you, my darling?'

'Faithless?'

'You forgot me quicker then I forgot you, didn't you? When you had so promised to remember.'

'Oh,' she said, wondering if she should admit so much, but unable to resist the ominous luxury of admission, 'oh, I didn't forget you.'

'Didn't you? How long did you remember me for?'

'Oh, how can one say,' she said. 'After all, there are degrees of remembrance.'

'Tell me,' he said, 'tell me. What harm can it do, to tell me now?'

She moved a little on the seat, away from him, but settling at the same time into a more comfortable pose of confidence: because she wanted to tell him, she had been waiting for years to tell him.

'I suffered quite horribly,' she said. 'Really quite horribly. That's what you want to hear, isn't it?'

'Of course it is,' he said.

'Oh, I really did,' she said. 'I can't tell you. I cried, all the time, for weeks. For a month. For at least a month. And whenever the phone went, I started, I jumped, like a fool, as though I'd been shot. It was pathetic, it was ludicrous. In the end I had to invent some bloody silly story about waiting for a call about a job, though what job could ever have got anyone in such a state I can hardly imagine, and each time I answered and it wasn't you I could hardly speak, I could somehow hardly make the effort to speak. It's odd how people don't notice when one doesn't reply. I would stand there listening, and they would go on talking, and sometimes I would say yes or no, as I waited for them to ring off, and when they did ring off I don't think they even noticed. And then I would sit down and cry. Is that what you want me to say?'

'I want to hear it,' he said, 'but it can't, it can't be true.'

'It's as true as that you came to this place to look for me,' she said.

'I did come,' he said.

'And I did weep,' she said.

'Did you ever try to ring me?' he asked, then, unable to resist.

'No!' she said with some pride. 'No, not once. I never tried, not once. I'd said I wouldn't, and I didn't.

'I rang you, once,' he said.

'You didn't,' she said, 'you didn't, and became aware at that instant that her knees under the table were trembling; they were, quite unmistakably.

'I did,' he said. 'It was just over a year ago, and we'd just got back from a party, about three in the morning it was, and I rang you. But you didn't answer. He answered.'

'Oh God,' she said, 'oh God. It's true, it's true, it't not a lie, because I remember it. Oliver said it was burglars. A Friday night. Wasn't it a Friday night?'

'Yes,' he said, 'my darling darling, it was. Did you know it might have been me?'

'I didn't think it could have been you,' she said. 'Not you, after so long a time. But I thought of you. When the phone rang and woke us, I thought of you, and when Oliver said there was no answer, I thought of you. Oh my darling, I can't tell you how I've had to stop myself ringing you, how I've sat there by the phone and lifted the receiver and dialled the first numbers of your number, and then stopped, and not let myself do it, and the receiver would be dripping with sweat when I put it down, but I stopped myself, I did stop myself. That was good of me wasn't it?'

'Oh,' he said, 'if you knew how I'd wanted you to ring.'

'I did write to you once,' she said. 'But I couldn't bring myself to post it. But I'll tell you what I did, I typed out an envelope to you, and I put one of those circulars from that absurd Poetry Club of mine into it, and I sent it off to you, because I thought that at least it might create in you a passing thought of me. And I liked the thought of something from my house reaching your house. Though perhaps she threw it away before it even got to you.'

'I remember it,' he said. 'I did think of you. But I didn't think you sent it, because the post mark was Croydon.'

'Oh,' she said, weakly. 'You got it. You did get it. Oh Lord, how alarmingly faithful we have both been.'

'Did you expect us not to be? We swore that we would be. Oh look, my darling here's your lunch, are you still eating cheese omelettes every day, now that really *is* what I call alarming consistency. And I haven't even ordered. What shall I have, what about some Moussaka, I always used to like that, it was always rather nice, in its own disgusting way. One Moussaka, please.'

'I *like* cheese omelettes,' she said. 'And after all, I don't see why one shouldn't have the same lunch every day. I mean, most people always have the same breakfast, don't they. Nobody complains when people go on eating toast and marmalade, do they?'

'I wasn't complaining,' he said. 'I was just remarking. I like your habits, I always did. You don't think I've changed, do you?'

'How should I know?' she said, and ate her first mouthful. Then she put down her knife and fork, and said, reflectively, 'You know, from my point of view at least, the whole business was quite unnecessary. What I mean is, Oliver hadn't the faintest suspicion. The thought of you had never even crossed his mind. Which, considering how ludicrously careless we were, is quite astonishing. We could have carried on forever, and he'd never have known. He was far too preoccupied himself with his own affairs to notice. I got it all out of him in the end, and I forgave him very nicely, and do you know what he said at the end of it all, at the end of all my forgiveness? He said that he'd had his suspicions that I'd been carrying on at the time with Robert Bennington. Have you ever heard of such a thing? I was so horrified by the very idea that I flew into a terrible rage and defended myself so vehemently that I quite frightened him. I mean to say, Robert, what a choice that would have been, what a ghastly mistake that would have been. I was never so offended in my life. What a pleasure it was, all that virtuous indignation, it was like getting rid of three years guilt, I can't tell you what a relief it was.'

'Robert Bennington,' he said, 'Robert Bennington. Who was he? Was he that tall fellow in films, with that fat wife?'

'Oh,' she said, 'he's nobody, just nobody, I mean he's quite nice, but as for anyone thinking him more than quite nice ...', and she noticed as she spoke that her voice had taken on, somehow, as with age-old habit, those provocative, defensive tones in which they would always discuss others, other people, the stray characters with which they would decorate from time to time their charmed and passionate dialogue and she knew that he, in reply, would use that note of confident and yet in some way truly, dreadfully suspicious jealousy.

'I seem to remember,' he said, sure enough, 'that Robert Bennington took you out to the cinema one evening, when Oliver was in Ireland. That was him, wasn't it?'

'You remember everything,' she said.

'And you said that you thought of me when you were in the cinema, but you didn't, I know you didn't,' he said.

'Oh, I did, I did,' she protested. 'I thought of you everywhere, and what better place to think of you than in the cinema, especially when with a dull fellow like Robert?'

'I thought you said he was quite nice,' he said, and she started to say, 'Yes, he is quite nice,' and then instead she started to laugh, and said,

'You are absurd, darling, it was Oliver that introduced that Robert motif, there's no need for *you* to start on it, especially so long after the event, I mean any concern you might now feel would be well and truly irrelevant.'

'After what event?' he said, incurable.

'No event, there wasn't any event,' she said, 'the whole point of the story was that Oliver had got it so wrong, so pointlessly wrong, I mean suspecting Robert instead of you...'

'It's no good,' he said, 'whatever you say, I simply can't prevent myself feeling annoyed that anyone might have had any reason for thinking that you were in love with anyone but me...' and then, the word love being mentioned, that final syllable, they were both reduced to silence, and they sat there, still in their ridiculous proximity, until she managed to take another mouthful of her omelette.

'You know,' he said, when the movement of her jaws had sufficiently disrupted the connection, 'all those continual threats of separation, that was really corrupt, you know, that was as bad as nagging. I feel bad about it now, looking back. Don't you?'

'How do you mean, bad about it?' she said.

'I feel we ought to have been able to do better than that. Though come to think of it, it was you that did nearly all the threatening. Every time I saw you, you said it was for the last time. Every time. And I must have seen you six days in every week for over a year. You can't have meant it, each time.'

'I did mean it,' she said. 'I did mean it. Though each time I stopped meaning it and fixed up the next time to see you, I felt that of course I hadn't meant it. By then again I did mean it, because I finally did it. Didn't I?'

'You mean we did it,' he said. 'You couldn't have done it without my help. If I'd rung you, if I'd written to you, it would have started all over again.'

'Do you really think so?' she said, sadly, without malice, without recrimi-nation. 'Yes, I suppose you might be right. I could never decide whether I could do it on my own or not. Evidently I couldn't. It takes two to part, just as it takes two to love.'

'It was corrupt, though,' he said, 'to make ourselves live under that perpetual threat.'

'Yes,' she said, 'but remember how lovely it was, how horribly lovely, each time that one relented. Each time one said I'll never see you again, all right I'll meet you tomorrow in the usual place at half past one. It was lovely.'

'Lovely but wicked,' he said.

'Oh, that sensation,' she said, 'that sensation of defeat, that was so lovely, every time, every time you touched me, every time I saw you . . . and I felt so sure, so entirely sure that what you felt was what I felt, that you were as weak as me, and as capable of enduring such ghastly self-inflicted wounds . . . Lord, we were so alike, and to think that when I first knew you I couldn't think of anything to say to you at all, I thought you came from another world, that we had nothing in common at all nothing at all except, well, except you know what, I feel it would be dangerous even to mention it, even now. Oh darling, what a disaster, our being so alike.'

'It was that that made it so hard,' he said. 'The reverse of the irresistible force and unbreakable object principle, whatever that might be.'

'Two objects most infinitely breakable, perhaps,' she said.

'I liked it though,' he said. 'I liked it, breaking up together. Better than having it done to one, better than doing it.'

'Better?'

'Perhaps even after all less corrupt,' he said.

'Yes, but more seriously incurable,' she said. And silence threatening to fall once more, she said quickly. 'Anyway, tell me what you're doing round here. I mean to say, one has to have some reason, for coming to a place like this.'

'I told you,' he said, 'I was looking for you.'

'You *are* a liar,' she said, smiling, amazed that she still even here could allow herself to be amused: indeed, could not prevent herself from smil-ing.

'What are you doing here then?' he said.

'Oh, I had a perfectly good reason,' she said, 'perfectly good, though rather embarrassing, I don't know if I'll tell you, but I suppose I will. You know that false front tooth? Well yesterday morning I lost it, and I've got to be on a television thing tonight, and the thought of being without a tooth was so alarming so I went to my dentist and he made them make me a new one, and I had to come round here to the warehouse to pick it up.'

'Have you got it in?'

'Yes,' she said, and turned to face him, smiling, lifting her upper lip. 'Look, there it is.'

'Do you mean,' he said, 'that if you'd had lunch *before* collecting your tooth, I would at least have seen you without it in?'

'Theoretically,' she said, 'but it wouldn't in fact have been possible, because how could I ever have had lunch in a public place without my front tooth?'

'I'd hardly call this a public place,' he said. 'What a vain woman you are. You always were.'

'I don't see anything wrong with vanity,' she said. 'And look, if you really want to see me without my tooth, there you are,' and she took it out, and turned to him, and showed him.

'You look lovely,' he said. 'You look like a school child. You look like my daughter, she's got three missing at the moment.'

'You still haven't told me what you're doing here,' she said, putting her plate back again. 'I bet you haven't got as good a reason as me. Mine is entirely convincing, don't you think? I mean, where else could I have had lunch? I think my reason clears me entirely of any suspicion of any kind, don't you?'

'Any suspicion of sentiment?'

'That's what I meant.'

'He thought for a moment, and then he said,

'I had to call on a man about my Income Tax. Look, here's his address.' And he got an envelope out of his pocket and showed her.

'Ah,' she said.

'You see,' he said.

'See what?' she said.

'I came here on purpose,' he said. 'To think of you. I could have had lunch at lots of places between London Wall and here.'

'Yes, I suppose so,' she said, 'but you always were rather conservative about eating places. Suspicious, almost. You didn't come here because of me, you came here because it's the only place you know about.'

'It comes to the same thing,' he said.

'No, it doesn't,' she said, firmly. She felt creeping upon her the familiar illusion of control, created as always before by a concentration upon trivialities, which could no longer even momentarily disguise the gravity of any outcome: and she reflected that their conversations had always so closely followed the patterns of their dialogues in bed, and that these idle points of concentration were like those frivolous, delaying gestures in which she would turn aside, in which he would lie still and stare at the ceiling, hardly touching her, not daring, as he said, to touch her, and thus merely deferring, in their own studiously developed amorous dialectic, the inevitable: and thinking this, and able to live only in the deferment, for now there was no inevitability, no outcome that she could see, she said, eating her last chip,

'And how are your children?'

'They're fine,' he said, 'fine. Saul got into Grammar School, and starts next year. We were pleased about that. What about yours?'

'Oh, they're all right too. I've had some dreadful nights with Laura recently, I must say I thought I was through with all that, I mean the child's five now, but she says she can't sleep and has these dreadful nightmares, so she's been every night in my bed for the last fortnight. It's wearing me out. Then in the morning she just laughs. And then at night it starts all over again. She doesn't kick, she's not as bony and awful as Fred used to be, it's just that I can't sleep with anyone else in the bed.'

'What does Oliver say?' he asked, and she said, without thinking, having said it so often to others,

'Oh, I don't sleep with Oliver any more,' and realizing as she said it precisely what she had said, wondering how she could have made such a mistake, and wondering how to get out of it. But fortunately at that instant his Moussaka arrived, and the depositing of the plate and the redeployment of cutlery made it unnecessary to pursue the subject. Though once it had become unnecessary, she regretted the subject's disappearance: and she thought of saying what was no less than the truth, what was the truth itself: she thought of saying that she had slept with nobody since she had slept with him, that for three years she had slept alone, and was quite prepared to sleep alone forever. But she was not sure, not entirely sure that he would want to hear it, and she knew that such a remark once made could never be retracted, so she said nothing.

He stared at his Moussaka, at the browned yellow crust.

'It looks all right,' he said, and took a mouthful, and chewed it, and then he put his fork down and said, 'Oh Lord, oh Lord, what a Proustian experience. I can't believe it. I can't believe that I'm sitting here with you. It tastes of you, that stuff, oh God it reminds me of you. You look so beautiful, you look so lovely, my darling, Oh God I loved you so much. I really loved you, do you believe me that I really loved you?'

'I haven't slept with anyone,' she said, 'since I last slept with you.'

'Oh darling,' he said: and she could feel herself fainting and sighing away, drifting downwards on that fatefully, descending eddying spiral, like Paulo and Francesca[1] in hell, helpless, the mutually entwined drifting fall of all true lovers, unresisting, finally unresisting, as though three years of solitude had been nothing but a pause, nothing but a long breath before this final acknowledgment of nature, damnation and destiny; she turned towards him, and said, 'Oh my darling, I love you, what can I do, I love you,' and he with the same breath said, 'I love you, I all the time love you, I want you,' and they kissed there, their faces already so close that little inclination was needed, they kissed there above the Moussaka and chips, because they believed in such things, because that was what they believed in, because, like disastrous romantics, they habitually connived with fate by remembering the names of restaurants and the streets they had once walked along as lovers. Those who forget, forget, he said to her later; and those who do not forget will meet again.

---

[1] Lovers in the 'Inferno' of Dante's *Divine Comedy*.

Angela Carter

1940 –

B orn in Sussex, and educated at Bristol University, Angela Carter now lives in London. She is one of the most highly acclaimed contemporary writers of fiction and short stories, but she has also written criticism, radio plays and a screenplay. Her novels include The Magic Toyshop *(1981),* The Passion of New Eve *(1977),* Heroes and Villains *(1981),* Infernal Desire Machines of Doctor Hoffman *(1982) and* Nights at the Circus *(1984).*

The following stories have been taken from The Bloody Chamber and Other Stories *(Penguin, London, 1986).*

The Company of Wolves

O NE beast and only one howls in the woods by night.

The wolf is carnivore incarnate and he's as cunning as he is ferocious; once he's had a taste of flesh then nothing else will do.

At night, the eyes of wolves shine like candle flames, yellowish, reddish, but that is because the pupils of their eyes fatten on darkness and catch the light from your lantern to flash it back to you – red for danger; if a wolf's eyes reflect only moonlight, then they gleam a cold and unnatural green, a mineral, a piercing colour. If the benighted traveller spies those luminous, terrible sequins stitched suddenly on the black thickets, then he knows he must run, if fear has not struck him stock-still.

But those eyes are all you will be able to glimpse of the forest assassins as they cluster invisibly round your smell of meat as you go through the wood unwisely late. They will be like shadows, they will be like wraiths, grey members of a congregation of nightmare; hark! his long, wavering howl . . . an aria of fear made audible.

The wolfsong is the sound of the rending you will suffer, in itself a murdering.

It is winter and cold weather. In this region of mountain and forest, there is now nothing for the wolves to eat. Goats and sheep are locked up in the byre, the deer departed for the remaining pasturage on the southern slopes – wolves grow lean and famished. There is so little flesh on them that you could count the starveling ribs through their pelts, if they gave you time before they pounced. Those slavering jaws; the lolling tongue; the rime of saliva on the grizzled chops – of all the teeming perils of the night and the forest, ghosts, hobgoblins, ogres that grill babies upon gridirons, witches that fatten their captives in cages for cannibal tables, the wolf is worst for he cannot listen to reason.

You are always in danger in the forest, where no people are. Step between the portals of the great pines where the shaggy branches tangle about you, trapping the unwary traveller in nets as if the vegetation itself were in a plot with the wolves who live there, as though the wicked trees go fishing on behalf of their friends – step between the gateposts of the forest with the greatest trepidation and infinite precautions, for if you stray from the path for one instant, the wolves will eat you. They are grey as famine, they are as unkind as plague.

The grave-eyed children of the sparse villages always carry knives with them when they go out to tend the little flocks of goats that provide the homesteads with acrid milk and rank, maggoty cheeses. Their knives are half as big as they are, the blades are sharpened daily.

But the wolves have ways of arriving at your own hearthside. We try and try but sometimes we cannot keep them out. There is no winter's night the cottager does not fear to see a lean, grey, famished snout questing under the door, and there was a woman once bitten in her own kitchen as she was straining the macaroni.

Fear and flee the wolf; for, worst of all, the wolf may be more than he seems.

There was a hunter once, near here, that trapped a wolf in a pit. This wolf had massacred the sheep and goats; eaten up a mad old man who used to live by himself in a hut halfway up the mountain and sing to Jesus all day; pounced on a girl looking after the sheep, but she made such a commotion that men came with rifles and scared him away and tried to track him into the forest but he was cunning and easily gave them the slip. So this hunter dug a pit and put a duck in it, for bait, all alive-oh; and he covered the pit with straw smeared with wolf dung. Quack, quack! went the duck and a wolf came slinking out of the forest, a big one, a heavy one, he weighed as much as a grown man and the straw gave way beneath him – into the pit he tumbled. The hunter jumped down after him, slit his throat, cut off all his paws for a trophy.

And then no wolf at all lay in front of the hunter but the bloody trunk of a man, headless, footless, dying, dead.

A witch from up the valley once turned an entire wedding party into wolves because the groom had settled on another girl. She used to order them to visit her, at night, from spite, and they would sit and howl around her cottage for her, serenading her with their misery.

Not so very long ago, a young woman in our village married a man who vanished clean away on her wedding night. The bed was made with new sheets and the bride lay down in it; the groom said, he was going out to relieve himself, insisted on it, for the sake of decency, and she drew the coverlet up to her chin and she lay there. And she waited and she waited and then she waited again – surely he's been gone a long time? Until she jumps up in bed and shrieks to hear a howling, coming on the wind from the forest.

That long-drawn, wavering howl has, for all its fearful resonance, some inherent sadness in it, as if the beasts would love to be less beastly if only they knew how and never cease to mourn their own condition. There is a vast melancholy in the canticles of the wolves, melancholy infinite as the forest, endless as these long nights of winter and yet that ghastly sadness, that mourning for their own, irremediable appetites, can never move the heart for not one phrase in it hints at the possibility of redemption; grace could not come to the wolf from its own despair, only through some external mediator, so that, sometimes, the beast will look as if he half welcomes the knife that despatches him.

The young woman's brothers searched the outhouses and the haystacks but never found any remains so the sensible girl dried her eyes and found herself another husband not too shy to piss into a pot who spent the nights indoors. She gave him a pair of bonny babies and all went right as a trivet until, one freezing night, the night of the solstice, the hinge of the year when things do not fit together as well as they should, the longest night, her first good man came home again.

A great thump on the door announced him as she was stirring the soup for the father of her children and she knew him the moment she lifted the latch to him although it was years since she'd worn black for him and now he was in rags and his hair hung down his back and never saw a comb, alive with lice.

'Here I am again, missus,' he said. 'Get me my bowl of cabbage and be quick about it.'

Then her second husband came in with wood for the fire and when the first one saw she'd slept with another man and, worse, clapped his red eyes on her little children who'd crept into the kitchen to see what all the din was about, he shouted: 'I wish I were a wolf again, to teach this whore a lesson!' So a wolf he instantly became and tore off the eldest boy's left foot before he was chopped up with the hatchet they used for chopping logs. But when the wolf lay bleeding and gasping its last, the pelt peeled off again and he was just as he had been, years ago, when he ran away from his marriage bed, so that she wept and her second husband beat her.

They say there's an ointment the Devil gives you that turns you into a wolf the minute you rub it on. Or, that he was born feet first and had a wolf for his father and his torso is a man's but his legs and genitals are a wolf's. And he has a wolf's heart.

Seven years is a werewolf's natural span but if you burn his human clothing you condemn him to wolfishness for the rest of his life, so old wives hereabouts think it some protection to throw a hat or an apron at the werewolf, as if clothes made the man. Yet by the eyes, those phosphorescent eyes, you know him in all his shapes; the eyes alone unchanged by metamorphosis.

Before he can become a wolf, the lycanthrope strips stark naked. If you spy a naked man among the pines, you must run as if the Devil were after you.

It is midwinter and the robin, the friend of man, sits on the handle of the gardener's spade and sings. It is the worst time in all the year for wolves but this strong-minded child insists she will go off through the wood. She is quite sure the wild beasts cannot harm her although, well-warned, she lays a carving knife in the basket her mother has packed with cheeses. There is a bottle of harsh liquor distilled from brambles; a batch of flat oatcakes baked on the hearthstone; a pot or two of jam. The flaxen-haired girl will take these delicious gifts to a reclusive grandmother so old the burden of her years is crushing her to death. Granny lives two hours' trudge through the winter woods; the child wraps herself up in her thick shawl, draws it over her head. She steps into her stout wooden shoes; she is dressed and ready and it is Christmas Eve. The malign door of the solstice still swings upon its hinges but she has been too much loved ever to feel scared.

Children do not stay young for long in this savage country. There are no toys for them to play with so they work hard and grow wise but this one, so pretty and the youngest of her family, a little late-comer, had been indulged by her mother and the grandmother who'd knitted her the red shawl that, today, has the ominous if brilliant look of blood on snow. Her breasts have just begun to swell; her hair is like lint, so fair it hardly makes a shadow on her pale forehead; her cheeks are an emblematic scarlet and white and she has just started her woman's bleeding, the clock inside her that will strike, henceforward, once a month.

She stands and moves within the invisible pentacle of her own virginity. She is an unbroken egg; she is a sealed vessel; she has inside her a magic space the entrance to which is shut tight with a plug of membrane; she is a closed system; she does not know how to shiver. She has her knife and she is afraid of nothing.

Her father might forbid her, if he were home, but he is away in the forest, gathering wood, and her mother cannot deny her.

The forest closed upon her like a pair of jaws.

There is always something to look at in the forest, even in the middle of winter – the huddled mounds of birds, succumbed to the lethargy of the season, heaped on the creaking boughs and too forlorn to sing; the bright frills of the winter fungi on the blotched trunks of the trees; the cuneiform slots of rabbits and deer, the herringbone tracks of the birds, a hare as lean as a rasher of bacon streaking across the path where the thin sunlight dapples the russet brakes of last year's bracken.

When she heard the freezing howl of a distant wolf, her practised hand sprang to the handle of her knife, but she saw no sign of a wolf at all, nor of a naked man, neither, but then she heard a clattering among the brushwood and there sprang on to the path a fully clothed one, a very handsome young one, in the green coat and wideawake hat of a hunter, laden with carcasses of game birds. She had her hand on her knife at the first rustle of twigs but he laughed with a flash of white teeth when he saw her and made her a comic yet flattering little bow; she'd never seen such a fine fellow before, not among the rustic clowns of her native village. So on they went together, through the thickening light of the afternoon.

Soon they were laughing and joking like old friends. When he offered to carry her basket, she gave it to him although her knife was in it because he told her his rifle would protect them. As the day darkened, it began to snow again; she felt the first flake settle on her eyelashes but now there was only half a mile to go and there would be a fire, and hot tea, and a welcome, a warm one, surely, for the dashing huntsman as well as for herself.

This young man had a remarkable object in his pocket. It was a compass. She looked at the little round glass face in the palm of his hand and watched the wavering needle with a vague wonder. He assured her this compass had taken him safely through the wood on his hunting trip because the needle always told him with perfect accuracy where the north was. She did not believe it; she knew she should never leave the path on the way through the wood or else she would be lost instantly. He laughed at her again; gleaming trails of spittle clung to his teeth. He said, if he plunged off the path into the forest that surrounded them, he would guarantee to arrive at her grandmother's house a good quarter of an hour before she did, plotting his way through the undergrowth with his compass, while she trudged the long way, along the winding path.

I don't believe you. Besides, aren't you afraid of the wolves?

He only tapped the gleaming butt of his rifle and grinned.

Is it a bet? he asked her. Shall we make a game of it? What will you give me if I get to your grandmother's house before you?

What would you like? she asked disingenuously.

A kiss.

Commonplaces of a rustic seduction; she lowered her eyes and blushed.

He went through the undergrowth and took her basket with him but she forgot to be afraid of the beasts, although now the moon was rising, for she wanted to dawdle on her way to make sure the handsome gentleman would win his wager.

Grandmother's house stood by itself a little way out of the village. The freshly falling snow blew in eddies about the kitchen garden and the young man stepped delicately up the snowy path to the door as if he were reluctant to get his feet wet, swinging his bundle of game and the girl's basket and humming a little tune to himself.

There is a faint trace of blood on his chin; he has been snacking on his catch.

He rapped upon the panels with his knuckles.

Aged and frail, granny is three-quarters succumbed to the mortality the ache in her bones promises her and almost ready to give in entirely. A boy came out from the village to build up her hearth for the night an hour ago and the kitchen crackles with busy firelight. She has her Bible for company, she is a pious old woman. She is propped up on several pillows in the bed set into the wall peasant-fashion, wrapped up in the patchwork quilt she made before she was married, more years ago than she cares to remember. Two china spaniels with liver-coloured blotches on their coats and black noses sit on either side of the fireplace. There is a bright rug of woven rags on the pantiles. The grandfather clock ticks away her eroding time.

We keep the wolves outside by living well.

He rapped upon the panels with his hairy knuckles.

It is your granddaughter, he mimicked in a high soprano.

Lift up the latch and walk in, my darling.

You can tell them by their eyes, eyes of a beast of prey, nocturnal, devastating eyes as red as a wound; you can hurl your Bible at him and your apron after, granny, you thought that was a sure prophylactic against these infernal vermin . . . now call on Christ and his mother and all the angels in heaven to protect you but it won't do you any good.

His feral muzzle is sharp as a knife; he drops his golden burden of gnawed pheasant on the table and puts down your dear girl's basket, too. Oh, my God, what have you done with her?

Off with his disguise, that coat of forest-coloured cloth, the hat with the feather tucked into the ribbon; his matted hair streams down his white shirt and she can see the lice moving in it. The sticks in the hearth shift and hiss; night and the forest has come into the kitchen with darkness tangled in its hair.

He strips off his shirt. His skin is the colour and texture of vellum. A crisp stripe of hair runs down his belly, his nipples are ripe and dark as poison fruit but he's so thin you could count the ribs under this skin if only he gave you the time. He strips off his trousers and she can see how hairy his legs are. His genitals, huge. Ah! huge.

The last thing the old lady saw in all this world was a young man, eyes like cinders, naked as a stone, approaching her bed.

The wolf is carnivore incarnate.

When he had finished with her, he licked his chops and quickly dressed himself again, until he was just as he had been when he came through her door. He burned the inedible hair in the fireplace and wrapped the bones up in a napkin that he hid away under the bed in the wooden chest in which he found a clean pair of sheets. These he carefully put on the bed instead of the tell-tale stained ones he stowed away in the laundry basket. He plumped up the pillows and shook out the patchwork quilt, he picked up the Bible from the floor, closed it and laid it on the table. All was as it had been before except that grandmother was gone. The sticks twitched in the grate, the clock ticked and the young man sat patiently, deceitfully beside the bed in granny's nightcap.

Rat-a-tap-tap.

Who's there, he quavers in granny's antique falsetto.

Only your granddaughter.

So she came in, bringing with her a flurry of snow that melted in tears on the tiles, and perhaps she was a little disappointed to see only her grandmother sitting beside the fire. But then he flung off the blanket and sprang to the door, pressing his back against it so that she could not get out again.

The girl looked round the room and saw there was not even the indentation of a head on the smooth cheek of the pillow and how, for the first time she'd seen it so, the Bible lay closed on the table. The tick of the clock cracked like a whip. She wanted her knife from her basket but she did not dare reach for it because his eyes were fixed upon her – huge eyes that now seemed to shine with a unique, interior light, eyes the size of saucers, saucers full of Greek fire, diabolic phosphorescence.

What big eyes you have.

All the better to see you with.

No trace at all of the old woman except for a tuft of white hair that had caught in the bark of an unburned log. When the girl saw that, she knew she was in danger of death.

Where is my grandmother?

There's nobody here but we two, my darling.

Now a great howling rose up all around them, near, very near, as close as the kitchen garden, the howling of a multitude of wolves; she knew the worst wolves are hairy on the inside and she shivered, in spite of the scarlet shawl she pulled more closely round herself as if it could protect her although it was as red as the blood she must spill.

Who has come to sing us carols, she said.

Those are the voices of my brothers, darling; I love the company of wolves. Look out of the window and you'll see them.

Snow half-caked the lattice and she opened it to look into the garden. It was a white night of moon and snow; the blizzard whirled round the gaunt, grey beasts who squatted on their haunches among the rows of winter cabbage, pointing their sharp snouts to the moon and howling as if their hearts would break. Ten wolves; twenty wolves – so many wolves she could not count them, howling in concert as if demented or deranged. Their eyes reflected the light from the kitchen and shone like a hundred candles.

It is very cold, poor things, she said; no wonder they howl so.

She closed the window on the wolves' threnody and took off her scarlet shawl, the colour of poppies, the colour of sacrifices, the colour of her menses, and since her fear did her no good, she ceased to be afraid.

What shall I do with my shawl?

Throw it on the fire, dear one. You won't need it again.

She bundled up her shawl and threw it on the blaze, which instantly consumed it. Then she drew her blouse over head; her small breasts gleamed as if the snow had invaded the room.

What shall I do with my blouse?

Into the fire with it, too, my pet.

The thin muslin went flaring up the chimney like a magic bird and now off came her skirt, her woollen stockings, her shoes, and on to the fire they went, too, and were gone for good. The firelight shone through the edges of her skin; now she was clothed only in her untouched integument of flesh. This dazzling, naked she combed out her hair with her fingers; her hair look white as the snow outside. Then went directly to the man with red eyes in whose unkempt mane the lice moved; she stood up on tiptoe and unbuttoned the collar of his shirt.

What big arms you have.

All the better to hug you with.

Every wolf in the world now howled a prothalamion outside the window as she freely gave the kiss she owed him.

What big teeth you have!

She saw how his jaw began to slaver and the room was full of the clamour of the forest's Liebestod but the wise child never flinched, even when he answered:

All the better to eat you with.

The girl burst out laughing; she knew she was nobody's meat. She laughed at him full in the face, she ripped off his shirt for him and flung it into the fire, in the fiery wake of her own discarded clothing. The flames danced like dead souls on Walpurgisnacht and the old bones under the bed set up a terrible clattering but she did not pay them any heed.

Carnivore incarnate, only immaculate flesh appeases him.

She will lay his fearful head on her lap and she will pick out the lice from his pelt and perhaps she will put the lice into her mouth and eat them, as he will bid her, as she would do in a savage marriage ceremony.

The blizzard will die down.

The blizzard died down, leaving the mountains as randomly covered with snow as if a blind woman had thrown a sheet over them, the upper branches of the forest pines limed, creaking, swollen with the fall.

Snowlight, moonlight, a confusion of paw-prints.

All silent, all still.

Midnight; and the clock strikes. It is Christmas Day, the werewolves' birthday, the door of the solstice stands wide open; let them all sink through.

See! sweet and sound she sleeps in granny's bed, between the paws of the tender wolf.

Wolf-Alice

COULD this ragged girl with brindled lugs have spoken like we do she would have called herself a wolf, but she cannot speak, although she howls because she is lonely – yet 'howl' is not the right word for it, since she is young enough to make the noise that pups do, bubbling, delicious, like that of a panful of fat on the fire. Sometimes the sharp ears of her foster kindred hear her across the irreparable gulf of absence; they answer her from faraway pine forest and the bald mountain rim. Their counterpoint crosses and criss-crosses the night sky; they are trying to talk to her but they cannot do so because she does not understand their language even if she knows how to use it for she is not a wolf herself, although suckled by wolves.

Her panting tongue hangs out; her red lips are thick and fresh. Her legs are long, lean and muscular. Her elbows, hands and knees are thickly callused because she always runs on all fours. She never walks; she trots or gallops. Her pace is not our pace.

Two-legs looks, four-legs sniffs. Her long nose is always a-quiver, sifting every scent it meets. With this useful tool, she lengthily investigates everything she glimpses. She can net so much more of the world than we can through the fine, hairy, sensitive filters of her nostrils that her poor eyesight does not trouble her. Her nose is sharper by night than our eyes are by day so it is the night she prefers, when the cool reflected light of the moon does not make her eyes smart and draws out the various fragrances from the woodland where she wanders when she can. But the wolves keep well away from the peasants' shotguns, now, and she will no longer find them there.

Wide shoulders, long arms and she sleeps succinctly curled into a ball as if she were cradling her spine in her tail. Nothing about her is human except that she is *not* a wolf; it is as if the fur she thought she wore had melted into her skin and become part of it, although it does not exist. Like the wild beasts, she lives without a future. She inhabits only the present tense, a fugue of the continuous, a world of sensual immediacy as without hope as it is without despair.

When they found her in the wolf's den beside the bullet-riddled corpse of her foster mother, she was no more than a little brown scrap so snarled in her own brown hair they did not, at first, think she was a child but a cub; she snapped at her would-be saviours with her spiky canines until they tied her up by force. She spent her first days amongst us crouched stockstill, staring at the whitewashed wall of her cell in the convent to which they took her. The nuns poured water over her, poked her with sticks to rouse her. Then she might snatch bread from their hands and race with it into a corner to mumble it with her back towards them; it was a great day among the novices when she learned to sit up on her hind legs and beg for a crust.

They found that, if she were treated with a little kindness, she was not intractable. She learned to recognize her own dish; then, to drink from a cup. They found that she could quite easily be taught a few, simple tricks but she did not feel the cold and it took a long time to wheedle a shift over her head to cover up her bold nakedness. Yet she always seemed wild, impatient of restraint, capricious in temper; when the Mother Superior tried to teach her to give thanks for her recovery from the wolves, she arched her back, pawed the floor, retreated to a far corner of the chapel, crouched, trembled, urinated, defecated – reverted entirely, it would seem, to her natural state. Therefore, without a qualm, this nine days' wonder and continuing embarrassment of a child was delivered over to the bereft and unsanctified household of the Duke.

Deposited at the castle, she huffed and snuffed and smelled only a reek of meat, not the least whiff of sulphur, nor of familiarity. She settled down on her hunkers with that dog's sigh that is only the expulsion of breath and does not mean either relief or resignation.

The Duke is sere as old paper; his dry skin rustles against the bedsheets as he throws them back to thrust out his thin legs scabbed with old scars where thorns scored his pelt. He lives in a gloomy mansion, all alone but for this child who has as little in common with the rest of us as he does. His bedroom is painted terracotta, rusted with a wash of pain, like the interior of an Iberian butcher's shop, but for himself, nothing can hurt him since he ceased to cast an image in the mirror.

He sleeps in an antlered bed of dull black wrought iron until the moon, the governess of transformations and overseer of somnambulists, pokes an imperative finger through the narrow window and strikes his face; then his eyes start open.

At night, those huge, inconsolable, rapacious eyes of his are eaten up by swollen, gleaming pupil. His eyes see only appetite. These eyes open to devour the world in which he sees, nowhere, a reflection of himself; he passed through the mirror and now, henceforward, lives as if upon the other side of things.

Spilt, glistering milk of moonlight on the frost-crisped grass; on such a night, in moony, metamorphic weather, they say you might easily find him, if you had been foolish enough to venture out late, scuttling along by the churchyard wall with half a juicy torso slung across his back. The white light scours the fields and scours them again until everything gleams and he will leave paw-prints in the hoar-frost when he runs howling round the graves at night in his lupine fiestas.

By the red early hour of midwinter sunset, all the doors are barred for miles. The cows low fretfully in the byre when he goes by, the whimpering dogs sink their noses in their paws. He carries on his frail shoulders a weird burden of fear; he is cast in the role of the corpse-eater, the body-snatcher who invades the last privacies of the dead. He is white as leprosy, with scrabbling fingernails, and nothing deters him. If you stuff a corpse with garlic, why, he only slavers at the treat: cadavre provençale. He will use the holy cross as a scratching post and crouch above the font to thirstily lap up holy water.

She sleeps in the soft, warm ashes of the hearth; beds are traps, she will not stay in one. She can perform the few, small tasks to which the nuns trained her, she sweeps up the hairs, vertebrae and phalanges that litter his room into a dustpan, she makes up his bed at sunset, when he leaves it and the grey beasts outside howl, as if they know his transformation is their parody. Unkind to their prey, to their own they are tender; had the Duke been a wolf, they would have angrily expelled him from the pack, he would have had to lollop along miles behind them, creeping in submission on his belly up to the kill only after they had eaten and were sleeping, to gnaw the well-chewed bones and chew the hide. Yet, suckled as she was by wolves on the high uplands where her mother bore and left her, only his kitchen maid, who is not wolf or woman, knows no better than to do his chores for him.

She grew up with wild beasts. If you could transport her, in her filth, rags and feral disorder, to the Eden of our first beginnings where Eve and grunting Adam squat on a daisy bank, picking the lice from one another's pelts then she might prove to be the wise child who leads them all and her silence and her howling a language as authentic as any language of nature. In a world of talking beasts and flowers, she would be the bud of flesh in the kind lion's mouth: but how can the bitten apple flesh out its scar again?

Mutilation is her lot; though, now and then, she will emit an involuntary rustle of sound, as if the unused chords in her throat were a wind-harp that moved with the random impulses of the air, her whisper, more obscure than the voices of the dumb.

Familiar desecrations in the village graveyard. The coffin had been ripped open with the abandon with which a child unwraps a gift on Christmas morning and, of its contents, not a trace could be found but for a rag of the bridal veil in which the corpse had been wrapped that was caught, fluttering, in the brambles at the churchyard gate so they knew which way he had taken it, towards his gloomy castle.

In the lapse of time, the trance of being of that exiled place, this girl grew amongst things she could neither name nor perceive. How did she think, how did she feel, this perennial stranger with her furred thoughts and her primal sentience that existed in a flux of shifting impressions; there are no words to describe the way she negotiated the abyss between her dreams, those wakings strange as her sleepings. The wolves had tended her because they knew she was an imperfect wolf; we secluded her in animal privacy out of fear of her imperfection because it showed us what we might have been, and so time passed, although she scarcely knew it. Then she began to bleed.

Her first blood bewildered her. She did not know what it meant and the first stirrings of surmise that ever she felt were directed towards its possible cause. The moon had been shining into the kitchen when she woke to feel the trickle between her thighs and it seemed to her that a wolf who, perhaps, was fond of her, as wolves were, and who lived, perhaps, in the moon? must have nibbled her cunt while she was sleeping, had subjected her to a series of affectionate nips too gentle to wake her yet sharp enough to break the skin. The shape of this theory was blurred yet, out of it, there took root a kind of wild reasoning, as it might have from a seed dropped in her brain off the foot of a flying bird.

The flow continued for a few days, which seemed to her an endless time. She had, as yet, no direct notion of past, or of future, or of duration, only of a dimensionless, immediate moment. At night, she prowled the empty house looking for rags to sop the blood up; she had learned a little elementary hygiene in the convent, enough to know how to bury her excrement and cleanse herself of her natural juices, although the nuns had not the means to inform her how it should be, it was not fastidiousness but shame that made her do so.

She found towels, sheets and pillowcases in closets that had not been opened since the Duke came shrieking into the world with all his teeth, to bite his mother's nipple off and weep. She found once-worn ball dresses in cobwebbed wardrobes, and, heaped in the corners of his bloody chamber, shrouds, nightdresses and burial clothes that had wrapped items on the Duke's menus. She tore strips of the most absorbent fabrics to clumsily diaper herself. In the course of these prowlings, she bumped against that mirror over whose surface the Duke passed like a wind on ice.

First, she tried to nuzzle her reflection; then, nosing it industriously, she soon realized it gave out no smell. She bruised her muzzle on the cold glass and broke her claws trying to tussle with this stranger. She saw, with irritation, then amusement, how it mimicked every gesture of hers when she raised her forepaw to scratch herself or dragged her bum along the dusty carpet to rid herself of a slight discomfort in her hindquarters. She rubbed her head against her reflected face, to show that she felt friendly towards it, and felt a cool, solid, immovable surface between herself and she – some kind, possibly, of invisible cage? In spite of this barrier, she was lonely enough to ask this creature to try to play with her, baring her teeth and grinning; at once she received a reciprocal invitation. She rejoiced; she began to whirl round on herself, yapping exultantly, but, when she retreated from the mirror, she halted in the midst of her ecstasy, puzzled, to see how her new friend grew less in size.

The moonlight spilled into the Duke's motionless bedroom from behind a cloud and she saw how pale this wolf, not-wolf who played with her was. The moon and mirrors have this much in common: you cannot see behind them. Moonlit and white, Wolf-Alice looked at herself in the mirror and wondered whether there she saw the beast who came to bite her in the night. Then her sensitive ears pricked at the sound of a step in the hall; trotting at once back to her kitchen, she encountered the Duke with the leg of a man over his shoulder. Her toenails clicked against the stairs as she padded incuriously past, she, the serene, inviolable one in her absolute and verminous innocence.

Soon the flow ceased. She forgot it. The moon vanished; but, little by little, reappeared. When it again visited her kitchen at full strength, Wolf-Alice was surprised into bleeding again and so it went on, with a punctuality that transformed her vague grip on time. She learned to expect these bleedings, to prepare her rags against them, and afterwards, neatly to bury the dirtied things. Sequence asserted itself with custom and then she understood the circumambulatory principle of the clock perfectly, even if all clocks were banished from the den where she and the Duke inhabited their separate solitudes, so that you might say she discovered the very action of time by means of this returning cycle.

When she curled up among the cinders, the colour, texture and warmth of them brought her foster mother's belly out of the past and printed it on her flesh; her first conscious memory, painful as the first time the nuns combed her hair. She howled a little, in a firmer, deepening trajectory, to obtain the inscrutable consolation of the wolves' response, for now the world around her was assuming form. She perceived an essential difference between herself and her surroundings that you might say she could not put her *finger* on – only, the trees and grass of the meadows outside no longer seemed the emanation of her questing nose and erect ears, and yet sufficient to itself, but a kind of backdrop for her, that waited for her arrivals to give it meaning. She saw herself upon it and her eyes, with their sombre clarity, took on a veiled, introspective look.

She would spend hours examining the new skin that had been born, it seemed to her, of her bleeding. She would lick her soft upholstery with her long tongue and groom her hair with her fingernails. She examined her new breasts with curiosity; the white growths reminded her of nothing so much as the night-sprung puffballs she had found, sometimes, on evening rambles in the woods, a natural if disconcerting apparition, but then, to her astonishment, she found a little diadem of fresh hairs tufting between her thighs. She showed it to her mirror littermate, who reassured her by showing her she shared it.

The damned Duke haunts the graveyard; he believes himself to be both less and more than a man, as if his obscene difference were a sign of grace. During the day, he sleeps. His mirror faithfully reflects his bed but never the meagre shape within the disordered covers.

Sometimes, on those white nights when she was left alone in the house, she dragged out his grandmother's ball dresses and rolled on suave velvet and abrasive lace because to do so delighted her adolescent skin. Her intimate in the mirror wound the old clothes round herself, wrinkling its nose in delight at the ancient yet still potent scents of musk and civet that woke up in the sleeves and bodices. This habitual, at last boring, fidelity to her every movement finally woke her up to the regretful possibility that her companion was, in fact, no more than a particularly ingenious variety of the shadow she cast on sunlit grass. Had not she and the rest of the litter tussled and romped with their shadows long ago? She poked her agile nose around the back of the mirror; she found only dust, a spider stuck in his web, a heap of rags. A little moisture leaked from the corners of her eyes, yet her relation with the mirror was now far more intimate since she knew she saw herself within it.

She pawed and tumbled the dress the Duke had tucked away behind the mirror for a while. The dust was soon shaken out of it; she experimentally inserted her front legs in the sleeves. Although the dress was torn and crumpled, it was so white and of such a sinuous texture that she thought, before she put it on, she must thoroughly wash off her coat of ashes in the water from the pump in the yard, which she knew how to manipulate with her cunning forepaw. In the mirror, she saw how this white dress made her shine.

Although she could not run so fast on two legs in petticoats, she trotted out in her new dress to investigate the odorous October hedgerows, like a débutante from the castle, delighted with herself but still, now and then, singing to the wolves with a kind of wistful triumph, because now she knew how to wear clothes and so had put on the visible sign of her difference from them.

Her footprints on damp earth are beautiful and menacing as those Man Friday left.

The young husband of the dead bride spent a long time planning his revenge. He filled the church with an arsenal of bells, books and candles; a battery of silver bullets; they brought a ten-gallon tub of holy water in a wagon from the city, where it had been blessed by the Archbishop himself, to drown the Duke, if the bullets bounced off him. They gathered in the church to chant a litany and wait for the one who would visit with the first deaths of winter.

She goes out at night more often now; the landscape assembles itself about her, she informs it with her presence. She is its significance.

It seemed to her the congregation in the church was ineffectually attempting to imitate the wolves' chorus. She lent them the assistance of her own, educated voice for a while, rocking contemplatively on her haunches by the graveyard gate; then her nostrils twitched to catch the rank stench of the dead that told her her co-habitor was at hand; raising her head, who did her new, keen eyes spy but the lord of cobweb castle intent on performing his cannibal rituals?

And if her nostrils flare suspiciously at the choking reek of incense and his do not, that is because she is far more sentient than he. She will, therefore, run, run! when she hears the crack of bullets, because they killed her foster mother; so, with the self-same lilting lope, drenched with holy water, will he run, too, until the young widower fires the silver bullet that bites his shoulder and drags off half his fictive pelt, so that he must rise up like any common forked biped and limp distressfully on as best he may.

When they saw the white bride leap out of the tombstones and scamper off towards the castle with the werewolf stumbling after, the peasants thought the Duke's dearest victim had come back to take matters into her own hands. They ran screaming from the presence of a ghostly vengeance on him.

Poor, wounded thing . . . locked half and half between such strange states, an aborted transformation, an incomplete mystery, now he lies writhing on his black bed in the room like a Mycenaean tomb, howls like a wolf with his foot in a trap or a woman in labour, and bleeds.

First, she was fearful when she heard the sound of pain, in case it hurt her, as it had done before. She prowled round the bed, growling, snuffing at his wound that does not smell like her wound. Then, she was pitiful as her gaunt grey mother; she leapt upon his bed to lick, without hesitation, without disgust, with a quick, tender gravity, the blood and dirt from his cheeks and forehead.

The lucidity of the moonlight lit the mirror propped against the red wall; the rational glass, the master of the visible, impartially recorded the crooning girl.

As she continued her ministrations, this glass, with infinite slowness, yielded to the reflexive strength of its own material construction. Little by little, there appeared within it, like the image on photographic paper that emerges, first, a formless web of tracery, the prey caught in its own fishing net, then in firmer yet still shadowed outline until at last as vivid as real life itself, as if brought into being by her soft, moist, gentle tongue, finally, the face of the Duke.

Further Reading

Abel, Elizabeth (ed.) *Writing and Sexual Difference*, University of Chicago Press, Chicago, 1982.

Anderson, Nancy Fix, *Woman Against Woman in Victorian England: A Life of Eliza Lynn Linton*, Indiana University Press, Bloomington and Indianapolis, 1987.

Babington Smith, Constance, *Rose Macaulay*, Collins, London, 1972.

Bailey, Hilary, *Vera Brittain*, Harmondsworth, Penguin, 1987.

Baker, Michael, *Our Three Selves: The Life of Radclyffe Hall*, Hamish Hamilton, London, 1985.

Barbera, Jack and McBrien, William, *Stevie: A Biography of Stevie Smith*, Heinemann, London, 1985.

Battiscombe, Georgina, *Charlotte Yonge: The Story of an Uneventful Life*, Constable, London, 1943.

——*Christina Rossetti: A Divided Life*, Constable, London, 1981.

Bell, Quentin, *Virginia Woolf: A Biography*, Hogarth, London, 1972.

Boll, T. E. M., *Miss May Sinclair: Novelist. A Biographical and Critical Introduction*, Associated University Press, New Jersey, 1902; reprinted 1973.

Butler, Marilyn, *Maria Edgeworth: A Literary Biography*, Clarendon Press, Oxford, 1972.

——*Jane Austen and the War of Ideas*, Oxford University Press, Oxford, 1975.

Campbell, Mary, *Lady Morgan: The Life and Times of Sydney Owenson*, Pandora Press, London, 1988.

Chitty, Susan, *Now to My Mother: A Very Personal Memoir of Antonia White*, Weidenfeld & Nicholson, London, 1985.

Collis, M., *Somerville and Ross*, Faber & Faber, London, 1972.

David, Deidre, *Intellectual Women and Victorian Patriarchy: Harriet Martineau, Elizabeth Barrett Browning, George Eliot*, Macmillan, London, 1987.

DiBattista, Maria, *Virginia Woolf's Major Novels: The Fables of Anon*, Yale University Press, 1980.

Dunn, Jane, *Moon in Eclipse: A Life of Mary Shelley*, Weidenfeld & Nicholson, London, 1978.

Easson, Angus, *Elizabeth Gaskell*, Routledge & Kegan Paul, London, 1979.

Ellman, Mary, *Thinking About Women*, Harcourt Brace Jovanich Inc., New York, 1968.

Forster, Margaret, *Elizabeth Barrett Browning: A Biography*, Chatto & Windus, London, 1988.

Franks, Claudia Stillman, *Beyond the Well of Loneliness*, Avebury Publishing Co., Avebury, 1982.

Fraser, Rebecca, *Charlotte Brontë*, Methuen, London, 1988.

Fromm, Gloria, *Dorothy Richardson: A Biography*, University of Illinois Press, 1977.

Gérin, Winifred, *Charlotte Brontë: The Evolution of Genius*, Oxford University Press, Oxford, 1967.

——*Emily Brontë: A Biography*, Oxford University Press, Oxford and London, 1971.

——*Anne Thackeray Ritchie*, Oxford University Press, Oxford and London, 1983.

——*Elizabeth Gaskell*, Oxford University Press, Oxford, 1988.

Gerrard, Nicci, *Into the Mainstream: How Feminism has Changed Women's Writing*, Pandora Press, London, 1989.

Gilbert, Sandra and Gubar, Susan, *The Madwoman in the Attic*, Yale University Press, New Haven, 1979.

——(eds), *Shakespeare's Sisters: Feminist Essays on Women Poets*, Indiana University Press, Bloominton, 1979.

Gittings, Robert and Manton, Jo, *Dorothy Wordsworth*, Oxford University Press, Oxford, 1985.

Glendenning, Victoria, *Edith Sitwell: A Unicorn among Lions*, Weidenfeld & Nicolson, 1981.

Goreau, Angeline, *Reconstructing Aphra: A Social Biography of Aphra Behn*, Dial Press, New York, 1980.

Greene, Gayle and Kahn, Coppelia (eds), *Making a Difference: Feminist Literary Criticism*, Methuen, London, 1985.

Haight, Gordon S., *George Eliot: A Biography*, Oxford University Press, Oxford, 1968.

Hanscombe, Gillian E., *The Art of Life: Dorothy Richardson and the Development of Feminist Consciousness*, Peter Owen, London, 1982; Ohio University Press, Athens, 1983.

Hanscombe, Gillian E. and Smyers, Virginia, *Writing for their Lives: The Modernist Women 1910–1940*, The Women's Press, London, 1987.

Hardy, Barbara (ed.), *Critical Essays on George Eliot*, Routledge & Kegan Paul, London, 1979.

Heineman, Helen, *Mrs Trollope: The Triumphant Feminine in the Nineteenth Century*, Ohio State University Press, Athens, 1979.

Hemlow, Joyce, *The History of Fanny Burney*, Oxford University Press, Oxford, 1958.

Homans, Margaret, *Bearing the Word: Language and Female Experience in Nineteenth-Century Women's Writing*, University of Chicago Press, Chicago, 1986.

Honan, Park, *Jane Austen: Her Life*, Weidenfeld & Nicolson, London, 1987.

Hopkinson, Lyndall P., *Nothing to Forgive: A Daughter's Life of Antonia White*, Chatto & Windus, London, 1988.

Howe, Susanne, *Geraldine Jewsbury*, Aberdeen University Press, Aberdeen, 1935.

Jacobus, Mary, *Reading Woman: Essays in Feminist Criticism*, Columbia University Press, New York, 1986.

Johnston, Joanna, *The Life, Manners and Travels of Fanny Trollope*, Constable, London, 1979.

Kaplan, Cora, *Sea Changes: Essays on Culture and Feminism*, Verso, London, 1986.

Kiely, R., *The Romantic Novel in England*, Harvard University Press, Cambridge, Mass., 1972.

Leighton, Angela, *Elizabeth Barrett Browning*, Harvester Press, Brighton, 1986.

Lewis, Gifford, *Somerville and Ross: The World of the Irish R. M.*, Faber & Faber, London, 1980.

Miles, Rosalind, *The Female Form: Women Writers and the Conquest of the Novel*, Routledge & Kegan Paul, London, 1987.

Millett, Kate, *Sexual Politics*, Avon Books, New York, 1970.

Moers, Ellen, *Literary Women: The Great Writers*, Doubleday & Co., New York, 1976.

Moi, Toril, *Sexual/Textual Politics: Feminist Literary Theory*, Methuen, London, 1985.

Monteith, Moira (ed.), *Women's Writing: A Challenge to Theory*, Harvester Press, Brighton, 1986.

Mulford, Wendy, *This Narrow Place: Sylvia Townsend Warner and Valentine Ackland; Life, Letters and Politics, 1930–1951*, Pandora Press, London, 1988.

Newton, Judith and Rosenfelt, Deborah (eds), *Feminist Criticism and Social Change*, Methuen, New York, 1985.

Pichanick, Valerie K., *Harriet Marineau: The Woman and Her Work*, University of Michigan Press, Ann Arbor, 1988.

Poovey, Mary, *The Proper Lady and the Woman Writer*, Chicago University Press, Chicago, 1984.

Pratt, Aniis, *Archetypal Patterns in Women's Fiction*, Harvester Press, Brighton, 1982.

Rich, Adrienne, *On Lies, Secrets and Silence*, W. W. Norton, New York, 1979.

Robinson, Lillian S., *Sex, Class and Culture*, Methuen, New York, 1978; 1986.

Russ, Joanna, *How to Suppress Women's Writing*, The Women's Press, London, 1984.

Salter, Elizabeth, *Edith Sitwell*, Oresko Books, London, 1979.

Schofield, Mary Anne and Macheski, Cecilia (eds), *Fetter'd or Free? British Women Novelists 1670–1815*, Ohio University Press, Athens, 1985.

Showalter, Elaine, *A Literature of Their Own: British Women Novelists from Brontë to Lessing*, Princeton University Press, 1977.

——(ed.), *The New Feminist Criticism: Essays on Women, Literature and Theory*, Virago, London, 1986.

Smith, Esther Marian Greenwell, *Mrs Humphry Ward*, Twayne, Boston, 1980.

Spacks, Patricia M., *The Female Imagination*, Alfred A. Knopf, New York, 1975.

——*Imagining a Self: Autobiography and Novel in Eighteenth-Century England*, Harvard University Press, Cambridge, Mass., 1976.

Spalding, Francis, *Stevie Smith: A Critical Biography*, Faber & Faber, London, 1988.

Spencer, Jane, *The Rise of the Woman Novelist: From Aphra Behn to Jane Austen*, Basil Blackwell, Oxford, 1986.

Spender, Dale, *Mothers of the Novel: 100 Good Women Writers before Jane Austen*, Pandora, London, 1986.

——*The Writing or the Sex? (Or why you don't have to read women's writing to know it's no good)*, Athene, Pergamon, New York, 1989.

Stubbs, Patricia, *Women and Fiction: Feminism and the Novel 1880–1920*, Harvester Press, Brighton, 1979.

Todd, Janet (ed.), *A Dictionary of British and American Women Writers 1660–1800*, Rowman & Allanheld, Totowa, New Jersey; Methuen, London, 1985.

——*Feminist Literary History*, Polity Press, Cambridge, and Routledge, London, 1988.

——*The Sign of Angellica: Women, Writing and Fiction 1660–1800*, Virago, London, 1989.

Tompkins, J. M. S., *The Popular Novel in England 1770–1800*, Constable, London, 1932; University of Nebraska Press, Lincoln, 1961.

Travitsky, Betty (ed.), *The Paradise of Women: Writings by Englishwomen of the Renaissance*, Westport, Conn.; Greenwood Press, London, 1981.

Wolff, R. L., *The Sensational Victorian: The Life and Fiction of M. E. Braddon*, Garland, New York and London, 1979.

Index

Index